Portrait of Moses Mendelssohn by Johann Christoph Frisch

Moses Mendelssohn

A BIOGRAPHICAL STUDY

by Alexander Altmann

THE UNIVERSITY OF ALABAMA PRESS
UNIVERSITY, ALABAMA

The Writing Of This Book Was Sponsored
By The Leo Baeck Institute
As Part Of A Research Project
In The History Of The Jews Of Europe
Through A Share It Received
In The
Erasmus Prize
Awarded To Martin Buber
In The Year 1963

FOR MY CHILDREN
AND
GRANDCHILDREN

Table of Contents

List of Illustrations

Moses Mendelssohn. Oil painting by Johann Christoph Frisch (1778; see p. 329). Original in the possession of Doctor Cécile Lowenthal-Hensel, Berlin. *Frontispiece.*

The *Mühlendamm*, Berlin, viewed from the Molkenmarkt, with Veitel Heine Ephraim's *palais* on the right. Steel Engraving by Finden after a drawing by Stock. In the possession of the Staatsarchiv Preussischer Kulturbesitz, Berlin.

Interior of the Synagogue in Berlin, consecrated in 1714. Engraving by Goblin; reproduction by Historia-Photo, Bad Sachsa (Südharz).

Gotthold Ephraim Lessing in his Early Twenties. Oil painting presumably by Christian Wilhelm Ernst Dietrich (see Heinrich Schneider, *Lessing,* Bern, 1951, p. 250 ff.). In the possession of the Herzog August-Bibliothek, Wolfenbüttel.

Friedrich Nicolai. "D. Chodowiecki del.—J. E. Hais sculp. A. V. 1780." In the possession of the Staatsarchiv Preussischer Kulturbesitz, Berlin.

Fromet Mendelssohn, née Gugenheim. Minature-painting by Doctor R. S. (1767). Original in the possession of Fanny Kistner, Erlangen-Nürnberg.

Thomas Abbt. Engraving in the possession of the Niedersächsisches Staatsarchiv, Bückeburg.

Johann Caspar Lavater, Deacon in Zürich. Engraving in the possession of the Zentralbibliothek, Zürich.

Facsimile of Mendelssohn's Letter to Lavater, dated December 24, 1769. Original in the possession of the Zentralbibliothek, Zürich.

Count Wilhelm of Schaumburg-Lippe. Engraving in the possession of the Niedersächsisches Staatsarchiv, Bückeburg.

Adolf Friedrich August Hennings. Engraving in the possession of the Staatsarchiv, Hamburg.

Doctor Marcus Herz. Painting by J. F. Weitsch; reproduction by Historia-Photo, Bad Sachsa (Südharz).

David Friedländer in his Old Age. Drawing by C. Bardua in the possession of the Staatsarchiv, Preussischer Kulturbesitz, Berlin.

Hartwig (Naphtali Herz) Wessely. From a painting reproduced in *Jüdisches Lexikon* (ed. G. Herlitz and B. Kirschner), 4/2 (Berlin, 1930):1415.

Ezekiel Landau, Chief Rabbi of Prague. Portrait in the possession of the State Jewish Museum, Prague.

Ernst Ferdinand Klein. Engraving by J. M. S. Lowe. Published in Lowe's *Bildnisse jetzt lebender Berliner Gelehrten mit ihren Selbstbiographien*, II (Berlin, 1806).

Joseph Mendelssohn. Oil painting in the possession of Angelika von Mendelssohn, Georgenhof, Tigerfeld, Kreis Münsingen.

Preface

———⟨∞⟩———

The present study seeks to present Moses Mendelssohn in strictly biographical terms. It does not attempt to assess his significance from the hindsight of historical perspective or to trace his image in subsequent generations, which have either idolized him as the most perfect embodiment of the modern Jew or abused him as the false prophet of a de-Hebraized, denationalized, assimilated Judaism. It is the *life* of Moses Mendelssohn, and nothing else, that I have tried to describe, and to this end my sole endeavor was to observe this life from within the period in which it was set. The picture that emerged will have to speak for itself and answer such questions as the historian or the partisan may care to ask.

In confining myself to a portrait of Mendelssohn I have not narrowed my vista to a single person or, for that matter, to a single society or culture. Mendelssohn's life is a kaleidoscope of the European intellectual scene, Jewish and non-Jewish, in the second half of the eighteenth century. In portraying his life I have had to populate my canvas with a great variety of people, famous and otherwise. No other Jew of his period was so deeply rooted in the sphere of Jewish tradition as well as in the Berlin Enlightenment. If, in Eduard Zeller's often quoted phrase, he was "the noblest representative" of German Enlightenment, he was, at the same time, a scholar versed in Talmud and Hebrew literature. In his time, the age of Frederick the Great, Berlin was teeming with statesmen, scientists, artists, and liberal theologians. Mendelssohn was part and parcel of the local scene, which included the Jewish community on its fringe. To what extent the two disparate worlds of Judaism and modern Enlightenment jostled each other in his mind and to what degree he could harmonize them are questions that admit of no facile answer. It is only in the aggregate of a multitude of accounts of experiences, reactions, and statements on his part that his attitude becomes fully articulate. His reply to Lavater's challenge, his formidable Bible project, his tussles with the rabbis, the formulation of his view of Judaism in *Jerusalem*, his response to Lessing's *Nathan the Wise*, the way he educated his children—these and many more items in his biography add·up to the final answer to the question: what was his Judaism like?

No less complicated and subtle is Mendelssohn's philosophy. Clichés such as *Popularphilosoph,* follower of the Leibniz/Wolffian school, and the like fail to do justice to him. Though his early metaphysical writings, which I analyzed in a previous study,* fixed the essential outline of his thinking, there remained scope for flexibility. The "strange illness," which started in 1771 and plagued him, more or less, until the end of his life, effectively barred any major development in his philosophical outlook, but it could not prevent fresh glimpses of creative insight. I have endeavored to trace his philosophical activity from his opus 1 down to the last great effort, the *Morning Hours,* and its sequel, *To Lessing's Friends.* His contest with Friedrich Heinrich Jacobi, which was the motivating force in his final outpouring of energy, has been analyzed in some detail and in the light of many hitherto unknown sources in order to clarify the rights and wrongs in this sad affair, which precipitated his end. In this connection the entire background of the conflict, viz. the confrontation between the Berlin Enlightenment and its opponents (notably Hamann, Herder, and Lavater) had to be illumined. Moreover, Mendelssohn's relationship with Lessing during the last phase of the poet's life had to be investigated.

Few will doubt that a new biography of Mendelssohn is an urgent desideratum. The one and only scholarly biography extant was written by Meyer Kayserling more than a century ago (it first appeared in 1862, and a second revised edition followed in 1888); that this book was able to maintain its monopoly for so long testifies to its merit. In the intervening period, however, a wealth of research has appeared, stimulated in particular by the bicentennial of Mendelssohn's birth in 1929 but stretching back over a long time and embracing over seven hundred items.** Moreover, the critical edition of seven out of the projected fifteen volumes of Mendelssohn's *Gesammelte Schriften: Jubiläumsausgabe*** placed the entire range of Mendelssohn studies on a new footing. It presented a considerable number of hitherto unknown sources, and the excellent introductions and annotations by the editors (Fritz Bamberger, Haim Bar-Dayan [Borodianski], Simon Rawidowicz, Bruno Strauss, and Leo Strauss) laid bare unsuspected dimensions in Mendelssohn's literary output.

---

*Alexander Altmann, *Moses Mendelssohns Frühschriften zur Metaphysik untersucht und erläutert* (Tübingen: J. C. B. Mohr (Paul Siebeck), 1969).

**See Herrmann M.Z. Meyer, *Moses Mendelssohn Bibliographie* (Berlin: Walter de Gruyter & Co., 1965), pp.119–74 (Nos. 685–1398). Since Meyer's work was published, many additional works have appeared.

***Berlin, 1929—. Cut short by the advent of the Nazi régime in Germany but now resumed to include twenty volumes under my general editorship, to be published by the Friedrich Frommann Verlag Günther Holzboog, Stuttgart.

The present work draws not only on published material, including some valuable research done in Israel in recent years, but also on many autographs (letters, drafts, and other documents) that have not yet seen the light of day. Herr Robert von Mendelssohn, owner of the precious Family Archive (now deposited in his name at the Staatsbibliothek der Stiftung Preussischer Kulturbesitz, Berlin) gave me his kind and generous permission to use and edit the entire hitherto unpublished material. To him my most grateful thanks are due. I also wish to express warm gratitude to the Leo Baeck Institute, New York, for having placed at my disposal xerographic copies of its very extensive collection of Mendelssohniana. Further unedited material was made available to me by the Staatsbibliothek der Stiftung Preussischer Kulturbesitz, Berlin; the Niedersächsische Landesbibliothek, Hannover; the Niedersächsisches Staatsarchiv, Bückeburg; the Goethe und Schiller-Archiv, Weimar; the Museen der Stadt Halberstadt, Das Gleimhaus; the Staats- und Universitätsbibliothek, Hamburg; the Staatsarchiv, Hamburg; the Royal Library, Copenhagen; the University Library, Amsterdam; and the Hebrew University and National Library, Jerusalem. Baron Hugo von Mendelssohn Bartholdy and Mr. Eric Warburg were kind enough to send me copies of autographs in their possession. My sincere thanks are extended to all these contributors. I feel a special sense of indebtedness to Professor Fritz Bamberger, who generously opened up to me his large and valuable collection of Mendelssohniana and accompanied the growth of the present work with a steady flow of relevant material. I also appreciate the ready help received from Dr. Rudolf Elvers, curator of the Mendelssohn-Archiv, Berlin, and Professor Heinz Moshe Graupe, director of the Institut für die Geschichte der Juden in Deutschland, Hamburg. Finally, I want to express my thanks to the owners of the various pictures reproduced in this book, in particular to Dr. Cécile Lowenthal-Hensel, Berlin for permitting me to publish for the first time Mendelssohn's (her ancestor's) superb portrait in oil by Johann Christian Frisch (1778) in color as the frontispiece.

As the preamble to the present work indicates, it was written under the sponsorship of the Leo Baeck Institute and, more especially, of its "Martin Buber Erasmus Prize Administrative Committee." I am greatly indebted to Dr. Robert Weltsch, London, and Dr. Hans Tramer, Tel-Aviv, leading members of the committee, for the unflagging interest they have shown in the progress of my writing. I am equally indebted to Dr. Max Gruenewald, president of the New York branch of the Leo Baeck Institute, for sponsoring an application for a grant in aid for the publication of the work. My sincere thanks are due to Mr. Harry Starr, president of The Lucius N. Littauer Foundation, New York, for his generous response to the request for a subsidy, and to Mr. Philip W. Lown, the well-known patron of Jewish studies, for making additional help available. It was my good fortune to have enjoyed the warm-hearted support of Dr. Abram L. Sachar, chancellor of Brandeis University, and I am truly thankful to him. Finally, I wish to express my appreciation of the enthusiastic and efficient manner in which The University of Alabama Press has undertaken to publish this volume. To its Senior Editor, Mr. Francis P. Squibb, I offer my special thanks for the splendid manner in which he discharged his responsibility. His queries and suggestions were of such a kind as only the most sympathetic understanding could have produced. I cannot conclude these acknowledgments without thanking my dear wife for having shared with me the growing pains and the joys experienced in the writing of this book, and also for many a valuable suggestion that helped to improve it.

A. A.

Moses Mendelssohn

CHAPTER ONE

Years of Growth

Childhood in Dessau

Moses Mendelssohn was born in Dessau, capital city of the small principality of Anhalt-Dessau, on September 6, 1729 (Elul 12, 5489), the youngest—probably—of the three children of Mendel (Menahem) Heymann and his wife Bela Rachel Sara. On his father's side he was of rather humble origin. In 1726, three years before Moses was born, Mendel Heymann appears in the list of Dessau synagogue officials as custodian (*Küster*) and *Schulklopfer*, as one whose job it was, early every morning, to knock at the doors of members of the community, calling them to the service.[1] Eventually he achieved the position of teacher and scribe (*sofer*). In a brief autobiographical note, written in 1774, Mendelssohn described his father to a non-Jewish public as "schoolmaster and writer of the Ten Commandments."[2] The office of sofer implies, of course, much more than this description indicates. It entails the writing of Tora scrolls and the mending of defective ones, and the preparation of legal documents such as bills of divorce (*gittin*) and of ritual objects such as phylacteries (*tefilin*) and doorpost capsules (*mezuzot*)—activities demanding considerable knowledge and skill. The sofer was also the secretary of the community. Until about 1706 this office had been administered in Dessau by the gifted Arye Löb Lipschütz, hailed as "the great scribe of our community," who translated into Yiddish the poetic Hebrew dirges (*kinot*) of the fast day of the ninth of Av. He had moved to Berlin where he died in 1736.[3] Compared to him, Mendel Heymann was a quite ordinary man, yet one qualified for his profession. The elegant handwriting of the "Sohn of Mendel" probably reflected a paternal influence.

On the maternal side, Mendelssohn was of truly aristocratic descent. Among the early Jewish settlers in Dessau, where Jews were first admitted

3

in 1672, was the family of Simha Bonem (Benjamin) Wulff. Its ancestor was the illustrious Moses Isserles, of Cracow (ca. 1520–1572), author of the glosses to the *Shulhan 'Arukh* ("The Prepared Table"), Joseph Karo's codification of Jewish laws and customs. Simha Bonem's father, Simon Wolf, was a grandson of Dresel, Isserles' daughter from his second marriage.[4] Simon Wolf had been the leader of the Jewish community of Vilna. When forced to flee the city after its invasion by the Cossacks, he found refuge in Hamburg. One of his daughters married Juda Wahl, grandson of Saul Wahl, who was the leader of the Jewish community of Brest-Litowsk (ca. 1545–1617) and, according to legend, ruled as king of Poland for one night. The Wahls' place of origin was Katzenellenbogen (Hesse). Rabbi Meir ben Isaac of Katzenellenbogen emigrated to Italy, where he achieved great fame as a rabbinic authority and was known as the Maharam of Padua. He was the grandfather of Saul Wahl. Juda Wahl's son Saul, named after his great-grandfather, lived in Dessau, where he was licensed to open the first brandy factory in the principality. His descent from the Maharam of Padua and Saul Wahl of Brest-Litowsk on the paternal side, and from Moses Isserles on the maternal, earned him wide respect. He died in 1717. The inscription on his tombstone lists his many illustrious ancestors and pays tribute to him personally as "one who belonged to the perfect who assemble for prayer morning and evening before Him who is enthroned on High" and as one whose "deeds were kindly" and were pursued "quietly and invisibly, as the pious and wise are wont to do."[5]

The man lauded in this epitaph was Moses Mendelssohn's maternal grandfather. Saul Wahl of Dessau had married Sisa (Susanna), daughter of Menahem Man of Kalisch. The daughter born to this couple was Bela Rachel Sara, the mother of Moses Mendelssohn. During his childhood years in Dessau, Moses must have read more than once the row of names engraved on his maternal grandfather's tombstone. No doubt, he was aware of the nobility of his descent. In a letter written by him in 1770, when he was forty-one, he introduced Rabbi Shelomo Zalman Lipschütz of Neuwied to his cousin Elkan Herz with these words: "It is a *mizva* [meritorious deed] to honor him and treat him with respect, for he is the son of a great father renowned for his works and a member of our distinguished family, descended as he is from the author of the Glosses [viz. Moses Isserles] of blessed memory, as his writings attest."[6] Mendelssohn was anything but a snob but he cherished his family tree and cultivated a close relationship with many members of his family throughout life. His Hebrew and Yiddish letters bear eloquent testimony to this fact.[7] When, in 1771, Elkan Herz challenged him to explain one of his utterances that had been construed to imply a denial of revelation, he took pains to refute the accusation,[8] for he would have regretted being suspected of unorthodox views by so dear a relative. Rooted as he was in his family, he became himself a very devoted husband and father. The apostasy of his children, with the exception of his daughter Recha and his eldest son Joseph, would have hurt him deeply, had he lived to witness it. The many attempts that would be made to draw him toward the baptismal font were doomed from the outset. The Jewish tradition remained the very core of his being, though the world of European culture tended to overpower it at times. *Moshe mi-Dessau* [Moses of Dessau], as he signed his name in Hebrew, and Moses Mendelssohn did not always seem to be identical. He lived in two spheres, as it were, and the drama of his life and its achievement is caught within the dialectic of these two realms. Whether he ultimately succeeded in merging them into a unified whole is a moot point. The philosopher and the Jew in him were felt by his opponents to be hardly compatible. He was the acknowledged leader of the German philosophy of the Enlightenment in the latter half of the eighteenth century. He was also the first great spokesman of the Enlightenment in modern Jewry. Yet his philosophic stance is one thing, his Jewishness another.

Dessau, his birthplace and the scene of his childhood, provided an ideal setting for the formation of such a dual outlook. The local community was imbued with old-time piety and learning but was, at the same time, veering toward a measure of the Enlightenment that had gripped the age. It was an intellectually alive community, "a city full of scholars and writers," as a chronicler described it.[9] Its character was largely due to the impact of the strong personality of a "court-Jew," the *Hoffaktor* Moses Benjamin Wulff, who lived in Dessau for over forty years. Mention has already been made of Simon Wolf of Vilna, who came to Hamburg in 1655, one of whose daughters married Juda Wahl. Another of his daughters became the wife of the celebrated Shabbatai ben Meir Ha-Kohen (1621–1662), author of *Sifte Kohen* ("The Priest's Lips"), an authoritative commentary on the second and fourth parts of the *Shulhan 'Arukh*. One of Simon Wolf's three sons, Barukh (Berend) Wulff, also called Barukh Minden, went to Berlin, where the Great Elector appointed him successor to the court-Jew Elias Gumpertz; he died in 1706 in Berlin, having moved first to Halberstadt, then to Halle, and finally back to Berlin. Another son, Solomon Wulff, married the daughter of the Hildesheim rabbi Samuel Hameln, brother-in-law of the famed Glückel of Hameln; he died at a ripe age in Dessau.

Much more dramatic was the life of the (probably) eldest son, Simha Bonem (Benjamin) Wulff. Fleeing from the Cossacks, he simulated, on arrival in Poland, conversion to Christianity in order to save his life. Having reached Hamburg, he revoked his "conversion." According to the record book *(pinkas)* of the "Portuguese" Jewish community of Hamburg, he was a follower of the "prophet" and "miracle worker" Shabbatai Raphael, a Sabbatian heretic, and was placed under the ban *(herem)* in 1668.[10] He went to Halberstadt and, subsequently, to Berlin, where he helped to establish a *hevra kadisha* ("holy fraternity") for the burial of the dead). He left Berlin for Dessau in 1686, when the Great Elector served an expulsion order on his son Moses Benjamin Wulff, called "the tall Jew" because of his imposing figure, who had become persona non grata as a result of intrigues by his competitor, the influential court-Jew Jost Liebmann. Fortunately, Prince Johann Georg II of Dessau offered him asylum, and so it happened that, together with his parents, wife, and two children, Moses Benjamin settled in Dessau. He was appointed court administrator (*Hoffaktor*), a position he continued to hold under the prince's son Leopold, famous as "the old Dessauer."

Benjamin Wulff was not the only *Hoffaktor* of the principality, but his outstanding achievements made him one of the most important court-Jews of the time. He improved the country's monetary system, established transportation and postal services, provided money for the pay and billeting costs of the army, and supervised the leasing of the prince's estates, the collection of custom fees, the buying of hunting grounds and mines, etc. He represented the prince in numerous lawsuits and often accompanied him on his journeys. His relations to the imperial court-Jews of Vienna enabled him to play a helpful role in the delicate negotiations between the emperor's court and Prince Leopold, who had married a commoner and wanted her to be elevated to the rank of an imperially recognized princess. Not all of his own enterprises succeeded, least of all a contract for the delivery of silver that he concluded in 1691 with the duke of Gotha and Altenburg, with the object of improving the country's currency. Wulff stood then at the peak of his economic power, his credit extending to Rome, Venice, Paris, England, Holland, and Brabant. He lent the government of Gotha hundreds of thousands of guilders, having raised the money by offering his jewels and private property as security. The result was the undermining of his credit, and he was several times imprisoned at the instance of his creditors. The protests raised on his behalf by the governments of Saxony and Prussia and even the personal intervention of Prince Leopold of Dessau proved ineffective. Gotha turned the tables, denying being indebted to Wulff and even suing him for alleged debts. The lawsuit dragged on for decades. Wulff died without having received redress from the trumped-up charge of having delivered coins of inferior metal. His death occurred on August 29, 1729, just a few days before the birth of Moses Mendelssohn.[11]

As a "type" the court-Jew represents one of the most interesting phenomena of seventeenth- and eighteenth-century Jewish history. There were several hundred of them, each living in two worlds, as it were. As a loyal member of the community, the court-Jew belonged to a society that prized the study of the Tora and the mastery of Jewish learning as the supreme value and the only true criterion of social standing. But as an employee and confidant of princes he had to cultivate standards that set him off from the rank and file of the ghetto community. He could not help imitating the courtly style of living. He built himself magnificent mansions, where he received, on occasion, the visit of his princely patron; it was by no means uncommon for the princely family to attend the wedding of a court-Jew's daughter. Long before the barrier separating the Jew of the ghetto from the environment was legally removed, there had been a partial de facto transition from exclusiveness to broader vistas in the case of the court-Jew. The pattern of a kind of dual existence, of a familiarity with two worlds, that we meet in Moses Mendelssohn is a repetition, albeit in different terms, of the phenomenon of the court-Jew.

Moses Benjamin Wulff was one of the finest specimens of this social type. His piety and generosity created two institutions that proved to be of immense value to Dessau Jewry and to Jewish culture in general. He founded a Beth Midrash ("House of Study"), also referred to as a *Klaus,* and a Hebrew printing plant. It was the ingenious combination of the two that helped to make Dessau a center of Hebrew scholarship. Otherwise, Wulff might have followed the example of other court-Jews, who merely endowed houses of study and occasionally subsidized the publication of Hebrew books. Thus, Elias Gumpertz, who died in 1689, had established the Beth Hamidrash in Cleve, and the *Hoffaktor* Behrend Lehmann founded the *Klaus* of Halberstadt in 1703. If a court-Jew was not himself a scholar, he often sought to gain vicarious merit and the reflected glory of learning by his support of scholarship. A *Klaus* was meant to offer impecunious men of rabbinic learning a carefree existence and leisure for their studies.[12] Moses Benjamin Wulff was by no means an ignoramus in rabbinics. He was able to entertain learned guests with *divrey Tora.*[13] His munificence was inspired by a true love of Jewish learning. Both the *Klaus* and the printing press were situated in his own mansion. Scholars who came to Dessau to deliver the manuscripts of their works to the press were at liberty to stay as honored guests, sometimes for months, to supervise the printing and, at the same time, to engage in study. The intellectual stimulus provided by the resident and visiting scholars of the *Klaus* was a boon enjoyed by the community as a whole. Moreover, each book produced by the press created a stir and was hailed as an event. Thanks to Wulff's beneficent endowments, Dessau had become "a city full of scholars and writers."

Many of the Jews of Dessau were related to Moses Benjamin Wulff. Isaac Gerson, head of the *Klaus,* was Wulff's nephew and a son-in-law of Reuben Fürst of Hamburg, who had married a daughter of Wulff's uncle, Barukh Minden. There were other members of the wealthy and distinguished Fürst family living in Dessau. One of them was the teacher and cantor Moses ben Yokel, who died in 1737. A daughter of the *Hoffaktor* married Menahem Man of Cleve, known also as Magnus Moses, and the couple lived in Dessau until 1700. Another daughter became the wife of Aaron Isaac Levi, who also lived in Dessau. Their son Barukh Aaron Levi was made *Hoffaktor* of the elector of Saxony in 1769. Yet another daughter married Isaac Wallich, member of a Koblenz family that produced a number of physicians. Isaac Wallich, a man well versed in the Talmud, received the doctorate of medicine at Leyden in 1675. After his marriage he settled in Dessau, where he died in 1716. Elija, Wulff's only son, was elected president of the Dessau community while still a young man (his father had refused this honor from a sense of modesty) and was also appointed as *Hoffaktor* by Prince Leopold. He followed in his father's footsteps insofar as charitableness and love of Hebrew letters were concerned, but he lacked the commercial talent required to reestablish the family fortune, and toward the end of his life he was dependant on his son Benjamin, who lived in Berlin; he died in 1754. One of Elija's daughters became the wife of Nathan ben Moses of Kalisch, whom Prince Leopold appointed chief cantor of the Dessau community in 1745.[14]

Bela Rachel Sara, Mendelssohn's mother, was a cousin of Elija Wulff. When she gave birth to a son at a time when the community was mourning the death of the *Hoffaktor* Moses Benjamin Wulff, he was named Moses in honor of both the deceased and the great ancestor Moses Isserles. His brother Saul bore the name of the maternal grandfather, who had died in 1717, and must therefore be presumed to have been older than Moses, since it was customary to name children after deceased grandparents. His sister Yente was named for the daughter of Simon Wolf, who had married the famous Shabbatai ben Meir Ha-Kohen; she too must have been older than Moses, for had she been born after him she would have been named after her maternal grandmother Sisa, who died in 1730, one year after Moses' birth. Yente remained a spinster and spent her entire life in Dessau. She was possibly the eldest of the three children. She died on August 12, 1769. The inscription on her tombstone praises the charity that she practiced toward the living and the dead. The brother Saul seems to have been a man of considerable rabbinic erudition but a bit uncommunicative, even brusque, which may account for his failure to achieve an adequate position. Moses found him temporary employment as proofreader and assistant to the eminent Hebraist Solomon Dubno, during the period in which the latter helped Mendelssohn edit his Pentateuch translation and commentary.[15]

Little is known of Mendelssohn's mother beyond the eulogy bestowed upon her in the epitaph. There she is described as "a woman appreciated and praised because of the virtue of 'quiet women'[16] [characteristic of her]," as "the modest and pious Bela Rachel Sara, daughter of the honorable Rabbi Saul Wahl of blessed memory," and the prayer is added: "Her virtue and charity may support her in the silence of the heavens above [*be-dom shahak le-ma'la*]."[17] One is struck by the absence of any reference to her as wife and mother. All by herself, as if her very being consisted in her virtue and noble descent, she is presented to eternity. As one of the "quiet women" she is said to have entered the "silence of the heavens." The silence of all literary documents (including the many letters her famous son wrote) strangely matches the poetic silence of the heavens above. One would have liked to know something of the relationship of Moses and his mother, who died on April 11, 1756, at a time when he had already

started his career as a philosopher. All we know is that he was unable
to attend the Schuch troupe's performance of Lessing's *Miss Sara Sampson*
because he was in mourning for his mother, a fact reported by Friedrich
Nicolai in a letter to Lessing dated November 3, 1756.[18] There is something
utterly poignant in the fact that this is the only mention of Mendelssohn's
mother in the many documents of the period. Mendelssohn honored her
memory seven years after her death by giving her name Sara to his first-born
child, a daughter born on May 29, 1763, who died on April 15 the next
year.[19]

We are somewhat better informed about Mendelssohn's relationship
with his father. A reminiscence from his early childhood is reported by
the biographer Itzig Euchel in the name of Moses' friend and disciple
David Friedländer, who had heard it from the master's own lips: Moses'
father used to rise in the small hours of the morning to awaken him and,
because of the boy's delicate health, to carry him on his shoulder to the
Beth Hamidrash.[20] Mendelssohn was anything but sentimental or self-
pitying, and in recalling this childhood memory he obviously wished to
pay a tribute to his father. A propos this story, the Protestant preacher
Daniel Jenisch remarked in his Mendelssohn biography: "Luther, too,
praised his father for having carried him on his arms to school: One might
say that the Luther of the Jews (for what else was Mendelssohn for that
nation but the torchbearer of enlightenment?) and the Luther of the Protestants were both initiated by their fathers into the great task for which
Providence had destined them."[21] Although the comparison is rather far-
fetched, Jenisch sensed the deep impression that the father's concern for
his son's Jewish education at a tender age had left on Mendelssohn's mind.
Yet it can hardly be said that the father initiated the son into the historic
role that the latter would play as the leading figure of the Enlightenment
among the Jews.

Mendel Heymann was scarcely the man to kindle such a spark in the
soul of his gifted son. Nor was there a particularly close relationship between
the two. In the letters Mendelssohn wrote to his fiancée, Fromet Gugenheim,
he mentioned his father several times with due respect yet with a touch
of light humor and without any evidence of deep affection. The father
was about forty-seven years of age when Moses was born and the boy
probably always felt him to be rather old and distant. In the letters to
Fromet the term "the old father" occurs many times and although it was
fully justified—Mendel was then almost eighty years old—one gets the
impression that Moses had always looked upon his father as "the old man."
His father, Moses wrote on April 3, 1762, was "a man from the old world,"
who had "his special whims." To spend the Passover that year with the
father in Dessau, as he was being urged to do, was a prospect not at
all relished by Moses, and in the end he did not do so. Mendel had planned
to attend his son's wedding but was physically unable to make the trip

to Hamburg. Moses informed Fromet of the father's regrets and added: "The good, venerable man, I would have liked to see him once more, but he can hardly drag himself to *Shool* [the synagogue]."[22]

Mendel Heymann died four years later, on May 10, 1766, at the age of eighty-three. His epitaph carries the inscription: "On the holy Sabbath, Sivan 2, 526, according to the abbreviated reckoning, there departed with honor Menahem called Mendel the scribe and he was buried on the following day, Sunday. Throughout his life he walked on the straight path. His deeds were performed with honesty, and he was one of the first to arrive in the synagogue every morning and evening. His soul departed in purity. May it be bound up in the bond of life."[23]

As a child Moses lacked neither the will nor the capacity for study. One of his early teachers, named Hirsch, whose father was a member of the Beth Din (rabbinic court) of Dessau, testified in later years to the piety, zeal, and brightness of the lad.[24] Euchel reports that at the age of six Moses had already begun to study "Halakha and Tosafot," i.e. the Talmud with its commentaries and the codes. The correctness of this statement need not be doubted. The teaching method prevalent in the *Heder* or Beth Hamidrash aimed at familiarity with the Talmud and neglected the Bible and its classical commentaries. Even as a child, however, Moses showed a degree of independence: he loved to read the Bible on his own and became so well versed in it that he came to know large portions of the Hebrew text by heart.[25] He also studied Hebrew grammar and strove to gain facility in writing Hebrew prose and poetry in the biblical style. He is said to have tried his hand at the writing of poetry at the age of ten but to have soon realized his lack of talent in that respect.[26] How successful he was in his linguistic exercises was to manifest itself later in his extensive literary output in Hebrew, which excels in both beauty and precision. One may say that already as a child he showed himself imbued with the love of classical Hebrew that was to become one of the distinctive features of the Haskala, the early phase of the Jewish Enlightenment in Germany. By the same token, the fondness for the Bible and for biblical studies, which led him to his German translations of the Hebrew texts of the Psalms, Canticles, and above all the Pentateuch, goes back to the strong attachment to the Bible that he developed as a child. And it is probable that he also commenced the study of Maimonides' philosophy while he was still a boy in Dessau.

In 1742 the Wulffian printing house, then located in neighboring Jessnitz, published a new edition of Maimonides' *More Nevukhim* ("Guide of the Perplexed"), with the commentaries of Shemtov, Efodi, and Crescas and with Ibn Tibbon's glossary of foreign terms. Since the 1553 edition of Sabbioneta the *Guide* had not been reprinted, and the publication of this embattled work in a handsome new format was a literary event of the first order, heralding as it did a thaw in the intellectual climate of German Jewry. Since the study of philosophy was still frowned upon by the pious (a ban pronounced in 1305 had made it illicit to engage in such study unless one was over the age of twenty-five), it was all the more remarkable that the new edition of the *Guide* appeared with the tacit approval of the chief rabbi of Dessau: the cost of printing had been defrayed by a relative of the chief rabbi, and the reading of proofs had been supervised by Aaron Hirsch, a member of the Beth Din.[27] Prior to the publication of the *Guide* the Wulffian Press had already brought out, in the various localities in which it was situated at different times, a whole series of works somewhat secular or scientific in character:[28] Excerpts from Eldad Ha-Dani's *Report* of his travels had appeared in a Yiddish version in Dessau, around 1700; a book entitled *Lashon Naki* ("Pure Language") on matters of Hebrew style had come out in Halle in 1713; a Hebrew grammar called *Derekh Ha-Kodesh* ("The Way of the Holy"), Cöthen, 1717; a Hebrew dictionary of Jehuda Arye Löb of Carpentras, Jessnitz, 1719; an encyclopedia of natural sciences and medicine by the physician Tobias Moshides, Jessnitz, 1721. A year after the publication of Maimonides' work, the press printed the astronomical and geographical treatise *Nehmad Ve-Na'im* by David Gans (1541–1613), whom Moses Isserles, his teacher, seems to have encouraged to study astronomy and who was on friendly terms with Kepler and with Tycho de Brahe, when he came to Prague.

Presumably these and other works published by the press in or around Dessau were known to Moses, more or less, and his intellectual development was no doubt stimulated by them in no small measure. They provided a mirror of the diversity of Hebrew literature, only a fraction of which had remained alive in the consciousness of the majority of his Jewish contemporaries. He may also have become acquainted with some kabbalistic writings. One of the old Dessau prints was Moses ben Menahem Graf's *Wayakhel Moshe,* a commentary on the Zohar's doctrine of emanation; and in 1723 an edition of Isaac Luria's *Sefer Ha-Kavvanot* appeared in Jessnitz with a new augmented edition coming out in Hanau the year after. The printing of such works indicates that the interest in Kabbala, though definitely waning, was still alive among German Jews of the period. The subtle impact of the Enlightenment, which went hand in hand with the slow rise of an industrial age and the breakdown of ghetto exclusiveness, was bound to corrode the mystical spirit. There was a world of difference between the spiritual climate in Dessau, where Mendelssoh grew up, and the atmosphere in Padua, where only a few years before Moses Hayyim Luzzatto and his circle were engrossed in kabbalistic speculations and messianic dreams. Both Mendelssohn and Luzzatto were adepts of pure biblical Hebrew. Both were steeped in traditional learning and piety. Yet they moved in different worlds. Mendelssohn tended toward a humanistic type of Judaism, and his inwardness was that of a lonely youth who sought to enlarge his horizon. Luzzatto was expecting salvation on a cosmic scale from the concentrated power of a mystical fraternity of prayer and meditation. Each member of his group could secretly regard himself as destined for messiahship, as the mystical diary of Moses David Valle, one of his confrères, reveals.[29]

The vistas opened to Mendelssohn through his study of the *Guide* were of incalculable value in his early intellectual development. The last year of his childhood in Dessau, during which he made the first groping effort to penetrate the world of Maimonides, was therefore of decisive importance for his future. He had to grasp new terms and concepts. A disciplined way of thinking, different from the talmudic one, had to be acquired. He was encouraged in this by his teacher Hirsch, it seems, but it is doubtful how much help he could receive from him. The boy was pretty much left to his own devices. In later years he used to say that he owed the curvature of his back to Rambam (Rabbi Moses ben Maimon), since the intensive study of the *Guide* had weakened the resistance of his body to the illness that caused the malformation. He would say this with a twinkle in his eye, adding that he felt compensated by the great benefits derived from his labors: the study of Rambam had brought refreshment to his soul and transformed many a trying time in his life into one of joy.[30] Long before he explored the works of John Locke, Gottfried Wilhelm von Leibniz, and Christian von Wolff, Moses Mendelssohn made himself at home in the world of Judaeo-Arabic philosophy, where many of the topics of seventeenth- and eighteenth-century metaphysics had been the object of incisive discussion. His familiarity with medieval thought facilitated his entry into modern philosophy, and it was in Dessau that he took the first steps in this direction. However, his interest in the *Guide* did not entail an estrangement from the more traditional type of study in which he had been engaged from early youth. The teacher to whom he owed a sense of balance and a healthy respect for the talmudic disciplines was David Fränkel, the brilliant young chief rabbi of Dessau. To him Moses looked up with unbounded reverence and enthusiasm. If he needed a "father-figure," he found it in Fränkel.

Fränkel had held no rabbinic post before being "called" from Berlin to Dessau in 1731. Like his father, Naftali Hirsch Fränkel, who enjoyed a considerable reputation as a talmudic scholar, he had been in the jewelry business. He had, at the same time, written *hiddushim* (*novellae*) to the Babylonian Talmud and the codes. He had also commenced work on his commentary on the Palestinian Talmud, which was to make him famous. In Dessau, his primary aim, like that of all the great rabbis of the time, was the raising of a generation of talmudic scholars. The memoirs of Abraham ben Joseph ben Aaron (Abraham Bri Bra), who studied under Fränkel in Dessau from 1739 to 1741, describe in some detail the curriculum, method, and personality of this outstanding teacher. Thirty students attended the lectures in the rabbi's house. The course in Talmud lasted the whole afternoon until the evening prayer. After a break of an hour and a half, study continued. It now concentrated on the first part of the *Shulhan 'Arukh* and the commentary *Magen Avraham*. Advanced students participated in a course on the more difficult second part of the *Shulhan 'Arukh,* which began at seven in the morning.

Fränkel took great pains to raise the students to his own level of under-standing and sought to convince himself, by persistent questioning, that they had grasped his interpretations. He insisted on thorough preparation and keen attention, and those who were remiss could count on their food rations being reduced. Among the sources he used were the Palestinian Talmud and old midrashic material, sources often ignored in other schools. Fränkel was also much concerned with the physical well-being of his pupils. For those from out of town he provided billets and scholarships; a room in his own house was put at their disposal for study during the night, and his well-stocked library was freely available to them. He published a new edition of Maimonides' great code, the *Mishne Tora,* so that his students could have access to this indispensable work, which had not been reprinted in its entirety since the Amsterdam edition of 1702 and was out of print. He commissioned the Wulffian Press in Jessnitz to produce a new complete edition, the cost of which was underwritten by his brother Solomon Fränkel and other members of his wealthy family. The first volume appeared in 1739 and three others followed during the next several years.[31]

Despite his heavy duties as rabbi and teacher, David Fränkel continued his prolific writing. His students knew that he usually rose at midnight to work on his commentary on the Palestinian Talmud. The very conception, let alone the execution, of so ambitious a project was bound to win him widespread admiration. The leading talmudists of German-Polish Jewry had hardly paid attention to the Palestinian counterpart of the Babylonian Talmud, which through the influence of the Babylonian academies had become "the" Talmud par excellence.[32] Among the seventeenth-century Sephardic Jews it was Joshua Benvenisti, in Turkey, who composed a com-mentary on the legal sections of the Palestinian Talmud. The first Polish scholar to approach such a task was Elija ben Löw Fuld, of Wisznice in Galicia. His commentary on the tractates comprising the first "order," viz. that of *Zera 'im,* appeared in Amsterdam in 1710. This rather terse commen-tary called forth the writing of marginal notes on the Palestinian Talmud by the illustrious David Oppenheim, chief rabbi of Bohemia (1664–1736), whose work Fränkel considered to be of sufficient merit as to render superfluous a new commentary by him.[33] Fränkel's own work, covering the remaining parts of the Palestinian Talmud, appeared in three volumes under the title *Korban Ha-'Eda* ("The Congregation's Offering").[34] He intended the title as an allusion to his desire to open up a hitherto more or less inaccessible text to the understanding of the people: to "bring near" (*korban*) the bound-up testimony (*te'uda;* see Isa. 8:16) to the congregation (*'eda*).[35] He wanted to render the text as intelligible as possible: difficult Aramaic terms are occasionally translated into Yiddish; textual emendations and dialectical attempts to harmonize the two Talmuds are omitted from the running commentary and are relegated to an appendix;[36] historical problems relating to the origin and growth of the Palestinian as well as Babylonian Talmud receive some attention.[37] There is, thus, a touch of modern scholarship discernible in this lucid and learned work.

When Fränkel arrived in Dessau, Moses was only seven years old and as yet unqualified to be admitted to the rabbi's courses. He probably began to study under him when he reached the age of ten. The bright lad must soon have caught Fränkel's attention, and he remained his pupil until the end of his childhood days in Dessau and subsequently as an adolescent in Berlin. The reverence that Mendelssohn felt for his teacher in Dessau is attested by the oldest extant specimen of his handwriting. It is inscribed on the cover of a rabbinic work,[38] is dated Av [5] 502 (1742), and states that the book is the property of Moses, son of the honorable Rabbi Mendel the Scribe. By remarking that this inscription was made in the house of Rabbi David Fränkel, the writer provided for himself an opportunity to heap epithets of fulsome praise upon the celebrated teacher: "Written in the house of the adept of the Tora, the distinguished and excellent scholar, the great Gaon, crown of our head, garland of beauty, diadem of holiness, lover of Israel, ornament of our generation, pillar of the exiled nation, our honorable teacher, Rabbi David (may his light shine forth), author of the commentary and the glosses on the Jerusalem Talmud . . ."[39] The ornate style follows the pattern usually found in rabbinic addresses and dedicatory inscriptions. Moses had obviously mastered the customary rabbinic phraseology even before he reached the age of thirteen. What strikes one is the enthusiasm he felt for his teacher and the poetic touches in the opening and closing lines.[40]

Mendelssohn retained his pride in having sat at such a master's feet throughout his life. It is reflected in a few sentences contained in an autobiographical note written in 1774: "Under Rabbi Fränkel, then chief rabbi in Dessau, I studied the Talmud. After this learned rabbi had acquired great fame among the Jewish nation by his commentary on the Jerusalem Talmud, he was, around the year 1743, 'called' to Berlin, to which place I followed him in the very same year."[41] Again, when in 1760 he reviewed Johann Jacob Rabe's translation of the Mishna in the *Literaturbriefe*, he drew attention to "the famous work of our local Rabbi Fränkel," which "ought to have been mentioned in particular" among the various editions of the Jerusalem Talmud. "This rabbi," he recalled, "was responsible for the printing, at his own expense, of the entire Jerusalem Talmud with his own commentary and ample notes."[42] It was not simply a pupil's pride in his master that caused Mendelssohn in his mature age to draw attention to Fränkel when writing for a non-Jewish public. He was eager to impress on the academic world the fact that Jewry was not bereft of scholars of high idealism who were not merely following the somewhat discredited pattern of rabbinic casuistry but were engaged in solid research and text editions of the most imposing character. To him personally the figure of his celebrated teacher represented talmudic studies as a search for the authentic meaning of the text in contradistinction to the prevalent exercise of futile dialectic *(pilpul shel hevel)*. Before joining Fränkel's classes Moses seems to have been exposed to the *pilpul* method and to have developed a strong distaste for it. Toward the end of his life he wrote to Herz Homberg, the tutor of his son Joseph: "As you know, a very special kind of education is required to find this exercise of the mind [viz. the *pilpul*] to one's taste; and though both of us received this education, we nevertheless agreed that we would prefer to see Joseph rather remain somewhat dull than trained in such a sterile kind of acumen."[43] He must have expressed himself in similar terms vis-à-vis his friend Friedrich Nicolai, for in his annotations to Mendelssohn's correspondence with Lessing, Nicolai remarked: "He [viz. Mendelssohn] learned in his early youth the art of talmudic/scholastic disputation and he acquired facility in it. This deplorable training increases the mind's subtlety but not sustained thinking, a deficiency that may be said to attach also to many a German speculative philosopher who indicates only endless and empty arguing."[44]

The strong boyhood attachment that Mendelssohn felt for Fränkel is most strikingly shown by the fact that, as his autobiographical note declares, he followed the teacher to Berlin. The exact circumstances of Moses' departure from Dessau can no longer be established. According to a report in David Friedländer's name, the boy begged his teacher to take him with him to Berlin; when this request was turned down because of his frail condition, the story continues, Moses stubbornly pursued his aim by walking a few miles ahead of Fränkel's coach, waiting for him on the road, and repeating his petition in so moving a fashion that it could not be resisted.[45] This report is flatly contradicted by Mendelssohn's own statement that he "followed" Fränkel to Berlin; had his teacher taken him with him, Mendelssohn would have mentioned it. Moreover, Fränkel did not go directly to Berlin. He moved first to Frankfurt an der Oder, where he was to occupy the rabbinate of the flourishing local community. He left Dessau for Frankfurt on June 10, 1743. On his arrival there, he learned that the acting chief rabbi of Berlin, the aged Rabbi Mordecai Tockeles, had died and that he, Fränkel, had just been appointed to succeed him as chief rabbi. This new "call" could be accepted without hesitation because the two communities of Berlin and Frankfurt had decided to unite under a single rabbinic head (as had been the case at some earlier period), with the chief rabbi residing in Berlin. Thus it came about that young Moses could begin to think of following his teacher to Berlin in order to continue his studies under him there.[46] In the autumn of 1743, shortly after the High Holidays, the fourteen-year-old Moses took leave of his parents and set out for Berlin.[47]

The Early Years in Berlin

By which of the many gates of the walled city[1] Moses of Dessau—as he now called himself—entered it, and precisely what happened at that gate, escapes our knowledge. The often-repeated story concerning the stern manner in which Moses was questioned by the gatekeeper[2] seems to be apocryphal, though such questioning would have been in accord with the legal provisions that governed the admission of nonprivileged Jews to Berlin in those days. For only the declaration that he intended to study under the chief rabbi could secure him the right of entry. The legislation then in force sought to prevent any "stealthy" increase of the local Jewish population. The maximum number of resident "protected" Jews had been fixed at a hundred twenty families and two hundred fifty domestic and public servants by the edict of 1737, when five hundred eighty-four persons were expelled. In 1743, the year in which Mendelssohn arrived, a check of the Jews' lists had just been undertaken. It had shown that three hundred thirty-three Jewish families were now resident in Berlin and that the total Jewish population amounted to one thousand nine hundred forty-five souls. No fresh expulsion had been ordered, but new restrictive measures had been devised. Jews in transit were admitted only for short periods, and the elders of the community were made responsible for implementation of the rules. They had to provide gatekeepers at the only two city gates, the Prenzlauer and the Hallisches Tor, through which Jews might enter.[3] These officials had to issue passes *(Passierscheine)* and to remove people whose presence was illegal.[4] The original of such a pass has been preserved. It is dated March 14, 1744, and signed by both the municipal gateclerk and the Jewish gatekeeper *(Thor-Steher)* Löbel Spier.[5] Since the gatekeepers were more or less permanent officials of the community,[6] it is possible to assume that it was this same Löbel Spier who had admitted the lad from Dessau a few months earlier.

By whatever gate, Moses came to Berlin in the third year of the reign of Frederick the Great and he died there in 1786, in the year of Frederick's death. Thus Mendelssohn's entire life, apart from his childhood years in Dessau, was spent under this monarch, who made Berlin the capital of the German Enlightenment but whose attitude toward the Jews was anything but enlightened. The purely economic considerations that had determined his predecessors' policy toward the Jews remained Frederick's guiding principle and were formalized in the edict of 1750.[7] The result of the measures enacted was a highly complex economic and social stratification of Prussian Jewry.[8]

Only a small group was in possession of a "general privilege," which conferred the right to settle in any of the localities open to Jews; the right to move from one place to another and to acquire houses; equality with Christian merchants in respect of commercial transactions; and the right of all children to inherit these privileges. A few members of this small class of Jews even possessed patents of naturalization, i.e., citizenship.

To the second class belonged the ordinary *Schutzjuden* (protected Jews), who had no right of mobility in settlement and in whose case only one son or daughter could inherit the father's status. A second son was granted "protection" only if he owned a sum of at least one thousand thalers, and a third son only if he owned two thousand thalers. A special fee had to be paid for the "concession."[9]

The third class comprised extraordinary *Schutzjuden,* i.e., Jews whose privilege was confined to their own person and was not transferable to a child. This group included physicians, painters, engravers, opticians, and other professionals.

The fourth group consisted of the officials of the community. When the Jews' lists were checked in 1743, the public servants of Berlin Jewry were one rabbi, two assessors to the rabbinic court, one chief cantor and one assistant cantor, three *Klöpper* (literally, "knockers," i.e., men appointed to call the male members of the community to the morning service by knocking at their doors), three beadles, etc., totalling forty-three people.[10] They were forbidden to engage in commercial activity but in other respects shared the status of extraordinary *Schutzjuden.*

The fifth class was not "protected" but merely "tolerated." Its members depended on the patronage of some member of the protected group. They enjoyed no "concession" of any kind, were barred from all commercial or professional activities, and were permitted to marry only into a family belonging to one of the two upper classes. To this group belonged those children of ordinary *Schutzjuden* who could not inherit the father's status, all children of extraordinary *Schutzjuden,* and the children of public servants.

The sixth and lowest class consisted of private employees. They were not permitted to marry and were allowed to stay in Berlin only for the duration of their employment.

When Moses of Dessau arrived in Berlin, he fell into none of the six categories. He was an unprotected foreign Jew whose sojourn was tolerated only because the community offered him board and lodging as a student of Talmud. Chief Rabbi Fränkel immediately took care of him by placing him in the hospitable home of the pious Hayyim Bamberg and his wife Gella, daughter of Senwil Halberstadt, a member of the rabbinic court.[11] The shy and lonely youth could not have found a kindlier foster home. Bamberg is mentioned in the record-book *(pinkas)* of the Berlin Jewish community as a man of wealth and Tora learning *(ha-kazin ha-torani)* and as one of the four dispensers of charity *(gaba'ey tsedaka)* who, according to custom, had also to take care of synagogue matters.[12] He was active in communal affairs from 1747 until 1753, and died in 1764.[13] The gratitude Mendelssohn felt for this man is reflected in the way his biographer Euchel described him, echoing praises he must have heard from Mendelssohn himself: he was "a generous, good-hearted man" who "loved the lovers of the Tora."[14]

As he had done in Dessau, Fränkel took charge of the physical welfare of his students in Berlin, though he does not seem in his new position to have presided over a Yeshiva. His letter of appointment makes no mention of his right to conduct a talmudic high school or of an obligation

on the part of the community to support students from out of town.[15]
The year 1743 in which Fränkel came to Berlin saw, however, the founding
of a Beth Hamidrash, which attracted a number of students from afar.
One of them was Naftali Levin (Rosenthal), of Raab, who later continued
his studies in Prague and eventually returned to his native Hungary.[16]
That he and Moses became close friends is evident from an exchange
of letters in 1776, long after their separation. From Mendelssohn's letter
one senses the atmosphere of piety in which they had studied together.[17]

It must be assumed that during his early Berlin years Mendelssohn
devoted most of his time to talmudic study in the Beth Hamidrash. He
earned a little pocket money by copying manuscripts for Fränkel, who
was then busy writing the second part of his commentary on the Palestinian
Talmud.[18] Moses' life was thus spent chiefly in a Jewish environment. But
this does not mean that he lived in a ghetto. Prior to the expulsion of
the Jews in 1572, the community was confined to a small piece of land
called "Judenstrasse" and "grosser Judenhof."[19] The new settlement was
no longer a ghetto in the physical sense. The area inhabited by Jews was
also the parish of Sankt Nicolai and of other churches in old Berlin between
the Spree and the Neue Friedrichstrasse, around the Molkenmarkt and
the Neuer Markt, in the large thoroughfares like the Spandauer- and Klos-
terstrasse and in the criss-cross of little alleys in this neighborhood. Here,
a few years later, Karl Ramler and Gotthold Ephraim Lessing were to
move from one apartment to another, and here, at the corner of the Mühlendamm and Poststrasse, Veitel Heine Ephraim, Frederick the Great's
Jewish mint-master, was to build for himself a palace in 1762–1765.[20]
Hayyim Bamberg's home, where Moses had his quarters, was situated in
this district, near the Molkenmarkt.[21] From here it was not a long walk
to the Heydereuther Gasse, where the synagogue, the Beth Hamidrash,
and the chief rabbi's residence stood.[22]

The synagogue must have pleased Moses' aesthetic sense. Fortunately,
we possess pictures of both its exterior and interior as they looked in
his time, before structural changes were made in 1818. A painting by
F. Calau shows a simple edifice which by its high and narrow windows
gives the impression of a church. The interior is presented in an engraving
that commemorates the visit to the synagogue by King Frederick William
I, the queen, and the crown prince (afterwards King Frederick the Great)
on April 20, 1718.[23] A contemporary of Mendelssohn described the Berlin
synagogue as one of the most beautiful in the whole imperial realm and
as not inferior to the famous Portuguese synagogue in Amsterdam.[24] Above
the entrance to the oblong edifice, we are told, a verse from Ezekiel (16:11)
was engraved in Hebrew letters. Inside there was delicately carved wood-
work, with many decorations and flowerpots. The holy ark contained a
hundred Tora scrolls, and the curtain hanging in front of it on festive
occasions was a gift to the community from Frederick William I. It had
been woven at the time of the Elector Johann Georg, and its silken texture

was emblazoned with the royal crown and coat of arms.[25] The report mentions the fact that the consecration of the synagogue in 1714 was combined with the wedding of the daughter of the *Schutzjude* Solomon Isaac, the embroiderer in gold and silver for the royal household, and that it took place in the presence of the royal couple and a large congregation. This was the synagogue in which Moses Mendelssohn worshipped for more than forty-two years, except for those occasions when he preferred to attend the shorter, less ceremonious service held at the chief rabbi's home.[26] In the same synagogue court-Jews, ordinary and extraordinary *Schutzjuden*, tolerated Jews, public and private servants—all prayed together. Here the unity of the Kehilla found visible expression.

It had taken a long time for the heterogeneous elements that had settled in Berlin (since the admission of the Viennese Jews in 1670) to overcome their rivalries and build one synagogue in place of the four previous houses of worship.[27] Even so, the Kehilla was oligarchic in its administration, governed by a group of wealthy and highly taxed members who constituted the "Council of the Parnassim," or elders, presided over by the senior elders *(Oberältesten).*[28] In this respect the Berlin Kehilla was no different from other communities of the period.[29] The democratic character of communal life expressed itself in the granting of voting rights to every taxpaying member. Not everybody, however, was eligible for election to office.[30] The premium bestowed upon wealth was, on the other hand, matched by the reverence paid to rabbinic learning.

Like other communities, Berlin was thoroughly imbued with the spirit of traditional piety. Rabbis of repute had exercised a considerable influence and created an atmosphere of Jewish culture. In 1701 Yehiel Michel, known as Michel Hasid, had come to Berlin to join Rabbi Aaron ben Isaac Benjamin Wolff in conducting a Yeshiva sponsored by the wealthy court-Jew Jost Liebmann, who was related to both rabbis. At that time Berlin was a center of talmudic studies. In 1709 Aaron Wolff was appointed chief rabbi of the community, and when he moved to Frankfurt an der Oder in 1714, Michel Hasid became his successor.[31] For a short while after the latter's death in 1728, the community had to put up with a rabbi imposed arbitrarily by the king,[32] but after this interlude there followed the glorious though brief period of 1731–1734, during which the famed Jacob Joshua of Cracow, author of the *novellae* on the Talmud called *Pene Yehoshu'a,* was rabbi of Berlin. And when he left Berlin for Metz, Mordecai Tokeles, a widely esteemed scholar and member of the rabbinic court, assumed the functions, though not the title, of a chief rabbi.[33] David Fränkel, himself a native of Berlin and a former disciple of Michel Hasid, needed therefore only to continue the old tradition. The establishment of a permanent Beth Hamidrash in the year of his taking office was clear proof of the community's desire to make Berlin a center of Tora learning once again. The atmosphere into which Moses entered was therefore conducive to the strengthening of his own desire for rabbinic study. That he used the opportunity offered

him is demonstrated by the competence that he achieved in rabbinic literature. The ease and lucidity with which he discussed halakhic topics in
his Hebrew correspondence with rabbinic scholars, and the expert manner
in which he phrased legal matters in his *Die Ritualgesetze der Juden* (1778),
were obviously the result of his studies under Rabbi Fränkel in Dessau
and Berlin.

The presence of his revered teacher in Berlin made the transition
from quiet Dessau to the hustle and bustle of the big city more tolerable
than it otherwise would have been. The change was nevertheless upsetting.
Having grown up in a poor family, Moses was used to hardship. His sense
of human dignity had, however, suffered no harm. Dessau was a compact
community, almost a large family, where all belonged together under the
patronage of the more privileged court-Jews. In Berlin the contrast between
rich and poor created social barriers. The cruel division of Berlin Jewry
into no less than six distinct classes accentuated the importance of wealth.
The government protected and tolerated Jews only for economic reasons,
not on humanitarian grounds. The result was that the Jews' self-esteem
became largely dependent on the economic factor, and the affluence produced in the upper strata of Jewish society was bought at the price of
a corresponding loss in spiritual refinement.

Moses was not insensitive to the defects he encountered among the
rich. His sympathies were with the poor. "I have found comparatively
by far more virtue among the poor, at least in my nation, than among
the wealthy," he wrote toward the end of his life.[34] With the *ketsinim* of
Berlin he had little in common, although eventually he himself achieved
a modicum of wealth, and he was on good terms with the financial aristocracy
once his standing as a world-famous philosopher was recognized as a great
social asset to the community. As a youth he was repelled by the ruthless
drive for material gain that he noticed in the ruling circles of the Kehilla.
He may have realized that it was stimulated by governmental policy, which
set a premium on successful industrial enterprise, the opening of new
factories, and the like. He deplored its effect nevertheless. He must also
have noticed that contacts between Jews and Christians in the economic
sphere did not entail any deeper human relationship. The situation brought
about by the government-sponsored mercantilism was well characterized
by Frederick William I's leading economic adviser, the Kammerdirektor
Hille: "*En matière du commerce* it makes no difference whether the trader
is a Jew or a Christian."[35] A kind of neutral ground of indifference to
religion was thereby established, but cooperation in the economic sphere
did not amount to any community of higher interests.[36] Contacts between
Jews and Christians remained on the commercial plane and lacked the
desire for a meeting of minds.

The purely instrumental character of the relationship was typical of
the Christian as well as the Jewish attitude. This essential mutual exclusiveness constituted the very nature of the ghetto as an inner form of existence.

There was missing the intellectual and spiritual bond that would have transcended the mere *matière du commerce*. What Mendelssohn achieved was the creation, within himself, of a rich interior world in which the Jewish heritage blended with the philosophy of the age, and which removed the barriers of the ghetto long before emancipation was considered in legal terms. What he dreamt of was not commercial success as the road to wider contacts but a wider intellectual horizon and the prospect of citizenship in the world of the Enlightenment. The vision of this goal did not come to him suddenly. Nor did he achieve it by his own unaided efforts: he was fortunate enough to find mentors to guide him. And yet the decisive impulse did come from within.

It was the continuation of his study of Maimonides that provided Moses' first link with the modern Enlightenment. The opportunity for such study was incomparably greater now because of the presence in Berlin of Israel ben Moses Ha-Levi Samoscz (ca. 1700–1772), a scholar named for the town in Galicia in which he had previously been active as a teacher. Mendelssohn could not have wished for a more competent guide to introduce him to a methodical study of Maimonides and other medieval Jewish philosophers.

An encyclopedic and penetrating scholar, Israel Samoscz was the last representative of the rabbinico-philosophical synthesis that had its heyday in medieval Spain but had survived into the sixteenth and, to a lesser degree, into the seventeenth century. Figures like Moses Almosnino (c. 1516–c. 1580) in Salonica and Obadya Sforno (1475–1550) and Juda Moscato (d. before 1594) in Renaissance Italy had worthily continued the Hispano–Jewish tradition. So had Joseph Solomon del Medigo (1591–1655), the disciple of Galileo, in the seventeenth century. A hostile attitude toward philosophy and secular learning had set in toward the end of the sixteenth century and continued into the eighteenth, due chiefly to the influence of Kabbala.[37] It is found in preachers like Menahem Lonzano, David de Bene, and Azarya Figo, to name only the important Italian figures.[38] But Israel Samoscz reincarnated the old spirit in a noble way. In his book *Netsah Yisra'el*, which appeared in Frankfurt an der Oder in 1741, he treated mathematical and astronomical passages in the Talmud. His commentary on the philosophical dictionary *Ruah Hen* (attributed to Jehuda ibn Tibbon) was published in Jessnitz in 1744. His excellent commentary, *Otsar Nehmad*, on Jehuda Ha-Levi's *Kuzari*, which he wrote in the house of the wealthy banker and patron of Jewish learning Daniel Itzig (Jaffe), was published together with the Vienna edition of the *Kuzari* (1796). He wrote a commentary on yet another celebrated work of medieval Jewish philosophy, Bahya ibn Pakuda's *Hovot ha-Levavot*, under the title *Tov Ha-Levanon*, which appeared, with the text, in Vienna in 1809. An astronomical treatise by him, entitled *Arubot Ha-Shamayim*, remains unpublished.

This remarkable scholar, Israel Samoscz, having come to Berlin in order to live in the more enlightened atmosphere of the burgeoning local

community, earned his living as a teacher at the *Lehranstalt* founded by
Veitel Heine Ephraim, the senior elder of Berlin Jewry from 1749 until
his death in 1775. Although Samoscz wrote only in Hebrew, he was known
in Christian circles. Nicolai described him as "a very able head and a great
mathematician who hit upon highly important demonstrations by his own
unaided thinking," and as one who also had "much poetic genius for Hebrew
poetry."[39]

Mendelssohn developed a close personal relationship with this eminent
scholar. He copied part of Samoscz' commentary on the *Kuzari*.[40] His own
masterful Hebrew commentary on Maimonides' *Millot Ha-Higgayon*
("Logical Terms") could hardly have been written had he not been a disciple
of Samoscz. Viewed in the historical perspective, Mendelssohn's preoccupation with Maimonides' philosophy signaled a return to the Enlightenment
spirit that had characterized medieval Judaism in one of its most significant
aspects. It is interesting to find that at about this same time an older relative
of Moses Mendelssohn, Naftali Hirsch ben Jacob Goslar (born in Halberstadt, ca. 1700), began to study Maimonides' *Guide*—at the age of fifty.
He too was a descendent of Simon Wolf of Vilna and Moses Isserles.
Having served as a *dayyan* on the rabbinic court in Halberstadt, he finally
settled in Amsterdam, where in 1762 he published a Hebrew philosophical
work entitled *Ma'amar Efsharut Ha-Tiv'it* ("Treatise on Natural Possibility"),
which seeks to refute the doctrine of prime matter and the deistic position.[41]

Mendelssohn soon realized that his intellectual curiosity was not completely satisfied by his immersion in the world of Talmud and medieval
Jewish thought. He sensed that Berlin had much more to offer him, once
he had acquired the intellectual tools needed to comprehend it all. In
1745 the Académie Royale des Sciences et des Belles-Lettres had commenced publishing its *mémoires* in French, the language patronized by the
king. Thus living in Berlin without knowing how to read and speak French
was tantamount to excluding oneself from participation in higher culture.
And if one desired access to both classical literature and learned treatises,
Greek and Latin had to be mastered. Above all, one had to learn to speak
and write a faultless German.

It was Mendelssohn's good fortune to be befriended by young Jewish
intellectuals who willingly guided him in his first halting steps toward the
realm of secular knowledge. Abraham Kisch, scion of an old and distinguished Prague Jewish family, became his tutor in Latin and for half
a year gave him daily lessons of about a quarter of an hour.[42] Born in
1728, Kisch was Mendelssohn's senior by only a year. He had left his
native city in 1745 to study medicine at Halle University, and then had
come to Berlin to frequent the *theatrum anatomicum* there. His stay in Berlin
lasted until the end of 1755. From 1756 until 1758 he was a medical
practitioner in Breslau.[43] He then returned to Prague, where he became
physician at the Jewish hospital. He and Mendelssohn remained friends
throughout the years. Doctor Abraham Kisch was one of the subscribers

to Mendelssohn's edition of the Pentateuch, and he is referred to in a Hebrew letter written by Mendelssohn on September 30, 1783, as "my friend and beloved, the expert physician, searching scholar, may God's mercy preserve and guard him."[44] Kisch's tutelage in Latin enabled the young Moses to make sufficient progress on his own, and to take advantage of a course in philosophy given in this language by Johann Philipp Heinius, rector of the Joachimsthalisches Gymnasium, who admitted him as a guest pupil.[45]

Another mentor of Moses' early years was Aaron Solomon Gumpertz, also called Aaron ben Zalman Emmerich (1723–1769), his senior by six years. In the autobiographical note written by Mendelssohn in 1774, only three people are mentioned: his father, Rabbi Fränkel, and Gumpertz—a clear indication of the importance that he attached to the part Gumpertz played in his life. After recording the fact that he had followed his teacher (Fränkel) to Berlin, Mendelssohn continued:[46] "Here, through my association with Herr Aaron Gumpertz, who later became a doctor of medicine (he died some years ago in Hamburg), I acquired a taste for humane letters [*die Wissenschaften*]. I also received from him some guidance toward them."

Gumpertz was descended from a much esteemed family of scholars, and his father occupied a leading position in the Berlin community.[47] In 1742 the young Gumpertz had commenced studying medieval Jewish philosophy, mathematics, and astronomy, besides Talmud, at the feet of Israel Samoscz. An ambitious and daring youth, he made himself known to some members of the Royal Academy and won their favor. The marquis d'Argens, a protégé of the king[48] and author of the *Lettres juives* (1736–1738) and *Lettres cabalistiques* (1737), among other works, took a liking to the intelligent young Jew. In his writings the marquis had praised Judaism as an essentially deistic religion that needed only a reformer, and it was not difficult for Gumpertz to win his confidence. Other patrons of Gumpertz were Pierre Louis Moreau Maupertuis, who became president of the Royal Academy in 1745, and the court chaplain, Isaac de Beausobre, whose critical history of Manicheanism had some influence on Gibbon and Voltaire.[49] Beausobre's son Ludwig invited Gumpertz to join him in Rector Heinius' Latin philosophy course at the gymnasium, at which Ludwig was a pupil from 1744 until 1748.

Originally, Gumpertz had planned to study under the famous literary theorist Johann Christoph Gottsched in Leipzig. In a high-flown letter, dated March 8, 1745, he had implored that "wondrous star" and "incomparable philosopher" to allow him the privilege to "suck the sweet milk of the humanities" under his direction. He offered in return his services as an attendant or secretary.[50] It was a rather pathetic application but Gottsched, with admirable generosity, invited the young man to join his household. Yet fate decreed otherwise. The outbreak of the Second Silesian War thwarted Gumpertz' hopes. Obtaining a permit for a Prussian

Schutzjude to stay in Leipzig would have required a petition to the Saxon court, an impossibility in the prevailing circumstances. Much to the relief of his parents—and to Mendelssohn's advantage—the young Gumpertz had to remain in Berlin. In his letter to Gottsched[51] he had mentioned the fact that, on the advice of his patrons at the academy, he had studied Latin. Since he did not refer to philosophy courses, it may be assumed that he started attending Rector Heinius' class only after his Leipzig project had come to grief. It was probably in the second half of 1745 that he accepted the invitation of the young Beausobre to study with him under Heinius. When he introduced Moses to his friend, all three young men took part in the course. This happened, it seems, early in 1746, after Mendelssohn had turned sixteen.[52]

Euchel reports that Gumpertz also taught Mendelssohn French and English,[53] but, according to Nicolai's testimony, Mendelssohn learned these languages "almost without any guidance," simply by plunging into the reading of easy texts with the help of a dictionary. In 1757 Nicolai encouraged him to study Greek by the same method.[54] Mendelssohn seems to have had the benefit of at least some initial guidance by Gumpertz in French and English. In his autobiographical note he said distinctly: "By the way, I never attended a university nor have I ever in my life listened to a *collegium* [university lecture]. It was one of the greatest difficulties that I took upon myself, to achieve everything by the force of strenuous effort and industry."[55]

The importance of the role that Gumpertz was destined to play in Mendelssohn's life lay less in the tuition received from him than in the contacts that Mendelssohn was able to establish through Gumpertz' help and, above all, in the example Gumpertz set. Here was a young Jew, rooted in community and tradition, who had ventured into the intellectual world and society outside them. "He who knows you more intimately, dearest friend," Moses wrote Gumpertz in June, 1754, "and he who knows how to appreciate your talents certainly does not lack an example of how easily happy minds bestir themselves without model [*Vorbild*] and education, develop their priceless gifts, improve mind and heart, and raise themselves to the rank of the greatest of men."[56] In Gumpertz, Moses possessed, in his most formative years, a *Vorbild*, an example that he, shy though he was, could strive to emulate. Moses' self-esteem as a Jew was strengthened by the combination of qualities he found in this accomplished young man. The rather exaggerated praise bestowed upon Gumpertz in the letter must be understood in the light of Mendelssohn's purpose in writing it. The letter was intended to rebut the denigration of the Jewish people by Michaelis (of which more will be said below),[57] and thus reflected the young Mendelssohn's deep concern about the image of the Jew in the eyes of the educated Christian. His Jewish pride was an essential part of his being, and a figure like Gumpertz raised his self-respect and inspired him by example.

Alas, Gumpertz never reached the goal he had set himself. He first

became secretary of the marquis d'Argens and, subsequently, of Maupertuis. In May, 1750, he went to the University of Frankfurt an der Oder,
where he studied medicine under Johann Friedrich Carttheuser. Medical
science being woefully underdeveloped in those days, it took him little
time to obtain a degree. Gumpertz was awarded the doctorate as early as
March, 1751, when he presented a dissertation entitled *De Temperamentis.*[58]
He returned to Berlin, started practicing as a physician, and took a lively
part in Jewish community life. In 1761 he moved to Hamburg. Suffering
as he was from a chronic bronchial disease and plagued by premonitions
of an early death, he wrote a tract *Megillat Setarim* ("Scrolls on Things
Concealed"), which tries to explain obscure passages in Abraham ibn Ezra's
commentary on the five scrolls of the Bible. The tract has attached to
it an essay on the value of science, entitled *Ma'amar Ha-Mada'.*[59] The work
is permeated with the spirit of traditional piety and, at the same time,
emphasizes the need to recognize the importance of the sciences.[60] It was
published at the time when the second edition of Mendelssohn's commentary on Maimonides' *Logical Terms* was about to appear. As a tribute to
his old friend, Mendelssohn inserted a reference to Gumpertz' work in
the introduction to chapter fourteen of the commentary: "Should your
soul, oh reader, long to know the nature and object of every science in
the way it has been enriched by modern scholars and has been augmented
by valuable discoveries since the time of the Master of blessed memory
[Maimonides], turn your attention to the *Ma'amar Ha-Mada'* composed
by the most learned master, the physician, our teacher Aaron Emmerich,
and knowing it will prove beneficial to your soul. . . ."[61]

Writing in Hebrew and for a Jewish reading public, Mendelssohn
could afford to be overly generous in his appraisal of Gumpertz' *opusculum.*
Besides, he recognized the pedagogical value of Gumpertz' effort to boost
secular studies and show their compatibility with religion. The spirit of
Israel Samoscz was reflected in Gumpertz' little tract, and it was to this
spirit that Mendelssohn paid homage.[62] Gumpertz died on April 10, 1769,
a disgruntled, bitter man who felt that he had become a burden to himself
and his environment. His depressions, Mendelssohn suggested, were due
to his physical sufferings.[63] Upon receiving news of Gumpertz' death, he
wrote with a sense of deep pity: "One is wont to judge an actor according
to the last tirade he declaimed."[64] The gratitude Mendelssohn felt toward
Gumpertz is well expressed in a letter he wrote to his fiancée in Hamburg,
where she had received some tuition from Gumpertz: "To him alone I
owe everything I have acquired in the sciences. It befits, therefore, nobody
but him to 'form' my other half and to make her conform to the first."[65]

The Budding Philosopher

According to Nicolai's report,[1] Mendelssohn caught his first glimpse of
a non-Hebrew philosophical work when, by chance, he came across Johann

Gustav Reinbeck's *Betrachtungen über die Augsburgische Confession:* "Here he found himself, all of a sudden, in a totally different world; for until then he had not the slightest conception of the theology of the Christians or of a philosophy more recent than Maimonides'. He was, therefore, irresistibly attracted by the philosophical part of Reinbeck's *Reflections* dealing e.g. with the proofs for the existence of God. He now wanted to know more about the new philosophy." This report has the ring of authenticity. Reinbeck's *Betrachtungen*[2] could well have aroused the interest of a young Jew brought up on medieval philosophy. Written in a lively style, the twenty chapters of part one treated the following subjects: that there is a God; that there is only one God who is One; that He is a Spirit; His infinity and immutability; His knowledge; His wisdom; His will; His power; His goodness and truth; His holiness and justice; His creation and providence. Only one chapter deals with the Trinity, while the Creation and Providence occupy seven. The whole work is written in a spirit of rationality and reflects the influence of the Enlightenment. In the preface to part three Reinbeck tells his orthodox critics that the truths founded on reason are "after all, likewise, precious divine truths," and that "one does not disgrace the truths of Holy Scripture by connecting them with the truths of reason." Should one denounce such a connection as "Wolffian," he would leave it at that.[3]

By a stroke of good luck, then, Mendelssohn's first encounter with Christian theology was with an enlightened specimen of it, one that had many points of contact with Maimonides and that had, at the same time, a contemporaneous quality. It gave him a sense of the clash between Wolff and his orthodox opponents and brought the Wolffian philosophy immediately to his attention. It also made him aware of the possibility of writing philosophy in German. For Reinbeck vigorously defended the use of the vernacular, rather than Latin, following again in the footsteps of Wolff, whose German writings had created a philosophical terminology in this language. It was in defiance of orthodox attacks upon Wolff's innovation that Reinbeck wrote: "If you speak of existence, concept, notion, or idea, one lets it pass; should you, however, be intent upon using your pure mother tongue, you are considered almost a heretic."[4]

We do not know how deeply the young Moses studied Reinbeck's work, but there can be little doubt that it made an impression on him. Otherwise he would not have spoken about it to Nicolai, whose report could have been based only on information supplied by Mendelssohn himself. It is not impossible, therefore, that his chancing upon the Reinbeck tract had a far greater impact on Mendelssohn than he himself realized. It may not merely have aroused his curiosity but may even have opened up definite vistas. We know what an ardent follower of Wolff he later became, and we also know how highly he praised Wolff's creativity in making the German language an adequate vehicle for the most precise philosophical thinking. In his appraisal of Wolff in these respects Mendelssohn was not far from Reinbeck's sentiments.

However, it was some time before Mendelssohn turned to Wolff. As Nicolai tells us, he discussed his newly awakened interest with Doctor Kisch, who emphasized the need to learn Latin, the lingua franca of philosophy. After mentioning that Mendelssohn received some Latin tuition from Kisch, Nicolai describes the immense labors that he undertook to master Latin texts. First, so he tells us, Mendelssohn applied himself to some of Cicero's writings, with which he had little success. He then studied a Latin translation of Locke's *Essay Concerning Human Understanding*, "which gave him much pleasure." Yet he had to look up almost every word in the dictionary, and often he had to guess at the correct meaning after long deliberation, before he could verify his guess by finding the appropriate term in the lexicon.[5] It was Locke, then, through whom Moses made his entry into the area of modern philosophy. For quite some time, as Nicolai points out in the sequel to his report, Mendelssohn remained unaware of any philosopher between Maimonides and Locke, until he was introduced to Leibniz and Wolff by Gumpertz. The lectures in Latin given by Heinius, an expert in the history of philosophy, no doubt helped Mendelssohn to gain a more comprehensive view of the subject.

When Mendelssohn met Lessing for the first time, in 1754, at the age of twenty-four, he had already acquired a firm orientation in philosophy. The hard, grinding years, during which he had had "to achieve everything by the force of strenuous effort and industry," lay behind him. His economic situation, which for some time had been extremely precarious, had taken a turn for the better in 1750, when he was appointed private tutor in the household of Isaac Bernhard, also named Berman Zültz, a prosperous silk manufacturer. The leisure and freedom from want that he now enjoyed enabled the budding philosopher to concentrate on the things he cared for most. We have no direct information on his daily life and pursuits during the period between 1746, when he attended Heinius' lectures, and 1754, when his friendship with Lessing began. There are, however, occasional remarks in his later writings and reviews that allow us some glimpses of that period. Some testimony to his struggles is provided, it seems, by a passage in one of his earliest works, the letters *On the Sentiments* (1755), which has an unmistakable autobiographical ring. Palemon (with whom Mendelssohn identifies his own mature self) assures his friend Euphranor:[6]

> These ideas are not merely the fruits of hard thinking in which the heart has no share. No! I speak feelingly, I speak from a live conviction.
> Ask our friend . . . who handed you this letter. He knows how near I once was to complete ruin. My feet slipped from the happy path of virtue. Cruel doubts in Providence tortured me like furies of hell; doubts even in the existence of God and in the worthwhileness of virtue, as I may confess to you without fear. I was ready to give rein to all base desires. Drunk with lust, I was in danger of falling into the abyss in which the slaves of vice descend to lower and lower levels as the hours pass. Come on, despisers of the true philosophy! Come on, shallow thinkers who regard every profound reflection as absurd! Save a single soul

from the jaws of perdition. Muster all faculties of your soul! Give good
advice! What was I to do? Nip the rising doubts in the bud? By what
means? Through faith? Wretched me! I tried, but can the heart believe
when the soul is in doubt? . . .

You fall into silence? Your loquacity, which had an answer to everything, is all of a sudden at a dead end. Your specious arguments have
evaporated into thin air, and you leave me to my misery? My thanks
are due to the faithful guides who led me back to true knowledge and
to virtue. To you, Locke, and Wolff; to you, immortal Leibniz, I set
up an eternal memorial in my heart! Without your help I would have
been lost for ever. I never met you in the flesh, yet your imperishable
writings—which are unread by the world at large and which I implored
for help in the hours of my loneliness—have guided me to the firm
path of the true philosophy, to the knowledge of myself and of my origin.
They have engraved upon my soul the sacred truths on which my felicity
is founded; they have edified me.

Here speaks the authentic voice of a young man who had found his
spiritual anchorage in the teachings of Locke, Leibniz, and Wolff. Having
passed through a period of severe crisis due to nagging doubts—something
perfectly natural in his case—he had been saved by his study of these
three philosophers. He was now sure of the "true philosophy," which
affirmed the truths of natural religion, viz. God, Providence, and virtue,
as the road to eternal felicity. His portrayal of the depravity that had
threatened to engulf Palemon need not be taken as a faithful mirror of
what he had personally experienced; it is difficult to say how much of
it is fiction, how much personal confession à la Augustine. At all events,
the salutary influence exercised upon him intellectually and morally by
the three thinkers had led him, as he points out, not only to the true
philosophy but also to a knowledge of himself and his origin. We interpret
this to mean that through natural religion he found his way back to himself
as a Jew. "I may say," he wrote in his *Letter to Lavater* in 1770, "that I
commenced examining my religion not just since yesterday. I recognized
very early the obligation to scrutinize my views and actions, and if, from
my early youth, I devoted my hours of leisure and recreation to philosophy
and belles-lettres, I did so solely and exclusively with the intention of preparing myself for this necessary scrutiny."[7] His sense of gratitude to Locke,
Leibniz, and Wolff was all the more sincere because the verities affirmed
by them agreed with what he considered to be the essence of Judaism.
He seems to have discovered this identity at the very start of his career
as a philosopher. A more explicit reference to it would have been out
of place in Palemon's account. The barest hint of the knowledge of himself
and of his origin had to suffice. Otherwise, the theme is indicated in its
broadest sense.

The conflict from which Palemon had suffered was the antagonism
between emotion and reason: "Those who have donned the armor of indifference are, perhaps, sufficiently safe against the attacks of reason and
are able to coerce their heart into submission, as it were. Did it, however,

rest with me to make myself happy in this way, or rather unhappy and enslaved? For is there any slavery harder to bear than the one in which reason and heart are at loggerheads with one another?"[8] In this formula the deepest concern of Mendelssohn's philosophy is expressed: to bring the cognitive and emotional forces of the soul into harmony. What repelled him in the "shallow" and "loquacious" *philosophes* of the French Enlightenment was their frivolity and their cult of reason at the expense of the heart. When he read Helvétius' *De l'Esprit* (1758), he entered these lines after the title in his copy of the book: "Die Eigenschaften dieses Bandes / Sind Witz, Geschmack, viel Phantasey, / Französische Sophisterey, / Und Wetterleuchten des Verstandes."[9] Locke, Leibniz, and Wolff had helped him to achieve peace of mind—to accept the just claims of reason without destroying religion. Pierre Bayle's subversion of natural religion no longer frightened him. When, in 1764, his friend Thomas Abbt conjured up the shade of Bayle, the "enemy of the systems" and "propagator of doubts," he replied by another invocation: "Oh spirit of the great Leibniz, who scatterest the doubts of the scribbler . . . even as the sun of the morn disperseth the shadows . . . lead me into the hall of eternal destiny."[10] Serenity of mind, widely acclaimed as a trait of Mendelssohn's mature years, is discernible in his very earliest writings. Certainly it is evident in Palemon's confession.

The books that "edified" him in his "hours of loneliness" were above all, we may assume, Locke's *Essay Concerning Human Understanding*, Leibniz' *Essais de Théodicée*, and Wolff's *Vernünfftige Gedancken* ("Reasonable Thoughts"), the last dealing with a variety of major themes, particularly in metaphysics and ethics.[11] He also studied Wolff's Latin writings, especially the *Ontologia*, his most fundamental work. An autobiographical reference to Moses' painstaking labors in this treatise may be seen in a passage in his *Philosophical Dialogues* in which two fictitious figures, Numesian and Kallisthen, discuss the fact that many authors go astray because they lack perseverance in their studies. "I for one," Numesian admits, "could never bring myself to read the entire *Ontologia* from start to finish with full concentration of mind," whereupon Kallisthen remarks: "From the very essay we have been talking about [namely a work by Prémontval (1716–1764)] examples can be adduced that show how easily the most subtle thinker can err if his knowledge of the *Ontologia* is inadequate."[12]

In another context[13] Mendelssohn quotes a passage from Alexander Gottlieb Baumgarten's preface to the third edition of his *Metaphysica* (1757): "I am glad it was my fate to have been brought up first among the opponents of this [Wolff's] philosophy, and to have grasped the arguments against it almost before I had understood its doctrines; for the result of this has been that I accepted several, indeed a great many, aspects of this philosophy only after careful and close scrutiny. . . . From this fact I now derive the advantage that I no longer have to waver and change my preferences every so often." Baumgarten then says of the principles of the Leibniz/Wolffian philosophy: "Once upon a time I rejected them; then I had my doubts about them; finally I pondered them and found them true." Mendelssohn's experience had been similar. In a postscript to this quotation he said: "Be glad! To us fate has been as well-disposed as it was to [Alexander] Baumgarten. Do you still recall the book of refutations we compiled after we had gone over Wolff the first time? Hardly had we reached the second half than we started to have our doubts. We read him through a second time, and our book was consigned to the flames." The person addressed and the story of the burning of the book are of course purely fictional, yet the gist of the remark is genuine. Like Baumgarten, Mendelssohn had passed through a period of rejection and doubt before he arrived at the conviction that the Leibniz/Wolffian philosophy was true, a conviction that left no room for further "wavering" because it was the fruit of much prior reflection and skepticism. The work by Wolff referred to by Mendelssohn is clearly the *Ontologia,* which consists of two parts.

Mendelssohn's attachment to Leibniz and Wolff was accompanied by a distinct feeling of contempt for the "superficiality" of the French *philosophes*. He conceded that the French "are in more recent times the best observers of human *mores*"; that "they describe the characters of men, and are sometimes capable of discovering hidden propensities and the recesses of the human heart that escape the most profound philosophers." They would do well, however, to keep within their limits. They ought to be stopped when they try to be philosophers *(Weltweise)* instead of remaining mere empirical observers.[14] It would be a thousand pities, Kallisthen tells Numesian, were Voltaire to triumph over Leibniz. "It altogether ill becomes our witty neighbors to set themselves up as judges in matters metaphysical. They are too fickle to read through a systematic treatise with due effort."[15] Not having produced a single metaphysical genius since Nicolas de Malebranche, the French realized that profundity was not in their line; therefore, Mendelssohn suggests, they made elegance of manner their only object and ridiculed those who gave themselves to profound reflections and who behaved somewhat clumsily in refined society. Even the few philosophers still left among them began to practice refined manners and, in the end, accomodated their thinking to the prevalent mode. They wrote books *pour les dames, à la portée de tout le Monde,* etc., and had a good laugh at the somber minds whose writings contained a little something more than things of interest to the fair sex.[16] This view of the French was fairly commonly held in Germany at this time,[17] but it is remarkable that Mendelssohn, a Jew, felt free to state it publicly as his own personal conviction—and to satirize those Germans who tried to copy the French.[18] He did not spare even Frederick II, a Francophile, when he reviewed the king's *Poesies diverses* (1760),[19] though he was careful enough to express his criticism in the most circumspect manner.[20]

Mendelssohn had a much higher opinion of the English who, he admitted, could boast of at least a few philosophers. David Hume he did not regard as one of the great ones. "Only Locke, [Samuel] Clarke, and perhaps Shaftesbury [the third earl] are in my view true philosophers," he wrote in 1758.[21] In general, he held the forte of the English to be psychological observation and analysis rather than metaphysics. "It would be desirable," he suggested in a review of Edmund Burke's famous enquiry into the origin of our ideas of the sublime and beautiful (1757), "that the English study our philosophy as profoundly as we consult their observations."[22] His summary verdict was that "the French philosophize with wit, the English with sentiment, and the Germans alone are sufficiently sober to philosophize with the intellect."[23]

Mendelssohn remained consistently of this opinion to the end of his life. In one of his last essays[24] he remarked: "In the first half of this century there reigned at German schools and in German writings a profundity [*Gründlichkeit*] of thought that became the distinctive mark of German literature. The Leibniz/Wolffian philosophy and the several controversies occasioned by it gave the concepts a solidity that our neighbors have not properly grasped even now. Sophistical writings of theirs, which they considered striking, had only to be translated into German to manifest all their feebleness and poverty." Mendelssohn must have developed this view of the relative merits of German, French, and English philosophy during his years of study prior to 1754, when he met Lessing and began to express it with the force of a long-held and deeply ingrained conviction. It seems that his thorough training in Talmud had so disciplined his mind that only a philosophy of the German type, a philosophy involving subtle distinctions and penetrating to the core of a problem, was able to satisfy him. Hence his praise of Wolff's ontology and his undisguised contempt for specious types of metaphysical discussion. Hence also his disgust with the Germans' lack of pride in their philosophers. When Isaac Newton died, he said, almost royal honors were paid him, while Leibniz, who was at least his equal, was buried with as little dignity as that accorded the lowliest inhabitant of a city.[25]

The thoroughness and precision with which Mendelssohn studied philosophy may be gauged from a remark he made in a critical review of contemporary trends in 1759:

Today one entertains the whimsical notion of teaching all sciences in an easy manner and *ad captum*, as one likes to call it. One believes in spreading the truth among the people thereby, and broadening it, at least, in all its dimensions, since one cannot add to its interior worth. Perhaps the Wolffians are somewhat guilty of this prejudice. Yet I think nothing is more harmful than this royal road to the sciences, which one claims to have found. Wolff presented geometry in an easier way than Euclid, and I wish I had never learned geometry from Wolff. The same great philosopher summarized his propositions and arguments concerning natural law to suit our convenience and has thereby mutilated them. Some of his followers have treated the most profound truths of his philosophy in an easy, perspicuous, and, *Deo volente*, also nice manner.

What was the result? One talked at all parties of well-bred people about the monads, the principle of sufficient reason, of the indiscernible, etc. These terms became fashionable. . . . Little did one care about the proofs of the propositions that had found acceptance, since one *wanted* to be convinced; still less did one consider the difficulties that the favored system solves and those following from it. Truth itself became a prejudice by the manner in which it was accepted. I would have preferred to see it attacked with utmost vehemence rather than to see it win a chilly approval by surreptitious means.[26]

The popularizing tendency of the Enlightenment could hardly have been condemned more severely than it was in this statement. Mendelssohn's stance was anything but that of a *Popularphilosoph*. All shallowness was anathema to him. Enlightenment itself, he believed, lost its value when passed around as a ready-made commodity instead of being the result of ever-renewed search and testing. For all his allegiance to the Leibniz/Wolffian school, Mendelssohn refused to be a slavish follower of its doctrines. In his very first published work he presented himself not only as an admirer of Leibniz but also as his critic.[27] Where there is a difference of opinion between Leibniz and Wolff, Mendelssohn takes a stand according to his own preference. What is even more important, he does not feel tied to the Leibniz/Wolffian school but is open to the influx of new ideas, particularly from the English empiricists. "It is one of the causes of the decay into which metaphysics has fallen," he wrote in 1759,[28] "that many followers of the great Wolff want to be mere professional metaphysicians. They possess a small stock of broad truths. These they classify at their convenience and arrange in chapters, now one way and now another. They explain, draw inferences, and demonstrate, perhaps correctly, according to the rules. One will, however, fail to come across any larger vistas of other sciences, any fruitful projects by which to give their coinage some wider currency in the republic of the learned. They dig in rich mines but leave the treasures where they found them."

Mendelssohn's earliest writings already opened up the larger vistas for which he pleaded in 1759. Though prompted by his metaphysical concerns, these writings cover such diverse fields as the nature of the sentiments, aesthetics, and the mathematical theory of probability. The many-sidedness of his interests was partly due to the stimulus provided by the annual publications of the Royal Academy. The subjects treated therein ranged over the entire field of knowledge: the physical sciences, mathematics, philology, belles-lettres, and "speculative philosophy," the last an area that a reform of the statutes (1744–46) had added to the other classes. Speculative philosophy comprised metaphysics (including cosmology, natural theology, psychology, and logic), natural law, moral philosophy, and the history of philosophy.[29] As a friend of Gumpertz, who for some time prior to 1750 was secretary to the marquis d'Argens and to Maupertuis, Mendelssohn certainly got to know some of the goings-on and behind-the-scene activities of the academy, which made its scholarly *mémoires* all the more attractive to him. His early writings show the extent to which the publications of the academy enriched and challenged his mind.

The earliest known literary effort of Moses Mendelssohn is a short fragment entitled *Von den ohngefähren Zufällen* ("Of Chance Happenings"),[30] which was found in one of his little notebooks[31] and is dated March 16, 1753. It shows the young philosopher—he was then twenty-three —brooding on the problem of theodicy, a subject that never ceased to engage his interest. Of the doubts that plagued Palemon/Mendelssohn "like furies of hell," those concerning Providence, we may recall, were mentioned first.[32] "One secretly reproaches the wise author of nature," says the fragment of 1753, "by holding this against him: would we not be happier if we were not subject to chance happenings, viz. (more precisely) if nothing unexpected came our way?" Mendelssohn does not say *which* philosopher, if any, formulated this particular objection to the workings of Providence. The conjecture that he was referring to an address delivered in 1752 by Prémontval to the academy[33] is refuted by the fact that whereas this philosopher saw in chance happenings the best proof for the freedom of God, he did not enter at all into the problem of theodicy.[34] It was probably Mendelssohn himself who "secretly" posed the question.

The answer he offered runs as follows: The unexpected is what follows from the total series of happenings and is, therefore, known only to God (the assumption being that the accidental is determined by an infinite causal series that only God can comprehend). To desire that nothing unexpected should befall us is tantamount, therefore, to desiring that God should have made us omniscient like himself. It may also be tantamount to desiring that the entire nature and nexus of things be such as to produce results pleasing to all human beings, in which case God would have had to create an entirely different world—one that might cause us to admire God's omnipotence but hardly his wisdom. Mendelssohn uses here notions borrowed from the Leibniz/Wolffian philosophy, viz., the definition of the contingent, the distinction between the power and wisdom of God, and the implied concept of this world as the best of all possible worlds. The notion of probability, which he later employed extensively in metaphysical contexts, is also found here for the first time.

This little fragment is important as a document of Mendelssohn's metaphysical preoccupations in his early phase (that before he met Lessing) but it gives only a very limited view of the range of problems that must have engaged his mind at the time. Considering that his "opus 1," the *Philosophische Gespräche,* was written in 1754, one has to assume that by 1753 his Spinoza studies, which led up to it, were already far advanced. The figure of Spinoza had a special fascination for him. Here was a fellow-Jew brought up, like Mendelssohn, in the tradition of medieval Jewish philosophy, who "despite his speculative doctrine could have remained an orthodox Jew, had he not, in other writings, contested authentic Judaism and thereby excluded himself from the Law."[35] Far from considering

Spinoza an outcast, Mendelssohn was attracted to him. He may even have dreamt of becoming a "second Spinoza," yet one who would avoid the mistakes of the original. He wanted neither to abandon his religion nor to teach a philosophy so controversial as Spinoza's. Lessing seems to have caught the sense of Moses' secret hopes when, in the autumn of 1754, he wrote about him: "I foresee in him the glory of his nation, provided his coreligionists permit him to mature. . . . His honesty and his philosophical mind make me anticipate in him a second Spinoza equal to the first in all but . . . his errors."[36] Mendelssohn was too deeply rooted in the Jewish community to be able to consider abandoning the fold, and Spinoza's apostasy most likely had the effect of strengthening his determination to remain loyal to the traditional way of life. Spinoza's metaphysical doctrine, however, seemed to him capable of an interpretation by which the stigma attached to it might be removed. It was with this idea in mind that he immersed himself in the study of Spinoza and the literature dealing with him.

Among Spinoza's critics Pierre Bayle had been the most damaging, though not the most severe. He had at least conceded the personal integrity and moral virtue of the much maligned thinker,[37] whom Pierre Poiret had described as an "abject" person and as a veritable incarnation of the "devil."[38] Bayle found in Spinoza's system "the most monstrous hypothesis imaginable, the one most absurd and most diametrically opposed to the most evident notions of our mind," and, precisely on that account, the one form of atheism least likely actually to mislead people.[39] This verdict he elaborated in his attack on the fundamental thesis of Spinoza's doctrine, which recognized God as the only substance in the universe and all other beings as merely its modifications. According to this view, Bayle maintained, God is no longer the perfect, immutable, blessed being that has always been held to be the essence of divinity, but rather an infinite being that embraces all the follies and iniquities of the human race. Bayle realized that Spinoza distinguished between the infinite and the finite, substance and modes, but he denied the merit of this distinction within the basic framework of Spinoza's system. Since all things are in God, Bayle argued, they are part of him, penetrate him, and cannot be separated from him. They are not like the changing costumes worn by comedians but inhere in God.[40]

Mendelssohn was not much impressed with Bayle's objections. In his opinion Bayle had, on the one hand, advanced a few sound arguments against Spinoza (e.g. by disproving the possibility of extension as an infinite attribute of God), but had, on the other hand, interspersed them with so many specious arguments and so-called consequences alleged to follow from Spinoza's presupposition that the force of his attack was thereby greatly weakened. He rightly accused Bayle of having been too facile in imputing to Spinoza views that Spinoza had explicitly disavowed, such as the one attributing imperfections to God.[41] It seemed to Mendelssohn that Bayle had, at bottom, only a superficial understanding of Spinoza, and that his critique had been motivated by "blind religious zeal," which in this particular instance is a term denoting anti-Jewish sentiment.[42] Because Bayle had not taken the trouble to prove his main charge against Spinoza, all his accusations, Mendelssohn suggested, served only to arouse the rabble against Spinoza.[43]

It is clear from these strong expressions that Mendelssohn felt almost personally involved in the hostility shown toward the Dutch Jew who "lived moderately, withdrawn, and blamelessly" and "denied himself all human pleasures and devoted all his life to contemplation."[44] He was glad, therefore, to find that Wolff, his revered master in philosophy, was not among those who abused Spinoza in the name of religion. "This great philosopher, before refuting Spinozism, shows it up to the best advantage. He presents its strongest points, and he thereby discovers its weakness in the best possible way. One who has read his refutation carefully will never feel tempted to agree with Spinoza."[45] As a follower of the Leibniz/Wolffian school, Mendelssohn could not but disagree with Spinoza. The best he could hope for was to find an angle from which to offer a new perspective for the evaluation of Spinozism. Here Wolff was of little help. Indeed, his strictures on Spinozism, though free from invective, were hardly less severe than Bayle's. According to Spinoza's philosophy, Wolff argued, religion has no place. To know God means to know the natural things through their causes. There is no divine Providence and no freedom of will, though man *is* more perfect when he lives according to reason, as Spinoza himself did. Hence Spinozism is hardly different from atheism; it is equally harmful and in certain respects even more harmful.[46] It was all the more imperative for Mendelssohn to try to show "the form under which Spinoza's doctrine is consistent with reason and religion."[47]

The time for a fresh approach to Spinoza, Mendelssohn must have felt, was propitious. In 1746 the Royal Academy had published a *mémoire* entitled *Examen du Spinozisme et des Objections de Mr. Bayle contre ce système* by Philipp Joseph Pandin de Jariges (1706–1770), an outstanding jurist, who would become Prussian chancellor and minister of state in 1755.[48] In this *mémoire* both Spinoza and his adversary Bayle were scrutinized. As the opening sentences of the essay explained, Bayle's objections had displeased several philosophers, some of whom had gone so far as to declare that Bayle had by no means understood the doctrine that he attacked and that, consequently, his objections were faulty. The author held no brief for Spinoza, whose system he regarded as "a tissue of impenetrable absurdities and monstrous contradictions,[49] yet he wanted to touch upon the principles that had escaped Bayle and to discuss Spinoza in terms of Spinoza's own notions. Mendelssohn was certainly familiar with de Jariges' calm and dispassionate attempt to settle accounts in the judicious way befitting a lawyer. It could, however, not satisfy him. The "purified Spinozism" that he ultimately discovered and the link between Leibniz and Spinoza that he believed himself to have established must have simmered in his mind before the friendship he struck up with Lessing gave him an opportunity to air them in debate and put them in writing.

Lessing

"In the year 1754," Nicolai reports,[1] "Moses Mendelssohn (recommended by Doctor Gumpertz as a chessplayer) became acquainted with Lessing, an event that turned out to be the most important step toward the cultivation of his philosophic mind and toward the proper use of his rare talents." In his annotations to the published Mendelssohn/Lessing correspondence he added the following details:[2] "Doctor Gumpertz had already been acquainted with Lessing at an early period,[3] and all I know is that Moses was introduced to Lessing at the beginning of the year 1754 by his friend Gumpertz. The junior Herr Lessing [Karl Gotthelf Lessing] says in the biography of his brother[4] that the latter's acquaintance with Moses came about through a game of chess suggested by a certain Isaac. This I never heard. I doubt, moreover, that the great chessplayer Isaac Hess (for he is obviously the person referred to) was in Berlin as early as 1754 or that he knew Lessing. So far as I can remember, he came to Berlin later, not before the Seven Years' War." Nicolai was right, for from Mendelssohn's letters to his fiancée written in November, 1761, we learn that Isaac (Itzig) Hess arrived in Berlin at just about that time.[5] It was, therefore, undoubtedly Gumpertz who brought Lessing and Mendelssohn together. Nicolai's dating of the event must also be correct, since he himself became the friend of the two "shortly after their relationship assumed a more intimate character"[6] and in all likelihood had a clear recollection of the time and circumstances of his first meeting with them.

The friendship that soon developed between Lessing and Mendelssohn, who were born in the same year (Lessing being the older by eight months), meant a great deal to both men. Though of entirely different background, temperament, and education, they had much in common: strength of character, a free and open mind searching for truth, and a sense of piety and respect for tradition. In a sense, both shared the critical spirit that Bayle had bequeathed to the eighteenth century and that tended to keep religion and philosophy apart. At the same time, both were averse to the flippancy and shallow sarcasm into which the *esprit* of the French *philosophes* had degenerated. In November, 1752, Lessing had returned to Berlin from Wittenberg, where he had earned a master's degree and, inspired by Bayle, had written his *Rettungen* ("Vindications") of misjudged figures of the Reformation period: Johannes Cochlaeus (1479–1552), Hieronymus Cardanus (1501–1576), the anonymous "Ineptus Religiosus," and Simon Lemnius. Cardanus had been stigmatized as an atheist and reproached, in particular, for having presented paganism, Islam, Judaism, and Christianity as four religions each of which contained a relative truth. Lessing showed that Cardanus' alleged statement "I leave it to chance which of these will be victorious" was a misreading of the text, yet he betrays a basic attitude of tolerance that anticipates, in a way, the fundamental thesis of his *Nathan the Wise*.[7]

Tolerance was in his blood, as it were. His grandfather, a city councillor and mayor of Camenz (Lessing's birthplace), had written a doctoral dissertation entitled *Über die Duldung der Religionsgemeinschaften* ("On Tolerating Religious Sects").[8] When Lessing, at the age of twelve, had to pass an entrance examination at the *Fürstenschule* at Meissen, he had to translate into Latin a text dealing with the question of how Christianity had modified the ancient prejudice against the "barbarians." Having completed his task, he added these sentences ex tempore: "Whatever we do, we achieve with the help of other people. Hence we are all 'neighbors' [*Nächste*]. For this reason we will not damn the Jews, although they damned Christ; for God Himself has said: Do not judge lest ye be judged. We will not condemn the Mohammedans, for among them, too, are good people. Hence, no one is a barbarian unless he be inhuman and cruel."

Small wonder that Mendelssohn immediately felt at ease in Lessing's company. His own plan to rehabilitate the much abused Spinoza was akin in spirit to Lessing's *Vindications,* and the two young men must have spent many an hour discussing Spinoza. The *Philosophische Gespräche* ("Philosophical Dialogues"), Mendelssohn's opus l, may be considered to reflect, to a considerable extent, the actual discussions they had on the subject.[9] To what extent Lessing had known Spinoza's thought prior to his friendship with Mendelssohn cannot be established with any degree of likelihood. It is possible that he had some inkling of Spinoza through Gottlob Mylius, with whom he had been closely connected for some time and who seems to have been a follower of Spinoza.[10] But it was undoubtedly Mendelssohn who introduced Lessing to a deeper understanding of philosophy in general and of Spinoza in particular.[11] Philosophy had not been Lessing's *métier*, it seems, though the only course of lectures he attended regularly as a student in Leipzig was a philosophical *disputatorium* conducted by Abraham Gotthelf Kästner. This teacher, who was at home in mathematics, the natural sciences, and philosophy, and who was also gifted as a poet, had instilled a love of philosophy into Lessing. The discussions with Mendelssohn revived this old love. They also helped to discipline his mind, which tended to roam freely about a vast variety of subjects and delighted in mental gymnastics, paradoxes, and novel ideas.[12]

For Mendelssohn the conversations with Lessing were of incalculable value, but not because they led toward "the cultivation of his philosophic mind," as Nicolai suggested. Mendelssohn was by far more advanced in philosophical training than Lessing. They benefitted him in another way. They set him free as a writer. He had acquired strong convictions in metaphysics and moral philosophy. He lacked, however, the courage to write because he was a yet unsure of the literary medium in which he might best express himself. How it happened that he composed the *Philosophical Dialogues*[13] is told in the well-known anecdote reported by his son Joseph:[14] Lessing gave Mendelssohn a certain treatise by Shaftesbury to read. When Moses returned the book and Lessing asked him how he liked it, he replied: Indeed, very much! This sort of thing I can, however, do myself. Lessing: Well, do it. Sometime later Mendelssohn handed him a manuscript with the request that he have a look at it. Several months thereafter he asked Lessing whether he had read it, whereupon the friend presented Mendelssohn with a printed copy of the *Philosophical Dialogues*. And thus, to his utter astonishment, Mendelssohn suddenly found himself launched as a German writer.[15]

That there is a kernel of truth in this anecdote can hardly be doubted. It becomes clear on closer inspection, however, that the turn of events must have been less dramatic than Joseph's story would have it. We may accept the first part of the story as true and assume, further, that the treatise by Shaftesbury was his dialogue entitled *The Moralists, or a Philosophical Rhapsody* (1709). It is also highly probable that Mendelssohn was enchanted by this exquisite piece of writing and felt that here he had come across a genre of philosophic prose that he could successfully imitate. Though he realized, as he was to put it later, that speculative matters are best presented in a "strictly systematic" form, he did not trust himself to do justice to this highly desirable way of expression.[16] When Shaftesbury showed him the possibility of using the dialogue form for a subtle philosophic inquiry, he immediately recognized his own ability to do "this sort of thing," and the result was his first book. Lessing probably arranged its printing without mentioning anything to his friend. But it can hardly be true that Lessing handed the printed book to the author: it must be assumed, surely, that he gave Mendelssohn an opportunity to correct, revise, and augment the text at the proof-stage.[17] It is unlikely, furthermore, that the book would have come out anonymously had not Mendelssohn insisted on this. Finally, Lessing was not even in Berlin when the book appeared and, therefore, could not have handed it to Mendelssohn at that time.

The book was published, at the latest, in the first week of February, 1755, for as early as February 14 an announcement in the official Hamburg gazette[18] reported that it had been published by Christian Friedrich Voss in Berlin. On February 18, Lessing sent Mendelssohn the page containing the announcement and inquired: "Have you read the review of your *Gespräche* in the gazette? Here it is. You may keep the paper."[19] The announcement briefly indicated the topics discussed in "this small, very well-written treatise," and remarked that the decay of metaphysics in recent times might be due, in some measure, to the soporific effect of most writings in this field: "We, therefore, present to our metaphysical authors these *Gespräche* as a model and, at the same time, as proof of the possibility of treating subjects of this kind in a graceful, ingenious, and attractive manner." The quality of Mendelssohn's style and the novelty of it in a work on metaphysical problems was recognized in the very first review. Lessing's notice appeared soon afterwards, on March 1, 1755, in the official Berlin gazette,[20] with which he was then associated as literary editor. It opened with this remark: "This small work . . . contains so many novel and profound things that it obviously must be the work of a man given more to reflection than to a desire to write. Perhaps another author would have made it into as many books as there are dialogues in it." There follows a pithy description of the major themes of the dialogues and Lessing's explicit approval of Mendelssohn's interpretation of Spinoza.[21]

It may be taken for granted that before sending the manuscript of the *Dialogues* to the publisher Lessing had gone over it carefully and improved its style. Although Mendelssohn had already mastered the German language by this time—in fact, both the fragment of 1753 and his earliest extant letters (dated 1754) prove that he wrote a correct and fluent German—he still found it hard, as Nicolai reports,[22] to express himself adroitly: "He labored with incredible tenacity to grasp, little by little, the character of this language, which was by no means his mother tongue. It is all the more admirable that, left entirely to his own devices, he achieved such considerable progress as the result of his exertions."

Nicolai saw a marked improvement in Mendelssohn's writings of 1757 as compared with those of the year before. In 1755, at Lessing's suggestion, Mendelssohn translated Rousseau's *Discours sur l'origine et les fondemens de l'inégalité parmi les hommes* (1753), partly in order to improve his facility in writing German. In July, 1756, he wrote to a friend:[23] "If the translation . . . did not displease you, attribute this to the intolerable carelessness that one is used to finding in all translations.[24] Yet I know full well that my ear is not yet sufficiently German to assess the weight of words and the regularity of syntactical construction. Herr Magister Naumann[25] has, on the other hand, been remiss in the correcting, which required due care. I shall certainly stop writing unless I find a Lessing who rebukes me in a friendly and tactful way whenever I am in danger of making a mistake." This letter shows how far from perfect Mendelssohn himself considered his German in 1756. It also confirms that Lessing had been most kind and helpful to him for as long as he stayed in Berlin, and that when Lessing left that city for Leipzig, around the middle of October, 1755, he had obviously asked his friend Naumann to take the polishing of Mendelssohn's Rousseau translation in hand.

Whatever the extent to which Lessing slipped phrases of his own into the text of the *Philosophical Dialogues*, the bulk of the work and the felicity of its tone belong to the author. It could only please and amuse Mendelssohn, therefore, when the reviewer in the highly esteemed *Göttingische Anzeigen* hazarded the guess that the anonymous author of the *Gespräche* was Lessing:[26] the "pleasant, sharp-witted, and entertaining" style of writing and some characteristic figures of speech would seem to indicate this. After a brief discussion of the topics treated in the book, the reviewer commented also on its forthright stand against the French *philosophes* and their German admirers: "For the French manner of scholarship or (in plain German) of well-bred ignorance, which finds so many servile imitators in Germany nowadays, the author seems to feel as much sympathy as we do."

The reviewer in the *Göttingische Anzeigen* was none other than Johann David Michaelis (1717–1791), the famous theologian and orientalist, who had been professor in Göttingen since 1745 and editor of the *Anzeigen* since 1753. He had a high appreciation of Lessing and had taken his side in the conflict between him and Samuel Gotthold Lange, whose translation of Horace's *Odes* (1752) Lessing had dared to condemn.[27] Michaelis' guess that Mendelssohn's anonymously published *Gespräche* were by Lessing amounted, therefore, to a great compliment. It was all the more satisfying to Mendelssohn because of an incident that had involved him, Michaelis, Lessing, and Gumpertz just a year before.

The *Göttingische Anzeigen* of June 13, 1754, had carried a review by Michaelis of Lessing's *Schriften* criticizing his early comedy *Die Juden* ("The Jews"), in which a Jew is portrayed as a man of culture and noble virtue. Lessing had written the comedy in 1749 during his first stay in Berlin, and the amiable figure of the Jewish traveler who saves the life of a Christian baron may have had Doctor Gumpertz for its model.[28] It was not the first time that the German theater had pleaded for fairness toward the Jew. In 1746 Gellert's *Swedish Countess* had presented the figure of a Polish Jew with the avowed purpose of showing that even among Jews there are good people.[29] In Lessing's drama the traveler answers the anti-Semitic invectives of a person who turns out to be a rogue by saying with a heavy heart: "I wish to God this was but the language of the rabble!" The magnanimity of the traveler prompts the baron to exclaim: "Oh, how worthy of esteem would the Jews be if they resembled you!" Whereupon the Jew replies: "And how worthy of love would the Christians be, if they all possessed your qualities!" The moral of the story is clear: good and bad people are to be found among both Jews and Christians. Lessing had made a serious plea for tolerance in the guise of a light-hearted comedy.

In his review Michaelis pointed out that there was a defect in this presentation: the traveler was too perfectly good, generous, considerate, and educated, for surely it would be most difficult though not necessarily impossible, to find such a noble character among a nation that was bound to be hostile, or at least cool, toward Christians as a result of its principles, manners, upbringing, and the bad treatment it was receiving at the hands of Christians. The more he wished that the play's noble portrait of the Jews were true and real, the reviewer continued, the more the improbability of the imaginary Jew of the play interfered with his enjoyment of it. Even an average degree of virtue and honesty was so rare among this nation, Michaelis added, that the few virtuous exceptions could not diminish the hatred of Jews generally to the extent that one would wish. Nor was honesty to be expected in a people that almost without exception had to make a living from trade, a way of life offering more opportunity and temptation to cheat than any other.

Mendelssohn's sense of dignity and pride was deeply hurt by Michaelis' review. He undoubtedly discussed the most appropriate manner of reply with Lessing and Gumpertz. It was decided that he would express his indignation in a letter addressed to Gumpertz, and that this letter would be published by Lessing, together with a rejoinder of his own, in his *Theatralische Bibliothek*—without, however, indicating the identity of either the writer or the recipient of the letter. No time was lost. Toward the end of June, 1754, Mendelssohn wrote his epistle of protest. After a brief summary of the review, he unburdened his heart:

> What a humiliation for our hard-pressed nation! What an exaggerated contempt! The rabble among the Christians has always regarded us as the scum of nature, as the sore of humanity. Yet of learned people I expected a fairer judgment.... In truth, how can a man in whom a sense of honesty is left have the impudence to deny a whole nation the probability of being able to show a single honest man? A nation from which all prophets and the greatest kings arose, as the author of *The Jews* declared? Is his cruel verdict justified? What a shame for the human race! Is it unjustified? What a shame for him! Is it not enough that we have to suffer the most bitter hatred of the Christians in so many cruel ways; are these injustices against us also to be vindicated by defamation? Let them continue to oppress us, let them restrict our existence among free and happy citizens, let them even go on exposing us to the derision and contempt of the world, so long as they do not altogether deny us virtue, the only solace of hard-pressed souls, the only refuge of the forsaken.

Mendelssohn admitted that a playwright had to take popular prejudice into account when devising his dramatic effects. The unexpected character of the Jew produced a dramatic effect and was, therefore, in place, although it was deplorable that the simple truth—that the Jews, too, are human beings—should be considered a startling discovery. The entire Jewish nation owed a sense of obligation to the author of the play for his attempt to convince the world of a truth of great importance to it. Since Michaelis' review was unsigned, Mendelssohn could feign ignorance of the identity of its author and all the more easily castigate the Christian theologians: "Is it possible that this review, this cruel damnation of souls, was written by a theologian? These people believe that they greatly promote the Christian religion by declaring all non-Christians to be foul assassins and highwaymen. I am far from imputing such a disgraceful view to the Christian religion; it would undoubtedly be the strongest proof against its truth if in order to establish it all humaneness had to be disregarded."

He then entered into a critique of the substance of Michaelis' view of the Jews. Was it really incredible that a noble character such as that depicted by Lessing could be found among this nation? Was not the addressee of the letter (Gumpertz) a shining example of a Jew's ability to elevate himself to lofty heights? Would he not have played the part of the Jew in the drama, had he found himself in a similar situation in actual life? It would, however, be tantamount to degrading the Jewish people if he were to go on offering individual instances of noble-minded Jews. He did not mean to deny that the Jews had their faults. Yet he maintained that certain human virtues were more common among Jews than among Christians. There was no case of homicide one could cite against them (professional thieves excepted). Jews were compassionate and charitable toward the poor of "both nations" (i.e., both Jews and Christians). Jews were industrious, temperate, and mindful of the sacredness of marriage. Their social virtues alone were sufficient to refute the *Göttingische Anzeigen,* "and I pity anyone who can read such a wholesale condemnation without shuddering," Mendelssohn said in conclusion.[30]

Lessing published the full text of the letter in his *Theatralische Bibliothek.*[31] By way of preface he expressed his own reaction to the review: one had to distinguish between two points, namely, the alleged improbability of the figure in the play and the improbability of finding an honest, noble-minded Jew in real life. In the play, the circumstances of the traveler were such as to remove any cause for ill-feeling toward the Christians, assuming that the reviewer's analysis of the causes of such animosity on the part of the Jews were correct. The traveler was a well-to-do, educated man, not a miserable, oppressed creature. To say that a man in his position was unlikely to be virtuous simply because he was a Jew indicated a prejudice, and Lessing had written the play precisely with the object of weakening this prejudice. It could be attributed only to pride or hatred, and it placed the Jew not merely among uncouth human beings but below the level of human kind. It had not been the purpose of the play to suggest that all Jews or the majority of them were honest and generous. The character of the traveler would be a rarity even if he were a Christian. Now, in the same way in which the traveler in the comedy was plausible in view of his particular circumstances, Jews of similar character were not improbable in actual life, if they were placed in a similar situation. "Of course, in order to believe this one has to know the Jews more closely than merely from the rabble that roams about the fairs." He then added: "I would, however, rather let another speak whom this matter touches to the heart, one of this very nation. I know him too well to deny him here the testimonial that he is a man as spirited as he is learned and honest. He wrote the following letter in response to the Göttingen review to a friend among his nation whose good qualities equal his. I anticipate a reluctance to believe this and an inclination to assume that this letter is a fiction of my own, but I am prepared to convince irrefutably anyone who is concerned about its authenticity. Here it is."

In a postscript to the letter Lessing wrote: "I also have the answer to this letter before me. I hesitate, however, to reproduce it here in print. It is written with too much heat, and the retorts to the Christians are a little too lively. Yet one should believe me when I say that both correspondents acquired their virtue and scholarship without the help of riches, and I am convinced that many more among their people would follow their example, if only the Christians permitted them to raise their heads."[32] In a personal letter to Michaelis, written on October 16, 1754, Lessing once more stressed the authenticity of the letter. Michaelis replied in the *Göttingische Anzeigen* for December 7, 1754: in sum, he left the final judgment to his readers. He had not suggested that the character in the play was impossible, merely very improbable. Experience had shown, moreover, that even Jews in happy circumstances were not free from a certain coldness toward Christians—a coldness caused by the way in which they were being treated by Christians.[33] Mendelssohn must have been pleased with the attention that (thanks to Lessing's warm-hearted cooperation) his impassionate plea had received. His letter to Gumpertz may be described as his first public utterance on behalf of his people and as a fitting prelude to his career.

When half a year later, on May 29, 1755, Michaelis' review of his book appeared, Mendelssohn felt impelled to thank him for his "kind judgment." On September 7 he wrote to him to this effect. In the meanwhile his opus 2, the letters *Über die Empfindungen* ("On the Sentiments"), had appeared. They were published in the late summer of 1755 and announced by Lessing in the official Berlin gazette[34] on September 4. With his letter to Michaelis, Mendelssohm enclosed a copy of the new work—"a few sheets *on the sentiments*," with which he had again recently "ventured into the world of the learned"—and he asked the professor for the favor of mentioning his view of it in one of his letters to Lessing. His approval would please the author, his censure would instruct him. Though seemingly trivial and threadbare, this compliment, he assured Michaelis, was candid, coming as it did from a Jew whose "temporal circumstances" made it imperative for him to be known to all but a very few friends as a mere clerk.[35] That is, he asked Michaelis not to disclose the identity of the author of the two books (the second work had also appeared anonymously).

Michaelis' response was a generous one. On October 2 he published the following note in the *Göttingische Anzeigen*:[36]

> We have since learned who the true author is and shall shortly announce another piece of writing by him. Though we still hesitate to disclose his identity (seeing that he himself informs us of the necessity, in view of his temporal condition, not to be known as a writer except to a very few friends), we should not conceal from our readers the fact that in respect of his way of life he does not by any means belong to the scholarly world, and that one should not look for him among those who profess Christianity but among the Jews. This information has still further enhanced our pleasure in his book, since we had previously paid attention only to the subject matter and style, not knowing from what an unexpected sort of author this accomplished book had come forth.

A highly favorable review of Mendelssohn's second work appeared in the *Göttingische Anzeigen* for October 9, 1755. The book, it said, revealed a most reflective and philosophical mind, and it showed the author to be a disciple and defender of Leibniz and Wolff. His love for the Wolffian philosophy was probably responsible in part for his praise of the Germans and for his deprecatory remarks about the French and even the English. The way he spoke of metaphysics was "very noble" and indicated, to a perceptive ear, "the language of the heart."[37] The reviewer marveled at the fact that at a time when being called a Wolffian was no longer considered an honor the Wolffian philosophy counted some of the finest minds among its followers, whereas before, when it commanded universal admiration, its only spokesmen were babblers. "The disciples Wolff has raised after his death are better than most of those he saw in his lifetime." Michaelis, whose strength lay in theology and linguistics, was not fully qualified to assess the significance of of Mendelssohn's writings. A few points of criticism that he raised were interesting but not very important. What mattered was the fact that the *Göttingische Anzeigen* had taken notice of the anonymous Jewish writer and had acknowledged him as one of the "finest minds" among contemporary philosophers. In this respect Michaelis had shown a remarkable degree of discernment. His judgment may have been partly influenced by Lessing's high opinion of Mendelssohn. That opinion helped, at any rate, to establish the reputation of the new star that had risen.

The second work reflected in an even larger measure than the first the impact that Shaftesbury's *The Moralists, or a Philosophical Rhapsody* had had on Mendelssohn. The fictional device of the preface makes this immediately apparent. Palemon, the dominant figure of the letters *On the Sentiments,*[38] is introduced as "an English philosopher and namesake of the amiable enthusiast known from the *Rhapsody* of the earl of Shaftesbury." He is said to have left his country in order to study philosophy in the most thorough way in Germany. To be sure, he had found that in Germany, too, a frivolous manner of philosophizing had begun to spread, but he had met, here and there, some honest philosophers who, living in seclusion, upheld the old tradition of preferring right thinking to free thinking. Palemon, the preface continues, made friends with some young noblemen, in particular with one named Euphranor, with whom he spent many hours of discussion in some remote little place. When they parted company, their exchange of views continued by way of correspondence. The subject of their debate was "the nature of pleasure." Their letters had happened to fall into the present writer's hands and now were being made accessible in print.[39]

Mendelssohn could not have expressed more clearly his intention to adopt the literary form of Shaftesbury's work. He was one of the first in Germany to be enchanted by the great Englishman, who "allowed emotion to permeate the whole of his personality."[40] In the stylistic device of epistolary discussion employed by Mendelssohn, and in the very color and tone of his writing (portrayals of rural scenery, profuse expressions of friendship), we easily recognize Shaftesbury's influence. The content of the work has, on the other hand, very little to do with the English model. Palemon has, after all, left his country, as the fictional preface tells us, to study German philosophy. In him we meet Mendelssohn's self-portrait as it were, and in Euphranor, who spent many hours of discussion with him, we hear echoes of Lessing. The philosophy that Palemon represents is, of course, of the Leibniz/Wolffian type, as Michaelis rightly diagnosed, but it has a texture far richer than that. As will be shown further below, Mendelssohn's work was to a large extent an answer to Johann Georg Sulzer's *Recherches sur l'origine des sentiments agréables et desagréables,* which had appeared in 1753–1754 among the *mémoires* of the Royal Academy.[41]

It was probably in the spring of 1755 that Lessing introduced Mendelssohn to Sulzer.[42] A happy relationship was to ensue from this meeting. Sulzer, a Swiss by birth, was chiefly interested in the philosophy of art, and had joined the Berlin Academy at the invitation of the king. He was a warm-hearted man and a great admirer of his royal patron, whose victories in the Seven Years' War (1756–1763) he described with gusto and a great deal of expertise in letters to his friend Martin Künzli in Winterthur.[43] He could recognize the quality of beauty in algebraic formulae, mathematical theorems, metaphysical systems, and military expeditions as much as in works of art.[44] An indefatigable letter writer, he corresponded with many such notable figures as Bodmer, Gleim, Zimmermann, and Haller. A letter written to Bodmer in November, 1755, records his meeting with Mendelssohn: "Herr Lessing visited me several times during the last six months. . . . Through him I made the acquaintance of a Hebrew young man, a most vigorous thinker [*einen starkdenkenden Kopf*]. He wrote the letters *On the Sentiments,* which I enclose herewith. This circumcised one should serve me as a tenfold substitute for Ramler, whom I see but rarely."[45]

That Lessing had visited Sulzer several times from about the beginning of May, as the letter indicates, makes it seem probable that Mendelssohn was introduced to Sulzer long before the appearance of the letters *On the Sentiments* caused him to mention to Bodmer his personal acquaintance with the young Jew. This seems all the more likely in view of the fact that by the time of Lessing's departure from Berlin in October, 1755, Mendelssohn was already on sufficiently good terms with Sulzer to be introduced by him to Maupertuis, the president of the academy. He reported this to Lessing in a letter written soon after he had gone to Leipzig: "Today I visited Sulzer. He is a thoroughly good man, and tomorrow we shall visit Herr v. M."[46]

Though Mendelssohn's book contained some obliquely polemical and slightly frivolous references to his *Recherches,* Sulzer was broadminded enough not to take offense.[47] The high opinion he had of the bright young man is evident also in his asking him to write some critical notes on the manuscript of his *Essai sur le bonheur des êtres intelligens,* which was to appear among the *mémoires* of the academy in the following year. This Mendelssohn did. His annotations[48] are similar in spirit to the objections to Sulzer's

Recherches found in the letters *On the Sentiments,* but they are cautiously prefaced by the remark: "It may well be the case that I have not properly grasped the highly abstract notions of the Herr Professor."[49] Mendelssohn obviously felt ill-at-ease in the role of critic when he was personally confronted with the one being criticized, whereas he had been completely uninhibited when dealing with Sulzer's views prior to meeting the author personally. In the case of a young man vis-à-vis a prominent academician this diffidence was perfectly understandable. It was characteristic of him, moreover, to be more outspoken in his writings than in personal conversation. Lavater said of Mendelssohn, in his diary on April 7, 1763, that he was "more modest in his talk than in his writings."[50] Sulzer appreciated his notes and made use of them in his *Essai.*[51]

Soon after they became friends Mendelssohn and Lessing undertook a joint literary venture. In 1753 the Royal Academy had announced the subject of a prize-competition for 1755: What was the precise meaning of the statement "All is good," made by the English poet Alexander Pope in his "system" (*An Essay on Man*)? How did it compare with the "system of optimism" or "choice of the best," i.e., Leibniz' doctrine that this world was the best of all possible worlds? And what arguments could be advanced for or against this "system"? The choice of subject was prompted by the hope that an essay refuting Pope would win the prize and that a blow would thereby be dealt to the prestige of Leibniz, whom an influential group within the academy (Maupertuis, Euler, Count Dohna, and others) regarded as too speculative. As in previous years, the anti-Leibnizian faction, which favored Newton, had succeeded in making the examination of a Leibnizian doctrine the crucial issue of the prize-competition. Sulzer, a Wolffian and thus an admirer of Leibniz, had opposed the choice of subject and, having been defeated, had asked his friend Martin Künzli to take up the cudgels for Leibniz by writing an essay and winning the prize. He was sure of victory, since the majority of members in the philosophic class of the academy was pro-Leibniz.[52] He had no inkling of Lessing's and Mendelssohn's plan to enter the competition. The two went about their project in all secrecy. They did not have much time, since the deadline for delivery of essays was January 1, 1755. They decided to satirize the theme as an illicit attempt to raise Pope, a didactic poet, to the rank of a philosopher on a par with Leibniz. Lessing would show the absurdity of ignoring the difference between philosophy and poetry, Mendelssohn would analyze the two distinct types of optimism represented by Leibniz and Pope. The plan was carried out most brilliantly, and the essay was given the challenging title *Pope ein Metaphysiker!* ("Pope a Metaphysician!").

The delightful irony displayed by Lessing is matched by a playful fiction devised by Mendelssohn. Against his better knowledge he denied that Pope's concept of the great chain of being, "Where all must full or not coherent be, / And all that rises rise in due degree,"[53] was shared by Leibniz. In fact, Leibniz had expressed this famous and widely prevalent notion in several of his writings and most forcefully in a letter to the mathematician Jacob Hermann. However, the authenticity of this letter had been publicly denied only a short while ago, in 1752, in a pronouncement of the Royal Academy. The reason for the denial was the wounded pride of Maupertuis, who actually had had no real cause to feel insulted. The Dutch Professor Samuel König, a member of the academy, had pointed out in an article that Maupertuis' theory known as "the principle of least action" had been anticipated by Leibniz in a letter to Hermann. No charge of plagiarism was involved, since the existence of Leibniz' letter had not been known before. Yet Maupertuis took it to imply just this and demanded that the letter be shown to him. Unfortunately, the original of the letter could not be produced—it has been discovered since[54]—and König was flatly accused of having committed a forgery. A scandal of the first magnitude ensued, as a result of which Voltaire, who had taken a strong stand on behalf of König and had vilified Maupertuis, was forced to leave Berlin.

Mendelssohn, who took a lively interest in anything that concerned the academy, may be presumed to have condemned the ruthlessness with which Maupertuis and his party had acted against König. Members of the academy like Sulzer and Prémontval held the same view: they were convinced that the letter was authentic. Its full text had been published by König, and Mendelssohn noticed that it contained, among other things, a striking affirmation of the concept of the scale of all creatures, from the lowest to the highest, as a continuous progression without a break. Therefore he could not have doubted that Leibniz and Pope agreed on this point. Incidentally, the very same notion had been expressed by Lessing in an unfinished manuscript entitled *The Christianity of Reason* (1753), which was intended as a rational vindication of the trinitarian dogma.[55] He and Mendelssohn seem to have spent many an hour arguing the legitimacy (or otherwise) of the speculative effort to prove the truth of Christianity, and to judge from a letter Lessing wrote to Mendelssohn many years later (on May 1, 1774),[56] Lessing had yielded to his friend's objections and abandoned his *Grillen* (fancy ideas). As for the concept of the infinite scale of being, one that knows no gap or leap, there was of course complete agreement between them. It is all the more astonishing to find that in *Pope ein Metaphysiker!* Mendelssohn rejected this view as un-Leibnizian.

One cannot explain this except by assuming that Mendelssohn did so deliberately in order to embarrass the faction in the academy that had mistreated König and set out, by its choice of subject for the competition, to undermine Leibniz' authority still further. Mendelssohn's strategy for playing this joke on the academy was apparently as follows: the text of the Leibniz letter published by König was widely known and it contained the doctrine of the great chain of being; by denying that Leibniz held to this doctrine Mendelssohn could expect to arouse protests from all those who believed the letter to be authentic. In this way the old conflict between Leibnizians and anti-Leibnizians in the academy would likely be renewed, to the discomfort of Maupertuis and his faction.

However legitimate this procedure may have seemed from a moral point of view, Mendelssohn and Lessing soon decided that it would be unwise to submit an essay of this kind to the academy. Lessing had good private reasons not to offend Maupertuis,[57] and Mendelssohn, whose published work had so far been shrouded in anonymity, had no desire to gain publicity, let alone to make enemies. They resolved, therefore, to forego the chance of winning the prize of fifty ducats and to publish their polemical tract anonymously on their own.[58] It appeared in the late autumn of 1755. In the meantime, the academy's prize had been awarded, much to Sulzer's chagrin, to a rather mediocre essay by a certain Adolph Friedrich von Reinhard, whose purpose was to refute Leibniz and the philosophy of optimism. But by publishing their essay before Reinhard's treatise had been edited and published by the academy, Mendelssohn and Lessing stole a march on the academicians. The anonymous work was like a bombshell and could only please the Leibnizians. Sulzer and his Swiss friends were dissatisfied, however, because Künzli had been defeated, and they accused "the author" of having tried to prove too much on the one hand and too little on the other. His way of reasoning, they felt, approached chicanery.[59] They apparently took the essay to be the work of a single author, despite a clear statement to the contrary in the preface. As Mendelssohn wrote to Lessing, on November 19, 1755, Sulzer had asked him several times whether there was anything good in the treatise, and he seemed to blush a little when Mendelssohn replied that it had pleased him. Nobody admitted having written *Pope ein Metaphysiker!*[60] On December 26, Mendelssohn inquired of Lessing: "Who can have told Prémontval that you are the author of *Pope ein Metaphysiker!* I said I knew nothing about it."[61] It seems that nobody suspected that Mendelssohn had written a large part of the work.

The joint prize-essay project gave Mendelssohn and Lessing ample opportunity for discussion and for the deepening of their respect and affection for each other. A little note found among the papers left by Lessing tells us of yet another joint enterprise, albeit one that did not come to fruition.[62] Lessing wanted to publish a periodical entitled "The Best Found In Bad Books." Mendelssohn contributed a few "beautiful" pieces from some "bad" compendia of the Cartesian philosophy, and the first number was ready for publication. Lessing was, however, afraid of not being able to sustain a flow of suitable material and therefore canceled the project.[63]

Before Lessing left Berlin in October, 1755, he made Mendelssohn promise to translate and critically evaluate Rousseau's *Discours* on the origin of inequality among men and on the question whether the natural law sanctioned this inequality (1753).[64] The translation as such was to be an exercise in the fluent use of the German language; the critical part was meant to follow up the discussions they had had on the subject. In order to commit Mendelssohn to the task, Lessing published in the official Berlin gazette for July 10, 1755, a rather premature announcement of the expected translation, referring to it as the work of "a man of understanding and good taste."[65] Toward the end of October Mendelssohn reported: "My Rousseau is completed. I shall present the promised appendix in the form of an epistle [*Sendschreiben*] addressed to Herr Magister Lessing, in order that you may read at least my appendix in case you are unwilling to read my translation."[66] On December 26 Lessing inquired about the progress of the work,[67] and on January 10, 1756, Mendelssohn sent him the manuscript, which was published anonymously by Voss.[68]

The epistle addressed to Lessing, which formed the appendix to the translation, was more than a commentary on Rousseau; it was also a paean to friendship and an expression of the sentiments Mendelssohn felt for Lessing.[69] It offers, at the same time, a glimpse of the happy hours the two friends had spent together and of some of the subjects they had discussed. Speaking about associative thinking, Mendelssohn gives this example:[70]

> I enter the garden in which I rarely sought you in vain, and at once your figure presents itself vividly to my mind. You, my friend, were once connected with the garden in terms of space. I pursue this image and remember the night that overtook us when, there in the pavillion, we had become oblivious of all else. Then I call to mind the death of Socrates, which we discussed at the time. . . . Socrates' death evokes the memory of Seneca's death, which was similar to his, and this, in turn, of the tyrant Nero, the tragedy *Britannicus*,[71] and, finally, the remarks you once made on this tragedy.

The paean to friendship is contained in a passage that criticizes Rousseau's "portrayal of human nature" and praises the perfection of the soul and the innocent pleasures of the senses. The passage continues:

> Have I forgotten thee, divine friendship! Thou art the sweet delight of the spirits, without which nature and art with all their glories would leave us languishing under extreme poverty. Pardon my neglect, dearest friend! What a disaster it would be were you to conclude that I have become indifferent to friendship! Yet, how could you! You know too well my sensitive heart and its openness to the sentiment of friendship. You noticed more than once not without pleasure how deeply a friendly glance from your eyes affected me; how it banished all sorrow from my breast and suddenly changed my mien to one of gaiety.[72]

It would be a mistake to regard this profuse expression of friendship as mere sentimentality. Mendelssohn was utterly sincere. As a Jew he could but marvel at Lessing's unreserved friendship for him. He cherished it as a wondrous gift throughout his life. Lessing's reply was measured but no less warm: "Permit me to refer in the first place to the printed epistle. So far I have read it only twice. The first time I was so much occupied with the friend that it made me forget the philosopher. I felt too deeply to be able to think. More I will not say to you; for I have not learned to babble on this theme. I would not dare to sing the praises of friendship after you; I only want to be carried away by it. May I be as worthy of your choice as you are of mine!"[73] Although in the course of time their lives and thoughts drifted apart, their friendship never wavered. In a letter to Herder written after Lessing's death Mendelssohn said that Lessing had been the only man whose friendship had been unwavering and who had remained his friend and benefactor "with a heart never divided and always true to itself."[74] Similarly, Lessing described Mendelssohn in 1769 as "my oldest and best friend."[75]

The Metaphysician

It was metaphysics rather than belles-lettres that formed the main topic of discussion between Mendelssohn and Lessing. Mendelssohn, who had Maimonides in his blood, was a metaphysician by nature. The study of Leibniz and Wolff had given him a firm orientation, and the figure of Spinoza, whom he admired yet could not follow, compelled him to define his position more clearly.

Mendelssohn's first work, the *Philosophical Dialogues*, was essentially an attempt to come to grips with Spinoza without sacrificing his loyalty to Leibniz and Wolff. In order to achieve this he had to show that Spinoza's system, if properly understood, was not so far from that of Leibniz as had been widely assumed. Another aim close to his heart was the rehabilitation of Spinoza. The two purposes were intertwined. If it could be shown that there were points of contact between the two thinkers, a reevaluation of Spinoza would ensue. In fact, strong assertions of Leibniz' dependence on Spinoza had been made previously by opponents of Leibniz and Wolff. At the beginning of the century a rabid foe of Wolff, Joachim Lange, had hurled the accusation of Spinozism at the Leibniz/Wolffian philosophy. Far from rehabilitating Spinoza, the affinities, imagined or true, between him and Leibniz only served as means for discrediting the latter. Times had changed, however, and the reputation of the "grand Leibniz" was now firmly established.[1] The efforts of a certain faction in the Royal Academy to undermine Leibniz' authority is evidence of the commanding position he had achieved. In this new situation, Mendelssohn felt, Spinoza could be "saved" if he could be shown to have paved the way for Leibniz. In a sense, therefore, his *Philosophical Dialogues*, which set out to do this, is a tendentious piece of writing. However, it would be wrong to label it as such. Mendelssohn's overriding motivation was his desire to clarify his own position, and to this end he entered into a searching analysis designed to put firm ground under his feet. One can sense the absolute sincerity with which he went about his task. The strength of his conviction was tested many years later, in 1763, when Lessing expressed doubts about one of the theses advanced in the *Dialogues* and said, "I believe you were being somewhat sophistical at the time you wrote this."[2] Mendelssohn's reply was a strong reaffirmation of the thesis in question.[3]

The first of the four dialogues comprising the work seeks to prove that the essence of Leibniz' famous doctrine of the "preestablished harmony" is already to be found in Spinoza and that Leibniz received it from him.[4] The proof proceeds as follows: Spinoza's as well as Leibniz' point of departure was Descartes' view that body and soul are entirely disparate and therefore cannot influence each other; that the body is determined by the laws of motion and, the soul motivated by concepts. The harmony that nevertheless prevails between the motions of bodies and the actions and passions of souls had been explained by the Cartesians as due to a coordination continually effected by the will of God. Spinoza, who denied that God possesses will, could obviously not accept the Cartesian theory and he had to assume that the series of changes in the physical world and the series of changes in the souls correspond to one another by virtue of an eternally proceeding order—by virtue, to use Leibniz' term, of a preestablished harmony. Mendelssohn found this notion expressed in Spinoza's proposition: "The order and connection of the ideas is the same as the order and connection of the things."[5] He admitted that Leibniz' fully developed theory of the preestablished harmony implied more than the mere assertion of two parallel orders chiming together: that it was intimately linked with his view of the universe as a system of monads, small nuclei endowed with a degree of perception however minimal, which was correlated with the world of bodies on account of the fact that the latter was the mere "phenomenal" (the apparent, not the real) representation of the former. However, Mendelssohn maintained, one could divorce the doctrine of the preestablished harmony from the doctrine of the monads in its simple form (as found in Spinoza), and Leibniz himself, Mendelssohn suggested, had occasionally presented it in this way. Wolff, who rejected the monadic theory, could therefore still uphold Leibniz' preestablished harmony. What Leibniz did was to adopt the notion from Spinoza and fit it into his own metaphysical system. When he had to defend it against Pierre Bayle, he took it in its simple form in order to make it more easily acceptable.

Mendelssohn, who resented Bayle's violent attack against Spinoza, obviously relished the thought that Leibniz, in his reply to Bayle's objections, stated his theory in the same form in which it had been expressed by Spinoza. As a matter of fact, however, it was in defense of his theory against Simon Foucher (1644–1696) that Leibniz had done this, whereas in his answers to Bayle he had made ample use of his monadology. Mendelssohn's slip was doubtless the result of his preoccupation with Bayle. Bayle was very much on Mendelssohn's mind, and whenever he mentioned him, the purpose was secretly or overtly polemical. The thesis that it was not Leibniz who first "invented" the preestablished harmony is introduced as a novel one, since "nobody has as yet contested his title to fame" and since "Bayle himself congratulated him in the name of the learned world on this great discovery." Between the lines one reads: Bayle should have congratulated Spinoza. The fact that Leibniz failed to acknowledge his indebtedness to the Jewish thinker is explained with a subtle irony: Leibniz was careful not to divulge it, for otherwise would he not have caused certain people to defame him as a Spinozist? Since it was well known that this charge actually had been laid at Leibniz' door, the implication of the defense is: Little did it help Leibniz that he cautiously refrained from mentioning Spinoza. To lead up to this ironical playfulness, the thesis of the Spinozistic origin of Leibniz' theory had to be introduced as a new idea. Nobody was likely to be misled by this claim, of course, inasmuch as the Leibnizian doctrine of the preestablished harmony had been stigmatized as being descended from "Spinoza's pseudophilosophy" by Joachim Lange and as "plagiarism" by the Dutchman Ruardus Andala.[6] In pretending that no one had ever contested Leibniz' title to fame as author of this theory, Mendelssohn used a fictional element that helped to bring out the irony of his defense of Leibniz' silence on Spinoza.

The second dialogue goes right to the heart of the matter of Spinoza's rehabilitation. The upshot is that Spinoza's view of the universe becomes acceptable if applied to the world as it existed solely in God's mind prior to its becoming real by his decree. The Leibnizians, Mendelssohn explains, attribute to the world a twofold existence, as it were: it existed first in the divine intellect as a possible world among other possible worlds, and then, having been chosen as the best of all the possible worlds, it was made the real world. Spinoza, however, acknowledged only the first of these two stages of existence. In his view—according to Mendelssohn's interpretation—no world outside God ever became real and all things are still only in God's mind. What the Leibnizians assert of the preexistent universe Spinoza says of the visible one: the particular things express the divine attributes in a certain limited way. In Leibnizian terminology: God knows contingent things as possibles by thinking his own perfections as limited to a certain degree. Moreover, the Leibnizians define the contingent things in God's mind as the effects of an infinite series of causes and Spinoza says the same thing of the particulars. All objections to the Spinozistic view of the universe disappear if the system is seen in this light. The step from it to the truth is but a small one. Mendelssohn was much enamored with this interpretation of Spinoza's *Deus sive Natura* as God not reduced to nature but as nature exalted to God[7] or, more precisely, as nature exalted to being in God's mind. Not that Mendelssohn himself subscribed to this view. On the contrary, he argued against it in the very last phase of his life, when the question of Lessing's alleged Spinozism troubled him greatly. Yet he saw in this "purified Spinozism," as he then called it, a means of freeing Spinoza's doctrine from the accusation of atheism.[8]

The third and fourth dialogues do not compare and relate Leibniz and Spinoza but do indirectly serve the two purposes Mendelssohn had in mind, namely, the clarification of his own position and the rehabilitation of Spinoza. Though ultimately agreeing with Leibniz, these two discussions make it their business to show the difficulties that beset Leibniz' contention that this world is the best of all possible ones. The implication of Mendelssohn's highlighting of the somewhat problematical character of Leibniz' view is clear: if the arguments for the doctrine are open to certain objections, the notion that the world that exists is the result of a divine choice among possible worlds is in jeopardy, and the Spinozistic view, which eliminates possibility and choice in favor of necessity, gains a measure of plausibility. To put it differently: by his critical approach to Leibniz, Mendelssohn diminished the distance between Leibniz and Spinoza. At the same time, he freed himself from a slavish adherence to Leibniz and thereby made his allegiance to him all the more valuable.

The third dialogue proceeds in two stages. It first criticizes a passage in Leibniz' letters to Samuel Clarke on the problem of the world's eternity or creation in time. In the fifth letter Leibniz admitted the validity of the question: Assuming God created the world in time, why did he not add to the chain of beings some more links *a parte ante*, i.e., why did he not start creation earlier? Leibniz' answer was: Since God created the best of all possible worlds, any addition to it would not have been part of the best possible world. In his correspondence with Clarke, Leibniz assumed that the world had a beginning, though he regarded the doctrine of an eternal world as compatible with the belief in God. Mendelssohn refuted Leibniz' answer to the question in the fifth letter in the following way: Every link in the series of things has a sufficient reason causing it. Assuming that b, c, d, and e represent the series of real things, e following from d, d from c, and c from b, it becomes possible to assume a thing a which, had it been real, would have caused b. This thing a might have been real and b, c, d, and e would have followed from it in a natural way. Hence a could have existed without detriment to the best of all possible worlds. Why then did God not start with it? This question can be pursued ad infinitum. It follows that Leibniz, in accordance with his own principles, had to admit the feasibility of proving the infinite duration of the world. In point of fact, Leibniz did incline to this view, as is apparent from his correspondence with Louis Bourguet, which was unknown when Mendelssohn's *Dialogues* were written.[9] What emerges from Mendelssohn's critique of Leibniz is the difficulty of reconciling the belief in creation in time and the concept of the possible that underlies the doctrine of God's choice of the best possible world. Once possibility was admitted, the series of instants in time could be infinite. Spinoza, who recognized only necessity, had no such problem; for him things could not have been produced by God in any order different from the one in which they were produced.

At the second stage of the third dialogue the problematical nature of Leibniz' doctrine of the best possible world is shown from yet another aspect. The objection had been raised that producing the "best" was impossible since no creature could be said to be perfect and producing something more perfect was conceivable. Leibniz answered this objection by drawing a distinction between the individual creature and the universe. A particular individual creature could be surpassed by another because it was finite; the universe could not be surpassed by another because it was infinite both in its future extension in time and as a composite of an infinite number of monads. It did not form a whole that could be compared to another whole.[10] Mendelssohn denied that the number of monads in the world was infinite. He also rejected the denial of the holistic concept of the world. His critique of Leibniz was in line with Wolffian concepts, and it implied that Leibniz had not succeeded in refuting the argument that a better world was possible.

In the revised form that the third dialogue assumed in the 1771 edition of Mendelssohn's *Philosophical Writings*[11] the criticism of Leibniz proceeds no longer on a Wolffian but on intrinsically Leibnizian basis. The world is indeed infinite but its infinity, Mendelssohn argues, is still different from the infinity of God. It is but an image of the divine infinity and possesses only a limited degree of perfection. Hence a more perfect universe is conceivable and the objection raised against Leibniz is not removed. The only way to uphold the concept of the best possible world is the recourse to the divine attributes of wisdom, power, and goodness and to the principle of sufficient reason. Once it is assumed that the world has been produced by God, it must be held to be the best world possible, since God could have chosen only the best, and if there existed an infinite number of possible worlds, each surpassing the other in its degree of perfection, God could have produced none of them because there would have been no sufficient reason for a choice. Mendelssohn thus accepted Leibniz' doctrine, but he did not regard the arguments supporting it as conclusive: "The objections I advanced against it serve to convince us how far from absolute certainty we still are in doctrines of this kind."[12] The critical attitude adopted by Mendelssohn contrasts with the more strictly Leibnizian stance taken by Kant in his "precritical" phase. Kant's *Essaying Some Contemplations on Optimism* (1759) follows Leibniz' doctrine unquestioningly.

The fourth and last dialogue begins with a discussion of Leibniz' view that no monad is exactly like another and that it is impossible for two things to be completely alike because there can be no choice between indifferent things and there would have been no reason for God, the author of nature, to put them in different places in time and space. Leibniz' radically pluralistic view of the universe is thus based on "these great principles of sufficient reason and of the identity of indiscernibles."[13] Voltaire had opposed Leibniz by pointing out that the production of things exactly alike required more "art" than the making of dissimilar things and that, consequently, it must have pleased God to create things that were completely alike. Hence the existence of indiscernibles was not in contradiction to God's wisdom.

Mendelssohn could not allow Voltaire to defeat Leibniz, but he did find it necessary to offer more convincing proofs for Leibniz' thesis than the ones advanced by Leibniz himself. In Mendelssohn's view, Wolff had offered a satisfactory argument: Assuming that everything in the world stands in a definite causal nexus with everything else, it would be impossible for two things exactly alike to appear in different places of the spatial and temporal connection unless they belonged to two causal series that were exactly alike, i.e. unless we assumed the existence of two worlds that were indistinguishable. According to Wolff such an assumption is refuted by the impossibility of explaining why the one rather than the other was in a certain place. According to Mendelssohn two worlds exactly alike are impossible because they are indistinguishable and their difference is chimerical. Even God cannot think of two things as two if they are totally alike. Therefore, God's choice of a particular world is not due to chance, and to accuse Leibniz of holding such a view was unjustified.

In rejecting such a misreading of Leibniz, Mendelssohn was referring to Prémontval's *Du Hazard sous l'empire de la Providence,* which had just appeared. According to Leibniz, Mendelssohn emphasized, the world was a product not of a chance decision by God nor of necessity but of an act of divine choice that was the choice of the best. The question whether the choice of the best did not imply a necessity had already been answered by Mendelssohn at the end of the second dialogue, where he had distinguished between Spinoza's and Leibniz' determinisms. Spinoza's denial of free choice was the logical consequence of his concept of freedom as the ability to choose in an equilibrium of indifference. Since, however, the possibility of choice presupposes motivation, i.e., a preponderance of reasons of one sort against another, a truly free choice was impossible. Leibniz also denied the possibility of an *equilibrium indifferentiae,* but he still regarded the act of motivated choice as a free act because freedom consisted in the choice of the best, which carried with it no compulsion.[14]

Christian August Crusius, Leibniz' great adversary at this time, did not accept Leibniz' modified determinism because, in Crusius' view, its being linked to the principle of sufficient reason nullified the notion of God's free will. Mendelssohn avoided a discussion of Crusius, whom he did not take too seriously,[15] and he concluded the fourth dialogue with a reaffirmation of God's free will. His loyalty to Leibniz remained unshaken, yet he had shown the problems in which Leibniz' system was entangled and had also brought Leibniz and Spinoza into closer proximity. He had done this in the most lively, witty, and attractive fashion, of which a précis can give no inkling whatever. The form of dialogue that he employed proved to be highly felicitous. The work has a truly Socratic flavor and conceals under its appearance of ease and elegance an immense amount of learning and incisive, independent thinking.

Mendelssohn's letters *On the Sentiments* are far less speculative and much more empirical, and yet they remain metaphysical in their ultimate concern.[16] They lead to the conclusion that the pleasure we find in contemplating the order of the universe imparts to us the tranquillity of soul in which our true happiness consists. It is in keeping with this metaphysical orientation that the letters devote considerable space to a discussion of suicide as the most radical expression of unhappiness. The question of theodicy, which formed the topic of Mendelssohn's fragment of 1753, still predominates in this work. The answer to it as given here lies in the recognition of a hierarchy of pleasures corresponding to a rising scale of perfections.

The way in which Mendelssohn's thinking on the subject developed can be traced by comparing the preliminary draft entitled *Von dem Vergnügen* ("On Pleasure")[17] with the text of the letters. His point of departure was Sulzer's stimulating essay on the origin of pleasant and unpleasant sentiments. According to Sulzer, pleasure arises from a sense of ease, whereas pain is caused by a sense of constraint. Like Wolff, Sulzer considered the faculty of thinking, i.e. of producing ideas, as the "essential power" of the soul. However, he disagreed with Wolff's belief (following Descartes) that pleasure and displeasure derived from an awareness of perfection and imperfection. In Sulzer's view, the soul resembled a river that flows peacefully so long as its waters are not dammed but swells and roars when the opposite happens. Whenever the soul was free to develop a flow of ideas in an easy way, without let or hindrance, it felt a sense of pleasure. The prospect of its being able to cope with a multitude of problems made this pleasure all the more vivid. Boredom Sulzer defined as pain caused by the soul's inactivity. The fulfilment of a long-standing wish created pleasure because the soul could now freely pursue a whole range of ideas that was hitherto out of bounds. It was therefore not the awareness of a perfection but the ease of thinking that, in Sulzer's view, was the origin of pleasure. There were, he suggested, three different kinds of pleasure, namely those of the senses, the heart (i.e. moral judgment), and the intellect. Yet all three were ultimately related to the thinking power of the soul. The pleasure of the intellect concerned the beautiful, which Sulzer defined as a quality resulting from "variety reduced to unity." An edifice, a piece of music, and a dance were beautiful in the degree that they contained both diversity and unity. The concurrence of the various parts produced a "totality" (*un Tout*), and the focal point that unified them was the "interest" (*l'intérêt de l'unité*) or, as we might say, the central theme. An object possessing this quality gave pleasure because it presented a multitude of ideas held together by the thread of unity and, therefore, offered the mind a rich "booty" that could easily be absorbed.

There were, then, two elements combined in Sulzer's theory of the beautiful: the concept of ease and that of unity in diversity, which was but another way of expressing the idea of perfection. The doctrine of the focal point and the theme as the necessary conditions of aesthetic perfection had already been developed by Alexander Baumgarten,[18] and the notion of ease was taken over from Louis de Pouilly's *Théorie des sentiments agréables* (1747), as Mendelssohn pointed out in his draft. The question that he posed from the very start was whether it was legitimate to characterize, in summary fashion, all kinds of pleasure in the way that Sulzer did.

It was Mendelssohn's critique of Sulzer that led him to his own theory. He raised two objections against Sulzer. Firstly, he asserted the purely sensual nature of a certain class of pleasures and denied their reducibility to the prospect of unimpeded thinking. Secondly, he rejected the view that the pleasure derived from unity in diversity required for its explanation the principle of "ease." For the love of perfection must be attributed to all intelligent beings and, in its highest degree, to God himself. Now, if the pleasure afforded by perfection (which was here identified with unity in diversity) were merely the result of the ease of its perspicuity, it would testify to the feebleness of our comprehension. By the same token, it could not be said of God that he took pleasure in perfection. Mendelssohn, therefore, redefined perfection as a unity in diversity that challenged our intellect to understand the reason for the harmonious coexistence of all parts. The pleasure in comprehending it belonged to God in the most eminent degree. The distinction between the perfection of beauty and metaphysical perfection is not yet clearly formulated in the draft but Mendelssohn, though still somewhat ambiguous, was already moving in this direction.

A great deal of attention is given in the draft to an analysis of the sensual pleasures, which had been neglected by Sulzer. They yield only "pleasant sentiments," it is said here, but no "delight" *(Lust)*. Mendelssohn obviously connected the term *Lust* with Wolff's *voluptas,* which relates to perfection and beauty. Sensual pleasures, it is further said, give the soul no opportunity for developing her own power. They produce, however, a condition in the body that the soul darkly perceives and enjoys. Here Mendelssohn followed Descartes' *Les passions de l'âme.* As examples of physiological processes that pleasantly affect the body and raise its well-being he mentioned two observations, one by Sanctorius as reported by de Pouilly, and one by Leibniz. According to Sanctorius (1561–1636), pleasant sentiments cause an improved transpiration, and Leibniz used the medical term "tone" in order to characterize the beneficial effect of pleasant sentiments upon the blood vessels. However, it is not only sensual pleasures that improve the "tone" of the body: every kind of perfection enjoyed by the soul benefits the body as well.

It follows from all this that there are three levels of pleasant sentiments: (1) The supreme delight that a clear and distinct understanding of some perfection produces in the soul and eventually also in the body. (2) The clear impression of a perfect whole, which conveys a sense of the beautiful but lacks in distinct knowledge of detail, is of the nature of pleasant sentiments rather than of delight. In this case the soul enjoys both the beauty of the object contemplated and, at the same time, the effect that its own pleasure has on the body. (3) A purely sensual pleasure does not require the cooperation of the soul yet indirectly causes the soul pleasure by virtue of her concern for the condition of her companion, the body. This scale of pleasures corresponds to the three degrees of clarity that the Leibniz/ Wolffian school assigned to the ideas or "representations" in the mind. A representation is dark or "obscure" if we are not conscious of its specific character and are therefore unable to recall it. Otherwise, it is a "clear" idea. There is, however, a difference between clear ideas that are "distinct" and those that are "confused." If we are able to point out the individual attributes of an idea in precise analytical fashion, we have a clear and distinct notion; should we, on the other hand, possess only a total impression, our knowledge, though it is clear and enables us to recognize its object whenever presented to us, can only be called "confused," i.e. blurred, lacking in precision. The importance of this hierarchical structure of types of knowledge for Mendelssohn's theory of the pleasures is already noticeable in the draft and is even more apparent in the letters *On the Sentiments*.

The work opens with Euphranor's enthusiastic praise of beauty and his displeasure at Palemon's efforts to investigate the nature of the sentiments. Is not an analysis of beauty bound to destroy the enjoyment of it? Euphranor considers beauty a perfection insofar as it is perceived indistinctly (i.e. sensually), a definition taken over from Georg Friedrich Meier's *Anfangsgründe aller schönen Wissenschaften* and going back to Baumgarten's *Aesthetica* (1750), in which beauty is said to be the "perfection of sensual knowledge."[19] The moment we try to obtain a clear and distinct concept of the beautiful object, our pleasure is gone. Once we begin to think, we cease to feel. Yet we are to feel, enjoy, and be happy, as Euphranor's "purified epicurism" demands.

In a series of letters (3–7) Palemon seeks to rectify his friend's purely aesthetic view of the nature of pleasure. In the first place, he modifies the radicalism of the aesthetic approach itself. True, aesthetic enjoyment and distinct, scientific knowledge through analysis do not go together, but neither do the feeling for beauty and an obscure idea of it. The clearer the representation, i.e. the richer it is in diversity, the more vivid the pleasure. The beauty of the total impression will be the greater, the more clarity has been previously obtained. Where there are serious gaps in our awareness of the parts comprising the whole, the "aesthetic wealth"—a concept developed by Baumgarten—will be missing and the enjoyment of beauty will be correspondingly less. To make a diversity of parts aesthetically perspicuous does not require a scientific type of thinking by logical reasoning but can be achieved by the "aesthetic light" of *bon-sens* or taste, which according to Baumgarten is a subrational faculty analogous to reason.[20] In this context Mendelssohn recalls a passage in Aristotle's *Poetics* in which the need for perspicuity is stressed, and in interpreting it he assigns to imagination the creative function of making a diversity perspicuous and its beauty visible at a glance. Thus he shows himself much more ready than Baumgarten to absorb the doctrine of the power and creativity of the imagination, a doctrine that Addison and Steele had advocated and that had found eloquent protagonists among the Swiss (Johann Bodmer and Johann Breitinger). Beauty, Mendelssohn sums up, is a perfection clearly perceived.

Aesthetic perfection is not, however, the only perfection. Above it in rank is the true, authentic metaphysical perfection, which alone can ultimately satisfy the soul and offer genuine delight. Beings of a higher order are happier than we because they can perceive distinctly a larger variety of ideas and are, therefore, the more powerfully affected by the objects of their contemplation. For them, Mendelssohn concludes from the nature of beauty as previously defined, there can be no aesthetic enjoyment, since aesthetic perception is subrational, sensual. He might have followed Baumgarten in admitting that apart from the "profundity" and "purity" of "intensive" distinctiveness of knowledge there existed also an "extensive" distinctiveness of knowledge, which consisted in the perception of a totality and which constituted the "beauty of the intellect." If he had adopted this view he might have found it possible to attribute aesthetic pleasure to the higher beings, including God. What precluded this possibility was his acceptance of Sulzer's definition of perfection as valid for the beautiful. Since he acknowledged that beauty was unity in the manifold that pleases because of its easy perspicuity, he could not ascribe aesthetic pleasure to God. The true perfection of the world does not consist in the "unity in the manifold" that is easily perceptible but in the "accord," "agreement," or "harmony" that reveals itself to intelligent beings when they comprehend the purposiveness of the manifold. "Nothing can be considered superfluous, discordant, or deficient" where the true perfection is known. Pleasure in this perfection follows from the "positive power of our soul," not from the feebleness of man. It is peculiar to rational beings to desire ideas that are concatenated and follow from one another. The pleasure in this kind of perfection far surpasses that which beauty affords. For God, who comprehends all parts of the universe with the highest degree of distinct knowledge, beauty does not exist.[21] He recognizes but the metaphysical perfection that is grounded in the mutual accord and purposeful unity of the constituent elements of the whole. We must not confound the "earthly Venus" with the "heavenly" one, Mendelssohn added in the revised edition (1761).

Almost the entire sixth letter is in praise of metaphysical reflection as a "source of happiness," and eulogizes Locke, Wolff, and above all Leibniz as teachers of "the true philosophy." As has been noted already, the whole passage has an autobiographical ring. The upshot of the discussion so far is a clear differentiation between the beautiful and the true, between the aesthetical and the metaphysical. Precisely because Mendelssohn (following Baumgarten) had vindicated the autonomous character of aesthetics, he was able to separate the pleasure found in beauty from that derived from the knowledge of truth. On the other hand, he established the closest connection between the true and the good. Ethics and metaphysics are twins. One who finds pleasure in the wise order of things because he sees everywhere evidence of design will also accept the place of evil in the world as a whole. The delight in metaphysical perfection will outweigh all pain and attune man to a recognition of his moral duties.

There still remained the task of explaining the nature of sensual pleasure, a knotty point that most philosophers either "cut or ignored altogether." Mendelssohn tried to solve it by the assumption that the origin of this kind of pleasure lies neither in the soul alone nor in the body by itself. The tenth and twelfth letters develop the theory, known to us already from the draft, that the sensual pleasures impart to the soul an obscure representation of the perfection of the body, and thereby give pleasure to the soul. It remains true, therefore, that every kind of pleasure derives from the representation of a perfection. Conversely, every indistinct representation of a perfection, i.e. every experience of beauty, improves the condition of the body, as Sanctorius and Leibniz had shown. The result of our inquiry is presented in the eleventh letter: There are three sources of pleasure that must be marked off from each other: unity in the manifold or sensuous beauty, the accord of the manifold or metaphysical perfection, and the improved state of the body or sensual pleasure. The distinction between pleasant feeling and delight, which we met in the draft, is dropped, and the threefold hierarchy of pleasures is established.

From here Mendelssohn passes on to his first attempt at a theory of the arts. It starts with a hymn to music as the only form of art that yields all three kinds of pleasure. In what sense music could be said to convey a distinct awareness of metaphysical perfection is not explained. Most probably Mendelssohn regarded musical harmony, the mathematical proportions of which he had studied, as symbolic of the metaphysical accord of the manifold. For he added the remark that possibly every one of the five senses might become aware of a specific kind of harmony no less capable of evoking delight than that which musical harmony evokes through the sense of hearing. Such harmonies had yet to be discovered, but perhaps a beginning had been made in Newton's suggestion (in his *Opticks*) that there was a mathematically determinable analogy between sounds and colors.[22]

Another theme that the draft had not discussed is that of the "mixed sentiments." How was it possible, Euphranor asked in the eighth letter, for men to find pleasure in contemplating and witnessing gruesome and terrifying spectacles? A picture showing the horrors of a shipwreck pleased us not merely on account of the painter's skill but also because the terrible as such had a certain fascination. How could this experience be reconciled with the theory that pleasure was caused by the awareness of some perfection?

As Euphranor indicates, this question was stimulated by Jean Baptiste Dubos' *Réflections critiques sur la peinture et la poésie* (1719), in which many striking examples of perverse pleasure were cited. But the author's explanation of this phenomenon did not satisfy Mendelssohn. Dubos had suggested that the predominant desire of the soul was to be occupied, moved, aroused, no matter by what means. Mendelssohn objected that according to this theory men ought to derive pleasure from manifestations of anger, remorse, or fear, since they also move the soul. He offered a different explanation. There were two kinds of mixed sentiments (i.e., sentiments in which pain and pleasure were combined). One kind was represented by the cases cited by Dubos (a ropedancer who jumps over two swords, a Roman gladiator who dies in a graceful pose, etc.). Spectacles of this sort could be enjoyed only after one had learned to repress one's sense of compassion. What caused pleasure in these instances was the perfect skill of the actors, i.e., a perfection of the body. The other kind of mixed sentiments included pleasure born of pity. Pity itself was a mixed sentiment, one combining the love of a person with the awareness of the misfortune that befell him. Love was based on the perfections of the loved and therefore gave pleasure. An undeserved misfortune saddened us and, at the same time, enhanced our appreciation of the loved one. Pity was the only unpleasant sentiment that held an attraction for us. What was known as "fear" in a tragedy was "nothing else but pity . . . for the danger spells a threat not to us but to our fellow-man, whom we pity."[23]

When in 1761 Mendelssohn published his *Rhapsodie, oder Zusätze zu den Briefen über die Empfindungen* ("Rhapsody, or Additions to the Letters on the Sentiments"),[24] he treated the problem of the mixed sentiments from an entirely new viewpoint that had been suggested to him by Lessing. On February 2, 1757, Lessing had written: "Surely we both agree, dearest friend, that all passions are either vehement desires or vehement detestations. We also agree that through every vehement desire or detestation we are made conscious of a higher degree of our reality. Hence all passions, even the most unpleasant ones, are pleasant as passions."[25] On March 2, 1757, Mendelssohn had replied: "You are perfectly right. The ability to love perfections and to detest imperfections is a reality and, therefore, a perfection. Exercising it is, hence, bound to afford us pleasure. What a pity that this fine observation was unknown to me when I wrote my letters *On the Sentiments!*"[26] In the *Rhapsody* he revised his previous position in the light of Lessing's remark: "I was wrong to find fault with Dubos' statement that the soul only desired to be moved, be it even by unpleasant representations." We had to differentiate between the representations and their objects. In the case of an unpleasant sentiment we detested in most cases not the representation but its object. We disapproved of the evil that happened, while the idea of it in the mind might be highly attractive, provided no guilt attached to us. After the earthquake at Lisbon countless people visited the site of the devastation and derived a horrid pleasure from the spectacle. The reason lay in the fact that displeasure and disgust as such were expressions of a positive power of the soul, hence perfections, which qua perfections evoked pleasure. A mixed sentiment was, therefore, composed of displeasure at the object and pleasure at the subjective representation of it.

The admissibility or inadmissibility of suicide was yet another topic discussed in the letters that had not been premeditated in the draft. The subject is one that commanded widespread attention in the eighteenth century. Hume's essay *On Suicide* was written between 1754 and 1756, the period during which Mendelssohn dealt with the matter in his letters, but was not published until 1777. The issue underlying the debate was the question whether man was *sui juris*, i.e., his own master and judge, or answerable to God. In the seventeenth century Samuel von Pufendorf had condemned suicide as contrary to natural law: life was a gift from God; man had no jurisdiction over it; like a sentinel, he had to remain at his post until it pleased God to recall him.[27] The simile of the sentinel was an old one: Cicero had already quoted it from Pythagoras.[28] Certain Puritans claimed that God had told them by an inner voice to take their life. Anglicans like Jeremy Taylor and John Sym tried to refute this kind of argument.[29] On the other hand, John Donne's famous treatise *Biathanatos* (1646 or 1647) defended the right to suicide by quoting numerous passages from the Bible, the Church Fathers, classical authors, canonical jurists, and scholastic writers. In Mendelssohn's time, members of the Royal Academy debated the subject. In his *Lettres juives* (1738) the marquis d'Argens had argued that "great men" were permitted to take their life to save their country or preserve their honor. Formey, the secretary of the academy, invoked the authority of natural law to prove the inadmissibility of suicide.[30] Maupertuis, the president of the academy, had taken the opposite view. In his *Essai de philosophie morale* he maintained that the sum of evil in the world surpassed the sum of happiness and that nonbeing was therefore preferable to being. Hence the Stoics were right to regard suicide as a permissible remedy. Although he also presented the Christian point of view, it was obvious that Maupertuis' sympathies lay with the Stoics. It was probably the essay by Maupertuis that stimulated Mendelssohn to deal with the subject, for his main argument against suicide was directed against Maupertuis' thesis of the preponderance of evil as a cause for preferring death.

Mendelssohn suggested that the problem of suicide had to be approached in different ways corresponding to the attitudes of a believer in revealed religion, a nonbeliever in the immortality of the soul, and a deist who affirmed immortality. A believer in revelation, he maintained, could not justify suicide. According to his concepts only patience and trust in God offered the assurance of felicity in the hereafter. It was different in the case of a nonbeliever. Here there was room for argument and counterargument. Mendelssohn skillfully employed the literary fiction of letting Euphranor report the various arguments for the legitimacy of suicide that he had heard "recently" at a party. The spokesman whose reasons Euphranor recalls was a certain Lindamour, and his motivation is said to have been the desire to save the honor of the "philosophical suicide Blount." In other words, Euphranor is presented as an ear-witness to the arguments that Charles Gildon had published in 1695, under the pseudonym Lindamour, in the preface to his edition of various writings of his friend Charles Blount, who had committed suicide on account of frustrated love for a woman.

A comparison of Euphranor's report with the original text shows that Mendelssohn did indeed make use of Gildon/Lindamour's preface, but that he partly paraphrased or amplified the arguments found there. An impressive array of arguments in defense of suicide, culled from many literary sources, is woven into the texture of the debate to which Euphranor is said to have listened.[31] Of particular importance is an argument that on close inspection turns out to be a revised form of Maupertuis': In algebraic terms one might compare the happy moments in our lives with a positive quantity, the unhappy ones with a negative quantity, and death with zero; if a positive quantity remains after the account is made up, the condition is preferable to death; should a negative quantity remain, however, zero would have to be preferred. It is this argument for suicide that Palemon makes the target of his attack in the fourteenth letter, and which offers Mendelssohn an opportunity to deal with the problem from the vantage point of the Leibniz/Wolffian philosophy.

Before approaching the matter from this philosophical aspect, however, Mendelssohn mentions an entirely new argument that he wants to dispose of first. Significantly, Euphranor does not claim to have heard it mentioned at the party but puts it forward as his own. This was a subtle way of indicating that it came from Mendelssohn himself. Its gist is as follows: how could it be said that suicide was contrary to human nature, considering the fact that when presented on the stage it does not evoke disgust but pity? Euphranor recalls the moving impression made by Orosman's suicide in Voltaire's *Zaïr* and Mellefont's suicide in Lessing's *Miss Sara Sampson*. That suicide on the stage produces mixed sentiments would seem to be irreconcilable with our moral condemnation of the act.[32] Palemon's answer distinguishes between true and theatrical morality: the stage has its own laws. The purpose of the tragedy is to arouse the passions. Hence suicide is "good" in theatrical terms. The poet would defeat his purpose if he moralized and denounced the suicide committed in his play as an immoral act. His holding up the mirror of true morality would prevent the audience from feeling a sense of pity. Yet it still remains true that in actual life suicide is immoral. Obviously, there is only one standard of true morality, in Mendelssohn's view. The somewhat ambiguous term "theatrical morality" is used only to establish the autonomy of the aesthetical realm. The task of poetry, he means to say, is not the preaching of morals but the arousal of our sentiments, our passions. "Theatrical morality," he wrote to Lessing in December, 1756, "is not to be arraigned before the tribunal of symbolic [i.e. abstract, nonsensual] knowledge."[33]

Maupertuis' argument, in the arithmetical form given to it by Mendelssohn, constitutes the subject of the fourteenth letter. Palemon denies the validity of a calculation of the sort suggested by Maupertuis. A negative quantity was as unreal as a mathematical point. Assuming that Maupertuis had merely intended to imply that in a wretched life the positive quantity of evil subtracted from the positive quantity of good amounted to less than zero, there was still no reason to prefer death. For death annulled the very quantities to which the calculation referred. Only so long as a man was alive did his drawing up a balance sheet have any meaning. Moreover, the statement "I prefer death to life" was meaningless. Palemon shows up its absurdity in a brilliant Socratic dialogue with Eudox, the Englishman who is an advocate of suicide (a malaise that was almost epidemic in his country at the time).

Reduced to a series of propositions, the dialogue expresses the follow- ing points: The soul never makes a choice without a motivation. Hence everything we choose is chosen because it appears to us to be better than what we reject. Death too, if preferred to life, must appear to us better than life. However, to be better can only mean "to promote our good, to be useful to our perfection." The soul is more perfect if it has a greater power of forming ideas. For the perfection of a soul consists in the degree of its reality, i.e., its thinking power. That which enlarges the boundaries of our reality or thinking power and prevents its limitation makes us more perfect and is, therefore, better than that which fails to do this. In reverse: that which is supposed to be better than something else must enlarge the boundaries of our reality and existence or prevent their limitation. If this is the case, is there any sense in saying that we might prefer annihilation, the absence of consciousness, in the belief that it could more effectively prevent the limitation of our reality than a consciousness of our imperfection or of a lesser degree of our reality could be expected to do? Could a rational being declare that our annihilation enlarged the boundaries of our existence to a greater extent than a small degree of our existence? It followed that our being conscious of even a small degree of reality promoted our perfection to a greater extent than our annihilation could possibly do. The terms "to be better," "to be more desirable," and "to prefer" were, therefore, inapplicable to our annihilation.

In his Hebrew commentary on *Kohelet* (1768) Mendelssohn expressed the same idea in a simpler form when explaining the sentence, "For the living know that they shall die; but the dead know not anything" (9:5): "Despite all pain and all sorrow that is caused by this knowledge it is better than the absolute nonbeing of the soul's knowledge. For the annihilation [Hebrew: *abadon*] of the soul is the worst evil that can happen to a rational substance."[34] Palemon's demonstration employs three princi- ples of the Leibniz/Wolffian philosophy. The first is the principle of freedom as the choice of the best; the second is the definition of the good as that which contributes to our perfection; the third is the notion that the perfec- tion or reality of the soul consists in its power of thinking.[35]

The final discussion on suicide considers the argument of those who do not regard death as the annihilation of the soul but as a transition to a new and more beautiful form of existence. Why should they be denied the right to divest themselves of the body in order to find greater happiness in the next world? Palemon advances a number of objections to this argument, of which the strongest is perhaps the following: We have to assume a connection between the future life and the present one. If the identity of the person is to be maintained, consecutive conditions must form a causal nexus. The manner in which we depart this world cannot be considered irrelevant to our future mode of existence. A person who does not allow the natural course of his life to proceed to its allotted end throws himself into a condition different from the one for which he was destined. He takes a step into the dark.[36] When Eudox describes the subtle reasoning against his view derisively as trifles and as "a tremendous mountain revolving around a hair, as a Hebrew poet says,"[37] Palemon takes the opportunity to reaffirm the authority of reason, especially for those who refuse to believe in a revealed religion. Before "thrice-holy reason" they have to bow their knee, no matter how subtle its arguments. They were still far superior to the arguments by which suicide had been defended.

The Bel Esprit

The void left in Mendelssohn's life by Lessing's departure from Berlin was to some extent filled by Friedrich Nicolai, the Berlin-born bookseller, publisher, editor, and writer (1733–1811), who was Mendelssohn's junior by only a few years and was, like him, a devoted follower of the Wolffian philosophy. A man of strong moral fiber, Nicolai had developed a distaste for pietism and all forms of religious enthusiasm. During his long and busy life he proved to be the most tenacious protagonist of the German Enlightenment.[1] He met Lessing toward the end of 1754 and made Mendelssohn's acquaintance in the early part of 1755. His autobiographical notes recall that at the time he felt in some respects closer to Mendelssohn because, like him, he was self-taught and a businessman. On the other hand, he shared with Lessing the same type of elementary education and the same interest in historical and philological research, a kind of activity that Mendelssohn was wont to dismiss as a waste of time.[2] To Nicolai belongs the credit for winning Mendelssohn over to belles-lettres and literary criticism. At the beginning of May, 1756, Mendelssohn wrote to Lessing: "I shall try to rid myself of as many old acquaintances as possible, except for Herr Professor Sulzer and Herr Nicolai. The latter I have come to know better, and I believe we have already become friends; the former certainly deserves that one seek his company."[3] His letter of August 2, 1756, carried some rather startling news:

For the time being, I have become unfaithful to meditative [*grübelnden*] metaphysics. I visit the Herr Nicolai very often in his garden. (I truly love him, dearest friend, and I believe that our friendship will thereby gain, because in him I love your true friend.) We read poems, Herr Nicolai declames to me his own work, I sit in judgment as a critic, admire, laugh, censure until nightfall. Then we once more remember you and part company, contented with our day's work. I am making a fairly good start toward becoming a *bel esprit*. Who knows whether one day I shall not write verse? Madam Metaphysics may forgive me. She asserts that friendship rests on the identity of [people's] inclinations, and I find that, on the contrary, identity of inclinations may, in reverse, rest on friendship. Your friendship and Nicolai's has tempted me to withdraw part of my love from that venerable matron and to give it to belles-lettres. Our friend has even elected me a contributor to his *Bibliothek*, but I am afraid that his choice will prove an unfortunate one.[4]

The garden in which Mendelssohn's transformation into a *bel esprit* was enacted had a *genius loci* of its own. It was the garden of the house in the Spandauer Strasse 68 (later 33), where Lessing had lived with his cousin Mylius from November, 1748, until the end of 1751. Nicolai occupied it from 1755 until 1757. After him the poet Ramler stayed there until 1759, and from 1762 on it was Mendelssohn's residence until his death in 1786. He did not become the owner of the house, but his widow bought it in 1787.[5] In Mendelssohn's and Nicolai's correspondence with Lessing and later, after Mendelssohn moved into the house, in his letters to Thomas Abbt, the garden of this house assumes distinctly idyllic features.[6]

As Mendelssohn's August 2 letter indicates, he was a little uneasy about his new "inclination." He felt it was a betrayal of his first and true love, metaphysics, but he assuaged his conscience by persuading himself that his flirting with belles-lettres would be only a temporary affair. As events turned out, it lasted longer than he anticipated, for his career as a literary critic extended over eleven years, from 1757 to 1768.[7] However, even during this period his libido was by no means "withdrawn" from metaphysics. Two major metaphysical works, the prize-essay on *Evidence* and his celebrated *Phaedon*, appeared in 1764 and 1767, respectively. Nor can his writings on aesthetic theory from 1757 onward be considered as divorced from metaphysics. Even so, a goodly portion of his time and energy were channeled into literary criticism and, though only to a very minor degree, into the writing of poetry, both secular and religious.

From a pure metaphysician Mendelssohn had changed into a more richly orchestrated being. His friendship with Nicolai helped to develop an "inclination" that must have been dormant in him. He even took lessons in piano playing. His teacher was Johann Philipp Kirnberger, a composer and the *Hofmusicus* (court musician) of Princesse Amalia of Prussia. What motivated him to go in for this was not so much his interest in the mathematical aspects of musical theory, as Nicolai ventured to suggest,[8] but, undoubtedly, a sheer love of music. "Divine musical art!," he exclaimed in the letters *On the Sentiments*, "thou art the only one that astonishes us with every kind of pleasure!"[9] Such was the excitement that music aroused in him that in later years he was forced to deny himself the pleasure of attending a concert in the evening.[10] He did not make much progress as a player of the piano,[11] but he did become an excellent theoretician of music. A treatise on the best method of constructing a well-tempered pianoforte, which was anonymously published twice (in 1761 and 1764) was his work.[12] It was based on a study of Leonhard Euler's *Tentamen novae theoriae musicae* (Petersburg, 1739).

As he had predicted in his letter of August 2, 1756, Mendelssohn also tried his hand at the writing of poetry, although he had realized even as a child that he was not born to be a poet. On April 29, 1757, he sent Lessing twenty lines of verse as a sample of a few hundred "such-like things" he had written and which "looked like verse."[13] They are no more than modest efforts in imitating the didactic poetry of Pope, Young, and, above all, Haller.[14] In November he sent Lessing some more verse, which he had written shortly before "out of chagrin over some adversities," and which Nicolai had urged him not to withhold from Lessing. Unfortunately, the text of this piece is lost. Lessing found the *Ode* very beautiful and reminded Mendelssohn to let him have the remaining part of the didactic poem.[15] He also praised a sermon that Mendelssohn had composed and sent to him. He added: "I positively want to see all your poetic works, though I do not want you to spend more time on poetry than on philosophy. For you are indeed right: only part of our youth should belong to belles-lettres; we have to address ourselves to more important things before we die."[16] Mendelssohn did not take his versifying too seriously. In later years he looked back upon it—and poetry in general—as no longer a matter of delight. "Your poetry does not please me," he wrote to August Hennings, a friend of his latter years. "Does one of my age perhaps lose the taste for poetic art altogether? I suspect something like this to be true. For I no longer love the best poetic works nearly as much as I used to. Even *Nathan the Wise*, I believe, would please me better if it had been written in prose, like *Emilia Galotti*..."[17] Mendelssohn's transformation into a *bel esprit* had, indeed, been only a temporary diversion from his natural path—but one that had lent an added quality of charm to his personality.

No account of Mendelssohn's exercises in ars poetica would be complete without some mention of his synagogal hymns and sermons. The young *bel esprit* was by no means averse to putting his talents at the service of the Berlin community. The chance to do so was provided by the Seven Years' War. When Austria and Saxony opened hostilities against Prussia toward the end of 1756, the Jews of Berlin added to their daily prayers the recital of certain appropriate psalms and a special prayer composed in Hebrew by Hartog Leo and translated into German by Mendelssohn.[18] Frederick II's surprising victory at Rossbach caused great jubilation and was celebrated by a thanksgiving service in the synagogue on November 12, 1757. Mendelssohn, again, translated a Hebrew text, a hymn written by Hartog Leo, into German. It was published by the community,[19] and it seems that it had also been planned to publish Mendelssohn's German version of the sermon preached by Chief Rabbi Fränkel.[20] Another great victory, at Leuthen, was duly celebrated on December 10, 1757. The same pattern was repeated, but this time both the hymn and the sermon were published in German.[21] According to the title page, the sermon had been "delivered" by Fränkel[22] and then "translated into German" (omitting Mendelssohn's name). In fact, however, Mendelssohn had written the sermon, as he remarked in a letter to Lessing that, on internal evidence, can be dated about December 15, 1757:[23] "I shall no longer swear to anything in the world after it has come to pass that I write a sermon and praise a king. I also translated some Hebrew thanksgiving hymns into German, and these are printed." This sermon, which is the one praised in Lessing's letter of December, 1757,[24] is the earliest known specimen of modern Jewish preaching in the German tongue.[25] It has a slightly philosophical flavor and reflects the spirit of the Enlightenment. The "light of knowledge" is said to be spreading to all civilized nations. Men had to be active and use their God-given talents to best advantage since, as a rule, God did not produce miracles "without necessity."[26] The heroic efforts of the king are praised as the true miracle of the time in which they lived.

When the Seven Years' War came finally to its end, Mendelssohn wrote the beautiful *Friedenspredigt* ("Sermon on Peace"), in which his multifaceted personality is perfectly mirrored. The metaphysician, the *bel esprit,* and the rabbinic scholar blend in this little masterpiece of homiletics. Its text is a saying of Rabbi Joshua in the minor talmudic tractate *Perek Shalom:* "How very great is peace, seeing that God himself chose for his name the designation 'YHWH of peace.' "[27] In explaining the meaning of this phrase, Mendelssohn recalls that "in our Holy Scriptures the name YHWH signifies the gracious concurrence and special governance of God, by which he directs all things in the world in the way required by his holy purposes." God's purposes in creating, preserving, and governing the world "are but the happiness of his creatures; for his motivation is love, and his final purpose is the bestowal of his infinite Light, the glory of his majesty." Now, war is a condition in which men hurt one another and seek to impede happiness, a condition that runs counter to God's purposes. When war obtains, the ways of Providence are obscured and God's holy governance of the world seems to have ceased. It is only when the world is at peace that the concurrence of God and his creatures is in evidence. Hence YHWH is truly the Lord when he is known as YHWH of peace.

The essence of this homily is completely in tune with Jewish thinking, but its terminology betrays strong Leibnizian influence. Particularly striking is the term "concurrence," which translates Leibniz' phrase *"concursus"* as used by him in his *"Causa Dei,"* an appendix to the *Essais de Théodicée.* This small tract, which tries to vindicate Providence, was used by Mendelssohn at a later period in order to present a Jewish version of a defense of

Providence.[28] It seems, however, that already at the time of writing his *Sermon on Peace* he was immersed in Leibniz' *"Causa Dei,"* many more traces of which can be detected in the sermon.

The *Friedenspredigt* was read at the thanksgiving service on March 12, 1763, by the new Chief Rabbi Aaron Mosessohn, who had succeeded David Fränkel after Fränkel's death in 1762. Judging from a report in the official Berlin gazette, the "edifying and well-constructed address" was favorably received, but Mendelssohn himself poked fun at it when replying to Lessing's request for a copy.[29] The sermon was published by Nicolai, but Mendelssohn permitted himself the joke of presenting it, on the title-page, as "Aaron Mosessohn's Sermon on Peace translated into German by R.S.K.," the initials representing the name "Rabbi Samson Kalir." A man of this name had published Mendelssohn's Hebrew commentary on Maimonides' *Logical Terms* in his own name.[30] "Since Rabbi Samson Kalir has appropriated my *Logic,"* Mendelssohn remarked with a sense of amusement, "let him also take my sermon unto himself."[31]

In a way, Mendelssohn had become the poet laureate of the Berlin Jewish community. Apart from his German translations of Hartog's Hebrew hymns, he wrote German poems of his own for patriotic occasions. When Frederick II returned to his capital on March 30, 1763, after concluding the peace treaty of Hubertusburg, his triumphant advent kept the poets quite busy. Thus Ramler composed an ode, and so did Mendelssohn at the request of the community elders, who presented a loyal address containing his poem to the king as he entered the city. Mendelssohn's ode must also have circulated in print, since Hamann told a friend of his in a letter that he had read it the day before, and he made a copy of the entire text.[32] The first six stanzas—there were seven in all—were also recorded by Lavater in his Berlin diary on April 18, 1763, after a visit to Mendelssohn.[33] Except for Hamann and Lavater the ode would have been lost to posterity. Other poems of this genre were written by Mendelssohn when joyful events in the life of the royal family were celebrated in the synagogue.[34] Mendelssohn the *bel esprit* proved to be a useful member of the community.

Of incomparably greater significance than his writing of poems[35] was his activity as a literary critic and theoretician of the arts. Nicolai's *Bibliothek der schönen Wissenschaften und der freyen Künste* was to be launched in the autumn of 1756, but the outbreak of the war delayed the first volume until May, 1757.[36] To the four volumes that appeared in 1757–1758 Mendelssohn contributed no less than twenty-one review-articles.[37] Prior to publication of the first number, Nicolai and he had engaged in the famous correspondence with Lessing on the theme of the aesthetic categories of the tragedy. The correspondence lasted from August 31, 1756, until May 14, 1757. It was stimulated by Nicolai's *Abhandlung vom Trauerspiel* ("Treatise on Tragedy"), which was scheduled to appear in the first issue of the *Bibliothek.*[38]

In this essay Nicolai set out to refute Aristotle's view of the cathartic purpose of the tragedy and to suggest that its true purpose was the stirring up of the passions.[39] Lessing, on the other hand, supported Aristotle's theory. He interpreted the much-debated twin objects of "fear and pity" as a feeling of compassion for the doomed hero of the play. In his *On the Sentiments*[40] Mendelssohn had described fear in precisely these terms. Fear was not pure horror (since we do not fear for ourselves but for the hero on the stage) but a blend of dread and pleasure, a mixed sentiment, inasmuch as pity is composed of both love (which affords pleasure) and pain.[41] Lessing held that the aim of the tragedy was to enlarge our capacity for pity. He claimed Mendelssohn as an ally who would agree with his proposition that "the most compassionate man is the best man." He obviously had in mind a statement by Mendelssohn, in his critique of Rousseau, to the effect that pity was not founded on a natural instinct but on love, and that love was based on the pleasure we derive from a sense of harmony and order.[42]

While Mendelssohn and Lessing certainly did agree on this point, the particular stand that Mendelssohn took in the correspondence concerned the role of admiration. He expressed the view that admiration was an essential ingredient in the effect produced by the tragedy, since it endowed mere pity with an ultimate sense of elation at the sight of heroic virtue. Lessing, on the other hand, contended that admiration served only as a respite from the oppressiveness of pity. He felt, moreover, that heroism had no place in tragedy, as ancient Greek tragedy clearly proved. To Lessing's exhortation, "Let us learn from the ancients," Mendelssohn replied:[43]

> With you I want to learn from the ancient poets, but after we have left their school, do come with me to learn from the ancient sculptors. I have never seen their works of art but Winckelmann . . ., whose fine taste I trust, tells us that their sculptors never allowed their gods and heroes to be carried away by an unrestrained passion. One invariably finds in them, he said, "nature at peace," and the passions accompanied by a certain tranquillity of soul by which the painful emotion of pity is varnished, as it were, with admiration and reverence. He mentions, for example, Laokoön, whom Vergil designed poetically and whom a Greek artist hewed out in marble. The former admirably portrays Laokoön's pain, while the latter presents him as conquering his pain, as it were, and he surpasses the poet to the extent in which mere compassion is inferior to pity mixed with admiration and reverence.

As Nicolai pointed out, this passage was destined to serve as the nucleus of Lessing's *Laokoön*. By drawing attention to Winckelmann's *Thoughts on the Imitation of the Works of the Greeks in Painting and Sculpture* (1755) and, more especially, by singling out the reference to Laokoön,[44] Mendelssohn prepared the ground for Lessing's masterpiece,[45] and indeed, without Mendelssohn the *Laokoön* might not have been written.[46] When the draft of the work was ready in 1762/63, Lessing invited the critical comments of

Mendelssohn and Nicolai.[47] The manuscript he sent them consisted of forty-two pages with a margin as wide as the text. The copious annotations he received were only partly heeded but a great deal of what Mendelssohn had written in his *Reflections on the Sources and Connections of Belles-lettres and the Arts* (1757) had been used and further developed in the *Laokoön*.[48]

When Nicolai began to publish the *Literaturbriefe*, early in 1759, it was Mendelssohn and Lessing, and from 1761 onward Mendelssohn and Abbt, who carried the main burden of the twenty-four volumes that appeared regularly until 1765.[49] To a subsequent tremendous undertaking by Nicolai, the *Allgemeine deutsche Bibliothek*, Mendelssohn contributed only sporadically from 1765 to 1775.[50] His reputation as a writer already stood high when he commenced his role as a critic, but it now grew by leaps and bounds as a result of the grace of style and competent manner in which he exercised his new responsibility.

The idea for the journal had come from Lessing, who thought the *Bibliothek* much too tame and too lenient toward mediocrity. It was his spark that kindled the daring spirit of the *Literaturbriefe* and made it the exciting and invigorating enterprise that it turned out to be. Although the review-articles were anonymous—they were signed by arbitrarily chosen initials that changed from time to time—the identity of the reviewer was usually recognizable from his way of writing.[51] Mendelssohn was an enthusiastic, hard-working member of the team. Nothing could have better suited his temperament than the epistolary form of reviewing. Addressing an imaginary friend, he could permit himself a degree of informality and emotion that enlivened his impeccably methodical observations. He could also introduce fictional devices, as he had done in his metaphysical writings. Thus, when reviewing Wieland's tragedy *Clementina of Porretta* he feigned regret at not having carried out his own long-standing plan to dramatize this theme; now that Wieland had forestalled him, he wanted to give the reasons that had deterred him from proceeding with his plan. He goes on to show that the principal characters of the play had hardly any theatrical quality, and he thereby makes his criticism of Wieland's work all the more pungent.[52]

Mendelssohn's review-letters show him to be equally at home in German, English, and French poetry, in aesthetic theory, and in philosophy. When evaluating German didactic poetry he draws comparisons with English writings of the same genre.[53] As a *bel esprit* who was at the same time a metaphysician, he was able to find fault with Withof's poetic portrayal of Leibniz' system.[54] He exhibited the same dual competence when reviewing Frederick II's *Poésies diverses* (1760). There was some piquancy in the fact that he, a Jew, was entrusted with this particular review.[55] In 1757 he had "praised" the king in a sermon (as he wrote to Lessing at the time),[56] but now he mixed praise with criticism of the most adroit and tactful sort. It ill behooved a subject, he declared, to be a panegyrist of his sovereign. He had to distrust himself, lest his heart take sides before the intellect had passed its verdict. Yet this much he could say: one could rarely find in a poet so much philosophy, sublimity of sentiment, psychological insight, felicitous imagery, tenderness of feeling, and naturalness of language as one could find here. But what a loss to the German language, that this monarch had made the French tongue his own! And how strange that he should have adopted the tone of a dogmatist advocating, in his denial of the soul's immortality, the shallowest of metaphysical systems, namely that of Epicurus! It seemed to him that a Frederick who doubted immortality was a mere chimera, a square circle or a round square.[57] There was no lack of irony, surely, in a Jew chiding the king of Prussia for having neglected the German tongue.

Mendelssohn's expertise in aesthetics and in the theory of art made him the ideal judge of writings in these fields. He could speak with the authority of a man who possessed not only good taste but also a decided viewpoint and theories of his own. He zealously defended Alexander Baumgarten's definition of a poem as "a perfect sensual way of speaking" (*sensitiva oratio perfecta*),[58] but he did not hesitate to criticize him for having based his aesthetics too narrowly on poetry alone.[59] Truly remarkable, and an indication of the extent to which Mendelssohn broke away from the conventional and arid thinking of the Enlightenment, was his understanding of what constitutes a *genie*, a man of genius. In his review of Curtius' *Critical Essays about the Sublime in Poetry* (1760) he asked: "How can I better understand the sublimity of a Homer or Shakespeare than by assuming that they possessed, by nature, a lofty audaciousness in thinking great thoughts, and had vehement and enthusiastic passion? Art taught them to order thoughts, figures, and words in a way most appropriate to the sublime. However, I have mentioned men of genius who, it seems, are not thought of too highly by Herr Curtius. Of the Englishman he says in his stubborn and disdainful manner: 'Shakespeare's tragedies, especially his *Hamlet*, are, according to Voltaire, a composite of immense faults and dazzling beauties.' Oh, here I lost all my patience. Is this the way to speak about one of the greatest geniuses in tragedy who ever lived? . . . Surely, only one knowing Shakespeare only through Voltaire could pass such a judgment."[60] The ordinary rules of dramatic art, says Mendelssohn, do not bind a genius, and who can, with impunity, imitate him? "What does Ulysses' bow profit me if I am unable to bend it? Shakespeare is the only dramatic poet who can dare to let jealousy in *Othello* and madness in *King Lear* arise, grow, and reach a climax before the audience without the use of intermediate scenes. . . . Yet who is bold enough to steal the club from a Hercules or dramatic devices from a Shakespeare?"[61] How, then, is one to define genius? Was Sulzer right in regarding it as a combination of sagacity, judgment, and presence of mind, and in explaining the *présence d'esprit* as the ability of reason to control enthusiasm and the tempest of the passions? Mendelssohn did not wish to see creative genius reduced to rectitude and faultlessness. He agreed with the Abbot Trublet, who preferred the faults of a genius to the perfection of the mediocre.[62]

Mendelssohn also rejected Resewitz' view that genius consisted in the ability to see things in the concrete, for in that case, he argued, writers who illustrated theories by concrete examples would be greater geniuses than the abstract thinkers who produced the theories in the first place.[63] Mendelssohn was perfectly content to recognize Homer, Shakespeare, and Newton as men of genius without trying to press the phenomenon of genius as such into neat categories.[64] It has been noted that Lessing frequently echoed Mendelssohn's views on poets and dramatists,[65] and that he seems to have owed his appreciation of Shakespeare to Mendelssohn.[66] Lessing rebelled, however, against the lawlessness of genius that the Sturm und Drang movement proclaimed in the seventies of the eighteenth century. Goethe's *Götz von Berlichingen* (1773) greatly displeased him. "We now have," he wrote, "a generation even of critics whose very criticism consists in making all criticism suspect. 'Genius! Genius!' they shout. 'Genius suspends all rules! What genius does is the rule!' "[67] He found the "degeneration" of the theater so annoying that he did not want to pick a quarrel with Goethe, "despite his genius, about which he brags so much," he wrote to his brother.[68] And he told Friedrich Heinrich Jacobi that once Goethe regained his reason he would be hardly more than an ordinary man.[69] At the very same time he said of Mendelssohn that he was the most lucid thinker, the most excellent philosopher, and the best literary critic of the century.[70]

Mendelssohn, in his plea for the sovereignty of genius, had been careful to point out that any imitation of the true genius was fatal. Like Lessing, he failed to recognize the genius of Goethe. The great protagonists of the Enlightenment obviously had their limitations! They abhorred the cult of genius to which the Sturm und Drang gave rise. We encounter the same attitude in Elise Reimarus, who adored both Mendelssohn and Lessing.[71] It is not surprising, therefore, to find that at the end of his life, long after he had ceased to be a *bel esprit,* Mendelssohn described Goethe's poem *Prometheus* as "a poor thing" (*diese Armseligkeit*). Perhaps it was just as well that he was by then no longer active as a critic.

The *Literaturbriefe,* far from restricting Mendelssohn's participation to the reviewing of belles-lettres, gave him ample scope to assert his authority as a philosopher. Herder called him "the first and foremost in profound philosophy among the authors of the *Literaturbriefe*." Only the reviews written by Moses, "the most impartial and most fair-minded philosopher," could lead an apprentice along the road of true *Weltweisheit* (philosophy). His judgments showed him to be a writer of whom one might say, in the words of Thucydides, that he "philologizes with accuracy and philosophizes without sentimentality." Herder's attitude toward Mendelssohn in his early period came close to being that of a disciple.[72]

The very first review written by Mendelssohn was a masterly survey of the philosophical scene, deploring the "revolution" that had dethroned metaphysics and caused a marked deterioration in the fiber of philosophizing.[73] One of his major efforts was an analysis and critique of Ruggiero

Giuseppe Boscovich's system.[74] (Boscovitch's "law of continuity" would be put to good use by Mendelssohn in his *Phaedon.*)[75] Some of his reviews were excursions into physiology. One of them dealt with the spermatozoons, a subject on which a follower of Anton van Leeuwenhoek had written,[76] and another was an elaborate appraisal of Hermann Samuel Reimarus' study of the instincts of animals.[77] The latter provoked a sharp rejoinder by Reimarus and a dignified reply by Mendelssohn, who had the highest regard for the man. Neither could have guessed at the time that Reimarus' son and elder daughter would be among Mendelssohn's most intimate friends in the later years of his life.

A Learned Society

On March 9, 1756, Mendelssohn wrote to Lessing: "In all my life I have not made so many acquaintances as I have done since you left. There is, however, not a single person among them in whose company I could spend my few hours of leisure as pleasantly and usefully as I would with you." Of those he had met he mentioned "Lieutenant Jacobi, a very able man, a good mathematician, and a thorough metaphysician."[1] The broadening of Mendelssohn's circle of friends is explained by a note that Nicolai wrote on this letter:[2]

> Toward the end of the year 1755 a coffeehouse for a closed society of a hundred people, mostly men of learning, was established in Berlin at the suggestion of the late Abbot Resewitz, then candidate [of theology] in Berlin. Jacobi, like Moses and myself, was a member. Every four weeks a paper was read by one of the members, the rest standing around a billiard table. I remember that Herr Johann Albrecht Euler[3] . . . read a thoughtful mathematical paper on billiards entitled: "On the motion of two balls on a horizontal plane." Resewitz too presented there his essay *On Genius* and Moses' treatise *On Probability* also owed its origin to this society and was read before it. . . . Once Herr Johann Albrecht Euler, Doctor Gumpertz, and Lieutenant Jacobi played a game of taroc in this society. They had some quarrel about the tarocs played and asked Moses, who happened to be close at hand, to act as arbiter. Moses exclaimed: How marvellous! Three mathematicians cannot properly count twenty-one!—This amiable society declined gradually. At the start of the Seven Years' War several members were drafted. . . . Others left Berlin on account of promotions elsewhere, e.g., J. A. Euler, Aepinus, Wilke, Resewitz, Bamberger, and in the end Müchler, too, who had a great share in the establishment of the society . . .

Recalling the past after more than fifty years—the note was written in 1810—Nicolai said of this short-lived society that it "contributed very much not only to social culture but also to the advancement of learning among its members."[4] According to his recollection, Resewitz was the founder of the society, while Müchler only "had a great share" in its establishment. A letter from Müchler to Georg August von Breitenbauch, dated April

2, 1756, gives a slightly different picture of his own role and of the character of the organization:[5]

> I must inform you of a new foundation that I have brought about here in Berlin. I have created a society of forty people, mostly men of learning, but artists too, who have rented two large rooms. In one we placed a billiard table. . . . Members go there every day. Coffee and whatever one wants is to be had at a cheap price, and one meets pleasant company. On one day every week all members assemble. One talks, jokes, and reads something to one another. One finds there all kinds of learned periodicals, *journaux*, and other things. Each member pays an entrance fee of only two thalers. Expenses are covered by the billiards. . . . Our society has secretaries, stewards, and supervisors. Every member is entitled to introduce a stranger . . .

Müchler's description stresses the social aspect of the society rather than its academic purpose. There were quite possibly two schools of thought about the objects to be achieved and, hence, two different claims to the title of "founder." Judging from the variety and standard of the papers presented, the "Learned Coffeehouse" was an academy in miniature and on a lower social level. To Mendelssohn this pleasant, unpretentious, truly democratic society of scholars and artists was a godsend. Though it could not replace Lessing, it provided him with a social milieu in which his philosophical pursuits were appreciated. The "few hours of leisure" that he could spare from his daily work were now spent in congenial company.

His employer, Isaac Bernhard, who had appointed him as a tutor of his children in 1750, had made him a clerk in his silk factory in 1754. Bernhard was a highly enterprising businessman, who knew how keen the Prussian government was to promote the rise of the silk industry in the *Kurmark* Brandenburg. He was one of the first Jews in Berlin to receive a "concession" to open a factory. This happened in 1752.[6] Two years later, when he made Mendelssohn a clerk in his business, he had just received a government loan of seven thousand thalers for the enlargement of his plant. In 1758 he took over a large factory in Potsdam, thereby increasing the number of looms to forty. The expansion of his business was in considerable measure due to the hard work that his clerk put in, and Bernhard recognized Mendelssohn's devotion and commercial talent by promoting him to the position of manager in 1761.

We need not pursue Mendelssohn's business career in the present context. Much as it satisfied his material needs, and in later years increasingly established his authority as an expert in this branch of industry, it tended to sap his energies and left him little time in which to do the things he loved most. There was something glaringly incongruous about the two sides of his life, one spent in the company of traders, the other in the atmosphere of the most refined culture. His letters to Lessing reflect the pain he suffered as a result of this dichotomy. Even after his marriage, when the necessity of making a living might have seemed more acceptable, he bitterly complained: "True, I consider myself happily married and, thank God, have no reason to complain about my circumstances. But the business! The bothersome business affairs! They wear me out and consume the energies of my best years. Like a beast of burden, I drag myself through the years with a heavy load on my back."[7] The happy hours he was able to spend at the Learned Coffeehouse eased the burden of the "heavy load."

Another society in which Mendelssohn would have felt equally at home, and which would have welcomed him gladly, was the Berlin "Monday Club" founded in 1749 by the Swiss theologian Johann Georg Schulthess. Lessing joined it in 1752. Its membership, limited to twenty-four, included Nicolai, Sulzer, Ramler, Quanz (the flutist at Frederick II's court at Sanssouci), Johann Wilhelm Meil (the well-known painter and engraver), and Thomas Abbt, among others. The members met for dinner every Monday evening, and it is obviously for this reason that Mendelssohn, who strictly observed the Jewish dietary laws, chose not to become a member.[8]

The Learned Coffeehouse furnished the inspiration as well as the setting for the delivery of Mendelssohn's important paper *Thoughts on Probability*.[9] The amusing story of the manner in which this paper was presented is told in two slightly different versions, one by Nicolai,[10] the other by David Friedländer, who had heard it from Mendelssohn.[11] According to the second version, which would seem to be the authentic one,[12] Mendelssohn's shyness caused him to devise a stratagem by which to avoid disclosing the fact that he was the author of the paper. The plan was simple enough: a friend would read the paper and Mendelssohn would admit to being its author only if it was well received. During the reading a member of the club, a certain Lord Middleton,[13] whispered into Mendelssohn's ear: You are the author! Mendelssohn denied it and pointed at the reader, but Middleton shook his head incredulously. Unfortunately, the reader had little understanding of the contents of the paper and, toward the end, he mispronounced zero (0) as "oh." Mendelssohn could not resist correcting him, whereupon the audience, particularly Lord Middleton, burst into laughter. The identity of the author was now apparent. Lessing referred to this funny incident in a letter dated October, 1756, when requesting Mendelssohn to let him have, by return of post, his treatise on probability: "Even though I may not grasp it completely, I shall not, I hope, mistake a zero for an oh."[14]

The delivery of this paper by proxy, though not in absentia, lent a touch of humor to what was a serious piece of work. The treatise, which in the *Philosophical Writings* is renamed *On Probability* but is also referred to by Mendelssohn as *Treatise on Probability*, shows his competence both as a mathematician and as a metaphysical thinker. Its purpose is to utilize the mathematical theory of probability in order to substantiate a metaphysical notion. His fragment of 1753 had already indicated such a tendency. The treatise proceeds in three stages.[15] At the first of them, the definitions of probability offered by Bernoulli, 's Gravesand, and Wolff are reviewed and a logical explanation of statistical probability is advanced. Then the concept of "hypothesis" as a tool of science is discussed, and the fruitfulness of Wolff's interpretation of probability as linked to the principle of sufficient reason is demonstrated. At the second stage, the treatise deals with Hume's skepticism. Looking at it from a new angle, which strikes us today as surprisingly modern, it takes Hume's intent to have been not to question the principle of causality as such but to cast doubt on the validity of inferences by induction. As a solution of the problem posed by Hume, Mendelssohn suggested the use of the theory of probability. At the third stage of the paper the metaphysical concern comes to the fore. Leibniz' determinism had been attacked, as we know,[16] by Crusius and some members of the Royal Academy. Mendelssohn seeks to prove the correctness of Leibniz' determinism with the help of the theory of probability. He does so by pointing out that the degree of probability attaching to God's foreknowledge of human actions would be zero unless one assumed its certainty. This assumption was impossible, however, if determinism was rejected.

It was the argument for determinism that involved Mendelssohn in a protracted polemic with another member of the club, Franz Ulrich Theodosius Aepinus, a respected mathematician and physicist, who was also a member of the academy. The only record we have of this controversy is provided by Mendelssohn's correspondence with Lessing to whom, early in December, 1756, Mendelssohn sent a copy of the treatise, with the remark: "Professor Aepinus delivered himself of a refutation of it in our society last Thursday. I shall let you have it, together with my reply, as soon as possible."[17] On December 18 Lessing wrote: "I have read your treatise on probability with very great pleasure; after having read it a few more times, I shall understand it sufficiently well, I hope, to be able to ask you for some clarification here and there. If it were only possible to chat about such matters as easily as about the subject of tragedy!"[18] On March 2, 1757, Mendelssohn remarked: "I still owe you Herr Professor Aepinus' refutation of my treatise on probability as well as my reply. I still believe myself to be right, though Herr Aepinus did not fail to retort. The man is a hot-headed opponent of Wolff and a partisan of the *Aequilibrii indifferentiae*.[19] It hurts him to see the principle of sufficient reason demonstrated in respect of voluntary human actions in so novel a way."[20]

The energy with which Mendelssohn stuck to his guns is evident from a letter he addressed on January 6, 1758, to Professor Alexander Gottlieb Baumgarten, whom he had already consulted on this matter in September or October, 1757, without receiving a satisfactory reply. The second letter contains a closely argued defense of his position and expresses the hope that Baumgarten would not leave it to Aepinus to have the last word.[21] This hope was not to be fulfilled, nor did Lessing express an opinion on Mendelssohn's first letter to Baumgarten and Baumgarten's answer.[22] Lessing felt incompetent to write on the subject, since he was not sure that he had properly understood the two opposing views.[23] Mendelssohn, on the other hand, remained perfectly convinced of the rightness of his claim. More than once he referred to his proof for determinism in his subsequent writings. He mentioned it in the preface to the first edition of his *Philosophical Writings* (1761) and in a note added there to his letters *On the Sentiments:* "In my *Treatise on Probability* I ventured a new proof of this proposition [viz. that all volitions are determined], that, if it be correct, has the advantage of not depending on any particular system."[24] In his prize-essay *Evidence in Metaphysical Sciences* (written in 1762) he used the proof without any qualification,[25] and toward the end of his life he recapitulated the results of his investigations in the *Treatise on Probability* concerning the legitimacy of the inductive method, without, however, touching on the proof for determinism.[26] It appears that the paper presented at the Learned Coffeehouse turned out to be one of his favorite writings. Certainly it was a most original piece of work.

Of lighter caliber was the literary activity in which Mendelssohn engaged jointly with Müchler, the cofounder of the club. Johann Georg Müchler (1724–1819) hailed from Swedish Pomerania and was, at that time, private tutor in the household of *Hofrat* Stahl. He later became a professor at the Collegium Groeningianum at Stargard but left his position in 1773 and passed through a difficult time until 1785, when he was appointed professor of Latin at the Berlin Académie Militaire and inspector of the Schindler Orphanage. He was a theologian by training, a *bel esprit* by inclination. His prolific output included many translations from the French and English.[27]

Mendelssohn agreed to become Müchler's anonymous coeditor of a moralistic weekly called *Der Chamäleon,* of which eighteen numbers appeared in 1756. The articles that he contributed to this pleasant but in no way remarkable journal show the serious philosopher in a more relaxed, almost frolicsome mood and thus present him from a new and unexpected angle. He himself never referred to the *Chamäleon,* let alone to his association with it.[28] His writing for this paper was merely an outlet for the lighter side of his nature. However, one should not underestimate the care that he bestowed on even the minor efforts of his muse. Some of them are replete with literary references and testify to the wide range of his reading.[29] Their sense of humor reflects his happy frame of mind in these years of youth and tranquillity of soul.

One of the essays offered instruction to young people on how they ought to read the ancient and modern poets. Taking his cue from Plutarch's treatise on this very theme, and presenting his own views in the form of a letter by Aristes to his grandson Hylas, Mendelssohn offers a kind of popular abstract of his letters *On the Sentiments* when, e.g., he distinguishes between theatrical and true morality.[30] A collection of his epigrams in the *Chamäleon* contains some pithy observations: "A philosopher who strives for a position of high honor is like an alchemist begging for alms in return for his invention of the philosopher's stone." "Princes are actors and those called wise men are people hired to applaud them." "A highly placed man whose tumultuous passions keep him from listening to the voice of humanity deserves our pity. A highly placed man who hears but cold-bloodedly silences the voice of reason deserves to be detested."[31] The letter (fictitious) of a young girl who is afraid of the month of May—that month whose "dangers" were a favorite topic in contemporary journals and formed the subject of a well-known poem by Johann Gleim[32]—is answered in a reassuring way: too much ado was being made about the overpowering effect of springtime. "We fail to see why the westerly winds playing around your face in spring should affect your heart more forcefully than the gentle blow of your fan which, surely, never spelled danger for you."[33]

A humorous parallel to Mendelssohn's translation of Rousseau's second *Discours* was published in the *Chamäleon* under the title "Reflection on the Inequality and Sociability of Men; also a New Plan to Make the Faces of Men reasonable and moral."[34] Rousseau is here treated in satirical fashion—Rousseau who had given "comfort to all fools" by proving that there was nothing more shameful that men could do than strive for wisdom. According to him, a man noticing such a propensity in himself ought to beat his head until this dangerous preoccupation, which makes one dizzy, is made to disappear. Curious readers desiring to know more about Rousseau's strange doctrine might profitably consult the German translation (i.e., Mendelssohn's), which had been published recently. Its keynote was that all civilized nations were degenerate and inferior to the orang-utans and pongos. It was timely, therefore, to publish an epistle, currently being circulated in Switzerland, describing the way in which Rousseau's *Discours* had been received in that country. According to this epistle [which was, of course, purely imaginary], some people had shown an eagerness to restore the highly desirable state of nature by abolishing private property, dissolving society, and returning everyone to the forests. But others, on the contrary, had reaffirmed the dignity of civilized human beings, who had raised themselves from merely sentient animality to the imitation of God and to true happiness. However, it was conceded by these advocates of intellectual and social culture that a return to nature might prove a blessing to social misfits. With this idea in mind, a successor of the famous Abbé de Saint Pierre (1658–1743), the social reformer, had devised a "Patriotic Design to Make Men Altogether Happier." It suggested measures by which the lot of the unhappy ones who suffered from civilization could be improved. Motivated by pure love, the government ought to apprehend and subject the sufferers to drastic measures (such as solitary confinement in dark caves, stupefying potions, etc.) that would obliterate from their minds all images held by them to be the perverse products of culture. Then, having been cured of their malaise, they should be sent to the forests to join, as human animals, similar species of the animal kingdom. This race would propagate itself, presumably, and our philosophers would then be in a position to study primitive man at close quarters without having to undertake arduous expeditions into distant lands. This rather cruel satire hardly agrees with Mendelssohn's gentle nature, nor does it represent his true understanding of Rousseau. But it suited the moralizing tone of the *Chamäleon* and made for entertaining reading.[35]

The irony displayed in Mendelssohn's contributions to the *Chamäleon* recalls the light-heartedness of anacreontic poetry, which had lately gained a considerable popularity in Germany. Lessing had already outgrown this sort of youthful exuberance but Mendelssohn, who had never before experienced the gaiety of youth, now felt a certain kinship with the anacreontic spirit and gave vent to it in his own way.

Mendelssohn also contributed to another Müchler-edited periodical called *Beschäftigungen des Geistes und des Herzens* ("Preoccupations of the Mind and the Heart"), of which two volumes appeared in 1755/1756, and for which he wrote German translations of medieval Hebrew poetry. One of these was of Jehuda Ha-Levi's beautiful elegy *Tsiyyon ha-lo' tish'ali . . .* ("Zion, dost thou not ask for the peace of thy captives?"), in which the age-old yearning of exiled Jewry for a return to the Holy Land is given sublime expression.[36] The other text translated by Mendelssohn at this time was Yedaya Bedershi's *Behinat 'Olam* ("A Scrutiny of the World"), a philosophical meditation on the vanity of earthly concerns. Mendelssohn translated two chapters of this popular work, which has run into more than seventy editions.[37] One is amazed to find that as early as 1755/1756 Mendelssohn was capable of rendering difficult Hebrew texts of a poetic character into German. According to both Nicolai's testimony and his own admission,[38] Mendelssohn's command of the German vernacular still left much to be desired in those years; but on reading the perfect German of these two translations one has to wonder whether there was much justification for this feeling.

Müchler well summed up the spirit of Mendelssohn's contributions to the *Chamäleon* when, more than thirty years later, he described them as "satirical and good-humored" and as "the fruits of some serene hours in his best years."[39] The two poetic pieces that appeared in the other journal reflect a much deeper layer of his personality. They were motivated, obviously, by a desire to convey to non-Jewish readers the nobility of sentiment to be found in medieval Hebrew literature of the Spanish period and, thereby, to raise the image of the Jew in Christian eyes.

Another member of the Learned Coffeehouse with whom Mendelssohn established happy relations was Friedrich Gabriel Resewitz. Born in Berlin in 1728, Resewitz had studied under Alexander Baumgarten in Halle and then returned to his native city in 1755 as a "thinking" theologian. In 1757 Princess Anna Amalie, the king's sister, who patronized the fine arts and was, at the same time, abbess of the Quedlinburg convent, offered him the position of preacher at a neighboring church, and he accepted the offer. Later he became German preacher in Copenhagen and, finally, abbot at Kloster Berge. Geographical distance did not prevent him from maintaining close contact with his Berlin friends. In 1759 Nicolai published his translation of John Conybeare's *A Defence of Reveal'd Religion* (1732), and in the period from January, 1764, to May, 1765, Resewitz contributed twenty major articles to the *Literaturbriefe*.[40]

As Nicolai recalled,[41] Mendelssohn and Resewitz were intimate friends when they were together in Berlin. The fact that Resewitz was the son of a baptized Jew apparently did not bother Mendelssohn. In Nicolai's words, they were both committed to the "love of truth." The son of the convert, unlike many a theologian in those days, was tactful enough not to try to win his Jewish friend over to Christianity. In an undated letter that he wrote to Nicolai during the Lavater controversy (September, 1769–May, 1770), Resewitz remarked that "Herr Mendelssohn once expressed to me his satisfaction at my not having sought to convert him, although I was a theologian."[42] When Lessing's publication of the *Fragments of the Unnamed* aroused the ire of the orthodox and Mendelssohn was falsely rumored to be the author, Resewitz wrote to Nicolai, on December 30, 1779: "The surmise that Moses M. is the author of the *Fragments* has not come to my notice; nor would I have believed it, had someone told me so. This treatise runs counter to his mentality, spirit, and style. He would have had to disavow his good and noble character to find it possible to express so much hatred against a religion that never insulted him and under whose protection he lives, and many members of which, moreover, honor him."[43]

Resewitz had, clearly, a high opinion of Mendelssohn's character. He was also an admirer of his style of writing. After the publication of the *Phaedon* he wrote to Nicolai on October 21, 1767: "I always held the view: if any German can write in the Socratic manner, it is Moses." He was less satisfied with Mendelssohn's effort to bring Plato up to date: "So long as Plato speaks in this work, I see Socrates' admirable stride; but when Socrates borrows his thoughts from our time, ... I perceive the synthetic gait of a modern philosopher, albeit of a Moses who makes everything go in an easy and intelligible way, and who so lucidly explains the truth he wants me to see that by its conspicuity it forces its way into my eye."[44] Mendelssohn was less enthusiastic about Resewitz' work. His *Essay on Genius*,[45] the paper he had presented to the members of the club, had not won Mendelssohn's approval. His review of its two parts in the *Literaturbriefe*,[46] though admitting the excellence of many of its observations and the originality of some of them, expressed disagreement with its principal thesis.[47]

An important letter, which almost amounts to a little tract, was written by Mendelssohn on May 15, 1756, in answer to a letter by Resewitz on the question of suicide.[48] Resewitz, who seems to have had an aversion to abstract reasoning, had criticized Mendelssohn's demonstration of the illegitimacy of suicide. How could one hope to restrain a person from taking such a step by proving the metaphysical truth that it violates the laws of nature? Would it not have been more helpful to offer thoughts that might soothe the mind of a distraught man? Mendelssohn agreed that metaphysical reasoning was no substitute for effective pleading. He contended, however, that before employing the powers of persuasion, one had to be sure of the theoretical rightness of one's own principles. To establish the principle of the matter had been his sole concern in the letters *On the Sentiments*. It was now the business of the practical philosopher to express the truth in a way likely to move the will in the right direction.

Resewitz had also attacked some specific points in Mendelssohn's argumentation. He had asked: does our thinking capacity make us happy because it produces clear and distinct ideas or because it produces distinct ideas of such objects as give us pleasure? According to him, the second alternative was true. Mendelssohn disagreed: "I would recall all of Palemon's letters to Euphranor, in which I have shown, I believe, that we find those ideas pleasant which conform to our striving for knowledge." When a person beset by passions achieves distinct ideas, the passions vanish because they are due to obscure ideas. Another objection raised by the critic was the following: if the quality of a person's condition is to be judged entirely in terms of his thinking capacity, irrespective of pleasure or pain, does it not follow that evil spirits and the devil himself possess ultimate perfection, since it is their intellectual ability, not their wretchedness, which counts? Mendelssohn replied: "What you say about the evil spirits is utterly incomprehensible to me. I believe that the d[evil] himself cannot desire anything *nisi sub ratione boni* [except under the aspect of the good].... When a mind has a distinct and live knowledge of good and evil it is bound to desire the good or else the Creator must have originally determined it for evil, i.e., for its own undoing. A monstrous idea that can be accepted as possible only in the realm of poetry!" According to our view of God and the nature of the mind, Satan is both a rogue and a fool. Were his intellectual capacity perfect, he would of necessity be an angel. As for the irrationality of suicide, Mendelssohn reaffirmed his thesis that annihilation by death, assuming there to be no afterlife, amounted to zero. Hence the lowest degree of reality, however unpleasant, was preferable to annihilation. "To be or not to be, that is the question."

Resewitz' theoretical objections and Mendelssohn's answers reflect an earlier correspondence on the same theme that has come to light only recently.[49] In October, 1755, a month after the publication of the letters *On the Sentiments*, Mendelssohn received the first intimation of how the reading public was reacting to his work. It took the form of an elaborate epistle addressed to Müchler. The writer's name was Willich, and the place where he lived was Sukow, in Mecklenburg.[50] It may be surmised that Willich was a tutor at the estate of Ernst Ludwig von Blücher at Sukow, but nothing definite, not even his first name, has yet been established concerning the identity of this person who, as the letter indicates, also corresponded with Sulzer. Willich's letter to Müchler, a friend of his, was meant to be brought to the notice of Mendelssohn. It opened with these words: "You know, esteemed friend, what sort of a zealous defender of suicide I have become in recent years, and how much my attention was aroused when I saw a philosopher as profound as Palemon condemn with strong arguments this exit from the world." Willich's counterarguments impressed Mendelssohn, who felt it necessary to rebut them in a lengthy epistle addressed to Müchler but intended for Willich. It yielded not an inch of ground but expressed the hope that he would hear more from this penetrating thinker. He seems to have shown Willich's letter to Resewitz, for his objections to the arguments advanced in the letters *On the Sentiments* are clearly based, in part, on those expressed by Willich, which gave Mendelssohn an opportunity to repeat the gist of his reply to the first critic in his epistle to Resewitz.[51]

Willich appears actually to have committed suicide after a visit to Berlin, where he had met Mendelssohn and became his friend. The reply to Resewitz' objections opens with this moving passage:

> I cannot possibly recall my argument against suicide without refreshing in my mind the sad memory of that honest friend who was the first to let me share his objections to it. He now enjoys the reward of his virtue in that glorious world in which he beholds the truth in an incomparably brighter light, and from which, perhaps, he looks down upon us with a tranquil pleasure, like a fighter who has won the prize and now sees two young men do their exercises in the valley. I shall never forget the way he bade me farewell the last time he was here, after we had met for the first time at the home of our Herr Müchler and had become fond of each other. "Take care of yourself," he said to me when he left me *unter den Linden:* "We shall be fond of one another but not in the way of the worldly!"[52]

In the tragic figure of Willich the three friends, Mendelssohn, Müchler, and Resewitz, shared a memory poignantly distinct from the jolly recollections of the Learned Coffeehouse.

Kohelet Mussar

In the year 1758[1] Mendelssohn and a young friend decided to edit a Hebrew Weekly called *Kohelet Mussar* ("Preacher of Morals"). Their purpose was twofold: to strengthen Jewish youth in their moral conduct and to arouse their love for the Hebrew tongue.[2] The two aims fore-shadowed the twin goals of the Haskala: an enlightened understanding of Judaism and the renaissance of Hebrew. Yet there was a marked difference between the Haskala and the earlier effort. In 1783, when the first number of *Ha-Me'assef*, the organ of the Maskilim, appeared, the contours of an emerging opposition to strict orthodoxy were clearly visible. In 1758 no antagonism to tradition was consciously implied in the modest undertaking of the two young men. Chief Rabbi David Fränkel, Mendelssohn's teacher, was then still alive. His mellow personality represented tradition at its best. What motivated Mendelssohn and his friend was the urge to counteract the disruptive influence of the Berlin Enlightenment upon young Jews and, at the same time, a desire to make them share their own enthusiasm for the beauty of the Hebrew language, especially of biblical Hebrew. They felt that a revival of the classical Hebrew style was bound to create a sense of aesthetic pleasure and, thereby, of national pride as well.

In reviewing Robert Lowth's *De sacra poesi Hebraeorum* in 1757 Mendelssohn had recorded the author's glowing admiration for the special quality of biblical poetry. Lowth had praised its "extraordinary tenderness, occasional power, and its sublime loftiness." No language, he had said, had celebrated in song the power, the justice, the infinite mercy and wisdom of God so persistently and in so worthy a manner as had the Hebrew tongue.[3] In 1758, when reviewing the medieval Hebrew work *Fables of Foxes (Mishley Shu'alim)* by Berakhya Ha-Nakdan (Berlin, 1756), Mendelssohn suggested that the biblical poets had followed certain metric rules by which they achieved an "excellent rhythmical melodiousness." Having lost the secret of this metric system, later Hebrew writers took to rhymed prose. In more recent times the "good Hebrew authors" flavored their sentences by the skilful quotation of biblical phrases, which often assumed a new meaning through the context in which they were placed. "The difficulty consisted, therefore, in finding in the poems of the old Hebrews, which are all of the genre of sublime poetry, such phrases as could be given a naïve, smiling, and at times jocular turn of meaning. Our poet did this in an inimitable manner."[4] This was an apt characterization of the very style Mendelssohn was just then employing in the Hebrew journal that he and his friend began to publish.

The journal was printed in quarto by Aaron ben Moses Rofe' in Berlin. Only two numbers, each containing eight pages, appeared, and only four copies of the first number and a single copy of the second are still extant.[5] Apart from the title *(Kohelet Mussar)*, they indicate neither the year and place of publication nor the names of the editors and contributors. Mendelssohn never publicly acknowledged his association with this journal. As in the case of his connection with Müchler's periodicals, he preferred anonymity in this instance too. The reason was not so much shyness as an understandable concern for his reputation. Having made a name for himself in philosophy and literary criticism, he saw no need to publicize his authorship of essays that were, in a way, below standard, according to his own judgment. In private, however, he must have referred to the short-lived venture more than once. His disciple and physician Simon Höchheimer, who was also his first biographer,[6] could not have recorded 1758 as the year of publication unless it had been told him by Mendelssohn; nor could Solomon Dubno, his close collaborator from 1778 to 1780, have derived his knowledge about the editors of *Kohelet Mussar* and their motivations from any one except Mendelssohn. Dubno had come to Berlin as late as 1772, when that youthful enterprise had long been forgotten. His copy of the first number, which is now preserved at the British Museum, may have been presented to him by Mendelssohn. The note in Hebrew that Dubro entered on the last page must date from the time before 1780, when he broke with Mendelssohn. It reads as follows:[7]

> The authors of this fascicle are two men of outstanding knowledge of the Tora, God-fearing men of truth, namely the famous scholar, our teacher and master, Rabbi Moses Dessau (may God's mercy keep and deliver him) and his friend, the excellent scholar, our teacher and master, Rabbi Tobias (of blessed memory). It happened in the days of their youth [that they edited it]. Their intention was thereby to awaken those asleep and to arouse those slumbering from the torpor of the age; to train them in the ways of morality and in the improvement of their character; also to enthuse their hearts with the beauty of the style of the holy tongue, seeing that because of our sins, which are many, it has perished from our midst; to make them seek it like silver and search for it as for hidden treasures [Prov. 2:4]. Their original idea was to write and print a fascicle like this one every week and to distribute it among young Jewish men in order that their ambition for writing be whetted; that their knowledge increase; that the gifted among them help each other in the study of the rules of the holy tongue; that they strengthen each other in the knowledge of the language transmitted to us by our fathers, prophets and sages (of blessed memory); so that the tongue of the stammering might soon speak with elegance. However, for some reason their design came to grief, and only this fascicle appeared in print.

Dubno's mistaken assumption that only one issue of *Kohelet Mussar* had appeared may have been due simply to his having obtained only the one copy. The importance of his entry lies in the information it conveys about Mendelssohn's colleague in the enterprise. The way in which Dubno speaks of him suggests that he had known the colleague personally, and that he was no longer alive when the note was written. If so, then, he must have died after 1772, the year in which Dubno came to Berlin. It is also possible, however, that his description of the man simply reflects the eulogies Mendelssohn bestowed upon him when reminiscing about the distant past, and that Tobias had passed away as a young man long ago. This would explain the fact that the official records of the Jewish community in Berlin contain no reference to a member called Tobias whose personal data fit the person who could have been the coeditor of *Kohelet Mussar*. All attempts to identify the man have failed.[8] Isaac Euchel, who is our only other source for the knowledge of the coeditor's name, spoke in similar terms about him as "his [Mendelssohn's] friend" and as "a man known as an enlightened and intelligent person, our teacher and master, Rabbi Tobias (the memory of the righteous be for a blessing)."[9]

It seems that Euchel also owed his knowledge to Mendelssohn, whom he visited in the summer of 1784 on his way from Königsberg to his native Copenhagen.[10] As editor of *Ha-Me'assef*, he published in 1785 three essays from *Kohelet Mussar*.[11] His editorial comment on the first of them reads as follows: "This letter is taken from the writing [*mikhtabh*] *Kohelet Mussar* which was published [*hubbar*] long ago in Berlin by men of clear mind and pure heart; it came into our hands through one of our friends there and we owe him thanks for it, for it is all sweetness."[12] The friend was probably Mendelssohn himself, for who else would have dared to submit these old essays for publication? Though he still felt the need to preserve their anonymity, he must have taken Euchel into his confidence and told him what he had mentioned to Dubno some years before: that his collaborator was the late *Morenu Ha-Rav* Rabbi Tuvya (Tobias), a man versed also in secular knowledge. In deference to Mendelssohn's wishes, Euchel's editorial note, though mentioning the journal by name, referred to the editors only in the vaguest terms. After Mendelssohn's death he felt free to record, in his biography of the master, all he knew about the editorship, and thus it came about that in addition to Mendelssohn's name that of Tobias was revealed. Unfortunately, this information only created a mystery, since the absence of any cognomen made the identification of Tobias impossible.

It should be noted that Dubno's and Euchel's only source of information concerning the coeditor of *Kohelet Mussar* seems to have been Mendelssohn himself. It is clear from Dubno's report that Tobias, like Mendelssohn, was a young man when he joined the enterprise. Therefore he could not have been identical with Tobias Soldin, who was a generation older than Mendelssohn and had died in 1755.[13] Nor could he have been identical with Tobias ben Moses Schwabach, who died as late as 1788.[14] It is equally impossible to assume that Rabbi Tuvya (Tobias) was identical with the great banker and spokesman of the Dutch Jewish communities Tobias Boaz, who acted as a Maecenas to a number of Hebrew writers and is referred to in letters by Mendelssohn in 1772 as *Ha-Katsin* Rabbi Tuvya or simply as Rabbi Tuvya.[15] For Tobias Boaz (1696–1782) was sixty-two years old when Mendelssohn edited his periodical and was still alive when Dubno wrote his description of the enterprise, in which he referred to Mendelssohn's friend as being deceased.[16] Besides, a Maecenas could have hardly been considered a coeditor and been given the title of "our teacher and master." As we noted, Mendelssohn spoke of Tobias Boaz only as *ha-katsin* ("the wealthy").

One may assume, therefore, that the Tobias in question died very young and never became a paying member of the community. The honorific title *morenu ha-rav*, which was accorded only to married men, could have been applied to him by Mendelssohn because of his rabbinic learning. He may have been a fellow student of his at the Berlin Beth Hamidrash. There is the further possibility that the young man had come to study in Berlin under David Fränkel, stayed for a while, and later returned to his native city—as did Mendelssohn's friend Naphtali Levin (Rosenthal)[17]—and was not listed in the community records because he never became a member. It was only in Mendelssohn's recollections that the memory of the young scholar Rabbi Tobias was preserved. One may wonder whether he existed at all.

To what extent Tobias actually contributed to the two issues of the journal is another question. One has the distinct impression that all six "chapters" bear the stamp of Mendelssohn's thinking, and one looks in vain for any evidence of cooperation. A single voice speaks throughout, and it is the voice of Mendelssohn. The first chapter *(sha'ar)*[18] interprets the talmudic injunction *(Berakhot,* 43b) to pronounce a blessing on seeing trees blossoming the first time in the year. Of all creatures only man can enjoy the beauty of the world. It is an innocent and pure kind of joy that we derive from beholding the flowers of the field. There is also purpose and wisdom to be observed in the phenomena of nature. The lower is created for the higher. There are degrees of being and man occupies the highest rank among those "formed out of clay" (Job 33:6). Yet he is not the end of the "tremendous and wondrous order." To contemplate it is a source of joy to the human heart.

The reference to the "chain of being," which Mendelssohn had discussed in his letters *On the Sentiments* and in the essay on Pope, is obvious. There are also unmistakable echoes of physico-theology, and all these philosophical motifs are declared to be alluded to in the rabbinically prescribed eulogy of God, "who hast made thy world lacking in nought, but hast produced therein goodly creatures and goodly trees wherewith to give delight unto the children of men." A similar talmudic passage *(Rosh Ha-Shana* 11a; *Hullin* 60a) and its interpretation by Maimonides *(Guide of the Perplexed,* II, 30) are quoted. Philosophy and rabbinic thinking are shown to converge.

The second chapter[19] opens with a fictitious letter voicing a moving complaint about the abandonment of "our holy tongue" by the Jewish people. How could it happen that Jews no longer cultivated the study and use of Hebrew, the language of prophecy and of God's creative word, by which the universe had been called into being?[20] There was no validity in the excuse that we were dispersed among nations who did not understand our language, and were like house servants compelled to speak the masters' language and to forget our own. Why, then, did the children of Israel preserve their native tongue during their exile in Egypt, as the rabbis tell us they did *(Mekhilta, Bo',* chapter 5)?

The tacit assumption of the complaint is that Jews have become estranged from biblical Hebrew and use in their learned writings a mixture of rabbinic Hebrew and Aramaic, while among themselves they speak Yiddish, an idiom derived from German. Mendelssohn, who had only recently achieved a full mastery of literary German, was far from decrying the Jews' study of the languages of their host countries. What he deplored was the lack of interest in biblical Hebrew. It was characteristic of his loyalty to Jewish tradition that he advocated a return to biblical Hebrew precisely at the moment at which he had become a full-fledged member of the circle of German literati. He felt that the beauty of the language of the Bible was equal, if not superior, to the finest products of world literature, and he wanted his fellow Jews, especially those impressed with German prose and poetry, to recapture a sense of pride in their own legacy. He realized that the study of the Bible on its own had come to be frowned upon by the orthodox—that a comment by Rashi on a statement found in the Talmud (*Berakhot* 28b) was being quoted as a warning to parents against allowing their children to overdo the study of Scripture and thereby neglect the study of Talmud. In Mendelssohn's view, this was a misreading of Rashi, who merely advised against an overemphasis on massoretic studies and rightly wanted the Jewish people to accept the massoretic text without any scruples. Here he expressed a viewpoint that was later to guide him in his approach to the text when he translated and commented on Scripture. The fictitious letter published in *Kohelet Mussar* was concerned, however, with more than mere textual understanding. It wished to show that biblical Hebrew was capable of expressing all moods of human life—sorrow, joy, anger, etc. In other words, classical Hebrew could serve as an organ of expression even in modern times. The essay printed immediately after this letter was meant to produce the evidence for this claim.

Its point of departure was the rabbinic saying (*Berakhot* 60b): "Everything God does, he does for the good." The average man trusts in God's power to grant him prosperity and is at a loss to understand why this trust should suffer disappointment. The wise man knows that all *is* to the good. Sorrow will be superseded by salvation or will save us from greater evils. An example of wisdom is seen in the way in which "our friend Ahitubh" reacted to the cruel fate that overtook him. Though he was smitten with disaster, his faith never wavered. The biblical name Ahitubh was probably substituted for the name of some hero in a widely known novel. Again, a talmudic passage (*Bava Kama'* 38a–b) is quoted in support of the belief that we have to accept God's decrees not because we are powerless against them but because they serve a good purpose that only his wisdom can discern. What is good? What makes us more perfect. Once more, Leibniz/Wolffian concepts blend with rabbinic piety. The language is predominantly biblical. Mendelssohn shows himself a purist to the extent that in referring to a talmudic passage he uses the biblical word *'aleh* ("leaf") for the commonly used term *daf* ("folio") because the latter is mishnaic. Chapter three continues the meditation on the problem of evil. Its heading is taken from the Mishna (*Berakhot* 9:5): "A man is obliged to bless God for bad things even as he blesses Him for the good." There are basically two kinds of evil, natural and moral. Natural evils are few in number compared with those that our moral depravity inflicts on others and on ourselves. Natural evils are apt to be forgotten once they have passed. Death is the worst of them, but should we not remember that we are but mortal? The differentiation between the two kinds of evil reflects Leibniz' distinction between metaphysical and moral evil.

Chapter four,[21] which opens the second number of the journal, consists of a letter allegedly received by the editor and his reply. The fictitious letter rejects the sermonizing tone adopted in the first number, and exhibits a decidedly anacreontic frame of mind. It speaks in the name of a group of young people who preferred holding drinking parties and enjoying life to pondering metaphysical problems. Their leader, named A., had been absent for a month, but upon his return he waved the "flying roll" (Zech. 5:1, 2), i.e. the first number of *Kohelet Mussar*, in his hand. He read it in a loud voice, and everybody broke into laughter, when D. said: "Now everything is clear. I saw X. [the editor] and found him to be angry for several days. Why? Because he was bursting with all this stuff inside him." The young Epicurean advises X. in his epistle to remove the solemn mask from his face. He would achieve nothing except to make himself a laughingstock. "I know your stubbornness. You will not listen to me. Perhaps you have been beguiled by the ambition to write things for the sake of seeing them in print in the *Kohelet,* for this is the way of essayists."

The editor's reply is a beautiful ode to true joy. To the pleasure-seeking, unbridled Epicureanism of the group depicted in the letter it opposes the innocent love of nature and the delights of metaphysical contemplation. The theme of the "chain of being" is resumed in greater detail. The wise man "considers the universe of beauty, the order [*ma'arekhet*] of creation, and his own glorious rank on the ladder of degrees." Every one seeks the good, perfection, but some pursue what is merely an apparent perfection, whereas others look for the true perfection. The former will experience a short-lived, transient joy, the latter will achieve eternal happiness. The writer's goal is "the joy born of true perfection." The love of God is the joy in the knowledge of his perfection. He quotes a talmudic passage (*Sotah* 31a): "Two disciples stood before Rabha'. One told him: In my dream they taught us, 'How great is thy goodness thou hast laid up for them that fear thee' (Ps. 31:20). The other told him: In my dream they taught us, 'So shall all those that take refuge in thee rejoice.... Let them also that love thy name exult in thee' (Ps. 5:12). He said to them: You are both perfectly righteous men, the one from love, the other from fear." Love and joy belong together. Again Mendelssohn had no difficulty in harmonizing philosophical and talmudic concepts. The distinction between true and apparent perfection was borrowed from Wolff's *Ontologia*.

Chapter five, entitled "Dwell in the land, and cherish faithfulness" (Ps. 37:2),[22] draws a sharp line between two types of people, the sincere and the hypocritical. Appearances are deceptive. We despise the poor man who committed theft to still his hunger, and we honor the knight in his shining armor who robbed the innocent. Another figure from some novel—here given the biblical name Elzabhad—is recalled to illustrate a type of man who, after a life of oppression and violence, seeks refuge in piety. Finally, the tragic hero of some other story, whose name is hebraized into Asah'el—another biblical name—is presented. Yet none of these types is new, nor do the novels tell us anything that has not in some form or another been discussed by the rabbinic sages of old and their successors. A passage from Jehuda Ha-Levi's *Kuzari* (II,50) is quoted that does not wish to see the acquisition of riches deprecated if it can be accomplished without detriment to the pursuit of wisdom and good deeds, and if it serves the purpose of the welfare of children and society.

The last chapter[23] also begins with a fictional letter. Its content may, however, reflect some element of truth. A friend writes to the editors: "I shall not conceal from you, my brothers, [certain misgivings that have been expressed about your advocacy of Hebrew as a medium of modern thought]. I have seen the first number of *Kohelet Mussar,* the first result of your labors. I visited my friend the scholar-physician Rabbi S. [a veiled reference, no doubt, to Doctor Aaron Solomon Gumpertz, the title "Rabbi" as used here being purely honorific and, more or less, equivalent to "Mister"], for I know him to be a lover of instructive speech and beautiful discourse.[24] The scholar Rabbi B., and the enlightened patron of good causes Rabbi H., were with him. All were men versed in books and connoisseurs of elegant and dignified style. All praised with one voice the sweetness of your expressions. Then Rabbi B. observed: They [the editors] were right in saying that our language is suited to every kind of occasion, be it sorrow or joy. Yet we are incapable of translating into it words spoken in the languages of the nations. Has not the 'father of the translators,' Rabbi Jehudah ibn Tibbon,[25] admitted that in translating a treatise from Arabic into our holy tongue the beauty and splendor of the phrase was lost.[26] If this be the case with the languages of the east, which are close to the land of Israel and are almost one and the same language, what shall we say of the languages of the west, north, and south? Who would not fear to approach the task? . . ."

The fictitious author of the letter also records the answer he gave to this gloomy view, and in doing so he in fact leaves no doubt about his identity: it is Mendelssohn himself who speaks. "I replied: the translator quoted by you was right insofar as works on Tora and wisdom are concerned, e.g. [Maimonides'] *Commentary on the Mishna;* the *Book on the Duties of the Heart* [by Bahya ibn Pakudah], [Maimonides'] *Guide,* [Joseph ben Shemtobh ibn Shemtobh's] *The Glory of God,*[27]and the *Book of the Apple.*[28] For in these books one is not permitted to depart from the [meaning intended by the] authors in any way. However, all languages are affected by this difficulty; none is excepted in this respect. If, on the other hand, belles-lettres are translated,[29] the translator will pay attention only to matters of style. In this regard the Hebrew tongue is not only well-equipped but there is hardly any language like it. Books like the *Epistle on the Animals*[30] and *Prince and Ascetic*[31] [which belong to the category of belles-lettres] prove me right."

In order to demonstrate the eminent suitability of biblical Hebrew to express, in its own idiomatic way, the most subtle forms of modern poetry, the "friend" (Mendelssohn) reads his translation of the first nine stanzas of Edward Young's *Night Thoughts* (1742–1746). One need not be surprised at his choice, for he was an ardent admirer of Young.[32] His Hebrew rendering of these verses shows a remarkable command of biblical poetry. From it the most felicitous parallels are drawn for the subtlest shades of meaning in the English text. An impression of his artfulness will be conveyed by a comparison of the first stanza in the original with a literal retranslation of Mendelssohn's Hebrew rendering. The original reads: "Tir'd Nature's sweet Restorer, balmy Sleep!/ He, like the World, his ready Visit pays / where Fortune smiles; the Wretched he foresakes: / swift on his downy Pinion flies from Woe, / and lights on Lids unsully'd with a Tear." The translation of the Hebrew version reads: "Slumber! Repose to the weary! Through thee is reensouled the bitter in soul. Yet art thou treacherous and lovest those brought up in scarlet (Lam. 4:5), and art negligent of the poor that are cast out (Isa. 58:7). Thou swoopest down upon the wings of the wind (Ps. 18:11) to rest on eyelids that have seen no tear, and fleest from eyes desolate from grief."

It is clear from the distinction laid down and corroborated by the "friend" what Mendelssohn's view of the forte of biblical Hebrew was. It lay in a superb capacity for rendering belles-lettres, especially poetry, but decidedly not in the precise expression of modern philosophical thought. In quoting Jehudah ibn Tibbon's utterance about the difficulty he encountered in rendering philosophical Arabic texts by Jewish writers Mendelssohn did not wish to disparage the immense linguistic achievement of the medieval translations and of the works composed in Hebrew. He merely wanted to point out that the genius of the Hebrew tongue was best suited for the free flow of poetic inspiration, and he felt that his own strength in the use of Hebrew was limited to precisely this particular sphere. Hence his hesitancy to use Hebrew for expressing his philosophy. It took him a long time to overcome this reluctance to some degree.

Perhaps the real reason that publication of *Kohelet Mussar* was discontinued so soon has to be sought in Mendelssohn's estimate of what could be accomplished by such a journal. At best he could cultivate through it the genre of belles-lettres in Hebrew and present popular essays on themes of a philosophical and, at the same time, talmudic nature. Yet all this was essentially an expression of the lighter side of his being. It was the *bel esprit* in him that had created this journal, as it had participated in other ventures of this kind. When the metaphysician in him gained the upper hand, he lost his taste for the enterprise. There may also have been some discouraging opposition, though he had found a warm echo in certain circles, as one gathers from the last chapter.[33] However, the abandonment of the project cannot belie the fact that there had been a strong upsurge of love for Hebrew in Mendelssohn's soul, that for a brief moment the two layers of his being had been fused into a perfect harmony, and that he had anticipated in one big leap the idea of a Hebrew renascence that was to become a historic force a half-century later.

CHAPTER TWO

Maturity and Fame

‹∞›

Marriage and Family Life

By traditional standards, Mendelssohn married rather late in life, at the age of thirty-two.[1] Toward the middle of May, 1761, after his return from Hamburg, where he met Fromet Gugenheim, his future wife, he wrote to Lessing: "I visited the theater, I made the acquaintance of scholars, and (this will sound rather strange to you) I have committed the folly of falling in love in my thirtieth year. You laugh? By all means! Who knows what may still happen to you? Perhaps the thirtieth year is the most dangerous one—and you have not reached it yet. The female I am willing to marry has no means, is neither beautiful nor learned, and nevertheless I, a gallant lover, am so impressed by her that I believe myself to be able to live happily with her."[2] On July 4, 1762, shortly after his wedding, he reported to Thomas Abbt: "During the last few weeks I spoke to no friend, wrote to no friend, stopped thinking, reading, and writing, did nothing but dally, feast, observe holy customs . . . ; for the hour came, my dearest friend, that the Muse of Abaelardus Virbius[3] had foretold me long ago. A blue-eyed girl, whom now I call my wife, has caused your friend's icy heart to melt, and has involved his mind in a thousand diversions from which he now seeks gradually to extricate himself."[4] The somewhat flippant tone of these letters to the two bachelor friends does not reflect Mendelssohn's deepest feelings. His true self is expressed in the sixty-six letters he wrote to his fiancée during their engagement, the first bearing the date May 15, 1761, the last dated May 25, 1762.[5]

Mendelssohn had spent four weeks in Hamburg becoming acquainted with Fromet, as Doctor Gumpertz and also his employer, Isaac Bernhard, had urged him to do. The latter's daughter Sara, who lived in Hamburg as the wife of Asher Götting, was a friend of the young lady whose praises rang in Mendelssohn's ears. The Gugenheim family was a distinguished one. Abraham Gugenheim, Fromet's father, was a great-grandson of the court banker Samuel Oppenheimer of Vienna, a patron of Hebrew learning and a descendent of Jehuda Löb Oppenheim of Heidelberg, who died in about 1572. Fromet's late mother was descended from Samuel Jehuda, founder of the Altona community, who died in 1621.

At the time of the prospective suitor's visit Abraham Gugenheim was in Vienna, where he remained for some time in order to settle the financial troubles in which he found himself. Thus it was Madame Vogel Gugenheim, Abraham's second wife and Fromet's devoted stepmother, who received the guest. It was rather unusual in Jewish society for a marriage to be arranged without the services of professional matchmakers, but convention was ignored in this instance.[6] During his stay in Hamburg Mendelssohn saw Fromet at her home for several hours every day. Although extremely shy, he allowed his feelings free expression as the time of his leave-taking drew near. "Forget it forever," he wrote from Berlin after his return. "I cannot adequately describe to you how disquieted my heart was at the time. Even the kisses that I stole from your lips were mixed with some bitterness, for the approaching separation made me heavy of heart and incapable of enjoying a pure pleasure."[7] The exchange of letters twice a week was another innovation, and prevalent custom was disregarded still further when Mendelssohn refused to have the financial provisions of the "betrothal terms" spelled out and submitted for approval to Fromet's absent father.

Yet for all these tokens of independence, Mendelssohn showed an eagerness to pay due deference to his prospective parents-in-law. After he met Abraham Gugenheim, who was passing through Berlin on his way home, he wrote to Fromet: "He is the kindliest, most sincere man one could find, a truly God-fearing man, without hypocrisy. In short, he deserves to be Vogel's husband and Fromet's father. . . . I shall not be able to part with him without tears."[8] He was, however, not too happy with Gugenheim's slightly old-fashioned ideas about the way to celebrate the wedding in befitting style: "To tell the truth, our kind father . . . still upholds principles of dignity [*principia von kevod ha-beriyot*] that have lost their currency in 'Berlin. For here everyone does as he pleases, and the way one does it is right."[9] He had to dissuade the old gentleman from presenting him with a damask *tallit* (prayer-shawl), since such ornateness was unusual in Berlin and he intended to wear a woolen *tallit* anyhow after the wedding.[10] Mendelssohn settled these delicate matters with perfect aplomb.

Regrettably, the letters written by Fromet during the engagement are lost. To some extent their content can be guessed from Moses' replies, and her personality comes alive through them and the loving portraits he drew of her in his letters. He addresses her variously as "dearest Fromet," "most beloved" *(aller-liebste)*, "dearest angel." Her "tender heart," he assures her, "is the most precious thing I possess and wish to possess on earth."[11]

Human life, he writes in his first letter, is a fairy tale that quickly flies away. His four weeks in Hamburg had been such a fairy tale, but one to last, he hoped, all his life. He was proud and happy to hear her praises sung by so many friends: by Madame Götting, who in a letter to her parents in Berlin had described her character in a charming way;[12] by Moses Wessely, who was inexhaustible in his praise of her;[13] by Johann Friedrich Loewen, poet and private secretary to Ludwig, the prince of Mecklenburg, who complimented him on his happy choice and sent her "a thousand compliments;"[14] and by his friend Löb Bing, who "speaks with enchantment of a certain person closer to me than to him."[15] "What could be more pleasant than having our friends' approval of our choice and being envied by experts?"[16]

Yet when Fromet's father, writing from Vienna, praised his daughter's beauty, Moses wrote to her: "The kindly man assures me that his daughter Fromet is as beautiful as she is virtuous. What do you think? That one can trust the word of an honest man? I heartily laughed about his well-meaning praise. . . . I know his Fromet better than he does. She is beautiful, but not so beautiful as she is virtuous; she is not as beautiful as she is sweet. I envy, dearest Fromet, the felicitous way in which you express your gentle love. Even your shortest letters are full of tenderness, full of sentiment. The language of the heart is your natural language. . . . Continue, dearest and most sweet Fromet, to delight me by your lovely letters."[17] What he appreciated most was her unspoiled naturalness, her lack of affectation and pretense: "One of your most estimable traits, in my eyes, is your having been brought up in the purest innocence, away from the world at large, away from wickedness, deceit, and flattery, away from splendor and luxury. You already know enough French, as I am pleased to gather from your letter, to understand these verses:

> Heureuse, heureuse l'enfance
> Que le Seigneur instruit et prend sous sa défense.
> Tel en un secret vallon
> Sur le bord d'une ombre pure
> Croit à l'abri de l'Aquillon
> Un jeune lys, l'amour de la nature."[18]

Mendelssohn's appreciation of his fiancée's character could hardly have been expressed more beautifully. It was her naïveté, her "taste of the natural" (as Schiller was to define this term), that deeply moved him. He told her more than once how much he enjoyed her letters. On August 28, 1761, he wrote: "When you write as exquisitely as you did in your last letter, I always want to kiss the hand that can put down such beautiful thoughts."[19] Their correspondence was full of love, but their letters were not love letters. They were free from romantic indulgence in passionate feeling or sentimentality. A humorous note and happy lightheartedness always appear, especially in the frequent postscripts addressed to Fromet's younger step-sister Brendel, who relished being teased by her prospective brother-in-law.

It would have been rather difficult to write romantic love letters in the Yiddish-German idiom (in Hebrew characters) employed by them. The constant interspersion of Hebrew words and phrases of a pious, traditional character would hardly have accorded with the romantic style. The letters are a quaint assortment of Yiddish, German, and occasional French. That a young Jewish couple should conduct a correspondence of this nature was quite a novelty in this period. Its special charm lies in the fact that Mendelssohn the philosopher and accomplished writer was enthralled by the letters of a young lady far below his level. He took every care not to make her feel intellectually inferior to him and to raise her self-confidence. When he sent her a medallion struck in celebration of the battle of Liegnitz, he referred to his part in designing it with pride feigned to amuse her and put her at ease: "True, battles are of little interest to you, but you will soon participate in the king's victories [as a Prussian subject after her marriage]; moreover, this medallion will not be a matter of indifference to you, since I suggested the design. You see, I consider myself a sufficiently important person to believe that something coming from me cannot be a matter of indifference to you."[20] On August 11, 1761, he wrote: "I would like to share with you not only my happiness and my life but also my ideas [*Gesinnungen*]. I remember you once wrote to me that you had never read anything of the trifles I have published. Since, however, a second edition of the little things I have written is now in the press,[21] I shall have pleasure in sending you a copy. Should you approve of my ideas, dearest Fromet, it will make me feel proud, for our happiness and contentedness are based on the harmony of our sentiments."[22] On October 16, 1761, he announced the dispatch of four sets of the edition, two bound and two unbound, the bound ones for Fromet and Madame Götting, the others for Doctor Gumpertz and her French teacher, Herr Bode.

While Mendelssohn had no ambition to marry an intellectual woman, he wanted his wife to possess the social graces and for this reason he encouraged her to study French, the language that "here has almost become the mother-tongue." He himself paid, through Gumpertz, the fee for her lessons. Her tutor was Johann Joachim Christoph Bode, an author, translator, and tutor in music and languages, whom Mendelssohn had met in Hamburg.[23] Fromet applied herself assiduously to her task and thereby greatly pleased her fiancé. Unfortunately, Bode showed himself little interested in his job. When in January, 1762, she reported that Bode had failed to appear for the lessons and suggested that a letter be written to him, Mendelssohn replied: "I have treated the gentleman with sufficient delicacy. If in his heart he is a Jew-hater, he does not deserve that one seek his company. . . . Nothing annoys me more than a Christian who makes me pay dearly for being an acquaintance of mine, and who thinks in his heart that he lowers himself by intimacy with a Jew. Whenever I notice a thing like this, I am revolted."[24]

Mendelssohn was much concerned to provide suitable reading matter for his wife-to-be. He arranged for the dispatch to Hamburg of Rousseau's *La Nouvelle Héloise* in a German translation that had just appeared (Leipzig, 1761) but that he had not yet seen and would criticize later in the *Literaturbriefe*.[25] Friebche Götting, who was engaged to Doctor Gumpertz, was eager to get the book from Fromet, whereupon Mendelssohn jokingly remarked that a bride should not read such dangerous books without the groom's consent.[26] In one of her letters Fromet suggested that Julie's epistles in this novel were far better than those of her lover. Mendelssohn agreed, and he added: "In the *Briefe über die neueste Literatur* someone has discussed Julie at some length. In case you so desire, I may send you these pages. This critic judges approximately like you."[27] The unnamed critic was, of course, Mendelssohn himself.[28] Other books read by Fromet were the *Lettres de Mylady Catesby* by Marie Jeanne Riccoboni (of which a German version appeared in 1761) and some work by the third earl of Shaftesbury, most probably his treatise *An Inquiry concerning Virtue*, of which a German translation had been published in 1747. "That you read Shaftesbury more than once pleases me very much," Moses wrote to her. "You can learn a great deal from this little book, and you have the good fortune of having Herr Doctor [Gumpertz] still staying for some time at the house as your friend who, I know it from experience, never refuses to teach."[29] In July, 1761, he wrote: "A propos! Please let me know whether I am to send you something to read. Since by now you will most probably have stopped your exercises in Shaftesbury with Herr Doctor, I would like to supply you with books according to your taste, if you deign to command."[30]

Religious matters are frequently mentioned in the correspondence. During the "three weeks" preceding the fast day on the ninth of Ab, Mendelssohn observed the traditional rules of mourning, which forbid the trimming of the hair and the shaving of the beard. In one of his humorous postscripts for Brendel he remarked: "Since I am wearing now ... a horrible beard, I do not wish to have anything to do with my dear sister [-in-law] Brendel. I know she detests a beard so much that during the *sefira* [viz., the period between Passover and Pentecost, when the same rules apply] she looked at me with fear and trembling, and asked whether, as a married man, I shall wear a full or half beard."[31]

Two other letters contain some remarks about a man's hair style, a ticklish subject at the time, since both wigs and fashionable coiffure were frowned upon by the orthodox as illicit imitations of non-Jewish custom. To illustrate the point: when in 1738 a certain Jeremias Cohn had dared to remove his beard and to show up in synagogue with a wig, he was severely reprimanded for his "breaching of the fence."[32] Some years later, another transgressor, named Abraham Posner, who was similarly punished for the same offense, appealed to the king of Prussia for redress, invoking his right to personal freedom. Frederick the Great reacted by writing this sentence in the margin of the letter: "The Jew Posner is to leave me and his beard unmolested [*ungeschoren*]."[33] Mendelssohn lived in a slightly more liberal period, and in his thirtieth year he began to wear a wig *(Stutzperrücke)*. In later years, starting with his illness in 1771, he wore his own hair, as the portraits show.[34] In a letter to Fromet dated September 22, 1761, he commiserated with Moses Wessely, whose coiffure was objected to by his father, but he thought this stiff hairdressing a "useless vanity." As the next letter, October 8, indicates, he preferred to wear a wig for this simple reason: one who has no time to visit the *coiffeur* every day, yet is anxious to have his hair always well groomed sends his hair to the *peruquier* so as to be able to occupy his head at home with more important things.[35] As all portraits show, Mendelssohn used to wear a more or less trimmed beard around his chin.[36] An anti-Semitic pamphlet, *Über Mendelssohns Bart* ("On Mendelssohn's Beard"), which was published by J.G.B. [Johann Gottfried Bremer] in Berlin after Mendelssohn's death (1787), satirized his beard but also saw in it evidence of his loyalty to the Jewish tradition.[37] It was, however, not only Moses who observed the Jewish custom by wearing a beard after his marriage; Fromet, too, kept the law according to which a married woman must not show her hair. In her letter of October 8, 1761, she excused her delay in writing to Moses by pointing out that she had been busy making "holy caps" *(heilige Kopf-Zeuger)*.[38]

The letters, far from being preoccupied with their feelings for each other, mirror their social life and bring the entire circle of their friends before our eyes: Doctor Gumpertz, Moses Wessely, David de Castro, Joseph Präger, Moshe Zülz, Josel Schwabach ("my best friend here," as Mendelssohn described him), even Veitel Heine Ephraim, the magnate *(ha-katsin)* par excellence, his son Benjamin, and others. The great financier, we hear, had assumed the role of Moses' "patron," inviting him to stay at his palatial home[39] and repeatedly seeking to enlist him as a collaborator in his enterprises. Moses resisted the temptation to work for Veitel Heine Ephraim because he considered the operations in process at the king's command— they concerned the royal mint—as not altogether in keeping with the highest moral principles.[40] On February 23, 1762, he wrote to Fromet: "I thank God, be He blessed, that I kept away from the mint. How easily I might have been carried away by the tide.... Everybody blames me for not having seized the opportunity to become a rich fellow."[41] His letters to Fromet are particularly outspoken in his low estimate of the wealthy. When she suggested that Veitel Heine Ephraim might use his influence to help procure their marriage license and settlement right, his answer was: "That much I cannot expect from his so-called friendship. Your way of thinking is too refined to be capable of correctly assessing a rich Berliner.

When I shall have the good fortune of seeing you here and to live with you—God willing—you will have to avoid associating with the local rich because your character does not at all agree with their mentality."[42]

The correspondence was more than a prelude to their married life. It set the tone of their relationship and of the home they established. Their love for each other grew in depth and tenderness as the years advanced and children were born and raised. Fromet gave birth to ten children, four of whom died early. Their first child, named Sara after Mendelssohn's mother, was born on May 29, 1763, and died on April 15, 1764.[43] "Death has knocked at my hut and robbed me of a child that lived only eleven months of innocence on earth but did so gaily and full of promise," Mendelssohn wrote his friend Abbt on May 1, 1764.[44] Sixteen years later he still recalled this child's memory amid tears in a letter to Avigdor Levi dated April 17, 1780.[45]

His daughter Brendel, called by the pet name Beniken, was born on October 24, 1764. Mendelssohn described her to his friend Joseph Meyer Schmalkalden, who liked to spoil the children, as "not at all comely but clever and well behaved."[46] It was Brendel who later became Dorothea von Schlegel. Next came a son, Hayyim, born on February 19, 1766, who died on April 3 the same year. Shortly afterwards, on May 10, Mendelssohn lost his father. And from a letter to Abbt written on June 11 we learn that his wife, "whom I love more than father and child," had been dangerously ill at about the same time.[47] On July 18, 1767, a daughter, Reikel (Rebecca, later called Recha), was born. Another son, Mendel Abraham, named after Moses' father, was born in January, 1769, but died in September, 1775.[48] On August 8, 1770, Joseph, the apple of his eye and one of the two of his surviving children to resist the lure of baptism, was born. Describing his family to Joseph Meyer Schmalkalden, Mendelssohn wrote of him: "The smallest, Joseph, I hope, will, with God's help, surpass them all."[49] Another daughter, Yente (Henriette), was born probably in 1775 on August 23 or 24.[50]

When in 1776 Mendelssohn wrote to his old friend Naphtali Levin a letter describing his "circumstances," he summed them up as follows: "I have a wife who comes from a good family and is God-fearing, three daughters, the eldest one being eleven years old, and a boy, may he live on, who is six years of age."[51] On December 10, 1776, another son, Abraham, arrived (he would become the father of Felix Mendelssohn Bartholdy). From his trip to East Prussia in 1777, Mendelssohn sent greetings to his "dear children" Brendel, Reikel, Joseph, Yente, and Abraham.[52] Another daughter, named Sisa after Mendelssohn's grandmother, was born on June 8, 1778 and lost on September 15 the same year.[53] The last child, Nathan, was born on January 7, 1782, and was four years old when Mendelssohn died. In Joseph, whose education was of great concern to him, Mendelssohn placed high hopes. "The rest of my children," he wrote to Herz Homberg, "all turn out, for the time being, as we expected and, for the most, desired:

'not long and not short, not wise and not foolish,'[54] except my little Nathan who calls himself the Wise, and whose wisdom consists at the moment in expecting sweetbread from Swa, gingerbread from R[abbi] Samuel, and all else he needs from the cook."[55]

The letters Mendelssohn wrote to Fromet when away on business or taking the waters at Pyrmont manifest his deep love for wife and children: "Kiss our dear children, may God preserve them for us!" "God, be He blessed, preserve you and our dear children for a long and good life. Keep well, my dear one, I am as long as I live your Moses of Dessau. I greet my much beloved children. You cannot imagine how I feel when remembering them." "My heart longs exceedingly for you and our dear children." "I greet . . . my dear children, God preserve them. Now I presumably love them all in equal measure, for they all come to my mind simultaneously when I think of home."[56]

Fromet's letters to her husband likewise reveal her tender love—and her native wit. In October, 1770, when Moses was guest of the prince in Braunschweig, she wrote: "I am still very fond of the prince because of the *éloge* that you, my dear Moshe, make about him, but he must not detain you any longer, even for one hour."[57] In July, 1773, Mendelssohn, on his way to Pyrmont, spent a day in Braunschweig with Lessing.[58] The letter from Fromet awaiting him there was full of charm: "My regards to Herr Eberhard and if Herr Lessing permits himself to receive greetings from a woman, you will not be remiss in conveying my compliments. . . . I am not lacking company, but I assure you that all is empty to me when you are away. Should you find it half as difficult to be away from me as I feel in your absence, we shall certainly not part from one another for a single hour in our lifetime."[59] On July 22, 1774: "You complain about my 'laconic' letter. Had the Lacedaemonians [inhabitants of Laconia (Sparta)] been so little 'laconic' [i.e. so talkative], the war with the Greeks would still be on. How can I write you more, my dear Moshe, having written every mailday. You always had a big, full letter from me. That it nevertheless seemed empty to you is not my fault, my dear child!"[60] She then reported on some business matters in an astute manner. Moses observed: "As R[abbi] Asher tells me, you are doing your job in the business very well."[61] His illness had obviously necessitated her taking a more active interest in commercial matters.

A graphic picture of their social life is provided by her letter of July 18, 1777: "In the evening after you had left us nothing pleased me. I quarreled with everybody in the house until, at last, Meir Warburg rushed in to bid you farewell. When I told him that you had already left, you should have seen the face chubby Meir put on. He stood before me like a pillar and was so upset that I had to laugh. Eventually, after much begging that he pull himself together, I invited him to join us for dinner. . . . After dinner our Brendel played the piano for us for an hour. . . . When I got up Thursday morning, I had visits from many good friends who came to inquire whether I had spent a good night. In the afternoon Herr Lessing[62] came to pick me up with Brendel and Reikel to have coffee with his wife. Professor Engel[63] was also there. So we drank coffee and gossiped about the French and German *troupes*. Every one maintained that he had no objection to enjoying such miserable actors. What do you think, dear Moshe, we did after coffee? We, the women, went to the French comedy, the men to the German. The best of the joke was that both parties enjoyed it."[64]

Thomas Abbt

Mendelssohn's friendship with Thomas Abbt marks the opening of a new period in his life. It was entirely different in quality from his relationship with Lessing, whose genius he had immediately recognized and to whom he looked up with unbounded admiration, even though he felt completely free to criticize and, if necessary, to lecture him. He knew how much he owed the man, and he valued his friendship as a priceless gift from heaven. Abbt, Mendelssohn's junior by nine years and not comparable to Lessing as a literary figure, could not be considered his equal, yet the relationship between Mendelssohn and the highly gifted young man assumed a depth all its own and played a most significant role in his life. Having achieved maturity and self-confidence, he could now exercise his powers as guide, philosopher, and friend to one who craved his friendship and was willing to be guided. As matters turned out, it was not only Abbt who benefited from the relationship. The challenge that the young man's inexorable intellectual honesty presented could not be ignored. It evoked a profound response on Mendelssohn's part. Without Abbt, the *Phaedon* would not have been completed and Mendelssohn would not have become famous as "the German Socrates."

Thomas Abbt (1738–1766) was a Swabian by birth. He had studied at Halle from 1756 until 1758 and, subsequently, lectured there until 1760. His teachers were Siegmund Jacob Baumgarten, a theologian (and also a brother of the famous metaphysician and pioneer in aesthetics Alexander Gottlieb Baumgarten); Johann Peter Miller, a philosopher; and Johann Andreas Segner, a mathematician. He was particularly fond of Georg Friedrich Meier, who through his German compendia had introduced Alexander Baumgarten the philosopher to a wider public unfamiliar with Latin, the language in which his major works were written. When still a student, Abbt contributed to Meier's journal, *Das Reich der Natur und der Sitten* ("The Realm of Nature and Morals"), and he also published a rather quaint tract, called *Inquiry as to Whether God Buried Moses* (1757), on Deuteronomy 34:6. His Master's dissertation, also concerned with a biblical text, explained the "Babylonian confusion of tongues" as the result of climatic and social conditions.[1] Both studies reflect the influence of the critical method in biblical exegesis represented, at the time, by Michaelis and Ernesti. From

May, 1760, until May, 1761, Abbt held a professorship of philosophy at the University of Frankfurt an der Oder.

At the time of his arrival there the Seven Years' War was being fought in the immediate vicinity of the city and Frederick II had just suffered a severe setback in the battle of Kunersdorf, in which Ewald Christian von Kleist was mortally wounded. Von Kleist, an officer in the Prussian army, was a celebrated German poet, whose ode *Der Frühling* had been inspired by James Thomson's *The Seasons*. The plight of the much-admired king roused the nation to a high pitch of patriotic feeling. Abbt, whose inaugural lecture *De Rege philosopho* was a glowing tribute to the great Frederick, expressed his patriotic feelings very movingly in a little book of a hundred and three octavo pages that made him famous overnight. It bore the title, *Vom Tode fürs Vaterland* ("On Dying for the Country") and appeared in 1761. Mendelssohn, who in 1757 had poked fun at himself for "praising a king" in a sermon,[2] now caught the patriotic fever and expressed his pleasure at Abbt's work. On February 11, 1761, he wrote to Lessing: "Herr Nicolai . . . publishes now a small treatise entitled *On Dying for the Country*. The author is Professor Abbt at Frankfurt, who has received a 'call' to Rinteln. It is a pity that the man will not remain in our state! The essay has pleased me so much that I find it wholly unexpected from a professor of mathematics. I like him better than Iselin."[3]

In order to appreciate this favorable comparison one has to take cognizance of the praise Mendelssohn had bestowed on Isaak Iselin (1728–1782), the most notable spokesman of the Enlightenment in Switzerland, whose *Philosophical and Patriotic Dreams of a Friend of Humanity* (1755) had won Mendelssohn's wholehearted approval. In his *Sendschreiben* to Lessing he had held up this work as a model of how to expose the corruption of society without falling into the errors of Rousseau.[4] He had been less satisfied by Iselin's *Essay on Legislation* (1760),[5] but his review of the *Philosophical and Political Essays* (1760), which Iselin had published anonymously, clearly showed his esteem for the author. One had to admit, he wrote in the *Literaturbriefe*,[6] that some Swiss authors were the first among the Germans to apply a philosophical outlook to man as a political being. The reason for this, he suggested, was the greater freedom enjoyed by citizens in a republic. An "unnamed Swiss writer following in the footsteps of the noble-minded Iselin" and who "perhaps went beyond his predecessor"—an artful way of saying that Iselin had excelled himself—had produced a work that one could not read without pleasure. The section describing the important role of the scholar in society is singled out as especially noteworthy: "Though the power of the princes be ever so great and extended, there exists a kind of man who, without power and external greatness, exercises a stronger and more extended influence upon the minds. I am referring to the scholars and, among them, in particular to the writers. Plato, Xenophon, Horace, Cicero, Tacitus, Fénelon,[7] Wolff, Leibniz, Bodmer, Pope, Bacon have, each one of them, ruled over more men in a variety of countries and in the course of time than did an Alexander

the Great, a Charles V, a Timur,[8] and a Louis XIV." Mendelssohn approved
the author's insistence upon the tremendous responsibility attendant upon
such power and his criticism of the pernicious use to which some gifted
authors had put their art. He chided, however, the onesidedness of Iselin's
criticism. It was not enough to attack the frivolous type of writer alone.
Was the mournful enthusiasm of the superstitious less deplorable? Perhaps
it was providential that one kind of poison rendered the other innocuous.
We might still groan under the yoke of the old superstitions, had not
the skeptics broken its chains and expelled one evil by another. A man
of reason, Mendelssohn suggested, should see the abyss at both extremes
and choose the middle-path. Leibniz was a model of the true man of reason
but one had to admit that without Bayle's challenge Leibniz' *Essais de Théodicée* would not have been written.

Abbt's patriotic treatise was reviewed by Mendelssohn in the *Literaturbriefe* on August 13, 1761:[9] "You read with pleasure the philosophico-
political writings of the Swiss? You like the patriotic tone that prevails
in their essays and gives ardor, boldness, and emphasis to all their
thoughts and turns of phrase? You will, then, be all the more pleased
with the tract under review, seeing that it has the very same merits
and was produced in our country. It deals with ... a matter that concerns you and certainly deserves to engage the pen of a patriot who is a
philosopher at the same time." True, in Sparta one would have told
such a writer: rather than praise dying for the country, do it yourself!
However, since not every man was called upon to bear arms, the unwar-
like philosopher might be permitted to extol the noble duty at least by
the exercise of his imagination.

The "exceeding pleasure" that Mendelssohn derived from Abbt's work
and that made him read it "more than once" was due to the "beauty and
profundity" with which the lofty theme had been treated. Iselin's somewhat
pedestrian political philosophy was no match for Abbt's soaring enthusiasm.
Nor could Johann Georg Zimmermann's treatise *On National Pride*,[10] which
Mendelssohn had reviewed at great length and with much sympathy,[11]
be regarded by him as equal to Abbt's work. Zimmermann (1728–1795),
who had studied medicine under the great physician Albrecht von Haller,
was from 1754 to 1767 medical counsellor of Brugg, the Swiss city of
his birth, until he became personal physician to George III, elector of
Hanover and king of Great Britain. Mendelssohn had bracketed him with
Iselin as one of the Swiss writers who had produced the "first fruits" of
political philosophy in the German tongue.[12] Zimmermann, who harbored
a grudge against the patricians of Bern, where he had lived before, had
pointed out the difference between "false" and "genuine" national pride.
His treatment of the subject was tendentious, overloaded with anecdotes,
and disjointed, while Abbt's tract, though in some respects indebted to
Zimmermann's,[13] was all of one piece and inspiring. It bore the marks
of the "great and new manner of thinking" that it preached.

It was this *grosse Denkungsart* that enchanted Mendelssohn. Zimmermann had defined a nation's legitimate pride as "the sum of loves with which each member of the nation loved himself." He had thereby atomized the collective sentiment of national pride. Mendelssohn wanted the self-love of the nation as a whole to be recognized as such. In his view, the national pride of the individual citizen expressed itself in a kind of participation in the collective sentiment. It arose from reflections upon the merits of ancestors and contemporary fellow citizens rather than from claiming credit for personal achievement.[14] One might say that in characterizing national sentiment as a kind of *participation mystique* (to use a phrase borrowed from Lucien Lévy-Bruhl, who applies it in a different sense), Mendelssohn transcended the individualism peculiar to the Enlightenment. His understanding of the nature of collective feeling and national pride stemmed primarily from his Jewish consciousness. Sharing in the merit of ancestors was a concept familiar to him from rabbinic literature.[15] Abbt's plea for patriotism as a unifying bond could, therefore, evoke a genuine response on his part. The patriotic upsurge in the country could do this only to a limited degree, since the Jews were excluded from the status of citizenship and were merely tolerated. However, like the rest of the community, Mendelssohn was aroused to a strong sense of patriotic fervor. He was moved by Abbt's glorification of the king and added to it his own praise. By its love of the country, he said, the nation had assumed "a new soul," as it were, and the king was, in a sense, "the soul of souls." The latter phrase he took from a medieval Hebrew poem, Ibn Gabirol's famous hymn *The Royal Crown,* in which God is said to be "the soul of the soul."[16] It is rather intriguing to find that the friendship of Mendelssohn, the Jew, and Thomas Abbt, the Prussian, started as a result of the deep impression that the young Swabian's Prussian patriotism had made upon him.

Early in 1761 Abbt had been invited by the small university of Rinteln in Westphalia to fill the vacant position of professor of mathematics at a salary of four hundred thalers. He had accepted the "call" on the condition that he would remain free until the autumn of that year, so as to be able to spend the summer in Berlin.[17] He arrived in the capital in April, stayed until October, and then traveled to Rinteln. In a letter written in Berlin on April 25 he reported: "Moses is in Hamburg,"[18] and on May 9 he wrote to his friend and former teacher Johann Andreas Segner: "Yesterday I was with Ramler at a party. Nicolai is very agreeable; ... and Moses has undertaken a pleasure trip to Hamburg, from which he has not yet returned."[19] Mendelssohn was at the time—from about the middle of April until about May 14—visiting his old friend Doctor Gumpertz and meeting his future wife Fromet Gugenheim in Hamburg.

Abbt was most anxious to make Mendelssohn's acquaintance. He had already become a member of the circle that contributed to the *Literaturbriefe,*[20] and in letters to Nicolai he had criticized two reviews written by none other than Mendelssohn. One review was too lenient in Abbt's opinion, while the other offered too narrow a definition of the sublime in poetry. His objections were expressed with fitting modesty: if he was in error, he hoped to be set right.[21] In replying to the second criticism, Mendelssohn wrote to Abbt on March 9, 1761: "In communicating to you my answer to your interpretation of the sublime I do so not in order to prove myself right after all, nor in order to transform a friendly censure into an interminable dispute, but merely because the matter is important enough and merits further clarification."[22]

On March 12, Abbt had addressed a direct letter to Mendelssohn offering two critical notes on the letters *On the Sentiments*. One of these dealt with the mathematical problem of negative quantities,[23] the other with the objection to punishing suicide. Mendelssohn did not reply since he expected Abbt to arrive shortly in Berlin, but he embodied Abbt's mathematical objection and his reply to it in a note when reediting his *Philosophical Writings* in 1771. He mentioned there that on account of Abbt's critical remarks he had rephrased the passage concerned in the second edition of the letters (1761) without introducing any substantive change.[24] (Nicolai published the entire letter containing the two objections and Mendelssohn's answer to both when he edited Abbts collected writings.[25]) The second criticism had been accepted and an appropriate change had been introduced by Mendelssohn in the second edition. Thus there had been some critical, albeit friendly, exchanges between Abbt and Mendelssohn before they met in May, 1761.

The happy summer months they spent together were nostalgically recalled later by Abbt and Nicolai. On November 10, 1762, Abbt wrote from Rinteln: "*Desiderium amicorum!* Shall I always have to add these words with a gnawing sentiment? Nicolai's garden, on Saturday at two o'clock the little man [Mendelssohn] in the distance; then, after a hug, having talked to my heart's content, leaving him as a cheerful and better man. Are my friends to tell this of me only as a tale about the year 1761?"[26] Nicolai expressed similar sentiments when writing to Abbt on November 12, 1765: "Oh! When will the cherished hours return that we gossiped away with Moses at the cool well in Frisch's garden!"[27]

It remained a source of wonder to Abbt that he should have so quickly earned the friendship of Nicolai (who first discovered him) and Mendelssohn. On February 20, 1764, he wrote to the latter: "My life will hardly become remarkable enough ever to appear in print; but in the account of the moments of my good fortune, my progress, and my faults that I have put down for myself it is written that my first treatise gained for me the precious acquaintance of Herr Nicolai and Herr Moses, and that my subsequent stay in Berlin won for me the friendship of both. It is a long time since I doubted this, however incomprehensible this quick gain remains to me, seeing that your character is so much averse to acting impulsively."[28] A trace of his earlier doubt is discernible in a letter he had written to Mendelssohn on July 21, 1762: "Your letter came to me quite unexpectedly, and it gave me almost more pleasure than all previous letters of yours. . . . I wish altogether that it will often occur to you to write to me in a happy hour. . . . Our friendship will thereby increase in warmth, and I flatter myself to have already discovered more signs of this being the case. You will, I hope, have gathered from my conduct hitherto that I, on my part, shall spare no effort to give you the strongest proofs not only of my esteem—for this I share with very many others—but also, and above all, of the most loyal friendship, which shall be my own privilege in common with but a few. Most esteemed friend, though I cannot teach you anything, I can love you."[29]

In actual fact, Abbt had never had reason to doubt Mendelssohn's friendship. He himself had previously—on June 23, 1762—thanked Mendelssohn for his "short but a friend's" letter, and on February 9 of the same year he had written to Nicolai: "Your friendship and Herr Moses' is one of the greatest pleasures I know."[30] Yet there was some distance between Mendelssohn—"the little man in the distance"—and the youthful, enthusiastic Abbt. It was only gradually that this distance in years and temperament was overcome and that the friendship, which had never been in doubt, became more intimate and meaningful for both.

In a sense, Abbt had to fill the void that Lessing's long periods of silence created. On March 26, 1765, Mendelssohn wrote to Abbt: "It is now three years that I have not written to Lessing, and it is four years that he has not written to me.[31] You are, therefore, the only person with whom I converse on literary matters; and if I am not to be blotted out entirely from the book of rational creatures,[32] I shall have to write you very long letters very often."[33] On June 14, 1765, he complained to Abbt: "Herr Lessing is indeed in Berlin[34] but he visits me so rarely that I yearn for rational conversation now no less than I did when he was still in charge of the governmental secretariat in Breslau."[35] Mendelssohn exaggerated slightly, for during his stay in Berlin in 1765 Lessing is known to have discussed with him thoroughly and, no doubt, on more than one occasion the copious notes that Mendelssohn and Nicolai had supplied to his draft of the *Laokoön*.[36]

Abbt may not have relished his role as a substitute for Lessing. He must have realized, however, that Mendelssohn appreciated him in his own right. He could have found confirmation of this in Mendelssohn's letter of July 22, 1766: "Herr Lessing has written to me. This is in order. But why did you not tell us [i.e. Nicolai and me] that you did meet him;[37] that his candid, spirited character pleased you; and that you made him a partner of our bond of friendship?"[38] Here the "bond of friendship" between Mendelssohn, Nicolai, and Abbt is recognized as having a character of its own, and Abbt is supposed to have introduced (*eingeflochten:* literally, "woven") the outsider Lessing into this intimate circle. This is a clear indication that the towering figure of Lessing had until then not been permitted to intrude into the sanctum of Mendelssohn's special friendship with Abbt.

Although he felt as miserable in Rinteln as Mendelssohn did in Berlin, Abbt was by no means starved for friendship locally. His letter of February 20, 1764, in which he marvels at his good fortune of having won Nicolai's and Mendelssohn's friendship, contains also the sentence: "I also have other friends, though not many, whom I love as much as you; but no letters are looked forward to as much as yours because of their instructive character."[39] One of the friends he dearly loved was Justus Möser (1720–1794), the leading citizen of Osnabrück and a representative of its "learned patriciate," in whose amiable personality the broad vistas of the Enlightenment were blended with a vigorous traditionalism and sense of historical individuality.[40]

At first blush there would seem to have existed no more glaring contrast than between Abbt's two friends, Möser and Mendelssohn—Möser, who in his magnum opus, the *History of Osnabrück* (1768 ff.), presented the model of a new method of historical research, brushing aside the generalities of universal history and the viewpoint of universal reason in favor of local history and "local reason" *(Lokalvernunft)*, and Mendelssohn, who had no inclination to immerse himself in the particularities of history but looked toward universal man and universal reason rather than to individual groups and local reason or man *in concreto*. Yet on closer inspection some common ground between the two is discernible. Both were heirs to the Leibniz/ Shaftesbury view that contemplated the beauty of the whole as transcending the individual features making it up: the total view was Möser's goal no less than Mendelssohn's. The insistence on patriotism as the soul of a whole nation was clear evidence, as we have noted,[41] that Mendelssohn had moved away from a rigid Enlightenment position. Even Möser's defense of "superstitious" customs as useful devices[42] has its counterpart in Mendelssohn's plea that superstitions not be discarded so long as they serve as props of morality.

Abbt occupied a position somehow intermediate between Möser and Mendelssohn. History was a subject into which he was drawn first against his will ("I am now forced to lecture on history," as he put it in a letter to Mendelssohn on November 10, 1762), and then, probably under Möser's influence, because of his increasing interest. His personal contact with Möser was established by way of a humorous letter he wrote to him in April, 1762, "To the author of the *Harlekin*[43] in the name of a small Berlin society," attaching a copy of the review that had appeared in the *Literaturbriefe*.[44] He had taken this step because in Rinteln he had made the acquaintance of Möser's sister-in-law and had, besides, heard the praises of the Osnabrück *advocatus patriae* sung by all who knew him. Anxious to meet the man, who lived only nine miles away, he wrote that epistle and as a result soon became his intimate friend. He had his own room in Möser's home and was considered by the family like a son and brother.[45]

In 1765, when Abbt began to write a "History of the human race, insofar as such a history has become known in Europe, from the commencement of the world down to our times,"[46] Möser welcomed the idea, though he warned his friend of the drudgery he had taken upon himself. It was Abbt's intention to condense the world's history into one large conspectus, rather than an aggregate of individual accounts. At the same time, he put the emphasis on Europe. He wanted to show how contemporary Europe had come into being. To this end he proposed to make an excerpt from the monumental *Universal History from the Earliest Account of Time to the Present* (London, 1763–1765). The work turned out to be anything but a labor of love,[47] and although Möser had offered him good advice on how to organize the project, he could, in the end, only deplore the inevitable deficiencies of a method of work that smacked too much of universal history à la *Aufklärung* and failed to give scope to original intuition.[48]

Mendelssohn and Nicolai received their first inkling of the work through the catalog of the Leipzig book fair, and they were rather horrified to learn that Abbt had imposed such a laborious task upon himself.[49] When Mendelssohn received the volume, he praised it but also remonstrated with the author for having wasted his talent on so thankless a job. He was glad that Abbt had no intention of continuing the work: "German historiography has as yet shown not a single philosophical writer, so far as I know. Do not let yourself be deprived of this fame. It seems to be reserved for you."[50] Alas! Fate had decreed otherwise. This was the last letter that Thomas Abbt received from Mendelssohn. It was dated July 22, 1766. He replied to it on August 28. On November 3, 1766, he died, shortly before his twenty-eighth birthday.

In the last paragraph of his July 22 letter Mendelssohn had asked him:

> Tell me, dearest friend, what am I to do if I want to form an idea of the history of ancient and modern times? Until now I regarded history more as a science of the citizen [*citoyen*] than of man. I was of the opinion that a man who has no country could not expect any advantage from [the study of] history. I notice, however, that the history of civil conditions merges with the history of mankind, and that it is improper to be totally ignorant of the former. But where am I to start? Do I have to go to the sources or may I be content with the universal world histories that have become the fashion in recent times? Which do you advise me to consult? Do not forget to answer me concerning this point.—Take care of yourself! And Nicolai sends you cordial regards.

Abbt's reply was: "So far as historiography is concerned, you would act wisely, I believe, if you read Hardion's ecclesiastical and secular history. It contains all the tedious drolleries with which all our universal histories are inundated; yet it is still the shortest, without being merely a compendium. Bossuet's *Discours* is useful as a general chart."[51] The fact that Mendelssohn had begun to interest himself in the study of history may have been due partly to Abbt's preoccupation with it. On February 16, 1765, he had written to his young friend: "You once consulted me, if I remember rightly, on some history you meant to write, and I failed to give you any reply whatever. I was not able to, for what do I know of history? Whatever goes by the name of history: natural history, geological history, political history, history of scholarship, is beyond me; I yawn every time I have to read something historical, unless the style cheers me up. I believe history to be one of the studies that cannot be acquired without instruction."[52] It is a far cry from this confession to the request of July 22, 1766.

A major topic in the Abbt/Mendelssohn correspondence, in which Nicolai had his share and which throws a great deal of light on Mendelssohn's (and Abbt's) role as editor of the *Literaturbriefe*, is the frequent criticism of Abbt's style of writing. One is struck by a certain censoriousness in Mendelssohn's strictures and by Abbt's meekness in accepting most of them. The criticism offered by Mendelssohn was not confined to Abbt's contributions to the *Literaturbriefe* but extended to practically everything he produced. One of the complaints concerned Abbt's fondness for bold metaphors. Mendelssohn felt that the metaphors were not merely "bold" but "affected and far-fetched."[53] Möser agreed with this observation,[54] and Nicolai elaborated on it in a letter written to Möser after Abbt's death:[55]

> His style seems to have sprung... from an unsuccessful imitation of Tacitus. He wanted to express important sentences in but a few words. At times, however, his ideas had not yet sufficiently matured or he lacked patience to give them the adequate natural form of expression. He rather assumed that the language was at fault and formed new words or lost himself in metaphors for the sake of presenting his ideas more clearly. He soon became so much accustomed to this way of writing that it became natural to him.

Abbt's prose, Mendelssohn said in similar vein, bordered too much on poetry.[56] There was, obviously, a deep cleavage between Abbt and his friends insofar as matters of style were concerned. They failed to recognize the creativity of the young writer and could not foresee that some of his phrases and metaphors, to which they so strenuously objected, would be adopted into common usage.[57] Herder showed an entirely different attitude to Abbt: he considered him his favorite writer and had enthusiastic praise for the originality of his pithy style.[58] It seems that the "sensualistic" revolution in prose writing, which French authors like Voltaire and Helvétuis represented, had had an effect on Abbt.[59]

On May 21, 1764, Abbt mentioned to Mendelssohn for the first time that he was writing a new book called *Vom Verdienste* ("On Merit").[60] It sought to implement a suggestion he had made when reading Helvétius' *De l'Esprit* (1759): "Should one not be able to write on the heart, a subject matter that in many respects is still so obscure?"[61] While Helvétius had shown how sensations lead to judgments and concepts, Abbt's intention was to trace the development of sentiment from sensation. Imagination transformed *Empfindung* (sensation) into *Empfund* (sentiment) or *Empfindnis*, the latter term having been considered less objectionable than the first when the manuscript of the work was subjected to the severe criticism of Mendelssohn and Nicolai. Mendelssohn wrote in August 1764:[62]

> Your work on Merit contains very good things in a very good order but in the most intolerable style. I read it twice with genuine pleasure at its content but with as much annoyance at the strange affectation of its style. On many occasions I had to drop the pages in exasperation and had to divert myself. For Heaven's sake! Do not disfigure your beautiful work by the vain ambition to create everything by yourself, to owe nobody a thing, not even words and phrases.

Abbt did not demur at these critical remarks. As Möser put it in a letter to Nicolai after Abbt's death:[63] "He raised no objection when one reproached him for his affected style and he candidly told me of the letter in which his friend Moses bade him throw his entire first draft of the book *On Merit* into the fire. Not only this. He actually rewrote the book." Mendelssohn was conscious of the impression of censoriousness that his strictures were bound to create. "Give me credit for my magisterial tone, best friend," he wrote on July 4, 1762. "I cannot entirely deny my being a writer of the *Literaturbriefe*, and I invariably talk down from my height as a critic without consideration of the one I am addressing. A critic must have the impudence of a dog.—This is true enough but it serves only as a mask as often as he appears on the stage and wants to entertain the audience. Yet away with the uncouth mask once he joins his friends behind the stage. Should he then still behave immodestly, he is unbearable. Hence forgive me!"[64] It seems that the role of critic in the *Literaturbriefe* had indeed imparted a certain magisterial attitude to Mendelssohn.[65]

Mendelssohn's own literary activity in the years 1761–1766 cannot be divorced from his friendship with Abbt. There is, at first, the joint enterprise of Mendelssohn, Abbt, and Nicolai to translate the entire *oeuvre* of the third earl of Shaftesbury into German. It had been devised during the happy summer months of 1761 and a promising start was made soon thereafter, but the project was never carried to fruition. Mendelssohn's task included, to begin with, a translation of the treatise *Sensus Communis: An Essay on the Freedom of Wit and Humor* (1709). He had been intrigued by this work as far back as 1755. On December 26 of that year he had referred to it in a letter to Lessing: if one saw the difference between the comical and the burlesque, there was some sense in Shaftesbury's remark that ridicule served as a "criterion" *(Prüfstein)* of truth.[66] How much this passage had caught his fancy is evident from the elaborate use he later made of it in the revised third dialogue of the *Philosophische Gespräche* (1761).[67] On November 3, 1761, he reported to Abbt that he had already commenced the translation and that he enjoyed the work despite the considerable difficulties it presented. He hoped to be able to proceed steadily throughout the winter and to submit the translation to Abbt's judgment before long.[68] He discussed the difficulty of finding the exact German equivalent for the French word *raillerie* ("jesting, making fun"), which Shaftesbury used repeatedly when referring to the frivolity and irreverence with which some modern writers treated serious matters. A glance at the manuscript of the translation[69] shows the uneasiness that Mendelssohn felt about the proper rendition of this term. There are frequent deletions and a variety of German words is used in the end side by side with *raillerie*.[70]

Abbt took his share in the enterprise no less seriously. On February 9, 1762, he wrote to Nicolai and Mendelssohn:[71]

> The Shaftesbury text allotted to me decreases steadily in the original and increases in the translation. I hope you still intend to print it. Otherwise, I would propose to persuade Herr Moses that we put our translation jointly up for sale. I am really anxious to see what our theologians will say when a Lord, a merchant, and a professor; a free-thinker, a Jew, and a Christian appear hand in hand: Shaftesbury, Moses, and Abbt. What an odd assortment!

Mendelssohn's reply of February 22 shows the same lightheartedness but gives some early indication of the waning of his interest in the project:[72]

> My Shaftesbury translation has bogged down in the last few weeks. It is, however, to be continued shortly. This labor is of little benefit. The Lord is a self-willed Englishman who many a time refuses to don a German outfit. How the company of a professor and a Jew will suit him I do not know. The nuance will, however, provide no harsher contrast than the one that was once presented when our friend Nicolai walked in his dressing gown between a priest and a Jew. Of the Lord we have, besides, proof that he was able to forget his nobility in the company of his coreligionists, for he is said to have once visited Bayle in Rotterdam as a *studiosus medicinae* in order to dispense with all formality. He may visit us as a *studiosus theologiae*.

One can well understand that Mendelssohn grew a little weary of the arduous task of rendering the difficult and subtle English of the earl of Shaftesbury into German. One can, however, only admire the way he did it. His translation, though faithful to the finest nuances of the original, reads like German prose in the eighteenth-century idiom. However "self-willed" the lord may have been, he wore the German "outfit" like a tailored suit. Judging from the size of the extant manuscript,[73] the translation did not get very far. It covered only the first five sections of part one. This segment included, however, the passages that held a special fascination for him. The one relating to ridicule as a criterion of truth has already been mentioned. Another passage, whose influence upon him can be discerned in many places, is the one in section two that reads: "For we can never do more injury to Truth, than by discovering too much of it, on some occasions. 'Tis the same with Understanding as with Eyes: To such a certain Size and Make just so much Light is necessary, and no more.

Whatever is beyond, brings Darkness and Confusion. 'Tis real Humanity and Kindness, to hide strong Truths from tender Eyes." Mendelssohn rendered the last sentence: "Starke Wahrheiten vor schwachen Augen zu verbergen, ist wahre Menschenliebe und Gütigkeit." Not to blare forth the truths of the Enlightenment if they are likely to injure morality; to be tolerant of ingrained prejudice and superstition, if they are props of social well-being; not to deprive the lame of his crutches—these principles, which he enunciated throughout his life, may have owed a great deal to the few phrases in which Shaftesbury warned against the harshness of the zealots of Enlightenment. The lord's cautionary remarks about the "darkness and confusion" caused by too much light is reflected in Mendelssohn's sentence: "On the dark path that man has to walk here below he is provided with as much light as he requires for the next steps he is to take. More of it would only blind him and any side-light would merely confuse him.[74]

Abbt kept inquiring: "What about Shaftesbury?"[75] The answer he received was—a rhapsodic praise of Plato:[76]

> Plato has a manner of writing that combines all the merits of Shaftesbury's style with an inimitable ease of phrasing. His prose, even where it becomes poetic, flows with such tranquil majesty that a non-expert might think the phrase had cost him no effort. I never read Plato without feeling ashamed at ever having put pen to paper, for I have written enough in my life at least to be able to see the busy hand of the artist through the veil of naturalness. I can sense how hard the man must have labored to give his noble and spirited thoughts the fine polish, the gentle curve that, taken by itself, makes a Fontenelle a writer of fame. We, being rather negligent, behave almost like women in child-bed. In their contentedness at having managed fairly well in giving birth to a child, they close their tired eyes and care little about cleansing the baby. I say: *we*, dearest friend, because I believe the two of us are equal in this respect. We do some measuring with the compasses and form our periods but we fail to know how to wipe from their faces the sweat of art with the final touch of the master.

This hymnic description of Plato's style chimes with the way in which Shaftesbury praises the writings of the ancients as "somewhat different from that of our days." The passage occurs in section five, the last one, so far as we know, to be translated by Mendelssohn: "Their Treatises were generally in a free and familiar Stile. They chose to give us the Representation of real Discourse and Converse, by treating their Subjects in the way of *Dialogue* and free Debate." It looks almost as if Mendelssohn had taken Shaftesbury's hint to turn to the writings of the ancients rather than bother to translate him. The letter glorifying Plato contains an ungracious reference to the lord's "somewhat awkward, stilted and, at times, timid" way of writing.[77]

Mendelssohn had obviously decided to abandon the Shaftesbury project and had to find a pretext. However, his enthusiasm for Plato was completely genuine. It stemmed from the pleasure he derived from his translation of Plato's *Republic*, in which he was immersed at the time. In

the years 1759/1760 he had studied Greek under the guidance of Rector
Damm. During the first year, when Nicolai participated in the lessons,
he had read Homer, in the second Plato.[78] From a letter he wrote to
Iselin on July 5, 1763—exactly a year after praising Plato in his July 4,
1762, letter to Abbt—we learn that he had translated three books of the
Republic.[79] Fragments of this translation have been preserved.[80] The love
for Plato spelled the end of the Shaftesbury project. It is possible, however,
that Nicolai still clung to the hope of seeing it realized someday. For as
late as March 21, 1767, he wrote to the dramatist Heinrich Wilhelm von
Gerstenberg:[81] "Moses, Abbt, and I once had the plan of translating the
entire Shaftesbury and to explain some pieces by way of essays. In fact,
all three of us made a beginning of it. Herr Moses finished the *Moralists*,[82]
most of it, but it may be a long time before anything is printed."[83]

The Prize-Essay

The awarding of the 1755 literary prize to A.F. Reinhard had not enhanced
the prestige of the Royal Academy. The Zürich circle had expressed its
resentment by charging two writers, Waser and Wieland, with the task
of refuting Reinhard and attacking the academy. The resulting polemical
tract,[1] published anonymously, spared neither Reinhard nor the academy
but overshot the mark by the rudeness of its tone. Mendelssohn expressed
his disapproval of the tract in a review that, for some reason, was not
published at the time.[2] In it one can hear echoes of Shaftesbury's complaint
about the "persecuting spirit" of former times that had raised the "bantering
one" of the present.[3] Neither Reinhard nor his adversaries had understood
Leibniz correctly.[4] A review of Reinhard's prize-essay was published by
Mendelssohn in the *Literaturbriefe* on March 8, 1759.[5] It reaffirmed the
principles of Leibniz' metaphysics, which Reinhard's *Examen de l'Optimisme*
had tried to refute without taking cognizance of the proofs offered. The
academy itself was silent. No one took its part publicly, but the extreme
ill-temper of its opponents worked in its favor; in the end its position
in the scholarly world remained unharmed, even though the blunder it
had committed in awarding the 1755 prize to Reinhard was readily apparent
to all.

In choosing the topic for its 1759 prize-essay competion the academy
prudently avoided the metaphysical. The question put was: "What is the
mutual influence of people's opinions on language and of language on
opinions?" Competitors were expected to make practical suggestions as
to how to bring languages up to date, as it were, by liberating them from
the influence of antiquated ideas. The prize was won by Johann David
Michaelis,[6] to whose essay Mendelssohn devoted a penetrating review in
the *Literaturbriefe*.[7] He described it as one of the most important writings
on the subject. Only a man like Michaelis could have done justice to the
theme, combining as he did a mastery of linguistics and an extensive knowl-

edge of "opinions" and philosophical judgment. Mendelssohn saw the chief value of the treatise in the examples it cited, and he made it clear that the author had not abstracted from them any general principle beyond the one presupposed by the very formulation of the subject (the interplay between language and opinion). Since no new principles had been brought to light, it was not surprising that the practical suggestions for improving the languages were neither new nor profound.

Mendelssohn's own opportunity came in 1761 when the academy invited entries for a prize-essay on the question: "Whether metaphysical truths in general, and the first principles of natural theology and morality in particular, are susceptible of the same evidence as mathematical truths, and in case they are not, what is the nature of their certitude; which degree can it attain; and whether this degree is sufficient to impart conviction?"[8] The competition was set for the year 1763, the final deadline for entries being January 1, 1763. The posing of this question was timely in view of the low esteem in which metaphysics was held by the public, and also in view of the objections being raised against the introduction of the mathematical method into metaphysics.[9]

Among the large number of philosophers who decided to enter the competition were Kant, Johann Heinrich Lambert, Mendelssohn, and Abbt. Mendelssohn had already completed three quarters of his treatise before he learned of Abbt's intention to compete for the prize. Abbt had been equally unaware of his friend's intent. He wrote him in all innocence on April 21, 1762: "I am rather resolved to work on the prize-subject of the academy concerning the difference in certainty to be obtained by the metaphysical and mathematical truths. With that the doctrine of intuitive knowledge ought to be expounded at some length. In the meanwhile I keep my thoughts to myself."[10]

Mendelssohn was embarrassed by this information. It was distasteful to him to be his friend's rival, but his own work was almost finished. When replying to Abbt toward the end of May, he avoided the subject.[11] His mind was, at the time, too much preoccupied with his forthcoming wedding on June 22 to be able to think decisively on this particular matter. On April 27 he had written to Nicolai: "And now good night to literature! I depart from the realm of belles-lettres for a while, and shall have to spend some weeks in an occupation totally removed from the Muses. First writing a disputation, and then getting married.[12] Do not laugh now at this strange custom. I find it very wise. What is the good of all the prizes offered for the benefit of the sciences? Would it not be better if nobody in the entire country could get married before he had answered a learned question?"[13]

Immediately after the wedding he discussed the delicate situation with Nicolai, who on July 2 wrote the following letter to Abbt:[14]

> You wrote . . . in your letter to Herr Moses that you wish to work for the prize of the academy. Since I am aware of the fact that Herr Moses' marriage will probably prevent him from writing to you at any length

for the time being, I merely want to inform you that Herr Moses has the very same idea and that about three-fourths of his treatise is already finished. He was now somewhat embarrassed, and his first reaction was to leave it entirely to you to work for the prize. This, however, I have prevented, and I likewise forbid you, on pain of my curse, to abandon your intention on account of Herr Moses' also having let himself in for it. Were you in Berlin, I would have advised that you write the treatise jointly, as Herr Moses and Lessing did when upon the occasion of the prize-subject of optimism they jointly composed *Pope ein Metaphysiker!* By correspondence, however, this would not do. I, therefore, suggested to Herr Moses that you both submit your treatises to the academy and afterwards exchange copies of them. This will be the best, for if you were to exchange copies beforehand, you would only confuse one another. Herr Moses thinks that his ideas will be different from yours. He believes himself able to conclude this from your *Programma*. There you are! So unexpectedly can one give himself away.

The reference to the *Programma* calls for some explanation. As mentioned in a letter to Mendelssohn dated April 21, 1762, Abbt had published a tract *On the Influence of the Beautiful on the Exact Sciences* that was to serve as a program of his public lectures on belles-lettres. In this *Programma* a "good-hearted enthusiast" talks about, among other things, "the soul's inclination to intuit extension," and a note adds the remark: "One who accepts the well-known system of the simple things [viz. Leibniz' monads] and knows the difficulties of intuiting without images will understand why we attribute to the soul an inclination to the opposite. One of the most specific merits of mathematics consists, perhaps, in this. However, the matter is too important and as yet too little explored to be permitted to creep into a note. Let this meager explanation of an almost imperceptible hint suffice."[15]

It was this "note" that led Mendelssohn to the conclusion that his and Abbt's respective views on the prize-subject were different. He was right in this assumption, as a comparison of the two treatises clearly shows. Abbt reduces all knowledge to the original data of sense perception, which carry with them a sense of certainty based on intuition of things extended. Abstract concepts, he holds, are therefore apt to be viewed under the aspect of extension: "I call this the soul's inclination to intuiting extension." The subject matter of mathematics, including algebra and analytical geometry, is said to be ultimately capable of intuition (*anschaulich*), which is not the case in metaphysics.[16] According to Mendelssohn, the decisive element in both mathematics and metaphysics is the analytical treatment of concepts.[17]

On July 4, Mendelssohn himself wrote a letter to Abbt in which he referred to the *Programma* and the contemplated prize-essay:[18]

> And should your honest old man [viz. the good-hearted enthusiast] appear a second time this year, do forbid him to betray anything further about the soul's inclination to intuit extension. What a chatterbox! Should Professor Abbt have allowed him to read what he intends to submit to the

academy, why did he have to tell tales out of school?—His note he should have kept to himself altogether. An English juggler will sooner creep into a bottle than this corpulent matter through the narrow neck of a note. Perhaps no one understood as well as I what this mystical note means to betray. Herr Nicolai has informed you already that I hit upon the same idea as you, namely to work for the prize. My treatise has four sections, three of which are already written. Had I not been interrupted by domestic affairs, the whole could have been finished and, perhaps, been translated into another language. For I intend to have it translated by Herr*** into Latin, unless possibly you advise against this. When I learned from your letter that you wished to compete for the prize, my first thought was to stop my work and dispatch the manuscript to Rinteln. The idea that my essay should compete with yours made me diffident. The counsel of our friend, however, and a more mature consideration on my part persuaded me to change this resolution. I admit that I would have preferred not to know the champion against whom I have to fight. Since he made himself known, however, the laws of chivalry demand that I too lift my visor and once more embrace my friend before the combat.——At the commencement of next year we shall exchange our weapons. I shall send you my essay and you send me yours, but not before lest we confuse one another; we shall then have the pleasure of seeing which road we take when, not knowing one another's work, we write on the same subject. If I am defeated, it is, nevertheless, my friend who is the victor.—As you see, I talk as if I knew that no one except you and I could compete for the prize.

Abbt's reply, dated July 21, evinces the same spirit of fair play that Mendelssohn had exhibited:[19] "Concerning our intention pursuant to the prize of the academy, you have said everything in this letter that should be written and I am therefore ashamed to copy yours. Hence I cannot say anything further in reply." Abbt gives, however, additional proof of his unselfishness by advising Mendelssohn not to take the trouble of having his treatise translated into Latin. The academy, he assured him, would be equally pleased with an essay in German. Mendelssohn accepted his friend's advice, completed the work and submitted it to the jury well before the January 1, 1763 deadline. Abbt, on the other hand, was rather dilatory. On November 10, 1762, he reported to Mendelssohn about the lectures on history that he was compelled to give and about the preparation they entailed. As soon as he had finished this task and sent in his contribution to the *Literaturbriefe,* he would start working on the prize-essay.[20] On December 26 he informed Nicolai and Mendelssohn that he had submitted his treatise to Herr Formey, secretary of the academy, through his friend Albert E. Euler. He was not sure whether it had been handed in by December 20.[21] On January 3, 1763, Mendelssohn expressed his astonishment at Abbt's tardiness and subsequent tour de force.[22] On January 11 he wrote to Abbt:[23] "I do not ask whether you want to read [my essay]; I am sending it. Here are my weapons which are probably worth a hundred oxen! ... Take care of yourself and return my essay fairly soon.—Nothing of the fifty ducats [viz. the prize-money] is to go to you!"

This bragging about being so sure of winning the competition was, of course, a mere cloak for his uncertainty. In an undated letter to Lessing, which would seem to have been written early in May, 1763, he expressed his doubts:[24] "You judge my treatise like a brother in Leibniz. The academy, I suspect, will have a different opinion." Abbt, who despite the haste with which he labored had in the end copied his essay for the sake of Mendelssohn—"for no prince would I have done this favor," he had written on December 26, 1762—was on a trip that extended from March, 1763, to November 7 of the same year and took him first to several cities in Germany and then to Switzerland. He spent three months in Geneva, where he arrived, after five weeks of travel in various parts of the country, on June 1.[25]

On May 26, 1763, the "Classe de Philosophie spéculative" of the Berlin Royal Academy held its session and awarded the prize to Mendelssohn. According to the minutes of the meeting, the treatises number twenty (Mendelssohn's) and number twenty-eight (Kant's) received the same number of votes on the first and second ballots. When treatise number twenty eventually carried the day, it was, at the same time, recorded that the other was also worthy of the highest praise and, hence, was accorded the second place of honor, termed the *accessit*. The decision in Mendelssohn's favor was due to the verdict of Sulzer, who was chairman of the philosophical class.[26] At a public session on June 2 the result of the voting was announced and the identity of the winner established. A summary of Mendelssohn's essay, written in French by Merian,[27] and read by him, concluded with these words: "Je crois m'être fidelement acquitté de la fonction d'abréviateur, et avoir donné une juste idée des choses. Mais je n'ai pû faire connoitre le style de cette Dissertation, qui est très élégant, et décele un des plus beaux Ecrivains de l'Allemagne."[28]

The official praise bestowed on Mendelssohn as a philosopher and as one of the finest writers of Germany was an unprecedented triumph for the son of the ghetto who had arrived in Berlin only twenty years before. On Saturday, June 4, the *Berlinische privilegirte Zeitung* carried the terse announcement: "On Thursday the academy held its public session. The prize was awarded to the local Jew Moses Mendelssohn, who is already sufficiently known by his writings."[29] Kant, who was then still little known and was outshone by Sulzer and Mendelssohn,[30] expressed (in a letter to Formey) his "pleasure" at having learned from the Berlin newspaper the "favorable judgment" accorded to his essay.[31] He obviously did not resent Mendelssohn's victory.

During eight months of travel Abbt's correspondence with Mendelssohn had suffered a complete rupture. The day after his return, on November 8, he recommenced writing to him, "without apology." His letter reported briefly on the contacts he had made on his trip. He mentioned, among other things, that in Ferney he had made the acquaintance of Voltaire, his family, and his theater,[32] but had not been able to discuss any important matters with him. He also recalled having met Vernet and Bonnet in Geneva and having found both of them much impressed by the Germans. With his letter he enclosed a translation into French of Mendelssohn's *Rhapsody, or Additions to the Letters on the Sentiments,* which had appeared in the second volume of the *Philosophical Writings* (1761). This translation had been written by him, with some help from Bonnet, during his stay in Geneva, where it had been published under the title: *Recherches sur les Sentiments Moreux traduit de l'Allemand de Mr. Moyse fils de Mendel par Mr. Abbt, Professor en Philosophie dans l'Université de Rinteln* (à Genève 1763).[33] As Mendelssohn's reply indicates, he was not altogether happy with the rendition: "You have fulfilled the duty of a translator perfectly, so far as I can judge; not so the duty of a friend. The metaphysical subtleties read so badly in French that they cannot possibly reflect credit on their author. I do not expect applause from a single Frenchman. What truly delights me is the evident fact that the treatise pleased you; for otherwise you would not have imposed so much trouble upon yourself, our friendship notwithstanding."[34]

In his letter Abbt had asked Mendelssohn to let him know what he thought of his essay for the academy.[35] Mendelssohn replied:[36]

> I had hardly read through your essay for the academy when Herr von Rohr requested it from me. I shall send for it and read it a second time attentively. That we differ *in principiis* to a considerable extent you will have gathered from my essay. Do not believe, however, under any circumstances, that I imagine myself as having won a victory because I was awarded the prize by the academy. I know full well that in a war the worse general is not infrequently the one who carries the day. We have to settle the dispute between ourselves. If I fail to convince you, it will be sufficient proof that my arguments lack the evidence desired.

The sensitivity with which Mendelssohn acknowledges the friend who was a loser in the contest to be his true judge is indeed admirable. He was in no hurry to "settle" the issue, however, and he probably saw little point in delving into the matter further. The difference between his approach and Abbt's was too obvious. On February 9, about six weeks later, he wrote:[37] "I shall send for your essay and retrieve it from Herr von Rohr, read it, and judge it with the candor for which your friendship gives me credit. But let me have my essay back also. I entreat you, however, upon the sanctity of our friendship, not to return it without telling me your honest opinion.... The academy is about to publish the prize-essay. If I receive the copy with your annotations soon, I can make up the leeway in an appendix." Abbt returned the manuscript on February 20 but commented only briefly on the subject.[38] Since January 11, 1764, the correspondence between the two friends had found a new focus of interest, one that absorbed them completely and for this reason alone put an end to discussion of the two essays.

The recognition bestowed on Mendelssohn's essay was well deserved. An analysis of the work shows how deeply he had entered into the subtleties of the Leibniz/Wolffian philosophy and its finespun variations in Baumgarten's *Metaphysica* and *Ethica;* how masterfully he had interwoven the materials he had found there with the results of his own independent investigations; and how cogently he had argued his case.[39] To be sure, Kant's treatise, which won only the *accessit*, was superior to his in originality and depth, but it was less rich in thought and expression. One is struck, however, by the many similarities between their basic concepts—and, indeed, the whole pattern of their thinking. At this time, Kant was still in his precritical phase, steeped in Baumgarten's ontology. In certain respects he was more dogmatic than Mendelssohn, whose stance vis-à-vis the school philosophy was infused with a marked degree of freedom, due in some measure to his aesthetic concerns.

On balance, Mendelssohn's essay had much to recommend it for the prize. Its introductory part put the academy's question in historical perspective and reformulated it with greater precision. There had been, he pointed out, much coming and going of metaphysical systems, but a relative constancy in mathematics. The fact that ancient and medieval philosophy had lost their currency was a clear sign of progress. Progress in mathematics was no less pronounced but not so spectacular because it did not entail the abandonment of the old teachings; new discoveries did not devalue previous ones because mathematics had the advantage of certainty, owing to the evidence of its truths. In order to achieve a similar degree of evidence in metaphysics modern philosophers had tried to make the principles of metaphysics as unassailable as those of mathematics. These attempts had failed. Even those who considered metaphysical demonstrations of certain truths to be convincing and irrefutable had to admit that they lacked the evidence of mathematical proofs. In other words, the use of the mathematical or geometrical method by Descartes, Spinoza, Leibniz, and Wolff had not succeeded in making metaphysics a strict science. As a result, there was fairly widespread skepticism about the general validity of metaphysics.

Given this situation, the question raised by the academy was a timely one. The term "evidence" should, however, be understood to refer not merely to certainty but also to "perspicuity" *(Fasslichkeit)*, i.e., the ability to carry immediate conviction and acceptance. Mendelssohn borrowed the word *Fasslichkeit* from Alexander Baumgarten, who used it both in the aesthetic sense of viewing the totality of a manifold through the power of imagination and in the intellectual sense of a clear comprehension. A case of certain knowledge without perspicuity, Mendelssohn explained, was the infinitesimal calculus. Bearing this distinction in mind, the problem was to show (1) whether metaphysical truths were capable of irrefutable demonstration (i.e., of evidence), and (2) whether they were capable of the same perspicuity as geometrical truths. In case the answer to the first question was in the negative, one had to establish (1) in what sense they could be said to possess certainty, (2) to what degree of certainty they could be developed, and (3) whether this ultimate degree sufficed to produce complete conviction. Anticipating the result of his inquiry, Mendelssohn concluded his introduction with the statement: "I daresay that the metaphysical truths are capable of the same certainty but not of the same perspicuity as the geometrical truths."[40]

The first two sections of the essay deal with evidence in mathematics and metaphysics, respectively. Mendelssohn makes the tacit assumption that the method applicable to both disciplines is the same: in both, concepts are analyzed in order to make explicit and distinct what they implicitly contain, in an obscure way. What he means by the use of the analytical method in mathematics (more precisely, in geometry) is hinted at but not satisfactorily explained when he says that the concept of extension contains implicitly all geometrical truths, i.e., all the manifold possibilities of geometrical figures and their properties. He compares the analysis of concepts to the use of a magnifying glass by which obscure and unperceived parts of an object become clear and distinct. Whereas Kant's essay assigned the analytical method to metaphysics only, characterizing mathematics as proceeding by way of synthesis, Mendelssohn was obviously trying to bring the two disciplines into close proximity to one another by postulating the same method for both. According to Kant, the principles of mathematics are axiomatic, i.e., they are not explained by an analysis of a given concept but consist in the synthesis of an object and its definition: e.g., one draws four straight lines which include a plane and are not parallel to each other; one calls this figure a trapezoid. Here the concept is not given prior to the definition but, on the contrary, arises from the definition.[41] Mendelssohn's advocacy of the analytical method in mathematics seems to be guided by the consideration that Leibniz and Wolff analyzed and thereby proved the Euclidean axioms, a procedure by which mathematics is made a part of logic.[42] For in his Hebrew commentary on Maimonides' *Logical Terms* he followed Wolff in proving by logical analysis the axiom that the whole is larger than its part.[43] In fact, Mendelssohn was more consistent in his preference for the analytical method than were Wolff and some older members of his school, who used the analytical as well as the synthetical method in both mathematics and metaphysics.[44]

Since Mendelssohn saw no significant difference between mathematics and metaphysics insofar as method was concerned, the question of why these disciplines presented different degrees of evidence was all the more acute. The criterion of this difference had obviously to be found in their subject matters rather than in the method they employed. For the purpose of his preliminary investigation Mendelssohn narrowed metaphysics down to ontology (as distinct from the metaphysical concern with reality) and mathematics down to pure (as distinct from applied) mathematics. He could now define mathematics as a science dealing with quantities and ontology as a science dealing with the qualities of things. Strange as the latter definition may seem to us, it represents a view common to eighteenth-century philosophers. The description of mathematics as the science of quantity and the designation of ontology (and even, in some instances, of philosophy) as a science of quality can be found in Wolff, Baumgarten, Georg Friedrich Meier, Adolf Friedrich Hoffmann, Kant, Lambert, and Abbt.[45] The term "quality" as used here derives from the ontological perspective, which views a "thing" or "entity" and its determinations. It signifies the characteristics or *notae* of a thing in their widest sense. Between mathematics as the science of extensive quantity and ontology as the science of quality lies the intermediate science of unextended or "intensive" quantity (Baumgarten's *mathesis intensorum)*, which deals with the "degrees" of qualities. The mathematicians, Mendelssohn pointed out, had hitherto treated almost exclusively of extended quantity, where it was not difficult to obtain clear and distinct notions. For here the "parts" were discrete and spread out in space. The planes, lines, and points of a figure were visible to the senses. Hence evidence was no problem. It was different with unextended or intensive quantity, for it presupposed "profound insights into the qualities of things." The way in which one had hitherto measured the degrees of light, warmth, color, hardness, etc. amounted to a transposition of intensity into the key of extended quantity. One simply expressed degrees through lines and figures, a procedure that would be superfluous if one knew the principles of unextended quantity. Mendelssohn, like Baumgarten, applied the term "unextended quantity," or "degrees of quality," not only to physical qualities such as light, gravity, and elasticity but equally to nonphysical qualities like moral values and cognitive acts. His emphasis on the *mathesis intensorum* in this context was motivated by two considerations. He wanted to show that quantity and quality were closely linked in this intermediate science, and that the apparent discrepancy of mathematics and metaphysics was not as radical as the question posed by the academy had assumed. Moreover, he was trying to point out that it was not only in metaphysics but also in dynamics and mechanics that "difficulties" existed which aggravated the problem of perspicuity.

The discussion of the difficulties inherent in the *mathesis intensorum* forms an essential part of the first section of the essay. It has its counterpart in the second section, in which Mendelssohn investigates the reason for the deficiency of metaphysical evidence. It had been suggested, he said, that the reason lay in the nonavailability of imagery such as that which aided comprehension in geometry, in which one operated with figures.[46] He disagreed with this argument. There were no pictorial aids in arithmetic and algebra, and yet the principles of these branches of mathematics were almost as easily comprehensible as those of geometry. Therefore, intuitibility *(Anschaulichkeit)* could not be regarded as the criterion of easy comprehension or perspicuity. The decisive factor was the availability of a language of signs adequate to the objects to be expressed by them. The lack of a similar language of signs in metaphysics was the primary reason for its deficient perspicuity. The terms and combinations of words used by the philosophers were still arbitrary and failed to correspond to the nature and combinations of the ideas they were meant to express. Hence the seeming futility of explanations and the prima facie impression of demonstrations as mere verbiage. Since the mind had to be constantly on the alert to remember the meaning of the terms used, the least flagging of attention was bound to make one lose sight of the object referred to and to retain merely empty signs, in which case even the most thorough philosophical discourse appears to be a mere playing with words.[47]

There was yet another reason for the lesser degree of perspicuity in metaphysics. It followed from the very nature of its subject matter, i.e. quality. The characteristics of things were so closely interwoven with one another that none could be understood without reference to the rest. Every analysis of a concept demanded, therefore, a host of explanations that had to be borne in mind all the time if the meaning was not to be lost in the shadow of words. Since a failure to clarify all characteristics entailed the presence of a residual obscurity in the mind, it was necessary to return again and again to first principles before one could proceed to new insights—a point that was also made in Kant's essay. Fundamentally, however, it was the lack of a symbolic language of signs that, according to Mendelssohn, was responsible for the difficulties of demonstrative proofs and conceptual analyses in philosophy.

This realization on his part explains, we may add, his great interest in the project of a universal language of signs that, following the lead given by Leibniz, was being pursued by Johann Heinrich Lambert and Plouquet. In his review of Lambert's *Neues Organon* (1764) Mendelssohn emphasized the importance of the attempt it made to express all kinds of logical inferences by figurative signs: this might be the first step toward a universal language of signs in philosophy. He preferred Lambert's signs to those suggested by Plouquet in his *Calculum in logicis* (1763).[48] His admiration for Lambert's effort is clearly expressed in a letter he wrote to Abbt on July 12, 1764: "Had I read Herr Lambert's new *Organon* some years ago, my prize-essay would certainly have remained in my drawer or else it might have experienced the wrath of Vulcan [i.e., been burnt]."[49] Mendelssohn perfectly understood that Lambert's and Plouquet's efforts had nothing to do with the many eighteenth-century attempts to solve all philosophical problems mathematically. He recognized that, in addition to the *mathesis universalis,* which was concerned with the measuring of intensive quantities, there was a need for a calculus of qualities such as had already been projected in Leibniz' *ars characteristica* and *ars combinatoria.*[50] In contrast to most of his contemporaries, who showed no appreciation of Lambert and Plouquet, Mendelssohn hailed their endeavors enthusiastically as a decisive step toward remedying the fundamental weakness of metaphysics and philosophy in general.

Ontology, though suffering from a deficient degree of perspicuity, was nevertheless capable of evidence. For example, the proposition "God is just in the highest degree" could be demonstrated with the same certainty as any mathematical proposition if one presupposed the existence of God as the being that comprised all realities, viz., all positive predicates. The problem of evidence in metaphysics arose only when one tried to make the transition from the world of concepts to that of external reality. In every science but one the real existence of an object was verifiable through the senses; the one exception was metaphysics. Here one inferred, in a single case, real existence from possibility. (The reference is obviously to the ontological argument for the existence of God.) Moreover, it was the task of metaphysics to verify the testimony of the senses and establish the existence of the external world against the skeptics and the idealists. While the mathematician could afford to remain indifferent to the problem of reality, the metaphysician could not. He had to secure the truth of reality, and it was at this point that evidence tended to elude him. We have here an admission by Mendelssohn that evidence in metaphysics was of a lesser degree than in mathematics, and that it was not perspicuity alone in which they differed. Kant described both metaphysics and mathematics as capable of a degree of certainty such as was required for conviction, and saw the superiority of mathematics to consist in the ease with which certainty could be obtained there owing to the intuitibility of the subject. In fact, Mendelssohn had taken a similar position at the end of his introduction, where he vindicated evidence, though not perspicuity, to metaphysics. And as we shall see, he recaptured this view in the end. It remains remarkable, however, that he had some qualms about the matter and was less dogmatic than Kant.

There is irony in the fact that Kant, in his precritical period, attributed to metaphysics the same evidence as he did to mathematics, whereas Mendelssohn showed an inclination to consider metaphysical truths as less certain than mathematical ones.[51] There were "two ways" in which philosophy had tried to justify the transition from concepts to reality. Both had been attempted by Descartes, one starting out from the inner certitude of the *cogito* ("I think") and concluding that I am; the other modifying the ontological argument by inferring the reality of the necessary being (God) from its possibility. Both ways, Mendelssohn conceded, were attended by difficulties. Neither could impart to metaphysics the degree of certainty that would silence all doubt. There was, finally, another reason that militated against evidence in metaphysics. It lay in the intrusion of subjective interests and motivations into the consideration of metaphysical truths. Since the issues at stake had a bearing on our conduct and ultimate happiness, everybody considered himself competent to judge and take sides. Mathematics, on the other hand, was viewed impartially. The question whether or not the tangent of a circle and its diameter formed a right angle had no disquieting influence on human behavior. In describing the subjective factors that impede progress in metaphysics Mendelssohn was guided, no doubt, by Francis Bacon's discussion of the *idola theatri,* the figments of blindly accepted views of outdated authorities,[52] and by Maimonides' chapter on the causes of metaphysical controversies.[53]

The third section of the essay deals with evidence in natural theology. The criterion of perspicuity plays hardly any part in this section. Mendelssohn opens his treatment of the subject by developing a doctrine of divine attributes, making the point that every one of the perfections of God can serve as the principle from which all others can be derived, since they all entail each other: "One single chain of inferences unites all perfections of this primary being; his independence, infinity, immensity, most perfect will, boundless intellect and unlimited power, his wisdom, providence, justice, holiness, etc. are mutually grounded in each other in such a way that each one would be self-contradictory without the rest."[54] Mendelssohn's list and characterization of divine attributes follows Wolff, Baumgarten, and Meier. He derives the unity of God not from his necessary existence (as Wolff did) but from his infinite perfections (as Baumgarten did). What Mendelssohn meant becomes clear from Baumgarten's statement on the subject: since unity consists in the inseparability of the essential determinations of a thing, God, whose perfections are infinite, possesses the highest degree of unity.

In following Baumgarten, Mendelssohn chose a path that lead him completely away from the doctrine of attributes known to him from his study of Maimonides. According to Maimonides, unity is not an attribute of God but merely expresses his incomparable uniqueness, which cannot be grasped by our intellect. Unity in this sense is entailed by the unique coincidence, in God, of essence and existence.[55] In deriving God's unity from his perfections Mendelssohn abandoned the traditional pattern of the *via negativa*, which Maimonides had inherited from Neoplatonism and, ultimately, from Philo. In so doing he completed the break with negative theology that had been initiated earlier by medieval Jewish philosophers like Gersonides and Crescas.[56]

The principles of natural theology, Mendelssohn asserted, have the certainty and "almost" the evidence of geometrical truths so long as one considers them within the realm of pure concepts having no necessary claim to external reality. It was the transition to reality that in theology, as in metaphysics, gave rise to doubts and put evidence in jeopardy. Of the "two ways" by which Descartes had tried to secure the required transition, the one starting from the *cogito* and concluding from it the reality of a necessary being (God) was the easier, since it was based on the principle of sufficient reason. The second way, viz. the ontological argument, was less convincing in the form in which it had been hitherto presented. Mendelssohn tried to remedy this fault by giving the argument "an easier turn." The formulation of the ontological argument presented by him presupposes Baumgarten's concept of existence as the completeness of the determinations of a thing. All that exists is completely determined, and everything completely determined exists. So long as it is still undetermined whether certain possible attributes do or do not appertain to the thing, it is merely possible. Only when all determinables are actually determined can it be said that the thing is real, i.e., that it exists. Existence, therefore, is conterminous with the sum total of determinations present in an actual thing. At the same time, it is a predicate that adds something to the content of the thing. As for the determinations that make up the existence of a thing, they are either realities (i.e., positive predicates) or negations. A thing that has a certain reality (a certain positive predicate) does not have its negation. Realities as such cannot contradict each other. Hence it is possible that all realities coexist in a single thing. We can therefore conceive of a being that contains all positive predicates in the highest degree. This most real being *(ens realissimum)* is God, the most perfect being *(ens perfectissimum)*.[57]

How does Mendelssohn prove the existence of such a being? He starts out with the assertion that the nonexistent is either the impossible or the merely possible. The impossible is that which contains contradictory determinations. Were the concept of the most perfect being to contain contradictions, i.e. determinations affirmed and denied at the same time, it would be nonexistent. Since, however, it is by definition free from all deficiencies, it is at least possible in the logical sense. On the other hand, it cannot, be considered to be "merely possible" because the "merely possible" achieves existence only when another being's existence causes it. Being "merely possible" means that its existence does not follow from its own essence but is contingent and hence dependent. Here the old argument that concluded God's necessary existence from the contingency of things is presupposed but given a new turn. Instead of inferring necessary existence from contingent being, God is put in opposition to the "merely possible"—how could the most perfect being be said to be contingent?—and his existence is directly derived from his logical character as the most perfect being. Since the concept of such a being involves no contradiction, it is possible for such a being to exist. Impossibility being thus excluded, and "mere possibility" being likewise rejected, it follows that the reasons for nonexistence are absent. Moreover, in view of the fact that existence is identical with complete determination of predicates, God must exist.

In addition to this a priori proof for the existence of God, Mendelssohn also develops the proof from the contingency of things (following Wolff in this case) and in this connection enters into a subtle analysis of the principle of sufficient reason, its compatibility with the recognition of the possibility of miracles, and determinism as its corollary.[58] His next step is the discussion of reality and phenomenal existence as a prelude to a further clarification of what kind of predicates are applicable to God. Following Leibniz' lead, he excludes extension from the realm of realities (as he does in regard to all phenomena) and sees in the faculties of our soul attributes that in their most perfect form may be said to belong to God. Among such attributes are reason, wisdom, justice, goodness, and mercy.

Finally, he advanced the physico-theological argument that concluded from the beauty and order in the cosmos and in the laws of motion that the universe was not the product of chance but of a wise Creator. Although this kind of argument could not establish a creation ex nihilo, it had a more vivid effect on the mind than the earlier, more stringent proofs. In fact, the physico-theological proof was highly popular in the late seventeenth and throughout the eighteenth century. Mendelssohn, who toward the end of the third section of his essay felt justified in attributing to the two main proofs "a completely demonstrative convincing power," nevertheless realized that they could not be expected to arouse a strong and vivid impression in the soul and impel men to conduct their lives in conformity to religion. To arouse "practical conviction" and a "life of knowledge," one had to utilize every kind of proof that might help to strengthen and energize religion. In putting stress on the primacy of practical conviction, he anticipated, in a sense, Kant's *Primat* of practical reason and the young Hegel's concept of religion as a "matter of the heart."[59] There are, besides, many striking similarities between Mendelssohn's and Kant's treatment of the theme in their essays for the academy.[60]

The fourth and last section is concerned with evidence in the principles of morality. In his *Essay Concerning Human Understanding* Locke had declared that morality was capable of the same degree of demonstration as mathematics,[61] and the Wolffian school had adopted this view. It had gone beyond Locke in considering the conviction obtained by demonstrating moral truths as essential for acquiring a "correct and certain" conscience. Baumgarten defined the correct conscience (*conscientia recta*) as one that reasoned correctly, and the certain conscience (*conscientia certa*) as one that was sure of the correctness of its reasoning. The only difference between Wolff and Baumgarten was this: according to Wolff, conscience was the ability to judge the result of our actions, since it was the result of our actions that was the criterion of morality; according to Baumgarten, conscience was the ability to judge our actions in the light of the moral law.[62] The rational character of morality could not have been stressed more forcefully than by the Wolffian school in which Mendelssohn had been reared.

A diametrically opposite view had been developed in England. Francis Hutcheson denied the legitimacy of founding morality upon reason. Our rational faculty enabled us to understand the true and the false but could never provide a motivation for action. This only an awareness of purpose could achieve, and purposes presupposed instincts, affects. These furnished the reason exciting to action. Beside exciting reason there was, however, justifying reason, which approved or disapproved an action, and this kind of reason could only be explained by the assumption that we possessed a "moral sense," i.e., a "determination of our mind" to approve every kind affect in ourselves and others without consideration of self-interest. Hutcheson's theory was reaffirmed by Hume in his *An Enquiry Concerning the Principles of Morals* (1751) but questioned by Richard Price in his *Review of the Principal Questions and Difficulties in Morals* (1758).

The impact of Hutcheson's theory upon German philosophers is noticeable in Formey's essay *De la conscience,* which appeared in the *mémoires* of the Berlin Royal Academy (1753). There an attempt was made to find a place for the moral sense within the framework of the Wolffian theory of morals.[63] Of particular interest is the fact that in his earlier period Kant was much attracted by the moral sense theory, which he rightly traced back to Shaftesbury. The essay he wrote as a competitor of Mendelssohn, in answer to the questions posed by the academy, has been shown to follow rather closely Treatise II of Hutcheson's *An Essay on the Nature and Conduct of the Passions and Affections with Illustrations on the Moral Sense* (1728), and in 1765 he referred to the moral sense theory as "a beautiful discovery of our times."[64]

Mendelssohn's attitude toward Hutcheson underwent subtle changes.[65] Much as he appreciated the psychological analyses offered by Hutcheson and, following him, by Edmund Burke, he opposed the assumption of special "senses" such as the moral sense or the sense of beauty. In his view, this was "coming close to cutting abruptly the thread of all reasoned investigation."[66] He welcomed, however, Hutcheson's and Burke's differentiation between two kinds of "passions," viz. those aimed at "self-preservation" and those motivated by a concern for "society." In this connection he criticized Wolff, who had based our duties toward others on the need for self-perfection.[67] Mendelssohn was inclined to recognize a kind of natural sympathy as the source of our benevolence. This concession to Hutcheson, which was made in a letter to Lessing dated February 27, 1758, was further developed in a fragmentary essay, probably of the same year, on the *Affinity of the Beautiful and the Good*.[68] Here the "moral sense" is recognized as something actually found to be present in the soul, but it is considered to be nothing more than a sensual, confused knowledge of the good in analogy to the aesthetic sentiment, which also belongs to the subrational faculties of the soul. In other words, the moral sense, though existent, does not represent the principle of morality, which can be established only by the clear and distinct rational understanding of good and evil. In Leibnizian terms, it is but a "phenomenon." That is to say: it represents the manner in which the rational or objectively real is reflected in sense perception. Hearing a three-note chord produces a sentiment different from knowing the ratio of vibrations, which is the reality causing the sentiment. Similarly, we have to distinguish between moral sentiment aroused by the experience of a virtuous act and the rational understanding of the nature of virtue. Mendelssohn added a further interpretation of the moral sense. Moral sentiment, as he called it, was *bon-sens*, a kind of moral taste, i.e. a capacity of grasping by way of quick intuition what reasoning was able to arrive at by a slower, more circuitous route. The two interpretations of the moral sentiment do not quite harmonize, but they show how eager Mendelssohn was in 1758 to come to terms with Hutcheson's theory without yielding even an inch of Wolffian ground.

The prize-essay gave Mendelssohn an opportunity to examine and further clarify his view of morality. With Locke and the Leibniz/Wolffian school, he regarded the principles of morality as capable of demonstrative proof. The ethical maxim that he sought to establish was Wolff's "general rule of human actions," which demanded: "Do what makes you and your condition more perfect, and refrain from what makes you and your condition less perfect."[69] He modified it, however, to read: "Make your and your fellow-men's inner and outer condition, in proper proportion, as perfect as you can."[70] In order to arrive at this rule he employed three kinds of argument, viz. one proceeding, a posteriori, from an observation of the tendencies of action common to all men; one arguing, a priori, from the concept of a free rational being; and one taking the concept of God for its starting point.

The a posteriori argument is based on the premise that the "thousand fold desires and wishes, passions and inclinations" of men had this in common: that they all aimed at the preservation or improvement of our own or other people's inner or outer condition. Even the most vicious desires had no other purpose, yet placed specious goods in lieu of true ones by misjudging the due proportion between the objects pursued. The very fact that the ultimate goal, however misunderstood, was identical in all as the *summum bonum, quo tendimus omnes*[71] made morality a "law of nature." According to the a priori argument, the same law could be deduced from the very concept of a being endowed with free will. An obligation *(Verbindlichkeit)*—Kant used the same term in his essay—implied a moral necessity to act or refrain from acting in a certain way. Since every free being was morally constrained to let himself be determined in his choice by the most pertinent motivations, he was "obliged" to produce as much perfection, beauty, and order in the world as he could. Though Mendelssohn's formulation of the argument also uses the a posteriori reflection on the pleasure that we derive from perfection, beauty, and order, his real meaning is clear: perfection as such, not the pleasure we derive from it, is the *summum bonum*.[72] The principle of morality consists, therefore, in the freedom with which rational beings make perfection the maxim of their choice.

Finally, the theological argument proceeded from the assumption that God created the world for a purpose. Since God could have created only from wisdom and goodness, his design could have been none other than the perfection of his creatures. Hence the "law of nature" agreed with the design of God, and we were imitators of God whenever we made ourselves or others more perfect.[73] In his review of the three proofs Mendelssohn underlined the concept of freedom as the decisive principle on which morality was founded. Freedom, he said, was "a fertile concept" from which we could derive the knowledge of all our duties and obligations. Moral philosophy was nothing but the science of the quality of a being endowed with free will insofar as he had free will. This emphasis on freedom as the root of morality foreshadows, in however modest a way, Kant's ethical theory in the *Critique of Practical Reason* (1788).

The concluding part of Mendelssohn's essay deals with practical morality. It was not difficult, he declared, to apply evident ethical maxims to particular situations, but it was different with rules of action that were of a derivatory character. In such cases two kinds of difficulty beset the proper choice of action. Firstly, the major premise, which contained the rule, might be in doubt when a conflict of duties existed. Such a conflict of higher and lower duties was to be expected when rules of a specific rather than general nature claimed our attention. Since we were obliged to do the best and not merely the good, we were sometimes hard pressed to decide which duty took precedence. The second difficulty concerned the minor premise stating the nature of the situation and the possible results of any action contemplated. Our experience was insufficient to enable us to foresee in all cases the consequences of our actions. Hence the moral dilemma in which we were placed at times. In such instances urgent decisions could not be arrived at through long processes of reasoning but by a combination of two subrational faculties, viz. conscience and *bon-sens*. Mendelssohn defined conscience as an ability to differentiate correctly, by indistinct conclusions, between good and evil, *bon-sens* as an ability to do the same concerning the true and false. Both together formed the "inner feeling." Through conscience we were able to determine the major premise in conflict situations, i.e., to decide which duty deserved to claim priority. Through *bon-sens*—"a happy sense of the truth" *(Wahrheitssinn)*—we guessed, as it were, the correct minor premise, i.e., the situation in all its circumstances. The combination of the two served as a substitute for the judgment of practical reason.

The relationship between conscience and *bon-sens* was now clarified in a way far superior to the hazy notions adumbrated in the fragment of 1758. Yet now as before Mendelssohn refused to adopt Hutcheson's concept of "moral sense." What he admitted was "inner feeling" as a faculty of moral judgment on a prerational level that was useful in urgent conflict situations but did not claim to represent the faculty by which the ultimate criterion of morality could be established. While "inner feeling" served practical morality, reason alone was the principle of theoretical morality. Mendelssohn thus introduced a novel kind of moral doctrine. His departure from the Wolffian school is most pronounced in his definition of the conscience. According to Wolff, demonstrative proof is necessary to produce a correct and certain conscience. In Mendelssohn's view, the conscience operates in precisely those situations in which demonstrative proofs are difficult or impossible.[74]

One may ask whether the admission of "inner feeling" as a combination of conscience and *bon-sens* did not in fact amount to the recognition of Hutcheson's "moral sense" in disguise. The answer is that it did not. The conscience, Mendelssohn insisted, depended on reason and resulted from the sustained exercise of reason. It was the product of training. The ways in which the formation of a potent conscience comes about are described in the very last section of the essay, which draws heavily on the passages in the *Rhapsody* (1761) dealing with the application of psychological observations to morals.[75] The prominence given to the time factor in evaluating the function of conscience and *bon-sens* had appeared already in Mendelssohn's early treatise *On Controlling the Inclinations* (1756–1757), in which the basic notions of his psychology of morals are found. To ensure virtuous conduct, he had pointed out in that treatise, it was not enough to demonstrate the laudableness of virtue by strict proofs. We needed to become familiar with a large quantity of motivating factors of the right kind, and we had to learn to reflect upon them quickly.

In the prize-essay Mendelssohn utilized the insights he had gained for a portrayal of the means whereby the training of our conscience could be facilitated or, put in different terms, whereby the lower faculties of the soul could be made subservient to reason. There were four such means.

(1) The number of reasons persuading us to choose virtue was an important factor. While the mathematician could be satisfied with a single proof by which to win assent for what was a mere theoretical proposition, the preacher of morals, who had to move the heart and the will, was in a different position. The more arguments he could produce, the more likely that his plea would be effective.

(2) By way of continued training *(Übung)* we acquired the habit of acting in conformity to reason. The more frequently we engaged in contemplating moral principles and motivations, the more easily were the lower faculties of our soul amenable to their impact. Experience showed that many kinds of activity that could at first be performed only with much deliberation became habitual and capable of almost unconscious manipulation. Examples of this were the skills of the pianist and the typesetter. A person striving for moral perfection had to continue practicing virtue until his principles had been transformed into inclinations and virtuous conduct into second nature. The almost hymnic description that Mendelssohn gave of moral perfection as the ability to fulfill the moral law without effort, unconsciously, as if the fulfillment flowed from nature, introduced a new tone into moral theory. It found a deep resonance in Schiller and is reflected in his concept of moral beauty as the characteristic of a man in whom duty has become nature.[76]

(3) The arts could play a helpful role in promoting morality by arousing sentiments and stimulating the imaginative faculty. Rational arguments were able to convince the intellect of the excellence of virtue but belles-lettres and the arts compelled the approval of imagination. Mendelssohn assigned to music, in particular, the task of aiding morality by the sentiments of joy, devotion *(Andacht)*, pity, and gentleness that it evoked, especially if allied to poetic texts. He did not mean to suggest, however, that the arts should be made subservient to ethics. He loathed all moralizing on the stage and had clearly differentiated between true and theatrical morality.[77]

(4) Lastly, intuitive perception could help to harmonize imagination and reason. By "intuitive perception" *(anschauende Erkenntnis)* Mendelssohn understood the grasping of general principles of reason in the light of concrete examples. In theoretical contexts the example served merely as

an illustration, and it became superfluous once the theory was understood. In practical morality, on the other hand, the example was more useful than the maxim. It called forth the assent of the heart because it moved the senses and the imagination. Hence the importance of history and of the Aesopian fable to morals.

The result of employing these four means, Mendelssohn summed up, was the "conviction of the heart," which was the primary purpose of moral theory. Achieving this vivid knowledge of the good required no demonstrative proofs. In saying this, however, Mendelssohn did not intend to disparage rational demonstration. Whenever the theoretical foundations of morality were questioned, only the strictest proofs could suffice to secure them. Moreover, some people possessed enough animation and vigor of intellect to perceive the system of moral truths in all its ramifications, and to be enraptured by its "divine harmony." People of this disposition did not need additional means to establish a happy concord of mind and heart. It was the average man who required them. He did not have to be a metaphysician to become morally perfect. Metaphysical truth and moral goodness were two different things. Previously, Mendelssohn had separated the beautiful from the true. Now he went a step further by establishing the autonomy of ethics, at least insofar as practical morality was concerned.

The Correspondence on the Vocation of Man

On January 11, 1764, Abbt wrote to Mendelssohn:[1] "You are the only man with whom I can and wish to talk about the things that matter most, and to which, in the end, all study has to relate. I wonder whether you will permit me to place my thoughts and doubts concerning them before you ... The point from which I want to start is the *Vocation of Man* which, to me, is shrouded in mystery." The *Vocation of Man,* which Abbt wished to be the point of departure for the discussion, was Johann Joachim Spalding's famous *Betrachtung über die Bestimmung des Menschen,* which had just appeared in its seventh edition (1763). Fichte was later to say of this meditation that it had planted in his soul the first seed of higher speculation.[2] Spalding's manner of treating the subject foreshadowed, in a sense, the idealistic approach of Kant and Fichte. It shunned the employment of metaphysical notions of a technical type and obviously impressed Abbt by the freshness and directness of its meditative thinking. At the same time, it provoked Abbt's criticism by the very quality of moral pathos that had been the secret of its success ever since its first appearance in 1748.

Mendelssohn accepted Abbt's proposition that they should discuss the subject. Though he had already touched upon it in his letters *On the Sentiments* and, only recently, in his prize-essay, it had not been specifically attacked by him before, and Abbt's suggestion came at the right moment, when he needed a focal point for the completion of his *Phaedon* (as we shall see below). On February 9, 1764, he informed Abbt that he was looking forward with extreme impatience to his notes on Spalding's work. He suggested that their disputation be conducted under the names of two Greek philosophers. "In this way we shall be able to advance our boldest doubts . . . without hesitation."[3] The curtain-raiser of the debate was an essay that Abbt wrote as a review of Spalding's meditation, which was eventually published in the *Literaturbriefe* under the title "Doubts concerning the *Vocation of Man*." Mendelssohn replied in an essay of his own entitled "Oracle concerning the *Vocation of Man*." The editorial preface by Nicolai introduced the two essays under the guise of a tract published in Schinznach—a place in Switzerland—and made available to the editor by some person unknown to him. According to the preface, it contained a discussion of Spalding's *Vocation of Man* by two friends, Euphranor and Theodul, who had put forward diametrically opposing views on the subject.[4] However, the publication of these two essays did not conclude the debate by any means. For two and a half years the *Vocation of Man* formed a major topic in the correspondence between Mendelssohn and Abbt, the significance of which for the completion of Mendelssohn's *Phaedon* cannot be overestimated.

Before analyzing the correspondence, we have to acquaint ourselves with Spalding's monologue, which served as the "text," as it were, for the comments of the two friends. Spalding had dealt with the problem of man's vocation in a series of introspective meditations.[5] First he reflected upon man's desire for pleasure: was man merely a pleasure-seeking animal? And was his vocation, therefore, nothing but the gratification of his desires? The answer was in the negative. Man soon discovered that the vehemence of his desires robbed his soul of the peace it needed for self-knowledge. Hedonism, even if refined and curbed by reason, ultimately left us with a feeling of emptiness. Contemplative man, therefore, turned to the perfection of his mental faculties: he acquired and stored up knowledge, clarified his notions, sharpened his wits, and enlarged his horizon. Yet even the pleasures of the mind could not give him ultimate satisfaction, since they only helped to build up his own self and left the happiness of others out of account. To his astonishment, man noticed in himself propensities and sentiments that caused him to seek the welfare of others besides himself. There was an essentially altruistic impulse in his soul that was more than a refined form of self-love and yielded a sense of happiness superior to both the pleasures of the senses and the cultivation of the mind. The difference between the decent and the disgraceful, between right and wrong, was naturally implanted in our soul; there was within us a lawgiver who demanded virtuous conduct.

From morality there was but a small step to religion. Spalding, who was one of the leaders of the Berlin theology of the Enlightenment, defined religion as a frame of mind in which we embrace the idea of an archetype of perfection. This most perfect being (God) we approach with reverence and adoration. Man, a small creature on this earth, which itself is but a tiny spot in a vast cosmos, is distinguished by his ability to perceive the harmony of the universe and to rise to the contemplation of its maker. It is this ultimate knowledge that sets man's mind at rest: "The spirit that watches over everything will also watch over me. He, whose wisdom and goodness manifest themselves everywhere, will not allow anything to happen that does not befit his dignity nor benefit his creatures." True, in this world everything is an enigma, and the riddle of man's destiny is not solved here below. It would contradict the "unchangeable rules of fairness," however, were a soul to be deprived of the natural consequences of its inner rectitude. Hence the idea of immortality presented itself with irresistible force to a reflective mind. The prospect of a future opened up in which all disharmonies were dissolved in a perfect harmony. "The predisposition to it seems to be discoverable in my nature. I sense within myself capabilities that have the potential of infinite growth and can equally express themselves without union with the body. Can it be assumed that my ability to know and love the true and the good is to come to an abrupt end? Having been trained below, should we not rise to greater perfection in the hereafter?" To think otherwise would be tantamount to assuming too much futility in the provisions of infinite Wisdom.

Spalding's meditation was a faithful mirror of the Leibniz/Wolffian philosophy, which saw in this world the best of all possible worlds and felt justified in declaring what was and what was not compatible with the notion of God. Mendelssohn felt in complete agreement with the tenor of Spalding's work. Both his rootedness in Judaism and his adherence to the Leibniz/Wolffian school of thought predisposed him to accept Spalding's theses. Abbt's reaction was different. He, too, had enjoyed the beauty of this meditation, he confessed, but he rebelled against its all too complacent attitude. He wanted to be guided by experience and history rather than by metaphysical ideas. Not so very long ago Pierre Bayle had dared to attack rational theology, and it had been in reply to his acid skepticism that Leibniz had written his *Essais de Théodicée*. The discussion between Abbt and Mendelssohn repeated, on a different level, the controversy that had taken place between Bayle and Leibniz. Abbt distinctly invoked the spirit of Bayle to strengthen him in his endeavor,[6] and Mendelssohn, on the other hand, called Leibniz up from the shades to support him.[7]

In Abbt's view, the question of man's place in the universe could not be answered by introspective meditations but only by considering the entire human race with its history of crimes, errors, and tragedies. He had studied history—*mores multorum vidi et urbes*—in order to catch a glimpse of what might be the vocation of man. Spalding's "monologue of a learned and reflective man" did not take into account "the immense multitude of people who were determined for happiness or its opposite almost exclusively by external things."[8] The refined experiences that had inspired Spalding's monologue had no application to primitive man, who felt no disgust at sensuality and was not terrified by the vehemence of his desires. The picture of the refined hedonist was incorrect, since he was not bereft of intellectual pleasure. Above all, it was mistaken to assume a natural altruistic propensity in man, and to base our understanding of his vocation upon it. "Is it true that universal love for the human species ever dwelt in the breast of the savage?" Was Locke not right in trying to derive the more complex inclinations from some primary experience of ease and comfort?[9] Spalding's demand that we make the universal good the lodestar of our own individual happiness presupposed a high degree of maturity. Yet where should the great majority of people find their vocation? Least of all was Abbt ready to admit that our faculties were capable of infinite growth and thereby pointed in the direction of immortality. Could memory, for example, grow ad infinitum?[10]

In addition to these doubts, which reflected a sensualistic orientation in philosophy, Abbt raised some objections that, in modern parlance, might be termed "existentialist." He felt that Spalding had closed his eyes to the absurd and disturbing aspects of the human condition. He expressed his doubts in the form of a story, allegedly to be found in a "rare book" published in 1586 under the title "Description of Some Military Expeditions and of Some Amusing Events that Happened."[11] The events narrated in this story are anything but amusing. A prince had brought regiments of soldiers from a distant land. To what purpose? This was unknown even to the general who had been appointed their commander. The progress of the march was slow indeed. For secret reasons, orders had been given to take up temporary quarters until further notice. As one would expect of soldiers, some lived aimlessly and negligently. Some of them disappeared—suddenly. It was said that they had been removed at night on secret orders. But to where? *That* was a question! The general himself and some of the more conscientious officers, although ignorant of the prince's secret plan—or perhaps precisely because of their ignorance—were in a state of alertness, as if expecting at any moment to receive an order to resume the march. Others were in doubt whether such an order would ever be given. Presumably, they contended, the troups would be disbanded, notwithstanding the elaborate provisions and the high cost of their maintenance so far. What had happened to those who had been secretly removed? No letters had been received from them. Some claimed to have received letters, but they were hardly to be trusted. Had the departed ones been called away by the prince in pursuance of his plans? Or had they been notified of a secret order permitting them to go home, having covered some part of the road? Or had they been prematurely released in recognition of their good conduct? Some officers that stayed behind had committed grave offenses. Yet though they deserved punishment and, on closer inspection, had already suffered it in a way, it was, at most, to be suspected that the prince would avenge their offenses at some future time. There was, however, no way to guess what destination and what kind of duty had been assigned to them.[12]

The meaning of the allegory is clear. Abbt intended to raise anew, in all its starkness, the very question that Spalding had tried to answer: what is the vocation of man? There is an almost Kafka-like air about this story. The rules of conduct imposed upon the soldiers and officers tell us absolutely nothing of their true vocation and future destiny. The meaning of human existence is utterly obscure, if not absurd. Reason seems incapable of solving the problem. Abbt considered the possibility that revelation might provide the answer. Yet revelation too, he felt, was silent on the ultimate question. The prince, in his remote castle, apparently preferred to keep us in the dark. All that remained was to follow certain rules of conduct that promised a modicum of happiness on earth. It was a consoling thought that man had "just enough light" for the road he had to travel.[13] As for the "great and difficult question of immortality," reason was incapable of reaching any definite conclusion. For who could, on the basis of reason, seriously maintain that the imbalance of destiny was or was not straightened out here below? The strange distribution of misery and happiness in this world was no valid argument for a future life in which compensatory justice would be meted out. Who could tell me that an act of injustice committed against me had to be redressed in another life? My desire to see all my suffering ultimately avenged proved nothing whatever. It was but a hope indulged in, a mere wish-dream on my part. Did the universal order have to satisfy my wishes? And how could one consider this world a place of training for the next when so many human beings died shortly after birth?[14]

Abbt's essay was a frontal attack upon the whole philosophy of the Enlightenment, especially in its Leibniz/Wolffian form. Mendelssohn's reply was a strong reaffirmation of that philosophy. Neither nature nor history, he maintained, could refute the assumption that all happenings in the world were both factual and purposive. It was mistaken to divorce these two aspects. In his words:[15] "The whole of nature is but an expression of the thoughts of God by signs that are identical with the things themselves. Every new form that comes into being is a thought of the infinite and as such indicates purposiveness. The animal moves and is sentient in conformity to the designs of God; and man's actions, no matter how extravagant, likewise conform to the designs of the Almighty." In other words, the events themselves bear the seal of an ultimate purpose and testify to the designs of the creator. The soldiers in Abbt's allegory, Mendelssohn suggested, might have guessed from their daily occupations what the intentions of the prince were, namely, that which they actually did. "In the divine order all purposes are part of a unified whole. All ends are means and all means are ends. Do not think that this life is merely a preparation for the next as the final purpose. Both are means to an end, and both are ends in themselves. The designs of God and the processes of change go hand in hand ad infinitum."[16]

Mendelssohn's affirmation that everything conforms to God's designs is not to be taken in the Hegelian sense of the "cunning of reason," all things being employed in the service of the ultimate purposes of "Reason" in "History." On the contrary, Mendelssohn denies the instrumental character of happenings, historical or natural. Nor does Mendelssohn wish to justify evil by declaring its conformity to God's purposes. The problem of evil is submerged in the recognition of the great harmony in which everything is either created or admitted as contributing to the perfection of the whole. The concept underlying his statements is closely akin to Wolff's idea of nature as the unfolding of divine designs:[17]

> Nature is full of divine designs, which God seeks to achieve through the essence of things.... Since God knows everything resulting from the essence of the things and since he knows the purpose for which he produced it, it follows that the necessary results of the essence of things are God's designs.... In this sense all happy and unhappy coincidences belong to the divine designs, since God chose this world as the one in which they accord with all other things as part of the world's perfection.... Since everything that happens in the world represents a divine design, it follows that God has arranged his designs in the world in such a way that the preceding ones serve as means to those that result from them.

In Wolff's concept, however, the emphasis is on the chain of causality that connects all things and makes the prior in time a means to the posterior, whereas Mendelssohn goes a step further in assigning to everything the character of both means and end. His view is reminiscent of Maimonides' statement that all beings are created for their own sakes and, at the same time, for the sake of God's will.[18]

Viewed from this perspective, all beings, no matter how incomplete and imperfect, may still be said to fulfil their particular vocation. In the divine economy of things there is room for an infinity of variation. Nothing fails in its purpose because everything conforms to a divine purpose. Yet there is more to the reality of purposiveness than the general idea of the great harmony of the universe. Every being actually lives up to its vocation in the measure of its capability. The urge for self-perfection inherent in every being takes care of this.

As a Leibnizian, Mendelssohn believed in the dynamism of each monad in the universe. Each monad was a soul-unit striving from darkness to light, from the unconscious to consciousness, from obscure and confused notions to clear and distinct concepts. The savage who looked at a tree to form some conception of it thereby trained and improved the faculties of his soul. In so doing he fulfilled the special vocation of man, which consisted in the perfection (or at least the improvement) of his mental powers. Life was a constant endeavor to evolve the capacities inherent in us. In accomplishing whatever degree of perfection we managed to achieve, we acted in accordance with God's design. We had been sent here to improve our capacities, and the very nature of our desires, passions, tastes, and even our vanity showed that the urge for improving ourselves was the will of God. "You may die as a suckling or as a hoary head, you will invariably depart this life in a more developed condition than the one in which you entered it. The distance between the embryonic stage and that of an infant attempting to speak is perhaps greater than the distance between a schoolboy and a Newton."[19]

All the absurdities and crimes in the world's history could not obscure the fact that both victims and evildoers traveled the way from mere embryonic existence to some degree of mental comprehension. A man was the happier the more his free will agreed with the "true vocation" of his natural instincts, i.e. with the designs of God. Mendelssohn understood by the "true vocation" of man his perfection as a rational and moral being. Yet every man fulfilled the vocation peculiar to him, even though his progress came to an early halt. To ask why only some men reached perfection in this life ignored the character of the world as unity in diversity, and also failed to take cognizance of the future life as a chance for further growth in intellectual and moral capacity.

Echoing Leibniz' idea of the city of God, in which all rational spirits are participants and of which God is the monarch,[20] Mendelssohn said: "Be not contemptible in your own eyes.... As members of the realm of spirits, as citizens in the commonwealth of God, you belong to the most glorious part of creation." The enigmatic "prince" of the allegorical story told by Abbt is now transformed into the monarch of the great city of the universe, in which all is wisely planned.

As a postscript to the *Oracle* Mendelssohn added a brief discussion of a theme that held a special fascination for him: are sociability and altruism an original propensity in man or are they, essentially, a mere refined form of egotism? Abbt had cited the case of the savage as proof that universal love could not be considered a natural inclination. Mendelssohn agreed that the desire to promote general well-being indicated a highly developed state of civilization, but he insisted that the germ of it was already found at the most primitive level of man. Habit, education, example, etc. could increase but could not originate any desire or propensity. The existence of the original urge toward altruism, therefore, could not be denied even in the savage. It expressed itself in his desire to avoid hurting others, and it was different only in degree from the universal love of the fully developed man. In his *Sendschreiben* to Lessing, which was attached to his Rousseau translation (1756), Mendelssohn had drawn attention to Rousseau's statement that the savage was capable of pity and possessed the faculty of *perfectibilité*.[21] Lessing had questioned his friend's interpretation of this term,[22] but to no avail. Mendelssohn firmly adhered to his view and to his understanding of Rousseau's. He believed that what Abbt meant to say was actually not opposed to his opinion. From the viewpoint of the moral philosopher it was irrelevant whether one assumed an inborn tendency to altruism, as he did, or a native propensity to self-perfection, as Abbt seemed to suggest.[23]

The "doubts" that Abbt had expressed were by no means stilled by Mendelssohn's *Oracle*. Rational perfection, he objected, was but a tool serving man's vocation, not the vocation itself. Assuming that man was destined to achieve a certain degree of intellectual capacity, how could the stage reached by the savage be considered as conforming to his vocation? It was impossible to refute Rousseau's main thesis if one held, with Mendelssohn, that the savage lived up to his destiny by contemplating a tree and similar mental acts of a primitive sort. In other words, Mendelssohn had taken two mutually exclusive positions. On the one hand, he had set up the highest goals for man. On the other, he had acknowledged all stages of development as conforming to the designs of God. He had declared that no one departed this life without having made some progress in the growth of his faculties, this being the answer to the disturbing question raised by the death of infants. From Mendelssohn's letter to Abbt, written May 1, 1764, we learn that this consoling thought was intended for his own benefit, since on April 15 he had lost his first child at the tender age of eleven months.[24] He had been badly shaken by this event.[25] The comfort that his Leibnizian philosophy afforded him could not therefore be dismissed as purely academic. "My friend," he wrote to Abbt at the time, "the innocent child did not live in vain. . . . Her mind made astonishing progress in that short period. From a little animal that cried and slept she developed into a budding intelligent creature. One could see the blossoming of the passions like the sprouting of young grass when it pierces the hard crust of the earth in spring. She showed pity, hatred, love, admiration. She understood the language of those talking to her, and tried to make her own thoughts known to others." Abbt referred to Mendelssohn's personal grief:[26] "I regret that thinking about this matter arouses distressing sentiments in you. However, when you are again able to rise from the individual case to the general aspect of it, you will probably see my point. It is precisely the denial of full development to this progress that feeds my doubt: not whether men have a vocation but what that vocation is."

The next round of the debate found Mendelssohn reaffirming his position. It was futile to push beyond intellectual and moral perfection toward an assumed ultimate purpose or vocation distinct from such perfection. It was equally mistaken to demand that the intellectual powers of all members in the realm of spirits be uniformly developed. The various degrees of perfection achieved in this life agreed with the concept of a universe in which everything had its distinct place. Mendelssohn was thinking, no doubt, of the "great chain of being" that Alexander Pope had poetically glorified in his *Essay on Man,* and which he himself had discussed in various contexts.[27] In this vast chain or ladder of beings, from God down to nothingness, everything had its place, and any change would disturb the order and harmony of the whole. It was this view of the universe that permitted Mendelssohn to look upon man in general, and upon individual men in particular, as part of a grand design. Uniformity would reduce the world to chaos. He was not disturbed, therefore, by such phenomena as "Brühl and Pompadour," who had been mentioned by Abbt,[28] nor by Jesuits, inquisitors, pirates, tyrants, poisoners, and traitors.[29] (Count Heinrich von Brühl [1700–1763] had been the unscrupulous and criminally deceitful prime minister of Saxony, who had died the year before; and Jeanne-Antoinette Poisson, marquise de Pompadour [1721–1764], the scandal-ridden *maîtresse* of Louis XV, had just passed away.)

As a true Leibnizian, Mendelssohn could say, with Pangloss in Voltaire's *Candide*, "This world is the best."[30] The thesis that in the works of God all means are designs and all designs are means was capable of the widest application, he asserted.[31] He disagreed with Maupertuis, who had said that the purpose of the wonderful construction of a fly was to whet the appetite of a spider.[32] In Mendelssohn's view, the artful construction of that "flying machine" was designed, first and foremost, for the sake of the life of that tiny animal. To what end? To the end that even flies should have life and be sentient. One could go on asking: to what purpose? Yet who could give a final answer? There might be a variety of uses for which nature employed the lives of flies, but we had to admit ignorance of them.

Mendelssohn, we may note, was not averse to investigations into the "usefulness" of natural phenomena, such as had been undertaken in Wolff's treatise on the effects of nature,[33] or in the various physico-theological tracts of the period, which "found God in the stars, in the insects, in the plants, in the water."[34] What he objected to was the narrowly utilitarian outlook of these champions of teleology, who were given the final coup de grâce by Kant.[35] In his view, the very fact of the existence of certain creatures indicated their conformity to God's designs. Men existed; hence we had the right to conclude that the world would have been less perfect without them. What was the purpose of men? To do what we actually did, namely to develop our capabilities. To look beyond this general purpose was futile.[36] One had to admit that our "natural knowledge" (as distinct from revelation) was indeed deficient. But we knew, at any rate, that man had a vocation, and he expressed his pleasure at the fact that in this respect Abbt agreed with him. We were, however, ignorant of the modifications of our destiny in individual cases. We did not know what degree of development the individual was going to achieve; which ethereal body was to serve his soul for a cover; where he was to dwell in the hereafter; etc. No revelation answered these and similar questions, nor could revelation be expected to furnish the answers. For what we needed was instruction, not mere edification by allegorical images.[37]

The last stage of the correspondence is too intimately linked with Mendelssohn's work on the *Phaedon* to be discussed at this point. However, it would seem not inappropriate to conclude this account of their correspondence by referring to another and more down-to-earth theme that figured in their letters and is of considerable interest from a biographical point of view. About a year prior to his untimely death on November 3, 1766, Abbt had left Rinteln to become a councillor to the court and government of Count Wilhelm of Schaumburg-Lippe in Bückeburg. He had preferred this post to a professorship at Halle, which had been offered to him at the time. The reason for this choice was undoubtedly his glowing admiration for the count, a man of great culture and dignity,[38] to whose attention he soon brought his friend Mendelssohn. In a letter he wrote (to Nicolai?) on February 9, 1766, Abbt reported:[39] "I showed my lord some of Herr Moses' letters to me which it was not indiscrete to let him read. You see from the enclosed letter[40] what he replied in his own hand. I would ask you, however, to return the enclosure to me. My lord has since read the *Philosophische Schriften.* They pleased him very much, and for six days we talked about Herr Moses: except that he finds his subtle metaphysics a little too much for his liking; for he cannot reconcile himself too well with the spirituality of the soul." On June 11, 1766, Mendelssohn discreetly inquired about the possibility of his leaving Berlin and settling somewhere near Abbt so as to be able to lead a life dedicated to pure scholarship. The passage of the letter to Abbt containing this startling inquiry has never been published, and Abbt's references to it in his reply were for the most part obliterated in Nicolai's edition of the Abbt/ Mendelssohn correspondence.[41] Mendelssohn wrote:

> Having reflected a long time upon the vocation of man as such, it seemed to me, at long last, timely to consider my own in particular. I do not think that I shall put up with Berlin much longer. You said that in order to begin great things one ought to do something that appears to be foolish to small minds. I find myself rather capable of something of this sort, which looks like foolishness. We shall see whether anything great will result from it. I am ready to relinquish all business and to live in a small place entirely on my own, if possible. I can count on about three hundred to four hundred fifty thalers as interest from my capital. I should greatly be mistaken if I could not count on a small subsidiary income of one hundred thirty thalers. Should there not be a small place in your vicinity where I could live with my small family on four hundred thalers per annum? Such a place would, however, have to meet the following requirements. 1) Some, not necessarily many, Jewish families must already live there. 2) I would have to obtain the sovereign's "protection" at low cost. 3) The place should not be entirely bereft of literature; it should, at least, have facilities for receiving news of what is going on in the learned world. Perhaps you know, dear friend, a place in or around Bückeburg that combines all these qualities. If Göttingen were of this description, that would be paradise! There is not too much of a hurry about this, for I have to put up with my present situation for another year or two. I have to make a start, though, to think about it. Otherwise, my years will roll by and in the end I shall have done nothing but vegetate. So much about myself.

Abbt's answer could not have been more encouraging:[42] "I feel my heart palpitating when I think of the prospect of having you here.... I sent your letter immediately to the count, who stayed at his summerhouse at Baum, and I let you have the reply which I received." The last letter Mendelssohn wrote to Abbt reflected his gratitude and hope:[43] "I herewith return to you the letter of your count, that truly great friend of humanity. Oh! How remote is his way of thinking from the general way of reigning monarchs! Between ourselves: The cloak of an absolute ruler is perhaps as foreign to a great soul as the cloak of a Jew is to merit.[44] Convey to him, dearest friend, my humble thanks for the protection that he granted. It cannot be but pleasant to live under such a lord; and next to a friend as you must be true happiness." In his last letter Abbt wrote:[45] "The count is looking forward to your treatise on the immortality of the soul with burning desire. I too, as you can easily imagine. We are all too deeply interested in this subject." Alas! The rest was silence. The death that removed Abbt from the scene also killed Mendelssohn's desire for a new form of existence.[46]

The Phaedon

The work that would establish Mendelssohn's world-wide renown and win him the title "the German Socrates" was the dialogue *Phädon oder über die Unsterblichkeit der Seele in drey Gesprächen,* which was published in 1767. No other work of his had a more difficult birth or occupied him for so long a time. The first mention of the project occurs in a letter to Lessing dated December 19, 1760:[1] "My *Phaedon* still engages my mind. As soon as the letters [i.e. the *Literaturbriefe*] cease to be a drag on me, I shall first arrange the second edition of my *opuscula* and then apply myself to writing this treatise." He had obviously already discussed the plan with Lessing, who had spent the summer and fall of that year in Berlin. On November 7 Lessing had left for Breslau to assume the post of governmental secretary to General von Tauentzien. How lost Mendelssohn felt in the absence of his friend is pathetically expressed in the opening part of the letter of December 19: "Since you left I live in this big city as in a hermitage." His feeling of loneliness had been intensified by the simultaneous departure of his friend Marcus Eliezer Bloch, who had gone to Frankfurt an der Oder to study medicine.[2] Nicolai, too, was unapproachable because his marriage had taken place on December 12 and his honeymoon could not be disturbed. In these circumstances Mendelssohn felt no inclination to start work on the *Phaedon* project that he had discussed with Lessing. Instead he busied himself with the editing of his *Philosophische Schriften,* which appeared in time for the Michaelmas fair of 1761. He was hopeful, though, that the stimulus to more productive work would be provided by correspondence with Lessing: "My mind is at a standstill unless you wind up its springs. Start out from any subject you like. I shall follow you with pleasure." The next sentence contained the reference to the *Phaedon* project.

Mendelssohn might have brought this literary plan to earlier fruition, had Lessing responded in an encouraging way. He failed to do this, however, and the correspondence between the two friends seems to have got stuck, as Mendelssohn's letter of February 18, 1761 indicates.[3] At that point the project was still a mere idea *(Vorhaben)*: "I have written . . . to Herr Professor Baumgarten in order to inform him of my idea to recast and edit the *Phaedon.*" Mendelssohn obviously needed some moral encouragement for his somewhat pretentious undertaking. Unfortunately, Baumgarten had not been too helpful either: "What a strange man! He sent me a reply that astonished me. I meant to send you his letter; seeing, however, I hear as little from you as if you lived on another continent, I hold back until you have written to me." Lessing did not reply to this letter either. When Mendelssohn wrote to him again on March 27,[4] he answered in a gloomy, desperate mood, without referring to Mendelssohn's items of information.[5] Mendelssohn's next letter, in the middle of May, contained the happy news about his trip to Hamburg and the excitement of a "thousand diversions" in connection with his choice of Fromet Gugenheim as his wife-to-be. From this point until the middle of 1762 the *Phaedon* project seems to have been left altogether in abeyance. The letters written during this period were, for the most part, addressed to his fiancée. And the correspondence with Abbt grew in frequency and depth. As for Mendelssohn's literary activity during that time, the *Literaturbriefe* and the Shaftesbury translation kept him too busy to leave much time for work on the *Phaedon* project. However, he found time to write a Hebrew commentary on Maimonides' *Logical Terms* (to which repeated reference has been made before).[6] Eventually he abandoned the Shaftesbury project altogether in order to be free to try his hand at translating parts of Plato's *Republic* into German. This shifting of interest augured well for a resumption of the *Phaedon* project. It was by no means his first attempt to come to grips with the Platonic manner of writing. There had been an earlier preoccupation with Plato, which had, in fact, first given rise to the idea of recasting the *Phaedon.*

When Mendelssohn discussed this idea with Lessing in 1760, he had already familiarized himself with some of the problems involved in its realization. In June and July of that year he had reviewed in the *Literaturbriefe* (113–119) three writings dealing with Socrates. The first of these was Johann Georg Hamann's anonymously published *Socratic Memorabilia for the Boredom of the Public,*[7] which he described as "a pamphlet of four small sheets written with uncommon wit." He quoted with approval the author's remark that Socrates' sentences were "a great many small islands lacking bridges and ferries for linking them methodically." "One cannot judge more accurately," Mendelssohn observed, "the great truths and untrustworthy arguments of Socrates."[8] Thus Mendelssohn's discontent with Socrates' (i.e., Plato's) proofs was already evident. Its natural corollary was a desire to substitute more convincing ones.

The second review concerned a book by "W . . ." published in Zürich under the title *The Last Dialogues of Socrates and his Friends*.[9] Mendelssohn radically condemned the book, whose author he supposed was none other than Christoph Martin Wieland.[10] The initial W represented, however, Jakob Wegelin (1721–1791), professor of philosophy and Latin at the gymnasium at St. Gallen, who was called a "second Montesquieu" by his admirers (including King Frederick II). Wegelin felt much hurt by the review, which he attributed to Lessing: only a Lessing could poke fun at so serious a theme. He defended himself against its strictures in the *Freymüthige Nachrichten*.[11] describing himself as a persecuted Socrates and his detractor as an Aristophanes and Melitos.[12] As late as 1775 Herder wrote to Hamann about Wegelin: "He is also said to be the author of the *Socratic Dialogues by W.*, concerning which Moses so severely reprimanded Wieland, who thereupon declared himself innocent."[13]

Obviously Mendelssohn's review had attracted some attention. He later realized that Wegelin, not Wieland, was the author of the book he had criticized.[14] His review is of special interest because it offered him an opportunity to express his own views about the way in which one ought to present Socrates. Wegelin had originally planned his work for the stage but then had decided to cast it in the form of thirty-three discussions. Mendelssohn remarked that these discussions showed nothing of the "great manner in the art of dialogue" that we so much admired in the ancients.[15] Of the special style of the Socratic dialogues nothing at all was noticeable. "All participants . . . speak in one voice; the characters are without life, their ideas [*Gesinnungen*] without truth, and the speech they utter is unnatural." An author of "Socratic dialogues" should know what his subject demanded of him, and what sort of earlier authors had preceded him. The multitude of flowerets, which robbed his language of all naturalness, was the opposite of the spirited tongue of a philosopher enthused by the truth, whose powerful eloquence flowed from the heart and moved the heart.

Mendelssohn had clearly given much thought to the specific character of the Socratic dialogue and had already formed a distinct view of the character of Socrates. The impetuous, conceited, and vain Socrates presented by W had nothing in common, he declared, with the character of the historical Socrates. With delicate irony he said of the author: "He did not want to owe anything to his predecessors, men like Plato and Xenophon." Here, too, he mapped out in advance the road that he wished to take in his own presentation of Socrates in the *Phaedon*. It is questionable, however, whether he managed to live up completely to his own demands, which he expressed in the words put into the mouth of Alcibiades by Plato: "The language of Socrates closely resembles the figure of a satyr, the outward appearance of which enshrines a god within. If you listen to his discourses you will feel them at first to be ridiculous; for they are clothed as in the hide of a clumsy satyr..."[16] Mendelssohn reproached W for having endowed Socrates with flowery and pretentious oratory that concealed the outward satyr but betrayed the inner one all the more. But when his own *Phaedon* appeared, a similar complaint was directed against him. It was said that his Socrates lacked the austerity of Plato's and was improperly clothed in a pleasant modish garb.[17]

The third review dealt with Denis Diderot's outline of a tragedy on the death of Socrates in Diderot's treatise on dramatic art.[18] Mendelssohn used a German translation that he described as excellent (without giving any reference) and offered Diderot's design as a lesson for the much criticized W. In case this author had never read Plato, he could at least have learned from Diderot how difficult it was to present Socrates on the stage. Of the five scenes sketched by Diderot the first two followed the *Crito,* the third the *Apology,* and the last two the *Phaedon,* where, however, Diderot did not go very far but stopped abruptly. Socrates' message to Evenus to follow him shortly if he was wise marked the sudden end of the scene. Diderot added the laconic remark: "This utterance offers an opportunity for the scene about the immortality of the soul. Let him who so desires try his hand at this scene. I hurry to my purpose." Mendelssohn was not too happy with this fragmentary scene. "What's that?" he asked. "Why does Herr Diderot bolt at this point? Why does he not at least tell us how this scene is to be arranged for the stage? I fear he was at a loss what to suggest. In fact, there are here two horns of a dilemma that cannot be avoided. Should Socrates convince his disciples by philosophical arguments, most of the audience will yawn; should he move the audience by his eloquence, philosophers will be dissatisfied. I also say, like Diderot, let him who so desires try his hand at this scene. I hurry to my purpose."[19] At a later date Mendelssohn did try his hand at this scene, though not in the form of dramatic art. His *Phaedon* was the "purpose" to the fulfilment of which he meant to hurry, not anticipating the long delay this work would suffer. At any rate, the thorough analysis and criticism that he bestowed upon the three works[20] proved to be useful to him, both stimulating the idea of the *Phaedon* and paving the way to its realization. It is to be noted that the review of Wegelin's work contained Mendelssohn's own translation of a passage from the *Crito* (50A–51E) that he later adopted into his biographical introduction to the *Phaedon.*[21]

The spadework of 1760 stood Mendelssohn in good stead about two years later when the old plan was revived. From July, 1762, until June, 1763, he worked concomitantly on the translation of parts of Plato's *Republic*[22] and on the *Phaedon.* He had reflected long enough on the literary aspects of this undertaking, and he had also realized the need to revise the Platonic arguments. It was probably in July, 1762, that he put down on two folio sheets, which are still extant,[23] his first draft of the proofs. They are arranged under two heads: "First Proof for the Immortality

of the Soul," and "Second Proof." The first proof is developed in a series
of twelve propositions that reflect, albeit vaguely, Plato's reasoning in the
Phaedon (70E ff.) that all things are generated from their opposites. Mendelssohn's argument runs, briefly, as follows: All natural things are subject
to constant change. All processes of change are gradual, never abrupt
in the sense of a "leap." No force in nature can annihilate a thing, since
no transition from being to nonbeing—which would amount to a leap—is
possible. Consequently, death cannot be a "real annihilation." It is but
a transition to a new condition of existence. The second argument makes
use of Plato's proof from cognition as recollection (72E ff.) but gives it
a Leibnizian turn by describing the soul as a "constantly efficient force."
Appended to this proof is a short reference to the noncomposite nature
of the soul as evidenced by its ability to conceive of the "realities" without
their limitations. Here again a Leibnizian thought, which occurs in the
Monadology (#30), is introduced. It is a far cry from this rudimentary sketch
to the finished product. About the progress of the work we are informed
by Mendelssohn's correspondence with Isaak Iselin and Abbt.

In April, 1762, Iselin invited Mendelssohn to become a corresponding
member of the recently founded Patriotic Society of Bern and to contribute
an article to a projected "Journal for Morality and Legislation."[24] Mendelssohn answered evasively at first: as a Jew condemned to civil disabilities,
he was incapable of "ever attempting the high flights of the freeborn."
Nor would his literary interests, which were devoted to metaphysics and
belles-lettres, be of much service to the purposes of the society. He proposed
Abbt as a much more qualified member and mentioned two more suitable
candidates: Professor Sulzer, who had reflected so much credit on his
native Switzerland, and Friedrich Karl von Moser, a man of talent who
had been led astray by Pascal's "melancholy whims" and was likely to profit
from contact with a man like Iselin.[25] Mendelssohn's refusal was not
accepted. In a letter dated June 25, 1762, Iselin renewed his invitation:
"Since metaphysics and belles-lettres are your main occupations in the
field of learning, there is nothing more suited to promote the aims of
our society."[26] Further resistance would now have been churlish, and on
August 27, 1762, Mendelssohn replied in the affirmative. Since the aims
of the society were not so remote from his learned occupations as he had
believed them to be, he was able to accept the honor offered him, with
his "humblest and sincerest thanks." However, he was still reluctant to
commit himself to a "proper contribution." His business activities left him
so little spare time. (Since 1761 he had been manager of Bernhard's firm.)
However, he would submit some small essay from time to time, after the
first issue of the journal had appeared.[27] About a year later, on July 5,
1763, he offered as a possible contribution either of two papers:[28]

> One of these papers is a translation, to wit, of Plato's *Republic*. It
> is a disgrace that the Germans have translated almost none of this
> philosopher's writings into their language and that, in particular, this

divine work, the *Republic*, which merits to be called a masterpiece from the aspect of inventiveness and composition alone, should not have found, it seems, a lover among us. I have translated three of its books as a sample. I doubt, however, whether the society will find translations acceptable.

The second paper represents an idea that I have cherished for many years, namely to write a *Phaedon* or *Dialogue on the Immortality of the Human Soul* in conformity to Plato's design [*Anlage*] but truly and definitely borrowing from him not more than the design, which is magnificent. His reasoning is unconvincing, however, and a modern reader finds nothing but obscurity and sophistry where Socrates' friends found light and conviction. Maybe our times are more difficult to satisfy, as some believe to be the case, or—as I hold—we have an incorrect understanding of their [the ancients'] metaphysical terminology because the critics and lexicographers have to gather the meaning of the words from the poets and historiographers. I resolved, therefore, to make Plato's arguments more emphatic and convincing by minor modifications, and, moreover, to add such arguments as are supplied by modern philosophy. Their number and weight are by no means small. The first part of this project is finished. It advances the proofs for the incorruptibility of the soul. The proofs concerning immortality are to follow in a second section.—Do you think that this subject is not too far removed from the purpose of the Society? I await your kind judgment.

This letter is an important testimony to the concept that Mendelssohn had of the task he had undertaken as well as to the stages of its development. It shows that at the beginning of July, 1763, only the first of the three dialogues, i.e. the one dealing with the incorruptibility of the soul, was finished. When more than four months later, on November 16, 1763, Mendelssohn sent Iselin "the first part" of the *Phaedon* for publication, he undoubtly meant by "the first part" the first dialogue. "Here arrives," he wrote in the covering letter, "at long last, the first part of my *Phaedon*. Your verdict will decide whether the work deserves to be continued, and I have sufficient confidence in your friendship to assume that you will be frank in dealing with me."[29] By "continuing" the work Mendelssohn obviously meant writing the "second section" to which he had referred in his letter of July 5. As it turned out in the end, this second section contained dialogues two and three. That only the first dialogue was submitted to Iselin in November, 1763, is clearly attested by Mendelssohn's letter to him four years later when, on May 7, 1767, he sent him a copy of the work, which had just been published: "I take the liberty of sending you a copy of the *Phaedon*, the first dialogue of which you were kind enough to read in the manuscript."[30] According to the plan mentioned in the letter of July 5, 1763, the first part of his *Phaedon* dealt with the "incorruptibility" of the soul, and the second section was to offer proofs for its "immortality." No such distinction had been made in the draft, but in the course of work Mendelssohn came to adopt this kind of differentiation, which is found in Leibniz' *Essais de Théodicée* (I, 89) and in Wolff's *German Metaphysics*.[31] As Wolff put it: "The incorruptible is immortal if it retains in perpetuity the condition of a person," i.e., if "the soul of a man recognizes its identity with the person it was previously." The problem of immortality as a state of alertness, in the hereafter, to both the present and the past is raised by Mendelssohn in the second dialogue and answered in the third. In this respect dialogues two and three belong together. They form the "second part" of the work.[32]

Iselin's reaction to the *Phaedon* is known from his correspondence with Zimmermann, who had asked him what he found to criticize "in the style of the venerable Hebrew." In his reply Iselin mentioned four passages that had seemed to him to be lacking in smoothness. "Perhaps," he added, "I had come across some more passages that appeared objectionable to me; but certainly not more that two or three.... Apart from these, I found the style in the *Phaedon* excellent."[33] In August, 1767, he entered in his diary: "Went to Marienfeld—on the way reread the *Phaedon*. The more I read this excellent work, the better I like it."[34] It may be taken for granted that his judgment was not dissimilar when he read the first dialogue in November, 1763. Unfortunately, the society that was to publish Mendelssohn's paper went out of existence in 1765, and the projected journal never appeared. Encouragement for continuing the *Phaedon* project was not forthcoming from Iselin.

The completion of the work was due entirely to Mendelssohn's correspondence with Abbt. While he was waiting—in vain, it seems—to hear from Iselin, Abbt, who had just returned from his long European trip, proposed on January 11, 1764, that they start a discussion of the vocation of man. The proposal came at just the right moment. It proved far more important than any word of encouragement from Iselin could have been, for it suggested to Mendelssohn the focal point for the completion of the *Phaedon*. Cebes' speech at the beginning of the second dialogue affirms that his notions about God and man's dignity left him in no "doubt concerning his vocation."[35] This is the first clear echo of the great debate that had begun between the two friends, and it testifies to the significance that the theme of man's vocation had already assumed in the second dialogue. It proves, incidentally, that the second dialogue was written after the correspondence on the vocation of man had commenced.

Additional evidence to this effect may be found in another passage that occurs in the opening part of the second dialogue: "Were our soul mortal, our reason would be but a dream sent to us by Jupiter to cheat us, miserable as we are; virtue would be bereft of all splendor, which makes it divine in our eyes; and we would be like the beast, placed here to seek food and perish..."[36] This passage is obviously modeled on a poem by Johann Jakob Dusch published in 1765 as part of his didactic poem *The Sciences* (i.e., in the section dealing with the immortality of the soul). Translated into English prose, Dusch's verses say: "In truth, were the soul called into being merely soon to be no more, like the body, its earthly home, ... virtue would be but a dream, born of folly; and the glutton would be wise in believing himself created ... for worshipping his belly." In his review of Dusch's *Poetic Works* Mendelssohn quoted these lines. The review appeared as late as 1767 but may have been written soon after the publication of the volume in 1765 or 1766.[37] The second dialogue, which contains this paraphrase of Dusch's poem, could, therefore, not have been written before 1765.

It seems that Mendelssohn resumed his work on the *Phaedon* in February, 1765, a year after his and Abbt's debate had started, for on February 16, 1765, he wrote to Abbt: "I meant to continue our correspondence on the vocation of man. Since I am writing, however, a little work on the immortality of the soul, as is known to you for some time,[38] I mean to fill the second part of it with reflections on our vocation. Hence I want to give myself time to think about it thoroughly. Do continue, dearest friend, to put forward objections and to raise doubts. I cannot help confessing in all frankness that your last objections seemed rather weak to me and that I expect far more vigorous attacks from you."[39] The debate went on. In his last letter to Abbt, Mendelssohn wrote a year and a half later, on July 22, 1766:[40]

> You say that I still owe you a reply to your theological questions. Maybe this is the case. But do you know that I am about to send you a printed one that will comprise about ten sheets and, therefore, keep you somewhat busy. For presumably you will not simply throw up the game, and ten sheets are not so easily refuted. Your questions encouraged me to complete a treatise on the immortality of the soul that I started many years ago. I put my arguments into the mouth of Socrates. Perhaps I run the risk of turning my Socrates into a Leibnizian. But this does not matter. I need a pagan in order to be absolved from having recourse to revelation. Besides, Plato already turned him into a Pythagorean; and who knows whether he does not gain through me, seeing that he really lost through Plato? You would hardly believe what sort of miserable metaphysics the son of Ariston [viz. Plato] attributes to him.
> These are the eggs that I have begun to hatch this summer and, for this reason, I must not abandon. I defer the pleasure trip that you proposed, and which tempts me not a little, until later. We must come considerably closer to resolving our controversy, before we debate it orally; and I am sufficiently vain to expect this to result from my treatise.

Abbt's untimely death shattered this expectation. The correspondence was sealed not by a genial talk but by an epitaph. Mendelssohn opened the preface to his *Phaedon* with this tribute:[41]

> The following dialogues of Socrates with his friends about the immortality of the soul were to be dedicated to my friend Abbt. It was he who encouraged me to resume work on this project, which had been commenced years ago and had been laid aside.... It pleased Providence to remove this flowering genius from the earth before his time. The career that he accomplished on earth was short-lived and glorious. His treatise *On Merit* will remain an unforgettable memorial to his own merits...

The *Phaedon* appeared in time for the Leipzig Michaelmas book fair, and Mendelssohn sent a note to his publisher, Nicolai, at Leipzig on the same day, May 7, 1767, on which he wrote the letter presenting the book to Iselin: "Here is the letter to Iselin [which Nicolai was to forward together with the book]. Please, do not forget, dearest friend, to dispatch copies also to the following friends, Messrs. Weisse, Gellert, Gleim, Doctor Hirzel, Herr Kant in K[önigs]berg, and a copy on Dutch paper to Lessing."[42]

Christian Felix Weisse (1726–1804), playwright and journalist, had been editor of the *Bibliothek der schönen Wissenschaften und der freyen Künste* since 1759. A friend of Lessing, he had a high regard for Mendelssohn's literary criticism and was instrumental in making his works known in France. It was Weisse who, on a trip to Paris in 1759–1760, handed Rousseau, at Montmorency, Mendelssohn's translation of the second *Discours*.[43] Christian Fürchtegott Gellert (1715–1769) was the author of the novel *"Life of the Swedish Countess von G.,* in which a Polish Jew is presented as one of the noblest of men. As an author of enlightened piety he had achieved a unique position of authority. As Goethe put it, "To believe Gellert, virtue and religion are almost identical in our society."[44] Whether Mendelssohn knew Gellert personally is not known, but from the note quoted above we may gather that he regarded him as a kindred spirit and was anxious to pay homage to him by the courtesy of a complimentary copy of the *Phaedon*. With the poet Gleim, Mendelssohn had established a warm personal relationship. As far back as July, 1757, he had been told by Lessing that Gleim was one of his "greatest admirers."[45] Hans Kaspar Hirzel, town physician of Zürich, had published a book called *The Farm of a Philosophical Peasant,* which became highly popular on account of its genre-portrayals and reformist tendency.[46]

The motley list of people—ranging from Hirzel to Kant—who were to receive copies of the *Phaedon* curiously anticipates the widespread impact that the book was destined to achieve. The first edition was sold out within four months, and second, third, and fourth editions followed in 1768, 1769, and 1776; reprints by other publishing firms appeared in 1767, 1768, 1769, 1776, 1778, 1780, 1784, and 1785. After Mendelssohn's death in 1786 many more editions came out.[47] A number of translations were published during his lifetime. A Dutch translation (1769) that greatly annoyed Mendelssohn was snubbed by him in a brief anonymous review.[48] Two French versions, one by Abel Burja (1772) and one by George Adam Junker (1772,1773), prompted Mendelssohn to write to Nicolai on October 13, 1772: "Herr Junker has delivered altogether foolish stuff. The nice addition [consisting of a French translation of the *Letter to Lavater*] to his *avertissement* I attributed . . . to a doctor of the Sorbonne, but the compliment he pays to my nation right at the beginning seems to be his, and it is, in my view, as *impoli* as the stupid addition by the cleric. They have made cuts, insertions, and distortions in passages in which they had a sense of their own power, with the result that in the end no common sense is left therein. I have no intention of accepting gifts in so sheepish a manner, and only await your return to say something publicly about it."[49] He may have had second thoughts, for no public pronouncement concerning the translation is known. In 1773 an Italian translation appeared, which also displeased him greatly. He considered it much inferior to Junker's French version.[50] A Danish and a Russian translation appeared in 1779.[51]

The extraordinary success of Mendelssohn's *Phaedon* was due to a variety of factors. The first was its form. The theme of the immortality of the soul—one of the few dogmas of natural religion—had been treated before. Johann Gustav Reinbeck's *Philosophical Thoughts on the Rational Soul and its Immortality* (Berlin, 1740) was certainly known to Mendelssohn.[52] He may have also come across the extensive review of Hubert Hayer's *La Spiritualité et l'immortalité de l'âme* (Paris, 1757) in the *Journal des Scavans*.[53] Hayer had made a gallant attempt to refute La Mettrie's doctrine of a thinking matter. None of these works, including Wolff's *German Metaphysics*, had approached the subject in a manner as inspired and felicitous as Mendelssohn's did. There were, of course, the didactic poets who had dealt with immortality: Young in his *Night Thoughts* (sixth and seventh night) and Dusch in *The Sciences* (Book Five), both mentioned by Mendelssohn in a review referred to earlier.[54] What he accomplished was something in between prose and poetry. Nobody before him had hit upon the magnificent idea of rewriting Plato's *Phaedon*. The great impression he made stemmed to a large extent from the dialogue form and the specific setting of the particular Socratic dialogue that he employed.[55] How he conceived of his task was best expressed by him in the preface to the book: "Following Plato's example, I made Socrates in his last hours expound to his disciples the arguments for the immortality of the human soul. The dialogue of the Greek author, which bears the name of *Phaedon,* is rich in exceeding beauty worthy of being used to the advantage of the doctrine of immortality. I have employed its setting, arrangement, and eloquence, and have sought to adapt to the taste of our times only the metaphysical argumentation.... In this way there arose, as will be seen in what follows, something intermediate between a translation and a work of my own."[56]

The ambiguity involved in this dual character did not escape the reviewer in the *Göttingische Anzeigen:*[57] "When the author puts our modern philosophy into the mouth of Socrates and makes him talk like an eighteenth-century philosopher, Socrates recedes into the background, and I see the Wolff/Baumgartian philosopher. The moment, however, I am ready to imagine a modernized Socrates, circumstances are presented that take me back to Athens and Socrates' friends." The "illusion" was thereby disturbed or weakened. Similarly, Resewitz remarked in a letter to Nicolai:[58] "It is somewhat out of tune,[59] when Socrates uses arguments that require knowledge or, at least, presuppositions of our present time, if they are to possess the strength of more than probable conjectures.... Or ought he to say everything that might be said convincingly in favor of immortality? Well and good, I let it pass. I like to hear from Socrates whatever can make the thought of immortality sweet in my eyes. I shall listen to his attractive speech and forget whether he himself knew it or not. Herr Moses, however, does not permit me to forget it entirely." Resewitz mentioned as a case in point Socrates' "Pythagorean or oriental prejudices against the body and the desires," which Mendelssohn did not repress, and which were reminders that now Socrates was talking, while before it was not Socrates—and the tone soon changed again. In his review of the first and second editions of the *Phaedon*,[60] Resewitz stated more specifically that Mendelssohn's Socrates spoke with a tone of assurance that presupposed a Christian mentality.

Mendelssohn answered his critics in the appendix to the third edition, provoked, it seems, by Resewitz' remarks in particular:[61] "I distinctly admit in the preface that I put into the mouth of Socrates arguments that could not have been known to him in his time, according to the then prevailing condition of philosophy.... My Socrates is by no means the Socrates of history." The critics, in other words, had missed the point. What Mendelssohn wished to present was not the historical Socrates but a Socrates redivivus who spoke the language of the modern Enlightenment; who talked in the way in which Socrates would have talked if he had lived in Mendelssohn's time. The author's overriding concern was to secure the notion of immortality against the sophists of the eighteenth century, that is, against the French materialists.[62] The critics had obviously ignored what he had stated in his preface:[63] "I preferred to commit an anachronism rather than omit arguments that could contribute to conviction."

Mendelssohn's Socrates spoke not only the language of eighteenth-century philosophy but, more particularly, the language of Mendelssohn. The success of the work was due to this fact in no small measure. It gave his Socratic dialogue a more elegant flavor than was found in the original. The austerity and grandeur of Plato's style were toned down to make the speeches more palatable to the taste of the period. Purists among the critics were not slow in pointing this out as a defect, as an illigitimate transformation of the Platonic Socrates into a "sweet," "Gallicizing," "courteous" *(galant)* figure.[64] Other reviewers found fault with some inaccuracies of Mendelssohn's translation in places where he followed the original text.[65] His Greek, being of recent vintage, was obviously not that of a trained philologist, and it has been shown that he availed himself to some extent of André Dacier's French translation.[66] From a philological point of view J. Bernhard Köhler's German translation of the *Phaedon*, which appeared at the same time,[67] was certainly superior to his. Mendelssohn showed himself highly receptive to the criticisms directed against faults in translation and certain turns of phrase that were too glaringly colloquial. He removed these minor blemishes in the second edition.[68]

Mendelssohn could not agree, however, with another critic who, oddly enough, had described his style as "stilted." Heinrich Wilhelm von Gerstenberg, who had awaited the publication of the *Phaedon* "with ardent desire,"[69] characterized its manner of writing as *steif*. Mendelssohn referred to this remark in a letter to Iselin (dated September 10, 1767):[70] "Herr von Gerstenberg wrote to one of his friends [Nicolai] that my manner of writing was stilted and incorrect. Here too self-knowledge is infinitely difficult. I thought to be anything but stilted." Nicolai told Gerstenberg in a letter written on September 6, 1767:[71] "In my view, you are somewhat unjust to Herr Moses in respect of his *Phaedon:* He has very good reasons for differing in his manner of writing from the Greek of Plato. . . . I should like to have some detailed explanation as to what it is that you call stilted in my friend's style. I have been asked by him to request this from you by return of post, if possible, the reason being that the first edition of this book is sold out, and that the second is to be started before the Michaelmas fair. Herr Moses would like to use your observations in case he finds them justified." Gerstenberg's answer, which was not forthcoming until December 5, 1767, evaded the issue: if he had, after the first reading of the *Phaedon*, written down some sudden fancy, he did not wish to make things worse by offering an elaborate explanation. "This much I can add, that to me the *Phaedon* is one of the most beautiful philosophical books I have ever read. . . ."[72] Mendelssohn, who had been pained to read the remark about his "stilted" style in Gerstenberg's private letter to Nicolai, must have been even more perturbed when the same criticism was voiced on October 15, 1767, in a review of his book in the *Göttingische Anzeigen:*[73] The attempt to speak the language of the Socratic dialogue in a non-Attic idiom had forced Mendelssohn to sacrifice his own style and to adopt "an awkward, stilted, and forced manner."

There was obviously a bewildering contradiction between this kind of criticism and the one that accused Mendelssohn of having presented Socrates as an elegant writer of the eighteenth century. The problem of form, which had caused him to write "something intermediate" between a translation and a work of his own, was certainly not glossed over by the critics. The intrinsic ambiguity of the form he had chosen was reflected in the contrasting views of the critics. Mendelssohn's *Phaedon* did not seem to fit any accepted pattern, and yet its success was phenomenal. Undoubtedly, it was the synchronization of the Platonic and the Mendelssohnian Socrates that was partly responsible for this success.

The content of the book was no less impressive than its form. No other work on the subject had presented a comparable array of arguments with such clarity and circumspection.[74] Since the fictional setting of the debate was ancient Athens, modern authors could not be quoted for or against. "Whether I said something new or merely put forth what has so often been said before, others may decide. It is difficult to be altogether original in a matter about which so many great minds have been thinking, and to affect originality is ridiculous," Mendelssohn said in the preface. "Had I been allowed to cite authors, the names of Plotinus, Descartes, Leibniz, Wolff, Baumgarten, Reimarus, and others would have been mentioned frequently. In that case, the reader would have more clearly noticed what I contributed of my own."[75] However, it was unimportant to the amateur, the statement continued, to which author an argument belonged, whereas the scholar already knew the property rights in such weighty matters. As it turned out, amateurs and critics alike were busy trying to disentangle the Platonic from the Mendelssohnian strands in the texture of the new *Phaedon*. The young Goethe did so in his diary of 1770 (the *Ephemerides*), when, at the age of twenty-one, he was certainly not more than an amateur.[76] The same thing was done in expert fashion by the anonymous reviewer in the *Göttingische Anzeigen*[77] and by Christian Garve, who wrote the anonymous review in the *Neue Bibliothek der schönen Wissenschaften und der freyen Künste*.[78]

The first major departure from the Platonic text occurs in the passage describing the need to rise from sense perception to the knowledge of the true essence of things (51–55.).[79] Whereas Plato spoke of the "true, absolute essence of things" in the sense of his doctrine of ideas or forms (65A ff.) and referred to the ideas of justice, beauty, and goodness, Mendelssohn described the knowledge to be achieved as the knowledge of God. In Him the "highest goodness," and the "highest wisdom" were real. He was the "highest perfection," which implied existence in the most eminent sense. In short, Mendelssohn introduced into his Socratic dialogue the Leibniz/Wolffian concept of God as the *ens realissimum et perfectissimum*. In a footnote appended to the later editions he expatiated on the meaning of positive and negative attributes of God. All this is still but a prelude to the main discussion. Socrates has explained why he, who had striven all his life to be a true philosopher, can be cheerful in the face of death. Cebes wants to know how we are able to prove that after death the soul can exist by itself and has "power and intelligence" (70B) or, as Mendelssohn put it: "still has will and intellectual faculties" (60).

The Platonic Socrates offers two proofs, one drawn from the generation of things from their opposites and one employing the notion of learning as remembering, which implies the preexistence of the soul prior to birth. The two proofs we met in Mendelssohn's draft corresponded to the Platonic pattern. In the finished work the second proof is dropped altogether, while the first follows rather closely the outline sketched in the draft. However, the Platonic concept of generation as a circular process, not a straight linear one (72B), which still figured in the draft, is abandoned. It was still part of the tacit assumption of the transmigration of souls that underlies Plato's first argument.

Mendelssohn's proof is built on a different presupposition, that there can be no absolute generation and corruption in nature. All changes proceed gradually, without a leap. Between being and nonbeing no transition is possible. Hence the soul cannot be annihilated through death. Since it, therefore, continues to exist, it must be assumed to continue in its functions —to continue to feel, think, and will (61–73). The fact that man's soul is affected during his life by the ills of the body is mentioned (72) but not considered to invalidate the argument. In the absence of all earthly, material concerns, the soul will desire only wisdom and virtue (75–77). As Goethe summed it up in his *Ephemerides* (22): "The soul can feel without the senses. It will have sublime, holy, spiritual feelings about beauty and order and, hence, of God." In the appendix to the second edition Mendelssohn defended his proof against doubts expressed by his critics, and he took the opportunity to refer to Father Boscovich, who had elucidated the "law of continuity" in excellent fashion. The famous Ruggiero Giuseppe Boscovich, S.J. (1711–1787), mathematician, astronomer, and philosopher, who was professor in Rome, had written two treatises on the subject,[80] and the second of these had been reviewed by Mendelssohn at length in the *Literaturbriefe* (1759).[81] Though Mendelssohn had disagreed with Boscovich on certain points, he had quoted with approval the "law of continuity," and his proof in the *Phaedon* was based on that theory.

The second dialogue has rightly been described as "the most beautiful" of the three "because of the conclusiveness, clarity, and order in the presentation of the arguments, and because of the felicitous use of some random thoughts in Plato."[82] It opens at the dramatic moment when, after Socrates' speech, "there was silence for a long time" (84B, C) and only Simmias and Cebes conversed quietly with each other (78). The stage is set for a further probing of the question. In Plato (85E ff.), Simmias advances the famous argument about harmony and a lyre with its strings, and Cebes, while agreeing that the soul existed before it entered the body, fears that it wears itself out in the course of its transmigrations: was it not, therefore, "a foolish confidence" to expect an afterlife, unless it could be shown that "the soul is altogether immortal and imperishable"? Plato's answer to Simmias' objection uses once more the notion of learning as recollection, by which the preexistence of the soul is proved. How then can the soul be a mere harmony of the elements mixed in the body? How can a harmony exist before the things from which it arises? (91E ff.) It takes much longer to satisfy Cebes' demand for a proof that the soul is "indestructible and immortal" (95B–107A). Plato's argument amounts, however, to the simple thought that the soul, which causes the body to be alive, can admit its opposite, death, as little as the odd can be even or fire be cold.

In Mendelssohn's *Phaedon,* both Simmias and Cebes figure as the spokesmen of further doubts. Simmias becomes the advocate of the French school of materialism: "Perhaps sense perception in the animals and even man's reason are nothing but qualities of a composite, just as life, health, harmony, etc. which . . . can last no longer than the combinations" underlying them. Is the harmony to continue when the lyre is broken? Plato's simile is retained but the thrust of the question is now the notion that the "incomprehensible mechanics" exhibited in the life of plants and insects suggests the possibility of attributing to matter more than extension and solidity. Our ignorance gave us no right to deny the thesis that matter could think (Voltaire, La Mettrie).[83] Cebes' question is completely reformulated. It now concerns the problem of immortality as the continuity of the person conscious of its past and active in the exercise of its intellectual functions. The previous argument, Cebes asserts, proves no more than the incorruptibility of the soul, and leaves open the possibility that after the death of the body the soul lives on in a kind of swoon or sleep (83). The answer to this question is given in the third dialogue.

The second dialogue is taken up by the elaborate and highly original reply offered to Simmias' objection. It proceeds from Plato's incidental remark (92E–93A): "Do you think a harmony or any other composite thing can be in any state other than that in which its constituent elements are?" The way Mendelssohn interpreted this passage can be best understood in the light of his own comments in the appendix to the second and following editions. The thesis that he had to prove concerned the immaterial nature of the soul or, putting it differently, he had to show why matter could not think. Descartes' theory provided the answer, but Mendelssohn preferred to deal with the question in a less dogmatic manner and without laying himself open to the objections that had been raised against Descartes' dualism of mind and matter. He had, therefore, followed Plotinus' argument for the immaterial nature of the soul: assuming the soul to be corporeal, consciousness would have to be attributed either to each part of the body or to some or to none. If one part possessed life, this part was the soul; additional parts were superfluous. In case each part was of itself soulless or inanimate, their composition could not be said to produce life or intellect. Plotinus' treatise *On the Immortality of the Soul* (*Enneads* IV.vii), quoted by Mendelssohn, used traditional arguments against Stoic and Epicurean materialism.[84] These arguments, Mendelssohn felt, were highly persuasive and yet not wholly convincing. One could still object that irregular parts could produce a symmetry, individual sounds could form a harmony, and powerless individuals could together represent a powerful state. Moreover, the Leibnizian school derived motion and extension from monads ("substances") that were in themselves unextended and motionless. Hence Mendelssohn saw the need to go beyond Plotinus, and it is here that his originality in answering Simmias lies.

In order to prove, he said, that "a thinking whole" could not arise from "unthinking parts," one had to investigate which qualities applied to the whole without applying to the parts, and which qualities did not. He noticed first that the qualities that designated the composition and order of the parts—e.g., figure, magnitude, harmony—were essentially distinct from the parts as such. He then observed that the impression of totalities differed from the reality of individual parts. A chord of three notes sounded differently than the three notes by themselves. He concluded that the qualities of a composite that are missing from the individual parts are due either to the order and arrangement of the parts or to their being mere phenomena (*Erscheinungen*), i.e., total and undifferentiated impressions of real things upon our senses. Applied to Plotinus' proposition, this meant that the ability to think belonged to neither of these two kinds of quality. For all these qualities were obviously either produced by our thinking or else presupposed it. The composition and arrangement of parts was a quality created by a mind that compared and juxtaposed the parts. The phenomena did not belong to external reality but to the reaction of our senses to it. In both cases the qualities concerned are produced by the soul and, for this reason, cannot be considered as the very being of the soul. Hence no thinking whole can be made up from unthinking parts (136–139; 152–154). In other words, the soul cannot be regarded as the result of a composition of material elements because its activity has to be presupposed in order to explain that a composite "appears" different from its parts. It seems that the argument for the immateriality of the soul had never before been advanced with a comparable precision.[85] This argument was widely applauded and was considered to be far superior to Plato's. Garve called it "a masterpiece,"[86] and the reviewer in the *Göttingische Anzeigen* wrote: "In all this the new Socrates is infinitely superior to the Athenian."[87]

The third dialogue follows Plato only toward the end where, starting with Crito's inquiry about any directions Socrates might wish to leave (115A ff.), the last moments are described (124 ff.). In Mendelssohn's *Phaedon* the dialogue form is otherwise abandoned. Socrates still addresses his friends but, rather than engage in conversation, he declaims his views. The tone is reminiscent of the *Oracle,* in which Abbt's doubts had been answered in a lofty style. The illusion of the Athenian setting does not dispel the feeling that it is Abbt who is being addressed, particularly in view of the fact that we hear many formulations familiar to us from Mendelssohn's correspondence with this friend. Cebes' question, for example, is answered in the same way in which the vocation of man and the destiny of all creatures was described in the correspondence. "All finite spirits have innate faculties that they develop and perfect through exercise." "No man . . . has not left this world more perfect than he was when he entered it" (105 f.). "By imitating God one may gradually come nearer to his perfections, and the happiness of the spirits consists in this approximation; yet the road to it is infinite and cannot be travelled in an eternity. In essence, every human desire projects itself into the infinite" (113). "We may, therefore, assume on good grounds that this striving for perfection . . . is the vocation of rational beings and, hence, the ultimate purpose of creation" (114). Viewed from this perspective, Cebes' question falls to the ground.

Mendelssohn offers, however, an additional argument, which he describes in the preface as an entirely novel one. We may call it the argument from the collision of duties. It runs as follows: Assuming the soul not to be immortal, the preservation of life becomes the supreme concern of every man. He has then the right to set aside all moral duties (the welfare of his children, friends, country) if fulfilling them implies the sacrifice of his life. Yet there are moral obligations that demand the supreme sacrifice. This contradiction indicates the presence of error somewhere, and it can only lie in the assumed cessation of the soul's life after death.

Mendelssohn had already expressed this idea as far back as 1756, in his *Sendschreiben an einen jungen Gelehrten zu B.*: "One who denies immortality must prefer to see the entire creation perish, if only he can preserve himself. When it is a question of life and death, his egotism has no limits, since neither God nor nature can oblige him to agree to his own annihilation."[88]

The *Phaedon* (117 f.) almost literally repeats this statement. The force of the argument is strengthened by the consideration that under the erroneous assumption of the annihilation of the soul at death all human beings have the same right to fend for themselves at the expense of all others. The result could only be a war in which every one is right, a universal war of all moral beings in which even God is unable to pronounce a fair judgment. In his review, Garve contended that this proof was fallacious: All moral principles followed from metaphysical truths. Hence it was wrong to derive metaphysical statements from moral ones. This way of arguing was circular. Our knowledge that we were obliged in certain circumstances to renounce life was based on our belief that there were higher purposes than life. Should this belief be disproved, those obligations would lose their validity, and, consequently, no contradiction would be found to exist.[89] Mendelssohn replied to this criticism in the appendix to the third edition (156 f.): The proof was not necessarily circular. Our social duties could be demonstrated without presupposing the immortality of the soul. Not even Epicurus, Spinoza, and Hobbes could deny the right of society to demand the supreme sacrifice of the individual if the welfare of the whole truly depended on it. One may, however, find in this statement the expression of a view that is at variance with the sentiment voiced at the beginning of the second dialogue: if our soul is mortal, our reason is a mere dream and virtue lacks all splendor (see above, page 146). It is this sentiment that represents the overriding concern of the book.

The success of the *Phaedon* was ultimately due to the pervasiveness of this moral concern, and Mendelssohn had mustered the strength to write the last two dialogues only after Abbt's questionings had provided him with the focal point, the "vocation of man," in which the issue of immortality converged upon the moral issue. The formula expressing this convergence was the term "infinite progress toward perfection." The Leibnizian idea of a deathless world in which each monad strives toward perfection was turned into the notion of infinite perfectibility, and this concept provided the "solace" for which the Age of Reason was yearning. Revelation could no longer be invoked to secure the belief in immortality. Abbt, in a mood of despair, had referred to revelation as a possible source of information on the question that troubled him. Mendelssohn shunned this approach. As he told Abbt, he had put his arguments into the mouth of Socrates because he needed a pagan in order to be absolved from having recourse to revelation. It did not matter that his Socrates had become a Leibnizian.[90] Plato, we may notice, did not entirely discard the possibility of relying on some revelation: he had Simmias say that in a matter as difficult as the one they were discussing one either had to discover the truth or take whatever human doctrine was hardest to disprove, "unless he can sail upon some stronger vessel, some divine revelation, and make his voyage more safely and securely" (85C–D). In Mendelssohn's *Phaedon* the mention of revelation is omitted and replaced by a reference to "this consoling doctrine . . . as transmitted to us by the oldest sages" (79). This exclusive reliance on reason was entirely in the spirit of the Enlightenment. It was also called for in view of Mendelssohn's avowed object to safeguard the belief in immortality against the "sophists" (read: materialists) of the eighteenth century (149).

Curiously enough, despite the emphasis on reason, the tone of Mendelssohn's *Phaedon* is self-assured and dogmatic, while Plato's is critical.[91] The impact of the German Socrates upon his contemporaries stemmed in no small measure from the confidence it exuded. Mendelssohn's *Phaedon* could become a tract for the times because it represented in the most eminent degree the sentiment of the Enlightenment. When Resewitz attributed the "serenity" and "tone of assuredness" in Mendelssohn's Socrates to the impact of Christianity,[92] Mendelssohn replied: "When I had to reflect upon the immortality of the soul and found it somewhat difficult to distinguish belief from conviction, I hit upon the idea: by which reasons would a contemporary Socrates be able to prove immortality to his and his friends' satisfaction? As a friend of reason, he would most certainly have accepted with thanks from other philosophers what was founded upon reason in their doctrines, no matter to which country or religious party they belonged. One can agree with somebody in respect of rational truths and yet find several matters untrustworthy, which he accepts through faith. Brotherly tolerance being so much recommended in the political realm, it ought to be, in fairness, cultivated first and foremost among the friends of truth" (151). It was the rationality of the doctrine, irrespective of its historical roots, that alone commanded his attention in the *Phaedon*. His Socrates was meant to represent the spirit of eighteenth-century Enlightenment.

In the preamble to the dialogue, the "Life and Character of Socrates" is depicted in a manner that clearly shows the extent to which Mendelssohn identified himself with the portrait of his hero found in John Gilbert Cooper's *The Life of Socrates* (1749). Cooper had described Socrates, in true Enlightenment fashion, as a teacher of natural religion, and Mendelssohn acknowledged in the preface that this book had served him as a guide.[93] The following passage from Cooper, which Mendelssohn adopted literally, conveys the image of Socrates as the ideal man. It is quoted here in the original (p. 21 f):

> Socrates therefore from the beginning labored under these disadvantages and difficulties, which to others would have been insurmountable. He had the prejudices of education first to overcome in himself, the custom-protected ignorance of others to enlighten, sophistry to confute, malice, envy, calumny, and continual insults of his adversaries to endure, poverty to undergo, power to contend with, and what was the greatest labor of all, the vulgar terrors and darkness of superstition to dissipate; all of which, we shall find in the sequel, he overcame with the true wisdom

of a philosopher, and the disinterested virtue of a patriot, the patience of a saint, and the resolution of a hero, at the expense of all worldly pleasure, wealth, power, fame, and lastly life itself, which he cheerfully laid down for the sake of his country; sealing with his blood a testimony of the love he bore to his own species, and his unchangeable duty to the Creator and Governor of all things.

Some of the features drawn in this picture applied to Mendelssohn himself, and his contemporaries could not help noticing this. The difficulties and disadvantages that he had to overcome were formidable enough to warrant the comparison. He was, however, a man of too much taste to have wished to indulge in a self-portrait. On the other hand, he could not help identifying his own aspirations with those of Socrates. He did not go as far as the Dutch philosopher François Hemsterhuys (1721–1790), who declared himself to be the reincarnation of Socrates.[94] Nor did he adopt Cooper's description of Socrates in all respects.[95] In translating the above passage, he inserted the following sentence after the reference to superstition: "On the other hand, he had to avoid offending the weaker minds of his fellow citizens, causing annoyance, and forfeiting the beneficial influence that even the most absurd religion has on the morals of simple minds" (16). The idea that "superstition" may have to be tolerated if it serves as a prop to morality occurs more than once in Mendelssohn's sketch of Socrates and runs as a leitmotif through many of his writings. "No religious system," he said in the paragraph preceding the long quotation from Cooper, "is so corrupt as not to impart a certain sanctification to, at least, some duties of humanity, which a friend of humanity has to respect, and which a moral reformer has to leave intact, if he is not to defeat his own purposes" (15). Hence Socrates, we hear later (19), did not attack doctrines that were "only theoretically false" and could not, therefore, harm morality. He realized that more damage than good might result from reforms, and he observed, for this reason, the ceremonies and religious customs based on those false doctrines. In other words, Mendelssohn preferred idolatry to atheism, since an idolatrous religion offered at least some incentives for moral conduct, whereas atheism, in his view, did not. He made this point very clearly in his unpublished polemics against Pierre Bayle's *Pensées diverses sur les comètes*.[96] By projecting his own ideas upon Socrates, Mendelssohn made his hero not only into a Leibnizian but into a Mendelssohnian. His description of the "character of Socrates" may be profitably read as a guide to an understanding of Mendelssohn himself.

Questions and Answers

It is a strange study in contrasts, while reflecting upon Mendelssohn's intellectual concerns, to glance at some of his more mundane and not always pleasant daily preoccupations. On April 28, 1766, for example, he submitted a petition to the king asking exemption from a duty that had become irksome to many Berlin residents. The army, despite the large number of regiments stationed in the capital, owned no barracks and billeted its soldiers in private homes. In his application Mendelssohn pointed out that the house he occupied could accomodate no soldiers because the *comtoir* of the silk factory from which he drew his livelihood was located there, with all the books, the cash-box, etc. The king was willing to grant exemption if a favorable report was forthcoming from the chairman of the *Servis-Commission* in charge of billeting. It was only after a revision of the first report, which had been unsympathetic, that Mendelssohn's request was granted.[1]

In his commercial activities Mendelssohn proved highly successful. After his appointment as manager in 1761 the two factories run by the firm of Isaak Bernhard had rapidly expanded. In 1764 the Prussian government, in recognition of Mendelssohn's talents, had tried to persuade him to establish a new silk manufacturing plant of his own, in Potsdam. The sum of twenty thousand thalers had been offered to him as a subsidy. He had declined to become a competitor of his employer, who was also his friend, and the sum had been given as a free gift to the firm. As a result, the number of looms had risen from forty to sixty. After Bernhard's death on April 21, 1768,[2] Mendelssohn ran the firm jointly with the widow and developed the business to such an extent that the number of looms grew eventually to a hundred and two. A radical reform of the system ruling the import of raw materials and credits, which Mendelssohn proposed, was adopted by the government and formally legalized in 1771. It produced a marked improvement in the silk trade by allowing individual manufacturers a wider range of initiative.[3]

We catch a glimpse of the atmosphere both at his office and at home in the following account of a visit to Berlin toward the end of 1768 by Christian Gottfried Schütz, professor of rhetoric at Halle and founder of the *Allgemeine Litteratur-Zeitung*. It is contained in a letter to an unknown addressee, dated January 13, 1769:[4]

> ... I visited Spalding twice ... and spent three hours with Teller. ... Sulzer and Ramler I could never find at home. Moses Mendelssohn I met the first time in his *comtoir*, where he is a clerk, surrounded by a multitude of more common merchants, moneychangers, and hagglers, among whom I discerned the philosopher at first sight. He received me in the most courteous way and entertained me for some time. I presented him with my Disputation [*de origine ac sensu pulchritudinis*, Halle, 1768] (*sit venia verbo*), which he accepted with embarrassing compliments, assuring me at the same time that a copy of it already lay on his desk, since he had ordered it from Halle after reading the Göttingen review. What he added was enough to make me feel safe against ten Bremen reviews. He invited me for the following day. I had hardly arrived when Herr Nicolai, the young Herr [Karl] Lessing, the preacher Eberhard (a very fine mind) also came. From 3 until 7 P.M. there was not the slightest slackening in the discussion. ... With all his great learning and acumen, Moses is also the most jovial man, the most noble character, and the

most pleasant company.... At 7 P.M. we dined with Moses, and that was the period of *galanterie.* He has a very nice wife and a grown-up niece,[5] whose whole demeanor and beauty seem to indicate that she owes her education to the philosopher of Germany. Here I also met the *demoiselles* Itzig,[6] very beautiful ladies ...

Thus, from the grinding routine of business Mendelssohn was able to retreat into the sanctum of a home made all the more enjoyable by the graces of hospitality. Otherwise, he could have hardly mustered the strength necessary for his literary accomplishments. His reputation as a philosopher had been greatly enhanced when the academy's prize was awarded to him in 1763. People began to address him as "Monsieur Moses Mendelssohn, Sçavant très célèbre à Berlin." Hamann used this form of address in letters dated November 6, 1764, and September 13, 1770. Christoph Friedrich Oetinger, the Swabian theologian and mystic, did the same when writing to Mendelssohn on September 7, 1770. So did Johann Friedrich Löwen, director of the Hamburg national theater, in his letter of November 4, 1766. In his *History of the German Theater* (1766) Löwen spoke of Berlin as a city "in which the most excellent German men of genius, a Sulzer, Moses, Ramler, Lessing, and Nicolai reside."[7]

Mendelssohn's fame reached its peak when the *Phaedon* appeared in 1767. Echoes of the impression created by the work can be found in private letters exchanged by various people at the time. Pastor Johann Samuel Krickende (1733–1797), a friend of Mendelssohn from the years he had spent as a tutor in Berlin, wrote on July 27, 1767, to Johann Georg Scheffner (1736–1820), an important political figure in Königsberg: "Moses' *Phaedon* is indeed excellent but I won't stand people who try to follow him."[8] He obviously considered only Mendelssohn as qualified to use the form of Socratic dialogue. Hamann's friend Johann Gotthelf Lindner (1729–1776), since 1765 professor in Königsberg, wrote to Scheffner on July 18, 1767: "Some literary news—Lessing's Minna [von Barnhelm] ... Moses platonizes in the *Phaedon,* he has beauty and religion."[9]

Far more interesting, however, are the letters that Mendelssohn received from a variety of people, friends as well as strangers, who were troubled by questions concerning the *Phaedon* and expected him to answer them. These letters compelled him to rethink some of the problems, to write two more minor treatises on the subject (one in German and one in Hebrew), and, in response to Herder in particular, to contemplate the rewriting of the third dialogue.

When on May 7, 1767, Mendelssohn arranged for a copy of the *Phaedon* to be sent to Iselin, he asked him in a covering letter for his "rigorous" judgment. Iselin's reply is lost but we know from his letter to Zimmermann what it must have been like: "Don't allow yourself to be deterred by thirty pages of subtleties or, if you prefer, of casuistry, from carefully reading the *Phaedon.* Yesterday I wrote to the sublime [*erhabenen*] Jew about his work and I told him, of course, how little the sentences on pages 130–160 (or 162) appear comprehensible or correct to me." The letter to Zimmermann containing this passage is dated July 31, 1767.[10] Fortunately, we possess Mendelssohn's answer, dated September 10, 1767, which gives us a good idea of the specific points that Iselin had raised,[11] for they clearly emerge from Mendelssohn's comments. What God's designs and final purposes were could be more easily inferred, he admitted, in the physical world than in the moral. The dogmatism that had characterized Mendelssohn's stand vis-à-vis Abbt is somewhat softened. The "law of continuity," which forms the basis of the first argument for immortality, is more fully explained, and Mendelssohn indicates his intention to clarify "these subtle scholastic notions" in the second edition of the work.[12] He makes the following important statement: "I myself believe—and here I entirely concur with you—that the soul must have a *vehiculum*. Nevertheless, I considered it advisable to leave this doctrine in abeyance, since it did not seem to be necessary for my purpose. Should the spirit of man always retain such a *sensorium* in which the changes in the world are reflected, the doctrine of immortality could only gain thereby."

The possibility that after the death of the body the soul might survive without retaining the faculty of thinking was another point made by Iselin (anticipating Riedel). Mendelssohn rejected this possibility in his letter and, subsequently, in the appendix to the *Phaedon* (133 f.; 146 f.). As a simple, immaterial force, he argued, the soul could not have faculties essentially differing from each other. To prove this the "subtleties" of the scholastic philosophy, which had become highly unpopular, would have to be employed. He had, however, tried to do without them unless, on occasion, the lines of escape of some subtle adversary had to be cut. Mendelssohn thus admitted that he found it difficult to combine the popular character of the *Phaedon* with the rigorous demands of strictness in argument. His letter to Iselin foreshadowed his defense against Riedel's charge that his subtleties had no legitimate place in a Socratic dialogue.[13]

It was probably toward the end of 1767 that Mendelssohn received a letter in Hebrew characters from a remarkable fellow Jew, Raphael Levi of Hanover. Born in 1685, in Weikersheim an der Tauber, Levi had received a traditional education in Frankfurt am Main. At an early age he had taught himself mathematics and physics, become a clerk in the banking firm of Simon Wolf Oppenheimer in Hanover, and caught the attention of an engineer, Mölling, who introduced him to Leibniz. Soon afterwards Leibniz invited the likeable young man to become his pupil and secretary, and offered him, at the same time, the hospitality of his home. Raphael Levi spent six years in Leibniz' household. It seems that he later made a living teaching mathematics and astronomy, and all of his known works, published and unpublished, deal with subjects from these two fields.[14] He was said to have submitted to the king of England, on the king's 1748 visit to Hanover, an invention that met with the approval of both the English Admiralty and the Royal Society. At the invitation of these bodies he arrived in London on April 13, 1748, prepared to clarify certain doubts. His invention was supposed to enable even mere beginners in arithmetic to determine, without recourse to any instrument, the longitude of any position of a ship at sea.[15] According to a remark in the preface to a Hebrew astronomical work by him,[16] he had also written a treatise on metaphysics,[17] and considering his long and close association with Leibniz his competence in metaphysics may be taken for granted.

Levi's letter to Mendelssohn is lost but its gist can be easily inferred from the reply.[18] "Could I have suspected to find only readers as knowledgeable as you," Mendelssohn wrote, "I would either not have written [the *Phaedon*] at all or, at least, in a totally different way. One who knows modern [*die neuere*] philosophy will have no doubt whatever that, barring miracles, nothing can be brought into being or annihilated in nature. The real substances in nature, insofar as they are finite, determine each other mutually. Yet their limitations and modifications cannot produce other substances, nor can they annihilate any. For this God's omnipotence is required. These propositions can be found in every compendium, and if one follows the system, nothing is easier than to demonstrate all this. I was, however, not in a position allowing me to invoke a system. I had also to address myself to readers who are not metaphysicians but do possess sound common sense and are eager to think. These I had to acquaint in the first dialogue gradually with metaphysical notions. The most important thing was to explain to them the law of continuity and the fact that there is no leap in nature. This had to be done without presupposing a single definition from the system of this or that metaphysician. I had, therefore, to proceed analytically—to take the phenomena as they appear to us and develop the correct definition by way of analysis. In speaking about time, e.g., I considered it as a mere phenomenon without taking into account what sort of a definition of its reality is given in this or that system."

Obviously, Raphael Levi had expressed astonishment at Mendelssohn's having taken the trouble to explain things that needed no explanation. Whereas critics like Iselin and Riedel found the *Phaedon* too subtle and esoteric, the opposite charge was made by the Hanoverian Jew. Mendelssohn felt probably the more exasperated by this latter critique since it implied the accusation of shallowness. Hence the incisive manner in which he tried to convince Levi that there was more below the surface of the book than met the eye. The rather lengthy and closely argued reply went on showing how the "language of the phenomena" used in the *Phaedon* was merely the exoteric way of saying what had to be capable of being "translated," as it were, into the "language of truth." He actually undertook this translation in the letter and thus offered a fascinating example of the way in which the first proof of the *Phaedon* might have been presented in the technical language of the school philosophy. If one needed proof that Mendelssohn was anything but a *Popularphilosoph* it is furnished here. His summing-up of the point he made reads: "My arguments must be capable of being translated into the language of abstract truth, and they must be found correct, if they are to be of any use. However, I am content to present them in a way in which they can be comprehended by the mere *bon-sens,* independently of all systems." He expressed the hope that Levi would try his hand at "translating" the *Phaedon* from the *Sprache des Scheins* (using Lambert's term) into the *Sprache der Wahrheit.* He reminded him that the ancients were well aware of the distinction between the esoteric and exoteric ways of teaching philosophy.

The final paragraph of Mendelssohn's letter replies to a rather touching suggestion made by Levi: "I am indeed pleased that you wish to continue with me the correspondence on the 'vocation of man' in place of Professor Abbt. I fear, however, that we shall reach agreement too soon, since our philosophy is tarred with the same brush." A philosophical correspondence between two Jewish Leibnizians would indeed have been somewhat pointless. Moreover, a debate between the thirty-eight-year-old Mendelssohn and Levi, who was eighty-two at the time, could not have been too fruitful. The proposal by the old man, who lived to the age of ninety-four (he died in 1779), was, at any rate, an indication of the vigor of his mind. Mendelssohn treated him with the respect due his age and accomplishments. When he stayed in Hanover in 1771 and 1777, he did not fail to visit the old gentleman, who had preserved his physical and mental robustness despite many blows of fate: of his seven children only a daughter had survived.[19] G. E. Guhrauer, Leibniz' biographer, describes Levi as a disciple, friend, and collaborator of the great philosopher, and reports that shortly before Leibniz died he presented an oil portrait of himself to Levi "as a present from his hand and for a memento." Levi "was a man of hoary age, remote from all selfishness and vanity. It was well known in Hanover that he possessed a highly treasured picture of Leibniz and that a very wealthy man, who was eager to obtain the portrait, once offered him a handsome sum of money for it but only got the permission to take a copy of it."[20] The person concerned was the prince of Waldeck and the price he offered was a hundred thalers.[21] Raphael Levi was the only mourner at Leibniz' unceremonious funeral in 1716, and it was through him that the exact location of Leibniz' grave could be established later.[22] It may safely be assumed that these facts were known to Mendelssohn, and that the old Leibnizian's response to his *Phaedon* inspired a deep sense of reverence in him.

The first testimony to the reaction of the general public of educated laymen to the *Phaedon* came in the form of an "Attempt of a Mathematical or Sensible Proof for the Immortality of the Soul." Nicolai transmitted to Mendelssohn a short *exposé,* bearing this title, which he had received from Doctor Phillip Gabriel Hensler, a well-known medical writer. Hensler's covering letter stated that the Danish general "Count of S.," the author of the *exposé,* would appreciate a "brief but unreservedly severe criticism" from Moses Mendelssohn. The author was Hermann Woldemar, count of Schmettow,[23] and his modest effort showed how much impressed he was by Mendelssohn's work. Though a Danish translation of the *Phaedon* did not appear until 1779,[24] the impact of the book began to make itself felt immediately. In about 1797 the Danish poet Schack Staffeld wrote to a friend: "If you read Mendelssohn's *Phaedon* before the critical philosophy [of Kant] emerged [in 1781] and still remember the impression that the book made on you, you will admit that you eventually did not *believe* in immortality but that you were *sure* of it. You thought: it cannot be otherwise."[25] The influence of Mendelssohn's writings on the Danish Enlightenment (1770–1780) seems to have been quite considerable.[26]

The count's proof was rather simple and unsophisticated:[27] Being able to coordinate the various kinds of sense perceptions (e.g. the scent of flowers, the beauty of a landscape, the sound of music, the taste of food) and to choose between them, the soul could not be composed of parts representing various senses but had to be a single, indivisible entity. Such an entity was not subject to annihilation and, hence, it was immortal. In his reply[28] Mendelssohn agreed with this proof in the most complimentary terms, but he made a few further comments. Firstly, immortality implied more than incorruptibility; consciousness of the soul's present condition and remembrance of its past were an essential part of it. Secondly, immortality could not be said to belong to the soul in an absolute sense, since this would contradict the contingent nature of the soul and make annihilation even by God impossible. We could only say that it would not befit the supreme wisdom of God to annihilate the soul but the possibility of doing so was open to him. Thirdly, the proof, though highly convincing, needed to be supplemented by a further proof showing that the *sensorium commune*, which supposedly coordinated the sense perceptions, could not be identified with the soul. Ralph Cudworth, using a passage from Plotinus, had tried to do this.

A lay correspondent of astounding intellectual vigor and refinement of style was H. D. von Platen, who described himself as a "poor country squire."[29] He lived in Lipsitz on the island of Rügen, where his farm kept him busy but did not prevent him from cultivating his mind. He was "no author" and could therefore assure Mendelssohn of brevity in his letters—a promise that was not kept. The epistles of both correspondents turned out to be almost little tracts, but Mendelssohn, though extremely busy in other respects, did not mind von Platen's persistent questioning. On the contrary, he seems to have relished the debate with this nobleman, whose trenchant mind compelled him to lay bare the ultimate presuppositions of his proof for the immaterial nature of the soul. Von Platen's first letter was dated January 25, 1769. Mendelssohn replied on April 7. His second letter was written on August 10, 1769, and Mendelssohn answered it on December 29. Beyond that date no further exchange of letters seems to have taken place.

"If a communication like the present one should cause you some inconvenience," von Platen began his first letter, "you have to hold to account your eminent merits on behalf of philosophy. It naturally follows from universal applause. In a book so much praised as is the case with your *Phaedon* one wants to understand everything, to clarify even the slightest doubt, no matter how little it affects the whole, and one likes to draw from the well if it is within reach." The point that seemed in need of clarification was the statement that "without the faculty of thinking there is no whole in nature," which led to the conclusion that thinking (i.e., the soul), being the cause of the composition and arrangement of the parts, could not be caused by it. Was it true, von Platen asked, that without thinking subjects who conceive of order and harmony there would be no such thing in nature? Was not the perception of a real order, proportion, purposiveness prior to the concept of the whole formed by the mind? Were not organic units such as plants and animals or the infinite solar systems real wholes, and not merely the sums of their parts, even without the activity of the mind that compared, juxtaposed, and arranged the parts? Von Platen illustrated his point by an eloquent description of wholes observable in nature and concluded that there was nothing to prevent the assumption that the soul itself might be a similar composite whole.

Mendelssohn was much impressed by the "subtlety" of the objection raised. How seriously he took von Platen's "love of truth" and "sagacity" is shown by the fact that his reply did not merely explain the argument given in the *Phaedon* but concentrated on the specific point made by his correspondent. The upshot of his answer was a clear affirmation of Leibniz' monadic doctrine, which saw the entire universe as a composite of simple and indivisible spiritual substances. In other words, Mendelssohn revealed to von Platen the esoteric aspect of his view of the soul: "I consider these ideas [of Leibniz' monadology] to be both true and great.... This philosophy seemed to me, however, too sublime for the purposes I had to pursue in the *Phaedon;* there I had to be content merely to touch its hem, as it were."[30] Before making this confession, he first drew attention to the "remarkable words" of Plotinus quoted in his appendix to the second edition: "There would not even be a body, if the power of the soul did not exist. For the body is in constant flux and its nature is changed in its motion. The universe would instantaneously perish, were there only bodies."[31] He took these words to mean that "without thinking beings no corporeal world, no system of harmonizing composite beings, would exist."

Viewed in the light of his subsequent reference to Leibniz, this interpretation of Plotinus was not intended merely to repeat what he had said in the *Phaedon* (and what had aroused von Platen's doubt); it was meant to establish a link between Plotinus and Leibniz. Having stated his esoteric view, Mendelssohn returned to what he was "content" to mention in the more popular Socratic dialogue: "I regarded it as sufficient that without thinking beings only isolated parts, no whole, let alone a system would be found in matter." He then reiterated the old assertion that the parts, taken singly, exhibited no harmony, and that the whole had no "subsistence" except in a thinking being. In the same way in which mere phenomena like the rainbow owed their subsistence to the limited capacity of our senses, the harmonious and systematic character of objective reality subsisted in the concepts of minds. Yet this was precisely the point at issue, and it was to be expected that von Platen would raise the subject once more.

He did this in the most amiable manner: Even without the proof in question he was convinced of the immaterial nature of the soul. Yet in a book like the *Phaedon* one wished to find everything as convincing as it was beautiful. He, therefore, dared to confess that Mendelssohn's answer had not completely satisfied him. The words quoted from Plotinus were unquestionably true if the thinking beings without which no system in nature could exist included "the infinite Spirit that is the origin of thinking power as well as the author of matter." It was obvious that the purposiveness found in nature derived from such a source. If, however, Mendelssohn understood Plotinus' statement not to refer to God—and von Platen suspected this to be the case—the question was whether there was not here some confusion of the system as such and the concept of system in the mind. In his view, only the concept of system presupposed thinking subjects, whereas the systems of nature existed in reality and not as mere shadows on a cosmic screen. Mendelssohn's argument in the *Phaedon* was based on the assumption that without the activity of human thinking there was no whole in nature. With this assumption he could not agree. Had not Mendelssohn himself admitted that the systematic, harmonious, symmetric whole was ultimately based on objective reality, on the laws of nature. How, then, could it be lacking subsistence and be only a concept about relations? The salient point of their controversy, von Platen suggested, might be formulated in the question: was it legitimate to call a subsistence of parts that by their very nature conspire to form a whole by the name "subsistence"?

Mendelssohn's reply went straight to the heart of the matter: The question was not merely one of terminology. The issue was the validity of his proof. The character of "wholeness," it had been conceded, did not exist by itself but merely inhered in the parts. It was, in the language of the schoolmen, a determination of those parts. According to the principle that the determination of a determination was implicitly a determination of the thing itself,[32] any further determination of wholeness applied also to the parts. Were we to say, therefore, that the power of thinking applied to the whole (as the materialists asserted and as was implied in the description of the soul as a harmony), this would be tantamount to saying that the power of thinking applied also to the parts, which is absurd. Mendelssohn continued: "Now we do find that in fact certain determinations apply to the whole that cannot be attributed to the parts. Of these I assert that they apply to the whole not[33] insofar as it is objectively considered but insofar as it is considered in relation to a thinking being, since objectively the whole inheres only in the parts and, therefore, can have only qualities that also apply to the subject in which they inhere. This is manifestly true of order, symmetry, harmony, etc."[34]

Mendelssohn obviously distinguished between the whole as such and the determinations of order, etc. belonging to it. Von Platen might have considered the whole as identical with order, etc. He may, however, have accepted the premise and the extremely subtle reasoning with which Mendelssohn tried to establish the validity of his proof. The reason that prompted him to secure the argument against any doubt was his realization that his correspondent had shown little interest in the esoteric references to the monadology. The "beautiful hypothesis of Leibniz," von Platen had written in his second letter, was "alas, nothing more than a hypothesis."[35] The second round of the correspondence also dealt at length with the validity of the "law of continuity," which von Platen had been inclined to doubt. Mendelssohn explained this theory in some detail and emphasized its compatibility with Leibniz' monadic doctrine. Boscovich, he said, had treated the matter from a mathematical rather than metaphysical aspect.[36] In this connection he mentioned the interesting biographical fact that about ten years before he had ceased to engage in mathematical pursuits, his "circumstances" (i.e., the pressure of business) having compelled him to do so. His review of Boscovich's *Philosophia Naturalis* had appeared ten years before.[37]

Of an entirely different order was Johann Gottfried Herder's reaction to the *Phaedon*. Herder, born in 1744, had studied in Königsberg under Kant but his real mentor (and intimate friend) was Johann Georg Hamann, the "Magus in the North," a pietist and critic of all abstract intellectuality, and inclined to be both profound and obscure at the same time. The sworn enemy of the Enlightenment, Hamann was the antipode of Mendelssohn. Herder, who in 1764 became preacher in Riga, combined his affection for Hamann with a deep respect for Mendelssohn, which, he knew, was shared by Kant. In his *Fragments on German Literature* (Three Parts, 1767) and in his *Critical Forests*[38] (1769) Herder referred to Mendelssohn several times in the most reverential terms.[39] The first part of the *Fragments* contains his essay "On the Ages of a Language" *(Von den Lebensaltern einer Sprache)*, which developed a new theory about the natural growth of languages and became the nucleus of his famous treatise *On the Origin of Language*, which won the prize of the Berlin Academy in 1771.

In that early essay Herder cited as his authorities "two blind pagans": Diodorus of Sicily and Vitruvius; "two Catholic Christians": Saint Gregory and Richard Simon; "and in modern times an academician and a Jewish philosopher: Maupertuis and Moses Mendelsssohn."[40] The same essay also includes his first reference to Mendelssohn's *Phaedon:* "And where is a translation of the divine Plato whose manner of writing burns like fire and refreshes like heavenly dew? The embellishments of his dialogue, even if introduced by Moses, hardly compensate for the simplicity [*Einfalt*] of the Greek: yet, nevertheless, what a work would he have accomplished who had given us Plato's most outstanding dialogues in the way in which Moses gave us the *Phaedon?*"[41] Mendelssohn wrote a review of the first two parts of Herder's *Fragments* that was to appear in the *Allgemeine deutsche Bibliothek* but never did because a revised edition had been announced and the withholding of the review, which was intended as a temporary measure, turned out to be its burial among Mendelssohn's papers. It was resurrected in the publication of his *Gesammelte Schriften* (IV. i, 1844, pp. 93–101).[42]

The review praised "Herr Herder of Riga" as the anonymous author "of these invaluable fragments," which showed "familiarity with the ancients, a well-digested philosophy, penetrating sagacity, and sound judgment," yet were not entirely free from blame: in matters of taste one ought to be guided not by principles but by sentiment, feeling. In other words, Mendelssohn reproached Herder for relying overmuch on his hypothesis of the "ages" in the life of a language. In his view, Herder had been misled by abstracting his theory entirely from the Greek language. Mendelssohn contended that the theory broke down if one tried to apply it to the Romans and Hebrews. He also took issue with him on certain points of detail. He denied that the strict definitions of philosophy harmed the synonymous wealth and the poetry of a language. Above all, he rejected Herder's interpretation of poetry as "wild simplicity." Poetry, he insisted, was no longer nature but the imitation of nature. Impetuosity did not make for poetry. One senses the clash between the sentiment of *Aufklärung*, which Mendelssohn represented, and the incipient revolt of Sturm und Drang, the forerunner of Romanticism. Mendelssohn recognized the "genius" of Herder from the start, while others still wondered whether he would become "a very great writer or a decided fool."[43] He saw in him both a philosopher and a *bel esprit,* who had, however, failed to reconcile the two.

Herder, not having any direct contact with Mendelssohn, was completely unaware of the views expressed in the unpublished review. He was, on the other hand, plagued by increasing doubts about the *Phaedon,* which had, at first, elicited his enthusiasm. An ardent admirer of the late Thomas Abbt,[44] his "brother in spirit," Herder assumed Abbt's role of the skeptic vis-à-vis the "oracle," but he did so in much more resolute fashion. Hamann may have had a share in driving him into opposition. In a letter to Herder on June 10, 1767, when the *Phaedon* had just appeared, Hamann remarked: "I just read Moses Mendelssohn's preface to the *Phaedon* and I think it is more beautifully written than thought."[45] When the second ("augmented and improved") edition came out, he wrote on August 28, 1768: "I do not know whether Mendelssohn's *Phaedon* is improved: yet I almost doubt that it can be improved."[46] In November, 1768 Herder confessed to Hamann:

> For some time I have, in melancholy hours, revolved in my mind, like Diogenes his barrel, the idea of becoming a pupil of Socrates and to write a fourth dialogue in addition to Mendesssohn's three, but one of doubts. Socrates is dead, his disciples celebrate his last supper, and a Simmias among them chews the cud of the doubts which beset me when reading Moses' *Phaedon.* Let him then rouse Socrates from the dead . . . to decide the issue. Not believing in Moses and the prophets, my concept of the immortality of the soul cannot go much beyond the Pythagorean transmigration of souls or the mere survival of soul; thereby the "knot worthy of a redeemer" *(dignus vindice nodus)*[47] is being tied up at once in the form of a phenomenon, and Herr Moses will have to flee to his philosophy as a city of refuge—will have to, but how he will get there I fail to see. It seems to me that the whole character of Socrates as depicted by Moses is looking two ways. A biographer of Socrates in our days ought to take up his position *between* Plato and Xenophon. Moses stands *behind* them and pulls now the one now the other or even the Englishman Cooper.

About two months later, on January 10, 1769, Herder wrote in a similar vein, yet with due decorum, to Nicolai: "No person in the world can have read Moses' *Phaedon* more intensely with heart and soul than I have done. . . . Time after time I promised myself to write about it to Herr Moses but after one of my letters miscarried I always laid my pen aside. I have a principal doubt that seems to me extraordinarily important. . . . I do not wish to appear even remotely importunate, otherwise I would have placed it before Herr Moses long ago in private letters. For the philosopher, I thought, must be pleased to reply when eternity and immortality are the subjects of discourse—and yet, I have still failed to do so. I intended to give my doubts the form of a fourth Socratic dialogue (so as to cause less offense) and to send you the manuscript. May it be presumed that Herr Moses might once more wish to become an oracle or could he rouse Socrates from the dead to teach me or, rather, to secure truth itself as he sees it? Your *Bibliothek* has not yet judged the *Phaedon.* Perhaps the dialogue could take the place of a review. . . ."[48]

On April 11, 1769, Nicolai replied: "Do not by any means forget to complete your dialogue on the immortality of the soul. Herr Moses also asks you, through me, to do this. I would suggest, however, that you write it as an independent treatise and not as a commentary on the *Phaedon.* This the reader will find more convenient. Surely, you have thoughts of your own, without having to borrow the occasion from other books."[49] Herder, who left Riga on May 23, 1769, for a long trip to France, still found the time in April (?) to write Mendelssohn, at long last, concerning his doubts about the *Phaedon.* The letter,[50] which bore no signature, was probably enclosed with one addressed to Nicolai. It opened with an apology: "Pardon me, highly esteemed friend, for robbing you of half an hour of your activities by this letter. It is, at least, not wasted by anything less unworthy than the subject of the immortality of the soul. In the whole of your *Phaedon* the speaker is not a demonstrator but a wise man who wishes to convince others, and must he not listen also to the voice of doubt, if some of these are as yet unconvinced? As for myself, I can at least assure you, Sir, that I raise objections not from a deliberate skepticism as your Socrates describes it in the second dialogue but from the heart, as it were, and as a concern of humanity." Herder admitted that the arguments for the incorruptibility of the human soul were "very strong." He could not agree, however, that the surviving "thinking substance" remained without a body. What did we know of a human soul without a body? Herder then moved on to an attack on the fundamentals of Enlightenment philosophy:

> You see, therefore, what sort of propositions and conclusions begin hereby to totter. With you and most philosophers and theologians it is the liberation from sensual perceptions and the entirely spiritual perfection from which the rewards of the future condition derive in the first place. . . .Yet what is a soul liberated from all sensual perceptions, and what is a purely spiritual perfection in a human soul? I must confess: I do not know. No matter how refined and ennobled the conceptions may become, the *caput mortuum* is still visible as a fine sensual *vehiculum* around all these spiritual phantoms, a man!

Herder emphatically rejected the idea that the spiritualization of man made any sense as a goal to be pursued in this world. In spite of the advocacy of this goal by Pythagoreans, Platonists, and Spaldingians, a desensualized soul was a monstrosity and certainly not capable of happiness. It seemed to him, he pointed out, that already in his *Oracle* Mendelssohn had put undue stress on the "training of the soul's faculties" as the true vocation of man. In Herder's view, our nature contained "more specific mass" of animality than of pure spirituality. We were created as "mixed beings" and destined to remain mixed beings. "My human substance becomes again a human phenomenon or, if we prefer Platonic language, my soul builds again a body for itself." True, we had no knowledge on this subject, but we might infer from our present situation that we shall be what we are: *"quidquid est, illud est*—I become what I am." Herder was particularly critical of Mendelssohn's notion of a progressive rise toward perfection:

> Your proof of progressive development—Oh that you could teach me that it is valid! We are here to train [*ausbilden*] ourselves, to develop ourselves. Yet every faculty [*Kraft*] develops only up to a certain stage and then gives way to another. The human soul decreases in the measure in which it increases on the opposite side. In our present existence we have exactly those ages [*Lebensalter*] of destiny that plants, animals, and we as animals so evidently possess. The training and development for the sake of this life is purpose and vocation. It is, however, an illegitimate viewpoint to live in order to leave the world more perfect than one was when entering it. We entered it to become more perfect *here*, to increase

and decrease, to learn and apply, and to enjoy ourselves and the world. That was the purpose of nature.

Herder's idea of the specific nature of the ages *(Lebensalter),* which played such a notable part in his concept of the life of languages and which, unknown to him, Mendelssohn had questioned in his unpublished review, asserted itself again on an even broader scale. Whereas Mendelssohn believed in linear progress, Herder considered each stage as *sui generis* and moving in circles:

> In the whole of living creation we see no trace of upward striving, ascent by stages, etc. but we do see forward striving, and this forward striving is a kind of cycle of enjoyment. . . . Everything perfects itself, everything is perfect—but perfect for the hereafter and becoming more and more perfect for the hereafter? . . . I see a process of change, a cycle that consumes itself, one that flows back into itself. With you, the stream flows uphill.

Hence the training of our mental faculties had no bearing on our future condition. All we could hope for was palingenesis, rebirth in another life. There was comfort in this expectation, Herder believed. If only he commanded the energy displayed in Mendelssohn's third dialogue, he would plead for the acceptance of this outlook with as much emphasis. From the point of view of social philosophy this doctrine was far more salutary than the other one. It bade man enjoy his life on earth to the full and yet justified the demand of society that for the sake of the whole the supreme sacrifice be made by the individual. Death was not annihilation but a transition to another life. Mendelssohn's argument from the conflict of duties was thus met on his own ground. Yet to die for a great cause, Herder suggested, was a "political," not a "human," duty. As for Providence, it was enough if at the end of his life a man could say: what is, is good. "The five acts are in this life, why should we peep behind the curtain that no eye has yet pierced to obtain information on what must in itself already form a whole?" The letter concluded: "As long as your *Phaedon* has been out, I have been preoccupied with the matter that might, perhaps, be of sufficient importance to you . . . to deem me worthy of a kind and instructive answer, as I hope. Philosopher of humanity, disciple of Socrates, you must answer where the immortality of the soul is the subject of discussion." What kind of answer Herder expected is not quite clear. He had obviously made up his mind on the matter and could hardly have hoped for an answer assenting to the points he had made.

Surprisingly, Mendelssohn's reply (written on May 2, 1769), tried to narrow down their differences:[51] "Sir, if I am not mistaken, our thoughts about the nature of the human soul are not so distant from each other as you seem to believe. We agree so much in principles that we must merely understand one another in order to concur also in our conclusions." There follows the remarkable admission that he too assumed the soul to live on with some kind of corporeal *sensorium:* "Delete, in the first place, all passages in the *Phaedon* that distinctly state that in the hereafter our soul will be altogether bereft of body. So far as I remember, my intention was to leave the matter undecided so as not to complicate the knotty question of immortality by too many side issues. Yet in my heart I was, and still am, completely convinced that no limited spirit can be entirely without a body."

Once again it becomes clear that in his *Phaedon* Mendelssohn had repressed his esoteric Leibnizian views, for his conviction about the continued union of soul and body was in fact based on Leibniz' doctrine. According to Leibniz, every monad has a body belonging to it, which functions as the monad's sensorium.[52] On the other hand, Leibniz rejected the Pythagorean notion of a transmigration of souls, which had been advocated by van Helmont and Scaliger. In his *Reflections on the Principles of Life and the Plastic Natures* (1705) he said of van Helmont's and Scaliger's theory of the soul's "building up its body"—the phrase used by Herder too — *Non mi bisogna e non mi basta* ("I do not need it, nor does it suffice me").[53] Neither did Mendelssohn share Herder's view of transmigration (which had been only vaguely expressed and had been distinctly differentiated from the Platonic and Pythagorean view). He did, however, emphasize his basic agreement with Herder, and in spelling out his "reasons" blissfully ignored the fact that their Leibnizian character was opposed to Herder's very principle of rebirth.

He came closer to the fundamental concern that Herder had voiced when disavowing the "separation of the sensual from the spiritual": "I am surprised that you should have attributed to me such a monstrous opinion. Taking into account what reason and intellect achieve in improving and correcting sensuality, I do consider the sensual element in human nature as the flower of its perfection. I would be disconsolate were a philosopher able to demonstrate to me that I should ever lose it. A soul liberated from all sensuality? ... I agree with you that in the future life, as in the present, such a thing is a mere chimera." The indignation with which Mendelssohn reacted to Herder's charge against him "and most philosophers and theologians" of the Enlightenment was justified. As a *bel esprit* and aesthetic philosopher he could not, in fairness, be lumped together with the advocates of arid intellectualism. On the other hand, the very fact that he immediately qualified his praise of sensuality by referring to the improving and correcting activity of reason placed him again in the camp that a Herder or Hamann viewed with grave suspicion. Mendelssohn had obviously underestimated the depth of the cleavage separating him from the new trend that Herder represented. As his unpublished review of Herder's *Fragments* had shown, he was alarmed by the extreme views being put forward, but he saw in them merely the *paradoxa* of an able mind seeking novelty at any price. He was more concerned about the effects they were likely to have on the public, which so easily mistook the "erratic paths of genius" for "paved roads" on which to walk.

"So far," Mendelssohn's letter continued, "we think, I hope, completely alike. This being the case, I fail, however, to understand how the statement that our vocation on earth was the training of the faculties of our soul could have appeared strange to you. You say: We are beings of a mixed nature. Indeed. Yet what this mixed nature produces has manifestly the soul for its ultimate purpose." All pleasure, Mendelssohn explained, consisted in the unconstrained exercise of our faculties, and, conversely, all pain resulted from the constriction of our abilities.[54] This was true even of the pleasure and pain of animals. "Here the most perfect harmony between our happiness and our vocation shows itself. Each of the faculties with which we are endowed wants to be occupied and produces an urge. The harmonious satisfaction of all these urges creates our happiness and is, at the same time, our vocation." Herder had questioned the legitimacy of seeing in the exercise of our abilities a way to perfection; in his view every increase in perfection entailed a corresponding loss. Mendelssohn disagreed: "I have to confess that neither in experience nor in reason do I find the least justification for this statement. What did the soul of a child lose in order to learn turning its eyes toward the light? . . . Here there is no equality of effect and counter-effect that might lead to the conclusion that the same quantity[55] is preserved. . . . I fail to see, therefore, why we cannot say: We live in order to leave this world more perfect than we were when entering it."

Herder's most emphatic point had been this assertion: We enter this world only to become perfect *here*, to increase and decrease, to learn and apply, to enjoy ourselves and the world. "I have a good deal to say against almost every word in this sentence," Mendelssohn retorted. Limiting the perfections acquired in this world to the world alone was taking too narrow a view of what perfection implied. Life, however short, showed an increase on the credit side; there was no antithesis between learning and applying or between acquiring and enjoying. In each case the one entailed the other. We enjoyed acquiring and acquired in enjoying, since pleasure presupposed a consciousness of the harmonious exercise of some function of our nature, i.e., a consciousness of a transition to a greater perfection. We live to acquire perfections, and in this perspective our horizon extends beyond this world. Compared with Herder's view of life as structured in antitheses and balances, Mendelssohn's outlook was dominated by the concept of linear or spiral progress. Yet were the perfections acquired here below of any use in another world? Herder had denied it, and Mendelssohn gave a rather circumspect answer to this question. Certain proficiencies and skills might prove useless even in our earthly careers, while those things we learned in infancy and when still in our prime remained with us for life. As for a well-proportioned enlargement of our human capacities, it certainly was a perfection also in the hereafter, whereas mere scholarship was not.

Mendelssohn was obviously trying to differentiate between two kinds of perfection, one relating to this-worldly skills, the other embracing the totality of the person. It cannot be said that he scored a point against Herder. In this context he even conceded that he "had nothing against palingenesis," provided rebirth meant progress: we must not become again what we were before. The "upward striving" of the human soul was undeniable. We shall indeed remain beings of a mixed nature, but we shall be better than we were. The ultimate issue between Mendelssohn and Herder was not, therefore, the question of immortality versus palingenesis but of transcendent purposes versus immanent ones. The conflict was between two fundamentally different "existential" attitudes, and Mendelssohn misjudged the situation when he concluded his letter with these remarks: "I should be surprised if we were to persist in dissent, seeing that we are so close to each other in matters of principle. Perhaps, I am still too much attached to the system [viz. the school philosophy], and perhaps you withdrew too far from it. One of these two is supposedly the reason why we are still in disagreement. . . ."

On May 19, 1769, Nicolai forwarded Mendelssohn's reply, together with a letter of his own, to Herder. As a clever publisher he had hit upon an idea which he mentioned in the letter: "A new edition of the *Phaedon* is being printed now. I wanted to make it especially attractive in comparison with the previous one (seeing that there will be two reprintings), and it therefore occurred to me to add to the new edition your letter and the reply (it being well understood that no one will be able even to suspect your name)."[56] Herder replied from Nantes on August 5/16 that he had found Mendelssohn's letter very pleasant but "not quite satisfactory." "In one half I was and am in agreement with him. As regards the main point, his answer fastened too much upon subsidiary ideas of mine, and I am still in the dark. I ask you, therefore, not to print my letter yet, for without a further reply and explanation a wrong complexion is put on it by Moses' letter. I shall first explain myself in more systematic language in order to get Herr Moses' answer. For the time being, however, I am not in a position to do so."[57] Nicolai had therefore to abandon his plan, and the third edition of the *Phaedon* appeared without the two letters. On November 30, 1769, Herder wrote from Paris: "I am most eager to see Moses' new *Phaedon* and very glad that my letter is not printed. We understood each other too little. How much I wished that this book, which is so important for humanity, society, state, and philosophy, became completely convincing for all the world."[58] Attached to the letter was one for Mendelssohn.

This second letter to Mendelssohn, dated December 1, 1769,[59] reformulated the points of agreement and disagreement between them, and did so in rather more technical language and with great precision: "According to your declarations, Sir, our views about the nature of the human soul closely concur in everything that concerns the prolegomena of our subject. Like myself, you are convinced that an incorporeal human soul is a mere chimera, and hence you reject all the nonsense that our Platonists conclude from a nonsensual human nature about our future bliss. On the other hand, I hold, like you, that, as you define it, the purpose of our present existence is the training [*Ausbildung*] of the faculties of our soul, presuming that the soul is our self [*Ich*] and our body is, as it were, merely the phenomenon of its existence and the mediating organ of its representations." Herder added that he was philosophically convinced of the indestructibility of the soul, which implied its immortality and continued existence as a thinking being. "All this is, however, not yet the knotty point that I see before me, and which I asked you to help me untie. Pardon me if I sometimes fail to speak in transcendental fashion and in the language of the system. Try to transpose my thoughts into your words, if I express myself imprecisely. In the end we are bound to agree with each other." Mendelssohn had spoken of human proficiencies as "realities" that, if developed in proper proportion, were "perfections" and as such endured in the hereafter. Herder felt that these terms required further clarification, if agreement was to be achieved. He was sure that all our training, learning, and increase in proficiencies was merely a "modification of what already existed before" in the soul—that it amounted to mere "changes in the quality, not in the being, of the soul." The "specific mass" of inner forces, no matter how much developed they were, remained constant. We acquired neither new senses nor new powers, realities, or perfections of the soul. What changed was merely position, figure, form, not the substance.

In stating this, Herder said nothing with which Mendelssohn could have disagreed. It was his conclusions that were controversial:

> I believe that these statements are hardly capable of being doubted, and now the conclusion follows easily. If our learning is nothing but recollection, and our becoming perfect is nothing but development, it follows that there is nothing but learning, training, and development in and for our condition here below. It is this condition that determines the quality, the measure, and the proportion of the development. It is also that which determines utility and purpose. Take any single small proficiency: it presupposes a situation in which it was formed and for which it is meaningful. Remove the situation and application—and the proficiency disappears; it ceases to be a perfection. Now take the sum of all our acquired proficiencies, the sum of all our recollections of concepts, the sum of all our acquired well-proportioned perfections, and assume the end of this life, which is the phenomenon of this condition—what remains? The naked human soul, the elementary stuff of its powers and faculties; all accidental qualities and contingent modifications of its condition have disappeared. It has drunk from the stream of forgetfulness. What was habitual in its representations is deleted. Why? Because the position in which it developed its representations of the universe has changed. It has lost nothing, it has gained nothing, it is what it had been.

This powerful viewpoint was driven home with relentless vigor. "All you said at length, Sir, about the measure in which we ought to develop the faculties of our soul applies only to the present condition of life and does not affect our question." The terms "reality" and "perfection" were mere abstractions, mere shadows and colors of things, and it was illegitimate to see in them the things themselves or proficiencies "that the soul collects like coins." They were, in Leibnizian language, but *phenomena substantiata*. What alone persisted was the elementary stuff of the soul, with its inherent powers. "My soul has built for itself, by its own powers, an organic world; this world wears itself out according to its laws, and reaches its end. My soul begins, at the behest of its powers, to prepare for itself another one . . . but one that, like the first, is a creation of the same nature, with the same powers, and therefore on the same level amid the series of beings. If there is a graded order among these, it would seem to be required . . . that everything remains in its elementary stuff what it is; hence that the things qua realities of the universe do not change their rank; that—using a bold expression—just as God remains God, so likewise man remains a man, the lion a lion, and the tree a tree." The letter concluded with a request for further clarification of the issue.

When Herder's letter from Paris reached him, Mendelssohn was deeply involved in the Lavater affair (which will be described in the next chapter).[60] As a result, he did not continue the correspondence. However, the points Herder had raised lay heavily on his mind. He seriously considered rewriting the third dialogue of the *Phaedon*, against which the thrust of Herder's objections had been directed. He must have mentioned this to his young friend Marcus Herz, for on September 11, 1770, Herz informed Kant, whose devoted disciple he was, that Mendelssohn's *Phaedon* was to appear shortly in a new edition "in which the third dialogue is greatly changed."[61] The fourth edition of the *Phaedon* did not appear until 1776, however, and it did not contain a revision of the third dialogue or indeed any substantive revision whatever.[62] The reason for Mendelssohn's failure to implement the plan must be sought in the serious and prolonged illness that befell him in the spring of 1771. On October 8, 1775, when the fourth edition was being prepared for the press, he wrote to Nicolai: "I find that the trifles that I meant to change in the *Phaedon* in response to a review in the *Göttingische Anzeigen* have already been taken care of in the third edition. More important changes and additions I promise for the fifth impression, which I still hope to see, trusting that in the meanwhile my health will improve somewhat."[63] Alas, he was not to see the fifth edition. It appeared as late as 1814 and was introduced by David Friedländer. Yet the correspondence with Herder was not altogether relegated to the shades. It is reflected in the *Notes to Abbt's Friendly Correspondence*, which Mendelssohn wrote in 1781 for Part Three of Abbt's *Collected Works* (1782) and which also appeared as a separate booklet of eighty-eight pages in 1782.[64] It is clear from Mendelssohn's short preface that these disjointed annotations were meant as a substitute for a more elaborate treatment of the theme ("the vocation of man") in the "second part" of the *Phaedon*. By the "second part" of the *Phaedon* Mendelssohn understood dialogues two and three,[65] but it was the third dialogue in particular that, as we know, was to be revised in the light of Herder's polemic.

It was an excellent idea to embody at least some hints of his final answer to Herder in the notes on his correspondence with Abbt. The similarity in outlook between Herder and Abbt fully justified this procedure. It is "Note (s)" which specifically concerns itself with Herder's objections. In his letter from Paris, Herder had taken up Mendelssohn's contention that in a child's learning to turn its eyes to the light or to identify its nurse's voice no corresponding loss was involved. He had written: "The child has learned to turn its eyes to the light and to identify the voice of its nurse: When eye and ear are no longer, when the organ of the representations has disappeared, the habitual character of these representations has likewise vanished."[66] The point that Herder wished to make was the uselessness of our acquired proficiencies for the hereafter. Mendelssohn obviously had this passage in Herder's letter in mind when he wrote in his note:[67] "One asks: . . . what will be the use of the proficiencies that we acquired here and that relate merely to our present quality and modification of organs? The child has learned to turn its eyes to the light . . . [quoting, with some slight changes, the passage in Herder]. I reply: The soul of the child has not merely learned to see the light but to turn the eye voluntarily toward the light, i.e., to direct the appetitive faculty under the impact of the strongest and most vivid sensation and to seek enjoyment from it. This is an inclination and proficiency of the spirit that may remain in the soul even if all sensation and recollection of light and color should disappear." Mendelssohn tried to show that the soul was an organic entity comparable to a tree whose trunk gathered up the vital sap that caused its rejuvenation despite the withering of its other parts. In the soul too, he suggested, all inclinations, capacities, and dispositions merged in one "trunk." By perfecting one faculty, the total unit of the soul was affected. How well Mendelssohn succeeded in refuting Herder need not be discussed here. What is significant is the fact that he held firmly to his view of the matter.

The tenacity with which Mendelssohn defended this viewpoint is attested also by a collection of questions and answers loosely strung together, and eventually published by a Viennese admirer of his, Joseph Grossinger, the author of a study comparing Berlin and Vienna.[68] Grossinger edited these papers first in a Latin translation under the title "De Immaterialitate Animae" in the first volume of his *Mosis Mendelssohn Opera Philosophica* (1784),[69] and in the following year he published the original German text as *Moses Mendelssohn's Treatise on the Incorporeality of the Human Soul*.[70] He mentioned in the preface that Mendelssohn had let him know through a friend R** [Carl Julius Redlich?] that his Latin translation had "not displeased him." "The origin of this treatise," he cryptically remarked, "we owe to a Prussian Royal Highness, while it is due to the extreme modesty of the author that it has so far been withheld from publication. To give an account of all that transpired in this matter would be offensive to the two distinguished personages . . . ." It has been surmised,[71] with what seems to be a high degree of probability, that the "Prussian Royal Highness" was Luise Ulrike, sister of Frederick the Great and the widowed queen of Sweden, who was in Berlin for some time around the turn of the year 1771 and had a long conversation with Mendelssohn. On January 4, 1772, she wrote to her son, King Gustaf III: "J'ai eu une conversation avec le fameux juif de près de 3 heures et je vous assure que le temps ne m'a pas paru long un moment."[72] Since the Queen Mother was greatly interested in matters of philosophy and theology, as is shown by the names of the savants she invited,[73] it may be safely assumed that her long talk with Mendelssohn concerned the *Phaedon*. She might have raised some of the questions that had been put to him before and he might have agreed to let her have a random collection of his thoughts. We know that in 1774 he allowed a copy of this titleless collection to be made by his friend August Hennings, and that same year he sent the collection (augmented by a fragmentary piece) to Count Wilhelm of Schaumburg-Lippe. A transcript of it made by the Countess Marie Eleonora was intended as a "most valuable present" for her husband.[74]

The *pièce de résistance* of what Grossinger named the *Treatise on the Incorporeality of the Human Soul* is the fourth and last section, in which Mendelssohn analyzed Jean Le Rond d'Alembert's ideas on the subject, as found in volume five of the second edition of his *Mélanges de littérature, d'histoire et de philosophie* (1768).[75] This section could not, then, have been written before the *Phaedon* had appeared; nor could it have been written before 1769, since it quotes from Charles Bonnet's *Palingénésie philosophique*, which was published in that year.[76] Moreover, there is an echo of the correspondence with Herder in this part: "I say that the soul can neither perceive nor think unless it has a portion of organized matter for an organ of its perception, and here most philosophers will agree with me." On the other hand, Mendelssohn disagreed with those philosophers "who do not admit any enduring qualities in the soul": "In their view, the soul acquires nothing . . . that remains. It retains no conceptions, proficiencies, or inclinations, for all these are modifications of the organs, not of the soul."[77] The reference to Herder is clearly noticeable. Question one representing the first section ("Can matter possess the capacity of thinking?") reads like a rehash of Mendelssohn's reply to von Platen's first letter.[78] Question two, which forms the second section, deals with a point that had only been briefly referred to in the appendix to the *Phaedon* (136 f.; 152 f.): It had to be shown that matter, being by its nature incapable of thinking, could not be said to owe such a capacity to God's omnipotence, as had been suggested by Locke. To illustrate this point Mendelssohn inserted a beautiful little dialogue between Hylas and Philoponous—he borrowed the names from Bishop Berkeley's *Dialogues* (1713)—in which the Socratic method is employed to prove that even God could not transform a rosebush into a lemon tree (167–71).

The third section elaborates the mere hints thrown out in the *Phaedon* (83; 103) concerning the effects of illness, age, etc. on the soul. It tries to show, in a painstaking discussion (171–76), that the decay of the brain does not touch the life of the soul. The four sections do not form a composite whole in a literary sense, nor does the short fragment serve as an introduction, as Grossinger presented it in the Latin edition. Yet there is an inner unity and consistency among these parts that testify to the strength of Mendelssohn's conviction. The amount of energy he invested in the clarification of this problem is astounding, and one cannot but admire the elegance and ease with which he disentangled the web of questions with which he was confronted.

Unfortunately, Mendelssohn did not live to see the objection that Kant would raise against the *Phaedon* in the second and revised edition of the *Critique of Pure Reason* (1787). The section "On the Paralogisms of Pure Reason" contains a part called "Refutation of Mendelssohn's Proof of the Incorruptibility [*Beharrlichkeit*] of the Soul."[79] "This sagacious philosopher," he pointed out, had sought in his *Phaedon* to disprove the "disappearance" of the soul, i.e., its annihilation, by attempting to demonstrate that a simple being could not cease to exist: being simple, it could not be diminished and gradually pass into nothingness, because there was no moment in time between its being and its nonbeing, which was impossible. Kant's objection was: the soul, though without extensive quantity, possessed intensive quantity, i.e., a degree of reality, and could, therefore, fade out by a gradual remission of its powers. Kant did not do full justice to Mendelssohn. He entirely ignored the highly original second proof, and he seems to have missed the point of the first. The "law of continuity," Mendelssohn could have objected to Kant's notion of intensive quantity, also ruled out the possibility of a fading out through a remission of powers.

Cognate Hebrew Writings

Mendelssohn's letter to Raphael Levi,[1] written toward the end of 1767, had concluded with these words:[2] "I wish I were able to write a treatise on the immortality of the soul in the Hebrew language. The *Phaedon* does not allow itself to be translated [into Hebrew]. At any rate, I am convinced that it would no longer be intelligible in a Hebrew version. For this reason I would like to choose another literary form in which to make our coreligionists understand these matters. We shall see. As yet my Hebrew is not good enough."

Mendelssohn's desire to treat the subject in a Hebrew work was of old standing. It seems that soon after he had abandoned the project of the *Kohelet Mussar* in 1758 he contemplated writing on the immortality of the soul. The earlier plan is described in a letter to Hartwig Wessely, written late in the summer of 1768:[3] "Originally it occurred to me to write in Hebrew, and it was not my intention to attribute the statements to Socrates—for what have we, the followers of the true religion, to do with the son of Sophroniscus [i.e., Socrates]? I wanted to depart completely from the way of Plato and write my own book on the nature and immortality of the soul. My idea was to base my teaching on the utterances of our rabbis of blessed memory as found in the haggadic portions of the Talmud and in the Midrashim, for most of them agree to a very large extent with what I have expounded philosophically [*be-derekh ha-emmet*] and in no way contradict the [philosophical] truth. Yet many obstacles prevented me from carrying out my intention. They persuaded me to choose the vernacular as men greater and better than I had done when they wrote their works, without protest, in Arabic.[4] The change in language entailed a change in the treatment of the subject, and I followed in the footsteps of Plato . . ."

Since the revised plan is mentioned in a letter to Lessing written on December 19, 1760, as one "still" occupying Mendelssohn's mind,[5] one has to assume that the original idea of a Hebrew treatise on immortality antedated the year 1760, which brings us close to the period of the unsuccessful *Kohelet Mussar* venture. When this first attempt at the cultivation of Hebrew had miscarried, Mendelssohn, it appears, had by no means abandoned his concern for the revival of Hebrew as a vehicle of literary production, and looking for a serious and worthwhile theme, he hit upon the problem of immortality. There is a close affinity between the way he originally meant to treat the subject in Hebrew—namely to draw mainly on rabbinic sources—and the way in which the essays in *Kohelet Mussar* had been written. His continued preoccupation with Hebrew as a modern literary language is highly significant. When he realized that the immortality of the soul was not a suitable subject at which to try his hand in Hebrew, he undertook the writing of a commentary on Maimonides' *Logical Terms*. Since this work appeared as early as 1761 (in Samson Kalir's pirate edition), it must have been written in 1760/61, which clearly indicates that Mendelssohn had lost no time in attacking his task, once he had given up the idea of a Hebrew treatise on immortality. His reasons for desisting from his original plan (or as he put it in the letter to Wessely, the "many obstacles" that "prevented" him) are fairly clear. They amounted to a realization that he was as yet unable to express in Hebrew his ideas on a theme that called for more than conceptual precision. As he wrote to Raphael Levi in 1767, Mendelssohn felt that his Hebrew was simply "not good enough." One sympathizes with this excuse, when one considers the superb eloquence of the *Phaedon* and the powerful appeal it had for the eighteenth-century mind. Considering Mendelssohn's excellent command of Hebrew, however, one wonders whether this excuse might not have been merely the rationalization of an overriding urge to place his ideas before a larger audience than he could ever hope to reach by means of a Hebrew treatise.

Now that the *Phaedon* had appeared and enjoyed an instant success, Mendelssohn seems to have felt a sense of obligation to present at least an outline of its arguments to the Jewish public. His words "I wish I were able . . . ," in reply to Raphael Levi's suggestion, were obviously not meant to dismiss the idea but simply to express a sense of incapability that still plagued him. A translation of the *Phaedon* into Hebrew seemed to him an utter impossibility. He had therefore to find a literary form that was manageable. "We shall see," he wrote in his letter, thereby hinting at a plan that was taking shape in his mind. It was probably in the latter part of 1769, after Herder had caused him to reconsider the third dialogue, that he produced an essay shorn of the setting and the trimmings of the *Phaedon* and yet presenting, in neat and precise terms, the essence of the work. The essay contains a puzzling reference to the third dialogue of the *Phaedon* that is understandable only if we assume that Mendelssohn had visualized certain changes in response to Herder's critique.[6] Since these intended revisions were never made, the Hebrew essay referring to them was not published by Mendelssohn. It was only after his death, in 1787, that David Friedländer edited it, together with another piece, under the title *Sefer Ha-Nefesh* ("The Book on the Soul").[7]

The second piece is a letter from Mendelssohn to his friend Hartog Leo, who was secretary of the Berlin community from 1736 until about 1773, and served in a similar capacity in Breslau until his death in 1784. A man of formidable rabbinic learning and also versed in philosophy, Hartog was occasionally consulted by Mendelssohn, his junior by many years, on matters of rabbinic jurisprudence, and he sought from Mendelssohn, in turn, clarification on philosophic topics. The Hebrew letters exchanged between them in 1765 were concerned with the juridical aspects, in terms of Jewish Law, of a business transaction in which Mendelssohn was involved.[8] The letter that was published in *Sefer Ha-Nefesh* was Mendelssohn's final answer to his friend's objections to Leibniz' doctrine of the preestablished harmony, and dealt at length with the various theories about the relationship between body and soul. In his preface to the book Friedländer revealed the fact that the "friend" addressed in the epistle was Hartog Leo.[9] A German version of the first of the two treatises by an unidentified writer signing himself "H. J." was published by Nicolai in 1787,[10] and one of the second by Solomon Anschel, "candidate of philosophy at Bonn University," appeared in 1788.[11]

The first treatise discusses the immortality of the soul under three headings that reflect the tripartite division of the *Phaedon*. Its Jewish orientation is stressed by the initial remark that the doctrine of immortality represents a "fundamental tenet" *(yesod)* of the Tora. The first chapter establishes the spiritual nature of the soul. While the body is a composite held together by the order and relation of its constituent parts, the soul is a simple substance and the single substratum of sensation, desire, and conceptual knowledge. "This simple substance qua substratum of perception is called *nefesh*, qua faculty of desire and abhorrence it is called *ruah*, and in respect of its being the substratum of reason and conceptual knowledge it is called *neshama*."[12] This was a novel way of linking the three familiar Hebrew terms with a philosophical doctrine of the soul. Saadya Gaon had related them to Plato's three parts of the soul, and Jewish Aristotelians had interpreted them as the equivalents of the terms 'vegetative', 'animal', and 'rational' soul.[13] The proof for the simple, hence spiritual, nature of the soul from its function to impart order and relation to composite beings recalls the particular turn Mendelssohn had given the Platonic simile of the lyre in the second dialogue of the *Phaedon*. What is added here is the spelling out of the threefold function of the soul, which facilitated the reference to the Hebrew terms.

The second chapter of the treatise demonstrates the incorruptibility of the soul, a subject treated in the first dialogue in the *Phaedon*. There the heart of the argument had been the stress on the continuity of all natural processes: nature produces no change abruptly and is therefore incapable of annihilating a thing. This argument, which had followed Boscovich's theory, is now replaced by an ontological line of reasoning. Composite things come into being through the composition of their parts, and they cease to be when the order of their parts is destroyed. The parts both precede and outlast the composite thing. A simple thing (the soul), on the other hand, can come into being only ex nihilo and ceases to be only by annihilation. Time has no part in either its genesis or its destruction. In the case of composite things, generation and corruption happen in time, except when God performs a miracle. By God's act of creation all beings arose "in their beauty and full stature" *(be-tsivyonam we-komatam)* out of nothing. Mendelssohn used here the talmudic phrase, which had also been quoted by Maimonides in his account of creation.[14] Natural causes, being limited and time-bound, can neither create a thing ex nihilo nor annihilate it. Only an infinite being (God) can do this by way of miracle. Man's body is generated in time through natural causes, and it comes to an end by natural causes. The soul, which is a simple substance, comes into being through a miracle by the will of God, and it can perish only through a miracle. God, however, annihilates nothing: "For all actions of God (be his Name blessed) are good in themselves, and if they sometimes appear to us as being evil, this is due, as is well known, to the deficiency of our comprehension. If they are, in fact, evil insofar as a part of creation is concerned, they are good in regard to the whole. Were we to know all happenings in the way they are known to Him (may his Name be exalted), we would give thanks and praise to Him for the occurrences that seem to be evil, for they are only apparent evil, as will be explained more fully in another place,[15] and as Maimonides observed in his book *The Guide of the Perplexed*.[16] Now, annihilation is a true evil, not an apparent one, as is obvious, and all consequences of true evil are truly evil, as will be explained elsewhere.[17] This being the case, God can never desire the annihilation of any creature. It is demonstrated, therefore, that the soul of man does not die a natural death when the body dies and does not suffer annihilation through the mere will of God, but lives eternally."[18]

In the final analysis, Mendelssohn's proof hinges on the view that God, because of his goodness, cannot be assumed to desire the destruction of the soul because destruction, in the case of the soul, would amount to annihilation. In his "Counterreflections" about Bonnet's *Palingénésie* Mendelssohn had written:[19] "I recognize no death of the soul. True, Maimonides, in his tractate on repentance,[20] assumed that the souls of the impious are destroyed, and he rightly considered this the most severe punishment imaginable. However, I agree in this respect with Nahmanides, who contradicted this doctrine in his *Chapter on Retribution,* and denied both the annihilation of the soul and eternal punishment."[21] Similarly, Mendelssohn wrote in August/September, 1768 to Hartwig Wessely:[22] "In my view it is not right to assume that God could wish to destroy, by way of miracle, one of his creatures and thus annihilate it. I am aware that my view is contrary to the opinion of Maimonides as found in the rules on repentance, but the utterances of Nahmanides and of other scholars support my view."[23]

The third chapter of Mendelssohn's treatise speaks about the "true life of the soul." It corresponds to the third dialogue of the *Phaedon,* in which the question of immortality in the more specific sense of the continuity of the individual was discussed. In this final chapter Mendelssohn abandons the demonstrative method as being incompatible with the nature of the problem. The question is: Are we to believe that after its separation from the body the soul continues to be a substance endowed with reason and will and possessed of all its acquired perfections? Or is it possible that it descends from its high level to that of an infant "before knowing to refuse the evil and choose the good,"[24] or maybe even to that of "untimely births of a woman, that have not seen the sun?"[25] The answer to this question cannot be stated in terms of propositions asserting either a necessary truth or an impossibility. In discussing the logical status of the problem Mendelssohn refers the reader to chapter four of Maimonides' *Logical Terms* and his own commentary on it.[26] He suggests that there are, altogether, five possible ways of answering the question, and that the answer we accept depends on our concept of what best agrees with our notion of God. The five possibilities are: (1) The souls remain eternally in the same condition. This assumption is ruled out by the very nature of a limited substance that is subject to change; truly speaking, the first "possibility" is an impossibility. (2) All souls rise eternally in rank through an increase in perfection and happiness. (3) All souls rise for a time and then descend to previous levels down to the low grade of merely sentient beings. (4) All souls repeat the process of rise and fall ad infinitum. (5) Some souls rise and increase in perfection, while others descend and decrease in happiness.

Mendelssohn seems to have considered a modified form of the fourth possibility as the most likely fate of the soul, since it best agreed with "the rules of wisdom and the infinite and abundant love" of God: "Even as rational living beings have commenced to rise on the ladder of perfection and happiness, so they will continue eternally; yet at times they will descend for some period and thereafter rise again to enjoy their felicity." It appears that the measure and duration of the soul's rise and fall are held to depend on the soul's merits and demerits, and that descents represent punishments it deserves. For he continues: "All happens according to righteousness and justice, love and mercy in the way the supernal and infinite wisdom decrees it, depending on whether the quality of severe justice or the quality of mercy is called for, 'since the world is judged in grace.'[27] Only in this manner are the ways of God well-balanced, while otherwise there would be 'one event to the good and to the wicked, to him that serveth God and to him that serveth Him not.'[28] 'The righteous would be as the wicked; that be far from the Judge of the earth not to do justly.' "[29] In the *Phaedon* Mendelssohn had tried to show that the immortality of the soul could be demonstrated by reason, without recourse to the authority of revelation. In the Hebrew essay, too, his arguments are based on reason alone, and most strikingly so in the last chapter, in which the criterion of rationality decides which possibility best fits our assumptions about God. The biblical and rabbinic quotations are not adduced as theological proof-texts but as stylistic devices that help to give the essay a decidedly Jewish flavor without changing its basic character.

The second treatise—the letter to Hartog Leo—is a penetrating analysis of the principal theories concerning the connection between body and soul and some moral issues arising from the Leibnizian position. The entire range of problems had been touched upon in the *Philosophische Gespräche* of 1755 but was now discussed methodically for the first time. The treatise is for this reason an important part of Mendelssohn's philosophical *œuvre*. Written, like the preceding essay, in a precise and graceful medieval Hebrew, it has a charm all its own, due to its epistolary form, in which Mendelssohn excelled. A passage such as the following illustrates the point:[30] "For the sake of clarity the presuppositions have to be set out more fully than would seem to be necessary vis-à-vis a scholar like you, who at the beginning of a discourse already visualizes its end.[31] Yet I know that your love for me is still greater than your wisdom, and 'love covereth all transgressions.' "[32] The presuppositions are indeed explained rather fully, and knowing that the addressee was well acquainted with them (as the references to his arguments against Leibniz show), one wonders why Mendelssohn chose to go to such lengths in presenting them. There is also a certain amount of repetition in the way in which the three theories on the body/soul relationship—namely, those of Aristotle, the Cartesians, and Leibniz—are expounded. The gusto with which this is done makes one feel that Mendelssohn relished the opportunity to discuss the entire subject in Hebrew for the first time, and that he particularly enjoyed the coining of Hebrew equivalents for philosophical terms of more recent vintage and, hence, not found in medieval Jewish writings. Not all his translations of terms are satisfactory: *ba'aley ha-geram* is not too good a rendering of "adherents of occasionalism," nor does *ba'aley ha-haskama* adequately express the term "adherents of the doctrine of the preestablished harmony." *Hizayon* for "phenomenon" is not an especially felicitous choice either.

These are minor flaws, however, in what must be considered a remarkably successful effort to render a highly complex philosophical debate in Hebrew. The lucidity with which the salient points of this debate were presented was an achievement in itself and would have commanded respect even if it had been done in German. Leibniz, Wolff, and Bilfinger were Mendelssohn's main sources,[33] but the sovereign manner in which he treats the theme reveals his own incisive thinking. There is also a certain playfulness about this epistle, which stems from his desire to bring the subject matter close to the understanding of a Jewish reader. (Mendelssohn may have contemplated publishing the letter, which could also account for his elaborate presentation of matters well-known to the addressee.) Thus he offers a biblical illustration in order to explain what the various theories (influxionism, occasionalism, and harmonism) had in common and wherein they disagreed: Jacob saw Rachel and fell in love with her. What happened was an impression of Rachel's figure being made on Jacob's heart as a result of seeing her; because of the power of his own idea of her a train of thought was set in motion that caused him to serve her father seven years, and they seemed to him but a few days. No philosopher would deny that it was the effect of the internal image of Rachel in Jacob's heart that produced his desire for her and all his subsequent actions. What was in dispute was the manner in which the image arose in the soul. There were three opinions concerning this matter: (1) the influxionists (Aristotle and his followers) held that the soul was affected by the power of an external object perceived through the senses; (2) the occasionalists (the Cartesians) believed that the external object was not the agent that affected the soul but merely the occasion for the activity of God upon the soul; and (3) the harmonists (Leibniz and his school) were of the opinion that even the first representation arose in the soul by its own limited power as a result of preceding representations and, at the same time, in harmony with the external object.

The point at issue in Mendelssohn's correspondence with Hartog Leo was the question of influxionism versus harmonism. Hartog Leo believed that Leibniz' doctrine of the universe as a system of monads—a doctrine that he accepted—made the assumption of a preestablished harmony unnecessary. Mendelssohn, on the other hand, considered the influxionist theory untenable and sought to convince his friend that Leibniz' view did not entail any corollaries injurious to religion and morality. In order to place his friend's objections in their proper setting, he outlined Leibniz' position more fully. According to Leibniz, nothing is real except the monads, which are unextended simple substances. The body and its modes (extension, motion) are merely the appearance or phenomenon of the monads.

The universe is a single whole of the utmost perfection, constituted of monads each of which reflects the totality of coexisting things. The monads have the power of perception and a desire to perceive. This power is real and it is limited by the representation of coexisting substances. All monads, therefore, affect each other by way of an ideal, not a physical, influence, and there is a harmonious connection between them. The influxionist theory, on the other hand, declares that body and soul influence each other. The desire of the soul causes a motion in the body, and the motion in the body causes sense perception in the soul. Mendelssohn reproduced the standard objection to this theory: since the influxionists assumed motion to be something real and since, moreover, they held motion and ideas in the soul to be totally disparate things—the one being a mode of matter, the other a mode of thinking—it was difficult to understand how the one could influence the other. The difficulty, he added, was aggravated by the fact that the influxionist theory was incompatible with a fundamental law of nature, namely, that governing motion. From the way he described this law under three heads it is clear that Mendelssohn was thinking of Newton's famous three laws of motion, the last of which stipulates that action and reaction are equal and opposite. If it were true that a desire in the soul produced a motion in the body, an outgoing influence *(actio transiens)* would operate without causing any reaction; in other words, there would be a motion without a resultant motion in the opposite direction, and the quantity of the "living force" in the universe would not remain equal. Hartog Leo had previously sought to refute this argument. For Mendelssohn wrote:[34] "Perhaps you mean to say that all these rules and laws apply only to physical motion, while the motion of the will is not subject to them, and since the matter has not been decisively proved, it is not impossible that the motion of the will operates in a manner far removed from that of physical motion. This, approximately, was your objection, dearest friend."

Mendelssohn replied: Firstly, it was not nature's way to vary general laws. Secondly, if desire could cause an increase in the "living force" of the universe, it ought to be able to produce anything it wanted. To argue that the motion of the will was not caused by the pure will or desire but by the degree of power in the idea and that, consequently, one could not expect desire to be all-powerful, accomplishes nothing, for no amount of power in the idea *a* could produce an increase in the power *b* (seeing that idea and motion were disparate entities). At this point, however, Mendelssohn had to face up to another objection raised by Hartog Leo—and a rather ingenious objection at that:[35] "It is true, dearest friend, that, according to your opinion and according to what follows from your words, motion is nothing real. You agree in this respect with the followers of Leibniz: it is something produced by the power of the monads and is, therefore, of the genus of the monads, albeit on a lower level [viz., a mere phenomenon]. For this reason you do not consider it impossible that one monad should arouse another and produce ideas in it; that the thinking power inherent in it should thereby be changed; and that, in case this happens in many substances, locomotion in the body should arise from them. According to this view we [are said by you to] escape many of the snares we have mentioned. These are 'but the outskirts of your ways and a small whisper I have heard from you'[36] in explaining the manner of the connection between soul and body. But the matter requires further explanation." "It is indeed true," Mendelssohn pointed out in reply, "that the power of the monads is of the genus of thinking power, and that its effort to be active is of the genus of voluntary desire, as you told me, dearest friend, in your last letter. Yet this fundamental desire does not produce spatial distance or nearness, for space and all its attributes are phenomena in the soul, whereas distance and nearness are attributes of space. Now, if love and hatred, which are contained in that fundamental desire, are real, how can they give rise to the phenomena of distance and nearness, i.e., to changes appertaining to phenomenal space?"

As for his friend's contention that it was not impossible for one monad to affect another and arouse ideas in it, it required some clarification: Did it mean to assert that an external object *a* produced ideas in the substance *b*? Or did it suggest that the idea of *a* aroused ideas in the substance *b*? In case the first alternative represented his friend's view, the question arose: How can something emanate from one monad as the agent and enter another monad as a passive recipient? Mendelssohn obviously alludes here to Leibniz' fundamental view of monads as self-contained, windowless, active substances. In case the second interpretation was correct, the view proposed was rather close to Leibniz' own, except that according to Leibniz the change of ideas in the substance *b* was due entirely to the power of this substance, this power being subject to a process of change that corresponded to its ideas, and these ideas being subject to change that corresponded to the changes of external objects. This latter correspondence was due to a preestablished harmony, not to any influence: "This harmony between soul and body has been arranged by the Creator of the universe [*yotser ha-kol*] in such a way that all motions of the body are in harmony with the ideas and desires of the soul, and vice versa. For motion is the phenomenon of the change of relation between monads forming a group."

The reason that had prompted Hartog Leo to oppose the doctrine of the preestablished harmony is clearly stated in the epistle:[37] "I have furthermore noticed," Mendelssohn wrote, "that you resent this doctrine because, in your view, it denies free will and reduces everything to a preordained decree, leaving no room for just reward and punishment. In my view, however, this is not the case. Permit me to argue my opinion, and you, my friend, will judge for yourself." Thus, the somewhat fantastic situation had arisen that, just as in the days of Wolff, the doctrine of Leibniz had to be defended against the accusation that it jeopardized morality and religion. Hartog Leo was a kind of Lange redivivus, without Lange's malice but not without his fears, and Mendelssohn had to play the role of Leibniz' advocate vis-à-vis a fellow Jew. The point he made was a simple one: The controversy between the influxionists and the harmonists had absolutely no bearing on the question of free will. What the notion of free will implied had been discussed by him before[38] and was reiterated here at length. Following Leibniz, he defined free will as the choice of the good, be it the true good or the apparent one. Once the will had made its decision, the event called 'exercise of free will' was over. The action by which the body implemented that decision was a free action only insofar as it resulted from free will. The manner in which the action was performed by the body—whether through physical or ideal influence —was completely irrelevant insofar as the initial act of free choice was concerned. Neither of the two theories—influxionism or harmonism—impinged on the question of free will. Nor did predeterminism, which was inherent in the doctrine of the preestablished harmony, invalidate free will. For the choice of the will was made through the consideration of the good. It was motivated by purpose. The preordained decree was not part of the motivation. It did not operate upon the will but was merely in harmony with it. The same applied to God's foreknowledge.

As for divine retribution, its purpose could never be the avenging of misdeeds. The belief that the moral evil committed by a fool obliged God to impose suffering upon the evildoer and thus add misery to evil was "very far removed from the ways of the Tora and of the fear of the Lord, and it was also strange in the utmost degree from the point of view of reason."[39] In Mendelssohn's view, there was no divine punishment except for the benefit of the sinner, that is, for the sake of his improvement. The epistle elaborated this idea, which Mendelssohn regarded as both rational and characteristic of Judaism.[40] In his view there was also a preestablished harmony between the Jewish religion and reason. The epistle could have been written in 1770, during the Lavater crisis, when the issue of religion and reason was uppermost in his mind. On the other hand, the absence of any reference to the *Phaedon* casts some doubt on such an assumption. One would have expected at least a cursory mention of this major work in a discussion of the relation between body and soul. However, no mention is made of the *Philosophische Gespräche* either, although the problem had there been a topic of debate. And so one is left completely in the dark: there is no internal or external evidence as to precisely when the correspondence between Mendelssohn and Hartog Leo took place.[41]

In his letter to Raphael Levi, toward the end of 1767, Mendelssohn had declared himself incapable of translating the *Phaedon* into Hebrew.[42] He doubted the very feasibility of such an undertaking. In August/September, 1768, he received the news that Hartwig (Naphtali Herz) Wessely (1725–1805), already well known as an outstanding Hebraist, was planning a translation. Wessely had conveyed this information to his brother Aaron, who lived in Berlin, together with the request that Mendelssohn be informed of his marriage, which had just taken place.[43] Hartwig Wessely and Mendelssohn had never met but regarded each other as friends nevertheless, especially since Hartwig's brothers, Moses and Aaron, were close to Mendelssohn. When Mendelssohn visited Hamburg as a suitor, from the middle of April to the middle of May, 1761, Hartwig was not there, though it seems that he went to Amsterdam as manager of Veitel Heine Ephraim's bank only at the beginning of 1762.[44] Mendelssohn's letters to Fromet clearly indicate that he and Hartwig were friends only *per distance*.

On October 8, 1761, he wrote:[45] "Regards to my beloved friend [*yedidi ke-nafshi*], the distinguished bachelor, who is perfect in every science, the honorable Rabbi Herz Wessely." On October 16:[46] "Herr Hartwig Wessely will have left, I suppose, when this letter arrives. I expect him here for the holy days." On October 24:[47] "Regards to . . . my friend Moses Wessely. His brother Herz will no longer be there, I suppose. Please assure him, by way of letter, of my friendship. It would be a matter of sincere regret to me if the opportunity of making his acquaintance were to elude me." On February 6, 1762:[48] "Please convey regards to Moses Wessely. Yesterday I received a letter from his brother Herz. I am glad that this good man is satisfied with his present position." From these remarks it is fairly clear that until October, 1761, Hartwig Wessely's residence was in Hamburg; that he meant to visit Berlin for the holy days, probably for Sukkot; that he left Hamburg to spend the festivals, most likely, with his parents in Copenhagen; and that he moved to Amsterdam early in 1762.[49]

The high esteem in which Mendelssohn held Hartwig Wessely in those early years, before he had published anything, was well-deserved, for he had accomplished a remarkable synthesis of rabbinic learning and pursuits in secular sciences. Versed in a number of modern languages, he was above all deeply in love with biblical Hebrew, which he mastered in superb fashion, having been trained in his boyhood by the Hebrew grammarian Shelomo Zalman Hanau, author of the treatise *Tsohar-Ha-Teva* (Berlin, 1733). He continued his talmudic training in Hamburg under the guidance of Rabbi Jonathan Eibenschütz, who became chief rabbi of the three conterminous communities of Altona, Hamburg, and Wandsbeck in 1750, when Wessely was twenty-five years of age.[50] The indirect contact Mendelssohn and Wessely had established in 1761/62 does not seem to have been maintained in the years following. It was Wessely who broke the silence when he sent word to Mendelssohn in 1768 that he had, at long last, got married and that he desired to translate the *Phaedon*. In the intervening years his reputation as a Hebraist had soared as a result of the publication, in two volumes, of his *Levanon*, also called *Gan Naʻul* (1765–1766), an investigation of the elements of Hebrew style.

Wessely's interest in the *Phaedon* took Mendelssohn quite by surprise. He had assumed, mistakenly, that Wessely, a man steeped in piety and in a passion for Hebrew, would look askance on one who had become so deeply involved in the German Enlightenment. The letter in which he expressed his congratulations on Wessely's marriage and his reaction to the other piece of news is an important document testifying to the dual orientation that constituted his inner being. It contains the confession (quoted above) that he had originally intended to write a Hebrew treatise on immortality, based on rabbinic sources and unconnected with Socrates, "for what have we, the followers of the true religion, to do with the son of Sophroniscus?" What motivated Mendelssohn to make this startling *confessio Judaica* was obviously his desire to convince Wessely that his attachment to tradition and to Hebrew was as strong as ever. For in the paragraph preceding his confession he wrote:[51]

> In the next few days a copy of the small treatise on the immortality of the soul, which I wrote in German, will reach you. Truly speaking, I was afraid to present it to you until now because I thought you might hold me in derision for having propounded and demonstrated a truth that is not doubted by anyone "called by the name of Israel,"[52] since it is an integral part of the principles of our holy faith. For according to those who deny immortality there is no reward or punishment. Besides, from your books, which are full of "goodly words" [*imrey shefer*][53], I received the impression that you despise this method of investigation altogether, and that you suspect it to be either "laboring in vain and being diligent for trouble"[54] or, God forbid, rank heresy [*harisa*]. I said in my heart: Undoubtedly, his "zeal for the Lord of hosts doth perform this,"[55] for "his heart is whole with our God."[56] Perhaps he saw, or knew of, people "wise in their own eyes"[57] calling themselves searchers or philosophers, and from them he drew conclusions of a general nature. "As for me, whither shall I go"[58] with my book, all the "pins" and "sockets" of which consist of the lead of research inlaid with the base metal of human reason? "I shall seem to him as a mocker."[59] I have now seen, however, that you do not "comprehend in a single measure"[60] all those who engage in speculative inquiry but that you discriminate "between him that serveth God and him that serveth Him not,"[61] between him that "gives heed to the works of the Lord"[62] in sincerity and him that blasphemes God ["overturns the dish"][63] with a heart "crooked and perverse;[64] that my intention is so pleasing in your eyes that you have graciously volunteered to render the text in your pure and beautiful style from the language of the gentiles in our holy tongue. "My heart fainted"[65] when I received the good news. I felt ashamed when beholding your humility surpassing your wisdom, since I know your high rank and "your frame was not hidden from me."[66] Be this as it may: My book will be before you; look at it, and then decide whether it deserves to be translated or not.

Wessely received Mendelssohn's letter in Copenhagen, where he spent the first years of his married life and was active in his own business until 1774, when he moved to Berlin.[67] It was inevitable that the apologetic note sounded in Mendelssohn's letter put him on the defensive and challenged him to define his attitude to philosophy. In his elaborate reply[68] he made several points. The rabbinic authorities of ancient times did not hesitate to adopt scientific opinions current in their days, and they would readily embrace modern theories if they were living today. In all matters outside the realm of Tora and tradition the searching for truth was left entirely to the devices of human reason.

Insofar as matters of religious belief were concerned, Wessely continued, their validity rested on Tora and tradition. Yet there was nothing prohibiting us from rationally or scientifically demonstrating their truth and, thereby, strengthening our faith. In a work called *Ma'yan Ganim*, which he hoped to publish (but never did), he had interpreted the biblical term *tokheha* ("rebuke, reproof ") as a synonym of the term *hokhaha* ("proof "). The duty of reproving our fellow-men implied the task of proving to them the error of their ways.[69] It had never occurred to him to impugn the piety of people whom God had endowed with such abundance of intellect that they could demonstrate the truths of the faith. He was not conscious of a single statement in his writings attacking men of such caliber, who were "good and righteous and physicians of the soul." His fiery zeal was directed only against those who denied religion, taunted God, and relied solely on human reason, identifying "wisdom" *(hokhma)* with the human intellect. He believed himself to have shown that the biblical term "wisdom" invariably referred to the "perfect wisdom" expressed in the divine laws. One who supported the laws of wisdom by rational arguments, and especially one who demonstrated matters of faith, as Mendelssohn had done, merited being called a "man of understanding" *(navon, maskil)*. By proving the immortality of the "image of God" in man Mendelssohn had rendered a great service to religion. He had borrowed the *Phaedon* from a friend who took it back after a day. He had, however, read it from beginning to end with the utmost avidity and admiration.

He was sure, Wessely declared, that there was no greater stylist than Mendelssohn in contemporary German literature, and he was equally certain that had Mendelssohn chosen to write the book in Hebrew, its style would have been no less graceful. Though not himself a philosopher, he had grasped its meaning, being somewhat familiar with Plato, and he had promised some scholars versed in philosophy to translate it for them into Hebrew as soon as the book was returned to him. Now that Mendelssohn had sent him a copy, he would apply himself to this task as best as he could as soon as he was free to do so. He hoped to produce a translation acceptable to the author. The letter concluded on a note of great cordiality and admiration: "One request I make of my beloved one, who is so dear a friend to me: Let your heart firmly trust in me; charge me in your graciousness with any task, and I shall be at your disposal. For since my youth til the present day, my soul attached itself to scholars and men of understanding, and to those that 'turn the many to righteousness.'[70] Thank God, I belong neither to the flatterers nor to the supercilious. 'My soul cleaveth unto the dust,'[71] yet I dwell on high with him that speaks righteousness and walks uprightly. Above the stars I will place his throne.[72] Let your seat be there, taking refuge in the shelter of the wings of God. . . ."[73]

Regrettably, Hartwig Wessely's projected translation of the *Phaedon* did not materialize. Whether his newly established business in Copenhagen left him no time to spare, or whether he found the task beyond his powers, we do not know. It would not be surprising if, like Mendelssohn, he considered the style of the book so impregnated with the eighteenth-century mode of thinking that it defied any attempt to translate it into classical Hebrew. Yet in 1787, a year after Mendelssohn's death, a Hebrew translation of the *Phaedon* did appear, with a preface by Hartwig Wessely testifying that Mendelssohn had seen and approved it. The translator was Isaiah Beer-Bing (1759–1805) of Metz,[74] a staunch protoganist of Jewish emancipation in France, whose *Lettre d'un juif de Metz à M. A.-D.* [the anti-Semitic writer Aubert-Dubayet] also appeared in 1787. Beer-Bing's Hebrew version is a little masterpiece in the way it recasts Mendelssohn's thoughts in an authentic Hebrew idiom that makes one forget that one is reading a translation. In a sense, it is a slightly abridged paraphrase of the original, and the flavor of the German style had to be sacrificed for the sake of the naturalness of the Hebrew. The relevant paragraph in Wessely's preface reads as follows:[75]

> Now a man of understanding, young in years and valiant, a writer and clear spokesman, our rabbi and teacher, Yishai Beer (may the Merciful One perserve and redeem him), one of the elite from among our brethren, the members of the holy congregation in Metz (may God protect it), took courage. He translated this German treatise [the *Phaedon*] into our holy tongue. In some places he added words so as to render more intelligible some difficult expressions therein. He sent the translation, through one of his friends who resides here, to the learned author (may the memory of the righteous be for a blessing), while he was still alive, in order to obtain his judgment, and it did find grace in his eyes. The author told me that he found it satisfactory and that he considered it a good piece of work.

An earlier, and less successful, translation of the *Phaedon* had been made by David Wagenaar of Amsterdam, a friend and ardent admirer of Hartwig Wessely. Wagenaar submitted his manuscript to Mendelssohn with a covering letter of which only the undated draft has been preserved.[76] The approximate date can be determined as August/September, 1775, since greetings are sent to Wessely (who had moved to Berlin in 1774) and reference is made to Wessely's commentary *Yeyn Levanon* ("Wine of Lebanon") on *Pirkey Avot* (which appeared at the end of the year 1774, and which Wagenaar had already studied). The letter could, therefore, not have been written prior to 1775. It is unlikely that it was written later than that year, inasmuch as Mendelssohn's illness was still considered acute, Wagenaar signing his name as that of a friend "having pity on him" and expressing the hope that the "forthcoming Days of Awe" (Rosh Hashana and Yom Kippur) will bring speedy salvation (which enables us to fix the date more precisely).

Wagenaar reported in his letter that he had intended to translate all of Mendelssohn's German writings into Hebrew in order to test his capacity for this type of work and gain proficiency in it. He seems to have imagined himself as a successor to the famous medieval translators like Samuel ibn Tibbon who, though "greater than me," had sought the author's approval of their translations. For a variety of reasons he had left his plan in abeyance until many adepts of science versed in the Tora urged him to translate at least part of the *Phaedon* for them. They regarded this as important, since the principles of their faith were bound up with the doctrine of immortality, as Wagenaar himself had demonstrated in a little treatise of his own. Having acceded to their request, he had been asked to complete the translation, which he had done, including a wealth of references to Scripture, rabbinic literature, and the *Zohar*, etc. His intention had been to prove that the *Phaedon* was in accord with Jewish teaching and that there was nothing "perverse or crooked" in it, a clear indication that some of the more rigidly pious had their misgivings about Mendelssohn's work. Now his friends wanted him to publish this annotated translation, but he was not sure that he had a right to do so, since translating was a ticklish job and he might have misunderstood the author's meaning in many places. His knowledge of German was deficient, he felt, and there was no one in his vicinity who could check his translation. Would Mendelssohn, therefore, be kind enough to look at the manuscript, which a friend of his was taking to Berlin, and feel free to change, delete, and add as he pleased. We have no documentary evidence of the way in which Mendelssohn responded to Wagenaar's request. The fact that the translation was not published suggests that Mendelssohn's reply was not encouraging.[77]

CHAPTER THREE

Turning Point:
The Lavater Affair

------◆◇◆------

"Juif de Berlin"

Considering the state of degradation in which the Jewish population lived in eighteenth-century Germany and, excepting Holland, elsewhere in Europe, Moses Mendelssohn's rise to fame and his acceptance into the republic of letters was an amazing feat of personal achievement. It indicated, at the same time, the awakening of a more liberal spirit among influential members of society: men of letters, aristocrats, even theologians. The humanist outlook of the Enlightenment had prepared the ground for a greater willingness to treat an individual Jew on his own merits. It had also, in conjunction with the emergence of modern industrial enterprise, facilitated closer contact between Christians and Jews. A Jewish elite group had come into being, comprising successful entrepreneurs on the one hand and literati on the other. Daniel Itzig (Jaffe), the banker, may be named as a representative of the first type, and Doctor Marcus Herz, Kant's pupil, of the second. David Friedländer, Itzig's son-in-law, was wealthy *and* learned.

Thus Moses Mendelssohn, although unique as a figure of European fame, was not a completely isolated phenomenon. It would be wrong, however, to assume that the rapprochement between Jews and Christians amounted to the coming into being of a kind of "neutral society" in which the distinctive elements of the two faiths were submerged or ignored. While it is true that overriding common cultural interests facilitated bonds of friendship that were hardly feasible at an earlier period,[1] the differences between the two "nations"—a term frequently used by Mendelssohn[2]—were never glossed over. Indeed, it was an essential prerequisite of Enlightenment tolerance to face up to the Jewishness of Mendelssohn, however odd it may have looked to his friends, let alone his more distant admirers. It was gratifying psychologically to acknowledge the Jewish character of Herr Moses and yet to love him. The practice of absolute tolerance vis-à-vis this outstanding and amiable man demanded no great effort from a person able to appreciate his accomplishments and predisposed to Enlightenment liberalism.

People imbued with Christian missionary zeal found it harder to accept his unrelenting Jewishness. They either hoped for his eventual conversion or else, having realized the futility of this hope, consoled themselves with the thought that this exceptional "Israelite in whom there was no guile" was a Christian "at heart." In a letter dated September 7, 1770,[3] the famous Swabian theologian Christoph Friedrich Oetinger told Mendelssohn to his face—so to speak—that he was, in the words of Saint Paul (Romans 2:29), "a Jew circumcised in the spirit." At all events, he was, in the telling epithet of the French, the *"Juif de Berlin."*[4]

It was no easy task for Mendelssohn to bring the two strands of his being into harmony. Living as he did in two worlds, as it were, he had to express his Jewishness with varying emphases and in different keys. In his relations with non-Jews he did not hesitate to refer to his observance of Jewish laws and customs, but he did so with grace and, sometimes, with a light touch of humor so as to avoid any embarrassment. One of his letters to Abbt suddenly breaks off with the remark: "But the Sabbath begins! Take care of yourself, my best friend!"[5] But for the arrival of the sabbath, on which writing is forbidden, he would have loved to continue the epistle. In one breath he professed his loyalty to Judaism and his friendship for the Christian Abbt. Another letter to Abbt ends with these words: "I must finish.... The Sabbath has arrived; and since the calf has long ago been ground into a tincture of gold, the laws are holy to me."[6] From Brunswick he wrote to Lessing on July 16, 1773: "Dearest friend! We just arrived here. Tomorrow is Saturday; that makes it impossible for me to visit you [in nearby Wolfenbüttel].... In case you can manage it, do come over to see me, since you don't have to observe a Sabbath."[7]

His sense of humor is pronounced in the letters to Nicolai. A case in point is the way in which, shortly before his wedding, he informed Nicolai of his farewell to belles-lettres in order to prepare a totally prosaic talmudic discourse.[8] An undated note to Nicolai reads: "As the heart panteth after the water brooks, my soul yearneth[9] for rational conversation. Miserable me! While I was praying and feasting, my business affairs piled up, and now I sit here the whole day, observing the fast[10] and going crazy. Ask Lessing to come to you. Perhaps I shall be free toward 5 P.M. and, disregarding all bigots, fast in your company."[11] From yet another letter only the part containing this passage has been preserved: "Now good health to you and Lessing and as many as there are who, uncircumcised, sit at the table and, to the annoyance of the circumcised, drink choice wine and still choicer wit to each other...."[12] The "annoyance" at having to forego, because of the Jewish dietary laws, being wined and dined at Nicolai's table on some apparently auspicious occasion is openly stated, yet the whole tone is that of good-natured and playful rebellion on the part of a Jew to whom "the laws are holy."

The jesting about the circumcised versus the uncircumcised reflects the same jovial mood. It had become a *façon de parler* among Christian literati of the period to refer to Jews as the circumcised without necessarily intending to be malicious. Sulzer, we noted,[13] wrote about the young Mendelssohn, whom he had just met for the first time and for whom he had great admiration, that "this circumcised one" would be a good replacement for Ramler. In the same spirit Hamann could speak of him as "mon ami Moyse, le philosophe circoncis."[14]

The same pattern of uninhibited frankness is noticeable also in Mendelssohn's writings. Rabbinic phrases are quoted, although not always identified as such. Thus, the letters *On the Sentiments* speak of the goodness of God "whose right hand heals while his left hand inflicts a wound"[15] without indicating the rabbinic source.[16] Describing a subtle way of reasoning, he uses a Mishnaic simile and credits it to an unnamed Hebrew poet: "A huge mountain revolving around a hair, says a certain Hebrew poet."[17] In his essay *On the Question: What is Enlightenment?*[18] he paraphrases another saying of the Mishna[19] and attributes it to a Hebrew writer: "The nobler a thing is in its state of perfection, the more awful it is in its decomposition." In the context of another essay discussing the question whether the terms "fool" and "rogue" are synonymous we read: "The rabbis say: Man never sins unless a spirit of foolishness has taken hold of him."[20]

No doubt there was a certain deliberateness in quoting Hebrew phrases of this kind. They were obviously meant to show the poetic flavor or, simply, the "wisdom" to be found in Jewish literature. Prejudice might slowly be defeated in this unobtrusive way. For the same reason Mendelssohn published "Samples from Rabbinic Wisdom" in Johann Jakob Engel's *The Philosopher for the World*.[21] When the project of a German translation of the entire Mishna by the Ansbach chaplain Johann Jacob Rabe was announced in 1759, Mendelssohn took the opportunity to break a lance for the much maligned Talmud. "I am as curious as you," he wrote in the *Literaturbriefe*[22] under the usual cloak of anonymity, "to see the German rendition of the Mishna announced by Herr Chaplain Rabe, but for a totally different reason. I expect something entirely distinct from what you seem to expect. We shall find out whose conjecture will be confirmed. You judge this work according to the common idea that we, as a rule, form of the Talmud, and in anticipation you already make fun of the inanities and eccentricities of which it is [allegedly] composed. I, for my part, think differently. On no account can I persuade myself that the best minds of a nation (and, surely, the Jewish nation is not short of very good minds) should have occupied themselves throughout so many centuries exclusively with a work consisting of insipid rubbish. The immense diligence with which they study it and the oriental ardor that I have so often seen displayed when they argue some of its subjects would seem proof to me that a man of genius can find all he needs for nourishment in this kind of study."

Mendelssohn continued his review-letter by using, as he so often did, an intriguing fictional device. He posed as a Christian who had once met a learned Jew at a watering place. From him, he pretended, he had received authentic insight into what the Talmud stood for. It was now his intention to ask this Jewish scholar's opinion of Rabe's Mishna translation as soon as it appeared. Over a year later, in *Literaturbrief* 122 (August 14, 1760),[23] we hear that the first volume of the work had been published,[24] and that the reviewer had consulted the rabbi's opinion on its merits. We are told that he expressed great admiration for Rabe's accomplishment and, at the same time, offered a number of critical annotations. These are, of course, duly recorded. The device was repeated the year after,[25] when the second volume came out. Rabe had welcomed, we are informed, the critical comments on his translation and had, in fact, incorporated them in the preface to the second part. It was patent to most readers, naturally, that the reviewer in the *Literaturbriefe* was none other than Mendelssohn and that the rabbinic authority consulted was likewise Mendelssohn.

How much Rabe appreciated his critical comments we may gather from a letter written by Abbt to his friend Blum on April 25, 1761, soon after his arrival in Berlin:[26] "Since you will hardly read the German version of the Talmud by Herr Chaplain Rabe, I want to let you know the judgment he passed on our Moses in the preface [of volume two]. Having inserted into it the entire review [of volume one], he continued: 'I can apply to him what was once said of [Moses] Maimonides: From Moses until Maimonides there was no Jew like him, and also from Maimonides until this Moses there was no Jew like him.'" It is indeed remarkable that it was a Christian who first applied (as early as 1761) to Mendelssohn the popular saying "From Moses until Moses there was none like Moses." There may have been an undertone, in Rabe's praise, of recognizing in Mendelssohn the exceptional Jew. If so, it was offset by his genuine interest in rabbinics and Hebrew literature. He later translated Mendelssohn's Hebrew commentary on *Kohelet* (Ecclesiastes) into German.[27] The striking thing about the review-letters on Rabe is the very fact that they appeared— that Mendelssohn the critic of belles-lettres and philosophical writings showed not the slightest hesitation to figure also as an expert in rabbinics. The literary fiction he employed was anything but camouflage, since nobody was likely to be deceived.

The liberal spirit that acknowledged the differences between Jew and Christian but tried to neutralize their effect on human relations was a product of the Enlightenment. However, its influence penetrated even circles that resisted the secularizing tendencies of the age of Enlightened reason. Even Hamann, the very incarnation of anti-*Aufklärung,* could develop a somewhat ambivalent attitude toward Mendelssohn and, at least overtly, profess friendship for him. He had met "the Jew Moses" as early as 1756 "by chance" in Berlin,[28] before going to London, where he led a life of debauchery and then experienced a conversion to Christian piety. When, after his return to Königsberg, he made his literary debut with his *Socratic Memorabilia* (1759), Mendelssohn wrote a favorable review.[29] About a year later Hamann published an anonymous critique of Mendelssohn's view on *Rousseau's Julie, ou la nouvelle Héloïse* as expressed in the *Literaturbriefe*.[30] It defended the new Héloise, "the philosopher in crinoline," in the name of a new Abélard called Abaelardus Virbius against the new Canon Fulbert (Mendelssohn), whose prototype, the uncle of Héloïse, had been so cruelly vindictive toward his niece's seducer. Mendelssohn found the little tract highly amusing, wrote a reply under the pseudonym Fulbertus Kulmius,[31] and published both in the *Literaturbriefe*.[32] He had immediately discerned the identity of the author: there was "no other German writer who combined this witty mood with so pithy a style, which is both figurative and rich in epigrams."[33]

Hamann had alluded to the Jewishness of the anonymous censor of Rousseau with a robust humor that might have been considered a bit offensive in a different intellectual climate: Mendelssohn is castigated as an "aesthetic Moses" who dared to prescribe "imbecile and paltry statutes" to citizens of a free state, bidding them "not to touch this, not to taste that." How could he try to subject the first-born affect of the human soul to "the yoke of circumcision"? It would be as unfair to restrain the aesthetic conscience of Rousseau as it would be to induce in an Israelite a desire for Pomeranian ham.[34] Mendelssohn took no umbridge at these digs ad hominem, for there was a certain playfulness in them that tempered malice.

In the correspondence that ensued between the two, a light-hearted, liberal spirit continues to hover over their differences. Hamann describes himself as Mendelssohn's friend and brother in Apollo but also reminds him of the ominous character of his name: "Since, unfortunately, you know that I am not called Mordecai, the old address remains at all events."[35] Mendelssohn responded in good humor but not without betraying a sense of alertness: "Our public as well as private character shows inborn trouble. Writer and critic, Abélard and Fulbert, Hamann and a stubborn Mordecai. . . . The golden days of which it is said, 'And the wolf shall dwell with the lamb, and the leopard shall lie down with the kid'[36] have not, I believe, yet arrived."[37] Hamann echoes these sentiments but gives the quotation a more innocuous interpretation: "The golden days, I believe, have not yet arrived when Mordecai and the wicked Agagite [Hamann] sit together and drink each other's health. The golden days, I believe, have not yet arrived of which it is said that in them the leopards that draw the triumphal carriage of Bacchus and the goats that spoil his vineyards share their lair."[38] In other words, writers and critics cannot yet associate;

"free-born" people cannot join a "strange gang of unknown people who shun the daylight"—who write anonymous reviews in the *Literaturbriefe*. (This was in reply to Mendelssohn's suggestion that Hamann become a contributor to the *Literaturbriefe*.)[39]

It was this friendly, civilized tolerance of diversity that enabled Mendelssohn to feel at home and relaxed in the world of German letters. It gave him a sense of freedom that was essential for the flowering of his creativity. Well he knew that the liberal spirit was still a tender plant, that it had not really succeeded in detheologizing the intellectual atmosphere even of the Enlightenment. He was sensitive to repeated hints that he was expected sooner or later to convert to Christianity. He appreciated Resewitz' tactfulness in this regard,[40] and he must have been pleased when Abbt described to him the way in which he had turned a deaf ear to Johann Arnold Ebert's question concerning this point. It seems that Ebert (1723–1795), a professor of English literature, had asked Abbt to let Mendelssohn know that he loved him exceedingly and wished him better, perhaps, than Mendelssohn wished for himself. "When he put the question to me," Abbt wrote on October 13, 1761, "whether there was any hope that you will become a Christian, I asked him to show me his English books, of which he has a fine collection."[41]

Mendelssohn could disregard the conversionist zeal of some of his admirers so long as it merely smouldered under the surface. He also could safely ignore scurrilous attacks by eccentrics like Carl Friedrich Bahrd (1741–1792), who in his *The True Christian in Solitude* (improved and augmented, 2 volumes, Halle, 1763)—referred to by Mendelssohn as Bahrd's "Improved Christian in Solitude"—had accused the Berlin Academy of having gotten Mendelssohn to contest the Christian religion.[42] It was a more serious matter when J. H. G. von Justi (ca. 1705–1771), one of the founders of political science in Germany, denounced the *Literaturbriefe* to the authorities with the trumped up charge that in them a Jew had blasphemed Christ and the Christian religion, and that a review published there had been disrespectful to the king's *Poésies diverses*. As a result of these charges the *Literaturbriefe* were put on the index on March 18, 1762 (the ban was lifted a few days later). A sharply critical review, by Abbt, of von Justi's political novel on Psammitichus was the cause of this commotion.[43] Mendelssohn, for his part, was completely guiltless: his review of the king's poetry was critical but in excellent taste.

The overwhelmingly favorable response that the *Phaedon* had evoked tended to confirm Mendelssohn's hope that he had finally "arrived" as a fully fledged citizen of the realm of German letters. He had the satisfaction of knowing that he had achieved his position without in any way concealing or playing down his Jewishness. How he had reconciled his philosophical convictions with the deeper layers of his soul, which remained tied to the world of tradition, was his personal affair. He saw no need to publicize the manner in which he interpreted his religion. But was it possible, over the long run, to keep the secular and the religious apart, treating the one as a public and the other as a private domain? Standing at the pinnacle of fame, was he not expected to declare his creed? In the *Phaedon* he had come closest to stating his religious beliefs without referring to revelation. Yet he was not a deist. He was a full-blooded Jew. To him, obviously, reason and revelation did not exclude each other. The questions that the *Phaedon* had elicited did not challenge him on this most intimate issue, except for one that has not been mentioned so far.

The Duke Ludwig Eugen of Württemberg told Mendelssohn in a letter that he had put down a large number of notes on the *Phaedon* and offered three critical remarks for his consideration.[44] In his reply, dated July 17, 1767,[45] Mendelssohn asked the duke to send all of his annotations, since he might be able to use them for the revised edition of 1768. The three suggestions contained in the duke's letter were, in fact, taken care of in that edition.[46] Of special interest is the first one. It concerned the phrase in the introductory section on Socrates' life, describing Socrates' love of virtue and his obedience to the laws of the Creator, "whom he knew in the most vivid manner by the purest light of reason." As a good Christian, the duke had taken umbridge at the term "purest light of reason," which to him seemed to imply that a human being (and a pagan at that) was capable of knowing God in a supreme way. Mendelssohn substituted the more innocuous expression "the pure light of reason." On the main issue, however, he remained adamant. This is what he wrote to the duke: "The term 'the *purest* light of reason in the *most* vivid manner' is indeed inappropriate, since the superlative may easily be taken in a strictness in which it cannot be applied to man on this earth. On the other hand, I am not disinclined to attribute to the light of reason the capacity of leading man to true virtue. . . . The motivations of reason seem to me entirely sufficient for promoting a steady progression in the love of the good and noble. Can it be true that the majority of the human race is so God-forsaken that the means of attaining to true virtue are denied to it? Should this be taught by religion, a reverential silence is imposed by it at the same time, but this is not what my religion teaches."

Mendelssohn here anticipated the stand he was soon to take in the Lavater affair. Such was the strength of his conviction that even the mild provocation by the duke put him on his mettle.[47] Reason, to Mendelssohn, was divine. It sufficed for the ultimate happiness of all men. As a philosopher, he required no revelation to teach him universal truths. As a Jew, he recognized the fact of revelation and lived by its laws. He saw no conflict between the two parts of his being. The letter to the duke rejected the Christian concept of faith as the only road to salvation and the denial of salvation to the "God-forsaken" majority of the unconverted. Judaism seemed to him the more tolerant religion. He had made up his mind on this subject long before the Lavater affair compelled him to state his view publicly.

The Prehistory of the Lavater Affair

Johann Caspar Lavater was no stranger to Mendelssohn. Introduced by Sulzer and Albrecht Friedrich von Arnim,[1] he had, as a young theologian, visited Mendelssohn in 1763, in the company of his friends Felix Hess and Heinrich Füssli, when the three, for reasons of personal safety, had to spend some time away from their native city of Zürich. An enthusiast by nature, Lavater was at that time under the influence of the theology of the Enlightenment.[2] He was, therefore, anxious to meet Mendelssohn, and he was deeply impressed by him. This is attested by a letter to his parents written on April 7, 1763, by an entry in his diary of the same date, and by a letter to Canon Breitinger in Zürich, dated April 18, which hardly differs from the note in the diary. The note reads:[3]

> At about 6 P.M. we went (with Arnim) to the Jew Moses [*Jud Moses*], author of the *Philosophical Dialogues* and of the letters *On the Sentiments*. We found him in his *comptoir* busy with silks. An affable, radiant soul [discernible] in the penetrative eye and in an Aesopian[4] hut; quick of speech, but all of a sudden impeded in its flow by nature's strings. A man of sharp discernment, delicate taste, and extensive knowledge. An admirer of thinkers of genius, and himself a brilliant metaphysician. An impartial judge of the creations of intellect and good taste, trustful and candid in conversation, more modest in his talk than in his literature, and unaffected by praise.... Generous and obliging. A brother to his brethren, the Jews, complaisant and respectful to them, loved and honored by them in return—but how little do his external circumstances correspond to his talents! He is employed as supervisor of a factory by a wealthy Jew, Bernhard, who pays him three hundred thalers per annum. He has to spend most of his time in the *comptoir* and has little time for extending the activities of his mind in due measure....

Another entry in the diary, dated April 18, records a second visit. On both occasions the conversation touched only upon literary matters and events connected with the king's entry into Berlin after the Seven Years' War, which had just come to an end. Mendelssohn mentioned the *Sermon on Peace* by "a Jew," not disclosing his own authorship, and he showed the visitors his *Ode on the King's Entry*. Lavater copied the text of it in the diary,[5] just as he had written down the poet Ramler's ode celebrating the same occasion in his diary entry for March 31. Mendelssohn was obviously in a talkative mood. He spoke of Lessing's flair for the comical and the tragic, and characterized *Miss Sara Sampson* as a "tragic farce." He described in graphic terms the effects that the famous English actor David Garrick (1717–1779) was able to produce by his pantomimic art, and he criticized the absurd educational methods by which one tried nowadays in Berlin to instil in young people a taste for belles-lettres before one had taught them to speak and write correctly.

During Lavater's second visit the conversation seems to have concentrated on contemporary literature. Klopstock's *Der Messias* and a critical review of it that had recently appeared in the *Bibliothek der schönen Wissenschaften*[6] set the discussion going. It then turned to Klopstock's odes and to Johann Andreas Cramer's poetry. Mendelssohn was rather severe on Cramer's prose writings (excepting those of his earliest period) but praised his religious odes, particularly his *Auferstehung* ("Resurrection"). He ventured the remark that a man who had been a preacher for twenty years could hardly be expected to rise above mediocrity. He thought that, next to Haller, Friedrich von Hagedorn was the greatest poet of his time. Füssli, Lavater's friend, objected that one might describe him as a man of talent rather than of true genius, since his forte consisted merely in the ability to express old truths in a nice and pleasant way.[7]

Religious matters were not discussed in these conversations, which took place in 1763. Mendelssohn showed himself as a *bel esprit* and literary critic, not as a metaphysician and certainly not as a theologian.[8] There undoubtedly was a good rapport between him and his visitors. Lavater's sketch of Mendelssohn conveys the genial atmosphere in which they became acquainted. His reference to the host as the *"Jud Moses"* was not intended as a slur, but it did carry overtones of the astonishment that Lavater and his friends felt on encountering the unusual phenomenon of a Jew so much at home in German literature.

On May 3 the three young men left Berlin for Barth, a small city on the Baltic Sea coast of Mecklenburg, to study theology under the guidance of Johann Joachim Spalding. In 1761 the first edition of Spalding's *Thoughts on the Value of Feelings in Christianity* had appeared and given rise to much discussion. In opposition to pietism, the book pointed out that the moral conscience and its sentiments were the sole evidence of the workings of God's spirit in man. An entry in Lavater's diary (April 8) shows that the question of whether or not the uniform Divine Power could express itself in special operations of grace had formed a topic of discussion among the theologians in Berlin. But despite Spalding's liberalism, Lavater was ready to study under him. However, he and his friend Hess returned to Berlin in January, 1764, because Spalding had in the meanwhile been appointed deacon and councillor of the Berlin consistory.

It seems that Spalding, while still in Barth, had had several discussions with his students about Mendelssohn's religious views. Lavater must have received the impression that Mendelssohn had begun to examine the truths of Christianity. For on February 2, 1764, after his arrival in Berlin, he entered the following account in his diary: "Spalding related that Court Chaplain Sack and his friends wondered why the Jew Moses . . . no longer concerned himself with the examination of Christianity. He [Sack] was confident that he [Moses] would find its purified conceptions, after the strictest scrutiny, in accord with reason and to be divine; for the time being, he was a deist in all respects. Court Chaplain Johann Samuel Diterich added the further remark: 'He [Moses] had once said that the Messiah had already come but that men's spirits did not believe in the true one. On another occasion he had said that he failed to discover in the writings of the Old Testament the prediction of a Messiah as commonly understood.' "[9]

The seriousness with which the Berlin theologians of the Enlightenment debated among themselves on the chances of Mendelssohn's conversion could not fail to impress itself upon Lavater's enthusiastic mind. It planted the seed of the challenge that he presented to Mendelssohn in 1769. Spalding, in particular, bore the ultimate responsibility for this step. In a letter to Friedrich Germanus Lüdke, the Berlin theologian who bore the brunt of the behind-the-scene activities during the crisis,[10] Lavater confessed that he would not have acted had he not been informed by Spalding of the willingness of some "philosophical Jews" to embrace a unitarian version of Christianity. He had taken it for granted that Mendelssohn belonged to this group.[11] Spalding was obviously obsessed with the idea of winning converts among educated Jews. As late as 1782 the young Dane Friedrich Münter found Spalding talking in the same terms. His diary has the following entry dated October 29, 1782, à propos a visit he had paid to Spalding: "After dinner we talked about matters of religion. About the system of Arianism . . . He told me about Jews, especially a Jewish physician, who had said to him that he would have no scruples against undergoing baptism in the event Christian teaching was confined to Socinianism, and that most enlightened Jews thought likewise."[12]

Mendelssohn might have ignored Lavater's rather clumsy attempt to convert him had he not realized that the true adversary was not the enthusiastic Swiss deacon but the phalanx of the Berlin Enlightenment theology led by Spalding. It apparently hurt the pride of this group that the famed Jewish philosopher had withstood all efforts by well-meaning Christians to win him over to their faith. They all felt what Resewitz wrote Nicolai at the height of the controversy: that Mendelssohn's mind and heart had been influenced by Christianity without his being aware of the fact.[13] Should it not then be possible to alert him to the need to see the light? Did they not teach a purified understanding of Christianity that the enlightened philosopher Mendelssohn was bound to accept? Not having recognized Christianity as yet, he was, in their view, a mere deist. Yet he professed Judaism, and while they could have condoned his deism, his continued and pronounced Jewishness was a thorn in their flesh. The antagonism they felt toward him was reflected in their annoyance with the truly enlightened preacher and philosopher Johann August Eberhard, who had become attached to Mendelssohn soon after he came to Berlin in 1763 as a private tutor in the household of the baron von der Horst, and who was appointed professor in Halle in 1778. Nicolai reported: "I am almost ashamed to say it [but] it is nevertheless true that one of the reasons offered in support of the view that Eberhard was not really fit to be a preacher was the fact of his being in almost daily contact with Moses Mendelssohn. It was found particularly objectionable that he was often seen walking in the street with the Jewish philosopher. He was admonished by word of mouth not to do this, but he was stubborn enough to smile at the suggestion."[14] Lavater's Berlin diary is, therefore, not without significance for an understanding of the prehistory of his challenge to Mendelssohn.

While still in Berlin, Lavater considered it worthwhile to pay another visit to the *"Jud Moses."* This time, he seems to have promised himself, he would not waste a precious opportunity on literary gossip but would try to clarify the philosopher's attitude toward Christianity. On February 27 he wrote to his parents: "Yesterday we dined again with Herr Diterich. In the evening we visited the Jew Moses, who is famous on account of his learning and philosophical discernment." The letter is reticent about the conversation that took place—the diary breathes no word about it—but hints that Mendelssohn had refused to make any concessions to Christianity: "The cover of Moses still lies firmly upon his countenance. Only God, their Father, can lead this people to the adoration of his Messiah."[15]

The trend of the discussion can be reconstructed from the documents of the controversy, particularly from Mendelssohn's *Notes on the Addenda Sent by Herr Lavater.*[16] From them it is clear that Lavater and his friends (Hess and, probably, Diterich) asked Mendelssohn to explain his view of Christianity, and that Mendelssohn tried to divert the conversation to other matters. His visitors had to press him hard before he ventured to state his opinion, and even then he did so only after he had been assured that his words would never be made public (as he recalled later) or that they would never be divulged in a manner likely to injure him (according to Lavater's recollection of the stipulation).[17] What he told his visitors after these solemn preliminaries was harmless enough. He declared that, notwithstanding his remoteness from Christianity, he felt a sense of respect for the moral character of its founder (i.e. Jesus of Nazareth). He qualified this statement by adding that he would have to withdraw his respect in case the founder had arrogated to himself the quality of a being sharing in God's nature and transcending that of a human being striving for virtue.[18] When Lavater asked him how he differentiated between a Socrates, a Plato, and a Jesus, he replied: "Socrates never wanted to be more than a man. Had he proclaimed himself a divine person or a mediator between God and men, let alone as the only mediator, I would have had to deny him all respect... pretensions of this sort appertain to the moral aspect of one's character and determine all moral qualities in a strange way.—Should Jesus, however, have at no time intended to presume that much—which

I sincerely believe to be the case—I stand by my avowal of philosophical respect."[19]

Thus, all that Mendelssohn had admitted was his "philosophical" (viz., nonreligious) respect for Jesus as a human being who had made no claim to divinity. In spite of the modesty of this nontheological admission, it tended to assume in Lavater's memory the aura of a great promise. This was not surprising, since Christians generally believed that Jews were wont to abuse Jesus. One of Mendelssohn's correspondents during the Lavater controversy alluded to this point, and this is what Mendelssohn replied:[20] "Permit me to utter a mild complaint about a certain point in your letter. You seem to give me credit for having acted in an extraordinary way because, as a Jew, I speak with respect of the religion of Jesus, do not hate the Christians, do not abuse them, etc. You must, therefore, imagine that very few of my correligionists are capable of this modesty.—Do us, however, justice! Aben-Ezra has only a few passing remarks that concern the Christian religion. Maimonides, so far as I know, never wrote against it. Orobio did do this, but with a moderation that does him credit."[21]

Mendelssohn oversimplified the situation. The figure of the crucified had become, in the course of the Christians' persecution of the Jews, a symbol synonymous with anything but Christian love.[22] Mendelssohn alluded to the historical aspect of the relationship between Jews and Jesus when he said in the same letter: "I willingly believe that a great deal of what the Christian rabbis [sic] preached throughout so many centuries, and for the sake of which they so often killed and allowed themselves to be killed, had not been taught by Jesus." As a philosopher, he was able to shed the purely emotional attitude generated by historical experience and could take a more dispassionate view of Jesus. He was, however, not alone in trying to be fair-minded and to bring about better feeling between Jew and Christian. Rabbi Jacob Emden (1697–1776), the rabbinic leader of Jewish orthodoxy in Germany, whom he highly revered, had also drawn a line between Jesus and the church and had tended to pay respect to the historical Jesus.[23] However, nothing in Mendelssohn's statement about Jesus could be construed to imply more than he actually said. Lavater's hopes in that respect were utterly unfounded.

What was it that caused Lavater to attempt in 1769 the mission that in 1764 he had entrusted to the hands of God? What motivated him to challenge Mendelssohn publicly either to refute or to embrace the Christian faith? We have noted the impact that the missionary zeal of Spalding and his Berlin circle had had upon him. Mention has been made of Spalding's letter to him. And due weight has been given to the lingering memory of Mendelssohn's "admission" of respect for Jesus, however hedged around. But these things surely would not have moved him to action had not powerful incentives been provided by two additional elements: his own chiliastic fantasies and Charles Bonnet's proofs for Christianity.[24] As for the first:

In 1768 Lavater published the first part of a work entitled *Vistas of Eternity*[25] in which he presented his idea of a millennial kingdom of Christ on earth, to be ushered in by the conversion of the Jews. The Second Coming of the Messiah would be for the benefit of the Jewish nation. It would inaugurate the restoration of the Jewish state and thereby fulfil the Jewish messianic expectations. "It is true, the kingdom of Christ was not meant to be a secular kingdom in the popular sense, as hoped for by the Jewish nation which, at the time, was utterly corrupt. . . . Nevertheless, the Jews had been promised a glorious kingdom on earth to be enjoyed, at the end of time, by the better part of the nation only. This promise is as yet unfulfilled. . . . Hence, my friend, it can be understood why highly intelligent Jews who are familiar with their prophets are waiting with so much confidence for an appearance of the Messiah totally different from the one that we want to obtrude upon them as the only one."[26] The last sentence clearly echoes what, according to Lavater's Berlin diary, Diterich had said on February 2, 1764: Mendelssohn had failed to discover in the writings of the Old Testament the prediction of a Messiah as commonly understood [by the Christians].

It was Mendelssohn whom Lavater had particularly in mind when referring to intelligent Jews who expected a Messiah different from Jesus. He felt constrained, therefore, to fit the Jewish messianic idea into his eschatological scheme, as other Christian chiliasts had done before him.[27] He undoubtedly hoped that this concession would facilitate the conversion of the Jews. In the long preface to the second part of his *Vistas of Eternity*,[28] written in 1769, he returned to his millenarian notions in order to defend them against objections raised by Christian theologians. "Those who were the most lenient in judging this supposition (for only as such a one did I offer it in my Letters)[29] called it a poetic dream; by far the most pronounced it the wild imaginings of an enthusiast, and still others rated me as a disciple of Cerinthus[30] or Mohammed." By characterizing his doctrine as a mere supposition Lavater hoped to calm the fears of his adversaries. How truly serious he actually was about it may be gathered from his intimate correspondence with the Duisburg theologian Johann Gerhard Hasenkamp, in which mystical speculations and experiences are openly discussed.[31] Missionary work among the Jews, moreover, continued to be a topic on which he invited Hasenkamp's cooperation: "Advice, ideas, coherent or fragmentary thoughts on how one might possibly facilitate the transition of the Jews to Christianity and a candid conversation with them, this is what I wish to receive from you soon," he wrote to him on February 20, 1773.[32] The Berlin theologians were dismayed by Lavater's heterodox, fantastic ideas and tried to dissuade him from pursuing the millennium in this philo-Semitic fashion. He was far too enraptured by his own thoughts to listen to their warnings.[33]

The project of setting in motion a general conversion of the Jews as the prelude to the millennial Kingdom of Christ was too fascinating to be dropped, especially in view of what Spalding had told him about the prospects of a wholesale conversion. Lavater imagined that the "philosophical," i.e., the enlightened, Jews would welcome a public invitation to embrace Christianity—to find that "a golden bridge" was offered that enabled them "to break with their rabbis."[34] He was confident that Mendelssohn's conversion, should it happen, would be the signal for the rest of the Jews to follow his example. For this reason he looked upon Mendelssohn, the most famous Jew of his time, as destined by Providence to start the messianic process. In Nicolai's words: "Lavater, whose cool calculation was always in inverse ratio to his uncontrolled imagination, had taken it for granted that Moses would . . . become a Christian. Presumably, he had no doubt that all Jews would follow suit, that the millennium by which he set great store would arrive as a result, and that he would be able to claim credit for having hastened its coming."[35] It obviously did not occur to him that Mendelssohn's clear and realistic thinking was poles apart from his chiliastic dreams, and that the very idea of converting to Christianity as a means of restoring Jewish statehood would strike Mendelssohn as preposterous. Even in a purely secular and political form, the idea of a Jewish state in the immediate future seemed to him completely unrealistic. This is attested by his response to an anonymous admirer who, in the strictest confidence, had submitted to him a plan for the reestablishment of the Jewish state.[36] The tone of his reply shows how skeptical Mendelssohn was about any attempt to realize Jewish messianic expectations in the foreseeable future. Least of all could he have been impressed by the manner in which Lavater proposed it.

Full of chiliastic fantasies yet still uncertain as to how to proceed, Lavater hit upon the treatise *La Palingénésie philosophique ou Idées sur l'état passé et sur l'état futur des êtres vivans*,[37] by Charles Bonnet (1720–1793), the Genevan scientist and philosopher.[38] Bonnet's personality was "a strange mixture of devotion to penetrating, sober research and of naïve and credulous indulgence in fancies."[39] Like Condillac, he derived even the most abstract notions from sensible representations. Cognition, he held, arises from sensations, and sensations are conditions of the soul produced by certain vibrations of the nerve fibers. He assumed that all nerves converge upon, and are coordinated by, a certain part of the brain. This part, whose location he admitted was unknown, he designated the "inner sense." He saw in it the medium by which the soul influenced the body. Bonnet's "psychology of fibers" had a considerable impact upon pre-Kantian German psychology.[40] In his *Palingénésie* he based a theory about the past and future conditions of living beings upon this psychological doctrine. Since man consisted essentially of body and soul, he concluded that the immortality of man, as an *être mixte*, applied to both body and soul. It could be assumed, therefore, that the preservation of a man's memory, which safeguarded his continuity in a future life, rested upon the fact that "the present brain contains within itself another [brain], which receives enduring impressions from the former and . . . is destined to develop in the life-to-come." In Bonnet's view, this "germ" was the proper seat of the human soul, the essence of the person, whereas the body was merely the "husk" or the "garment" eventually to be shed. The "germ," preformed for some future state of being, was imperishable.[41]

These ideas, which are elaborated in the first section of the *Palingénésie,* were offered as "mere conjectures or, at best, as having a high degree of probability."[42] Bonnet was at pains to make it clear that neither our intuitive nor our deliberative knowledge are capable of furnishing moral, let alone demonstrative, proof for a future life. Man's immortality cannot be inferred from the idea of the goodness and justice of God because we lack a precise knowledge of what these attributes signify in the case of the Supreme Being.[43] In view of the fact that man is incapable of obtaining the knowledge of his immortality by the natural light of reason, he could receive "this so greatly desirable certitude" only "at the hands of the Author of his being" Himself. Hence only a revelation could supply the "moral certitude" of it.[44] The criterion of a true revelation is the miracle. It provides "the credentials of the Messenger, and the purpose of the Messenger's mission is to make life and immortality evident."[45] Bonnet saw in the miracle no infringement of the laws of nature but some extraordinary event preordained by God and prearranged in the "special economy of the laws of nature."[46] Since the facticity of the miracle is authenticated by eyewitnesses, Bonnet devoted a whole chapter to a discussion of "testimony." He suggested that the reliability of witnesses depended upon their capability of observation and upon the degree of their honesty. He contrasted the miracles attributed to Jesus and the "subtle tricks" of an Alexander of Ponto and Apollonius of Tyana, concluding that the acts reported of Jesus were infinitely superior in respect of their number, duration, public nature, importance of purpose, magnitude of consequences, and strength of testimony.[47] Further chapters treat of the weight of literary sources, prophecies, and "some vague conjectures concerning the bliss of the future life."

The impression that Lavater received from reading Bonnet's work was overwhelming. He had already been enthusiastic about Bonnet's *Contemplation de la Nature* (1764–1765), as we learn from the first letter of his *Vistas of Eternity:* "Bonnet's *Contemplation of Nature* came into my possession by chance. The principal section about the highest perfection of mixed beings rekindled my imagination . . . I immediately wrote some dozens of rhymes expressing several of Bonnet's boldest ideas intermingled with a few similar ones; and at once I resolved to compose a song or an ode for philosophical Christians in the meter of Cramer's *Resurrection.*"[48] What caught Lavater's fancy in the *Palingénésie* was, of course, the christological second part. This book, it seemed to him, offered incontrovertible proof of the truth of Christianity. Here then, he thought, was the means whereby to convince a Moses Mendelssohn. He made haste to translate the relevant parts of the *Palingénésie*[49] into German and to add annotations of his own. In the preface he wrote:[50]

> When reading this excellent work, I wished a thousand times that all the world appreciate the truth and conclusiveness of the arguments for Christianity as much as they were evident to me. Never before, I thought, had logic been used so well for an examination of Christianity, and philosophy for an elucidation of some specific doctrines. Such a pure, straight, simple, firm logic of intellect and heart! A philosophy so manly, sublime, and intimately combined with the art of observation!

The stage was set for an appeal to Mendelssohn.

Lavater's Challenge and Mendelssohn's Reply

When Lavater's translation appeared, toward the end of August, 1769, a surprise was sprung upon the public. The book contained the following dedicatory epistle addressed "To Herr Moses Mendelssohn in Berlin":[1]

> Most venerable Sir! I know no better way of expressing the respect instilled into my mind by your excellent writings and your even more excellent character, which is that of an *Israelite in whom there is no guile*, nor a better way of repaying the pleasure I enjoyed some years ago in your amiable company than dedicating to you the best *philosophical* examination of *Christianity* known to me.
>
> I know your profound discernment, your steadfast love of truth, your incorruptible impartiality, your tender regard for philosophy in general and for Bonnet's writings in particular. I shall never forget the sweet modesty with which you look upon Christianity despite your remoteness from it; nor shall I forget the *philosophical* respect which, in one of the happiest hours of my life, you expressed for the *moral* character of its Founder; so unforgettable and, at the same time, so important to me that I dare to ask you, to ask and entreat you before the GOD of truth, your Creator and Father and mine: not merely pleading that you read this treatise with philosophical impartiality; for this you will certainly do without a request on my part: but to refute it publicly in case you find the *essential* arguments adduced in support of the facts of Christianity to be incorrect: in case, however, you find them correct, to do what prudence, love of truth, and honesty bid you do;—what *Socrates* would have done, had he read this treatise and found it irrefutable.
>
> May GOD grant that still more truth and virtue be spread through you; that you experience all the good which my whole heart wishes for you. Zürich, August 25, 1769. Johann Caspar Lavater.

Fresh from the press, an unbound copy of the edition containing this dedication (which was *not* included in the edition intended for sale in Switzerland) and a brief covering letter[2] were sent to Berlin on September 4, 1769, reaching Mendelssohn during the Jewish autumn festivals, which fell that year between October 2 and October 23. As it happened, he received at about the same time two Hebrew volumes by Rabbi Jacob Emden, sent to him with the renowned author's request that they be passed on to the Berlin Beth Hamidrash and some private address.

Mendelssohn informed Emden on October 27 that having regaled himself with the reading of the books during the festival of Tabernacles (October 16–23), he would like to raise a question concerning a point Emden had made in one of them, viz., his commentary on the Mishna.[3] Arguing in the authentic style of rabbinic discussion, he proposed a different solution of the relationship between two texts. On November 1, Emden expressed his joy at the learned letter which, he said, showed both a clear mind and a love of the study of the Tora for its own sake. Though he disagreed with Mendelssohn's proposed solution,[4] he subsequently published it, together with his reply, in volume two of his collection of responsa.[5]

It is certainly not purely accidental that Mendelssohn displayed such gusto in discussing a completely nonphilosophic talmudic theme with a champion of Jewish orthodoxy at the very moment that he received Lavater's challenge. One may even find some symbolic meaning in the fact that he chose as his topic of talmudic discourse one connected with the ritual of purification through immersion in water. It looks almost as if he wanted to mock Lavater's challenge to undergo baptism. How close he felt to Emden and how deeply he revered him may be gathered from the titles he bestowed upon him in the letter: "Prince of wisdom and of Tora," "Pillar of the defenses of the true religion," "Who proclaims to God's people the ways of God . . .", etc. Far from drawing Mendelssohn toward Christianity, Lavater had only reinforced his anchorage in Judaism.

On October 26, the day before Mendelssohn wrote his letter to Emden, Karl Gotthelf Lessing, who had been living in Berlin since 1765 and was close to Mendelssohn,[6] informed his brother in Hamburg of the situation:[7] "Moses has a strange encounter with Lavater, who was here some years ago. They [then] had a conversation on matters concerning religion. Harking back to it, the epic poet of the future life[8] takes the opportunity to challenge Moses either to refute Bonnet's arguments for the Christian religion or publicly to profess it. This printed challenge annoys that good man Moses not a little, and, as he told me, he is going to prove to Lavater with arguments taken from Bonnet's own that he is nothing but a Jew, and that the fanciful imaginings of a Polish Jew who, some years ago, pretended to be the Messiah[9] could be defended with the same reasons; he will, at the same time, make it clear to him that he is not going to enter into religious disputes. To me it seems that Moses could, once and for all, declare his creed in the clearest terms straight to the point. Is sound reason contraband in theology, I wonder? The enlightened theologians and the *Deutsche Bibliothek*[10] will not say so; modestly, they will, however, pass only their own reason and declare that one should make reason a captive not, to be sure, of faith but of *their* reason. If only the unenlightened as well as the enlightened remained unconcerned about the salvation of the souls of men like Moses! It has, however, fallen to their lot to chatter when others so much prefer to be silent."[11]

Lessing's brother was obviously well informed about Mendelssohn's reaction to the challenge presented to him. His letter tells us a number of things. We hear that Mendelssohn was not a little annoyed. Considering his ability to keep his emotions under control when talking to friends and foes alike, we may assume that he was, in fact, furious.[12] The next thing we learn is that Mendelssohn was prepared to refute Bonnet with his own arguments. In other words, his immediate reaction was to respond to Lavater's challenge by disproving Bonnet. The reference to the Polish Jew whose alleged miracles were those of an impostor and showed the worthlessness of this kind of proof indicates that the main argument against Bonnet's line of reasoning had already taken shape in Mendelssohn's mind as early as October 26, and probably before. While he was then eager to give battle, he was, at the same time, curbing his militancy; as he told Karl Lessing, he was not going to enter into religious disputes. The inconsistency of his statements reveals a state of uncertainty in his mind: should he publicly refute Bonnet or should he seek a way to avoid controversy? Lessing, we gather, urged him not to be shy but to declare his creed, viz. his adherence to "sound reason." He well understood that what Mendelssohn meant by the religion of reason was considered "contraband" by the Berlin theologians. Both he and Mendelssohn were aware of the charge of deism that his position had incurred, though neither the theologians nor the *Deutsche Bibliothek* would say anything of this sort publicly. Their concept of reason was, however, somewhat different from Mendelssohn's, who identified the essence of Judaism with natural religion.

The militant mood attested by Lessing dominates Mendelssohn's first rough draft of his reply to Lavater, which is fortunately still extant.[13] It commences with the words: "What moved him to take this step? Not friendship. Among all heretics known to him personally I cannot be his one and only friend. Not the best interests of his religion. A Christian who undergoes circumcision proves more for Judaism than a hundred Jews who submit to baptism prove for Christianity." There follows an outline of several observations and ideas that reappear, down to details of formulation, in Mendelssohn's *Letter [Schreiben] to Lavater* dated December 12, 1769. The conjecture that this undated draft was composed in March, 1770,[14] is untenable; writing the draft would have made no sense after the formal *Letter* of reply had already been in print for three months!

The draft was undoubtedly the expression of Mendelssohn's immediate reaction and provides eloquent testimony to his strong impulse to refute Bonnet: "Having been publicly challenged, I am under an obligation to declare myself publicly; but I call God as witness that I do so with the greatest reluctance and that off my own bat I would never have had the insolence to do so. I hate all religious disputes, especially those conducted before the eyes of the public. Experience teaches that they are useless.

They are productive more of hatred among men than of clarification."
His sense of outrage at Lavater's attempt to convert him is particularly
noticeable in this passage: "To be sure, the fact that this despised, scattered
little band [of Jews] still exists—Blessed be the ashes of that humane
theologian who was the first to declare that God was preserving us as
a visible proof of the truth of the Nazarene religion.[15] But for this lovely
brain wave, we would have been exterminated long ago, humanly speaking.
True, it is a strange fact that this visible proof fails to consider itself as
such. I confess to being unable to comprehend why the Nazarenes want
to convert us, since thereby they [would] annihilate the visible proof of
their faith." The bitter sarcasm of this remark reflects the deep indignation
he felt.[16]

While Mendelssohn still debated with himself which line to follow
in his reply, an unexpected event came to his aid. The hereditary prince
Karl Wilhelm Ferdinand of Brunswick, who had won glory as a general
in the Seven Years' War and was now devoting himself to the arts and
sciences, visited Berlin and invited Mendelssohn to see him at his palace.
The *Berlinische privilegirte Zeitung* of October 31, 1769, reported: "Monday,
October 30 the hereditary prince of Brunswick asked the celebrated scholar
Herr Moses Mendelssohn to visit him at his palace; he conversed with
him on philosophical and moral subjects and manifested particular grace
and respect toward him." Coming as it did on the heels of the Lavater
challenge, this show of princely favor met with particular attention.
Mendelssohn's friends were delighted. Johann Arnold Ebert (1723–1795),
who held a professorship in Brunswick, informed Lessing on November
3 that, as the prince himself had told him, he had "met our excellent
Moses Mendelssohn; and . . . was greatly pleased with this new acquaintance.
[Moses] promised to send [the prince] the new edition of the *Phaedon,*
and the . . . prince will then start a correspondence with him on the subject.
He is most anxious to bring him also here, if possible [viz. in addition
to Lessing, who had just been appointed librarian in Wolfenbüttel near
Brunswick]. Perhaps you could be of some help in this respect."[17] Lessing
replied on November 7: "There is nothing in the world by which the
prince could more effectively have ensured my wholehearted devotion
and reverence than by his desire to meet in Berlin my oldest and best
friend. One could not doubt that they would take a liking to one another,
and I would give the world to see a way whereby the prince could draw
him away from that place [viz. Berlin] to which, I know, he has such an
aversion."[18] A reference to the prince's "extraordinary grace" and his promise to enter into correspondence with Mendelssohn about his *Phaedon* occurs
also in Nicolai's letter to Herder dated November 4.[19]

To Mendelssohn personally the honor he received at that particular
moment in his life tended to assume a kind of providential significance.
It reinforced his stance as a philosopher and made him realize that he
had to resist the temptation to deliver a theological counterblast. The dislike

of religious disputation that he had felt all along now gained the upper hand, and his fighting mood, born of anger and resentment, gave way to a measure of philosophical calm. Nicolai's letter to Herder expressed the decision that Mendelssohn had reached: "You know that whoever wrote in Germany about religion until now did so in a certain theological tone. Moses is now compelled to speak differently, and this is sure to have some effect in the future. At the same time, he will put his reply in such a way as to obviate any necessity to answer further challenges."[20] He wrote in similar terms to Lessing on November 8: "Have you seen Lavater's strange challenge to Moses? He will reply; but presumably his answer will not please either Lavater or many another theologian."[21]

In deciding to refrain from theological controversy Mendelssohn abandoned the idea of refuting Bonnet's arguments. His "Counterreflections on Bonnet's *Palingénésie*," which he had jotted down on forty pages as a first draft,[22] were not to be elaborated and published. Sections of it were used by him in the *Epilogue* to Lavater's *Reply* to his *Letter;* in his correspondence with Bonnet; and later in his *Jerusalem*. However, the manuscript of this unpublished text was guarded by him almost like a secret document. On January 2, 1770, the prince of Brunswick wrote to him: "How much I wish I could see the Reflections on Bonnet! For nothing can be more important to one of our faith than to note how a philosopher living under the Law of Moses establishes historical proof concerning Moses—with which we agree—and how, at the same time, the historical proofs upon which the Christian faith rests are side-stepped.... I leave undecided whether I should wish that you be pressed to publish these Reflections." In a letter written about January, 1770, Mendelssohn replied: "I would not hesitate to send your Highness most obediently my Reflections on Bonnet, did they not still exist in my head rather than on paper. What I have written down consists of fragmentary reflections that have to shun the eyes of an enlightened connoisseur. I have good reason to hope that it will be unnecessary to elaborate them and to put them in proper order.—However, in obedience to your Highness's gracious command, I shall, in answer to the questions put to me, quote some relevant points from my Counterreflections, firmly trusting that your wisdom will prevent the candid confession I am making to you alone from coming to the notice of anybody who might be annoyed by it or who might misuse it."[23]

The "confession" contained in Mendelssohn's letter to the prince expresses, under two main heads, some of the ideas found in the extant manuscript of the "Counterreflections." Since Mendelssohn referred to this text when sending the prince a copy of his *Letter to Lavater* in December, 1769,[24] we have clear evidence that the manuscript was in existence by that time. Bearing further in mind that the crucial argument against resting one's faith on miracles and the specific reference to the miracles attributed recently to a Polish Jew were already mentioned in Karl Lessing's letter of October 26, it is reasonable to assume that the "Counterreflections" were written down even before December and shortly after the early first draft of the reply to Lavater in which Mendelssohn had envisaged a refutation of Bonnet. In view of the fact that the conversation with the prince took place on October 30, and the fact that Nicolai's letters to Herder and Lessing announced Mendelssohn's nontheological stance on November 4 and November 8 respectively, the dates of both the draft and the "Counter-reflections" have to be pushed back to the fortnight immediately following the receipt of Lavater's book. Mendelssohn had obviously lost no time coming to grips with the challenge facing him.[25] The manuscript of the "Counterreflections" was subsequently worked over several times. It contains no less than three hundred and fifty corrections, deletions, and marginal glosses.[26] In 1771, when his friend Elkan Herz asked to be shown the text, Mendelssohn declined on the grounds that it was legible to no one but himself, everything in it being "untidy and incoherent," and also because he was determined, as he clearly admitted, not to let it pass out of his hands.[27]

On December 24 Mendelssohn sent Lavater his printed *Letter*[28] in answer to the challenge, together with a covering note that admirably summed up the attitude he had taken: his letter was only "a kind of reply" to the challenge since it by-passed the alternative placed before him. He *could* not accept Christianity and, on the other hand, he *would* not refute Bonnet's arguments for it. All that was left for him to do was to state his reasons for not attempting a refutation. This should be enough to persuade Lavater to retract the step he had taken so rashly.[29] Having decided to assume a philosophical stance, Mendelssohn rightly felt that the historical question of the facticity of miracles lay altogether outside his province. Therefore, he shifted his ground to a discussion of his reasons for refraining from any kind of religious controversy. These reasons amounted to an affirmation of the principle of tolerance, and in this way he managed in the most skillful manner to launch a counterthrust against Lavater's patent lack of tolerance.

Before entering into his subject proper, however, Mendelssohn had something to say on the professed kindness of his adversary, which he did not doubt, but which strangely contrasted with his knowledge of the fact that a public challenge of the kind he presented was bound to be distasteful to a man of Mendelssohn's cast of mind. Besides, a promise had been given never to divulge in public the words spoken by Mendelssohn in the privacy of his home. He preferred, however, to impute a faulty memory to himself rather than a breach of promise to Lavater. In a subsequent passage Mendelssohn referred once more to the conversation of 1764: "My remoteness from your religion, which I indicated to you and your friends, has in no way diminished since, and my respect for the moral character of its founder?—You should not have passed over in silence the condition that I expressly added."[30]

Thus, Mendelssohn reproached Lavater on two counts, namely, for disclosing a conversation that he had promised to treat as confidential, and for giving a misleading account of what had been said on that occasion. This dual charge represented a severe indictment and, in effect, nullified the passage about Lavater's doubtless having been motivated by kindness. Echoing the opening question of his first draft ("What moved him to take this step? Not friendship"), he asked Lavater: "What, therefore, could have moved you to lead me, against my inclination, which was known to you, to a public arena that I so greatly desired never to have to enter?"[31]

His reluctance to engage in religious controversy, Mendelssohn explained, was due neither to fear nor to shyness but was founded upon his religion, his philosophy, and his station in civil life. His plea for tolerance took the form of an elaboration of these three viewpoints. In order to present his credentials as a spokesman for Judaism, he stated in the broadest possible terms that a prolonged scrutiny lasting over many years had convinced him of the truth of his religion. Had the result of his search for truth been different, it would have been "the most abject baseness" to withhold his allegiance from another religion held to be superior. On the other hand, were he indifferent to both Judaism and Christianity, or were he a despiser of all revelation, prudence would have indicated where some advantage was in store. Fear of his coreligionists would not have deterred him, since their secular power was too meager to frighten anyone. Nor would stubbornness, inertia, or attachment to habit have stood in his way, seeing that he had devoted the major part of his life to the pursuit of truth.[32]

The almost brutal realism with which Mendelssohn argued his conviction of the truth of Judaism was a sarcastic retort to Lavater's challenge to do what prudence, love of truth, and honesty bade him do. At the same time, he used the opportunity to remind the Christian world of the oppression and indignities suffered by his people. His occupation with philosophy and belles-lettres, he declared, could have had no other purpose than the examination of his religion: "In the situation in which I found myself I could not expect the least temporal advantage from learned pursuits. I knew full well that for me no prosperity of a wordly nature was to be found on that road. And pleasure?—Oh! my esteemed friend of humanity! The station assigned to my coreligionists in civil life is so remote from all free exercise of mental strength that one, surely, does not increase contentedness by learning to see the rights of man in true perspective."

Summing up this *confessio Judaica*, Mendelssohn declared that having convinced himself of the truth of Judaism he had quietly continued on his path. He felt that he had the right to do so without being answerable to the world for his innermost convictions. He could not deny, he added in true Enlightenment style, that he had, in fact, noticed in his religion certain "man-made additions [viz. to "divine," i.e. natural religion] and abuses [viz. corruptions of natural law] that, alas!, obscure its splendor by far too much." However, the disfigurement of the essential character of natural religion was not peculiar to Judaism: "Which friend of the truth could boast of having found his religion free from harmful man-made

statutes? We all know this poisoning breath of hypocrisy and superstition."
Yet of the "essential core" of his religion he declared himself to be as
firmly assured as Lavater or Bonnet were of theirs. "I herewith testify
before the God of truth . . . that I shall adhere to my principles so long
as my entire soul does not assume a different nature."[33] The last clause
was certainly not intended as a *reservatio mentalis* but clearly meant to rule
out any possibility of a change of mind. A parallel passage in his "Counterreflections"[34] is even more explicit. There he testified before God that
his entire soul would have to be changed, should he at any time change
his mind in this respect, for the dogmas of Christianity contradicted everything taught by sound reason and holy script. It is in this context that
the *Letter* reproached Lavater for having omitted to mention the conditional
character of Mendelssohn's respect for Jesus, and reaffirmed, at the same
time, that his remoteness from Christianity had in no way diminished since
the time of their conversation. The first draft, it may be noted, contains
the sentence: "My remoteness from the Christian religion has not
diminished since, and so long as God allows me the use of my reason,
it cannot diminish."[35] The *Letter* concludes this section with the statement:
"One has to put a stop to certain inquiries sometime, if one wishes to
advance. I may say that in regard to religion I did this already some years
ago. I read, compared, reflected, and took sides."

Having presented himself as a Jew, Mendelssohn could now turn to
a discussion of his reasons for not attacking Bonnet's arguments. First,
however, he had a word to say about his preference for silence even insofar
as the defense of Judaism was concerned. The contempt in which the
Jew was held was best refuted by virtue, not by polemical tracts, and it
was beneath his dignity to enter into arguments with any "expert or half-
expert of rabbinics" who drew his knowledge of the subject from "trashy
volumes neither read by, nor known to, any sensible Jew." This blast was
directed against such notoriously anti-Semitic works as Johann Andreas
Eisenmenger's *Entdecktes Judentum* (1711), Johann Christoph Wagenseil's
Tela ignea satanae (1681), and others of a similar nature. That ground
being cleared, Mendelssohn proceeded to show that his reluctance to disprove Bonnet's arguments for Christianity was warranted, in the first place,
by his religious principles. "According to the principles of my religion
I am not permitted to seek to convert someone not born under our Law."
Since Judaism was averse to missionary activity, it discouraged, by implication, any attempt to show somebody not of the Jewish faith to be mistaken
in arguing the truth of his religion. Such an attempt might be construed
as an oblique effort at conversion.

Insofar as Mendelssohn described Judaism as being free from conversionist zeal he unquestionably had rabbinic law on his side; he could quote
Maimonides' codification of the talmudic ruling on the matter. Insofor
as desisting from any refutation of arguments was concerned, he could
not point to any explicit law. Here he had to rely on his own interpretation

of the well-known rabbinic dictum that assigns to the "righteous" or "pious" of the Gentiles a share in the world-to-come. Maimonides had codified this statement and thus made it the accepted Jewish doctrine, but he had defined the term "the pious of the Gentiles" as applying to those who observed the "seven laws given to the sons of Noah" and did so from obedience to God's command as expressed in the Tora; he had clearly stipulated that those who kept the seven Noachian laws merely on rational grounds, (namely, as the basic ethical precepts following from human reasoning) could be called "wise" but not "pious" and were, therefore, not entitled to the bliss of the hereafter. A corrupt version of the Maimonides text denied to this category of Gentiles even the character of "wise" men. Spinoza, who knew only the corrupt text, concluded from it that according to Jewish doctrine "true beliefs and a true principle of life make no contribution to blessedness so long as men embrace them by the light of nature alone and not as precepts revealed to Moses by prophetic insight."[36]

Mendelssohn, too, knew the Maimonides passage only in its corrupt version, but the conclusion he drew from it was different from Spinoza's. He declared the limitation of the meaning of the term "pious" to those who observed the Noachian laws as revealed laws to be devoid of validity, since the rabbinic source that constituted Maimonides' authority contained no such rider. According to it, the pious of all nations were assured of their portion in the next world; they all were *Kinder der ewigen Seligkeit*. He quoted Maimonides' own unqualified avowal of this doctrine, as expressed in his responsum to Hasday Ha-Levi,[37] as well as some other authorities including "Rabbi Jacob Hirschel, one of the most learned rabbis of our time [who] deals with this subject extensively in several of his writings."[38] Jacob Hirschel was none other than Jacob Emden. It is not quite clear to which of his writings Mendelssohn referred.[39] He asked Emden repeatedly for a statement of his view concerning the validity of Maimonides' ruling.[40] When Emden eventually replied in November, 1773, long after the Lavater controversy, he justified Maimonides' verdict as being supported by a closer scrutiny of the sources.[41] This reply did not please Mendelssohn, but neither did it change his opinion. Had he foreseen Emden's vindication of the Maimonides passage, he would not have included him among the authorities who spoke in favor of the more tolerant view. As he saw it, and stated in his reply to Lavater, the Noachian laws, which he also termed "the religion of the Patriarchs," are identical with the essence of natural law. In advocating this equation, he followed the theory laid down by John Selden in his *De jure naturali et gentium juxta disciplinam Ebraeorum libri VII* (1640).[42]

What compelled Mendelssohn to oppose Maimonides' idea of restricted tolerance is clearly stated in his letter to Jacob Emden of October 26, 1773: "Should all inhabitants of the earth except ourselves be doomed to perdition unless they believed in the Tora, which was given as an inheritance to the congregation of Jacob alone; especially as it [viz. the Noachian

law] is something not even expressly written down in the Tora but is transmitted only through the tradition of the chosen people or exegetically
derived by its sages from the words of the Tora? ... What, then, shall
the nations do who are not recipients of the light of the Tora and who
received no tradition except from untrustworthy and unreliable ancestors?
Does God, then, treat his creatures in the way of a tyrant, annihilating
them and blotting out their names [by denying them a share in the world-
to-come], though they committed no injustice?"[43] Excluding the righteous
of the Gentiles from salvation would be tantamount to injustice on God's
part. Eternal happiness, in Mendelssohn's view, was a philosophical, not
a theological concept. It was a corollary of his notion of the vocation of
man as a destiny bound up with his rational nature. In the *Phaedon* he
had deliberately argued the case for immortality in the name of a pagan,
Socrates, in order to place the concept outside the boundaries of
revelation.[44] The letter to Emden stresses another aspect intimately linked
with his universalism, namely that of God's justice. The full consequences
of his basic outlook are drawn in the reply to Lavater. Missionary activity
is alien to Judaism because man's eternal happiness does not require his
conversion to a revealed religion. "Should a Confucius or Solon happen
to be a contemporary of mine, I could love and admire that great man,
according to the principles of my religion, without hitting upon the ridiculous idea of wanting to convert a Confucius or Solon. Convert? To what?
Since he does not belong to the congregation of Jacob, my religious laws
are not obligatory upon him, and about doctrines we shall soon come
to terms with each other. Whether I believed that he could attain to eternal
happiness?—Oh! It seems to me that one who, in this life, leads men to
virtue cannot be damned in the next."[45]

In pointing out the absurdity of wanting to convert a Confucius and
in expressing the view that virtue was pleasing to God wherever it was
found, Mendelssohn was not saying anything new or startling. The educated
world of Europe had been nurtured on anticlerical ideas of this sort for
almost a hundred years as the result of the widening of horizons brought
about by, among other things, the numerous travel reports about the civiliza-
tions of the Far East. François de La Mothe Le Vayer (1588–1672) is said
to have been restrained only with difficulty from exclaiming: "Sancte Con-
fuci, ora pro nobis!"[46] In his *Émile, ou de l'Éducation* (1762), Rousseau had
advocated similar ideas. His famous chapter entitled "La Profession de
foi du vicaire savoyard" made the point that two-thirds of mankind were
neither Jews, Christians, nor Muslims, and had never even heard of Moses,
Jesus, or Mohammed; that we were led to absurdities by pride and the
spirit of persecution in believing that we possessed a greater share of reason
than the rest of mankind: "I call to witness that God of peace whom I
adore, ... that my researches have always been sincere; but seeing that
they were and always must be unsuccessful, and that I was launched out

into a boundless ocean of perplexity, I returned the way I came, and confined my creed within the limits of my first notion. I could never believe that God required me, under pain of eternal damnation, to be so very learned; and, therefore, I shut up all my books. The book of nature lies open to every eye. It is from this sublime and wonderful volume that I learn to serve and adore its Divine Author."[47]

In his profession of faith, Mendelssohn echoes these very sentiments. Traces of Rousseau's fervent calling upon God as witness are discernible in his *Letter*. They are even more obvious in the "Counterreflections." In saying there, "I thank God every day that He did not make my eternal happiness dependent upon exegetical inquiries,"[48] he obviously rephrased Rousseau's sentence about not having to be so very learned in the scriptures in order to escape eternal damnation. What was new and startling about Mendelssohn's avowal of tolerance was its presentation as the doctrine of Judaism. The *Letter* to Lavater is sufficiently explicit in contrasting Christian missionary zeal and Jewish restraint: "We are not to send missions to the Indies or to Greenland to preach our religion to these distant nations."[49] The "Counterreflections" are even more outspoken: "Why should both Indies have to wait until it pleases the Europeans to send them some clerics [*Pfaffen*] who bring them the good news without which they cannot live either virtuously or happily in the hereafter? To bring them news that, in their circumstances and way of thinking, they can neither understand nor put to use."[50] "The divine religion in which I was born teaches me that all nations of the earth attain to eternal felicity if they live by the laws of reason, i.e. practice virtue, and that God, for special reasons, imposed certain special duties . . . upon my nation exclusively."[51]

In thus describing Judaism as a religion of tolerance, Mendelssohn was sure to strike a note consonant with the sentiments of many of his contemporaries. But he was equally certain to antagonize those opposed to such broad tolerance. He referred in the *Letter* to the case of Jean François Marmontel (1723–1799), whose philosophical novel *Bélisaire* (1767) had just been condemned by the Sorbonne. His own advocacy of tolerance, Mendelssohn assured his readers, would have nothing to fear from a "venerable collegium" of rabbis objecting to his view. Nothing could have illustrated better the point he was trying to make than this reference to a case that happened just then to have aroused widespread discussion. The censure of Marmontel's successful novel by the Sorbonne concerned four topics: the eternal happiness of pagans, the relation of revealed to natural religion, universal tolerance, and the nature and certainty of Christianity. Marmontel had depicted the celestial "court" of God as hospitable to some of the Roman emperors. He had not felt he was offending God by expecting to find in the hereafter men who had been the delight of this world, and he refused to believe that an eternal gulf separated his Christian soul from the souls of Aristides, Cato, and Marcus Aurelius.

Only a religion that preached a benign God was a true religion, and doctrines conflicting with the notion of the goodness of God had no place in the true religion.[52]

All this was after Mendelssohn's own heart, and he did not hesitate to speak, in the *Letter*, of "honest Marmontel."[53] His friend Johann August Eberhard was to publish, in 1772, a spirited defense of Marmontel's belief in the future happiness even of pagans, trying to explain how the contrary doctrine had crept into the church and how certain theologians from Jerome down to the Quakers, Cambridge Platonists, and Arminians had opposed it. As a theologian of the Enlightenment, Eberhard contended that the exclusion of the multitude of pagans from eternal bliss could not be reconciled with the wisdom and justice of God. He also attacked the dogma of eternal punishment in hell on the same grounds. His work[54] was certainly inspired by Mendelssohn.[55] It met with severe criticism by Johann Christian Ernesti, the biblical scholar, on the one hand, and by Lessing on the other. Ernesti found that Eberhard had ignored the scriptural sources. As an exegete, he had little sympathy for imputing eighteenth-century universalism to church doctrine, which was founded on the Bible.[56] Lessing took issue with the neologistic tendency of the book in his famous essay *Leibniz on Eternal Punishment* (1773).[57]

In unequivocally siding with Marmontel, then, Mendelssohn espoused a cause that was by no means applauded by all and sundry. He was convinced, however, that his plea for tolerance was both timely and in accord with the teachings of Judaism. He concluded his outline of the Jewish position with the often-quoted statement: "I have the good fortune of having for a friend many an excellent man who is not of my faith. We sincerely love each other, though we suspect that in matters of religion we hold totally different opinions. I enjoy the pleasure of their company, which benefits and delights me. Never did my heart secretly whisper to me: What a pity that such a lovely soul is lost! One who believes that there is no salvation outside his church is bound to heave a sigh like this very often."[58] The contrast between his liberalism and Lavater's pietism could not have been more strikingly expressed.

Mendelssohn's next task was to explain on what grounds his philosophy was opposed to all religious controversy. Was it not the duty of a philosopher to disprove erroneous opinions, and was he not obliged, therefore, to refute Bonnet's proofs for Christianity, if he considered them inconclusive? His answer to these questions testifies to an extraordinary degree of candor: Not all "prejudices" were equally harmful. Those that had a pernicious influence on the state of morals in a given society had to be attacked. Prejudices of this kind were fanaticism, hatred, the spirit of persecution on the one hand, and levity, luxury, and immoral freethinking on the other. But prejudices and doctrinal errors that did not give rise to moral corruption of the kind described could be left in peace. Though theoret-

wrong, they were harmless in practice. Some of these "prejudices" had to be "tolerated" as part and parcel of a nation's moral fabric. "To contest such doctrines publicly because we regard them to be prejudices is the same thing as undermining, without proper safeguards, the foundation of a building in order to ascertain whether it is firm and secure. One who cares more about the welfare of men than about his own glory will hesitate to express his view about prejudices of this kind ... in order not to overthrow a principle of morality that he considers doubtful, before his fellow-men have accepted the truth that he would like to put in its place."[59] So long as the truth was not known or generally recognized as such, one had to look upon prejudices that happened to be beneficial in their effects upon the population as being "almost holy" to every friend of virtue. One was all the more obliged to feel that way, "if the nation that entertains such erroneous beliefs—erroneous, that is, in our judg-ment—has otherwise earned our respect because of its virtue and wisdom, and contains many great men who deserve to be called benefactors of the human race.... Who is to have the audacity to disregard the excellent qualities of such an exalted nation and attack it at a point where he believes himself to have discovered its weakness?"[60]

Mendelssohn had expressed the same notion in his *Phaedon,* when describing Socrates' attitude toward Greek popular religion,[61] and it remained his guiding principle throughout his life. He reaffirmed it in his essay *On the Question: What Does Enlightenment Mean?* (1784),[62] and he defended it against the strictures of his friend August Hennings, who had criticized his view.[63] Mendelssohn prized morality above theoretical truth. The philosophical reason offered by him for not wanting to ex-pose the weaknesses of Bonnet's proofs was not, therefore, an ad hoc argument but expressed a firmly held and repeatedly expressed principle. Even so, one is struck by the frank and fearless manner in which he re-ferred to the dogmas of Christianity as "prejudices" that had to be "toler-ated" because the morality of the nation was largely based on religious foundations.

The third reason for his avoidance of religious controversy, Mendels-sohn pointed out, was his position in civil life. His situation was a rather delicate one. He was "a member of an oppressed people that had to implore the ruling nation for patronage and protection, which it did not receive everywhere, and which was nowhere without restrictions." The "tolerable conditions" granted to his coreligionists in Prussia, particularly the freedom of religion, were no mean boon. It would betray a lack of gratitude were he to attack the Christian religion.[64]

Had Mendelssohn concluded his *Letter* at this point, he doubtless would have saved himself much unnecessary trouble. He added, however, some observations on Bonnet's *Palingénésie* that he later regretted. He had taken it for granted that Lavater had obtained Bonnet's consent before dedicating the translation of part of his work to him.[65] This assumption, which proved to be mistaken, had caused Mendelssohn to believe that Bonnet, too, had considered his arguments for the truth of Christianity to be sufficiently strong to convince Mendelssohn. Since Bonnet was a philosopher of some importance in Mendelssohn's view, his presumed partnership with Lavater could not simply be passed over in complete silence. Here, clearly, one philosopher stood against another. While Lavater's attack had no bearing on Mendelssohn as a philosopher—Lavater was, after all, known as a theologian and "enthusiast"—Bonnet's authority did carry some weight, and there was a prima facie case, Mendelssohn must have felt, for replying, especially in view of the fact that no counterarguments were to be delivered. "I have read the treatise by Bonnet, which you translated, attentively. Whether I have been convinced is obviously no longer a question.... I must, however, confess that it did not seem to me as important a defense of the Christian religion as you think it to be. From other works I know Herr Bonnet as an excellent author, but I have read many a defense of the same religion by our German fellow countrymen—leaving the English aside—that seemed to me much more profound and philosophical than this particular one by Bonnet, which you recommend to me for the sake of my conversion. If I am not mistaken, the philosophical hypotheses of this writer stem largely from German soil, and the author of the *Essai de Psychologie*,[66] whom Herr Bonnet follows so faithfully, owes nearly everything to German philosophers. Where philosophical principles are concerned, a German rarely has to borrow from his neighbors."[67] Far from being impressed by Bonnet's treatise, Mendelssohn criticized its lack of logical conclusiveness in its attempt to apply philosophical concepts to religion. He would not put it beyond his own powers, he declared, to demonstrate the truth of *any* religion by the very same arguments that had been advanced in the *Palingénésie*. Bonnet had obviously written this book not with the intention of converting non-Christians but merely to confirm convinced Christians in their faith.

So far the *Letter* had avoided open polemic and had kept in check the sense of indignation that had been Mendelssohn's initial reaction and had continued to simmer beneath the surface. However, the concluding paragraph did strike a sterner note: "I have given you the reasons that prompt my strong desire never to have to enter into arguments about matters of religion. I have also indicated to you my firm belief that I am able to offer arguments in opposition to Bonnet's treatise. If pressed, I shall have to disregard my hesitancy and shall have the resolve to make publicly known in Counterreflections what I think about Herr Bonnet's treatise and the cause it pleads." He hoped, he said, that Lavater would spare him the necessity of taking such a step and would permit him to return to his "peaceful condition."[68] The threat was clearly intended to impress Lavater with the advisability of withdrawing his challenge. All that Mendelssohn desired was a return to the peace of mind he had enjoyed before.

First Reactions and Behind-the-Scene Activities; *Lavater's* Reply *and Mendelssohn's* Epilogue

Before sending his *Letter* to the press, Mendelssohn asked the Berlin consistory whether he should submit the manuscript to one of its councillors or to the council as a whole. He took this precautionary step from fear lest the censor stop publication of his reply. He received the answer: "Herr Mendelssohn may print his writings without submitting them in part or in toto to the consistory, since one trusts his wisdom and modesty to write nothing likely to give public offense."[1] On December 24, 1769, the printed *Letter* was sent to Lavater. On January 3, 1770, Mendelssohn received a letter from Lavater that had been written on December 26.[2] Had this letter arrived before Mendelssohn took action, the course of events might have been different.

Lavater informed him that Bonnet and his friends in Berlin considered his challenge an "indiscreet" step, that he was now waiting for a "hint" from Mendelssohn whether and how he might remedy his mistake, and that he would be content if Mendelssohn were merely to consider Bonnet's arguments worthy of an inquiry. The short note concluded with these words: "Will you forgive me—what? That I love you, highly esteem you, and sincerely wish for you to be happy in this world and the next; forgive me if I took the wrong path to express this to you." The unrelenting conversionist zeal manifested at the end of the letter must have repelled Mendelssohn. On the other hand, Lavater's readiness to withdraw the public challenge was pleasant news. So was the report about Bonnet's disapproval. Bonnet himself later informed Mendelssohn that he had notified Lavater of his displeasure as early as September 26 and October 24.[3] It was improper, he had told Lavater, to dedicate to a Jew a book intended for Christians only, and to suggest to him the prickly alternative of either refuting the book or converting to Christianity; to expose him, moreover, to the censure of his fellow Jews by mentioning the respect he had expressed for the founder of Christianity. He had, at the same time, betrayed a certain fear of getting involved in a literary feud with Mendelssohn. He had reproached Lavater for challenging the Jewish philosopher to turn against him; "c'etoit le provoquer au combat contre moi." After the publication of Mendelssohn's *Letter,* Bonnet wrote to Lavater in a particularly severe tone: the *Letter* was anything but a *billet-doux,* love letter, for him, yet it had pleased him as much as Lavater's dedicatory epistle had displeased him; he admired in Mendelssohn's *Letter* the "wisdom, moderation, and capability of the famous son of Abraham."[4]

Mendelssohn's *Letter to Lavater* had been eagerly awaited by the general public and was widely discussed. "The whole fashionable world in Berlin, and even people who are otherwise hardly interested in the quarrels of scholars and literati in general," found the controversy an exciting topic for conversation, as Friedrich Lüdke informed Lavater on January 23.[5] The degree of public interest may be gauged from the fact that a new edition of Lavater's challenge and Mendelssohn's reply was published and republished in 1770 "at the expense of good friends" whose identity remains undisclosed.[6] The humorous tone of the preface suggests that some people were more amused than alarmed by the affair. The preface reads:

> Mendelssohn's *Letter* is by now in almost everybody's hands, while many people do not know the *Epistle* which provoked it. Here both make their appearance. Who will thereby be the loser, Lavater or Mendelssohn?—This question may be decided by the public which alone is to gain by comparing these two writers. A great many people wished to have these two letters together. This wish we want to satisfy. We have no other aims. Mendelssohn did not want to convert us to Judaism, for he has no conversionist zeal; and Lavater had no intention of making us angry with Mendelssohn, for he shows that he loves him dearly. We remained, therefore, indifferent, which is not difficult in the case of polemical writings of such modesty and calm. Besides, who will blame us if we just now remember Gellert's moral teaching.[7]

> So streiten unstudierte Velten
> Um Sachen, die sie nicht verstehn,
> Und endigen den Streit mit Schelten.
> Die Thoren sollten erst zu den gelehrten Velten
> Und Kunzen in die Schule gehn!
> Die streiten dialektisch schön,
> Und ohne Wortkrieg, ohne Schelten,
> Um Dinge, die sie ganz verstehn,
> Und fehlen ihres Weges selten,
> Weil sie den Weg der Schulen gehn;
> Denn da lässt sich kein Irrlicht sehn.

> Thus unlettered Valentines quarrel
> About things they do not understand,
> And finish the quarrel with scolding.
> The fools should first learn from
> The literate Valentines and Konrads!
> They quarrel beautifully in dialectic order,
> Without verbal squabbles, without scolding,
> About things they fully comprehend,
> Rarely losing their way,
> Because they follow the way
> of the schools;
> And there no *ignis fatuus* can be seen.

Gellert's poem did not exactly fit the case, since Velt and Kunz, alias Lavater and Mendelssohn, did not dialectically debate an issue. What Mendelssohn had tried to do was to avoid a debate. Nor were all observers of the scene as impartial as the editor of the two letters. Opinions *were* divided. Lavater's pietistic enthusiasm and the clumsiness of his attack raised many an eyebrow. "Nothing antagonizes me more," wrote Georg Christoph Lichtenberg, the Göttingen physicist, astronomer, and satirist, "than to see a young, importunate, injudicious babbler like Lavater upset the peace of mind of a thinker like Mendelssohn in order to gain heaven. It is better to serve the world with one's hands and head, as Mendelssohn does, than to assail it with volumes full of enthusiasm.... One Mendelssohn is worth more than a hundred Lavaters."[8] Johann David Michaelis, whom Mendelssohn might least have expected to be on his side, sent him on January 27 Part One of his *Mosaisches Recht* (1770) with a covering letter that finished with these words: "With enduring respect, which was further enhanced recently by your *Letter* to the far too hasty Herr Lavater, I remain, Sir, your most obedient servant Michaelis."[9] Another Göttingen scholar, the philologist and mythologist Christian Gottlob Heyne, thanked Nicolai for sending him Mendelssohn's *Letter,* saying: "How the moderation, dignity, and fitness with which Mendelssohn's *Letter* expresses itself puts to shame the hasty and enthusiastic Lavater!"[10] The poet Ramler, who was shown a copy of the *Letter* by Mendelssohn himself prior to its publication, wrote to Johann George Scheffner in Königsberg: "Moses is greatly embarrassed. Just now, however, he showed me a letter in reply... which is full of gentleness and sound reason. It has the effect that one loves the tolerant Jew and denies respect, to say the least, to any intolerant zealot for religion."[11] Another of Scheffner's friends, Johann Gotthelf Lindner, was less sympathetic to Mendelssohn, though he disapproved of Lavater. On January 27 he wrote to Scheffner: "Lavater's proselytizing zeal with which he tries to convert the crafty Moses Mendelssohn... arouses attention." And on March 3: "Lavater is an enthusiast, and Mendelssohn is a crafty Jew."[12] Goethe, the "great pagan," who was himself a target of Lavater's missionary zeal, recalled in *Dichtung und Wahrheit* how annoyed he was with the "vehement importunity" with which Lavater went for him as well as Mendelssohn and others in order to make them into Christians of his own type.[13]

Herder, too, deplored Lavater's action. In reply to the letter that Nicolai sent him on November 4, 1769,[14] he had written a letter from Paris on November 30 in which he described Lavater as "an enthusiast and often deluded" in spite of "all his honesty and zeal."[15] In a personal letter to Mendelssohn, dated December 1, he wrote: "And Lavater has sent you a *défi* concerning his religion and yours? However, Sir, if a third party, which does not wish to be an umpire, be permitted to make a request concerning your reply, it is this: that you reply not merely to Bonnet, whom, judging from certain Christian utterances in his physical writings, I cannot credit with entertaining the very clearest notions on the subject; but that you face the issue as such and tell us not merely why you cannot become a Christian but *why you remain a Jew*. A philosophical refutation of an argument for the Christian religion (which, by the way, is unknown to me) is only half the work: a philosophical proof for the truth of the Jewish religion would be something more, and I would like to see it not as an axiomatic presupposition but to see it demonstrated in the first place or in the end."[16] This request reached Mendelssohn too late to be given due consideration. It is more than doubtful that it would have been heeded even if it had been received earlier, for Mendelssohn had resolved neither to refute Bonnet nor to offer proofs for Judaism. Herder could hardly have been satisfied with his performance.

Hamann must have found himself in a similar position. On January 27, he wrote to Nicolai: "Our German Phaedon [i.e. Mendelssohn] seems to have forgotten me completely. The news about his *Letter to Lavater* made me sleepless for half a night, like Pilate's wife. I don't know why. I could not rest until I had set eye on Lavater's dedication. The German Bonnet I could not stand; the French one pleases me better. Lavater himself is like a Phaëton who is so much absorbed in the flight of his imagination that he seems to lose the tramontane.[17] Here we might have to wait a few more mail-days before we receive Herr Mendelssohn's *Letter*.—In such a case, a sense of embarrassment on both sides appears to be inevitable, and a sincere declaration seems to me as impossible as it is necessary and proper in my view."[18]

Like Herder, Hamann obviously would have welcomed a full "declaration" of the philosophical reasons for Mendelssohn's loyalty to Judaism. Why he was skeptical about Mendelssohn's willingness to offer such a "sincere declaration," is somewhat obscure. Did he, like Rousseau, believe that fear of persecution prevented the Jews from candidly expressing their views on Christianity? The Savoyard Vicar had declared: "Those among us, also, who have an opportunity to converse with the Jews, have but little advantage. These unhappy people know that they are at our mercy.... What, therefore, can they venture to say to us, without running the risk of incurring the charge of blasphemy?... Among the doctors of the Sorbonne it is as clear as daylight that the predictions concerning the Messiah relate to Jesus Christ. Among the rabbis in Amsterdam it is just as evident that they have no relation whatever to him. I shall never believe that I have acquired a sufficient acquaintance with the arguments of the Jews, till they compose a free and independent state, and have their schools and universities, where they may talk and dispute with freedom and impunity. Till then we can never really know what arguments they have to offer."[19]

Among the theologians, Resewitz regretted Lavater's action for reasons of his own: "What do I think of Lavater's quarrel with Herr Moses?", he wrote Nicolai on March 10, 1770, from Copenhagen. "I was not happy with his challenge, and I told him so myself. In such a case, it becomes a matter of attack and defense, not of conviction. Herr Lavater does not know either that this is not the way to win Herr Mendelssohn over. He has absorbed much that has its origin in Christianity; his philosophical inquiries and writings benefit rather than harm our religion; his mind and heart are, moreover, influenced by it unknowingly. If now, as a result of a formal challenge, this unperceived influence is upset, and if his indifference to the Christian religion, or what he regards as such, is changed into an aversion . . . and, in the end, the purpose is not achieved, I see no sense in attempting such a conversion. Importunity is, altogether, not the way to make any truth acceptable; and Herr Mendelssohn is, perhaps, the last person to be won over in this fashion."[20]

The attitude of the Berlin theologians of the Enlightenment expressed itself in behind-the-scene activities in connection with Lavater's *Reply*. It had been Mendelssohn's hope that his *Letter* would settle the matter in a way that would enable Lavater to withdraw his challenge. A letter by Nicolai to Lessing, written on January 13, 1770, reflected this expectation: "Everybody, even all local theologians, disapproves of Lavater's step. Bonnet too wrote Lavater that this step was indiscreet. You have presumably read Moses' *Letter to Lavater*. It may now be assumed that Lavater will leave our Moses in peace. The theologians themselves would like to see this happen. A controversy might place some theological points in too glaring a light, and, truly speaking, Moses would be most reluctant to have a go at it."[21]

This hope was premature, however. As a result of Mendelssohn's *Letter*, Lavater's position stiffened. When Bonnet reprimanded him anew on January 12,[22] he admitted that the dedication had been indiscreet in certain respects, but he rejected the charge of injudiciousness. From now on, he declared, the matter would be exclusively his own affair. He was not going to deny either the truth or his conviction, though he would admit his mistake in a free and easy manner. He regretted his step only because of Bonnet, not for his own or Mendelssohn's sake.[23] Lavater was resolved, it appears, not to let the matter rest where Mendelssohn had left it. In his view, it would seem, the *Letter* called for an answer on two counts: it had accused him of breach of promise, and it had put Judaism in such a favorable light that he had to straighten out the record. During the latter half of January he informed Spalding that his *Reply* was ready.[24] Spalding passed this piece of news on to Lüdke, who wrote to Lavater warning him against taking yet another rash step. The time, he pointed out, was not yet ripe for discussions of this kind. Would Mendelssohn not want to know which brand of Christianity he was supposed to declare himself about? Would he not ask: Is it your Lutheran or your Heidelberg catechism? Is it your Augsburg or your Helvetian confession?

There was, Lüdke suggested, a further reason to move slowly. "Purified Christianity" *(geläutertes Christentum)* and the "true religion of Israel" were, perhaps, not too far apart, and a conversation with Mendelssohn in private might soon lead to some agreement.[25] Mendelssohn had himself used the term "purified" in his "Counterreflections," when discussing the unitarian creed which, as he put it, was much closer to Judaism than to Christianity.

Having firmly rejected the trinitarian concept of the Athanasian creed, he had written: "I know, however, that several teachers of high repute, and some congregations too, as I am told, deviate from this doctrine.... These pride themselves on having purified [*gereiniget*] the religion of the Christians of erroneous views and on having led it back to its pristine simplicity, which is said to have nearly agreed with natural religion."[26]

Mendelssohn was certainly not prepared to let Unitarianism replace Judaism. To him, this purified form of Christianity was but a welcome sign that enlightened Christians were moving in the direction of Judaism. In reverse, Lüdke and his friends, particularly Spalding, saw in it some possibility of attracting enlightened Jews like Mendelssohn to Christianity. They possibly knew that Mendelssohn regarded Unitarianism as akin to the Jewish religion, and they considered it feasible to bring about a rapprochement between the two faiths via Unitarianism. Hence their plan to entice Mendelssohn to engage in private talks rather than in public debate. They realized, at the same time, that "purified Christianity," as they understood it, was too hazy a concept to be discussed in the full glare of publicity, and that it might be embarrassing to them were Mendelssohn, upon further provocation, to demand a clear definition of it. Nicolai hit the nail on the head when he wrote to Lessing that the theologians would prefer that Lavater leave Mendelssohn in peace in order to prevent a theological debate in public. Mendelssohn's threat to publish his "Counterreflections" in case of further pressure seems to have frightened them.

To Lavater's conciliatory note of December 26 Mendelssohn replied on February 9. The letter expressed regret at his having attacked Bonnet. Had he known that Bonnet was innocent of the dedication and that his book was not aimed at the conversion of Jews, he would have worded certain passages in his *Letter* differently. He assured Lavater that the "Counterreflections" had not been sent to the printer, as some reviewer had falsely alleged, and concluded with an earnest appeal for an end to the controversy: "Believe me, Sir, it does not befit either of us to become the sport of hucksters dealing in anecdotes, nor, through the publication of polemical tracts, to amuse the idlers among the public; to annoy the simple-hearted, and to give a malicious kind of joy to the enemies of all that is good. It is my sincere view and my heart's wish that we try as best as we can to escape from the trap into which we have fallen. First, let us wait till the truths we hold in common are sufficiently spread; then only, let us continue, with even greater zeal, the debate on the points that divide us."[27] How hopeful Mendelssohn was that his appeal would be heeded is apparent from a letter written a few days later, on February 13, by his friend Krickende to Scheffner: "About his involvement with Lavater he speaks quite gently, and he hopes that the fairness of the man will cause him to withdraw his *défi*. 'I declare on this occasion,' he added, 'that I am a Jew and intend to remain a Jew. To you, who have known me so long as a Jew, and as a peaceable Jew for that matter, my *Letter to Lavater* cannot contain anything new.' "[28]

Lavater answered Lüdke's letter on February 10, before Mendelssohn's reached him. He informed his friend that the manuscript of the *Reply* was on its way to Berlin via Leipzig, where Zollikofer[29] would check it. His friends' fears would be allayed, he was sure, once they saw what he had written. He had exercised the greatest care, but he wanted Lüdke to "delete, change, and add" as he liked, and his only request was for a copy of the final text.[30] What was more, he enclosed a letter addressed to Mendelssohn authorizing him to modify the *Reply* as he saw fit or else to add an *Epilogue,* and thereby let the curtain go down before the public. He had made a mistake, and the *Reply* was meant to be the "sacrifice of atonement." Hence, he had repressed his self-love and done "what prudence, honesty, and love of truth counseled me to do; what Socrates, in my view, would have done in my circumstances."

Quoting his own words from the unfortunate dedication, he clearly implied, in spite of his professed modesty, that he, not Mendelssohn, had lived up to them. He put it to Mendelssohn to absolve him from the grievous charge of indiscretion that insulted his innocent heart. His failure to mention the stipulation attached to Mendelssohn's respect for Jesus had been motivated solely by the desire not to violate the promise he had given.[31] On February 20 Lavater wrote to Mendelssohn again, in reply to Mendelssohn's letter of February 9, and appealed to him, most urgently, to drop the charge of indiscretion. It had been this particular reproach and nothing else in the *Letter* that caused him anguish. "Put yourself in the position of a Christian preacher in a city not a fourth the size of Berlin, who battles week in and week out against vice and prejudice, who frequently makes enemies, and who is now publicly accused, at least obliquely, by none other than a Jew, of having failed to keep a promise—and you will forgive me if I desire to receive an exoneration from you, in one form or another. I ask you to do this, if it can be done without hurting your conviction and without the least damage to you." So far as he could remember, he went on, he had urged Mendelssohn at the time to tell him all of his objections to Christianity, and he had promised to treat those objections confidentially. This promise, he submitted, had been kept.[32]

Early in March Lavater's manuscript arrived. A covering letter to Nicolai, who was to publish it, requested him to supervise the printing with particular care and to send free copies to a specified number of friends. Spalding was to receive six copies, Mendelssohn a dozen.[33] Lüdke's letter of acknowledgment, dated March 4, reflected the sense of relief felt by both the theologians and Mendelssohn. The vivid account of events found therein is worth quoting: Lüdke took Lavater's manuscript to Spalding first. They read it through together, and both felt satisfied. The next person to read and approve it was Nicolai. Lüdke then went to the preacher Diterich, and "again, there was not a single word that displeased the dear man." In the meantime it had been getting dark, and Lüdke could hope to find Mendelssohn at home. The report continues: "Now, at last, at seven P.M., I was with Herr Moses, whom I had to call away from a large company of old and young people of both sexes to hand to him your *Reply* and the letter, which he opened and read in my presence. He approved, at once, your alternative proposal, namely to print an epilogue containing some notes and explanations addressed to you and Herr Bonnet. I told him vaguely what was written in the *Reply*, which pleased him very much, left the manuscript with him so that he might read it in the evening, and returned him to his company." On the following day, Lüdke's report continues, Mendelssohn came to see him "in a very cheerful mood," and declared himself "perfectly satisfied." He suggested leaving the manuscript intact and omitting some changes that had been proposed by Zollikofer in order to please Mendelssohn. "Therefore, my dearest friend, you will receive your *Reply* to Herr Mendelssohn printed without any changes, except for a few words, at the earliest possible moment. He [i.e. Mendelssohn] has the manuscript, and he asked me to give him a week in which to write the notes or epilogue. The week has almost passed by, and then Herr Nicolai will speedily attend to the printing, and I shall read the proofs." In the *Epilogue,* Lüdke assured Lavater, Mendelssohn was not going to discuss particulars. He would confine himself to a public withdrawal of the charges that he had made against Lavater and Bonnet. "All your friends are pleased that the matter has been brought to such a happy end."[34]

The actual course of events was not, however, quite so smooth as Lüdke and his friends had anticipated. Having finished his *Epilogue (Nachbemerkung)*, Mendelssohn composed a cordial letter to Lavater.[35] It had not been sent off, when the situation took a turn for the worse. On February 22, or possibly 27, Lavater had dispatched some addenda *(Zusätze)* to his *Reply*, which he wanted Lüdke or Mendelssohn to insert in the text.[36] As he later confessed, his Swiss friends had urged him to take this step.[37] The text of these addenda—there were five in all—can be reconstructed in part from Mendelssohn's notes on them, which alone are extant.[38] The sharp language used by Mendelssohn in criticizing some of the addenda reflects the anger he felt at Lavater's last minute revisions.

The first of the additions displeased him because its style betrayed some outside influence, which he resented. The second he allowed to pass. The third concerned the delicate subject of his attitude to Jesus. This addendum, Lavater tried to explain later, was meant to protect Mendelssohn against possible reproaches by his coreligionists. Since it had come to his notice that Mendelssohn had been taken to task by a rabbi because of his respect for Jesus,[39] Lavater had considered it appropriate to liken his respect for Jesus to the esteem he had for Socrates, to which no one could possibly object. Mendelssohn reacted with this retort: "I wish this addendum did not contain several sorts of statements that I cannot allow to stand without some qualification. They lead me to discussions I would very much prefer to avoid." He then gave an account of the conversation of the year 1764: he had drawn a line between a Socrates, who never pretended to be more than a human being, and Jesus, for whom he could have respect only if he had had no pretensions to being divine.[40] "Why, then, is this question thrown into such full relief? A pagan?—a Jew—It is shameful to suggest that we ought to reproach Socrates and Plato for having been pagans! Did this amount to a flaw in their morals? And Jesus a Jew?—Yes indeed, if he had no intention to do away with Judaism, which I believe he had not. One ought to consider whereto this consideration would lead me."

It is evident from these remarks that what Lavater had wanted to add was a sentence to the effect that to accord esteem to the pagan Socrates and deny it to the Jew Jesus made no sense whatever from the point of view of a Jewish philosopher. Mendelssohn's answer shows how firmly he stood his ground both as a Jew and as a philosopher of the Enlightenment. His indignation at the last addendum was even fiercer. We may infer from his note that it asserted the beneficial influence of Christianity upon philosophy and morals. Most probably it contained an oblique suggestion that Mendelssohn himself owed much of his philosophical and ethical culture to Christianity. Lüdke had expressed this view in a letter to Lavater on January 23,[41] and Resewitz said the same in his letter to Nicolai on March 10, 1770.[42] Mendelssohn attacked this opinion with all the vigor at his command: "Who are these people who, *all* of them, admit this without qualification? I don't. I ask the gentlemen who will read what I am writing here not to be indignant because of the liberty I take. An authoritarian dictum of this kind, so positively stated, seems to me highly inappropriate in a letter to a Jew, unless it is meant as a signal for battle.—On the influence of religion upon philosophy ... I could write a large chapter that might appear rather paradoxical to many. It seems that in Germany there is some tacit agreement on certain propositions that, in my view, merit examination. I sincerely wish, however, not to be prompted to such investigations."[43]

It is not hard to guess what Mendelssohn would have written in such a chapter. In 1763 he had remarked to Lessing that the retrogression of philosophy in the period between classical Greek thought and modern times was probably due to the impact of religion. "You know what sort of effect it produces when it becomes enthusiastic."[44] He always regarded Christianity as particularly prone to enthusiasm, and the summary view he expressed was undoubtedly meant as a characterization of Christian philosophy. Bearing in mind also that in his view Christianity was permeated with intolerance and the spirit of persecution, we may be sure that his "chapter" on the influence of Christianity upon philosophy and morals would have been anything but complimentary.

He concluded his notes[45] with the announcement that in case Lavater insisted on the insertion of the addenda in their totality he would feel compelled to withdraw his *Epilogue* and to express his thoughts in a separate treatise. In other words, he renewed his threat to publish the "Counter-reflections" and, thereby, enter the arena of battle against his will. The reason for his startling irritability lay probably in the fact, reported by Nicolai,[46] that he suspected Lavater of a plot to coerce him to fight. The *Reply* contained a passage imploring him to refute Bonnet's arguments and to state the reasons that caused him to remain a Jew. This passage could be interpreted as a lure to battle, and if Mendelssohn did harbor a suspicion of this sort in his mind, the addenda were likely to confirm it. His threat to publish his "Counterreflections" might have been intended to have a deterrent effect and to promote the chances of a peaceful solution.

The threat was, however, a gamble. As Nicolai put it in a letter to Lessing on April 3, 1770: "That much I know: had he published his *Gegenbetrachtungen,* he would have stirred a wasps' nest and would have incurred many painful stings."[47] Mendelssohn seems to have sensed how critical the situation was at that particular moment. His Hebrew letter to Avigdor Levi, which was written on March 30, reflects this awareness: "Having begun to speak out and answer the words of that hasty person [Lavater's dedicatory epistle], all theologians of that particular faith and those supporting them 'have set themselves against me round about' [Psalm 3:7]. Some show fierce anger, others speak with soft, kind, and smooth words; some are enraged, while others smile; for this is their way. Yet all the time they belabor me with their speeches and imaginings. However, I trust in God who is my fortress. He will gird me with strength for the battle on his behalf. He will put into my heart what I am to say, and I know that I shall not be ashamed."[48]

Mendelssohn was obviously facing again the possibility of an open battle. Nicolai, who was entirely on his side, discontinued the printing of Lavater's *Reply,* and on March 10 informed Lavater accordingly. At the same time, he sent him the text of Mendelssohn's *Epilogue,* and returned the original of the addenda, without having made a copy of them, together with Mendelssohn's notes. In his letter he minced no words in telling Lavater that the controversy would be rekindled without fail, should he insist on the insertion of all the addenda submitted. Mendelssohn, he pointed out, did not want a fight. "He can leave many things undiscussed that you want to be closely debated. You wish he ceased to be a Jew, whereas he does not object to your remaining a Christian."[49] Nicolai added that he was prepared to cede the copyright for the *Reply* to Lavater's Swiss publisher on condition that Mendelssohn's *Epilogue* not be included in the publication. It now depended on Lavater whether the affair was to be amicably settled, or not.

Mendelssohn's fears turned out to be unfounded. In a letter written to him on March 19, Lavater admitted that the addenda had been a mistake. They were the careless work of half an hour and they had been occasioned, perhaps, by a desire to please his Swiss friends or, possibly, by his own mistrust in his views. Some points, he thought, had been misunderstood by Mendelssohn, yet he was willing to drop those objected to. Of Mendelssohn's *Epilogue* he was highly appreciative. He felt it was "too kind" and almost embarrassing. Lavater's letter ended on a note of utter irresoluteness and perplexity: was it altogether right for him to publish the *Reply*? He almost wished, in all sincerity, to repress the publication. "I foresee inevitable objections, if I do not print it; I think it is my duty to print it for *your* sake—on the other hand, I feel ashamed having—God knows, unintentionally—caused so much of a sensation. . . . Do what you like. I give you full authority."[50]

Mendelssohn, who had girded himself for battle, felt almost like a Don Quixote. His reaction is expressed in a hitherto unpublished note to Nicolai; it bears no date but was unquestionably written under the impact of Lavater's letter. It reads as follows:[51] "Through Herr Councillor Spalding I received yesterday a letter from Herr Lavater about which I would like to talk to you tomorrow. Herr [Karl Gotthelf] Lessing, however, took it with him by mistake. Would you be so kind as to have it fetched from him. If my messenger knew where Herr Lessing lives, I would have saved you the trouble. Herr Lavater is most irresolute, and gives himself up to us blindly, as he says. I think we shall have to speak once more to Herr Lüdke before we print. I would not like to do anything without the consent of his local friends." It may be safely assumed that he and Nicolai discussed the matter with Lüdke and Spalding, and that the four agreed to publish Lavater's *Reply* together with Mendelssohn's *Epilogue*, but without the controversial addenda, of which, in any case, they had no copy. Only now could Mendelssohn dispatch the letter he had written to Lavater early in March.

The postscript to this long-detained letter, dated April 9, commences with these words: "Thus far my letter was complete when your addenda arrived and delayed the actual ratification of peace by four weeks."[52] At long last, peace had been achieved. Lavater's letter of unconditional surrender must have arrived between April 4 and April 9, for in a letter written by Nicolai to Lessing on April 3 a happy ending of the affair was still only forecast as being most likely; had Lavater's letter already been received by that date, Nicolai's report would have been different. On April 20 Lavater declared himself satisfied with the decision taken: "The matter is now settled. . . . I most cordially embrace you. . . . No more word now about the old sins. . . . Yet anew I offer you all, my whole soul." He was longing to receive the printed text of the "pacification," and wondered how soon it would arrive.[53] On May 9 he sent a note to Nicolai: "From one mail-day to the next I am waiting for the promised copy of the *Reply* to Moses—but, to my utmost astonishment, always in vain." By that time, however, a copy was already on its way.[54] Lavater's *Reply* and Mendelssohn's *Epilogue* had appeared in time for the Easter fair of 1770.[55]

Nicolai's postscript to the whole affair took the form of a letter to Lessing: "You receive herewith the pieces belonging to the Moses/Lavater quarrels, which are now ended. Moses has acquitted himself honorably, without too much effort on his part."[56] Whether he was right in saying that Mendelssohn's moral victory had cost him but little is more than questionable. Nicolai revised his own judgment when he remarked, many years later, that chagrin at having been forced out of the tranquil mode of his existence had affected Mendelssohn's health and led to the severe illness that eventually became the cause of his premature death.[57] In the spring of 1770, when the issue seemed to have been settled for good, none of his friends could have foreseen the cumulative effect that the affair and its repercussions would have on his life.

Reverberations of the Conflict

Even before Lavater and Mendelssohn publicly composed their differences, the affair had begun to provoke others to join the fray. During the years 1770–1772 a small library of pamphlets of varying viewpoints cropped up.

The first to appear was an anonymous sixteen-page tract published in Hamburg that described Lavater's challenge as an "unreasonable demand" *(Zumuthung)*: Mendelssohn could not be expected to abandon the religion of his fathers, seeing that he believed in its divine origin. The Founder of Christianity had purified the Jewish religion of error and superstition, and he had thereby restored its original light. He could not, therefore, be denied respect by the "gentle and rational Mendelssohn." On the other hand, the Jewish philosopher who had found man-made admixtures in his own religion could easily discover accretions of this sort in Christianity too. Were such disfiguring elements removed on both sides, without touching the harmless prejudices common to all religions, the author would find himself with Mendelssohn on the same road leading to the God of Truth. Christianity was, no doubt, a gentler religion than Judaism. However, if the seed of Jacob was unwilling to accept the easier way of grace, it was evident that the time of its "complete illumination" had not yet arrived.[1]

Lavater took notice of this pamphlet in his letter to Mendelssohn dated February 20: it proved to him, he wrote, that it was not opportune for them to continue their appearance as combatants in public.[2] He was obviously afraid of the possibility of more Christians expressing disapproval of his importunity.

Another early pamphlet, dated February 26, 1770, was Johann Balthasar Kölbele's *Letter to Herr Moses Mendelssohn on Lavaterian and Kölbelean Affairs against Herr Mendelssohn*, which resumed, in the most scurrilous manner, the aggressiveness toward the Jewish philosopher that Kölbele had exhibited in previous publications. In his April 9 letter of reconciliation Mendelssohn wrote Lavater: "Herr Dr. Kölbele of Frankfurt am Main has assailed me, as is his wont, in such unmannerly fashion as one may only expect of a Jena student. But who is to worry about Kölbele?" He might simply have ignored this rude opponent, but he decided to expose his manner in the final section of his *Epilogue*. He informed Lavater in advance of his having taken this step: "I have replied to his rude *Letter* at the end of the *Epilogue* in the way he deserves. Have no fear, I have carefully distinguished between the fool and the wise by devoting to him an appendix separate from the *Epilogue*, and I say expressly: The following does not concern Herr Lavater but Herr Kölbele."[3]

It was only right and proper to draw a clear line between the reply to Lavater and the one to Kölbele. Yet it was equally justified to bracket the two together. Kölbele's unbridled anti-Semitism revealed, as it were, the true nature of the anti-Semitic sentiment that also underlay Lavater's more subtle and mellifluous *Reply*. Lessing, the sworn enemy of all hypocrisy, was contemptuous of both: Lavater's *Reply* he characterized as "treacherous caressing after so crafty a blow," and Kölbele he derided as "the *Kälbele* [young calf] of Frankfurt."[4] By juxtaposing Lavater and Kölbele, Mendelssohn deliberately placed the two in the same camp, despite the fact that he technically discriminated between them. It seems, however, that Lavater allowed Mendelssohn's strategic move to pass unnoticed. In his letter of April 20, he even applauded the step and expressed his severe condemnation of Kölbele: "Never before have I read anything so rude and vulgar by a sick Christian, whose sickness is notorious." Kölbele, he reported to Mendelssohn, had sent him his *Letter* with a covering note "oozing with intolerable vanity," and he had answered him briefly, drily, and in a tone such as he had never before permitted himself toward anybody: "In short, I declined friendship and correspondence."[5] It seems, however, that Lavater did not break off relations with Kölbele. When two young Jews from Germany were baptized by Lavater in 1771, he assured Kölbele "in a friendly letter" that this particular conversion had been an extraordinary event.[6] This in spite of the fact that on July 14, 1770, Kölbele had published a *Second Letter* against Mendelssohn that in size and vituperation outbid the first.[7]

Since Kölbele turned out to be the most annoying and troublesome among the dramatis personae of the Lavater affair, some information on his life and background is not altogether out of place.[8] Born in Frankfurt in 1726, he was related to Goethe (his mother was a sister-in-law of Anna Maria Textor, sister of Goethe's mother), and it is possible that Goethe belonged to the circle of young people who received instruction from him in philosophy and mathematics preparatory to their undertaking university studies. In 1765 Goethe described to his friend Riese the impression that Gottsched made on him: his feet were like Kölbele's *(Hinc ego Kölbelüs imponens pedibus magnis)*. Goethe's sister Cornelie wrote on July 28, 1768, to her friend Katharine Fabrizius in Worms that among the group of people whose company she enjoyed "le plus aimable est Mr. le Docteur Kölbele."[9] He must, therefore, have possessed some attraction for young people. He had studied law at the universities of Giessen and Halle and obtained his doctorate in 1748. His practice as a lawyer in Frankfurt lasted less than a year, however; as a man of considerable means inherited from his parents, and supported also by an aunt, he could afford to retire from professional life and devote himself to his studies.

Religious scruples about the admissability of oaths had been one of the factors prompting him to give up his legal practice. "I had ... taken the oath as a doctor, as a citizen, and as an advocate. Thereupon, however, I doubted for many years whether I was permitted as a Christian to continue taking oaths. For this reason I sought no promotion during that entire period." He wrote (but did not publish) a tract in which he violently contested, on theological grounds, the admissibility of oaths. Eventually, however, he convinced himself that the taking of oaths was an expression of "Christian freedom," and in 1767 he published a treatise to this effect entitled *The Admissibility of Oaths according to the Principles of the New Testament and Following the Direction of the Greek Text,* and dedicated the work to Emperor Joseph II. Kölbele's obsession with this subject reflected itself later in his attacks against Mendelssohn. It was part of the pietist trend that his thinking took after he left Halle.

His *Second Letter* against Mendelssohn contains an autobiographical paragraph that reads: "As a deist I left the university, could find no peace in this way of thinking, yet hated all blind faith. ... I abandoned the juridical practice, busied myself many years with inquiries into religion, and went back, from conviction, to Christianity. I examined its truth from many points of view, and studied several sciences by teaching myself. On the ocean of the sciences I navigated not all small islands, and I have been living now twenty-two years after leaving the university purposely unattached to any profession and preoccupied with many sciences. Some of these serve to confirm me in my religion. Others—I confess my human weakness—I studied from a scholar's ambition. About six years ago I began to learn enough Hebrew to understand correctly a passage of the Old Testament with the help of the Elder Buxtorf,[10] by consulting good exegetes, and with other aids. I have not yet been urged to study rabbinics."[11]

Kölbele's studies are reflected in a number of works, the earliest of which is the *Proof of the Universality of Sufficient Reason* (1750). A tract on Flavius Josephus' testimony on Christ, written in 1763, remained unpublished. In the following year he published a work called *Outline of Religion (Grundriss der Religion),* written in the form of letters to a young girl, "Mademoiselle R." (Lorgen Rost, his niece), offering proofs for the truth of Christianity and warning against the foes of religion. The book is prefaced by a letter of thanks to the "Royal Society of Great Britain and Germany at Göttingen University" for having elected him an honorary member twelve years before (1752).

In 1765 he published a study entitled *Sketchy Comparison between Philosophy and Mathematics, judging at the same time briefly the Treatises which appeared in answer to the Berlin Prize Question about Metaphysical Evidence."*[12]

This treatise was dedicated to the Princess Amalia of Anhalt, who lived in Frankfurt and had frequent conversations with Kölbele on matters of religion and philosophy. The treatise postulated a stricter mathematical foundation for philosophy, and in it Kölbele launched his first attack against Mendelssohn. As Mendelssohn disclosed in his *Epilogue,* Kölbele sent him a copy of the work with a covering letter in French. Mendelssohn did not reply because the treatise contained a reference to his hoped-for conversion— which had little to do with the subject of the prize-essay (as he wittily remarked)—and also because Kölbele himself had called his treatise a "sketchy" *(flüchtige)* comparison, thus permitting one to expect the appearance of something more solid at a later date.[13]

In 1765 Kölbele published an autobiographical account of a fictional young Jewish lady, Jungfer Meyer, who converted to Christianity and caused her wealthy parents to follow her example. In a second *roman,* published in 1769, he used the same literary medium to describe the moral steadfastness of Philippine Damien, the daughter of a fraudulent financier. Both novels are tendentious, and Kölbele himself pointed to his models in English and French literature.[14] In the same year, 1769, he also published *Duties of the Christian Poet in Dramatics and Judgment of Miss Meyer, Philippe Damien, and Marmontel's "Belisaire."*[15] In the preface to this work, Kölbele mentions his *Antiphaedon,* a critique of Mendelssohn's *Phaedon,* which (contrary to an earlier announcement) was not yet ready for publication: "Herr Mendelssohn furnishes an erroneous history of Socrates. . . . I know the soul's immortality from revelation. But Herr Mendelssohn? Let him reflect." The book itself is a mixture of literary references and anti-Jewish remarks. Kölbele's two anti-Mendelssohn *Letters* appeared in 1770, followed in 1772 by his *Little Essay on Miracles . . . with some Additions on the Mendelssohnian and Kölbelean Religious Controversy,* another essentially anti-Jewish treatise of some two hundred and eighty-five pages.[16] He died in 1778.

The strange combination of learning and abusiveness that is found in Kölbele's writings, especially in those directed against Mendelssohn, both repelled and intrigued the public. In an age that prided itself on its civility and courteousness, the coarseness of Kölbele's tone created a sensation. Some there were, no doubt, who actually relished the way in which Mendelssohn was anatomized without the slightest regard for his human dignity. Others felt ashamed and grieved. Yet all wanted to be kept informed. Even Lessing, who spoke of the "young calf" *(Kälbele)* as an "ox," nevertheless asked Nicolai to collect for him "everything that is published in this affair."[17] And Kant wrote to Marcus Herz on September 27, 1770: "Herr Friedländer has sent me a new piece by Kölbele. I beg you to let me share anything new that could reach me through channels of this kind."[18]

There was clearly a pathological streak in Kölbele's make-up, which accounted for the lack of control and inhibition in his writings. Lavater was right in describing him as sick, and so was the reviewer of his *Little Essay on Miracles,* who wrote: "We who have occasion to observe the physical

condition of Herr Doctor Kölbele at close quarters would have liked to ascribe the tone that he assumes . . . to hypochondria and a sick soul."[19] He
himself mentioned, in his first *Letter* against Mendelssohn, the fact that his
physical debility was "notorious in Frankfurt am Main," and that his doctor
had forbidden him to engage in "sustained thinking." Yet some of his remarks on Mendelssohn evoked a rather favorable response. The review in
the *Göttingische Anzeigen*, for example, though taking Mendelssohn's side,
was not altogether critical of Kölbele: "However well-intentioned Her
Doctor Kölbele may be, the context [of his *Letter*] seems to us rather hard.
Herr Mendelssohn is clearly put under suspicion of being a naturalist. At the
same time, various religious questions are formally laid before him to be
answered, e.g., what he meant when saying that he believed in the essential
core of his religion; whether he considered Moses alone or the prophets
too as divine; what he thought of the Messiah; etc. If Herr Mendelssohn
were, perhaps, a preacher or professor of theology in the Lutheran Church,
and his religion had incurred some suspicion, we would understand that
someone might put such questions to him. . . . Who, however, has a right
to demand a public religious confession of one who is not a theologian
and does not wish to write about religion? And even granting such a right,
how can a Christian publicly examine a Jew, without provocation by the
latter, on articles of orthodoxy? What if a Catholic did this to us? This
too is hard: Herr Mendelssohn, who wished to assure us that he was convinced of his religion, wrote: I testify before the God of Truth etc. Herr
Kölbele replies on page twenty-two: Why this solemn affirmation? Christians
have little trust in oaths taken by Jews. Some of the things said by Kölbele
make sense, e.g., that it was not entirely impossible for a Jew to remain
attached to his religion for the sake of temporal advantages, despite the
present circumstances of his people; moreover, that at certain times the
Jews were eager to proselytize. . . . It seems that Herr Mendelssohn will
eventually be compelled, against his will, to do what Herr Lavater and
Kölbele demand. We have so much confidence in the good case of our
religion that, in fact, we would not mind if he did so; yet we would not
like to be the ones who compel him to do this."[20]

Considering the rudeness of Kölbele's tone, especially in his attack
on Mendelssohn's solemn invocation of the God of Truth, the review was
far too uncritical. Surely Kölbele's insinuation that Mendelssohn might
have remained a Jew for mere reasons of expediency should have been
repudiated as an affront to his moral integrity rather than condoned as
a suggestion that made sense. The dishonest way in which Mendelssohn
was urged, and at the same time not urged, to state his case against Christianity was no improvement on the review of his *Letter to Lavater* that had
appeared in the *Göttingische Anzeigen* a few months earlier.[21] There the
reviewer, Gottfried Less, had said: "Now that the author [i.e. Mendelssohn]
has declared himself to be able to offer some arguments against the case
defended by Bonnet (and not only against Bonnet's defense), we make
bold to ask him to make his Counterreflections known. Rousseau might

otherwise regard as proven what he has hitherto offered as a mere conjecture: that the Jewish teachers know important arguments against Christianity, which they suppress only because they live under Christian oppression."

If Mendelssohn ever toyed with the idea of entering into polemic against Bonnet's arguments, the appearance of Kölbele's *Letter* killed any such intention. He disregarded the plea of the Göttingen reviews and of Lavater's *Reply* that he publish his "Counterreflections," and he confined his *Epilogue*, with one exception, to the clearing up of personal matters. To Lavater he was all kindness and magnanimity, praising his moral character and piety, even his "burning zeal for the good," and attributing the "hastiness" of Lavater's urgent dedication to the "love of truth." There had been no breach of promise on Lavater's part, he declared. He had no reason to doubt the accuracy of the account given of the conversation by Lavater in his *Reply:* the assurance offered on that occasion was to the effect that Mendelssohn's statement would never be reported in a manner harmful to him. That promise had not been violated.

This complete withdrawal of all charges was prompted, in the first place, by Lavater's letter of February 20, in which he had implored Mendelssohn to rehabilitate him in the eyes of the public and (especially) his Zürich parishioners. Mendelssohn was obviously moved to pity by this *cri de coeur.* That his chivalrousness went beyond this act of exoneration and led him to adopt an attitude of excessive friendliness may have been due to his sense of relief at Lavater's withdrawal of the challenge. That Lavater's *Reply* was as importunate as ever, in its urging him to convert, did not bother him. He had learned to expect nothing else from Lavater's exuberant pietism and conversionist temper. He was all the more grateful to have been liberated from the nightmarish prospect of a "long period of disquiet and anxiety."[22] As he put it in the *Epilogue:* "I thank Herr Lavater sincerely for having done justice to my hesitancy and for having absolved me from the necessity of engaging in a controversy that is so much opposed to my mentality. In the few hours of leisure that my business activities allow me, I like to forget all divisiveness, all discord that ever turned man into an enemy of man, and I try at such times to erase from memory the experiences of this kind that I had during the day. In these happy hours I like to abandon myself to the free, undivided sentiment of the heart, which I have not yet learned to reconcile with a polemicist's state of mind. Neither in a moral nor in a physical sense am I born to be an athlete."[23]

The *Epilogue* was also overflowing with kindliness toward Bonnet, whom Mendelssohn was eager to placate after the rather harsh manner in which he had treated him in the *Letter* replying to Lavater's dedication. The issue had already been settled by private correspondence, and the *Epilogue* merely recapitulated for the benefit of the public some of the points contained in Mendelssohn's letter of February 9.[24]

It had been his erroneous assumption, Mendelssohn declared in the *Epilogue*, that Bonnet was a party to Lavater's challenge that had caused him to misjudge the true intent of the arguments for Christianity offered in the *Palingénésie*. Since he had believed that they were meant to convert non-Christians, he had compared them with those of other treatises dedicated to Christian apologetics. Now that he realized that Bonnet's sole purpose had been to strengthen the faith of Christians, Mendelssohn's critical remark had become pointless. He was particularly anxious to assure Bonnet that he had never intended to accuse him of plagiarism (a charge that had in fact been laid at Bonnet's door by someone else, as Mendelssohn had recently discovered in a learned German journal).[25] In his view, Mendelssohn explained, it made little sense to insist on originality in metaphysical works. The pros and cons of every question had been debated for so long that one had almost to utter an absurdity in order to say something brand new. Thus, Bonnet's hypothesis of preordained miracles,[26] he pointed out, could already be found in Maimonides,[27] and his theory of a subtle, ethereal body as the seat of the soul was anticipated in kabbalistic doctrine.[28] A philosopher could claim a measure of originality if he clarified concepts and presented truths from new angles and within the context of other truths—as Bonnet had done. In referring to German predecessors of Bonnet, Mendelssohn had merely meant to say that the philosophical principles contained in the *Palingénésie* were not new to a German who had studied Leibniz and the Leibnizians, for they had evolved by speculative methods the concepts that Bonnet had developed by way of empirical observation. This last remark particularly pleased Bonnet.[29]

Both Bonnet and Lavater had taken umbrage at Mendelssohn's statement that any religion might be defended by the argument from miracles offered in the *Palingénésie*.[30] In his *Reply*, Lavater had urged Mendelssohn to show on what grounds the mission of Moses could be shown to be superior to Jesus', and the *Epilogue* could not avoid answering this question. It had already been posed by the prince of Brunswick, and Mendelssohn had dealt with it in his "Counterreflections." The passage concerned said of Moses' mission that its content was uncontested by reason, and went on to stress the public character of the Sinaitic revelation as something unique.[31] A lengthy marginal note in the manuscript of the "Counterreflections"[32] quoted Maimonides' disquisition on the subject:[33] The Jewish people believed in Moses' divine mission not on account of the miracles performed by him, for miracles produce no sense of certainty, but on account of the manner in which he was appointed at Sinai. If the Law bade us obey prophets who could produce miracles in support of their teachings, it was not because of any intrinsic evidence to be found in miracles as such but simply as an ordinance comparable to the one that declared a testimony by two witnesses to be sufficient evidence in court proceedings.

In his February 9 letter to Bonnet, Mendelssohn had expounded this viewpoint at great length,[34] and in the *Epilogue* he gave it an even preciser formulation: The Sinaitic revelation was not "to confirm truths by historical facts or doctrines by miracles; one was supposed to believe that the divine manifestation had appointed this prophet as its messenger, because everyone had himself heard this appointment announced by God."[35] In other words: Judaism was not a system of doctrines to be accepted on the strength of miracles but a body of laws publicly revealed. Two pairs of antitheses are involved in this formulation, namely, the contrast between miracle and revelation on the one hand, and the contrast between doctrine and legislation on the other. The latter distinction was to be elaborated later in Mendelssohn's *Jerusalem.*

Mendelssohn's answer was sympathetically summed up in the *Göttingische Anzeigen.* This time the reviewer was none other than Michaelis, as is evident from a number of indications to this effect.[36] He wrote a postscript of his own, as it were, on the Lavater affair in reviewing the *Reply* and the *Epilogue:*

> Herr Lavater recognizes his well-intentioned precipitousness. He no longer demands that Herr Mendelssohn must write against Christianity unless he is resolved to become a Christian. Herr Mendelssohn will, therefore, write nothing against Christianity, and it may be hoped that naturalists will in future refrain from uttering the improbable conjecture that external compulsion in Berlin prevented him from making known secret documents or reasons against Christianity. His answer, though he meant to say but little, contains, all the same, some of the things we were anxious to know.... As much as the present reviewer can make out within the limits of his understanding of Judaism, he recognizes in Herr Mendelssohn ... a Jew who is attached to his religion, and who, if we may say so, is an orthodox Jew, except that he presents the case of the synagogue in a philosophical garb and in modern style.... He does not deny the miracles upon which our religion is founded and which the Jews partly admit, but he denies the conclusion from miracles to the truth of the religion. The Jewish religion, he says, is not founded upon its miracles but upon the fact that God himself spoke from Sinai and appointed Moses as his messenger before the entire people. This is the authentic Jewish system, and we can testify to Christians and Jews alike that Herr Mendelssohn answered in the way in which a Jew who understands its teachings and believes in them has to answer.... Herr Mendelssohn also speaks to some extent about that which Herr Doctor Kölbele wrote against him.... He is sensitive to the injustice done to him, but in his answer he remains within the bounds of modesty and thereby he gains a great deal.... As for Herr Mendelssohn's reference to a teacher of our local university quoted against him by Herr Kölbele (although, so far as we can remember, nothing of the sort can be found in any of his writings), we can openly state that he agrees with Herr Mendelssohn; that he considers as trashy volumes [*Scharteken*] the Jewish writings designated as such by Herr Mendelssohn; and that he finds the writings of the learned rabbis replete with matters that, although not always true, are not identical with the wicked teachings one collects from those *Scharteken.* Eisenmenger's *Entdecktes Judentum* ["Judaism Unmasked"], about which Herr Kölbele speaks and whose remarks Herr Mendelssohn answers, is, to the best of our knowledge, hardly a book through which one can become acquainted with the way learned or honest Jews think. Were a Jew to write a book "Christianity Unmasked" and to present as the principles of Christianity what is e.g. written in a Jesuit casuistic treatise, how would we like it?

Mendelssohn was greatly pleased with Michaelis' review.[37] Now, it seemed to him, the affair was completely settled: "Herr Lavater is a friend of humanity and spares me all embarrassment; and Herr Kölbele—he is certainly not going to make me take a single step further than my comfort permits. One who shows so obviously his intention to incite me shall find it difficult to achieve his purpose."[38] Mendelssohn felt that, at long last, he could again give his undivided attention to literary projects.

Literary Concerns and Another Lavater Episode

Either at the end of 1769 or early in 1770 Mendelssohn's Hebrew commentary on Ecclesiastes appeared.[1] The work had been written in 1768. Though drawing largely on the classical Jewish commentators, it also made use of the exegetical works of Johann David Michaelis and A. V. Desveux,[2] and allowed, moreover, his own philosophical views to express themselves in a more popular vein, on occasion. The introduction closed with a promise to write similar commentaries on Psalms, Proverbs, and the Book of Job, should the present work be favorably received.[3] Regrettably, this laudable intention did not come to fruition. It should be noted, however, that Mendelssohn wrote his commentary on Ecclesiastes and conceived the plan of further works of this kind before the onset of the Lavater affair—that his concern with biblical scholarship was not a reaction to the traumatic experience of the Lavater controversy but antedated it. Yet in a way the controversy did have an effect on his literary production in the biblical field. It stimulated his desire to write a new German translation of the Psalms.

The first intimation of this project is found in a letter that Karl Lessing wrote to his brother on April 17, 1770: "Moses Mendelssohn has finished the controversy with Lavater and is now occupied with a translation of the Psalms. I get from it a conception of David the singer and of the entire Hebrew poetry completely different from what I gathered from Luther's version or Cramer's versified paraphrase. What will people say about his interpretations of the psalms that we Christians have hitherto considered to be predictions of Jesus?"[4] Lessing clearly perceived Mendelssohn's main purpose in offering a new translation of the Psalms: he wanted to present them as literary documents of pure religious sentiment, shorn of dogmatic or any other extraneous elements. This is how Mendelssohn himself described the intent of his version to Elise Reimarus in 1783, when the completed work appeared: "As has been known to you for a long time, the Psalms do not contain what Christians and Jews have until now tried to find in them, with so much critical acumen and learning. To show this was, in fact, my main purpose in translating them and in publishing the translation."[5]

Mendelssohn's original intention was to insert a selection of Psalms, under the title "Samples of the Lyrical Poetry of the Hebrews," in the second edition of his *Philosophical Writings*, which he prepared for the press in 1770 and which came out in 1771. Karl Lessing, who enjoyed Mendelssohn's confidence and was well informed, wrote at the end of his April 17 letter: "He will augment his *Philosophical Writings*, of which a new edition is to be brought out by Voss, by adding the *Treatise on Evidence*, revised though, and an essay about the lyrical poetry of the Hebrews."[6]

The most explicit information about the project is provided by Mendelssohn himself in a letter to Professor Michaelis, which is extant in two versions, one undated and the other dated November 12, 1770.[7] The first version was written shortly after Michaelis' review of Lavater's *Reply* and Mendelssohn's *Epilogue* had appeared on May 17, 1770, for the initial paragraph expresses Mendelssohn's pleasure in the review and the sense of relief that he felt at the time.[8] However, this letter was not mailed to Göttingen (it may have been intended to serve as a mere draft),[9] and the text had to be modified by the time the letter was rewritten in November, when Mendelssohn decided to send it. The introductory paragraph was then no longer current and had to be dropped. It was replaced by a brief report on a journey to Brunswick and Hanover, from which Mendelssohn then had just returned.

According to this report, Mendelssohn had met several of Michaelis' friends: "His Excellency the [Frei]herr von Münchhausen,[10] that great patron of learning, was gracious enough to admit me, and I was fortunate enough to find this worthy old man at an hour that was serene, and almost youthful considering his age. His first suggestion was that I travel to Göttingen 'to meet his Bible translator' [i.e. Michaelis]. I would have loved to travel ten more miles for this purpose, had my business activities and the group with which I traveled permitted it."[11] When Michaelis replied on December 27, 1770, he wrote à propos the baron von Münchhausen: "In the meantime the gentleman who encouraged you, Sir, to travel to Göttingen has passed away. Our university has suffered a very great and irreparable loss. . . ."[12] The fact that Michaelis' reply referred to the report contained in the dated letter proves that this letter and not the other was sent to Göttingen. In both versions, however, the main section deals with the projected translation of the Psalms in almost identical terms, except for slight changes due to the progress made between May and November, and some omissions.

The following is a précis of the original version: Having been informed of Michaelis' intention to edit a new translation of the Psalms,[13] Mendelssohn would like to know how soon it was to be published. The matter concerned him personally, since he had rendered about twenty psalms in German and was "not disinclined to publish them as 'Samples of the lyrical poetry of the Hebrews.' " He had to confess that he was "very little satisfied" with the translations that had come to his notice. In particular, those employing rhyme spoiled the intrinsic character of Hebrew poetry. He expected much help from Michaelis' interpretation because it would undoubtedly make use of Semitic linguistics. He was sure that Michaelis would treat the Psalms as poetry and disregard the prophetical and mystical exegesis of both Christians and Jews who were neither philosophers nor literary critics. A passage omitted in the final letter read: "Some thirty years ago someone dared to interpret the 45th psalm as a *Epithalamium Salomonis* [a nuptial song of Solomon], and he was therefore branded as a heretic by the Wittenberg theologians. This does not surprise us; but I am greatly astonished to find that Herr Cramer, too, still sees in the bridegroom the Messiah. It is perhaps dangerous to contest these ingrained prejudices publicly; yet we have to take this road at long last, if the Psalms are to be read with a sense of edification that is reasonable. Long enough has the clear meaning of Scripture been obscured by mystical casuistry."

In the final version of the letter Mendelssohn wrote that he awaited Michaelis' translation "with the greatest impatience." He himself had translated about twenty psalms "some time ago," among them some of the more difficult ones, and he had used a free meter that approximated to the sound of the original text. He had decided to publish them as "A Sample of the Lyrical Poetry of the Hebrews" but was now resolved to wait until Michaelis' rendition was available. He quoted his own translation of the 91st psalm in full and invited Michaelis' comment. In his reply Michaelis wrote: "As you, Sir, rightly demand, I have treated the Psalms as poetry. My remarks concerning the sample of the metrical translation of the 91st psalm, which you communicated to me, I must save for the previously mentioned conversation when we meet, because they concern for the most part things related to hearing, which I cannot discuss in writing without intricacy."[14]

Thus Mendelssohn found in Michaelis an ally who approved the undogmatic exegesis of Scripture. This does not mean that they shared the same ultimate motivation. Michaelis' interests were of a purely scholarly nature. To Mendelssohn the unbiased humanistic approach to the Psalms meant the breaking down of the barriers of prejudice. He was anxious to demonstrate the poetic character of the Psalms in order to dispel the cobwebs of exegesis that prevented Jews and Christians from enjoying the beauty of sentiment and expression in the text. In recoiling from the obtuseness of pietistic fanaticism such as that encountered in his most recent experience, he grasped for a freer, more open-minded approach to Scripture. Without the impetus of the Lavater affair he might have produced more Hebrew commentaries on books of the Bible but hardly his translation of the Psalms.

Mendelssohn's plan to include samples of the lyrical poetry of the Hebrews in the 1771 edition of his *Philosophical Writings* shows the extent to which his mind was engaged in searching for ways to combat religious divisiveness and intolerance. As matters turned out, this particular plan was not carried out. The new edition appeared without the essay on the Psalms because Mendelssohn wanted to use Michaelis' work, which was not ready in time. On the other hand, his preoccupation in 1770 with the second edition of the *Philosophische Schriften* indicates the degree to which he reimmersed himself in his own being as a philosopher. Despite the many upsets that he suffered throughout that year—all due to the reverberations of the Lavater affair—he managed to apply himself assiduously to the revision and enlargement of the essays contained in the philosophical work. The number of changes introduced in the second edition is quite extraordinary,[15] and one appreciates the eagerness with which Mendelssohn wanted to extricate himself from the Lavater affair which, apart from its intrinsic distastefulness, was interfering with his work.

A summary account of the changes made for the 1771 edition can be found in the remarks Mendelssohn added to the preface. It is interesting that the treatise *On the Sublime and Naive* shows the largest number of revisions, as he himself pointed out.[16] In 1762 Lord Henry Home had published his *Elements of Criticism,* in which he discussed, among other things, the nature of "dignity and grace,"[17] and a German translation of the work, by Johann Nicolaus Meinhard and Christian Garve, had appeared in 1763–1766; Mendelssohn mentioned the work as early as 1763, in a letter to Abbt.[18] He was particularly impressed by the concept of grace *(Grazie)* as described by Home, and he worked the concept into the texture of the revised treatise *On the Sublime and Naive:*[19] "Grace, or the high degree of beauty in motion, is likewise allied to the naive, since the movements of that which is graceful [*reizend*] merge in a natural, easy, and gentle way, and indicate, without being deliberate and conscious, that the springs of the soul and the stirrings of the heart, from which these free movements flow, operate in the same unforced manner, harmonize with each other in the same gentle way, and develop in the same unartificial fashion. Hence the ideas of innocence and moral naturalness [*Einfalt*] are always allied to noble grace.—The more this beauty in the movement is allied to consciousness, and the more it appears to be performed deliberately, the more it deviates from the naive and attains the character of the studied, and if the interior harmony of the propensities is missing, that of the affected."

To what extent Schiller's famous essay *On Grace and Dignity (Über Anmut und Würde)* is indebted to Mendelssohn (next to Home) has been a matter of debate among scholars;[20] that Mendelssohn's treatise in the 1771 revised edition occupies an important place in the history of the aesthetic understanding of grace in its relation to the moral sphere is undisputed. Thus, while Mendelssohn was involved in a highly public controversy in which religious fanaticism played an ignoble role, his mind was really focused, as we can see, on philosophical and aesthetic issues.

In the summer of 1770 he read with pleasure an anonymous edition of an annotated Dutch translation of his treatise *On the Sublime and Naive* by Rijklof Michael van Goens, professor of history and belles-lettres at the University of Utrecht.[21] A letter from van Goens, dated November 26, explained to Mendelssohn that he had undertaken the translation solely for the benefit of his compatriots. Otherwise, he would have submitted it first to Mendelssohn. To his surprise, however, the work had found its way into Germany, and his own name had been mentioned as that of the author in learned reviews. Van Goens asked Mendelssohn's forgiveness for his lack of courtesy, and expressed his readiness to withdraw any of his notes that might have caused the least annoyance.[22] Mendelssohn replied on December 14 expressing his pleasure at the fidelity of the translation and his warm approval of most of the comments.[23]

On May 8 he wrote to Nicolai that he was ready to contribute a review to the *Allgemeine deutsche Bibliothek,* provided the weather was bad: "With the sun out in spring, the reviewing of books can be a very tedious task." In the same letter he urged Nicolai to prevail upon Garve to write a defense of the theater, a subject hitherto treated unsatisfactorily even by a d'Allembert, a Rousseau, and a Marmontel. The letter was apparently addressed to Nicolai at Leipzig, where he was then staying for the spring book-fair, and where Garve occupied a professorial chair.[24] It concludes with the request that he be sent any important new publication, especially by Wieland, and "things that concern me in particular," by which he meant pamphlets or tracts bearing on the Lavater controversy. They were, as he put it, "not altogether, but relatively important," and belonged among the things that he expected to receive.[25] Here we have a clear formulation of Mendelssohn's attitude. His main interest lay in matters that had nothing to do with the public debate about him; while he could not help being curious about what was being written for or against him as a Jew, all this was not really, only "relatively," important.

In the spring of 1770 there began a series of developments indicating that the ghost of the Lavater affair still hovered about. The first of these developments was a letter from Bonnet to Mendelssohn dated June 24.[26] It acknowledged in the most amiable terms Mendelssohn's letter of February 9 and his public response in the *Epilogue.* The "objections" to the proofs for Christianity, Bonnet remarked, had pleased him because of their candor; he was, however, not trying to answer them now. He had done this in a new edition of the chapters of the *Palingénésie* that dealt with the subject, a copy of which had already been sent to Mendelssohn. These *Recherches*[27] had been amplified by many footnotes, including some that sought to resolve the difficulties raised by "the wise son of Mendel." However, Bonnet continued, in his anxiety to avoid the semblance of polemics, he had presented Mendelssohn's objections as if they had occurred to himself. He regretted, Bonnet said, having had to deprive himself, through this procedure, of the pleasure that direct references to Mendelssohn and the merits of the "virtuous *Phaedon*" would have given him.

Mendelssohn's reaction to this letter, and to the *Recherches* when the work reached him, was one of bitter consternation. He had considered the affair as settled. The reply he had given to Bonnet was not meant as an attack but as a simple explanation of why he, as a Jew, had remained unconvinced by Bonnet's arguments. It hardly called for a rebuttal. And had not Bonnet himself admitted that his "proofs" had never been intended for the consumption of non-Christians? Now, all of a sudden, Bonnet's ardor and zeal to fight back had been awakened. The *Recherches* tried to show that Judaism, contrary to Mendelssohn's assertion, was founded upon the evidence produced by miracles. The Sinaitic revelation was itself a miracle. Bonnet's insistence on the essential soundness of his thesis looked very much like an attempt to reopen the question. Moreover, certain passages of the *Recherches* were undisguised appeals for the conversion of the Jews. They left Mendelssohn with the impression that Bonnet had decided to assume the role that Lavater had played with so little success—that, in a sense, the mantle of Lavater the missionary had fallen on Bonnet.

Considering Bonnet's high prestige as a philosopher, the situation now appeared even more dangerous than before. In point of fact, Bonnet had been urged by some German savants of repute to renew Lavater's challenge on his own behalf,[28] and it is quite possible that Mendelssohn had an inkling of this. He suspected something of this kind, at any rate, for unless his worst fears had been aroused by the appearance of the *Recherches,* one could hardly understand the intensity of his annoyance with Bonnet's letter and the new edition of Bonnet's proofs for Christianity. Despite the cordial tone of Bonnet's June 24 letter, Mendelssohn was so upset, indeed, that he denied him even the courtesy of a reply or simple acknowledgment. In a letter to Lavater, dated December 4, Mendelssohn complained of Bonnet's "inconsistent" behavior: having disapproved earlier of Lavater's presentation of the *Palingénésie* as a work designed to convert Jews, Bonnet now did the very same thing himself.[29] This complaint indicates clearly the direction in which Mendelssohn's thoughts were moving, though the full extent of his fears and suspicions could hardly be expressed vis-à-vis Lavater.

There was, however, an additional reason for complaint that Mendelssohn did not hesitate to bring to Lavater's notice. It concerned Bonnet's suppression of Mendelssohn's name in rejecting his objections. Without even considering the possibility that Bonnet had acted in good faith and was motivated by a desire to avoid giving the impression of an attack upon him, Mendelssohn saw the procedure adopted by Bonnet as a calculated move to defeat him without even acknowledging him as the adversary: "Is this not tantamount to using one's weapons against an unarmed opponent?" Perhaps Mendelssohn would have interpreted Bonnet's silence about him more charitably had not a further circumstance aroused his misgivings. The preface of the *Recherches* was dated April 29. Lavater's *Reply* and Mendelssohn's *Epilogue* had appeared at approximately the same time. Was it possible, then, that Bonnet had deliberately antedated the preface in order to create the impression that the *Recherches* owed nothing to the objections raised in Mendelssohn's *Epilogue*?

In Mendelssohn's view this assumption was not only possible but inevitable. It did not occur to him, apparently, that Bonnet already knew his objections from his letter of February 9. Or perhaps he felt that precisely in view of the private character of the letter Bonnet ought to have credited him with the objections, instead of pretending that he, Bonnet, had tentatively raised them himself. In short, Mendelssohn was convinced that Bonnet's dating was simply a dishonest maneuver designed to bypass him. An insufficiently informed reader, Mendelssohn feared, might easily believe that he had borrowed his arguments against Bonnet from Bonnet himself. "And was this, in fact, *all* I could have said in refuting Bonnet?," he asked Lavater angrily in his letter. His reticence looked somewhat futile in retrospect; he now felt that if he had been more outspoken and bold in his objections, Bonnet could not have disposed of him in such cavalier fashion. The "unexpected behavior" of Bonnet, he frankly confessed to Lavater, had "so completely upset" him that he felt incapable of replying to Bonnet's letter.[30] Mendelssohn's violent reaction to Bonnet was shared by Lessing, who wrote him on January 9, 1771: "I return to you herewith... the letters Bonnet sent you. His name has become so nauseating to me that I would not want to learn from him even the truth. I could not refrain from telling the abbot Jerusalem[31] the circumstance of the antedating of the preface... The abbot said repeatedly: This is not decent. I replied each time: This is worse than not decent; it is vile."[32]

Lessing's condemnation of Bonnet can be fully understood only if one bears in mind that the founding of religion on the basis of historical proofs was utterly repugnant to his way of thinking. The same letter contained his much-debated passage about "the most detestable edifice of nonsense" that ought to be subverted—a reference not to orthodox Christianity but to the efforts of men like Bonnet and Lavater to "prove" Christianity by historical arguments.[33] As for the charge that Bonnet had antedated his preface from ulterior motives, neither Mendelssohn nor Lessing seems to have weighed the evidence with sufficient care. Since Bonnet's *Recherches* appeared as early as May, 1770, he probably did write his preface on April 29.[34] Mendelssohn unquestionably overreacted to Bonnet's *Recherches* on the mistaken assumption that another challenge à la Lavater was in the offing. The fact that he was so completely carried away by his fears can only be explained as due to a failure of nerve.[35] Unfortunately, it caused an abrupt break in the relationship between him and Bonnet. The latter was at first bewildered by Mendelssohn's silence and later felt deeply hurt, when he learned from Lavater the reason for it.[36] The rupture was not altogether complete, however. As Bonnet reports in the final paragraph of the section of his *Mémoires* dealing with his relations with Mendelssohn, he received, from time to time, publications of "the modern Phaedon," as they appeared, but never a single line addressed to him by their author; and he sent him, in return, the complete edition of his own *Oeuvres*. This paragraph of the *Mémoires* was written on October 28, 1786, when Mendelssohn's death, which had occurred early that year, was still fresh in Bonnet's memory. The last few words are a moving tribute to the man "who had served the republic of letters so well by his moral writings," and a valediction: "Vale, carissime, et ama Bonnetum tuum."[37] That Mendelssohn should have so grossly misjudged Bonnet's character was one of the tragic results of the Lavater affair.

Mendelssohn's stamina was further tested by the continuing appearance of pamphlets and tracts taking sides on the issue. For the most part they attacked, in varying degrees of virulence, both Mendelssohn and Judaism.[38] Particularly disconcerting was Kölbele's *Second Letter* (dated July 14, 1770),[39] which displayed considerable forensic skill and produced some alarm in Jewish circles because of its attempt to expose Mendelssohn as a deist whose unbelief in revelation was barely disguised. By quoting certain passages from the *Philosophical Writings* and the *Phaedon* Kölbele sought to create the impression that Mendelssohn had completely substituted reason for revelation. The doubts and misgivings aroused by Kölbele's insinuation seem to have lingered for a whole year. As late as July 22, 1771, Mendelssohn found it necessary to explain his position in a letter to Elkan Herz:

> As for Kölbele, dear friend: I shall be very cross with myself, if I permit myself in future to waste any time on him. Some upright people feel unhappy at my having replied to him the first time. It is to people like him that the saying refers: 'Answer not a fool according to his folly [lest thou also be like unto him].'[40] His accusations are so impudent, and his proofs so stupid, that I would feel ashamed to answer them.
>
> You say that many of our own people might believe him. Dear Rabbi Elhanan, by the Kölbele-minded of our own people I am heartily amused, for a sensible person is bound to perceive quickly the inanity of this foolish babbler. Christians, especially the theologians among them, are altogether easily inclined to accuse one of deism, because their revealed religion has to add to natural religion a tremendous lot that is above and contrary to reason. But blessed be the Lord, who gave us the Tora of Truth. We have no principles ['ikkarim] that are contrary to, or above, reason. Thank God, we add to natural religion nothing except commandments, statutes, and righteous ordinances. As for the principles and fundamental tenets of our religion, they are based on reason and agree in every respect and without any contradiction or conflict whatever with the results of inquiry and true speculation.
>
> Herein lies the superiority of our true, divine religion over all other false religions. The Christians will accuse all our principles of deism or naturalism. Doctor Ernesti in your locality [i.e. Leipzig] has already said in his *Bibliothek*[41] that in his view present-day Judaism was a refined form of naturalism, because I had shown that according to the Law of our Tora the Gentiles were obliged to keep only the seven commandments in order to share in the world-to-come. I do not wish to prolong my discourse on this matter, for in things of this kind 'the talk of the lips tendeth only to penury.'[42] Our people ought, in fairness, to understand this by themselves, for here lies our praise and our glory, and all the books of our philosophers are full of it.[43]

Another charge against which Mendelssohn had to defend himself vis-à-vis his fellow Jews concerned a passage in his *Letter to Lavater* in which he spoke contemptuously of "trashy volumes" *(Scharteken),* neither read by nor known to any sensible Jew, from which self-styled experts in rabbinics took their armor in attacking Judaism. He was, of course, thinking of such notorious anti-Semitic textbooks as those of Eisenmenger and Wagenseil.[44] In his first *Letter* against Mendelssohn, Kölbele had interpreted this passage, either wilfully or mistakenly, as a reference to rabbinic writings: "Most rabbinic writings are perhaps not to your taste; and you call them, for this reason, *Scharteken?* Yet the majority of your people is educated according to these 'trashy volumes.' The Synagogue invokes the authority of these 'trashy volumes.' And the rabbis quote these 'trashy volumes' more frequently than the divine books." Christian scholars too, he added, described Judaism on the basis of these *Scharteken.* He mentioned Michaelis, Semler, the two Buxtorf, Lightfoot, Eisenmenger, and others, without discriminating between the savants of rank and the mere virulent scribblers.[45]

Michaelis, as we saw,[46] agreed with Mendelssohn that certain writings deserved to be called *Scharteken,* and he differentiated between them and "the writings of the learned rabbis." He also rejected Eisenmenger's *Entdecktes Judentum* as a source of valid information on the mentality of learned or honest Jews. Rather ambiguously, however, he called the *Scharteken* spoken of by Mendelssohn "Jewish writings," which could mean writings by or about Jews. And his repudiation of Eisenmenger was likewise rather ambiguous, as Kölbele was not slow in recognizing:[47] only the mentality of an elite among the Jews could not be found in Eisenmenger's portrayal of the Jew, whereas the common run of Jews conformed to the image drawn there.

Although Kölbele's *Second Letter* did not raise again the question of the validity of the term *Scharteken,* it revived the debate about what Mendelssohn had meant by this term of abuse, since people who had paid no attention to the *First Letter* were prompted to read it now. That Mendelssohn felt the impact of the questioning is evident from a letter he wrote to Elkan Herz during the summer of 1770. After making brief reference to his "final reply [to Lavater: the *Epilogue*] and the end of the conflict," he went on to say: "From this reply you will clearly see that I am far removed from declaring a single utterance of our sages, of blessed memory, to be a *Scharteke,* God forbid. There is not a single Gentile scholar who has leveled this charge against me or misinterpreted my words to this effect. Had this been my opinion, I would have had to declare myself a Karaite, not a Rabbanite. I do not wish to speak at great length about this, for one who has the capacity to understand will interpret me correctly, and, thank God, the great men in Israel, the princes of the Tora, agreed with me and expressed their appreciation of all I wrote."[48] This letter seems to have been written in answer to a fairly widespread discussion as to where he stood. Such a discussion was undoubtedly provoked by

Kölbele's misreading of his intention, and perhaps also by Michaelis' ambiguity. Mendelssohn did not consider Kölbele a "scholar," and was therefore not misrepresenting the facts when he denied that any scholar among the Gentiles had misinterpreted him. Actually, an anonymous tract,[49] which Kölbele described as more vehement than his own *First Letter*,[50] had expressed indignation at Mendelssohn's contemptuous designation of *Christian* works on Judaism as *Scharteken*, and took revenge by calling the Talmud and the rabbinic codes of law "trashy volumes."[51]

The anti-Semitic outbursts provoked by the Lavater affair were viewed with dismay in the Jewish community, and the question was raised whether Mendelssohn had acted wisely in answering Lavater at all. It was in response to criticism of this kind that Mendelssohn wrote to Elkan Herz on November 16, 1770:

> You ask me why I allowed myself to get involved in the dispute? I only wish I had got involved more deeply. Thank God, I have not yet regretted it. I pay no attention to any of the *Scharteken* that are being written against me. A person who has a little brain in his head clearly understands that they are without rhyme or reason. I wish I had again an opportunity of this kind: I would do again what I did this time. If some people thought that one had better keep quiet in the face of it all, I for one did not think so. When I consider what one is obliged to do in order to sanctify the Holy Name,[52] I fail to understand why a good many of our people continually clamor against any further writing on the subject by me. God knows, I was not happy when I disengaged myself from the dispute. I "nullified my will before the will of others."[53] Had it depended upon me, I would have given an entirely different answer.[54]

In trying to avoid an open fight, Mendelssohn had been motivated, of course, by his deep-seated aversion to theological controversy. Even so, he might have yielded to his original impulse to give battle, had not the timidity of some of his Jewish advisers, as we gather from this letter, swayed him in the opposite direction. Therefore, there was some justification for his claim that without the pressure exerted upon him by Jewish fears his attitude would have been different. It seems that he purposely overemphasized this point in order to put part of the blame for his leniency upon his friends. He rebuked them, at the same time, for their timorousness. The bold stance that he now assumed was rather at variance with the peaceable attitude he had displayed before. It would be mistaken, however, to dismiss it as insincere and purely diplomatic. The appearance of Bonnet's *Recherches* had changed his mood to one of militancy. Mendelssohn now felt a certain regret at his having failed to attack Bonnet's proofs more forcefully.

This change of mood also owed something to the invigorating effect of his trip to Brunswick and Hanover in October. The letter to Elkan Herz was written upon his return from this journey, with its impressions still fresh in his mind. In Brunswick he had spent a whole evening at the palace with the hereditary prince, and also had met the prince's mother, the duchess Phillippine Charlotte, sister of Frederick the Great. At the request of his host, he paid him another visit the following day.[55] The Lavater affair must have figured prominently in the conversation, and Mendelssohn probably tried to show that Bonnet's *Recherches* had not met the objections he had raised, especially those formulated in the "Counter-reflections" and submitted confidentially to the prince in the January précis. Even more exhilarating than the cordial reception at the palace were the hours Mendelssohn was able to spend with Lessing, who came to Brunswick to take him to his new domicile in Wolfenbüttel.

In May Lessing had commenced his duties as librarian of the famous Bibliotheca Augusta and already he had discovered, among the six thousand manuscripts under his care, Berengar of Tours' hitherto unknown treatise *De Sacra coena* (eleventh century), which had been written in reply to Lancfranc's *De Corpore et sanguine Domini*, and which, as Lessing mentioned in a letter to his father, anticipated Luther's concept of the Eucharist. Mendelssohn congratulated Lessing on this discovery, but he could see no great value in the resuscitation of works that were of purely historical interest, especially if they concerned subjects of this kind, and he frankly confessed that he did not envy Lessing this particular find. Nor did Mendelssohn evince much enthusiasm for "those beautiful coffins," as he called the old tomes on the shelves of the library. He was much more eager to talk about matters of living concern.[56] Some of these we can infer from letters written after Mendelssohn returned home. "Herr Moses has assured me," Lessing wrote to Ramler on October 29, 1770, "that soon we shall have the second part of your *Odes*. What a good fellow you are! How small and contemptible I appear to myself, beguiled as I am by my evil spirit to go astray with people like Berengar and similar nonsense." Had Mendelssohn, perhaps, mentioned the pending publication of Ramler's new *Odes* in order to call Lessing back to his true vocation?

On November 11, 1770, Lessing wrote to his brother Karl: "Above all, I want you to ask Herr Moses to send me the two promised books... John Bunckel, or however he spells his name, and Ferguson. He made me extremely curious to read the first of these, and I would also like to read the other in English rather than in German." The books referred to were Thomas Amory's *The Life of John Buncle, Esq.* (1756, 1766), an extravagant and amusing autobiography, and Adam Ferguson's *An Essay on the History of Civil Society* (1767), a German translation of which had appeared in 1768. (Ferguson's *Institutes of Moral Philosophy*, which was published in 1769, became available in a German version by Christian Garve only in 1772, and thus could not have been the book Lessing wanted.) There was some misadventure in connection with the mailing of the *John Buncle*, and it is not clear from the correspondence whether it ever reached Lessing. It probably did. On February 16, 1771, Lessing reminded Nicolai to send him the book: "Don't let me pine for it any longer." On January 10, 1779, in a letter to Herder, he mentioned Wieland's critical review of Nicolai's translation of this work (in *Teutscher Merkur,* 1778) and the ensuing controversy between Nicolai and Wieland.[57] Ferguson's *Essay* is known to have reached Lessing eventually, but to what extent it contributed to the shaping of his *The Education of the Human Race* is a moot question.[58]

It was during Mendelssohn's visit in Wolfenbüttel in October, 1770, that Lessing showed him the manuscript from which, starting in 1774, he would publish the highly controversial *Fragments of the Unnamed.* There can be hardly any doubt that Lessing had received this manuscript in strictest confidence from the author's children (Doctor Johann Albrecht Heinrich Reimarus and Elise Reimarus) before leaving Hamburg to take up his position in Wolfenbüttel. The deceased author, Hermann Samuel Reimarus (1694–1768), a radical deist and prominent schoolman, had bequeathed to his family a work of some four thousand handwritten quarto pages entitled *Apologie oder Schutzschrift für die vernünftigen Verehrer Gottes* ("Apologia in Defense of the Rational Worshippers of God") that, according to his instructions, was to be kept secret until the time was more propitious for it to be disclosed to the world.[59] Copies of sections of the work nevertheless circulated in Hamburg and Berlin.[60] The copy in Lessing's possession contained the preface and three hundred and thirty-five quarto pages,[61] and its text differed considerably from that of the final version.[62]

When publishing the first of the *Fragments,* Lessing stated that the manuscript from which it had been taken belonged to the ducal library, that it bore no title and gave no hint who its author was, and that he had been unable to find out how and when it had come into the possession of the library.[63] This was, of course, a deliberate mystification designed to conceal the fact that he had himself obtained the copy from the Reimarus family, probably with the purpose of placing it in the library. There is nothing that invalidates the assumption that the manuscript had been entrusted to him by the extremely cautious children of the late author. He had stayed in Hamburg from April, 1767, until May, 1770, and must have spent many hours in Doctor Reimarus' home. He had been not only a patient of the doctor but also his friend,[64] and had made ample use of Reimarus' well-stocked library, as the lists of books returned clearly show.[65]

Among the items returned on April 10, 1770, was a "bundle" *(Konvolut)* of manuscripts by the late Reimarus No. 271 in quarto. This might have been the *Schutzschrift.* Although Elise seems to have played down the closeness of her and her brother's friendship with Lessing in these years (on April 12, 1802, writing to the Swedish diplomat and poet von Brinckmann, she declared that they had then met Lessing only "rarely and accidentally in society," and that their close and intimate acquaintance did not commence much earlier than 1778),[66] the evidence suggests that Lessing was indeed entrusted with the manuscript. Thus, when thanking Lessing for a complimentary copy of the *Berengarius Turonensis,* in a letter written in November or December, 1770, Doctor Reimarus showed himself well aware of the fact that his father's manuscript had found its way into the ducal library at Wolfenbüttel. For he wrote at the end of a letter in which he tried to persuade Lessing to refute Mendelssohn's insistence on the historicity of the Sinaitic revelation:[67] "I have learned that in your library a manuscript is found in which several matters concerning the Jews are investigated; perhaps, still more [than mentioned in the letter] could be quoted from this source . . ." How could Doctor Reimarus have known that this particular manuscript, in which the veracity of the biblical stories was the main target of attack, was extant in the ducal library, unless he himself had recently presented it to Lessing, to be placed there unobtrusively?[68] Even more eloquent testimony is provided by the later correspondence between Lessing and Doctor Reimarus on the one hand and Elise on the other.[69]

It bespeaks the intimacy of their friendship that Lessing revealed to Mendelssohn the secret of the Reimarus *Fragments*. This is evident from the discreet allusions to the subject in their subsequent correspondence. On November 29, 1770, Mendelssohn wrote:[70] "Please let me know in your reply whether the person in question [the hereditary prince of Brunswick] has persisted in urging you to show the manuscript, or whether the keen interest displayed was but short-lived and a mere passing whim." Lessing replied on January 9, 1771:[71] "The curiosity of the person in question could be kept in check. He did not think of the matter again until he caught sight of me a few days ago. I am afraid that his desire to have a close look at the thing itself [the text as distinct from the preface, which had already been left with the prince] does not amount to much. For this very reason I sent him only the preface, using the pretext that the rest of the manuscript was in your hands. Let him not think that I want to force things of this kind upon him."

Mendelssohn seems to have advised Lessing to inform the prince of his "discovery" of the anonymous manuscript before he ventured to publish it. The degree of trust that Lessing placed in Mendelssohn may be gauged from the fact that he gave him the copy of the Reimarus manuscript to take with him to Berlin. He obviously wanted him to read it at leisure in order that he might have the benefit of Mendelssohn's considered judgment of its merits. Some passages in the manuscript bore a striking resemblance to some of the things that Mendelssohn had written in reply to Lavater. Religious truths, Reimarus had said, cannot be verified by miracles. It is fallacious to conclude that because a prophet produced a miracle, he spoke the truth—that because Jesus restored sight to a blind man, the person of the Godhead is triune and Jesus is both God and man. The criteria of the true and false are determined by logic and also must be applied to revealed doctrines.[72] In pleading for tolerance toward deists, Reimarus referred to the Mosaic legislation as having set a precedent: The "strangers in the gates," whom the Israelites were commanded not to oppress but to love, were, according to rabbinic tradition, the descendants of Noah, i.e., general humanity, who observed the fundamental laws of morality and religion. The "seven Noachian laws" had been shown by "the learned Seldenus" (John Selden) to form the basis of "the law of nature and the law of nations," and Maimonides, "the most judicious of all Jews," had declared that those who kept them were assured of the bliss of the pious in the next world.[73]

In the preface to his work Reimarus had struck a somewhat different note. Old Testament figures like Abraham, Jacob, Joseph, Moses, Samuel, and David, he said, "seemed to deviate from the rules of virtue and, indeed, [from] the law of nature and of the nations" and to be guilty of "deceit, craftiness, maliciousness, and cruelty."[74] Having taken the manuscript with him to Berlin, Mendelssohn wrote to Lessing on November 29, 1770:[75]

> I am not yet returning your manuscript, my dear friend. I have as yet not had the time to peruse it with critical eyes. It seems to me that in some places the author was unfair. He is as much biased against certain characters as other people are [biased] in their favor. He traces everything to malicious, cruel, and misanthropic designs, without taking into consideration that even the leader of a band of robbers must be presumed to combine at least some good intentions with his malicious designs. If everything [in the biblical stories] is to have happened in a human way, we have to take the people as they actually were in those times, as acting in accordance with the then prevailing exceedingly limited notions about the law of nations, universal justice, and love of the human race. Viewed from this angle, things will appear in a light totally different from the one in which your Unnamed conceives them. . . . If one wants to consider man as man and to judge him in accordance with the morals, habits, and the culture of his time and in comparison with his contemporaries, one ought to have no prejudice and one should not, out of disgust with prejudice, permit oneself to be misled into unfairness. One ought to know the limitations of man's capacities and not indulge in phantoms that make us dizzy in the head. All the same, the manuscript is very important in every respect, and it alone was worth a trip of thirty miles, even if I had no other reason to recall with so much pleasure the brief period I spent in Brunswick and in Wolfenbüttel.

This letter gives the impression that Mendelssohn had read only the preface and had merely glanced over the rest of the manuscript. It made, however, a telling point: if the biblical personages were to be reduced to human size, as the author insisted, they ought to be considered in their historical setting and not be judged by the abstract yardstick of Enlightenment ideas about natural law. In his reply of January 9, 1771, Lessing defended the Unnamed against the charge of unfairness.[76] Though it was true, he wrote, that historical conditions had to be taken into account, this applied only to ordinary men, not to "patriarchs or prophets," who were supposed to be models of sublime virtue. Since they were presented with the halo of the divine despite certain inexcusable actions on their part, modern scholars were justified in treating them with contempt. Lessing added: "The reason why such procedure by our Unnamed startled you must be entirely due to the fact that you were never obligated to view those blameworthy actions in the light of divinity in which we are supposed to regard them." He probably meant to say: whereas Jews looked upon the heroes of the Old Testament as mere human beings whose moral frailties might be excused or somehow explained, Christians had been taught to see them as "types" prefiguring Christ. Hence latter-day scholars were bound to be much more severe in judging their actions.

While Lessing defended Reimarus against Mendelssohn's charge of unfairness, he by no means wished to adopt the negative attitude toward biblical religion expressed in the manuscript. According to Reimarus, the inevitable conclusion from the nonhistoricity of the biblical reports, which he believed that he had demonstrated, was the nonvalidity of the biblical teachings. Lessing was not prepared to draw this conclusion. He fully accepted the historical criticism of the Bible but refused to make the "inner truths" of the Christian religion dependent on either the veracity or lack of veracity of the historical reports. His letter to Mendelssohn contained the memorable passage about the need to retrieve lost truths.[77] Not just "since yesterday" had he been afraid, he said, that in discarding certain prejudices he might have discarded a little too much, which he would have to "retrieve." Only the fear of "dragging all the rubbish back into my house" had so far prevented him from doing this. "It is infinitely difficult to know when and where to stop, and for the overwhelming majority of people the result of their reflections is the point at which they grew weary of reflection." He would not wish to deny that this had also been the case with the Unnamed in certain places.

Being himself sure that the "inner truths" of the Christian religion could not be affected by the results of historical research, Lessing detested all the more the frantic efforts by Enlightenment theologians and scholars like Bonnet to secure Christian belief by "proving" the historicity of Jesus' miracles and his resurrection. To some extent it had been Lavater's attempt to compel Mendelssohn either to disprove Bonnet's arguments or to convert to Christianity that had served as a catalyst in Lessing's thinking and stimulated his interest in Reimarus' critique of the Bible. He felt that it was high time to expose the fallacy of the alleged historical proofs, and thus it had been his hope that Mendelssohn would vigorously attack Bonnet's arguments. It is highly probable, indeed, that he lent Mendelssohn the Reimarus manuscript with just this idea in mind. He meant to prod Mendelssohn into taking a bolder stance than he had adopted so far. Mendelssohn's letter must have come as a disappointment but a postscript to a subsequent letter, which referred to a seemingly fresh attack by Lavater, gave Lessing another opportunity to urge his friend to speak out without any inhibition:[78]

> Please be so kind as to send me the sheet by the first mail. And I have something further to ask of you. If you answer this attack, do so with all possible frankness and all conceivable emphasis. You alone, in this affair, may and can speak in this manner and are therefore infinitely

more fortunate than other honest people who can further the downfall of the most detestable edifice of nonsense only under the pretext of giving it a new foundation.

The "most detestable edifice of nonsense" that Lessing wanted to see openly attacked was Christianity in both its rigidly orthodox and its shallow neological forms. For the orthodox he had far more respect than for the modern theologians who acknowledged only rational truths and yet affirmed revelation as a positive sanction of those truths and sought to prove the historicity of the biblical reports. It was these theologians that he had in mind when he spoke of "other honest people" who furthered the collapse of the dogmatic system under the pretext of giving it a rational basis. In his "Counterreflections" Mendelssohn had referred to the same group of theologians as "some excellent gentlemen" who explained the trinitarian dogma as mere "human additions" on account of its incompatibility with reason but did so only secretly.[79] Lessing's appeal was not heeded. Mendelssohn preferred not to become involved in theological controversy.

The postscript that had occasioned Lessing's attempt to arouse his friend to an all-out attack indicated, however, a new and disturbing development that could not be ignored. It was appended to a letter written probably in December, 1770, and read as follows:[80] "Have you seen in the *Jenaische Zeitung* what Herr Lavater wrote about me in his travelogue and submitted to the Zürich Consistory? I have written to him concerning the matter and am awaiting his reply; for I could hardly remain silent on this issue, and what I am going to say will be annoying to both him and me." What had happened was the following:[81] In its December, 1770, issue the *Jenaische gelehrte Zeitung* published an account of the conversation that had taken place between Mendelssohn and his visitors in 1764, together with an editorial introduction that stated: "What follows is an excerpt of the travelogue written at the time by Herr Lavater about his first meeting with Herr Mendelssohn." The Latin text was thus presented as an authentic composition by Lavater. It was well known that, according to a custom prevalent in Zürich, theological candidates were obliged, upon returning from trips to other countries, to render an account, in Latin, of the most remarkable experiences they had encountered.[82] The *Report*[83] opened with a glowing description of Mendelssohn's erudition in philosophy, physics, mathematics, and humane letters. His Leibnizian sublimity of thinking, it said, was immediately recognizable. He was not merely learned but possessed of a most lucid mind, and he was far removed from vanity and ostentation. He honored and modestly revered all men of greatness. His utterances were full of wit and loveliness. The *Report* continued:

> We observed in him great piety toward God and the greatest desire to promote the virtue of his fellow-men . . . and, indeed, the highest piety toward his Jewish brethren as well as a singular candor in all his deportment. Yet, though he is averse to the heinous prejudices and blasphemies of the Jews against our Jesus; though he calls him the best man and

free of vices; . . . though he condemns and abhors the Jews of the time and the invectives of the Sadducees and Pharisees against him and the way they treated him; though he deplores the continuing invectives of his brethren against Jesus; though he expects least of all some terrestrial, but a truly spiritual Messiah, that is to say one most perfect, free from all prejudices and vices, a man pure and inaccessible to them [i.e. prejudices and vices], one so lofty by highest, divine authority as none of the prophets ever before him, king of the entire orb of the earth, the future supreme legislator and judge of all nations; . . . he is nevertheless so much surrounded by an impregnable custody and garrison as it were of prejudices against our divine religion that none except God seems to be able to ever guide him to the fortress of the true Messiah.

Mendelssohn lost no time in taking action. As early as December 4, 1770, he wrote to Lavater:[84]

The string that we had but softly touched continued to vibrate for a while in public, and now it is being struck by clumsy fingers to the point of tearing it up. What sort of annoying gibberish still appears on this subject at every fair! All these consequences I have foreseen, more or less, my friend, and I have also foreseen that you will be spared as little as I. . . . The enclosed sheet I could not read without exceeding displeasure. Is this essay authentic? And has it been published with your consent? I fail to recognize myself either in the prodigious compliments paid to me or in the views attributed to me. . . . They are contrary, in part, to my concepts of religion, and, in part, to my philosophical principles, and I believe myself bound in conscience not to permit any views to be ascribed to me in public that I do not hold. I expect to receive your kind reply in the nearest future, and it will give me infinite pleasure to learn that this description is either falsely attributed to you or, at least, is falsified in part, in which case I shall be spared the necessity of referring again to this awkward point.

Lavater replied on December 15 that he was equally upset by this publication: "I have no words to express my regret, and I testify before the Omniscient that I am completely innocent of this unfortunate publication, and that I neither know nor am able to guess how it reached Jena." This emphatic declaration could have left no doubt in Mendelssohn's mind that Lavater bore no responsibility for the appearance of the Latin *Report* in the Jena paper.

The mystery of who did submit the *Report* for publication remains unsolved to this day. Nicolai's inquiry at the time produced no result beyond the editor's reply that a Jena "public teacher, who was free to insert what he wanted," had handed him the article without intending to cause any unpleasantness to Mendelssohn or to Lavater.[85] It is possible that the instigators of the publication were those same Swiss theologians who had urged Lavater to write the ill-fated addenda to his *Reply*.[86] While Lavater thus bore no share of blame for the publication, in his answer to Mendelssohn he did admit the authenticity of the *Report*: "Whether it is genuine?—I believe, insofar as I can remember (for I have tried in vain to find the original), that it is fairly genuine; though some not very important phrases appear rather strange to me."[87] This admission seems to indicate that Lavater was indeed the author, for he relied on his memory, he had been looking for the original, and he disowned only certain phrases. Yet the next paragraph of his letter reads:[88]

> But this essay is not by me—it is by my friend [Felix Hess] (God rest his soul), who travelled with me; I do not find, however, that my admittedly spirited and precipitate, yet very honest and truthful friend really entered in his diary anything that was substantially at variance with what could be inferred, so far as I can remember, from your demeanor and words. Nor could I have assumed that your concepts of religion and philosophical principles were thereby contradicted. Should my honest friend have erred, or should I be in error, and should you find this error to be harmful to you in the least degree, you are free, in God's name, to justify yourself. I surely never write lies, deliberate lies, either for public consumption or in my diary, nor did my friend, God rest his soul. . . . Take any action, dear friend, you desire and consider appropriate for the cause of truth and virtue as well as to the complete settlement of all conflict. Yet I beg of you before God— not to spare my friend or me but tell the whole truth with that sort of artlessness with which we hope not to have credited you without reason.

This part of the letter could only strengthen Mendelssohn's suspicion that Lavater was in fact the author of the *Report*. Though attributing it to his friend, he so completely identified himself with the friend, and so strongly deprecated any suggestion that either of them wrote "lies" in his diary, that the dividing line between the two became virtually meaningless.

Lavater seems to have sensed the unsatisfactory nature of his reply, for three days later, on December 18, 1770, he sent Mendelssohn an essay with the request that he check it and forward it, in case it met with his approval, to the editor of the Jena paper, for publication. He hoped thereby to have done "everything demanded of me by honesty and fairness."[89] Mendelssohn passed the essay on to Jena, and on January 25, 1771, the *Jenaische gelehrte Zeitung* published it as *Herr Lavater's Declaration*, with an editoral note explaining that Mendelssohn's misgivings about the previously published *Report* had given rise to this statement. The *Declaration* read:[90]

> With utter dismay I have learned through Herr Mendelssohn that the ninety-second number of the *gelehrte Zeitungen* contained a Latin excerpt of the traveller's diary that I was said to have written, and that concerned my first meeting with that venerable man. I have no words to express my astonishment at this occurrence.—I myself had publicly characterized the step taken by me recently against Herr Mendelssohn as precipitate. I almost reproached myself for having mentioned the conversation with him, though this had been done in the most general and, I believe, the most innocuous terms.
>
> And now a third party had the audacity to drag into the limelight, without my knowledge, an obsolete, immature, unpolished private essay that was not even written by me but by one of my former traveling companions, as if it were my work. . . . I fail to see the right of anyone

to thrust upon the public the manuscripts of an author still alive without
his knowledge, especially when they contain personal opinions that might
entail important consequences. . . . And what would Herr Mendelssohn
have to think, were he not a wise man who understands that certain
phrases in a diary, which the author can amplify in his own mind, may
easily and without the least dishonesty assume, in a foreign language,
too strong and vague a meaning. . . .

Did Lavater give himself away when he contested anybody's right to
publish manuscripts of an author who was still alive without his consent?[91]
Not necessarily. Since the *Report* had been ascribed to him, the editor
could rightly be blamed for having committed to print an article whose
presumed author was alive and available for consultation. However, the
suspicion that Lavater was not so innocent as he pretended is well-founded.
Certain phrases describing Mendelssohn's character are reminiscent of passages in his diary of April 7, 1763.[92] Although an examination of the
diary has shown that it contains no entry about Mendelssohn's views on
Jesus,[93] this does not prove that the Latin *Report* for the consistory could
not have been written by Lavater on the basis of the diary and his recollections of the conversation. Nor does the ascription of the *Report* to his
friend Felix Hess sound too convincing. Since the two companions shared
the same experiences on their trip to Germany, it may be assumed that
they gave a joint account of their remarkable experiences. If Hess also
kept a diary, as Lavater asserted, they could have drawn on both sources
when compiling the *Report*. It is also conceivable that it was Hess who
actually wrote the Latin composition, based on one or two diary records,
and that Lavater could for this reason state in good conscience that his
friend was the author of the document. At all events, Lavater was deeply
implicated in the genesis of the *Report,* and this accounts for the tortuous
manner in which he pleaded both innocence and truthfulness.

Mendelssohn, who of course knew nothing of the diary, felt nevertheless, with sound instinct, that Lavater had had a great deal to do with
the *Report*. His letter acknowledging the *Declaration* makes little effort to
disguise the fact that he identified the author of the Latin text with Lavater:
"I heartily thank you for having spared me the necessity of speaking publicly
about this matter. I may, however, confess to you in particular what, in
fact, offended me in the excerpt from your, or rather your friend's, diary."
That the reference to "your" diary was not a mere slip of the pen becomes
clear from the way Mendelssohn tries, in the next paragraph, to disabuse
Lavater's mind of the "prejudice" against the Jews underlying the *Report*.
He pleads with Lavater as if there was no doubt that he was guilty of
that particular prejudice:[94]

It is an ingrained prejudice of your coreligionists that the Jews, all of
them, incessantly slander the religion of the Christians and its founder,
and thereby a great many things are conveniently explained in dogmatics,

and much that is both irreligious and unrational is thereby justified in ordinary life. Yet it does not befit you, most worthy friend of humanity, even to seem to favor suchlike prejudices, which are but relics of the old barbarism, and to reawaken, albeit by mere figures of speech, the religious hatred that we ought to put to sleep in increasing measure. I say: by mere figures of speech, for I know that in your heart you are far removed from these misanthropic sentiments, and that the emphatic expressions "the heinous prejudices and blasphemies" and "the continuing invectives of his brethren against Jesus" are mere ornaments of speech. Yet even this I could not stand as coming from you, and least of all allow to be put so firmly on my account.

This letter, which bears the date January 15, 1771, is not only the last that Mendelssohn addressed to Lavater in connection with the "affair"[95] but is in every sense, an epilogue to it. The publication of the Latin *Report* had shown that its author harbored the same prejudices and ill feelings against Jews that had been more forcefully expressed in some of the virulent pamphlets that had been appearing. Mendelssohn, who refused to dignify such writings by a reply, could not help rejecting accusations against Jews of which Lavater himself seemed to be guilty.

The prejudice that Mendelssohn was particularly anxious to refute was the Christians' belief that the Jews continually slandered Jesus. An anonymous pamphlet,[96] of which Lavater had said, in his letter to Mendelssohn on December 15, 1770, that it went to his heart,[97] contained the sentence: "He who tenderly and fraternally loves the enemies and slanderers of Jesus Christ; who seeks their friendship and commends them as exceedingly wise and virtuous men is not a Christian, and if he pretends to be one, he is a false brother and a hypocrite."[98] This was a personal attack on Lavater, who had praised and sought to befriend Mendelssohn. Kölbele's *Second Letter,* to which Lavater had referred in the same context as one that had caused him "a great deal of annoyance," repeatedly mentioned the "slandering" of Jesus by the Jews.[99] Provoked by Rousseau's conjecture about some secret knowledge of the historical Jesus that the Jews might possess,[100] Kölbele challenged Jewish scholars to produce any evidence that would invalidate such authentic testimonies as that of Josephus.[101] He rightly denied that the "slanderous book *Toledoth Yeshu*"[102] was of historical value, since it was of medieval origin, and he mentioned the fact that modern, enlightened ("deistic") Jews repudiated it.[103] He also spoke, however, of the "slanders of the talmudists against our Jesus"[104] and implied that the vilification of Jesus was an essential part of the Jewish tradition.

Mendelssohn felt it necessary, therefore, to clarify the position in his final letter to Lavater. He did not deny that a strain of hostility toward Christianity existed among Jews, but he saw in it merely a reaction to the persecution they had undergone: "When the powerful still spilled blood for religion's sake, the weak had left to them no other means of retaliation than, as the saying goes, to snap their fingers in the pocket, that is, to slander their foe's religion behind closed doors. In the measure that the spirit of persecution ceases on the one side, hatred ceases on the other, making room for appreciation, and it is now the duty of all good men to relegate the old feud to oblivion."[105]

Mendelssohn continued:[106]

> The same applies to the wrong done to the person of Jesus by the Sadducees and Pharisees. It would seem, though, that one still takes us to account on this score. Do I know what sort of just or unjust sentences were passed by my ancestors in Jerusalem 1700 or 1800 years ago? I should be greatly embarrassed were I to be held responsible for the sentences passed, e.g. by the Royal High Court in Berlin, during my lifetime. Besides, we on our part possess no reliable information concerning that great event, no legal documents, no reports that we could oppose to yours. The notorious *Toledoth Yeshu* is a monstrosity from the age of legends. It fits into it, and it is looked upon as such by my brethren. Some traces of reports are found here and there in the Talmud. But it is uncertain whether they refer to the same event, and they are, surely, insufficient to allow us to judge.
>
> How then are we in a position to offer a decisive judgment in a case about which we know so little? All of my coreligionists who have but the least sense of fairness are bound, at least, to suspend judgment, and to leave it to the great rewarder of the good and avenger of evil to judge the accusers and persecutors of Jesus according to their deserts. I have the pleasure of knowing many people of my faith who are possessed of this wise moderation and permit themselves neither blasphemies nor slanders.
>
> I also know many a Jew who, like me, go a step further and, basing themselves upon the statements of Christian testimonies (for, I repeat, we have no reliable Jewish ones), acknowledge the innocence and moral goodness of that founder's character, yet do so on the clear condition (1) that he never meant to regard himself as equal with the Father; (2) that he never proclaimed himself as a person of divinity; (3) that he never presumptuously claimed the honor of worship; and (4) that he did not intend to subvert the religion of his fathers...

In his final utterance vis-à-vis Lavater, Mendelssohn thus completely reaffirmed the stand he had taken from the very start. While he disavowed, in the fairest and most judicial manner, any kind of anti-Christian sentiment and pleaded for an end of all hatred in response to an end of all persecution, he made his respect for Jesus as a moral teacher dependent on four stated conditions.

To the theological tone of the pamphlet-literature that had denounced him as a mere deist he turned a deaf ear. Characteristic of his nontheological stance is the way in which he replied in a private letter to Pastor Hesse, the most moderate and thoughtful of his opponents, who had sent him, with an apologetic covering note, the pamphlet he had written on Mendelssohn's *Letter to Lavater*.[107] Mendelssohn told Hesse that he would probably have included a reply to this pamphlet in his *Epilogue*, had it reached him in time. One wonders whether he would have entered into the substance of some of the more theological points raised by Hesse.

It seems likely that he would have refrained from doing so. For in his letter to Hesse he cited an example of the kind of refutation he would have included in the *Epilogue*. He would have answered "the argument, e.g., from our civil misery to the untruth of our religion—I am astonished that one still upholds this proof." Hesse had written: "No Israelite groaning [under oppression] can deny that it is a very severe curse that oppresses his nation. . . . It is necessary to assume that a national crime, and for that matter a continuing national crime, underlies this continuing harsh decree imposed on Israel. The justice of God and the purpose of all his acts of punishment in this life leave no doubt concerning this."[108] Mendelssohn's letter continues: "This kind of drawing of conclusions seems to me not only unphilosophical but even contrary to the spirit of the Gospels. What is it that Jesus and the Apostles have sought to drive home with greater emphasis than the inadmissibility of concluding from the temporal to the eternal? Could we not enjoy all civil advantages and privileges, if only we were ready to simulate, as our brethren in Portugal and Spain did? . . . The strangest thing is that everything possible is being done by the Christians in order not to lose this argument. One keeps us carefully under pressure so as to be able to refute us the more triumphantly."

Clearly, Mendelssohn was unresponsive to purely theological reasoning but was immediately aroused when a moral issue was at stake. As a Jew and as a philosopher he was struck by the absurdity of the stock clerical argument that Hesse had dished up again. The Lavater affair had sharpened his awareness of the menace presented by the spirit of clericalism, and had caused him to cherish all the more the free spirit of inquiry that he saw being fostered in philosophy.

CHAPTER FOUR

Changes in the Pattern of Life

The Strange Illness

The year 1771 began rather auspiciously for Moses Mendelssohn: the Royal Academy in Berlin decided on February 7 to propose to the king that the vacant place of a "membre ordinaire de la classe de philosophie spéculative" be filled by the appointment of *"le juif Moses."*[1]

Johann Georg Sulzer, who had moved the resolution, announced it to Mendelssohn that same day in an official letter:[2] "The Royal Academy has directed me to inform you that it desires to have you as a regular member of the philosophical class. It is its desire and hope that you will not object to such a position, although, for the time being, it carries no stipend. Should this be the case, the proposal will be dispatched to the king tomorrow. Kindly let me know whether this meets with your approval. To have you for a colleague would be a particular pleasure to me."[3] On February 12 Nicolai wrote to Lessing:[4] "Our friend Moses was elected a regular member of the academy (albeit without a stipend) last Thursday. True, the king's confirmation has not yet been received from Potsdam, but no one doubts it."

The king had *his* doubts, it seems, and chose to veto the appointment by the simple expedient of ignoring the letter. His ominous silence was attributed first to the pressures of state business,[5] and when the academy convened on September 26, 1771, a majority of the academicians voted to resubmit Mendelssohn's name to the enlightened monarch. But this resolution was not carried out. In the end, the academy preferred not to risk offending the king. A list of three names from which he might choose was submitted, and Mendelssohn's name was not one of the three. Mercifully, Mendelssohn did not learn of this cowardly act on the academy's part. When no news of any response by the king was forthcoming, he seems to have asked Sulzer about the situation, and Sulzer's reply indicated that the academy's letter proposing Mendelssohn's name, as well as that of Garve and some others, had been dispatched to Potsdam on September 27, as Sulzer's inquiries had shown. The matter was all very puzzling, he suggested, and the only person likely to be able to shed light on it was Privy Cabinet Councillor Köper. Yet Sulzer did not offer to proceed with further inquiries. It is hardly likely that he was unaware of the omission of Mendelssohn's name from the final list. He probably wanted to hide the embarrassing truth under the cloak of an assumed mystery.[6] The names included in the list were those of Garve, Spalding, and Privy Councillor Gualtieri.[7] Since no appointment was made at this time—the king kept the vacancy open until 1783[8]—Mendelssohn at least had the consolation of knowing that he had not been bypassed in favor of someone else.

There can be hardly any doubt, that King Frederick the Great's action (or inaction) in this matter was due to anti-Jewish sentiment.[9] How Mendelssohn felt about the rebuff may be gauged from two remarks of his. The first is found in a letter he wrote to Joachim Heinrich Campe, Basedow's successor as head of the Dessau *Philanthropin*. Mendelssohn saw nothing extraordinary or novel in the school's policy of admitting Jewish pupils and masters, since there was a whole string of precedents for the promotion of Jews even to the highest academic ranks: a Royal Prussian Academy of Sciences had elected a Jew to membership, the Berlin Gesellschaft naturforschender Freunde included Jews among its fellows, Mendes d'Acosta had been secretary of the London Society [of Sciences] a few years ago, and early in the century the elector of the Palatinate had invited Spinoza to occupy the chair of philosophy at Heidelberg.[10] It is obvious from this that what mattered to Mendelssohn was that the *academicians* had elected him, and he did not conceal his pride. Even more outspoken was the consolation he offered his friend Herz Homberg, whose appointment to a post in the Austrian public school system had been vetoed by the emperor: it would have been worse, Mendelssohn told him, to have been approved by his Majesty but rejected as unfit by philosophy. "As you know," he continued, "I had a similar experience. The academy elected me a member but his Royal Majesty did not ratify the election."[11]

The recognition Mendelssohn had won from his peers compensated him for the disappointment he had suffered. Yet the king's veto of his appointment was nevertheless a cruel blow at the time, for it killed Mendelssohn's last hope of freeing himself from the burdens of business and being able to give his undivided attention to the things he loved most. Although the position at the academy had entailed no stipend "for the time being," the prospect of becoming a salaried member was by no means precluded. Nicolai may have expressed not only his own hope but Mendelssohn's when, in his letter announcing the news to Lessing, he envisaged the possibility of a "stipend in the future" that "would give him the leisure he does not have as yet."[12]

No one was better qualified to read Mendelssohn's mind than Nicolai, and he well knew that Mendelssohn was beset by a deep sense of frustration. Only a few months earlier, on October 1, 1770, Mendelssohn had written to him in an outburst of despair:[13] "When I reflect on my past life, [I realize that] I have perhaps acted wrongly, at least too hesitantly, in failing to make greater sacrifices for the sake of my inclination toward the humanities. Resoluteness, resoluteness! This I lacked at all times. Always I slid along with the times, not knowing whither. Now it is too late to make plans. What is left undone by the age of forty, my friend, can be written off and remain untried forever." He had reached the decisive age of forty in September, 1769.

Mendelssohn had made an effort to start a new life in 1766, when he approached Abbt for advice and received an encouraging response from him and the count of Schaumburg-Lippe.[14] But Abbt's sudden death had buried Mendelssohn's hopes. On June 12, 1767, he had written to the count:[15] "Last year I entertained the confident hope of living in the near future under the protection of your Grace *in otio litterario* near my friend, your governmental counsellor Abbt. Since that time my particular circumstances have undergone such a change that I had to renew my association with the merchant to whose business I attend. For the time being I shall have to be content to devote only some hours of leisure to the Muses and to revere an admirable prince but from afar."

In accusing himself of a lack of "resoluteness," Mendelssohn was probably thinking not merely of this particular missed opportunity. It seems that he blamed himself for not having taken a bolder initiative to change the course of his life at various times. We know, on the other hand, that he did not always regard his commercial activities as an unmitigated evil. A contemporary of his, Karl Gottlieb Bock, wrote in a letter to a friend, long after Mendelssohn's death:[16] "I remember that Mendelssohn used to say that without the toil of the silk shop and the clerkship he would never have felt the taste of happiness in philosophizing to quite that same degree." However in October, 1770, when he confided his sense of failure to Nicolai, he was not merely in one of his frequent moods of lament over the little amount of time he could spare for the "Muses," although he felt this too.[17] As the letter to Nicolai reveals, he was suffering even then from a sense of nervous debility. Having requested Nicolai to order for him two English books from abroad, he wrote: "I have no more desire for mathematical works. . . . I am fully aware that in the condition in which Providence has placed me I have to keep away from what is too abstract. It is sad if one has to resolve to make a halt in whatever it may be, and even to retrogress, as is bound to happen in the end." It was at this point in the letter that Mendelssohn burst out into the self-recrimination quoted above. His despair was obviously caused by the realization that his mental stamina had declined and that he was no longer capable of the highly abstract thinking required for mathematics.

A letter that Mendelssohn wrote to Kant on December 25, 1770, provides further evidence that he was already aware of a nervous debility and its effect on his power to cope even with the subtleties of philosophy. The occasion for the letter was the return to Berlin of the young Mordecai ben Hirz Levi, known as Marcus Herz (1747–1803), who in 1766, at the age of nineteen, had begun to study philosophy under Kant. It was he whom Kant chose to be his "respondent" in 1770 when he presented his famous dissertation *De mundi sensibilis atque intelligibilis forma et principiis*, which marked the breakthrough to his new phase. As is well known, Kant's letters to Herz during the decade in which the *Critique of Pure Reason* (1781) took shape are the principal sources of our knowledge of Kant's thinking during that decisive period. After his return to Berlin, Herz wrote Kant an enthusiastic letter of thanks for all he had done for him—for his having made him into a new person—and mentioned that the first visit he had paid was to Mendelssohn. They had spent four hours together, he reported, discussing some of the topics treated in Kant's dissertation, which Mendelssohn admired without agreeing on all points. The impression one receives from Herz' account of Mendelssohn's critical observations would seem to belie the idea that his entering into Kant's way of reasoning put a strain on him. What Mendelssohn was most fond of, Herz wrote, was "to develop metaphysical topics," and he announced to Kant a letter by Mendelssohn—albeit a short one, since Mendelssohn believed that subtle points could not be settled by correspondence.[18]

A somewhat different picture emerges from Mendelssohn's own letter to Kant:[19] "I took hold of the dissertation with the keenest interest and read it through with very great pleasure, though for some time [*seit Jahr und Tag*] I have hardly been in a position, owing to the considerable weakness of my nervous system, to think through, with due effort, speculative matters of such high caliber." The letter contains a number of pertinent remarks on "side issues" of the dissertation. It expresses satisfaction at the fact that Kant's ideas about infinity in extension were similar to what had been said by Mendelssohn in the revised third dialogue of the *Philosophische Gespräche*, which was about to appear in the 1771 edition of his *Philosophische Schriften*.[20] It disagrees with Kant's notion of the subjectivity of time and rejects the charge that Leibniz' definition of time implied a *circulus vitiosus;* etc.[21] Above all, Mendelssohn immediately perceived the significance of the dissertation as "the fruit of prolonged meditations" that "must be considered as part of a complete system" worked out by the author who, for the time being, had wanted to reveal only samples of the whole. He urged Kant to publish his entire work as soon as possible, life being so short.

The elegiac note is even more pronounced in the introductory part of the letter. Speaking of the happy lot of the young Marcus Herz, who had had Kant to guide and develop his gifts, Mendelssohn wrote with a tinge of melancholy: "Many a one who did not have this good fortune was left to his own devices in the immeasurable realm of truth and error, and had to consume his precious time and best energies in a hundred futile attempts. In the end he lacked both time and energy to continue on the road that he had at long last discovered, after much groping. If only I had had a Kant for a friend before I was twenty!" The last sentence makes it perfectly clear that the odyssey Mendelssohn described was meant to portray his own life. He bewailed his own fate: having found his way at long last, he no longer had the time and energy to progress along it further.

No doubt Mendelssohn took too gloomy a view of his situation: much important work still lay ahead of him, even in the area of philosophy. Yet his premonition was essentially right: his creative powers as a philosopher were indeed on the wane. At the very moment that his contact with the rising star of Königsberg was firmly established through Marcus Herz, Mendelssohn was already more or less *hors de combat*, though Kant was not aware of it;[22] an epistle by Mendelssohn or Lambert, Kant wrote to Herz on February 21, 1772, carried more power to induce an author to reexamine his views than ten feather-weight reviews in the *Göttingische Anzeigen*.[23] But Mendelssohn was fully aware of his own condition, and out of this disconcerting knowledge of the limitations imposed upon him grew the desire to serve his people. A reorientation evolved that made him, the philosopher of the German Enlightenment, also the initiator of a new era in Jewish history. This development might not have taken place had not a severe and drawn-out illness forcibly changed the pattern of his life.

One night in the early spring of 1771 Mendelssohn awoke after a short and restless sleep to find himself incapable of moving his limbs, making a sound, or opening his eyes. The paralysis was accompanied by a sensation of a burning mass pushing downward along his spine, or of someone lashing his neck with fiery rods. His heart was palpitating and he was in a state of extreme anxiety, yet fully conscious. This agony lasted until some external stimulation of the senses broke the spell. Throughout the following day there remained, however, a measure of agitation that made any kind of mental effort impossible. Attacks of this kind reoccurred whenever he tried to resume even moderate intellectual activity.[24]

Doctor Marcus Eliezer Bloch, Mendelssohn's friend and physician, diagnosed the illness as due to a congestion of blood in the brain, and attributed it to excessive mental strain during the previous year, recalling that there had been a series of similar (though less severe) attacks in the year 1758.[25] Doctor Bloch prescribed a therapy designed to prevent the rush of blood to the brain, but both his diagnosis and the measures he applied were contested by two other physicians, who considered the cause of the illness a debility of the nerves and prescribed tonics for the nerve fibers. When the medication taken on their advice resulted in a worsening of the patient's condition, Doctor Bloch's rather radical therapy, which had frightened the family, was finally adopted.[26] It seems that an important contributing factor in the acceptance of Doctor Bloch's viewpoint was the fact that it was supported by the Hanoverian court physician, Doctor Johann Georg Zimmermann, who was consulted by letter. Mendelssohn had met him for the first time in October, 1770, when he spent a few days in Hanover.[27] Zimmermann's reply, an undated copy of which has been preserved,[28] reflects his deep concern for the patient and is an interesting document of eighteenth-century medicine:

> Oh, how sincerely I pity dear Herr Moses, concerning whose illness I have no doubts. It consists indeed in too strong a rush of the blood to the head. If it were a mere debility of nerves, Herr Moses would surely be unwell, but since things are as they are, for Heaven's sake (and this is the reason that I reply on the spot), for Heaven's sake, no [iron] filings, no cold baths, which would terribly aggravate the illness and bring about the apoplexy we want to prevent. China bark and other invigorating measures would at best be of no help. Anything, however, that can reduce the rush of the blood to the head seems to be useful. Blood-letting on the foot, leeches applied to the ears, enemas, foot baths in water containing boiled grains of mustard seed, mustard plaster under the soles of the feet, daily use of cream of tartar, and lemonade as regular beverage, no wine, no coffee, little or no meat at all, principally vegetarian food. No mental effort whatsoever, and when all this has been done for a month or two, perhaps China bark. I hope that all this will be of some help and avert all danger, though the dear patient will be somewhat weakened in the process.

Doctor Bloch's therapy was almost identical with that suggested by Zimmermann, but slightly more rigorous. It included daily blood-lettings; cold fomentations of the head; foot bathing in river water containing wheat bran; at bedtime, an ample dosage of a powder in which cream of tartar and salpeter were mixed; sleeping in an upright position; no meat, coffee, spices, or fermented beverages in the diet; no smoking of tobacco; and a strict order to refrain from all reading, writing, sustained thinking, and learned discussion.

According to Bloch's medical report,[29] two months of treatment so improved the patient's condition that he was able to resume his business activities, though not his learned pursuits. However, this information is contradicted by what Mendelssohn himself wrote to Elkan Herz on July 22, 1771, about four months after the onset of his illness; according to this letter he had not yet attended to his business at all.[30] At any rate, the therapy had the effect of preventing a worsening of the condition, and it even produced some improvement. But it did not cure the illness. There was a reduction in the frequency and severity of the paralytic attacks, but it was six years before the patient was back to a relatively normal condition. As late as November, 1776, Mendelssohn had to tell a friend that he was unable to read his book, since "my fibers still resist the least strain."[31]

Yet in all these years Mendelssohn did read a great deal. He wrote many important, thoughtful letters. He began publishing again, he undertook many journeys, he engaged in many learned conversations. Thus his illness seems not to have been a continuous state of extreme disability. It occurred in spasms and permitted him a considerable amount of activity in between. But he was prone to attacks whenever he overexerted himself, and strictly speaking the illness was never cured. Until the end of his life he had to take care not to expose himself to any excessive stimulation of his nerves. In a letter to a composer, written on December 14, 1784, he expressed deep regret at his not being able to attend a musical performance, since in the evening "every lively sensation has the direst effects on my sickly nervous system, and music that touches the heart is deadly poison to me" (the performance was of Mendelssohn's rendition of Psalm 65 set to music). The letter concludes with the sentence, "Keep well and pity your neurasthenic friend M. Mendelssohn."[32]

Nicolai had his own theory about the nature of this erratic sickness. In his notes on his letters to Lessing (published in 1794) he commented on Mendelssohn's illness from the vantage point of one who had long been a close observer of the scene and now could look back on the entire range of events. On April 26, 1773, he had told Lessing: "Moses has the cold fever; one hopes that this will dispose of his illness." His comment reads: "Unfortunately, this did not happen. It was the illness that he had contracted through too much effort; that the physicians first failed to recognize; that gradually consumed him, and eventually brought about his premature death. This illness is described in Doctor Bloch's *Medicinische Bemerkungen*...; yet not all circumstances that are psychologically important are mentioned nor are subsequent events. For the recovery announced [by Doctor Bloch] was not of long duration, notwithstanding the fact that some improvement took place. The philosophical resignation with which this extraordinary man bore his suffering is hardly comprehensible. Out of friendship I did not visit him at that time for a whole year, because the interesting and lively character of our conversation immediately aggravated his condition."[33]

Nicolai obviously shared Doctor Bloch's view that the illness was due to excessive mental strain, but his reference to additional causes of a psychological nature is quite striking, reflecting an insight that one would not expect from an eighteenth-century writer. What he meant may be inferred from a comment of his concerning an earlier letter to Lessing, which mentioned Mendelssohn's moral victory in the Lavater affair. In explaining Mendelssohn's decision to arm himself for battle, Nicolai pointed out that "this peace-loving man" had been placed in a situation of great embarrassment and that his "annoyance at having been dislodged from his quiet life affected his health and dealt it the blow that later produced his severe and psychologically so strange illness, which was to become the cause of his premature death."[34] It is clear from this passage that the decisive factor in Mendelssohn's "strange" illness was not simply overexertion but the "blow" to his health caused by the emotional upheaval he had suffered during the Lavater controversy. As Nicolai saw it, it was irritation at being forced to become a fighter that had so upset the "peace-loving" man.

In accepting Nicolai's psychological emphasis one need not go so far as to imply that Mendelssohn's strange illness was essentially psychological. Not the slightest warrant can be adduced in favor of such an assumption. On the contrary, the calm and pious resignation with which Mendelssohn reacted to his tribulations testifies to a remarkable inner stability. The elegant, steady, and flowing handwriting in his letters of the 1770's is sufficient evidence of a mind at peace with itself. Doctor Bloch's report indicates that Mendelssohn had experienced similar attacks before, and Mendelssohn's letter to Kant mentioned that he had suffered from a nervous debility for a long time. It has also to be remembered that since childhood he had been afflicted with kyphoscoliosis, a curvature of the spine.

Taking all the recorded symptoms into account, one may infer that Mendelssohn suffered attacks of paroxysmal auricular tachycardia. Such fits of abnormally rapid heart-action in the auricle may result from nervous, emotional, toxic, or digestive stresses. They are accompanied by a smothering sensation in the chest and in the throat, and by a sense of congestion in the neck and head. There ensues a general weakness caused by diminished cardiac output and giddiness caused by cerebral ischemia. It is typical of such attacks that they often start after a short sleep. It is evident from the description of the attack that no true paralysis occurred. Some etiological factor may be found in the circulatory stresses caused by Mendelssohn's kyphoscoliosis. Thus on no account can the nature of his illness be considered as psychosomatic.[35] This diagnosis would not seem to be contradicted by the fact that mental strain, such as hard thinking in abstract terms, tended to have an adverse effect on him. Strenuous activity of this kind is nowhere said to have brought on attacks of illness as such. It resulted merely in sleeplessness and the discomforts following from lack of sleep (particularly headaches) the morning after.

Unfortunately Mendelssohn's doctors were not capable of understanding the nature of his disease; not only were they helpless in dealing with cardiac conditions, they may have even done some harm by blaming his troubles on mental overexertion and putting him on an intellectual starvation diet. Fortunately, his ailment, protracted though it was, put him out of action for only limited periods, and after 1777 it settled down to a still more tolerable pattern.

Ups and Downs: A Chronicle of Events

Though illness cast a large shadow upon Mendelssohn's life, there were bright spots and happy interludes that helped to sustain his morale. The

1770's were not a uniform grey in grey or an unrelieved tale of woes. In tracing the course of events from 1771 to 1778 we shall encounter new friendships created and old ones deepened. Enforced abstinence from literary activity allowed Mendelssohn to give these human relationships their full due. It also facilitated a reappraisal of his life and a reorientation toward new goals. Far from being tedious or barren, the years of illness were both dramatic and rich in terms of inwardness.

A testimony to the high regard in which Mendelssohn was held by the Jewish community of Berlin was the honor paid him on April 1, 1771, immediately after the start of his illness. Its obvious purpose was to uplift his spirit. At a meeting held on that day, the elders, assessors, and fifteen communal officers, headed by the chief rabbi, resolved to make Mendelssohn eligible for the honorary position of *parnass* (elder) by suspending in his case the strict rules governing the election of communal dignitaries. Ordinarily only members of high-income groups who paid a correspondingly large sum in community taxes, and who also already had to their credit years of service in the lower echelons of office, could aspire to the rank of *parnass*.[1] Mendelssohn had met neither of these statutory conditions. Yet "although this [resolution] contradicts the statutes of the kehilla,"—the minutes of that special session recorded[2]—"all rules are suspended in the case of a great man like him."

It was most probably on account of his prolonged illness that for almost a decade Mendelssohn was not actually elected to a position of leadership in the community. Not until the elections of May 1, 1780, did he become a dignitary of the kehilla for the first time: he was made one of the five treasurers *(govim)*. In the minutes of April 6, 1783, he figures as an "assessor" *(manhig)* elected to membership on a committee dealing with budgetary matters. In the elections held on April 21, 1783, he became one of the five high dignitaries called *tovim*.[3] Toward the end of his life Mendelssohn thus played an active part as a communal leader. The resolution of 1771 had not been an empty gesture, nor had it been the first token of esteem shown him by the community. The services he had rendered during the Seven Years' War as a translator of hymns and writer of sermons had been duly recognized. At a meeting of the community leaders held on March 26, 1763, a decision had been taken to exempt him from taxation and a document embodying this resolution was entered in the minute-book *(pinkas)*. Written in poetic style, replete with biblical quotations, it made him in fact an honorary member of the community.[4]

The honor awarded to Mendelssohn in April, 1771, came at a moment of considerable anguish. A letter to Lessing dated April 9 describes his situation in his own words:[5] "Since recently my condition has been so miserable that reading and writing has been strictly forbidden to me. I am to spend this entire summer in such a prosaic [*musenlos*] fashion and, like that king,[6] to be deprived of humanity in order to regain my reason among the wild beasts." However, the fact that Mendelssohn did write to Lessing and sent him a copy of the second edition of his *Philosophical Writings* shows that by the date of this letter the worst seemed to be over. On April 10 he felt sufficiently strong to write a long letter to Professor Michaelis, a letter so full of learning and humor that it seemed to belie his illness altogether.

The letter of April 10 was in reply to two epistles from Michaelis dated December 27, 1770, and March 8, 1771, respectively; obviously Mendelssohn was anxious not to delay his answer, though writing it must have cost him some effort. In December Michaelis had asked for information on the author of the *Recherches sur les Américains,* a book that had been published in Berlin,[7] and in March he had invited Mendelssohn to visit him in Göttingen:[8] "Since Herr Gumprich, the most distinguished member of the local Jewish population, heard at the Brunswick fair as well as from me that we may hope to see your Honor here this year, he asked me to offer you the hospitality of his home; and since I advised him to do this himself in writing, he sent me the enclosed letter for transmission to you. His house is the third next to mine. I should therefore have the good fortune to be as close to your Honor as is possible, for I believe that my own house, which I would have offered most willingly, might be less convenient to your Honor than a Jewish one, having regard to the difference in food and drink." The same letter also inquired about the purpose of circumcision, a subject that Michaelis wanted to discuss in his book on the Mosaic Law; it seemed to him, he pointed out, that a certain explanation offered by Herr von Haller[9] was mistaken.

Mendelssohn's letter of April 10 began with a brief account of his illness, of which Michaelis had been unaware:[10] "I was unable to write hitherto because I had to abstain from all writing and reading. Whenever I dared to read or write a single page, I was immediately attacked by giddiness, which was not without danger. I am not yet completely free from this complaint, but a gradual improvement has set in and I hope that I shall not forever be forbidden to enjoy my life." He regretted his inability to visit Michaelis that summer: in his doctors' opinion, a long journey would prove harmful. "I am, however, infinitely obliged to your Honor for your kind endeavors, and I thank Herr Gumprecht[11] in the enclosed note for his friendly offer. . . . I would have been greatly pleased to discuss with your Honor several points, particularly the Psalms and the prophecies allegedly found in them. This cannot be done in writing. Perhaps the doctors will permit me to make the trip at the end of the coming summer, if not before." He then offered a great deal of biographical and bibliographical information on Corneille de Pauw and his work on the Americans, refuted Albrecht von Haller's opinion on circumcision, and drew attention to an amusing howler made by Johannes Buxtorf I.

The improvement hoped for did not materialize during the summer. On July 6, 1771, Nicolai reported to Herder:[12] "He undergoes this summer a therapy that necessitates a mere vegetating on his part; it may hardly be hoped that he will be able to write anything for a year." In a letter to Kant on July 9, 1771, Marcus Herz mentioned his desire to discuss with Mendelssohn some points in his *Rhapsody* that he found difficult; unfortunately he could not talk to him on account of a "nervous disease" that incapacitated Mendelssohn from reading, writing, and thinking about philosophical matters. In contrast to the consistently pessimistic Nicolai, Herz expressed the hope that as a result of his "strict diet of both body and soul," which had already brought about some degree of improvement, Mendelssohn would be able to resume work that winter.[13]

During the summer of 1771 Doctor Zimmermann came to Berlin to undergo a hernia operation, a medical procedure that created something of a sensation at the time. It was described by the surgeon, Professor Meckel in a tract called *De morbo hernioso singulari et complicato* (Berlin, 1772), and Zimmermann himself gave a vivid account of the trials he had endured in his book *Über Friedrich den Grossen und meine Unterredungen mit Ihm kurz vor seinem Tode,* written much later.[14] He also recorded with some pride the visits he received from the intellectual elite of Berlin:[15] "Men of the first magnitude, Spalding, Sack, Mendelssohn, and Eberhard devoted many hours to me every week." Sulzer and Nicolai are mentioned as daily visitors, and the list includes many more luminaries.

After his recovery, Zimmermann visited Mendelssohn frequently at his home.[16] Their discussions seem to have touched, among other things, upon Mendelssohn's translation of selected Psalms, a favorite occupation of his since the year before. For on November 6, when still in Berlin, Zimmermann wrote to him as follows:[17] "My dearest and most revered Sir, In order that I may not write to Herr Consistorial Councillor Jacobi in Celle[18] anything unworthy of you, I ask you kindly to reply in a few lines to the following [inquiry by Jacobi]: 'I would like to know how Herr Mendelssohn could have said that he understood only three or four Psalms, seeing he has demonstrated in printed works of his that so far as Moses [the Pentateuch] and Solomon [Ecclesiastes] are concerned, he not only believes that he understands them but actually does so.[19] There are more than four Psalms that consist entirely of words and combinations of words found also in Moses [in the Pentateuch] and other simple historical books of Scripture, and which do not contain any sublime and difficult poetry either. Many Psalms can be understood more easily than the books of Solomon.' "

Mendelssohn answered the doctor's question in a lengthy epistle that must have been written prior to Zimmermann's return to Hanover in December, for it concludes with the words:[20] "Have a good journey, my best, dearest friend! My best wishes accompany you, and I am looking forward with extreme longing to the news of your safe arrival." The letter itself is not only clear evidence of Mendelssohn's mental vigor at the time of writing but is also a remarkable document of his sustained effort to find a new approach to the Psalms. The letter reads as follows:

True, my friend Nicolai has slightly exaggerated my ignorance.[21] Herr Consistorial Councillor Jacobi is perfectly right. Many more than four Psalms are as easily comprehensible as any passage in the historical writings of the Old Testament. Yet I have to confess that there are many, very many, Psalms that I simply fail to understand. Among the easily comprehensible ones are many that I must consider very mediocre poems: verses without any connection, now repetitions ad nauseam of the very same thought, now leaps and deviations that no enthusiasm can justify. One could arrange the verses in any different order without causing a worse disarray. Yet of the excellent poems, which are true models of lyrical poetry, I know but a few that I can fully understand.

I have published a commentary on Ecclesiastes that has been translated into German by Herr Rabe. However, I confess to you and Herr Consistorial Councillor Jacobi that there are many passages in Ecclesiastes that I do not understand. I did what all commentators do. I offered an interpretation that somehow agrees with the meaning of the words, and the reader has to be satisfied with this. However, I cannot be satisfied. I know that the meaning given to many passages is so unnatural that no good author wanting to say this would have expressed himself in this way. Is Solomon supposed to have expressed himself in this fashion?

I feel the same about many Psalms. Were I willing to follow the ordinary way of the commentators, I could comment on the Psalms just as well as I did on Ecclesiastes, but I would not satisfy myself. I have translated fifteen or twenty of the most outstanding Psalms, and these I believe I understand. I shall continue this work as soon as your art will permit me to do so, my excellent friend. At the moment I am hardly allowed to think about it.

Herr Michaelis is an outstanding exegete, but I believe him to have the least reason to be satisfied with his Psalms,[22] and who knows whether he would not be equally dissatisfied with my interpretation. Some difficult Psalms are of such a nature that you can read into them what you want; probably because one is ignorant of the situation that occasioned them; because author, time and circumstances are unknown; because some passages are possibly corrupt, etc. I could adduce two Psalms that have been considered by commentators of both nations [Jews and Christians] as messianic prophecies. I investigated them more closely, and believe one of them to be a satirical ode to avarice, the other a flattery written for David by a court poet when his general laid siege to Rabba. Let this be enough.[23]

This letter shows that Mendelssohn had not progressed with his Psalms translation beyond what he had reported to Michaelis in 1770, but it also indicates how much he desired to go on with the work, and how little Michaelis' translation had satisfied him.

It was in September, 1771, that Mendelssohn traveled to Potsdam for the famous interview at the royal palace.[24] The king had invited the baron von Fritsche, a cabinet minister of Saxony, to stay with him. When his guest was about to take his leave, he mentioned that he intended to visit Berlin before returning home. Asked for his reason, he explained that he was eager to meet the famous Moses Mendelssohn. The king suggested that he delay his departure by another day and meet Mendelssohn at the palace. Thus it came about that Mendelssohn received an invitation from the court to present himself on the following day in order to meet von Fritsche. The date of the meeting was September 30, 1771, as we happen to know from a letter written on that day by a certain C. F. Behn in Potsdam to Zacharias Veitel Ephraim in Berlin. It reported the unexpected appearance of Mendelssohn on the very day it happened. That particular date coincided with the Jewish festival of Shemini Atseret, on which travel is not permitted. Nicolai's report on the episode[25] mistakenly assumed that the day in question was a sabbath (on which the prohibition of traveling is even stricter). He wrote as follows: "Moses [Mendelssohn] observed the wise restraint of never divorcing himself arbitrarily from the laws kept by his whole nation. Hence a meeting of experts in Jewish law was convened by the chief rabbi, at which it was decided that in this particular case, in which a definite command had issued from the monarch, a dispensation from the law was in order. However, in view of the possibility that some people might be ignorant of the [special] circumstances, he was requested to walk through the gate of Berlin and to alight from the carriage before it entered Potsdam."

The scene at the palace gate, at which the stocky, hunchbacked philosopher had to present the letter of invitation to the tall officer in charge before being admitted, has been immortalized in Daniel Chodowiecki's beautiful and humorous print.[26] To the officer's question on why he was described in the letter as "famous", Mendelssohn puckishly replied: "Ich spiele aus der Tasche" ("I am a conjurer"). On his arrival in the palace, Mendelssohn was introduced to the baron. The king was not present at the interview, as we know from a letter in which Karl Lessing replied from Berlin to his brother's question from Brunswick: "How is our Moses? Is he well? Did he talk to Fritsche alone or also to the king?" Karl's response, dated November 9, was: "Moses is well, and he talked only with the Saxonian minister Fritsche."[27] The king may have deliberately avoided facing the man whose appointment to the academy he had blocked earlier in the year. It so happened that the revised list of candidates had just been submitted by the academy. It was dated September 26, 1771, four days before Mendelssohn's appearance in Potsdam.

Nothing is known of the conversation between the baron and his visitor, but it may be taken for granted that philosophical topics were discussed. Fortunately, the invitation came at a time when Mendelssohn was relatively "well," as Karl Lessing testified, and as the event itself proves: the excitement it entailed could not have been withstood with such equanimity and humor if Mendelssohn had been in poor shape physically. That the improvement in his condition was rather fickle is evident from a letter that Nicolai wrote to Doctor Zimmermann, December 16, 1771, reporting that "Herr Moses' health" was "not such as I desire it to be. He cannot even attend to his business, and I almost fear that he might not summon up the strength for scholarly work in the near future. He himself predicts this, and when I am alone with him, I notice how sad he feels at this prospect. I do not wish to comfort him, nor am I able to do so, because my comfort would be poison. I infer from my sentiments what his must be. He is my most devoted and most trusted friend. I know the worth of his talents and of his heart better than anybody else—even Lessing hardly knows him so intimately—and I therefore know how much the world loses as a result of his illness."[28] Yet such was the erratic pattern of Mendelssohn's malaise that around the turn of the year he was able to accept an invitation from Luise Ulrike, queen mother of Sweden, to visit her in Berlin. He must have been extremely fit on that occasion, since he conversed with her on philosophical matters for nearly three hours in such an animated and interesting way that she failed to notice the passage of time.[29] The improvement of his condition in the early part of 1772 is confirmed by a letter from Nicolai to Herder, written on January 25, 1772:[30] "Herr Moses' health is somewhat tolerable, but he will not so soon be able to start something of a serious nature. He wishes to be remembered to you."

The respite may have allowed Mendelssohn to return to more regular business activities, but it was not sufficient to permit him the pleasure of sustained reading. When Herder's prize-essay *On the Origin of Languages* was published by the academy, Nicolai wrote to him on February 18, 1772:[31] "Herr Moses has not yet been able to read it on account of his illness." How Mendelssohn felt about his intellectual deprivations may be gathered from a rather grim undated note that he sent to Nicolai in reply to an invitation to attend a recital by Ramler of Lessing's new play *Emilia Galotti:*[32] "I shall not have the honor of visiting you, the reason being that Herr Ramler will recite a new tragedy by Lessing. Who am I to allow myself such a pleasure with impunity? For me there remains but—how does the New Testament say?—'standing outside and gnashing of teeth'." However, the summer of 1772 saw a marked upward trend in his health, as is evident from his vigorous correspondence during that period with the Jewish community leaders of Schwerin and with Rabbi Jacob Emden, about which more will be said later. His sense of relief was expressed in a letter to Doctor Zimmermann on June 25, 1772:[33]

> I am no longer a patient who requires your help in a hurry. I am, thank God, for the most part restored, and if your Honor were now kind enough to offer my physician, as hitherto, small hints from time to time how to guide me in future, I would be most hopeful—more than last time when I had the pleasure of writing to you—considering that I notice now a daily increase in alertness and strength. As I find it difficult to take pills, my physician gives me the roots suggested by you in a different form, which I hope will not vitiate the expected effect.
>
> I am staying now in the most pleasant part of the Thiergarten, attend to my business in town at the same time everyday, and return in the evening to the graceful country house of a friend, which is situated at the bank of the Spree opposite Sulzer's garden in the land of the Moabites.[34] A trip to Pyrmont[35] is precluded by my domestic circumstances. Your Honor advised me last summer to take the waters [of

Pyrmont] preferably not at the well, since it would better suit my condition if the gas had somewhat evaporated. Bearing this in mind, I asked the last time whether your Honor would consider it advantageous to drink the Pyrmont waters this summer here, away from the well. I shall continue with the valerian root for a while and then try the waters unless, in the meantime, you prescribe something different.

From a letter to Elkan Herz written a few days later, on June 30, we learn that the friend with whom Mendelssohn and his wife were staying at the time was Eisik Dessau, called Isaak Benjamin Wulff, a brother-in-law of Daniel Itzig, banker and senior alderman *(Oberältester)* of the Berlin Jewish community; that the "graceful country house" was located on the grounds of Eisik Dessau's silk factory; and that Fromet was taking the Pyrmont waters there.[36] What the "domestic circumstances" were that made a trip to Pyrmont impossible is explained in a letter written to Michaelis on June 25—the day on which he also wrote to Doctor Zimmermann—:[37] "I meet again obstacles and hindrances that render my trip to Pyrmont impossible, no matter how strongly some of my doctors advise me to undertake it. My private circumstances seem to rule out any journey of much length. I have to attend to my work almost every day, if it is not to pile up to such an extent that it will eventually be beyond my capacity to cope with it."

The letter to Michaelis was dictated by the necessity of informing him that, contrary to expectation, there was as yet no prospect of combining a trip to Pyrmont with a visit to Göttingen. On November 16, 1771, Michaelis had written in reply to Mendelssohn's letter of April 10:[38] "I regret that another year has passed without seeing the fulfilment of the hope that your Honor had given me concerning a visit to Göttingen. I had in fact intended to travel to Berlin in September; however, my lectures finished so late, and I was so overwhelmed with work, that I had to desist from it. I would very much like to be in Berlin for once, since I have never seen the capital city of my own country. I have planned it so many times, and always it miscarries. Now I have it in mind for 1772, and the desire to meet your Honor makes my wish the keener."

Mendelssohn's reply, dated December 3, 1771,[39] had been as vigorous as ever. It gave some factual information requested by Michaelis, and spoke at length about Johann Jacob Rabe's German translation of his Hebrew commentary on Koheleth: "This man is a strong talmudist, and I admire his patience.... This very same man also translated the first three parts of both the Babylonian and Palestinian Talmud into German, as he wrote me. They are ready for print but he cannot find a publisher." Mendelssohn expressed his desire to help Rabe find an enterprising man to undertake the job. He regretted that a work of this kind had no chance of Jewish support: "In my view, one cannot count in the least on my own nation, though only it [the Jews] could really make use of the translation and derive benefit from it." He meant to say that Christians, being unfamiliar with the talmudic idiom, could not hope to become scholars in this field by way of a translation. He saw some advantage, however, in a German rendition of the text for Jews. His judgment foreshadowed, in a way, his own later project of a German translation of the Pentateuch. The letter concluded: "Many of your friends and admirers entertained the hope, last autumn, of seeing you here. I hope to visit you in Göttingen, however, before the next fall. My health is improving gradually, though somewhat slowly. If it continues to do so, I shall be able to visit Pyrmont with profit next summer, and that place is not far from Göttingen. Perhaps I shall then have the pleasure of taking my return trip to Berlin in your company." Since this hope did not materialize, Mendelssohn had to inform Michaelis accordingly. Fortunately, it was due to "domestic circumstances" rather than to a deterioration of his health that the trip had to be canceled.

The situation was more propitious in 1773. A letter from Johann Jacob Engel to Nicolai, written from Leipzig on January 23, 1773, contains some information on Mendelssohn's condition at the time:[40] "Recently I had Herr [Marcus] Herz here. I talked with him a great deal about all of you and especially about Herr Moses, whose recovery gives me great joy. God grant that he be soon restored to complete health." The journey to Pyrmont had also become a more feasible proposition. It so happened that Zacharias Veitel Ephraim, son of Veitel Heine Ephraim, the aged leader of Berlin Jewry, had to take a cure at Pyrmont, and he invited his friend Mendelssohn to travel with him. The offer was gladly accepted, and on July 12 the two friends departed. After a stay of twenty-four hours in Magdeburg, where the coach had to undergo repairs, they arrived at Brunswick on July 16.[41] Mendelssohn immediately sent a note to Lessing in nearby Wolfenbüttel, inviting him to come over.[42] The two old friends celebrated a happy reunion. On July 19 Mendelssohn wrote to Fromet that Zacharias and he were still in Brunswick, but shortly after midnight he added a postscript saying that the departure had been fixed for three A.M. The last sentence of the postscript read:[43] "I have much hope that the traveling will be very beneficial to me." After arriving in Pyrmont he wrote home:[44] "The traveling entails many exertions but, thank God, I always feel better the more I fatigue myself." The letter mentioned that Doctor Zimmermann also happened to be staying at Pyrmont and had already visited him.

The news of Mendelssohn's trip to the spa seems to have attracted wide attention. A letter written on August 21, 1773, by Zollikofer in Leipzig to Garve in Breslau contained a reference to it:[45] "As you probably know, Moses was in Pyrmont, but so far I have not been told whether the waters did him much good. Is it not sad that our best philosophers are nearly all sick and feeble? Is it because we are as yet incapable of accepting instruction from them? Is it because we cannot as yet suffer the light they would spread over us?" A rather melancholy meditation!—and one that seems to reflect thoughts akin to Nicolai's about the possible connection of Mendelssohn's illness and his anguish over the Lavater affair. It had been Zollikofer through whose hands Lavater's letters to Mendelssohn had passed.

Mendelssohn's stay in Pyrmont ended ahead of schedule because nearly all of the guests had left by the first of August. His letter to Fromet announcing the change of plan was written in a happy frame of mind:[46] "I expect much more from the traveling than from the water of the well, though I enjoy it very much and derive great benefit from it." The return trip was arranged in the following way: he and his friend would leave on August 3 for Hanover, where they would part company for a while; he would then "wander around a little," by which he meant to say that he would make a detour, visiting Göttingen at long last. His intentions were good, but fate decreed otherwise. What happened he described in a letter to Michaelis on August 9, 1773:[47] "It looks as if I am definitely not to have the pleasure of visiting Göttingen and of meeting the worthy gentlemen I so much revere. On the third of this month I left Pyrmont to travel as far as Hanover in the company of a friend who had taken me to the spa. The idea was to part company with him there and to rejoin him in Brunswick via Göttingen and Kassel. However, not far from Hameln I suffered an attack of tertian fever, which kept me in bed until yesterday and so weakened me in these few days that I have to think of journeying home to recover under the care of my family."

Mendelssohn had overestimated his stamina and had paid the price. It appears that the trip had a good effect in the long run, however, for in October he felt sufficiently strong to visit the Leipzig fair, and he passed the winter in a tolerable condition.[48] Yet the spring of 1774 was marred by frequent recurrences of paralytic attacks, and once again he had to reduce his mental exertions to a minimum.[49] A letter written on February 8, 1774, to an as yet unidentified addressee ("Herr Doctor") graphically describes his condition at the time:[50] "I find myself . . . in such feeble health that reading and writing have become very arduous to me. Letter writing, a recreation in the past, has . . . become a labor; not infrequently I have to wait several months for the hour in which I feel fit for it."

That his spirits were at a low ebb at this time is evident also in the way that he answered Johann Jacob Spiess' request to send him an autobiographical note for a book he was about to edit. Spiess was head of the public library and collection of coins and medals in Ansbach, and he had already published four volumes on famous men, in which their likeness was shown through reproductions of medals. The fifth volume was to contain a half-length portrait of Mendelssohn (from the silver medal engraved by Jacob Abraham), an autobiographical note, and an appraisal of Mendelssohn by the editor.[51]

Mendelssohn replied on March 1, 1774, that he was not in a position to fulfill the request. The circumstances of his life were so ordinary that they had little entertainment value for readers; he himself had considered them so unimportant that he had failed to record them in the least, and now it would cost him a terrific effort to recall and describe particular events. He then stated the "principal facts" he could remember. Only three people are mentioned by name: his father, Rabbi Fränkel, and Aaron Solomon Gumpertz. He had never attended a university or a lecture course. He had to "force everything by his own effort and industry." He had in fact "gone too far and through excessive study contracted, in the last three years, a nervous debility" that had made him "generally incapable of any learned occupation."[52]

It is indeed a pity that Mendelssohn was in such a depressed mood when he wrote to Spiess; we might otherwise possess a more substantial and revealing statement about his life, especially in its early phases. What is most revealing and significant in his short note is the importance that he attached to the basic elements of his existence: the home he came from, the traditional education he received, his love of the humanities, his earning a livelihood, his marriage and family. Not a word of the books he had written, the honors he had received, the interesting people he had met. Was it the illness that had relegated all of this to the background, at least temporarily, or was it modesty that forbade him to say more of himself than he considered absolutely essential?

During his stay in Pyrmont in 1773 Mendelssohn had had conversations with Johann Georg Heinrich Feder, professor of philosophy at Göttingen, who visited him in Berlin more than once in the following year. On the last visit Feder and Engel had debated in his presence the nature of the moral and aesthetic sentiments. Mendelssohn had intervened but then immediately slapped himself on the forehead and said in a terrified voice: "Now the night is lost." Feder wrote to him from Göttingen on July 8, 1774: "I thank you once more with all my heart for the inestimable pleasure that talking to you, my dearest Herr Mendelssohn, has given me. Is it true, however, that my loquaciousness caused you a sleepless night and some indisposition on the following morning? ... So as not to repeat my sin, I will say no more to you about the subject of our last talks (which occupied my mind long afterwards) except that I misquoted Wolff's doctrine concerning the origin of property but was not mistaken when I said that he had failed to state the sufficient reason." The letter then goes on to refer to Christoph Martin Wieland's *The Golden Mirror,* a pedagogic work in the guise of "oriental" stories, which Mendelssohn had found delightful. "In *The Golden Mirror,* parts of which I have reread with extraordinary pleasure, I came across passages that you would certainly not approve or imitate." Finally, the letter introduced a young man, "Herr Salzmann of Strassburg, *lic.jur.* and tutor of Baron von Stein," who wanted to meet Mendelssohn.[53]

Feder's epistle shows that, despite his debility, Mendelssohn still received guests, risked the perils of learned debate, had a clearer recollection of Wolff's doctrine of property than the professor from Göttingen had, and so infected Feder with enthusiasm for Wieland that Feder reread the stories. A propos this particular work, Mendelssohn had written to Doctor Zimmermann on June 25, 1772:[54] "What an extraordinary man is your friend Wieland! Not for many years has any book given me so much delight as the third part of his *Golden Mirror* has done.... Here the philosopher, the worshipper of divinity, the teacher of virtue, and the most inimitable author manifest themselves in their brightest light." As late as 1781 Mendelssohn wrote in a letter to Madame Nicolai that he was "a great admirer of *The Golden Mirror*, though I cannot otherwise reproach myself for admiring either mirrors or gold."[55]

In July, 1774, Mendelssohn visited Pyrmont for the second time. He accompanied Madame Rösel Meyer, wife of Aaron Meyer and sister of Zacharias Veitel Ephraim, who had been his host the year before. Aaron Meyer (Joresh), banker and son-in-law of Veitel Heine Ephraim, was a man of culture and a friend of both Mendelssohn and Lessing.[56] The party included Madame Rösel's daughter Särchen (Sara), a charming young girl, who was not at all surprised to learn that Fromet was a little jealous of her. "Even if I were the frostiest Stoic," Mendelssohn wrote to Fromet, after their arrival in Pyrmont, "she would still believe in her power to triumph over male frostiness, and if you had the greatest illusions about your beauty, she would still believe in her power to triumph over female illusions." Of Madame Rösel he reported: "The friendly concern she has for my comfort and pleasure I cannot sufficiently describe, and I have become so used to it that I let it pass without protest and even without a compliment."[57] Mendelssohn took the waters and sulphuric baths of Pyrmont and felt very well indeed. Rösel told Fromet in a postscript to a letter Mendelssohn had written:[58] "I must tell you that you will have a most healthy husband when he is back home." She also informed her of the pleasure that Mendelssohn derived from the friendliness shown him by two illustrious visitors at Pyrmont, Count Wilhelm and Countess Marie Eleonora of Schaumburg-Lippe.

It was an exhilarating experience for Mendelssohn to meet the count who had patronized his late friend Abbt and had acted so graciously toward him. Seven years had passed since he had finally declined the invitation to settle in Schaumberg-Lippe's county. Now he had an opportunity to become more closely acquainted with the man for whom Abbt had felt such glowing admiration. The count and his lady were no less eager to meet Mendelssohn. We possess a precious record of the encounter between the Jewish philosopher and this remarkable couple in one of the notes Mendelssohn wrote on his correspondence with Abbt (1782).

Commenting on Abbt's portrayal of the count, Mendelssohn wrote:[59] "I later had the opportunity to meet this extraordinary count and to enjoy his company at the well of Pyrmont. He seemed indeed capable of instilling into the mind of a young man ... the high sense of enthusiasm that he [Abbt] felt for him." The picture Mendelssohn drew of the count was one of contrasts. In his outward appearance he was far from attractive: tall of stature, strong of build, he looked emaciated, severe, and "strange." On closer acquaintance he revealed himself to be a man full of gentleness and sympathy, "the finest Greek soul in a rough Westphalian body." "He loved hard and dangerous physical exercises, the sciences, great deeds. *Dévouement à la mort* was his watchword. . . . Death for the sake of freedom and justice, the future life, and Providence were the topics of his ordinary conversation. I never heard a man talk with more warmth about the truths of natural religion. Free from all the prejudice that leads to discord and hatred of men, he was permeated to the degree of enthusiasm with the true, beneficial teachings of religion."

Mendelssohn was equally impressed by the countess: "He had with him his lady, the countess, or more precisely: he had come to Pyrmont for her sake, for he did not himself take the waters. She was a lady of rare beauty and extraordinary gifts of soul. In matters of doctrine and belief she was of one mind with the count, on whose will and opinions she seemed to rely completely. In conversation, however, she was not of the same profoundly serious disposition, but rather of a sweet and soft youthfulness. Both appeared to have lost some of their natural vivacity owing to the recent death of their only child, a three-year-old daughter. They had resigned themselves to God's will, yet this blow of fate was too severe to be accepted so soon. There remained in their hearts an elegiac melancholy. . . . Though of different age and, it seemed, opposite temperament, they loved each other with a tender and almost romantic amorousness that was perhaps too pronounced to make for happiness in marriage. . . . The death of the countess a few years later so depressed the splendid man that he could find no further happiness in this life. Sunk in grief, he decreased in vitality day by day, and soon followed her."[60]

The mutual affection that sprang up between Mendelssohn and this pair can be sensed from this warm-hearted portrayal and is also attested in other ways. Rösel reported to Fromet: 'Everybody seeks to meet him [Mendelssohn], and the count and countess of Bückeburg in particular enjoy him very much. A few minutes ago the coach and the attendent of the count came to fetch him for a breakfast. Now, dear Fromet, you have no more reason to be jealous of my daughter. Now you may be so of the countess of Bückeburg."[61] Another observer, Johann Gottfried Herder, was somewhat less elated at Mendelssohn's intimacy with the count and countess. Herder, at this time, was the consistorial counsellor and leading minister of religion at Bückeburg. Though he admired the countess ("a holy, sweet angelic apparition") and respected the count, he felt oppressed by his philosophizing ("all speculation and metaphysics") and had written in 1772:[62] "My situation vis-à-vis the count is still the same: indistinct, remote, one of incompatibility." From July 7 until July 21 Herder stayed at Pyrmont, taking the waters and meeting Mendelssohn for the first and only time.[63]

Writing from Bückeburg, Herder informed Hamann that Mendelssohn was now "the idol of my count, to whom he sent his picture by Chodowiecki"[64] with a Latin inscription of two verses that had been written in Celle by Frau von Ompteda, lady-in-waiting to the exiled queen of Denmark: "Vir bonus et sapiens, quem vix ex millibus unum————tulit consultus, Apollo."[65] He could not remember the missing words and admitted not being sure whether the picture bore the inscription when it arrived. In another letter to Hamann he remarked sarcastically that in Pyrmont "Mordecai [Mendelssohn] had a retinue like a grand vizier."[66] To Lavater he wrote:[67] "I have also met Mendelssohn, the clearest, brightest head I ever saw, I might say, on a human trunk—one that in itself is most distinct. Maybe it is just because of this that I found no grounds for feeling drawn to him. Yet he is, I think, very happy in himself, albeit in a seemingly artificial way, resting as he does on a bulwark that he has built for himself (I don't know how)." Herder's distaste for Mendelssohn here appears undisguised and in marked contrast to his earlier attitude of respect. It was only in his Weimar period that his attitude would change, and it took Lessing's death—in addition to a temporary break with Lavater—to cause him to seek Mendelssohn's friendship.

Before his departure from Berlin for Pyrmont, Mendelssohn had received a letter from a distinguished Dutch gentleman named van der Hoop—he later became minister of the navy—asking for advice on how to educate in philosophy a young man between fifteen and twenty years of age. The question had been prompted by a genuine concern to provide the proper kind of curriculum for his own son, who was then still an infant. Mendelssohn had been obviously quite touched by this rather premature request from the provident father, for toward the end of his stay in Pyrmont he sat down and wrote a four-page letter to van der Hoop, which is preserved at the Royal Library at the Hague and indicates at the bottom that it was written in Pyrmont on July 24, 1774.[68] The reply was limited to directives in speculative philosophy although, in Mendelssohn's words, "practical philosophy is of far greater importance since it has a direct bearing on the happiness of man." He excused himself, however, by pointing out that owing to the treatment at the spa his memory was weak and his time too much occupied to allow him to mention the many excellent works in this field. The ancients, he added, were here the best guides—an interesting admission, because Mendelssohn had no high opinion of ancient metaphysics. The English, too, he remarked, had accomplished a great deal in practical philosophy.

The major part of the letter to van der Hoop outlines a curriculum in speculative philosophy that is broadly based yet clearly focused. One could hardly wish for a more balanced statement on the order of priorities that he assigned to subject matters, authors, and writings in this area. To begin with, he suggested, a young man ought to study the principles of geometry in the works of Euclid and thereby prepare himself for the study of logic. The more difficult synthetical method followed by Euclid was more suited to this end than the simplified presentation offered by the moderns.[69] Of logical works he gave a short list of three: Wolff's German Logic, 's Gravesande's Latin Introduction, and the famous French Logic of Port-Royal. Turning to metaphysics, he first recommended Wolff's German treatise on the subject. "This author," he said, "is the most distinct and profound among all I know." Reimarus, Samuel Clarke, and Bilfinger are cited next. "Thereupon one may advance to Locke's *Essay Concerning Human Understanding,* a work that ought to be read several times and collated with Leibniz' *Nouveaux Essays sur l'Entendement humain.* I daresay that these two works alone suffice for philosophical training, if studied with due attention." In addition to these basic texts he mentioned an early work by Condillac and the *Traité des sensations* of Claude-Nicolas Le Cat, both representing the sensualistic approach to the theory of knowledge, as well as Thomas Reid's *Inquiry into the Human Mind on the Principles of Common Sense,* a book that Mendelssohn had asked Nicolai to obtain for him in 1770.[70]

Before proceeding further in philosophical study, Mendelssohn remarked, the young man should make himself at home in algebra and higher mathematics in order to master the analytical method. Thus prepared, he should apply himself assiduously to Descartes' *Discours de la méthode,* to Francis Bacon's works, and "particularly and with all possible attention" to Lambert's treatises. There follows a list of nine "minor sagacious writings" that could be read with profit, all leading up to the "excellent *Théodicée* of Herr von Leibniz," which should be collated with Bayle's articles, to which it replies. Baumgarten's *Metaphysics* and Hansch's presentation of Leibniz' monadology are recommended in this connection. Interestingly enough, Mendelssohn also suggested the study of the Cambridge Platonist Ralph Cudworth's *The True Intellectual System of the Universe* (1678) in its annotated Latin version by Johann Lorenz von Mosheim. The history of philosophy, he went on to suggest, might best be studied through Thomas Stanley's and Johann Jacob Brucker's works on the subject.

The final paragraph reads: "Thereupon the writings of the paradoxical philosophers such as Spinoza's posthumous works, the *Système de la Nature* [by d'Holbach] and other well-known skeptics and so-called *strong spirits* might be read for the training of the mind. Sound philosophy having been firmly ingrained, nothing is to be feared from the specious arguments of these teachers of heretical doctrine [*Irrlehrer*]. On the contrary, they can serve to confirm the mind in the true principles of reason and of natural religion." Clearly, true philosophy and true religion were identical in Mendelssohn's view. Hence he could apply the term "heretical" to misguided philosophers. Sensualists, skeptics, and enthusiasts ("strong spirits") are included in the curriculum only as aids for the training of the mind and as challenges to be met. Spinoza is introduced as one of the "paradoxical" philosophers, a characterization that agrees with what Mendelssohn had said about him in the *Philosophical Dialogues* of 1755. There was no need in this context to go into the positive aspects of Spinoza, which mitigated his "errors."

That Mendelssohn took off time at the spa to write a letter of this kind is ample proof, if proof is needed, that his illness had in no way diminished his concern for philosophy.

Hebraica and Judaica

How deeply Mendelssohn was committed to his project of a new German translation of the Psalms is evident from his letters to Michaelis and Zimmermann.[1] Indeed, his strong desire to meet Michaelis was chiefly inspired by the hope of clarifying, in conversation, some of the problems related to this plan. His correspondence with the unidentified "Herr Doctor," to which brief reference has already been made,[2] was also concerned with the Hebrew Bible. That the addressee was a learned clergyman of high rank can be inferred from the form of address used in the letters. The correspondent had translated into German some rabbinic commentary on the Pentateuch and was now approaching Mendelssohn in the hope of obtaining his help in finding a publisher. Mendelssohn regretfully informed him on February 16, 1773, that he had been unsuccessful in his efforts, and he remarked:[3] "Indeed, who is supposed to buy a rabbinic commentary in our clever age, when every beginner in Hebrew is permitted to change the text at will? In case *le-fetah hatt'at rovets* [Gen. 4:7: sin coucheth at the door] seems unintelligible, an English emendator is immediately at hand, who reads *le-fallot hata'ta revatz;* and rabbinic skills are no further required. Is *esh dat lamo* [Deut. 33:2: a fiery law unto them] difficult to explain? No problem. Read *'or* instead of *dat* and everything is clear. I really fail to see where this recklessness is going to end. However, here too one has to allow fashion to run its course for as long as it has the lure of novelty. As time goes on people lose the taste for it, and then the time has come to lead them back to the path of sound reason."[4] We have in this letter clear evidence of Mendelssohn's negative attitude toward the textual criticism of the Bible that had just begun to spread.

Mendelssohn's scorn for facile changes of the masoretic text is reiterated in his second letter to the same correspondent.[5] Dated February 8, 1774, it touches on a variety of interesting matters. The learned clergyman had criticized the way in which the Anglican Hebraist Benjamin Kennicot (1718–1783) and his followers treated the biblical text: They were taking liberties that "modest critics" should not permit themselves even when dealing with ordinary authors of antiquity. Mendelssohn agreed with this complaint. Kennicot, it may be explained, had undertaken the gigantic task of establishing the original text of the Old Testament by collating manuscripts from all parts of Europe. With the help of friends, he had managed to compare more than six hundred manuscripts and old prints. The fruits of these labors were eventually presented in his *Vetus Testamentum Hebraicum cum variis lectionibus* (1776–1780). The net result of this grand undertaking was far from startling: it proved only that most of the variants were negligible.

In 1774 Mendelssohn could not foresee precisely this result, but he was guided by a sound instinct when he wrote to his correspondent: "The great clamor with which some followers of Kennicot announce the collection of variants has been very annoying to me at times, when I saw the carelessness with which these gentlemen snatch up everything they can lay their hands on. Yet I believe it is all to the good. The more fuss and puff they make at the start, the greater will be the expectations they raise, and the more difficult it will be for them to satisfy the public. The harm done by their recklessness will be correspondingly less. Perhaps some incidental advantages will accrue from the grandiose efforts we have seen being made over so many years with the object of collating manuscripts. Even if I had the power to put a spoke in their wheel, I would hesitate to do so since, in my view, every scholarly effort is bound to have some good effect either directly or, at least, indirectly."[6]

Kennicot's selection of manuscripts had been critically reviewed by Olaf Gerhard Tychsen (1734–1815), professor of oriental languages at Bützow and Rostock, who was also active as a missionary in Hamburg. Mendelssohn's letter also refers to him: Tychsen's critique of Kennicot was sound and did not deserve to be treated in a "supercilious manner" by the Kennicot group. Mendelssohn was in a position to judge the merits of Tychsen's strictures because he knew both his critical treatise and the work written in its defense;[7] the two books were part of his library.[8] However, though he repudiated the attacks against Tychsen, he expressed astonishment at the man's "very limited knowledge of rabbinics." Not a single passage quoted by Tychsen from the Talmud had been correctly translated. Such glaring ignorance, Mendelssohn wrote to the clergyman, weakened the credibility even of those of his statements that were nearer to the truth than Kennicot's. In the future, Mendelssohn suggested, Tychsen should get the help of some learned Jew.

Mendelssohn's lenient, though critical, attitude toward the Rostock professor and Hamburg missionary shows a remarkable degree of objectivity, considering Tychsen's past behavior toward the Jewish community. In 1769 Tychsen had accused the rabbinic court (Beth Din) of Altona of complicity in the defamation of Christian holidays in the current Altona Jewish calendar, and had demanded that punitive action be taken by the state authorities. An official investigation had been ordered but was suspended when the editor of the calendar died and the innocence of the Beth Din was established. While the Altona community had been threatened with court proceedings, its leaders had asked Mendelssohn for advice and intervention. What action he took in response to this request is not known, but a letter of thanks dated December 12, 1769, and signed by the secretary of the community testifies—in the most ornate Hebrew—to the Community's gratitude.[9] At all events, although Mendelssohn had every reason to look askance at Tychsen, his letter to the unknown clergyman betrays no animosity toward the man.[10]

Unbeknownst to Mendelssohn, Tychsen was also responsible for the trouble in which the Jews of Mecklenburg-Schwerin found themselves in 1772. On April 30 of that year Duke Friedrich issued an order to his Jewish subjects prohibiting the religious custom of burial on the day on which death occurred and requiring a waiting period of three days to ensure that no seemingly dead but actually living person was buried. The edict had been occasioned by a memorandum submitted to the duke by Tychsen, in an indirect way, on February 19, 1772.[11] It had urged the duke to put an end to the "cruel and inhuman" practice followed by the Jews and had quoted some of the rabbinic and kabbalistic sources upon which this practice was founded. The duke was advised by his cabinet to take no action, since the legal protection granted to the Jewish community did not permit any interference with Jewish law and custom. Moreover, the Jewish burial rites, which included the cleansing of the body, seemed likely to ensure that no still-living person would be committed to burial by mistake.

The duke was not satisfied with this opinion and decided to abolish the practice unless it could be shown, in a convincing way, that the practice was an integral part of the Jewish religion. He forthwith commissioned a Jewish convert to Christianity to prepare a memorandum on the subject. On receiving a statement that the custom in question did not follow from fundamental Jewish beliefs, the duke proceeded to act; the cabinet no longer resisted, though it was not convinced of the consistency of the arguments offered in the memorandum, and the edict was issued. The Jewish community of Mecklenburg-Schwerin was in a state of alarm and consternation. On May 15, 1772, a petition was sent to the duke asking him to rescind the order, since it was contrary to Jewish traditional law and custom. Proof to this effect would be submitted as soon as testimony had been received from noted authorities; in the meantime no burial would take place without a death certificate from the local physician. The duke agreed to suspend the order for a period of three weeks. The authorities to whom the Schwerin community had turned for help were Rabbi Jacob Emden and Moses Mendelssohn.

The question put to him placed Mendelssohn in a moral dilemma at a time when he was supposed to avoid all mental strain, and the incident led to some brushes with Emden, whom he revered as the guardian of rabbinic tradition, but whose views he could not always accept. In writing to Mendelssohn, the acting rabbinic head of Schwerin Jewry, Mordecai Jaffe, had failed to mention that Emden had also been approached. He had merely asked Mendelssohn to act as their "intercessor and patron" and by his powerful command of the German tongue deflect the duke from the course he had taken. In a Yiddish postscript to the Hebrew letter Jaffe urged a quick response and expressed the fear that the duke's edict might be the forerunner of more trouble.[12] The letter was written on May 18. On June 9 Mendelssohn responded to the request by sending the draft of a memorandum (unsigned), with a covering letter to the Jewish community of Schwerin.[13]

The memorandum gratefully acknowledged the duke's concern for the welfare of his subjects, which had occasioned the edict, but declared the edict to be at variance with Jewish law, which did not permit leaving a dead person unburied any longer than necessary. Though the literal observance of the Mosaic laws of purity had ceased, the spirit of those laws demanded the quick removal of dead bodies, and the rabbinic law distinctly forbade the retaining of the dead in the home overnight.[14] The derivation of this law from the Bible was admittedly open to doubt, but the authority of the rabbis was binding upon Jews and the duke had assured them of protection in the exercise of their religion. The certainty that death had occurred was obviously a precondition of burial. Yet in most cases a few hours were sufficient to establish the fact. Nevertheless, in order to satisfy their conscience the Jews of Schwerin would in future ask for a medical certification of death prior to burial. The memorandum pleased the duke, and a new regulation along the lines suggested by Mendelssohn was substituted for the previous edict.[15]

Though Mendelssohn had acceded to the request of the Schwerin community—and done so with striking success—he expressed his own personal view of the matter in the letter addressed to the community leaders, with which the memorandum was enclosed.[16] He came close to chiding them for what he considered an unwarranted reaction to the duke's order. He noted that they "were grieved and pained by it as if he [the duke] had, God forbid, desired to make them change their religion or offend against a prohibition laid down by the Tora or a rabbinic decree." It might be due to his ignorance, but he failed to see any reason for their alarm. The rabbinic head of Schwerin Jewry was known to be a competent talmudic scholar, yet he felt it necessary to state his own opinion, which was, of course, open to correction. Obeying the duke's edict would, in his view, involve no transgression whatsoever. True, the rabbis had declared that leaving the dead unburied overnight violated a prohibition by the Tora; yet the rabbis permitted it when time was needed to provide the necessities for decent burial or to make it possible for relatives to attend the funeral. Seeing they legalized delay for such minor reasons, was it not also permissible, *a fortiori*, in cases where there was a possible doubt that death had actually occurred and the possible saving of a life was at stake? There was no danger of burying a seemingly dead person in the ancient period, when the deceased were not interred but were placed in caves and watched by guards for three days.[17] But under present conditions, the danger of burying someone alive could not be entirely ignored. According to the physicians, there was no absolute criterion by which the occurrence of death could be established. Mendelssohn quoted a passage from the Talmud[18] that seemed to him relevant to this point. For the reasons stated he felt that the Schwerin community should not oppose the duke's edict, in the event that he chose not to revoke it. The remedy lay in a return to the ancient Palestinian custom. Mendelssohn realized that his suggestion would be ignored, and that it might well be frowned upon, but he had at least satisfied his conscience by stating it.

Toward the end of June, 1772, Mendelssohn received a letter from Rabbi Jacob Emden from which he learned that representatives of the Schwerin community had visited Emden in Altona in order to obtain a memorandum from him.[19] Emden mentioned that he had first tried to avoid acting in the matter, pointing to his lack of experience in dealing with princes and writing memoranda in German, and advising them to approach Mendelssohn, "who enjoyed a high reputation at the courts of princes and kings, was a master of the vernacular, and knew how to explain and present matters in a convincing way." Mendelssohn would no doubt do much better than he. But when the men from Schwerin, the letter continued, refused to budge from their request, Emden wrote in great haste a Hebrew responsum on the subject, handed it to his visitors without retaining a copy, and added some oral comments. He obtained their promise that the original would be returned after it had been translated into German and that Mendelssohn would be sent at least the translation. Since he had not heard from them, despite several letters asking for information, Emden wondered whether his responsum had been passed on to Mendelssohn, in which case he requested the return of the original or else a copy of the translation.

Upon receipt of Emden's letter, Mendelssohn immediately replied on June 30:[20] He had been astonished to learn of the strange manner in which the men of Schwerin were behaving. They should have returned the responsum by now. And he, at any rate, had never received it. Nor had he been told that they had requested a memorandum from Emden as well as from him, for if he had he would have refused to draft one of his own. In his innocence he had sent them a statement as requested, but he had received no acknowledgment so far, and he too was anxious to know how the matter stood. Mendelssohn's letter continued: "I greatly desire to see my master's and teacher's responsum [so as to learn] how he justified the [prevalent] Jewish practice [of early burial] by true and irrefutable arguments. For I, in my ignorance, do not know how to justify it and why we departed from the practice of our saintly forebears of blessed memory. They laid their dead to rest in caves and sepulchral chambers, and observed them three days." The letter repeated the arguments stated vis-à-vis the community leaders of Schwerin, and concluded with the suggestion that the ancient practice be restored.

In his reply, dated July 3, 1772,[21] Emden rebuked Mendelssohn in a stern, paternal manner for the view he had expressed "through mere error, no doubt, and without premeditation." He referred him to his responsum, where he would find the answer to his question. It would be passed on to him as soon as it was returned from Schwerin. As for the specific points raised by Mendelssohn, Emden's rebuttal was outspoken. How could he have questioned the legitimacy of a practice that had been adopted by Jewry as a whole, by Ashkenazim as well as Sephardim, in the East and in the West? Burial in caves had been abandoned long ago, even in the Holy Land. The risk of burying a seemingly dead person was negligible. The sages of Israel required no reminder of their duty to concern themselves with the saving of life. Quoting the opinion of physicians was out of place, since paying attention to medical views would disrupt the texture of Halakha.[22] Besides, the Jewish people was not permitted to abandon its distinctive time-honored customs for the sake of adopting the ways of the Gentiles. The talmudic passage adduced by Mendelssohn had been wrongly interpreted. Emden went into a detailed discussion of it in order to prove this point. He warned Mendelssohn against taking insufficient care when invoking rabbinic sources and expressed the hope that the suggestion that the practice of early burial be abolished had not been meant seriously. For how could he wish to abolish a law clearly stated in the Mishna? A similar rejection of Mendelssohn's arguments—prefaced by a highly flattering form of address in rabbinic style—was contained in the reply written on July 15 by Mordecai Jaffe of Schwerin,[23] who drew on the arguments set forth in Emden's responsum and exhibited a sense of unquestioning loyalty to tradition—in marked contrast to the daring tone that Mendelssohn had adopted.

Emden's rebuke was keenly felt by Mendelssohn. His reply, which is lost, can be reconstructed in part from Emden's answer, dated August 14, 1772.[24] Emden opened his letter by expressing his joy at Mendelssohn's recovery: "Blessed be the Merciful One who has given us great joy, for I have noticed that your power in debating issues of the Tora is as strong as it used to be in former days." However, the polemical tone was immediately resumed: "I see that you make every effort to maintain your view with vigor and that you feel astonished, in a way, by what I wrote in my previous letter, in which I did not suppress the truth." It seemed, Emden added parenthetically, that Mendelssohn was angry with him and failed to understand that his warning was meant to save him from incurring slander. This point is reiterated toward the end of the letter: Mendelssohn would be hurting himself were he to ignore Emden's advice, which had been prompted by "special love and affection (not to be misconstrued as enmity!) so as to remove from you 'a froward mouth and perverse lips'[25] [malicious charges] and prevent any opportunity for derision." More and more people were complaining, Emden declared, that Mendelssohn was cultivating heretical views.[26] Continuing in this vein, he wrote: "I had assumed that your affection for me would be the stronger [viz. as a result of the rebuke offered], as it is written, 'Reprove a wise man and he will love thee,'[27] since I did not intend to engage in a quarrel and fight with you but meant to promote your well-being and to ensure that you are not attacked by embittered people when they hear that you are turning to the 'vanities of strangers'[28] and mean to change the custom of Israel, the altogether holy nation."

The seventy-five year-old Emden, who was Mendelssohn's senior by a generation, felt justified in using such blunt language: "For this is my way. In matters concerning the Tora I am not a respecter of persons, not even of the great ones of former times, compared with whom I am but a dwarf, let alone of young men of worth, whom I consider as my children and who regard themselves as my disciples.[29] I do not hide from them what is in my heart, for I want to teach them and, free from flattery, guide them toward the true and right path. . . . Why then are you angry, and why did you tell me that I had spoken harshly? . . . Did I not use mild language and did I not put a favorable complexion on your first letter by treating it as an inadvertant utterance?"

Obviously Mendelssohn's second letter had reaffirmed his viewpoint and even dared to refute Emden's rebuttal of the arguments he had brought forward from rabbinic sources. For Emden wrote: "As I noticed from your second letter, you find it difficult to change your mind and admit the truth. . . . It seems to me that you are not free from the manner characteristic of our present-day students of the Tora who engage in vain dialectics [*pilpul shel hevel*] (a manner, I believe, abhorred by you!), and who twist the plain meaning in an effort to prevail by force." Emden's letter concluded: "My dear son, you have indeed taken great pains and apparently spent many hours in preparing your statement; yet all your labor was to no purpose. No one will listen to you, and I fear that the matter will become one of derision and contumely. . . . Consider and understand this . . ."

The personal relationship between Mendelssohn and Emden was not adversely affected by this incident. On October 26, 1773, Mendelssohn wrote again to the venerable defender of orthodoxy, describing himself humbly as his "disciple" and "loyal servant ready at all times to 'run before' him," as the biblical phrase has it.[30] The earlier clash had obviously left no hard feelings. The issue that had divided them had been amicably settled by the duke's decision. Since the suggestion offered in Mendelssohn's memorandum had been adopted, the raison d'être for a change in the traditional custom no longer existed and in retrospect the whole halakhic dispute had become purely academic. Yet there can be no doubt that Mendelssohn had expressed an attitude that ran counter to traditional sentiment. The tenacity with which the community of Schwerin had sought to preserve the old practice derived not merely from halakhic considerations but also from deeply ingrained mystical notions that, in turn, reinforced allegiance to the halakhic rule. It was believed that the soul could not enter paradise until the body had been laid to rest, and that prior to burial both body and soul were assailed by demons.[31] As an adept of the Enlightenment, Mendelssohn had emancipated himself from beliefs of this kind and regarded them, no doubt, as "superstitions." In pointing out that the rule of early burial laid down in the Mishna *(Sanhedrin* 6:5) had admitted exceptions for "minor" reasons, he implied that fear of demons was one of those late accretions to the "pure" religion that "disfigured" its pristine beauty.[32] Hence his desire to see a return to the old Palestinian practice of deferring burial until all risk of interring a person alive was removed.

Mendelssohn's cast of mind was strictly conservative, and he had no intention of twisting Halakha to suit modern ideas. Yet here was a case in which an apparently misguided custom seemed to violate humanitarian principles and to tarnish the image of Judaism as a religion of reasonableness and concern for humanity. It therefore appeared to him that the "alarm" felt by the Schwerin community was quite unwarranted. So convinced was he of the rightness of his stand that he was not afraid to uphold it even against Jacob Emden. The learned debate between the two had all the aspects of a sham battle, however, the outcome having been fixed in advance: both had their predetermined positions, which were irreconcilable because Mendelssohn, owing to his Enlightenment philosophy, had shifted his ground from pure Halakha to extraneous considerations such as medical opinion and, more generally, a distaste for the current burial practice. The episode was therefore a portent of more clashes to come. Emden's outspoken and rather harsh references to the slander that lay in store for Mendelssohn, should he persist in his attitude, clearly indicate an awareness of a certain cleavage that had arisen between them. Judging from one of Emden's remarks, the watchdogs of the community had already begun to cast doubts on Mendelssohn's orthodoxy.

The issue of early burial remained dormant until 1787, a year after Mendelssohn's death. It was raised anew in Mecklenburg-Strelitz, and a memorandum submitted in 1788 by the court physician Dr. Hempel quoted the letter Mendelssohn had written to the community of Schwerin. A German translation of this letter had appeared as early as 1772, in an obscure periodical, and had been republished in 1787 in the *Berlinische Monatsschrift,* where Hempel probably read it.[33] The community again rose in protest, and the matter rested until 1793, when the Jewish director of a public school in Breslau and professor of philosophy Joel [Brill] Loewe, a former member of Mendelssohn's circle and coeditor of *Ha-Me'assef,* the literary organ of Haskala in Germany, brought it up again by writing a letter echoing Mendelssohn's viewpoint to the members of Jewish charitable societies. As a result, the governments concerned held hearings in Strelitz, Schwerin, and Berlin, but in response to Jewish representations took no action. However, in 1794 the "Berlin Society of Friends," founded by disciples of Mendelssohn in 1791, made arrangements of its own to ensure that no early burials of its members took place.[34] The struggle against the old burial practice was pursued vigorously by the Maskilim, who saw in it a kind of test case in their confrontation with unyielding orthodoxy. The authority of Mendelssohn was invoked by them in their prolonged efforts to introduce moderate reforms.[35]

When Mendelssohn wrote to Emden on October 26, 1773, he was again motivated by a desire to see confirmed his belief in the rationality of Judaism. It was almost four years since he had quoted Emden ("Rabbi Jacob Hirschel, one of the most learned rabbis of our time") as an author who had amply dealt with the rabbinic doctrine promising eternal bliss in the hereafter to "the pious among the gentiles" or, as Mendelssohn paraphrased it in the spirit of the Enlightenment, to "the virtuous men of other nations."[36] The occasion for referring to Emden and several other rabbinic authorities was, as we recall, his *Reply to Lavater*.

What had irritated him then, and what still weighed on his mind, was Maimonides' definition of the term "the pious among the Gentiles" (*hasidey 'ummot ha-'olam*) as applying only to those non-Jews who acknowledged divine revelation as the reason for observing the Seven Commandments of the Sons of Noah.[37] This limiting clause sharply contradicted his portrayal of Judaism as a religion that distinguished between the revealed laws binding upon Jews and the "law of nature" valid for all men.[38] According to Maimonides, following the laws of nature and of reason was not sufficient to assure a Gentile of eternal happiness; belief in the revealed sanction of these laws was also required. In the absence of such belief, a Gentile could be termed "wise" but not "pious." A corrupt reading of the Maimonides text in some editions, including the one used by Mendelssohn, denied a nonbeliever even the title to wisdom. Mendelssohn could not simply ignore this statement, since it had been widely advertised by Spinoza, who also had only the faulty text. In the fifth chapter of his *Tractatus Theologico-Politicus* Spinoza had quoted Maimonides to prove that in the Jewish view "true beliefs and a true principle of life [viz. a philosophically true religion] make no contribution to blessedness so long as men embrace them by the light of nature alone, and not as precepts revealed to Moses by prophetic insight."

In the context of Spinoza's interpretation of the Jewish religion, the Maimonides passage (and a similar one quoted from Joseph ben Shemtob's *Kevod Elohim*)[39] made perfect sense. Mendelssohn could not reconcile his own view of Judaism and Maimonides' stipulation, which he declared (in his *Letter to Lavater*) to have "no authority in the Talmud." He was able to say this because no talmudic or midrashic source on which Maimonides could have based his clause was known[40] and Joseph Karo, in his commentary on the passage, had distinctly stated that it represented Maimonides' personal opinion. Though Karo himself expressed agreement with this view, Mendelssohn could feel on safe ground so long as it could be considered merely as a personal viewpoint of a rabbinic authority (no matter how great a one). What mattered to Mendelssohn was that the Talmud was free from this particular bias and could be said to propound a concept of tolerance unfettered by demands of a dogmatic nature. Yet it was precisely this comfortable feeling of a kind of preestablished harmony between classical rabbinic Judaism and enlightened opinion that was shattered in 1773 by a letter from Jacob Emden. Mendelssohn must have asked Emden for his view in the matter several times without receiving an answer. His inquiries probably dated back to the period of the Lavater affair. The brief but disconcerting reply that he received in 1773 was probably due to a reminder that he had sent Emden during that year or the year before. There would have been good reason for him to renew the inquiry because in 1772 his friend Johann August Eberhard had published his *New Apology of Socrates,* which dealt in great detail with the church's doctrine of the denial of eternal happiness of pagans and nonbelievers and tried to show that such exclusiveness was contrary to the wisdom and goodness of God.[41]

The situation that prompted Mendelssohn to write Emden on October 26, 1773, is well summed up in his opening sentence: "As for the question concerning which I have inquired several times, and upon which my teacher and master has now made some observations, thereby impelling me to bring it up again, it relates to what Maimonides wrote . . ." Having stated his objections to Maimonides ruling with the greatest possible emphasis,[42] Mendelssohn referred to the obnoxious statement that had occurred in Emden's recent letter: though Emden agreed with Mendelssohn about the rational character of the moral law, the words of Maimonides were nevertheless borne out by the talmudic discussions.[43] In other words, Maimonides' verdict represented the thinking of the Talmud on the subject. Mendelssohn's consternation can easily be imagined. But he was far from being convinced. The purpose of his letter of October 26 was to elicit further information: "[My teacher and master] has not mentioned the passage in the Talmud from which he deduced the proof. Now, if I have found favor in his eyes, let him not turn me back empty-handed."

Emden wrote a full-length reply[44] in November, trying to substantiate his point by a wealth of references and arguments. Whether Mendelssohn accepted them as valid is hard to say. What mattered to him was his conviction that eternal blessedness could be attained by *all* men through the light of reason. If it was correct to say that a streak of intolerance ran even through classical rabbinic Judaism and colored even so beautiful a statement as the one he had quoted to Lavater, the truth was not thereby altered an iota. The ideal Judaism to which Mendelssohn aspired possessed a kind of Platonic reality for him, and there were more occasions still in store for him to defend this vision.

The Chronicle Continued

His prolonged illness was a heavy drain on Mendelssohn's purse. Before leaving for Pyrmont in 1774, he wished to settle his account with Doctor Bloch. The sum he owed was fourteen hundred thalers, and since he held a debenture from Nicolai in this amount, he made payment by transferring it to his physician. The Nicolai Archive still has a note by Bloch, dated July 19, 1774, informing Nicolai of the situation and adding: "Since I need the money, I most obediently wish to inquire whether it is convenient to you to honor this bond." Nicolai was seemingly in no hurry: the reply he wrote at the bottom of the note merely indicated that he would settle his account with Mendelssohn after his return.[1] Back from Pyrmont, Mendelssohn sent Nicolai a note on August 11: "What about our money-matter? I would so much like to pay Herr Doctor Bloch what I owe him, and would therefore ask for your kind reply whether you can manage to supply me this week with no more than eight hundred or a thousand thalers."[2] Nicolai was again unresponsive. On January 13, 1775, Mendelssohn wrote to him: "The bond that I gave Doctor Bloch [Nicolai's debenture] is payable on the twentieth of this month. Surely, I can count on receiving from you by that date at least eight hundred thalers. I shall contribute the balance and honor the bond." And on January 24, he sent a further note: "Since my bond is due for payment today, I ask you to remit to me through the messenger the amount you can spare."[3] In the absence of any further record we do not know whether this last appeal settled the matter. We only know that in April, 1775, Mendelssohn was short of cash and asked Nicolai for a loan of one hundred or at least fifty thalers, and that he received thirty louis d'or.[4]

In 1773 Nicolai had published the first part of his *Life and Opinions of Herr Magister Sebaldus Nothanker*, the first German novel *(Roman)*, as it has been called, which immediately became a bestseller owing to the trenchant manner in which it satirized conditions in the church, and in society generally. The work had provoked instant attack on the part of the famous pietistic writer Johann Heinrich Jung (known as Jung-Stilling) who accused the anonymous "taunting Philistine" of anti-Christian sentiment and kinship with the Voltairian spirit.[5] In 1774 Nicolai prepared the second part for the press and asked Mendelssohn, to whom he sent the manuscript, for his candid opinion.

In his answer, dated October 3, 1774,[6] Mendelssohn expressed the view that Nicolai had overdone the theological aspect and given the impression that Berlin was talking of nothing else than the dogmatic ("symbolic") books. He admitted that he was "perhaps already tired of the controversies" of this kind, whereas other readers might find the subject more attractive. One senses Mendelssohn's strong distaste for theological quibbles even when treated sarcastically. The only thing in this section that pleased him had been the conversation of Sebaldus with the *Herrnhuter* [i.e., a member of the Moravian Brethren], which is not surprising because this conversation is a biting satire of the morbid type of pietism with which Lavater was infected. But Mendelssohn found much to praise in the dramatic section: "Here is action, here are characters." He only regretted that no female figures participated in one of the more moving scenes; their presence might have added warmth and a blending of the colors. The schoolmaster's wife, he realized, could not have served that purpose because, as a silk-reeler, she surely had no feeling or warm blood—and Mendelssohn was good-humored enough to quote his assistant clerk's observation that no warm-blooded person was fit for the job of disentangling silk. In a second letter, dated February 20, 1775,[7] a more serious tone is evident. He was not altogether sure, he told Nicolai, that the continuation of the novel kept within the bounds of justifiable sarcasm. In the eyes of "the friend of revelation"—a category to which Mendelssohn belonged—the open rejection of revelation was "harmful unbelief." Why this excessive frankness when "enlightened [*vernünftige*] people already got your point and the rest of mankind is perhaps better off if it does not understand you." It would be wrong to read into this letter a plea for hypocrisy. It merely warned against a reckless presentation of Enlightenment ideas without due regard to the possible harm that might be done.

In the spring of 1775 Lessing sent Mendelssohn the proofs of the *Philosophical Essays by Karl Wilhelm Jerusalem*, which he was editing (with an introduction and supplements of his own) as a tribute to the memory of his brilliant young friend, whose suicide in October, 1772, had shocked the world and moved Goethe to write *Die Leiden des jungen Werthers*. A son of the Abbot Johann Friedrich Wilhelm Jerusalem (who was probably descended of Dutch Jews), the young Jerusalem, born in 1747, had studied law and philosophy in Leipzig and Göttingen, and from May, 1770, until the end of August, 1771, had held a juridical post in Wolfenbüttel, where Lessing became his mentor. When he moved to Wetzlar and, a lonely soul, had to contend with intrigue, a deep passion for Elizabeth Herd, the wife of a colleague, took hold of him. Bereft of all hope, he shot himself. Nobody could have been more upset by this tragedy than Lessing, and when Goethe's *Werther* appeared, Lessing rejected the novel as a distortion of the character of the young man whom he had known as a seeker after truth—not as a mere victim of passion. He felt a sense of obligation to present Jerusalem's true image to the world.[8]

One of the essays included in the collection dealt with Mendelssohn's theory of sensual pleasure. It was natural, then, for Lessing to invite Mendelssohn's comments, though doing so meant delaying publication. He had intended to put the finishing touches on the work in Vienna, but his trip to Italy together with Prince Leopold of Brunswick prevented this, and the book could not appear until 1776.[9] In his supplements Lessing obviously incorporated a note Mendelssohn had sent him. It pointed out that the question raised in Jerusalem's essay was no longer valid since the new edition of Mendelssohn's *Philosophical Writings* (1771) had revised the earlier theory.[10] On June 16, 1776, Lessing wrote from Brunswick: "My brother will have given you a copy of the Jerusalem essays, and I wished you could be satisfied with the way I acted. . . . Whether I correctly understood your note on the first essay, you will see. Otherwise, you will not take it amiss, I hope, that I made no further use of it. It would have been impolitic to point out all the weak points of my author."[11] It seems that Mendelssohn had a great deal to remark à propos Jerusalem's essays, but Lessing rightly felt that the purpose of his memorial volume might be defeated if criticism was given too much scope in the supplements. Marcus Herz, too, had written Lessing a long letter offering a defense of Mendelssohn's theory of sensual pleasure as against Jerusalem's critique.[12] Lessing replied toward the end of April, 1776, that he had "not wished to weigh Jerusalem's reflections too minutely on the scales."[13]

Mendelssohn's own disgust with Goethe's *Werther* is attested by a letter reporting a rather amusing episode from the year 1776. The letter, written as late as March 20, 1797, was addressed to Goethe himself. The episode was recalled by the writer of the letter, Frau Sara von Grotthus, the wife of a Prussian army officer (she having been divorced from the merchant Lipmann Wulff, to whom she had been unhappily married). Sara von Grotthus, as it happened, was none other than Särchen, the daughter of Aaron and Rösel Meyer, who as a girl of eleven had enchanted Mendelssohn during his second stay in Pyrmont.[14] In 1776, when she was thirteen, she had—so her letter tells us—a romance with a very handsome young man from Hamburg. "Once he sent me the solace of frustrated lovers, the divine *Werther;* having devoured it, I returned it with a thousand passages marked, together with a glowing note. This message was intercepted by my dear father, I was punished by confinement to my room, and Mendelssohn, my mentor, appeared: he bitterly reproached me. Could I have forgotten God and religion, he asked, and amid foolish reproofs of this sort he took the dear *W*[*erther*], the innocent corpus delicti, and threw it out of the window...." The continuation of the story is that she fell ill but recovered when Lessing happened to appear for a visit. He was indignant at Mendelssohn's behavior and brought her a new copy of the *Werther* ("which, however, he contemplated a long time with a shiver"). In her view, Lessing's only fault was his leniency, especially toward "Moses," and she assured Goethe that if ever Lessing said anything against the *Werther*," it came from that source."[15]

Another interesting letter of Sara von Grotthus to Goethe may be quoted in passing, since it concerns Lessing, Mendelssohn, and her father:[16] "As it happened, Lessing believed that he owed my father a sense of obligation, since the gallant man supported the young scholar by word and deed. Consequently, he was for a long time a friend of the family, was pleased to see me when I was a small goodlooking child, and obtained a promise from my father to send me as often as possible to Wolfenbüttel, where he would guide and judge my progress." On three occasions she stayed with Lessing for four weeks. She was proud when Lessing asked Mendelssohn to show her the final page-proofs of his *Nathan the Wise*. "All persons in it," she wrote in her letter to Goethe, "were familiar portraits: Nathan himself, a liberal merchant, representing my father, and as a thinker representing Mendelssohn . . ." Her metamorphosis into Sara von Grotthus had certainly not diminished the love she felt for her father.

One of those who were curious to meet the author of the *Phaedon* was Rochus Friedrich, count of Lynar, who, after a distinguished career as Danish royal governor of Oldenburg and Delmenhorst, lived in retirement (yet busy as a writer) on his family estate in Lübbenau (Niederlausitz), not far from Berlin.[17] It seems that he visited Mendelssohn several times and also became friendly with members of his circle, particularly Nicolai and Johann August Eberhard. When Christian August Crusius, the well-known metaphysician, published an essay expressing his misgivings about the spiritualist experiments of Johann Georg Schröpfer, who had created some *furore* in Dresden and Leipzig and then committed suicide,[18] the count sent Mendelssohn a copy of this essay, with the request that he jot down his thoughts about it. Mendelssohn obliged with some "Notes on an Essay Concerning the Miracles of the Notorious Schröpfer," which were published in the first number of the *Allgemeine deutsche Bibliothek* of 1775.[19] It was Mendelssohn's first appearance as a writer since the onset of his illness. The *Notes* left no doubt that Mendelssohn placed little confidence in Crusius' judgment, which had relied on someone's eyewitness report; had Crusius personally attended the séance, his inquisitive mind might have embarrassed Schröpfer, despite the fact that he was not averse to recognizing the "cooperation of evil and good spirits."

The clever impostor—Mendelssohn considered Schröpfer to be such—had picked his witnesses carefully from among those who were predisposed either to hope or fear. One who hopes is easily deceived, one who is terrified does not see reality but the thing feared. The awesome borders upon the sublime and for this reason has a certain attraction. Crusius' reporter, Mendelssohn suggested, had been both hopeful and fearful—and also swayed by a lively imagination, as the nature of his report indicated. Having thus disqualified Crusius' witness, Mendelssohn refrained from examining his essay and ventured instead some conjectures of his own. He suspected that Schröpfer had achieved his effects through optical illusions produced by a magic lantern, and he went into considerable detail to explain just how certain apparitions could be conjured up. Guyot, he pointed out, had given examples of this in his *Physical and Mathematical Amusements* (Augsburg, 1773). Mendelssohn handed a copy of his "thoughts" to the count on a visit he paid him, probably in January, 1775, and on that occasion he became involved in a discussion of the "affinities" as well as the differences between enthusiasts, visionaries, and fanatics. He offered, offhand, a lucid delineation of these three types, which greatly pleased the count.

On February 6, 1775, the count sent Mendelssohn a letter of thanks for the "very profound thoughts" he had expressed on Doctor Crusius' essay: they were a "highly estimable present." Yet something else was bothering the count. Mendelssohn's lucid definition of the three types had made "their differences and gradations" perfectly clear to him at the time, but he was now at a loss to recapture them in his mind. "Would it be too immodest if I asked you to put them down on paper in a few words?"[20] Mendelssohn lost no time. On February 12, 1775, he sent the count a short essay entitled *Enthusiast, Visionary, Fanatic,* with a covering letter explaining that his previous *extempore* definitions were now replaced by an attempt to analyze the concepts in greater depth.[21]

The essay offered, to begin with, some general observations on the effects of ideas on men. Mathematical propositions illumined the mind but left the heart cold. They were too abstract to affect us, whereas notions of a sensual character engendered the warmth required for action. Ideas conveyed by signs were less powerful than intuited or sensually experienced objects of knowledge. Reading a musical score will move the expert, but listening to the music will have a far stronger impact on him. All this was rather commonplace. The interesting point Mendelssohn made concerned the different effects produced by the same ideas upon different people. He formulated a kind of law to account for the difference. The force of ideas depended (1) upon the degree and proportion of our mental faculties, inclinations, skills, etc.—in short, on our total personality,[22] and (2) upon the accidental circumstances in which we found ourselves at a given time (i.e., upon our mood). In certain people the most feeble ideas could produce the most powerful and extraordinary effects if they hit upon the appropriate type of character and mood. An enthusiast was one whose soul was so strongly moved by feeble notions of a certain kind that all of his mental faculties were excited and activated for the sake of a single overriding purpose. We all were more or less sensitive to certain ideas—virtue, religion, country, friendship, and the like—even though they were general and abstract and feeble as such. The mere sound of these words could kindle enthusiasm in the soul and move it to action of an apparently inspired nature, provided the total personality was attuned to them and happened to be in the right mood. A visionary, on the other hand, was a person who reacted to ideas of a certain kind so rapidly that his creative imagination was moved by the mere signs (words, letters) to transform the signs into pictures *(phantasmata)* and the pictures into sensations. Finally, the fanatical person was described as one upon whom the ideas congenial to his personality had the effect of producing far more heat than light. These ideas set the most hidden springs of the heart into violent, sustained motion and caused strong and extraordinary kinds of action, action that would in most cases be evil because it originated in an impure source, in delusion and dreaming, rather than in truth. Lastly, Mendelssohn referred to the kind of enthusiasm found in the fine arts and in belles-lettres, complimenting the treatment of this species of enthusiasm *(Begeisterung)* in Sulzer's *Allgemeine Theorie der Schönen Künste.*[23]

The significance of this little essay lies in its sharp distinction between enthusiasm *(Begeisterung)* as a positive value and fanaticism *(Schwärmerey)* as an evil. Previously Mendelssohn had followed the lead of conventional speech, which often used the two terms indiscriminately as synonyms. How pleased the count was with the essay may be gauged from a hitherto unpublished letter that he wrote to Nicolai on May 15, 1775.[24] The relevant paragraph reads: "I could not refrain from inserting the valuable essay, which Herr Moses Mendelssohn wrote at my request, in a treatise on enthusiasm that you will find in the second number of the new *Miscellanies* that is now being printed. Since I mentioned no name, I hope he will not resent my having done this without his knowledge. The high esteem I have for this excellent man deserves at least some clemency."[25]

It may be taken for granted that Mendelssohn had no objection to the piracy. If he had wanted to publish the essay, he could have done so easily. The fact that on May 20, 1775,[26] he sent a copy to the count of Schaumburg-Lippe, with whom he had remained in friendly contact by correspondence, was unconnected with the pending publication of the count of Lynar's new *Miscellanies*. Mendelssohn had planned to send Schaumburg this particular essay and the earlier pieces on Schröpfer before the count of Lynar had informed Nicolai of the action he had taken. We may infer this from a note dated May 1, 1775, in which he asked Nicolai to return to him the copy of Crusius' *Misgivings* and of his own "little essay" (obviously the one entitled *Enthusiast, Visionary, Fanatic*).[27] Having retrieved the two copies, he sent them (together with his essay on Schröpfer and with a copy of Marcus Herz' letter to Lessing thrown into the bargain) to the count of Schaumburg-Lippe, with a covering letter explaining the various items.[28] It was rather fortunate that he sent this material to the count. Had he not done so, the "little essay" would have been lost to posterity. It is extant only in a copy made by the count's secretary, which was preserved in the *Haus-Archiv* of the *Fürstliche Hofkammer* at Bückeburg.[29] In 1774 Countess Marie Eleonora herself had copied Mendelssohn's papers on the incorporeality of the human soul.[30]

Mendelssohn's stay in Pyrmont had again failed to produce a permanent cure: the unnerving attacks reoccurred. A letter to the count of Schaumburg-Lippe, written by Mendelssohn in the early part of 1775, described his condition.[31] The count had sent him an essay of his own (from among several of his writings that they had discussed in Pyrmont),[32] and Mendelssohn had intended to offer his comments, but as he explained: "My health has not permitted me to . . . [comment on the essay]. The stay in Pyrmont has been extremely important to me in another respect, and it will remain memorable to me as long as I live. God grant that her Grace the countess will experience better results from the use of the waters than I obtained this time. I am still incapable of any mental effort and have to be careful to avoid any opportunity for meditation [*Nachdenken*]. However, so long as I feel physically well I do not give up the hope of returning to my favorite occupation someday. Yet I am firmly resolved not to force nature, not to wrest from her the least advance, but to follow her bidding with childlike obedience wherever she leads me. Should she restore me to philosophy, the former companion of my life, I shall embrace her with the ardor one bestows upon a regained mistress. But should I finish my career in idleness, I shall bless Providence even for such a fate, hoping to pick up the thread in the hereafter at the very point at which I had to tear it off so abruptly in this world." This letter must have been written in one of Mendelssohn's less optimistic moments, for as his responses to the count of Lynar's requests show, he was far from incapable of mental effort, and he disproved himself when on May 20 he sent the two pieces he had written to Bückeburg.

It seems that Mendelssohn sometimes used his illness as a pretext to avoid commenting on writings that he could not praise but was unwilling to criticize. The count's essay may have been in this category. And yet we cannot discount the possibility that at certain periods Mendelssohn was indeed in a state of helplessness. There is no evidence that he had developed traits of hypochondria. The utterly resigned and other-worldly tone of his letter may have reflected a desire to help the count and countess to overcome their grief by conveying to them a sense of acceptance of the decrees of Providence. That he himself lived up to his preaching cannot be doubted. In a letter to Nicolai he had declared with assumed boastfulness that one could learn from him how a patient had to conduct himself.[33] And he and Fromet were themselves in need of comfort when in September, 1775, they lost their son Mendel, who had been named after his paternal grandfather, at the age of six.

An academic figure whose friendship Mendelssohn valued was Ernst Platner (1744–1818), since 1770 a professor of medicine at Leipzig, who also lectured with great success on forensic medicine, physiology, logic, metaphysics, moral philosophy, and aesthetics. The two volumes of his *Anthropology for Physicians and Philosophers* had appeared in 1772–1774, and in 1776 he published the first volume of his principal work, the *Philosophical Aphorisms* (the second volume came out in 1782). Platner was at this time a follower of Leibniz; when later he reworked his *Aphorisms* for the second edition (1793–1800) he was a skeptic who had relegated Leibniz' notions to the realm of "subjective ideas" and combated Kant in a very astute way.[34] His letters to Mendelssohn in 1775 and 1776 show him to have been a glowing admirer of the Jewish philosopher. On December 18, 1775, he wrote:[35] "Dearest, best man, again a student of mine and admirer of yours, a friend of philosophy, versed in philosophy (without being very gifted for it), a good, well-educated, modest man, eager to learn [is herewith presented to you]. Do grant him the happiness to have talked to you, to the man whom many people only want to see, being totally incapable of talking to a philosopher. Since I am largely responsible for our young people's desire to meet you in person, it is only fair that I do all I can to satisfy [the desire]. Your most devoted friend Platner." He continued to send students of his to Mendelssohn. On July 8, 1776, he introduced another one:[36] "Herr Le Grand is one of those apprentices who give an academic teacher courage and his profession a certain dignity. Irrespective of me, he deserves that you have a talk with him.... Yet what must you think of me, best and most beloved man, seeing that I constantly send my students to you? You cannot think anything worse than that I esteem you very highly and love you. This I surely do with all my heart." There is an undated third letter introducing two more students.[37] It also inquires about Mendelssohn's health: "How is your health? *Leidlich* [not too good], this is what I always hear. Do come to Leipzig for the fair. There you feel invariably well. Should this reason appear too selfish to you, do come for the sake of your friends. Now, however, my interest in your health becomes selfish, seeing that I am not your physician but only *your friend.*"

Mendelssohn reciprocated Platner's sentiments of friendship. He never forgot to send him greetings when Nicolai visited the Leipzig fair.[38] And on November 14, 1776, it was his turn to introduce a young friend to Platner:[39] "The bearer of this letter, my estimable friend, is a physician and lover of philosophy, who has been a frequent visitor to my house for several years. Hence you need not be surprised that he is most desirous of meeting you personally. He asked me for the favor to make it possible for him to do so, and I trust your kindness that you will not deny him free access to you during his short stay in Leipzig. Please accept at the same time my sincere thanks for the *Aphorisms* you were good enough to send me. I hope to be in a position to read them in the course of this winter. For the time being, my fibers still resist the least strain. Keep well, my dearest friend, and do continue to teach reason and wisdom despite all the prevalent mysology [science concerned with trivia]." The young friend of this letter was most probably Marcus Herz, who had received the doctorate of medicine at Halle in 1774 and was to publish his *Letters to Physicians* in 1777. It would have been natural for him to have wished to meet the physician-philosopher Platner. How interested Mendelssohn was in the *Aphorisms* is evident from the fact that on October 8, 1775 he had written to Nicolai:[40] "As soon as Platner's *Aphorisms* are available, I would like to receive a copy by mail [from the Leipzig fair]." He must again have been in poor condition when, on receipt of a complimentary copy from the author, he had to defer reading it. The zigzag pattern of Mendelssohn's illness had not changed to any considerable extent.

Mendelssohn's periods of enforced idleness were not entirely sterile, however. He was able to continue his old habit of writing down in a pocket notebook ideas that suddenly occurred to him or that he had pondered for some time. We know three such entries from the year 1776. The first, written in March, deals with François Hemsterhuis' *Lettre sur la Sculpture* (Amsterdam, 1769), which defined the beautiful as "that which imparts the maximum of ideas in the minimum of time."[41] Mendelssohn agreed but suggested certain modifications: the "maximum of ideas" had to be understood not only extensively as the greatest number of ideas but also intensively as the greatest clarity, power, etc. Moreover, in addition to the shortest space of time, the definition had to include minimum of effort. He made further observations on the essential points of difference between painting and sculpture, a subject with which he had been intimately acquainted ever since Lessing, Nicolai, and he had discussed the problems dealt with in the *Laokoön*.[42]

The other two entries are dated June, 1776.[43] The first concerns what Mendelssohn calls the objective and subjective "capacity for entertainment" *(Unterhaltungsfähigkeit)* and what, according to his exposition of the theme, amounts to aesthetic enjoyment and its opposite. Objects, we are told, are able to arouse in us certain "thoughts and sentiments" that may or may not lead to action, and we have a subjective capacity to be entertained by them. Both capacities are differentiated according to the quantity and quality of the thoughts and sentiments produced. The various ratios between the objective and subjective factors result in beautiful, sublime, or tedious thoughts and in a scale of sentiments which includes the pleasant and that which causes dizziness and nausea. What is remarkable in these observations is his concern with a capacity of the soul that is neither cognitive nor directed toward action but stands midway between them.

The second entry for June, 1776, pursues this line of thinking further: "Between the capacity of cognition and that of desire lies the capacity of sentiment [*Empfindungsvermögen*], by virtue of which we feel pleasure or displeasure about a thing, approve or disapprove of it, applaud or reprove it, find it pleasant or unpleasant. There are thoughts and representations that leave us unmoved, to which no sentiments attach. There are likewise sentiments that do not pass over into desire as yet. We are able to find music or a painting beautiful, and to be moved by it, without desiring anything." By thus assigning to the sentiments a role on a par with knowing and desiring Mendelssohn brought to full fruition what was already implied in his distinction between the true and the beautiful in his letters *On the Sentiments*. He thereby replaced the traditional division of the soul into "cognitive" and "practical" faculties by a tripartite pattern. In that same year (1776), Johann Nikolaus Tetens did the same in his *Philosophische Versuche*, in which he introduced the doctrine of the three *Seelenvermögen*—intellect, will, and sentiments—and designated the last group as *Fühlungen* or *Gefühle*.[44]

Mendelssohn's notebook entry owed nothing to Tetens and put an entirely original complexion on the function of the sentiments by describing it as an act of approbation or disapproval. The element of pleasure or displeasure in the sentiments was due to an act of discerning the good or bad, the beautiful or ugly aspects of a thing, an act different from both the act of knowing and that of desiring. The focus of the knowing capacity, Mendelssohn explained, was the true, whereas the capacity of sentiment or approbation was concerned with the good and beautiful. There was this further difference: in exercising our cognitive faculty we tried to make our concepts of things consonant with their objective reality. When we allowed our sentiments to operate, the reverse happened: we endeavored to make objective reality conform to our notions of goodness, order, and beauty. Sentiment, therefore, ultimately issued in action but was in itself neither desire nor action. It was, as Mendelssohn put it, "connected" with a desire to bring the qualities of an object, including our own personal qualities, into harmony with our sense of the approvable, and Mendelssohn tried to lay down the rules determining the chances of sentiments to pass over into action.

That the ideas expressed in the little sketch of 1776 were taken very seriously by Mendelssohn is evident in the fact that he took them up anew in a more polished form in his *Morgenstunden* (1785), and the fact that the tripartite division of the faculties of the soul came to be reflected in his favorite album inscriptions. The first such inscription is dated July 6, 1776, and reads:[45] "To *think* the true, to *love* the good, to *do* the best." Thinking, loving, and doing denote the three faculties of cognition, of sentiment or approbation, and of desire or action. Mendelssohn's album inscriptions in the 1780's define the "vocation of man" under four heads, the last two merely spelling out the dual aspect of the third faculty. The motto now reads:[46] "To search for truth, to love beauty, to desire the good, to do the best." The differentiation between the beautiful and the good need not be taken as evidence of a shift in the concept of sentiment or approbation, for in the *Morgenstunden*[47] the formula reads: "Man searches after truth, approves the good and beautiful, desires all that is good, and does the best." Though it was Immanuel Kant who firmly established the tripartite division of the functions of the soul (representation, feeling, willing), Mendelssohn's share in this development is not to be disputed.[48]

The year 1777 was one of many travels for Mendelssohn. He had invested some money in a business in Memel, which was run by his brother-in-law and partner Joseph Gugenheim. There were reports that Joseph had been negligent, that serious losses had been incurred, that claims for damages had been filed. Mendelssohn decided to travel to Memel to deal with the situation, planning to be away for about five weeks.[49] Benjamin Veitel Ephraim and David Friedländer were his travel companions, and the trip, which was begun in mid-July, proved to be very enjoyable,[50] though they were glad when they had left Poland.[51] On July 24 the party arrived at Königsberg, where Mendelssohn was entertained royally by the local Jewish community and cordially received by Kant, Hamann, and some civic dignitaries. He stayed in the city until July 31 and revisited it on his return trip from Memel.

Joseph Gugenheim arrived in Königsberg on July 29, and on August 1 the two traveled to Memel via Tilsit, where they spent the sabbath. "One cannot imagine a more pleasant journey than one through Prussian Lithuania," Mendelssohn wrote Fromet from Tilsit. "I assure you that the *Tiergarten* [the most salubrious district in Berlin] is not much more pleasant."[52] Mendelssohn stayed in Memel from August 4 to August 10, satisfying himself that Joseph had been the victim of intrigues, that he had not squandered the money, that his bookkeeping had been somewhat negligent and that this had caused some friction with another quarrelsome partner (who had to be dismissed), and that there was every hope for the business to improve. Mendelssohn kept assuring Fromet and his mother-in-law (who lived with them) that all was well with Joseph, both physically and morally. The tenderness of his concern for their feelings is manifest in all his letters.[53] His confidence in Joseph remained steadfast in later years even when the business in Memel came to grief. A letter he wrote some years later (on June 5, 1781)[54] to Elkan Herz testifies to his sense of fairness and nobility of character: "May I tell you how pleased I am that my brother-in-law Joseph is doing business with you. . . . I have every confidence in his well-proven honesty. True, the business that he ran for me in Prussia miscarried. It was not his fault, however, nor has anybody, God forbid, suffered any loss except we ourselves. By the way, he does not owe any one a penny, so far as I know."

On his return trip from Memel, Mendelssohn stayed again in Königsberg, from August 10 to August 20.[55] It seems that his second stay was more enjoyable than the first. On the first occasion he had written home that three days of receiving and paying visits was more than he could stomach; that everything between heaven and earth, and these included, was much more pleasant in Berlin than at any place he had so far seen on his long trip. "This is my whole diary of my journey to Königsberg," he wrote on July 27, "and even in Königsberg I have nothing to add." He had as yet made no new acquaintances among the Christians, and would probably make only a few, apart from Kant and some people recommended by Kant. He was not keen on meeting more; he realized that there might be good and able men among them, but he could enjoy better Christian friends in Berlin. He asked Fromet to warn Professor Engel against accepting any kind of post in Königsberg.[56] It seems, however, that during his first stay in the city Mendelssohn did become quite friendly with Kant, for on August 8 he wrote Fromet from Tilsit:[57] "I have to tell Herr Doctor Herz much too much from his friend Herr Kant to be able to write it down."

What Kant felt about Mendelssohn by the time of his departure on August 20 is stated in a letter he wrote to Marcus Herz on that very day:[58] "Today your worthy friend and mine, as I flatter myself, departs from here. Having a man of such gentle disposition, cheerful temper, and bright intellect for a permanent and intimate companion in Königsberg would be the kind of nourishment for the soul that I miss here so completely. . . . I could not arrange, however, to take full advantage of this unique opportunity to enjoy so rare a man, partly from fear lest I might disturb him . . . in the business he had to attend to locally. Yesterday he did me the honor of being present at two of my lectures, *à la fortune du pot*, as one might

say, since the table was not prepared for such a distinguished guest. . . .
I beg you to keep for me the friendship of this worthy man in the future."

On August 4 Hamann announced Mendelssohn's arrival to two
friends:[59] "On July 24 my dear Phaedon Moses Mephiboseth arrived and on
the last day of the month he left with his brother-in-law. . . . In a week
I expect Moses back and I hope to enjoy him even more." Why he dubbed
Mendelssohn "Mephiboseth," after the lame son of Jonathan, King David's
friend, is not clear. He did this not only behind his back but in a letter
of the same year addressed him as "my dearest best Moses Mephiboseth."[60]
Hamann seems to have enjoyed Mendelssohn's presence, for he visited
him "every day, *nolens volens*, at the right time and at the wrong time."[61]
He wrote to Lavater:[62] "I have spent more than one sweet hour with him.
I also read his *Philosophical Writings* during his stay here, as well as the
Platonic correspondence between the two of you. This man is really the
salt and light of his race, and he would have lost all his merit and dignity
had he become one of us like Adam."

On the day following Mendelssohn's departure from the city a "farewell
greeting" was published in the local gazette:[63] "At about four yesterday
afternoon, Herr Moses Mendelssohn left this city on his return trip to
Berlin. We had long revered him as a profound philosopher and as a
man of good taste who is at home with belles-lettres. Now we admire in
him, more than all learning that is vain, transient, and useless, a good
and noble heart capable of friendship and open to all gentle sentiments
associated with it. He did not shun any society eager to meet him . . . nor
did he obtrude himself upon any. For a special reason he spoke to some
of the greatest men of our city, such as his Excellency Herr Count von
Keyserling and his Excellency Herr Chancellor von Korff, and everywhere
he exceeded all expectations . . ." The party traveled via Danzig and early
in September Mendelssohn was reunited with his wife and children, after
a separation of more than six weeks. Never before had he been away
from home for so long a time, he remarked in his last letter from Königsberg.[64]

It is not difficult to guess the nature of the "special reason" that had
prompted Mendelssohn to seek an interview with the high dignitaries mentioned in the Königsberg gazette's farewell message. He had no doubt
been asked by leaders of the local Jewish community to intervene on their
behalf in a case then under investigation by a government commission.
Its origin lay in a royal edict of August 28, 1703, which forbade the recital
of a certain phrase, "for they bow down and prostrate themselves before
what is vain and futile and pray to a god who cannot help," in the '*Alenu*
prayer at the conclusion of each service. A Jewish convert to Christianity
had testified that this particular phrase was meant as a slur against Jesus.
To ensure the omission of this sentence from the prayer, the edict demanded
that the text be recited aloud by the cantor and that the services be inspected
by government-appointed Christian supervisors familiar with the Hebrew

language, who would report any failure to comply with the law. The punishment threatened for such failure was expulsion from the country.

This utterly ludicrous edict had actually been observed by the Jewish communities, so as to avoid giving any imagined offense, but the duty of supervising the services was no longer taken seriously by local authorities except in the city of Königsberg. In that city the office of governmental inspector of the synagogue had become a much coveted post, one that carried a stipend of a hundred thalers per annum and was entrusted to a series of respectable university professors of theology or oriental languages. From 1755 onward the office had been administered by one Georg David Kypke, a mediocre and somewhat pedantic orientalist, who had his reserved seat in the synagogue and attended services with the punctuality of a Prussian official. This already farcical situation was made the more absurd in 1777, when the community, in all innocence, decided to move Kypke from his accustomed seat to another one that he chose to regard as less dignified. Offended, he lodged a complaint with the Royal Ministry of State on April 5, 1777, airing not only his personal "grievance" but also reporting that the *'Alenu* prayer was being recited in a sort of "muttering," rather than aloud, and that the community had failed on certain special occasions to notify him in advance of the order of service, thus making it impossible for him to prevent the recital of psalms that were in his view most unsuitable. Thus Psalm 49 (verse 13: "But man abideth not in honor; He is like the beasts that perish," etc.) was read at the memorial service for Elizabeth, empress of Russia, and Psalm 17 was recited at the service celebrating the birth of the hereditary prince of Prussia, although it was capable of a disrespectful application.

In self-defense the community submitted a testimonial written (at its request) by Mendelssohn a few weeks before his departure for Königsberg. It was entitled "Thoughts on Jewish Prayers, Especially on the *'Alenu* Prayer" and did not bear his signature. The dignity with which he dealt with the subject was in stark contrast to the petty suspicions of the orientalist Kypke. "The prayer *'Alenu*," Mendelssohn pointed out, "is one of the oldest prayers of our nation. It was originally instituted only for New Year's Day, as a solemn introduction to the homage paid to the Supreme Lawgiver and Judge of the World. Because of its important and sublime [*erhabenen*] content it has been adopted as the daily concluding prayer. It can be shown irrefutably, on a number of grounds, that only the heathens and their idolatrous worship are referred to in it, and not, as some enemies and slanderers of the Jewish nation falsely contend, the Christians, who like ourselves worship the King of Kings, the Holy One, blessed be He; that, moreover, no kabbalistic allusions to their [the Christians'] Messiah are found in it." The last remark was directed against the allegation that the numerical value of the word *va-rik* ("and futile") alluded to *Yeshu* (Jesus).

Mendelssohn then undertook to prove that this prayer had originated in pre-Christian times and thus could contain no anti-Christian passages.

Indeed, some authorities had attributed its authorship to a figure of such remote antiquity as Moses' disciple Joshua the son of Nun. Yet this much was certain, that the prayer must have existed at least at the time of the Second Temple. For had it been composed later one should find there some expression of hope in the rebuilding of the Temple and the restoration of the Jewish state. The text had remained unaltered, and the fact that Jews in Muslim lands recited it in exactly the same way as Jews recited it in Christian lands was a clear indication that no anti-Christian reference was intended.

As for the recital of Psalm 49, Mendelssohn pointed out that it described, rather movingly, the brevity of man's life, the vanity of all temporal power, the victory of life everlasting over death, and the reward and punishment to be meted out in the hereafter. Hence the psalm had been chosen for reading during the week of mourning for a deceased person, and its recital at the memorial service for the Russian empress was entirely in keeping with Jewish ritual. Mendelssohn quoted his own beautiful German rendering of this psalm. It was incomprehensible to him, he said, how Kypke could have considered it disrespectful.

Kypke's angry rejoinder to this impressive testimonial was submitted to the royal commissioner on July 16, 1777 (just as Mendelssohn was starting his trip to the East). It tried to disprove Mendelssohn's arguments as "unscholarly" and insisted that the prayer, irrespective of its origins, had come to be associated with anti-Christian sentiment. At the time of Mendelssohn's arrival in Königsberg the case was being studied by the authorities, and it is quite understandable that the community leaders were anxious to use his presence for the advancement of their case. What they wanted was nothing less than the abolition of the degrading practice of inspection. The personal impression that Mendelssohn made upon the count von Keyserling and the chancellor was no doubt an important factor in bringing this about. On September 2, 1777, a strong memorandum opposing Kypke's rejoinder was submitted, and in the following year a petition addressed to the king finally achieved the termination of the undignified practice. Kypke, who had a vested interest in it and had made a last minute effort to thwart the opposition, was absolved from his duty as inspector and charged merely to administer an oath to newly appointed cantors whereby they agreed to recite the prayer in the fashion laid down in the royal edict of 1703. A rise in salary compensated Kypke for the loss of his stipend, and the sum of four hundred thalers, which the community had raised by selling his former seat in the synagogue, was accepted as a gift by the local university. At long last the curtain had descended on this strange comedy.[65]

About two months after his return from Königsberg, Mendelssohn went on another trip. Together with his wife and a friend, Dr. Joseph Haltern,[66] he traveled to Hanover, intending to stay there eight or ten days, and with a view to visiting Lessing en route back to Berlin. Originally,

Lessing's brother Karl was to join the party.[67] On November 3, 1777, Mendelssohn sent Lessing a note from Hanover informing him that he was being detained, "for who knows how long," and that he was therefore mailing to him two letters and a box of flowers: the letters he had meant to hand to him, and the flowers he had hoped personally to deliver to Madame Lessing in order to predispose her to a friendliness that she might otherwise not have felt toward a "strange bearded face." Lessing's marriage to Eva König had taken place on October 8, 1776, and Mendelssohn was looking forward to making her acquaintance.[68] The letters as well as the flowers came from Karl. He had been asked by his brother to buy on his behalf "three little bouquets" of "silk flowers" *(Florblumen)* for his wife who assumed that they could be had in Berlin.[69] Lessing's reply to Mendelssohn's note is lost, but we know from the letter Mendelssohn wrote to him on November 11, and the one that he wrote to Nicolai on the following day,[70] that Lessing sent him a "very interesting letter" and enclosed with it the manuscript of his *Dialogues for Freemasons*[71] which he had just completed.[72]

Lessing had conceived the plan of this work as far back as 1767, when he began his efforts to be received into the mystically inclined and most powerful of the German masonic systems, the Order of the Templars (or the "Strict Observance"). His efforts failed but his continued interest in Freemasonry is evinced by his research into the origins of the order. The theory that he evolved traced the etymology of the term *masonry* back to the term *massony* (round table). The first draft of his *Dialogues* was ready in 1771. On October 14, 1771, he was initiated, more or less privately, into one of the semi-official lodges *(Winkellogen)*, i.e., the one called "At the Three Golden Roses," which had been founded by Baron Georg Johann von Rosenberg.

When Lessing and Mendelssohn had met in July, 1773,[73] the conversation had turned quite naturally to the subject of Freemasonry. Lessing admitted having joined the order and explained somewhat apologetically that his oath of secrecy debarred him from revealing anything. Mendelssohn assured him that nothing was further from his mind than to elicit any Masonic secrets from him. Yet he could hardly help expressing a sense of bewilderment: "From our early youth we have been seeking the truth. Ever since we became friends we have sought it jointly, with all the faithfulness [with which] it wants to be pursued. Now there might be truths that Lessing swore in the most solemn fashion not to reveal to his friend of twenty-five years standing, and yet I am supposed not to be even curious to know these truths. However, if it is not truths that the order transmits to its adepts, you will all the more concede that I—— [can have little respect for Freemasonry]." Lessing, who was greatly amused by his friend's zeal, interrupted him, saying: "Stop, dear Moses; now I have compromised my order to no purpose."[74] When Lessing spent some time in Berlin in the early part of 1776, he discussed his theory of the origin of Freemasonry with Nicolai, who was an eminent expert in this field, and Nicolai in turn frequently discussed it with Mendelssohn.[75] Hence the manuscript of the *Dialogues for Freemasons* that Lessing sent Mendelssohn in November, 1777, came as no big surprise to him. "Your discovery concerning the origin of the name [Freemasonry] you must have disclosed to our Nicolai at some time," he wrote in his reply on November 11. "If I am not mistaken, he has spoken to me about it several times already—at least I remember quite distinctly having heard something like this more than once from one of my friends, and except for you and Nicolai I have discussed Freemasonry with no one."

It is obvious from the last remark that Mendelssohn had never made an effort to enter the order, as many Jews of the next generation would do with varying success.[76] Some indication as to how he felt about the Freemasons is found in his notes on Crusius' essay dealing with Schröpfer:[77] "The Freemasons, to whom he [Schröpfer] was wont to turn for the most part, are said to be directed, at their meetings, toward great expectations by means of mysterious practices and rituals. Their entire soul is excited, as it were, to a high pitch of expectancy; and I seem to have noticed that the more amiable and benevolent the members of this society are, the more chimerical the hopes by which they allow themselves to be deceived."

Lessing's manuscript did not change Mendelssohn's fundamental attitude of distrust of Freemasonry, but it did help him understand the idealistic motivations that had caused Lessing to join the order. For many individuals of high spiritual caliber the order served as a kind of substitute for the pre-Reformation church, as a hierarchically constructed secular community of searchers after truth in which the individual was no longer lonely and isolated but was part of a noble-minded society of kindred souls.[78] Lessing, who had experienced a keen sense of frustration following his acceptance into the order,[79] tried to distinguish between the true essence and the imperfect manifestation of the masonic idea. The distinction between accidental historical truths and necessary, timeless truths of reason, which led him toward a view of the church as a mere precursor of the ultimate kingdom of autonomous reason, also lay at the root of his *Dialogues on Freemasonry*.[80] Mendelssohn's reaction to the manuscript was clear and to the point:[81] "I have read your *Dialogues on Freemasonry* with very great pleasure. Not that they satisfied my curiosity. . . . On the one hand, I had rid myself of this demon long ago. I am convinced that what men conceal from men is rarely worth being searched for. On the other hand, you know best that your *Dialogues* are not meant to satisfy curiosity. What they did do to me, however, was produce more proper ideas about an institution that for some time past had begun to appear almost contemptible to me."[82]

The date of their impending reunion was still uncertain when Mendelssohn wrote his letter on November 11: "I shall visit you in Wolfenbüttel without fail, though I cannot yet determine the day. . . . Surely, no business shall stand in my way, for in fact none is as urgent to me as the desire to see you and chat with you." On November 19 he replied to a letter from Lessing, not extant, which must have contained the question as to whether his stepson Theodor König could join the party on their return trip to Berlin. Mendelssohn answered on November 19:[83] "I have a spacious coach with four seats, and there are only three passengers. A comfortable seat is therefore available for your son, and I [will be] glad to have it occupied by a person so close to you. I believe that I shall have to stay here about another three weeks at most, perhaps only two weeks. We are sure to pick up our traveling companion then. What about your coming to Hanover in the meantime, and searching with me in Leibniz' papers [at the library]? The thought is so attractive, so comforting in the boredom under which I am smarting, that I prefer to receive no answer to this question rather than have a refusal. I herewith return your *Dialogues*. The principal idea is so important and, to me at least, so novel that I am most eager to see it fully elaborated."

Precisely what kind of business kept Mendelssohn in Hanover for so long a time remains a mystery. Eventually the return journey via Wolfenbüttel could take place. On December 19, Lessing informed his brother Karl that Mendelssohn was expected to arrive in Brunswick that very day (a Friday) or the following day (he forgot that his friend would not travel on a Saturday), and would spend Sunday with him.[84] That this plan was carried out, we know from the entry of Mendelssohn's name in the guest book of the Wolfenbüttel library. It is dated December 21, 1777.[85]

Lessing's newly found happiness at the side of Eva, a woman of remarkable qualities of heart and mind, was patent to all, and Mendelssohn had already noticed the change in his friend's demeanor when he wrote to him on November 11. It was the happiest year in Lessing's life. He looked forward to the birth of his child by this beloved woman, and he was ready to move into a new home. His and Mendelssohn's talks were attended, at least partly, by a certain Captain Rothmann, who had lived for several years in America and was eminently qualified to take an active part in the discussion of Corneille de Pauw's *Recherches philosophiques sur les Américains*.[86] In Lessing's view almost all the references in that book were false, and the correct ones did not prove what they were meant to prove.[87] Freemasonry was no doubt another subject discussed.

This was the last meeting of Mendelssohn and Lessing. It took place only a few days before Eva's confinement. The child died two days after its birth on December 27, 1777, and the mother having been unconscious almost all the time since her labor began, died on January 10, 1778. Lessing never recovered from this mortal wound inflicted on his soul, and Mendelssohn, who had caught a last glimpse of his dearest friend's short-lived happiness, must have been deeply shocked and grieved when the sad news reached him.

Some Philosophical Preoccupations

The anonymous treatise *Reflections on the Universe*,[1] which had appeared in 1777, was remarkable in two respects. It had something of the quality of a Renaissance work on metaphysics in the way that it combined Leibnizian ideas and the Platonism of Shaftesbury and Hemsterhuis; and it drew on a wide-ranging knowledge of the sciences in order to substantiate its metaphysical doctrine. Its author was Baron Karl Theodor von Dalberg (1744–1817), a Roman Catholic priest who had become governor of Erfurt in 1772, a position he held until 1787, and later rose to dazzling eminence in both church and state: in 1802 he was appointed elector and archchancellor of the German Reich, in 1806 he became archbishop of Ratisbon and prince primate of the Rhine Confederation, and in 1810 he was made grand duke of Frankfurt.[2] One of his early admirers was Count Johann Eustach von Görz (1737–1821) at Weimar, who in 1777 held no office but in the following year was appointed Prussian chargé d'affaires, then minister of state, and eventually ambassador by Frederick the Great. Mendelssohn had been introduced to von Görz by Johann Gabriel Marson, a professor of engineering in Berlin, and on May 11, 1777, the count sent Mendelssohn a letter recalling their meeting and topic of conversation, and enclosing a copy of the anonymous *Reflections on the Universe*. Would Mendelssohn let him know what he and Eberhard thought of this work.[3]

It is possible that the count approached Mendelssohn at von Dalberg's request. We know that it was at the author's request that Herder sent Hamann a copy of this book on September 4, 1777,[4] and in the covering letter Herder openly mentioned von Dalberg as the author. The count von Görz does not seem to have revealed the identity of the writer (since Mendelssohn's reply dated June 10, 1777[5] mentions no name), but soon after being informed by the count of the content of Mendelssohn's letter, von Dalberg wrote to him. The date was July, 1777, and the letter arrived in Berlin after Mendelssohn's departure for Königsberg. Mendelssohn replied to it on September 5, immediately upon his return. Apologizing for the long delay, he explained that he had given orders not to forward letters unless they were of an urgent nature, and that his people had not considered a metaphysical inquiry all that urgent.[6]

In his first letter—the one addressed to von Görz—Mendelssohn characterized the anonymous author's method as one that had been prescribed by Francis Bacon but had so far not been properly (*gehörig*) applied. It required "a man who combines the profoundest insights into the sciences and a fervent [*feurigen*] love for the good and beautiful." Neither of these qualities seemed to be lacking in this author, and yet he had not convinced Mendelssohn that the principle laid down in the treatise was a universal one. According to von Dalberg, the universal law governing the coexistence of things is to be found in their tendency to assimilate to each other, to become more and more similar. In and by itself each thing is an individual manifold to which a limited quantity of qualities is allotted. These qualities are partly alert ("a living force"), partly dormant. They would persist in their condition if they did not coexist with other things. It is coexistence that elicits change and assimilation within the limits of the capacities inherent in the things. The assimilatory tendency in bodies von Dalberg called "affinity," the same tendency as operative in human souls he called "sympathy" or "love."[7]

Mendelssohn's critique concerned the meaning of the terms "similarity" and "assimilation." In his second letter—to the author himself—he wrote: "In my letter to the count von Görz I clearly indicated my conjecture that the author of the *Reflections* used the word 'similarity' in a sense different from the one I am accustomed to, and that we ought first of all to come to terms about the semantic aspect. If the noble author means by 'similarity' what I have called 'nondiscernibility,' the difficulty is removed, and my observation was purely grammatical." Having cleared up this point, Mendelssohn added another critical remark. Though he modestly played down its significance, it amounted to a radical attack upon von Dalberg's main thesis. "I hold that unity [*Einheit*] is to be clearly distinguished from sameness [*Einerleiheit*]. The latter cancels the manifold, the former connects it. Sameness opposes the manifold; unity is the greater the more of the manifold is connected and the more intimately this is done. When this connection of the manifold is brought about in a harmonious fashion, unity passes into perfection. . . . Now, the forces and tendencies of nature seem to me to aim not so much at the obliteration of differences as at the connection of the manifold. They do not seek so much to do away with the variety of things as to bring them into a union, that is to say, into a harmonious union, *ad consensum*. Everything aspires not to a real [*dingliche*] identity but to a unity of final purpose; and the principle that underlies all natural forces is the tendency toward the *harmony* of the manifold, i.e., toward perfection."

Mendelssohn had distinguished in somewhat similar fashion between two kinds of unity in the manifold when he discussed the difference between aesthetic and metaphysical perfection in the letters *On the Sentiments*.[8] In his critique of von Dalberg the thrust of the distinction was directed against what he considered a mistaken concept of the principle of unity in metaphysics. One may see a connection between his subsequent fight against "religious union" (*Glaubensvereinigung*), in his *Jerusalem* (1783), and his rejection of the assimilatory principle in metaphysics. His own awareness of this connection is apparent in the phrasing of the argument he used in the *Jerusalem*: "Let us not falsely pretend to be in agreement, seeing that the manifold is obviously the plan and purpose of Providence."[9] When discussing metaphysics in his letter to von Dalberg he was, of course, motivated by purely metaphysical considerations. How much the baron had been impressed by Mendelssohn's letter to count von Görz, is apparent from the last paragraph of the letter addressed to him: "I now come to the request which your Excellency condescended to put forward with such exceptional modesty and love for truth. For many years past I have been completely incapable of abstract investigations of any sort, and I have to make a maximal effort to read, with understanding, profound reflections such as yours. All I can hope to offer your Excellency are the meager remarks above, and some more of the same kind. What use you decide to make of them depends entirely on you. Should they appear to your Excellency to merit being inserted as an appendix to the new edition of your 'Reflections,' I shall be glad to feel that even in my present condition I am able to produce, from time to time, ideas that seem to an enlightened mind to be not entirely lacking in worth."[10]

Von Dalberg's request shows that Mendelssohn, despite his illness and his long inactivity as a writer, was still regarded as a towering figure in philosophy. To obtain his comments and the permission to incorporate them in one's own work seems to have been regarded as a kind of imprimatur and as a mark of distinction. In 1778 it was the famous physicist Jean André de Luc (1727–1817) who was anxious to receive Mendelssohn's critical observations on the draft of a work to be entitled "Traité sur le matérialisme." De Luc, a lecturer to the queen of England, had written *Lettres à la reine*, which his friend Doctor Zimmermann had shown to Mendelssohn and which had won the latter's approval. Their concern was a refutation of materialism, and Mendelssohn had asked Zimmermann "what it was that constituted the bridge on which de Luc crossed over from geology [his proper field of research] to materialism." On May 3, 1778, Zimmermann told Mendelssohn by letter how pleased de Luc had been with his judgment of the *Lettres* and that he had answered his question at length. Unfortunately, his epistle had been mislaid, but it would be forwarded to Mendelssohn as soon as it was found. Zimmermann then went on to say:[11] "Because of the feelings of the most sincere reverence that Herr de Luc has for you, dearest Herr Mendelssohn, he commissioned me on April 10[12] to transmit to you the "Esquisse d'un traité sur le matérialisme," which is to appear as an appendix to his *Lettres* [*physiques et morales sur l'histoire de la terre et de l'homme*],[13] and to implore you to express your definite opinion about it. 'We have to deal with adversaries that are strong through their reputation; it is therefore necessary to meet them with the shield of Minerva and the club of Hercules,'[14] de Luc tells me."

The *esquisse* had been in the hands of François Hemsterhuis, who had dispatched it to Zimmermann from The Hague on April 24. Zimmermann admitted that he had been rather dismayed by de Luc's request, "because I fully understand that in view of your health labors of this kind are of little benefit to you." Yet the draft was short, he pointed out, and it mattered greatly to the "honest de Luc" to be told by Mendelssohn where he had possibly gone astray. De Luc, who had already commenced his trip to Germany, was hoping to have Mendelssohn's notes in French (underlined) waiting for him in Hanover by the end of the month. Would Mendelssohn, as soon as he had finished his work, pass the *esquisse* manuscript on to Professor Sulzer, whose comments de Luc also wished to have. On May 10 Zimmermann sent the manuscript to Mendelssohn with a covering letter[15] in which he again urged him to "help the honest man achieve his great purpose" and to prevent his becoming an object of derision to the materialists of England and France. In the same letter Zimmermann quoted, in lieu of de Luc's answer to Mendelssohn's question (which he seemed to have lost), some interesting remarks he had made about him in another letter: "Having read the *Phaedon*, [I assume] you can well imagine how much Herr Mendelssohn's judgment [of my work] interests me. After reading this precious work, I found myself almost entirely of the same religion, while he is, at the same time, a true Jew. We [Christians] admit a revelation over and above the one he admits; but the morality, the hopes, and other motifs of this new revelation are not foreign to him. What this new dispensation has added to the ancient one, which serves him as his prime base, and which the world was in need of as it advanced in age, blends so well with what preceded it in the path of Providence that a true Jew who knows Christianity unwittingly adopts it."[16]

On May 12, 1778, Mendelssohn acknowledged receipt of de Luc's manuscript and Zimmermann's letter.[17] He promised to fulfil the request but held out no hope that he would write his annotations in French: "I have to summon the entire stock of my best thoughts to converse with this excellent man, and in a foreign language I am only half as rich." As for de Luc's utterances on their common religion, he would dare to express his opinion on some other occasion. He obviously regarded it a futile undertaking to discuss the matter.

Mendelssohn lost no time in formulating his critical notes. On May 22, 1778, he wrote a few pages, "On an Essay by Herr de Luc concerning the Immateriality of the Soul,"[18] opening his discussion with Voltaire's observation that Malebranche had employed the most brilliant imagination when declaiming against imagination.[19] Herr de Luc declaimed with the most subtle metaphysical arguments against the subtleties of the metaphysicians. In fact, he suggested, de Luc had used the very same arguments that several metaphysicians had advanced against the materiality of the soul. His main argument was hardly different from Descartes', but he had not only left unanswered some questions arising from Descartes' premises but had exposed the argument to further attacks by the materialists because of his assertion that motion, elasticity, and gravity were not properties of matter. Could not the materialists, taking their cue from de Luc, place consciousness or thinking in the same category as motion, etc., and conclude that matter was as capable of thinking as it was of motion? De Luc ought, therefore, to have shown that there was a difference between thinking and motion. In raising this objection Mendelssohn was harking back to his earlier discussion of d'Alembert's arguments against the immateriality of the soul.[20]

Nor was Mendelssohn satisfied with de Luc's theory that the soul's operations were unconnected with the phenomena of matter. What he wholeheartedly approved of, however, was de Luc's refutation of the "popular theory of vibrations" by which David Hartley (1705–1757) had reduced all mental processes to sets of vibrations produced in the brain by sensory stimuli. Mendelssohn found de Luc's counterarguments both thorough and decisive. He added a few observations of his own, which he used later, in 1784, when he took issue with Condillac's sensualism.[21] It was not until the fall of 1778 that de Luc received Mendelssohn's notes. His geological explorations had prevented him from visiting Hanover earlier. And it was not until about a year later that he wrote a letter directly to Mendelssohn asking him to check a French paraphrase of the latter part of his notes, which he had by now decided to incorporate in his *Lettres physiques et morales* (Twelfth Discourse).[22] Mendelssohn replied in French,[23] expressing surprise at Zimmermann's failure to translate his notes and asking de Luc to insert a more elaborate version of his thoughts, which would make for greater clarity. He hoped that de Luc would correct and polish the text submitted by him in French. De Luc introduced the text as "remarks" that Mendelssohn "had been good enough to make on the draft of this *Discours* that I had sent him."[24]

De Luc's request played only a secondary role in the letters that Zimmermann wrote to Mendelssohn in May, 1778. Of infinitely greater concern to him was the support that he wanted to make sure he had received from Mendelssohn in a feud with Georg Christoph Lichtenberg, the brilliantly satirical Göttingen physicist and astronomer. The issue at stake was the evaluation of Lavater's *Physiognomic Fragments for the Promotion of the Knowledge and Love of Men,* which had appeared in four volumes in 1775–1778.[25] Goethe, who visited Lavater in Zürich when the first part of "this strange work" was about to appear, described it in *Dichtung und Wahrheit*[26] as *"genial-empirisch"* and *"methodisch-kollektiv,"* and gave a vivid picture of the tremendous effort Lavater had invested in it. He had tried to make "the whole world his coworkers and participants." It certainly was the most elaborate attempt ever made to make physiognomy into a science, and it created a great stir at the time.

Doctor Zimmermann had become an ardent partisan of Lavater's theory from the moment the new science had been first outlined in his treatise *On Physiognomy* (published in Zürich in the early 1770's). He had it reprinted, with enthusiastic annotations, in the *Hanoverian Magazine* (February, 1772).[27] Later he had endeavored to enroll subscribers for the large work.[28] Lichtenberg, who had never been an admirer of Lavater's and who had satirized his conversionist zeal in the grimly humorous tract *Timorus* (1773),[29] was alarmed by the uncritical manner with which the general public embraced the new discovery. In October, 1777, he published an essay *On Physiognomy* in a yearly almanac that he edited in

Göttingen, and in 1778 he republished it as a booklet under the title, *On Physiognomy against the Physiognomists, For the Promotion of the Love and Knowledge of Men.*[30] In this essay he expressed his doubts concerning the scientific merit of Lavater's method and suggested in its place a new science, which he called "pathognomy," that would be content to read character traits from the changes of expression in the human face.[31] Although Lavater replied to Lichtenberg's critique in a moderate tone,[32] Zimmermann considered it a personal affront, and published an extremely rude article against Lichtenberg in the *Teutscher Merkur* (November, 1777).[33]

This was the state of affairs when Mendelssohn arrived in Hanover at the beginning of November. To Zimmermann his advent seemed a perfect godsend. He showed him Lichtenberg's essay and begged him to let him have an article that would put things in proper perspective and restore the balance.[34] Mendelssohn was placed in a quandary. He did not want to disappoint his friend, but he had no desire to become embroiled in a personal controversy between the two men, both of whom he respected. Moreover, he himself took a dim view of Lavater's exaggerated claims, though he saw some meritorious features in his theory.[35]

Shortly after the publication of Lavater's first volume, in 1775, Mendelssohn had expressed his thoughts on the subject in an essay entitled *Random Ideas on the Harmony of Inner and Outer Beauty*, which he left unpublished.[36] In this essay he had admitted that, in contrast to works of art ("artificial machines"), natural organic beings ("natural machines")[37] have a physiognomy in the sense that their outer appearance corresponds to their inner quality. Beauty was goodness and ability made visible. This had been Lavater's central thesis. Mendelssohn added, however, several riders to this sweeping assertion that severely restricted its applicability. The correspondence between interior fitness and exterior beauty could not be considered a general rule of nature. Both beauty and its absence could be deceptive. The head of Medusa was adorned with serpents, symbolizing dangerous beauty, and the statue of Hermes represented excellence, though it bore ugly features. One had also to distinguish between beauty as mere form and beauty as expression. Something could be beautiful regarded from the mere aspect of its aesthetic appearance. It represented the "dead beauty of natural machines." "Living beauty" was of a different kind because it "expressed" an inner perfection, be it the health of a plant, the natural propensities of an animal, or the moral and rational quality of a human being. There was also "accidental beauty," which was purely subjective because it was projected, by way of association, upon a person that reminded us of another we happened to love. The correspondence between "dead" and "living" beauty was not something that could be taken for granted. There were frequent exceptions to the rule. Nor was there an absolute ideal beauty. Each being had, objectively speaking, its own mixture of capacities and inclinations that formed its specific character and determined its specific type of beauty. At the same time, beauty lay to a large extent in the eye of the beholder. The proverb was right in saying that everybody had his own taste and that in matters of taste there could be no dispute.[38]

Yet subjectivism was not his last word. It was the "high office of criticism" to show us which taste was the best (i.e. agreed with the "true destiny of man") and to guide us in the cultivation of our faculties so as to enable us to achieve the refinement of our taste. A man who enjoyed the grotesque and ridiculous had to be educated toward an appreciation of the sublime, for so long as his soul was incapable of finding delight in the sublime he was incapable of true happiness. Mendelssohn felt that national character played a part in the preferences of taste. The French seemed to love good manners and brightness more than truth, the sublime, and nature. The English had the opposite taste.

In addition to these general observations, the essay contained also some specific remarks about Lavater: "The empirical approach requires cool-headed circumspection, perhaps a spirit of moderate warmth, if some subtlety is to be achieved. It soon vanishes altogether in the heat of Lavater's imagination. . . . Enthusiasm presents to us the symptoms [*Zeichen*] as more expressive than they really are. Such a disposition of soul [which was characteristic of Lavater] must dispose us toward reading in the physiognomies by far more than is contained in them. . . . However, the fault may not be Lavater's alone. It seems to me that our language and our psychology are as yet not sufficiently developed for [the purposes of] physiognomy. . . ."[39]

The thoughts that Mendelssohn expressed in this essay were new only in part. What he said about the subjective element in the appreciation of beauty and about the varieties of taste he had already expressed in identical fashion in an unpublished series of notes on Friedrich Justus Riedel's book *On the Public, Letters to Some of Its Members* (1768).[40] His remarks on Lavater's enthusiasm were, perhaps, to some extent provoked by the manner in which his own features in the silhouette had been described:[41]

> Supposedly you know this silhouette? I can hardly conceal from you that it is exceedingly dear to me! Most expressive! . . . Can you say, can you hesitate a moment as if wanting to say: "Perhaps a fool! A vulgar, tactless soul!" One who could say a thing like this or could bear another saying so should close my book, throw it away—and permit me to stop thinking lest I pass judgment on him! I revel in this silhouette! My glance welters in this magnificent curve of the forehead down to the pointed bone of the eye. . . . In this depth of the eye a Socratic soul is lodged! The firmness of the nose;—the magnificent transition from the nose to the upper lip—the height of both lips, neither protruding beyond the other, oh! how all this chimes with one another to make the divine truth of physiognomy perceptible and visible to me. Yes, I see him, the son of Abraham, who some day, in unison with Plato and Moses, will recognize and worship the crucified Lord of Glory!

When in November, 1777, Mendelssohn was asked by Zimmermann to express his views on Lavater's *Physiognomic Fragments,* he could have told him that he had already done so in his unpublished essay. He preferred not to mention this piece of writing, however, since it was outspokenly critical of Lavater, and he promised to let Zimmermann have an article that might help restore peace between the contending parties. His idea was to show that the controversy could be reduced to a mere *Wortstreit,* a lack of agreement on the meaning of the terms used—that, in other words, Lichtenberg and Lavater had been talking at cross-purposes. The article he intended to write was to be, in the main, a précis of the old essay, shorn of its polemic against Lavater but otherwise retaining the distinctions and qualifications that amounted, in fact, to an implicit critique of Lavater's claims. As later events proved, it was very unfortunate that he failed to mention the earlier essay to Zimmermann and to point out to him the serious reservations he felt about Lavater's theory.

Several times during his eight weeks' stay in Hanover Mendelssohn met Heinrich Christian Boie, editor of the *Deutsches Museum,*[42] who declared his readiness to publish the essay. It eventually appeared in the issue of March, 1778, and it might have served the cause of peace had Zimmermann not acted foolishly. Enraged by the reprinting, in book form, of Lichtenberg's essay and the wide acclaim it enjoyed, Zimmermann announced, in advance, the forthcoming refutation of his adversary, and when Mendelssohn's article appeared, anonymously, in the *Deutsches Museum,* he introduced it, also anonymously, by a highly bombastic kind of preface in which he declared that the privilege of infallibility claimed by the Göttingen anti-Physiognomy was going to be rendered ineffective by a philosopher of the first rank, one whose fame throughout Europe was second to none. This man would show, with sublime tranquillity and impartial love of truth, where Zimmermann's famous colleague (Lichtenberg) had erred. As a result, Herr Timorus (Lichtenberg) might be made to understand what he was saying in his malicious attacks against Lavater's assertion of the harmony between beauty and virtue.

The disproportion of Zimmermann's tasteless announcement, of which Mendelssohn had not the slightest warning, and the calm and lucid essay that followed it was patent to all, and Lichtenberg could rightly claim that the analysis of concepts offered in the essay, far from refuting him, had actually vindicated his position. Moreover, Nicolai, who had become increasingly suspicious of Lavater's physiognomy as a smoke screen for religious purposes, informed Lichtenberg on April 15, 1778, that Mendelssohn's essay in the *Deutsches Museum* had not been written against him; that it had originated a year and a half ago in response to his, Nicolai's, request for clarification of the issue ("Lavater's babble about beauty"); and that Mendelssohn's statement was, on closer inspection, tantamount to a complete refutation of Lavater.[43] Thus Nicolai let the cat out of the bag, probably without prior consultation with Mendelssohn. In his review of Lavater's work in the *Allgemeine deutsche Bibliothek*[44] he had quoted some passages from Mendelssohn's earlier essay but without attributing them to him.[45] Nicolai drew Lichtenberg's attention to these quotations, as further evidence that Mendelssohn's article in the *Deutsches Museum* was anything but an attack on him.

As the news conveyed by Nicolai spread, Zimmermann's position became increasingly uncomfortable. As early as March 12 Boie had written to a friend:[46] "The preface to No. 1 in March causes a great deal of noise here." Zimmermann was seized by a sense of panic and implored Mendelssohn to come to his rescue. His letter of May 3, 1778,[47] asked Mendelssohn to forgive him for having written a preface that was "rather sharp" in its attack against Lichtenberg. However, he had been provoked by Lichtenberg's essay in the almanac and its republication. Zimmermann now expected Lichtenberg to take his revenge for the preface, and in order to be prepared for the fight he needed some information from Mendelssohn. He had been told, Zimmermann said, that his adversary "maintained with his fist toward everybody in Göttingen who wanted to hear it" that he had "found no line and no syllable in your notes . . . that was directed against him." This was going to be the main point of Lichtenberg's polemical tract. "Should this be also your opinion, dearest Herr Mendelssohn, I have lost the battle." He added that Lichtenberg also claimed to have learned from a friend in Berlin that Mendelssohn's essay had been written prior to the publication of Lichtenberg's almanac, and that Zimmermann had no right to present it as having been directed against Lichtenberg.

Zimmermann admitted that Mendelssohn's essay could not have been written for the purpose of picking a quarrel with Lichtenberg or anyone else. "You, as a wise man, expressed your opinion on a controversial issue . . . without prejudice or sympathy vis-à-vis either Lichtenberg or Lavater." He also admitted that the manner in which he had presented Mendelssohn's essay in his preface could only be blamed on him. Yet it seemed to him absurd, he pointed out, to maintain that he had completely misunderstood the burden of Mendelssohn's remarks and that they contained nothing that contradicted Lichtenberg's view. He would be grateful for a clarification of this point, so as to be able to answer any doubts raised on this score in a manner most appropriate to Mendelssohn's position. He realized that his quarrel with Lichtenberg was rather ridiculous, that he was himself far from enthusiastic about Lavater's theory, and that the whole controversy was in fact no more than an *affaire d'honneur,* a kind of English cock-fighting designed to show the public which of the two cocks was the more combative and virile. On May 10 Zimmermann renewed his request for Mendelssohn's help,[48] asserting that Lichtenberg's "rage" against him was "boundless," and that he had threatened to publish in the very near future a tract against him "in a tone hitherto unparalleled in Germany." "Hence it is necessary, as you can see, for me to be provided with everything required for a successful campaign against this little devil [an unkind reference to Lichtenberg's small stature]."

Mendelssohn's reply, a long letter dated May 12, 1778,[49] was calculated to defuse the quarrel by making Zimmermann aware of the responsibility he bore for the ill-feeling that had been generated. It also amplified on the purport of his essay without, however, admitting the full facts of its history; he probably saw no point in weakening Zimmermann's morale by telling him that Lichtenberg had been correctly informed. On the other hand, he did not deny that he had written down his thoughts on Lavater's work at a much earlier date. There was a deliberate vagueness in his account: "Since I conceived [lit. "made"] part of these notes immediately upon my first reading of Lavater's work, it is possible that I communicated them orally to my local friends, with whom I am in the habit of discussing things I have read. When I had the pleasure of receiving Lichtenberg's essay from you in Hanover, my thoughts came back to me through the stimulus of his ideas to the contrary; and you know what caused me to write them down.—This, then, is the story of the ill-fated essay."

The impression that Zimmermann was bound to get from this report could not hurt his feelings, since nothing was said in it about the notes having been written down previously.[50] In fact, however, Nicolai hardly could have quoted from the original essay had Mendelssohn merely mentioned "orally" what his ideas on the subject were. It seems that once having suppressed certain facts in order to spare Zimmermann's feelings, Mendelssohn decided to maintain the fiction for the very same reason, and also so as not to appear inconsistent. He could hardly have felt comfortable when he wrote the letter, however, and the partly humorous, partly moralistic tone he adopted in it, as well as the elaborate account he gave of the way in which Lavater's and Lichtenberg's views were not mutually exclusive, clearly show how much he sought to be helpful in restoring the peace. Unfortunately, the facts revealed by Nicolai were fully exploited by Lichtenberg, who mercilessly used his sharp satirical pen to the detriment of Zimmermann, ridiculing him and praising all the more "the famous Berlin scholar."[51] The real culprit, it seems, was Nicolai, whose indiscretion on this occasion was in strange contrast to his otherwise impeccable liaison with Mendelssohn.

Quite another kind of philosophical matter that preoccupied Mendelssohn in 1778, for a time, was the reformulation of the ontological argument. How he came to recast the a priori proofs for the existence of God offered in his prize-essay of 1763 has to be pieced together from a number of letters and documents, of which only some have so far been published, and of which only two are dated, the year 1778 being attested by one single witness. This crucial testimony is provided by the mention of June 13, 1778, as the date of a letter to Mendelssohn from Doctor Schumann of Hanover. The letter in question was attached to a copy made of Mendelssohn's reformulation of the arguments and Schumann's elaborate refutation of them in his own hand.[52] The covering letter is no longer extant, but the folder containing Mendelssohn's arguments and Schumann's rebuttal tells us its date, June 13, 1778. We also have the undated original, in Mendelssohn's own hand, of the text of the new two proofs and a postscript *(Nacherinnerungen)*, three and a half pages altogether, entitled "The Existence of God a priori Demonstrated."[53] The text of the original completely agrees with that of the copy sent to Doctor Schumann and returned by him on June 13, 1778. That Mendelssohn wrote this text in 1778 is confirmed by the rather intriguing circumstance that he used the empty space of the last page to record the names of the first eight subscribers to the Pentateuch edition, which was just then, in 1778, being announced. He later deleted the list as not belonging there, but the testimony it furnishes stands. It is clear beyond doubt, therefore, that in 1778 (probably during the month of May) Mendelssohn wrote a short essay entitled "The Existence of God a priori Demonstrated," and that he sent a copy of it to Doctor Schumann, asking for his comments.

That Mendelssohn was interested in Schumann's reaction to the essay is not surprising. In 1771 Schumann had published an anonymous essay on the ontological argument, in which he offered some critical notes on the "new turn" that Mendelssohn had given to it in the prize-essay.[54] During his stay in Hanover in November and December, 1777, Mendelssohn probably met Schumann, who was director of the gymnasium in the old part of Hanover. Johann Daniel Schumann (1714–1787) was the author of the polemical treatise *On the Evidence of the Proofs for the Truth of the Christian Religion*,[55] which has been immortalized by Lessing's famous rejoinder *On the Proof of the Spirit and the Power—To Herr Director Schumann in Hanover* (1777).[56] It was only natural that Mendelssohn was curious to know whether his reformulation of the ontological argument commanded the assent of his former critic.

Mendelssohn also sent his little essay to two other people who had previously expressed objections to his a priori proofs. They were Johann Bernhard Basedow (1723–1790), the Rousseau-inspired pioneer in pedagogy, and his friend Doctor Marcus Herz. Basedow had voiced his criticism in his *Methodenbuch*,[57] which first appeared in 1770. Both forms of the a priori argument had been described by him as fallacious *(Scheinbeweise)*. Though he did not mention Mendelssohn by name, it was obvious that "the great philosopher" who had varied the older form of the argument, and with whom he had discussed the matter in conversation, was none other than Mendelssohn.[58] The letter in which Basedow replied to the refurbished proofs sent to him by Mendelssohn in 1778 is, happily, still preserved.[59] It bears an incomplete date, May 27, but one can hardly doubt that the year was 1778. It replied, albeit only briefly, to the same set of arguments to which Doctor Schumann had responded. The date of his reply, May 27, roughly corresponds to that of Schumann's, June 13. Mendelssohn may have written to both on the same day.[60] As for Marcus Herz, he had opposed Mendelssohn's a priori arguments as early as 1770. On September 11 of that year he had written to Kant:[61] "Just now I am busy writing for him [Mendelssohn] a little essay in which I want to show him the fallacy of the a priori proof for the existence of God. He is biased in favor of this proof." The Mendelssohn family archive has preserved a short essay refuting Mendelssohn's a priori arguments, which the archivist described on the folder as having probably been written by Herz ["according to the handwriting by M. Herz (?)"].[62] It bears no date. Assuming that Marcus Herz was its author—and there seems to be no reason to doubt it—this essay cannot be the one mentioned by Herz in his letter to Kant and may be assumed to date from 1778 and to represent an answer to the reformulated proofs. Evidence for this assumption lies in the fact that the objections raised follow closely the outline and partly new terminology of Mendelssohn's short essay of 1778.

What emerges from our survey of the material mentioned so far is that in May, 1778, Mendelssohn rewrote his proofs for the existence of God and submitted copies of the draft to at least three of his former critics, Schumann, Basedow, and Herz. The question that arises is: what caused him to recast his arguments at a time when he had already begun—as will be shown in the next chapter—to concentrate his energies on his Pentateuch project? Why this sudden return to the old theme?

The clue to answering this question lies in a letter to a Dutchman, Doctor Allard Hulshoff (1734–1795), a Baptist minister in Amsterdam and author of many learned works in philosophy and theology.[63] The letter[64] was written by Mendelssohn in reply to one received from Hulshoff, and it refers to a publication, *"Dissert. Leg. Stolp.,"* that Hulshoff had sent to him. Two essays contained in that volume are commented upon in Mendelssohn's letter, namely, one by Hulshoff and one by a certain Herr Goeden. The abbreviation *"Dissert. Leg. Stolp."* stands for *Dissertationes Latinae et Belgicae ad Theologiam Naturalem Spectantes. Pro Praemio Legati Stolpiani Conscriptae,* and, more particularly, for volume two of the series. The Legatum Stolpianum was a fund, established in 1743 by Jan Stolp, a citizen of Leiden, which offered a gold medal once every two years for an essay on natural religion, Christian ethics, or both. The prize-essays were published in volumes appearing at certain intervals. Volume two, which contained a Latin treatise by Goeden (Goedenius), a citizen of Bremen, and a Dutch essay by Hulshoff, came out in 1776 at Leiden.[65]

It was this volume that Hulshoff had sent to Mendelssohn, together with a covering letter (now lost). Mendelssohn's reply is undated but the year 1778, tentatively suggested by the editor of *Moses Mendelssohn's gesammelte Schriften* (5:551), would seem to be correct. It cannot be far off the mark, since the date of publication, 1776, gives us that year as *terminus a quo.* Assuming that Mendelssohn received the volume in 1777 and replied within the year—his letter does not apologize for any delay in his acknowledgement—there would still be a clear connection between the receipt of the volume and his rewriting of the a priori arguments in 1778 in the form in which he submitted them to his former critics. In order to see this connection, we have to take cognizance of the two essays that are referred to in Mendelssohn's reply to Hulshoff.

Goeden's Latin inquiry (pages 1–66) describes itself in the title as a "dispassionate investigation" (*modesta disquisitio*) of the arguments by which Descartes and his followers had tried to prove the existence of God a priori from the idea of a most perfect and necessary being.[66] Included in the survey, if only briefly, are Descartes' predecessors (Anselm of Canterbury and Nicholas of Cusa) and a number of opponents such as Johann Lorenz Mosheim and Christian August Crusius. Goeden set out to complement the earlier survey of the discussion by the Lutheran classical scholar and bibliographer Johann Albert Fabricius (1668–1736).[67] The philosophers presented and analyzed by him are Descartes, Leibniz, Michael Gottlieb Hansch, Christian Wolff, a few less well-known figures—and Moses Mendelssohn, whose treatment of the ontological argument in his prize-essay is given extraordinary prominence. The introductory part already refers to the "twofold demonstration" by which "this most learned author" had tried to defend the a priori argument, and declares: "Since his reasons seem to contain more solidity and acumen than those of all the others, we shall mention them below in a special discussion."[68] This discussion (pages 49–61) takes the form of a Latin translation of the relevant passages in the prize-essay,[69] followed by critical analyses.

Goeden reduces Mendelssohn's first argument to the following syllogism: that which does not exist is either impossible or merely possible; the most perfect being is neither impossible nor merely possible; hence it exists. The assumption underlying this syllogism is twofold: the most perfect being is not impossible and it cannot be merely possible. The second of these assumptions rests on the following syllogism: the existence of a merely possible being is contingent; but the existence of the most perfect being cannot be contingent; hence the most perfect being cannot be merely possible. Goeden observed that the force of the whole argument rested on the proposition: the most perfect being cannot exist contingently. But in his view the proposition could be stated only in this form: the most perfect being, should it exist, cannot exist contingently. Once this limiting clause is added, nothing real is posited by this demonstration and the conclusion is subject to a certain condition being fulfilled. In the major premise, too, the term existence ought to be qualified by the conditional clause: if given as such. Otherwise the argument amounted to a *petitio principii*. It was begging the question.[70]

In his letter to Hulshoff,[71] Mendelssohn commented on this criticism: "I am astonished at Herr Goeden. On page fifty-three he objects to my argument: if one enunciates the minor proposition likewise in a conditioned manner, the conclusion will likewise be merely conditional. He forgot that the condition obviously belongs to the middle term, which must never appear in the conclusion." Clearly, Mendelssohn was not too happy with Goeden's critique, which extended also to the second argument. On the

other hand, he must have been pleased to find how seriously his proofs
had been treated, and could hardly resist the challenge contained in the
last paragraph of Goeden's essay: "We would indeed wish that the most
sagacious man himself [Mendelssohn] candidly examine what we observed
against his two-fold demonstration and inquire whether our observations
are of any significance. We surely owe much to the capacity [*ingenio*] of
Mendelssohn, whose outstanding discernment [*insignem perspicaciam*] in
philosophical matters, and whose acumen in other respects, we hold in
sufficient respect." Mendelssohn's reformulation of his a priori arguments
in 1778 was, it seems, in direct response to this challenge.

The way in which Mendelssohn recast his two proofs and rebutted
possible objections bears unmistakable traces of Hulshoff's Dutch essay,
which he had apparently read with a great deal of appreciation, though
it made no reference to him. The essay[72] described itself in the title as an
"inquiry to prove God's existence a priori" written in answer to the question:
"Can one demonstrate a priori the actual existence of a Necessary Being . . .
from the mental image [*Denkbeeld*] of it?" It pointed out that the word
Denkbeeld was an ambiguous term. It could be understood in a subjective
sense, as something imagined by the soul, and it could also denote something
objective, namely truth insofar it was an object of thinking.[73] In his letter
to Hulshoff, Mendelssohn wrote:[74] "The distinction between imagined
[*bildlichen*] and real [*dinglichen*] existence, which all opponents of this argument invoke, is entirely irrelevant. These gentlemen, who discriminate
so subtly, clearly confuse imagined existence and subjective existence. The
presence of a concept in a thinking being is called an imagined existence;
from it nothing can be inferred concerning real existence. Yet real existence,
insofar as it is an object of thought and insofar as it is attributed, in thought,
to a certain notion, is called subjective existence. From it a great deal
can be inferred concerning objective existence; for every truth must be
capable of being thought."

Mendelssohn thus adopted Hulshoff's term *Denkbeeld,* translating it
"imagined existence" (*bildliches Daseyn*); but whereas Hulshoff identified
the intramental existence with subjective existence, Mendelssohn drew a
line between two kinds of intramental existence: one that signified the
mere presence of a concept in the mind, and one that reflected real existence
in the form of a notion. Only the latter could be termed subjective existence,
and objective reality could be inferred from it. It is precisely this set of
distinctions that we meet in the postscript to Mendelssohn's two refurbished
a priori arguments:

> Both kinds of argument infer external existence from the connection
> of concepts. It is said that this procedure is fallacious. One argues that
> although real things hang together in a manner similar to the way in
> which ideal things are connected with each other one could nevertheless
> infer only ideal things from *idealia*, and could infer *realia* only from presup-
> posed *realia*. This argument can, however, be answered easily. We

see that, despite this boundary, the transition from the imagined [*bildlichen*] world to the real one [*sachliche*] is not wholly impossible. In particular, the following propositions cannot be denied: (1) What is incapable of being thought as an idea [*idealiter*] does not exist in reality [*realiter*] either; (2) if the statement A is B is *idealiter* unthinkable, it is *realiter* untrue; (3) if the statement A is not B is *idealiter* unthinkable, the statement A is B is also objectively true.

[One objects, however:] Still, in the final resort we infer the existence of God merely from our ability to think certain attributes as coexisting without any contradiction. How absurd! I reply: we infer the existence of God from the fact that otherwise truth would be at the same time untruth, and contradiction would be at the same time no contradiction. What sort of absurdity does one find here? Our opponents say, further, that from conclusions of this kind there follows only ideal existence, not real and objective existence. Although this objection has been refuted in what has been said before, I throw the following observation into the bargain. Should one wish to call the presence of a concept in a thinking being an imagined existence [*bildliches Daseyn*], I will let it pass, provided one differentiates between ideal and subjective existence. The mere concept which is being thought has ideal existence. The object of this concept outside the thinking being has real and objective existence. However, when the concept is being thought as objectively existent, it attains to a subjective real existence. No inference can be drawn from imagined existence [*bildlichen Daseyn*] to real existence. However, a great deal can be inferred from subjective existence concerning objective existence, as mentioned before.

The text quoted reads like an elaborate commentary on the letter to Hulshoff, from which it even makes a literal borrowing. In view of this no doubt can remain that Mendelssohn's concern with the ontological argument in 1778 was inspired by the volume sent to him from Holland. Though his mind was already fixed on a new project, and one of absorbing interest, his philosophical Eros was reawakened when he read the two essays, and he could not help putting pen to paper, reformulating his two arguments and adding a rather sophisticated postscript. The negative replies he received from Schumann, Basedow, and Herz did not deter him later from again taking up the subject in his *Morgenstunden* (1786). On the other hand, he was not insensitive to the opposition the argument had encountered. When he congratulated Hulshoff on having managed to steer clear of some of the objections and to remove others, he wrote wistfully: "The strongest objection to this argument is to be seen, I think, in the fact that there are still philosophers who consider it inconclusive."[75]

The agility that Mendelssohn displayed by his journeys of 1777 was more than matched by the evident upsurge of fresh energy and joie de vivre of 1778. The zest with which he responded to Hulshoff's letter fits into the picture. One has only to read a letter that he wrote to Zimmerman on January 29, 1778, to be aware of the change that had occurred after years of mere "vegetating" or "tolerable" health. He had still to be extremely careful, but he felt alive again, he relished the theater, and he sat for a painter, Frisch, in the most jovial mood. The letter to Zimmermann was written shortly after Mendelssohn's return from Hanover. Its major topic was the great actor Johann Franz Hieronymus Brockmann:[76]

> It is perfectly true what is being said about the spell that Brockmann was able to cast on the otherwise rather frigid Berliners. When I returned from Hanover, everybody was so much taken and enchanted by his performance, particularly as Hamlet, that nothing else was being talked about, even in the kitchens and servants' quarters. The playhouse was so crowded in those days that I had difficulty in finding a seat. . . . I, too, was completely enraptured by him, and he seemed to surpass all expectations I ever had entertained about a good actor. . . . Only during the third or fourth performance it seemed to me that I had discovered the possibility of Garrick's superiority. The Englishman, I said to myself. . . . may have been the less active and for this very reason the more effective. It appeared to me as if Brockmann was too agile, too vivacious in his movements and gesticulating more than the character of the Prince permitted. At times I seemed to find an awe-inspiring scholar where I expected the noble demeanor of a prince. Finally, I believed myself to have noticed that he had not sufficiently studied the gradations and various changes in mood and sentiment in which the poet presents this inimitable character.
>
> In short: if I lend an ear to my criticism, the Englishman surpassed the German not, to be sure, in the convincing manner in which he expressed the passions but in his familiarity with high society and in the profundity of his study of the author. Yet I dare not publicly state these thoughts of mine since they contradict the inscription on the medal that has been struck in honor of this great actor.

Mendelssohn's attendance at the theater was widely noted. Zimmermann had already learned from the Hamburg newspaper that he had "watched a performance of *Hamlet* in Berlin."[77] Brockmann was certainly pleased to see the Jewish philosopher in the audience and he asked Mendelssohn to enter an inscription in his album. The inscription reads:[78] "He strives on the stage, as in life, to please everyone; yet he is content to please there [on the stage] but *a few*, and here [in life] but ONE." The date of this inscription is January 7, 1778.

As for Mendelssohn's portrait by Frisch, for which he sat in the same year, its exact date is provided by a note he sent to Nicolai on September 3, 1778.[79] "Do tell me how I can manage to see you for once. In your home you can never be found. You don't visit me either, and the weather is too miserable to make it possible for me to visit you in the garden. Yet I have to tell you a thousand things of which I want to rid myself. Tomorrow morning I shall be with the painter Frisch, where I shall be painted in cameo. Where does one find you in the afternoon at approximately three o'clock?" Nicolai replied:[80] "I am sitting in the garden where, having recovered from a rather severe illness, I am to gather some strength. . . . In accordance with your wish, my dearest friend, I shall be happy to welcome you tomorrow afternoon at three o'clock in my garden. . . . Give my best regards to Herr Frisch, and thank him on my behalf for a beautiful drawing he sent me."

Johann Christoph Frisch (1738–1815) made a very large number of pictures of Mendelssohn in 1784 and 1786.[81] In his biography of his father, Joseph Mendelssohn mentioned one painted by Frisch and engraved on copper by Müller in Stuttgart when Mendelssohn was between forty and fifty years of age. He was forty-nine on September 6, 1778, and we may assume that the painting referred to by Joseph was the one for which he sat then. The engraving on copper made of this picture was chosen by Joseph as the frontispiece for the edition of *Moses Mendelssohn's gesammelte Schriften* (Leipzig, 1843–1845) because it seemed to him truer to life than any other.[82] The magnificent original, a colored painting in oils, reproduced for the first time as the frontispiece of the present work, reflects the radiant spirit of Mendelssohn, which had returned to him after the years of bewildering trials.[83]

Friends in Unexpected Quarters

In January, 1773, August Hennings, at twenty-six a councillor at the Danish legation in Berlin, presented himself to Mendelssohn with a letter of introduction by his brother-in-law, the Hamburg physician Doctor Johann Albert Heinrich Reimarus. Hennings had obviously expected to take up his post early in 1772, for Reimarus' letter bore the date January 24 of that year, but his patent of appointment had not been forthcoming until the end of the year, and it was soon after his arrival in the Prussian capital that he paid his first of many visits to Mendelssohn.[1] Doctor Reimarus' letter read:[2]

> I cannot let pass the opportunity of my brother-in-law's stay in Berlin when he can hand you this letter. He desires to enjoy the pleasure of being in contact with you, and you will find in him a man worth talking to. I would like to receive some instruction from you, and therefore take the liberty of suggesting a friendly correspondence between us. My professional duties cannot entirely divorce me from philosophical reflections. At the moment, however, I merely want to inquire whether your health permits you at present to enter into matters of this kind. Subjects that immediately occur to me are, for example, the arguments against a voluntary departure from this world, which have failed to convince me.[3] True, *in dubio*, I consider it better to stay here, but the freedom of choice would, it seems to me, meet many complaints against fate. Of still greater importance would be an inquiry into the kind of concept that the Infinite Being can have of progressive time, seeing that everything is simultaneously present to It and that, consequently, everything must be determined, without any further addition in the future as well as in the past. As mentioned, I expect, however, first only some indication whether I may set forth my ideas on these matters. Your Honor's most devoted servant J. A. H. Reimarus.

Mendelssohn did not feel inclined to start a correspondence on such random topics, especially at a time when his health condition forced him to keep exercises of this kind to a minimum. He left the letter unanswered but referred to it when two years later, after his return to Hamburg, Hennings wrote him a letter of thanks for his kindnesses to him in Berlin, and expressed a desire on his part to enter into correspondence.[4] Mendelssohn replied:[5] "Let your good intention to write to me from time to time be of long duration. . . . Should my answer sometimes be long in coming, kindly hold my weak state of health accountable. It makes letter writing, which used to be a recreation to me, into a laborious task. As you know, I kept for no other reason delaying my reply to the very kind letter of Doctor Reimarus (though twelve months out of the total you have to charge to your own account).[6] I wish I could reply to the questions of this excellent man with something worthy to be read by him, and this requires more effort of the mind than I can now afford. Do, however, assure this philosopher of my highest esteem."

Mendelssohn could hardly have imagined at this time that during the last years of his life he would engage in a most lively exchange of letters with Doctor Reimarus and, particularly, with his sister Elise (Margaretha Elisabeth) Reimarus. The dramatic story of those years is reflected in this correspondence. One might say that it was this very correspondence that constituted the history of his closing years, for it was Elise's enthusiastic veneration of Mendelssohn that goaded Jacobi to write the fateful letter in which he alleged that Lessing, unbeknownst to Mendelssohn, had embraced Spinozism in his later years—a letter that initiated a chain of events that ended in agony and disaster for Mendelssohn.

The prelude to the intimate contact between Mendelssohn and the Reimarus circle was Hennings' two years' stay in Berlin, from December, 1772, until December, 1774. Adolph Friedrich August Hennings (1746–1826), the son of an old Schleswig-Holstein middle-class family, had studied law and political economy at Göttingen. Voltaire's *Essai sur les moeurs,* with its orientation toward universal historiography, had been mediated to him through August Ludwig von Schlözer, the historian, and he remained an admirer of Voltaire all his life. Yet he had also been moved by Rousseau. He spent his last night in Göttingen reading the *Émile.* His dream was to transform his country, Denmark, into a stronghold of advanced, liberal ideas. A restless spirit, full of ambition and idealism, he was badly in need of a mentor to guide, encourage, and restrain him. In Mendelssohn he met the man he needed. The first post he held was that of secretary at the archives of the revenue office in Copenhagen. After his downfall, the all-powerful Johann Friedrich Struensee was succeeded as prime minister by Øve Höegh-Guldberg, professor at the academy for young noblemen in Sorö, who offered Hennings a diplomatic post at the Danish Legation in Berlin. A good dancer, fencer, horseman, and swimmer, fluent in conversational French and English, biased against the Jews (owing, in part, to his study of Voltaire),[7] he might have seemed the last person to carry with him to Berlin a letter of introduction to Moses Mendelssohn. However, such was the attraction Mendelssohn held for all sincere adepts of the Enlightenment that he had cast his spell on the young diplomat.

Hennings established many contacts during his sojourn in Berlin. He became friendly with Nicholas Bernoulli, the mathematician, and other members of the Royal Academy, whom he met at the salon of the Russian Prince Dolgorucky. He frequently visited the home of Daniel Itzig, the banker and senior alderman of the Jewish community, whose daughters he found charming. Obviously he was discriminating between Jews in general and those who appealed to him. He befriended the writer Moses Wessely. Above all, he sought the company of Moses Mendelssohn.[8] Many years later, in a kind of autobiography (unpublished), in which he spoke of himself in the third person, Hennings wrote of his days in Berlin:[9] "During his stay in Berlin he frequently met some local savants, particularly Mendelssohn, whose spirited conversation and philosophy of life meant to him everything he looked for in thinkers.... At that time, he had as yet no intention of making a name for himself as an author, and he used to laugh when Mendelssohn's wife occasionally interrupted him, saying that for once, at long last, something ought to appear in print out of his many philosophical conversations with Mendelssohn and others."

The letter Hennings wrote to Mendelssohn after his return to Hamburg acknowledged his indebtedness:[10] "Now I write to you merely to thank you for your kind and friendly conversations with me during my stay in Berlin. The best thanks I can give you is the assurance that you have made me a better man.... I shall often feel the need for the pleasant hours I spent in your company, and remembering them will not always suffice. Should I then appear with a philosophical petition, you may perhaps think that it is not always as easy to be a benefactor as it is by way of conversation and as one assumes it when sharing your leisure hours and being imperceptibly formed by your mind." In his reply Mendelssohn welcomed Hennings' avowal of loyalty as an indication of his resolve to abandon the "rhapsodic disorder" (*odenmässige Unordnung*)[11] of the current fashionable philosophy—a reference to *Sturm und Drang*—and to rally to the flag of sound common sense. "If my representations have contributed toward this resolution, I am proud of the brave recruit I have won for philosophy, or rather of the able deserter I have brought back to it at a time when I myself am no longer able to do battle for it."

The remark about the "rhapsodic disorder" in contemporary thought may have been occasioned by the sense of outrage that both Mendelssohn and Hennings felt at Goethe's *Werther*, which had just appeared.[12] In this novel the poet had woven together his own experience of unrequited love with that of the young Karl Wilhelm Jerusalem. Goethe himself had been in love with Charlotte Buff, the fiancée of his friend Johann Christian Kestner in Wetzlar, and Jerusalem's love had been for Elizabeth Herd, the wife of a colleague of his. Hennings had been a fellow-student and friend of Kestner at Göttingen and immediately recognized him in the portrayal of Lotte's husband in the novel. He wrote him a letter inquiring about his fate, and Kestner showed the letter to Goethe as proof that the poet had been indiscreet in the way he had presented him and Lotte to the public. Mendelssohn, who read the *Werther* at the same time as Hennings, remarked sarcastically that Goethe had "found it poetically more beautiful to shoot oneself, and prosaically better to live."[13]

The antipathy that Hennings felt toward Goethe on account of the *Werther* persisted for a very long time. "Satires, epigrams, and *xenia* may sprout forth in this way, yet no Pindar, Horace, Homer, or Klopstock flowers and matures in such fashion." In his view, Goethe lacked cultivated bloom; he was all exuberance of nature, uncritical toward its excrescences. Lessing's judgment was not strikingly different for the most part, and Mendelssohn told Boie, when he met him in Hanover in 1778, that what he appreciated in the *Werther* was merely the language.[14] Elise Reimarus shared this dislike of Goethe and, for that matter, of other "geniuses" such as Matthias Claudius and Lavater: "Claudius enjoys himself in Darmstadt as much as any genius enjoys himself, that is to say, as long as it lasts. You will presumably know what kind of nonsense [*närrisches Zeug*] Goethe is engaged in at Weimar. How quixotic a world composed only of geniuses, headed by a Lavater, would be!" She wrote this in a letter to Hennings on March 31, 1776, after Lessing had published Jerusalem's essays, and there is a reference to this act of piety in the same letter: "Perhaps you have seen the philosophical essays of the unfortunate Jerusalem, with Lessing's preface. How different is the stride of a great mind from the wry swerves of the big and small sham geniuses, how unwavering in its fidelity to itself!"[15] A letter of hers written to Hennings on August 20, 1776, contains the important information:[16] "He [Lessing] admits that it was chiefly in defiance of Goethe that he considered himself obliged to present to the world Jerusalem's authentic intellectual image through his philosophical essays."

There was, then, a remarkable community of sentiment between Mendelssohn and the Reimarus/Hennings circle. At a time when the legacy of the Enlightment was being threatened by the inroads of Sturm und Drang, the cult of genius, and incipient romanticism, the adepts of pure reason felt the need to draw together, and Mendelssohn assumed more than ever before the role of accredited spokesman of the Enlightenment.

There was some irony in the fact that Mendelssohn had become the guide, philosopher, and friend of the Reimaruses. Professor Hermann Samuel Reimarus, the celebrated patriarch of the family, who had died in 1768, had angrily reacted to Mendelssohn's review of his *General Reflections on the Instincts of the Animals* (1760).[17] Doctor Reimarus, his son, had been indignant with Mendelssohn when reading his *Reply to Lavater*. In a letter to Lessing, written toward the end of 1770, he voiced his misgivings:[18] "Since you now work for religion (something rarely met with in a man of your genius),[19] I must draw your attention to one more thing that just occurred to me. You know Herr Moses, son of Mendel. He seems to be a very good man. Yet all the same, it must annoy us that he is a Jew, and I wonder whether we should tolerate the way in which he scorns us Christians and paints in such glowing colors the certitude claimed by his sect. 'It is founded not on mere miracles,' he says; 'it is the public giving of the Law in the presence of the entire nation that furnishes undeniable proof.' What is it, however, that renders the proof from miracles so weak? . . . It is only the *report* about miracles transmitted by men that we doubt. How then can he boast of his sect's certitude as being superior to the Christians'?" After a detailed discussion of the biblical passages describing the Sinaitic revelation, Reimarus continued: "Has not the Christian religion a much better claim to acceptance? The miracles on which it is founded happened, after all, in far more enlightened times, and the witnesses are at least fifteen hundred years younger." There followed the veiled reference to the copy of his father's *Schutzschrift* in the possession of the Wolfenbüttel Library, which has already been noted.[20] The letter concluded with the suggestion that Lessing might use this work for the purpose of converting Mendelssohn.

Little did Doctor Reimarus know that Lessing had shown the manuscript to Mendelssohn when the two met at Wolfenbüttel in October, 1770, and that Mendelssohn had taken it with him to Berlin.[21] Ironically, it was still in his possession when Doctor Reimarus wrote his letter to Lessing.[22] The tone of the doctor's remarks about the Jew Mendelssohn was anything but friendly. Yet only a bit over a year later, in January, 1772, Reimarus recommended his brother-in-law Hennings to the Berlin philosopher and expressed a desire to start a friendly correspondence with him. We may surmise that Lessing had replied to Reimarus' letter in a way that radically changed his mind. Once a happy relationship between Mendelssohn and Hennings had been established, the friendship with Doctor Reimarus and Elise soon followed.

After his return to Hamburg, Hennings stayed with his brother-in-law until the summer of 1775, when he was appointed Danish chargé d'affaires at the court in Dresden. His term of office there lasted until October, 1776. He spent sixteen memorable months amid Dresden's art treasures; went to neighboring Meissen, where he hired craftsmen in porcelain manufacture for Denmark; studied Winckelmann's *History of Ancient Art* (1768); and enjoyed exchanging letters with the learned and sparkling Countess Brühl, who lived on her estate near Dresden.[23] Yet he was restless and felt the need to continue his correspondence with Mendelssohn, which he had kept up while in Hamburg.[24] On August 9, 1775, he wrote:[25]

> For a long time I have been seeking the quietude necessary for conversing with you. Sometimes I think I have found it, sometimes I think that I shall never find it—at least not in the full measure that I believe you possess, and which I desire to possess. . . . Tell me what you think of Lavater's folly [i.e. his *Physiognomic Fragments,* the first part of which had

just appeared]. Had he only not admitted being a fool, which makes
it reprehensible to repeat this after him! The thing itself may be good,
but what a long or thick nose, a large or small eyelid means in physiognomy
can be said on a few sheets, without so many exclamation points, as
if we were all deaf, and without so many dissimilar profiles, as if we
were all blind. . . .

In September, 1775, Mendelssohn replied:[26] "What you say about Lavater has my full approval. It is true that undigested philosophy and insipid,
sentimental twaddle *à la mode* form the major part of his work. Yet if
one discounts all this, there still remain good observations in larger number
than have ever been made on physiognomy. I admit that much in it is
still incomprehensible to me, and I find, after all the tests suggested by
Lavater and applied by myself, that I have not the least talent for physiognomy. From the little I understood, however, which pleased me I draw
conclusions as to the rest, and I wish I could read more often the things
that are good in this excessively expensive work." On September 13, 1775,
Hennings communicated this well-balanced judgement to Elise,[27] who
replied on September 22:[28] "Mendelssohn's verdict on Lavater was doubly
welcome to us because we are just now engaged in glancing over the *Fragments* of this honest enthusiast in our small circle."

Hennings reverted to the subject of physiognomy in a letter written
to Elise on February 28, 1776:[29] "One who knows Mendelssohn will love
him with the warmth of the heart that pervades and invigorates all veins,
not with the feverish effervescence that goes to the head and dulls reason.
When I compare what Mendelssohn wrote about Lavater and what [Count
Friedrich Leopold] Stolberg[30] says about him, I find it striking that the
true and almost infallible thinker [Mendelssohn] candidly admits not being
a physiognomist, while Stolberg, without giving himself time for investigation, believes that he comprehends everything, merely because his heart
overflows and finds mysteries and effects of physiognomy in the whole
creation." On March 31, 1776, Elise replied:[31] "I would like to know what
Mendelssohn says about the second part of the *Physiognomy,* in which
Basedow is appointed to be the bodyguard of reason."[32] Mendelssohn visited
Dresden in August, 1776, and Hennings could put the question to him.
The account of the days he spent with the master included this passage:[33]

> Remembering your request, I asked him for his opinion on the continua-
> tion of Lavater's *Physiognomy.* He believes that we owe Lavater [credit
> for] several new observations in physiology and, in particular, an enrich-
> ment of physiological terminology. He especially likes the idea that the
> bones, seeing they are solid and less subject to change, indicate more
> accurately the natural character than the soft fleshy parts, which can
> be made flexible through assumed habits; [he also likes the idea] that
> in the contrast of the two, one may suspect a contradiction between the
> natural and the moral character. Otherwise, Mendelssohn thinks that
> Lavater has written a pathognomy rather than a physiognomy, and that
> he is not so much concerned to recognize the inner man from his physiog-
> nomy but rather wants to point out the miracles of God in the formation

of man. He invariably adds the remark that he [Mendelssohn] is no physiognomist, and since he, the expert judge of human character and seeker after truth, talks in this way, what else can he mean but a disavowal of physiognomy?

Hennings sensed that Mendelssohn's critical attitude dominated his appraisal of the merits of Lavater's theory. His report to Elise shows that in drawing a line between physiognomy and pathognomy and in characterizing Lavater as being motivated by religious rather than by scientific interests Mendelssohn anticipated the essentials of Lichtenberg's critique by well over a year.[34]

A number of other interesting subjects are raised in a letter that Hennings wrote to Mendelssohn on October 16, 1775:[35]

> For many weeks I have been wanting to write to you, dearest Mendelssohn, for your letters are a real nourishment and tonic to my mind, but a particular small reason has so far prevented me. I meant to talk to you about Haller's *Letters* against Voltaire but could not yet get hold of the book in this nice but hardly inquisitive place. You have probably read it and can satisfy my wish to hear your opinion. All I know about it is a review in the *Göttingische Anzeigen,* which displeased me precisely because of what it praised. Haller believes himself sufficiently rewarded if he can lead a youth back from the wrong path that Voltaire had made him choose. This is the style of a preacher and babbler, not that of a philosopher. A philosopher does not play with the imagination and frivolity of a wayward youth. He seeks to convince men. His criterion is reason, not the heart. . . .
>
> Professor Büsch of Hamburg told me, when passing through Dresden, that the author of the *Poems of a Polish Jew* is being kept in strict seclusion by his corelegionists in Breslau because of their fear lest he, like other brethren of his, convert to the Christian religion. Yet another proof that people invariably want to impose their folly upon others and grudge them the right to be fools according to their own fashion. It is really too bad that a man loses his freedom because of a little water or foreskin. Perhaps you could, without difficulty, set the poor proselyte free in the freethinking Frederick's state, in which freedom of thought is granted. I know that you do not object to his being what he wants to be, and that you do not wish to coerce him to return to Abraham's lap as Lavater wanted to lead you to the Lamb's throne. . . .

In 1775 Albrecht von Haller (1708–1777), the great anatomist, physiologist, and poet, had published the first part of his *Letters on Some Contemporary Freethinkers' Objections to Revelation,*[36] in which he took issue with Voltaire's attacks upon Judaism and Christianity. The work dealt point by point with the "sophistries" and "sneers" found in Voltaire's *Questions sur l'Encyclopédie par des Amateurs,*[37] and evinced a deep sense of piety, but it was rather rambling and not conspicuous for philosophical depth. When Mendelssohn visited Dresden in 1776, Hennings renewed his question about the book and this is what he reported to Elise:[38] "Like myself, he found Haller's *Letters* against the freethinkers miserable. What a decline of a poet who was so spirited in his youth!" This verdict need not be

taken at face value. Mendelssohn might have found Haller's rebuttal of
Voltaire wanting in certain respects, but he could hardly have found nothing
to admire in Haller's gallant and painstaking attempt to defend religion
against the famous scoffer. His recognition of the merits of the work was
bound to increase when the second and third parts of it appeared in 1776.
They extended the criticism of Voltaire to the entire gamut of his writings
and obiter dicta, and made some striking points in vindicating the honor
of Judaism.[39]

After Haller's death Mendelssohn urged Doctor Zimmermann to
rewrite his biography of his former teacher, which had been published
in 1755.[40] On January 29, 1778, he wrote to him:[41] "It seems to me that
Germany's genius looks upon you and expects, nay demands, of you a
second *Biography of Herr von Haller*. When you wrote the first, Haller had
not yet completed his career and you had hardly started yours. Now he
has finished his, and you occupy a position from which you can survey
both beginning and end in an equal light. The task, large though it be,
cannot cause you as much trouble as there would be annoyance on your
part if it were undertaken by a bungler, and that is inevitable unless you
soon take care of your great countryman." Zimmermann pleaded lack
of time as an excuse,[42] but Mendelssohn continued to encourage him to
give his undivided attention to this work:[43] "If you will be able to apply
yourself with the necessary tranquillity and concentration of mind to this
task, Haller will be the first German scholar whose life has been described.
Biographies of Leibniz and Wolff are still to be written." Unfortunately
Zimmermann bore too much resentment toward his teacher to summon
up the love and energy required for the work.[44] Viewed from the perspective
of the reverence that Mendelssohn had for Haller, the disparaging remark
to Hennings about the *Letters* carries little weight. He knew that Hennings
was a partisan of Voltaire, and he probably saw no point in taking up
the cudgels on behalf of a work that by its very nature could not impress
a philosopher, let alone a Voltairean. Moses Mendelssohn's overriding concern was to strengthen Hennings' respect for natural religion.

How little the young diplomat cared for either Judaism or Christianity,
and how pronounced was his view that tolerance had to be absolute, may
be gathered from his observations about the author of the *Poems of a Polish
Jew*.[45] To Mendelssohn the piece of news that he conveyed in the letter
must have come rather as a shock. Isachar Falkensohn Behr (1746–1814),
the author of the poems, was a native of Courland who had grown up
in poverty and ignorance of secular culture. His phenomenal rise is
described in a letter written by Karl Lessing to his brother on July 11,
1771:[46]

> His fate is quite extraordinary. He has been in Berlin for about three
> years. In the beginning he dressed like a Polish Jew and knew not a
> word of German. In Königsberg, where he had arrived some four or
> five years ago to buy merchandise, he suffered the misfortune that a
> piece of velvet, in which his whole fortune consisted, was stolen from

him. Out of fear that he might be scorned because of this mishap if he went home, he decided to stay and to attend the local university. He gained access to some professors and learned the German language from Wolff's mathematical writings. Eventually he was recommended to our Moses, who gave him much support. At first, I could talk with him only a little. Because he was studying also Latin, I asked him to translate into Latin something from a German author; and lo and behold, he brought me a whole act from Wieland's version of *Romeo [and Juliet]*. True, this translation was more absurd than my amazement would admit, and I could not help regarding his audacity as a sign of ignorance rather than as an expression of genius. But soon I had to undeceive myself. He now writes a rather good German, he understands a Latin and a French book, and he is no stranger to mathematics, philosophy, and medicine. If he continues in this way, he will achieve much."

Karl Lessing mentioned prior to this biographical sketch that Behr was going to publish poems, "some of which are very nice." He was probably referring to the *Poems of a Polish Jew*, which appeared in 1772. A few poems had already been published in the *Almanac of the German Muses for the Year 1771.*"[47]

On December 30, 1771, Heinrich Christian Boie wrote to Karl Ludwig von Knebel: "The poems of the Lithuanian [Behr] are said to be now in print. You are right, the Jewish nation promises a great deal, once it wakes up."[48] The *Poems of a Polish Jew* was reviewed by the young Goethe in the *Frankfurter gelehrte Anzeigen* of September 1, 1772.[49] Goethe confessed to a sense of disappointment. He had expected to find a distinct reaction to "our world" on the part of a man who had spent his former years "under a strange and bleak sky." What he found in fact, he complained, was merely another conventional, handsome young man who described himself as "powdered" and as having a "smooth chin" and a "green, gold-embroidered jacket." Goethe's review then passed on to an evocation of his own dream of a true lyrical poetry—this was his first important utterance on this subject—and concluded with the wish that he might meet the Polish Jew once more in the future, "on those paths where we seek our ideal."

In 1772 Behr went from Berlin to Leipzig to study medicine. On September 27, 1772, Mendelssohn sent him regards through Elkan Herz and promised to write him a letter before long.[50] Having obtained the doctorate of medicine in Halle, Behr decided to return to Courland, there to practise his medicinal art. It was on his way home that he stayed for some time in Breslau, where, according to the information Hennings received, he aroused a suspicion that he was thinking of becoming a convert to Christianity. In point of fact, he did convert to the Greek-Orthodox faith in the year 1781, while practicing as a physician in Mitau, Courland.[51] It would seem, then, that the Jews of Breslau were not mistaken in their estimate of the man. Even so, it is hardly credible that they held him "in seclusion."

Whether Mendelssohn took any action is unknown. He seems to have been fond of this gifted young man, who during the Lavater controversy had written an ode to him (dated April 15, 1770):[52] "Time, blotting out all, spares thee, Mendelssohn, who, elected to eternal glory by the Infinite, hast done away with men's fear of death. / Thou bestowest holy comfort upon every soul which, too proud to deceive itself with transient earthly goods, constantly longs for immortality. / ... / Blind envy believes that thou art unarmed, perplexed, and is sure of victory by surprising thee; but in vain. To thee truth is a lodestar. Protected by Minerva's aegis / thou walkest in glory. The baying of Cerberus never dispels from your face the gentle smile; though poisonous breath rise from his jaws, / it never despoils the splendor of thine eternal fame. Filled with noble delight, knowing [thee] to be immortal like the celestial gods, souls greet thee in undying joy."[53]

The highlight of Hennings' stay in Dresden was Mendelssohn's visit of 1776. "Mendelssohn is in Dresden. Thus I have found refreshing drink in a parched desert," he wrote rapturously to Elise Reimarus on August 21, 1776.[54] The long letter describing his memorable conversations with his friend and master is a veritable mine of information and deserves to be quoted in full:

> For the last three days I have been busy with him alone. It is impossible to tell you everything that happened during this time, to describe to you all the practical philosophy, all the reduction of small ideas, the total obliteration of unessential concepts, the very healing of the wounds that the consciousness of [one's] smallness inflicts upon the soul; in short, to describe to you the whole leap from the world to Mendelssohn, from folly to understanding.
>
> I found him little changed. His condition of health has not yet permitted him to do work in philosophy; he communicates his thoughts to his friends Nicolai, Eberhard, Engel, and Friedländer, to be worked out by them. His external appearance has gained by the fact that he wears his own hair. You know how refined and gentle his facial expression is. The various visits and the many conversations seemed to fatigue him a little, but one clearly perceives that the weariness is due to the body and that his mind invariably manifests itself in the finest equilibrium of quietude. His judgment is so clear and so straight, his expression is always so equal to itself, that no better proof of the independence, autarchy, and immateriality of the soul can be found than in his manner of thinking, talking, and being.
>
> [Here follows the discussion of Lavater's *Physiognomic Fragments* quoted above, p. 334 f., whereupon Hennings continues:] Mendelssohn praised and recommended to me [Christoph] Meiners' philosophical writings.[55] When we discussed Hume, whom I dislike on account of his coldness, he mentioned an idea of his that had particularly pleased him: to wit, that despite all the varieties in the religions there was one principle of virtue in which all nations agreed. I asked him to name it to me but he refused to tell me and suggested that I read this idea in its context.[56] He is very satisfied with the German translation of Hume's *Essays* in which Sulzer, he said, succeeded in resolving the skeptical doubts of the author.[57] [Here follow the two sentences about Albrecht von Haller quoted above, p. 335.] We glanced over the second part of the doublettes offered for sale by the electoral library, and found much excellent material in

the chapter [of the catalog] dealing with heterodox books. The librarian was present and we asked who the author of the catalog was. He told us that he was the author and wondered whether we had noticed any inaccuracies. Mendelssohn replied: no, the catalog is exactly as it ought to be, and the heterodox works are among the most beautiful.

On the day preceding the day of his departure I found him in the company of the farmer Palitzsch,[58] who pleased him immensely, and whose biography will appear with an engraving made from Grafs portrait of him. Zingg has very neatly drawn Mendelssohn's picture in profile. He wants to engrave it and present also the engraving of Palitzsch'.[59] Now that Mendelssohn has left, I am again as poor in spirit and as lonely as before.

Elise Reimarus' response more than measured up to Hennings' warm-hearted report. On August 20, 1776, she had informed her brother-in-law that Lessing was on a visit to Hamburg. On August 28, having received the letter about Mendelssohn's presence in Dresden, she replied:[60]

Happy for us, we have Moses and the Prophets,[61] and it is these we want to hear. For your *Te Deum* about Mendelssohn's stay in Dresden could not have come at a more appropriate time, when our souls were more sympathetically attuned, than just at that moment. Lessing was with us, to wit, all by himself, for otherwise one cannot really enjoy this heavily besieged man nor warm oneself through at the fire of his exuberant spirit but has almost to suffer thirst at the well, if I may change the metaphor. We read to him some passages from your penultimate letter, discussed the immortality of the soul and the mortality of certain opinions —and then your letter arrived. You know what Lessing thinks of Mendelssohn. He was amazed that he was in Dresden at this time and that he wears his own hair, but he was not amazed at your joy to have had him with you. I feel so deeply what it means to be in Mendelssohn's presence that I would gladly give up one part of my life to sit, during the other, at the feet of this Gamaliel and to learn truth from his mouth and spirit. Thirst in a sandy desert is a mere trifle compared with the thirst of the mind . . .

That Dresden and Hamburg should have appeared as "parched" and "sandy" deserts and Mendelssohn's spirit as the water of life illustrates in striking terms what the Jewish philosopher had come to mean to August Hennings and Elise Reimarus. The avidity with which Hennings absorbed his every word is attested by what Hennings further reported in letters to Elise. On September 26, 1776 he wrote:[62] "Mendelssohn once told me that Providence follows steadfastly a wise plan and leads it to fruition, taking, however, more time than men are prepared to grant it. Often they spoil much by premature intervention." Hennings added: "There may be much truth in this, but when does the plan mature, and when is intervention premature? Who can tell?"

Having left Dresden, Hennings wrote in October, 1776, from Berlin:[63] "You see, I am a true admirer of the religion of Christ, though not of our Christian religion, to which I am unjust, according to Mendelssohn's reproach, because I judge it by the sight of the papal religion (which is,

admittedly, hideous to me) and by the principles of some French authors.
He thinks that nowadays the Protestants teach nothing but natural religion,
which, however, they derive from revelation (the Bible). He, therefore,
believes that one ought to be content to show them that natural religion
is not founded upon what they teach to be its foundation. To prove this
he recalled that Basedow had built in Dessau a Temple of Providence
in which all nations worshipping Providence could pray, and that all sections
hold their peace about it. I retorted by telling Mendelssohn that perhaps
he judged things more than I did by the people he saw around him.
Not all pulpits were filled with Berlin clergymen, and even Berlin had
its Silberschlag.[64] In proof of his contention he showed me the catechism
in which the court preacher Diterich examines the young. When I looked
up the article about redemption, I was admittedly able to find there—with
Mendelssohn's help—the natural truth; and yet one could also interpret
everything in a mystical sense." Hennings report gives us an excellent
insight into Mendelssohn's view of the Berlin Enlightenment theology.
To him it was to all intents and purposes identical with natural religion,
and yet it refused to acknowledge the fact and pretended to be based
on revelation—but without taking revelation seriously.

Hennings continued in the same letter: "Our conversation led us also
to discussing the rationality of moral goodness, the definition of the concept
of beauty, and the immortality of an immaterial soul. Mendelssohn considers
the morally good to be founded upon the harmony [in which it finds
itself] with our vocation [*Bestimmung*]. He conceded, however, that there
were collisions between the universal vocation of man and the more specific
societal and individual vocations. He admitted that these collisions made
for the most difficult situations. He calls beautiful that in which we find
the greatest harmony between our sentiments and our imagination.[65] Three
teachings, he suggested, had to be upheld as sacred without challenge
because without them no covenant could be concluded, no trust was possible,
and no social bond could survive. These teachings were the belief in the
deity, in the necessity of virtue, and in a future life in which there was
reward or improvement through punishment. So far as the first two
[teachings] were concerned, we carried within us not merely a sense of
their necessity but also a sense of disgust with those who denied them
or held them in contempt. We could gladly say with Voltaire: Si dieu
n'existait pas il faudrait l'inventer; and with another poet: La vertu, je
la nomme et son éloge est fait. But if someone has the misfortune being
in doubt as to continued existence after death, what proofs can we offer
that will give him certainty? I recalled Plato's and Mendelssohn's *Phaedon*.
They might persuade a searching and willing mind but they do not furnish
proofs. Mendelssohn appealed to the moral sentiment, nothing more. It
makes no difference to me, he said, *how* I shall continue my existence
and *what* its form and organization is going to be. Only it *has* to be. This
follows from the teaching about God and Providence. I remarked: if the

soul is a being of its own encompassed by the body and hence confined, it is not immaterial, for where there is a boundary, there must be matter that comes to an end, or something material. What my Mendelssohn said in reply about the immaterial nature of an infinite being that dissolved or weakened in the process of its expansion and thereby differed from the Supreme Being, which never changed, was not sufficiently comprehensible to me. In the same way in which the moon is not in my eye, he added, when I look at her, though she affects my eye, so my soul is not included in my body, though it exercises its effect primarily upon the body. An external object, I objected, admittedly affects me and becomes known to me, and yet it never becomes part of me. True, I appreciate that I am nothing that subsists individually or as a substance but that I am an organization upon which the whole of nature has a vivifying effect; that, moreover, there is no reason why this transient, almost dreamy organization called human life should not reappear in variously modified forms. Yet who can explain how there should arise an individual with a particular being and continued existence? Ideas similar to those I heard from Mendelssohn I have found in a treatise about the gods and the world by Sallustius the Philosopher, which I took with me for my entertainment on the journey. The immortality of the soul, this philosopher says, follows of necessity from the soul's knowledge of the gods, for the mortal has never known the immortal."[66]

It is not necessary to analyze the discussion reported by Hennings. Some of Mendelssohn's statements may have been imprecisely reproduced by him. However, we do recognize the general outline of his thoughts on immortality as found in the correspondence with Herder. What is missing is the insistence on the upward striving of the soul, not merely on its continued being in some form or another. Yet one has to remember that Mendelssohn had to accommodate himself to the level of Hennings' philosophical standpoint, and that his prime concern was pedagogical. How successful Mendelssohn was in his presentation of the three main teachings of natural religion is indicated by the fact that Hennings, in his book *Olavides* (1779), which is devoted to a plea for tolerance, declared that there were three truths that must never be sacrificed for the sake of tolerance: the truths about God, providence, and the reward of virtue. They took precedence over tolerance because those who denied them gave free rein to all the vices.[67]

After his return to Copenhagen, Hennings remained in contact with Mendelssohn, with Elise acting as transmitter of messages and letters. In December, 1776, Hennings had been appointed to an important post in the State Department of Economic Affairs with the title of *Justizrat,* and he was also made inspector of industrial enterprises in Copenhagen. His ambition was, however, far from satisfied and his restlessness continued. He felt the need to promote the ideals of the Enlightenment, which the conservative trend in the Danish government seemed to stifle, and wrote a treatise *On Reason*[68] that he hoped would produce some practical results. He wanted Mendelssohn to judge and correct the manuscript and then persuade Nicolai to publish it. On November 18, 1777, Elise wrote to him:[69] "Do you know, à propos, that we expect that good man Mendelssohn to arrive here any day? We shall personally hand to him your treatise and the letters as well as soon as he comes. . . ."

Mendelssohn obviously intended originally to return from Hanover via Hamburg. The unforseen extension of his stay[70] spoiled this plan. On December 30 Elise informed Hennings of the situation:[71] "Since the hope of seeing Mendelssohn here has vanished like a beautiful dream, your manuscript will probably be dispatched [to Berlin] as early as this week. . . ." On January 24, 1778, Mendelssohn wrote Hennings a letter acknowledging receipt of the manuscript and complimenting the author:[72] "I accept with pleasure the role of godfather of this beautiful first-born of your spirit. It is a word fitly spoken in its season, for in my view reason was never in greater need of an apologia than in this philosophical century." The letter was forwarded on February 11, 1778, by Elise, who commented:[73] "It does one good to hear a word of unalloyed reason from such an authentic philosophic source. . . ." Because Nicolai felt unable to act as publisher, Mendelssohn arranged for the book to appear under the impress of "the harmless Voss, publisher of the Royal Academy, who does not annoy the theologians." If Hennings had chosen Nicolai in order to secure for his work "the odor of heresy," he need not worry:[74] "I hope that readers who have a good sense of smell will notice what kind of man he is who could deliver this eulogy of reason and of the simplicity of Homeric morals." On May 8, 1778, Mendelssohn could send Hennings six copies of his printed treatise.[75]

The book created hardly any impression, and Hennings for a while considered retiring from public life. Elise tried to restore his faith in the ultimate victory of the good in terms reminiscent of what he had once told her about Mendelssohn's trust in the workings of Providence:[76] "What else is it you so often admire in Providence and nature but the fact that notwithstanding the little, vile rebellions that try to thwart its great plan it pursues its path unperturbed and uses even fools and their deeds for its final purpose? The true sage does not act otherwise in his small world. He takes it [Providence; nature] for his model amid the people whom he meets on his [actual] path, not on a chimerical one in which everything happens by itself and in which virtue would no longer be virtue because no vices are possible."

She went on holding up the image of Mendelssohn as an example to emulate, and in so doing revealed the negative attitude toward Judaism and the Jews that was prevalent even among the most enlightened non-Jews, particularly among those in whom "pure reason" had taken the place of religion: "Were you to abandon the world as early as now, how would you be able to face Mendelssohn, who spends his life, day in and day out, in physical distress and soul-degrading business, amid the indignities of a religion the compulsion of which he feels every day; ready to serve every haggling Polish Jew, and who despite all this, is a contented, happy father and friend." The portrayal of Mendelssohn as a man who stoically bore the "compulsion" exerted upon him by his religion was rather grotesque, though infused with sympathy and admiration. In the course of time Elise, her brother, and Hennings became increasingly aware of Mendelssohn's deep-rooted loyalty to Judaism. They also eventually realized that his ideas about enlightenment versus prejudice differed somewhat from theirs. It is to their credit that they never wavered in their reverence and affection for him.

On March 10, 1779, Elise informed Hennings that Mendelssohn's health had suffered another setback—that he could not even merely listen to any discussion of "serious matters" without incurring sleeplessness and indisposition the next day. A certain visitor from Berlin had mentioned this to her brother.[77] This disturbing news caused Hennings to resume his interrupted correspondence with Mendelssohn. In a letter dated March 20, 1779,[78] he expressed his regret at the alarming situation and assured Mendelssohn of his friendship. He took the opportunity of inquiring whether a manuscript of his had reached him via Hamburg. In case it had, he wanted it destroyed.

This reference concerned, no doubt, the manuscript of Hennings' new work, *Olavides,* which Elise had indeed forwarded to Mendelssohn, as is evident from a letter she wrote to Hennings on September 29, 1778:[79] "Since Mendelssohn does not answer you, I assume that he is having your treatise printed on the quiet, and as you object to this, I wish you would write to him about this, the sooner the better. Or perhaps his overloaded schedule of work is to be blamed for his inability to read it at his leisure." The request to destroy the manuscript was due, however, to the fact that the book had appeared in the meantime.[80] Hennings' letter continued: "If you have the time, show me the favor and read the enclosed little work that Olavides occasioned. Your judgment will stamp it for me. The world always praises and reproves in a distorted way. This I have learned in connection with the little I have written. Yet for the sake of the cause I attach great importance to the approval or rather cooperation of certain men." Olavides, a Peruvian born in 1724, had emigrated to Spain, where he studied the humanities, wrote some plays, and in 1763—motivated by a high sense of idealism—founded a model colony at the foot of the Sierra Morena. Inspired by Rousseau, he sought to bring his people back to nature and the religion of nature. He incurred the wrath of the Holy Inquisition and was condemned, on trumped-up charges, to eight years imprisonment. Hennings' book described the fate of Olavides in the form of a poem in hexameters, with explanatory notes and an appendix entitled "Something on Unrecognized Virtues" (namely courage, freedom, honor).[81]

Contrary to Hennings' expectations, the book met with a fierce response in some quarters, while others praised it as "the most reasonable statement that one could make on prejudices." Those who attacked it the most indignantly were Schönheyder, the court preacher, and Lauritz Smith, a professor of philosophy. Hennings was accused of superficiality, of failure to differentiate between Roman Catholicism and Protestantism, and of a hatred of religion. As a result of the furor, Hennings' position in Copenhagen was placed in serious jeopardy,[82] but when he asked Mendelssohn for his opinion the storm over *Olavides* had not yet broken out. The atmosphere was still calm when, in the absence of a reply from Mendelssohn, Hennings wrote to him again on June 22, 1779.[83] At that time Mendelssohn was himself involved in difficulties arising out of the announcement of his plan to publish the Pentateuch with a German translation and a new Hebrew commentary, and Hennings offered him his help through government intervention.

This proposal and the circumstances that gave rise to it, as well as Mendelssohn's reaction, will be discussed in the next chapter. What belongs here is the famous section in Mendelssohn's letter of June 29, 1779, in which he described his new involvement as a result of the changed pattern of life brought about by his illness. The letter was written before he received Hennings' letter of June 22. The passage that reveals so much about the reorientation that had taken place in Mendelssohn reads as follows:[84]

> According to the first plan of my life, as I designed it in my better years, I was far removed from ever becoming an editor or translator of the Bible. I wanted to confine myself to having silken materials manufactured during the day and to being in love with philosophy in my free hours. However, it has pleased Providence to lead me toward a different path. I lost the ability to meditate and, as a result, initially, the major portion of my happiness. After some examination I found that the remainder of my strength might still be sufficient to render a useful service to my children, and perhaps [also] to a considerable part of my nation, by giving into their hands a better translation and explanation of the holy scriptures than they had before. This is the first step toward culture, from which, alas, my nation is kept at such a distance that one might almost despair of the possibility of an improvement. However, I considered myself obliged to do the little that lies in my power, and to leave the rest to Providence, which as a rule requires more time for the execution of its plan than we can see at a glance. . . .
>
> But I have talked enough about myself and my great accomplishments. In reality, I have not done by far as much for my brethren as Olavides did for his, and therefore I cannot expect as much ingratitude in return. It seems to me that you have made very good use of the fate of this man, my dearest Hennings, in urging salutary truth upon the small circle, as you call it. You are perfectly right. One has to constrict one's sphere of activity, for otherwise one hovers, like a meteor, in the upper regions, viewed and enjoyed by the curious, without imparting warmth and noticeable light. . . .

Looking back, from the perspective of this letter, to the way Mendelssohn had reacted to his illness during the seventies, one may notice a gradual development. At first he adapted himself, with a sense of resignation, free from any resentment or bitterness, to what seemed to be a temporary condition. Characteristic of this early phase was the answer he gave to Doctor Bloch, who had asked him: "What do you do, confined to your room and not permitted to think?" "I go to the window," Mendelssohn replied, "and count the tiles on my neighbor's roof."[85] There followed a period of deep anxiety and depression as the illness persisted and he began to fear a permanent loss of his capacity for sustained abstract thinking. It was Nicolai, more than anybody else, who observed his sense of despair and expressed himself in extremely pessimistic terms. The next stage was one of reconciliation to whatever Providence had decreed, but also of recapturing, at the same time, a glimmer of hope that one day he might be able to return to his old love, philosophy. His letter to the count of Schaumburg-Lippe, in the early part of 1775, contained the most moving expression of this attitude of resignation combined with hope. The element of cautious optimism came to the fore in a note he sent Nicolai on October 3, 1775, "promising" important changes and additions for the fifth edition of the *Phaedon* "which I trust I shall live to see, and in the meanwhile my health is supposed to improve in some measure."[86] On the other hand, the note of resignation was dominant in the letter he sent Hennings in September, 1775:[87] "The condition of my health is still unchanged, without the least deviation toward either improvement or worsening. I feel well so long as I neither write nor read. This very letter, despite its shortness and poverty of thought, tires me and is an intellectual effort sufficient for the whole day. Still, I can carry out my daily business without difficulty, and for the rest let everything happen as God wants it. I shall not be less contented as a result. Why should I not be able to live in the same way as my neighbor, the pastry-cook?"

Such astonishing serenity was possible so long as in his heart of hearts Mendelssohn could still cling to the hope that philosophy would someday again become the preoccupation of his leisure hours. When this hope began to fade, he was forced to plan his future in a realistic way. The letter he wrote to Hennings on June 29, 1779, reflected the decision he had reached. Having "lost the power of meditation," he had resolved to dedicate what strength he still possessed to a practical purpose whose importance he fully realized. He had discovered that by constricting his sphere of activity he might dispense more warmth and light where it was needed than he could by hovering like a meteor in the upper regions of pure philosophy.

Thus the figure of Olavides assumed a symbolic significance for Mendelssohn: one had to take action for the sake of an ideal and be ready to pay the price for it. Hennings' ardent desire to promote reason and tolerance in his own circle had been evident to Mendelssohn for some time. It is not impossible that the practical outlook of his disciple had proved somewhat infectious or had at least reinforced Mendelssohn's new orientation.

CHAPTER FIVE

The Teacher

———◦∞◦———

The Avant-Garde of Haskala

In the 1770's, the decade of Mendelssohn's illness, the number of gifted, "enlightened" Jews in Berlin increased considerably. For the most part, they were newcomers to the city, where they remained for different periods of time. Almost without exception[1] they looked upon Mendelssohn as their chief spokesman and leader, although they represented various shades of conviction within the burgeoning Haskala and went their own several ways in many respects.

Berlin was now fast becoming the center of West-European Jewish Enlightment. There had been Maskilim in Berlin long before, of course. In the 1740's, men like Israel Samoscz (who died in the year 1772 in Brody, where he had finally settled), Abraham Kisch, and Aaron Gumpertz had been Mendelssohn's teachers when he was a mere youth. There was Marcus Eliezer Bloch (1723–1799), Mendelssohn's physician and a friend from the early days, about whom he had written to Lessing on December 19, 1760 (a week after Bloch had registered as a medical student at the University of Frankfurt an der Oder): "What makes my sojourn here still more lonely is the fact that Herr Bloch, to whose company I had become accustomed, has departed for the *Hohe Schule*...."[2] Bloch achieved world-wide fame as an ichtyologist, and his magnum opus in twelve volumes, with four hundred and thirty-two magnificent illustrations, counted King Frederick the Great among its sponsors. He remained a loyal member of the Berlin community, and throughout his life retained a keen interest in Hebrew literature.[3]

These men were extraordinary figures, however. As avant-couriers, they indicated the shape of things-to-come but did not constitute a movement. In the 1770's the picture changed: a more or less cohesive group of Maskilim began to come into being.

This development had a visible effect on Mendelssohn's role in the community. He was now the acknowledged head of a group, and he was well aware of it. Moreover, the influx of men of great talent enabled him to embark upon a bold project of cultural reform. The German Pentateuch translation and the new Hebrew commentary became a feasible proposition because his circle provided him with the necessary scholarly and administrative manpower. His decision to devote his energy to the advancement of his people came at the right moment.

Who were the people who formed Mendelssohn's circle in the 1770's and after? Presenting them in chronological order, according to their appearance on the scene, we first meet Marcus Herz,[4] who returned to Berlin (where he was born in 1747) in the autumn of 1770. He was the son of a sofer and had been educated in Berlin at the Beth Hamidrash founded by Veitel Heine Ephraim. At the age of fifteen he had left Berlin for Königsberg to be apprenticed to business, but at the age of nineteen he entered the university and soon became the favorite student of Kant, at whose feet he sat from 1766 until 1770, finishing with a flourish as Kant's chosen "respondent" at the defense of the famous *Inaugural Dissertation* of 1770. Herz published a résumé of Kant's thesis in the form of a book entitled *Betrachtungen aus der spekulativen Weltweisheit* (Königsberg, 1771).

Mendelssohn had followed Herz' progress with keen interest, and in 1769 he had sent him a copy of the third edition of the *Phaedon* with the inscription:[5] "In jenem Leben ein mehreres" ("More on the subject in the next world"), an epigram he had also inscribed in the copy presented to the poet Ramler. Returned to Berlin, in 1770, Herz went straight to Mendelssohn, with whom he discussed Kant's dissertation and other matters for four hours,[6] and with whom he remained in the closest contact. On December 25, 1770 Mendelssohn wrote to Kant:[7] "Herr Marcus Herz, who by your teaching and (as he assured me) in even larger measure through his personal contact with you, has become a philosopher, continues to follow, in the most laudable fashion, the path that he commenced to enter upon under your guidance. Whatever my friendship can contribute to his progress shall not be withheld from him. I sincerely love him, and I enjoy the pleasure of his very entertaining company almost day by day. Nature has endowed him generously indeed. He has a bright intellect, a tender heart, a moderate imagination, and a certain subtlety of mind that seems to be a trait of the [Jewish] nation. What luck ... that these natural gifts were guided so early in his life toward the true and good." How highly Mendelssohn thought of young Herz' talents as a philosopher is further attested by the sentence he inscribed in a copy of the revised edition of his *Philosophical Writings* that he presented to him in 1771: "To his friend Marcus Herz these essays are committed for further elaboration, since the author will hardly be able to accomplish this in this life."[8]

There are numerous references to Mendelssohn in Herz' correspondence with Kant. On May 1, 1781, when Kant's *Critique of Pure Reason* was about to appear, the author informed Herz that four copies would be sent to Berlin: one for him and the other three for the cabinet minister von Zedlitz, Mendelssohn, and Doctor Sell.[9] He would "take the liberty of writing more concerning this matter" both to him and to Mendelssohn.[10] Kant's next letter (or draft of a letter)[11] to Herz contains the following passage:[12] "It is most disagreeable to me that Herr Mendelssohn has put my book aside, but I hope that this is not final. Among all those who could explain its point to the world, he is the most important, and I have counted on him, on Herr Tetens[13] and on you, my very esteemed friend." Kant realized that it would take time for the "total change" in philosophical outlook represented by his work to win acceptance, and it is pathetic to read how disappointed he was when Mendelssohn, for reasons of health and on account of other preoccupations, declined to study and review his "system." He expressed gratitude to Herz for his promise to study the book despite his involvement in a "medical encyclopaedia" (probably a reference to the *Grundriss aller medicinischen Wissenschaften*, which Herz published in 1782). In the end neither Mendelssohn nor Herz was converted to Kant's new philosophy.

In 1774 Herz was awarded the doctorate of medicine at Halle University and he subsequently combined his medical practice (he became physician-in-chief at the Berlin Jewish Hospital) with psychological and physiological research.[14] His book *Briefe an Ärzte* ("Letters to Physicians")[15] led Kant to write to him on August 20, 1777:[16] "The observing and practical mind excels so much in it, apart from the finely spun more general concepts that I had known you to be capable of, that you are bound soon to attain to a high rank among physicians, if you continue to pursue the medical art with the searching mind of an experimental philosopher and, at the same time, with the commitment of a humanitarian. . . ." Mendelssohn must also have admired Herz' concern for human welfare and the lofty concept he had of his profession. Herz translated the apocryphal (?) *Prayer of Maimonides*[17] from Hebrew into German and published it in the *Deutsches Museum*[18] under the title: "Daily Prayer of a Physician before visiting his patients; from a Hebrew manuscript of a famous twelfth-century Jewish physician in Egypt." Herz obviously relished the opportunity to acquaint the Christian world with the profound spirituality of this medieval prayer. The warm affection his patients felt for him is reflected in a poem addressed to him by Leopold Friedrich Günther von Göckingk.[19]

Marcus Herz was a worthy heir to the many notable Jews of medieval times who combined the practice of *ars medica* and the practice of philosophy. An interesting exchange of notes between Mendelssohn and Herz illustrates how the latter's philosophical thinking impinged on his medical writing and also offers proof of Mendelssohn's interest in his work.

The exchange had to do with the definition of "illness." The question had been discussed at an evening party on February 10, 1780, and Herz' objection to the definition suggested by Mendelssohn had had a bad effect: "The difficulty that you raised last night," Mendelssohn wrote to him the following day, "drove me out of the good company in which I would have loved to spend the evening. Now my brain is (forgive the unphilosophical expression) like granulous powder. A single spark thrown into it by a constable like you instantaneously kindles the entire mass, and I have to throw mud on it to extinguish the fire. *Do* answer me—but not in the evening! Whenever the sun rises, I am yours M. Mendelssohn."[20] The opening part of this note quotes Mendelssohn's Latin definition and asks whether Herz found anything objectionable in it: "Illness is an unnatural condition of an organic body, which lasts for some time and impedes some function of the body." Herz' elaborate reply amounted to the distinction between illness in its wider sense and illness strictly speaking—between being afflicted with some illness and being ill (i.e. feeling indisposed).[21] Mendelssohn agreed with this distinction but was not satisfied with Herz' other remarks and thereby provoked a further memorandum.[22]

It seems that it was in connection with Herz' *Grundriss aller medicinischen Wissenschaften* ("Compendium of all Medical Sciences") that this particular discussion arose. It also led Mendelssohn to write his "Observations on the Draft of a Materia Medica by Marcus Herz,"[23] in which Mendelssohn remarked, inter alia, that Herz had allowed the philosopher in him to sway the medical writer:[24] "Yet, my friend, are you not too wide-ranging for a compendium? The theory of classification is ingenious but would seem to belong more to logic than to the materia medica. It appears that you seize every opportunity to engage your mistress [philosophy]."

As early as 1778 Herz commenced to give public lecture courses on philosophical and scientific matters. One of his "students" was Baron Karl Abraham von Zedlitz (1731–1793), minister of justice in the Prussian cabinet since 1770 and, in addition, minister of "cultus" and education since 1771. On August 1, 1778, the baron wrote to Kant:[25] "This winter I shall take a course in rational anthropology with your former pupil, Herr Herz. I promise myself much good from this course of lectures. Since I have no time to learn from bunglers, I am always most wary in starting something like this . . . ; Mendelssohn has vouched for Herz' talent, however, and on this man's voucher I might undertake anything, especially since I know that you respect Herz and are conducting a kind of correspondence with him." Herz' lectures became increasingly popular and attracted even members of the royal family. In 1787 King Frederick William II awarded him the title of professor. His marriage in 1779 to the very young and dazzling Henrietta de Lemos, daughter of a physician of Sephardic descent, made his home a center of Berlin high society, but Mendelssohn died before the salon of the "tragic Muse" stood in full bloom.

Marcus Herz remained steadfast in his loyalty to Judaism. His moving report on Mendelssohn's last illness and death[26] documents his love for "our Mendelssohn," the "pious man," whose endeavors had his full support.

In 1787 he published in the German appendix to the periodical *Ha-Me'assef,* the literary organ of the Maskilim, a treatise on the custom of early burial in which he supported Mendelssohn's earlier plea for its abolition.[27] He sent a copy to Kant who graciously acknowledged the gift and in return for it and some previous complimentary copies presented Herz with his *Critique of Practical Reason,* which had just appeared.[28] Among Mendelssohn's intimate friends Herz was one of the most distinguished.

David Friedländer (1750–1834), son of a wealthy Jewish family in Königsberg, came to Berlin in 1771, joined the business firm of the powerful community leader Daniel Itzig, and married Itzig's daughter Blümchen in 1772.[29] He established a silk factory in 1776 and eventually rose to great prominence as a merchant and Berlin city councilor. According to . his own testimony, he met Mendelssohn for the first time in 1771, the year of his arrival in Berlin, and he could not, therefore, have accompanied him on his visit to the prince of Brunswick in October, 1770, as has been alleged on the mistaken assumption that the "Herr Friedländer" who, together with a certain Herr Samson of Brunswick, escorted Mendelssohn to the palace and was "also known" to the prince[30] was identical with the "twenty-year-old David Friedländer."[31]

In Königsberg, the young Friedländer had been the friend of Marcus Herz, who had introduced him to Kant. How long and to what extent Friedländer had studied under Kant is by no means clear, but it seems that after Herz' departure he had come somewhat closer to Kant and become aware of the revolutionary turn in his thinking. "Herr Friedländer has sent me a new piece by Koelbele," Kant remarked in a letter to Herz on September 27, 1770,[32] and Herz wrote to him on July 9, 1771:[33] "My friend, Herr Friedländer, told me on [his] arrival [here] that you are no longer so great an admirer of speculative philosophy as you were before . . ." Herz was so disconcerted by Kant's changed attitude to metaphysics that he demanded, as it were, an explanation. The result was a correspondence in which Kant provided such an explanation and thereby set down the only documentary evidence we possess concerning the genesis of the *Critique of Pure Reason.* Without Friedländer's report to Herz this priceless correspondence might not have been started. However, the young man had arrived in Berlin not merely as a harbinger of disturbing news but also as the bearer of a gift for Herz: a picture of Kant. The happy recipient wrote in his letter of July 9 how "infinitely obliged" he was to Kant and to his friend. Kant's portrait above Herz' desk would remain a constant reminder of his "instructive hours" at the master's feet.

Friedländer continued to cultivate his friendly relationship with Kant[34] but it was Mendelssohn whose devotee, disciple, and friend he became. Among Mendelssohn's many admirers none was so deeply and unreservedly attached to him as David Friedländer, and Mendelssohn responded with equal warmth. It was to Friedländer that Mendelssohn would reminisce about his early childhood,[35] and it would not have been surprising if he had appointed Friedländer his literary executor, had he appointed anyone. As matters turned out Friedländer did act in such a capacity when he published the Hebrew book *Sefer Ha-Nefesh*[36] in 1787 and the fifth and sixth editions of the *Phaedon*[37] in 1814 and 1821. As a collector of autographs he acquired Mendelssohn's correspondence with important personages from his *Nachlass*,[38] and he took care to indicate that certain annotations in books originally belonging to Mendelssohn had indeed been entered by him and in his own hand.[39] The same attitude of almost filial piety inspired his essay "Something on Mendelssohn's Translation of the Psalms" (in the *Berlinische Monatsschrift*, 1786)[40] and the German translation of *Ecclesiastes*, which he wrote on the basis of Mendelssohn's Hebrew commentary on the book and which appeared with notes by Joel Brill Löwe in 1788.[41] It was in the spirit of the master that he contributed "Samples of Rabbinic Wisdom" to Johann Jakob Engel's *Der Philosoph für die Welt*[42] and short pieces of the same genre to the *Berlinische Monatsschrift*.[43] Friedländer's memory was a store-house of anecdotes from Mendelssohn's life, and his point in telling them was to show the wisdom and nobility of the man. One is almost tempted to draw an analogy to the way the Hasidim delighted in story-telling about their great masters. "Wordly Wisdom of a Sage" is the title of an anecdote that he published in the *Neue Berliner Monatsschrift*,[44] and a letter written by him at the age of seventy-nine, on December 9, 1829, tells the following story:[45]

> Mendelssohn was taking a walk with Professor Engel in the so-called *Lustgarten* in Berlin. A drunken soldier, a Pole, as his dialect indicated, stops in front of them, his arms akimbo, and utters the most vulgar insults against the hunchbacked Jew. Being ignored, he follows the men and, judging from his posture and the motion of his hand, is about to pluck the little man by the lobe of his ear while continuing his abusive language. In outrage, Engel, walking on the right side of Mendelssohn, raises his stick to ward off the impudent one, but the calm philosopher quickly seizes him by the arm. "Don't! Allow the wretched slave the pleasure of teasing a Jew a little." Engel could never tell this incident without deep emotion. He would add: "I cannot imitate the amiably ironical tone of this noble man."

"Tell me," Friedländer wrote by way of postscript, "assuming Plutarch had reported this anecdote of a Greek philosopher, would we not listen to it with a melancholy love?"

As Daniel Itzig's son-in-law, Friedländer wielded considerable influence even as a young man. Being of genial disposition, he used his connections for the benefit of people who were in need of help. When the learned Isaac Ha-Levi Satanov[46] arrived in Berlin, Friedländer found him a position as private Hebrew tutor for some wealthy Jewish families.[47] He took care of David Friedrichsfeld, a young man of roughly his own age, who had been educated at the Berlin Beth Hamidrash founded by Veitel Heine Ephraim and had to suffer great hardships. Almost three decades later, in the preface to his Hebrew biography of Naphtali Herz (Hartwig)

Wessely,[48] Friedrichsfeld recalled the kindnesses he had received at the hands of his protector: "Who was it that introduced me to the home of the 'diadem of Israel,' the 'light of the exile,' our teacher Moses Mendelssohn (may he rest in paradise)? . . . Who made it possible for me to establish an enduring covenant of friendship and great love with that man of valor and leader in the sciences, the honored Rabbi Mordecai [Marcus Herz] the physician? Who but you acted as a father to me, shaped my intellect, and founded my spirit." Another protégé of Friedländer and, through him, of Mendelssohn was the highly educated Ephraim Hirschel of Karlsruhe, who came to Berlin in 1779 and left two years later. Friedländer employed him as a clerk and tutor, and Mendelssohn gave him a warm letter of recommendation when he took his leave on August 13, 1781. Mendelssohn could not have guessed that the young man, who had been a frequent visitor to his home, would embark on a rather strange career—that he would abandon the philosophy of the Enlightenment and, assuming the name Hirschfeld, turn to the mystical theology of a branch of Freemasonry known as the "Asiatic Brethren."[49]

As a man of affairs, Friedländer co-founded (together with his brother-in-law Isaac Daniel Itzig) the Berlin Jewish *Freyschule* (Free School), which offered free tuition in Hebrew and secular subjects such as German, French, geography, and bookkeeping. The decision to establish the *Freyschule* was taken, probably with Mendelssohn's encouragement, if not at his suggestion,[50] in 1778, and the school was opened in 1781.[51] It served as a model for similar schools in Wolfenbüttel (1786), Dessau (1799), Seesen (1801), etc.[52] In 1779 Friedländer published a *Lesebuch für Jüdische Kinder* ("Reader for Jewish Children") and in 1786 an annotated German translation of the prayer book in Hebrew characters (as a companion volume to the edition of the Hebrew text [*Tefillot Yisra'el*] with grammatical notes by Isaac Satanov).[53] The reader was hardly designed for the benefit of children. It presented a collection of short pieces of a moralizing nature culled from Hebrew and Greek sources in addition to translations of the Principles of Judaism by Maimonides and of the Ten Commandments. Most of the material was supplied by Mendelssohn. The booklet was attractively produced and sold on commission by Voss, the net profit accruing to the *Freyschule*. Soon however the school had its own printing press; a royal concession for the establishment of an "oriental printing-office and bookstore" was granted on February 3, 1783, and from 1784 until 1796 the works published appeared under the impress of the Jewish Free School (*bi-defus hevrat hinnukh ne'arim*). In 1796 the name was changed to "Oriental Printing Office."[54] The press was a powerful instrument of cultural reform and owed a great deal to David Friedländer and his brother-in-law.[55]

The scholar who directed the school's printing office from its inception until 1788 was Isaac ben Moses Ha-Levi Satanov (1732–1804), an immensely gifted and incredibly prolific writer who by his own works alone could keep a small press quite busy.[56] Born in Satanov (Podolia), he came to Berlin in 1771/72 at about the age of forty.[57] In a short time he acquired an encyclopaedic range of proficiency in the natural sciences and some knowledge in modern philosophy. His outlook in philosophical thinking remained, however, essentially geared to the concepts of medieval Hebrew literature, and his relationship to Mendelssohn was therefore hardly that of a pupil to his master.

In his *Sefer Ha-Middot* ("Ethics"), published in 1784, Satanov developed his own religious and moral philosophy in terms borrowed from medieval works and employed with an astonishing degree of competence. In a brief appendix (pages 138–44), he discussed the nature of the soul and its immortality in a manner reminiscent of the medieval writings on the subject, notwithstanding the fact that in the introductory paragraph he referred to Mendelssohn's *Phaedon* as his source: "Many of the most accomplished Maskilim among our people are longing to behold the beauty of [Mendelssohn's] Book on the Soul[58] ... and they said to me ... 'make his words available to us that we may know them' ... I could not refuse their strong plea and therefore saw fit to attach some remarks on the nature of the soul ... and its survival after death, and to verify all this by reliable proofs taken from the words of earlier investigations ... before there appeared the all-encompassing teacher [*ha-rav ha-kolel*], the famed sage, the lamp of Israel, our teacher Moses Dessau and taught the truth in his treatise, the Book on the Soul, in which he explained the nature of the soul, its incorruptibility and eternity by new proofs ... and this book of his may be considered [to underly] the second part [viz. the appendix] of this *Sefer Ha-Middot*." However, one looks in vain for traces of the *Phaedon* in Satanov's treatment of the subject. One finds, on the other hand, a reference to the kabbalistic doctrine of transmigration,[59] which is not surprising since Satanov edited in 1782 Hayyim Vital's *Ets Hayyim* and *Peri Ets Hayyim*.[60] His affinity to Kabbala is attested also by his publication, in 1783, of a specimen of a new Zohar (with a fictitious approbation), and by his work *Imrey Bina* (1784), which sought to show the basic accord between philosophy and Kabbala (invoking once again fictitious approbations by rabbis long deceased).[61]

Mendelssohn could not have felt too happy about Satanov's type of philosophy and literary practices. Yet he must have recognized the genius of a man who was equally at home in all strata of Hebrew literature and could imitate all styles with perfect ease. Satanov's *Sefer Ha-Hizayon*, published in 1775,[62] was written in the style of Immanuel ben Solomon of Rome's *Mahbarot*, a work that Satanov would reedit, with additions of his own, in 1796. His *Mishley Assaf* (1789) is hardly distinguishable from biblical wisdom literature. In 1794 Satanov published a commentary on the Psalms, presenting it as a work by Rashi's grandson, Rabbi Samuel ben Me'ir (Rashbam). Mendelssohn died long before Satanov's half-humorous, half-fraudulent production of modern pseudepigrapha came to an end, and he probably did not condemn Satanov as harshly as some nineteenth-century historians (with the exception of Steinschneider)[63] would do; the eighteenth-century rather fancied literary fictions and anonymous publications. Satanov was certainly a character *sui generis,* yet he intrinsically belonged to the age of transition, just as the rest of Mendelssohn's followers did. We know next to nothing about his and Mendelssohn's personal relationship. From an incident reported by Euchel[64] we learn only that Satanov visited Mendelssohn's home occasionally, at least. At all events, Satanov's presence in Berlin undoubtedly gave considerable strength to the forces of the Haskala.

Less brilliant but outstanding as a biblical scholar and as an authority in massoretic studies was Solomon ben Joel of Dubno (1738–1813)— Solomon Dubno for short—who arrived in Berlin in 1772. As a youth he had been a pupil of "the Gaon Rabbi Naphtali Hirz" in his native city,[65] which could boast of a long and illustrious history. In Lemberg he studied under Rabbi Solomon ben Moses Helma, author of the commentary *Mirkevet Mishne* on Maimonides' *Mishne Tora*[66] and of an investigation into the musical rendition of the books of Job, Proverbs, and Psalms entitled *Sha'arey Ne'ima.* Solomon Dubno published the latter work with notes of his own and an introductory poem.[67] It was to this remarkable teacher that Dubno owed his transformation into a Maskil. In the introduction to his *Mirkevet Mishne,* Solomon Helma revealed himself as a fearless opponent of all those who shunned the strictly methodical study of the Talmud. He grouped them under three headings: the adepts of mere edification through haggadic works, the kabbalists, and the new type of Hasidism that was forming in Wolhynia and Podolia.[68] Helma's approach to Jewish learning was modeled on Maimonides'. As he pointed out in his introduction, he had studied algebra, geometry, and astronomy in addition to logic and the art of poetry.[69] His opposition to Hasidism was shared by his disciple Solomon Dubno,[70] as was his scientific cast of mind. From 1767 until 1772 Dubno lived in Amsterdam, where Hebrew poetry flourished and great libraries were available to him. The leading figure of the Hebraists' circle was David Franco Mendes, a disciple of Moses Hayyim Luzzatto, who had spent eleven years in Amsterdam and had written there an allegorical drama, *La-Yesharim Tehilla.* Solomon Dubno reedited this work in 1780,[71] and Mendelssohn sent a copy of it to Herder. In a covering letter dated September 24, 1781, he described it as follows:[72] "An allegorical drama. The author, who lived fifty years ago in Amsterdam, was in some respects a man of great genius, but being deterred by the jealousy of some rabbis, he could not develop his gifts. He was ill-treated, withdrew into solitude, and died a premature death. His kabbalistic manuscripts are now being assiduously studied in Poland. He is said also to have written new psalms, but they have not come to my notice." Solomon Dubno, himself a poet, published in 1776 a dirge entitled *Evel Yahid* in honor of Rabbi Jacob Emden, whose death had occurred on April 19 of that year.

Mendelssohn had deep respect for Dubno's learning and piety, and when his own interests veered toward biblical studies he could hardly have found a more congenial companion. It is fair to say that without Dubno, Mendelssohn's great Bible project would probably not have come about. Dubno's contributions to the project will be discussed below; for present purposes it is enough to say that his involvement in the project began, in a sense, even before the project as such existed, i.e., when Mendelssohn appointed him as a tutor of his son Joseph. The exact date of the appointment is not known, but a clue is found in Mendelssohn's introductory essay to the Pentateuch edition, in which he stated:[73] "The Lord sent me our teacher and master Rabbi Solomon of Dubno (may his light shine forth) to teach my son, the only one left to me at the time (may God strengthen his heart for serving and revering Him), the science of [Hebrew] grammar one hour every day." Mendelssohn had lost his son Mendel, aged six, in September, 1775, and his son Abraham was born in December of the following year; thus Dubno's appointment as tutor must have been made in the interim, for it was only then that Joseph was the "only" son "left" to Mendelssohn.

Joseph, then a boy of five or six hardly needed a scholar such as Dubno to teach him Hebrew grammar.[74] We may surmise that Mendelssohn gave him the job as a way of supporting an outstanding scholar with dignity. It seems that he also employed, besides Dubno, a learned young man, Rabbi Samuel, as resident teacher for the children. When writing to Fromet from his trip to Königsberg in July, 1777, he twice sent regards "to my friend, our teacher and master, Rabbi Solomon [Dubno] (may his light shine forth); to the honorable Rabbi Samuel the bachelor (may his Rock and Redeemer preserve him); and to all members of our household."[75]

The happy relationship between Mendelssohn and Dubno during this period is apparent from the token of friendly remembrance that Mendelssohn sent Dubno in August, 1777, from Königsberg. It took the form of a riddle in fourteen Hebrew stanzas, to which Dubno replied on September 23 with a rather intricate and highly learned solution.[76] In a letter written in 1770, Mendelssohn had confessed to another correspondent that he was neither used to solving nor fond of posing riddles, since he always strove to express his ideas with as much clarity as possible.[77] In the light of this remark it is all the more noteworthy that vis-à-vis Dubno he broke his rule in a happy mood of playfulness.[78] It must have been in a similar spirit that he wrote Dubno a letter from Strelitz in June, 1779; the letter itself is lost, but its tenor may be gauged from the postscript of his epistle to Fromet of the same date:[79] "To Rabbi Solomon [Dubno] I send the enclosed letter for pleasure's sake."

Naphtali Herz (Hartwig) Wessely moved to Berlin from Copenhagen in 1774. His business in that city having fallen on evil days, he gladly accepted an offer by Joseph Ephraim, a son of Veitel Heine Ephraim and brother of Benjamin, his former employer in Amsterdam, to become manager of his firm in the Prussian capital. Wessely's arrival in Berlin constituted an important accretion of strength to the circle around Mendelssohn. He was closest in spirit to Solomon Dubno, whose friend he had been when they both lived in Amsterdam in 1767–1768. They shared, no doubt, nostalgic memories of the lovers of Hebrew poetry in that city of Ashkenazic and Sephardic Jews who were rivals in Jewish studies.[80]

Like Dubno, Wessely formed a bridge between the old world of pure, untarnished faith and the new era of secularism. There were revolutionary stirrings in him too: his dissatisfaction with the usual type of Jewish education revealed itself as early as 1778 in the poem *Mahalal Re'a*, in which he glorified Mendelssohn.[81] Yet his rebellion grew out of the very fabric of his Jewishness. Intoxicated as he was with the love of biblical Hebrew, he tried to evolve the whole realm of tradition from the nuances of the Hebrew tongue as employed in the Bible.

Philosophy played hardly any role in Wessely's thinking. He knew the works of the great medieval Jewish philosophers, but he did not allow himself to be guided by them. When discussing, for example, the meaning of the term *hokhma* (wisdom) in the Bible, he rejected the views of Maimonides, Gersonides, Isaac Abrabanel, and others.[82] Toward the end of 1774[83] he published in Berlin an extensive commentary on the mishnaic tractate *Avot* under the title *Yeyn Levanon* ("The Wine of Lebanon"). In opposition to the numerous commentaries that had linked this text with various philosophical notions, Wessely made the point that in the entire tractate philosophical speculation was conspicuous by its absence, and that it was generally not the way of the sages of the Mishna and the Talmud to raise philosophical questions.[84] He greatly stressed the importance of faith in its twofold aspect: as assent to an inner awareness and as acceptance of authority, as "believing some one" and "believing in some one."[85]

The naive piety of Wessely and the sophisticated religious philosophy of Mendelssohn were worlds apart, yet Mendelssohn was able to appreciate the sincerity of a faith so much aglow with passion for biblical Hebrew. He was not a man to underestimate any sincere, unpretentious believer, nor was the emotional experience of religion alien to him.[86] Above all, he fully shared Wessely's enthusiasm for classical Hebrew (though not Wessely's reasons for such enthusiasm). Wessely, on his part, revered Mendelssohn as the most illustrious Jew of the time, as a man whose towering intellect was matched by his amiable character and by his strict observance of the Jewish Law.

The confidence that Wessely enjoyed for many years among the custodians of orthodoxy is apparent from the approbations *(haskamot)* accorded to his earlier writings. His *Levanon* (1765–1766) carried eloquent eulogies by Saul Löwenstamm, chief rabbi of the Ashkenazic community in Amsterdam; by Saul Ha-Levi, chief rabbi of the Sephardim at the Hague; and by Solomon Ayllon, Sephardic chief rabbi of Amsterdam, all of whom were men of great renown.[87] The commentary *Yeyn Levanon* was praised by Saul Löwenstamm, Solomon Ayllon, and two more authorities: Ezechiel Landau, the celebrated chief rabbi of Prague, and David Tevele, chief rabbi of Lissa, both of whom would later attack him.

Ezechiel Landau departed from his self-imposed rule to refrain from writing approbations:[88] "Since the words of your Honor please me very much, and since from the day when I saw the first part of his book *Gan Na'ul* ["A Garden shut up," Canticles 4:12], 'I went down into his garden, I gathered my myrrh with my spice' and I drank the waters from 'the flowing streams of Lebanon,'[89] and sang his praises everywhere, 'for love abolishes the rule.' "[90] He felt certain that the author's future works would be written in the same spirit of the fear of the Lord. He approved their publication, provided Wessely adhered to his accustomed ways and based "all his words . . . upon the truth of our revealed Tora as received, generation after generation, from the Teachers of the Mishna and the Talmud."

Landau referred specifically to a work that was to be published by Wessely in 1780: his rendition, in magnificent biblical Hebrew, of the apocryphal "Book of Wisdom," which he mistook for an authentic work by King Solomon. He had "discovered" this book at the age of seventeen in a German Lutheran Bible, and encouraged by his uncle Joseph Wessely in Copenhagen he had translated the text from Luther's German version or else a French version (he knew no Greek). It was his sincere belief that in so doing he had restored the book to its original language. He also wrote an elaborate commentary, *Ruah Hen,* on the book. Landau expressed his approval of the projected publication of this work much in advance of its actual appearance, seeing the *haskama* to Wessely's *Yeyn Levanon* is dated the eighth of Av, 1771. He agreed with Wessely that the book was by King Solomon and mentioned the fact that Nahmanides (thirteenth century) had quoted it in the introduction to his commentary on the Tora.[91] Wessely distinctly referred to Nahmanides' acceptance of the Solomonic origin of the book on the title-page of his edition,[92] and this assumption was poetically expressed in laudatory hymns by David Franco Mendes, Solomon Dubno, and Isaac Cohen Belinfante.[93] In Dubno's happy phrase: " . . . thou didst find a book written by our King Solomon; yet it had become a stranger to us; thou didst have mercy on it, and didst say: 'This is one of the Hebrews' children'[94] . . . " Wessely had given beautiful poetic voice to his conviction in an early poem, but in a poem written much later he betrayed some doubts: he asked the reader to accept the work irrespective of whether it was by King Solomon. He was sorry if he had exerted his strength to no purpose, if he had taken hold of a thorn instead of a rose; but it was, at any rate, an artful work by a man of understanding and pure hands.[95] Mendelssohn did not accept the authenticity of the work.[96]

In the year 1777 a remarkable figure of the early East-European Haskala, Baruch of Shklov (Russia), visited Berlin. Born in 1752, the son of Jacob of Shklov, a learned preacher *(maggid)* and author, Baruch traced his descent from Samuel Jehuda Katzenellenbogen of Padua (Maharshik),

the famous sixteenth-century halakhic authority. Baruch received his rabbinic authorization from Abraham Katzenellenbogen, chief rabbi of Brisk
since 1760 and a vigorous opponent of Hasidism since 1772. Having served
as a member *(dayyan)* of the rabbinic court in Minsk, Baruch, who had
been cultivating some of the secular sciences as well, felt an overpowering
desire to travel and broaden his horizon. He went finally to England where
he studied medicine. It was on his way back from England to Lithuania
that he spent some time in Berlin.

Baruch was well received by the Mendelssohn circle, particularly by
Wessely. Hirschel Levin, chief rabbi of Berlin since 1772, also showed
him much kindness, putting at his disposal two manuscripts, owned by
him, of the as yet unpublished astronomical work *Yesod 'Olam* by Isaac
ben Joseph Israeli of Toledo (thirteenth–fourteenth century). Baruch published an annotated edition of this important text on the basis of the two
(unhappily deficient) manuscripts, with a preface by Wessely (Berlin, 1777).
In the same year he published in Berlin an astronomical work of his own
under the title *Sefer 'Amudey Shamayim* in the form of a commentary on
Maimonides' "Rules Concerning the Sanctification of the New Moon"
(Hilkhot Kiddush Ha-Hodesh); and he added to it an anatomical treatise,
Sefer Tif'eret Adam.

In 1778, after his return to Lithuania, Baruch was received by the
great "Gaon of Vilna," Rabbi Elija ben Solomon Zalman, who asked him
to translate into Hebrew as many scientific works as possible, for Tora
and science were "bound together" and ignorance of the sciences made
one "a hundredfold more ignorant of the Tora." Baruch related this utterance by the Gaon in the preface to his annotated Hebrew translation of
the first six books of Euclid, which appeared in 1780 at the Hague. Baruch
continued to cultivate his scientific interests and even conducted chemical
experiments. He spent his last years as Dayyan and private physician of
Prince Radziwill in Sluzk, where he died in 1810.[97]

Baruch was an outstanding representative of the scientific orientation
that was part of the educational program advocated by the Gaon of Vilna
and that went hand in hand with the latter's opposition to the Hasidic
movement.[98] His presence in Berlin in 1777 must have been considered
quite an event. The Gaon of Vilna himself is said to have visited Berlin
as a young man, when wandering from place to place in self-imposed
"exile" as was the custom of holy men. He was reported to have made
a profound impression on a professor of astronomy by solving with ease
a certain problem that had baffled the astronomers of the period.[99] Since
he returned to Vilna in 1748, his visit could have taken place in that year
or shortly before, when Mendelssohn was about eighteen years old. The
importance of the image of the Gaon as a master of all the sciences[100]
does not depend on its highly questionable historical veracity. It lies in
the fact that this image was woven into the legend of this rabbinic saint,
and that the study of secular sciences as aids to the full understanding

of the Tora was thereby legitimized. It is strange that Mendelssohn nowhere refers to the Gaon of Vilna.

Naphtali Herz Homberg (1749–1841), a more radical adept of the Enlightenment than Dubno, Wessely, and Baruch of Shklov, and rather akin in spirit to David Friedländer, returned to Berlin in 1778/79 (having been there previously in the years 1770–1772).[101] He was born in Lieben (near Prague) and studied Talmud under Rabbi Ezechiel Landau and at the Yeshivot of Pressburg and Gross-Glogau. In secret, he taught himself to read and write German and left Glogau when his secular pursuits brought him into conflict with the rabbinic authorities; his later fierce antagonism to the traditional type of education was obviously a reaction to his personal experience. He went to Breslau, where the study of Rousseau's *Émile* kindled his enthusiasm for pedagogy. After a stay of two years in Breslau (1768–1770), he spent another two years in Berlin, devoting himself to Latin and mathematics. From 1772 until his return to Berlin we find him in Hamburg, where he concentrated on pedagogical studies.

In Berlin after 1778/79 Mendelssohn took a particularly warm interest in Homberg, appointing him tutor to his son Joseph (then about nine years of age), a position that Homberg held until 1782, when he left Berlin for Vienna. An "elective affinity" developed between Mendelssohn, then in his early fifties, and Homberg who was thirty-three when he departed from Berlin. A similar relationship had sprung up between Mendelssohn and David Friedländer, who was Homberg's senior by only a year. Both young men endeared themselves to the aging master because they tried to imbibe his philosophical teachings and made him feel that they were his true disciples. None of the older Maskilim of his circle shared his philosophical concerns in any comparable degree. Of the younger ones, Marcus Herz owed first allegiance to Kant. No wonder, therefore, that Mendelsshon considered Friedländer and Homberg as the most worthy of his affection and confidence.

As late as 1841 Joseph Mendelssohn, then over seventy years of age, could still recall the intimate friendship between Homberg and his father:[102] "You were his friend to such a degree," he wrote to Herz Homberg, who was ninety-two years old and still agile, "that he opened his heart to you about many a thing concerning which he kept it closed vis-à-vis others. I still remember this, and letters of yours found among the papers he left, testify to this fact." When Homberg took his leave of Mendelssohn in 1782, he received as a token of affection a silhouette of the master drawn by the artist Hasse, with the following inscription:[103] "My friend, my son, and my son's father![104] If this silhouette fails to reveal the heart's whole gratitude, blame the limits of art, blame Hasse's inability, but on no account [blame] Moses Mendelssohn."

A colleague of Homberg was Aaron Zechariah Friendenthal of Jaroslav (Galicia), known as Aaron Jaroslav, whom Mendelssohn entrusted with the task of writing the commentary *(Bi'ur)* on the fourth book of the Pentateuch, while the fifth book was assigned to Homberg. In his introduction Mendelssohn described the two men as "expert scholars [*meviney mada*'] at home in Tora and secular learning," whose modesty was responsible for the anonymity of their contribution.[105] In 1784 Jaroslav published the third edition of Maimonides' *Logical Terms* with Mendelssohn's commentary, which had gone out of print and which Jaroslav enriched by glosses based on oral remarks by the master.[106] In 1791 Jaroslav brought out a new edition in Lemberg.[107] Shortly after Homberg's departure from Berlin, Jaroslav had been invited to go to Breslau as teacher at the newly established primary school,[108] and he took later a similar position in Lemberg.[109] He shared neither the ambitions nor the radicalism of Homberg, and he was Mendelssohn's disciple in the truest sense of the term.

In 1778 Aaron Joel of Halberstadt introduced himself to Mendelssohn with a letter of recommendation from Kant. Joel had studied medicine at Königsberg and now wished to settle as a physician in Berlin. Kant wrote of him:[110] "Though he is not endowed with a talent as outstanding as Herr Herz's, his sound intelligence, industry, orderliness, and above all, the friendly disposition of his heart permit the expectation that he will establish himself before long as a skillful and respected physician. I know that these qualities alone are enough to induce you, my most honored friend, to devote some effort to promoting the chances of this promising young man." Kant mentioned Joel also in a letter to Marcus Herz,[111] and there can be little doubt that this protégé of his was well received by the Mendelssohn circle.

The very opposite of the orderly but not outstandingly bright Aaron Joel was Solomon Maimon (1754–1800), a rather disorderly and somewhat uncouth but undeniably brilliant Lithuanian who arrived in Berlin in 1779 and caused a furor as well as some embarrassment among the Jewish intelligentsia. As his autobiography tells us,[112] Maimon had tried in vain to enter the city some three years before when, after a grueling journey via Königsberg and Stettin, he had reached the Rosenthaler Gate in a destitute and exhausted condition. His plea for admission was turned down when, lodging among the beggars at the gate, he revealed to a rabbi his plan of writing a commentary on Maimonides' *Guide of the Perplexed*. He had thereby laid himself open to the suspicion of being a freak and a dangerous person. When he returned in 1779, he did so by coach and entered the city without difficulty. But even on this occasion things were not so simple:[113]

> The Jewish police officer, L.M., came and examined me in the strictest manner. I told him that I wished to enter into service as a family tutor in Berlin, and that the length of my stay could therefore not be precisely determined. I appeared suspicious to him; he believed he had seen me before, and evidently looked on me as a comet that comes nearer earth the second time than the first and so makes the danger more threatening. But when he saw I had a *Millot Ha-Higgayon*, or Hebrew Logic composed by Maimonides and annotated by Mendelssohn . . . he went into a perfect

rage. "Yes! yes!" he exclaimed, "that's the sort of book!" He turned to me with a threatening look and said, "Pack! Out of Berlin as quick as you can, if you don't wish to be led out with an escort!" I trembled and knew not what to do; but as I had learned that there was a Polish Jew residing in Berlin for the sake of study, a man of talent, and received in the best houses, I paid him a visit.

It was through the good offices of this countryman—Isaac Satanov?— that Maimon obtained permission to stay in Berlin and soon became acquainted with people who appreciated him despite the strange jargon he spoke. He was a highly accomplished Talmudist and had acquired the rudiments of some of the sciences. In Königsberg he had astounded some young Jewish students by the ease with which he translated passages from Mendelssohn's *Phaedon* extempore into Hebrew, although, to their great amusement, he could barely pronounce the German words.[114] In Berlin, too, he provoked both amusement and admiration. He was obviously a man of genius, but nobody could foresee that in 1790 he would publish a critical evaluation of Kant's *Critique of Pure Reason* under the title *Versuch über die Transcendentalphilosophie*, about which Kant wrote to Herz that none of his opponents had understood him and the main problem so well as Herr Maimon, and that few possessed the acumen necessary for such subtle inquiries.[115] Maimon's first philosophical efforts after his arrival in Berlin were concerned with Wolff's German work on metaphysics, a copy of which he had discovered by chance in a butter shop where it was being "anatomized" to serve as wrapping paper. He bought it from the "barbarous" dealer for two groschen, and was "in raptures" at the very first reading of the book, though he could not agree with Wolff's a posteriori argument for the existence of God in accordance with the Principle of Sufficient Reason. Maimon failed to see how this principle, which was abstracted from particular cases of experience, could establish the existence of an object beyond all experience. Nor could he reconcile Wolff's metaphysical propositions with those of Maimonides (or, rather, Aristotle).

In the dilemma in which he found himself Maimon turned to Mendelssohn, about whom he "had already heard so much" but whom he had not yet dared to approach. Maimon put his doubts in writing and sent the little essay, which was in Hebrew, to Mendelssohn, who replied immediately: his doubts were indeed justified, Mendelssohn wrote, but they should not deter him from continuing his studies.[116] Encouraged by Mendelssohn's reply, Maimon wrote a metaphysical treatise (again in Hebrew) in which he expressed his doubts about the teachings of both revealed and natural religion. In his autobiography he reports:[117]

All the thirteen articles of faith laid down by Maimonides I attacked with philosophical arguments, with the exception of one, namely that on reward and punishment, to which I conceded philosophical relevance as the necessary consequence of freely willed actions. I sent this dissertation to Mendelssohn, who was quite amazed that a Polish Jew who had scarcely got so far as seeing Wolff's *Metaphysics* was so soon able to penetrate into their depths to the point of questioning their conclusions by means of a correct ontology. He invited me to call, and I accepted his invitation. But I was shy, and the manners and customs of the Berliners were strange to me, and it was with trepidation and embarrassment that I ventured to enter a fashionable house. When I opened Mendelssohn's door, and saw him and other gentlefolk there, as well as the beautiful rooms and elegant furniture, I shrank back, closed the door, and had a mind not to go in. But Mendelssohn had noticed me. He came out and spoke to me very kindly, led me into his room, placed himself beside me at the window, and paid me many compliments about my writing. He assured me that if I persisted, I should in a short time make great progress in metaphysics; and he promised to resolve my doubts. Not satisfied with this, the worthy man looked after my maintenance also, recommending me to the most eminent, enlightened, and wealthy Jews of Berlin, who made provision for my board and other wants. I was given the freedom of their tables, and their libraries were open to me.[118]

Of the members of Mendelssohn's circle who showed particular kindness toward him Maimon mentions a few by their initials. In H... we recognize Marcus Herz, in Herr A. M. Aaron Meyer (Joresch), son-in-law of Veitel Heine Ephraim, and in "the young Herr S. L. (who is still my Maecenas)" we suspect Samuel Levy, who is mentioned by Mendelssohn in a letter to Homberg.[119] Marcus Herz and Maimon had vehement discussions on all kinds of philosophical topics, which led to a happy and enduring relationship. It was Herz who recommended Maimon's *Versuch über die Transcendentalphilosophie* in 1789 to Kant.[120]

Mendelssohn himself was exceedingly kind to the somewhat exasperating genius, who was lacking in all refinements of culture and was rather undisciplined. He invited him to his home,[121] and occasionally took a stroll with him. He soon realized that Maimon was not likely to become his disciple, but this in no way affected his friendly concern for him. He tried to interest him in belles-lettres and was glad when, after some initial resistance, Maimon began to find pleasure in poetry. To his great consternation, however, the young man soon went to the extreme of also seeking less refined pleasures. According to Maimon's version of the story, some tutors of French and other secular subjects, who were jealous of his growing reputation, conspired to lead him morally astray and their plan succeeded only too well, whereupon they spread ill reports about him. Eventually, Mendelssohn asked him to come and see him, and Maimon realized that his position in Berlin had become untenable. He decided to leave the city. Mendelssohn gave him a "very favorable testimonial" as to his abilities, and he went via Hamburg to Holland, where he spent almost a year. Afterwards he stayed for about two years in Hamburg, where he became a rather irregular "pupil" at a grammar school and acquired a firmer grounding in the humanities.

After an absence of about three years Maimon suddenly reappeared in Berlin. Assuming that his first stay lasted from 1779 until the end of 1780, his return must have occurred in the early part of 1784. Mendelssohn was again faced with the problem of helping this brilliant but erratic man find the means to make a living. He discussed the matter with a few friends, who are referred to in Maimon's autobiography as Doctor B., F., I. and L., these initials standing most probably for Doctor Bloch, (David) Friedländer, (Isaac Daniel) Itzig, and (Samuel) Levy. Maimon's report of the discussion is of considerable interest. It reflects the difference of opinion among this group on the possibilities of spreading the Enlightenment to the Polish Jews, most of whom "still lived in darkness."[122]

The conferees agreed that Maimon should translate into Hebrew some important book that would bring some light to the ignorant Jews of Poland. The question remaining was which work to choose for this purpose. Herr Itzig felt that what was needed at the outset was a history of the Jewish people, and he proposed that Maimon translate Jacques-Chrétieu de Beauval Basnage's *L'histoire des Juifs* (Paris, 1710). It was decided that he should present a sample translation before any further discussion took place. The sample he produced turned out to be excellent, but then an objection was raised by Friedländer. For the purpose of enlightenment, Friedländer averred, a book on natural religion, such as Reimarus' famous treatise on the subject,[123] was preferable. Mendelssohn wisely withheld his opinion, "for he believed that whatever was undertaken in this line, though it would do no harm, would also be of little use." Since no agreement could be reached, Maimon was asked to go to Dessau, where he would soon receive instructions and carry on his work at leisure—whatever that work might be. It is obvious that his continued presence in Berlin was considered undesirable, and that Mendelssohn himself had grown tired of the burden that this man presented.

When no word reached Maimon in Dessau, he wrote to Berlin that in his view the most beneficial influence could be expected from a Hebrew work in the mathematical sciences, and that he therefore proposed to write a mathematical textbook. Friedländer, who jointly with Itzig was responsible for the printing office of the *Freyschule,* gave his consent. Within a few months Maimon finished the work and went to Berlin to present it for publication. Itzig informed him, however, that the large size of the manuscript and the required copperplates would make the production too costly, and he returned the copy to the author. In the ensuing conflict, Mendelssohn remained neutral. He sympathized with both parties and suggested only that Maimon get the book printed by subscription. He himself and others actually subscribed, but nothing came of the plan, and he could not induce his friends to pay Maimon a remuneration or to provide for his subsistence. In anger, the frustrated author left Berlin and went to Breslau, where, amid other occupations, he translated Mendelssohn's *Morgenstunden* (1785) into Hebrew.[124] When he next returned to Berlin, Mendelssohn was no longer alive.[125]

Although Maimon was hardly a member of the Mendelssohn circle—he was too independent a spirit to fit into any group—he had the highest respect for Mendelssohn, to whose memory he dedicated a special chapter in his autobiography.[126] Louder than his praise speaks the fact that he took every opportunity to follow Mendelssohn's example in defending the honor of Judaism. "I would have to write a [whole] book," he said in a rebuttal of Eisenmenger, "if I wanted to refute all the unjust recriminations and calumnies leveled against the Talmud by Christian authors and even by would-be enlightened Jews. One who has penetrated into the true spirit of the Talmud . . . will surely not find there . . . the absurdities that these gentlemen are so readily inclined to find. . . ."[127]

It is quite imaginable that without Mendelssohn's steadying influence Solomon Maimon might have strayed completely from the Jewish path. His Hebrew contributions to *Ha-Me'assef,* the organ of the German-Jewish Haskala, are further evidence of his desire to enhance the cause of Judaism. One of his essays he republished in German in the *Berlinische Monatsschrift* under the title "A Sample of Rabbinic Philosophy."[128] It starts with this sentence: "Our lamented [*seliger*] Moses Mendelssohn conceived the idea, some years ago, of presenting translations of several moral maxims and anecdotes under the title 'Samples of Rabbinic Wisdom.' I intend to imitate this useful idea with your permission. Here you have the first instalment: the translation of a passage from the Mishna, together with Maimonides' commentary and my own interpretation of the latter." As a result of this publication, in which Maimon had publicly proclaimed himself as a Jew following in Mendelssohn's footsteps, he was invited by the society responsible for the publication of *Ha-Me'assef* to write a commentary on Maimonides' *Guide of the Perplexed* in Hebrew. He accepted this task and produced the outstanding commentary *Giv'at Ha-More.*[129] Belatedly, Maimon had become a member of the group that formed the vanguard of Haskala.

Two more members of Mendelssohn's circle should be mentioned here: Joel Brill Loewe and Isaac Abraham Euchel. Both commenced their activity not long after the "meteor," Maimon, had hit Berlin in 1779.

Joel Brill Loewe (Joel ben Rabbi Jehuda Leb Levi, 1762–1802) was born in Berlin and even in early childhood displayed a love for Hebrew studies. In 1782, at the age of twenty, he became a tutor in David Friedländer's house and thereby joined the group around Mendelssohn. In 1785 he published the first volume of *Sefer Zemirot Yisra'el,* an edition of the Hebrew text of Psalms with Mendelssohn's German translation (in Hebrew characters), Sforno's introduction and commentary, and a short additional commentary *(Bi'ur)* by himself. On March 6, 1784, Mendelssohn mentioned this edition (referring to Loewe as "a young man," without naming him) in a letter to Rabbi Moses Fischer in Vienna, as about to appear.[130] The work was printed by the *Freyschule* and came out in four volumes (1785, 1786, 1788, 1790). Volume two is prefaced by a Hebrew poem in which the enthusiastic Loewe paid a glowing tribute to his teachers. When he was still a "small and tender child of nine" they had taken care of both his bodily and intellectual needs. In his estimation they deserved his gratitude even more than his parents. Loewe also edited other books of the Bible with a *Bi'ur* and he became one of the editors of *Ha-Me'assef* when Euchel took charge of the printing office of the *Freyschule* in Berlin. In 1891 Loewe was appointed director of the Royal Wilhelm-School in Breslau, and two years later the title of "Royal Prussian Professor" was conferred upon him. He lectured on Kant, but at heart he remained a disciple of Mendelssohn. In 1794 Loewe published *'Amudey Ha-Lashon,* the first part of a Hebrew grammar based on Mendelssohn's idea that linguistic studies should be connected with logic *(Vernunftlehre).*[131]

Isaac Abraham Euchel, a close friend of Loewe, also seems to have grown up in Berlin, though his birthplace was undoubtedly Copenhagen. In his "Letter to Joel Brill, my intimate friend who is like a brother to me," which precedes his magnum opus (his Mendelssohn biography), Euchel recalled the admiration, if not envy, he felt when watching the friend's steadfastness in study when still a boy, while he himself preferred to roam the streets and idle his days away. "It is now fifteen years," he wrote in this letter, which is dated Berlin, 1788, "since I went out from here at the age of seventeen to wander around and sojourn in a strange land without knowing what my future would be like." According to this precise information, he must have been born in 1756. If Loewe was born in 1762, the two could hardly have been "brothers from youth on," as Euchel says in the letter, especially if he left Berlin at the age of seventeen when Loewe was only a lad of eleven. However, the testimony of friendship leaves no doubt that they were roughly of the same age.

Euchel seems to have passed through difficult times before summoning up the courage to change the pattern of his life. In the letter, he rejoiced at his having entered the fold of scholarship in Hebrew and secular studies. We know that he settled in Königsberg and became a student of Kant, who proposed him as a lecturer in Hebrew at the university. He was rejected because of his being a Jew and subsequently became a tutor of David Friedländer's nephew Michael Friedländer, who would qualify as a physician and write a book *De l'éducation physique de l'homme* (Paris, 1815).

The great moment in Euchel's life came when, together with Menachem Mendel Breslau and others, he founded the "Society of the Friends of the Hebrew Tongue" *(Hevrat Doreshey Leshon 'Ever)* in 1783. A prospectus entitled *Nahal Ha-Besor* (I Samuel 30) announced the news *(besora;* a pun on *Besor,* the name of a river) that a Hebrew monthly called *Ha-Me'assef* ("The Collector") was to be published. The first issue appeared in 1784.

In the same year Euchel undertook a trip to Copenhagen and other places, including Berlin, in the company of the ladies Friedländer. The Hebrew letters he sent to his pupil Michael during this journey, which make delightful reading, were meant to prove to the boy that even the most trivial matters could be expressed in the Hebrew language. The purpose of the trip, Euchel explained, was "to pay honor to my father's house and to show love to my relatives," as well as to study the conditions of

Jews in various localities. The letters were published in *Ha-Me'assef*.[132] On their way to Copenhagen, the party spent some time in Berlin, where Euchel was no doubt a frequent guest in Mendelssohn's house. The animated debate between Euchel and Wessely, described in David Fried-länder's "second fragment" of reminiscences of the master, reflected the widening gulf between the conservative and the more radical wings of the Berlin Haskala. The debate could only have taken place when Euchel was visiting Berlin on his way to Copenhagen. Friedländer reports:[133]

> One day a venerable old man joined the unusually large evening party. He was a friend of the family, though a zealous supernaturalist. He was an excellent poet and happened to be occupied with a commentary on the Genesis story in Hebrew,[134] and being deeply immersed in the subject, he spoke with great eloquence. This scholar, whose name was W[essely], was attacked by another man of younger age E[uchel], a great admirer of Mendelssohn, who took pride in calling himself his disciple. He [Euchel] started arguing with him [Wessely] in lively fashion, and the difference between their respective viewpoints did not seem to permit any reconciliation. Mendelssohn was sitting quietly on his chair with downcast eyes, keeping silent.

The "lively" debate does not seem to have produced any ill feeling between the two adversaries, for on June 1, 1784, probably a few days after the encounter, Wessely wrote a most cordial inscription in Euchel's album.[135]

On June 15, 1784, Mendelssohn wrote the following letter of recommendation on Euchel's behalf to two of his own relatives in Copenhagen, his brother-in-law Joseph Gugenheim and Moses Fürst, the husband of one of Fromet's sisters:[136]

> Dearest and faithful brothers, If I recommend some one to you, be assured that he is not a man who wants to rob you of your money or your good name; nor one who wants to be master in your house or in your kitchen, in your wine cellar (in case you have one) or in your bedroom; nor one who offers you a Hebrew book that you don't need, and in return takes from you money that you do need. I recommend a man who wishes to find your door, not your purse, open at all times; who at most will cost you a little time, which in any case one is in the habit of wasting, and which in this instance is anything but lost. For his conversations are so useful and instructive that they doubly compensate for the loss. Such a man is Rabbi Itzig Euchel, who will hand you this *billet* or this pastoral letter or this cabinet order from your good brother Moses of Dessau.

When writing this delightful letter of recommendation, Mendelssohn was obviously in one of those relaxed and happy moods that came to him naturally when he felt himself to be in congenial company. Euchel must have sensed that, although he resided in Königsberg, he had been fully accepted into the elite of Mendelssohn's intimate friends. The words that Isaac Satanov wrote into Euchel's album were true also of Mendelssohn's feelings for him: "For a fleeting moment we met in love, my brother, yet very quickly we parted in great affection, for nearness and separation were riding as a pair, like sun and moon, which meet and move from each other."[137]

Finally, mention must be made of two pre-Haskala Maskilim with whom Mendelssohn was in touch only by correspondence: Jehuda ben Mordecai Ha-Levi Hurwitz, "physician of the holy community of Vilna" (as he called himself),[138] and Avigdor Levi of Glogau.

Hurwitz, who was not only a medical practitioner and writer on medicine but also a philosophical author, poet, and translator, had asked Mendelssohn to forward to Hartog Leo the manuscript of a treatise of his entitled *'Amudey Bet Yehuda,* a moralistic work modeled on al-Harizi's *Tahkemoni.* He was no doubt anxious to receive Mendelssohn's appraisal of his work and must have been pleased to read his acknowledgment:[139] "Every man of understanding [*Maskil*] possessed of the fear of the Lord and free from hypocrisy and deceit will find joy in your book. He will admit that most of its words are 'overlaid with sapphire,'[140] polished by wisdom,[141] and 'set with beryl'[142] of virtues. 'The inside thereof is inlaid with love,'[143] the true love of the Law, and with the glory of the Tora and the commandments. If the sages of our time will but consider the decline of wisdom and virtue among us, they undoubtedly will give their support and approbation to the printing of this work in order that our children may learn to know wisdom, moral instruction, and the fear of the Lord 'without being of double heart.' "[144] Hurwitz inserted Mendelssohn's letter in the preface of his book, which was published in Amsterdam in 1766. He introduced it with these words:[145] "I will present to you that which was 'written uprightly'[146] by the scholar and prince, the head of the pious among the philosophers and faithful disciple of the Sages [of Israel], political philosopher, astronomer [sic!], logician, who is versed in the Tora, in rabbinic learning and law, etc., our teacher and master, Moses of Dessau, may his light shine."

A brisk and colorful correspondence developed between Mendelssohn and Avigdor Levi of Glogau, who had spent six years (1762–1768) as a private tutor in Berlin but, being very shy, had met Mendelssohn on only a few occasions. From Prague, where he settled as a teacher, he wrote Mendelssohn a letter in 1769, followed by another in 1770, which included a rhymed Hebrew riddle of the genre customary in that period, and also a Hebrew elegy for the Prague scholar Meir Fischels. Replying on March 30, 1770, Mendelssohn explained the long delay as due to his preoccupation with the Lavater controversy. He had words of praise for the elegy but confessed his inability to solve the riddle: he had never cultivated this kind of writing and had always tried to express his thoughts as clearly as possible.[147]

The next letter Mendelssohn received from Avigdor Levi was written in the jail of Pirna, where the unfortunate man had been detained without trial for ten months on a trumped-up charge of theft. Beginning with a rhymed Hebrew eulogy of Mendelssohn, the letter went on to relate

Levi's experience as a man falsely accused but who had been morally sustained by a Christian minister's visits; happily, the clergyman knew Hebrew and was an admirer of Mendelssohn. Levi's main solace, however, had been the study of medieval Jewish philosophy. In conclusion, he asked Mendelssohn to explain a difficult passage in Jehuda Ha-Levi's *Kuzari* (IV, 1).[148] Immediately upon receipt of this letter Mendelssohn replied (on January 13, 1774) in German but using Hebrew characters, guessing correctly that the letter would pass through the censor of the prison and prove helpful to the addressee. He expressed his confidence in the final triumph of justice, promised assistance to the prisoner's family, and offered a learned exposition of the difficult passage.[149] Levi was released when the judicial authorities realized that he enjoyed the personal esteem of the famous Berlin philosopher.

Levi remained in contact with Mendelssohn and kept him abreast of events in Prague when the announcement of the new Pentateuch translation and its subsequent publication aroused opposition.[150] A marked cooling-off in Mendelssohn's friendship for Levi was caused by some impious remark he had permitted himself in the preface to his *Davar Tov,* a book on Hebrew grammar (Prague, 1783). In a letter dated September 30, 1783, Mendelssohn admitted that his feelings toward him had changed when he noticed how they differed in their principles:[151] "You express and print certain comments on passages in Holy Scripture [*be-divrey kodesh*] that you know to be false, and you speak on a variety of things against your better knowledge. All this hurts me, and although I can imagine a situation in which all this might be consistent with the duties of an upright and honest heart, I have my reasons for avoiding all semblance of approval." When Levi retracted his statements, Mendelssohn resumed the warm relationship of former days. He found words of praise for the expertise and fine sensitivity that Levi had shown in commenting on his Psalms translation (1783).[152]

The German Translation of the Pentateuch

We do not know exactly when Mendelssohn commenced his German translation of the Five Books of the Tora. When he started to translate the Book of Psalms, in April, 1770, Karl Lessing recorded the fact in a letter to his brother,[1] and there are references to the work and the problems encountered in Mendelssohn's correspondence with Michaelis and Zimmermann.[2] But no reporter was present when he began to produce his German version of the Pentateuch, a translation destined to become a landmark in the history of the Jews in modern times. Nor did the progress of his work leave any traces in the letters he wrote at the time. It appears that Mendelssohn kept the matter secret until he considered it ripe for disclosure.

Mendelssohn probably started the translation in about 1774, when his son Mendel was five years of age, for the introduction, *Or Li-Netiva*

(1782), to his edition of the Pentateuch contains the following account:[3] "When God in his grace gave me sons and the time arrived to teach them Tora and to instruct them diligently in the words of the living God, as Scripture bids us do,[4] I took it upon myself to translate the Five Books of the Tora into decorous and refined German such as that spoken in our time, and I did this for the benefit of the children. I put the translation into their mouth when teaching them the [Hebrew] text, rendering it sometimes word by word, sometimes according to its meaning[5] or according to the context,[6] so as to introduce them to the intent of Scripture, its idiomatic figures of speech, and the fine points of its teaching, all in the hope that as they grew older they would by themselves achieve the right understanding." There follows the passage about Solomon Dubno's appointment as Joseph's teacher, which has already been quoted.[7]

The appointment must have been made sometime between September, 1775, when the elder son Mendel died at the age of six, and December, 1776, when Abraham was born.[8] Prior to September, 1775, Mendelssohn himself had tutored Mendel and Joseph, and since Dubno's task was confined to teaching Hebrew grammar, he continued to give Joseph lessons in the Pentateuch in the way just described (i.e., using his German translation). This is clearly stated in the partly identical account of the genesis of the translation given by Mendelssohn in a letter to Avigdor Levi on May 25, 1779.[9] Thus we have his own testimony that he put his German translation "into the mouth" of his sons Mendel and Joseph when the one was six years old and the other five. Mendel's lessons had probably started when he was five, in 1774. We may conclude, therefore, that work on the Tora translation was commenced in that year.

As Mendelssohn saw it, there was a pressing need to provide a German version of the Tora for use of the younger generation. He described the prevailing situation both in the prospectus, *'Alim Li-Terufa* (1778),[10] which was largely his work (though signed by Dubno),[11] and in the introduction, *Or Li-Netiva*.[12]

The passage in the Hebrew prospectus reads: " . . . We, God's people, who are dispersed in all the lands of Greater Germany and grew up under the impact of the language of the dominant peoples, 'came down wonderfully' and there is 'none raising us up.'[13] For the ways of our holy tongue have been forgotten in our midst; the elegance of its phraseology [*tsahut melitsoteha*] eludes us; and the loveliness of its poetry is hidden from our eyes. No one takes care to render our Tora in the German tongue as spoken today among our own people. True, the books of the Bible have been translated into German by Yekutiel ben Isaac Blitz of Witmund (printed in Amsterdam, 1679) but the translator, though motivated by good intentions, did a poor job, for not only was he ignorant of Hebrew, he did not know German either, and so 'with stammering lips did he speak to his people.'[14] In his preface he [Blitz] mentioned that he had seen the German version of the Tora by the famed grammarian Rabbi Elija Bahur Ashkenazi[15] . . . and he heaped abuse on this translation, declaring it unfit for use. He went so far as to deny that it had been produced by the Ashkenazic grammarian. I myself have not come across it, for it is not extant in this part of the world." A parallel passage in *Or Li-Netiva* makes the same statement in less poetical language and puts yet another Judeo-German Bible on the list, viz. the one by Josel Witzenhausen (Amsterdam, 1678–1687). Though Mendelssohn passed no judgment on this work (which was eventually incorporated in the *Biblia Pentapla* [Wandsbeck, 1711]), he was obviously not satisfied with it.

In support of his claim that a new translation was called for, Mendelssohn might have quoted the words of a fellow Jew of Berlin, Jehuda Leb ben Joel Minden, who had published in 1760 a lexicographical work, *Sefer Millim Le-'Eloah* ("The Book of Words on God's Behalf"), which carried a warm approbation *(haskama)* from Chief Rabbi David Fränkel and his Beth Din.[16] In his preface Minden had written: "I have heard the complaints of many of our people who voiced dissatisfaction with the teachers of Scripture by saying of them that they caused Jewish children to stumble 'before knowing [enough] to refuse the evil and choose the good'[17] [viz. they put confusing notions into their heads at an early age]. The reason given was that they sought to explain the Tora of Moses, the 'man of God,' and the book of the Prophets in German, but they understood neither the ways of the holy tongue and the elegance of its phraseology nor the grandeur of its resplendent beauty, which excels that of the language of the Gentiles into which they translate the word of God and the vision of his prophets. [In rendering the texts] they rely on 'a staff of reed,'[18] i.e. on the authors of [such Hebrew–German dictionaries as] *Melammed Siah*[19] and *Be'er Moshe*[20] as well as on other translators. Yet who does not know that these authors frequently erred in their interpretation of Scripture and that, to make things worse, they spoiled the beauty of the words of our Tora by [rendering them in] a clumsy kind of German remote from the language of the Gentiles that is in use among us?"

Here it is clearly stated that German Jews—that is, the educated upper classes—spoke German and wanted their children to study the Hebrew text of Scripture with the help of an adequate German translation. The complaint that "many" people lodged against the general run of teachers, according to Minden, was a twofold one: the teachers were said to be deficient in their knowledge of Hebrew and also in their knowledge of German. The phrase "the ways of the holy tongue and the elegance of its phraseology," found in Minden's preface of 1760, reoccurs literally in Mendelssohn's prospectus of 1778. Minden considered a proper German translation not as an end in itself but as an indispensable tool for teaching the Hebrew text. Mendelssohn held exactly the same view. In translating the Tora for the benefit of the young he responded to Minden's request, which had met with the whole-hearted approval of Mendelssohn's late teacher, Rabbi Fränkel. However, the pedagogical objective was only part of a larger and more far-reaching cultural program whose roots can already be discerned in his youthful *Kohelet Mussar* project.

According to the account given in Mendelssohn's letter to Avigdor Levi,[21] which reappeared with only slight variations in *Or Li-Netiva*,[22] Mendelssohn might not have committed his Pentateuch translation to print had not Solomon Dubno urged him to do so. The passage in *Or Li-Netiva* reads: "When the afore-mentioned rabbi [Dubno] saw the Tora translation in my hands, he liked it and found it useful. He therefore asked for my permission to have it printed for the benefit of students who, by the grace of God, were able to appreciate poetic language.[23] I consented [to his proposal] on condition that [in a commentary to be written by him] he carefully point out where in my translation I had decided to follow the view of some earlier commentator and where I had departed from all previously expressed views and had chosen a different interpretation that seemed to me to be more in accord with the ways of the [Hebrew] language, as well as with the context and the massoretic marks of intonation. He was to examine all these points, argue with me [if necessary],[24] and embody all this in a book explaining the verses [of the Pentateuch] in language readily comprehensible to the reader.[25] At the same time, I faithfully promised to help him to the best of my ability in the composition and writing of this commentary [*Bi'ur*]."[26]

According to this report, it was Dubno who took the initiative in editing Mendelssohn's translation. The letter written to Hennings on June 29, 1779 (see above, p. 344) does not contradict the story as presented to Avigdor Levi, and as repeated in the introduction, but adds another perspective. Having lost the ability to meditate, Mendelssohn told Hennings, he found that what remained of his strength might be sufficient to render useful service to his children, and perhaps to a considerable part of his nation, by supplying them with a better translation and interpretation of Scripture than they had had before. According to this account, his translation was meant from the very start to be published. Moreover, it was to be the "first step toward culture, from which my nation is, alas, kept at such a distance that one might almost despair of the possibility of an improvement." Yet he considered himself obliged, he said, to do what lay in his power, leaving the rest to Providence, which as a rule took its time in implementing its designs.

If Mendelssohn did indeed consider his translation as conforming to a providential scheme for the cultural improvement of the Jewish people, it is not surprising that in his letter to Avigdor Levi and in *Or Li–Netiva* he described Dubno's appearance on the scene as an act of God: "The Lord sent me [*hikrah le-fanay*] our teacher and master, Rabbi Solomon of Dubno ... to teach my son."[27] The providential character of Dubno's arrival in Berlin obviously did not relate to the fact that in him Mendelssohn had found a teacher of Hebrew grammar for his little son; it was clearly understood to have been revealed in the immediate sequel to the story, namely, in Dubno's request for permission to publish the translation and in the subsequent arrangement that gave birth to the *Bi'ur*. The theme of Providence thus plays a part in both versions of the story, the German and the Hebrew one, and may be said to serve as a link between them.

What actually happened may be described as follows. To start with, the need to teach Tora to his sons led Mendelssohn to translate selected passages. He found pleasure in the work and it occurred to him that a German version of the entire Pentateuch, if not of the Bible as a whole, would be very much in the interest of a growing sector of Jewish youth. Therefore, he applied himself vigorously to this task. After a time he came to realize that a bare translation without a commentary would not do. Only a combination of translation and commentary could open up and articulate the full meaning and beauty of the Hebrew text. To awaken in the more refined young people an awareness of the moral and aesthetic values of the Bible was in his view tantamount to a cultural rebirth. By "culture" he did not mean "enlightenment" in the purely intellectual sense; he meant moral and aesthetic refinement.[28] Hennings, the all-out *Aufklärer*, may have wondered what Mendelssohn could mean when he characterized a new Bible translation as "the first step toward culture" among the Jews. Hennings and the Reimarus circle were convinced that reason had to be established in place of the Bible, and they were far from happy with Mendelssohn's biblicism.[29]

What Mendelssohn had in mind, but conveyed neither to Hennings nor to Avigdor Levi, was an educational program aimed at a renascence of the biblical spirit and its broad humanism in the way in which the Haskala movement would conceive it. In his view, two things were required as the first step toward this goal: a new translation and a new commentary. The revolutionary character of this seemingly retrogressive project was well understood by its orthodox opponents as soon as it was launched, while Hartwig Wessely, the pious and tradition-bound Maskil, gave it an enthusiastic welcome. By the time of Dubno's appointment as a tutor to his son Joseph, Mendelssohn had completed a sizeable part (if not the whole) of his Pentateuch translation; what was still missing was the commentary. He could hardly envisage the possibility of coping single-handedly with an additional task of such magnitude, and Dubno's arrival must therefore have appeared to him as part of a providential design. When he showed his translation to this outstanding biblical and rabbinic scholar, he most probably did so in the hope of eliciting a response that would lead to some form of cooperation. Not knowing in advance how Dubno would respond to his German translation, he had to act in a circumspect manner. Dubno's reaction, happily, could not have been more forthcoming, for his request for permission to publish the translation gave Mendelssohn the opportunity to ask him to write the *Bi'ur*.

It is not quite clear whether the inclusion of textual (massoretic) notes by Dubno was discussed at the initial stage or arose as an afterthought at some later time, The report to Avigdor Levi[30] and the introduction[31] seem to suggest that the latter was the case: Dubno "added"—we are told —to his commentary and "placed at its side" his work *Tikkun Soferim*, which was "very useful" to students of Massora and grammar but not really essential to the purpose of the edition. Since Dubno was a specialist in massoretic studies and would have been disappointed had the common enterprise shown itself inhospitable to this particular concern, Mendelssohn had little option in the matter.

As we gather from Mendelssohn's account, only one more thing had been arranged from the outset: "I stipulated yet another condition: He [Dubno] was to make my learned brother, our teacher and master Rabbi Saul (may his light shine forth), his associate in the supervision of the printing and in proofreading. The two men were to receive the same fee for their labors. They could also look forward to the reward [in the next world] that is 'stored up' for those who do what is good and right in the eyes of the Lord, since they were to 'magnify the Tora and increase its honor,' and since they were to keep the minds of the children of 'the house of Israel' away from the translations[32] with which they had supplied themselves hitherto."

It was also understood as part of the initial arrangement that Dubno would figure as the editor of the work:[33] "It never occurred to me, nor did I ever expect, to reap either material benefit or honor from this enterprise. I did not even want my name to be associated with it, and I gave my consent to it [viz. the use of his name] only when Rabbi Solomon Dubno asked for my permission to do so in order thereby to attract more subscribers." Mendelssohn, who was fully conscious of the opposition the work was likely to incur among the orthodox, obviously wished to calm any rising fears by launching the venture under the flag of Dubno, whose orthodoxy had never been questioned even by the most orthodox.

In actual fact, however, Mendelssohn was not only the moving spirit but also the chief editor and contributor to the commentary, and even the publisher, of the work. He decided to raise the money required to defray the cost of production by inviting the public to subscribe to the project, and he organized the collection of the amounts due, all of which were payable in advance. He appointed agents in all the larger Jewish population centers, and the response was encouraging. About eight hundred people, Jews and also non-Jews, in many parts of Europe sent in their subscriptions. (In the end, however, a deficit in the amount of a thousand thalers had to be met out of Mendelssohn's private purse.)[34] His principal administrative assistants were Jeremias Bendit, Jr. and David Friedländer, each of whom received honorable mention in the introduction. Of the first he wrote:[35] "I found a friend close to me like a brother in the wealthy and learned Jeremias Bendit, a respected member of this [Berlin] community and one of the overseers of aid to the needy. He proved to be a tower of strength in supervising those engaged in the work,[36] in examining expense accounts and receipts, and even in the distribution of the copies to the subscribers. These tasks, in which I lacked experience, required much zeal and energy." In fact, Mendelssohn showed himself remarkably astute in handling matters of this kind, and he often attended personally to minute details of an administrative nature.[37] Of David Friedländer, Mendelssohn wrote in the introduction that he had been his "first and foremost helper and supporter" and that he had been active in enrolling subscribers through his influential brothers in Königsberg.[38]

Exceptional care was exercised in the preparing and printing of the prospectus announcing the projected edition of the Pentateuch and inviting interested persons to subscribe to it. As Mendelssohn confessed in a letter to Avigdor Levi, written in the summer or early fall of 1781,[39] he had realized from the start that his enterprise would run into trouble: "As soon as I had permitted Rabbi Solomon [Dubno] to publish my translation, 'I put my life in my hand,' 'I lifted up mine eyes unto the mountains,' and 'I gave my back to the smiters.'[40] Alas, I knew how much opposition, hatred, persecution, etc. is engendered among the public by the least innovation, no matter how important the improvement it seeks to foster."

The employment of pure and refined German, albeit in Hebrew characters, in translating the Tora was an innovation, of course, and as such it seemed strange and alarming to strict traditionalists who knew only Hebrew and Yiddish. The rendition of the Tetragrammaton, the holiest name of God, as "the Eternal One" (*der Ewige*) had an alien ring. The printing of the German version side by side with the Hebrew text seemed an intrusion of the profane into the realm of the sacred. It was all the more necessary to show in the prospectus that there was nothing heterodox in either the translation or the Hebrew commentary. To this end a few specimen chapters of the projected edition were presented, along with an elaborate introductory essay outlining the character of the work. At the same time, no attempt was made to play down the novelty of the undertaking. The very title given the prospectus clearly indicated that the work about to be published was meant to remedy a sad state of affairs; it read: *'Alim Li-Terufa* ("Leaves for Healing").[41] The introduction emphasized the role of Hebrew as the only authentic language of the Jewish people and lamented the fact that, as a result of exile after exile it had to yield to foreign languages (Aramaic, Greek, Arabic, etc.). Again and again the Bible had to be translated into the language of the environment so as to make the Hebrew text intelligible to the masses of the people. In their own time the few available Judeo-German translations were utterly deficient. The question arose, therefore:[42] "How are we to deal with Jewish children 'running to and fro to seek the word of the Lord'[43] and desiring to understand the Scriptures and to taste the savor of its poetic style in a language with which they are familiar, who find nothing [wherewith to satisfy their desire]?"

The specter of Jewish youth being sorely tempted to use Christian Bible translations is raised in an obvious attempt to justify the presentation of this new version of the Pentateuch: "In their narrow straits they 'turn to vainglory and alluring deception,'[44] that 'changes into wormwood'[45] the Law of our God. They supply themselves with the works of the Gentiles,[46] using the translations of non-Jewish scholars who disdain the trusted interpretations of our sages of blessed memory and who refuse to accept their unblemished tradition, while interpreting Scripture according to their own fancy and spoiling the vineyard of the Lord of hosts." The allusion is of course to both christological and "critical" exegesis. Having painted a somewhat lurid picture of the contemporary situation, the account, which bore Dubno's signature, continued: "All this has been taken to heart by the famous scholar Moses of Dessau, our teacher, may the Merciful One preserve and redeem him. He observed and understood [the prevailing situation], and he took mercy on his people. He bestowed his care upon a translation of the Five Books of the Tora into the most splendid and yet simple and clear German. This translation pays attention to grammar, considers every word in its context, and heeds the massoretic signs which, as has been pointed out by Rabbi Abraham ibn Ezra, are of great importance for the interpretation of Scripture."

The principal authorities consulted by the translator were said to have been the classical commentators who belonged to the French and Spanish schools of the "literalists" (*pashtanim*), and the reader was advised not to expect traces of homiletical, allegorical, or mystical exegesis in the new translation. It was stated plainly that whenever a novel interpretation had the advantage of suiting both the context and the massoretic signs it had been incorporated in the new translation even though it was unsupported by any authority. (As has been noted above, Dubno's commentary was to signal such departures from earlier exegetical views.) Fidelity to the text and to the massoretic directives was thus spelled out as the overriding concern of the new version.

The translation was not an end in itself but was meant to facilitate a proper understanding of the biblical text. Hence the translator had been careful not to copy the imagery and syntactic form of the Hebrew original but to use idiomatic German phraseology and sentence structure. Only in this way could the true intent of the text be conveyed to the German reader. To illustrate this point Dubno discussed at some length certain semantic differences between German and Hebrew. Finally he referred to the instructions he had received concerning the writing of the commentary[47] and the nature of his massoretic notes (*Tikkun Soferim*), which were based on three outstanding works: Me'ir Ha-Levi Abulafia's *Massoret Seyag La-Tora*,[48] Menahem di Lonzano's *Or Tora*,[49] and Yedidya Solomon Norzi's

Minhat Shay.[50] He acknowledged also his indebtedness to Mendelssohn for having put at his disposal a Bible manuscript of 1689, which contained valuable massoretic notes.[51]

Many points made in the introduction to the prospectus were later elaborated in Mendelssohn's *Or Li-Netiva,* and there can be no doubt that Dubno's share in the initial essay was confined more or less to its literary form.[52] In addition to the essay, the prospectus contained thirty specimen pages of text (Exodus 1 and Numbers 23–24), with Mendelssohn's German translation in Hebrew letters, and Dubno's *Bi'ur* as well as *Tikkun Soferim.* These would enable the public to judge the quality and merit of the work and would demonstrate that the new edition of the Tora, notwithstanding its innovatory character, was thoroughly imbued with the traditional reverence for the Pentateuch as God's gift to Israel through Moses. In particular, the critical approach, which was then gaining momentum in biblical scholarship, had not been allowed to intrude into what was meant to be a work of unquestioned piety, a work destined to take its rightful place alongside the well-established versions and commentaries of old.

The traditional flavor would have been spoiled by the slightest explicit reference to the documentary hypothesis and proposed textual emendations. Yet Mendelssohn was well aware of the problems raised by critical scholarship, and the principles that he followed in his translation were designed to meet them without resorting to solutions contrary to the assumption of the unitary origin of the Tora.[53] But the rank and file of the Jewish community, including the rabbis, untroubled as they were by biblical criticism, could hardly appreciate a traditional stance that was taken for granted; they were more likely to be struck by the novelty of the work than by its loyalty to accepted standards. Hence the prospectus, though signed by Dubno, was unlikely to allay their misgivings and fears. Mendelssohn was enough of a realist to foresee the reaction to this enterprise and he felt it all the more incumbent upon him to present the work in the most favorable light.

The third and final section of the pamphlet *'Alim Li-Terufa* had no apparent connection with the announcement of the Pentateuch translation. It contained the Hebrew text of Jehuda Ha-Levi's moving elegy "Zion, dost thou not ask for the peace of thy captives?," with an introduction and notes, accompanied by Mendelssohn's German translation, which had been published many years before by Müchler,[54] and which now reappeared in Hebrew characters. This gratuitous appendix was nothing unusual in itself: it was customary with Jewish authors not to leave unused any redundant space on the last sheet of a book. Yet in this case there was symbolic meaning in the choice of this text, which bewails the Jewish people's exile and estrangement from the Holy Land. Precisely at the moment when Mendelssohn was seeking to legitimize yet another foreign tongue within the orbit of Judaism he reminded his nation of Zion and struck a chord of lament over its past glory. By reciting Ha-Levi's poem he reminded his readers not only of the land but also of the language that had been lost as a living tongue; his translation was intended to bring home to them the poignant beauty of Hebrew. Inclusion of the elegy *Tsiyyon ha-lo' tish'ali* in the prospectus heralding a German Tora translation thus had a deep significance: it reaffirmed Hebrew as the authentic language of the Jew and designated the German version about to be published as a necessary makeshift and nothing more. This gesture gave the lie to any suspicion that Mendelssohn's translation was designed to dislodge the study of Hebrew in favor of German.

The planning of the prospectus was done with loving care. The printing was entrusted to Abraham Proops of Amsterdam, then the head of the leading Hebrew printing house of the eighteenth century. In 1773 Joseph Proops had published a new edition of the Tora, with Rashi's commentary and the old Spanish translation that had first appeared in Constantinople (1552). Mendelssohn was greatly impressed by this edition. It was, he remarked,[55] the ultimate in perfection of craftsmanship, and he knew no other Hebrew book that could compare with it. Small wonder that he chose this firm for the production of his prospectus. The way the work was done fully met his expectations. The title page was in itself a little masterpiece, displaying nine different Hebrew type faces printed in black and red. Each of the four sections making up the text was printed in different type.[56] The prospectus appeared in the summer of 1778 and it carried the announcement that the typesetting of the Pentateuch would commence following the Sukkot festival.[57]

The handsome pamphlet created quite a sensation. Mendelssohn's friends and admirers rallied to his support by ordering the set, which, it was hoped, would be completed over the next few years. The largest number of subscribers came from Berlin (one hundred twenty-four), Copenhagen (fifty-nine), Frankfurt am Main (forty-nine) and Königsberg (forty-eight). Some wealthy individuals ordered up to twenty copies to bolster the enterprise. Austria and Bohemia presented fifty-seven subscribers, Poland, Lithuania, and Russia fifty-five altogether. Johann Friedrich Hartknoch, Kant's publisher and bookseller in Riga, ordered six copies for sale among Jews.[58] There were some anonymous supporters and an appreciable number of non-Jewish subscribers.[59] This was a fairly good response, considering the disfavor and opposition that the project had to face either openly or clandestinely. It has also to be borne in mind that the major part of Jewry in central Europe was incapable of understanding, let alone appreciating, the German translation. The situation was well described by Johann Christoph Doederlein, the editor of the *Theologische Bibliothek*, in a review of the prospectus:[60] "We doubt that the author will find many people among his coreligionists in Germany who understand his German. We showed the sample [of the translation] to several Jews of considerable learning. They had difficulty reading the German and making sense of it. As yet only a few are sufficiently advanced in the humanities [*an Geist, Genie und Sprache*] to derive pleasure and benefit from reading good and polished translations."

Ironically enough, the anonymous reviewer of volume one of Mendelssohn's Pentateuch in the *Allgemeine deutsche Bibliothek*,[61] though praising the translation, declared it not to be of such purity (*nicht so rein deutsch*) as might have been expected, and Mendelssohn felt rather piqued by this remark.[62] It is not known how he reacted to the point made by Doederlein, but he could have replied that his work was addressed to the needs of the rising generation rather than of the old one. Little did he know that it was precisely his concern with the young that alarmed the rabbinic guardians of the tradition. The Maskilim, on the other hand, greeted his prospectus as the dawn of a long overdue educational reform.

The hopes of the Maskilim found enthusiastic expression in Hartwig Wessely's *Mahalal Re'a* ("In Praise of a Friend"), an essay combined with a poem, which hailed Mendelssohn's objective.[63] The essay said in prose what the truly magnificent poem expressed in a rapturous outburst: Hebrew as a spoken language had vanished like the holy vessels of the Temple when the Romans destroyed it. When the Jewish nation adopted foreign tongues, it became increasingly alienated from the true understanding of the Scriptures. The prevalent system of Jewish education was utterly wrong, since it treated the study of the Hebrew language and of the Scriptures as of no importance compared with that of the Talmud. The minds of the young were burdened with highly sophisticated interpretations of the biblical texts before they had learned to grasp the rules of the language and the literal meaning of Scripture itself, in all its clarity and beauty. This defect in educational method was due largely to the teachers' inability to convey the exact meaning of the scriptural texts in precise and impressive language. "For we, who dwell in Germany and Poland, fail to speak the German language in proper fashion. Every one has his own way of speech, as it were." Mendelssohn's translation would, at long last, cure this malaise.

The poem following this discourse opened with a paean to the Tora, in which many biblical, midrashic, and philosophical motifs were intertwined:

Fiery Law,[64] Eternal Splendor, thou illuminest darkness;
High above God's heavens thou art enthroned,[65]
And from the light of thy garment radiance went forth to the lower
    regions.[66]
From the well of thy wisdom the pure-hearted draw inspiration.
They love the purity of thy righteousness above all wealth.[67]
Thou art the Law of the living God,[68] thou art the life of every
    spirit.

In the thirteen stanzas that follow the fate of the Tora and the decline of the Jewish spirit are movingly described. In bygone ages, the poet tells us, the teachers of Israel planted the seed of Tora in the hearts of the young by articulating its poetry in clear language. Now the seed falls on stony ground because no one speaks in compelling, soul-stirring terms. If the "ladder of wisdom"[69] is to reach heavenward, it must rise from the knowledge of Hebrew. Yet ever since we were exiled from the Holy City we have been bereft of vision and wisdom because we have abandoned the holy tongue and there is, at present, no language that we master. This lamentable state of affairs will be remedied by Mendelssohn's accomplishment. Moses will lead his flock to the well that he himself has dug. Now the children of Israel will apply themselves to the study of Hebrew.

Far from regarding the German translation as a threat to Hebrew studies, Wessely, who fully understood Mendelssohn's intentions, saw the translation as a help in the revival of Hebrew. As the elder statesman of the growing Haskala, which was bent upon the rebirth of classical Hebrew, he felt in complete accord with Mendelssohn. No one was more conscious of the historical significance of the new Bible project than he was, and no one was more anxious to translate its vision into reality. His "ladder of wisdom," i.e. the gradual ascent in Hebrew learning by a methodical progress, foreshadowed the educational program that he would adumbrate in his fiercely contested *Divrey Shalom Ve-Emmet* (1782).

In Berlin, Mendelssohn enjoyed not only the acclamation of his project by the Maskilim but also the support of the chief rabbi, Hirschel Lewin (1721–1800), who had become an admirer of his when still rabbi of Halberstadt (1764–1770).[70] In 1772 Lewin had been elected the rabbinic head (*Oberlandesrabbiner*) of Berlin and the provinces, and happy personal relations with Mendelssohn had immediately ensued. In 1773 the Jewish philosopher sent him as a Purim present a manuscript volume of Hebrew translations of some of Aristotle's works.[71] This gift was not out of place, for Lewin was an unusual type of rabbi, well read in secular literature, versed in Hebrew grammar, while famous as a talmudic scholar who presided over a flourishing yeshiva. When the prospectus *'Alim Li-Terufa* appeared, he had no qualms about writing an approbation (*haskama*). It was issued on Elul 12, 5538 (September 4, 1778) but not published by Mendelssohn until 1783, at the beginning of the first Book of the Tora in the complete edition. The deferment was probably due to the fact that—contrary to custom—no other leading rabbi had been asked for an approbation. The text of Lewin's *haskama* is notable for the striking manner in which it echoed certain of the thoughts and sentiments expressed in the opening essay of the prospectus:[72]

> Nowadays there are many Gentile nations that, by God's grace, believe in the Tora of Moses and in the holy prophets, and do understand the Scriptures. God inspired them to undertake the translation of the Bible into their several languages, "making it savory food"[73] to their heart's delight. Yet we, the people of the children of Israel, and particularly those of us who dwell in these lands and are called *Ashkenazim* [Germans] ... speak with a stammering tongue. For we are "surety for a stranger,"[74] and there is none among us who knows his way about the foreign tongue[75] [well enough] to make himself understandable in it. We merely "went

about and gathered"[76] words from the books of the Gentiles, and there resulted a very "grievous mixture."[77]

I have seen the Bible [*ha-biblia*] printed in Amsterdam with the approbation of renowned rabbinic authorities of the [Council of the] Four Polish Lands in 1679,[78] and also the one published in Amsterdam, the translation of which had taken about twenty years.[79] Neither of them is in any way satisfactory so far as establishing the correct meaning is concerned, least of all in the Hagiographa. These were the only ones available to Jews desiring to understand the words [of Scripture] in such a way that they were "established upon their lips"[80] and that their language was sweet in their mouth. "Lo, their prosperity is not in their hand";[81] they fetch "counsels from afar"[82] and supply themselves with the works of the Gentiles.[83] These [non-Jewish Bibles] have become "a rock of stumbling"[84] for young Jews who [thereby] drink deep of strange notions alien to the children of Israel.

Now, however, "mine eye seeth every precious thing"[85] since there arose and took courage "a wise man of strength,"[86] the outstanding rabbinic scholar, the accomplished sage, our honored master and teacher Rabbi Moses of Dessau (may the Merciful preserve and redeem him), who is "known in the gates"[87] and has achieved fame[88] in the realms of Tora, Talmud, and the natural sciences as well as in Hebrew grammar and, above all, in the German tongue, in which he excels. "Therefore peoples praise him,"[89] and "they bring their witnesses that they may be justified"[90] [in praising him]. For there is not one in a thousand among them like him, who is a master of the word, and who speaks and writes their languages with grace and clarity. His heart has impelled him to design the holy work of explaining the entire Five Books of the Tora in clear language. I know the man ... and I am certain that nothing short of ultimate perfection proceeds from his labors.

I am looking forward to the benefit that will accrue from it to all who come in the name of the Lord, desirous of knowing the clear language of Scripture and the interpretation offered by him. No longer will our young rush to drink of the wells dug by strangers, [for now] they will find refreshing water flowing down from the mountains of Israel; waters that do not fail nor lead astray from the path of the righteous. Knowing all this, I have departed from my rule [of withholding requested approbations] and "my hand shall be established and mine arm shall strengthen him"[91] in giving my consent to the printing of the Five Books of the Tora in the manner referred to.

It is understandable that neither the aesthetic aspect of Mendelssohn's effort (which stressed the "beauty" of Hebrew) nor his role as a philosopher are mentioned in this approbation. It would not have behooved a chief rabbi to introduce a humanistic note into his recommendation of a new edition of the Tora. While the sciences had achieved recognition within the ambit of faith and piety, philosophy was frowned upon, and purely aesthetic categories had no *locus standi* at all. Hence Lewin's emphasis on "clarity" rather than beauty. Notwithstanding these tacit reservations, the warm approval accorded Mendelssohn and his project was remarkable. It was not extended to Wessely when a few years later, spurred by Joseph II's Edict of Tolerance, Wessely published his plea for educational reforms.

Lewin then reacted with a sense of outrage and with stern action that compelled Mendelssohn to rush to his friend's aid.[92] By that time Mendelssohn's relationship with the rabbis had become rather strained, and Lewin himself may have had second thoughts about the wisdom of the approbation he had granted in 1778. Though nothing so dramatic as the issuance of a ban (*herem*) had taken place anywhere,[93] a number of prominent religious leaders had expressed strong misgivings in regard to the Pentateuch translation, and Mendelssohn was seriously concerned about the possibility of drastic action such as a ban.

It seems that the main centers of agitation against the new work were Prague and Altona. On May 14, 1779, less than a year after the prospectus had come out and almost a year before the First Book of the Tora appeared, Avigdor Levi wrote Mendelssohn a letter from Prague,[94] which indicated that the opponents of the project had directed their attacks also against Dubno.[95] The main purport of the letter was, however, to express surprise at the fact that Mendelssohn had failed to ask Ezekiel Landau, the renowned chief rabbi of Prague and the foremost religious leader of the time, for his approbation. The criticism implied in Avigdor Levi's confession of astonishment at Mendelssohn's failure to do this was obviously prompted by his first hand observation of the hostility that the project had engendered in Prague; as an admirer of Mendelssohn, Levi felt aggrieved by this reaction and in trying to account for it he put part of the blame, it appears, on what seemed to him a disregard of the time-honored custom of requesting a *haskama* from the leading authorities. In his reply on May 25[96] Mendelssohn, who was most sensitive to the requirements of etiquette, was at some pains to explain his reasons. He gave a detailed account of how the project came about [97] and made two decisive points. First, he had no financial interest in the project and hence he did not require the protection of copyright (for the sake of which rabbinic approbations were usually sought, since they contained a threat of sanctions (*herem*) against the publishers of any pirate editions): "Why, then, should I knock at the doors of the great leaders of Israel and petition their *haskama* or *herem* for an enterprise from which no material gain will accrue to me?" Second, this book was, insofar as his part, [the translation] was concerned, a German book designed for the benefit of children and teachers. He had not been aware of patronage ever having been bestowed by rabbinic authorities upon books written in Judeo-German.[98] Should he publish a Hebrew work at a future time, he would feel obligated to ask the sages of Israel for their consent.

Mendelssohn's own position was therefore quite clear. As for Dubno, his reason for not applying for an approbation was also simple enough. He had not produced a brand-new Hebrew commentary and massoretic treatise but had, for the most part, drawn on the classical exegetes and grammarians. In deference to the custom of inviting an approbation from the local rabbinic head he had nevertheless asked the chief rabbi of Berlin for his approval, and such approval had been granted. However, he was anxious to consult the chief rabbi of Prague on a scholarly matter in connection with his work. It concerned a certain massoretic problem[99] with which Landau had dealt in his responsa.[100] Dubno's letter had been written some time ago but its dispatch had been delayed by the war between Prussia and Austria (viz. the so-called War of the Bavarian Succession). Now that peace had just been restored,[101] the letter was about to be sent off. "We hope," Mendelssohn added significantly, "that our words will find favor in his [Landau's] eyes and will cause him to show us kindness and to give support to our teacher, Rabbi Solomon Dubno, with 'the arm of his righteousness' against all who rise up against him, and also to command one of his disciples to let us have a reply."[102]

Mendelssohn's letter to Avigdor Levi leaves no doubt as to how he felt. He was obviously much concerned about the opposition in Prague and yet hoped that it was still possible to rectify the matter by placating Landau. His elaborate account of the reasons that had prevented the request for a *haskama* was clearly meant to be brought to the chief rabbi's notice. Moreover, there is evidence that Dubno inserted such a request in the letter that was belatedly dispatched to Prague, and that no reply was received at the time. It was only some years later, in 1786, when after his break with Mendelssohn Dubno had embarked on an independent edition, that Landau, now willingly granting an approbation to Dubno's project, referred to his rejection of the earlier petition:[103] "I refused because in the work printed at the time the holy [the biblical text] and the profane [Mendelssohn's German translation] were joined together; for he [Dubno, who had figured as editor] had included a [sort of] commentary in a foreign tongue, called by its author [Mendelssohn] *Targum Ashkenazi* ["German Translation"]. We fear that this foreign element will prove a stumbling block to Jewish children and lead to the neglect of the study of the Tora. For this reason I declined to give my consent."

This statement not only proves that in May, 1779, Dubno did belatedly ask Landau for an approbation, but also shows the nature of the misgivings felt by Landau from the very start. Like many other rabbis, he saw in Mendelssohn's translation—dubbed by him a "commentary" as distinct from a simple, literal rendition—a serious menace to the study of the Tora. While he would not hesitate in 1785 to write a *haskama* for the rather primitive word-by-word rendering of the Pentateuch and the Five Scrolls by Sussmann Glogau, Landau looked with disfavor upon Mendelssohn's work:[104]

> It possibly was the author's [Mendelssohn's] intention to prevent a rush after [Christian] Bibles, and he may have intended to improve the situation. Yet we can see that in actual fact this offers no improvement. . . . For the translator deeply immersed himself in the language using as he did an extremely difficult German that presupposes expertise in its

grammar. Now since the children will find it hard to understand it, the teacher will have to spend most of the time in explaining German grammar. . . . Moreover, the translation does not follow the text word by word but renders units of meaning. . . . This would have been the right procedure had he made it clear that his version was meant for mature people at home in Bible and Mishna. Seeing, however, that it is in demand by teachers of children, it induces the young to spend their time reading Gentile books in order to become sufficiently familiar with refined German to be able understand this translation. Our Tora is thereby reduced to the role of a maidservant to the German tongue. . . . The intention of the translator may have been good, as I have said before. We have to assume this since we must "judge every man in the scale of merit,"[105] especially one who is famous as a scholar. Yet we cannot rest satisfied with the intention that prompted him if the result of his action is so devastating.[106]

Whereas Ezekiel Landau's opposition was marked by considerable restraint, Raphael Kohen, the greatly respected chief rabbi of the three communities Altona, Hamburg, and Wandsbeck,[107] seems to have been more inclined to resort to drastic countermeasures. The agitation fostered by him was particularly pronounced in Altona, where he resided, the city being then under Danish jurisdiction.

Obstacles on the Road

Most of what we know about the events in Mendelssohn's life from the summer of 1779 until the autumn of 1780 is based on his lengthy correspondence with August Hennings and on the letters written to Hennings by his sister-in-law, Elise Reimarus.[1] We have already quoted the section of Mendelssohn's letter of June 29, 1779, in which he explained to his Danish friend how he had arrived at the idea of presenting a Bible translation.[2] That letter was written about a month after he had replied to Avigdor Levi, and it dealt to a large extent with the situation that had arisen in Altona. Though the danger of some hostile activity could not be ignored, Mendelssohn tended to "play it cool"; he probably wished to discourage any precipitate action by Hennings, whose anticlericalism would have made him only too willing to exercise his political influence on Mendelssohn's behalf and possibly to go too far in the process.

Mendelssohn wrote this letter, dated June 29, in the quiet atmosphere of Strelitz, where he and his wife had spent about ten pleasant days the year before as guests of a good friend,[3] and where he was now on his own.[4] "I have come here for a few days to visit a friend," he told Hennings in the letter.[5] "Here I do no business and have no books, and so there is nothing to distract me. I can collect my thoughts and reflect, at leisure, upon matters close to my heart. You, my dearest, shall be the first with whom I wish to converse in such circumstances." As the letter shows, the matters close to his heart were not, for a change, of a philosophical nature but had to do with his Bible project and Hennings' interest in being of help.

"I was greatly pleased by the affectionate concern for my health and peace of mind, which you expressed to my brother-in-law [Moses] Fürst,"[6] Mendelssohn wrote."It is proof of your sincere friendship which, in fact, I never doubted." The letter continued:

> Yet, in truth, the little thunderstorm that has gathered around my poor book has not caused me the least disquiet. No zealot shall so easily succeed in stirring up my cold blood. I look upon the play of human passions as a natural phenomenon that merits observation. One who is fearful and trembles at every electric spark is unfit to be an observer. By and large, my heart shows little susceptibility to anger, worry, remorse, and such disagreeable affects. I am sensitive only to love and friendship, and even to these only in such moderate degree that my friends often accuse me of being lukewarm. . . .
>
> For the time being, the rabbi of Altona keeps his thunderbolts in abeyance. I do not know his intentions. Perhaps he means to strike with all the more rumbling at a more propitious time, when he has the finished work before him. Let him do so! I want him to be left alone, without any outside interference, so that we can see what truth on its own, untrammeled by any extraneous considerations, is able to accomplish among my nation. As soon as external factors such as threats, interdictions [by the government], etc. come into play, the compasses are shifted and observation is lost. A little ferment may possibly benefit the cause that I really have at heart, and I might jeopardize it by interference.

At this point there follows the long passage that has already been quoted, leading up to this final statement: "The more resistance my modest effort encounters, the more necessary it appears to me, and the more eagerly I shall try to carry it through. Yet I shall not permit the fanaticism of the zealots to entice me to any kind of unbecoming measures. The youthful vehemence that so often carries us away, despite the best of intentions, left me early in life and I hardly regretted the loss. At my time of life, when I am so close to the shore, it would be foolish to expose my sail to every whim of impetuosity."

This letter was a rather belated reply to one that Hennings had sent to him on March 20, 1779,[7] which in point of fact had contained no reference to the Bible project or the problems it faced. What had moved Mendelssohn to break his silence was the news he had received from Fürst. As his letter indicates, he had heard from his brother-in-law in Copenhagen that Hennings was greatly concerned about his "health and peace of mind," and thus it was to reassure Hennings on this score that Mendelssohn now hastened to write to him from Strelitz. As a councillor of state it would not have been difficult for Hennings to find ways and means of restraining the chief rabbi of Altona from any action harmful to Mendelssohn; it was to prevent any such step that Mendelssohn wrote to his friend. His emphatic rejection of any "outside interference" by "threats, interdictions, etc." suggests that, according to information received from Fürst, Hennings had been considering certain plans along such lines, and, in fact, a letter from Hennings in precisely this vein had crossed Mendelssohn's and was waiting for him in Berlin upon his return from Strelitz. Henning's letter, dated June 22, 1779, contained the following passage:[8]

> Should . . . the Altona rabbi become too bothersome to you, and should the peace and quiet, which every citizen in a country governed by Reason should enjoy, seem to be in peril, it would require no great effort to stop the fanatical zeal of the chief rabbi of Altona. Even as theological controversies ought not to be resolved by despotic verdicts, theological despotism must likewise be precluded by sound police measures on the part of the government, and assertions of power embroiling the secular sphere and seeking to disturb the safety, peace, and civil position of one of the finest members of the state must be curbed.
>
> Since you are better qualified than I am to indicate in precise terms an appropriate course of action, I leave it to you to instruct me to what extent the chief rabbi of Altona can be directed to adopt an orderly and priest-like conduct without infringing upon his freedom of conscience and his right of dissent (which his church is entitled to exercise in common with all other churches), it being understood that it does not give rise to civil discord, persecution, and intolerance. Knowing as I do the mind of our ministers [of state], I am convinced that a request from you (to which you might call my attention in private) will be carried out without difficulty out of sheer respect for your name and for the sake of justice.

In replying to this letter on July 13, 1779,[9] Mendelssohn reiterated his aversion to repressive measures, but he conceded that there was a philosophical angle to the problem that Hennings' suggestion had posed: "What you say about the limits of tolerance toward intolerant people . . . seems to me very true and surely deserves to be explored. The question has always appeared to me rather complicated and hard to decide: to what extent is a state obliged or justified to extend civil protection and tolerance even to men who can be presumed to be domineering and intolerant? How should the Peruvians have behaved, had they been aware of the character of the Spaniards and had the latter come to them asking for the right of settlement?[10] Humanitarianism would have demanded that they be received, but prudence and the duty of self-preservation would have necessitated certain restrictions, ones that, to my mind, cannot be easily defined. I thank you once more for you kind offer to protect me in every possible way against civil persecution. However, things have not yet come to such a pass, and I do not think they ever will, although the seemingly quiet thunderclouds are not to be fully trusted."

In view of the unpredictability of the "weather" in Altona, Mendelssohn proposed an extremely clever course of action: "If it could be arranged that a subscription to the work be taken out in the name of His Majesty the King,[11] or in the names of some of the Great of the Realm, a prospect which Herr Fürst described to me as feasible, this would serve the rabbi of Altona as a hint to behave in a more orderly way in future. To go beyond this kind of warning I consider, for the time being, both ungracious and unnecessary."

Hennings lost no time in acting on this suggestion. It was probably on July 19 that he discussed the matter with the powerful secretary of state, Øve Höegh-Guldberg, who submitted it to Crown Prince Frederick and, having obtained his answer, sent the following message (written in French and bearing the date July 19, 1779) to Hennings:[12] "His Majesty the King and Msgr. his brother are pleased to subscribe to the translation of Monsieur Mendelssohn, if you are perfectly certain that it contains nothing [directed] against the majesty and truth of Holy Scripture. His Royal Highness has expressly commanded me to ask for an assurance from you to this effect so as to avoid any consequences in case the Jews of Altona should later demonstrate [when the work is published] that our philosopher belongs to the religion of Berlin ["*la religion de Berlin*" = radical Deism]. As a friend I also ask you to bear this in mind, since I know how distrubed His Royal Highness would feel if he were to have [unwittingly] bestowed his favor upon the printing of a scandalous work. I myself subscribe to it in any event, and I ask you to take care of the matter." On July 20 Hennings sent this note to Mendelssohn, with a covering letter of his own:[13] "What has happened here at court in respect of your translation you will gather from the enclosed original letter of our secretary of state, Höegh-Guldberg, which I ask you kindly to return to me. You will not take amiss the scruples expressed in it by people who can have no knowledge of the matter as such. In order to make the thing more weighty in the eyes of laymen through observing formalities, I have handed the sample of your translation [viz. the prospectus] to Professor Kall, the librarian, who is competent in philological studies, and whom I had asked to subscribe on behalf of the university library. I hope our leading clergymen will do likewise in their individual capacities. In order that I may arrange this business in proper fashion I would ask you to inform me how the prepayment of the subscription is to be handled, and in case I need special forms on which to enter the names, do let me have some. Herr Fürst told me that the imperial library in Vienna and some of the Great there have subscribed. The procedure adopted there could serve us as a model."

A day or two later Hennings wrote Mendelssohn again,[14] this time in a philosophical key: he was planning the publication of two volumes of essays, one of which was to deal with his views on prejudice, and it was to discuss in this context the case mentioned by Mendelssohn. The Chinese emperor had shown the way, in 1724 or thereabouts, when he politely but firmly expelled the Jesuits from his dominions. This was the only way to treat intolerant people so long as the government still had the power to overwhelm them. He would therefore, had he the authority to do so, politely suggest to the rabbi of Altona that he leave the country in which he was a source of disquiet by reason of his intolerance. If the intolerant faction grew so strong that the government was rendered powerless, then no remedy was possible. Yet who could foretell that this was going to happen? Could the Moors in Spain have foreseen that after seven centuries they would be exterminated by the Goths whom they had tolerated among them? It was part of the civil order to leave everyone unmolested so long as he caused no unrest. The state had no right to interfere in theological disputes so long as they did not upset the peace and endanger the safety of its citizens. The letter ended on a more practical note: "Why do you not print your translation also in German characters? Many people who cannot read the new Hebrew [*neuhebräisch*][15] would welcome this. And it would be more useful than three editions of [Klopstock's] *Messias*." Some valuable comments on Hennings' letters are found in one which Elise Reimarus wrote to him toward the end of July, 1779:[16]

> I hope I acted in the right way, dear Hennings. I posted your letters to Mendelssohn last Friday evening, after permitting our dear trusted ones[17] to share them with me. Very many thanks for letting this correspondence pass through our hands. It is of extraordinary interest, and you need not be afraid that improper use will be made of it. Who could have been so impertinent [*fürwitzig*] as to write the newspaper article about the ban [alleged to have been issued] by the Altona chief rabbi? I was worried when I saw it because I feared that Mendelssohn might feel anxious, and I was therefore pleased to read the denial [*Wiederspruch*] [in the column] "From the District of Brandenburg" [*aus dem Brandenburgischen*]. It might actually be all to the good that the matter is being aired in public so that reason can utter its verdict before unreason can do so.
>
> It was an excellent idea on your part to give a sample of the translation to Professor Kall. Who knows how far the clergymen will extend the border line *de la secte de Berlin*. Now Kall will be responsible, not you. Another good thing is that you suggested a German edition, or rather one printed in German letters. I too know several people here who would welcome this, your mother being among the first. Rumor has it that such an edition is already being prepared, but I have no idea by whom. As soon as Mendelssohn sends you the subscription forms for his first edition let me have one also. I do not mean to say that I can pretend to be actually collecting money for this purpose. However, I might do something occasionally. By the way, I am a little surprised that Mendelssohn chose the method of advance subscriptions. Why? If the thing is worth the price, it will undoubtedly sell. Otherwise, the subscribers will grumble when the price has to be reduced later on.

Elise's reference to the "newspaper article" is the only extant contemporary testimony to the appearance of a false report in the *Hamburger Correspondent* of July 17, 1779, which read as follows:[18] "*Altona*. The local chief rabbi has placed under a ban any Jew who reads the translation of the Pentateuch by Herr Moses Mendelssohn in Berlin." Only some irresponsible hothead could have supplied this announcement, which made very little sense at a time when Mendelssohn's translation had yet to appear! It was rather strange, however, that the denial had been issued in Berlin (in the "district of Brandenburg"), not in Altona itself. Raphael Kohen might not have been too displeased that a "warning shot" had been fired. On July 19, when Höegh-Guldberg and Prince Frederick discussed Hennings' suggestion of a royal subscription, the note in the *Hamburger Correspondent* may have played some part in the formulation of the answer; being made keenly aware of the agitation against Mendelssohn's work, the prince may have thought it desirable to receive an assurance such as that spelled out in the letter to Hennings. The fact that no ban had actually been proclaimed is attested not only by Elise's letter but also by Mendelssohn's own clear statement in a letter to Hennings dated September 20, 1779.[19] By that date his strategic winning of royal support had forestalled any radical action that the chief rabbi of Altona may previously have had in mind.

We resume the thread of the story where we left it. Mendelssohn's reply to Hennings' two letters and the ministerial note attached to the first was written on July 29:[20]

> I herewith return the minister's letter concerning my translation of the Books of Moses. The difficulty of promoting a work accused of irreligion is a bother that, in my eyes, honors the statesman who is troubled by it. However, I hope that you will have assured him without hesitation that your friend Mendelssohn is incapable of publishing a scandalous work and that his translation of Holy Scripture is aimed at anything but the denigration of the majesty and truth thereof. So far as the term "religion of Berlin" is concerned, I consider it to be a mere *façon de parler*. For if your noble-minded minister . . . knows Berlin through you and more than by hearsay, he must be aware that in Berlin—as indeed in all great cities—belief and unbelief, fanaticism and reason, enthusiasm and frostiness, etc. are intermingled . . .

If Hennings had been hesitant to give the prince the required assurance, this declaration by Mendelssohn was to settle all doubts. Besides, Hennings had protected himself, as Elise acutely noted, by taking shelter behind the authority of Professor Kall. The result of the assurances produced was the gracious bestowal of the royal patronage, which was not kept a secret by any means, and which prevented the chief rabbi of Altona from taking any overt action against the Pentateuch translation. When the complete edition of the work appeared in 1783, the list of subscribers was headed by "His Royal Majesty, Christian the Seventh King of Denmark" and "His Royal Highness, the Hereditary Prince of Denmark."[21]

Mendelssohn's July 29 letter to Hennings also provided a detailed reply concerning subscription procedures. Subscribers were to receive a certificate (*Schein*) signed by Mendelssohn. Enclosed with the letter were twenty certificates, of which ten were for the "large median size" edition at the price of seven and a half Dutch guilders, and ten for the "large royal size" edition at nine guilders. The letter also informed Hennings of other matters related to the work: it was to comprise at least a hundred sheets, and it was being printed in Berlin at Mendelssohn's expense "for the benefit of some indigent scholars" who were writing the commentary and the "critical notes" (a reference to Dubno and his assistant Saul Mendelssohn). He hoped to bring out the first part toward Easter 1780, and he was confident that "the experts among my nation [would] be pleased with it."

An edition of the translation in the German alphabet was contemplated, Mendelssohn told Hennings, and someone had been found who would provide an extract from the Hebrew commentary in German. For this edition, too, subscriptions would be invited. However, it would be a considerable time before this difficult and rather thankless task could be completed by the scholar who had embarked on it. "How well or how badly he will do his job remains to be seen. I hardly have the time to read even my own proofs perfunctorily, and [then] only once. I have to rely on others. The right kind of people are helping me, fortunately, and I hope to present a text second to none so far as exactness goes." The unnamed editor of the German edition was Josias Friedrich Christian Löffler (1752–1816), professor of theology in Frankfurt am Main.[22] He had, we are told,[23] the assistance of a Jewish scholar but he managed to publish only Mendelssohn's translation in German characters and had to abandon the project of also producing extracts from the commentary. However, his edition contained a valuable introduction and, as a special feature, Mendelssohn's translation of the Song of Deborah (Judges 6).[24]

The Jewish scholar whose help Löffler enjoyed was none other than Mendelssohn himself. This is evident from a brief note written by Mendelssohn on March 14, 1780, to Nicolai, the publisher of Löffler's edition (of which only volume one appeared):[25]

> Of the specimen sheets of the German translation, sheet A is missing. I had returned it to you with some notes for Herr Professor Löffler. Please send me another in its place so that I can compile the list of *errata* that we shall have to append at the end. Some of the misprints cause a change of meaning. Should we perhaps add to the introduction or at the very end my translation of Deborah's Triumphal Song, so as to enhance the value of our edition,[26] or is this not the right place for it?[27]

Mendelssohn's July 29 letter concluded with some observations in reply to the philosophical discourse in Hennings' second letter: "I entirely agree with what you say about tolerating the intolerant. However, the problem seems to be applicable also to a case that you failed to discuss in sufficient detail and that I had principally in mind [viz.]: to what extent may a sound police permit the tolerated party to win people over to its side by using the force of persuasion [*Überredungsgründe*]? On the one hand, it seems to be harsh and contrary to the natural liberty of man to limit the exercise of his capabilities, and one might think that the authorities ought to allow the enthusiast a free hand to hoodwink people by phantoms [*Meteoren*] in the same way in which the rationalist is permitted to convince people by the force of reason [*Vernunftgründe*]. On the other hand, one can easily perceive the danger to which one is thereby exposed. Experience has shown, and it corresponds to human nature, that the less powerful religious party shows greater conversionist zeal and explores the avenues to people's minds more efficiently than the powerful ruling party, which takes its superiority for granted. Under such circumstances, to what extent is the ruling religious party entitled to insist strictly on its prerogatives and to use its superior power when the less powerful make the slightest attempt to usurp it?"

Mendelssohn apologized for having adumbrated his thoughts in what he described as a somewhat confused manner and he half promised to revert to the subject on another occasion. Elise, who read the letter before passing it on to her brother-in-law, found this passage most disturbing indeed. "As for Mendelssohn's letter," she wrote to Hennings on August 31, 1779,[28] "it is not only *inexplicable* to me in many places, but it also appears different from a letter such as I would have wished to see written by Mendelssohn. This latter [impression] must be [due to] a misunderstanding. Let me talk therefore only about its inexplicability. What is meant by the question: to what extent may a sound police permit the tolerated party to win people over to its side by using the force of persuasion? Limits are limits, it seems to me, and hence all toleration is thrown to the winds if the ruling party is to have the right, at some time or another, to maintain its superior power over what people *think*. Who is to determine the limit at which interference by the police becomes legitimate? Such interference is warranted, I believe, only when a public disturbance of the peace occurs, and you stated this clearly in your letter when mentioning the Altona chief rabbi." In another letter to Hennings, dated September 7, 1779,[29] Elise returned to this point: "I would also like to know what you are going to reply, or have already replied, to Mendelssohn's question. I confess that I would not have suspected this kind of intolerance . . . in such a right-minded philosopher." She added: "I now understand why you do not consult Mendelssohn about your *Philosophical Essays.*"

Elise was merely projecting her own indignation upon her brother-in-law, for Hennings had, in fact, consulted Mendelssohn and sent him many of his earlier drafts.[30] As to how he reacted to Mendelssohn's question, we do not know: a letter that he wrote to Mendelssohn—to which Mendelssohn replied on September 20, resuming the theme of tolerance—has unfortunately not been preserved. Elise's sense of bewilderment was justified, however, and the view that Mendelssohn expressed in that July 29 letter does call for an explanation.

We suggest that the hypothetical case that Mendelssohn had stated in general terms reflected his own personal concern. The ruling religious party in the Berlin Jewish community favored the rationalist trend, of which he was the leading exponent, while the rank and file was opposed to the spirit of the Enlightenment and inclined to support the zealous defenders of the status quo. The agitation against the new edition of the Pentateuch was not confined to Prague and Altona. It must have been noticeable even in Berlin, despite the fact that the chief rabbi had endorsed the enterprise. Precisely because the Enlightenment had gained considerable ground among the socially advanced Jews of Berlin, the clash between the Maskilim and their opponents was all the more pronounced. A *Kulturkampf* seemed inevitable, and Mendelssohn was caught between his love and respect for tradition on the one hand, and his desire for educational reform on the other. The threat of a *herem* from Altona had subsided but the vehemence of the opposition must have shaken him. The terms "zealots" and "fanatics" in his correspondence with Hennings show that he was somewhat alarmed. Even his effort to appear unruffled and calmly observing "weather-clouds" and "electric sparks" betrayed an underlying nervousness.

Although the reaction that he was encountering came as no surprise to him,[31] it was nevertheless upsetting, and it raised in his mind the question that he posed in the letter to Hennings and that Elise found so objectionable: was it right to allow a "tolerated" group of "intolerant people" to intimidate others and try to prevent them, through the unbridled use of the "force of persuasion," from reading his Pentateuch translation? The "force of reason" was clearly of no avail in such a situation. A "sound police" might, after all, be the only means by which to curb excesses of intolerance. Previously he had rejected Hennings' offer of "sound police" protection and governmental intervention of any sort. He had considered it better to let things take their natural course. Had he now changed his mind?

He had not. He was merely thinking aloud, as it were. Having posed the question, he dismissed it once and for all. In fact, his next letter to Hennings was a complete disclaimer of the preceding one. It squarely and unequivocally rejected the notion that in certain situations force might legitimately be used in the service of religious tolerance or religion as such. Out of the anguish of his personal dilemma there emerged a purified concept of religion as the very antithesis to force. This concept was to find its classical expression in two of his subsequent writings, viz. in his preface to *Manasseh Ben Israel* and in his *Jerusalem*. It inspired his impassionate appeal to the rabbinic authorities to renounce the weapon of the ban as incompatible with the essential character of religion.

The important letter that Mendelssohn wrote to Hennings on September 20, 1779,[32] urged tolerance even toward prejudice, the bête noire of the Enlightenment: "Let us not on our part be biased by prejudice against prejudices. I believe that in certain circumstances their indispensability cannot be doubted. I look upon them as mistakes in calculation. It should please us if our bookkeeper remedies a miscalculation, which would have caused us considerable loss, by making a mistake of the opposite kind, though it does no credit to the bookkeeper, nor does it excuse him, if by chance his errors cancel each other out. The case of prejudices is similar. For a time they may repair the damage that would be inflicted on society by prejudices of a contrary nature, and they are indispensable so long as we are too weak to eliminate the latter."

It had been an old and cherished idea of Mendelssohn's that in certain instances prejudice might be preferable to enlightenment,[33] and although he was only too familiar with the ugly manifestations of prejudice, this did not prevent him from trying to be objective and fair-minded. He admitted, however, in pursuing the analogy introduced in the letter, that in most cases it might be better to suffer a loss than to see it prevented by another error. Assuming the bookkeeper was my friend or my son, his proneness to miscalculation would hurt me more than any tolerable loss. Hennings had declared[34] that he could almost hate someone who dared to speak in favor of prejudice. In quoting this statement Mendelssohn said humorously: "You see the danger to which I am exposing myself. However, you are the kind of friend whom I would not like to see cancel out one mistake by another. Besides, I know that you take the word [prejudice] in a practical sense [as indicating a mode of conduct], in which its meaning is far more restricted than in the general theory. Therefore, we actually differ only in words. As for the thing itself, we shall soon come to terms."

The word "prejudice," Mendelssohn had explained earlier in the letter, derived from jurisprudence, where it signified a previous verdict passed by a competent judge in a similar case. The preceding judgment could have been right or wrong. In philosophical thinking, too, it was admissible to rely on principles previously established by ourselves or others, and this explained why a prejudice was invariably located in a premise and never in a conclusion. Here again prejudices might be true or false. What had discredited prejudice was the abuse of *praejudicia* by hypocrites who sang the praises of inherited false principles, claiming that they were beneficial to society. Thus they heaped error upon error, and all this in the name of God.

As Mendelssohn explained in a covering letter addressed to Elise,[35] his remarks were meant to restrain Hennings from being too outspoken in his attacks against prejudice. "He is one of those spirits who, as the saying goes, need the rein rather than the spur,[36] and it seems to me that in the profession he has chosen one can never be too careful."

It is remarkable that Mendelssohn should have counseled restraint at a time when he might have been tempted to join in attacks upon prejudice. The final part of his letter, which referred to his own situation, was written in the same vein:

> My rabbis have been rather quiet of late. What has caused their silence I do not know. It was surely not some better understanding on their part. Judging from a correspondence that came into my hands by chance they seemed to be rather determined not to change their mind. As for me, I have no intention of either challenging or ridiculing them. After all, what would it profit me to put the scholars of my nation up to ridicule? You, my dearest friend, have rendered me an important service by obtaining subscriptions from the highest quarters. The people of Altona are thereby at least prevented from taking the rash step of condemning a book before they have seen it. What they will want to do later, when the work has appeared and can be judged by everyone, is left entirely to their discretion, and I do not wish their judgment to be influenced by any external measures on my part.

The rabbis who had been "rather quiet of late" were the chief rabbi of Altona and the members of his rabbinic court (Beth Din) referred to subsequently as the "people of Altona." The correspondence that had come to Mendelssohn's notice and was proof of their determination to persevere in their attitude might have been an exchange of letters between the Beth Din of Altona and the chief rabbi of Berlin. The moral support he had given Mendelssohn by his *haskama* could easily have led to an acrimonious correspondence. This is, however, purely conjectural. How seriously Mendelssohn had taken the threat of a *herem* is evident from the way he acknowledged the "important service" Hennings had rendered him. The thing that prompted him to decline once more any "external measures" was an offer by Hennings, in his letter of September 7,[37] to insert some appropriate remark in his forthcoming philosophical writings, in the event that the harassment continued. Mendelssohn made it clear that he was averse to using any outside pressure.

On the other hand, he welcomed the active interest that both Hennings and Elise had taken in the "business" of winning advance subscribers. On August 24 Elise had informed Hennings that she had placed one certificate at nine guilders with the Hamburg municipal library and that she hoped to sell a few more to local preachers, at least to Goeze and Krohn.[38] Of Krohn she had an amusing story to tell:[39] "When I approached him the other day, he said that he was pleased to have proof through this [Pentateuch] translation that Mendelssohn was truly a Jew; now he could hold him in high esteem, while there could be no mercy for the deist. I continued in the same vein by saying that but for Mendelssohn half the Jewish population of Berlin would, to the best of my knowledge, have long ago embraced naturalism. Bravo! he exclaimed applauding me!!!" The three exclamation marks show how much Elise, herself a radical deist, relished the conversation. On September 10 she informed Mendelssohn of the subscriptions by the library and by Pastor Krohn, and she added:[40] "If you are patient, perhaps some more connoisseurs will be found. At least, I shall gladly use every opportunity of making my own small contribution, as an outsider, to the advancement of your salutary project, and I trust that you will reap in peace the harvest of the full reward. My brother wishes to be remembered to you, and so do I, since my esteem for you is as high as his."

Elise's misgivings about Mendelssohn's "intolerance" had obviously been brushed aside but his subsequent letter in defense of prejudice was again hard to swallow. Mendelssohn, too, "slightly panders to prejudice," Hennings had remarked,[41] and she agreed: "How can such a glorious mind expect to get away with such a metaphor as the one about miscalculation?"[42] There were indeed true and false prejudices, but one could not warn loudly enough against the damage that resulted from adhering to prejudice when a more mature judgment was available. She told Hennings that in this instance she had "taken the liberty" of letting Mendelssohn know what she thought. Her letter has not been preserved, but she quoted from it a simile suggested by her brother: prejudices were like the scaffolding of an edifice, which had to be torn down when the building was completed.

Despite her disagreement with Mendelssohn, Elise sought to explain his attitude to her brother-in-law: "You should put part of the blame on his character, which is gentle and peace-loving by nature and bids him fight the evil in the world through [the influence of] his life rather than his writings; it causes him to expect the same from his friends." She then expressed her regret at not having been able to obtain subscriptions for the German edition for the simple reason that she did not know the price. Her letter concluded with this interesting observation:[43]

> On the whole, however, I fear that he [Mendelssohn] will lose the reward of his labor, i.e. the beneficial impact that this translation of the Bible was meant to have on his nation. For the Portuguese [the members of the Sephardic congregation in Hamburg] no longer read Hebrew, and the German [Jews] do not read *him*. "He is a Mameluke! We hold him in little esteem." This is how almost every one to whom my brother talked spoke about him. I am sorry for the sake of Mendelssohn and also from a general point of view because it shows how much of human toil is being wasted. It seems, on the other hand, that Mendelssohn has risen in the esteem of truly orthodox Christians, for what this may be worth. When I told my Pastor Krohn that the German translation was to benefit a couple of poor families, he immediately offered to buy a copy, irrespective of whether these families were Christians or *Jews*.

Elise Reimarus was certainly right in suggesting that Mendelssohn had little chance of influencing either of the groups she mentioned. What she failed to realize was that the translation was intended neither for assimilated Sephardic Jews nor for Ashkenazi upholders of the status quo but for those Maskilim who were genuinely concerned with a revival of Hebrew culture. She could not know that what gave Mendelssohn the strength to carry his enterprise through was his vision of the rebirth of Hebrew, which he shared with men like Dubno and Wessely, and which was destined to create the Hebrew Haskala movement in Germany and Eastern Europe. It created the school of the "Biurists" who completed the Bible project begun by him, and it culminated in the monumental new edition of the German translation and the *Bi'ur* by the Hebrew poet and grammarian Abraham Bär Lebensohn (1794–1878), known by his pen name Adam Ha-Kohen.[44]

But to Elise it looked as if Mendelssohn's only gain would be an enhanced reputation among orthodox Christians who welcomed his interest in the Bible. She must have wondered how he could be so cheerful amid all the toil and adversity. Her letters to Hennings remarked on his excellent spirit. On August 31 she wrote:[45] "By the way, it seems that his Bible business is giving him a new lease of life, and I am very happy about this." On February 18, 1780:[46] "I hear that Mendelssohn's health is now better than it had been for a long time. [Moses] Wessely, who just arrived from Berlin, told us this. He also said that he is very satisfied with the subscriptions." She added that she herself had been able to sell no more than two copies of the Hebrew and two of the German edition. In a previous letter, dated January 28, 1780,[47] she had mentioned that her brother was not favorably impressed by the specimen of the German edition that had been published in a newspaper. On March 31, 1780:[48] "Mendelssohn seems to be in a happy mood, and this pleases me all the more because it shows that his labors have not weighed him down. I feel ashamed at not having brought him more than five subscribers, namely two for the Hebrew and three for the German edition." On September 7, 1779, Hennings had informed Mendelssohn that Pastor Schiemeyer, superintendent general in Lübeck, an old admirer of his, had joined the ranks of subscribers.[49] In his letter of March 24, 1780[50] he reported that seven certificates had been placed, that the money had been remitted to Fürst, and that the unused forms were being returned via Hamburg. When on April 4 Elise informed her brother-in-law that she had forwarded the "package" to Mendelssohn, she wrote as a postscript:[51] "May he reap some benefit from his work. It is extremely sad for friends to see an excellent mind undertake, with the best of intentions, . . .[a] work that is useless. How else can one assess this Bible translation?"

The winding-up of the "business" by Hennings and Elise had been prompted by a letter which Mendelssohn sent to his friend in Copenhagen on March 14, 1780:[52]

> Herr Fürst will have the honor of presenting to you, on my behalf, the first instalment of the Five Books of Moses in three copies of large royal size for the king, the hereditary prince—His Royal Majesty and His Royal Highness—and the minister [of state]. I was unable to have them bound because the second instalment, which is due to appear in the near future, is part of it. To save expense the remaining copies will be dispatched when the tide comes in. The work turns out to be larger, more expensive, and more troublesome than I had anticipated. According to my present estimate, it will comprise about one hundred twenty sheets. At the [Leipzig] Fair volume one, printed in German letters and published by Nicolai, will also be available. Perhaps my work will meet with approval even among Christians. A readable extract from the elaborate Hebrew commentary is being arranged and has been taken care of by a Christian scholar.[53] Keep well, dearest Hennings. May the Lord protect you, and me also, in future against all quarrels with heresy hunters. They have a pretty strong crowd on their side. One ounce of sound common sense surely outweighs the whole lump, but only in the spiritual scales of a Homer, according to which the scale of the victors rises toward Olympus, while that of the vanquished descends toward Orcus. The common people, however, know only their ordinary cheese scales, as the good old Rector Damm used to say when explaining Homer to us.[54]

Now that the first volume of the Pentateuch was available in print,[55] one had to expect that "heresy hunters" would get busy, and it was difficult to forecast the turn of events. The last paragraph of Mendelssohn's letter reflects his anxiety, and clearly indicates his acute awareness of the opposition to the project. It also shows his growing contempt for his adversaries: they might be numerically strong but they lacked "sound common sense." The cleavage between him and the rabbis was widening.

Fortunately, the exacting task of distributing the work to the subscribers left little time for brooding. Errors had to be rectified. On March 15, a day after he had written to Hennings, he had to inform him that his *homme d'affaire* had mistakenly sent two copies to Hennings instead of three to Fürst: "That's the way it is, the booksellers say, when scholars interfere in the trade."[56] On March 28 Hennings acknowledged receipt of the first two copies and reported that they had been presented, by the minister, to the king and the prince.[57] This was the final act in a little play that owed its origin to some rumblings of rabbinic thunder behind the stage.

On April 17, 1780, Mendelssohn wrote to Avigdor Levi in Prague:[58] "I assume that the first instalment consisting of the Book of Genesis has arrived from Leipzig. I expect from you a candid statement as to how you like it." No doubt he also hoped to be informed about the impression the work had created in Prague. Levi's reply is unfortunately lost. More than a year later, in the summer of 1781, with the second volume already published and the third in press,[59] disturbing news about developments in Prague reached Mendelssohn from a source other than Levi, with whom he had been in correspondence as recently as May/June of that year.[60] He assumed that his friend in Prague had been afraid to tell him the truth. "I hear from Fürth," he wrote to him,[61] "that it has pleased the renowned chief rabbi[62] of your community [Ezekiel Landau] and his rabbinic court to prohibit, or even put under a ban, the edition of the Pentateuch that includes my translation, without having indicated to me any reason whatever that would justify this action. I have to confess that I find this kind of procedure most astonishing. Can you, my friend, let me know 'what they have seen concerning this matter and what has come unto them'[63] when they sentenced me without trial and lawful process? The renowned chief rabbi is surely not wont to act so hastily. I expect your reply through the trusted bearer of this letter. Be utterly frank, without trying to spare my feelings." At this point there followed the statement[64] about his having realized from the very start how much opposition, hatred, and persecution was in store for him. The letter concluded with the words: "Let them curse. I shall bless. To their use of force I shall not oppose the least display of force on my part. However, I would like to know their reasons for condemning me."

The friend in Fürth who had sent Mendelssohn word about the action alledgedly taken in Prague was most probably Doctor Wolf, physician at the local Jewish hospital and father of Aaron Halle (Wolfsohn) who became a prominent member of the group of Maskilim known as the *me'assefim*.[65] Doctor Wolf was one of the three Jews in Fürth who had subscribed to Mendelssohn's Pentateuch edition.[66] As it turned out, he had been misinformed about the situation in Prague. The fact that the false alarm emanated from a Jewish resident in Fürth offers no support to the conjecture that a *herem* had first been proclaimed in that particular locality,[67] though Hirsch Janow, who had become the rabbi of Fürth in 1778, was most probably opposed to Mendelssohn's enterprise. Janow was a son-in-law of the chief rabbi of Altona and despite his interest in mathematics and science his outlook differed little from that of practically all other rabbinic authorities. However, the minutes of the Fürth community contain no record of any public announcement or ban issued by him.[68] Moreover, had the rabbi of Fürth taken any action, Doctor Wolf would have reported it and Mendelssohn's letter to Avigdor Levi would not have passed it over in silence. As the letter shows, he was rather shaken by the news he had received. Notwithstanding his assurance that he had braced himself for attacks, he seems to have been genuinely puzzled by the hostile reaction now that two volumes had already appeared and to the best of his knowledge contained nothing to which a pious Jew could possibly object.

Avigdor Levi's reply has not been preserved but may be guessed from a note that he appended to his reproduction of Mendelssohn's letter when, many years later, he published a selection from his Hebrew correspondence.[69] There he testified that Ezekiel Landau had refused to listen to the "whisperers" and had rebutted their complaints and their clamoring for action against Mendelssohn.[70] This had been the case when the prospectus had been published, and Avigdor Levi had obviously no reason to assume that Landau's attitude had in any way changed since the first two volumes had come out. The serious misgivings that had prevented Landau from granting a *haskama* to Dubno's *Bi'ur*,[71] and which stemmed from his disapproval of Mendelssohn's translation, were one thing; outlawing the translation was another. He was urged to do so, and he refused. As Avigdor Levi reports in his note, the chief rabbi's son, Rabbi Samuel Landau, resolutely endorsed his father's restraint. In view of these circumstances, Levi was obviously in the fortunate position of being able to refute the news from Fürth that had caused Mendelssohn so much anguish. He might have replied as follows: The chief rabbi is certainly opposed to using your translation in schools. In his view, it is bound to take time and attention away from the study of the Tora, for in order to understand the refined literary German of your version the children will have to immerse themselves in German belles-lettres, and the inevitable result will be an increasing neglect of Hebrew learning. Your good intentions are not in doubt, however, and there is nothing heretical in either the translation or the commentary. Hence the chief rabbi's reluctance to take any action. His personal respect for you as a scholar of renown is likewise unquestioned. Yet he found it necessary to rule that your Pentateuch must not be introduced into our schools. He hopes that another word-by-word translation in very simple German will shortly be produced. On the other hand, he has no objection to the use of your Pentateuch edition by adults who have already mastered the basic elements of Hebrew traditional learning.

Assuming Avigdor Levi was well enough informed about Landau's attitude, a letter of this kind could have been written by him in response to Mendelssohn's request that he be utterly frank in reporting the situation in Prague. At all events, no ban had been issued, and any anxiety on this score could easily be allayed. The fact that the chief rabbi and his son Samuel were opposed to the issuance of a ban and held Mendelssohn in high respect is borne out by additional witnesses. There is, in the first place, Ezekiel Landau's *haskama* for Sussmann Glogau, which contains a complimentary reference to Mendelssohn's fame as a scholar.[72] Moreover, Jehuda Löb Jeiteles (1773–1838), scion of a notable Prague family and a friend of Rabbi Samuel Landau, wrote in the preface to his *Introduction to the Aramaic Language (Mevo' Lashon Aramit)*:[73] "Our great master of blessed memory [Ezekiel Landau], recognizing as he did his [Mendelssohn's] high rank, protected his honor and silenced those who spoke arrogantly against him." He quoted the testimony of Landau's elder son, Rabbi Jacob of Brody, who had written the following statement in the margin of the manuscript of his father's biography:[74]

> I remember that some thirty years ago I was called to come and see our father, and that I spent ten days with him. At that time the German translation of the Tora by the famous scholar, our teacher Rabbi Moses of Dessau of blessed memory, had just appeared. Many rabbis considered it an evil thing and "they looked [disapprovingly] after Moses,"[75] and they were ready to condemn his translation, particularly his rendition of the Holy Name.[76] They derided him in an unbecoming fashion but "they were afraid to come nigh unto him"[77] so long as they lacked support by the "powerful pillar"[78] [viz. Chief Rabbi Landau]. They therefore addressed to my father and teacher (the memory of the righteous be for a blessing) an appeal written with "black fire" imploring him to kindle the fire of zealousness. Yet he placated their fierce spirit by gently replying: Stop imputing blemishes to the "fruit of the lips"[79] of [a man of] understanding. I find nothing wrong in him, and why should we put a veil on the beams of his glory?[80]

This testimony can hardly be questioned. There is no discrepancy between Landau's anxiety about the possible ill effects of the translation on the one hand and his endeavor to protect Mendelssohn on the other. It was not until an increasing secularism among Prague Jews, coming in the wake of Joseph II's educational reforms, had made serious inroads into the traditional pattern of life that Landau felt it necessary to write and preach about the dangers of treating the Bible as mere literature and saw fit, in this connection, to warn publicly against the use of Mendelssohn's translation in schools and generally.[81]

A crisis that threatened to wreck the whole enterprise from within occurred in the autumn of 1780, when Solomon Dubno dissociated himself from the project. Nine years later, in a letter to Wolf Heidenheim,[82] Dubno would ascribe the break to religious scruples, but such scruples were by no means the sole or even the major reason for his withdrawal from a partnership that he had prized so highly. The decisive factor was clearly stated in a long letter that Dubno wrote to Mendelssohn on September 22, 1780.[83] The source of contention was Mendelssohn's refusal to print in full a rather extensive introduction, dealing principally with matters of Hebrew linguistics, that Dubno had prepared for publication in the second volume. It appears that the excuse offered by Mendelssohn was the prohibitive cost of production, but this explanation failed to convince Dubno. As he pointed out, he had declined to accept, for three years past, the annual fee of eighty thalers due to be paid to him out of the subscription fund; thus he had saved Mendelssohn a great deal of money. If Mendelssohn persisted in his refusal, Dubno was going to claim a year's fee and use the money to publish the introduction on his own. For how could he permit his work to remain on the shelf or to appear in a truncated form? He had spent more than ten weeks of painstaking labor on this particular essay. He had consulted over a hundred books and invested more concentration of effort in the essay than in his entire commentary and in the massoretic notes. Besides that, when Mendelssohn had urged him to be as brief and concise as possible in the writing of the *Bi'ur* and the *Tikkun Soferim,* he had stipulated no such restriction in regard to the introduction. Would Mendelssohn now go back on his word? Surely he was the last person to act in this way. Yet irrespective of the legitimacy of his claim, Dubno implored Mendelssohn to honor his promise as a mere personal favor. Dubno assured Mendelssohn of his eternal gratitude, if he acceded to this request and explained to his administrative associates the merits of his introduction. Dubno obviously suspected Jeremias Bendit and David Friedländer, whose names occur in an earlier part of the letter, of trying to dissuade Mendelssohn from including the costly introduction in volume two.

What Dubno failed to understand was the true nature of Mendelssohn's objection, which was perhaps pointed out to him with less candor than was required. It was not merely the inordinate length of the essay that compelled Mendelssohn to cut it mercilessly and to publish only the opening part;[84] his overriding concern was its suitability as an "introduction." In his view, Dubno's essay was too technical and specialized for such a purpose.[85] He therefore decided to step into the breach and write an introduction of his own. The eventual result was his masterful introductory essay *Or Li-Netiva* ("A Light unto the Path"), written in 1782.[86] In the circumstances, Mendelssohn had no choice than to publish Dubno's piece only in part, since omitting it completely would have been too harsh a measure.

Unfortunately, Mendelssohn's decision so wounded Dubno that his sense of allegiance to their common enterprise began to waver. Hitherto he had brushed aside his religious scruples about being associated with a project that had met with so much rabbinic disapproval. In his letter he alluded to the agitation that had been aroused but expressed the hope that a time would come when "jealousy and hatred" would have vanished

and their joint work would be studied with love and affection. The reference
to the "opposition" indicates that Dubno was quite well aware that he was
involved in a controversial undertaking. Though torn by conflicting
loyalties, he still managed to repress his own misgivings, but his attachment
to the common cause was hanging by a thread. In making his last attempt
to change Mendelssohn's mind Dubno declared that all joy would go out
of his work if his introduction were to be cut short. His health had already
suffered as a result of the anxiety he had been caused. He asked for an opportunity to discuss the issue with Mendelssohn.

As can be clearly discerned from Dubno's letter, there were other
grievances contributing to the overwrought state of mind in which he now
found himself. His relations with Mendelssohn's brother Saul, who was
associated with him as proofreader, were quite strained. Moreover, an
aspersion, he felt, had been cast upon him in connection with a ridiculously
small amount of money claimed by Saul.[87] The financial arrangements,
he complained, had been altogether unsatisfactory. Dubno considered himself the victim of exploitation, and he asked for some form of redress.

When no agreement between Mendelssohn and Dubno could be
reached, Chief Rabbi Hirschel Lewin was asked by Mendelssohn and his
friends to adjudicate in the matter. A report on this development is contained in a letter written on Shevat 4, 5543 (1783) by David Friedländer
to his friend Joseph Elias, a banker in Vilna:[88]

> I was personally present with Rabbi Solomon Dubno [when called] before
> the chief rabbi of our community to hear his complaints against the afore-
> mentioned honored scholar [Mendelssohn]. After he had presented all
> his claims, we came to an arrangement whereby all the work should
> be his responsibility and the entire amount of money in our hands should
> be given to him. Only a small sum—I have forgotten how much pre-
> cisely—was to be given to the brother of the afore-mentioned scholar.
> The condition was clearly stipulated that he [Dubno] resume his sacred
> work and bring it to completion. All profits from the publication of the
> Pentateuch that the Lord would grant us were to be his. Having made
> this arrangement, we saw him no more . . .

Mendelssohn's own comments on his conflict with Dubno are to be
found in a letter to Avigdor Levi and in his introduction to the Pentateuch.
To Levi he wrote on June 5, 1781:[89] "Indeed, I did become involved
in a quarrel with our teacher and master Rabbi Solomon Dubno (may
his light shine forth). God knows and is witness that I am not to blame.
Time will tell whether I shall again be able to come to terms with him."
As we know, the breach was indeed final.

In his own introduction[90] Mendelssohn expressed a sense of bewilderment over Dubno's sudden withdrawal. First he told the story of how
the project came into being[91] and praised the conscientious and competent
manner in which Dubno had discharged his obligations. Dubno had written
the entire commentary *(Bi'ur)* on Genesis, except for the first pericope
(parashat bere'shit), which was Mendelssohn's work. Dubno had also written

the massoretic notes *(Tikkun Soferim)* on Genesis as well as on Exodus, the volume that was being prepared at the time of his departure. In addition, he had left behind some material for the commentaries on Exodus and Numbers. Mendelssohn mentioned that, having been left in the lurch, he had himself to write the commentary on Exodus "in its entirety from beginning to end," but that he had inserted Dubno's notes in the appropriate places, marking them as such by enclosing them within brackets.

Mendelssohn's reference to Dubno's introduction was deliberately fictitious in order to avoid any criticism. It would have been in bad taste for him to record the fact that he had felt constrained to curtail it, and he believed, it seems, that his way of explaining the truncated form in which the introduction was published had the advantage of safeguarding Dubno's dignity as author. He wrote as follows: "He [Dubno] had begun to print his introduction at the beginning of the book, but he did not complete it [the printing of the full text]. For prior to its completion a 'strange spirit' *[ruah aheret]* came upon him. I do not know what happened to him. He left me and returned to his native country. Maybe this was the reason: when he agreed to undertake the work, he may have believed himself able to complete it within a year or two and to receive the full reward of his labors. I, too, imagined that this would be the case. Yet when it became plain that the work was protracted and exceedingly heavy, that it required much toil and assiduity day by day, that the cost of printing was constantly rising and that all the money so lavishly contributed by my supporters would not suffice to pay for the high quality paper and the high cost of production (which amounted to over thirty five hundred thalers), he grew weary, his strength flagged, and he despaired of receiving any reward whatever."

Mendelssohn's tentative explanation was, obviously, at variance with the facts. Dubno had made it clear in his letter that his principal grievance was the radical shortening of his introduction, and that the financial aspect, though calling for redress, played only a secondary role. Had his principal worry been his monetary reward, the agreement reached in the presence of chief rabbi Lewin would have settled the matter. The reason for Mendelssohn's decision to attribute Dubno's "strange" behavior to frustration over money matters is easy to guess: he wanted to offer a rationale for Dubno's action that avoided the delicate subject of their dispute over publishing Dubno's introduction.

How Dubno felt upon reading Mendelssohn's version of the story in the introduction *Or Li-Netiva* when it appeared has been described in a letter written to David Friedländer by Joseph Elias of Vilna on Adar I, 1, 5543 (1783):[92] "His face darkened when he saw the words said about him [as quoted in Friedländer's letter to Elias][93] ... While I was discussing the various aspects of the matter for the sake of restoring peace between these two perfect men—for in my humble view Rabbi Solomon, too, may be called a whole-hearted and perfect man—he grew impatient and displayed a whole file of documents . . . in an effort to refute by an abundance of arguments what our teacher Rabbi Moses had said in his *Or Li-Netiva*."

Joseph Elias, who had offered Dubno the hospitality of his home,[94] found himself in a difficult position. He was the son-in-law of Rabbi Samuel ben Avigdor, chairman of the rabbinic court *(rosh bet din)* of Vilna, and was himself a fine rabbinic scholar. Like others of his group who were inspired by the Gaon of Vilna, he was imbued with respect and love of the sciences. He admired both Dubno and Mendelssohn. He saw nothing objectionable in Mendelssohn's translation, yet he approved Dubno's plan to reedit and continue his *Bi'ur* and *Tikkun Soferim* without the German translation, which was at any rate of little use in Lithuania. Dubno's project envisioned a new edition of the entire Pentateuch, which would also contain the *Targum Onkelos* and Rashi's commentary.[95] While Dubno was staying with Elias in the early part of 1783, he had already begun to mobilize the support of prominent rabbis in several countries for his grandiose undertaking.[96] Having left Berlin in the fall of 1780, he apparently went first to Brody.[97] He then traveled widely in Poland, Lithuania, and Germany, everywhere arousing great enthusiasm for his idea and obtaining rabbinic approbations galore. When writing to Friedländer, Elias drew attention to Dubno's success and offered the suggestion that Mendelssohn try to appease rather than blame a man who had so many powerful supporters. Some sided with Dubno from genuine love, he remarked, while others did so from hatred of Mendelssohn. There was enough paper and type for the printing of all sorts of things. Elias, who wanted to be helpful and to prevent anything that might hurt Mendelssohn, did not suggest any specific action that might heal the breach. He did say, however, that few people believed the version of the story as told by Mendelssohn in his introduction.

In reply, Friedländer reiterated the facts as reported in his previous letter. Dubno, in the chief rabbi's presence, had agreed by his handshake to abide by the agreement arrived at—and then he had simply disappeared. He ought to feel ashamed of himself! Friedländer expressed astonishment when he was advised that, in view of the strong support that Dubno had marshaled, every effort should be made to bring about a reconciliation. "Dubno lived with us for a long time. He knows that 'we have a little sister,'[98] whose name is 'love of truth.' Though her paths are 'paths of pleasantness,' strength lodges upon her neck." In conclusion Friedländer's letter cited Isaiah 54:17: "No weapon that is formed against thee shall prosper," substituting "him" (i.e. Mendelssohn) for "thee." Elias thereupon apologized for having occasioned a misunderstanding. He had not doubted the *truth* of Mendelssohn's version of the story; he had merely appealed to his generosity. What was "a small thing for Moses"[99] was not so small for Dubno. For the sake of peace, the elder sister of truth, he hoped that the two men, for whom he bore an equal love, would be reconciled.[100]

This hope was not to be fulfilled. The rift had become too wide, especially in view of Dubno's dazzling success in gaining rabbinic support in the form of highly complimentary approbations.[101] Those extolling his enterprise included the Gaon of Vilna, Rabbi Noah Mendes of Vilna, Chief Rabbi Ezekiel Landau of Prague, the Sephardic and Ashkenazic chief rabbis of Amsterdam, the chief rabbi of Nancy, and the rabbinic heads of many German communities. In many cases the praises lavished upon Dubno implied a condemnation of Mendelssohn's project. Thus Dubno became the darling of the orthodox opposition, and it was inevitable that he came to look upon his divorce from the Mendelssohnian circle as primarily due to religious scruples that he had suppressed for a long time but that prevailed in the end.

Any compunction that Dubno might have felt about the competitive character of his effort was probably stilled by the applause he received from the rabbinic leaders. How formidable the competition was may be gauged from the fact that his appeal for subscriptions brought in no less than twelve hundred individual orders from thirty-two communities, whose secretaries verified the signatures. The money was to be paid upon delivery of the projected work. In 1788 Dubno made a second appeal for the loan of a large amount of money that would permit the start of the actual printing. The response was insufficient and the whole plan had to be abandoned. Thus a tremendous outpouring of effort and enthusiasm had been wasted.[102]

In retrospect it would appear that a reconciliation with Mendelssohn, whose circumspection and organizing capacity ensured the success of his enterprise despite all opposition, would have benefited Dubno, and benefited Mendelssohn's Pentateuch as well. It was to be expected that the shattering experience of his failure would cause Dubno to reevaluate his past association with Mendelssohn. Since nothing had come of his own ambitious project, he was bound to look upon his share in Mendelssohn's Pentateuch as a creditable achievement untainted by the setting in which it had appeared, and to dissociate himself from any disparagement of Mendelssohn's translation. A letter written by Dubno in 1789, when the failure of his own plan had become manifest, seems to reflect the impact that this sad fact had had on his thinking. The letter was addressed to Wolf Heidenheim, the noted massoretic scholar, who had asked Dubno for the loan of the Worms manuscript of Rashi's and Rashbam's commentaries on the Pentateuch, which he had used when writing the *Bi'ur*.[103] In his reply (dated Amsterdam, Siwan 8, 5549/1789) Dubno wrote:[104]

> To my regret I am unable to fulfil your request; for the Worms manuscript on parchment, which contains Rashi's and Rashbam's commentaries and which I used when writing the *Bi'ur*, is not in my possession but in the possession of the heirs of the wise Mendelssohn of blessed memory. Since my departure from Berlin I no longer have any connection with the place, and I cannot apply to the people there, however much I wish to be of service to you. My old teacher in my youthful years, the Gaon Rabbi Naphtali Hirz of Dubno (may his memory be for a blessing), who was passing through Berlin, reproached me in the words of II Chronicles 20:37 ("Because thou hast joined thyself with Ahaziah, the

Lord hath made a breach in thy works") for cooperating with people whose aim was to uproot our sacred tradition, as he had been informed in writing by the rabbis of Prague and Hamburg. I thereupon promised him to break with this group and to leave Berlin.

I have no reason to regret my cooperation or the fact that I was the one who induced Mendelssohn to publish his translation. Every person of intelligence recognizes that this beautiful translation and the *Bi'ur* are of great benefit to our youth, teaching them as they do to appreciate the splendor of the Word of God. Yet some of those who had been invited to assist in the execution of the work and, especially, those who had been entrusted with the dispatch of the First Book of Moses to the subscribers, were so much under suspicion of having thrown off the "yoke of the Tora" that it was indeed necessary to draw away from them: "Depart, I pray you," etc.[105] I have no doubt that by writing to Mendelssohn's heirs you will receive the desired manuscript on loan.

The ostensible purpose of this passage is to explain why he found it impossible to get in touch with Mendelssohn's heirs: he had irrevocably severed his connections with those (notably David Friedländer) who might prove helpful in the matter of Heidenheim's request. In elaborating this point Dubno took the opportunity to tell the story of his departure from Berlin. In so doing he offered a rather tendentious mixture of fiction and truth. Obviously he wished to create the impression that he had left Mendelssohn only because of Mendelssohn's entourage, which had become repugnant to Dubno on account of their religious laxity. In order to make the force of this argument stronger and more convincing he invoked the authority of this old teacher Naphtali Hirz, who had allegedly urged him to dissociate himself from such company. There may be a kernel of truth in this statement. Naphtali Hirz, who died in 1777,[106] could have visited his former pupil shortly before he passed away. In that year the Pentateuch project was already well under way, and Hirz could have expressed misgivings about some of the people who were close to Mendelssohn. However, he could not have received any letters from the rabbis of Prague and Hamburg-Altona denouncing the Pentateuch project. The opposition to it began only after the appearance of the prospectus in the summer of 1778. The two rabbis might, on the other hand, have written to Hirz about the Berlin "freethinkers" among whom Dubno was moving, and the advice to leave Berlin might have been independent of the literary effort in which Dubno was engaged. Dubno's mention of Mendelssohn's fellow workers who were under suspicion of having thrown off the yoke of the Tora—the reference is clearly to Herz Homberg on the one hand, and to David Friedländer and Jeremias Bendit on the other—occurs in the context of his personal reflections and is not part of the observations relating to the early period when his teacher visited him. No anachronism can be detected here.

That Dubno waited some three years before acting on his teacher's advice (assuming that he ever received such advice) need occasion no surprise. He was too deeply involved in the project to be able to abandon it without more compelling pressures. It was only when his pride as an author was hurt by Mendelssohn's refusal to publish his long introduction in its entirety, and when additional reasons of a financial character pressed upon him, that he decided to withdraw. Dubno's distaste for Mendelssohn's administrative associates was undoubtedly a contributory factor: he abhorred them both on religious grounds and because he suspected them to be the real culprits in the matter of his literary setback. This is evident from the letter he wrote to Mendelssohn on September 22, 1780. Nine years later, recalling the past in his letter to Heidenheim, Dubno presented them as the sole villains of the piece, while he had only nice things to say about Mendelssohn and his translation and about his own work, the *Bi'ur*. The praise he bestowed on their common enterprise reads almost like a précis of his prospectus. By reemphasizing the beauty of the translation and the splendor of the Word of God that the work would bring home to Jewish youth he reverted to the old pattern. He had obviously not become alienated from the spirit of Haskala that had given birth to the new edition of the Pentateuch. Had he remained at his post, the work produced would have been more even and, in parts, superior to what was accomplished in the end. He would also have spared both Mendelssohn and himself a good deal of trouble.

Completing the Work

The first volume of the translation, Genesis, to which Dubno contributed both the commentary and the massoretic notes, appeared in the spring of 1780.[1] The second volume, Exodus, came out a year later, in the spring of 1781.[2] Dubno's share in it consisted of the massoretic notes and glosses to the commentary, which were identified as such by being placed within brackets and marked by an asterisk. The bulk of the commentary was by Mendelssohn.[3] It cannot be assumed that Mendelssohn started writing his commentary after Dubno's departure in the fall of 1780. A work of such magnitude and subtlety could not have been written and printed in just over six months. He must have begun working on it not later than in the summer of 1779, about a year after the publication of the prospectus. He had begun to realize, he said in the introduction (1782), "that the labor was too heavy for Rabbi Solomon Dubno—that he could not bear it alone."[4] He had therefore entrusted the writing of the *Bi'ur* on the third volume, Leviticus, to Wesseley.[5] We assume that he decided at the same time—presumably the summer of 1779—to take personal charge of the commentary on Exodus. It may be taken for granted that under the new schedule Dubno was to supply the massoretic notes for the entire Pentateuch and to compose the *Bi'ur* on the last two volumes, Numbers and Deuteronomy. This would explain the fact that at the time of his dissociation from the project he had completed not only the massoretic notes on Exodus but had also started work on the Numbers commentary.

Our assumption that Mendelssohn commenced writing the *Bi'ur* on
Exodus long before Dubno left him is strikingly confirmed by a document
whose true nature and significance have not been recognized before. The
collection of manuscripts in Dubno's *Nachlass,* preserved at the Hebrew
University Library, Jerusalem, contains four, partly damaged, folios of
notes (thirty-two in all), in Dubno's own handwriting, offering penetrating
observations on various points in Mendelssohn's *Bi'ur* on Exodus. The same
sheets also contain, in the margin or between lines, brief comments (twelve
in all) on those notes, in Mendelssohn's handwriting.[6] The notes in Dubno's
hand are of varying length, some being extremely long and others very
short indeed, and they concern highly intricate and technical matters related
to the vestments of the High Priest (Exodus 28), the form of his anointment
(Exodus 29:7), and the construction of the Sanctuary (Exodus 26, 27).
The notes are based on a text presented on thirteen folios, as is clear
from the exact references to the text in the notes. According to these
references the text discussed the subject matters, more or less at random,
following this order: Exodus 28, 29, 26, 27, and again 26. This haphazard
arrangement suggests that the text underlying the notes was not Mendelssohn's *Bi'ur* as such but selected passages from it, perhaps ones that
seemed to call for further discussion.

The scholar to whom Mendelssohn sent these sheets, and probably
many others like them, was not Chief Rabbi Hirschel Lewin or Hartog
Leo, as has been variously suggested,[7] but Solomon Dubno. For several
reasons it has to be concluded that Dubno, in whose hand the notes are
written, did not merely copy them but was their author. The most glaring
evidence to this effect is provided by the quotation of one of the notes
in the *Bi'ur* on Exodus 28:17. The note in our document that declares Nahmanides' rejection of a certain interpretration by Rashi to be unjustified[8] re-
appears word for word in the *Bi'ur* and is there identified as Dubno's both in
the customary way (brackets and asterisk) and by the words, "Solomon said."
Now, seeing that one of the notes found in the document has been established as having Dubno for its author, it follows that all the other notes in that
context are probably also by Dubno.[9] At the very least, the assumption that
Dubno merely copied someone else's notes is surely untenable: what could
the purpose of such copying have been? There is further evidence of
Dubno's authorship in the style of the notes: the extremely deferential manner in which both approval and disapproval are expressed is typical of
Dubno, and reminds one of the self-deprecating manner of some of the
passages in his September 22, 1780, letter to Mendelssohn. Finally, the
underlying text, the notes, and Mendelssohn's brief comments on the notes
make sense only if one assumes a close working partnership between the
two men.

The document at our disposal shows in the most circumstantial manner
how that partnership worked. We see Mendelssohn sending a few sheets
to Dubno. He had done his research into the meaning of certain difficult

phrases, and having consulted the talmudic sources, the Targumim, Maimonides' Code, and the classical medieval commentators, he had formed an opinion; but he still had his doubts and so was anxious to hear Dubno's view. Dubno repeated the labor of digging up all relevant sources and, after long deliberation, put down his findings in notes of varying length. Mendelssohn then studied those notes and finally made up his mind. When he found Dubno's objection convincing, he would revise what he had previously written in the manuscript of his *Bi'ur*, as he did, for example, in the case of a note by Dubno[10] concerning Exodus 28:33, to which Mendelssohn reacted by admitting in the margin: "You are right, and I have deleted this expression [in my manuscript of the *Bi'ur*]." In other cases his comment made it clear that he rejected Dubno's view. For example, he had suggested that a certain phrase in Maimonides' Code was a misprint, as could be seen from the context. Dubno's note tried to uphold the printed text, but Mendelssohn did not budge from his position, as his comment and the *Bi'ur* indicate.[11] When Dubno, most apologetically, took issue with him on the thorny question of the manner of anointment and remarked, incidentally, that the Greek letter Ξ was to be pronounced *gsi* and not *ksi*, as Mendelssohn had indicated in his transliteration, Mendelssohn ignored both Dubno's lengthy discussion and the correction.[12] Sometimes Dubno confessed to not having understood Mendelssohn's way of expression; for example, what did Mendelssohn's term "the angles between the circles" signify? In answer to this query Mendelssohn drew a graph in the margin, but he did not include the graph in the published commentary.[13]

The document, which gives us such a revealing glimpse of the close cooperation between the two scholars, bears no date but, since it reflects a rather advanced stage of the work on the Exodus commentary,[14] it could have been written as late as the summer of 1780. At that time their mutual relationship was still unclouded. Dubno had not yet written his grammatical introduction,[15] and so the controversial issue of its publication had not yet arisen. He obviously had no doubt that once it was written it would appear at the beginning of the second volume. According to his announcement in the prospectus, it was due to appear in the first volume in order to give the reader a clue to the grammatical references in the *Bi'ur*.[16] How Mendelssohn felt about the matter is clearly stated in his own introduction:[17] "Rabbi Solomon Dubno wrote at the end of his preface to the treatise *'Alim Li-Terufa* that he was going to write an abridged grammar ... and use it as an introduction to the Pentateuch. Yet I did not fancy this idea. We are not short of books on grammar, and I shall not add one more to their number." So long as Dubno was still unaware of Mendelssohn's opposition to his plan, he had no reason for resentment insofar as literary matters were concerned. True, Mendelssohn had complained about the excessive length of some of Dubno's comments in his *Bi'ur* on Genesis and also of some of the massoretic notes.[18] A mere glance at the printed text shows, however, that despite his grumbling Mendelssohn had been rather lenient. As he explained in a letter to Moses Fischer, rabbi of Vienna, in a letter dated March 6, 1784, he had not considered himself sufficiently competent in grammar and had therefore invited Dubno (and later other scholars) to supply the grammatical passages in the *Bi'ur*.[19] When working with Mendelssohn on the commentary on Exodus, Dubno thus had a rather free hand. In such circumstances there could hardly have been strained relations between them.[20]

Two highlights of Mendelssohn's *Bi'ur* on Exodus are his interpretation of the Divine Name (YHWH) and his introduction to Moses' Song. In his translation he renders the Tetragrammaton either as *der Ewige* ("the Eternal One") or as *das ewige Wesen* ("the eternal Being"), and his commentary on Exodus 3:14 offers the reason for this translation, which has no precedent in traditional Jewish sources but is found in its Greek form (*ho Aionios*) in the apocryphal Book of Barukh and in its French form (*l'Éternel*) in Calvin's Geneva Bible.[21] In two places in the commentary Mendelssohn incorporates glosses by Dubno[22] that are in complete conformity with his own explanation. The text of the commentary, including the glosses, which are marked as such with asterisks and brackets, reads:

"I am that I am." According to the Midrash, the Holy One, blessed be He, said to Moses: Say unto them, I am the One that was, and now I am the same, and I shall be the same in the future, [*and our rabbis of blessed memory said furthermore: I shall be with them in this plight as I shall be with them in ther servitude under other kingdoms. They meant to say that*] because the past and the future are all in the present for the Creator, for "there is neither change nor any fixed time for Him"[23] and none of His days are ever gone. Hence for Him all times are called by one Name that comprises past, present, and future. Consequently, it [sc. this Name] indicates the necessity of [God's] existence, and it also indicates [His] perpetual, unceasing providence. By this Name He says, as it were: I am with the children of men to be gracious and merciful unto whom I shall be merciful. Now say unto the Israelites that I was, am, and shall be, ruling all and exercising providence over all, I am in truth and shall be with them in all their miseries, I am with them in their present plight and I shall be with them whenever they call unto Me.

Now there is no word in the German language which expresses the meaning of [being] at all times and the meaning of necessity of existence and the meaning of providence all combined in one term as does this Holy Name (the eternal, necessary, provident Being). We translate it: the Eternal or the Eternal Being. [*Onkelos rendered *ehye asher ehye*: I shall be with whom I shall be (according to the text quoted by Nahmanides of blessed memory) in the sense of "I shall be gracious unto whom I shall be gracious, and shall be merciful unto whom I shall be merciful" (Exodus 33:19). His intention was to translate it in the sense of providence only, and in accordance with the second Midrash. Saadya Gaon wrote that its interpretation is: Who did not cease to be and shall not cease to be, for He is the First and the Last. His words come close to those of the first Midrash, which refer to (His) eternity. Maimonides explained it in the *Guide of the Perplexed* to mean the Existent that exists (sc. of necessity). He had the meaning of necessity of existence in mind. In reality, it comprises all three meanings, but Onkelos, who wrote Aramaic, and Saadya, who wrote Arabic, and Maimonides, who likewise wrote Arabic, could not find in their respective languages a word that would comprise all these significations as does this Holy Name. Hence each one rendered it in his own way by choosing one of these meanings, and the German translator (sc. Mendelssohn) saw fit to render it in the sense of eternity, seeing that from it the other significations derive. I found that (the Targum of) Jonathan ben Uzi'el translated it in the same sense: I who am and shall be has sent me to you.*][24]

Dubno's gloss merely elaborates Mendelssohn's interpretation by pointing out that the three aspects of divinity implied in the Tetragrammaton appear singly in the respective explanations of it by Onkelos, Saadya, and Maimonides. He justified Mendelssohn's emphasis on the attribute of eternity ("the Eternal One" or "the Eternal Being" as the translation of the Holy Name) by declaring that the other two significations derived from it. Here, too, he simply followed Mendelssohn's commentary, which said that the Name expressing God's eternity thereby ("consequently") indicated the necessity of his existence and his providence. The philosophical background of this view is to be found in Mendelssohn's assertion that all attributes of God are so intimately connected with each other that from one of them all the rest can be derived, a concept that Mendelssohn had adopted from Baumgarten's *Metaphysica*.[25] The term "eternity" (*nitshiut*) is used only in Dubno's gloss, but the notion is clearly defined in the commentary: past and future are for God in the present, there being no change nor any fixed time for him. This concept of an eternal Now is what differentiates between eternity and an infinitely long time or the sempiternal. While avoiding the dryness of philosophical jargon, the essential elements of the philosophical idea of God are not lacking. It was characteristic of Mendelssohn to prefer the poetical flavor of a quotation from the Book of Job (10:17) to the technical term "eternity." We may add that the older German translations of the Bible by Yekutiel Blitz and Josel Witzenhausen rendered the Tetragrammaton in the same way as the name *Elohim*, namely by *Got* (God). Where the text has both names together (*YHWH Elohim*), they translated *Got der Her* (the Lord God), being totally unconcerned about the christological flavor that the term *der Her* had acquired.[26]

Mendelssohn's introduction to Moses' Song (Exodus 15:1–18) fulfils the promise he had made in his commentary on the first pericope of Genesis (4:23) to explain some of the rules of biblical poetry. The Genesis passage had given him an opportunity to refer to what Robert Lowth (in his famous *Lectures on the Sacred Poetry of the Hebrews*)[27] had designated synonymous and antithetic parallelism. As Mendelssohn put it: "Sometimes the meaning of the first member of a period [*delet; haruz*] is repeated in the second with but a verbal change... and sometimes it is opposed to the meaning of the second member while there is a correspondence in language." An example of the first type of parellelism is Lamech's speech (Genesis 4:23):

"Adah and Zillah, hear my voice; / Ye wives of Lamech, harken unto my speech; /For I have slain a man for wounding me, / And a young man for bruising me." The other kind of parallelism is illustrated by Proverbs 27:6: "Faithful are the wounds of a friend; / But the kisses of an enemy are importunate."

Mendelssohn had been familiar with Lowth's great treatise ever since he reviewed it in 1757 and 1761,[28] and he also knew Lowth's *Isaiah, A New Translation* (London, 1778).[29] In his introduction to Moses' Song he again made use of the subtle analyses by which the Englishman had enriched Hebrew prosody, but he mentioned by name only Azarya dei Rossi (1513–1578), whose discussion of the subject in chapter sixty of his *Imrey Bina* had furnished Lowth with more ideas than might appear from his references to him.[30] The following is a brief synopsis of Mendelssohn's introduction, which for the first time in the history of Hebrew Bible commentaries dealt with the formal aspects of biblical poetry.[31]

Ancient Hebrew poetry, Mendelssohn pointed out, was neither governed by the metrical rules based on the number of long or short syllables nor did it employ rhyme. These devices, he contended, achieved nothing more than sounds pleasant to the ear when the poem was recited, and became useless and even cumbersome when the poem was set to music and chanted. Moreover, the charm produced by the metric system and by rhyme was utterly lost in translation. "Our ancients" had followed rules of a superior quality. Mendelssohn here paraphrased Jehuda Ha-Levi's statement in the *Kuzari* (II, 70–74), which rejected the notion that melodies required the use of meter, and which saw the superiority of ancient Hebrew poems in their power to enhance the understanding rather than to flatter the ear. As Mendelssohn put it, their words entered not merely into the ear but into the heart of the listener, creating strong and enduring sentiments.

In a passage not alluded to by Mendelssohn, Jehuda Ha-Levi had deplored the imitation of the metrical systems of Arabic poetry by Hebrew writers as alien to the Hebrew tongue and causing only disharmonies—a view that seems a bit strange when uttered, as in this case, by a great Hebrew poet who had used this method himself.[32] What Mendelssohn emphasized in this connection was that a great deal of biblical poetry, notably the Psalms, was intended to be chanted to the accompaniment of instrumental music. One had to assume that the art of music was highly developed in ancient Israel and that it was intimately wedded to poetry. There follows this startling remark on contemporary music:

> Do not compare our contemporary art of music to the magnificent art cultivated by those perfect ones [i.e. the leaders, sages, and prophets of Israel], for it seems that there is no comparison between them at all. To this art happened what happened to the art of poetry. Excellence of meaning and thought, in which the improvement of the rational soul lies, has been abandoned in favor of excellence in sound, which makes only for sensual pleasure and the delight enjoyed by the ear . . .

Mendelssohn here reiterated a view about the function of instrumental music that he had expressed several times before, although it hardly represented a consistently held opinion. In his *Letters on Art* [33] he had defined the purpose of music as being closely allied to that of poetry. The meaning of the words combined with the affect produced by the music created a powerful enchantment. Alas, music had been led astray: "It has become divorced from poetry and it has been treated as an independent art. Its frontiers have been infinitely expanded, instruments upon instruments have been invented, melodies upon melodies have been composed that are no longer guided by reason but are a mere jingling of sounds that flatter the ear. All effort has been directed to the end of pleasing the senses without enlightening the understanding, without improving the heart, without trying to make us happier."[34]

It is remarkable how tenaciously Mendelssohn sometimes adhered to theories evolved at an early period of his life. By its very nature his work on the *Bi'ur* tended to reinforce ideas of a conservative character. Reflecting on ancient Hebrew poetry, he suddenly realized how much its alliance with music conformed to the ideal picture of the two arts that he had formed in his mind. It is not impossible that his concept had owed something from the very start to Jehuda Ha-Levi's contempt for poetic art that merely pleased the ear.

The function of Hebrew poetry, Mendelssohn went on to suggest, helped to explain its formal structure, i.e. both the "measures and proportions," which had been discovered by Azarya dei Rossi and mentioned by Lowth, and the various nuances of parallelism, which Lowth had found. Whereas Rossi was content merely to describe the specific rules, and whereas Lowth had attributed the difference between Greek and Latin poetry, on the one hand, and Hebrew poetry, on the other, to formal aspects of the languages concerned,[35] Mendelssohn linked form to purpose. Since the poem wanted to impress the mind with a certain idea or sentiment, it had to present clearly intelligible units of meaning arranged in a certain measure not of syllables but of words, and it had to do this in a way that allowed for caesuras or rest-periods at the right time so as to enable the listener to absorb the idea, to ponder it, and to commit it to the memory. The breaking up of the verses into short component parts was also designed to facilitate their musical rendition.

Mendelssohn quoted the entire passage in which Rossi had formulated his theory of the particular kind of Hebrew "meter" and its variations. It consisted not in the number of long or short syllables but in the number of terms or parts of a proposition. A phrase containing two terms is, as a rule, joined by another likewise comprising two terms, the two phrases together forming what Lowth called a tetrameter, and two tetrameters forming a single verse. Moses' Song, Mendelssohn remarked in a gloss, was built almost exclusively on this kind of meter: "Thy-right-hand, O-Lord / glorious in-power, // Thy-right-hand, O-Lord / dasheth-in-pieces the-enemy" (Exodus 15:6). (The words here connected by hyphens render what are single words in the Hebrew text.)

Another form of biblical "meter" uses two phrases consisting of three terms or measures. Moses' Farewell Song (Deuteronomy 32:1–43) is constructed in this fashion: "My-doctrine shall-drop as-the-rain, / My-speech shall-distil as-the-dew" (verse two). The two combined phrases form what Lowth termed an hexameter, and a single verse may contain one or two such hexameters. Tetrameters and hexameters may alternate in one poem, and Mendelssohn dwelt at some length on the different possible variations and on the inspiring effect produced by certain changes in meter. He also elaborated other fine points suggested by Lowth, and might have gone on in this vein, had he not remembered that he was engaged in the writing of a commentary. His final paragraph reads as follows:

> I have already gone beyond the limits set by my purpose. I have transgressed the law of brevity which I had laid down for my *Bi'ur*, and this I did from love for the subject. For I have not found in any of the commentaries on the Tora a statement that sufficiently explains the matter and makes the reader aware of the glorious beauty of the poems in the Holy Scriptures. I notice how the young of our people "supply themselves with the products of the Gentiles" and take pride in the poetic art of alien nations, as if to them had been given the splendor and precious grace of poetic art. Hence my heart was burning with the zeal to show that "as far as the heavens are high above the earth," so are the ways of our sacred poetry high above the ways of secular poetry. This is true not only in regard to the excellence of the poets (the efficient cause), or the exalted phrases (the material of the poems), or the purpose that is to guide us to eternal happiness and true felicity through the sublime matters they deal with, viz. the prophecies, promises, blessings, and praises of God that lead man to life eternal. It is true also in regard to the form, i.e. the arrangement, composition, and order of the words. In this respect, too, our sacred poetry is vastly superior in splendor and beauty to all other poems that are so highly praised.

The sincerity of the sentiments expressed in this postscript cannot be doubted. Mendelssohn discussed Hebrew prosody not because he wanted to foist a secular type of aestheticism upon the understanding of biblical poetry but because the element of form was for him part and parcel of a sacred entity in which—speaking in Aristotelian terms—the four causes (efficient, formal, final, material) were inextricably intertwined. Aesthetics and theology are happily married in this introduction. How much Mendelssohn felt indebted to Lowth may be gauged from the fact that immediately after the Exodus volume appeared, he sent him a copy of it together with a copy of the Genesis edition. The gift was accompanied by a letter written in ornate Hebrew on April 26, 1781. It reflected a sense of solemnity befitting the occasion: the *Juif de Berlin* addressing the Lord Bishop of London. The text of the letter, which bore also the Hebrew date, read as follows:[36]

> To the Cedar on Lebanon, Prince of Tora and Wisdom, the Priest that is highest among his brethren in the Royal City of London (may

God protect it), my honored Teacher (*kevod rabbi*) Lowth (may he be granted children and length of days, Amen) from the hyssop out of the wall,[37] Moses son of Rabbi Mendel of blessed memory [the greeting of] peace.

Wherewith shall I come before thy face,[38] my lord! We who take pleasure in the language of thy country and love her dust![39] Wherewith shall we render thanks unto thee for all the good thou hast bestowed upon us by thy loved and cherished books: the one on sacred poetry in general, which I read and which was to my palate like the best wine,[40] and the one of Isaiah's prophecy in particular, which is well known and highly esteemed. When I saw that thou has fully understood the character of that precious language and mastered the depth of its style, I promised myself and vowed to send thee the Book of the Tora that I am now committing to print, namely the Book Genesis and the Book Exodus, which I recently finished. My Prince, kindly have a look at it, for thine is the judgment upon having examined it. Thou wilt know if thou didst find in it a word of truth and rightness or not. I will not trouble thee, my lord, with a reply to this letter. For I realize the multitude of business besetting a man of affairs like unto thee, and who am I to come thus far?[41] I regard as sufficient glory, and it will be deemed an honor by the elders of my people, if thou wilt accept this present, which is being brought to thee by my trusted friend, the enlightened physician Doctor Mires. I shall thereby know that the servant who wants to reconcile himself unto his lord[42] has found favor in thine eyes. Peace unto thee.[43]

The third volume of Mendelssohn's edition of the Pentateuch, the Book of Leviticus, was published in quick succession. As early as September 24, 1781, Mendelssoln was able to send a copy of it to Herder. In a covering letter he described it as "the third Book of Moses, with my translation and a commentary by my learned friend Herr Wessely, which to my financial detriment and to many a reader's boredom turned out to be much too learned."[44] He failed to mention that the many scholarly glosses added by him had contributed to that result, which, in fact, he was far from deploring. He was undoubtedly pleased with the magnificent job Wesseley had done. We may note that this volume was held in high esteem by many leading rabbis of the time and of the subsequent period. Rabbi Mordecai Benet (II) of Nicolsburg (1753–1829), who was chief rabbi of Moravia, had special praise for Wessely's *Bi'ur*.[45] In his introduction, *Or Li-Netiva*, Mendelssohn offered a brief account of his cooperation with Wessely. After mentioning the fact that he had realized the urgent need to take part of the load from Dubno's shoulders, he continued:[46] "Because of his esteem and great love for me, the afore-mentioned rabbi [Wessely] relinquished his occupations and devoted himself to the writing of a commentary on that entire book [Leviticus] from beginning to end. He embodied in his *Bi'ur* valuable investigations of halakhic matters, of the characteristics of the [Hebrew] language, of the traits of [human] souls, and of the varieties of moral qualities. There is no pericope in which he has not something new to say on one of these subjects, in accordance with the method he has followed in his well-known and celebrated works. 'His modesty hath made us great,'[47] for in his broadmindedness he permitted me to express views different from his own, and he inserted into his commentary my polemical glosses and arguments (enclosed within brackets), leaving it to the reader to choose what is right in his eyes."

One cannot but admire the delicacy of feeling with which Mendelssohn described Wessely's acceptance of the task allotted to him. Judging from his account, one might have thought that in response to the call Wessely had given up his business in order to write the commentary, whereas in reality he was in dire financial need at the time and welcomed the invitation as a godsend. His employer Joseph Veitel, at whose request he had moved to Berlin in 1774, had liquidated his business and gone into retirement without making any provision whatever for Wessely, who was then well past the age of fifty and had a wife and six children to support. This sudden change in his fortunes must have occurred in 1778.[48] Deprived of his livelihood, he had to depend on whatever income he could earn by his pen. It seems that David Friedländer proved helpful by employing his services in certain ways that are not quite clear.[49] Jeremias Bendit invented another means of benefiting the man without hurting his pride, inviting him to deliver lectures on the Tora for young people two or three times a week. At first the attendance was overwhelming; many people of different ages were attracted by Wessely's learned and enthusiastic exposition, which dealt with the first chapters of Genesis. Soon disillusionment set in, however, because the lecturer's approach, ostensibly sophisticated, seemed to take insufficient account of modern scientific theories. The audience became smaller and smaller until in the end Wessely found himself deserted completely. The only redeeming feature of this sad story is the fact that the lectures prompted Wessely to write a Hebrew commentary on Genesis.[50] He must have been very happy indeed when, probably in the summer of 1779, Mendelssohn asked him to write the *Bi'ur* on Leviticus.

Mendelssohn was no less tactful in his reference to Wessely's "modesty" and "broad-mindedness" in permitting him to express his own viewpoint when it differed from the one expounded by Wessely in the *Bi'ur*. In actual fact, Wessely's commentary is interspersed with numerous glosses of various kinds. Some of them elaborate on Wessely's comments. Their purpose in others is to explain the translation. Sometimes Mendelssohn draws attention to a point he had made in his own *Bi'ur* on Exodus, and frequently he takes issue with Wessely's exegesis. Thus the commentary was greatly enriched by Mendelssohn's contributions. Two polemical glosses will be discussed here.

Following his rule of letting the context determine the meaning of a phrase, Mendelssohn had translated Leviticus 19:17 as follows: "Thou shalt not hate thy brother in thy heart; thou mayest rebuke thy neighbor (if he hurts you) but thou shalt not bear him a grudge because of his offense."[51] Ignoring this translation, which was at variance with the traditional rabbinic understanding of the verse as enjoining the *duty* to rebuke one's fellowman for *any* sin committed by him, Wessely commented: "Thou shalt surely rebuke thy neighbor, make clear to him that he sinned, and speak to his heart words of reason teaching him the right path so that he may acknowledge his sin and depart from his way. In so doing you will bear no sin on his account, as I shall explain. The precept refers to matters obtaining between man and God as well as between man and his neighbor."[52] Wessely's comment on the following verse (Leviticus 19:18) reads: "And thou shalt love thy neighbor as thyself... This should be properly rendered, Love thy neighbor, for he is thy equal [all men being created in the image of God].... The regular Hebrew phrase denoting the love of someone else as oneself is *ohavo ke-nafsho*, as for example in 1 Samuel 18:1 ..." To this exegesis Mendelssohn replied in a gloss: * "Says the translator: All these words of his are utterances of grace and good understanding to those who do thereafter.[53] Happy is everyone who hearkens to his rebuke, but the literal meaning of the verses does not bear them out. In my opinion this is the sequence of their meaning: ... *Thou shalt surely rebuke they neighbor,* if he inflicted evil upon you, rebuke him to his face and make clear to him the evil nature of his deed; you will then not bear any grudge against him because of the sin which he committed against you.... *And thou shalt love thy neighbor as thyself,* viz. in the same manner of love with which you love yourself. The verse refers only to the quality, not to the degree of love." Mendelssohn explains that there are both various kinds and various degrees of love, and that the Tora commands us to benefit our neighbor not for selfish reasons but for the sake of his own good. The linguistic point made by Wessely is not taken up.

The other gloss occurs in the context of the Warnings of Divine Punishment in Leviticus 26:14–46. Mendelssohn translated verse thirty-nine in the following sense: Those of you that are left shall pine away in your enemies' lands, partly because of their own sin, and partly because of the sins of their fathers they shall pine away with them. In his *Bi'ur*, Wessely quoted the old rabbinic interpretation,[54] reproduced by Rashi, which tried to reconcile this verse with the injunction (Deuteronomy 24:16) not to punish the children for the misdeeds of their parents: *Because of the sins of their fathers with them* bore this meaning: if the sins of their fathers are still with them, i.e. if they cling to the deeds of their fathers, they will bear guilt and receive punishment. Wessely considered this interpretation a bit forced, yet he did not dismiss it entirely. He merely invested the rabbinic phrase "if they cling to the deeds of their fathers" with a new meaning: if the children of sinful parents are inclined to repeat the evil acts of their forebears, they will be punished, even though they did not actually commit the acts. For God, "who searcheth the hearts," knows that the evil desires they harbor would cause them to sin, should the opportunity present itself.

To cling to the deeds of their fathers is understood by Wessely to mean being predisposed to imitate their fathers. Divine justice is therefore meted out because of God's knowledge of how the children would act in certain circumstances.[55] It was for this reason, Wessely pointed out, that the punishment that befell our forefathers (viz. the destruction of the Temple and the nation's exile) continued generation after generation. Mendelssohn was outraged by this exegesis: * "Says the translator: God forbid that He should hold a man responsible for a sin that he has not actually committed. Onkelos' translation agrees with the [old rabbinic] opinion expressed by Rashi, but this was not the view indicated by the massoretic accents, which connect the word *ittam* ("with them") with [the following word] *yimmakku* ("they shall pine away"). According to Rashi, it should have been connected with the preceding words."

Having thus established the correctness of his own translation, Mendelssohn proceeds to explain why the children should have to bear the iniquities of their forefathers. Implicit in his little discourse on the subject is the view that there are two kinds of divine retribution, namely one that works through natural causes without requiring a miraculous intervention,[56] and one that represents a supernatural and miraculous act. No punishment of the second kind is ever inflicted on children because of their fathers' sins. This is what the principle enunciated in Deuteronomy 24:16 amounts to. However, the evil inflicted as punishment for grave sins by a supernatural and miraculous divine intrevention does not vanish with the generation upon which it was decreed. Its effects remain with their descendants, and what was once a miraculous event turns into a natural condition with natural consequences. It takes another miracle to undo these effects and restore the previous condition. Thus, Israel's exile from the Holy Land was not a natural punishment: it happened as the result of a special divine intervention. Once the Jewish nation was exiled, however, the fate of being in exile became a natural situation, and the children born in foreign lands bear the "yoke of exile" as a natural consequence of what once happened. The termination of *galut* requires a divine miracle. From the fact that such a miracle has not yet happened we must conclude that our merits are as yet insufficient to warrant a supernatural suspension of our plight.

The meaning of the verse is therefore perfectly clear: the children do bear the natural consequences of the supernatural retribution decreed upon their fathers because of severe iniquities. It is difficult to reconcile the theory of supernatural acts of retribution as expressed here with Mendelssohn's philosophical theodicy as formulated in his treatise *Sache Gottes oder gerettete Vorsehung* (1784), where a single eternal decree of God is said to take care of all changes in the fortunes of men.[57] What is of particular interest in this gloss is the fact that despite his happy "symbiosis" with European culture Mendelssohn still shared the traditional sentiment, which regarded the "yoke of exile" as a punishment and expected a divine act of redemption.

The *Bi'ur* on the two remaining volumes, the books of Numbers and Deuteronomy, was in the main written by Mendelssohn himself. The introduction *Or Li-Netiva* is quite explicit on this point:[58] "In the commentaries on Numbers (which, thank God, I completed last summer) and Deuteronomy (which, by the grace of God, I shall complete this winter) I had the assistance of other men, [viz. of men other than Dubno and Wessely, who had been mentioned before], trusted friends, expert scholars competent in matters of Tora and Wisdom, but because of their great modesty they did not permit me to reveal their names." Mendelssohn added another important piece of information: "The author of the massoretic notes [*Tikkun Soferim*] to the last three books is the grammarian, our master and teacher, Rabbi Shalom of Mezerich (may his light shine)."[59] According to this statement, the fourth volume was completed in the summer of 1782, seeing that the introduction is dated Kislev 1,5543/1782. Its coauthor was Aaron Zechariah Friedenthal of Jaroslav,[60] a tutor in Mendelssohn's household, who in July, 1782, expected to be offered a teaching job in Breslau. By that time his work on the commentary had been completed.

Mendelssohn's hope of finishing the *Bi'ur* on the last volume during the winter of 1782/83 is also reflected in the inscription he entered in a fourteenth-century Pentateuch manuscript lent to him by its owner Ulamo (Ullmann) of Hamburg. It reads:[61]

> A thousand thanks to the owner of this glorious book, this precious treasure and heirloom, for the favor he did me in letting me have it on loan for the purpose of the printing of the Pentateuch, with which I am occupied at the present time and which I hope to bring to its conclusion in the coming month of Nisan. . .

The date of this inscription is Tebet 20, 5543 / December 25, 1782, almost two months later than the date of the introduction. Mendelssohn's expectation that the *Bi'ur* on Deuteronomy would be completed during the winter and that the volume would be in print by he spring proved to be an accurate forecast.

The final stages of the work are recorded in his correspondence with Herz Homberg, the coauthor of the last volume. On June 20, 1782, he had invited the former tutor of his children, who had left for Vienna, to assist him: "I would like you to tell me before long whether you are able and willing to decide to continue the commentary on the Pentateuch. [The first two pericopes] *Devarim* and *Va-Ethanan* are finished, and [the two last ones] *Ha'azinu* and *Ve-zot Ha-Berakha* are also practically ready. I want to reserve for myself also *Nitsavim* and *Va-Yelekh*. There remains therefore *'Ekev, Re'eh, Shofetim, Ki Tetse', Ki Tavo'*, which are still open. You should soon be able to see whether your situation permits you to engage in work of this kind."[62] Apparently Homberg's answer was in the affirmative, for on July 1 Mendelssohn wrote to him: "I [shall] see to it that you receive a copy of the German translation of the five chapters [viz. pericopes] of the Pentateuch. I wonder whether you have the requisite books in your place. As to the honorarium, we shall come to terms with God's help. You are my brother and shall not serve me for nothing."[63]

By July 16, however, Homberg had not yet finally committed himself, as appears from Mendelssohn's letter bearing that date: "I have the chapters ... copied for you, as mentioned already, and am now looking forward to hearing from you whether and how I am to send them to you. I have no doubt that you will receive permission to work in the Imperial Library. Kindly let me know as soon as possible whether you can take charge of the work. For I would not like to waste time."[64] Three months later Homberg had already finished and delivered his part of the *Bi'ur*. Mendelssohn wrote to him on October 15, 1782: "I received the continuation of the commentary and express to you, for the time being, my best thanks. I do so only for the time being because I have not yet been able to read any part of it, as I do not want to be disturbed in the writing of some other work in which I am currently engaged."[65] The "other work" in which Mendelssohn happened to be so absorbed was the *Jerusalem*. When he eventually found the time to examine Homberg's contribution he was far from satisfied and had to invest some effort in revising it. On January 1, 1783, he wrote to Homberg: "As you will see, I took considerable liberties with your commentary, but I hope you will be satisfied with what I did. Now state your honorarium so that I may pay it."[66] Homberg seems to have suggested the amount of ten louis d'or; this, at any rate, was the fee that Mendelssohn sent him on June 27, 1783, together with a little postscript: "Your first production is, indeed, not worthy of you. If you want to atone for your sin, I know no better advice than to wipe it out by better works."[67] Unfortunately, the ill-repute that Homberg later acquired not only among strict traditionalists but also among the more moderate Maskilim[68] helped to feed the opposition of certain orthodox circles to the *Bi'ur* as a whole. The price Mendelssohn paid for making Homberg an associate was far heavier than ten louis d'or.

Mendelssohn named his Pentateuch edition *Sefer Netivot Ha-Shalom* ("The Book of the Paths of Peace") in allusion to Proverbs 3:17: "Her ways are ways of pleasantness, and all her paths are peace," the well-known praise of wisdom traditionally applied to the Tora. In keeping with this title, he gave to the introduction the name *Or Li-Netiva* ("A Light unto the Path"), which is borrowed from Psalm 119: 105: "Thy word is a lamp unto my feet, and a light unto my path." It was at the end of his introduction, which bears the date Kislev 1, 5543 (November 7, 1782), that he announced both titles for the first time.[69] Neither in the prospectus nor in any of his letters prior to that date do we find any indication that the projected edition of the Pentateuch was to be called *Sefer Netivot Ha-Shalom*. There can be no question that this choice of title was inspired by the same sentiments that caused him to conclude the *Jerusalem* with the appeal "Love the truth! Love peace!"[70] The appeal was directed to "the rulers of the earth" and implored them to be tolerant toward the Jewish nation. "Peace" was for Mendelssohn synonymous with tolerance.

The introduction was written after he had completed the *Jerusalem*,[71] and it concludes with the same words: "As for you, love truth and peace!"[72] Here the exhortation follows the customary request to the reader to let the author know of any misprint, error, or ambiguity he may discover in the text so that the necessary corrections may be made. Yet there is obviously more to this request and the rather startling final sentence than meets the eye. The work had already encountered a great deal of opposition and had been threatened with ostracism by *herem*, a weapon of "ecclesiastical power" that Mendelssohn had recently denounced[73] as irreconcilable with the very nature of religion. He had appealed to "the rabbis and elders of my nation" to renounce the use of this weapon and to practice the tolerance they expected from the secular authorities in their own conduct toward fellow Jews.[74] The words "As for you, love truth and peace" at the end of the introduction therefore clearly meant to say: Be tolerant toward this book! Tell me of any error you find in it, and I shall be happy to put it right. Yet do not condemn it from the outset! The introduction is clearly intended to convey such an appeal. At the same time, the title Mendelssohn gave to the work implies that the ways of the Tora are "ways of pleasantness, and all her paths are peace." In other words, the precepts of the Tora are designed to promote tolerance rather than militancy. Thus there is an intimate connection between the whole tenor of the *Jerusalem* and the concept of Tora as enunciated in the title chosen for the new edition of the Pentateuch.

As the introduction indicates,[75] three hundred copies of it, dated Kislev 1, 5543, were printed as a separate advanced edition. It appeared in December, 1782, and Mendelssohn sent a copy of it to Homberg on January 1, 1783.[76] The text was reprinted in the format of the Pentateuch, with the date changed to Nisan 1, 5543/1783, and distributed together with the last volume. The title page was also sent to the subscribers at the same time. The printing of the work was completed around Passover, 1783.[77] On May 20 Mendelssohn could finally inform Elise Reimarus that "the last parts of the Five Books of Moses" had already been dispatched by freight to Pastor Krohn, together with the introduction.[78]

Within the short span of three years all five volumes had been published. It is most astonishing indeed that Mendelssohn managed to produce the Pentateuch edition according to plan despite the fact that during the same period he was working on his preface to Manasseh ben Israel's treatise (1782) and on two other major books, namely the *Jerusalem* and a translation of the entire Book of Psalms, both of which appeared simultaneously with the completion of the Pentateuch.

All things considered, Mendelssohn had ample reason to feel rather satisfied with himself. But, if he felt any sense of elation he failed to show it when sending out copies of his latest works to a number of people. As was his wont, he was entirely unpretentious, almost casual, about what must be judged a tremendous achievement. Characteristic in this respect is the letter he wrote to Ferdinand Kindermann Ritter von Schulstein, the famous educator and dean of the Collegiate Church of Prague, who had written to him on January 5, 1783.[79] In his reply[80] Mendelssohn announced that he was going to send him his Pentateuch translation, the final volume of which was expected to appear in a few days, together with his German translation of the Book of Psalms and "a treatise *On Ecclesiastical Power and Judaism*,"[81] both of which were due to come out in time for the Easter book fair. In similar vein he wrote to Homberg on June 14:[82] "Herr Arnstein[83] will bring you (1) my translation of the Psalms; (2) *Jerusalem* etc. . . . and (3) the Five Books of Moses, or *Netivot Ha-Shalom*."

Moses Mendelssohn had vowed to use whatever energy he still possessed for the benefit of his nation. He had redeemed this promise in superb fashion. In addition, he had embarked upon a literary campaign for the promotion of Jewish civil rights and written his long awaited statement on the philosophy of Judaism. His intense occupation with the Bible and the rabbinic commentaries, on the one hand, and the opposition to his enterprise, on the other, had fortified his resolve to carry the struggle for his people's well-being into the political sphere.

CHAPTER SIX

Political Reformer

———◁◦❦◦▷———

Spokesman of his People

The role that Mendelssohn played in promoting the civil rights of Jews
was wholly unpremeditated. The initiative he took in activating Dohm
on behalf of the cause and his own literary efforts in this field were inspired
by the flow of events. Unlike his Bible project, they were not the results
of long-term planning. Even so, they did grow out of deep-seated, life-long
concerns, and they by no means reflected a newly awakened interest or
a shift in his attitude. On the contrary, on many previous occasions Mendelssohn had acted as intercessor when Jewish communities were threatened
with special measures of a cruel kind.

Most such appeals had been addressed to him in his unofficial capacity
as the most widely respected and influential Jew of the time. On him
had fallen the mantle of the *shetadlan* ("intercessor"), the one who from
the sixteenth to the middle of the eighteenth century stood up before
kings and princes in defense of Jewish life and limb in Germany and
Poland. This function had been exercised, in the majority of cases, in
an honorary capacity by Jews outstanding in wealth, command of language,
and personal dignity. Famous representatives of this type were men such
as Joselman of Rosheim, Samuel Oppenheimer, Samson Wertheimer, Leff-
mann Behrend Cohen, and some members of the Geldern and Gomperz
families. Mendelssohn was a modern version of those *shetadlanim*. The
influence he wielded was based on the admiration he commanded as a
writer and on the affection he inspired as a human being. In certain instances
his fame was sufficient to induce sympathetic action. In contrast to the
old-time defenders of Jewish interests, who were powerful court-Jews of
high financial standing, he was a man of rather moderate means, yet he
was greatly respected even on account of his commercial talents.

As has been mentioned previously,[1] when after his employer's death in 1768 he took charge of the business jointly with the widow of the deceased, Mendelssohn raised the number of looms in his silk factory from sixty to one hundred two. Reference has also been made to the fact that the Prussian government adopted his proposals for a complete overhaul of the rules governing the importation of raw materials and the credit system. In the late seventies import restrictions imposed by other states and a change in fashions away from heavy silk dresses caused a decline in business and by 1782 the number of looms in his factory had to be reduced to seventy-eight, and later to sixty. In 1781, after the death of his former employer's widow, the name of the firm was altered to "Gebrüder Bernhard & Company" (referring to two sons of the original owner, who had become partners). Another designation used was "Gebrüder Bernhard & Moses Mendelssohn." The decline in the trade in no way reflected on Mendelssohn's reputation as one of Berlin's leading experts in the field. In 1782 the government required an elaborate report on the state of the silk industry. The exposé prepared by Mayet, a ministry official, was submitted for comment to Mendelssohn and two Christian experts. The memorandum worked out by Mendelssohn shows his intimate knowledge of the technical as well as commercial aspects of the trade. In terms of broad policy, it advocated the greatest possible amount of freedom for private enterprise.[2] One wonders how, in addition to his many literary preoccupations in 1782, he could have found the time and energy to write this memorandum. From the point of view of the impact that his ideas about the "civil improvement" of the Jews were meant to exercise, it was of no mean importance that he was regarded as a man of practical good sense and not merely as a philosopher and scholar.

Mendelssohn's great prestige as a man of letters was nevertheless the most decisive factor in his being able to intervene on behalf of his fellow Jews, sporadically over the years and in a more concentrated and far-reaching way after he established a cooperative relationship with Dohm. Only a man of his authority in the intellectual realm could, as a Jew, hope to be listened to with the degree of respect necessary to achieve tangible results, immediate or long-term. Even among the literati he was admired not only because of his merits as a writer but also for his eminently sound judgment. Mention has already been made, for example, of the trust that Baron Karl Abraham von Zedlitz, the most important member of the Prussian cabinet, placed in Mendelssohn's recommendations.[3] We know, moreover, that Zedlitz, who held, among his other portfolios, that of minister of education, frequently consulted him when he had to fill academic vacancies. A letter written by Christian Jakob Kraus, one of Kant's close disciples, contains some information to this effect. It reports Mendelssohn's arrival in Königsberg in the summer of 1777 and then goes on to say: "On Sunday Kant called for me and told me that Mendelssohn had visited him and had, among other things, spoken also about me. Would

I wish to succeed the late Maier as professor in Halle. He said that Minister von Zedlitz had charged him [Mendelssohn] to propose someone for this position, and he wanted to leave the decision to Kant."[4] Subsequently, Zedlitz made strenuous efforts to persuade Kant himself to accept the post, but Kant refused it.[5] Later he offered the chair to Marcus Herz, who also declined.[6] A direct testimony of Zedlitz' practice of seeking Mendelssohn's advice is provided by the following letter, heretofore unnoticed:[7]

> You, my dear Herr Mendelssohn, know Professor Buesch in Hamburg.[8] Can you possibly tell me what his standing there is, and whether one might be able to attract him to our land, also whether you consider it worthwhile making the effort. Some weeks ago he passed through here when traveling to Silesia. I would like to know for what reason, and whether he has already returned.
>
> I find it really annoying that I live in the same place as you do and practically never get to see you. The short morning that I spent with you in Freyenwalde has infinitely increased my desire to be more often in your company. Perhaps someday your doctor will prescribe for you a diet that will cause you to relax your strength of mind (what for people like me is a natural rest is, in reverse, tension for you) and in such a situation, it seems to me, I would be your man—Zedlitz 28.7. 75

It is possible that Mendelssohn had his reasons for not wishing to see the powerful cabinet minister too often. Much as he valued the confidence placed in him, he may have tried to avoid being asked too many questions. He was not, after all, an intelligence agent of the government. Zedlitz, on the other hand, was a man of high culture and was immortalized as such in Kant's dedication of the *Critique of Pure Reason* (second edition, 1787) to him, as the protector as well as a lover and adept of the humanities. Still, Mendelssohn most certainly preferred to be consulted by scholars.

How greatly his counsel was sought after even by men working in fields different from his own is illustrated by a letter written to Christoph Martin Wieland by the famed philologist Friedrich August Wolf (1759–1824). Reminiscing about his early days and recalling the struggles preceding his epoch-making *Prolegomena ad Homerum* (the first volume of which did not appear until 1795), he wrote on May 8, 1795:[9]

> It is strange how these ideas of mine [concerning the origin of the Homeric poems] developed, and perhaps I may, therefore, be excused for having become more and more entangled. At the outset, I looked upon the matter purely from the viewpoint of a historical task, roughly corresponding to the way in which theologians sometimes regard Moses and the Prophets. Unconcerned about the final outcome, I searched for light, committed random results to paper, and did this for nine years without indicating to anybody what I saw, or rather sensed, I was heading for. Yet the late Moses Mendelssohn, besides three or four other scholars, was responsible for my going deeper into the matter. I asked him to tell me his opinion: assuming a nation had as yet nothing in writing, and assuming that it was customary to publicize by way of recitation nothing but cantos lasting from four to six hours, would a bard—be he even the greatest and most extraordinary man imaginable—ever have

been able to hit upon the idea of constructing such a tremendous edifice as the Iliad and the Odyssey without a basis on which the human mind must rest itself in such cases? Mendelssohn answered drily: No! He expounded, besides, several ideas about Hebrew poetry that wholly coincided with my own. The other scholars were all the more skeptical . . .

What Mendelssohn's judgment meant to Wolf at the time can be fully appreciated only if one considers the consensus of opinion he had to contend with. Robert Wood's thesis,[10] that the art of writing was not yet common in Greece at the period of Homer and that his poems, like Ossian's, were orally transmitted by bards, was hardly contested in Germany. Wolf's doubts were not thought to merit much attention, and Nicolai refused to publish a major work of his, in which he tried to show that without script a poem as large as the Iliad could not have come into being. Having left Göttingen in 1779, Wolf negotiated with Nicolai in 1780, and it must have been around this time that Mendelssohn's firm support strengthened Wolf's resolve to "go deeper into the matter."[11]

Mendelssohn's practical sense was put to a particular kind of test when, immediately after the publication of his *Reply to Lavater,* a "Man of Rank" submitted to him, under the seal of secrecy, a document that suggested—judging from Mendelssohn's reply—nothing less than the reestablishment of the Jewish state. It was accompanied by a letter dated January, 1770, and signed "Your devoted, though unknown, admirer."[12] The letter asked Mendelssohn to open the attached document only when nobody was around, and to refrain from trying to discover the identity of the writer and from communicating its contents to anyone, should he consider the idea foolish or impracticable. Would he, please, send his reply through the same channels through which the letter and its enclosure had reached him. The person concerned was a friend but had no inkling what the document was about. The motivation that had inspired it was a love of humanity. In case, however, Mendelssohn considered his brainchild a monstrosity, he would accept his judgment without demur. The friend who had passed on the mysterious letter and the still more mysterious document was George Detlef Friedrich Koes, director-general of the Royal Bank at Berlin. In a covering note dated January 23, 1770, Koes described the anonymous correspondent merely as "a Man of Rank" *(ein Mann von Stande),* whom he knew and loved as "a friend of humanity."[13] Mendelssohn probably never learned the man's identity. His verdict on the plan was negative and he returned the papers "with the most solemn vow of eternal silence" and the promise to repress his natural desire to know a person who was worthy of high esteem.[14]

From a few clues offered in the letter and from other data a most convincing case has, however, been presented for the theory that the "Man of Rank" was none other than Count Rochus Friedrich of Lynar, at whose request Mendelssohn had formulated, some five years later, his ideas about Crusius' essay on Schröpfer and about the terms "enthusiast," "visionary," and "fanatic."[15] The count, who was deeply involved in New Testament studies, may have been influenced by chiliastic ideas such as propagated by the Danish mystic Holger Paulli[16] and by Lavater, who expected the restoration of a Jewish state under the rule of Christ.[17] As a former states-man and diplomat, he undoubtedly had some concrete and down-to-earth suggestions for the implementation of such a scheme, and it was with these that Mendelssohn had to deal when he was asked for his judgment.

In his reply[18] Mendelssohn declared, in the first place, his incompetence to judge a project that presupposed "the most profound knowledge of statistics" (viz., data relating to matters important to the state, such as the numbers of the population, taxation, the value of trade, etc.).[19] The idea as such, he admitted, seemed to him majestic and indicative of a mind conscious of its powers. The zeal for tolerance, the detestation of hierarchical power, and the views expressed about religion and morality were proof to him that the author was used to thinking in a wise as well as a grand manner. Even the confidence with which so bold an enterprise had been outlined had filled him with an uncommon measure of respect. But if his own mind possessed any courage at all, it was related to speculative matters. So far as practical things were concerned, he had been confined to a sphere too narrow to permit him to rise to the planning of great pro-jects or to ignore difficulties of the ordinary kind. Who can increase his height even by a span?

Having disqualified himself from pronouncing judgment on a scheme of such magnitude as the one being proposed, Mendelssohn pointed out why, in his view, the restoration of the Jewish state was impossible under prevailing circumstances. The "greatest difficulty" militating against it was "the character of my nation." Jews were not sufficiently prepared for any big undertaking. Centuries of pressure had deprived "our spirit" of all *vigueur:* "It is not our fault, yet we cannot deny that in us the natural urge for freedom has become atrophied. It has been transmuted into a monkish virtue, and it finds expression only in praying and enduring, not in action." Nor could one expect that the widely dispersed Jewish nation would rally to the cause in a united effort. The "spirit of unity" required for the success of such a project hardly existed. Mendelssohn may have been thinking of the cruel manner in which the Portuguese Jews of Bordeaux had behaved toward Ashkenazic Jews in 1760, and he may have remembered, in particular, the contempt with which Isaac Pinto (1715–1787) had looked down upon non-Sephardic Jewries when defend-ing the honor of Judaism against Voltaire's slanderous attacks.[20] How he felt about Pinto's parochial arrogance came out in a letter that he wrote on June 14, 1774, to a friend at the Hague who had sent him, on its author's behalf, a copy of Pinto's treatise against the materialists.[21] After expressing thanks and acknowledging Pinto's merits as a writer, he con-tinued: "Could the [Jewish] nation show ten authors like Pinto, the Voltaires would speak about us in a different vein. Pinto must not take offense if we Ashkenazim, too, are proud of his achievements. We are still children of One Father, notwithstanding the fact that in his apologia he hardly admitted it."[22] Pinto's apologia had appeared in 1762, and seeing that Mendelssohn made a biting reference to it as late as 1774, it may be reasonably assumed that he could have had it in mind in 1770 when deploring the lack of unity in the nation.

Another counterargument offered by Mendelssohn to the count's proposal was the immense cost of such an undertaking: "Knowing as I do that the wealth of my nation consists in credits, rather than in actual assets, I cannot believe that its means are sufficient to raise the sums of money required." His final point was a political consideration: "Apart from all these difficulties, it seems to me that such a project has a chance of realization only at a time when the major powers of Europe are involved in a general war and each one has to take care of itself. In a quiet period such as prevails now a single jealous power (and there would be not a few of them) could bring the project to grief. The unsuccessful crusades seem to justify this fear only too well." Mendelssohn's judgment was undoubtedly correct. The Jewish people had first to be emancipated before it could embark on the scheme placed before Mendelssohn by the well-meaning but somewhat unrealistic count. Mendelssohn's role in Jewish history was formed by the conditions of his time. It consisted in promoting emancipation. Even before the propitious moment for applying himself to this task arrived, he used his prestige to alleviate Jewish suffering or distress of various kinds on a number of occasions.

In 1769 he interceded with the authorities in the case of charges leveled against the Altona community.[23] In 1772 he answered the call of the community of Schwerin.[24] When in 1775 the tiny Jewish community in Switzerland appealed to him for help, he did not hesitate to ask Lavater, with whom he had been out of touch since writing to him in January, 1771,[25] to intervene. The letter he sent him on April 14, 1775, was couched in the most moving terms:

> Venerable Friend of Humanity! With unfeigned confidence, which I have never ceased to place in your humaneness, I turn to you, my dearest friend, in a matter which concerns me, because it regards my coreligionists, and is not foreign to you, because it regards human beings. It concerns essentially the few Jews who are tolerated in Switzerland, i.e., in Lengly and Endingen. True, I have no detailed knowledge of the particular circumstances of these people and of the conditions under which they are permitted to stay there. I can, however, faintly imagine their wretched subsistence considering the general attitude toward my nation, which is almost everywhere looked upon as strangers on God's earth, and bearing in mind the special situation in your country. I am told that the authorities to which they are responsible are just now planning to impose further restrictions upon them and, among other oppressive measures, to forbid them procreation and increase, the Creator's first commandment to mankind. The people concerned—some of them, and the rabbi in particular, are known to me by reputation as honest men—tell me that you, venerable

friend of humanity, are in a position to contribute much to their preservation and welfare by using your influence, and having heard of the friendship between us, of which we publicly assured each other, they turn to me and ask me to intercede on their behalf.

The letter concluded with a fervent appeal for help and assured Lavater of Mendelssohn's perpetual gratitude for any action taken. Lavater's response was most satisfactory and resulted in the cancellation of the contemplated measures.[26]

In the summer of 1777 Mendelssohn proved himself a tower of strength on behalf of Königsberg Jewry who pleaded for the abolition of a degrading legislation.[27] When in November, 1777, he traveled to Hanover,[28] he received there a letter from the Jewish community of Dresden imploring him to come to their aid.[29] According to the *Judenordnung* (regulations concerning Jews) of 1772, an exorbitant sum of money had to be paid annually as a poll tax by rich and poor alike. Those who failed to pay the tax by a certain date were to be expelled. Many decent people in strained circumstances had been unable to make the prescribed payment that year and had been mercilessly driven out of the city. Indeed, almost half the Jewish population had been exiled and did not know where to turn for refuge. The letter describing the situation and entreating Mendelssohn to help in whatever way he could had been written by the leader of Dresden Jewry, the educated and wealthy Samuel Halberstadt, who commanded a beautiful Hebrew style replete with biblical allusions that made his tale of woe all the more poignant. The form of address and the introductory part abounded in praise for Mendelssohn, who was the ornament and glory of his nation and who, at the same time, enjoyed the high esteem of the Gentile world. The letter recalled that the baron von Fritsche [who had met Mendelssohn at the Palace in Potsdam in 1771][30] never tired of speaking about him in glowing terms. Therefore, could Mendelssohn not use his influence with the baron, who wielded great power and might be willing to exercise it on behalf of the expelled in order to please a man he so much admired?

Mendelssohn lost no time in responding to the appeal, but he preferred to approach not the baron but another highly placed friend, with whom he had been in touch more recently. When visiting Dresden in August, 1776,[31] he had met the baron von Ferber, privy counsellor to the elector of Saxony, and the circumstances that had occasioned the meeting of the two men were not unrelated to the plight of the Jews in Saxony. Soon after his arrival in Dresden, a community official appeared at his lodging demanding the payment of twenty groschen as *Leibzoll* (custom for importing a person). Mendelssohn took it in good humor, joked about being treated like an ox, and paid the prescribed duty. On the following day he visited the library together with Hennings, whose letter to Elise Reimarus contains some interesting details about the conversation he had with the librarian.[32] His name was Karl Wilhelm Dassdorf and at the time he was busy editing Johann Joachim Winckelmann's letters to his friends.[33] He was horrified when Mendelssohn mentioned his experience of the evening before and reported the matter to the baron von Ferber, whose protégé he was. The baron, annoyed at the insult to a person of such high rank and fearing some repercussions in the press, took the necessary steps to repair the damage insofar as was possible. An order by the elector himself commanded the College of Finance to return the twenty groschen to "the Berlin scholar of the Mosaic religion, Herr Moses Mendelssohn," and to inform him of his right to stay in Dresden without paying any fee for as long as he pleased. Thereupon Mendelssohn paid a visit to the baron to assure him of his esteem. The incident led to the establishment of a most happy relationship between the two. When a year later Mendelssohn asked Dassdorf to take care of one of his friends who was a "lover of the arts,"[34] the baron added a few lines to Dassdorf's reply, promising to take Mendelssohn's protégé under his wings.[35] It seems that in the same letter he assured Mendelssohn of a readiness at all times to fulfil requests of his.[36] Such manifestation of good grace could not be left unacknowledged. On September 22, 1777, Mendelssohn wrote a letter of thanks to Baron von Ferber for the "exceedingly precious lines" he had sent him. Replying to a remark made by the baron, he pointed out that he (the baron) had least cause to envy a man like him, one who spent his time in mere contemplation: "The highest degree of wisdom is undoubtedly the *doing of what is good.* Speculation is a lower degree and mere stepping stone to that higher one.... Happy is he to whom Providence imparted the will and the power to spread, through works and actions, morality and brotherly love among the children of men, and to oppose prejudice whenever it stands in the way of human happiness!"

When Mendelssohn received the cry for help from the Dresden Jews, it was obvious that the baron von Ferber was the man to be approached. The letter he wrote to him from Hanover on November 19, 1777, contained more than a petition for redress in a particular case. It condemned the entire system of oppressive regulations:[37]

> In the state of extreme consternation and despondency in which I find myself I dare to turn to you, magnanimous friend of humanity, with childlike trust, and in deepest sadness I implore your help. My lord, I hear as the latest news that many hundreds of my brethren are to be expelled from Dresden. Among them are many who are personally known to me and of whose honesty I am convinced; who have become impoverished and may not be in a position to bear the burdens imposed on them; who, however, have come down in the world not through their own fault, not through extravagance or laziness, but as a result of misfortunes.
>
> Good and beneficent God! Where are these wretched ones to go with their innocent wives and children? Where are they to find shelter and protection after having been thrown out by the country in which they lost their possessions? Expulsion is for a Jew the hardest punishment: It is more than mere banishment, it is, as it were, extermination

[*Vertilgung*] that removes him from God's earth, prejudice turning him away, by force and arms, from every frontier. Must human beings suffer this hardest of all punishments, without any guilt or trespass, merely because they are committed to different tenets of belief [*Grundsätzen*] and through misfortune are reduced to poverty? And the Israelite, who is punished for poverty as hard as for dishonesty, is still expected to be honest?—

No, I refrain from all further contemplations in order to spare the heart of a friend of humanity, which might be too much hurt by them. I still have hope, well-founded hope that consoles me in my anguish. Under the government of the best and kindest sovereign, under the administration of wise friends of humanity, it is impossible to fear punishment without crime . . .

The crux and challenge of this impassionate plea, which erupted from Mendelssohn with elemental force and almost without deliberation,[38] lie in the sentence asking how the Jew could be expected to be honest when his poverty was treated as a crime. This was more than a rhetorical question. It implied that Jewish dishonesty was, as a rule, to be blamed not on the Jews but on the governments that treated only wealthy Jews, more or less, as human beings. Mendelssohn here anticipated the essential thesis of Dohm's plea for the "civil improvement" of the Jewish people. The corollary of this thesis was the moral right of the downtrodden to resort to cunning in order to eke out an existence. This was a dangerous theory, but Mendelssohn had spelled it out as far back as 1755, when at the time of translating Rousseau's second *Discours* he entered the following remark in his notebook:[39] "One whose rights are violated in an illicit manner is made war against. Hence the Jews are incessantly being made war against. If the party that wages war is of superior power, the other party may employ cunning." In writing to the baron as he did, he had allowed his feelings free rein, and he apologized for this in his final paragraph. He felt a sense of uneasiness about having permitted himself so much candor, but he nevertheless dispatched the letter without toning it down. He enclosed it with a brief note addressed to Samuel Halberstadt in Dresden, who was to deliver it to the baron. The note reflects the state of mind in which he found himself after having written the letter:[40]

I made haste and did not tarry to act according to your words, my friend. I enclose herewith my letter to the lord, Baron von Ferber. I wrote to him in bitterness of spirit. My knees were indeed shaking from the great fear and terror that befell me when reading your beautiful letter. The situation makes me feel exceedingly bad and bitter. It is possible that I offended the count, yet "let come on me what will"; "I wearied myself to hold it in", but "who can withhold himself from speaking?"[41] Besides, I know that the lord will forgive the offense of a sorrowful spirit, for he is an amiable person, and in his letters he has promised me many times to show me true kindness, should I ever call upon him. May God the Almighty give you mercy before the lord, the elector. May he take pity on the poor and destitute people, and repent of the evil that he said he would do unto the torn and battered nation.[42]

As a result of Mendelssohn's intervention, the expulsion order was revoked.[43] Another instance of the effectiveness of his pleading concerned the Jewish community of Warsaw. The second edition of Euchel's biography of Mendelssohn contains, as a supplement, the following piece of information:[44]

> Our master, of blessed memory, averted the blood libel that had [in the past] cost many lives among God's people in Poland due to the enmity of the priests, who incited the leaders of the provinces to take revenge upon the Jews by slaughtering and spilling the blood of poor and innocent people. This is the story: One day, our learned master and teacher, Rabbi Isaac Ha-Levi, known as Itzig Satanov, visited him. They discussed the subject of improving the lot of the Jews,[45] and the conversation turned to the blood libel that had just been renewed. Somebody brought a newspaper and read aloud from it. One of the items reported was the fact that in the city of Warsaw two Jews had been arrested on the charge of ritual murder. Satanov was so terrified that he fainted. When he came round, he bitterly lamented: how long shall we be like sheep being led to the slaughter? He said to the master [Mendelssohn]: Find ways and means to help; perhaps they will prove effective.
>
> Thereupon the master called for some of the devoted leaders of the nation, including the well-known dignitary Rabbi Ephraim, son of Rabbi Veitel (may his light shine),[46] and the late communal leader [*parnas u-manhig*] Rabbi Abraham Strelitz.[47] They took counsel together and wrote a letter in French to one of the princes of Poland. The letter was couched in the most refined and ornate style. It was signed by all of them and it stated the following: We, the House of Israel, have been assailed by the blood libel at a moment that seemed propitious for doing so, and it has cost us many lives [in the past]. Perhaps you could use your influence to prevent the spilling of innocent blood in your country. We do not suspect the prince of entertaining any doubt whether or not there is any substance—God forbid—to this accusation, for the prince is a wise man who knows that the thing is a pure fabrication. We petition, however, the prince, knowing as he does that the accusation is groundless, to remove this belief from the minds of those holding it so as to prevent the shedding of innocent blood in their land.—
>
> The prince listened to their words and acted as his wisdom demanded. He decreed that this libel be forever abolished and made it part of the written laws of Poland that uttering it was a punishable offense. He wrote a friendly letter to the master. May his reward be perfect for having shown kindness to the Jewish people.

The above account, which Euchel declared to have found among his old papers, gives us no clue as to the date of the reported event or the identity of the Polish prince who responded to the plea. Since Satanov is mentioned as a participant, the story must be dated after 1772/73, when he arrived in Berlin. We know that in 1775 Christian middleclass citizens forced the Crown Marshal Lubomirski to expel the Jews from Warsaw.[48] The arrest of Jews on the charge of ritual murder may have been the prelude to the agitation against permitting further Jewish settlement in Warsaw. The happy ending to this particular incident as recorded by Euchel obviously had no bearing on the fate of Warsaw Jewry. It is known, however, that the king of Poland tried to protect the Jews, and the "prince" of Euchel's document may have been this monarch. Whatever trimmings the account may have added to the story, its historicity cannot be doubted. It is vouched for by Mendelssohn's own testimony in his preface to Manasseh ben Israel's treatise. After mentioning a case of blood libel in Posen not so long ago, he wrote:[49] "Only a few years ago the same story would have been repeated in the environs of Warsaw, had not, fortunately, the wise king of Poland and some enlightened magnates delayed juridical procedure long enough to enable the Jews to expose the libel." The reference to the "wise" king of Poland sounds very much like the repeated reference to the "wise" prince in Euchel's source. Since Mendelssohn wrote the preface in 1782, the time of the event, said to have happened "only a few years ago," could well have been the year 1775. What remains doubtful is the identity of the person to whom the petition was submitted. It could have been sent to one of the "magnates" to whom part of the credit is given. It is equally possible that the king (Stanislaus II Augustus) himself was approached. That the happy outcome of the story was due to Mendelssohn's prompt action we know only through Euchel.

Even before the Edict of Tolerance was promulgated Mendelssohn had reason to believe that the abolition of the civil disabilities of the Jews was only a matter of time. The least sign of progress in this direction was gratefully acknowledged by him. He was extremely happy when his friend Hennings reported a modest dent he had been able to make in the wall excluding Jews. In a letter of June 22, 1779, Hennings wrote:[50]

> A small point scored by tolerance is the following: Consequent upon the abolition of a guild, permission has been granted to Jewish manufacturers to admit, as well as dismiss, Jewish apprentices and journeymen. What I liked best was the fact that this permission was given without any effort to obtain it, merely as a natural result of the prevalent mentality. This is but a small step, true, but small things of this kind help to promote a good spirit, and once it is aroused, the greatest things can be accomplished. Another small matter that has given me much pleasure is this: The Danish court has settled eighty free peasants at the expense of the crown around its rural castle at Friedensburg and endowed them with cattle and arable land.

On July 13, 1779, Mendelssohn replied:[51]

> A thousand thanks for the news about the small and yet in my view very important step that civil and religious liberty has taken in your regions. Seeing that even under the rule of a philosopher-king one seems to entertain principles concerning this matter that are still very shaky—day by day I witness examples of the most offensive kind—I shall take the liberty of publicizing this information . . . without, however, mentioning your name.
> Forgive me, dearest friend, if I do not wait for your permission to do so. The occasion is urgent, and after a period of two weeks it might be lost forever. As far as one can humanly foresee, one need

have no fear that the matter will cause you the least embarrassment, and how greatly will your patriotic heart rejoice, should Denmark stimulate other states to follow her example! In such matters the first step is always the most difficult and the most important one.

In his letter of July 20, 1779,[52] Hennings described more fully how the new regulation had come about. The guild concerned was that of the stocking weavers. Owing to its abolition, for reasons that are not mentioned, the distinction between former members of the guild and "privileged" (i.e. licensed) weavers was no longer maintained, and complete equality resulted. The "privileged" factories of Wessely and Warburg now enjoyed the same rights as those that had belonged to the guilds, and they soon achieved great prominence. Their success called forth a "national resistance" and "several disturbances," the outcome of which was the granting of permission to Jewish factories to employ Jewish workers as apprentices and journeymen. Hennings emphasized that this privilege had been introduced on Höegh-Guldberg's initative, which was motivated by the intention "to make the Jews true citizens of the state, which they have not been until now, and which they could not be, since they did not engage in civil occupations [*bürgerliche Gewerbe*]." He had heard this from Guldberg himself. Now it all depended on whether the Jewish nation itself had the courage and determination to use its advantages. It seemed to him, Hennings told Mendelssohn, that while the forces of oppression put obstacles in the way of progress toward culture among the Jews, they themselves were spoiling their cause by being acquiescent and timid. As for Mendelssohn's publicizing the news, no objection could, Hennings believed, be raised by the government, and he himself could look upon it only with pleasure. However, he hoped that the announcement would be couched in such terms that even those acquainted with the matter could not suspect any share on his part in either the announcement or the thing itself. Nobody should be given the impression that he was claiming credit for someone else's achievement.

Why Mendelssohn was in such a hurry to advertise the new Danish regulation is not clear. Nor do we know what kind of action he took in mid-July, 1779, when he told Hennings that a two weeks' delay might mean the loss of a unique opportunity. It is obvious, however, that he was pursuing some scheme that would permit young Jews to train for certain crafts. A letter written to Nicolai precisely at that time (July 8, 1779) makes distinct reference to the matter.[53] With it he enclosed Hennings' letter of June 22 which, as he pointed out, showed that "the man has indeed good intentions" and that he "also carried them, partly, into effect insofar as his influence in Denmark permitted." He urged Nicolai to write a review of Hennings' *Olavides*[54] for the sake of the good cause, and he added: "Oh, could I, by means of a review, make fifty Jewish children into journeymen and thirty serfs into free peasants, I would ask good taste to excuse me and would try to spend half an hour in the adjacent

The *Mühlendamm*, **Berlin,** viewed from the Molkenmarkt,
with Veitel Heine Ephraim's *palais* on the right

Interior of the Synagogue in Berlin

Gotthold Ephraim Lessing in his Early Twenties

FRIDERICVS NICOLAI
Berolinensis.
A.C. MDCCLXXX.

Friedrich Nicolai

Fromet Mendelssohn, née Gugenheim

Thomas Abbt

ΑΛΗΘΕΤΕΙΝ ΕΝ ΑΓΑΠΗ.

Johann Caspar Lavater

Facsimile of Mendelssohn's Letter to Lavater, dated December 24, 1769

Count Wilhelm of Schaumburg-Lippe

Adolf Friedrich August Hennings

Doctor Marcus Herz

David Friedländer in his Old Age

Hartwig Wessely

Ezekiel Landau, Chief Rabbi of Prague

Ernst Ferdinand Klein

Joseph Mendelssohn

room." The last sentence refers to Nicolai's reluctance to review the *Olavides,* whose style he considered too "sweet" and offensive to "good taste."[55] Quite probably Mendelssohn wanted Nicolai to include in his review a reference to the hopeful beginning of Jewish civil improvement in Denmark; this would explain why he treated the publicizing of it as a matter of urgency. Nicolai did not fulfil this particular request, however, assuming that it had been made, as the review itself shows.[56]

Cooperation with Dohm

In 1780 yet another call for help reached Mendelssohn. The situation of the Jews in Alsace had become critical owing to the unscrupulous machinations of the fanatical anti-Semite François Hell, the author of a tract called *Observations d'un Alsacien sur l'affaire présente des Juifs d'Alsace* (1779), in which the Jews were represented as an accursed and criminal people. Its clear purpose was to bring about their extermination or, at the very least, their expulsion from the country. In February, 1780, Hell was arrested by royal decree when some of his fraudulent practices came to light, but his removal from the scene did not of itself cure the ills of the community, which was exposed to virulent hatred and suffered under a most oppressive legislation. It was, therefore, decided to submit a memorandum *(mémoire)* to the Council of State offering a historical survey of the position of the Jews and asking for the lifting of the restrictive measures. Herz Cerfberr, the most distinguished Alsatian Jew, who in 1775 had been granted citizenship by King Louis XVI,[1] turned to Mendelssohn with the request to write the *mémoire* for them, there being no Jews in France both capable and willing to compose a document such as that required. Certainly no help could be expected from the educated Sephardic Jews of Bordeaux and Bayonne, who had only shown enmity toward their non-Sephardic brethren. It may be assumed that Cerfberr supplied Mendelssohn with some material and rough notes but otherwise left the drafting of the memorandum entirely to his discretion and superior judgment.

Mendelssohn was at this time quite busy writing his commentary on Exodus, but he could not refuse the call. It seems, however, that in order to comply with the request without upsetting his schedule he invited the young ministerial councillor *(Kriegsrath)* Christian Wilhelm Dohm to organize and, possibly, augment the material submitted by Cerfberr. In the absence of any documentary evidence it is impossible to determine the exact nature and extent of the share that Cerfberr, Mendelssohn, and Dohm, respectively, had in the finished product. It may be assumed that it was Mendelssohn who put the final touches on it, for otherwise Dohm, notwithstanding the clandestine character of his cooperation, could not have written a year later in his own book:[2] "A *mémoire* that was submitted last year to the Royal Council of State by Alsatian Jewry and that has come to the author's notice, has been added as an appendix to the present treatise. Both the interesting facts reported therein and its refined and dignified diction would seem to make it worthy of some larger publicity." Despite the concealment of his own part in the document, Dohm would not have bestowed such praise on its stylistic merits had he himself been responsible for them. It is obviously Mendelssohn to whom the compliment was paid. It is equally certain that some of the points made in the *mémoire* were taken over from the original draft presented by Cerfberr and reflected the viewpoint of neither Mendelssohn nor Dohm. Thus, the plea for a reconfirmation of the rabbis' right to impose the ban on certain types of transgressors[3] was contrary to Mendelssohn's way of thinking, and was retained only because it had been in the initial draft. Since Mendelssohn had voiced no objection, Dohm took it for granted that it had his approval. Hence the reappearance of the same claim in his own treatise. It was only then that Mendelssohn expressed his protest.[4] Similarly, the account of the events leading up to the royal decree of May 27, 1780, referring all law suits concerning usury to the *conseil souverain* of Alsace, was considered by Dohm to be still sub judice. It did not represent his own considered view of the matter. He had simply adopted it from Cerfberr's draft.[5] All that can be said, therefore, is that the *mémoire* was the joint work of Cerfberr, Mendelssohn, and Dohm.[6] It was dispatched to its sponsor, Cerfberr, some time in 1780 and submitted that same year to the Council of State.[7] Its eventual, rather disappointing, result was the issuance, as late as July 1784, of Louis XVI's *Lettres Patentes*.[8]

Of infinitely greater significance than the *mémoire* itself was the cooperation between Mendelssohn and Dohm that it helped to establish. Wilhelm von Dohm (1751–1820)[9] was born in Lemgo (Lippe), the son of a preacher. After studying at Leipzig University, he had come to Berlin first in 1773, when Prince Ferdinand offered him a post as *Pagenhofmeister* (tutor) in his household. Dohm was soon at home in the circles of the Berlin Enlightenment (Sulzer, Spalding, Teller, Nicolai, etc.), and he probably met Mendelssohn for the first time in the course of that year. At Lavater's suggestion, he had translated Bonnet's *Essai de psychologie* into German, and the book was published in Lemgo (1773). From 1774 until 1776 he continued his studies at Göttingen. The subjects to which he devoted himself were constitutional law, modern history, and statistics.[10] Together with Heinrich Christian Boie he founded the periodical *Deutsches Museum*. As its joint editor from 1776 until 1778 his aim was "to make Germany better acquainted with herself and more alert to her various constitutions; to arouse among us a sense of public spirit; and to offer political and statistical data and inquiries."[11] In September, 1776, he was appointed professor of the sciences of finance and statistics at the Collegium Carolinum at Kassel, a post that he held until he was "called" to Berlin in 1779. There he entered government service in a dual capacity, as registrar of the secret archives and as a councillor in the department of foreign affairs (the title of *Kriegsrath* was awarded to him on account of the latter position). He enjoyed the full confidence of his superior, the minister von Hertzberg, but he had to put up with a great deal of animosity and intrigue (due to envy)[12] and he tended, therefore, to be rather cautious in whatever he undertook.

It could not have been very easy for Mendelssohn to persuade Dohm to work on the *mémoire,* and the secrecy with which his collaboration was guarded would seem to have stemmed from scruples on his part rather than from Jewish reluctance to reveal the fact. Besides, he was an extremely busy man, what with his professional duties and a variety of literary projects on which he was working on his own. Even so, he yielded to yet another request by Mendelssohn, which had the wholehearted support of Nicolai.[13] It concerned the writing of a treatise on the desirability of admitting the Jews to citizenship. The subject was, as we have shown, exceedingly close to Mendelssohn's heart, and the exemplary manner in which Dohm had done his part in composing the *mémoire* seemed to call for a continuation of their cooperation on a larger and more general scale. It was an act of uncommon far-sightedness, to put it at its lowest, when Mendelssohn proposed this plan to Dohm, and Dohm's acceptance of the plan was a veritable coup, considering the historic impact of the work he produced. Without Mendelssohn's inspired vision the epoch-making treatise *Über die bürgerliche Verbesserung der Juden* ("On the Civil Improvement of the Jews") would surely never have been written. True, Dohm mentioned in the preface to the first part of his work that as long as "several years ago" he had planned "to study the history of the Jewish nation since the destruction of their own state." It had been his intention, he declared, to investigate the moral and political conditions of the Jews in the various periods and countries in which they found themselves; the influences that shaped their character and changed their original mentality; and also their influence upon the industry, trade, and mores of their environments. All this he had intended to present to the public not merely in order to fill a lacuna in historical knowledge but with the principal object of showing "that the oppression under which they still live in most countries is but a relic of the impolitic and inhuman prejudices of the dark centuries, hence unworthy of being continued in our times." It is most unlikely, however, that this literary plan would ever have materialized. Dohm's lively mind was constantly preoccupied with all kinds of designs, only few of which could ever be implemented. Thus, in 1773 he meant to write a "history of Germany" conceived "in the spirit of Hume," but in the same year he began collecting material for a work on the history, literature, religion, etc. of the Indians.[14] What was in the foreground of his interests at the time when Mendelssohn suggested that he write a treatise on the Jews were subjects of an entirely different sort: while he was working on the treatise, volumes three and four of his collection of materials for statistics and political history appeared, and at the end of 1781, after he had finished the treatise, he started collecting material for a book on commercial treaties.[15] It is quite reasonable to assume, therefore, that without Mendelssohn's push Dohm's work on Jewish civil rights probably would not have been written.

No one could have been better qualified to write this work than he. Dohm could not describe himself as being particularly fond of the Jews,[16] but he considered humaneness *(Menschlichkeit)* and "true politics" to be one and the same thing.[17] He combined sound political realism with an incorruptible sense of justice. His deism facilitated the impartiality with which he analyzed the anomalous situation of the Jews and proposed its remedy. Free from any dogmatic bias, he looked at the facts objectively, and thanks to his political and historical training he could apply scientific catagories to their interpretation. He belonged to no particular school of political economics. An essay he published in 1778[18] criticized the physiocratic system, which was then being revived in France and also had a following in Germany and Switzerland. Nevertheless, he felt akin in spirit to the concept of natural law that formed the basis of that system. In his portrayal of Joseph II, which he wrote toward the end of his life,[19] he traced the emperor's politics of tolerance to the influence of physiocratic ideas. Speaking of the emperor's tolerance toward the Jews in particular, Dohm said: "The attention of the emperor was also attracted by the nation of the Jews, that peculiar people which for thousands of years has lived among all peoples of the earth without becoming incorporated into any of them; which rather endures contumely and oppression than give up its ancient faith, its ancestral customs and habits. Joseph II believed that this people was no exception to the rule of human nature; that originally it was morally not more corrupt than other human beings; that the only reason for its refusal to become integrated into civil society and to fulfil its duties was the denial to them of all the rights and privileges thereof; that in order to overcome its resistance one ought not to apply oppression and persecution, as had been done, without effect, for such a long time; but that the only means toward its gradual improvement consisted in offering it the enjoyment of the rights of citizens on condition that the duties of citizens be fulfilled. He actually conceded to them these rights to an extent such as the Jews had never enjoyed in any Christian state."[20]

One has the impression that in describing Joseph II's motivations Dohm projected upon the monarch his own trend of thought as he remembered it from the time when he was engaged in the task suggested to him by Mendelssohn. That the Jewish people was no exception to the rule of human nature; that its deplorable position in the world was not due to its rejection by God but to its persecution by men; that it was incumbent upon the rulers of the earth to restore to it the natural rights of human beings; all this was but an epitome of what Dohm had stated in his famous book. Viewed against the full panorama of his long political career and impressive bibliography, the treatise of 1781 and its sequel of 1783 were only a brief interlude, to which his biographer devoted no more than seven out of seven hundred seven pages. Yet in his latter years Dohm himself used to recall this episode with obvious pleasure.[21]

Concerning the progress of the work and some of the circumstances attending it we are informed by a number of letters—eleven to Nicolai, his publisher, and eight to Mendelssohn, who closely collaborated with him.[22] We do not know exactly when he commenced his research and writing on the subject, but a letter to Nicolai dated May 11, 1781, shows him already immersed in his task. It also reveals the fact that he had originally intended to have the treatise printed outside Berlin but had changed his mind:[23]

> I am now working most diligently on my apologia on behalf of my circumcized brethren, and provided there is no major intervention, I hope to finish it by the beginning of July. I told you that I wanted the printing of the treatise to be done elsewhere and you know my reasons. On reflection, however, I hesitate to implement this plan because (1) I want to read the proofs myself, and (2) a Saxon or other foreign censor might possibly object to some of the things as being too liberal in respect not so much of my political as of my religious ideas. For it is very easy to cause offense even though, believe me, I am writing with as much tact and caution as is possible. In order, therefore, to take care of everything I have asked Herr Councillor Teller[24] whether he was prepared to act as censor, since the treatise dealt with matters on the border line between theology and politics, and since one could easily explain that something concerning the Jews had been brought before the theological forum, should the political censor stake his claims. In case, therefore, you raise no objection, the treatise can be printed here and will be submitted to Herr Teller's censorship. Kindly let me know your view.

The work took him about two months longer than had been anticipated. On August 24, 1781, he wrote to Mendelssohn:[25]

> At long last I have the pleasure of sending you the concluding part of my treatise. The appendix [viz. the text of the French *mémoire*] and the preface will not exceed one and a half sheets. With your permission, I shall send you these, too, and ask you to read the proofs of them since I do not sufficiently trust my eyes [to spot any errors] in the French text. In case the proofs were returned to me today, the printing could be done tomorrow.
>
> Seeing that a treatise makes, after all, a greater impression if it bears the author's name; seeing, moreover, that mine contains nothing to be disowned by me and, besides, has been passed by the censorship; considering also that the identity of the author invariably becomes known, I have decided to put my name on the title page. Herr Nicolai will greatly welcome this. . . .

We gather from this letter that Dohm was sending Mendelssohn parts of the book as he finished them. He obviously valued Mendelssohn's comments and suggestions. In this particular instance he asked him to assist also in the proofreading. The inclusion of the *mémoire* was probably designed to keep the still unresolved issue of the Alsatian petition before the public eye in France. For this very reason a French translation of Dohm's treatise was considered desirable. Of particular interest in Dohm's letter is the paragraph announcing his decision to waive anonymity. Having abandoned the idea of printing the work outside Prussia, and knowing that Teller had raised no objection to its publication, Dohm felt safe enough to acknowledge his authorship of a humanitarian plea that fully corresponded with his ideas. The preface, dated August 3, 1781, must have been written after he had arrived at his decision; otherwise, it could hardly have struck such a personal note. The book must have appeared in September, 1781,[26] for on October 23 Dohm sent Mendelssohn the first review:[27] "I do not know whether Herr Moses[28] reads Büsching's journal, and I therefore enclose the final instalment of a review that is as favorable as we could rightly expect of him. I also attach a letter by the prince of Dessau, which will be of interest to you because it deals at such length with the matter." Anton Friedrich Büsching (1724–1793), theologian, geographer, and director of the Gymnasium zum Grauen Kloster in Berlin, was a friend of Dohm.[29] In his weekly he had published a review of the treatise in three consecutive issues,[30] and seeing that the last instalment had appeared prior to October 23, the date of Dohm's letter, the book could not have come out later than the end of September. The letter of the prince of Dessau is unfortunately lost.

Immediateley after the German publication of the treatise steps were taken to arrange for its translation into French. The job was entrusted to Johannes (Jean) Bernoulli, a member of the famous family of scientists, who was director of the Mathematics Class of the Berlin Royal Library. On October 2, 1781, Dohm wrote to Mendelssohn:[31] "I have heard nothing about our French translation for some time. I assume Herr Bernoulli is all the busier for that. News has come to me from Dessau that the *Librairie des auteurs [et des artistes]*[32] will be pleased to take the matter over and that, besides, the printing there will be twenty-five thalers less expensive than here." Progress was more rapid than might have been expected. In his letter of October 23, Dohm could tell Mendelssohn that together with Bernoulli he had already checked more than half of the translation; that in response to their criticism Bernoulli now tended to be less literal and "slavish" in rendering the text; and that, anticipating a suggestion they were going to make, he had asked "a good French grammarian" to put the finishing touch upon his work. Dohm was hopeful, therefore, that within a short time he would be able to dispatch the first sheets to Dessau. At the same time, he requested Mendelssohn to let him have, for insertion "at the appropriate place" in the French edition, "the extract of a letter about the maritime services of the Jews in Holland."[33] He was referring to a report on the outstanding bravery shown by a Sephardic (Portuguese) Jew in the battle between the English and Dutch fleets on August 5, 1781. Conscious of the humane attitude toward Jews on the part of the Dutch government, many Dutch Jews had volunteered for service in the navy and had done so with the blessing of the Sephardic chief rabbi of

Amsterdam. Mendelssohn sent the interesting news item to Dohm, who included it both in the French version and in the second part of his German treatise.[34] On November 1, 1781, Dohm sent Mendelssohn a considerable part of the translation in its final revision:[35] "I would be happy if Herr Moses were to go over it once more and tell me his opinion. Should I receive it back the day after tomorrow, I shall immediatley send it to Dessau." The French version appeared early in 1782 under the title *De la réforme politique des Juifs.*[36]

As the letters show, both the German treatise and the French translation were heavily indebted to Mendelssohn. Traces of his consultative role are easily noticable in the text itself. The "great Jewish scholar" whose statement about military service on the sabbath is quoted in a footnote (I, 144) was clearly Mendelssohn. The remarks about Eisenmenger and the Talmud were undoubtedly inspired by him.[37] The same may be true of the passages culled from Josephus (I, 42; 139–41). Of special interest is the revision that Dohm applied to his advocacy of the rabbis' right to impose the ban.[38] In the German treatise he had written (I, 124): "Like every other ecclesiastical society, the Jewish one should also have the right of excommunication [*Ausschliessung*] [as a punishment extending] for limited periods or permanently. In cases in which the rabbinic verdict is challenged, it ought to be upheld by the civil authorities. The exercise of this *Bannrecht* should not be of any concern to the state, since it never transcends a religious society and is of no effect in political society: a person expelled from membership in any church can still be a most useful and respected citizen."

Mendelssohn did not share this view. He wanted to see the *Bannrecht* of the rabbis abolished on both religious and civil grounds, and took an early opportunity—in his preface to the German translation of Manasseh ben Israel's *Vindiciae Judaeorum* (1782)—to say so publicly. When reading Dohm's manuscript and, subsequently, the proofs, he must have come across this passage and could have asked the author to change or qualify it. It seems, however, that he left the text as it stood in order to use it as a target of friendly attack. In his preface to Manasseh ben Israel's treatise Dohm's words proved to be the ideal cue to enable him to make his point. Yet originally he felt that someone other than he should raise this issue in public. Having himself narrowly escaped being put under a *herem*, he probably wanted to avoid the impression of entering a plea on his own behalf. (Later he would abandon these scruples.) Therefore, he arranged with Moses Wessely, who lived as a merchant and author in Hamburg, to write some critical observations on Dohm's work—which had not yet appeared but whose proofs had been made available—and to include among them certain objections against the use of the ban by the rabbis.

This was done, of course, with the knowledge and consent of Dohm. In his letter of August 24, 1781, Dohm wrote to Mendelssohn:[39] "Herr Wessely could either send me his critical annotations to be used as an appendix [to the treatise] or else publish them later in a separate tract, in which he would duly express agreement with my main thesis. I personally consider the second course the better one, since following the first would delay matters. It depends, however, on what has been agreed to by you and Herr Wessely. I very much want him to write on this matter, and this alone will make my treatise worthwhile." On December 14, 1781, when Dohm had completed the revision of the French translation, it occurred to him that in order to meet Mendelssohn's objection to the paragraph on the *Bannrecht* he might insert a few lines of clarification in the French edition. Accordingly, he wrote a last minute addendum and sent it to Mendelssohn with the following note:[40] "I would like to include in the French translation of my treatise the enclosed little addendum concerning the issue of the ban, and only want to know whether it meets your approval, dearest Herr Moses. I believe that this addendum suffices to prevent all misunderstanding of what has been said about the right of excommunication (which I had improperly called *Bannrecht,* not realizing that according to your principles the term 'ban' implies much more). The more elaborate discussion of the matter I expect from Herr Wessely. I shall certainly make use of it in a second edition." It seems that Mendelssohn agreed to the insertion of the proposed rider, though he was by no means satisfied that it met his objection (and said just that in his preface to *Vindiciae Judaeorum*). The text of the addendum as found in the French edition[41] and in the revised German edition[42] reads as follows:

> In accordance with it [the principle of the separation of church member-ship and citizenship], the civil authorities should never permit a rabbi to pronounce against a member of his community such a ban as excludes him from all social contact with the rest of his coreligionists outside the synagogue, degrades him in their eyes, interferes with his business, or even exposes him to persecution by the mob. It appears that fines imposed for transgressing presumed commandments from heaven are likewise improper. The wrong use of power in imposing these penalties that can be made and, in fact, has often been made by rabbis makes it necessary for the government to keep the exercise of this power under constant supervision. When punishing the Jew who is a transgressor, this power must never punish the man and the citizen. Nothing but exclusion from ecclesiastical society and its benefits should follow from a violation of its precepts.

It was precisely this caveat that Mendelssohn, in his preface, described as totally unrealistic: "To admit a churchly regimen and to keep civil happi-ness inviolate seems to me a problem that still awaits its solution in politics. It is tantamount to the order given by the Most High Judge to Satan: Let him be in thy hands, but spare his life! Break the cask, but don't let the wine run out—as the commentators put it."[43]

Mendelssohn's categorical rejection of the use of ecclesiastical power had been anticipated by Wessely's pamphlet, which seems to have appeared in February, 1782, for on February 15 Dohm sent Nicolai a copy.[44] The pamphlet bore the title *Notes on Herr Dohm's treatise on the Civil Constitution* [sic!] *of the Jews* and the initials J. C. U. [Johann Christoph Unzer].[45] Unzer was a well-known physician and poet in Altona, where he held the post of professor of natural science at the local gymnasium. A friend of Wessely, he was pleased to lend his name to a tract that had a better chance of success, it was felt, if it was launched under a Christian writer's flag. Its purpose was twofold. It was to express, in the first place, moral support for Dohm's plea, and it was, secondly, to voice strenuous objection to the idea that Jewish "autonomy" as practiced heretofore should be continued. It attacked, in particular, Dohm's defense of the rabbis' right to "excommunicate" anybody. As promised, Dohm referred to this pamphlet in the revised edition of his work.[46]

Though Mendelssohn played a highly important role in the writing of Dohm's treatise from its very inception, he cannot be regarded as its coauthor.[47] And yet he was certainly more than its "godfather."[48] Apart from having persuaded Dohm to undertake the work, he gave it every possible assistance. As Dohm put it, in a letter written during the course of his work on the second part,[49] Mendelssohn had helped to make his treatise "more perfect." What he had *not* done was to try to exercise undue influence where Dohm's basic attitude toward Jews was concerned. The harsh tone in which Dohm spoke of the moral decline of Jewry must have offended Mendelssohn; he had repudiated the idea of the moral inferiority of the Jews when he rebutted Michaelis' charges to such effect,[50] but he did not attempt to soften Dohm's language in the treatise. Nor did he prevail upon Dohm to change the ambiguous title of the book to one that he would surely have preferred. The term "civil improvement of the Jews" suggested not merely the desirability of granting the Jews civil rights but also the need to improve their moral character. In his preface to *Vindiciae Judaeorum*[51] Mendelssohn adopted the inoffensive term "civil admission" (*bürgerliche Aufnahme*), which had been current in the older juridical literature on laws concerning the Jews in its Latin form (*ius recipiendi*).[52] It is possible that the misquotation of the name of Dohm's work in the title of Wessely's (Unzer's) pamphlet was deliberate and was intended as a camouflaged snub. Mendelssohn's noninterference was due, in the first place, to the respect he had for an author's right to speak his mind. It may also have been dictated by the consideration that only a work that shared the general view of the Jews' corruption stood any chance of being taken seriously and of achieving any success. And Dohm himself had to forestall any accusations that his treatise had been bought and paid for by wealthy Jews, a charge that had been leveled against Lessing's publication of the *Fragments*.[53]

It can hardly be doubted that Cerfberr paid Dohm an honorarium for his services in connection with the *mémoire*, that he rewarded Bernoulli's labors as translator, or that he also paid Dohm a certain fee for his protracted work on the treatise, seeing that its French version was to assist the cause of the Jews in Alsace. Dohm received no honorarium for the second part of his treatise. In view of the fact that Dohm's services were being rewarded by a Jewish sponsor, Mendelssohn had to be doubly careful not to encroach on his freedom. The honorarium paid by Cerfberr was over and above what Dohm received as an author's fee from his publisher, Nicolai. Evidence to this effect is provided by Dohm's letters to Nicolai.[54] When asked to state what he considered an appropriate fee for the first edition of his treatise, Dohm replied on January 9, 1782, that one ducat per sheet was the minimum he could agree to. When a second edition as well as a second part of the work were contemplated, Dohm requested one louis d'or per sheet of the new edition and two louis d'or per sheet of the second part. Nicolai thought this too high and suggested that Part Two be published by another firm. In a letter dated November 15, 1782, Dohm expressed astonishment that his modest claims had been rejected. He reminded Nicolai of the unusual amount of profit the book had brought him as the publisher. Two hundred copies had been bought immediately upon publication and seven hundred and fifty more had been sold through booksellers in the first six months. It was now up to Nicolai to pay him either one ducat or nothing for the second edition. On no account could he agree to a change of publisher, which was bound to give rise to all kinds of rumors and suspicions. (He had mistakenly assumed that Nicolai's suggestion had been made with reference also to the second edition.) He then continued: "So far as the continuation [Part Two] is concerned, you will understand that, this being a task requiring my attention for most of my available time throughout the winter and concerning which the circumstances surrounding Part One no longer exist, I cannot reduce the price mentioned but would rather work gratis, which my economic position does not really permit me to do." The special "circumstances surrounding Part One" that had allowed Dohm to accept the low fee of one ducat per sheet and had now ceased to exist must be understood as the payment of an honorarium by someone other than Nicolai—an obvious allusion to Cerfberr's role as sponsor.

The purchaser of the two hundred copies was undoubtedly Dohm himself, who hoped to sell them at a profit in France and asked Cerfberr to assist him in this endeavor. In a letter written to Mendelssohn on November 25, 1781, about two months after his treatise had appeared, Dohm betrayed some anxiety about not having heard from his sponsor:[55] "I do not wish to bother Herr Cerfberr with yet another letter. I would, however, ask you to request him to kindly let me know as soon as possible (1) whether he has duly received all the copies mentioned in my letter, (2) whether a license for the sale has been granted, and what kind of arrangements he has made with booksellers, and (3) how the cause of the Alsatian Jews now stands." Fortunately, Dohm had taken the precaution of urging Cerfberr to apply to the Chambre Syndicale de la Librairie for a license. As a result, he seems to have encountered no difficulty in selling the books. It was different in the case of the six hundred copies of the

French translation, which, at the request of Cerfberr, he had sent to his Strassbourg office. A letter written by Dohm to Mendelssohn as late as December 28, 1784,[56] tells a tale of unmitigated woe: Cerfberr's employees in Strassbourg had delayed the dispatch of the books to Paris "for years," without ever writing to Dohm. When they eventually sent the consignment to the capital, it did not reach Cerfberr but was confiscated by the Chambre Syndicale. Cerfberr was too busy to pursue the difficult task of obtaining its release, and he suggested that the embassy and other influential agencies be set in motion by Dohm. After endless negotiations and thanks to the intervention of Nicolai, the astronomer Lefrançais, and others, permission for the release of the six hundred copies was eventually granted. It came too late. The books had already been sent to the Bastille and destroyed.

The anguish and frustration that Dohm suffered on account of the bad luck of the French edition were of minor significance compared with the satisfaction he felt over the great stir to which his work gave rise. He expressed this feeling at the opening of his introduction to the second part of the treatise (1783): "I have been fortunate enough to achieve the purpose I had set myself in this work as completely as is, perhaps, not often the case with writers. My purpose was none other than to alert the public to a subject worthy of attention, yet hitherto unnoticed." A public debate on the pros and cons of his plea had been initiated, and the second part was intended to appraise it. In October, 1781, immediately after the publication of the treatise, Büsching's favorable review had appeared.[57] On December 1, 1781, the supplement to the *Göttingische gelehrte Anzeigen* (Number 48) published a hostile and rather scurrilous attack by Michael Hissmann, professor of philosophy at Göttingen. Dohm referred to it in the introduction to Part Two as hardly deserving a serious refutation.[58] In an undated note to Mendelssohn Dohm wrote:[59] "Here is my first adversary. His utterances will astonish you as little as they did me. On account of the first impression they make they could hurt our cause. Is it possible that the statement about Eisenmenger is justified? I shall consult the archives, where some reference must be found concerning the action allegedly taken in this matter by King Frederick I. I heard that several of our theologians are also not satisfied with my treatise. But their approval was not the purpose I sought to achieve."

The "first adversary" mentioned in this note could not have been Hissmann, for his review contained nothing about Eisenmenger. Nor is anything known about an earlier critical review.[60] One has to assume, therefore, that Dohm was referring to the extensive review-article by Michaelis in which Eisenmenger figured quite prominently. The article appeared in Michaelis' *Orientalische und Exegetische Bibliothek*[61] in March, 1782. It was on March 13 that Dohm sent Nicolai "Michaelis' Recension meiner Judenschrift," and on the twenty-seventh of the same month that he informed him of his intention to write a retort.[62] If our assumption is correct, Dohm's note to Mendelssohn was also written in March, 1782.

It called Michaelis the "first adversary" because his was the first serious critical discussion of the treatise, and it described Michaelis' attack as not surprising because he was known to be anything but a friend of the Jews. The review admitted that Eisenmenger's *Entdecktes Judentum* was a slanderous piece of writing *(eine Lästerschrift)* but did not entirely discredit the author. Michaelis wrote:[63] "Eisenmenger is not unjustified in complaining that it is highly doubtful whether a Jew considers what we think is an oath to be one." Dohm was evidently perturbed by Michaelis' support of Eisenmenger's accusation. In Part Two of his treatise, in which he reproduced the entire text of Michaelis' review,[64] he devoted a long section[65] to a refutation of this particular charge. The arguments he advanced had been largely supplied by Mendelssohn. The undated note may be regarded as an invitation to Mendelssohn to provide the answer. The reference to the action taken by Frederick I on behalf of Eisenmenger, about which nothing is mentioned in Michaelis' article, must have been due to information received when Dohm made some inquiries about Eisenmenger. He learned, no doubt, that the king had intervened in the trial concerning the sale of the abusive work by pleading with the Emperor Leopold I to lift the prohibition.[66]

During the summer of 1782 Dohm prepared both the second edition and the second part of his treatise. He had received, and was still receiving, a large number of letters from readers, some of them welcoming his proposals, others rejecting them on various grounds. He planned to include a selection of them in the second part, and eventually did so.[67] He also kept in close touch with Mendelssohn. We catch a glimpse of their personal relationship from a note written by Dohm on June 19, 1782:[68] "Should you spend this afternoon in your garden, dearest Herr Moses, I shall visit you there together with my brother-in-law. On no account do I want to inconvenience you. Hopefully, we shall have many more beautiful days this summer." A note at the bottom of the page in Mendelssohn's hand expresses hearty agreement.

It had been Dohm's intention to publish both the revised edition and Part Two by the spring of 1783, but something went wrong.[69] On June 16, 1783, he wrote to Mendelssohn that things were now moving again:[70] "The printing of my second part has now been resumed. Herr Professor Poppe[71] reads the second proofs, and since he lives in your neighborhood, I have instructed him to send you the sheets regularly. As the printer hurries me, I ask you to return them to Herr Poppe as soon as your preoccupations permit it; also to put down separately all comments you might wish to make, and to send them directly to me so that I can make use of them when reading the third proofs. May I, moreover, ask you for a precise list of all your festivals and the extent to which they interfere with your work. Forgive me for bothering you so often, but I know that, as hitherto, you still like to contribute toward making my little treatise more perfect. You would do me an additional favor if you were to correct, at the same time, blemishes in style and any printer's errors that have not been caught. There were a great many of them in the first proof." The letter clearly shows the extent of Mendelsshon's continuing cooperation with Dohm.

A Momentous Event and a New Tract for the Times

In May, 1781, when Dohm was already immersed in his "Apologia" for the Jews,[1] the Austrian Emperor Joseph II requested his Council of State to comment on certain proposals for the liberalization of laws restricting the economic activities of Jews.[2] These proposals of the emperor foreshadowed the famous Patent of Tolerance, and they gave rise to a lively public debate. A number of tracts and pamphlets discussing the pros and cons of the matter appeared in Vienna and Prague during that year.[3] Whether the proposed measures concerning Jewish trade would be passed and perhaps lead to a more broadly based reform of the legal position of the Jews in the Austrian monarchy was a matter of conjecture for some time. The patent applying to the Jews in Bohemia came out first. It was issued on October 19, 1781, and the Austrian version of the edict followed on January 2, 1782.[4] From May until October, 1781, Jews were in a state of extreme tension. Some Maskilim were already dreaming of obtaining teaching posts under government auspices.

It must have been during this period of suspense that Mendelssohn wrote the following undated letter to Avigdor Levi:[5]

> The more I think about it, the more firmly I stick to my idea that too much agitation by certain people will only hurt the cause. If "the thing proceedeth from the Lord,"[6] and if it is the monarch's true and sincere resolve to improve our condition, it will come somewhat more slowly but all the more surely and beneficially. Should it, however, be a mere casual fancy on his part without any propelling force behind it, or should fiscal considerations have been at its root, as some suspect, we should refrain from goading them. This will be of no avail, and you, my friend, stand to gain nothing from arousing animosity against you. In the event that the thing materializes, people as educated as you will be in great demand.

As this letter shows, Mendelssohn viewed the situation with a great deal of equanimity. Despite his concern, he remained remarkably calm, leaving it entirely to Providence to decide the outcome. He had little faith in trying to force any issue. The fact that Dohm's plea coincided with a pending reform by the Austrian emperor was exciting but a strong dose of skepticism put the brake on his emotions. When the text of the Austrian Patent of Tolerance was published and many of his friends were swept off their feet, Mendelssohn immediately saw its flaws. He was by no means as enthusiastic as might appear from his preface to Manasseh ben Israel's treatise, which he completed on March 19, 1782.[7] On the contrary, there is evidence that he had serious misgivings about the purpose of the edict, and that Dohm was also disappointed. On February 8, 1782, Mendelssohn wrote to Nicolai, who was the publisher of the Manasseh ben Israel treatise:[8]

> I enclose herewith the Vienna Patent in its full text [*in extenso*]. What Herr Dohm says about it, I have deeply felt myself. Shall we perhaps take the opportunity of reproducing the entire patent at the end of our pamphlet? The excerpts published by the newspapers were far too warped. However, let us leave this rather in abeyance. After all, I cannot express my view as plainly and candidly as I would like. Hence I prefer to be altogether silent.

This rather gloomy note makes it abundantly clear that Mendelssohn did not join in the widespread jubilation over the edict. What must have disturbed him was the openly displayed tendency of the new legislation to lure the Jews into the pale of the Christian church. There is no reason to doubt that he carefully studied the text of the edict when it became known in Berlin toward the end of January, 1782, and that he found in it indisputable evidence of this tendency. Nor was he the only one to notice it. Among the letters that Dohm received in February, 1782, and subsequently published in Part Two of his treatise there was one voicing the same impression:[9]

> The emperor's edict concerning the Jews, which you will have seen in the meanwhile, hardly lives up to your expectation [as expressed in the postscript to the treatise (I, 151–54)]. In essence, it seems to be a *political attempt at the religious improvement* of the Jews, and it obviously has for its purpose to make them into Christians within twenty or, at most twice twenty, years, i.e., by the time the present generation has died out. I doubt, however, whether it will achieve its purpose. Such an edict may tempt many Jews to emigrate.
> G., February 23, 1782. M.

There can be little doubt that the writer of this letter was none other than Professor Michaelis (M.) of Göttingen (G.), whose review of Dohm's treatise, which had appeared in March, 1782,[10] referred to exactly the same paragraph in the edict and drew the same conclusion. It mentioned the clause stipulating that the leasing of real estate to Jews was to be limited to a period of twenty years, and that an extension in perpetuity was to be granted only if the Jewish tenant converted to Christianity.[11] Michaelis' distinct reference, in the review, to the twenty years' limitation helps us to understand the cryptic remark about conversion within twenty or twice twenty years in the letter. In his review Michaelis also stated the opinion that the purpose of the edict was a missionary one.[12]

It may be assumed that the paragraph noticed by Michaelis had not escaped the attention of Mendelssohn and Dohm. In the following year their doubts about the emperor's liberalism were confirmed when a deistic sect of Bohemian peasants was expelled and deported to the Turkish border. Reports of this cruel act of religious persecution appeared in the newspapers in March, 1783, and caused Dohm to insert a lengthy note and a postscript in Part Two of his treatise.[13] In Dohm's view the phrase "the only saving faith" in the text of the compulsion order was "wholly unworthy of the 'official style' [*Canzleystil*] of an enlightened government."[14] Mendelssohn's reaction was expressed in a letter dated April 4, 1783, to Carl Julius Redlich in Vienna:[15] "The enclosed cutting from a newspaper, which contains an alarming piece of information from your country, has confused me completely and disturbed me not a little. I take comfort in the fact that the diction departs so much from 'official style' and that the contents depart so markedly from Emperor Joseph's way of thinking that the whole story looks like a pure fabrication. Forgive my forwardness, but may I expect to hear the facts from you?"[16]

Even prior to the promulgation of the Patent of Tolerance Mendelssohn had decided to make a contribution of his own to the cause of Jewish civil rights. He felt that certain views expressed by Dohm called for comment and amplification, and that others called for modification. He also considered it necessary to expose the prejudices that the public debate of Dohm's proposals had brought to light, and he regarded it as altogether desirable to keep the discussion going by introducing fresh viewpoints. He was not entirely happy at the prospect of entering the arena of discussion. In his opinion it was preferable, on the whole, to leave it to the Christians to plead the cause of justice for the Jews. In 1785, when the baron von Hirschen invited him to write an essay for a periodical designed to combat prejudice against the Jews, Mendelssohn declined: he had always liked it best when the Christian prejudices against the Jews were contested by Christian authors.[17] For the same reason Moses Wessely's "Notes" on Dohm's treatise were published under Unzer's name. However, this was not the way that Mendelssohn could adopt.

Mendelssohn found a solution to his problem when he reread the moving tract written in 1656 by the celebrated Amsterdam Rabbi Manasseh ben Israel pleading for the readmission of the Jews to England, whence they had been expelled in 1290. It occurred to Mendelssohn that the solemn and authoritative manner in which the author had refuted the age-old prejudices against the Jews had lost none of its pungency; that presenting the tract in a German translation would be a matter of literary interest and, at the same time, a service to the cause he had at heart; and that he could give utterance to his own views in a preface to the German edition. The publication could take the form of a supplement to Dohm's treatise. This plan was carried into effect with much success. The original text had been reprinted in an old periodical called *The Phenix, or Revival of scarce and valuable Pieces, no where to be found but in the Closets of the Curious* (London, 1708), where its title was given as *"Vindiciae Judaeorum: Or, a Letter in Answer to Certain Questions Propounded by a Noble and Learned Gentleman, Touching the Reproaches Cast on the Nation of the Jews; wherein all Objections are Candidly, and yet Fully Clear'd."*[18] It has been generally assumed that it was at Mendelssohn's request that Doctor Marcus Herz translated this text into German,[19] and this assumption is confirmed by a contemporary source: Doctor Simon Höchheimer, a medical practitioner in Berlin until 1785, who also attended to Mendelssohn,[20] wrote in 1786 that "in the year 1782 there appeared in Berlin *Manasseh Ben Israel Rettung der Juden* translated from the English (by Doctor Marcus Herz) with a preface by Moses Mendelssohn."[21] That Dohm assisted in the proofreading is evident from a note Mendelssohn sent Nicolai on February 8, 1782.[22] The note also sheds light on the sense of urgency he felt about the publication of the work:[23]

> Dearest Friend! I enclose herewith a part of the manuscript that you kindly promised to print, together with a letter by Herr *Kriegsrath* Dohm, in which he indicates the procedure he wants to follow in regard to the proofreading. I ask you to see that this brochure is printed as soon as possible. I think that at the present time one ought to keep the public constantly *en haleine* [in suspense] in regard to this matter, and that the pros and cons of this issue should continue to be a subject of debate.

Mendelssohn completed his preface on March 19, 1782,[24] and the book appeared soon afterward; as early as April 27 Hennings acknowledged the complimentary copy that had been sent to him.[25] The work bore the title: *Manasseh Ben Israel's Vindication of the Jews Translated from the English, with a preface by Moses Mendelssohn. Being a supplement to Herr Kriegsrath Dohm's Treatise: On the Civil Improvement of the Jews (Berlin & Stettin, 1782).*[26]

Mendelssohn's preface opened with a prayer of thanksgiving reminiscent of the Hebrew benediction prescribed for festive and other joyful occasions: "Thanks be rendered to a kind Providence for having allowed me to reach, at the end of my days, this happy season in which a beginning has been made to consider human rights from a truly universal aspect." Despite his misgivings about the Edict of Tolerance, Mendelssohn appreciated the historic significance of the event. He felt no urge to write an ode in praise of the emperor (as Klopstock and Hartwig Wessely had done), nor a rapturous essay (such as the one that Rabbi Isaac Alexander of Regensburg had produced),[27] but he was alert to the fact that a new era had been ushered in. In the past, he said,[28] one had heard talk of tolerance only from the weak and oppressed. Yet it was the duty of the stronger party to take the first step toward brotherly love. He recalled the moving scene in Corneille's *Cinna* (V, 3) in which Augustus speaks the words: "Let us be friends!" To him this simple sentence had always represented the noble spirit of magnanimity at its best,[29] and notwithstanding the fact that the Edict of Tolerance offered only the rudiments of plain justice, he was generous enough to see in it a magnanimous gesture. He noted further that previous debate about tolerance had been exclusively concerned with dissident Christians, with pagans, Jews, Muslims, and believers in natural religion hardly entering into the picture at all. The "Fragmentist,"[30] for example, had probably been the very first man in Germany to demand tolerance for those who adhered to radical deism.[31]

In this passage, drawing attention to groups other than the Jews who stood to benefit from the awakening of a more liberal spirit, Mendelssohn lifted Jewish claims out of the confines of a special problem and presented them as part and parcel of a universal clamoring for justice; however, he immediately returned to the specific situation of the Jews. Lessing in his *Nathan the Wise* (1779)[32] and Dohm in his treatise had given thought to "the great purpose of Providence," which embraced the "prerogatives" *(Gerechtsame)* of humanity as a whole, and "an admirable monarch" had commenced to implement them. With obvious deliberateness Mendelssohn described the edict as a mere beginning, and he hinted at the tremendous obstacles it had to overcome by saying that its realization required "more than human powers."[33] Here he was alluding to the resistance that the emperor's plans for educational reform had already encountered among the Jews themselves.[34] In March, 1782, when Mendelssohn was finishing his preface, Hartwig Wessely's pamphlet *Divrey Shalom Ve-Emmet* ("Words of Peace and Truth") had appeared, seeking to allay the fears of the traditionalists and strongly supporting Joseph II's projects. Judging from his own experience, Mendelssohn foresaw the storm of protest that Wessely's pamphlet would arouse.

As one whose life had been spent in quiet meditation, Mendelssohn went on to say, and lacking both the desire and the opportunity to take an active part in world affairs, he was powerless to influence the course of events. Even so, he wished to reflect on the arguments that Dohm had advanced in favor of the civil admission of the Jews. As he modestly remarked, there was in fact little he could add, Dohm having all but exhausted the philosophical and political aspects of the matter. His first point concerned the fundamental purpose of Dohm's work: it was not an apologia on behalf of Judaism or the Jews but a defense of the cause of *humanity* and thus only incidentally a plea for Jewish rights; as a philosopher of the eighteenth century, Dohm had transcended the barriers created by doctrinal differences and considered every individual simply as a human being. Mendelssohn did not further elaborate this point in the preface, but it deserves a closer look, considering its central importance for an understanding of the position held jointly by Dohm and Mendelssohn.

All religions, Dohm had stated in his treatise (I, 24), were more or less exclusive as a result of the different "opinions" they professed. The state could not consider adherence to certain views a sufficient reason for withholding the privileges of citizenship. It had to grant tolerance either to a single religion or to none, both alternatives being absurd. "Can it be true that a large number of industrious and good citizens are less useful to the state because they are of Asian descent and differ from others by being bearded and circumcised and by revering the Supreme Being in a particular manner inherited from their ancestors?"[35] Mendelssohn wholeheartedly agreed with this line of reasoning. Johann David Michaelis, on the other hand, voiced strong objections to it in his review of Dohm's work. The Mosaic laws, he argued, were designed to maintain the Jews as a separate nation, and so long as the Jews kept those laws they would not be able to "merge with us in the same way that Catholics and Lutherans, Germans, Wends, and Frenchmen living in the same state did." Such a separate nation might perhaps become useful to the state, but it could not be expected to coalesce with the other citizens. The mere fact that the Jews still hoped to return one day to Palestine precluded this.[36]

In a spirited reply that Mendelssohn published in Part Two of Dohm's treatise (pages 72–77) he took issue with the points raised in Michaelis' review. Mendelssohn did not deny that the Jews wanted to maintain their separate identity as a nation. However, in his view a group's readiness to "coalesce" with other groups was no criterion of worthiness so far as civil rights were concerned. The only legitimate question was: can the Jews be expected to discharge the duties incumbent upon citizens? Michaelis had asserted that the answer to this question was in the negative; military service on the sabbath, for example, was sure to be refused by the Jews. Mendelssohn, rather amazingly, anticipated no serious difficulties. It was up to each individual to adjust his "particular views" to his duties as a citizen. If the defense of the country was at stake, everyone called to arms had to serve. With a strong dose of realism, he suggested that people knew how to "modify their views" in specific circumstances. Dohm had put forward similar arguments: the benefits flowing from a just and impartial political system had the effect of weakening the hold of religious principles, and the bonds connecting fellow citizens had a greater influence than expectations related to the life in the beyond (I, 28–29). As for the hope for a return to Palestine, history had shown, Mendelssohn pointed out, that wherever Jews enjoyed tolerance, they had felt quite at home. It was part of a man's nature—unless one happened to be an "enthusiast"—to love the place where he was well treated and to confine the expression of certain "religious opinions" to the liturgy. Besides, the talmudic sages had warned the Jewish nation against a forcible return to Palestine for the purpose of restoring their state before the divinely appointed time had arrived.[37] The burden of Dohm's as well as Mendelssohn's argument was the nondifference of the Jews in their human nature, reactions to circumstances, and conduct as citizens.

The opposition that Dohm's proposals had encountered was, in Mendelssohn's view, proof of a new kind of prejudice against the Jews. "It is strange to see," the preface continued, "how prejudice changes its form in successive centuries in order to suppress us and place obstacles in the way of our civil admission."[38] With a deft move Mendelssohn drew attention to the barbaric type of defamation that had been the legacy of past ages, and with which Manasseh ben Israel had had to cope. Dohm, he said, had rightly disdained to deal with those relics of the past, which bore the marks of the "monkish cells" where they originated. Yet new and no less insidious accusations had taken their place. "In those superstitious times it was said of us that we desecrated wafers, pierced crucifixes and and made them bleed; that we secretly circumcised children and dismembered them to our eyes' delight; that we required Christian blood for Passover; that we poisoned wells; etc. . . . Now times have changed. Those defamations no longer produce the desired effect. Now it is superstition and stupidity, of all things, with which we are charged; lack of moral feeling, taste, good manners; an incapacity for the arts, sciences, and useful occupations, particularly for military and civil service; an irrepressible inclination toward fraudulence, usury, and lawlessness." Even the medieval prejudices still lingered on, as the revival of the ritual murder charge some time ago in Posen and, more recently, in Warsaw showed.[39] Arguments were of no avail when the adversary was not prepared to listen.

Mendelssohn did not deny that Jews were in need of "improvement." Centuries of persecution had left many scars, and oppressive legislations had fostered an outlook of narrow parochialism in many quarters. It had been for the sake of a cultural regeneration that he had initiated his Bible project, and it was for the same reason that he so ardently desired the civil equality of the Jews. He resented, however, the accusation that Jews were morally inferior to Christians. Michaelis had tried to prove statistically that in respect of thievery (to him, the lowest of all vices) Jews were twenty-five (or more) times corrupt as the Germans. Mendelssohn did not mince his words in rebuttal:[40] if a nation's depravity was to be assessed, he declared, it was necessary to take into account murderers, highwaymen, traitors, arsonists, adulterers, harlots, infanticides, etc.—not thieves alone. But even under the erroneous assumption that only thieves and dealers in stolen goods were an index of a nation's depravity, Michaelis' statistical method was wrong. The number of Jews in that category was not to be compared with general population figures but with non-Jews of the same description among small traders and second-hand dealers. A comparison would then show that there were twenty-five times more German than Jewish offenders of this kind. He added grimly: "Besides, the Jew resorts to such a way of life from sheer necessity, while the non-Jew has a chance to become a field marshal or cabinet minister and by his free choice became a small trader, second-hand dealer, mousetrap vendor, magic lantern operator, or curiosities huckster." He remembered from his early years in Dessau that people of blameless character had in their younger days, out of despair, joined bands of thieves in order to raise the money required to buy the right of residency from the government. Their misdemeanor had been entirely due to the inhuman policy that denied protection to destitute Jews. In the Middle Ages, Mendelssohn said in the preface, Christians had made every effort to convert the Jews. Now conversionist zeal was on the wane—and Jews were neglected entirely. Now they found themselves excluded from all access to cultural improvement and at the same time blamed for their cultural backwardness. "Our hands are tied—and we are reproached for not using them."[41]

Yet even under present conditions, Mendelssohn maintained,[42] the Jews were "useful" to the state, and one had no reason to fear that permitting them to increase their number would prove detrimental to the Christian population.[43] One could still read with profit what Manasseh ben Israel had had to say on this subject.[44] Holland offered the most convincing proof that even under restricted conditions the Jews could make a considerable contribution to the prosperity of the commonwealth. It was unworthy of a statesman to declare that some group was of no use to the country. Under a wise government no one could be considered superfluous or unfit for service. True, Dohm had mentioned the theoretical possibility that a further increase in population was harmful; that there was a limit to the absorptive capacity of a country; but this limit had not been reached as yet in any large European state (I, 5). Mendelssohn could not agree that restrictive measures to curb an increase in population were justifiable at any time. Legislation to this effect was bound to do more harm than good. One should trust to the "wise provisions of nature." Men chose to live in places where they could find their sustenance. They increased in numbers and accumulated where free rein was given to their activities. Increase in population continued so long as people's ingenuity discovered new means of earning a livelihood; when the sources of gainful occupation dried up, diminished increase ensued naturally. It could safely be said, Mendelssohn declared, that whenever a part of the population felt the need to emigrate, the fault lay with the government; it was invariably bad laws that produced such a situation.

This view echoed a theory that had been propounded by Johann Heinrich Gottlob von Justi (died 1771),[45] according to which the principal asset of a state was its population, whose increase meant a growth in power, security, prosperity, and culture. This doctrine had been taken up by the politician Josef von Sonnenfels, a leader of the Viennese Enlightenment,[46] who insisted, however, that an increase in population was to be welcomed only if economic measures could secure an adequate standard of living.[47] Considerations of this kind had been the point of departure for Dohm's advocacy of more liberal laws concerning the Jews, whose growth in numbers had been severely restricted. In Part Two of his treatise Dohm made reference to Mendelssohn's critical comment on his observation that a point of saturation was conceivable, explaining that this was a purely hypothetical assumption and that for all practical purposes he found himself in full agreement with Mendelssohn.[48] Noninterference by the state was indeed the best policy.

Mendelssohn discussed yet another point that had been raised against permitting any increase in Jewish population. It had been said that in their present condition the Jews were merely consumers, not producers, since their sole economic function was that of middlemen; that their role, moreover, was a harmful one, because it unnecessarily made goods much dearer than they would be without their intervention. As Mendelssohn recalled,[49] a writer of good repute had made this point only recently and had gone so far as to advise governments either not to tolerate Jews at all or to permit them to become farmers and artisans.[50] Mendelssohn himself was greatly in favor of the second alternative,[51] but he was realistic enough to see the difficulties of putting such a scheme into effect, and he was not prepared to admit that under prevailing conditions the role of the Jews was in any way harmful. He challenged the whole conception underlying the negative appraisal of the Jewish part in the economy. If it were indeed true that in order to be regarded as productive one had to create or improve some tangible thing, then the majority of citizens would have to be considered mere consumers. For example, neither teachers nor soldiers could claim to be producers of tangible things. And from among those concerned with trade and industry, one would have to exclude merchants, porters, coachmen, and navigators, among others. In the end, the class of so-called producers would comprise, for the most part, only ploughmen and journeymen, since landowners and masters rarely engaged in manual labor. The absurdity of such a conclusion being manifest, the premise had to be suspected of being false.

In Mendelssohn's view, productivity designated not merely an act of "making" but also one of "doing,"[52] not merely manufacture[53] but any action that promoted utility and pleasure. The merchant who devised commercial projects at his desk was more productive than the laborer. The soldier helped to produce a state of peace and security. The scholar produced goods of an intangible nature. Rousseau, Mendelssohn remarked, must have been in a bad mood when he suggested that a Parisian confectioner "produced" more than the Academy of Sciences did. The welfare of the state and of the individual depended on a great variety of things material and spiritual, and whoever helped to promote any of these was not a mere consumer. Nor could middlemen in trade be called superfluous consumers. By channeling the flow of goods from manufacturer to customer they saved an enormous amount of time and energy for increased production, which resulted in cheaper prices and a higher standard of living. The much-abused middleman was, therefore, a "true benefactor" of the state. As for the forcing up of prices by greedy and unscrupulous jobbers, this could be prevented by increased competition through the suspension of all monopolies. Viewed from this angle, the smallest Jewish tradesman was an asset to the country. Mendelssohn's resolute defense of the "smallest Jewish tradesman" implied a criticism of Dohm's suggestion that Jews be eliminated from small trade and transfered to agriculture and the crafts.[54]

In the fall of 1781 Mendelssohn had immersed himself in the study of natural law, a topic that had always held a special fascination for him. His prize-essay of 1763 had already touched on certain aspects of it,[55] and the first fruit of his renewed occupation with the subject had been the short fragment *On Perfect and Imperfect Duties*,[56] written in November, 1781. The ideas sketched therein became the nucleus of his theory of the relationship between church and state, which appeared in its developed form in the *Jerusalem* (1783) but also played a decisive role in the *Manasseh* preface. Dohm had proposed that a certain amount of autonomy in juridical matters be left to the Jews even in the event of their being admitted to full citizenship, and that their autonomy included the right of enforcing religious observance. Mendelssohn subjected these proposals to a close scrutiny, modifying the first and rejecting the second.

As for the first, Dohm had suggested that Jews should have the right to bring cases of litigation between themselves before a rabbinic court to be decided according to Jewish law, as had been the practice hitherto. In some countries the rabbinic verdict was considered on a par with judgments administered in the first instance at the ordinary courts, in others it was accorded only the status of an arbitration.[57] If a rabbinic verdict was appealed, the matter was referred to the ordinary court of appeal. In Fürth, no appeal against a rabbinic judgment was possible. In Metz, the appellate court passed judgment according to Jewish law in order to avoid the misuse of the court by plaintiffs who saw a better chance of winning the case by turning away from rabbinic jurisdiction. In Berlin the rabbinic court had (after 1750) only the right of arbitration,[58] and an appeal was permitted. In order to enable Christian judges to decide cases between Jew and Jew in accordance with Jewish law, Chief Rabbi Hirschel Lewin of Berlin had been asked by the government to write a German digest of the Jewish laws concerning inheritance, testaments, guardianship, and matrimonial matters insofar as they had a bearing on property rights. The rabbi had approached Mendelssohn for help, and the work that ensued, bearing the misleading title *Ritual Laws of the Jews Concerning Inheritance etc*, had appeared in 1778. Mendelssohn's role in its production was tantamount to that of an author.[59]

Dohm proposed the following legal provisions. If litigants preferred to go to the ordinary court, no objection should be raised, but the judges would be enjoined to pass judgment in accordance with Jewish law, and to do this in all instances, including the higher courts of appeal. Christian judges could inform themselves about Jewish legal concepts by consulting the work published under Chief Rabbi Lewin's supervision. But it was preferable, Dohm pointed out, to have Jewish judges decide cases in the first instance, since Christians would find it difficult to cope with the intricacies of rabbinic law, whose source material was available only in Hebrew.[60] Mendelssohn seems to have felt a bit uneasy on this point. He obviously did not want to ask for too many favors and perhaps jeopardize the entire project. In his view, it was enough to ask for the application of Jewish legal principles in the adjudication of lawsuits between Jews. To insist, even guardedly, on Jewish judges as the only ones qualified to pass judgement in the first instance appeared to him to be going too far: "To the question: 'should Jewish or Christian judges decide?' I reply: It does not matter whether the judges belong to the Jewish religion or any other so long as they are magistrates. Once the members of the state enjoy equal human rights, no matter to which religion they adhere, this difference is irrelevant."[61] All one had to ask of a judge was conscientiousness and legal competence. His religion did not enter into the picture. Did we not entrust our health to a physician irrespective of his religion? Why then could we not entrust our claim to certain property to any qualified judge? For all practical purposes, Mendelssohn must have agreed that if Jewish jurisprudence was to be employed in the administration of justice to two Jewish parties in a lawsuit, few Christian judges would have the necessary competence. He was dealing with principles, however, and here he could not permit the question of religion to intrude.

But was the claim to a separate system of jurisdiction compatible with the claim to civil equality? Could it not easily be misrepresented as a desire on the part of the Jews to have the best of both worlds—to continue, in a way, their medieval system of self-government while at the same time enjoying the privileges of full citizenship? The term "a state within the state" had already been applied to the Jews by the notorious François Hell,[62] and both Dohm and Mendelssohn must have been aware of it. Dohm justified his proposal for Jewish juridical autonomy on two grounds. First, the Jews considered their system of law as divinely revealed and a part of their religion. To deny them the application of their legal ordinances would therefore be tantamount to a curtailment of their religious freedom and, hence, of their human rights. In other words, the Jewish motivation in wanting to maintain their own juridical system was not political but religious. Second, the separateness produced by the granting of such a privilege should not be exaggerated as to its degree. It was analogous to the distinctive character of certain towns and communities that lived according to special statutes.

Mendelssohn quoted the first of these arguments with approval but he felt it necessary to add a third reason. The Jews asked for juridical autonomy only in matters concerning property rights. Matters of this kind depended on freely entered contracts, and every group was free to adopt certain rules by which the transfer of property became valid or—to use the terminology of the natural-law school—by which imperfect duties became perfect (compulsory) ones. Therefore, should a group of people prefer to have litigations among its members settled according to its own well-defined rules, there was no reason why the state should object. The Jews, who believed in the divine origin of their laws, were such a group. Mendelssohn, who usually spoke of the Jews as a "nation," used in this context the term "colony."[63] This term had a familiar ring in Berlin, with its "French colony," and Jews liked to compare their status to that of the Frenchmen.[64]

The point on which Mendelssohn disagreed with Dohm concerned the question whether the Jewish "colony" should have jurisdiction over its members to the extent of having the right to enforce adherence to religious beliefs and practices. In other words, was the rabbinate to be left in the possession of coercive power analogous to that of the church? Should it be permitted to excommunicate recalcitrant offenders? As already mentioned in a previous passage,[65] Mendelssohn strongly objected to the continuance of this kind of autonomy. He did so not merely for tactical reasons, that is, in order to please the government, which had always regarded the ecclesiastical *Bannrecht* as a thorn in its side[66] and could easily construe it as an infringement of its sovereignty. He was motivated, in the main, by philosophical considerations concerning the nature of religion, on the one hand, and of power, on the other. His reflections on the subject were reinforced, however, by an acute awareness of experiences in recent times,[67] and the fervor of his plea for the renunciation of force as an instrument of religious conformity bore witness to it. The arguments he put forward anticipated to a large extent his reasoning in the *Jerusalem* and will be discussed later. Certain striking passages in the preface have to be mentioned, however, because they evoked a response of a kind that compelled Mendelssohn to write the *Jerusalem*. Never before had he defined the peaceable nature of religion in such ringing terms as these:[68]

> Every society, it seems to me, has the right to be exclusive, the only exception being any churchly society, for exclusiveness is diametrically opposed to such a society's purpose. Its aim is the joining together of people for the sake of edification and the sharing in the effusion of heart with which we express thankfulness for God's bounties and our childlike trust in his goodness. With what kind of a heart can we deny to a dissident, heretic, or nonconformist the right to participate in this edification? The laws and the police will deal with disturbers of the peace. Disorders must and can be checked by the secular arm, but even a criminal should not be prevented from quiet participation in the assembly, unless we deliberately wish to block to him all roads of return. Reason's house of prayer requires no closed doors. It is not meant to guard anything inside nor is it to deny entry to anyone outside.

In accordance with his belief that Judaism in its pristine form was identical with the religion of reason, Mendelssohn pointed out that "the wisest of our [Jewish] ancestors" had never excluded anyone from joining religious services in the Jerusalem Temple. As a biblical witness he quoted King Solomon's prayer at the inauguration of the Temple, which invited strangers (i.e. heathens) to come and pray in there, and which implored God to harken to their call (I Kings 8:41–44). Manasseh ben Israel had cited the same passage in order to prove that we pray for the "conversion of the Gentiles," an interpretation that Mendelssohn repudiated in a lengthy note.[69] As a rabbinic law testifying to a spirit of broad tolerance and nonexclusiveness Mendelssohn quoted the injunction *(Hullin* 5a) to accept offerings to the altar from heathens and from Jewish transgressors who had not entirely removed themselves from religion. By not rejecting their offerings one was likely to facilitate their improvement.[70] Denying any connection between religion and power, Mendelssohn had said in a previous passage:[71]

"True, divine religion does not arrogate to itself any power over opinions and propositions; it neither confers nor assumes any claim to earthly goods or any right to enjoyment, possession, or property; it knows no power other than the power to convince by reasoning and to make one happy through convictions held. True, divine religion needs neither arms nor fingers to be effective. It is all mind and heart."

The renunciation of all force, in Mendelssohn's view, was indispensable if abuses of ecclesiastical power were to be avoided. He referred in this connection to a recent incident: he was not going to investigate, he said, to what extent the complaints that had been voiced in public against a certain famous rabbi had been justified; the published report was onesided and he was prepared to believe that the severity of the measures taken by the rabbi had been exaggerated; and the matter was now before the highest tribunal of the country.[72] The case to which Mendelssohn referred concerned Chief Rabbi Raphael Kohen of Altona, who had felt it necessary to impose some rigorous penances on a certain Samuel Marcus jun. in Hamburg, who had been placed under the minor ban and threatened with the major ban if he failed to comply with the penances. Marcus had lodged a complaint with the Danish authorities, and the rabbi had been ordered to rescind his measures and to refrain from similar acts of persecution and despotism in the future. A protest by the rabbi was still sub judice (the matter was finally decided against him in May, 1782).[73] The "report" mentioned by Mendelssohn was an anonymously published tract *On the Misuse of Ecclesiastical Power*,[74] the doing of August Friedrich Cranz, more a scribbler than a serious author, who had been relieved of his post as *Kriegsrath* and lived by his writing. He had fallen out with Dohm, who was the government's officially appointed censor.[75] In some of his previous writings Cranz had advocated greater tolerance toward the Jews,[76] and the tract accusing the chief rabbi of Altona had probably been written by him at the instigation of some Jews in Hamburg-Altona. Mendelssohn had therefore to be extremely cautious in alluding to this rather "partial" piece of writing, but he could hardly have ignored it, considering the widespread attention it had attracted.[77]

Mendelssohn concluded the preface with an impassioned appeal to the "most enlightened [*erleuchtetsten*] and most pious rabbis and elders" of his nation to renounce the "sword of vengeance" that the weapon of *herem* and all diciplinary penances represented. It was time to relinquish this last vestige of power that their oppressors had allowed them to retain. All nations had hitherto believed that religion required for its maintenance the exercise of "iron power" and that true conceptions about the God of love could be secured only by the force of hatred. This misguided notion had invaded Jewish thinking and it may have given some sense of satisfaction to Jewish authorities to treat their own people as intolerantly as their persecutors treated them. Vengeance invariably craved an object, and if it could not be turned against others, it sought to devour its own flesh and blood. Now the nations[78] had begun to tolerate each other and even to show a measure of love and forbearance toward the Jews, which—with divine help—might grow into true brotherly love. "Oh, my brethren, follow the example of love, even as hitherto you followed the example of hatred. Imitate the virtue of the nations whose vices you hitherto thought it necessary to copy. If you wish to be sheltered, tolerated, and spared by others, you ought to shelter, tolerate, and spare each other. If you offer love, you will be loved in return."[79]

The Issue of Educational Reform

The Jewish nation, the Edict of Tolerance declared,[1] was to be made "more useful to, and usable by, the state principally through better instruction and enlightenment of its youth and its employment in the sciences, arts, and crafts." The Jews were given the choice of either sending their children to Christian schools or establishing, at their own expense, Jewish primary schools, which would enjoy equal status and operate within the state-controlled educational system.[2]

Even prior to the edict, Jewish children in the Austrian monarchy had been admitted to high schools,[3] but attendance at primary and nonclassical secondary schools[4] now became compulsory. A decree of the Vienna court chancery issued on October 19, 1781,[5] permitted the training of qualified Jewish teachers and headmasters in Christian schools, prescribed the supervision of curricula and examinations, and ruled that, in consultation with the Jews, textbooks containing reading material would be prepared for use in Jewish schools. While textbooks dealing with grammar, geography, history, geometry, etc. were to be uniform, the readers currently in use required some modification to make them acceptable to Jews. The revised readers should teach a "philosophical morality" and omit everything offensive to the Jewish faith. In Christian schools teachers were to refrain from any interference in the religion of their Jewish pupils. A decree of the court chancery issued to the government of Lower Austria on March 6, 1782,[6] recalled the emperor's resolution "according to which the Jews themselves were to write their moral books and submit them for approval." Reinterpreting the imperial order, it pointed out that the Jews might "also touch upon such moral principles as bore a special relation to their religion, provided these were not in conflict with the principles of universally ordained tolerance and the citizens' duties toward each other and the state." A Jewish reader that had appeared in Prague might be used for the time being. And when the Jews in Vienna showed themselves unwilling to produce a new reader of their own,[7] a rescript of February, 1783,[8] legalized the continued use of the moral textbooks that had come out in Prague.

The emperor had not realized that the problem of providing suitable readers did not admit of an easy solution. It highlighted, at a single flash as it were, the cultural situation of the Jews at the time. The immense spiritual wealth contained in a vast amount of Hebrew literature was suddenly of no avail when the need arose for Jewish reading material in German. The *Lesebuch für Jüdische Kinder,* which David Friedländer had published in 1779,[9] was a first step, but a feeble one, and Mendelssohn's great Bible project, of which the first three volumes had already appeared when the Edict of Tolerance was issued, was anything but a German reader, for it was far too ambitious and learned a work to qualify for use in primary schools, and the translation was printed in Hebrew characters. One wonders to which Jewish textbooks published in Prague the two rescripts of the Vienna court chancery (March, 1782, and February, 1783) referred, seeing that a reader for Jewish children by Moses Wiener, teacher at the Prague Jewish *Normalschule,* did not appear until 1784.[10] The answer to this question is provided by a hitherto unpublished letter written to Mendelssohn on January 5, 1783, by Ferdinand Kindermann *Ritter* von Schulstein.[11]

Von Schulstein, a priest and educationist who had been raised to nobility by Maria Theresa in 1777 and was highly regarded by Joseph II on account of his outstanding merits as the leading reformer of primary and industrial education in Bohemia,[12] was a truly progressive pedagogue, a warm-hearted human being, and a friend of the Jews.[13] He it was who organized the "German Jewish schools" in his country in response to the emperor's wishes and in accordance with his own humanitarian principles. The esteem in which he was held by the Jews of Bohemia was largely responsible for the smooth manner in which the educational reforms were enacted. In 1782 Joachim Edler von Popper, the president *(Landesprimator)* of the Jewish communities of Bohemia, was able to effect the transformation of the existing educational establishments *(hadarim)* into German elementary schools.[14] This step was taken with the consent of the deputies of the communities concerned, and with the blessing of Chief Rabbi Ezekiel Landau, who composed and read a Hebrew poem in honor of the occasion.[15] When von Schulstein wrote to Mendelssohn at the beginning of the year 1783, he did so chiefly to invite his comments on the textbooks that had been introduced. His letter is interesting not only because it sheds light on the nature of the "moral readers" that had been produced in Prague, but also because it offers a vivid picture of the principles that guided the efforts of the man:

> Sir, You see how freely I conduct myself toward you. I do so, however, merely with the intention of being treated by you in like manner without special courtesy. Were you less kind, great master and admirer of the humanities, I would take fewer liberties, let alone dare to impose on you an examination of the German textbooks [*Schulbücher*] written for Jewish [youth]. Our textbooks for primary schools have already been favorably reviewed everywhere, with the exception of two that a year ago, at the very commencement of the Jewish school reform, were re-created from our so-called reading exercises for the children of country schools into the German album [*Stammbüchlein*] for Jewish children, and

from part two of the reader for the Christians into the German reader for the second and third form of the German *Judenschulen*.

What caused us some embarrassment at the time was the fact that the work was attacked the moment it was started. In addition, there was the need to retain the uniformity of the existing institution of primary schools, and the necessity of giving Jewish children in Christian schools an opportunity for joint readings with the Christian children. The principal purpose in modeling the reader on part two of our own was to instruct Jewish youth in the social[16] virtues and to guide them toward this end in community with others. We surely wish to labor to achieve this. This surely is the great purpose: to make this nation more refined in manners [*sittsamer*] and more sociable toward us, having hitherto been at such a distance.

We, therefore, tried to eliminate from part two of the reader, the re-creation of which had been proposed, everything that was peculiar to the Christian religion. We inserted after every moral chapter ... a moral story by some highly reputed author, and we did this not only in order to make the tuition more concrete, entertaining, and comprehensible to the Jewish children, but also because, first, the Jewish nation is descended from people who were fond of instruction by imagery and parable, and, second, a totally raw youth ought to sense moral truths through familiar imagery that is endorsed by revealed religion. Jewish youth finds in the album and also in its reader stories about things that lie in its horizon. . . .

In selecting the moral stories we invariably considered the prevalent faults of our Jewish population, and we never lost sight of its impregnation, at an early age, with the social virtues. . . . The chapter on patriotism . . . was allowed to remain, though it looks more like a philosophical dissertation than a piece for children, only because it offers material for common reading exercises. . . .

Altogether, our endeavor in the reader and in the entire constitution of this work of school reform was to start the thing in a manner suited to the spirit, mental capacity, and present needs as well as future destiny of this nation. . . . All other textbooks the Jewish children use in common with us in German schools, almost all of them being listed in the attached catalog. I also enclose two of our public announcements so as to enable you to form some idea of the entire constitution of the school reform. I would ask you to regard it ... as a mere child in the cradle and pass your judgment accordingly. Should you be so kind as to examine these books ... kindly let me have your comments; they will surely be put to good use in the second edition. . . .

So pronounced was the success of von Schulstein's efforts in Prague that Joseph II, when told by the Jews in Pressburg that they could not reconcile themselves to the new school system, retorted: "Look to Prague; there I am thoroughly satisfied with the school."[17] Protagonists of Czech culture accused von Schulstein of having created, through the organization of Jewish schools, centers of Germanism in a Czech environment.[18] In Vienna, Jewish reaction to the emperor's measures was recalcitrant in more than one respect. Having been denied the right to form an officially recognized community and to erect a synagogue, the Jews in the capital city felt an understandable resentment toward the suggestion that they should establish a school at their own expense and produce the requisite textbooks. In a statement submitted on their behalf in 1782 by Adam Isaak Arnsteiner and Löw Isaak Leidesdorf the following points were made: (1) the local Jews form no community and have no communal purse, (2) wealthy Jews keep private tutors for their children, (3) the children of less wealthy Jews attend the German *Normalschulen,* (4) these children are provided with the Prague reader for primary schools, and (5) the cost of maintaining a school was prohibitive. The refusal to comply with the suggestion that the establishment of a Jewish primary school was desirable was perhaps intended as leverage for the attainment of community status. It may have been primarily due to a policy aimed at full integration into the surrounding culture. Separate Jewish schools were probably considered an impediment rather than a help toward achieving this end.[19]

The Jews of Trieste, on the other hand, responded enthusiastically to the challenge presented by the edict. The city was under Austrian rule but its cultural climate was Italian, and the local Jewish community reflected the broader intellectual outlook of Italian Jewry and its strong Sephardic ingredient. Isacco Formiggini, chief rabbi of Trieste and a noted talmudist, welcomed the prospect of enhanced secular training in Jewish schools as something adding to the honor of the Jewish nation.[20] He certainly supported the efforts of Elijah Morpurgo, scion of an illustrious Jewish family and a devoted champion of Hebrew culture,[21] to alert the community to the opportunity offered. Morpurgo, who had written a dirge at the death of the Empress Maria Theresa, had also published an essay, *Discorso alla nazione Ebreo* (Gorizia, 1782), in celebration of Joseph II's edict. [22] It was doubtless at his suggestion that the Trieste community informed the governor, Count Zinzendorf, of its readiness to establish a primary school and asked his advice about the provision of textbooks for religious and moral instruction. Zinzendorf counseled an approach to Mendelssohn as the obvious authority on a matter of this kind. Thus it happened that Joseph Hayyim Galico, the learned secretary of the community, wrote to Mendelssohn, probably in February or March, 1782, asking for his guidance and requesting copies of relevant works by him.[23]

Both Galico's letter and Mendelssohn's reply of April, 1782, are lost,[24] but his answer to a second letter from Galico (alas, also lost) has been preserved.[25] It is dated May 7, 1782, and indicates that the books requested had been mailed a month ago to Nathan Arnstein in Vienna, who was to have sent them on to Trieste; they should have reached their destination by now, and Mendelssohn was expecting to hear from Galico in what other way he might be of service. He was also anxious to learn whether the Jewish school had been established, and whether the new textbooks for moral and religious instruction mentioned by Galico had been produced. The remaining part of the letter deplored the violent attacks that some prominent rabbis had launched against Wessely on account of his plea for educational reform. Mendelssohn, who had recommended Wessely's pamphlet to the leaders of the Trieste community, assured them of the man's unquestionable piety. Galico's second letter had acknowledged receipt of the Wessely pamphlet with warm acclaim,[26] and the Jews of Trieste as well as many Italian rabbis subsequently showed themselves to be his staunch supporters.

The pamphlet, *Divrey Shalom Ve-Emmet* ("Words of Peace and Truth")[27] had appeared in January or February, 1782,[28] and was meant to boost Jewish support for Joseph II's educational reforms. Written in haste and with the obvious desire to present its case as forcefully as possible, the work suffered from a certain imbalance of judgment and an aggressiveness that did not represent Wessely's true self. He began from the thesis that religious tuition presupposed a humanist and secular education to be effective and meaningful. To embrace the revealed law of God, one had first to imbibe the law of man, which was derived from reason alone. Had not the rabbis taught that *derekh erets* (refinement of morals) preceded the Tora (the revealed legislation) by twenty-six generations (i.e., those from Adam to Moses)?[29] Wessely took this statement to mean that the law of man was not only "prior in time" but also the essential prerequisite for the applicability of the divine law. In other words, one had to be a good man before one could lay claim to piety. As Wessely himself put it rather beautifully:[30] "The human law prepares the soul for its eventual perfection by the higher studies [viz. of the divine law]." There was nothing objectionable in this doctrine as such. The distinction between commandments flowing from reason and commandments sanctioned by revelation was one of long standing in Jewish tradition. Wessely was well aware of it,[31] and he identified *derekh erets,* which "preceded" the Tora, with the Seven Noachian laws,[32] much in the way in which Mendelssohn, following earlier examples, had equated the "laws of the Patriarchs" with natural law.[33]

What did give offense, though, was the injudicious manner in which Wessely broadened the meaning of the rabbinic term *derekh erets.* Having declared it to be synonymous with what he called the law of man *(torat ha-'adam),* he subsumed under it nothing less than the totality of secular culture, especially the "moral, mathematical, and physical sciences."[34] Having described the law of man as the sine qua non of religiosity, it seemed to follow that without a wide-ranging secular education one was neither a human being in the true sense of the word nor qualified to embark on the study of the divine law. Unfortunately, Wessely made it easy for his opponents to impute this conclusion to him. He quoted a hyperbolical statement from rabbinic literature that, judging from its context, meant simply to point out the need for modesty: ("As for a scholar who lacks sensibility [*da'at; de'a*], a carcass [*nevela*] is better than he"),[35] but he interpreted it to mean that a scholar bereft of social grace was incapable of benefiting anyone, no matter how profound his knowledge of the divine law. Lacking savoir faire, owing to his inexperience in mundane matters, such a scholar was of no use to his fellow-men. Even his rabbinic learning was untrustworthy since he was ignorant of the secular sciences, which were the stepping stones to the higher wisdom of the Tora.[36] Though Wessely was right in interpreting the passage as condemning mere rabbinic scholarship bereft of *derekh erets,* he left the meaning of this latter term somewhat ambiguous; more precisely, he understood it in the sense of secular culture. The quotation was obviously aimed at the prevalent type of rabbinic scholar, and it was bound to cause anguish and protest.

Wessely bestowed unqualified praise upon the "great emperor" who by his edict had not only improved the economic position of a downtrodden nation but had also opened up the prospect of cultural rehabilitation. He urged his fellow Jews to show gratitude by wholeheartedly complying with the emperor's request. The establishment of Jewish primary schools was best designed to bolster both secular and Hebrew training. By mastering the German language Jewish youth would not only gain access to the realm of secular knowledge but would also acquire the means of understanding the Hebrew Scriptures more accurately.[37] Here Wesseley advanced an argument that Dubno had already put forward with great force in the Pentateuch translation prospectus. Mendelssohn's translation, the argument ran, would usher in a renascence of Hebrew learning. Hitherto teachers had tried to explain, with a "stammering tongue," a text barely intelligible to themselves, biblical studies having been almost totally neglected. Mendelssohn's translation now offered a remedy for this melancholy state of affairs.[38] It would also serve as a means of teaching the German language at its best.[39] Whereas neither Mendelssohn nor Dubno had looked upon the Pentateuch translation as an instrument for teaching German to the Jews, Wessely, writing as he did under the impact of the emperor's edict, introduced this additional viewpoint. At the same time, he clamored for "new books on doctrines and beliefs [*emunot ve-de'ot*]" that would explain the principles underlying the Jewish faith. It was hopeless to expect children to imbibe an awareness of these principles through the mere study of the Scriptures. To understand the depth of the figurative language of the Bible one had to be a competent scholar. It was also necessary, he pointed out, to write manuals on ethics expounding moral teachings on rational grounds and linking them to such divine commandments as "Thou shalt not covet," "Thou shalt not take revenge or bear a grudge," etc. All these textbooks ought to be written in simple Hebrew and translated into German.[40]

The proposals listed so far kept more or less within the bounds of Joseph II's reform program, which sought to integrate the Jews into German culture. Wessely found himself in sympathy with this aim,[41] provided it could be reconciled with a thoroughgoing education in Hebrew culture. The prevalent system of Jewish tuition seemed to him not only out of tune with the measures imposed by the Austrian ruler but intrinsically ill-conceived, odd, and reprehensible. He therefore considered it timely and necessary to suggest radical changes. The prime requisite, he felt, was the introduction of a graded system of teaching. There was nothing of a heretical nature in this proposal as such. The complaint about the unsatisfactory condition of the teaching methods employed in the German and Polish *hadarim* and *yeshivot* was an old one. Rabbi Isaiah Horovitz, in his celebrated work *Sheney Luhot Ha-Berit* ("The Two Tablets of the Covenant"), which was completed in 1623, suggested that before studying the Talmud one ought to be versed in the Mishna;[42] and his son Sheftel recalled nostalgically his father's admiration of the educational system of the Sephardic Jews in Amsterdam, when he visited their yeshiva; he had wished that a rabbinical synod, convened by the German and Polish rabbis, would introduce the methods used by their Sephardic brethren, who cultivated in systematic progression the study of the Bible, the Mishna, and the Talmud.[43]

Wessely referred to these precedents when he was accused of willfully tampering with the traditional method.[44] However, he had laid himself open to severe criticism when he wrote:[45] "Take care also to divide the pupils into sections and grades. A child should not leave the class in which he learns the reading and grammar of languages for the class in which the Tora and the faith as well as some of the moral doctrines are taught, before he has been examined and found to have completed his course. Likewise, the pupil should not leave the class in which he studied the written Tora and ethics for the class in which Mishna and the Baraita are taught, before he has been found to have completed his course. In case he is found not to be fit for studying Mishna and Talmud, it will be more beneficial for him not to engage in such study but to learn, instead, one of the crafts to which he feels attracted, and also to continue with the study of the Tora and of ethics so as to learn to fear the Lord, and to become a good neighbor and by his conduct and work help his brethren." It seemed preposterous to bar a child from the study of the Pentateuch before he had passed an examination in "languages," and it appeared equally wrong to withdraw a pupil from the study of Mishna and Talmud on the easily mistaken assumption that he was not "fit" for it. Wessely later reinterpreted and modified his proposals,[46] but he steadfastly maintained the principle of gradual advance and of concern for the individual aptitude of students. He also advocated a recognition of the need for set periods of leisure and recreation. His whole philosophy of education was at variance with that of the old-timers, inspired as he was by the philanthropinist pedagogy of the period.[47]

Wessely's pamphlet, though basically sound, scandalized many rabbis. They saw in it a treacherous attack upon the very citadel of the faith, viz. the future of Jewish religious education, which had already been placed in jeopardy by the Austrian secular-reform measures. They considered it outrageous that at such a critical moment a fellow Jew should not only urge the unqualified application of these measures but should also assail the prevalent system of Jewish religious education. The indignation aroused by the pamphlet expressed itself with a vehemence far in excess of the manner in which Mendelssohn's translation had been condemned. Two sermons preached toward the end of March, 1782, on the "Great Sabbath," by Ezekiel Landau and by David Tevele, chief rabbi of Lissa, respectively, reflect the deep anger evoked by Wessely's plea. Both rabbis managed to combine their stern repudiation of the offensive pamphlet with elegant professions of gratitude to Joseph II. In Landau's case, his position as chief rabbi of Prague made it imperative that he do this. David Tevele, whose city was under Polish rule, could better afford to be outspoken, but he considered it advisable, apparently, to praise both his own king and the Austrian emperor for the "kindnesses" they had shown their Jewish subjects. Landau referred to Wessely, without naming him, as a "wicked" and "impudent" man to whom the Tora was "worth nothing" and who had vilified those engaged in its study. By way of contrast, he described the educational measures introduced by the government as designed to benefit the Jews by making them more proficient in the German language and in the conduct of their businesses without infringing upon their prime vocation, the study of the Tora. Quoting Proverbs 24:21 ("My son, fear thou the Lord and the king, and meddle not with them that are given to change"), he exhorted his community to carry out the sovereign's wishes but to be on guard lest the study of the German language lead them on to the reading of books detrimental to the faith. There were now many Jews who no longer believed in the divine origin of the oral law. He did not suspect teachers at the new Jewish school of spreading such views, for in so doing they would contravene the purpose for which they had been appointed (to teach secular subjects without undermining religion).[48]

Landau did not mention Mendelssohn's translation, though Wessely's pamphlet might have tempted him to speak out against it, seeing it contained so strong a recommendation of the work. It is therefore surprising to find that in a private letter to the leaders of the Trieste community Wessely reported Landau's sermon as having attacked not only him ("in language sharp like a razor blade") but also Mendelssohn's translation.[49] Whoever Wessely's informant in Prague had been, he probably had read a veiled reference to Mendelssohn into Landau's warning against harmful literature. If so, he had surely been mistaken, for by no stretch of the imagination could the German version of the Pentateuch have been considered a book injurious to the faith. It should be noted that David Tevele's by far more aggressive sermon also refrained from making any reference to Mendelssohn.[50]

Wessely's letter to the community leaders of Trieste was written on May 7, 1782 (Iyyar 23, 5542), the day on which Mendelssohn dispatched his second letter to Galico.[51] Its purpose was to let his Italian friends in Trieste know how he and Mendelssohn felt about the harassment to which he was being subjected. Enclosed with the letter, which was meant to be private, was a pamphlet, twice as long as the first, entitled *Rav Tuv Le-Vet*

Yisra'el ("Abundant Goodness to the House of Israel") and designated as *Mikhtav Sheni* ("Second Epistle").[52] It sought to amplify and explain crucial passages in the pamphlet (the *First Epistle*),[53] especially those that had come under fire, and pretended to have been written in reply to the letter which Wessely had received from Trieste.[54] Unfortunately, the text of David Tevele's sermon, which fully specified the charges that had been bandied about, had reached him only after the *Second Epistle* had already left the printer's office.[55] He dealt with them in great detail in his *Fourth Epistle*, which was the final effort he made to vindicate his essential points.[56] In these epistles Wessely repeatedly made reference to "three Polish rabbis"[57] who had abused and taken action against him. He would not retaliate, he declared, by disclosing their names in public.[58] He named them, however, in his private letter on May 7:[59] "The first is the rabbi of Posen [Rabbi Joseph Ha-Tsaddik], who is the son-in-law of the rabbi of Prague; the second is the rabbi of Lissa [Rabbi David Tevele]; and the third is a man who resides in Vilna and is called Rabbi Elijah Hasid [undoubtedly none other than the famous "Gaon," who in Vilna was always referred to as "Rabbi Elijah Hasid"].[60] All three were domiciled in Greater Poland. The indignation of these Polish rabbis[61] had reached such a pitch, Wessely reported,[62] that they had ordered the burning of his pamphlet. This allegation was repeated in another letter, dated June 28, 1782 (Tammuz 16, 5542), which he wrote to the Trieste community.[63]

It seems, however, that Wessely had been misinformed once again, for the rabbi of Lissa, in his sermon, had merely expressed his approval of the drastic step that, according to news received, had been taken by the rabbinic authorities in Vilna: they were said to have condemned Wessely's pamphlet to be attached to an iron chain (the pillory) in the courtyard of the synagogue and then publicly burned.[64] He also indicated his intention to consign Wessely's earlier works to the store-chamber *(geniza)* for discarded books.[65] He uttered no word about the desirability of following the precedent set by Vilna (i.e., by the Gaon, without whose consent no measure of any consequence was thinkable). Nor can it be taken for granted that he was properly informed of events in Vilna. While the Gaon was sternly opposed to the ways of the hasidic sect and sanctioned such steps as the issuance of a ban and the burning of their writings,[66] he could not have taken serious offense at Wessely's proposals. The advocacy of secular studies and of a graded system of Jewish education actually conformed to his own views. The Gaon's appreciation of Wessely's *Bi'ur* on Leviticus, which had appeared only recently, could have dated from a later period, when Wessely's reputation had been restored.[67] More relevant to our point is the Gaon's alleged counsel to Mendelssohn's opponents to refrain from any condemnation of the translation of the Pentateuch.[68] One has to assume, therefore, that the rabbi of Lissa or his informant confounded the public burning of the hasidic book *Toledot Ya'akov Yosef*, which had appeared in 1780 and given rise to the second wave of anti-hasidic measures by the Gaon in 1781,[69] and the purely imaginary *auto-da-fé* of Wessely's *First Epistle*.[70] This surmise would seem to offer the only possible explanation of David Tevele's statement, though it is difficult to see how the confusion could have arisen in the first place.[71]

Immediate action of a different and more sinister kind was, however, taken by the rabbis of Lissa and Posen.[72] They tried to bring pressure to bear upon Chief Rabbi Zevi Hirschel Lewin of Berlin to use his authority to prevent the publication of any further writings by Wessely and to threaten this author's expulsion from the city if he failed to comply. Since the consent of the lay leaders of the local community was required to make such a threat tangible, they expected Lewin to initiate the necessary steps. It appears that the chief rabbi, despite his generally tolerant attitude, was about to yield to the expostulations of his zealous colleagues. A letter written on March 30, 1782, by the cabinet minister Zedlitz to Daniel Itzig, the lay head of Berlin Jewry, expressed serious concern about the action contemplated and asked for more specific information. It would be sad, he remarked, if a man were driven out of the city on account of a well-written book that he had produced.[73] On April 17, Mendelssohn wrote to his friend David Friedländer, who was Daniel Itzig's son-in-law:[74]

> I hear that the rabbi [Lewin] has indeed transferred the case of our friend Hartwig Wessely to the leaders of the community. Whether or not he submitted the letters that he received in this matter I do not know. I hope, however, that no one will permit himself to be pressurized into issuing any orders, however minimal, that might cause discomfort to the honest Wessely. I ignore all other aspects and do not wish to investigate who is right in this matter. I only want this point to be considered: What will the Christians have to say about it? What will people think about us if we arrogate to ourselves such power over authors and seek to prevent them from publishing their ideas?

Mendelssohn recalled in this connection how courteously he had been treated by the Berlin consistory when, at the time of the Lavater affair, he had "dared to come up against the Christian faith."[75] Everyone residing in the realm of "our gracious king" enjoyed complete freedom of literary expression, be he circumcised or not. How could we Jews stop the publications of an author who merely criticized our methods of teaching and education? Mendelssohn suggested that Friedländer and his brother-in-law Isaac Daniel call upon Daniel Itzig and place this consideration before him. He would himself see the rabbi, were he not afraid of causing a rift, which would not be opportune at the moment. He felt, however, that one ought to dissuade him from mentioning the matter in his sermon. In case Lewin wished to clear himself vis-à-vis the rabbis (of Lissa and Posen), he could do so simply by pleading the freedom of the press in Germany.

Apparently Lewin was not to be so easily deflected from the course he had decided to take, for as late as June 4, 1782, Zedlitz found it necessary to address another letter to the lay leaders of the community requesting a full report on the "persecution" to which, according to hearsay, the author of the pamphlet *Words of Truth and Peace* (sic!) was being subjected.[76] It may be safely assumed that Zedlitz' action on both occasions was due to Mendelssohn's discreet intervention. His professed ignorance of precise details of the case was mere pretense, of course, designed to conceal his actual *démarche*.[77] In July Mendelssohn could already speak about the whole episode as a thing of the past. In a letter dated July 11, 1782, he told Wolf Dessau, who had himself incurred severe criticism on account of a remark found in his recently published manual of the Jewish religion:[78] "Some months ago a most terrific thunderstorm had gathered around our good brother, the famous Hartog [sic!] Wessely. As you probably know, his innocent *Words of Truth and Peace*[79] [sic!] gave rise to it. From all regions of Poland anathemas [*Bannstrahlen*] were hurled against him, and it was a matter of touch and go whether his German brethren were also to be up in arms against him. By composure and calm response he silenced most of them in a short time, and the more reasonable part of the nation[80] is completely convinced of his innocence."

In his *Second Epistle*, which was completed on April 24 (Iyyar 10), Wessely had challenged his adversaries to specify their charges against him within three months so that the "whole House of Israel" may be able to judge who was right; should they fail to answer his appeal, this would indicate their inability to indict him.[81] When the full text of David Tevele's sermon reached him on May 2 (Iyyar 18), there was no longer any point in waiting for a detailed accusation. The sermon was sufficiently explicit. He therefore decided to rebut the charges in another pamphlet, and he announced his intention in the *Third Epistle*, called *Eyn Mishpat* ("Fountain of Judgment"), which he finished on April 30, 1784 (Iyyar 9, 5544).[82] In his letter to the Trieste community on June 28, 1782, he mentioned that the lay leaders of Berlin Jewry had lodged a severe protest against the rabbis of Posen and Lissa by writing to the communities concerned and demanding a specification of the charges in order to enable the public to judge the issue.[83] The letter of complaint must have been dispatched at the time when Wessely threw out the identical challenge in his *Second Epistle*, i.e. before May 2, when the text of David Tevele's sermon became available in Berlin.

The letter of complaint was far more aggressive than Wessely's account of it seems to indicate. It was signed by seven people and demanded that the communal leaders of Lissa and Posen reprimand their respective rabbis on account of their vilification of Wessely. A threat was added to the effect that in the event of noncompliance the case would be submitted to the state authorities. This ultimatum so outraged the chief rabbi of Prague that he sent a letter of severe condemnation to the heads of Berlin Jewry, in which he insisted that the seven signatories be compelled to tender an apology to the rabbis of Lissa and Posen.[84] Landau's intervention, which most probably occurred around the middle of May, 1782, was bound to cause some friction within the various elements of the Jewish lay leadership in Berlin. This explains why Daniel Itzig moved cautiously and why Mendelssohn chose to work behind the scenes, through the good offices of his friend Zedlitz. To increase pressure on the Lissa community, Friedländer and his friends sought the cooperation of the Christian writer August Friedrich Cranz. It was at their instigation, no doubt, that he wrote a sequel to his anonymous denunciation of the "misuse of ecclesiastical power" by the chief rabbi of Altona,[85] this time making the rabbi of Lissa the target of his attack and dedicating his pamphlet to Prince Sulkowsky, the ruler of that Polish town.[86] Wessely was anything but happy about the retaliatory measures of his friends. In his *Third Epistle*[87] he wrote: "It never occurred to me to retaliate; no epistle of a vexatious character was written by me; only two epistles have come from my pen. Everything else was written either by some fellow-Jew or by writers not of our faith. I did not ask for this in any shape or form." The restraint that he had shown was acclaimed by Mendelssohn in his letter to Wolf Dessau.[88]

In his *Second Epistle* Wessely had given much prominence to his close liaison with Mendelssohn: he repeated his praise of the Pentateuch translation,[89] referred several times to his own *Bi'ur* on Leviticus,[90] spoke in glowing terms of the honor that men like Mendelssohn, Doctor Bloch, and Doctor Herz had brought to the Jewish people,[91] and concluded the epistle by quoting, in Hebrew translation, the last three paragraphs of Mendelssohn's preface to *Vindiciae Judaeorum*.[92] Mendelssohn, whose shadow had already loomed large behind the first pamphlet, now appeared as the real patron saint of Wessely's plea for educational reforms. By citing Mendelssohn's appeal to the rabbis imploring them to forgo all exercise of power, Wessely had touched a most sensitive spot, and some reaction was to be expected. The counteroffensive that had been taken in the meanwhile by the seven Berlin lay leaders aggravated the situation. It looked as if Wessely was but the spearhead of a laymen's onslaught upon the authority of the rabbinate. The brunt of the battle against Wessely had hitherto been borne by rabbis outside Germany, viz. those of Prague, Lissa, and Posen. The chief rabbi of Berlin could not be expected to take forceful action. In these circumstances it fell to Pinhas Ha-Levi Horowitz (Hurvitz), chief rabbi of Frankfurt am Main, to enter the fray.[93] A celebrated talmudic scholar[94] and a devoted follower of the hasidic master Dov Bär of Mezerich (the "Great Maggid"), he shared his colleagues' sense of outrage, and he summoned his congregation to listen to a sermon on the otherwise inconspicuous occasion of the eve of Rosh Hodesh Tammuz, 5542 (June 12, 1782).[95]

Unfortunately only some of the key passages of this sermon are known,[96] but they suffice to show that Horowitz' attack was as ferocious as the previous ones had been. Its target, however, was no longer a single individual, Wessely, but the whole group of which he was representative.

True, in most cases the indictment refers to one man, who remains unnamed
but can easily be identified with Wessely. He is the "wicked one and heretic"
who had caused the rabbi distress "previously," i.e. by his pamphlet, and
who had now published "a little book" (i.e. the *Second Epistle*) in which
he misinterpreted the biblical verse (Lev. 19:17) "thou shalt surely rebuke
thy neighbor." Horowitz could not have had in mind Mendelssohn's translation of this verse,[97] since he mentions distinctly "a little book" in which
he had found the "lengthy" discussion of the duty of rebuking one's
neighbor. Such a discussion is contained in the *Second Epistle*.[98] Had
Horowitz looked up Wessely's *Bi'ur* on the verse in question he would
have discovered that it disagreed with Mendelssohn's translation. The
reason that he imputed to Wessely a denial of the principle of moral responsibility for one another must be sought in the citation of Mendelssohn's
appeal for tolerance at the end, following upon the discussion of the right
kind of rebuke. Far from denying the duty of taking one's neighbor to
task and trying to lead him back to the right path, Wessely had in fact
emphasized this obligation. Yet the fact that he quoted Mendelssohn's call
for tolerance obviously misled the rabbi as to his true intent. In condemning
Wessely, then, the rabbi actually indicted Mendelssohn. It must be assumed
that he deliberately refrained from referring to the said quotation. His
doing so would have involved him in crossing swords with Mendelssohn
on a most delicate issue. He did however allude to Mendelssohn and his
circle when speaking in the plural of those who had "written a new commentary on our holy Tora" that was pure fantasy and nonsense, when warning
against reading "their books," when declaring that their "association"
(*havuratam*) was an ugly thing, and when remarking that their "dispersal"
(*pizzur*) would be desirable.[99] The tenor of the sermon was a fierce protest
against their attempt "to lay down improvements and rules of conduct
[*tikkunim ve-hanhagot*] for rabbinic scholars." Such an endeavor on the part
of people bereft of talmudic training was disgraceful. Horowitz could not
have included Mendelssohn in this category, since Mendelssohn's talmudic
erudition was well known. The wholesale condemnation uttered by him
reflected, however, his annoyance at the "heresies" and lay interference
that had emanated from the group close to Mendelssohn.

Rabbinic animosity toward Wessely soon subsided, whereas the anxiety
aroused by Mendelssohn's translation tended to persist. The chief rabbi
of Prague now began to express his misgivings in public. His *novellae* on
the talmudic tractate *Berakhot*, which were completed in 1783,[100] contain
the following comment on Rabbi Eli'ezer ben Hyrcanos' (second century
C.E.) exhortation, "Keep your children away from *higgayon*:[101]

> According to Rashi, it means: Do not permit your children to overindulge
> in the study of Scripture, which holds so much attraction. I believe his
> intent in interpreting the statement thus to be as follows: Even freethinkers
> [*apikoresim*], who deny the divine origin of the Tora, study it from a
> linguistic interest in precisely the same way in which they study other

languages [and literatures]. This is particularly true in our time in which the German translation [by Mendelssohn] has gained currency. It *attracts* people to the reading of Gentile books and serves as a tool of becoming more conversant with the language. Hence the exhortation: Train the children by the [traditional] method of Tora study.

In a sermon preached during the Ten Days of Penitence,[102] Landau bewailed the attitude of parents who curtailed the Jewish education of their children in order to provide them with a "useful" knowledge of languages. To the young generation reared in this fashion he applied the verse (Psalms, 73:9): "They have set their mouth against the heavens, and their tongue walketh through the earth," i.e., through the training of their tongue in the languages and literatures of the Gentiles they forgot the Tora and abandoned faith in the miracles recorded therein. Since using Mendelssohn's translation was considered by Landau as a training in the German language, his complaint was in all likelihood aimed against it too. Landau's concern was shared by his disciple Rabbi Ele'azar Fleckeles, a member of the rabbinic court of Prague and a distinguished talmudist and preacher.[103] One of his published homilies[104] contains a spirited assault on the new Bible translation: Jews were now spending their hours of leisure in the study of modern languages and failing to allot to the "holy tongue" so much as the rank of "dessert after dinner."[105] By an exegetical twist Fleckeles interpreted the Mishna (Shabbat 16:1) as forbidding the reading of Bible translations if doing so leads to the neglect of Tora study; thus only a simple translation, which avoided "deep" language, was permissible.[106] Jews who looked upon the books of the Prophets as mere "literature" deserved to be denounced in the words of Ezekiel (13:9): "They shall not be in the council of My people, neither shall they be written in the register of the house of Israel." To such Jews, he said, applied the words of King David (Psalms 69:29): "Let them be blotted out of the book of the living, and not be written with the righteous." The harshness of this attack provoked a fierce protest from Avigdor Levi[107] and caused David Friedländer to publish a rebuttal in his *Epistle to the German Jews*.[108]

That the new Pentateuch translation had aroused great interest among the Jews of Prague is attested by Mendelssohn himself. In his reply to Schulstein's letter of January 5, 1783,[109] he announced the imminent publication of the last volume and added:[110]

My Books of Moses have been welcomed also in Prague. I have, however, no one there who could act as a commissary to whom the sale might be entrusted. Maybe the local primary school also has a bookstore at its service, as many public schools in the Prussian States do. In such an eventuality it might not be disinclined to take the books on commission and charge a small fee. Permit me, Very Reverend Sir, to be audacious enough to inquire about this. Since you give credit to many a coreligionist of mine for impoliteness,[111] you will forgive me also in case I am too importunate. I think that a considerable sale can be expected in your locality, and I offer a fee of ten percent apart from expenses.

Schulstein's immediate reply has not been preserved and we are therefore not in a position to know how he reacted to this commercial proposition. All we learn from a subsequent letter, which he wrote to Mendelssohn on December 15, 1784,[112] is that he had received the "valuable" Books of Moses through a certain Gunzenhausen, whom he praised as an enthusiastic and able teacher. It may be assumed that Schulstein gave his wholehearted patronage to the use of Mendelssohn's Pentateuch in the Jewish primary school in Prague. But even without his support the progressively minded Jewish teachers would have succeeded in introducing the translation as a text for study. The opposition offered by Landau and Fleckeles must be seen against this background.

We catch a glimpse of the struggle between the teachers who were devotees of Mendelssohn and the rabbinate from a letter written by Moses Wiener, who had been extolled in Schulstein's first letter as "a very good teacher of German grammar and composition," and who, according to the other letter, was to submit to Schulstein a "report on the rising enlightenment and education of the local Israelites." He published a *Reader for Jewish Children*[113] and a *Report on the Origin and Progress of the German Jewish Prime School in Prague,* the latter dedicated to Schulstein.[114] On October 12, 1785, Wiener sent Mendelssohn a copy of his first work with a covering letter[115] informing him that most Jews in Prague had taken offense at some passages of the book said to be "contrary to religion." No action had been forthcoming, but he was anxious to know whether the charge was justified. Since he had little confidence in the objectivity of his opponents, he hoped that Mendelssohn would let him know whether he had indeed transgressed propriety, in which case he would make amends. On November 1, 1785, Mendelssohn replied[116] that he considered his book to be excellent for its purpose and suited to the requirements of "our brethren." He was not surprised that some had found in it suspicious passages. "Where has one not tried to find things of this sort?" His only criticism, a mild one, related to the exaggerated praise of the emperor in which the author had indulged. He had bestowed on the sovereign epithets that the Jewish nation customarily applied to "its true Redeemer" alone. In case his opponents had taken umbrage on this account, it was pardonable. Had they been motivated by envy or malice, however, the only fitting answer was contempt.

To what extent Mendelssohn himself had by that time come to be annoyed by even so great a rabbinic figure as Ezekiel Landau is apparent from a letter he wrote in 1785 to one of his admirers, a certain Rabbi Hanokh,[117] who had sent him a copy of Landau's *haskama* for Sussmann Glogau's primitive Pentateuch translation:[118]

> My hearty thanks for the nice approbation of the Pentateuch that you were good enough to send me. I was amused by it, and I was surprised at your nervousness about it. Someone so familiar with Hebrew as the author of this approbation and so "deep" in the language . . . cannot

possibly fail to care if the merest nuance of beauty is lost in translation or if our young are prevented from studying the elements of the language. Hence his zeal comes most natural to him, and only his great virtue of "judging everyone in the scale of merit" has inspired his kindly conjecture that I myself regret my undertaking and only desire an opportunity of remedying my mistake. Such excessive goodness is eloquent testimony to the humble spirit of the rabbi who wrote this approbation. Who could, then, be indignant or, God forbid, contemplate paying back in the same coin? In all seriousness, dear Rabbi Hanokh, you must not think of retaliation by doing or even wishing him harm.

My answer has so far been: had my translation been accepted by all Jews without demur, it would have been superfluous. The more it is opposed by the so-called "sages of the generation" [*hakhmey ha-dor*], the more necessary it is. Originally I wrote it only for the man in the street [*dalat ha-'am*], but now I find that it is still more important for the rabbis, and I intend—God willing and His grace allowing it—to edit also the Prophets and Hagiographa. Keep your temper under control and be but calm, my good Rabbi Hanokh!

The Summer of 1782

On June 20, 1782, about two months after the publication of Manasseh ben Israel's treatise, Mendelssohn wrote to Herz Homberg:[1] "All Christian theologians are extremely satisfied with my preface. Teller, Spalding, Zollikofer, Büsching, and others take every opportunity to recommend it. Only the Christians in Hamburg have nothing good to say about it, because of the stand it takes in regard to the so-called ecclesiastical law. What it is that our own people really hold against it I do not know; it may be a case of injured vanity on the part of the officials—the Parnassim—as you justly remarked. The erroneous belief that my thesis contradicts Holy Scripture first predisposed some intelligent people against it; however, after due reflection it disappeared completely."

This rather smug letter makes strange reading. Was Mendelssohn not a little naive to note the theologians' approval with such satisfaction? Did he not realize that some of his utterances might have been interpreted as evidence of a lessening of his "distance" from Christianity? No less puzzling is his confession of ignorance as to the reason for Jews to object to some of the things he had said in his preface. He could not have expected the latitudinarian way in which he had portrayed Judaism to go unchallenged. He might have asked himself whether he had not overstated his case by tacitly equating Judaism with a religion that was "all mind and heart," devoted purely to the purpose of "edification" and in no need of disciplinary measures. He had disregarded the punitive aspects of the biblical law, and his critics were right in finding some contradiction between his thesis and Scripture. His plea for the renunciation of all forcible means in dealing with dissidents had fallen on deaf ears, as he knew only too well from the harsh manner in which only recently a number of prominent rabbis had sought to discredit Hartwig Wessely's appeal for educational reforms.[2] He himself had to intervene when the chief rabbi of Berlin was about to take steps for the suppression of Wessely's right to issue any further publications.[3]

That Mendelssohn could write to Homberg in the way he did shows that neither the warm approval of the Protestant theologians nor his growing alienation from the upholders of orthodoxy in his own community was bothering him. He was convinced that the ideas he had expressed were not only philosophically sound but also in agreement with what "the wisest of our ancestors" had taught. To him "reason's house of prayer" was the synagogue, nonexclusiveness and tolerance were the hallmark of authentic Judaism, and the notion of ecclesiastical power was a foreign importation. He considered himself to be as firmly anchored in the Jewish tradition as before. He was critical of the Edict of Tolerance because it set a premium on conversion. He asked for civil admission on the grounds of human rights and not as a reward for religious conformity. What he failed to notice was that in his zeal to fit the Jewish "colony" into the framework of civil society he had allowed the political orientation to override the religious one. He had not given serious thought to the question of how to reconcile the halakhic norm with civic duties. In his answer to Michaelis, which was not to appear until 1783 (in the second part of Dohm's treatise), he treated the matter rather cavalierly. The preface to the *Vindiciae Judaeorum* gave hardly a clue as to the way in which Mendelssohn envisaged a solution of the problem. The only statement that had a bearing on it was his advocacy of the admission of any state-appointed magistrates in lieu of rabbinic law-courts in the first instance. He had obviously moved toward the concept of a more or less spiritualized Judaism. It required strong reactions from outside to make him aware of the need to define where he stood more clearly.[4]

The first challenge came from August Hennings, in a letter dated April 27, 1782.[5] He welcomed Mendelssohn's plea for tolerance, which he hoped would not expose him to the usual fate of peace-makers, that of being maltreated by both parties. He was happy to find that his own treatise *On Tolerance*[6] had anticipated Mendelssohn's point about the social consequences of ecclesiastical excommunication. On the other hand, he was far from being enamored with Manasseh's epistle. The arguments advanced therein might have been suited to the purpose of impressing the Lord Protector of England but could hardly serve, in Henning's opinion, the cause that Mendelssohn had at heart. Civil rights could be claimed by the Jews on general human grounds only, not because of any special Jewish virtues. Manasseh's attempt to base the Jews' case upon historical evidence of their own tolerance toward non-Jews was without foundation. The Old Testament was "full of proofs of how little tolerant the Jews were," and his reverence for God forbade him to make allegedly divine orders responsible for certain atrocious acts reported in the Bible. He could attribute them only to the character of the Jewish nation, which showed traits of ruthlessness. How could Judaism be described as a tolerant religion when the biblical law demanded the penalty of death-by-stoning for certain offenses? How could one believe in a God who "preached with stones"?

Hennings' attack, probably inspired by Voltaire's invectives against the Old Testament,[7] ostensibly took issue only with Manasseh ben Israel, but it was in fact a frontal assault upon Mendelssohn's claim that Judaism was essentially a tolerant religion. The attack was pursued with unrelenting vigor. Manasseh had quoted passages from the Bible, the Apocrypha, rabbinic sources, Philo, and Josephus, all in an effort to document the tolerant nature of the Jews.[8] Hennings could see in these sources only evidence to the contrary. Exhortations to be peaceable permitted the inference that those being admonished were anything but peaceable in fact, just as one could infer from Juvenal's satires the virtues in which the Romans were most lacking. The submissiveness of the Jewish high priests toward Alexander the Great and the Roman emperors was no sign of tolerance but of fear and political prudence. Had not Mendelssohn himself taken the precaution of praising his own king (who had expelled the Jews from western Prussia) after he had lavished his admiration upon the Austrian emperor? Such evidences of cleverness had to be judged within their context but were no proof of the virtue of tolerance or sociability. Nor had the character of the Jews changed in any way. They were no more tolerant and conciliatory now than they had been in the desert and in Palestine. True, they could not show their character so openly, but what one saw of them was sufficient for a shrewd guess. Mendelssohn had had some personal experience of their "barbarism" when he announced his Bible translation; and hearing some of the most respected Jews in Copenhagen talk about the Marcus affair[9] could cause one to believe that the rabbi of Altona had suffered great injustice because he had been prevented by the government from maltreating his opponent.

Most striking of all, Hennings suggested, was the Jews' opposition to the Austrian emperor's educational reform plans, as the case of Hartwig Wessely amply demonstrated. It was one thing to cling tenaciously to old customs, but why did they refuse to participate in the "general refinement and development of the soul's faculties," in regard to which they were "totally behind." Even in Berlin, where the Jews were more polished than in other places, and where they had a Mendelssohn among them as an example to follow, there were very few of them who did not consider themselves superior to him because he was interested in the public weal, while they knew how to enrich themselves. (There is a note at the bottom of the page, entered by Hennings in later years, when he revised his copy: "In Berlin I have heard more than one intelligent Jew say: Mendelssohn is a *Phantast* [one indulging in fantasies].") He did not think he was prejudiced against the Jews, Hennings pointed out. For assuming he had to plead the right of Christians before the emperor of Japan, he would not rest their case on the virtues of the Christians (which were not preferable to Jewish morals) but on general humanitarian grounds. What he regarded as the authentic Christian religion was probably identical with what Mendelssohn considered as authentic Judaism. The upshot of Hennings' argumentative and by no means friendly letter is contained in this paragraph:

> And to what end do we need Judaism and Christianity? We have teachings common to all religions that sound reason must recognize everywhere. The more we spread these principles or doctrines, the more firmly do we establish tolerance, which without this universal enlightenment is always in danger of becoming infected by the poison of partiality, and of demonstrating folly rather than the truth. If we could all unite in the worship of the one true God—to quote from a Jewish prayer[10]—and then leave it to everybody's discretion to discover for himself the road to such worship—something that neither Christians nor Jews ever did—the result would be this: we would, each one of us, seek to achieve preeminence by serving God in a truly reverential spirit, i.e. by imitating his goodness and love, and not by indulging in spiritual pride and in considering ourselves better than others.

If Mendelssohn had imagined that his preface would strike a sympathetic cord in all enlightened minds, Hennings' letter disabused him of any such notion. Despite his efforts to underline the universalist teachings of Judaism, a freethinker like Hennings had found his outlook still too particularistic. Nothing short of a complete renunciation of all that was characteristic of the Jewish tradition would have been considered acceptable. The portrayal of Judaism as a tolerant religion had only had the effect of provoking Hennings to his unbridled denunciation of the character of the Jewish people. All his latent anti-Jewish feeling came to the surface and produced a caricature of the Jew devoid of the least understanding of the Jewish spiritual legacy. Hennings' reaction was fully shared, behind the scene and without Mendelssohn's knowledge, by Elise Reimarus and her brother Doctor Reimarus. In Elise's words, Hennings' letter contained "some harsh truths" (*derbe Wahrheiten*) about Mendelssohn and the Jewish nation.[11] Even less restrained was a letter that Hennings had sent Elise on April 18, when he had just received the copy of the book through Gugenheim:[12] "I ask Mendelssohn's pardon, but his treatise seems to me ridiculous. For when I picture to myself the next best *Mauschel* [vulgar Jew] as personifying the whole spirit of the Jewish nation, which I have come to know on many occasions, I find in all that Mendelssohn says nothing that concerns us more than if he had written for the moon." Having tried hard to write a tract for the times, Mendelssohn had obviously not gone far enough to please people like Hennings and the Reimaruses, who held that "the improvement of the Jews *as Jews* was a self-contradictory proposition."[13]

Two weeks after the arrival of Hennings' letter Mendelssohn received an equally long and no less disquieting epistle from a stranger who introduced himself in the following way:[14] "Although the preface to *Manasseh Ben Israel: Vindication of the Jews* was not the first of your invaluable works that I read, it offers me a pleasant opportunity of making myself known to you. You will ask why this work of all? Because, Sir, it appeared at a time when it has become the duty of all good men to straighten out, as they say, everything of this kind and to promote the spreading of a healthy public spirit. Do not expect or fear to receive from me a polemical piece of writing or to be assaulted by me for the sake of your soul's greater felicity. I lack both the skill and vocation for either. What seemed to me important when I read and examined your work was merely an exchange of views and an endeavor to add to your large store [of ideas] a further widening of the horizon." The author of this letter (dated May 9, 1782) was Baron Friedrich Eberhard von Rochow (1734–1805), who had frequented the academy for young noblemen *(Ritterakademie)* in Brandenburg, served as a lieutenant in the Seven Years' War, and then devoted himself to agriculture in administering his estates. For a time, he had been canon *(Domherr)* at Halberstadt. In 1773, he had established a pedagogical academy in Rekahn near Potsdam and become rather active in propagating a philanthropic type of enlightened education.[15]

The first part of Rochow's letter contained some pithy observations on statements in the preface, such as the following: prejudice against the Jews antedated the Christian era, and the spirit of exclusiveness was a legacy bequeathed to Christianity by the Jews. Alluding to Mendelssohn's reference to King Solomon's prayer, Rochow remarked: "Among the rare Solomons of all centuries there were indeed some who, if only in prayers, expressed different ideas. Yet temples are not consecrated every day." A problem whose solution would require all of a Mendelssohn's sagacity, Rochow pointed out, was the reconciliation of the Jewish law and the duties of citizenship. It was not enough to reject the charge that Jews were unsuitable for service to the state in all its ranges, without admitting the necessity of abandoning certain customs that were held to derive from holy sources. Rochow touched here on a question that, it will be recalled,[16] had not bothered Mendelssohn very much. The Dark Ages that accused the Jews of impossible deeds treated the Christians no more gently: the history of every country abounds in trials of witches and conjurers. It was not fair, Rochow asserted, to deride Christian missionary efforts. One who considered the condition of the Jews in countries other than Holland, particularly in Poland, could only wish, on purely humanitarian grounds, that they were all Christians. It was not true that in all Christian lands the Jews were excluded from all of the arts, sciences, and other useful trades and occupations. The charge was refuted by the very being of men like "the noble author of the [*Manasseh*] preface himself" and like Marcus Herz, Bloch, et al. Rochow rightly saw a contradiction between Mendelssohn's statement that the Jews in Holland were nearly as restricted as in many a province in Germany and his subsequent praise of Holland as a country in which there was "nothing but liberty, gentle rule, fairness of laws, and the acceptance with open arms of men of every sort, dress, opinion, custom, and religion."[17]

In Rochow's view, Berlin was more tolerant than Amsterdam, and Holland's prosperity had to be attributed to its geographical position. Mendelssohn had said that it was unworthy of a statesman to declare anyone unfit to serve the country. Indeed so, Rochow retorted, if the person concerned permitted himself to be used for service. Assuming, however, that certain people desired, on account of their institutions, to be of no use in certain respects, assuming that they wished to enjoy all the commodities of society and yet refused to help protect the country, as was the case with the Jews, would it be unworthy of a statesman to declare: I cannot use the Jews in all of the respects in which I can use the Christians? So long as the Jews shunned military service because of their observance of the sabbath, they seemed to be fit only for Palestine. Rochow expressed the hope that Mendelssohn would clarify his remark about the Jewish belief that both the written laws of Moses, which related to Judaea and the ancient juridical and ritual constitution, and the orally transmitted laws, which could be exegetically derived from the written text, were of divine origin.[18] Had the Jews ever attempted to separate those aspects of the written law that applied to Judaea and ancient times and those that were of universal validity? Furthermore, were the contents of the divine oral law identical with the laws derived from the written text by exegetical means? In Rochow's view, unless this was held to be the case, many later derivations could hardly stand the test of critical scrutiny.

It is interesting to see to what extent Rochow concerned himself with matters that had formed a subject of methodological discussion among Jewish scholars for a long time past. Rochow's letter highlighted some of the points that called for discussion at a time when the integration of the Jews into the polity had become an issue of debate. Though the author was obviously poorly informed and not a little biased, he did share Mendelssohn's political philosophy, and a fruitful exchange of views might have developed but for the second part of the letter, in which its real purport was disclosed. This was all the more disappointing in view of the enthusiastic approval that Rochow had expressed for Mendelssohn's rejection of ecclesiastical power. In his words, all that "the true philosopher" had said on this score was "beautiful to the point of deserving to be memorized."

Yet occasional hints at what the letter had ultimately in store were not lacking even in its first part. Thus, commenting on a remark in the *Manasseh* preface ("the Law-giving God of our fathers or, as the fashionable term has it, Moses the Law-giver"),[19] Rochow said: "I wish . . . it had occurred to the noble-minded Mendelssohn that it is not the Christians but the naturalists, who are so close to the Jews, who employ this kind of language, which he seems to hate. This proves nothing more and nothing less than that much sound philosophy has obviously been preserved by the Christians." He defined a naturalist as "a man who believed that to receive instruction from Christ about God and our duties was at least dispensable." Rochow's opportunity to give free rein to his feelings came when he commented on the concluding passage of Mendelssohn's preface: "Who will not approve, with all his soul, the sincere final apostrophe, kneel down and paraphrase, with great devotion, the beautiful philosophical expression of the Christian model prayer, Thy kingdom come, O Lord."

Mendelssohn's fervent appeal for brotherly love and tolerance had struck Rochow as reflecting a Christian spirit, and without much further ado he suggested that Mendelssohn would presumably be "completely satisfied" with the definition of a Christian in terms compatible with "what the true philosopher considers him to be," freed from "what has been added here and there." In other words, he imputed to Mendelssohn a religious philosophy indistinguishable from the essence of Christianity, and taking this assumption for granted, he challenged Mendelssohn to reply to the following question: "What valid objection can be raised against one who asserts that the Christian religion is more capable [*geschickter*] than any other of leading man to moral perfection?"

The arguments advanced by Rochow in support of this thesis were the following: (1) Christianity contains everything good to be found in other religions; (2) it is free from all the "unbearable burdens weighing upon the conscience" that are part, to one degree or another, of all other faiths; and (3) if fits best into all climes and political constitutions and, being suited to all of mankind, is the ideal universal religion. It was superfluous, Rochow believed, to offer "learned proof" for his assertions. He was sure that Mendelssohn was in agreement with Jesus' purpose to make God lovable and virtue desirable, to arm the poor and humble against all the terrors of life and death, and to equip them with the means of enjoying all pure pleasures. He concluded his letter with this appeal:

> In short, the Christ who was descended from your fathers in the flesh, and who has become, to be sure, a source of happiness to both of us in trying to argue correctly in true philosophical fashion; he, without whom you would not have written your preface nor I this letter; he is of greater worth to the most unprejudiced thinker than anything of worth. Now, seeing that one can be a Christian without becoming a coarse or refined polytheist (according to my rather mild definition of a Christian as opposed to the naturalist), and having regard to the fact that very disparate things such as a Christians' state and the Jewish constitution cannot be reconciled, I ask you, in accordance with Christ's own interpretation (St. John 4:23), whether the wise Jew cannot obtain by a shorter route all the benefits of humanity and civil advantages of the Christians if, subject to all conditions which, in his view, true philosophy must lay down, he—becomes a Christian? I expect impatiently your esteemed reply. Whatever its verdict, it will be instructive to me, and perhaps also grant me the joy of regarding you, if this be possible, even more highly than hitherto. *Vale fave!*

Thus in May, 1782, Mendelssohn was again face to face with a Lavater! However, both the content of the challenge and its circumstances were different. Unlike the Swiss pietist, Rochow was a layman and an adherent of the Enlightenment philosophy, and he sought to convert Mendelssohn not to a full-fledged Christianity but to a pale, abstract version of it, to a Christianity shorn of the trinitarian dogma and implying that only a belief in the moral teachings of Jesus was necessary to salvation. And the challenge was not made a public issue but was confined to the privacy of a letter. Furthermore, its motivation was quite different. Lavater had pursued a chiliastic dream: Mendelssohn's hoped-for conversion was to signal the beginning of the millenium, a Jewish kingdom under Christ in Palestine. Rochow, though no less enthusiastic and devout than Lavater, was a pragmatic philosopher. He wanted the Jews to become Christians in order to facilitate their integration into a Christian state. In his view, adherence to the Jewish "constitution" *(Verfassung)*—the term had been adopted from Mendelssohn[20]—was incompatible with citizenship in a European country. A "wise Jew," therefore, would have to choose a short-cut to a better life, which happened to be the only road to civil rights.

What must have disturbed Mendelssohn was not so much the naïveté of this proposal as its outspoken assumption that Mendelssohn was, to all intents and purposes, already a Christian, that the *Manasseh* preface had a Christian flavor in its final apostrophe, and that all that was now needed on his part was to draw the full conclusions from his premises. What a strange thing that both Hennings and Rochow should urge him to be consistent with himself, Hennings suggesting that he shed Judaism to become a naturalist, Rochow proposing that he become a Christian. Twice within two weeks he had been told that the goal of civil admission could be attained only at the cost of the abandonment of Judaism.

Just how Mendelssohn answered these two correspondents is not known. It may be safely assumed that he combined his firm rejection of their respective suggestions with a renewed plea for true tolerance. His friendship for Hennings was by no means affected by the latter's unkind letter: Mendelssohn knew the impetuosity of the man. And he seems to have established some personal contact with Rochow, for Ferdinand Kindermann *Ritter* von Schulstein, in his letter of January 5, 1783,[21] asked him to convey regards to Herr von Rochow (and to Herr Royal Councillor von Dohm).[22] If the two letters suggested to Mendelssohn the advisability, if not the necessity, of further clarifying the issue, any literary plan that he may have considered was incapable of implementation, at least for the time being, in view of a more pressing task in which he had just then become involved.

On May 25, 1782, the Prussian high chancellor, the count von Carmer, who had initiated a reform of the rules of court proceedings, instructed one of the principal counsellors in the ministry of justice to seek advice from some prominent Jewish leaders such as Moses Mendelssohn and the rabbi of Breslau, Joseph Jonah Fränkel, about the best way of revising the procedure of oath-taking by Jews. The councillor entrusted with this task was Ernst Ferdinand Klein (1744–1810), a distinguised lawyer whose criticism of various legal practices had helped to stimulate the trend in favor of reforms. As a solicitor in Breslau, his native city, Klein had written a series of provocative essays that had been edited in three volumes by his relative and friend the philosopher Christian Garve.[23] The essays had so impressed the count von Carmer, then minister of justice in Silesia, that upon his appointment as high chancellor of Prussia he decided to make a sweeping effort to improve the entire system of legislation, inviting Klein to cooperate in the capacity of assistant councillor *(Assistenzrath)*, first in Breslau and soon afterward in Berlin.

Thus it happened that in the winter of 1781 Klein came to the Prussian capital to join the department of the ministry headed by the eminent lawyer, Karl Gottlieb Suarez.[24] Garve's recommendation opened to him the homes of the leading figures of the Berlin Enlightenment, including that of Moses Mendelssohn.[25] In the late spring of 1782 Klein was given leave of absence to spend the summer in Breslau working on proposals for a reform of the marriage laws,[26] when the order to consult with Jewish leaders on the administration of oaths interrupted his schedule. No one was better qualified for this mission than he. In the first volume of his essays, published in 1779, he had shown the injustice of the law that disqualified a Jew for the so-called *Erfüllungseyd,* i.e., for substantiating his claim for damages from a Christian by taking an oath.[27] It was probably in connection with the mission entrusted to him that he wrote Mendelssohn a letter from Breslau inquiring about the truth of the allegation that rabbinic law permitted a *reservatio mentalis* in case an oath was administered under duress.

In his reply Mendelssohn pointed out that the rabbinic sources had been misquoted; that the sanctity of oaths being inviolate, neither the Talmud nor the codes permitted false oaths with the subterfuge of a *reservatio mentalis* in any lawsuit. Only in cases of coercion by usurpers of authority (brigands, unauthorized tax-collectors, rebels) was one allowed to resort to evasive action.[28]

It seems that Klein was anxious to clarify this particular point before discussing with Mendelssohn the issue of oath-taking procedures. He wanted to be satisfied that there were no grounds for distrusting the veracity of Jewish oaths because of any duplicity sanctioned by rabbinic law, as had been suggested by slanderous authors. Having received Mendelssohn's assurance, he traveled to Berlin for a detailed discussion of the specific problem on the agenda. The manner of oath-taking prescribed for Jews involved in lawsuits before the civil courts was a relic of past ages of hate and prejudice, a fantastically absurd and repugnant procedure designed to terrify and degrade the Jew.[29] Mendelssohn lost no time in working out a memorandum on the subject. On June 4, 1782, he presented the document to Klein who on June 5 sent him a list of queries and suggested

that Mendelssohn enter his replies in the margin. The next step consisted
in the drafting, by Klein, of "Directives for Administering Jews' Oaths"
(undated). Once again, Mendelssohn entered his comments in the margin.
The information so received enabled Klein to formulate, in twenty-two
paragraphs, new rules of procedure and to suggest a drastically revised
text for the admonition.[30] All this was done with remarkable speed. As
early as June 7 Klein could dispatch all four documents to the king. In
a covering letter he reported on his conversations with "the famous Moses
Mendelssohn" and summarized his proposals. He concluded the letter with
the observation that Jewish youth, while being instructed in the ceremonial
laws, received no tuition in the moral laws per se. As a result, their moral
principles were bound to be shaky, and he wished to leave it to the king's
superior wisdom to consider measures for improving the situation. It seems
likely that this paragraph was added at Mendelssohn's suggestion. It implied
a gentle reminder to the king that, following the precedent of the Austrian
emperor's active interest in educational reform, similar action ought to
be taken by Prussia.[31]

Mendelssohn's memorandum, which was one of the documents submitted to the king, was based on the relevant passages in the Talmud and
the rabbinic codes.[32] It showed once again his mastery of the sources,
but it was not altogether free of minor errors, doubtless the result of
the haste in which it was composed.[33] What has to be deplored, however,
is the unfortunate answer he gave to one of Klein's queries concerning
oath-taking by Jews in criminal proceedings involving the death penalty.
In his memorandum[34] Mendelssohn had rightly stated that Jewish law
admitted no oaths in trials of this kind because self-incrimination was considered invalid. Klein had inferred from this statement that a Christian
court could not demand an oath from a Jew in a case of criminal proceedings
—an erroneous inference, for Jewish law did not prohibit Jews from taking
an oath if the law of the state demanded it. Mendelssohn could simply
have pointed out the mistake, but he chose to add the following remark:
"The second kind of oath [viz., an oath by which the suspect person clears
himself] may be imposed upon a Jew if, by taking the oath, he is to free
himself from a fine or some other minor penalty; ... In case, however,
it is a matter of severe corporal punishment, let alone of life and death,
I would hardly trust a Jew."[35] What he probably meant to suggest was
that in view of the nonadmissibility of oaths in criminal cases according
to Jewish law, a Jew might erroneously question the legality of such oaths
even in non-Jewish courts, and that it was therefore preferable not to
permit Jewish oaths in such cases. He certainly did *not* mean to suggest
that Jewish law actually invalidated oath-taking of this kind before a state
court. It was, however, bad enough that he voiced the possibility that the
trustworthiness of Jewish oaths in criminal proceedings might be suspect
and thereby facilitated the objections to the granting of emancipation.
As late as 1811 his remark was being quoted as proof of the "untrust-
worthiness" of the Jews.[36]

Since Mendelssohn never wrote in a slipshod manner, his remark must be attributed to a ruthless sense of honesty: the government had sought his advice, and only the truth as he saw it would do. He recognized that a certain amount of demoralization had set in and was afraid that perjury for the sake of evading severe penalties affecting life and limb could be construed by some as permissible. He was equally outspoken in his rejection, at a somewhat later date, of Rabbi Fränkel's suggestion that the use of the "Jewish-German idiom" and the intermingling of German and Hebrew should be permitted in the admonition prior to the oath and in the administration of the oath. His often-quoted reply was:[37] "I am afraid that this jargon has contributed not a little to the immorality of the common people, and I expect some very good results from the use of the pure German way of speech that has been coming into vogue among my brethren for some time. How annoying to me it would be for the law of the land to speak in favor, as it were, of the misuse of both languages! Herr Fränkel might rather make an effort to translate the entire admonition into pure Hebrew so that it may be recited, according to the circumstances of the case, in pure German or in pure Hebrew or even in both languages. But let there on no account be a mixture of tongues!" One has only to read the barbarous text of the old admonition to appreciate the justice of Mendelssohn's fierce rejection of Fränkel's proposal. Whether or not the "jargon" had had a demoralizing effect is quite another matter. Certainly it had not demoralized Mendelssohn. As an aesthete and purist in matters of style he was, however, convinced of the morally corrupting influence of linguistic carelessness, and he felt that the time had come to call a halt to it. If he loved pure German, his love for pure Hebrew was even greater.

On June 13, 1782, while Klein was still in Berlin, he conveyed to his immediate chief, Suarez, Mendelssohn's answers to some minor points that Suarez had raised.[38] On August 21, after returning to Breslau, he wrote a letter to Mendelssohn beginning with these words:[39] "Revered Man! The high chancellor could not have better rewarded me for my work than by providing me with the opportunity of coming into closer contact with you without being guilty of an immodest obtrusiveness, which so often becomes a bother to great men. It is with pleasure, therefore, that I avail myself of an occasion, which offers itself, to enter into correspondence with you." The occasion was Rabbi Fränkel's suggestion that more Hebrew words be introduced into the German text of the admonition in order to make it more intelligible and impressive to Jews insufficiently acquainted with pure German. In his answer of August 29—its contents have already been noted—Mendelssohn responded to the warm tone of Klein's letter: "Your modesty, revered Herr *Assistenzrath*, comes close to humility and it made you use expressions that put me to shame. A man of your talents may confidently expect that every person of intelligence must take real pleasure in being on friendly terms with him and in having an opportunity to discuss with him matters of concern to humanity."

It is not hard to guess what subjects of general concern, apart from Jewish legal problems, Mendelssohn had discussed with Klein in June, 1782. A note in the *Jerusalem*[40] à propos the theory of contracts reads: "This very plausible exposition of the concepts has been suggested to me by my highly esteemed friend, the philosopher-jurist Herr *Assistenzrath* Klein, with whom I have had the pleasure of discussing this matter." Klein was an expert in natural law, and in 1789 he would publish, in the form of a letter to Garve, a treatise on the difference between compulsory duties and duties of conscience,[41] the very subject that Mendelssohn expounded in the first part of the *Jerusalem*. When later he became *Kammergerichtsrath* (councillor of the Supreme Court of Justice) in Berlin, Klein acted as private tutor to the Humboldt brothers, introducing them to Christian von Wolff's *Institutiones juris naturae et gentium*.[42] His talks with Mendelssohn in June, 1782, must have ranged over a wider field than the mere theory of contracts. They certainly stood Mendelssohn in good stead soon afterwards when he wrote the *Jerusalem*. Klein, in turn, benefitted from Mendelssohn's superior competence in philosophy. As he tells us in his autobiographical essay, he was much attracted to the kind of philosophical theory that saw the source of every pleasure in activity, considered virtue to be the most sincere and most consistent type of activity, and defined happiness as the sentiment derived from energy. Among the philosophers who represented this outlook and, therefore, appealed to him most he named Mendelssohn.[43] After his return from Breslau to Berlin he had ample opportunity to cultivate his friendship with the Jewish philosopher.[44] Free from all bias and a truly enlightened man, he was bound to arouse deep respect and affection in Mendelssohn. Klein's tolerance was inherited from his father, whom he lost when he was young and remembered with great reverence. Reminiscing about him, he wrote:[45] "He used to have conversations with a venerable old man of the Jewish nation, whose honesty, expertise in trade, and sensible religiosity he praised, and who was greatly esteemed by the whole family. My father spoke altogether respectfully about every kind of worship." Klein was, no doubt, a man entirely after Mendelssohn's heart, and their friendship deepened with the years.[46]

On May 27, 1782, a few days before Klein's first visit, Mendelssohn had written the following letter to Nicolai:[47]

> *Littera non erubescit*, says Cicero.[48] I can, therefore, confess to you in writing what I would not have the audacity to tell you viva voce. I find it is time to edit my translation of the Psalms. I dare, however, to lay down conditions to which neither you, my friend, nor any other publisher known to me are likely to consent. You, in particular, publish so many and such precious works that you are surely not going to agree to my conditions. For I insist on a format like that of Ramler's *Florilegium*, with the same type and on the same paper.[49] The work will consist of two volumes of twenty sheets each. The first is to contain the bare translation in verse form. The second is to offer essays and notes, and it will not follow until next year, since the manuscript is not ready as yet.

Nor is this all. The publication, at my own expense, of the Five Books of Moses in Hebrew has left me with a deficit that I would like to wipe out, in part, through the Psalms. I expect, therefore, five louis d'or for every sheet of verse and half that amount for the prose, i.e., approximately one hundred fifty louis d'or for the entire work. What an impudence, you will say, or at least think, and I cannot say you are wrong. Yet I would like to find out whether the German language can possibly repair the damage done by the Hebrew one. As I mentioned, I fully understand that this cannot be regarded by you as a feasible proposition, and my purpose in writing to you is merely to ask your friendly advice. You are sincere enough not to withhold it even in such a case. I am your sincere friend, Moses Mendelssohn.

It was twelve years earlier, in the midst of the Lavater affair, that Mendelssohn had begun his translation of the Psalms as a means of escape from theological controversy and as an exercise in scholarship and pious devotion. What the Psalms meant to him he expressed most movingly in the last letter he wrote to a friend, Sophie Becker, on December 27, 1785, a few days before he died (see below, page 719).[50] Mendelssohn was not prone to indulge in sentimentality and pietism, but he was a deeply religious man who discovered the nature of true prayer when he was still a very young man. In a letter to Lessing written as early as October, 1775, he criticized Hutcheson's occasional "shallowness":[51] "Especially so far as prayer is concerned, the man has trivial notions." When in May, 1782, he decided to publish his translation of the Psalms, it was a great moment in his life, and the financial considerations mentioned in the letter to Nicolai were of marginal importance. In a sense, the de-theologized presentation of the Psalms as a reflection of a kind of universal human piety[52] was a counterpart to his *Manasseh* preface. It was meant to draw attention to an important legacy shared by the synagogue and the church. Perhaps, it was meant to suggest that in the Book of Psalms one might recognize the liturgy of "reason's house of prayer." The plan of publishing the fruit of twelve years of devoted labor matured at the right moment.

As Mendelssohn had anticipated, Nicolai was not prepared to accept the conditions proposed, but Mendelssohn came to agreeable terms with a young publisher, Friedrich Maurer, who shortly afterwards consented to bring out the *Jerusalem* as well. As it turned out, both works appeared at the same time. Mendelssohn was highly satisfied with Maurer's performance. He recommended him to Hennings, then searching for a publisher for his *History of Liberty in England,* to whom he wrote on September 9, 1783:[53] "Maurer is a man with whom one can easily get along. He knows his trade, and it seems that he will do well. For the time being his bookstore is still new and making a start. He has published my Psalms and also my treatise *Jerusalem,* and I am quite satisfied with both the printing job he did and with the way he deals with the author." A somewhat belated testimony to Maurer was written by Mendelssohn's son Joseph on May 4, 1840, to his nephew, Felix Mendelssohn Bartholdy:[54] "I know it from the mouth of my late father that he never received an honorarium for his writings prior to the year 1783. A present consisting in good books was the only thing offered by the gentlemen who were his publishers. The *Jerusalem* was published by a young bookseller, Maurer, who had just set up business at the time (in 1783, three years before father's death), and he surprised him by an honorarium of a hundred louis d'or, which were the only golden fruits he reaped from a lifetime of literary activity."

What caused Mendelssohn to write the *Jerusalem* was the impending publication of an anonymous tract of forty-seven pages in small octavo entitled *The Searching for Light and Right in a Letter to Herr Moses Mendelssohn occasioned by his remarkable Preface to Manasseh Ben Israel.*[55] It was signed "Your most sincere admirer S***—Vienna, June 12, 1782," and thereby inevitably created the impression of having been written by the celebrated Josef von Sonnenfels, a high-ranking politician and leader of the Viennese Enlightenment, whose esteem for Mendelssohn was well known. In a lecture at Vienna University he had declared only recently:[56] "I was certainly one of the first to imbue people in Vienna with respect for men like Ramler, Sulzer, Mendelssohn, Gleim, Spalding, and others [in Germany]. These men belong among the ancestors, the *Imagines majorum,* of German literature, whom my compatriots ought to revere as well as emulate." Mendelssohn, for his part, had mentioned Sonnenfels' name more than once in his correspondence with Herz Homberg: "Did you visit ... Sonnenfels? How did he receive you?," he asked in his letter of June 20, 1782, and on July 16 he remarked: "The advice that Sonnenfels gave you seems to indicate great friendliness, but can you entertain the hope that he will be able to fulfil his promise of helping you obtain one appointment or another?"[57] It was most natural, therefore, for Mendelssohn to assume that the small tract signed by an "admirer" in Vienna with the initial "S" had for its author none other than Sonnenfels. The booklet was to be published by the same Friedrich Maurer who would bring out his translation of Psalms. Hence it is not surprising that Mendelssohn knew well in advance the content of the public "letter" addressed to him by "S***." What Maurer did not tell him was that the true author was the rather notorious scribbler August Friedrich Cranz who, it seems, used the misleading initial and place name in order to make sure that his work received maximum publicity and Mendelssohn's serious attention. In this he fully succeeded. Mendelssohn wrote his *Jerusalem* in the mistaken belief that he was replying to Sonnenfels.

Evidence to this effect is provided by a contemporary witness of events. The young Danish theologian Friedrich Münter, son of the well-known Copenhagen court chaplain Doctor Balthasar Münter, a subscriber to Mendelssohn's edition of the Pentateuch,[58] had undertaken an educational trip to some European countries and happened to be in Berlin at the time. His stay in Berlin extended from August 22 until September 12, 1782.

His father's reputation and his own pleasant demeanor gave him entrée into many homes, and the diary he kept and the letters he wrote make extremely interesting reading.[59] Münter was anxious to become acquainted with Mendelssohn but managed to see him only twice during his sojourn in the Prussian capital. In a letter written from Dresden to Herder he explained why he had not been able to visit Mendelssohn more often:[60] "I talked a great deal with Moses Mendelssohn, but he was too busy replying to Sonnenfels' question as to why he had not yet become a Christian to make it possible for me to see more of him." Thus it was no secret in the Berlin theological circles in which Münter moved that a tract by Sonnenfels challenging Mendelssohn to convert to Christianity was about to appear and that Mendelssohn was engrossed in writing a reply to it.

Münter saw him on August 26, shortly after his arrival in Berlin, and on September 10, when he took his leave. On the first occasion they talked about some prominent contemporaries (Hennings, Feder, Meiners, Heyne), Mendelssohn speaking with great frankness. During the second visit the Moravian Brethren came up for discussion. Münter noted in his diary:[61] "I gave him a better idea concerning them than he had had previously." The excitement aroused by the new challenge to Mendelssohn is reflected in the conversations Münter had with Johann Erich Biester and some leading ecclesiastics. Biester, who was just then about to launch the *Berlinische Monatsschrift* (jointly with Friedrich Gedike), told Münter of the widespread intolerance toward the Jews. Even Spalding, he said, was not free of it, as was shown by the resentment he bore toward Eberhard because he used to take walks together with Mendelssohn; Spalding ardently wished Mendelssohn to be converted to Christianity.

The discussion then turned to the Lavater episode insofar as Biester could remember it.[62] It was no mere chance that this particular topic commanded fresh interest. The appeal to Mendelssohn that was held to have come from Sonnenfels struck everyone as a revival of Lavater's challenge of thirteen years before. In the course of an after-dinner conversation at his home Spalding told Münter that few enlightened Jews would hesitate to undergo baptism if only the Christians were to forego the trinitarian dogma and embrace Socinianism.[63] Dean Teller, on the other hand, tried to explain to Münter that Mendelssohn could do more good by remaining a Jew. His moral influence upon the Jewish community was effective only so long as he was a member; hence one should not press for his conversion.[64] It is obvious from the remarks recorded by Münter in August/ September, 1782, that the theologians in Berlin considered Mendelssohn's present situation to be reminiscent of what it had been in the Lavater affair. And this view prevailed for as long as Mendelssohn's reply was still everybody's guess. It is reflected in a letter that Eberhard wrote to him on January 13, 1783:[65] "Up to now I have watched the game that your preface to *Manasseh* occasioned, and which is somewhat cruel to you. I have done

so with interest but not without annoyance and chagrin. A hundred times
I meant to interfere—had I only known how you felt about it—to give
the proselytizers a piece of my mind."

How did Mendelssohn himself interpret his situation? What impelled
him to write *Jerusalem* in reply to a tract presumed to have been the work
of Sonnenfels? As the whole tenor of *Jerusalem* shows, the question he
sought to answer was not at all concerned with his own person. The Berlin
theologians were gravely mistaken in imagining that he was busy replying
to Sonnenfels as to "why he had not yet become a Christian," as Münter
put it. This was a question he could safely ignore. What Mendelssohn
felt to be at stake in 1782 was not his personal situation but the civil admission
of the Jews as a matter of right and with no strings attached. He realized
that his preface to *Manasseh ben Israel* had not served its avowed purpose
of adding strength to Dohm's proposals and had been misconstrued as
an admission that Judaism had to be de-Judaized as a precondition of
civil equality for Jews. Hennings had challenged him to take the ultimate
step of reducing the Jewish religion to a deistic formula, and von Rochow,
no mean figure in the German educational world, had urged him to be
consistent with his claims by adopting a liberal form of Christianity. Both
Hennings and Rochow had disputed the Jews' right to citizenship so long
as they adhered to their separateness. Mendelssohn had seen no need
to rebut these private overtures in public. Now a new situation had arisen
as a result of the "open letter" addressed to him—as he believed—by
Sonnenfels.

There was a certain piquancy in the presumed authorship of the
pamphlet about to be published. Josef Edler von Sonnenfels (1732–1817)
was a Jewish convert to Roman Catholicism. His father, Perlin Lipmann,
was the son of the Berlin Rabbi Michel Hasid[66] and had changed his name
to Alois Wiener upon undergoing baptism together with his two sons.
He became a teacher of oriental languages at Vienna University, was
nobilitated, and died as Alois von Sonnenfels in 1769. His younger son,
Franz Anton, was made a *Hofrath* (court councillor), and Josef had achieved
fame in both politics and literature.[67] The latter had reached the zenith
of his political career during the reign of Empress Maria Theresa (died
1780), as her most trusted adviser. Under Joseph II his political influence
declined. He played no important role in the promulgation of the Edict
of Tolerance: all the emperor had asked him to do was to polish the
wording, and Joseph had been quite annoyed when Sonnenfels objected
to the use of the phrase "most gracious will" on the ground that "it seemed
inappropriate for the monarch, whom the legal document presented as
speaking in the first person, to pay compliments to himself."[68] Sonnenfels'
influence in the literary sphere grew by leaps and bounds. He made a
determined effort to improve the quality of the theater, and he extended
his patronage to the arts in general.[69] As the leader of the Enlightenment
in Austria he was responsible for the abolition of torture as part of judicial

procedure. He pleaded for the closing of the monasteries, which he considered "useless," and argued against the exemption of the clergy from general civic duties. He attacked the prerogative of churches to grant asylum to criminals, and he raised his voice against the "encroachments" *(Anmassungen)* of the Vatican.[70] He was a humanist and liberal at heart. To his enemies he was a Jew and a freethinker, both, despite his conversion.

To prove himself a true Christian Sonnenfels occasionally stressed the superiority of the New Testament over the Old, but he did so in contexts criticizing the shortcomings of the clergy. Thus he contrasted "the commandment of the Old Testament: Thou shalt never appear before the priest with empty hands" with "the excellence of the New," which disassociated the priesthood from wealth. He deplored the failure of many members of the clergy to live up to New Testament teaching.[71] His fondness of Old Testament imagery somewhat belied his stress on the superiority of the New. When exhorting the priests to make themselves "venerable," he wrote:[72] "Moses' countenance reflects the glory of Him whom he has seen face to face.... He has to veil its splendor in the sight of laymen. This miracle symbolizes the venerability that the altar must reflect upon those who minister before it." When Pope Pius VI made his sensational visit to Vienna in 1782, with a view to mitigating any possible ill effects on Roman Catholic supremacy as a result of the tolerance granted to the Protestants, a flood of pamphlets debated the event. Sonnenfels took the opportunity to shield the pope against the attack made upon him by a certain Landrath Eibel in a pamphlet entitled *What is the Pope?*[73] He did so in a brochure *On the Arrival of Pius VI in Vienna, Fragment of a Letter by* ****, *edited by J. v. Sonnenfels* (Vienna, 1782).[74] In it he accused Eibel (but not by name) of having disregarded the particular circumstances of the time and the kind of reader he was addressing. His censure of Eibel was denounced as sheer hypocrisy by the reviewer in Nicolai's *Allgemeine deutsche Bibliothek,*[75] who was an outright foe of papism and had no stomach for the ambivalent attitude of the Viennese politician.

The sharp tone of the review reflects, no doubt, the resentment that Mendelssohn and his intimate circle also felt toward the half-liberal, half-clerical tone of the challenge contained in what was mistakenly considered to be yet another tract by Sonnenfels, viz. the pamphlet about to be published by Maurer. Sonnenfels' defense of the pope obviously reinforced the impression that the pamphlet could indeed have been written by him. The review must be considered, therefore, as evidence of the angry reaction that both writings had inspired in Mendelssohn and his friends. It clearly indicates the estimate they took of Sonnenfels' character at the time. The following passages of the review will help to make the deception about the authorship of the second pamphlet more plausible:

> The reviewer was eager to read this little tract [*On the Arrival of Pius VI*]. He knows the author's talents; but how great was his astonishment when he found it to be wholly unworthy of Sonnenfels.... Herr von

Sonnenfels often puts on a strange countenance unbecoming to him.
He considers himself the first reformer in Vienna. He does, indeed,
deserve well of Vienna. He was the first to peruse the good writers of
Protestant Germany and dared to propagate them in Vienna at a time
when all heretics were considered there as damnable.... The way he
answers the question "What is the Pope?" is by no means instructive
but declamatory and rhetorical.... Herr v. S. is confident that Pius VI
has the best intentions; he thinks it impossible that he should be engaged
in a plot to make the subjects waver in their loyalty to their monarch....
The concluding part of this treatise reminds the reviewer of Don Quixote
who, upon seeing the shepherd's hazel nuts, delivered an emotional speech
that astonished all listeners. We shall see whether Herr von Sonnenfels'
prophecy will be fulfilled: "that starting from the time of his journey
the system of the Roman cabinet will be transformed"... Vienna and
Austria are in need of more men like Eibel to wake them up by loud
shouts, not a Sonnenfels who puts them to sleep by sweetly chanting
that everything there is in perfect shape.

Sweet chanting and quixotic prophesying were also part of the makeup
in the pamphlet *The Searching for Light and Right*. There had been a time,
the author said in his opening words, when he blamed Lavater for his
importunity and disregard of privacy, whereas now he almost wished that
Lavater would risk another assault upon Mendelssohn. For some of the
latter's utterances in his "excellent preface" to *Manasseh ben Israel* entitled
everyone in search of truth to expect some further clarification. When
Lavater had embarrassed Mendelssohn by his indiscretion, everybody had
enjoyed the deftness with which Mendelssohn had avoided answering the
questions then put to him. Now it was a different story. Mendelssohn
had made an important public statement, and surely he was obliged to
explain its meaning more fully. When replying to Lavater, like Moses of
old, he had put a veil on his face. In his preface, however, he had revealed
himself without a mask, for a brief moment, and had thereby kindled
the hope of seeing him again in full view. Employing a rather "declamatory
and rhetorical" style, the author addressed Mendelssohn with these words:
"You have presented us with a preface that cut across the darkness like
a flash of lightning. Permit us now to read a complete epilogue, which
will be the aurora of truth heralding a beautiful day, and which will help
the friends of light walk in the light, desirous as they are of taking certain
steps under the guidance of the hand of truth."[76] Less poetically phrased,
the author expressed the hope that Mendelssohn's next pronouncement
would be an affirmation of Christianity and would lead him and his fellow
Jews to the baptismal font. In so doing, he added, Mendelssohn would
not be forsaking "the faith of his fathers," to which he felt a deep attachment,
as he had told Lavater.[77] For the essence of Christianity was identical with
the faith of his fathers in that it consisted in the worship of the One
God, in the observance of the divine commandments revealed through
Moses, and in the gathering of all nations into one flock ruled by the
scepter of the Messiah. What Christianity rejected was the statutory system

based on the rabbinic interpretation of Scripture, by virtue of which the Jews were separated from all other nations.[78]

So far the author had spoken only in dark hints. He had not explained in what way Mendelssohn's preface had exposed his closeness to Christianity. Now he elaborated his point. By rejecting all manner of religious compulsion, Mendelssohn had removed himself from the faith of his fathers as understood in a narrow sense and had dealt a decisive blow to the statutory system of the synagogue and the Mosaic Law. His denial of the compatibility of religion and power was commendable from the point of view of reason but was utterly irreconcilable with Judaism. According to the Law of Moses, nonobservance of certain commandments was punishable by death, and although the loss of temporal power now prevented the synagogue from inflicting such penalty, it did not imply the abrogation of the law. "Your lawgiver Moses is always the drover with the stick, who led his flock to pasture with an iron rod." The biblical stories gave ample evidence of the severity of Jewish theocratic rule. The arm of the "church" in biblical and subsequent times was "equipped with the sword of the curse": "Cursed be he that keepeth not all the words of this Law to do them."[79] The curse had been placed in the hands of the "first ministers of the church." It was they who imposed the penalties and the ban of excommunication. Mendelssohn had been perfectly right in declaring that the church required no sword and no scourge, but if this was the case, what was to become of the very laws of Moses which were said to be authorized by a direct revelation? "To what extent can you, my dear Herr Mendelssohn, abide by the faith of your fathers and, by removing the cornerstones, shake the whole edifice, contesting as you are the churchly system of law that was given by Moses and that claimed the authority of a divine revelation?" It was this question that hit Mendelssohn and forced him to write an answer, as he confessed in *Jerusalem*.[80]

But the author was not content merely to ask for clarification. He felt justified in drawing conclusions from the way Mendelssohn had defined religion: might one not discover here some evidence of second thoughts about the desire that Lavater had once expressed? Perhaps he had come closer to the Christian faith after he had "torn himself away from the servitude of iron churchly bonds" and begun to teach a system of religious freedom based on reason, which was the hallmark of Christian worship. In the author's view the freedom and rationality of the Christian religion consisted in an "escape" from compulsory laws and burdensome ceremonies. Christian worship was no longer tied to either Jerusalem or Samaria but was a worship of God "in spirit and in truth."[81] It was also possible, he suggested, that Mendelssohn regarded the faith of his fathers in the way in which all religions of the world had to be looked upon, namely as imperfect edifices that had constantly to be improved. In this case, it seemed to him, ecclesiastical power might not be the only article that Mendelssohn wanted to see removed from the faith of his fathers.

It was at this point that the author raised the issue of the civil admission of the Jews. "Permit me, worthy man," he addressed Mendelssohn, "to submit for your consideration some remarks that seem important to me precisely in the present age, in which a great revolution has started for your nation's benefit." The preface to *Manasseh Ben Israel* had been right in drawing attention to the "unjust oppressions" suffered by the Jews ever since Jerusalem was destroyed and the nation had been scattered. Yet remarkable changes had occurred in more recent times, to which Mendelssohn had himself alluded in his prayer of thanksgiving at the opening of the preface: "You rejoice that at the end of your days you have reached a time when some of the Christians who rule over your nation have begun to become human beings and to recognize the Jews as human beings. . . . You rejoice in the happy revolution in the imperial states in which the orphaned children of Israel have found a father in the enterprising Joseph, who accords to them too a portion and an inheritance[82] in his country by placing them on the same level of humanity with the rest of his subjects."[83] The wise and intelligent among the Christians were now ready to love the noble-minded among the Jews as their brethren, and unprejudiced Christians had taken up the case of humanity by pleading on behalf of Jewish rights.[84]

Why was it, the author wondered, that the two nations, the Jews and the Christians, though of equal nature and worshipping the same God, were nevertheless still divided? His answer was: "Dear Herr Mendelssohn, the blame for the separation and exclusion from the privileges of the polity . . . does not attach to the Christians alone. The faith of your fathers is in itself a powerful barrier that removes your nation from unrestricted sharing in the general and private benefits of society."[85] The author cited as examples the laws of the sabbath, which in his view were a hindrance to the complete fulfilment of civic duties, and which, he suggested, should be modified to suit the conditions in which Providence had placed the Jews. Had not the ancient sacrificial cult to be abandoned after the destruction of the Temple, though it had been considered holy and sacrosanct? Still more urgent, he felt, was a change in the laws that put obstacles in the way of social contacts between Jews and Christians. The dietary rules were a case in point. Their original purpose had been a legitimate one, namely the separation of the Jews from the heathens and their idolatry. These laws had outlived their usefulness because the Christians were not idolators. Nor was it to be feared that by participating in common meals Jews might be induced to accept "certain mysteries of the Christian church," which alone divided the two faiths. "It is absolutely necessary that all barriers separating the two nations in civil life be lifted, if the Jews are to become more closely integrated into the state so as to enjoy, as inhabitants and citizens, equal advantages with the Christians."[86] In other words, the author regarded the Jews' renunciation of their exclusiveness as the necessary precondition of their being granted citizenship. He did not wish, however, to force the "mysteries" of the church (i.e. the trinitarian dogma) upon the Jews. Nor did he insist on formal baptism as a *conditio sine qua non* of civil equality.

Returning to his starting point (Mendelssohn's rejection of ecclesiastical power) the author asked: "If it be possible, without detriment to unalloyed Judaism, to abolish churchly privilege [i.e. the right of excommunication], which is based upon positive Mosaic laws, why should it be impossible to cancel, for the nation's benefit, mere rabbinic measures of late vintage, which create such detrimental barriers between Jews and Christians? Should, however, the allegedly revealed legality of churchly power necessarily belong to the very essence of the Jewish religion, there could be no objection to considering all the rest as of equal standing. Yet in this case you, my most worthy Herr Mendelssohn, have abandoned the faith of your fathers. One more step and you have become one of us."[87] So long as Mendelssohn did not take this second step the public had a perfect right to expect one of two things: either an explanation of how Mendelssohn could reconcile the tenor of his *Manasseh* preface with the religion of his fathers or else a statement of the reasons by virtue of which he was opposed to joining the faith of the Christians publicly, and which caused him to reject the "true" (i.e., the unalloyed and enlightened) form of Christianity as such.[88] Mendelssohn understood this sentence as a "challenge either to accept the Christian religion as the religion of freedom or else to refute it."[89] It sounded to him not very different from the alternative once posed by Lavater. Yet there was a difference in nuance and in the circumstances. It was an enlightened, liberal form of Christianity—a Christianity shorn of its mysteries—into which the author of the pamphlet sought to lure Mendelssohn.

Having formulated his challenge, the author hastened to assure Mendelssohn that his decision would be respected by Christians even if it turned out to be "unfavorable"—even if he resolved to remain a Jew. Should he, on the other hand, wish to join the true Christianity by simply dismissing certain parts of Judaism that were, after all, of secondary importance, he had no reason to be afraid of the rabbinate ("the priesthood of your nation"), since he lived in a state that protected dissidents. "By explaining yourself more fully you will either contribute toward relieving your nation of many a compulsory law . . . leading your coreligionists closer to us, or you will lead us closer to you by dispelling our errors. In either case a foundation will be laid for the fulfilment of the prophecy (unless it be a mere dream) that before the end of days God shall be the universal Shepherd and all men shall be but one flock. The truth alone can lead to this goal—be it your truth or ours, or perhaps it will be found to lie midway, if we advance toward it from both sides." It seemed, the author added, that now the time was still propitious for the victory of truth. Freedom was still unimpaired. Yet the danger of "new monsters" arising from the recrudescent spirit of fanaticism was a real one, and it only required a reactionary regime to suppress reason for the sake of reinstating the old superstitions. "Yet at this remarkable juncture nothing should prevent you from revealing your total conviction. Having forced the iron gate of churchly power, what can hinder you from entering into the realm of truth?"[90]

This plea was bound to evoke a response. Apart from its intrinsic persuasiveness, there seemed to be no doubt that the pamphlet had been written by Sonnenfels, whose standing in the political and intellectual world commanded Mendelssohn's respect. The actual author had employed great skill in his pseudepigraphical venture. The tract was not only signed "S***—Vienna" but it also referred in a footnote to "our Vienna, Germany's capital" and to a lawsuit then pending there. Moreover, the explanation offered for two printer's errors in the text was "the indistinct handwriting of the distant author"—yet another attempt to reinforce the deception. Finally, the spelling employed in the tract was not the one in vogue in northern Germany but had a distinctly southern flavor that was rather overdone.[91] This was a risky procedure, in view of the fact that the spelling in Sonnenfels' authentic writings by no means deviated from the standards observed in Berlin. Superficially, at any rate, the impression was created that the pamphlet was of southern origin. The seriousness with which Mendelssohn treated the issue of the Viennese lawsuit in his *Jerusalem*[92] makes it clear that he believed himself to be dealing with an author who knew the emperor's mind and wielded some influence.[93] Likewise, the fervor with which he rejected as premature the proposed union of Jews and Christians clearly stemmed from his assumption that he was addressing Sonnenfels and, through him, the emperor whose Edict of Tolerance Mendelssohn had long suspected of conversionist tendencies.[94]

Exactly how long Mendelssohn held the mistaken belief that Sonnenfels was the "unnamed Searcher for Light and Truth"[95] is a question that cannot be answered with certainty. He apparently labored under this assumption throughout the period during which he wrote *Jerusalem*. He commenced the writing of this treatise not later than the time of Münter's arrival in Berlin, that is, in the latter half of August, 1782. The pseudo-Sonnenfels pamphlet could not have appeared in print before mid-September, since a postscript added to it by David Ernst Mörschel, a military chaplain, is dated September 3, 1782. On October 15 Mendelssohn was still busy writing, as we know from a remark in a letter he wrote to Herz Homberg that day.[96] In his undated reply to Schulstein's letter of January 5, 1783,[97] which must have been written in March,[98] he announced the forthcoming publication of his Psalms translation as well as his treatise "On Religious Power and Judaism" for the Easter book fair. In this letter he betrayed his awareness of the pseudepigraphical character of the pamphlet, referring to it as a treatise "alleged to have been written in Vienna."[99] It was probably at about the same time that he added the clause "allegedly written in Vienna" to the first reference to the "little tract" in his *Jerusalem.*[100] We know from his letter to Carl Julius Redlich in Vienna that on April 4, 1783, both his Psalms translation and his *Jerusalem* were still in press.[101] Hence there was still time in March to enter that small correction. Eberhard, who in his letter of January 18 had deplored the "cruel game" of the "proselytizers" (Sonnenfels and the Berlin theologians?), wrote on April 19, (when the identity of the author of the pamphlet had been discovered):[102] "I have asked Herr Nicolai to request from you the proofs of your Psalms translation and of your treatise against Cranz. Yet he sent me nothing. Now I apply to you personally and adjure you to send me everything that is printed. It is impossible for me to wait until the book fair."

The tension had clearly been eased by the discovery that the "proselytizer" was not Sonnenfels but Cranz. Mendelssohn must have felt a certain embarrassment upon realizing that the illustrious Viennese was innocent of conversionist zeal. When in September, 1784, Sonnenfels launched a grandiose scheme for a "Private Association of Men of the Sciences"[103] and invited Mendelssohn to join this academy, the reply he received opened with this effusive address:[104] "Most beloved Confrère! I do not hesitate to call you this; for I appreciate the honor you wish to bestow upon me with the warmest gratitude and I accept it with pleasure. Since Sonnenfels wants to be my leader, I no longer ask: in what direction?" Mendelssohn's enthusiastic response was his previous misdirected answer in reverse.

Cranz' authorship of *The Searching for Light and Right* is attested beyond doubt by a statement that has come to light only recently.[105] In a treatise published by him in 1798 he spoke at length and with remarkable candor about the motivations behind his past literary activity, especially his fight against "religious and political superstition" and his advocacy of a fair chance for the Jews. "The evidence of all this," he said, "can be found in my earlier writings such as my *Searching for Light and Right,* which was addressed to Moses Mendelssohn and provided the occasion for his excellent work entitled *Jerusalem.*"[106] There are no valid grounds for casting an aspersion on so clear an utterance made fifteen years after the publication of *Jerusalem* and at a time when Sonnenfels was still alive. On the contrary, it is only by accepting the fact of Cranz' authorship that the admission of Mörschel's postscript can be satisfactorily explained. Had Sonnenfels been the author, the publisher would have hardly dared to add to the work of so famous a writer a *Nachschrift* by an unknown, mediocre army chaplain. There is no difficulty in assuming that Cranz and Mörschel, who resided in the same city, were hand in glove with one another.

What requires some explanation is the meticulous care with which Cranz tried to make his pamphlet appear to be a work by Sonnenfels. The answer to this question must be sought, chiefly, in his desire to secure Mendelssohn's serious attention. Cranz was obviously afraid that a work appearing under his name would simply be dismissed as carrying little weight. He must have known that his reputation as an author stood rather low. Nicolai described him in a letter to Baron von Gebler as "a scribbler [*Schmierer*] esteemed by nobody here,"[107] and although Nicolai had an axe to grind,[108] his view was widely shared and rightly so. August Friedrich Cranz (1737–1801) had studied theology and jurisprudence but had to make a living by his pen after being forced to resign a position as a high civil servant (*Kriegs-* and *Steuerrath*) in Cleve on account of certain irregularities committed by him. He tried hard to become a second Voltaire by writing in a satirical, if not scurrilous vein, and his prolific output ran into many editions, though scandalizing the more serious-minded (especially clerical) circles. Frederick the Great seems to have been amused by his writings and granted him freedom from censorship for a while.[109] He revoked this privilege when Cranz announced a publication entitled "Austrian Realities and Charlataneries," which was likely to cause political trouble. Dohm was charged with the responsibility of acting as censor of Cranz' further writings, a task that Dohm did not relish.[110] Thus in 1782, when Cranz wrote his pamphlet *The Searching for Light and Right,* he knew that if he sought to publish it under his own name he would first have to submit it to Dohm; it seems quite likely that one of his reasons for ascribing the pamphlet to the Viennese celebrity, Sonnenfels, was the desire to evade this censorship. For had the little tract been submitted to Dohm, the identity of the author would have become known to Mendelssohn—and this is what Cranz wanted to prevent.

There may have been still another consideration on Cranz' part: he was on excellent terms with Mendelssohn's friends and he greatly admired Mendelssohn himself.[111] It would have been embarrassing to him had the challenge presented in the pamphlet been recognizable as his.[112] Just recently he had published a polemical tract, *The Misuse of Ecclesiastical Power and Secular Dominion,* against the chief rabbi of Altona, and its sequel, which was directed against Rabbi David Tevele of Lissa,[113] was dated June 24, 1782,[114] twelve days after the fictitious S*** had signed the pamphlet addressed to Mendelssohn. The two anti-rabbinic brochures had been commissioned by David Friedländer and his group. As a professional writer, who compared his calling to that of an advocate working for a client, Cranz had no compunctions about delivering literary "merchandise" for an appropriate fee.[115] Yet he must have been afraid that his Lavaterian challenge to Mendelssohn would be suspected of being custom-made and dismissed as such. In this instance, as it happened, he had employed his pen from no ulterior motive, for he was genuinely interested in promoting what he considered to be a noble, even a sacred, cause. In his previous works, too, one can detect evidences of an underlying seriousness, though they are as a rule submerged in a flood of frivolity, cynicism, and vulgarity.

In *The Searching for Light and Right* Cranz' better self is in full control, almost as if his addressing Mendelssohn had compelled him to rise to the occasion. Yet some of the thoughts and phrases used in the pamphlet have their parallels in his other writings. A case in point is the striking image of the one Shepherd and the one flock, which expresses his ultimate concern. How fond he was of this particular phrase can be seen from a passage dating from 1781, which notes with regret the divisions within Christianity:[116] "There is no one Shepherd and no one flock but there are many shepherds and many flocks. One shouts: Right!, the other Left! —whom are the poor sheep to follow?" The theme of Jewish/Christian reconciliation had been portrayed to him in his youth under this very image, as he tells us in his treatise of 1798:[117]

> A pious and very orthodox teacher of the young commended to me at an early age the universal love of men, especially of the Jews, who were being unjustly hated and whose defects he attributed solely to their oppression under Christian governments. He ardently clung to the old theological view that a time would come when they would "seek their king (Jesus)" and a general conversion of the Jews would take place so that there would be "one Shepherd and one flock." This faith motivated his desire to contribute, on his part, to this conversion and, in case it failed, to take comfort in the thought that the time preordained by Providence had not yet arrived.

Cranz' personal creed had been expressed before in terms similar to those found in the pamphlet. In answer to a critic, who had described his satirical treatment of biblical stories as injurious to religious faith,[118] he had spoken of the "simple, purified religion of those who worship God in spirit and in truth"; of the "light" of truth, which even among enlightened Protestants was still enveloped in an "artificial darkness of mystical ideas totally alien to true religion"; of the need to remove "mere human statutory laws" (*blosse Menschensatzungen*) and to preserve the essence of religion (i.e., the worship of God); and of the lack of courage on the part of liberal theologians who did not assail the "crumbling walls of the old orthodox system."[119] A disgust with the ambivalent attitude of the theologians of the Berlin Enlightenment had been voiced by Cranz (in a manner somewhat reminiscent of Lessing) in the ditties of his *Berlin Chronicle*,[120] and his appeal to Mendelssohn was as much a call for help as it was a challenge to convert. He sincerely expected Mendelssohn to "lead" not only the Jews toward the Christians but also the Christians toward his superb enlightenment by which their "errors" might be removed. True, he put this dual aim in the form of an either/or,[121] which could be taken as a mere token of respect, and Mendelssohn's ear did not catch its full meaning, believing as he did that it was Sonnenfels, the Jewish convert to Roman Catholicism, who addressed him. How far Cranz was from the zeal of the true proselytizer can be seen from the way he memorialized Mendelssohn in 1786: "He remained a true Jew until his end. He loved Christians, and he was loved by Christians. . . . for he was too good and noble a man to be oblivious of the *man* in both the Jew and the Christian."[122]

Jerusalem

I

In May, 1783, both the Psalms translation and the treatise *Jerusalem or On Religious Power and Judaism* were published.[1] Those who had hoped that Mendelssohn might succumb to the "Searcher's" plea were disappointed. The treatise did not yield an inch of ground. As the subtitle indicates, it resumed the theme of ecclesiastical power that had already been briefly discussed in the preface to *Vindiciae Judaeorum,* and it also contained the long delayed philosophical interpretation of Judaism. The avowed object of the work was to show the compatibility of Mendelssohn's political liberalism and his loyal adherence to the faith of his fathers, which he now calls "Judaism." The title *Jerusalem* may have been chosen in proud defiance of the New Testament passage quoted in the pamphlet, which dissociated the worship of God from both Samaria and Jerusalem and described it as one in spirit and in truth. As his first draft of the outline of the book shows, the quotation of this militant phrase had aroused Mendelssohn's ire, for he wrote rather caustically: "Christianity is a yoke in spirit and in truth. It has transformed thirty-nine corporal floggings [Deut. 25:3, according to rabbinic exegesis] into as many spiritual ones"—an allusion to the thirty-nine articles of the Anglican Church, which he was going to mention in his treatise. The harsh sentence in the draft was not repeated in the book but the sentiment remained alive and was articulated, not in the least, by affirming in the title the undiminished significance of Jerusalem. His critic Hamann missed the point when he remarked, in a note to his *Golgatha and Sheblimini:*[2] "Why he gave his treatise the name of a destroyed[3] city no critic has hitherto bothered to ask, and the author himself, perhaps, did not know either." If our interpretation is correct, Mendelssohn chose the name in order to indicate that Jerusalem, though destroyed and bereft of power, was still the symbol of the true worship of God.[4]

Fortunately, the first rough draft outlining the structure and topics of the work has been preserved.[5] It very much resembles the first drafts we have of the letters *On the Sentiments* ("On Pleasure")[6] and of the *Phaedon.*[7] Like them, it contains no more than mere guidelines and barely a hint of the wealth of fine points and embellishments that emerged in the process of writing.[8] It is also similar to the initial outline of his *Reply to Lavater,*[9] showing as it does his immediate reaction to the Searcher's challenge. According to this original plan, the treatise was to consist of three parts. The first was to deal with the relationship between church and state, the second with the juridical presuppositions of Mendelssohn's denial of the legitimacy of ecclesiastical power, the third with the assertion, rejected by Mendelssohn, that a plea for tolerance and the teachings of Judaism could not be reconciled. In its final form, the *Jerusalem* presented the first and second parts as a unified whole in the first section *(Abschnitt)*. In the first edition of the work (1783) sections one and two are treated almost as two books (since the pagination starts afresh in section two). Attached to the original draft are two pages containing, in Mendelssohn's own hand, some excerpts from Latin treatises of which use was made in the *Jerusalem*. They were taken from Canz' manual of practical philosophy and jurisprudence[10] and Hobbes' *Leviathan*.[11] Critical remarks are interposed between some of the excerpts. There were probably many such sheets digesting relevant source material that are no longer extant. The small sample that has been preserved testifies to the pains that Mendelssohn took in gathering and critically analyzing his material before he began the actual writing of his treatise. The text of the first draft reads as follows:[12]

1

Church and State. Borderline disputes between them have caused enormous evil[13]—Hobbes—Locke—The latter limits the state to the care for temporal welfare.—A makeshift intended for the protection of dissidents against persecution.—But wrong, for the temporal cannot be separated from the eternal, and ineffective—for the Church employs the secular arm.—The true dividing line is [the difference between] compulsory duties and persuasion. The former belong to the state, the latter is the privilege of religion.—When the church arrogates to itself property and compulsory rights, it usurps them.

2

The origin of compulsory rights. Only the duties of omission are perfect. The duties to do something become, as a result of contract, duties not to do [what violates the contract]. Contracts relate to dispensable goods which are used for the benefit of others. Opinions confer no rights nor can they be brought into any connection with rights. Nobody must be asked to testify under oath that he holds a certain opinion. Confirming articles of faith under oath amounts to a misuse of God's name, is a vain oath, never a false oath.—Consolation to all those who confirmed symbolic [i.e. dogmatic] books or established articles of faith under oath and have a guilty conscience. The state needs religion only as a safeguard of oaths; hence the state presupposes faith and cannot have someone confirm his faith under oath. To the extent that religion does not safeguard the state, it has to limit itself altogether to persuasion.

3

It has been objected to these rational arguments that they run counter to the Jewish religion—*Searching for Light and Right*. Challenge to accept the Christian religion as the religion of freedom or else to refute it.—Inconsistency of this unfair suggestion. He who finds the foundation of his edifice to be unsafe, will not save his belongings by moving them from the lower to the upper floor.—Christianity is a yoke in spirit and truth—It has transformed thirty-nine corporal floggings into as many spiritual ones. The modern Reformation of the 18th century is no longer founded on revelation, leaves everything to reason, yet arrogates to itself a name [that of a Church] in order to use the privileges attached to this name—Not so Judaism.

[Additions in the margin at the bottom of the page:] History of religion. Union of faiths. Divorce of Marriage. Faith of my fathers.

As this first draft shows the third part—his answer to the *Searcher*—was overwhelmingly polemical in tone and content, while the first and second parts set forth the essential elements of his political doctrine. In its final form the *Jerusalem* faithfully reflects the outline of the first two parts in section one but differs vastly from part three of the draft in section two. It seems that originally Mendelssohn had been content to remind the challenger of the heavy burden that Christian dogma and ecclesiastical law placed upon man's conscience, by comparison with which the practical commandments of Judaism were an easy yoke. In the unpublished "Counterreflections" on Bonnet's *Palingénésie*, Mendelssohn had reacted in a similar way:[14] "The more closely I look upon this religion, which is so much recommended to me, the more repulsive it becomes to my reason. . . . What a fetter to my reason!" Yet in the course of the writing polemics receded more and more into the background and gave way to a philosophical discourse on Judaism. Mendelssohn himself mentioned this change of direction in a letter to Herz Homberg on June 14, 1783:[15] "*Jerusalem* is a booklet of a special kind, about which I would like to hear your opinion. This much is certain: it is of a sort such as neither the orthodox nor the heterodox of both nations [viz., Christians and Jews] expected. For both expected a quarrel about religion, whereas I, following my bad custom, look at every step for speculative matters that I can weave together, and in the meantime allow the club to drop from my hands. This displeases most readers. Yet who wants to write for most readers?" The speculative matters that he developed in section two were all related to his theory of Judaism as natural religion and revealed law. Here he could draw on a wealth of ideas that were partly old and well-tested and partly of more recent vintage, such as his view on human progress in history, which had formed the subject of his latest correspondence with Hennings. His "Counterreflections" on Bonnet also came in handy, after having been locked away for a long time. The urge to theorize and neatly classify the respective domains of state and religion in the first section, and of natural religion and revelation in the second, did not cause him to forget the Searcher's challenge and the need to rebut it. The *Jerusalem* concluded with a spirited rejection of the proposed union of faiths and a fervent appeal to his fellow Jews to remain loyal to the religion of their fathers at no matter what cost. Better to forgo the benefits of civil equality, if they had to be paid for by disloyalty to Judaism.

While the ideas "woven together" within each of the two sections form a coherent whole, the question remains whether the two sections reflect a completely unified outlook. In other words, was the plea for absolute freedom of conscience in the first section reconcilable with the upholding of religious authority in the second? A Leipzig professor had rudely declared:[16] "In the first section Mendelssohn is a sophist and in the second an arrant Jew [*ein Stockjude*]." Kant was of a different opinion:[17] "Herr Friedländer will tell you," he wrote to Mendelssohn on August 16, 1783, "with what admiration I have read your *Jerusalem,* noting as I did its acumen, subtlety, and good sense. I consider this book the manifesto [*Verkündigung*] of a great reform which, though slow in starting and advancing, will affect not only your nation but others too. You have known how to reconcile your religion with such a degree of freedom of conscience as one would not have imagined it to be capable of, and as no other religion can boast of." Unless one wants to read between the lines some sarcasm about the hitherto unsuspected degree of Jewish tolerance, Kant was evidently much impressed by Mendelssohn's achievement.

Whether the political reformer and the Jew in Mendelssohn were really unified cannot be decided by quoting opinions such as these. Only by analysis of the work in question can we hope to clarify the issue.[18] Such analysis will benefit from some of the reviews and pamphlets in which Mendelssohn's contemporaries reacted to the treatise.[19] Judging from the intimate and very frank letter that he wrote to Herz Homberg on March 1, 1784, Mendelssohn was not conscious of any inconsistency in his position. He knew that he had been accused of it, of course, and of other things besides. "All this was not unexpected. Still, I took pleasure in the fact that some of the brightest minds and best people expressed agreement in regard to the most important points; and what else is required to compensate for all the distorted judgments that have been passed and may yet be passed upon me?"[20] Although he was confident as to the rightness of his position, he was determined not to discuss it with anybody: "I must candidly admit, however," he wrote in the same letter, "that I dislike debating the content of my *Jerusalem* [even] with my most intimate friends. My intention from the start has been to decline all private discussion, written or oral, and to suggest to those desiring to raise some objection that they raise in it print." He had several reasons for this reluctance, he declared.[21]

> On the one hand, I had to contradict many a prevalent prejudice and false principle in such forthright fashion that I had naturally to expect attacks from all sides, and what is more, attacks of various kinds, since I was well aware that I had failed to please any of the parties demanding to be heard. The clergy was surely going to be displeased. Yet even the secular authorities, should they find it necessary to argue, were bound to oppose me, for the abolition of ecclesiastical power does not fully serve their purposes; all that suits them is Hobbes' system, which takes the incense from the altar and burns it for their glory. Moreover, the idea that it was Christianity that first made commandments and laws out of matters of doctrine and belief—an idea that is to me self-

evident—must of necessity somewhat upset many a system; and my notions about Judaism can, in fact, satisfy neither the orthodox nor the heterodox.

I took it for granted, therefore, that I would find most opinions opposed to me. Hence I wished to avoid all private controversy so as not to waste too much time and energy over this matter. I also desired to see the controversial points publicly investigated in order to enable the public to share in the discussion. For it seemed to me that the subject, however deficient in practical value at the moment, nevertheless has a useful aspect, especially in our times.

Impressive though these reasons are, they are not entirely convincing. One suspects that there were deeper motivations for Mendelssohn's reluctance to discuss the *Jerusalem*. Did he perhaps sense that the views he had expressed in this work were in the final analysis held together less by the force of incontestable logic than by a concatenation of personal convictions and loyalties?[22]

Section One of the *Jerusalem* seeks to clarify the concepts of "state and religion" or, as the draft had put it, of "church and state." The terms "church" and "religion" are used as synonyms in both the draft and the book. Sometimes they are replaced, in the book, by a third term: "religious society." It was this indiscriminate use of the three terms that permitted Mendelssohn to make some of his most radical statements about the limited rights of the church, and his contemporary critics were not slow in blaming them on the strange shifts in his terminology. The problem of church (religion, religious society) versus state did not exist so long as there was a Church (with a capital C) endowed with undisputed authority in the Western world. In pre-Reformation times, Mendelssohn pointed out, the "despotism" of the Roman Catholic Church secured "perfect peace," albeit "that dreadful calm that, in Montesquieu's phrase,[23] prevails during the evening in a fortress expecting to be taken by assault during the night." Without hesitation, Mendelssohn applied Montesquieu's characterization of "the principle of despotic governance" as tranquillity achieved by fear to the Church of Rome and the states submitting to its rule.[24] The Reformation had abolished churchly despotism and aroused a sense of freedom but had as yet been unable to establish recognized borderlines between state and religion. The trouble was that one still pretended to possess independent churches with some form of constitution, though one no longer recognized a supreme pontiff.

Mendelssohn detected this basic inconsistency even in the more recent textbooks of ecclesiastical law.[25] The textbooks he had in mind were most probably those expounding the theory of collegianism, which divested the church of its character as a divinely founded body and considered it, in analogy to the state, as a free association of like-minded individuals, as a collegium established by contract.

This theory goes back to Hugo Grotius (1583–1645) and Samuel Pufendorf (1632–1694) but was developed and designated "collegianism" by

Christian M. Pfaff of Tübingen in his *Academic Addresses on Ecclesiastical Law* (1742). J. H. Boehmer's monumental *Jus ecclesiasticum Protestantium*[26] reflected the fundamental outlook of collegianism, as did also Canz' *Disciplinae morales omnes*, from which Mendelssohn made excerpts in preparation for writing the *Jerusalem*.[27] One of the excerpts reads: "The right [*facultas*] belonging to the prince to take care lest the state be injured by the institutions of the church is called right of majesty [*jus majestatis*]. To the contrary, the right belonging to the church to direct everything appertaining to it so as to preserve [public] order is called *jus collegiale*."[28] Mendelssohn made a note of Canz' demand upon the church to share in the responsibility for seeing to it that "the three truly illustrious rights (the *jus collegiae*, the *jus majestatis*, and the right of conscience)" be brought into harmony with each other. On the other hand, he discovered an inconsistency in Canz' provisions for the treatment of dissidents: while they are not to be deprived of their civil rights, they have to forgo the ecclesiastical rights enjoyed by the members of the church.[29] As we know, this position was strongly contested by Mendelssohn, and his criticism of Canz is a good illustration of what he meant when he accused the textbooks on ecclesiastical law of clinging to the pretense that there still existed a Church or churches endowed with compulsory rights. Yet while he rejected the ecclesiastical claims that were kept on the agenda, he tacitly adopted the fundamental tenet of collegianism, namely, the view that the churches were freely established religious associations.[30] What he strenuously denied was the contractual origin of religious societies. Only the state had come into being as a result of a social contract. From this basic difference Mendelssohn derived the essentials of his theory of state and church, civil and religious society. Everything depended therefore, he insisted, on a clear understanding of what was implied in the concept of the social contract.

According to Hobbes' *Leviathan*, the social contract brought an end to man's natural state of anarchy in which there was a war of all against all. To secure peace and order man surrendered all his rights to the sovereign, the absolute ruler who demanded conformity to his will even in matters of religion, insofar as external worship was concerned. Only private interior thoughts and modes of worship remained inviolate.[31] Mendelssohn denied Hobbes' assumption that in the state of nature man was bereft of all morality and that only the social contract established and secured it. If it were true that natural man was under no moral obligation, what could prevent him from breaking contracts at any time, when he had the physical power to do so with impunity? The validity of contracts[32] presupposed a moral duty preceding all agreement, i.e., a natural obligation to abide by contracts.[33] Mendelssohn believed that he had found additional evidence of an implied admission on Hobbes' part that even natural man was not devoid of morality.[34] He underestimated, however, the force of Hobbes' thesis that it was the fear of a relapse into a state of anarchy, not any moral principle, that constituted the validity of contracts and set certain bounds to monarchical rule. What Mendelssohn dreaded most was the justification of despotism in matters civil and religious that was the raison d'être of Hobbes' theory.[35]

The complete freedom of public worship as Mendelssohn envisaged it for all religions in the state was precluded, however, not only by Hobbes' doctrine but also by the teachings of Spinoza, Rousseau, and others.[36] All these thinkers were unanimous, albeit on different theoretical grounds, in holding that only interior worship as a matter of conscience was free. Mendelssohn probably saw no need to discuss the others beside Hobbes who held this intolerant view. That he was familiar with both Spinoza's *Tractatus Theologico-Politicus* and Rousseau's *Du Contrat Social* can hardly be doubted. The latter work may have provided Mendelssohn with his notion of the inseparability of ecclesiastical sanctions and civil disadvantages.[37] The influence of the *Tractatus* on Mendelssohn, most pronounced in the second section, was also not inconsiderable in the first.[38] So far as his theory of state and religion was concerned, it had to be based on premises different from those used by any of the political philosophers mentioned. Nor was Locke of much use to him, though Locke's advocacy of the separation of state and religion seemed highly commendable. Locke's neat demarcation of the "commonwealth" as "a society of men constituted only for the procuring, preserving, and advancing their own civil interests" from the church as "a voluntary society of men" devoted to "the public worshipping of God in such a manner as they judge acceptable to Him, and effectual to the salvation of their souls"[39] was in Mendelssohn's view no safeguard against intolerance. For if the state concerned itself exclusively with the temporal welfare of its citizens and left their eternal felicity to the church, it was inevitable that the church, being in charge of men's ultimate vocation, would claim superiority and would, in cases of colliding duties, assert its higher authority. Mendelssohn quoted the famous work *De Romano pontifico* by Robert Cardinal Bellarmine,[40] which had vindicated to the pope ("at least indirectly") jurisdiction over everything temporal in order thereby to advance the spiritual. All objections that had been raised against the cardinal's "fallacious arguments," Mendelssohn declared, missed the point once the state relinquished responsibility for the spiritual welfare of its citizens.[41]

Locke's theory, Mendelssohn suggested, suffered from yet another shortcoming. It was neither true nor in man's best interest to distinguish so sharply between the temporal and the eternal. "Eternity can, in fact, never be man's portion; his 'eternity' is merely an infinitely prolonged temporality. His temporality never ceases; it is an integral and essential part of his continuity."[42] Mendelssohn had expressed this idea as early as 1755, and again in his *Phaedon*.[43] In addition to these early statements of a metaphysical character, he had also stressed, from a practical point of view, the danger inherent in upholding a sharp dichotomy between the temporal and eternal life of man. "If I may quote myself here: 'On the dark path man has to travel here below, he is granted just as much light as he needs for taking the next steps. More would only blind him, and any lateral light would merely confuse him.' "⁴⁴ The passage quoted was meant to reaffirm Abbt's confident view that, despite the darkness in which man's exit from this life into the next is shrouded, there was still enough light for the path he had to travel on this earth.⁴⁵

Mendelssohn's *Notes to Abbt's Friendly Correspondence*, which contains this passage, had appeared early in 1782, and Hennings had shown himself deeply affected by the work. In an undated letter eighteen pages long, to which Mendelssohn replied on June 25, 1782,⁴⁶ Hennings had asked for the privilege of continuing the debate by "walking in the *umbra cogitationis* of your late friend," and he had cited the very passage that Mendelssohn himself quoted a few months later when writing the *Jerusalem*. What he meant to assert was the need to concentrate on the tasks of this world rather than to fix one's gaze upon life in the next. It seemed to him that Locke's radical separation of the temporal and the eternal represented a contrary viewpoint, one that encouraged men to neglect their duties as citizens on earth "in the hope of thereby becoming better citizens of heaven." Rousseau, rather outspokenly, had voiced the fear that a truly good Christian might lose all interest in the mundane affairs of state, believing that it was only life eternal that mattered.⁴⁷ Against such undue emphasis on the world-to-come Mendelssohn illustrated his viewpoint by a well-known rabbinic saying (*Abot* 4:12), which he paraphrased as follows: "This life is a vestibule in which we have to conduct ourselves in the way in which we want to appear in the innermost chamber." His objections to Locke foreshadow his own theory, which advocates anything but an absolute separation of state and religion.

Mendelssohn set the stage for his intricate discussion of the juridical concepts underlying his theory by first outlining his ideas about the relationship between church and state. It is here that his opposition to Locke can be seen most clearly. The common welfare for the sake of which man associates with his peers comprises spiritual as well as temporal concerns, both of which spring from a sense of duty and are, for this reason, inseparable. What caused man to abandon the state of loneliness and to enter into association with others was his awareness of the impossibility of fulfilling his various duties (viz., those toward himself, his God, and his fellow-men) so long as he lived in isolation. The happiness that he obtains as a result of doing his duty is the very opposite of his wretchedness before he became a member of society. Mendelssohn thus considered the origin of society to lie in a moral necessity or sense of duty inherent in the very nature of man. The term "social contract" is not mentioned by him in this particular context. Society, it seems, is considered to be the matrix of both state and church, and in his view it is only the state, as we shall see later, that is based on a social contract.

The bifurcation of society into state and religion is explained in the following way. For the fulfilment of our duties two things are required: action (*Handlung*) and the appropriate sentiment (*Gesinnung*). *Handlung* carries into effect what duty demands; *Gesinnung* ensures that the action is motivated by right-mindedness. Society will live up to its purpose if it creates the institutions needed to direct actions that serve the common good and instil into people's minds such sentiments and convictions as will lead to proper actions. The responsibility for ensuring that beneficial actions are performed rests with the governing body of society, and the formation of good character as a source of lawful deeds is the business of the educational agencies of society. Both institutions belong to the state, and a state will be the happier if it manages to govern the nation through the impact of education, without having to use force for the promotion of the common weal.

Man's education comprises, however, not merely the cultivation of his interhuman relationships. It extends also to the development of his relation to God. The type of "public institution" designed to educate man in this respect is called by Mendelssohn a "church," no matter whether it belongs to Christians, Jews, Muslims, heretics, or dissidents.[48] The state has no interest in religion insofar as theological tenets are concerned, but it is vitally interested insofar as religion teaches morality and social conduct. If the nation is to be, ideally, governed by the inculcation of moral principles, the church will prove an invaluable asset to the state. Since, according to an old theory of Mendelssohn's,[49] moral convictions need powerful support of an emotive kind to become truly effective, the importance of religion cannot be gainsaid. It provides "authority and example" for the strengthening and stimulation of ethical maxims.[50] It is in this area, Mendelssohn said, that

> religion can come to the assistance of the state and the church can become the support of civic welfare. The task of religion is to convince people, with all the emphasis at its command, of the truth of noble-minded principles and sentiments; to show them that duties toward men are also duties toward God and cannot be violated without incurring the deepest misery; that serving the state is a true service of God; that law and justice are commandments of God; that charity is his most sacred will; and that the true acknowledgment of the Creator cannot leave even a residue of hatred in the human soul. To teach this is the business, duty, and vocation of religion; to preach this is the business, duty, and vocation of its ministers. How was it possible, then, that men ever permitted religion to teach, and its ministers to preach, exactly the opposite?[51]

By emphasizing moral teachings presumed to be common to the various religions Mendelssohn found a way of integrating the church into the state's sphere of interest without permitting any interference by the state in the affairs of the church. Religion retains its autonomy and at the same time becomes a pillar of the state. This theory avoids the pitfalls of both Locke's radical separation of the two societies and the complete subordination of the church to the state advocated by Hobbes and Spinoza. What Mendelssohn took over from Locke was the postulate of a completely free and uncontrolled worship, and what he shared with Hobbes and Spinoza was the inclusion of religion in the state's sphere of interest.[52] He also agreed with the commonly accepted notion that the social contract entitled the state to the use of coercive power to produce right action. He saw in this right of law enforcement "the dividing line," as his draft had put it, between church and state: "The state will . . . be content with mechanical deeds—with works without spirit, with conformity of action without concurrence in thought. Even though a person may have no regard for laws, he must obey them as soon as they have been enacted. . . . Not so with religion. It recognizes no act not founded on sentiment, no work without spirit, no conformity in deed without concurrence in the mind. Religious actions without religious thoughts are mere puppetry,[53] not service of God. . . . The state gives orders and coerces; religion teaches and persuades. The state issues laws; religion issues commandments. The state possesses physical power and uses it when necessary; the power of religion is love and charity."[54]

Mendelssohn expressed this difference between church and state in the following juridical terms: "Civil society, viewed as a moral person, has the right of coercion; in fact, it has secured this right through the social contract. Religious society neither demands the right of coercion nor can it possibly obtain it by any conceivable contract. The state possesses perfect rights, the church, imperfect rights."[55] By using the technical terms "perfect rights" and "imperfect rights" Mendelssohn provided the cue for the next stage of his discussion, in which he sought to establish his political theory upon the "first principles" of natural law. In the words of the reviewer in the *Göttingische Anzeigen*,[56] he performed his task "with a thoroughness and lucidity not readily to be found elsewhere." He was well prepared for it. In his prize-essay of 1764 he had already used the definition of a "right" that he used here.[57] How well he had studied Wolff's works on natural law[58] is attested by Feder's letter of July 8, 1774.[59] His 1781 fragment "on perfect and imperfect rights and duties" had been the forerunner of the discussion of the subject in the preface to *Manasseh Ben Israel*,[60] and in the summer of 1782 he had debated the relevant issues with Klein;[61] Garve's translation and annotation of Adam Ferguson's *Institutes of Moral Philosophy*[62] had figured largely in their conversations.

Mendelssohn contrasts man's legal position in the state of nature and his legal position after the social contract is established. In so doing he does not wish to imply that there ever was a stage in human history during which man actually lived in a pure state of nature. As early as 1775, and later in 1767, he had interpreted Rousseau's portrayal of such a stage as a mere "abstraction" or, as one might say, a kind of philosophical myth intended to describe man's essential nature.[63] We have already noted that in Mendelssohn's view "natural man" is not destitute of morality, as Hobbes had asserted. Hobbes' statement that according to natural law everybody had a right to everything, right being nothing but might, had been attacked by Richard Cumberland as absurd, for if it were true, the law of nature would be self-contradictory.[64] In his prize-essay[65] Mendelssohn had recalled Cumberland's critique of Hobbes, and the *Jerusalem* echoes the same argument:[66] "If I have a right to do something, my fellowman cannot have the right to prevent me from doing it, for otherwise the same action would be morally possible and impossible at the same time." Hobbes had also been criticized by Leibniz for defining the justice of God as his power to dispense curse and blessing and for seeing in God's goodness only a part of his power to ingratiate himself with his creatures. According to Leibniz, the justice of God and man alike conforms to "the eternal laws of wisdom and goodness."[67] Mendelssohn had quoted this definition of justice in his prize-essay,[68] and said, likewise, in our passage in the *Jerusalem:*[69] "Wisdom, coupled with goodness, is called justice." What then is man's position according to natural law? He has a moral right to use certain goods for the promotion of his happiness, provided this right is just—provided, that is, that it does not contradict "the laws of wisdom and goodness."

Mendelssohn, unlike Wolff, assumed that even in the state of nature man has an exclusive right to goods that he produces or improves through the use of his capacities and that become his private property thereby.[70] However, man has not merely rights but also duties, i.e., obligations to do what the laws of wisdom and goodness demand and to refrain from doing what contravenes them. There are perfect and imperfect rights as well as duties. If a right or a duty is of such a nature that it may be exacted by force, it is a compulsory (perfect) right or duty. On the other hand, if a right is only in the nature of a claim directed to another person's goodwill (such as asking for charity), it is an imperfect right; and a mere duty of conscience, being nonenforceable, is an imperfect duty. Omitting to fulfil a compulsory duty is tantamount to injustice, but noncompliance with a duty of conscience is merely unfair.[71]

Having clarified these elementary concepts, Mendelssohn continues: "Man cannot be happy without beneficence, whether it be passive, through receiving it, or active, through extending it. He cannot attain perfection except through mutual assistance, through reciprocity of service, through active and passive connection with his fellowman."[72] Man is therefore obligated to use for the benefit of his fellowmen as much of his property as he can spare without detriment to his own well-being. Conversely, he may expect to be supported by others, should he find himself in need of help. In the state of nature it is left entirely to the individual's discretion to decide the amount, the timing, and the nature of his benefactions. There may be competing claims on his beneficence, and seeing a person's means are limited and not all claims can be satisfied, the benefactor must have the choice in the matter. "Hence, in the state of nature I—and I alone—am entitled to decide whether, to what extent, when, to whose benefit, and under what conditions I am obliged to practice benevolence. In the state of nature I can at no time be compelled to bestow benefits. My duty to do so is a mere duty of conscience, concerning which I am not beholden to anyone to render an account, just as my right to the beneficence of others is merely a right to petition and may be rejected."[73] It follows that in the state of nature all *positive* duties are nonenforceable, imperfect duties, just as positive rights are merely imperfect rights. In the natural state only duties and rights of omission are perfect: I am perfectly (i.e., absolutely and unconditionally) obliged *not* to injure anyone, and I am just as perfectly empowered to prevent anyone from injuring me.[74]

In making these distinctions Mendelssohn followed closely the precedent set by Garve's notes on Ferguson, in which exactly the same terms and ideas, including the reference to charity, occur.[75] He added, however, one particular nuance that would be of crucial importance in his subsequent discussion of the nature of the social contract: he defined the individual person's right to decide on whom, when, and how to bestow his beneficence as a right to "settle cases of collision." This term, "collision," crops up again and again,[76] and it becomes a key term in his thinking. It expresses the idea that, in the state of nature, it is the prerogative of the individual to make his decision when a conflict of duties of conscience arises. The term implies, furthermore, that it is precisely through situations of moral conflict that man's freedom can assert itself. Where there is no conflict ("collision") of duties, beneficence is merely a matter of moral impulse. In the state of nature, Mendelssohn sums up,[77] man is the master of all that is his, and he alone has the right to decide how he is to dispose, for the benefit of others, what goods he can spare. His fellowmen have merely an imperfect right to his surplus goods. They have the right to solicit them, while he, as the absolute master, is bound in conscience to set aside a portion of his goods for the benefit of others. At times he may even be obliged to sacrifice to others what he has set aside for his own use, insofar as the practice of beneficence makes one happier than selfishness does—provided this sacrifice is made voluntarily and spontaneously.

This situation, which is characteristic of man's natural state, changes if a contract is concluded that transfers the ownership of certain goods to another person—if, by means of a freely entered contract, one surrenders his right to the goods concerned. In this case, one's fellowman's imperfect right to the goods has become a perfect right. But it is precisely one's initial freedom to dispose of one's goods as one sees fit that makes such a contract valid and binding. Having been originally the exclusive owner of the right to dispose of the goods, one can cede this right to another, and one's decision to do so, if clearly indicated by a promise and accepted by the other party, must be legally binding. A contract has to be kept not merely because a breach of faith would be immoral (as Ferguson and Garve had argued) but also, and primarily, because a person's freedom to use his goods according to his discretion would be nullified if the contract were held to be devoid of *legal* force.

Mendelssohn acknowledged his indebtedness to Ernst Ferdinand Klein, who had suggested this "simple and fruitful theory of contracts." He objected to Ferguson and Garve on the ground that according to their theory contracts would be nonenforceable, since they implied only duties of conscience. It was only through deriving the validity of contracts "from the nature of man's freedom" (as Mendelssohn succinctly put it in a letter to Herz Homberg)[78] that one could satisfactorily explain how contracts transformed duties of conscience (imperfect duties) into compulsory (perfect) duties.[79]

By concluding contracts, Mendelssohn pointed out, man left his natural state and entered into a state of social relationships. His own nature urged him to do this so as to change his undecided, unsettled rights and duties into something more settled and decided. Marriage contracts obviously reflected such a desire for stable relations.[80] The social contract was not essentially different from all other privately concluded agreements. Though the right to decide on the merits of competing claims and to dispense his goods rested with the individual, it seemed advisable to renounce the right of autonomous decision by means of a social contract, that is, by a legal agreement specifying what portion of his rights a person could be compelled to give up for the good of society. By virtue of the social contract a certain part of the person's duties of conscience became compulsory duties that were enforceable by the state.[81] Mendelssohn had, in a previous passage,[82] entered a plea that the state not take over all humanitarian tasks, including charity, but leave as wide a margin as possible for private agencies and initiatives: "Man becomes conscious of his worth only when he himself performs charitable acts. . . . If he gives only because he *must,* he will be conscious only of his fetters." There was also room for freedom and the exercise of ethical motivation in the very fulfilment of one's compulsory duties: by acting from a sense of civic responsibility, one was not merely externally complying with one's duties but also following the interior dictates of one's conscience. If inner springs of action were missing and duty remained unfulfilled, the state had the right to compel action. This right derived from the social contract that had come into being either by tacit agreement or, in rare cases, by explicit compacts.[83]

This right did not apply, however, to religion. The notion of a surrender of one's natural prerogative to decide in cases of competing claims explained how the social contract arose. The coercive power of the state was the corollary of the social contract. In the case of religion or church there could be no right to coercion because the raison d'être for a social contract was lacking. The idea of a transference of the right to settle conflicting claims to one's benevolence had simply no place where religion was concerned. Nor could a conflict of duties vis-à-vis God be conceived, the settling of which was to be passed on to the church. For in Mendelssohn's view there existed no specific "duties" toward God, just as God could not be said to receive any benefits from man:

God is not a being who needs our good will, demands our assistance, or claims any of our rights for his use. Nor can his rights ever collide or be confused with ours. False notions of this kind are the result of the fact that duties have been divided into those toward God and those toward man, a kind of division that is an awkward one in certain respects. The parallel has been extended too far by juxtaposing the duties toward God and those toward man. It has been assumed that just as we make sacrifices for the benefit of our neighbor in compliance with duty, we must do the same out of a sense of duty toward God. Men demand service, so does God. My duty toward myself may conflict with my duty toward my neighbor; in the same way my duty toward myself may conflict with my duty toward God. . . .

In reality, there is no subdivision in the system of human duties that could be entitled "Duties Toward God."[84] *All* of man's duties are obligations to God. Some of them concern us, others our fellowmen. . . . Nor does religion, the relation between God and man, demand any other duties [than those demanded by reason]; religion merely gives solemn sanction to those duties and obligations.[85]

From these "maxims" Mendelssohn drew the conclusion that the church had no claim upon our property and possessions, that it could not demand contributions and renunciation of rights, and that there could never be a case of collision between membership in the church and citizenship. It followed that there was no place for a contract between church and citizen, for all contracts presupposed cases of collision that had to be settled.[86] What Mendelssohn denied were the claims, the demands, the coercive powers of the church, not the right of the church to accept voluntary contributions and to own property. He said distinctly: "No man-made contracts could, therefore, have endowed the church with a right to property and possessions, since by its very nature it cannot advance such claims or have an imperfect right [which could become a perfect, compulsory right through a contract]. The church can never acquire the right to use coercion, nor can its members be compelled to submit to coercion by the church."[87]

Those among his critics who defended the right of the church to own property and to lay down commonly agreed rules of membership[88] misjudged Mendelssohn's real intent. The thrust of his argument was his denial of any legitimate coercive power to the church. He conceived the possibility, however, of a church functioning, and perhaps ideally so, without owning property. In his view there was no need for any funds to be owned by a religious society since "the church must not remunerate nor must religion buy anything, pay anything, give any wages." Teaching virtue and preaching the fear of God were activities incompatible with accepting of a salary for so doing. Those who devoted themselves to these noble tasks could expect at most some compensation for their time, but the payment of such compensation was the business of the state, not of the church.[89] It was this proposition that perplexed and annoyed many critics, who saw nothing degrading in the remuneration of ministers of religion and considered Mendelssohn's distinction between a salary and compensation for time lost to be mere sophistry.[90] As Michaelis rightly pointed out in his review,[91] Mendelssohn's advocacy of mere compensatory payment for the time spent in religious teaching reflected a rabbinic concept.[92] This concept had arisen from the notion that no price could be charged for the teaching of Tora.[93] Mendelssohn actually quoted the biblical passage (Deut. 4:5) from which the rabbis inferred this.[94] He thus found in Jewish tradition support for his theory that religious services could not be "bought, hired, or paid for."

Having established the "dividing lines" between state and church, Mendelssohn drew yet another important conclusion from the basic concepts he had outlined. The right to use coercion, which the state has obtained through the social contract, applies to actions only. So far as sentiments and convictions are concerned, neither church nor state possesses such a right. They both can instruct, teach, encourage, and suggest,[95] but neither may reward or punish, employ force, or use bribery to make a man subscribe to certain ideas or beliefs *(Gesinnungen)*. Mendelssohn did not merely plead for "freedom of thought" (as Hobbes, Spinoza and Locke had done before him); he repudiated the right of the state to give *any* favorable treatment to a particular religion. He described such favoritism as an "indirect bribe" and every curtailment of the rights of dissidents as an "indirect punishment."

Mendelssohn also gave a novel turn to the argument for freedom of thought. Locke had stated that "no man can, if he would, conform his faith to the dictates of another,"[96] and Spinoza, similarly, had declared that "no one can transfer to another his natural right or his faculty to think freely."[97] Mendelssohn wrote: "No contract could have given the state the least right to use coercion in matters of sentiments and convictions [*Gesinnungen*]. Altogether, *Gesinnungen* can be neither swayed by benevolence nor compelled by force. I cannot renounce any of my ideas or beliefs out of love for my neighbor, nor can I relinquish and cede to him any part of my faculty of judgment out of benevolence. By the same token, I must not arrogate to myself a right over his ideas or beliefs, nor can I acquire it in any way. The right to our own ideas or beliefs is inalienable and cannot be transferred from person to person."[98] In other words, there are no imperfect duties or rights insofar as sentiments or convictions are concerned. In the state of nature no one is obliged to sacrifice any of his ideas for the benefit of others, nor has anyone the right even to ask for such a sacrifice. There is therefore nothing that the social contract could have surrendered so as to make it into a compulsory duty or right.

All religions, therefore, including heretical faiths, have an equal right to toleration. This doctrine had already been enunciated by Locke.[99] Yet Locke had excluded atheists, on the theory that "promises, covenants, and oaths, which are the bonds of human society, can have no hold upon an atheist."[100] The question of whether atheism and morality could go together had been a major topic of debate for some time past. Bayle and Toland, taking their cue from Plutarch, had argued that superstition and idolatry were far more injurious to morality than atheism, but Mendelssohn, in a few notes on Bayle's *Pensées diverses,* had strenuously contested this view.[101] In the *Jerusalem* he wrote: "I grant that the state must be vigilant [literally: see to it from afar], so that no doctrines will be spread that are detrimental to public welfare or that, like atheism or Epicureanism, might undermine the happiness of society. Let Plutarch and Bayle question whether a state might not be better off with atheism than with super-stition. . . . What they are doing is basically not different from what a man does when he examines whether a slow fever is more fatal than a sudden one."[102] Mendelssohn's critics pointed out that by conceding to the state the right to prevent, albeit by the most judicious indirect means, the spread of certain ideas, he had abandoned his fundamental thesis, which demanded perfect freedom of thought.[103] However, this objection ignores the fact that Mendelssohn did not vindicate to the state any right of *coercion* in respect of atheists; that he included atheists among the beneficiaries of toleration; and that he considered vigilance of the kind described not as a right but as a duty flowing from the very purpose of the state as guardian of the public good. The same consideration that prompted him to integrate religion into the sphere of the state's interests also caused him to limit tolerance insofar as atheism was concerned.[104]

In this connection Mendelssohn permitted himself a trenchant attack on the validity of a practice that was then prevalent in most Lutheran principalities in Germany. By order of the state, ministers of religion had to testify under oath that they believed in the dogmas ("symbols") laid down in the "symbolic books" and collected in the *Konkordienbuch* (Dresden, 1580). Similarly, the clergy of the Anglican Church had to subscribe to certain articles of faith. Nicolai, in his famous novel *The Life and Opinions of Herr Magister Sebaldus Nothanker* (1773–1776),[105] had satirized the dire consequences that followed from this practice in Germany. Mendelssohn's objections were spelled out in philosophical terms. Basic principles common to all religions required no confirmation by oaths, he declared, and specific doctrines of a particular religion were of no concern to the state, since they had no bearing on the moral well-being of society. Hence the state had no right to intrude upon a man's conscience and to compel him to confessions unrelated to the public good. Moreover, it was a mistake to assume that opinions could be subscribed to under oath. Quite often people understood different things by the same words, and many a dispute revealed itself in the end as having been due to talking at cross-purposes (as Men-delssohn used to say, a mere *Wortstreit*). How then could it be considered legitimate to demand an oath testifying to so personal and elusive a thing as an opinion? It was in order to impose an oath when some fact of a tangible nature had to be established before a court. It was different in the case of matters of belief. Even granting that a good legal case could be made for requesting a clergyman to take an oath of office, should one not consider the results of such procedure: "Count the bishops sitting in the Upper House, count all the truly great men who hold high office and occupy positions of honor in England but can no longer unconditionally accept the Thirty-nine Articles that they had initially affirmed under oath. Count them all—and then tell me that it is not feasible to grant civil rights to my oppressed nation because so many among it have little regard for an oath! Alas, may God protect my heart from misanthropic thoughts."[106]

It is easy to surmise that the whole passage about oaths was brought in chiefly for the purpose of leading up to this final remark. We remember that the draft contained a biting reference to the Thirty-nine Articles as a "yoke in spirit and truth." Now they are cited for a different purpose. Mendelssohn had just worked, jointly with Klein, on proposals for a reform in Jewish oath-taking procedures. He had been forcibly reminded of the aspersions cast on Jewish credibility. It was impossible not to reflect, at the same time, on the many breaches of faith arising from Christian oaths attesting to beliefs. Yet it might have been wiser for Mendelssohn to have resisted the temptation to enter this tendentious comparison and to make reference to the Anglican bishops in particular, for his powerful critic Michaelis immediately took up the cudgels for the bishops. In his review he censured Mendelssohn severely,[107] and he followed the matter up in a subsequent postscript:[108] His—Michaelis'—personal inquiry of a highly placed English clergyman (who wanted to remain anonymous lest mention of his name be unpleasant to Mendelssohn)[109] had established that none of the Anglican clergy were sworn to the Thirty-nine Articles; that all "inferior clergymen" merely subscribed to them and that bishops were neither sworn nor subscribed; that it might be affirmed with a good conscience that there were no dissidents among the bishops; and that Mr. Mendelssohn might have been misled by a recently published anonymous pamphlet, "when some of the clergy were uneasy under their subscriptions." The Englishman quoted by Michaelis had concluded his statement with this remark: "But what shall we think of Mr. Mendelssohn, who upon so slight a ground, if he had even that slight ground, ventures to stigmatize the whole Bench of Bishops, of whom he probably knows *not one* as PERJU-RED men?"

When Michaelis announced in his review that he was planning to make a personal inquiry into this matter, Mendelssohn became somewhat alarmed. On November 12, 1783, he sent a note to Nicolai:[110] "Dearest Friend! Where could I possibly find the Thirty-nine Articles of the English church and the form that its clergy is expected to sign? You would greatly oblige me, were you to supply me with these. *Ritter* Michaelis wants to deal me a blow, which I must evade. Yet first I have to get some more precise information about the true situation." The information was furnished by the English clergyman's letter, which Michaelis still managed to publish in the 1783 volume of his journal,[111] whereupon Mendelssohn issued a long article explaining the points he had made. The article appeared in the *Berlinische Monatsschrift* (January, 1784), and he sent one of the few reprints he had ordered to Elise Reimarus. It offered an extremely effective reply. He had never accused even a single Anglican of perjury but had merely pointed out that oaths of the kind described tended to bring the practice of oath-taking into general disrepute; that he could not see any real difference between subscribing and being sworn; etc. He repudiated, in particular, Michaelis' epilogue to the postscript, in which some vile remark about oaths by Jews had been made.[112]

In the final part of the first section Mendelssohn reaffirmed, in the most solemn way, the stand he had taken in the preface to *Manasseh Ben Israel* against excommunication and all forms of coercion by the church. In so doing he drew an ideal picture of religion, one that he did not identify with any existing faith or religious community but that was supposed to represent "divine religion" *(die göttliche Religion)* or natural religion as the archetype, as it were, inherent in all positive faiths as their normative essence. In this sense it was possible to speak of "religion" not merely as an abstract concept or pure idea but also as a "moral person" distinct from the state (which was also a moral person). The basic distinction between these two entities was now summed up:[113]

> Divine religion . . . does not prod men with an iron rod; it guides them "with bands of love."[114] It draws no avenging sword, dispenses no wordly goods, arrogates unto itself no right to earthly possessions, and usurps no external power over any person's mind. Its sole weapons are reason and persuasion; its strength is the divine power of truth. The punishments it threatens, as well as the reward it promises, are but manifestations of love—salutary and beneficial to the person who receives them. It is by these signs that I recognize you, daughter of God, religion, who alone, in truth, are all-saving on earth as well as in heaven!

Here the concept of natural religion was stated with a fervor probably unmatched by any other work of the Enlightenment. The treatise might have ended on this note, with nothing further needing to be said, had not Mendelssohn been faced with the particular task of replying to the "Searcher for Light and Right."

II

Section Two begins with a rapid survey of the reaction that the disavowal of all religious coercion in the *Manasseh* preface had produced. Mendelssohn expressed "true joy" at the "seriousness and sincerity" with which "some worthy members of the local clergy" had responded to it.[1] Others, while detecting no flaw in his arguments, had been startled by his conclusions. The reviewer for the *Göttingische Anzeigen*, Michaelis, had declared:[2] "All of this is new and harsh. Where first principles are negated, all discussion has come to an end." By "first principles" Michaelis had meant the validity of ecclesiastical law and the right of the state to confer certain privileges upon adherents of certain faiths. But in Mendelssohn's view it was precisely the old established axiomatic rules that needed investigating. He was quite conscious of the fact that he had broken new ground. He knew of no author, he said, who had ever examined the legitimacy of ecclesiastical law and the right of excommunication. One generally assumed that there was such a thing as a *jus circa sacra* ("a right appertaining to holy things") and limited one's discussion to the question of whom it should be entrusted to, the church or the state. But what if the meteor that everybody was busy trying to locate did not exist at all? Pythagoras' golden thigh was a matter of much speculation among members of his school; should they not have asked, first, whether this legendary thing actually existed?[3]

Following these initial remarks—a kind of preliminary canter—Mendelssohn approached his real task: "Let me now proceed to a far more important objection that has been raised against me and is the principal reason for this essay." An anonymous author had written a tract *The Searching for Light and Right,* addressed to him, in which "the sacred authority of the Mosaic religion that I profess" was said to contradict the views expressed in the preface to *Manasseh Ben Israel.* In this case, too, no attempt had been made actually to refute his arguments. Mendelssohn thus characterized the pamphlet as an attempt, in the first place, to show that his thesis, no matter how rational it might be, was in flagrant contradiction to the Mosaic Law and could not for this reason be upheld by a loyal Jew. He candidly admitted:[4] "This objection cuts me to the heart." He could not deny, he said, that the picture that the Searcher had painted of Judaism corresponded, by and large, to the idea that many Jews did have of their religion. Should that idea indeed prove to be the authentic one, he would have no choice but to retract his statements and subordinate reason to the yoke of faith. But this would not do. Authority had the power to humble a man, but not to instruct him. Authority could suppress reason, but not shackle it. If the results of his reasoning were found to be clearly contradicted by the word of God, Mendelssohn might silence his reason. Yet in such an event his unrefuted arguments would continue to trouble his mind, turning into disquieting doubts and eventually giving rise to fervent prayer for illumination *(Erleuchtung).* He would cry out with the psalmist, "Lord, send me thy light, thy truth, that they may guide and bring me unto thy holy mountain, unto thy dwelling place" (Ps. 43:3).[5]

It comes as a surprise that Mendelssohn considered a prayer for illumination as a last resort, and one of his critics was quick to notice this seeming departure from his usual deprecation of all supernatural revelation of truth.[6] Mendelssohn did not actually utter this prayer, however, since he had not the slightest doubt that Judaism was essentially in harmony with reason, or as he put it later,[7] that "one truth cannot clash with another." What he emphatically rejected from the outset was the "offensive" accusation that it had been his "odious intention" to overthrow the religion that he professed and to renounce it covertly, if not overtly. He made the interesting statement: "Not everyone who holds a certain view is prepared to agree with every conclusion that may be drawn from it, no matter how correctly inferred. Imputations of this kind are hateful and lead only to bitterness and strife, by which truth rarely stands to gain anything." In other words, Mendelssohn, with his characteristic frankness, did not deny that some inconsistency might be discernible in his overall position, but he deplored the inquisitorial attitude that tried to pin a person down to all conceivable consequences that might follow from a particular view he held. Such inexorability *(Consequenzerey)*, he declared, was unbefitting scholars.[8]

Mendelssohn's reply to the Searcher (and Mörschel) had concerned itself so far with the assertion that his liberalism and the Jewish religion were irreconcilable. His answer had been that in his own search for "light and truth" (quoting Psalms) he would always strive to harmonize the two; that his personal concept of Judaism was different from that of his challenger (and, for that matter, from that of a great many fellow Jews); and that it had been utterly wrong to impute to him an open or tacit withdrawal from his religion. Yet the Searcher, he continued, had gone even further: he had suggested that a careful reading of the preface to *Manasseh Ben Israel* showed a definite tendency to come closer to the Christian faith. Mendelssohn cited at length the peroration addressed to him, characterizing it as "solemn and moving enough." We know from the draft quoted earlier what his initial reaction to this apostrophe had been, and how he had commented on the final passage quoting from St. John. In the published *Jerusalem* he deleted all traces of bitterness, but the ingenious reply already jotted down in the original draft was retained and stated in the most humorous and graceful way:[9] "Shall I, my dear one, take this step [of converting to Christianity] without first pondering whether it will really extricate me from the confusion in which you think I find myself? If it were true that the cornerstones of my house were so out of alignment that the entire building threatened to collapse, would I be acting wisely if I attempted to save my belongings by moving them from the lower to the upper floor? Would I be safer there? Now Christianity, as you know, is built upon Judaism and must necessarily collapse along with it. When you say that my conclusions undermine the foundations of Judaism and you offer me the safety of your upper floor, must I not suspect that you mock me? Surely the Christian who is seriously concerned with light and truth will not challenge the Jew to a fight when there seems to be a contradiction between one truth and another, between Scripture and reason. He will rather join him in an effort to discover the groundlessness of the contradiction. For this is their joint concern. The discussion of what divides them may be postponed until later."

Mendelssohn's meaning was clear and simple enough: if Judaism could be considered to be undermined by the disavowal of ecclesiastical law and power, what about Christianity? Kant would read too much into this passage. After describing it as a "very adroit way" of meeting the challenge of conversion, he went on to say that Mendelssohn's real intent was apparently as follows: "He meant to say: if you yourselves remove Judaism from your own religion, . . . we shall consider your proposal. (In fact, all that would then remain would be a purely moral religion, without any admixture of statutes.) By throwing off the yoke of external observances our burden is not made easier in the least if another [burden] is imposed on us instead, namely, that of articles of faith concerning a sacred history, which presses a conscientious person much harder."[10] Mendelssohn most certainly did *not* wish to imply that once Christians had divested themselves of Judaism, Jews would join them in a purely moral religion! It is amazing, however, to find that Kant almost paraphrased Mendelssohn's remark about the far heavier yoke of Christian dogma. Since Kant had not seen the unpublished draft in which that remark was made, the similarity must be considered a pure coincidence.

If he had wished to dodge the issue, Mendelssohn playfully continued, the simile of the two-storied building would have been the answer to the Searcher. Unfortunately, however, Herr Mörschel's postscript did not permit such an easy escape. With his keen eye, this kind-hearted letter writer had spotted the fact that Mendelssohn was neither a Jew nor a Christian but a "naturalist." Had he not spoken of pagans, Jews, Muslims, and adherents of natural religion in one breath—and asked tolerance for them all? "Reason's house of prayer" constituted another indictment, and the good man, though not desirous of converting him or anxious to see Christianity refuted and his own peace of mind disturbed, merely demanded a declaration as to where he, Mendelssohn, really stood. To ease the man's mind at the outset, Mendelssohn assured him that he had no intention of contesting the Christian religion and that he had at his disposal no secret documents that would throw an unexpected light on the origin of Christianity.[11] As for his own religious position, he had to admit that Mörschel was not entirely wrong in what he imputed to him. Here follows the famous passage in which Mendelssohn defined his concept of Judaism as a revealed legislation rather than a revealed religion:[12]

> It is true that I recognize no eternal truths other than those that are not only comprehensible to human reason but also demonstrable and verifiable by it. Yet Herr Mörschel is misled by a misconception of Judaism when he supposes that I cannot make such a statement without departing from the religion of my fathers. On the contrary, I consider this an essential aspect of the Jewish religion and believe that this doctrine constitutes a characteristic difference between Judaism and Christianity.
>
> To say it in one sentence: I believe that Judaism knows nothing of a revealed religion in the sense in which Christians understand this term. The Israelites possess a divine legislation—laws, commandments, ordinances, rules of life, instruction in the will of God as to how they should conduct themselves in order to attain temporal and eternal felicity. What was revealed to them through Moses were rules and precepts of this kind, not doctrines, saving truths, or universally valid propositions of reason. These the Eternal One reveals to us and all other men at

all times through the nature of things[13] but not through the spoken or written word [of revelation].

Mendelssohn thus completely identified the doctrinal part of Judaism and natural religion. Already in his Hebrew letter of July 22, 1771, addressed to Elkan Herz, he had said that all that Judaism added to natural religion was commandments, whereas Christianity added dogmas that contradicted reason.[14] In his answer to Lavater he had implied the same thing: Judaism was the religion of the Patriarchs (which he equated with natural law) plus laws given to the Jews alone in a special revelation. The Gentiles who adhered to natural religion required no revelation for their eternal happiness. For this reason Judaism was not concerned with proselytization.[15] In the "Counterreflections" he had been more explicit,[16] and in the *Jerusalem* he developed his doctrine with perfect clarity:[17] "I do not believe that human reason is incapable of perceiving those eternal truths that are indispensable to man's happiness and that God had therefore to reveal these truths in a supernatural way."

Mendelssohn offered two arguments in support of this statement. First, assuming that God's goodness revealed to man the eternal verities necessary for salvation, was God not sufficiently powerful or benign to endow man with the capacity to discover them for himself? Second, assuming that a supernatural revelation was indispensable for man's bliss in the hereafter, why was it granted only to a small portion of humanity? Why should the larger part of mankind have lived from time immemorial without the benefit of true revelation, and why should the two Indies have to wait until it pleased the Europeans to send missionaries? It was this moral argument that weighed most heavily with Mendelssohn, as his letter to Jacob Emden makes abundantly clear.[18] Zöllner's objection that the same question might be asked about Europe's preeminence in the sciences[19] was beside the point, for man's eternal felicity did not depend on scientific progress and no injustice on the part of God involving the ultimate good was here at issue.

Another critic[20] attacked not so much the arguments as the thesis itself: was it true that human reason, unaided by divine revelation, was able to discover such a truth as the unity of God, and even assuming that reason did possess this capacity, why could God not have chosen to reveal it at an early period before reason had sufficiently matured to arrive at the truth by its own efforts? This view, that reason and revelation propounded the same truth and that a revelation of rational truths in a popular form was necessary for the philosophically untutored, had long been in vogue, from medieval times down to the modern Enlightenment.[21] Mendelssohn had assailed the formidable phalanx of this tradition by his flat denial that it had been the purpose of revelation to disclose any truths; the sole concern of divine revelation, he had stated, was legislative. The argument that God might have deemed it necessary to reveal certain truths for the benefit of the unsophisticated rank and file did not impress him. He had no use for the medieval distinction between "esoteric" and "exoteric" truth in religion. One did not have to be a trained philosopher to attain eternal happiness. While demanding the strictest standards in science and metaphysics,[22] Mendelssohn was satisfied that in the sphere of religion the essential truths could be perceived by "sound common sense."[23] The same tendency that caused Rousseau to base religion on "sentiment" and Kant to anchor it in "morality" made Mendelssohn recognize common sense as sufficient for the apprehension of the truths necessary for man's eternal happiness.[24] He preferred the simple, unsophisticated man who heard and saw the all-pervading power of the deity "in every sunrise, in every rainfall, in every flower" and played no "deceptive game" with the term "nature," as an Epicurus or a Lucretius, a Helvétius or a Hume, did.[25] In Mendelssohn's view, man's moral conduct probably benefited as much from primitive notions about the deity as it did from more refined concepts.[26] The essential truths of religion having been available in all ages and at all levels of human development, there had been no need whatever for God to "reveal" them.

Nor could it have been possible, Mendelssohn contended, to convey such truths by means of a supernatural revelation unless man had already formed a conception of them. Assuming that God had wanted to reveal to the Israelites the truth of his existence and attributes, who would have been convinced of these eternal verities upon hearing them announced to the sound of thunder and to the blast of trumpets? "Surely not the unthinking, animal-like man whom his own reflections had not yet taught to acknowledge the existence of an invisible being that governs the visible world. The miraculous voice could not have infused any such concept into this kind of person and, consequently, could not have convinced him. Nor could it have convinced the sophist, whose ears are buzzing with so many doubts and brooding questions that he can no longer hear the voice of common sense. He demands rational proofs, not miracles."[27] This passage clearly reflected the way in which Spinoza had described the Sinaitic revelation in the *Tractatus Theologico-Politicus:*[28] "Although that Voice could not give any philosophical or mathematical certainty about God's existence, it was sufficient to inspire them with admiration for God as they had known him before [viz. by name only] and to rouse them to obedience; and the purpose of this spectacle was precisely this. For God did not want to teach the Israelites all the attributes of his essence—in fact, He then revealed none of his attributes—but He wished to break their stiff-neckedness and to lead them toward obedience. For this reason He impressed them not with arguments but with thunder and lightning." In a previous chapter Spinoza had pointed out that conviction could be obtained by rational arguments only and that hearing or repeating words affected the mind as little as the words of a parrot or automaton. He had advanced the notion, moreover, that the election of the Jewish people by God consisted merely in the establishment of a commonwealth through special laws revealed at Sinai,[29] and the statement that the "spectacle" at the mountain was meant to instil a sense of obedience in the people's minds becomes fully intelligible only if it is remembered that it was laws, not doctrines, that were revealed.

In interpreting the Sinaitic revelation as having commandments rather than eternal truths for its content, Mendelssohn was obviously following Spinoza's precedent. But he was far from adopting the corollaries of this theory as found in the *Tractatus*. Thus Mendelssohn refused to accept Spinoza's thesis that the purpose of the Mosaic legislation was purely temporal and political. In his view the laws were intimately related to the promotion of virtue and true opinions, and their ultimate aim was to guide the Jew to eternal felicity. Yet in limiting revelation to the legislative aspect he shared Spinoza's point of view:[30] "The voice that was heard at Sinai on that great day did not proclaim, 'I am the Eternal, thy God, the necessary, independent being, omnipotent and omniscient, who rewards men in a future life according to their deeds.' This is the universal religion of mankind, not [specifically] Judaism; and this kind of universal religion—without which man can become neither virtuous nor happy—was not and in fact could not have been revealed at Sinai." What the voice did proclaim were commandments, and they were introduced by a preamble that established the authority of the Lawgiver: "I am the Eternal One, thy God, who brought thee out of the land of Egypt, the house of bondage" (Exodus 20:2).

Elaborating traditional sources,[31] Mendelssohn described the first of the Ten Commandments as the statement of "a historical truth, on which this people's legislation was to be founded." By paraphrasing the terse language of Exodus 20:2 he unfolded the whole panorama of salvational history that culminated in the Sinaitic legislation: "I am the Eternal One, thy God, who made a covenant with thy fathers, Abraham, Isaac, and Jacob, and who swore unto them to raise a people from their seed unto Myself. The time for the fulfilment of this promise has finally come. To this end, I have redeemed you from the Egyptian slavery—redeemed you with unheard-of miracles and signs. I am your Redeemer, your Sovereign and King. I now make a covenant with you and give you laws by which you are to live and become a happy people in the land that I shall give you." What compelled Mendelssohn to amplify the meaning of the first commandment—which he considered not a commandment at all but the foundation of the legislative act—was his desire to explain the function of miracles as authentications of historical truths: "All these are historical truths that by their very nature rest on historical evidence, must be verified by authority, and can be confirmed by miracles."[32]

Historical truth, Mendelssohn had explained in an earlier passage, was to be differentiated from both the eternal, necessary truths of reason, which were grounded in God's intellect and were therefore unchangeable, and the eternal yet contingent verities, which derived from the will of

God and were not immutable. The laws of logic and mathematics were of the first kind, the laws of nature of the second. He had adopted the distinction between the two classes of eternal verities from Leibniz,[33] and like Leibniz he admitted the possibility of ad hoc suspensions of the laws of nature.[34] The class of historical truths, which Mendelssohn added, was characterized by him as "passages that occur only once, so to speak, in the book of nature." Truths of this kind had to be accepted upon the testimony of reliable witnesses, and in cases in which historical events had to be safeguarded against doubts, God's wisdom had seen to it that this was achieved by means of scriptural narrative and miracle: "It seems to me that only with regard to historical truths does it befit God's supreme wisdom to instruct men in a human way, i.e. by the spoken or written word, and to cause extraordinary things and miracles to happen in nature, whenever this was required to confirm the authority and credibility of the event."[35]

These formulations are far from clear. How can miracles authenticate historical events if the chief event to be authenticated is the miracle itself? There is also some ambiguity about the description of the Sinaitic revelation: "A historical truth, on which the legislation of this people was to be founded, and laws were to be revealed here." Which historical truth was to be revealed at Sinai, in addition to the laws? As one critic remarked, the fact of the Exodus from Egypt, mentioned in the first commandment, required no authentication. The people assembled at Sinai knew it, and so far as subsequent generations were concerned it was the miracle itself that stood in need of authentication.[36] What Mendelssohn probably meant to convey was that the miracles accompanying the Exodus and the heavenly voice at Sinai served to invest the series of events that led up to the Giving of the Law with a more than ordinary significance, endowing them with the aura of the divine. In brief, their purpose was to pronounce the story from Abraham to Moses as "salvational history" *(Heilsgeschichte)*.

The appearance of such theological concepts as covenant, redemption, and miracles in the essentially nontheological, metaphysically oriented, and rational context of the *Jerusalem* may seem to constitute a departure from Mendelsssohn's normal frame of reference. It is demanded, however, by the fact that he had excluded all purely rational tenets from revelation and defined the specific character of Judaism in terms of a revealed law. It was precisely his equation of Jewish religion (in its doctrinal aspect) and natural religion that opened the way to doing justice to the historical and legal perspective of Judaism, which medieval Jewish philosophers had tended to neglect. Though Mendelssohn did not pursue this line of thinking, it stood him in good stead when, toward the end of the *Jerusalem,* he formulated his answer to the Searcher's characterization of Judaism and reaffirmed his allegiance to the Sinaitic legislation. The historicity of the convenant, on the one hand, and the recognition of the historic changes that the Jewish people had undergone, on the other, played a decisive part in what he had to say.[37]

By way of contrast, history did not assume any significance in Mendelssohn's thinking about natural, universal religion. His firm belief that the means for achieving eternal felicity were freely available at all times and in every clime militated against assigning to history any essential role so far as religion and morality were concerned. In a sense, Mendelssohn denied the validity of the belief in universal progress. When in the spring of 1782 Hennings had expressed consternation at the fact that human progress in technology and the arts was not accompanied by any advance in the moral sphere,[38] Mendelssohn replied on June 25 that there was indeed no such thing as a steady linear progress of mankind as a whole; only the individual was destined to proceed on the road to perfection, while the species "man" oscillated between periods of bloom and decay and moved in cycles.

In Mendelssohn's view, this was a wise arrangement of nature, for it provided the individuals of successive generations with the challenge to exercise their capacities to the full:[39] "Assuming we continued to improve our crafts to such an extent that the worker needed no mental effort or routine to produce his work; assuming we purified our religious notions of all prejudice, developed trade to the point of making the products of all countries available everywhere at all times, eliminated tyranny from governments, chicanery from courts of justice, drudgery from customhouses, and all maliciousness from book reviews—what would there be left for our children to accomplish? . . . It is manifest that the human species has to retrogress here and there if individuals are to have any chance to progress. . . . Our existence on earth resembles a boy's stay at school. If freshmen are to be trained, the teacher has to repeat the same beginners' course from time to time." Mendelssohn expressed the same viewpoint in some reflections he wrote on an essay by Klein:[40] "Without exercising their faculties neither states nor individuals can be happy. The faculties must . . . meet resistance if they are to be set in motion. Once the spring has overcome resistance and is in full swing, tension has ceased and motion comes to an end. Hence a cycle is required by the nature of things. When the fathers have acquired honor and fortune and have bequeathed these to their children, nothing but tedious enjoyment without effort is the children's portion. When they [the fathers] fought for freedom and secured it against all attack, the children will indulge in languidness and slavish mentality as a result. . . . The pinnacle of perfection is in danger of a recession that will wind up the spring. . . . The ultimate purpose is not the progress of society but of men."

This sharp distinction between the linear progress of individuals and cyclical movement in the history of societies, states, and the human species as a whole is not found in Mendelssohn's earlier writings. At the time of the Lavater affair the Swiss physician and mystic Jacob Hermann Obereit (1725–1798) had asked Mendelssohn in which religion virtue was most perfect. Mendelssohn's answer included the following:[41] "The ultimate purpose of virtue is to improve what can be improved; and in the case of

man the whole genus as well as every individual is capable of infinite progress." Nevertheless, even while he was speaking of the possibility of historical
progress, Mendelssohn denied that cultural changes had any bearing on
religion. The primitive inhabitant of Greenland could be as virtuous as
the most highly cultured man. He also expressed, even then, skepticism
concerning the durability of progress. The degree of prejudice to be found
in the various religions was far from constant, dependent as it was on
time and circumstances in each century: "Now here, now there, a flash
of reason appears and then, sometimes, disappears. For the last fifty years
a small minority among your coreligionists has made a beginning on the
removal of prejudices. Mine will certainly follow suit. Perhaps one party
will have to do away with more weighty and the other with more numerous
prejudices. May God cause these efforts to produce speedy and permanent
results."

To Obereit's question whether it was right and proper for an honest
patriot to prefer the quiet of his home to the public marketplace, Mendelssohn replied: "Only, it seems to me, if he is certain, in a moral sense,
that he can achieve the greatest amount of good in a quiet way. Otherwise,
there is a time to speak and a time to keep silent, as the wise man said.[42]
If the honest-minded always keep their mouth shut, the power of the
word is surrendered to corrupt demagogues who misuse it." Thus, Mendelssohn considered it a moral duty to work for progress, though he had
his doubts as to how long the results achieved would last. With this reserva-
tion in mind, he could then admit the possibility of infinite progress for
the human race as a whole. If it was not linear, it could be assumed to
be spiral. His cyclical theory was not articulated until 1782. It first appeared
in the June 25 letter to Hennings, and it found its classical expression
in the *Jerusalem:*[43]

> For my part, I cannot conceive of an education of the human race
> as my late friend Lessing imagined it under the influence of I-
> don't-know-which historian of mankind. One pictures the collective entity
> of the human species as an individual person and imagines that Providence
> sent it to school here on earth, as it were, in order to raise it from childhood
> to manhood. In reality, mankind is—to use the same metaphor—child,
> man, and a hoary head at the same time, though in different places
> and regions of the world. . . . Progress applies only to the individual man
> who is destined by Providence to spend part of his eternity here on
> earth. . . . However, I do not believe it also to have been the purpose of
> Providence to let mankind as a whole advance steadily and perfect itself
> in the course of time.
>   . . . If you take mankind as a whole, you will not find constant progress
> in its development that brings it steadily nearer perfection. We see, rather,
> an oscillating movement; mankind as a whole has never taken any step
> forward without soon, and with redoubled speed, sliding back to its pre-
> vious position. . . . Individual man advances, but mankind continually fluc-
> tuates within fixed limits, while maintaining, on the whole, about the
> same degree of morality through all periods—the same amount of religion
> and irreligion, of virtue and vice, of happiness and misery . . .

It is clear from this passage that Mendelssohn's denial of any progress in history, so far as religion was concerned, had been provoked by Lessing's famous essay *The Education of the Human Race*. The first fifty-three of the one hundred paragraphs of this work had been published by Lessing in 1777, at the conclusion of his comments on Reimarus' fragment "That the Books of the Old Testament Were Not Written to Reveal a Religion." Lessing had pretended that these paragraphs had been copied by him from a manuscript that had circulated among friends. When the complete essay appeared at Easter, 1780, Lessing maintained its anonymity in order to save himself further trouble in the already sufficiently turbulent last phase of his life.[44] (He died shortly afterwards, on February 15, 1781.) The identity of the author was of course no secret to Mendelssohn. The Reimarus fragment to which the first fifty-three paragraphs had been attached tried to show that the Old Testament could not be considered a revelation of religious tenets since a religion implied a belief in an afterlife and such a belief was unknown to the Hebrews.[45]

Reimarus' notion that the Old Testament was not meant to teach a religion had been taken over from Spinoza,[46] as had been Mendelssohn's thesis that the Sinaitic revelation was not concerned with doctrines but with laws. However, the difference between Reimarus and Mendelssohn was a profound one. According to Mendelssohn the Hebrew Bible presupposed the truths of natural religion, including the belief in the immortality of the soul. Lessing accepted Reimarus' thesis and was even prepared to admit that prior to the Babylonian captivity the Old Testament writings did not have the true notion of the unity of God. He refused, however, to draw Reimarus' conclusion that the Old Testament was not of divine origin and was not a revelation of religious truths. In his view, a revelation could be divine without containing the truths of natural religion, while natural religion could be found in many ancient books that were not of a revealed character. In the divine economy, the Old Testament was meant to train a people in "heroic obedience to keep God's laws simply because they were God's laws," and the purpose of "this education of so untutored a people" as the Jews were then was to train "the future educators of the human race."[47] As an "elementary textbook" the Old Testament served its purpose: it suited the stage of childhood. But "a better pedagogue had to come"—Christianity, which represented in Lessing's view the manhood of the human race. The "time of perfection," in which the good will be done because it is good, was still to come. Lessing recalled the promise of a "new, eternal gospel" as found in the Apocalypse of John (14:6) and in certain medieval enthusiasts, an allusion to Joachim of Fiore's heretical doctrine of a third age, that of the pure Spirit.[48] The impact of Lessing's essay became pronounced in the philosophy of German idealism, which responded enthusiastically to the prediction of the coming age of man's ultimate maturity and interpreted Joachim of Fiore's third church as the rule of autonomous morality.[49]

Mendelssohn, who regarded natural religion as timeless, eternal, and divine, was bound to reject the view that Judaism and Christianity represented successive stages in the development of the religious consciousness of the human race.[50] He refused to see in Judaism "a mere early revelation of religious tenets and teachings required for man's salvation,"[51] and he denied the validity of the childhood/manhood/old age metaphor. In speaking of human history as a school in which the elementary lessons had to be repeated again and again,[52] he may have consciously tried to vary Lessing's image of man's education as a process in the course of which the elementary textbooks had to be discarded. He had Lessing in mind, finally, when he wrote:[53] "You want to divine what designs Providence has for mankind? Do not frame hypotheses! Simply look around and observe what actually happened." There follows the paragraph about the absence of any linear progress of mankind as a whole.

In one of his essays Kant discussed Mendelssohn's opposition to Lessing's "hypothesis" and found it wanting.[54] The cyclical view of history as propounded by Mendelssohn was simply a new version of the Sisyphus myth. The eternal recurrence of the same things was a tragedy that tended to become rather tedious, and was at variance with the concept of a moral author and governor of the world. Kant professed a belief in a steady progress of culture and in a continuing, though at times interrupted, progress of morality. "This hope of better times . . . has always had an influence on the activities of benevolent people; and that good man Mendelssohn must surely have relied on it when he put so much effort into the enlightenment and welfare of the nation to which he belonged." Mendelssohn, had he lived to see Kant's essay, might have replied that one was morally obliged to work for progress, but that one could never be sure how long it would last once it was achieved; that the civil improvement of the Jews, for instance, might be accomplished, but that relapses had to be expected. He was perhaps more of a realist than Kant, and it may be noted that Kant, in a later work in which he inquired afresh into the question *Whether the Human Race is Continually Progressing toward the Better?*,[55] took a more cautious view. What was increasing, he now said, was the quantity of legality, not morality: "For we must not expect too much of men's progress toward the better, if we are not to incur, and justifiably so, the scorn of the politician who is inclined to consider such hopes as the reveries of eccentrics." On the other hand, Mendelssohn betrayed, in a rather indirect and curious way, his belief in Jewish messianic hopes when in Section One of the *Jerusalem* he mentioned the year 2240 as the time when one might expect the principles of natural religion to have gained universal currency.[56] The year 2240 of the common era corresponds to the year 6000 in the Jewish chronology and according to rabbinic tradition has some messianic significance.[57] In Section Two Mendelssohn made an even more distinct reference to the messianic future when he expressed the hope that he himself might live to see the day on which Zecharia's prophecy (8:19) would be fulfilled.[58]

For Mendelssohn the Jew, therefore, there was no "eternal recurrence" of things but rather a dramatic climax on the plane of *Heilsgeschichte*.

Nor was the dichotomy of Judaism into a timeless, generally valid part (i.e., the truths of natural religion) and a history-bound, specifically Jewish element (i.e., the laws of the covenant of Sinai) tantamount to a tearing asunder of doctrine and commandment. Having established the difference between the two spheres, Mendelssohn took great pains to bring them together by showing their interrelatedness:[59]

> Although the divine book that we received through Moses is essentially a book of laws ... it also includes, as is well known, an inexhaustible treasure of rational truths and religious teachings. They are so intimately connected with the laws as to form an indivisible whole. All laws refer to, or are based upon, eternal truths of reason, or remind us of them and induce us to ponder them. ... The experience of many centuries also teaches that this divine law book has become a source of knowledge from which a large segment of the human race draws new insights or corrects old notions. The more you search in it, the more you will be astounded at the depth of the insights hidden in it. At first glance, to be sure, this book presents truth in its simplest attire, as it were, free from any pretentiousness. Yet the more closely you approach it and the purer, the more innocent, the more loving and longing is the glance with which you look upon it, the more it will unfold its divine beauty, veiled lightly so as not to be profaned by vulgar and unholy eyes.

This rapturous description of the Tora, the "divine law book" that reveals its beauteous truths only to the persistent lover, is a simplified version of a simile that played an important role in Jewish mystical literature.[60] Mendelssohn used it not merely as a rhetorical embellishment but as an apt expression of what he himself had experienced in his lifelong study of the Pentateuch and, more recently, as its translator and commentator. One senses the deep sincerity with which he sang the praises of this lawbook, which enshrined the most precious truths in the simplest of language. A wide chasm separated Mendelssohn, after all, from Spinoza. He marveled at the fact that this book of laws contained not a single commandment enjoining belief. All the truths contained therein, he pointed out, were presented as matters to be reflected upon and they were not forced upon our faith. Ancient Judaism knew no "articles of faith," and when medieval Jewish philosophers laid down the principles (*'ikkarim*) of the Jewish religion, they did so without bandying about recriminations of heresy.[61]

Mendelssohn had touched upon this subject in a letter he had written on July 11, 1782, to Wolf Dessau, the author of a commentary on the book of Job (1777) and of a work on the principles of Judaism that had appeared in 1782.[62] The passage in the *Jerusalem* dealing with the matter made use of what had been stated in the letter:[63] "Present-day Judaism, like the ancient one, possesses no proper creed. Only a very few principles and doctrines are prescribed to us. Maimonides enumerates thirteen, Albo only three, and nobody will accuse him of heresy on this account. Laws, customs, rules of life, actions are prescribed to us, [but] so far as doctrines are concerned, we are free. . . . The spirit of Judaism demands conformity in action and freedom in respect of doctrine, except for a few fundamental tenets on which all our teachers are agreed, and without which the Jewish religion simply could not exist." In his "Counterreflections" Mendelssohn had declared that in Judaism there was "no conflict between religion and reason, no rebellion of our natural knowledge against the oppressive power of [dogmatic] faith." The Jewish religion, he held, contained essentially only three principles: God, Providence, and the Giving of the Law.[64] He thus followed Albo's view,[65] and he made it a special point, in both the letter to Wolf Dessau and the *Jerusalem,* to declare that nobody, so far as he knew, had ever charged Albo with heresy for having reduced the number of fundamental Jewish doctrines to three.

Having outlined the bifocal yet unified character of "ancient, original Judaism, as I conceive it," Mendelssohn devoted a substantial portion of his book to a discussion of the ceremonial law, which the Searcher (and also Hennings and Rochow) had urged him to discard as an obstacle on the road to civil equality. He made an elaborate effort to show the extreme importance that the ceremonies—using this term to designate the two hundred forty-eight positive commandments *(mitsvot)*—had in safeguarding the monotheistic religion.

He began by pointing out that Judaism had entrusted its "doctrines" and "sentiments" not to rigid written formulae but to living oral instruction. He described the early rabbis' reluctance to permit the writing down of the oral traditions[66] as due to a keenly felt desire to keep the interpretation of the laws fluid and responsive to changing times and circumstances. Rather than commit the doctrinal aspect of Judaism to cold script, they left it free to be expressed in a living way: "The ceremonial law is itself a living script, stirring mind and heart, full of meaning, stimulating contemplation at all times, and offering constant opportunity for oral instruction." The student brought up in the tranditional environment learned far more through intimate contact with his master than he did from his books. Our modern civilization, Mendelssohn complained, had become a mere bookish world and was lacking in that personal relationship between teacher and pupil, between man and man, that only a society nurtured on a living tradition could create: "All is reduced to the dead letter; the spirit of living dialogue no longer exists anywhere." The preacher read his sermon, the teacher his lesson; we quarreled and became reconciled in letters, and our entertainment consisted in recitations; what we knew came from books, and the wisdom of old age counted no longer. In short, we had become mere literati.[67] This critique of modern society no doubt owed something to Rousseau's influence. Rousseau had deplored the decline of language; no one, he had said, understood the language of the heart any longer. For easy chattering *(babil facile),* the language had words; for noble sentiments, it did not. People were talking without saying anything, etc.[68] Mendelssohn's characterization of his period as a "paper age" seems to have impressed Schiller and Hegel.[69]

At this point Mendelssohn permitted himself a digression that turned out to be a circuitous road to his ultimate goal, the vindication of the ceremonial law. He launched into a discussion of the origin of language and script, and from there he ventured on some flights of speculation into the connection between the changes in script and the history of religion. He realized that his remarks on the origin of language were rather sketchy, but he wisely refrained from elaborating the copious notes he had prepared, the subject being too vast to be adequately dealt with in the present context.[70] The theme had occupied him on and off ever since he had translated Rousseau's second *Discours* and set down his thoughts about it for Lessing.[71] As a philosopher he sought to explain the origin of language in a natural way, while as a Bible exegete he accepted the traditional view that Hebrew was the *lingua Adamica* in which God addressed man.[72] Similarly, Rousseau had offered a naturalistic theory to account for the first "invention" of language and yet as a *philosophe chrétien* had professed to believe Moses; Rousseau had even tried to reconcile his theory with the biblical view,[73] something never attempted by Mendelssohn. It is strange to find that his brief allusions to the subject in the *Jerusalem*[74] omit all reference to traditional concepts. Apparently he did not want to lay himself open to criticism and perhaps even ridicule by so much as mentioning a belief that had been discarded by the Enlightenment. Leibniz had still upheld the notion of a *lingua Adamica,* but in his view that language had been irretrievably lost; certainly it was not Hebrew. Christian Wolff had considered language the arbitrary product of society. Lichtenberg, that irrepressible cynic, had mocked the notion of Hebrew as the primordial tongue. Reimarus, Lessing, Michaelis—all had scrapped the traditional concept.[75] Only Hamann saw in language a divine revelation.[76]

Mendelssohn derived the origin of language from the need to attach concepts formed in the mind to sensible (audible) signs in order to arrest, as it were, their elusiveness—in order to retain them in the memory and to be able to communicate them to others. The visible signs (script), on the other hand, were invented out of a desire to be able to recall, at will, abstract notions that ordinarily would not arise by associative thinking. At first, animals representing clearly defined characters functioned as such signs or symbols. Later, images of animals or mere allusions to their shape were substituted and hieroglyphic script came into being. Mendelssohn assumed that alphabetic writing developed from hieroglyphic signs, and he found evidence for this in the forms and names of the Hebrew script, from which he believed all other alphabets had derived. The Phoenicians had transmitted the art of writing to the Greeks.[77] Mendelssohn then tried to show, in true Enlightenment fashion, how first from misunderstanding and later through abuse and priestly fraud the signs and symbols, especially those of hieroglyphic script, gave rise to mythological beliefs and, eventually, to various idolatrous practices: animal worship, deification of heroes, human sacrifice on the altar of animals held to be sacred and divine (as Plutarch, for example, reported,[78] and as Hosea expressed in the phrase "they that sacrifice men kiss calves"),[79] and other abominations.[80] Mendelssohn, who had declared idolatry to be a lesser evil than atheism,[81] now had second thoughts on the matter: "The notions of the deity lingering on in folk religions were so distorted by superstition, so corroded by hypocrisy and priestcraft, that one had reason to wonder whether atheism would not actually have been less harmful to human happiness; in other words, whether godlessness, so to speak, would not have been less godless than such a religion."[82]

It cannot be said that Mendelssohn made a very plausible case for the idea that abuses of script led to idolatry. Even if one conceded his point that men tend to take the sign or image for the thing itself, the question of why the worship of animals should have developed via the corruptive influence of hieroglyphic writing, and not more directly, would still remain.[83] Mendelssohn's "hypothesis" that "the need for written signs was the first cause of idolatry" is the least substantiated of all theories he ever advanced. His only reason for putting it forward, no doubt, was to contrast the image worship of paganism and the imageless ceremonial acts of Judaism, the perilous hieroglyphic and the safe living script of Jewish ceremony. The comparison is drawn at the next stage of the discussion, in which Mendelssohn suddenly reintroduces the matter of salvational history against the background of the natural history of religion he had just outlined:[84]

> And now I am at the point where I am in a position to explain more fully my surmise about the purpose of the ceremonial law in Judaism. Our nations' patriarchs—Abraham, Isaac, and Jacob—had remained faithful to the Eternal and sought to preserve pure religious concepts free of all idolatry, for their families and descendants. And now these descendants were chosen by Providence to be a priestly nation, a nation that through its constitution and institutions, through its laws and conduct, and throughout all vicissitudes and changes of life, was to point out continually wholesome and unadulterated ideas of God and his attributes—and to teach, preach, and preserve these ideas among the nations by virtue of its mere existence, as it were. Initially they lived under extreme pressure among barbarians and idolators, and their misery made them nearly as insensitive to the truth as their oppressors had become because of their arrogance. But God liberated them from their slavery by extraordinary miracles. He became the savior, leader, king, lawgiver, and judge of the nation that He himself had fashioned, and He designed its entire constitution in accordance with the wise purposes of his providence.

The election of Israel is here portrayed as a saving act of Providence by which natural religion, which had been distorted by gross aberrations, was to be restored and safeguarded. Nothing is said of the period between Adam and Abraham as a preliminary to *Heilsgeschichte*. Neither the Adamitic revelation nor the covenant with Noah is mentioned. The tower of Babel is not referred to in connection with the theory of language. The only hint of a link between Adam and Abraham is found in the statement that Abraham had remained faithful to the Eternal. Yet this faithfulness is understood as adherence to "wholesome and unadulterated ideas about God and his attributes," that is to say, to natural religion. The recognition of an original monotheism conforms, of course, to the traditional view,[85] and so does the doctrine of the gradual corruption of the earlier pure faith.[86] However, Mendelssohn treats both of these on the plane of natural history, as it were. Adam's religion was *natural* religion, and the rise of idolatry was a *natural* development. The striking thing is that even *Heilsgeschichte*, which irrupts with Abraham's election, is meant to serve natural religion.

The way in which Mendelssohn explains the function of the ceremonial law clearly points in this direction:[87] "The truths necessary for the happiness of the entire nation, and of its individual members, were to be utterly removed from all imagery. For this was the main purpose and the fundamental law of the constitution. Those truths were to be associated solely with deeds and practices, and these were to take the place of the symbols without which truth cannot be preserved. Men's actions are transitory; there is nothing permanent or enduring about them that, like hieroglyphic script, could lead to idolatry through misuse or misunderstanding." In a sense, Mendelssohn offered a new version of Maimonides' doctrine that "the first intention of the Law as a whole is to put an end to idolatry" and that the commandments specifically concerned with this purpose "are meant to bring about deliverance from those unhealthy opinions" that hinder man's perfection.[88] Mendelssohn was careful not to present his interpretation of the meaning of the ceremonial law as an authoritative doctrine. Rather he stressed its hypothetical character:[89] "Who can say, 'I have entered the sanctuary of God,[90] comprehended all his plans, and am therefore able to determine the measure, goal and limit of his purpose'? Yet the humble searcher is permitted to form conjectures and to draw conclusions from results, so long as he remembers that he can but surmise."

To the categorical denigration of the ceremonial law by the Searcher for Light and Right Mendelssohn opposed his "conjectures" in the unassuming role of "humble searcher." The "results" from which he felt entitled to draw conclusions were the beneficial *effects* of the ceremonies, which were not merely preventing idolatry but were fostering a close and intimate union of doctrine *(Lehre)* and life.[91] What Mendelssohn failed to explain was why Providence left the rest of mankind without a comparable legislation that would serve it as a safeguard against idolatry and as a bond between doctrine and life. The same moral considerations that caused Mendelssohn to deny the revealed character of eternal verities should have suggested the need for a universal revealed legislation.

We now approach Mendelssohn's final answer to the charge that Moses' "churchly system" was a "theocracy" armed with the sword and based on the "severest ecclesiastical law," and that by denying the validity of ecclesiastical law and power he had implicitly abandoned the religion of his fathers. In reply he pointed out that in the Mosaic constitution there was no such thing as ecclesiastical law distinct from civil law. The two were identical. Man's relation to society, which was normally the concern of the state, and his relation to God, which was normally the province of religion, here converged on a single point. God was the king of this nation and, being a sovereign without any wants, he demanded only what benefited his people. Mendelssohn did not particularly emphasize the covenant between God and Israel as the characteristic feature of the Mosaic constitution, but he had referred to the covenant idea before[92] and had mentioned it again in the present context.[93] Yet what his description of this constitution amounted to was nothing but a spelling out of what was implied in the biblical notion of the covenant between God and the people of Israel.

Mendelssohn may have been hardly aware of the fact that the modern doctrine of the social contract was but a secularized form of the biblical covenant idea, and that the original, authentic concept had in fact reemerged in Calvinist Protestantism in the sixteenth and seventeenth centuries.[94] It is clear, however, that in his view the Mosaic state, unlike all others, did not come into being through a social contract that conferred certain rights upon the sovereign. He also refused to see in it a theocracy,[95] as the Searcher and Locke[96] had done. If "theocracy" is only a euphemism for hierocracy, the term can certainly not be applied to the ancient Jewish commonwealth, in which the priesthood was kept separate from political administration. What Mendelssohn was emphatic about was the union of the civil and religious aspects of life under this constitution:[97] "Every civil act, therefore, was invested with sacredness and religious authority, and every act of civic service became ipso facto a true act of divine worship. The community was God's community; its concerns were God's; public taxes were an offering to God;" etc. Hence every offense against the Mosaic Law was a political crime, lese majesty, punishable under state law. For example, the desecration of the sabbath was an infringement of the constitution of the state and was punishable as such, for it denied the validity of the covenant of which the sabbath was "a perpetual sign" (Exod. 31:17). Under the terms of this polity all kinds of transgressions had to be punished not as heresies or unbelief but as misdeeds, as crimes against the state, as acts tending to weaken the authority of the Lawgiver and thereby to undermine the state itself. The actual carrying out of the prescribed punishments was, however, so much hedged around by legal provisions of the oral law that it happened only in rare cases. Humane considerations largely neutralized the severity of the laws, which was more a matter of theory and principle than of practice. "It is therefore evident that a man must be unfamiliar with the Mosaic laws and the constitution of Judaism if he believes that they bestow rights and power upon the church or authorize temporal punishment for unbelief and heresy. The 'Searcher for Light and Right,' as well as Herr Mörschel, are obviously far from the truth when they think I have abrogated Judaism by my arguments against ecclesiastical rights and ecclesiastical power."[98]

Mendelssohn refused to label the Mosaic constitution a theocracy or describe it by any other generic term. It existed only once and had no parallel. In its pristine purity it was, like Plato's heavenly love, an idea, a blueprint as it were, of heavenly politics that had little chance to endure for more than a fleeting moment. Soon the people were clamoring for an earthly king of flesh and blood, the prophet Samuel had to yield to their request, and the Mosaic constitution was abandoned: state and religion ceased to be one and the same thing. A collision of duties was now possible, though this was unlikely to occur under the rule of kings obedient to the Law.

Mendelssohn refrained from tracing the vicissitudes of Jewish political history in biblical times and down to the destruction of the second Temple and commonwealth. With a grand sweep he pointed to the "sorrowful period" of Roman rule in Palestine, when Jews had to serve two masters and the founder of Christianity "prudently counseled," "Render unto Caesar what is Caesar's, and unto God what is God's" (Mark 12:17). In this formula the inevitable split between state and religion was acknowledged as a reality, and Mendelssohn suggested that no better advice could be given to the "House of Jacob" even today:[99] "Adapt yourselves to the customs and conditions of the country in which you find yourselves, but also be steadfast in upholding the religion of your fathers. Bear both burdens as well as you can. True, on the one hand, the burden of civil life is being made a heavy one for you because of the religion to which you remain faithful; and, on the other hand, in the present clime and period the observance of your religious laws has become more burdensome than it used to be. Persevere nevertheless; stand firm in the place assigned to you by Providence; and submit to everything that may happen, as you were told to do by your Lawgiver long ago."

In Mendelssohn's view, then, the split between state and religion, which had been sealed by the destruction of the Temple, did not by any means signify the end of the covenant between God and the Jewish people. The Law had remained as valid as before. Transgressions were no longer crimes against the state (which had become defunct) and were therefore no longer punishable as such. Mendelssohn recalled in this connection the rabbinic statements that denied to Jewish courts the right to impose bodily and capital punishment as well as certain fines after the Sanhedrin had ceased to function within the Temple precincts.[100] He saw in this ruling evidence that once the union of state and religion had been dissolved, Judaism had become a mere religion and that all coercive power had been renounced.[101] Yet as a religion it was still bound by the laws of the covenant, even though those parts of the legislation that presupposed the existence of the state and of the Temple were no longer capable of fulfilment. Mendelssohn emphatically affirmed the duty of every Jew to observe all remaining laws strictly, for "what God has joined together, man may not tear asunder" (Mark 10:9)—a reminder intended more for the benefit of Christian readers than for the strengthening of Jewish loyalties. Differently expressed: no Jew had a right to question the continuing validity of the Mosaic Law unless God abolished it "as openly, publicly, and beyond any possibility of doubt and uncertainty as He gave it."[102]

Christian critics did not take too kindly to this argument. Zöllner pointed out that if the thunderous voices at Sinai had confirmed the Mosaic constitution, the destruction of the Jewish state proved no less impressively that its continuance was no longer in accordance with God's designs.[103] This was the old Christian "proof" for the rejection of Israel. Uhle remarked ironically that "a legislator would not, as a rule, abolish his legislation with the same solemnity with which he introduced it."[104] They missed Mendelssohn's essential point: without an "authentic dispensation from the Law," without "authorization by the Lawgiver," no Jew could "in good conscience" exempt himself from the binding force of the commandments.

The concluding part of the *Jerusalem* showed Mendelssohn's strength of character at its best. Addressing his "dear brethren and fellowmen who followed the teachings of Jesus," he asked them why they rebuked the Jews for keeping to the Law of Moses and the statutes of the rabbis that Jesus of Nazareth had himself observed. Did they seriously believe that civil rights had to be denied to the Jewish people so long as it remained loyal to the ceremonial laws and thereby maintained certain social barriers? If this was indeed the case, if civil equality had to be paid for by "our departing from the Law that we still consider binding," the answer was clear: "We sincerely regret having to declare that we renounce our claim to civil union." All that Dohm the humanitarian had written would then prove to have been in vain, and everything would remain in the hardly tolerable condition in which it was now or [—a reference, perhaps, to Joseph II's Edict of Tolerance, which had put a premium on conversion—] into which the Christians' love of humanity might find it appropriate to put it. If one remembers that Mendelssohn believed that he was addressing Sonnenfels, the tenor of this forthright statement becomes fully understandable.[105] Mendelssohn was aware that Sonnenfels' political influence had declined under Joseph II,[106] but he rightly identified him with the spirit of the edict, especially after he had read the tract, which mixed praise for the emperor's intentions and an open appeal for Jewish conversion.

Mendelssohn gave an equally shattering reply to the Searcher's plea for a union in faith in fulfilment of the prophecy that some day there would be only one Shepherd and one flock. He had himself written in his "Counterreflections":[107] "All prophets of the Old Testament agree, and reason delights in the hope, that the differences between the religions will not last forever; that someday there will be a single Shepherd and a single flock,[108] and the knowledge of the true God will cover the whole earth as the waters cover the sea."[109] However, in a lengthy note on Manasseh Ben Israel's treatise[110] he had sounded a strong warning against calls for a union of faiths; he saw in such calls only intolerance in disguise. The Searcher's plea had confirmed his suspicions. "Do not let yourselves be deceived!," he implored his "well-meaning brethren." "To belong to this universal Shepherd, it is not necessary for the entire flock to graze on one pasture or to enter and leave the master's house through one door. This would be neither in accord with the Shepherd's wishes nor conducive to the well-being of the flock."[111] The apostles of such union might outwardly feign brotherly love while secretly being already at work forging the chains with which to shackle our reason. Besides, it was impossible to reach agreement on the exact shades of meaning of doctrines to be held in common. Formulations of a unified creed were bound to give rise to endless debate and heresy-hunting of a new sort. Mendelssohn had quoted Michaelis' view in support of his stand in the note on *Manasseh*, and Michaelis, in turn, fully corroborated this position when reviewing the *Jerusalem*.[112]

What Mendelssohn feared most was the dissolution of Judaism as the result of the will-o'-the-wisp that the lure of a union such as that proposed in the pamphlet represented. It was "the wolves' system of union," as he put it in a letter to Homberg on September 22, 1783.[113] Wolves were so desirous of union with sheep that they liked to transform the flesh of lambs into wolves' flesh. It would be fatal, he pointed out to Homberg (who was inclined to doubt the necessity of the ceremonial law), to relent on this issue. Even if it were true that the ceremonies no longer served the purpose of conveying religious truths in symbolic fashion, the need for them as a "bond of union" serving to keep the Jewish people together was unimpeachable. That union would lose none of its significance so long as polytheism, anthropomorphism, and usurpation of power by religions still ruled on earth. So long as those tormentors of reason were united among themselves, it was incumbent upon Jews, as the true theists, to remain a distinct group. In his view, the distinctiveness of the Jewish people was still in accord with the design of Providence. In other words, the aspect of *Heilsgeschichte* that attached to the Sinaitic covenant was still valid. Union among Jews being founded not on dogmas but on actions, the ceremonies served as the only possible bond of unity. Their importance should not be belittled. Rather, efforts should be made to rediscover the authentic meaning that lay at their root, to make the living script again legible after its having been overlaid for so long by "hypocrisy and priest-craft"—a reference, probably, to kabbalistic interpretations of the meaning of the commandments.

The *Jerusalem* ended with an appeal for the kind of tolerance "for which reason still longs in vain." "Reward and punish no doctrine; hold out no allurement or bribe to anyone for the adoption of a particular faith. . . . Permit no one in your country to search someone else's heart or to judge someone else's thoughts. Let no one usurp a right that the Omniscient has reserved to himself. If we render unto Caesar what is Caesar's, then let us also render unto God what is God's. Love truth! Love peace!"[114] Thus, the renunciation of force by religion and nondiscrimination by the state insofar as religion was concerned, the two basic themes of Section One, were reiterated as the final message of the book, lending emphasis to the unity of the treatise as a whole.

The extent to which the different elements of which the *Jerusalem* is composed can be harmonized into an organic whole is another question. It cannot be doubted that Mendelssohn's profile emerges in distinct outline, without any haziness or confusion. It is the profile of a man who lives up to the image that one would expect to find at the closing stage of a life steeped both in the Enlightenment and in the Jewish tradition. Section One presents the philosopher, Section Two the loyal Jew, and the two levels of existence, though by no means blending into an organic unity, at least do not fall apart. They are held together by a strong tendency to interpret the one in the light of the other, to infuse philosophy into Judaism and to allow Judaism to color philosophy. The way in which *Heilsgeschichte* and all that it implies (miracles, revelation, covenant) is permitted to intrude into the timeless realm of natural religion might indicate a break in the structure of Mendelssohn's thought, but the subordination of salvational history to the designs of Providence and to the purposes of natural religion restores the compactness of the vision as a whole. It took a man of the upbringing, training, experience, and energy of a Moses Mendelssohn to write this strange, powerful, and unique book, the *Jerusalem*.

CHAPTER SEVEN

Strains and Stresses

———————•⟨∞⟩•———————

Friendship with Lessing: The Last Phase

I

Lessing's essay *Leibniz on Eternal Punishments,* published in 1773,[1] with its reaffirmation of the view that sinners were subject to eternal and infinite punishments, caused some alarm in Berlin Enlightenment circles. Just the year before Johann August Eberhard had criticized Leibniz' defense of this doctrine and had done so, no doubt, under the influence of Mendelssohn's strenuous rejection of the concept.[2] Lessing's essay sounded a discordant note.

In Leibniz' view, as expressed in the *Essais de Théodicée,*[3] the cause of ever-renewed suffering was the infinite continuity of sinning by the damned. Eberhard had denied the possibility of such infinite sinning on the part of finite creatures and had suggested, moreover, that Leibniz' argument was intended only to strengthen the faith of individuals already predisposed to accept the dogma of eternal punishment. Lessing vigorously contradicted this interpretation of Leibniz. What Leibniz had had in mind, Lessing said, was not to please all parties but to discover the esoteric truth concealed in the shell of the dogma. Pretense and insincerity had been utterly foreign to Leibniz: "He struck fire from the flint, but he did not conceal his fire in the flint."[4]

At the beginning of his essay Lessing published the Latin text of a short note that Leibniz had written as a preface to his projected new edition of a treatise on the subject by Ernst Soner (1572–1612), a Socinian who had argued: sins are finite; there is no proportion between the finite and the infinite; punishments, therefore, must also be finite. Leibniz' prefatory note had been discovered by Lessing in the ducal library. It stated: "Even if we were to admit that no sin as such is infinite, one may nevertheless truthfully say that the sins of the damned are infinite in number, since the damned persevere in sin throughout eternity. If, therefore, the sins are eternal, it is appropriate that punishments also be eternal."

Lessing agreed with Leibniz' view, which he interpreted to mean "that nothing in the world is isolated, that nothing is without consequences, [and] that nothing is without eternal consequences." He concluded from this assumption that if punishments were the consequences of sin, they had to be eternal. According to Lessing, it was this "great esoteric truth" that Leibniz had confirmed. Even Eberhard had admitted the eternality of "eternal damage" caused by sin, without recognizing, however, the notion of "infinite hell." Yet once the eternality of the evil effects of immoral acts is conceded, Lessing argued, why deny the eternality of hell? Was "hell" anything but a popular term designating the consequences of evil acts? The endlessness of punishment, taken in the esoteric sense, could even coexist with the notion of the improvement of those punished. The "improved" sinner remained in "hell," so to speak, by virtue of his perceiving the bliss of the righteous who were far ahead of him and could not be overtaken. The very concept of progress by infinite degrees applied equally to heaven and to hell. If it was true that the best man was not without much evil, and the worst not bereft of all goodness, the consequences of evil would accompany the good man into heaven, and vice versa. Every one would find his hell even in heaven and his heaven even in hell.

The thrust of Lessing's interpretation of Leibniz was aimed against Eberhard's attempt to soften the harshness of the doctrine of eternal punishment. Eberhard had been at pains to show that Leibniz could not have wished this doctrine to spoil his view of this world as the best one possible; that he had in fact intimated his disapproval of the doctrine; that the assumption of a "more lenient fate of sinners" was "too deeply ingrained in his principles" to be ignored, and that he assumed the world to be constantly growing in perfection.[5] Lessing's denial of this facile interpretation of Leibniz struck at the very roots of Enlightenment optimism. Karl Lessing wrote to his brother on January 16, 1773:[6]

> Your view of eternal punishment in hell is philosophy, is heresy to both the orthodox and heterodox. . . . Necessary consequence of every act of man instead of the positive punishment in hell—a beautiful thought! Moreover, a true thought! Yet who is to thank you for this Christian or ingenious volte? Reason or Christianity?

Karl seems to have grasped his brother's point. He also clearly foresaw the resistence it would meet. On the other hand, a subsequent letter of his (referred to in Lessing's reply of April 8) suggests that Karl himself had joined the opposition camp by echoing Eberhard's view that the essay was meant to please the orthodox. Still later, on March 20, Karl wrote:[7] "You will hear nothing further from me about Eberhard's *Apology*. Eberhard and Moses wish to do this themselves. That Moses has not yet done so is due to his infirmity." It is obvious from this remark that Mendelssohn and Eberhard were allied in their opposition. And Nicolai was completely on their side: in a jocular vein he rebuked Lessing for his "unauthorized attack on Eberhard's [*New*] *Apology of Socrates,*" of which he was the publisher. In the end, Nicolai continued, a heretic would get away equally well if he was eternally damned à la Lessing or not eternally dammed à la Eberhard.

On April 8, after a long silence, Lessing told his brother that his intentions had been misinterpreted. The orthodox were of no concern to him: he despised them as much as Karl did. Yet he despised "our modern clergymen" even more. As theologians they had too little, and as philosophers they had by far not enough.[8] Karl assured him, in a letter dated April 17, that Eberhard was quite unlike those unorthodox theologians who sold their paltry stuff in place of the old, and that he was going to reply to Lessing's polemic with the respect with which he treated all of Lessing's writings.[9] Nicolai's April 26 letter conveyed regards from "Moses and also from the preacher Eberhard, notwithstanding the fact that the latter ought, in fairness, to hurl a little excommunication as a *foudre de poche* at you." It was in the same letter that he reported: "Moses has the cold fever, and one hopes that this will dispose of his illness."[10]

Had it not been for his physical debility Mendelssohn would doubtless have been more articulate on the subject under discussion. However, it formed the major topic of conversation between him and Lessing when they spent a few days together at Brunswick in July, 1773.[11] Lessing's letter to Karl (July 14, 1773) contains the following report:[12]

> My compliments to Herr Eberhard. I had reason to hope that I was going to have the pleasure of seeing him here with Moses. I feel certain that we would have composed our quarrel with a dozen spoken words. What Moses said concerning the matter convinced me in part and left me unconvinced in the other part. Yet, however profound both are or may be, they would hardly affect me, if they were written down black on white. For I would not allow myself to be deflected from the main point: the hell, the eternality of which Eberhard denies, does not [even] exist, whereas the hell that is real, is eternal. Why should we not rather contest the insipid and meaningless notions about the nature of this hell, be it eternal or not, instead of attacking the duration that admits of a good way of interpreting it? However, I am looking forward to what [Eberhard] himself has to say.

It is clear from this account that Mendelssohn did not accept Lessing's esoteric interpretation of Leibniz' view. Though Lessings' concept of the eternal consequences of sin appealed to Mendelssohn personally, he could not accept it as the authentic interpretation of Leibniz' defense of eternal punishment. Even so, that he agreed with the notion as such, and that he considered it compatible with his belief in the soul's infinite advance toward greater perfection and happiness, is apparent from a letter he

wrote on March 24, 1780, to Peter Adolph Winkopp (1759–1813), a
Benedictine monk in Erfurt, who had been troubled by doubts about the
doctrine of eternal punishment and had solicited his help. Mendelssohn's
letter contains the following paragraph:[13]

> I admit that the consequences of sins are eternal; for the consequences
> of all causes persist eternally. This is true, however, only of natural con-
> sequences . . . and even natural consequences are not eternal misery, since
> they can be outweighed by the good. And this is my hope. The conse-
> quences of my sins will remain eternally and leave traces by which they
> can be recognized, but they will not render me eternally miserable. . . .
> The sentiment of the good will yet prevail in my soul, and I, like you
> and all men, our brethren, will be eternally happy.

Mendelssohn recommended that Winkopp read Eberhard's *New Apology
of Socrates,* where he would find this doctrine thoroughly investigated and
very profoundly treated.[14]

   That in his view Leibniz had to be taken literally is obvious from
the way Mendelssohn described, and repudiated, Leibniz' notion in a treatise
entitled *"Causa Dei," or Providence Defended,* which he wrote in 1784 (it
seems), and in which he tried to rewrite, as it were, Leibniz' *"Causa Dei"* for
the benefit of his fellow-Jews.[15] The relevant passage reads:[16]

> According to our system, the greatest difficulty that Leibniz had to meet
> in respect of the future life will disappear. One accuses Providence, he
> said, of allowing even in the hereafter more evil to exist than good,
> seeing that most men are destined for damnation and only a few are
> said to be elected for bliss. The Christian philosopher [Leibniz] who
> accepted the eternal damnation of the impious . . . as an article of faith
> found here indeed insoluble difficulties. In order to save his system Leibniz
> resorted to an infinite variety of angels and inhabitants of other planets
> who might have been elected for eternal happiness in far larger num-
> bers. . . . Yet neither our religion nor our reason acknowledges this prepos-
> terous presupposition: not a single individual capable of happiness is
> elected for damnation, nor is any citizen in the commonwealth of God
> destined for eternal misery.

The difference between Mendelssohn and Lessing was clearly not one
of their personal beliefs but of their differing interpretations of Leibniz'
belief. They both rejected the notion of eternal punishment in its crude
literal sense. They both accepted the idea that evil acts had eternal consequences. But whereas Lessing took the Christian dogma and Leibniz'
defense of it in an esoteric sense, Mendelssohn did not. Underlying Lessing's
esotericism was his growing desire to establish the "inner truths" of the
Christian religion in a way that would transcend both orthodoxy and neolo-
gism. This problem did not exist for Mendelssohn, who believed in a kind
of preestablished harmony between Judaism and natural religion. He could
hold to such a belief only because he chose to ignore those elements in
the Jewish tradition that tended to contradict his rationalistic assumptions.[17]

   Lessing's next theological essay, *Andreas Wissowatius' Objections To the
Trinity,*[18] followed the pattern of the previous one. It started out from

Leibniz' refutation of the arguments that Wissowatius (another Socinian theologian) had raised against the trinitarian dogma. Its purpose was to show that Leibniz' defense of the dogma was more philosophical than the Socinian's vacillation between the rejection of the divinity of Christ, on the one hand, and his worship of Christ, on the other.[19] Lessing produced an improved version of the badly mutilated first edition of Leibniz' *Defense of the Trinity by Means of New Logical Inventions,*[20] and he published for the first time Wissowatius' *Objections,* to which Leibniz had referred without actually quoting the text.

On February 1, 1774, Mendelssohn sent Lessing a letter in which he suggested an emendation of a difficult passage in the Leibniz text:[21] "I cannot help finding fault with [what I think is] a minor mistake . . . in your second volume, be it merely to give you some proof of my existence, and to show you that even in my illness I cannot endure leaving unread your contribution to a branch of literature [viz. theology] that I used to hold in poor esteem." There followed an acute and penetrating discussion of the Leibniz passage. Mendelssohn agreed that the printed version was "pure nonsense." And yet he felt that the text substituted by Lessing could not be the correct one either, and he offered a conjectural emendation that made very good sense, fulfilled Leibniz' promise of presenting something new in logic, and proved useful to the defense of the trinity.

Apropos of Lessing's reference to the trinitarian interpretation of the *intelligible,* the *intelligens,* and the *intellectus* by the medieval scholastics,[22] Mendelssohn wrote in his letter: "Among the essays you wrote in your youth you must still have preserved the one in which you explained this distinction with much ingenuity." The old essay was the one entitled *The Christianity of Reason,* Lessing's earliest attempt to interpret the Christian dogma philosophically.[23] Lessing replied:[24]

> I thank you, my best friend, for your kind instruction. You are perfectly right: thus and in no other way could Leibniz have written. . . . Yet is it not strange that you should restore the correct reading in a treatise that must appear to you as complete nonsense from beginning to end—and, indeed, is complete nonsense? It is complete nonsense to me also, and was undoubtedly considered as such by Leibniz himself. I am convinced nevertheless that Leibniz was thinking and acting here too in a way befitting a Leibniz. For it is unquestionably better to defend something unphilosophical in a very philosophical manner than to want to reject or reform it unphilosophically. My own former fanciful ideas on this subject I still remember very well, and I also remember the objections you then raised against them, as a result of which I was at once dissuaded from taking them seriously myself henceforth.

As Lessing's latest essay showed, his former disavowal of speculative arguments for the trinitarian dogma had not prevented him from again trying his hand at the same theme, though he admitted that Leibniz' effort was "complete nonsense." One senses the spirit of the former youthful days of gaiety in this correspondence, which contains some lively bantering about the trinity of one ducat and the unity of three ducats. It is also apparent from Mendelssohn's postscript that he shared Lessing's low opinion of the neologists: he offered "congratulations" on the "considerable interest" that the theological faculty in Göttingen had of late evinced in Lessing's publications. "Herr Less said the other day in the *Göttingische Anzeigen* that depriving the Christian religion of its principal proof (i.e. the miracles) was tantamount to depriving the human race of all virtue. I suggest that you start demonstrating the truth of miracles. You would then undoubtedly receive the doctorate in theology that, as Ernesti assures us, you already deserve."

The third volume of the Wolfenbüttel series appeared toward the end of 1774, and it comprised, in addition to an essay by Lessing on Adam Neuser (a sixteenth-century Protestant theologian who had converted to Islam), the elder Reimarus' chapter *On the Toleration of Deists*.[25] The latter was Lessing's first step in launching the *Fragments of the Unnamed*. In order to protect the Reimarus family, he suggested that Johann Lorenz Schmidt (1702–1749 or 1751), the translator of the Wertheim Bible,[26] might have been the author of the fragments he had discovered in the ducal library.[27] It was this particular "fragment" that contained the reference to the rabbinic concept of the "proselytes in the gates" or "resident proselytes" (*gerey sha'ar; gerey toshav*) who were assured, according to Maimonides, of the bliss of the next world.[28]

Karl Lessing warned his brother that neither the essay on Neuser nor the fragment would please "the terrestrial bodyguard of God," but his letter reflected his own delight,[29] which was shared by Mendelssohn. Lessing wrote in reply:[30] "I recall that Herr Moses once wrote for me a special note on the *'proselytae portae'*—which, however, I no longer remember. Please ask him about it and give him my best regards. I hope his improvement continues." Karl answered the inquiry on November 30, 1774:[31] "Moses cannot recall any note on the *proselytae portae* that would differ from what is found in the fragment on the toleration of deists. With all his heart he wishes for you as much serenity as he wishes a healthy mind for himself. For he cannot do any reading for an hour without feeling the ill-effect for a whole week." How greatly impressed Mendelssohn was with the fragment may be gauged from the fact that in his preface to *Vindiciae Judaeorum* he would laud the "Fragmentist" for having been the first to advocate the toleration of "naturalists," of radical deists.

In January, 1777, after an interval of more than two years, the fourth volume of the Wolfenbüttel series appeared. The intervening period had seen the publication, by Lessing, of the *Philosophical Essays of Karl Wilhelm Jerusalem*,[32] his journey to Italy, and his marriage to Eva König on October 8, 1776. The new volume, *Some More Things from the Papers of the Unnamed Concerning Revelation*,[33] contained the remaining five fragments of the manuscript in his possession but presented the last and most challenging fragment only in part (II.#10–#32), under the heading "On the Story of the Resurrection." Lessing knew that he was heading for trouble, but he decided to take the plunge anyway. In August, 1776, before setting out on a trip to Hamburg, he sent the first batch of proofs to Doctor Reimarus. In a letter to Hennings dated August 20, 1776, Elise reported:[34]

> Prior to his coming, he sent a letter and a printed enclosure to my brother.... In the letter he said: "For what has to be done must be done soon or never. What sense would there be in letting the arrow fly at a target that has been moved?"—Well then, let a start be made to hit the target and move it until there is no target any more.

Elise was obviously caught up in Lessing's militant mood and his sense of urgency, though the true meaning of his phrase about the arrow that might lose its target could hardly have been understood by her. For what Lessing had in mind was a situation in which Reimarus' historical critique of the Bible would no longer be meaningful. He was alluding to his own view of the "education of the human race" through revelation in stages. On September 18, 1776, Elise wrote to Hennings:[35] "[While a premature disclosure of the identity of the Unnamed would produce more harm than good], a general subversion of the edifice will no doubt soon lead to its total collapse and do away with any thought of reconstructing it. This is the reason that Lessing has adopted the form that you call a mask." Her phraseology ("subversion of the edifice") strikingly recalls the expression used by Lessing in his letter to Mendelssohn of January 9, 1771. Lessing had obviously spoken in similar terms to Elise during his stay in Hamburg. Whether she fully grasped what he had meant by "subverting" the prevalent systems of Christian doctrine is another matter. Her attitude toward Christianity was as negative as her late father's had been, whereas Lessing was groping for the "inner truths" of the Christian religion. The "objections" that he appended to the five fragments clearly indicated this. When she read the volume, her verdict was far from being enthusiastic. She felt that Lessing had assumed a stance that neither the orthodox nor the heterodox could approve.[36] Nicolai expressed a similar view when writing to Lessing on April 24, 1777:[37] "The theologians believe that you are a freethinker, and the freethinkers hold that you have become a theologian." Lessing considered himself neither the one nor the other, and in his reply to Nicolai he recalled that "in a similar way" he had been considered during the last war "an arch-Prussian in Leipzig and an arch-Saxon in Berlin" because he was "neither of the two."[38]

Mendelssohn had too clear an insight into Lessing's position to misjudge him. Yet precisely because he understood him so well, he felt that there was room for criticism on another score. While staying at Hanover in November, 1777, he read, as we recall,[39] the manuscript of *Ernst and Falk: Dialogues for Freemasons*, which Lessing had sent him. On November 11 he replied:[40]

> If you say that you are a Freemason in the same way in which you are a Christian, I must confess that I would say the exact opposite: you are a Freemason of a kind such as you disapprove of in a Christian

[in his approach to Christianity]. For compared with an authentic Freemason, your position looks very much like Eberhard's vis-à-vis Goeze [the spokesman of strict orthodoxy]. In the very fashion of the heterodox you do away with the charm that holds a spell for the senses; exactly like them you explain everything that enchants the orthodox and carries them to the third heaven by reducing it to human and earthly size; like them you preach righteousness, say that Socrates was a Christian without having known the fact, and maintain in the name of God that no honest man can be found outside Christianity.

Lessing had characterized Freemasonry as a kind of "invisible Church" comprising the noblest and least prejudiced men of all ages. Mendelssohn accused him of idealizing the order in the same way in which Eberhard had idealized Christianity as embracing "all men of good will." Masonic orthodoxy, he suggested further, had been treated by Lessing in precisely the same manner in which Christianity had been despoiled of its supernatural charm by a neologist like Eberhard. Its myth and ritual had been dissolved into pure humanitarianism. Not that Mendelssohn objected to such procedure. He wished simply to note a certain inconsistency on Lessing's part.

When Mendelssohn eventually visited Lessing in Wolfenbüttel on December 21, 1777, he may have touched on yet another point of difference. Lessing, in his "objections" to Reimarus' fourth fragment, had included the first fifty-three paragraphs of his (Lessing's) essay *The Education of the Human Race,* representing this material as being from an as yet unpublished treatise by someone other than himself. (When Lessing published the complete essay in 1780, he still maintained this fiction.) The fifty-three paragraphs published in 1777 gave only a hint of Lessing's thesis as a whole, but they were enough to inspire some disquiet in Doctor Reimarus, who eventually expressed his misgivings in a letter to Lessing dated March 19, 1778:[41] " Some friends [have] failed to understand what you really had in mind when mentioning, in your 'objections,' the education of the human race [by way of revelation]. And, seriously speaking, was this essay written by another friend, a would-be sophist, who wanted to move the target at which the arrows [of the Fragmentist] are aimed?" Doctor Reimarus suspected Lessing of being the author, and he also realized that the historical perspective that the essay had opened up threatened to "move the target" against which his late father had shot his arrows.

Lessing's somewhat cryptic reply was:[42] "The *Education of the Human Race* was written by a good friend who likes to construct all kinds of hypotheses and systems in order to have the pleasure of tearing them down again. So far as this particular hypothesis is concerned, it would indeed cause a tremendous shifting of the target at which my Unnamed took aim. Yet never mind. Let everyone tell what he believes to be the truth, and let truth itself be taken care of by God." Lessing thus admitted that the new orientation advocated in the essay had rendered the *Fragments of the Unnamed* largely irrelevant. Doctor Reimarus could not accept the notion of revelation as a progressive gradual unfolding of truth. As a man of the Enlightenment he believed in the selfsameness and self-sufficiency of reason to discover the eternal truths without the aid of revelation. Mendelssohn's attitude was exactly the same, and in his *Jerusalem*, we noticed,[43] he outspokenly rejected Lessing's concept. When he met Lessing in December, 1777, he may well have voiced this opposition in person.

Lessing had wondered whether the orthodox theologians might not react more fiercely to his "objections" than they would to the *Fragments*.[44] He could read a clear answer to this question in an article by Johann Melchior Goeze, chief pastor at the Church of St. Catherine in Hamburg:[45] "Generally speaking, I must confess that I read Herr Lessing's objections with far greater sorrow than [I do] the fragments of the [unnamed] author who displays so much hostility to our most holy religion, and utters such impudent and coarse blasphemies." Goeze's article bestowed high praise on Johann Heinrich Ress, superintendent in Wolfenbüttel, who had attempted to refute the Fragmentist's attacks on the New Testament stories about Jesus' resurrection.[46] The "crusade" against Lessing had been opened by the still moderate effort of Doctor Johann David Schumann, director of the gymnasium in Hanover, who tried to disprove the fragments in his treatise *On the Evidence of the Proofs for the Truth of the Christian Religion*.[47] Goeze commended this work in a review published on January 9, 1778.[48] Lessing had seen fit, he declared, to publicize blasphemies and to offer "objections" that were anything but satisfactory.

It was in his spirited reply to Schumann (*On the Proof of the Spirit and of Power*)[49] that Lessing made the famous statement that "accidental historical truths can never become the proof of necessary truths of reason"; that the transition from one species of truth to another was illicit; and that this was "the broad, ugly ditch" that he could not get across.[50] With even greater force and brilliance Lessing devastated Johann Heinrich Ress' claim that he had resolved the contradictions in the Gospels' accounts of the resurrection. This *Rejoinder*,[51] written at the most cruel time of Lessing's life—his newly born son had just died and his wife was struggling with death—mercilessly scorned the "narrow-chested, lame, squinting, Thersites-like harmonizers" and exhibited their fallacies with a grim sort of wit. When Karl described this work as "a theological comedy," Lessing wrote in reply:[52] "I am very pleased that my *Rejoinder* appealed to you. I am particularly glad that you begin to enjoy the *haut-comique* of the polemic, which makes all other theatrical projects so insipid and wishy-washy." But Mendelssohn had been the first to diagnose Lessing's temper. As early as January 29, 1778, he had written in a postscript of a letter to Doctor Zimmermann:[53] "Yesterday I read Wieland's *Rosamund*, and today Lessing's *Rejoinder*. If the former betrays the aging poet, the latter reveals the rejuvenated fighter in all his alertness. Though I am hardly a friend of polemical writings, I nevertheless beg of you to read this *Rejoinder*. In my view, it equals the best of Lessing's comedies."

One can almost see Mendelssohn watching the theological battle and enjoying Lessing's superb performance—and yet regretting his friend's increasing involvement in what he considered useless polemic. This dual strain in Mendelssohn's attitude persisted for as long as the "comedy" lasted and Lessing's freedom of expression was not curbed. He was kept abreast of the course of events by Lessing's brother Karl. When the situation took an adverse turn, he at once offered his help, and in the end even he somehow became involved in the affair, ironically enough. It may be taken for granted that Mendelssohn cared little for the purely theological issues of the controversy but took an intense interest in it insofar as it affected Lessing and called forth the exercise of his literary genius.

On March 16, 1778, Lessing sent his brother two pieces in reply to Goeze: the *Parable* and the *Axiomata*.[54] Both abounded in striking similes and scored point after point. The *Axiomata* offered the most elaborate statement of his position. Goeze had singled out as targets for attack[55] ten sentences in the preamble to Lessing's "objections" to the Fragmentist. The *Axiomata* offered a kind of commentary on these key sentences. They expressed the view that the Bible contained more than what concerned the Christian religion as such; that the "letter" was not the same as the "spirit," and that the Bible was therefore not identical with the Christian faith; that objections to the Bible were not ipso facto objections to Christianity, which existed prior to the writing of the New Testament; and that the Scriptures had to be interpreted in the light of the "inner truth" of Christianity rather than as the sources of this truth. In support of his thesis Lessing quoted a statement by Johann David Michaelis, according to which the Christian religion did not "stand or fall" with the authenticity of the gospel stories.[56] Lessing may have considered it advisable to invoke the authority of a recognized Christian scholar because Goeze had raised the specter of the Jews as gleeful beneficiaries of New Testament criticism: "The Jews will welcome the last fragment in particular. By confirming them in their unbelief and hostility toward Jesus and his religion, it will be more useful to them than even their *Toledot Yeshu*." This was not the only anti-Jewish reference in Goeze's polemic against Lessing.[57]

The battle was moving toward a climax. "A new fighter has arisen, a certain Rector Mascho," Karl Lessing wrote to his brother on March 14, 1778.[58] Friedrich Wilhelm Mascho, a schoolmaster, had just published a *Defense of the Revealed Christian Religion against the Fragments from the Wolfenbüttel Library*, in which he denigrated the Unnamed as a "miserable prig,"[59] and a glowing review of this treatise appeared on March 17 in the Hamburg *Freywillige Beyträge*,[60] which Lessing erroneously attributed to Goeze. In the same issue, however, Goeze had linked Lessing's theological writings to those of the notorious Karl Friedrich Bahrdt (1741–1792), against whom the Imperial Court Council in Vienna had begun to take action:[61] "Herr Lessing will have to start believing that it is no trifling matter to publish fragments in which the holy apostles . . . are denounced as rogues, thieves of corpses, and liars."

Doctor Reimarus was greatly concerned by this implied threat, since Goeze was the prime mover in the fight against Bahrdt. Lessing was enraged but not at all intimidated. On the contrary, he decided that the time was now ripe to publish the balance of the fifth fragment *On Jesus' Purpose and That of His Disciples*. He informed Doctor Reimarus of his intention and as further proof of his determination sent him the first number of his *Anti-Goeze*, a "drollery" *(Schnurre)* dealing with both Mascho and Goeze. He promised to write such a drollery every time Goeze made rude remarks in his paper. The promise was fulfilled. No less than eleven numbers of the *Anti-Goeze* appeared. But Goeze had not given in either. On April 7 he signed the preface to a volume of polemical essays *(Etwas Vorläufiges . . .)* in which Lessing's "direct and indirect hostile attacks against our most holy religion and its unitary source, Holy Scripture" were to be rebutted. Soon there followed Part One of his *Lessings Schwächen*, an attempt to show the "weak points" in the reasoning of Lessing's *Parable* and other writings.

Early in June, 1778, the last fragment, *On Jesus' Purpose and That of His Disciples*, of which only a section had been published hitherto, appeared in Brunswick. It exploded like a bombshell. Never before in Germany had the New Testament been subjected to such radical criticism.[62] The fragment portrayed Jesus as a political adventurer who, jointly with his "cousin" John, plotted the overthrow of both secular and spiritual authority in order to establish himself as the messianic king of the Jews. He had no intention of abolishing the Jewish ceremonial law and he opposed only the hypocrisy of the Pharisees. Nor did he wish to extend his rule beyond the confines of his nation. The apostles and evangelists shared his aspirations until his death. When they realized that he had failed miserably in his purpose, they conceived the idea of imputing to his mission on earth an entirely different goal, namely the redemption of the human race through his suffering. The new eschatological "system" that they applied to Jesus also had its origin in the Jewish tradition. In order to invest their apocalyptic theory with credibility, they cleverly removed Jesus' body and invented the story of the resurrection.[63] Lessing explained in his preface that he had deemed it necessary to present the last fragment in its entirety so as to make a full inquiry into the subject possible. To fear the collapse of Christianity as the result of an open discussion showed little faith in its truth. Pastor Goeze, who attempted to stifle debate and who called Lessing *raca (rasha'*, "wicked") so as to bring down upon him the punishment of the Great Council, had a proud and yet poor opinion of the Christian religion.[64]

Both orthodox theologians and neologists were shocked by this new publication. Goeze noted that this time Lessing had appended no "objections" to the "monstrosities" that he had dared to commit to print; he deserved thanks for this omission, Goeze continued, Lessing's previous comments having been more poisonous than the fragments themselves. To see the founder of Christianity treated like a Sabbatai Zevi could only cause every Christian to shudder.[65] The neologist Friedrich Lüdke asked in his review-article:[66] "What useful purpose can such a book serve in the interests of the Christian public? . . . We shall never invent a better religion for men than the religion of Christ, which apart from its inner rationality has also an external positive sanction. Can we want to deprive the people of the latter? Is this not tantamount to exposing the ship to the open sea without rudder, mast, or sail?" As Karl Lessing reported to his brother on June 7, Mendelssohn also felt serious misgivings. He had pointed out "that if we desired to overthrow the whole of Christianity, the priests would hold before us, as it were, morality—the innocent child —and say that we ought to refrain from attacking Christianity lest morality should get lost too."[67] It had always been Mendelssohn's conviction, we recall, that religious doctrines should be left inviolate if they were closely interwoven with the texture of a nation's moral life. His remark to Karl Lessing indicates that he was watching the course of events with growing anxiety.

The identity of the Unnamed had continued to remain a well-kept secret, but an unguarded remark of Lessing's in the *Rejoinder* had betrayed the fact that he, at least, knew who the author was. He had advised the polemicists to tone down the shrillness of their voice, lest they incur ridicule "when [they] eventually learned who the honest and blameless man was whom they had scorned." Goeze inferred from this remark that Lessing knew more about his Unnamed than he had seen fit to tell his readers, and that "all he had pretended about the Wertheim Bible translator was dust thrown in our eyes."[68] In March, 1778, rumors circulated in Hamburg that the late Professor Reimarus was the author of the *Fragments,* but a review of Mascho's *Defense,* which appeared in Altona on March 9, helped to clear Reimarus of the charge.[69] The rumor persisted however, and on April 24 Goeze declared that it was now Lessing's "duty" to name the author.[70] Doctor Reimarus grew alarmed and wrote an angry letter to the editor of the Altona *Reichs-Postreuther,* which had published a note about the author as a person "only too well known," a clear reference to his late father. As a result of his action, a paragraph appeared in the paper that read:[71] "We take this opportunity to deny publicly the very widespread rumor that a certain famous teacher at the Hamburg gymnasium, now deceased, was the author of the *Fragments.*"

In his *Anti-Goeze IX* and *Anti-Goeze X* Lessing condemned the idle curiosity about the identity of the Fragmentist, but the curiosity continued unabated and speculation continued. Professor Reimarus' name was not the only possibility considered. Johann Friedrich Kleuker, author of a lengthy polemical treatise attacking Leibniz and Wolff in addition to Lessing and the Unnamed, suggested that certain literary, orthographical, chronological and other clues pointed to the ex-Rector D[amm].[72] Christian Tobias Damm, who died on May 27, 1778 (and thus was still alive when Kleuker wrote his treatise), had been forced to resign in 1776 from his post as rector of the Cölnisches Gymnasium in Berlin; he had expressed dissident theological views and had paid for his candor. Mendelssohn, who had profited from Damm's lessons in Homer and enjoyed his pithy asides, remembered the rector with deep affection.[73] He compared Damm's fate as a martyr to that of Johann Christian Edelmann (1698–1767), whose radical ideas about the Bible and Jesus had wrecked his life.[74] In a letter to Hennings dated July 29, 1779, Mendelssohn described the agonies in store for freethinkers in Berlin:[75]

> Such a one will perhaps not be persecuted; he will be permitted to breathe the air, to drink water gratis and eat bread for money; but, like Edelmann, Damm, and others who were innocent victims of their old-time German outspokenness, he will walk about like a shadow, misunderstood and abandoned among his fellow men and, eventually, he will be forgotten. I still saw and talked to Edelmann, who had to live here under a false name. I have known no more miserable figure than his, as he timidly sneaked into the room for fear of being recognized.

Another writer suspected of being the author of the *Fragments* was Ludwig August Unzer, a brother of Johann Christoph Unzer who in April 1778 had taken up the cudgels on Lessing's behalf in the *Neuer gelehrter Mercurius*, a journal he edited in Altona.[76]

Eventually suspicion turned even to Mendelssohn. Thus on October 20 Lessing could write to his brother Karl:[77] "Have you read the *Epistle of a Layman*[78] in which Moses is said to be the author of *On Jesus' Purpose and That of His Disciples*? I wish the thing were not so exceedingly poor, so that he could defend himself. Perhaps the accusation will be taken up by others too, and I shall laugh heartily if he is at long last compelled to stand up for his good name." Karl replied:[79] "Moses is, it seems, as yet unable to repudiate the accusation because, according to this fool, circumcised friends are supposed to be assisting you." That the suspicion was indeed taken up by others and persisted for a considerable time is shown by Mendelssohn's postscript to a letter he wrote to Herder on September 24, 1781:[80]

> I suppose there is no need for me to reassure you at length that I am not the author of the *Fragments*. Even assuming I was able and willing to write something of this sort, I would not have done it anonymously. However, you will find it hard to believe that up to this hour I have not yet read that much-quoted, famous, notorious, refuted, and yet not often enough refuted fragment [*On Jesus' Purpose* . . .]. It is nevertheless a literally true fact. I never read Lessing's altercations for the sake of the subject matter. It was only his style and manner that compelled one to read them.

We know of no other attempt by Mendelssohn to defend himself against this particular accusation. Probably he preferred simply to ignore it. Lessing's remark must be understood as a good-humored comment on his friend's stubborn refusal to get involved in theological controversy. When Hennings complained about the annoyance that his conflict with ecclesiastics was causing him, Mendelssohn wrote to him on June 20, 1780:[81] "Did I not tell you from the beginning, dearest friend, that your quarrel with the theologians would soon become bothersome to you? One has to be a hardened fighter like Lessing to be able to stand them. I for one would be patient and steady enough to protect my skin against a furious swarm of bees rather than against these bellicose apostles of peace." From a hitherto unpublished letter of Friedrich Resewitz to Nicolai it appears that the rumor about Mendelssohn's authorship of the *Fragments* had not reached him. Nicolai had asked Resewitz to review the entire literature appertaining to the *Fragments* for the *Allgemeine deutsche Bibliothek*, but Resewitz had declined and Lüdke had stepped into the breach (his review covered no less than twenty-nine books and pamphlets); Resewitz did, however, write a review of Johann Salomon Semler's devastating attack on the *Fragments*.[82] As the letter to Nicolai shows, it originally contained the conjecture that some modern Jewish writer might be responsible for them. When asked by Nicolai whether he was alluding to Mendelssohn, who was rumored to be the author, Resewitz replied on December 30, 1779:[83]

> I have heard nothing about the surmise that Moses Mendelssohn is the author of the *Fragments* nor would I have believed this if I had been told it. This treatise is far too contrary to his mind, spirit, and style. He would have had to renounce his good and noble mind to be able to utter so much hatred against a religion that has not insulted him and under whose protection he lives, and many of whose members hold him in high regard. Hence, when I wrote that the author of the *Fragments* expressed a neo-Jewish view I was not thinking of him nor could I have done so, but I wrote this because I had a feeling that this was the case and because of the impression that the author's mind had made upon me. He really seems to know the mentality of the latter-day Jews better than the mind of the ancient Jews at the time of Jesus, and he is obviously unable to put himself in the then prevailing context. He speaks in the manner of latter-day Jewish writings rather than in accordance with the locale and frame of mind of the people of the time. Hence I did not consider it impossible that it was written by a latter-day Jew, though obviously by one unlike Mendelssohn, or that it had, at least, been supplied with material by such a one. However, if a remark of this kind is apt to cause even the least annoyance to Herr Mendelssohn or to give rise to unkind interpretations, I give my full consent to the omission of the passage concerned from the printed review.

In the remaining section of the letter Resewitz replied to the disclosure by Nicolai that the late Professor Reimarus was actually the author. Resewitz refused to believe this and argued at length that a work of this kind was utterly foreign to the character of the man. It seems that the rumor about Reimarus' authorship had come to Resewitz' ears previously and that he had made up his mind to discredit it. His theory about the Jewish origin of the *Fragments* was a convenient solution to the problem. Just a year earlier Mascho, in a new treatise *(Beleuchtung der neuesten Angriffe . . .),* had taken the same line, that of blaming the *Fragments* on the Jews. His suggestion had been that the Fragmentist's source was "a poisonous old Jewish book," identified as the *Sefer Milhemet Hova,* extracts from which had been published in [Siegmund Jacob] Baumgarten's *Hallische Bibliothek.*[84] A reviewer of Mascho's work had expressed his pleasure at the fact that the evidence produced had completely "nullified" the "slanderous" assumption that "a late Hamburg teacher of merit" was the author.[85]

The turning point in Lessing's controversy occured in July, 1778. The Wolfenbüttel consistory prevailed upon the old Duke Karl, at a time when the hereditary prince was abroad, to clamp down on Lessing. A rescript dated July 6 ordered the local publishing firm not to print any more theological writings by him; to stop the sale of volumes three and four of the Wolfenbüttel series and of the subsequent publications; and to surrender the remaining copies for confiscation.[86] A letter addressed by the duke to Lessing on July 13 accused him of having contravened the condition under which he had been granted dispensation from censorship: he had published writings injurious to religion and morality. The dispensation was canceled, and he was ordered to return the manuscript of the Unnamed and to refrain from any further publication of the *Fragments* or of similar writings.[87] Lessing had been informed of the rescript by his publisher before the duke's letter reached him. On July 11 he wrote to the sovereign, expressing his consternation and defending himself against the charge of having acted against the interests of the Lutheran Church. While submitting to the order forbidding any more publications from the *Fragments,* he pleaded for the right to continue his self-defense vis-à-vise Goeze. After receiving the duke's letter of July 13, Lessing reiterated his petition but was informed that all his writings were now subject to censorship.[88]

When early in July the disturbing news reached Berlin that Lessing was being prevented by the authorities from continuing his theological writing, it was not clear whether the prohibition had come from the Brunswick government or from the Imperial Corpus Evangelicum, which comprised the German Protestant Estates *(Reichsstände).* Karl, who was greatly disturbed, asked his brother for precise information by return mail. His letter continued:[89] "Our friend Moses sends his regards and asks you to let him have a copy of the official document containing the prohibition, if the rumor is indeed true. He will then write to you concerning the matter, and he will publish the letter in printed form so that you and others may find it easier to read. He has always predicted that things would come to such a pass. I believe that he knows the Christian theologians only too well from his powerless rabbis. The gentlemen in this world who hold office and draw salaries for the sake of the eternal bliss of others resemble each other in their behavior to the same extent that they are dissimilar in their dogmatic assertions." When replying to his brother on

July 23, Lessing did not enclose the requested copy. Karl asked for it a second time on August 1:[90] "Do send Moses a copy of the prohibition that has been issued against you. He will use it on your behalf." Lessing seems to have responded to the request, for it was he who told Elise Reimarus during his stay in Hamburg in September of Mendelssohn's plan. In a letter to Hennings, dated September 15, 1778, she reported among other thing that Lessing (who "had just been here") had told them:[91] "All rumors about investigations and testimonies at the behest of higher authorities concerning the author of the *Fragments* are false. However, it is true that Mendelssohn will soon publish a philosophical letter about this sort of prohibition of writing on ecclesiastical matters. I am eager to see it." He never did, however, for the project failed to materialize.

How strongly Mendelssohn felt the urge to be of assistance to Lessing is attested by yet another offer on his part. In his letter to Karl dated July 23[92] Lessing had informed him that he was not aware of any action taken by the Corpus Evangelicum or the Imperial Court Council. Nor was he afraid that the Roman Catholic majority of the council would be swayed by the condemnation of his writings by the Lutherans. For he could easily present his case in a way that would appeal to the papists: had he not shown that Christianity was founded upon the tradition of the church rather than on Scripture, and were not Lutheran attacks on this view tantamount to attacks on the Catholic position? With this strategy in mind Lessing had written a reply to Goeze's recent point-blank question: "What kind of a religion did he [Lessing] mean by the Christian religion; and what kind of religion did he recognize and accept as true?" His reply bore the title *A Necessary Answer to a Very Unnecessary Question by Herr Chief Pastor Goeze in Hamburg.*[93] A copy of it was enclosed with the letter. Lessing had sent another copy to Hamburg to be printed there, and he left it to his brother's discretion to have the work printed in Berlin as well. On August 1 Karl reported: "Moses, who sends his regards, was of the opinion that the manuscript that you sent me should be printed without prior inquiry and distributed gratis; he was most willing to defray the cost. I was not too happy with this proposition, however, and I handed the manuscript to Herr Voss, who immediately received permission from Chief Consistorial Councillor Teller to have it printed and sold publicly." On August 4 Karl was able to send his brother twenty-four copies of the printed *Answer.*[94] The Berlin and Hamburg editions appeared simultaneously, and on the title-page both named Wolfenbüttel as the place of publication.

Following this act of defiance, Lessing wrote a letter to the duke on August 8, asking for clarification of the purpose of the rescript. He assumed, he said, that only works of his that were actually printed in the duchy of Brunswick were subject to censorship. But if his interpretation was erroneous, he had to inform the duke that a pamphlet printed in Berlin, where it had the approval of the censor, had just appeared in contravention of the rescript. Since he planned to publish further writings of this kind, he implored the sovereign to instruct the ministry to let him know precisely what the terms were. The nature of the reply received would determine whether or not he could obey.[95] The last sentence implied a threat to resign from his post. Lessing refused to believe that the duke would take a rigorous stand, and he took a calculated risk. At the same time, he considered the possibility that his resignation might become inevitable, as is evident from his letters to the brother and Elise.[96] On August 17 the duke informed Lessing that he was not permitted "to print anything appertaining to religious matters either locally or elsewhere, be it under his or any assumed name, without prior sanction by the Ducal Secret Ministry."[97] The controversy, which had become Lessing's "hobby-horse," was forcibly ended. Only as a last act of defiance did Lessing publish a sequel to his *Answer* in reply to the third part of Goeze's *Lessings Schwächen*.

As Elise reported to Hennings on September 15, Lessing was not really afraid of unpleasant consequences, since the old duke had permitted him to travel to Hamburg and written in his passport: "To my dear Lessing . . ." What led him to stay in Wolfenbüttel was a combination of factors: dire economic necessity, the importance of the library as his "arsenal," and the creative compensation of a new and exciting project, *Nathan the Wise*.

II

Lessing's youthful comedy *The Jews* had helped to initiate his friendship with Mendelssohn. His last play, *Nathan the Wise*, became the crown and glory of their relationship. *The Jews* had been written before Lessing had met Mendelssohn. *Nathan* without Mendelssohn would have been like *Hamlet* without the Prince of Denmark. One does not have to assume that Lessing wished to immortalize his friend.[1] It was quite natural that in drawing the character of the wise Jew (from his *Vorlage* in Boccaccio's *Decameron*) Lessing should endow the character with the familiar features of his closest friend Mendelssohn, the merchant-philosopher.

In so doing, Lessing did not idealize his friend, nor did he produce an exact replica. As a dramatist, he took, added, and omitted whatever suited his artistic purpose. Yet Mendelssohn's personality is clearly recognizable in the character of Nathan. And some of the other figures of the play were also drawn from life, more or less. The old arithmetical wizard and chess-player Abram, known in Mendelssohn's circle as *Arlequin sauvage*, served Lessing as a model for Al-Hafi,[2] and Chief Pastor Goeze enriched the character and vocabulary of the Patriarch. On June 3, 1779, Elise Reimarus wrote to Lessing:[3] "I just received the following written verdict about your *Nathan:* 'A noble Mendelssohnian character; yet my hero is Lessing. It is him that I found in the Templar, the Friar, the Dervish, and the Wise. In all the various traits that he scattered abroad I find a truth on which I like to reflect with all my soul. . . .' " The enthusiastic judge quoted by Elise was certainly right in finding Lessing himself in many of the figures, including Nathan. But he was equally justified in describing Nathan as a "Mendelssohnian character," notwithstanding the needlessly heated efforts of some later scholars and critics to minimize, or to deny altogether, the similarity of Mendelssohn and Nathan.[4]

It was during the period of acute anxiety, when as a result of his risky letter to the duke he had to envisage the possibility of a bleak future, that Lessing decided to resume work on his *Nathan*. He had originally planned to do this immediately upon his return from the Italian journey, but had abandoned the idea.[5] On August 11 he wrote to Karl:[6]

> I do not yet know how the matter will turn out, but I want to be prepared for every eventuality. You well know that there is no better way of achieving this than by having as much money as one needs. Well, a bizarre idea occurred to me last night. Many years ago I sketched a play whose content has a sort of analogy to my present quarrels that could have hardly been dreamt of then. Provided I have your and Moses' approval, I want to have the thing printed by subscription, and you may—the sooner the better—have the attached announcement printed in a few hundred copies on a single octavo page and have it distributed to the extent you deem necessary. Though I do not wish the content of my play to become known prematurely, I suggest that if you and Moses would like to be acquainted with it you look up Boccaccio's *Decamerone*, Giornata I, Nov. III: Melchisedech Giudeo. I think that I have invented a very interesting episode for it, that it will read very well, and that I shall, no doubt, thereby play the theologians a trick worse than ten more fragments.

"At all events, complete your Nathan," Karl replied on August 18.[7] "There will be no lack of subscribers. Our Moses, who is returning from a two-week trip today,[8] very much approves of your plan, as I already know. He had often found fault with you for not having employed your labors in this fashion." Mendelssohn, it may be gathered from this remark, was relieved to see Lessing return to his true métier. The theological controversy had put a certain distance between the two friends, but the prospect now opened up for a restoration of their unanimity. Karl, being still in the dark about the manner in which Lessing proposed to treat his theme—the *avertissement* spoke merely of a dramatic work of "a somewhat unusual kind" entitled *Nathan the Wise, in five acts*—expressed the hope that in the guise of a "theological comedy" he would continue to pursue his adversaries.[9] As long ago as July he had urged his brother to conclude his quarrels with a "merry afterpiece."[10] Mendelssohn, he reported on August 25, held a different view:[11] subjecting the "follies of the theologians" to scorn and laughter would only play into the theologians' hands. They would be able to discredit his work as a mere comedy and stigmatize him as a Voltaire. But if he were to sustain in the play the serious tone of his recent *Answer* to Goeze, any attempt to disparage the work would fail. What he should write, then, was a theatrical piece unrelated to the current controversy.

Lessing agreed with Mendelssohn in this. On October 20, following his return from Hamburg, he wrote:[12]

Even you, dear brother, have gotten an entirely wrong idea about it [*i.e., Nathan*, which had already aroused concern in Wolfenbüttel]. It will be nothing less than a satirical piece with which to leave the arena mockingly. It will be as moving a piece as any I have made, and Herr Moses was perfectly right in his judgment that ·derision and laughter would not fit with the tone sounded in my last paper (and which you also find in the enclosed "sequel"), unless I wanted to give up the entire controversy. Yet to do this I have as yet not the least inclination, and he [Mendelssohn] will no doubt realize that I am doing no harm to my cause as a result of this dramatic swerve.

During his stay in Hamburg, Lessing had told Elise in exactly the same terms that his new play would turn out to be one of his "most moving ones."[13] He had abandoned the *haut-comique* of the polemic but not his polemical intent. "I have to find out whether I am still permitted to preach undisturbed at least in my old pulpit, the theater," he had written to Elise on September 6.[14] The "sort of analogy" between *Nathan* and his theological writings was still in force, though he warned the reader in an unfinished draft of a preface not to expect more allusions of a topical nature than could have possibly been worked into the play. After all, its outline had been fixed at a time prior to his involvement in theological controversy. He added, however, that "Nathan's attitude toward *all* positive religions has always been the one I took."[15] His *Nathan,* he wrote to Jacobi, was "a son of his beginning old age, whom polemic had helped deliver,"[16] and similarly he told the baron von Gebler in Vienna that the play was "the fruit of polemic rather than of genius."[17]

When *Nathan the Wise* was banned in Vienna, Nicolai tried to minimize its connection with Lessing's theological writings: "I do not believe," he wrote to von Gebler on October 10, 1779,[18] "that Lessing's *Nathan* has anything in common with the *Fragments* and the controversy about them. His friends know that he had finished the sketch [of the play] long before. . . . The only relation . . . lies, perhaps, in the association of the Patriarch with Goeze in Hamburg." Yet the "analogy" went far deeper than Nicolai suggested. Lessing, like his hero, faced danger in speaking the truth; and like him, he had to resort to poetry to be free to express what he had to say. Nathan used the parable form; Lessing chose for his medium a "dramatic poem," and he indicated its theological intent by adopting as its motto Heraclitus' line (which he had found in Aulus Gellius): "Introite, et hic Dii sunt" ("Do enter, for here too are gods"). Moreover, both Nathan and Lessing affirm the truth of a religion transcending divisiveness.[19]

As early as November 7, 1778, Lessing could inform his brother that the play was more or less ready to be printed but that he now wished to put the finishing touches upon it. He hoped to start making a fair copy about the end of the year and to see it published in the spring.[20] On December 7 he announced to Karl that *Nathan* was written in verse, and he attached the first batch of the manuscript with his letter. He wished to know what Ramler thought about his choice of meter, and how Mendelssohn felt about "the tone of the whole."[21] Ramler was the reigning master of the art of versification, and since Lessing had never before used verse in his dramas and was, moreover, introducing as a novelty the English blank verse of five iambic feet,[22] he was anxious to have Ramler's approval.[23] The procedure adopted for checking the manuscript was as follows: Lessing sent it in six successive batches (following the first)[24] to Karl, who passed it on to Ramler, who in turn sent it to Mendelssohn;[25] Karl returned the manuscript to Lessing, who considered the suggested revisions and in due course sent the work to the printer.

Mendelssohn, though immersed in his Pentateuch project, took the time to read the manuscript with care. It was probably due to his heavy schedule that he sometimes kept it too long. We get a glimpse of the situation from a hitherto unpublished note addressed to him by Johann Jacob Engel on March 13, 1779.[26] It urged him to return the manuscript of the fourth act, which Karl Lessing and Voss had promised him. Karl had tried in vain to contact Mendelssohn, and now Engel had been authorized by Voss to "demand" the manuscript back. "Would you be kind enough," Mendelssohn is asked, "to hand it to the bearer of this note? I would have liked to pick it up myself, but I know I would not have been able to get away from you so soon, yet would not have had the time to stay long." As it turned out, Mendelssohn's close reading of this act did pay dividends. On March 19, 1779, Lessing wrote to his brother:[27] "The most recent [batch of] manuscript has just come back.... By the next mail I shall personally thank our Moses for the good suggestion he has offered." According to information supplied by David Friedländer,[28] Mendelssohn had objected to a scene in the fourth act in which Saladin had asked the Templar whether his mother had ever stayed in Eastern lands (presumably because he wanted to explain to himself the Templar's resemblance to his late brother), and he replied: "Not my mother, but my father." Mendelssohn felt that this passage should be deleted because it was reminiscent of a well-known short story and, in his view, unworthy of Lessing.[29] It is unknown whether he conveyed his suggestion in a letter of his own or through either Ramler or Karl, nor whether Lessing's letter of thanks was ever written. However, Lessing did accept the suggestion.

On May 1, 1779, with the last batch of clean proofs returned and publication near, Karl wrote to his brother:[30] "Moses sends his warmest regards. He believes that your *Nathan* is the best play you have ever written." Lessing probably agreed. Though aware of certain flaws in the work, he did not regret them; they were the price he had to pay to achieve the purpose closest to his heart. He made this point clearly in a fragmentary essay that may have been written during the winter of 1778/79:[31] "Should one say that a play devoted to such a particular tendency is not sufficiently rich in particular beauty, I shall keep silent but not be ashamed. I am conscious of a goal that, kept in mind, enables one honorably to hold his own.... As yet I know of no place in Germany where this play could now be put on the stage, but all hail and cheers to the one in which it is first performed."

The goal of which Lessing was conscious was the promotion of toler- ance. For its sake he had been willing to violate a rule of dramatic art that he had himself laid down in his *Hamburgische Dramaturgie:* to reserve reasoning for the comedy and to make passion preponderant in the tragedy.[32] Knowing well that his play was neither comedy nor tragedy, he called it a "dramatic poem." Mendelssohn was probably not at all troubled by critical considerations of this kind. The noble tendency of the work filled him with deep admiration, and he relished the deftness of the plot, the wisdom and humor of the dialogue, and the pungent allusions to current affairs. As later utterances of his show unmistakably, he was in deep accord with the point Lessing had made (or seemed to him to have made). He described the play as a "magnificent poem in praise of Providence,"[33] and as an affirmation, therefore, of one of the principal tenets of natural religion. He was no less in agreement with the way in which Lessing had elaborated the parable of the three rings that he had found in Boccaccio. We shall discuss this aspect first.

Lessing knew the three-rings story both in Boccaccio's rendering and in an older version found in the German translation of the *Gesta Romanorum* printed in Augsburg in 1489.[34] In this version, which was a literal translation from the early fourteenth-century Latin text of the popular collection of stories, an emperor is said to have bequeathed different things to his three sons. To the first he gave the right of inheritance, to the second his treasures, and to the third a ring more precious than the other two gifts. The first two sons also received rings, but they could not compare in value with that given the third. The story is here told as an authentic parable that discloses the ultimate truth on a religious plane.[35] Of the three sons (the Jews, the Saracens, and the Christians), the first received from God the promised land, the second received wealth, and the third received the Christian faith—which excels all else. In Boccaccio's *Decameron* (1349–1351) the story-teller describes the parable as "dangerous" (*dubbioso*), and quite daring it is, considering the relativistic position it takes. Saladin, desiring to lay a trap for the rich and avaricious Jew Melchisedek, asked him which of the three religions he considered to be the true one. The Jew answered the question by telling the story of the three sons who were alike in handsome appearance, virtue, and obedience to the father. According to an ancient family rule, only one in every generation was to possess the most beautiful and precious ring. But the father wishing to please all three equally loved sons, had two additional rings fashioned by a skillful master; they so closely resembled the original that the father could "hardly" tell which was which. On his deathbed, the father secretly gave each son one of the rings, and after his demise each claimed the right to be acknowledged head of the family, for each had "the" ring. Yet because the sons could not distinguish the original ring from the copies, the question of who was head of the family had to remain undecided. In the same way, Melchisedek told the Sultan, the question as to who professes the true religion is undecided. This version has all the marks of a Renaissance story: the father still knew which ring was the true one, the sons did not. God knows the truth, but it is beyond the power of men to determine with certainty which religion is to be preferred. Only unmitigated skepticism is justified.

This rather crude solution did not commend itself to Lessing, and though he followed the outline of the story closely, he infused a new spirit into it. The old medieval affirmation of simple faith could not be resuscitated, but echoes of it can be heard in Lessing's version. There is an intimation of eternity in its opening lines: "In days of yore, there dwelt in Eastern lands / A man, who from the hand of his most dear beloved / Received a ring of priceless worth . . ."[36] The ring was a gift from its very inception, then, and its power, which resided in its wondrous stone (an iridescent opal), made him who wore it "of God and man beloved." Yet faith of a kind was required for the stone to show forth its magic: its owner had to wear it with a sense of trust *(in dieser Zuversicht)*. Trust in its efficacy to render its owner beloved is also trust in the father's judgment, which ordained that, generation after generation, the most beloved of his sons should inherit the ring. This principle of election, which implies favoritism and perhaps supernatural grace, breaks down in the situation of a father who, though not wishing to abrogate the old rule, makes it ineffective. Loving all three sons equally, he fails to exercise his prerogative and "with good-natured weakness" promises the ring to each. He has two more rings of the same quality made, and when they are brought to him not even he can see any difference among the three. Thus the truth is lost even to the father, the divine mystery of yore is dissolved, and the supernatural order is replaced by the human. Now everyone wants to be the prince of the house. "Question arises, tumult and debate— / But all in vain—the true ring could no more / Be then distinguished than—the true faith now." Yet are there no distinctive marks between the religions? Do they not differ in their ways of life? To this question, which concerns the positive religions, Lessing has the answer: they are all built on history, traditional or written. In this respect they are all alike. But history must be taken on trust—it has no other credentials—and each religion claims to be the true one because it trusts its own tradition most. In other words, all that makes it a positive religion (revelation, miracles, law, and ritual) has historical roots and rests on a body of traditions received on trust *(auf Treu und Glauben)*.

Nathan's parable is not yet ended. Since each son claimed to have received the ring directly from his father's hand—as, indeed, each had—mutual recrimination was inevitable. The judge, exasperated, asked the three to bring the father before his tribunal, if they wanted him to pronounce a verdict. "Am I to judge enigmas? Do you think / That the true ring will here unseal its lips?" This feature of the story is found neither in the *Gesta Romanorum* nor in Boccaccio. It is, however, the final answer in the early sixteenth-century Hebrew version of the parable as it appears in Solomon ibn Verga's popular work *Shevet Yehuda* ("The Rod of Judah").[37] In this version a fictitious king, Pedro the Elder, asks a fictitious Jew, Ephraim Sancho (Santob; Shemtob), which of the two religions, the Christian or the Jewish, is the better one. At first Sancho gives an evasive answer: the Jewish religion is the better one for the Jews because it fits their condition, since they had been slaves in Egypt and had been redeemed by God amid wonders and signs; Christianity, on the other hand, is the better religion for the Christians because it wields power in the world. The king rejects this answer; he wants to hear which religion is intrinsically better. Sancho asks for three days' grace in which to reflect on the question. His request is granted. After three days he returns, his face showing distress and anger. Asked by the king what it was that had upset him, Sancho tells this story: his neighbor, who had gone abroad, had given each of his two sons a precious stone. The sons had now come to ask his opinion as to which stone was the more valuable. He had told them that there was no one as well qualified to answer their question as their own father, who was the most expert of jewellers; they should send someone to him if they wanted to find out the truth. Whereupon Sancho had been insulted and beaten up by the sons! When the king expressed indignation at such behavior, Sancho said: Let thine ears, O King, listen to what went forth from your mouth. Esau [the symbol of Rome and of the Roman Church] and Jacob [representing Israel] were brothers, and to each a jewel was given. Now my lord asks which one is better. Let the king send a messenger to our Father who is in heaven. He is the great jeweller, and He will tell the difference." The king thereupon turned to his councillor, Nicholas of Valencia, who had denounced the Jews as hostile and impudent, and told him that he was exposed as a liar. Lessing's "If the father is not brought / Before my seat, I cannot judge the case" is obviously based on the Solomon ibn Verga story, which could well have been brought to Lessing's notice by Moses Mendelssohn, who was of course familiar with it.

On second thought Nathan gives his final answer: if the authentic ring has indeed the power to make the man who wears it beloved both by God and man, let that decide. Since none of the three is best loved by the others and each seems to love only himself, all three are deceived deceivers; all three rings are false—and the real ring has disappeared! Perhaps the father wished to end "the tyranny of the one ring in his house" and had three rings made to take the place of the one. As things now stand, the only way to prove one's religion to be true is to imitate the father's love: "So, free from prejudice, let each one aim / To emulate his brethren in the strife, / To prove the virtues of his ring by kindness, / By cordial understanding, charitable acts, / Accepting God's decrees in perfect love." In his dialogue *The Testament of John,* written in 1777, Lessing had asked the question: "Which of the two would seem to be the more difficult thing?—To accept and profess the Christian dogmas? Or to practice Christian love?" The words, "Little children, love one another," which according to Jerome were John's last words, occur again and again in this dialogue.[38] They are the burden of Lessing's message in Nathan's parable, and in the additional exhortation to be "free from prejudice" they contain the flavor of Enlightenment philosophy. Nathan has now answered Saladin's question, "which faith or law you deem best." The only truth of positive religion that is capable of proof is the practical truth: deeds of love begetting love. The verification of this kind of truth has no limit in time, and the final verdict has to be postponed: "And when in days to come the magic powers / Of these fair rings among your children's children / Brighten the world, I call you once again, / After a thousand thousand years are lapsed, / Before this seat of judgment. On that day / A wiser man shall sit on it and speak. / Depart! So spake the modest Judge."[39]

Mendelssohn could and did agree with every nuance of this parable. Like Lessing, he vindicated to the positive religions only a historical foundation and the right to accept their own inherited traditions on trust. In his *Epilogue* to Lavater's *Reply* he had said[40] that by employing the historical proof from miracles he could defend any religion "because I know of no religious party that does not produce testimonies from miracles, and each one must have the right to consider his forebears trustworthy. Every revelation is transmitted by tradition and documents; herein we agree. According to the principles of my religion, however, the source of the tradition must be a public act of legislation, not mere miracles." When an unidentified French correspondent asked him to explain why he saw no need to make proselytes for Judaism, he replied on August 20, 1770:[41]

> The interior worship of the Jews has no precepts other than those of natural religion. We are indeed obligated to propagate these. . . . Our external worship, however, is by no means meant to be propagated, the reason for this being that it contains precepts that are connected with certain persons, times, and circumstances. True, we believe that our religion is the best, seeing we regard it as divine [revealed]; but it does not follow that it is the best in an absolute sense. It is the best for us and our descendents, the best for certain times and circumstances, and under certain conditions.
>
> Which external worship is the best for other nations God has perhaps made known to them through prophets or has left to their reason to decide. I know nothing about this, and I cannot make out anything concerning it. But this much I do know: no external [positive] worship can be universal. . . . This too I know: I sincerely love all friends of virtue and wisdom.

The affinity between the sentiments expressed here and Lessing's views need not be spelled out. As the passage about "the best [religion] for us and our descendents" clearly indicates, Mendelssohn wrote it with Solomon ibn Verga's story in mind. Ephraim Sancho's on-the-spur-of-the-moment reply seems to have appealed to him because it was another way of saying that each positive religion is historically conditioned and adheres to its own tradition from a natural sense of loyalty. Remarkably enough, Mendelssohn's letter and Lessing's central piece in *Nathan* go back to the same source, the ring parable.

The justaposition and simultaneity of the three religions are what the parable is all about, and because Lessing had made the parable the very heart of his play,[42] the idea had to be worked out in the plot itself. This Lessing did with a great deal of ingenuity, and in the end the representatives of the three faiths are happily united as members of one family. Mendelssohn was right to describe *Nathan* as a paean to Providence. Lessing had followed the rule he had laid down in his *Hamburgische Dramaturgie*:[43] In the infinite connection of all things in history "that which appears as blind fate and cruelty in the few parts selected by the poet is [in the larger perspective] wisdom and goodness. From these few parts he ought to fashion a whole . . . [and] the whole of this mortal creator's making ought to be an image of the whole of the eternal Creator. It ought to accustom us to the thought that in the same way in which all turns out for the best in the play it will happen also in the world." The happy ending of *Nathan* was intended to portray the workings of Providence in a Leibnizian universe in which there was a preestablished harmony between the two realms of efficient and final causes—in which natural causality served the purposes of divine grace.[44] This is what Lessing meant by "accepting God's decrees with perfect love" (*innigster Ergebenheit in Gott*) and by the lecture on the "true miracles" that are concealed in natural events such as Recha's rescue by a human Templar rather than by a winged angel.

Mendelssohn had a good ear for discerning the Leibnizian overtones in the play. Notwithstanding the fact that the word "Providence" did not occur in it, the theme was there, and it was not mere coincidence that Lessing did use the word in his very first *avertissement*: it might not be the fault of Providence, he said, if the world as he imagined it was not as real as the world outside, though he believed it to be just as natural. In later years, in a polemic against Jacobi, and with Lessing's belief in natural religion a hotly contested issue, Mendelssohn would point to the evidence provided by *Nathan*:[45] "What Horace said of Homer in regard to morality,

> Qui, quid sit pulcrum, quid turpe, quid utile, quid non,
>   Plenius ac melius Chrysippo et Crantore dicit[46]
> ["Who said more fully than Chrysippus and Crantor what is beautiful and what is unbecoming, what is useful and what is not"]

I would venture to say of Lessing's masterpiece in regard to certain truths of natural religion. Especially insofar as the doctrine of Providence and

God's governance is concerned, I know of no author who recommended these great truths to the reader with the same purity, power of conviction, and concern as he did." Mendelssohn suggested[47] that Lessing might even have intended *Nathan* to be a kind of "Anti-*Candide.*" "The French poet [Voltaire] gathered all the powers of his ingenuity, spurred the inexhaustible humor of his satirical mind, in short, put to work all the extraordinary talents with which Providence had endowed him, in order to satirize that very Providence. The German [Lessing] did the same thing in order to vindicate it [Providence] and with the aim of showing it to the eyes of mortals in its purest transfiguration. I recall that my late friend, soon after *Candide* appeared, had the passing idea of writing a counterpart to it, or rather a continuation of it, in which he meant to show by a sequel of events that all the evils that had been multiplied by Voltaire at the expense of a defamed Providence in the end turned out for the best and were found to be in accord with the most wise designs."

Even before his controversy with Jacobi prompted Mendelssohn to write in this vein, he had interpreted *Nathan* as a poem whose theme was "the great purpose of Providence: the vocation of man and the prerogatives of humanity."[48] He had then emphasized the idea that all men had the duty and the right to fulfil their own particular destiny, a concept that must have seemed to him the natural corollary of the ring parable, and that, in the play, Saladin formulated in the words:[49] "I have never desired / That one bark grow on all trees of the wood." Similarly, Mendelssohn said in his *Jerusalem* that in order to belong to the omnipresent Shepherd it was not necessary for the entire flock to graze on one pasture.[50] "True happiness" could not be bought by disingenuous agreement, viz. a union of religions, since "diversity" was the "plan and purpose of Providence."[51]

In his own fragmentary essay on *Nathan,* Lessing wrote:[52] "Should one say: this play teaches that not of yesterday there have been people among diverse nations who disregarded all revealed religion and were good people nevertheless; should one add that it had obviously been my intention to present people of this kind as less repulsive than vulgar Christians generally consider them: I shall have little to object." He went to say: "Should one contend, however, that I did violence to poetic fitness by claiming to have found such people among Jews and Muslims, I shall recall the fact that Jews and Muslims were the only scholarly people at the time [of the crusades, during which the play is set] . . ."

It would appear that Michaelis' criticism of his early comedy *The Jews*[53] still lingered in Lessing's mind, and his fears on this score were not unfounded: the theologians maintained a sullen silence,[54] but anti-Semitic sentiment soon asserted itself. On November 17, 1779, Elise drew Lessing's attention to a report in the Altona *Reichs-Postreuther* according to which Amsterdam Jewry had made him a present of a thousand ducats for having published the *Fragments*. "Had it at least been an award for *Nathan*, I might have believed it," wrote Elise.[55] As Lessing informed her on January 22, 1780, the report had originated in the official Viennese gazette, the *Wiener Diarium*, and a refutation had been published by him under the name of his stepson, who happened to be staying in Vienna at the time.[56] Although the story mentioned nothing about *Nathan the Wise*, the fact that Lessing had presented a Jew in such a favorable light could have given impetus to the ugly defamation.

The spokesman for the Christians who were offended by Lessing's play was the old Breslau physician and poet Doctor Balthasar Ludwig Tralles. On December 18, 1779, Karl Lessing, who had left Berlin in July to assume the directorship of the mint in Breslau,[57] wrote to his brother:[58] "I assume that you have read the pious physician Tralles. He proves only that you are no Christian and are ignorant of German. Perhaps more trifles of this sort have appeared without your knowing it." In a letter of December 12, which crossed Karl's, Lessing had written:[59] "A few days ago I received Doctor Tralles' publication. What do you say? What do people in Breslau say? Only his advanced age spares the man a merry dance that I would otherwise perform with him."

Lessing was obviously irritated by the hostile reception that *Nathan* was receiving on many sides. Years later Mendelssohn gave the following description of the animosity shown toward his friend on account of the play:[60]

> How dearly our immortal friend had to pay for this magnificent poem in praise of Providence . . . ! Alas, it embittered his last days, and it may well be the case that it shortened his precious life. When editing the *Fragments* he was prepared to see himself attacked by the whole crowd of writers who would want to refute the *Fragments*, whether or not they were qualified to do so. He considered himself strong enough to defend his guest against all rude assaults by his adversaries. . . .
>
> In the end, the controversy, however lively the manner was in which it was conducted by him, remained a purely scholastic affair that was able to create on both sides many an enjoyable and disagreeable hour but could, as he thought, have no appreciable effect upon the happiness of his life. But how the scene changed after *Nathan* appeared! Now intrigue penetrated from studies and bookstores into the private homes of his friends and acquaintances and whispered into every one's ear that Lessing had insulted Christianity—though he had dared to utter some reproaches only against some Christians and Christendom, at most. In reality, his *Nathan*, let us admit it, redounds to the honor of Christendom. The degree of enlightenment and education attained by a people must be high indeed if one of its members can soar to such sublimity of sentiment . . .
>
> Posterity, I believe, will think thus. Yet Lessing's contemporaries thought otherwise. Everyone considered as a personal insult whatever reproach he had directed against some of his coreligionists or had expressed through the dramatis personae when castigating self-conceit or

narrow-mindedness. He, who used to be made welcome everywhere as a friend and acquaintance, now found everywhere unfriendly faces, reserve, frosty glances, a cold reception, and a ready farewell. He saw himself deserted by friends and exposed to the snares of his persecutors.

It is strange: among the superstitious French *Candide* did not have, by a long way, the evil consequences for Voltaire . . . that Lessing incurred by his *Nathan* among the most enlightened Germans, and the results this produced in his mind were sad. Lessing, who despite his scholarly work was the most pleasant companion, the most cheerful guest at a dinner party, now lost his jovial mood completely and became a sleepy, insensitive machine.

Karl Lessing similarly deplored the widespread hostility toward the play. In his biography of his brother he wrote:[61] "How the public received *Nathan,* how some reviews treated it, would make a nice chapter in church history. In the history of reason silence will be the better part." However, he saw the cause of Lessing's depression and physical decline not in the impact that malevolence had upon him but in the progressive illness (dropsy of the chest) that ravaged his body.[62] Mendelssohn, who no longer had the benefit of being kept informed about his friend through the brother, was apt to imagine more than the facts warranted. He increasingly felt that Lessing was becoming a martyr of his convictions and associated his ailing condition with the hostility that he was encountering. It was for the purpose of cheering him up that on February 18, 1780, he sent him a little note introducing the young Joseph Fliess[63] and his traveling companion, the Swabian mathematician, astronomer, and botanist Steudel.[64] The note read as follows:[65]

> Herr Fliess, who is about to travel to Italy in the company of Herr Steudel, desires first to make your personal acquaintance, and asks me to introduce him to you, since he is probably unknown to you personally. I gladly take this opportunity to give you at least written evidence of my existence, after you have given to your friends so many, and in part such magnificent, printed evidences of yours. Herr Fliess is a man of great means, who for the sake of pleasure studied medicine in Göttingen and would like to be instructed in other useful branches of knowledge as well. . . .
>
> I do not really know what his purpose in visiting you is. Presumably it is to meet you and to be informed by you about the sights in Italy. Were I in his position, I would certainly leave Italy and all its rarities to the last when chatting with you in Wolfenbüttel. Take care of yourself, my best friend, and show Herr Fliess that I have some influence with you.

We know from a letter that Lessing wrote to Karl on February 25, 1780,[66] how much he enjoyed this visit. Lessing returned the favor in December, when he wrote a letter of introduction for his friend Alexander Daveson, an art dealer who had lived in Brunswick since 1778. This letter dated December 19, 1780, was his last to Mendelssohn, and it makes poignant reading. The first part deals with the visitor he is presenting. Taking his cue from the humorous classification of travelers in a well-known story,[67] Lessing described Daveson as an "emigrating" traveler—a category not listed by the author—who by his very nature fit into the two groups of "unhappy" and "innocent" travelers, whereas Doctor Fliess, whom Mendelssohn had sent to him, was a "curious" traveler. He went on to say:[68]

> This emigrant's proper name is Alexander Daveson, and I can testify that our people, incited by yours, behaved abominably toward him. All he wants of you, dear Moses, is that you show him the shortest and surest way to a European country where there are neither Christians nor Jews. I hate losing him; but as soon as he safely arrives there, I shall be the first to follow him.

In the second part of the letter Lessing reacted to the enthusiastic praise Mendelssohn had bestowed on some of his work in recent years. Since perfect honesty had always marked their relationship, Mendelssohn could not have pretended that all of Lessing's literary output had pleased him. We know that he found the polemics against Goeze hardly to his taste.[69] Lessing had sensed this long ago and was far from resenting it. His objectivity in evaluating other people's reactions can be gauged from a letter he had written on April 19, 1778, at the height of the battle, to his Christian friend the poet Matthias Claudius:[70] "I would have liked to send you a book in return for yours, perhaps my polemical writings against Goeze. Yet can they be of any use to you? If I were you, I would surely not read them." One has to bear this almost self-depreciating attitude in mind if one is to understand correctly what Lessing wrote in reply to both the glowing praise and the veiled censure in Mendelssohn's letter:

> I still chew and suck on the short letter from you that Doctor Fliess brought me at the time. The juiciest word in it was the most generous one. In truth, dear friend, I very much need such a short letter from time to time, if I am not to become totally dejected. I believe you know me not as a man avid for praise. Yet the coldness with which the world is in the habit of demonstrating to certain people that nothing they do is right has, if not a deadening, at least a stupefying effect.
>
> That you did not fancy everything I wrote in recent times does not surprise me at all. Nothing should have pleased you; for nothing was written for you. At most, the remembrance of our better days might have been able to deceive you in one passage or another. I too was then a healthy slim young tree; and now I am such a rotten knotty trunk. Alas, dear friend, this scene is finished. I would love, though, to talk to you once more.

How deeply moved Mendelssohn was when reading these lines he recalled some four years later in the "Notes and Additions" to his *Morgenstunden:*[71] "The words used by my unforgettable friend in the last letter, which a traveler brought me from him, still pierce my soul.... For as long as I knew him, and in whatever external circumstances and varying conditions I knew him, Lessing had never complained of his contemporaries' ingratitude, of not being treated justly, of the nonrecognition of his merits. . . . I had been accustomed to find him in a variety of moods, but never dejected or ill-humored. At all times he was the friend who offered, but did not seek, comfort. Now, however,—I cannot describe the disconcerting state of mind in which I found myself when these lines showed me an entirely different man, a cast-down, weary, finally succumbing fighter." He wrote him a letter toward the end of December 1780, possibly early in January 1781, of which only the quotation of single passage has been preserved.[72] A few weeks later, on February 15, 1781, Lessing died at the age of fifty-two.

A Projected Essay on Lessing's Character

Upon receiving the news of Lessing's death—letters announcing it had been sent out to friends by his devoted stepdaughter Amalie König, with the postscript "no reply, please"[1]—Mendelssohn expressed his grief and paid homage to the memory of the deceased in a letter of condolence addressed to Karl:[2]

> [Let] not a word [be said], my very dear one, about our loss, about the great defeat that our heart has suffered. The memory of the man we have lost is now too sacred to me to be profaned by lament. It appears to me at this time in a light that diffuses quiet and a refreshing serenity upon all objects. No, I no longer count what I lost by his demise. Deeply moved, I render thanks to Providence for the blessing it conferred upon me by introducing me so early in life, in the flower of my youth, to a man who formed my soul; whom I pictured as friend and judge in whatever action I was about to take, in regard to every line I was about to write; and whom I shall continue to picture as friend and judge at all times, whenever I am to take an important step.
>
> If a touch of melancholy affects these reflections, it is due to a sense of regret at not having made sufficient use of his guidance; at not having been covetous enough of his inspiring company; at having missed many an hour in which I might have held conversation with him. . . .
>
> If all is duly considered, my dearest, it would seem that your brother departed this world just at the right time, not merely according to the plan of the universe (in which, properly speaking, nothing happens at the wrong time) but also from the perspective of our narrow sphere. Fontenelle said of Copernicus: he introduced his new system and died. Your brother's biographer will be able to say as fitly: he wrote *Nathan the Wise* and died. I cannot conceive of a work of the human mind that surpasses *Nathan* as much as this play surpassed in my eyes all he had written before. He could not rise higher without entering a region hidden from our physical eyes; and this he did. Now we are left behind, like the disciples of the prophet, and we marvel at the place whence he ascended and vanished from sight.
>
> Only a few weeks prior to his demise I had occasion to write to him [that] he should not be surprised that the majority of his contemporaries failed to appreciate the merit of his work. Fifty years after his

death a better world would find in it much on which to chew and to digest. Indeed, he was more than one generation ahead of his century.

Shaken though he was, Mendelssohn could bear the loss because he had so integrated the image of Lessing, his "friend and judge," into his own being that death could not rob him of it. Herder, who had only lately begun to establish closer personal relations with Lessing, was more disconsolate by far. "I cannot tell you," he wrote to Gleim, "how his death has made me feel empty; it is as if all stars had set and the wanderer faced a dark, clouded sky."[3] In this mood of despondency he turned to Mendelssohn, whom he had admired in his younger days, treated cavalierly at Pyrmont, and yet had once more sought to befriend of late. On October 10, 1779, he had sent him a theological work dealing with the Apocalypse of John,[4] and Mendelssohn had responded on June 20, 1780, with a copy of the first volume of his Pentateuch translation, just off the press. In his letter Herder had dedicated his book to the "honest Israelite," whom he "heartily esteemed." He had expressed the hope that Mendelssohn, who was "the best judge" of a book "written in *his* language and using the imagery of *his* prophets and teachers," would let him know whether he agreed with the way in which the images had been interpreted.[5]

In his reply Mendelssohn disclaimed being competent to judge the work. It would be a different matter were Herder to invite his opinion on *The Oldest Document of the Human Race*[6] or the "invaluable little book *Songs of Love.*"[7] Since Herder had shown himself very knowledgeable in Hebrew and might also have some acquaintance with rabbinics—he seemed, at least, not to despise it—he would be qualified to judge the Pentateuch edition. That work, he remarked, owed its origin to considerations not dissimilar to those that had inspired Herder's treatise on the Apocalypse. "I too have children to educate. For what vocation? Whether to pay poll tax with a game of dice whenever passing through Saxe-Gotha, or whether to tell a little satrap the tale of the indistinguishable three rings, is known only to Him who has apportioned our paths to us all. It is my duty so to educate them that they bring no shame upon themselves in any situation and bear resignedly the unmerited contumely to which their fellow-men expose them. This was the purpose of the translation, when it was first envisaged. The rest has been occasioned by the circumstances when I resolved to publish it."

There was indeed a faint analogy between Mendelssohn's and Herder's motives. To simplify the understanding of the Bible by a clear translation and so to make the text speak to the heart had been Mendelssohn's first aim. To read the Bible as a document of piety rather than as a textbook of theology was what Herder recommended. Lessing's *Testament of John* and his other polemical writings had evoked a deep echo in Herder, and he was enchanted with *Nathan.* He disagreed about the indistinguishable three rings but accepted the criterion of practical love.[8] Mendelssohn must have been pleased to find a spirit of tolerance advocated in Herder's book, but in view of his past experience of the man he was skeptical and felt it necessary to refer to the harsh realities that his children might have to face.

Lessing's death prompted Herder to approach Mendelssohn again. As early as February 21, 1781, he wrote him the following letter:[9]

> Undoubtedly, dear and revered Mendelssohn, you are aware, as I am, of Lessing's death. Having been preoccupied with it for the last two days, and having no one to whom to pour out and unburden my heart, I cannot help writing to you, dearest Mendelssohn, whose friend he was to such a very large degree, and whom, in my younger years, I so often fondly pictured together with him. . . .
>
> I certainly need not tell you what Germany, the humanities, and the noble and manly striving in the humanities have lost in him and will not retrieve in a long time. Though we were distant in our work and thought, I still feel a sense of emptiness, as if I were in the midst of a vast barren desert.
>
> Do yield to my entreaty, dear Mendelssohn, to fill, as it were, his place within me, and to come a little closer to me than you have been hitherto. A series of accidental happenings and circumstances, for which I am not entirely to blame, has created—so it has seemed to me, at least, for some time—a greater remoteness from me on your part than I ever desired. The unfortunate time when we met in Pyrmont and so little enjoyed each other, coming as it did on top of Nicolai's action,[10] was a contributory factor. . . .
>
> I do not ask for your friendship . . . but your favor, your unreserved good will with regard to certain things, since we have to promote, more or less, the same purposes, albeit in so different spheres. This I ask of you, because I esteem and love you so truly and sincerely with a love that increases with every year of my life. . . .

Mendelssohn was wary of Herder's emotionalism—future events would show how right he was in this respect—but his reply, though candid, was more than a grudging response.[11] The letter, written on March 15, 1781, immediately struck a conciliatory note: "This too, my best Herder, is the way of Providence that Lessing's death had to bring closer together two minds that had been separated, as is now manifest, by a deplorable misunderstanding." Mendelssohn agreed that the ill-fated meeting in Pyrmont was largely to blame. He had then received the distinct impression that Herder wished to shun his company, that he implored him with his eyes to leave him alone. This kind of attitude had not come as a complete surprise to him. He had become used to the experience of seeing former friends desert him when their station in life changed and prudence suggested that closeness to a Jew might be embarrassing. Lessing had been the only man in more than thirty years whose friendship had never wavered, the only one who had remained true to himself and never ceased to be his wholehearted friend and benefactor. "The death of this friend . . . has inflicted a deep wound upon my soul, and it is truly comforting that you feel the same sense of loss in your heart and wish to fill the gap by drawing closer to mine. Accept my sincere thanks for having taken the first step in this direction. You will surely find me meeting you halfway. I walk somewhat slowly but uninterruptedly. Everyone has his own way, and I trust your judgment of people not to misunderstand my apparent coldness. It is, in fact, more moderate than cold; and I hope you will, in the course of time, find it increasingly genuine, proven, and worthy of your love."

Herder had concluded his letter of February 21 with an appeal of an eminently practical nature: "Please help ensure that Lessing's papers [*Lessing's Nachlässe*] are saved and come into good hands. You are in the most excellent position to accomplish this through your own and your friends' efforts." In his reply Mendelssohn could put Herder's mind at rest on this score, but he did not tell him what steps had already been taken, on his initiative, even before Herder's appeal had reached him. On February 20 Mendelssohn had written Nicolai:[12] "Best Friend! Our Lessing is gone! Should not we his friends write to the duke [of Brunswick] and ask for his papers?" Nicolai agreed and at Mendelssohn's request drafted the petition and sent it to Mendelssohn, with the following note:[13] "Here is the requested draft. After due consideration it seems to me more appropriate that you write the letter in your name, and that I am merely mentioned. Should you, however, find it more appropriate that we both sign it, you can easily change *I* to *we* in the places concerned and send me the letter for signature. If you alone sign it, mail it to the address indicated above. Your intention of describing Lessing's character seemed to me a reason [for desiring the papers] that might sufficiently impress the duke as to induce him to grant the petition. But if you do not consider it right to add this, simply omit it." Upon hearing from Mendelssohn, Nicolai himself—as the draft clearly shows—changed the singular to the plural, except in the sentence referring to Mendelssohn's intention of writing a "memorial" to his late friend; there he added, in his own hand, Mendelssohn's name, making it read: "I, Moses Mendelssohn." The draft also suggested that the signatories to the letter include Ramler as well, and there can be no doubt that Ramler agreed. The petition was dispatched on February 20, the same day on which Mendelssohn had conceived the idea and sent his first note to Nicolai. It read as follows:[14]

> To His Highness the reigning Duke... at Brunswick. Your Highness, most gracious Sir,
> We, the undersigned oldest and most intimate friends, believe to owe it to the memory of our late friend to ensure that his correspondence and the manuscripts that form his *Nachlass* are preserved for posterity, that nothing of it gets lost, and that nothing of it is published in any way other than is to the advantage of the humanities [*Wissenschaften*] and to the honor of our friend's memory. We ourselves conducted with him an interesting correspondence, and since various cases of indiscreet publications of letters left behind are known to have happened, it is a matter of concern to us that our correspondence be spared a similar

fate. A further reason is that I, Moses Mendelssohn, desire to erect a memorial to my dearly beloved friend by publicly describing his character to the world, for which purpose I need to have all requisite papers in my hands.

The balance of the letter contained a formal petition that all manuscripts and letters of the late Lessing be handed over to the signatories and gave the assurance that nothing would be published without the prior consent of the legal heirs and without having first satisfied their financial claims.

The duke's answer to this letter has been lost. It is known, however, from extant documents that on February 16 the duke had ordered that Lessing's "*Nachlass* of effects, books, and writings" be put under seal.[15] In his letter of March 15 Mendelssohn informed Herder that the *Nachlass* was, he trusted, in good hands; that Professor Konrad Arnold Schmid of Brunswick had, at the duke's command, placed everything under seal and that it would be "opened" only by the brothers and other heirs; and that Karl Lessing would soon visit Wolfenbüttel. "Papers of a private nature and letters from friends, wrote the duke [in his reply to the three friends?], are to be set apart from Lessing's own manuscripts by Professor Schmid, and they are to be returned to their original owners. In view of our contemporary fondness for [letter] writing this precaution will please many a correspondent." From April 6 to April 20 Karl stayed in Brunswick and Wolfenbüttel. Upon his application Lessing's estate was unsealed and an inventory was drawn up. Karl had to sign a declaration on behalf of the family promising to indemnify creditors that might present themselves, but even so he was permitted to take with him only four manuscripts from one of some twenty-six packages. The rest was put into crates, sealed up once more, and deposited in the house of the prefect von Döring.[16]

It took a long time for Karl Lessing to get posession of these precious crates. The Wolfenbüttel court of justice moved with a slowness that, as Karl had later reason to remark, was excelled only by Prussian offices of justice.[17] In his despair, he turned to Mendelssohn, and it seems that the triumvirate Mendelssohn/Ramler/Nicolai wrote yet another petition to the duke, asking him to expedite matters.[18] On January 21, 1782, Karl was still "sighing" for the manuscripts of the *Nachlass*, which he was eager to publish.[19] We do not know exactly when the legal procedures terminated, but a letter he wrote to Mendelssohn on April 22, 1783, shows him already deeply immersed in his editorial work.[20] Questions related to the editing occupied a major part of his correspondence with Mendelssohn through August, 1784.[21] Karl's letters, which alone have been preserved, make it abundantly clear that his edition of the *Nachlass* was greatly indebted to the consultative role played by Mendelssohn. Initially, Karl was groping in the dark as to how to proceed. He wanted to know whether the posthumous works ought to be published in chronological order or whether those dealing with theological matters should be edited in a separate volume.

He asked Mendelssohn to tell him "candidly and without trying to spare his feelings" what he thought about the theological manuscripts and the order in which he intended to publish them. He would print nothing without his "approval."

When Karl was preparing to edit the miscellaneous writings of his brother, he again wished to be guided by Mendelssohn: "Any deletions or additions you suggest, I approve unseen." On the other hand, he occasionally departed from advice given him. Mendelssohn proposed (for reasons to be discussed later) that the volume containing the theological writings in the *Nachlass* (including the early essay *The Christianity of Reason*) should be published last, and Karl agreed, at first. Later, however, he objected. Now was the time, he argued, to put theological books on the market. Ten years later they would hardly arouse any interest, if tolerance continued to progress at the present pace. Karl also dismissed the suggestion that he start with the "literary" pieces; he preferred to give precedence to the theatrical ones. What happened was that the theatrical *Nachlass* appeared as Part One (1784), followed a year later by the theological Part Two.[22] Mendelssohn's suggestion that he omit the essays *On the Origin of Revealed Religion* and *My Arab's Proof that the Arabs, not the Jews, are the True Descendants of Abraham* was accepted at first, but eventually Karl decided to publish the first of the two essays vetoed by Mendelssohn. In the end, quite rightly, Karl allowed his own judgment to prevail. Yet there can be no doubt that he leaned heavily on Mendelssohn's suggestions. In one of the letters he pointed out that he was trespassing on his friend's time only because he was "in distress." As it turned out, all the material from Lessing's *Nachlass* that was published by Karl had been submitted to Mendelssohn.[23]

In May, 1781, Mendelssohn was ready to apply himself to the task he had promised to undertake, that of writing about Lessing's character. The time was propitious. The first two volumes of his Pentateuch translation had appeared, and the third volume was being printed. In April he had sent complimentary copies to Robert Lowth, the lord bishop of London,[24] putting the seal as it were on a major portion of his effort. He now enjoyed a little breathing space and could give undivided attention to the solemn obligation he felt toward the memory of his friend. On May 8, 1781, he wrote to Hennings:[25]

> I am now occupied by one single thought: Lessing's death. It does not make me sad or abstracted, but it is always before my mind, like the image of a mistress. With this thought I go to sleep; of it, I dream; with it, I awake, and I thank Providence for the blessing it bestowed upon me by allowing me to meet this man so early in my life and to enjoy his company as a friend for such a long time.
>
> The world knows his merit as a writer, but few people know his merit as a friend. I find, moreover, that his merit as a moral character is entirely misjudged by many. Notions of virtue and morality, too, are subject to changing fashions, and whoever is unable to adapt himself

to the notions fashionable in his century is misjudged and decried by
his contemporaries. But this much seems to me beyond doubt: if there
ever was a man who was better than he allowed himself to appear in
his writings, it was Lessing.

Mendelssohn went on to describe Lessing's aversion to all superficial politeness and his genuine readiness to be of help, a readiness completely free
from selfishness and conceit; his sarcasm toward all affectation and pretense; his kindness and modesty toward every one who sought the truth.
The letter was a kind of first attempt at a characterization of Lessing.

On May 18, 1781, he informed Herder of his plan and, in similar
vein, drafted a preliminary sketch of Lessing's traits of character:[26]

> This summer I intend to write something about Lessing's character,
> provided my health permits it. It seems to me that from this aspect he
> is still widely misjudged. Only his most intimate friends know him as
> one of those rare people who are better than they want to appear....
>
> I gather from Lessing's letters, which I have been going over again
> on this occasion, that with you, too, he exchanged some that must have
> been of the most intimate kind and of the sort in which he used to
> correspond only with few. Should they contain something that sheds
> light on his moral character and is suitable to be submitted to the eyes
> of the public, I would ask you to copy the passages concerned whenever
> it be convenient and, if I may add a further request, to write a few
> notes of your own commenting on them.
>
> In case your circumstances make it imperative that your name not
> be mentioned, you may be sure of my discretion. I promise, if you so
> desire, to tone down your hardly mistakable manner of writing to such
> an extent that nobody will be able to guess the author, if you were willing
> to present to me your thoughts about the morals of our friend for my
> use.... In case my request is too bold, do refuse it with the same
> uninhibited candor with which I make it.

It is somewhat surprising to find that Mendelssohn felt it necessary
to make a request of this kind to Herder. He was not short of either
material or points of view for the work he was planning to do that summer.
Nor did he have to wait for Karl to send him the letters he had written
to Lessing, as he told Nicolai in a note dated May 23, 1781:[27] "From [Karl]
Lessing I have so far neither heard nor seen anything. As soon as I receive
the letters that I wrote to him [the late Lessing] I shall start the work."
All that really mattered were Lessing's letters to him, and these were already
in his possession. As he mentioned to Herder, he had reread them, and
there is little doubt that the rough sketch entitled *Principal Traits (Hauptzüge)*,
which Karl Lessing published in his biography of the brother (1795),[28]
was written by Mendelssohn in May, 1781, under the impression made
upon him by these letters. No less than ten letters are referred to in
chronological order.[29] Nevertheless, he hesitated to elaborate on the points
he had jotted down.

Obviously there was some psychological inhibition that caused him
to delay the project, and the nonavailability of his letters to Lessing served

merely as a convenient pretext for postponing the work. Whether it was the closeness to his late friend or an excessive perfectionism arising out of a sense of special obligation that impeded his effort is hard to determine. His strange request to Herder admits of both interpretations. He did not feel sure of himself somehow, though his sketch did contain a wealth of pertinent ideas. It mentioned Lessing's "favorite inclination to espouse the case of the weaker party"; his readiness to accept criticism and correction from friends; his charitableness; his view that man's vocation lay in the search for truth, not in its possession. It alluded to Nathan's monologue (III:6): "He asks for truth—for truth! / And wants it paid in ready cash, as though / The truth were coinage. Yea, even as if / It were old coinage that was told by weight." Mendelssohn interpreted this passage to mean: "Truth paid like coinage, without inquiry into weight and alloy, is harmful." He added: "Hence the perpetual circle in sciences and arts. The way of Providence." He thus ascribed to Lessing his own cherished notion of the way of Providence: for the perfection of the individual to be possible, mankind as a whole has to retrogress and start over from time to time.[30] He characterized Lessing's imagination as rational rather than sensual: Lessing could think in terms of passion but not put himself in the position (hence the artificiality of his love scenes); he was most felicitous in depicting characters similar to his own, such as Tellheim and the Templar.

No one waited for Mendelssohn's essay on Lessing with greater eagerness than Elise Reimarus. His letter to Hennings had seemed to her full of promise and in itself worthy of publication: "No man can fail to recognize in it the stamp of Mendelssohn; no man can deny Lessing's character his reverence." She felt that the relevant passage of the letter should be published in the *Deutsches Museum*, but this idea was not acted upon. Though Mendelssohn had not mentioned the plan of his essay in his letter to Hennings, Elise had obviously heard about it, and she expressed the hope that he would not hesitate for long to set up this monument to himself and his friend. This was written to Hennings on May 29, 1781.[31] On September 18, 1781, she wrote to her brother-in-law: "That Mendelssohn does not yet publish anything of Lessing's biography is Lessing's brother's fault."[32]

While Mendelssohn remained silent, Herder published—in the October, 1781, issue of the *Teutscher Merkur*, which appeared toward the end of September—a magnificent essay on Lessing in which he delineated in masterful, congenial strokes the literary accomplishments of the deceased and offered an appreciative account of the aims that had motivated his theological writings.[33] The passage discussing the significance of Lessing as "originator and father" of the *Literaturbriefe* also paid due tribute to Mendelssohn: "Good fortune brought him a noble helper, Moses Mendelssohn; as is evident from several utterances, the two men esteemed and loved each other as philosophical friends. One may gather this from Mendelssohn's *Letter to Lessing* at the end of [his translation of] Rousseau's *Discours*[34] and from the respect with which Lessing mentioned Mendelssohn on every occasion. Two such men of bright mind and pure heart, free from political impediments and accessory circumstances, jointly approached this work, which for a considerable time was to be called 'the German Journal.' . . . Lessing remained with it up to its seventh part. Mendelssohn retained his tested character until the end." The essay concluded with an enthusiastic apostrophe to "the noble seeker after truth, knower of truth, and fighter for truth," at the end of which Herder asked the reader's forgiveness: "The final situations of his life carried me away, and it had not really been my intention to say anything about his character, which can and will be described far better by his closer friend."

Herder could not have acted in a more friendly and generous manner. He lost no time in sending a copy of the essay to Mendelssohn, enquiring in a covering letter about his work on Lessing's character. Mendelssohn's reply, dated September 24, 1781, clearly indicated that, far from begrudging his having been anticipated (in a sense), he was overjoyed by the way in which Lessing—and he?—had been treated:[35]

> Accept a thousand thanks, best and most revered Herder, for the good feelings that you aroused in me this morning. My high esteem for you is of long standing, but this essay about Lessing causes me to draw closer to you, to love you, and ardently to desire to be loved by you in return, and to be called your friend. For the friendship of such a man can replace the loss of a Lessing for the rest of my days. . . . You ask me about my essay on Lessing's character. I am still waiting for my letters, which the brother has promised to send me from the estate. When I receive them, shall I be able to produce something that merits being put side by side with yours? We shall see.

Karl Lessing was himself still "sighing" for his brother's *Nachlass*, but even in 1782, when he eventually took possession of it, he was seemingly in no great hurry to return the requested letters to Mendelssohn. Since he intended to publish a volume, or more than one, of letters, he was loath to part with his treasures. On April 22, 1783, he wrote to Mendelssohn:[36] "What to do with his letters I myself do not know as yet. I found all of them, up to 1778, alphabetically arranged, and yours in a separate package. I would have returned them to you already, had I not been told that you would be coming here yourself." On May 8, 1783, at long last, he fulfilled Mendelssohn's request:[37] "Here are your letters and also those of Herr Nicolai. . . . I still pursue the idea of publishing a collection of the letters of his [Lessing's] friends." Two years had passed during which the plan to write about Lessing's character had been held in abeyance. Mendelssohn had been far from idle during this period: he had completed the Pentateuch edition, taken an active part in Dohm's work, published his "notes" on Abbt's correspondence with him, edited Manasseh Ben Israel's treatise and provided a preface, and written and published both his *Jerusalem* and the Psalms translation. Once having allowed the months of May and June, 1781, to slip by without acting on the impulse and favorable mood that animated him then, he had no chance of redeeming his vow, it seems, until all the other work had been accomplished.

By the spring of 1783 Mendelssohn was again free to turn his attention to the long overdue project. Happily, a fresh impetus had just then been given to his desire to apply himself to the task. On April 22, 1783, Karl had sent him the manuscripts found in his brother's theological *Nachlass,* including the youthful essay *The Christianity of Reason,* which Mendelssohn remembered vividly from the time—1754—when Lessing had showed it to him, and to which he had referred in his February 1, 1774, letter to Lessing.[38] The sight of the familiar manuscript awakened nostalgic feelings. It also forcibly reminded him of a characteristic feature of Lessing's mind: his tendency to interpret the Christian dogma in terms of a speculative metaphysics inspired by Leibniz. Mendelssohn's interest in the project, which had gone somewhat stale, suddenly revived. He wrote Karl a letter[39] in which he announced his intention to get down to business: he was now resolved, he said, to "devote his morning hours"—the only time when he was capable of creative work—to the memory of his friend. He also urged Karl to send him the long-awaited letters and to defer the publication of Lessing's theological *Nachlass* until after his essay had appeared. This request, which would not be fulfilled, was obviously prompted by his desire to be the first to present to the world some relevant parts of *The Christianity of Reason.* One can sympathize with his wish to disclose to the public his late friend's early *opusculum,* which had lived in his memory for thirty-nine years. How eager he was to make use of this particular fragment is shown by the fact that he at once copied the paragraphs that interested him. We still possess the two sheets containing paragraphs 1–5 and 13–18 (leaving out paragraphs 6–12, which deal with the trinity, and paragraphs 19–27) in his handwriting.[40] Thus the stage was set once more for the fulfilment of his promise, especially after Karl had sent him the letters on May 8 and had written:[41] "I am very happy that you wish to devote your morning hours to the memory of my brother. For what has been written about him until now has not entirely pleased me. . . . May Heaven preserve you in your intention and permit no hindrance to intervene except a trip to Breslau at most."

Even prior to the arrival of the theological *Nachlass* Mendelssohn had thought of resuming the abandoned project as soon as Karl had returned his letters. He had mentioned this to Elise Reimarus when she visited him in Berlin on March 24, 1783. It was the first time they had ever met in person. Elise had traveled to Berlin in the company of her friends Joachim Heinrich Campe and his wife. On March 25, the day after her visit to Mendelssohn, she recorded her impressions in a letter to Friedrich Heinrich Jacobi:[42]

> Yesterday I saw Mendelssohn, my dear Mendelssohn. He is entirely as I had imagined him: irresistibly captivating in the goodness of his heart, which is strikingly manifest, and in the radiant clarity of his mind. We talked a great deal about Lessing and you. Lessing's bust, which bears a fairly good resemblance, was the first thing I noticed when I entered. . . .

To date, Mendelssohn has not yet managed to get hold of his correspondence with Lessing, but the brother has promised to send him before long a package of papers, which is to include this particular correspondence. Mendelssohn promises to subsequently keep his word about "Something on Lessing's Character." May Heaven grant him the requisite health and serenity of mind so that we may yet read something about our friend that is worthy of the man.

The intrusion of Jacobi into the present context will become fully clear in due course. Let it suffice for the moment to say that Jacobi's answer to Elise's well-intentioned letter initiated a sequence of events that would cast a deep shadow upon Mendelssohn's life and that undoubtedly hastened his end. The answer was not forthcoming until the end of July, and it reached Mendelssohn only at the beginning of August, 1783. If only he had written his promised essay in the interval, he could have spared himself a great deal of trouble later. Unfortunately, he failed to do this. Perhaps, after his amazing outpouring of energies in recent years, he simply needed some rest. His mind was also absorbed by the response to the *Jerusalem* and the Psalms translation. As we have seen, the manifold echoes, both private and public, produced by these two works claimed much of his attention.

Elise Reimarus had left with Mendelssohn some of the letters that she had received from Lessing, hoping that they might prove a useful addition to the source material on which the Lessing essay would draw. On May 20, 1783, Mendelssohn wrote to her:[43]

> Dearest Friend! I dare to call you thus, for our friend Lessing has appointed me heir of his rights in this respect. Should you not trust my word for it, I can advance yet another reason: the identity of our views [*Gesinnungen*] that I could infer, I believe, from what you said, and even more so from your meaningful silences in the few hours in which I had the pleasure of seeing you. Many thanks for sharing the Lessing letters with me. As soon as I have sufficiently perused them, they will be safely returned. Herr [Moses] Wessely will send you in my name a copy of a treatise entitled *Jerusalem* about which some words were spoken when you were here. I would also have sent you the Psalms, but I suspect that they will be of little interest to you . . .

Elise replied on June 20, 1783:[44]

> I cannot allow our friend Wessely to go on his journey to Berlin, dearest Mendelssohn, without sending along with him my cordial thanks for the letter and the book that you presented to me through him. Both were a highly important gift to me and could not have come at a more appropriate time so far as my feelings were concerned. I had just then lost my mother, who was very dear to me and whose loss will grieve me for a long time to come. In such a situation nothing, I am sure, is more capable of giving our sentiments a different direction than the words of a friend whose mind and heart interest us in equal measure.
>
> How much you are this kind of friend, dearest Mendelssohn, I need not prove to you. You understood me from my silence as well as from my speech, and I am glad of this. I would have liked to have seen you

and spoken to you more often during my stay in Berlin, but you are too high in my esteem for that. Suffice it that I may hope not to have become more of a stranger to you as a result of this personal acquaintance, the memory of which still remains so valuable to me. God grant that you long remain a blessing to the world and to your house. I shall be pleased to stand at a distance and rejoice in all the good things, and thank you for all the good things, that He dispenses through you.

The letter went on to express her and her brother's thanks for the "many a pleasurable hour" that reading the *Jerusalem* had given them. She wished she could indicate the many passages that commanded their full assent, and wondered "to what extent this first treatise of its kind" would "mark an epoch." She also thanked Mendelssohn for his Psalms, a copy of which she had evidently received. There were two reasons for her sense of gratitude on account of this work: "First, because in it, too, you illumined the truth in a new and beautiful way. . . . Secondly, because in the preface to it you erected a worthy memorial to our Lessing. How much I long to see the day when you will tell the world something about his character that you alone can tell."

The passage in the preface that pleased Elise so much reads as follows:[45] "When engaged in writing, I am used to imagining as reader a friend whom I particularly wish to please. In philosophical matters it *was* our friend Lessing,—it is and continues to be our friend Lessing, for whose approval and encouragement I [shall] strive so long as the breath of life is still within me. For although zeal for the freedom of inquiry wore him out before his time, he will never be dead to me. He will always be present to my mind, and at every line I write in philosophical matters I shall ask myself: would Lessing approve this?" How much Mendelssohn appreciated the friendship shown him by Elise and her brother, and what the correspondence with Elise meant to him, was expressed in a letter he wrote to Hennings on December 5, 1783:[46] "This time I only want to add that last summer[47] I had the pleasure of making the personal acquaintance of Madam Reimarus, that I have since entered into closer correspondence with her, and that I esteem her exceedingly."

It was Elise Reimarus who would have the unenviable task of acting as mediator between Mendelssohn and Jacobi in their ill-fated contest over Lessing's ultimate creed.

Jacobi's Attitude toward Mendelssohn: Antecedents of their Conflict

In 1761, when Friedrich Heinrich Jacobi (1743–1819) returned to Düsseldorf after a two-year stay in Geneva, the Berlin Academy had just announced the theme of its latest prize competition: whether metaphysical truths, especially the first principles of natural theology and morals, could be demonstrated with a certitude comparable to that of mathematical truths, and if not, with what degree of certitude could metaphysical truths be demontrated. Jacobi, the son of a well-to-do manufacturer, reared in a pietistic atmosphere, a devoted disciple of Charles Bonnet and an ardent admirer of Rousseau, was fascinated by the question posed by the academy. Indeed no question, he would confess later, could have aroused his interest to a greater degree, and he looked forward to the publication of the essays with intense longing. "The moment came and turned out to be doubly memorable. The prize-essay [by Mendelssohn] did not fulfil the expectations that the name of the then already very famous author had provoked in me. I was all the more surprised when in the second essay [by Kant], which had been awarded only accessional recognition, I found hints and information that could not have been more in tune with my requirements."[1]

Jacobi's first impression of Mendelssohn was, therefore, one of disappointment. This was counterbalanced, however, by the effect that Mendelssohn's *Phaedon* produced upon him in 1767. Jacobi's extraordinary interest in this work is attested by his correspondence with the Amsterdam bookseller and publisher Marc-Michel Rey, which has only recently come to light.[2] On October 21, 1768, he wrote to Rey:[3] "Have you not heard of the masterpiece of our famous Moses Mendelssohn? It revolves around the immortality of the soul. It is a notable effort of the human mind. Three editions have come out within the space of one year; it seems to me that this is quite something for a book of profundity." On November 25 he proposed that a French translation be entrusted to somebody who was adequately trained in philosophy and had sufficient command of both languages. He himself would gladly undertake the task of checking and correcting the translation. In case a suitable translator was found, he would request a sample rendition of two marked passages in the copy of the work that he would send to Rey. In the German revised edition of 1768 the book had no more than two hundred and twenty-eight pages, which would amount to about three hundred and fifty pages in a French version printed in the format of the *Journal des savans*.[4] On March 16, 1769 he asked Rey how much he was prepared to pay for a good translation of the *Phaedon*,[5] and on July 14, 1769 he reported:[6] "I have carefully examined the translation of the *Phaedon*, and I am very sorry to have to tell you that it is absolutely worthless. Since, unfortunately, I wrote to Moses about six weeks ago that I was seeing to a translation of his book, I shall have to keep my word. Hence I am resolved to undertake the translation myself, however hard the effort is. As soon as it is accomplished, I shall send it to Le Sage and Bonnet so that they can correct flaws of style and Germanisms that might have slipped in. Let me know by return mail whether you are satisfied with this proposal, and whether you wish to accept responsibility for bringing out a nice edition of this work."

On July 28 Jacobi expressed astonishment at the fact that his last two letters had been left unanswered. In the meantime he had heard from Mendelssohn that he would gladly check the French translation in the event that Jacobi himself undertook it.[7] Shortly afterwards Jacobi assured Rey of his intention to commence the work as soon as he had completed the translation of some poems by his brother (Johann Georg Jacobi), which were to be printed in Paris.[8] It was almost three months, however, before he remembered his promise. On October 20, 1769, he informed Rey that the praise that the Homer translator Paul Jérémie Bitaubé and other members of the academy had bestowed upon his translation of his brother's poems had encouraged him to apply himself to the *Phaedon* project.[9] Yet the plan fell through. Subsequent letters make no reference to it, and one has to assume that the Amsterdam publisher had learned of another translation already underway and had informed Jacobi of it.[10]

The seriousness with which Jacobi pursued the *Phaedon* translation project, and the fact that he was prepared to step into the breach when the quality of the work seemed to require it, furnish ample evidence of his favorable opinion of this work. As the correspondence with Rey shows, he was in direct contact with Mendelssohn in July, 1769. His respect for the Berlin philosopher was seemingly undiminished in 1772, for on October 27 of that year he tried to impress Wieland with the blameworthiness, from a moral point of view, of Wieland's enchanting novel *The Story of Agathon:*[11] "I cannot imagine, dearest brother, that I am overly timid in this case, since I know the views that Mendelssohn, Lessing, and several other renowned men of learning, whose names I hesitate to mention, have expressed concerning the morality of *Agathon.*"[12] In another letter to Wieland, written only a day later, he referred to Mendelssohn's satirical verses about Helvétuis' *De l'esprit,* which, he assumed, were known to Wieland.[13] Even when he became Goethe's friend in July, 1774, and was caught up in the radical spirit of Sturm und Drang, Jacobi's respectful attitude toward Mendelssohn was not tangibly affected. (Goethe himself, when staying for a short while in Berlin in 1778, showed his respect for the Jewish philosopher. As Anna Louise Karsch [the poetess known as "die Karschin"] reported to Gleim on May 18, 1778,[14] Goethe, who would not pay court to any poet, did pay a visit to Moses Mendelssohn.)

When Jacobi published the first part of his *Vermischte Schriften*[15] in 1781, he sent Mendelssohn a complimentary copy with the following startling inscription:[16] "To the reverend [*Ehrwürdigen*] Mendelssohn from his grateful pupil of many years standing, the author. Pempelfort, October 23, 1781." Considering that the book contained two quasi-philosophical pieces diametrically at variance with the disciplined thinking and lucid style of Mendelssohn, the dedication was somewhat out of place. The first of the two items was a novel *(Roman)* entitled *Der Kunstgarten,* "a philosophical dialogue," which had been published previously in the *Deutsches*

Museum[17] under the title "Woldemar" (by which it is generally known). The second was called *Eduard Allwills Papiere,* a glorification of titanic striving ("All Will").[18]

In 1779 Goethe had derided *Woldemar* as indicative of self-deification and Jacobi had felt deeply insulted.[19] Lessing, on the other hand, had encouraged him. On May 18, 1779, when sending him a copy of *Nathan the Wise,* he had written:[20] "The author of *Nathan* would like to requite the author of *Woldemar* for the instructive and emotionally enriching [*gefühlvolle*] hour that he afforded him." Jacobi was extremely elated by this warm-hearted praise. In his reply of August 20, 1779, he promised to visit Lessing, who to him was "a king among the spirits," in the following year:[21] "What is estimable about me," he wrote in an odd mixture of conceit and lack of self-confidence, "you will see at once, and I hope it will win for me your friendship. I am yearning for these days more than I can express in words; also because I want to conjure up through you the spirits of some seers who do not sufficiently answer me, and whom I want to become articulate through you."

During an eleven-week journey in the summer of 1780 Jacobi visited Lessing twice: from July 5 to July 10 on his way to Hamburg, where he became friends with the Reimarus family, and on his return, when he took Lessing on an excursion trip to visit the old Gleim in Halberstadt. In an elaborate report about this "great journey," which Jacobi sent to his friend Wilhelm Heinse on October 20, 1780, with memories of it still fresh in his mind, he mentioned that Lessing seemed to consider Mendelssohn "the most lucid mind, the most excellent philosopher, and the best art critic of our century." He added that this was also the view of Lichtenberg, with whom Jacobi had talked for six "magnificent hours in Göttingen."[22] On November 28, 1780, Jacobi sought to fortify himself again by turning to Lessing. He informed him that a review in the *Allgemeine deutsche Bibliothek* had referred to "the unnatural, bombastic stuff called *Allwills Papiere.*" He felt "astonished and pained" by the "tone" of this verdict.[23] Lessing again restored his spirit by encouraging him to write a sequel to *Woldemar.*[24] On March 15, 1781, a month after Lessing's death, Jacobi informed Elise Reimarus that—as he had learned—Lessing had reread *Woldemar* and had liked it so much that he felt impelled to urge him to continue the novel; moreover, that shortly before he died Lessing had sent word to him repeating the advice, since *Woldemar* was "an excellent piece of work," and exhorting him not to leave *Allwills Papiere* in abeyance either.[25] How much Lessing's encouragement meant to Jacobi is also attested by a letter he sent to Lavater on October 10, 1781, together with a copy of his *Vermischte Schriften:*[26] "In *Allwills Papiere . . .* is found something in which I believe more than in myself. Lessing sensed in them something similar, and he sent me a message shortly before his death, when he was already blind, bidding me to change nothing therein." It was about two weeks later that Jacobi inscribed the complimentary copy for Mendelssohn.

The reverential tone of the dedication was obviously designed to evoke more than a mere polite acknowledgment. In the preface to the volume Jacobi had stated that he was anxious to learn what "serious thinkers" thought of the book, especially about the second half of *Woldemar*. Did he expect Mendelssohn, the leading figure of the Berlin Enlightenment, to show an understanding sympathy for the dethronment of reason in favor of pure feeling, as *Woldemar* had proclaimed it? The fact that Lessing had, in his view, "sensed" the truth affirmed in that dialogue could hardly have made it seem likely to Jacobi that Mendelssohn would react in a similar way. In his conversation with Lessing, Jacobi had gathered the impression that some rift had developed between the respective philosophies of the two friends. He had inferred this from certain utterances of Lessing's that he kept a closely guarded secret, to be revealed at the appropriate moment.[27] Believing Lessing to have abandoned the stance of the Enlightenment and to have shown himself open to his more radical type of thinking, it was not difficult for Jacobi to imagine that a failure to appreciate his work proved at the same time a certain remoteness from Lessing. Hence Jacobi's seeking to test Mendelssohn's response to his book was in a sense tantamount to his seeking to gauge the distance not only between himself and Mendelssohn but also between Lessing and Mendelssohn. During Jacobi's stay in Wolfenbüttel, Lessing had urged him to travel to Berlin in order to meet personally Mendelssohn, "whom he esteemed highest among his friends."[28] Jacobi had not acted on this suggestion, nor did he give due weight to Lessing's tribute to his old friend. The notion that he had a profounder understanding of Lessing than Mendelssohn did was probably already firmly fixed in Jacobi's mind.

An opportunity for Jacobi to present Mendelssohn with an inscribed copy of his work arose through his growing friendship with Dohm. On September 20, 1781, with his treatise *On the Civil Improvement of the Jews* fresh from the press, Dohm wrote a letter to Jacobi, whom he had met briefly in Münster during the summer, expressing his high esteem (particularly on account of an article Jacobi had published in the *Deutsches Museum*) and presenting him with a copy of the treatise. Dohm expressed the hope that Jacobi would agree with the principles underlying it.[29] The assumption that Jacobi, when sending his volume to Mendelssohn a month later, did so through Dohm,[30] is corroborated by a letter that Dohm wrote to Mendelssohn on November 25, 1781.[31] By a stroke of good fortune this brief letter, which deals largely with matters concerning the sale of the treatise in France, contains a final paragraph that yields information on Dohm's role as a channel of communication between Jacobi and Mendelssohn and—what is far more important—on Mendelssohn's reaction to Jacobi's book. The paragraph reads: "Herr Jacobi had dedicated his book to you; hence it is herewith returned. Since he desired at all events truth and austere criticism, your remarks, which to me seem exceedingly appropriate, should be acceptable to him." We interpret this passage to mean that Jacobi had asked Dohm to pass on to Mendelssohn the inscribed copy of his *Vermischte Schriften,* with the distinct request that Mendelssohn offer him his honest opinion, however severely critical. Thereupon Mendelssohn replied as requested, and his "remarks" *(Anmerkungen)* turned out to be anything but complimentary. He asked Dohm to forward his letter to Jacobi and enclosed the copy of the book so as to give Dohm an opportunity to compare his critical remarks with the text. Dohm found Mendelssohn's censure fully justified and expressed confidence in Jacobi's fairmindedness: having asked for a candid opinion, Jacobi was sure not to bear his critic any grudge. He returned the copy to Mendelssohn, to whom it had been dedicated.

A letter written by Dohm to Jacobi on December 18, 1781, offers a clue to the sequel of the story:[32] "Mendelssohn is very satisfied with your letter, yet he desires more simplicity of style. He thinks that you had overly aimed at brilliant phrases, antitheses and, particularly at the end of a discussion, at making a *pointe.*" It seems that Jacobi had answered Mendelssohn's objections in a conciliatory manner but without admitting to any shortcomings of style. Mendelssohn, therefore, felt it necessary to reemphasize his criticism of the somewhat bombastic manner of Jacobi's writing. His whole reaction was exactly as Jacobi had expected. It confirmed his view of Mendelssohn as one incapable of appreciating the merits of *his* work and as, therefore, worlds apart from *Lessing.* Jacobi remained outwardly polite, but his true feelings are revealed in the opening paragraph of Dohm's letter of December 18, where a remark of Jacobi's is quoted with some astonishment:[33] "Your warning against what you call the Berlin mentality [*berlinischen Geist*] I consider proof of your confidence and friendship, and I shall therefore be on my guard. However, I confess to being at a loss to understand in what way this mentality is expressed in my treatise on the Jews—it would be too bad, I dare say, had this happened unconsciously." It is clear, then, that Jacobi had warned Dohm against the insidious influence of the Berlin school of the Enlightenment—the influence of Mendelssohn.

Evidence of Jacobi's growing conviction that he had a profounder understanding of Lessing than Mendelssohn did is provided by a minor literary skirmish that, in a way, foreshadowed the real fight. In 1782, the historian Johannes von Müller published a little tract entitled *Journeys of the Popes (Reisen der Päpste),*[34] which was occasioned by Pius VI's famous trip to Vienna in the spring of that year, and which sought to prove the beneficial results accruing from the high dignity of the papal office. The fact that the Protestant Swiss historian had raised his voice on behalf of the papacy reminded Jacobi of a certain utterance he had once heard Lessing make, and he lost no time in writing and publishing a small work of his own called *Something that Lessing Said, A Commentary on the "Journeys of the Popes," as well as Reflections by a Third Party.*[35] He stated: "This I heard Lessing say: What Febronius[36] and his followers contended was a shameless flattery of the princes; for all their arguments against the privileges of the pope were either not valid arguments or applied with double and triple force to the princes themselves. Everyone was able to grasp this; it was, however, strange enough and an extremely bad symptom that among so many whose most urgent business it would have been to speak out nobody had as yet said so with all the conciseness and sharpness befitting the subject."[37] One single man, Jacobi remarked, had said it at long last, and since this man (Johannes von Müller) was in danger of being misunderstood, if not ridiculed, he might be joined by the "shade of a noble one" (Lessing) for his protection.[38]

When Jacobi's work appeared in the fall of 1782, it aroused a great deal of misapprehension. Doctor Reimarus suspected that its purpose was to defend churchly despotism, and this interpretation was shared by Campe and Mendelssohn, among others. As Jacobi's letters to Doctor Reimarus and Campe show, he was rather perplexed and dismayed by this reaction.[39] He realized that a clarification of his true intent was called for, and in order to provide himself with a convenient opportunity for a reply he resorted to a somewhat unusual stratagem: he fabricated an article directed against himself and asked Dohm, in the strictest confidence, to publish it anonymously in the *Deutsches Museum,* of which Dohm was a coeditor. The article, entitled "Some People's Thoughts à propos a Noteworthy Treatise," appeared in the January, 1783, issue of the periodical.[40] It was composed of two letters in French (dating from 1770 and not directly related to the subject) and some German comments on Lessing's statement about Febronius. The French correspondence, we gather from Jacobi's confidential letter to Dohm on December 3,.1782,[41] had passed between him and the baron von Fürstenberg. It dealt with the question of whether the closing of the monasteries would be beneficial, and Jacobi's letter was outspokenly anticlerical. Although the article mentioned no names, it did point out that the writer of the anticlerical letter was identical with the anonymous author of *Something that Lessing Said.* The letter, it was suggested, probably represented his true opinion.

As for the German comments contained in the article, they were written partly by Mendelssohn and partly by Dohm. As Jacobi revealed much later,[42] upon reading *Something that Lessing Said,* Mendelssohn had formulated some critical remarks that had been forwarded (with his permission) to Jacobi and later inserted (again with Mendelssohn's permission) in the article. When sending the manuscript to Dohm, Jacobi had left a broad margin so as to enable him to "make changes and additions ad lib.,"[43] and Dohm had added an entire section. This fact is attested by Jacobi's letter to Hamann, dated October 18, 1784:[44] "When you read 'Some People's Thoughts à propos a Noteworthy Treatise' [*Something that Lessing Said*] in the January, 1783, number of the *Museum,* you will be interested in learning that the proprietors of these 'thoughts' are Dohm and Mendelssohn. I myself committed them to print at the time."[45] Jacobi's reply followed in the February, 1783, number of the *Museum* under the title, "Objections to the Thoughts on a Noteworthy Treatise, Which Appeared in the January Issue of the *Museum*."[46]

What objections had Mendelssohn raised and how did Jacobi deal with them? The treatise, Mendelssohn pointed out, had failed to deal with the theme that it had set out to discuss. By its very title *(Something that Lessing Said)* it had given the impression that its subject was confined to the problem of papal versus princely power, whereas its actual subject was the advocacy of government by the people as distinct from monarchical rule. One wondered, therefore, whether the author was unable or unwilling to keep to "his first idea" as announced. Jacobi had suggested that perfectly virtuous characters were more easily formed under a despot. Mendelssohn found this observation very true and fruitful. "Viewed from this perspective, Lessing acted wisely when he set his *Nathan* in Turkey. Socrates developed in Athens at a time when the form of government inclined toward tyranny." A question posed by Mendelssohn was: can we transform our monarchies into governments by the people, and supposing we can, should we? He invited Jacobi's reply to this question. In his own view, such a change would only worsen the evil. "Hence what is the purpose of all declamations, which are pointless in practical terms? We tell the patient, with all the embellishment of rhetoric, that he is dangerously ill; we do not tell him what he has to do to recover his health or even how he could reduce his suffering. Let him rather believe that he is in good health than listen to a truth that cannot be of any use to him." Lessing's statement that the arguments against papal power applied with double and triple force to the princes was typical of his fondness of paradox: "Lessing held that an exaggeration, if widely acclaimed, had to be opposed by another exaggeration. I dare explain all paradoxes that occur in his writings as flowing from this principle, and perhaps all the paradoxes that have ever been asserted [by anyone], derived from no other source. It seems that our author [Jacobi] is also prepossessed in favor of this principle. For, truly speaking, his arguments for government by the people are rather exaggerated and are merely intended to tilt the balance from one extreme to the other. I believe, however, that this principle can be considered valid only in conversation, where the dialogue will be more lively if each of the partners kicks over the traces, as the expression goes. As soon as simple common sense takes over and applies the ruler, the dispute vanishes and the conversation comes to an end. It is otherwise in the case of an author who wishes not merely to entertain but to instruct. He has to look for distinct and pure concepts, and he has to adhere to them."

How did Jacobi's anonymous "objections" *(Erinnerungen)* in the February issue of the *Museum* reply to Mendelssohn's likewise anonymous "thoughts"? In exactly the same fashion in which he later would attack Mendelssohn's *Erinnerungen* in the pantheism controversy: by claiming, in the first place, that Mendelssohn's arguments completely missed the point, and by rejecting, in the second place, the way in which Mendelssohn explained the intent of Lessing's paradoxical statements. There is a striking similarity between his article in the *Museum* of 1783 and the letter he would write to Mendelssohn on April 26, 1785.[47] The same basic pattern of argumentation is discernible in the two documents. In the letter Jacobi wrote: "Before looking for weak spots, one must first find, and keep in check, the adversary's blade. You were looking for mine and brandished your weapon in a circle without meeting any resistance, for my presence was not over against there." In the *Museum* article he said:[48] "The preface [of *Something that Lessing Said*], the motto alone, Lessing's comment and Möser's gloss as well as the concluding passage indicate clearly enough, it seems to me, what was the one and only point at issue. . . . The adversary's [Mendelssohn's] objections, all of them, miss this point and hence prove nothing except his having misunderstood the author."[49] Moreover: "The logical order of our thoughts, said Lessing, is not always followed when we communicate them to others. Yet it is the adversary, above all, who must look for it, if his attack is to be fair. From this point of view there was hardly any justification for reproaching our author by saying: one wondered whether he was unable or unwilling to keep to his first idea. As said before, in this treatise everything revolves around a single point, and the first idea, like the last, is none other than to investigate the Gordian knot that has at all times so inextricably entangled the external freedom of man."[50]

The salient point, Jacobi explained, was his demand that the power of the state be restricted to the prevention of any infringement of its citizens' property rights; in other respects, the state should grant its citizens perfect freedom, including far greater freedom even to their passions. Reason could be trusted, Jacobi believed, to promote what benefited the whole of man and the common weal. In its external form and as a "machine of compulsion," society *(die Gesellschaft)* had for its sole object the negative function of holding off damage.[51] Thus, Jacobi repudiated every kind of despotism, and the question which form of despotism was the best did not merit being discussed by a wise man.[52] It was incomprehensible, therefore, how the adversary [Mendelssohn] could have accused the author of having entered an exaggerated plea on behalf of democracy *(Volksregierung)*—which could still be a despotism wielded by the multitude—and how he could have described this alleged plea as "the principal idea of *Something* [*that Lessing Said*]." All that was wanting was for him to pose the question whether the papacy was a democracy.[53] In point of fact, this particular question *had* been put to Jacobi in Mendelssohn's written remarks, but it had been omitted from the printed text.[54] It is obvious, therefore, that in Jacobi's view Mendelssohn had simply not grasped the point of his treatise.

Jacobi also took issue with Mendelssohn's interpretation of Lessing:[55]

What the adversary said . . . about paradoxes could be objected to in several respects, and I could document the objections by good examples. However, I shall mention only what Lessing told me concerning this point. It once

happened in his presence that I was accused of being paradoxical. I
explained myself to this effect: never would I attack the truth of a matter
of which I was convinced, yet I was wont to attack the wrong arguments
that caused others to be convinced of that very same truth. Love of true
belief bade me combat false belief. As a result, such people learned to
understand better the real connection of their ideas; they rid themselves
of an error—the error of thinking that they believed something that
they actually did not believe—and came, no doubt, in reality closer to
the truth even if they momentarily dismissed something that was true. . . .
Lessing, who in the meantime had come closer and was leaning on me,
repeated several times: This is precisely how I feel. Witnesses who heard
him say this are still alive.

Jacobi's point was that Lessing would assail views that he shared if
they were wrongly argued but was otherwise not indulging in paradoxicalness for its own sake, as Mendelssohn seemed to have implied. Yet Mendelssohn had made no such sweeping statement. He had merely said[56] that
Lessing wished to oppose an exaggeration, "if widely held," by another
exaggeration. A somewhat kindred observation occurred in the very first
paragraph of his preliminary draft *(Principal Traits)* when he set about
to write on Lessing's character in May/June, 1781:[57] "Favorite inclination
to espouse the weaker party." In other words, Lessing was apt to espouse
any cause or opinion that was under attack. Mendelssohn would fully elaborate this point in his *Morgenstunden* (1785),[58] which Jacobi would quote
with approval.[59] In his *Objections* to Mendelssohn's *Thoughts,* however, Jacobi
took umbridge at his "adversary's" remarks. He clearly considered himself
more competent to interpret Lessing's character than Mendelssohn was.

The little skirmish left no ill feelings on Mendelssohn's side, or so
we may infer from a letter written by Dohm to Jacobi on January 27,
1783:[60] "Let me reply to your letters. The first I showed to Mendelssohn.
It made him sad that his criticism had hurt you. He had written his verdict,
he explained, point-blank, as I had expressly asked him to do, without
sugaring it. Nowadays, he said, people were so used to sugaring all criticism
that everyone took it for granted and, therefore, added in thought something to what had been written. But he had added nothing at all in his
mind, and your arguments have really convinced him that he had looked
upon the thing from the wrong angle."

Mendelssohn was obviously not offended by the charge that he had
missed the point concerning Jacobi's political theory and had failed to
understand Lessing's fondness of paradox. How could he possibly have
guessed the depth of Jacobi's antipathy toward all he stood for? He may
even have gathered the impression that Jacobi harbored the friendliest
sentiments toward him personally, for the two passages in the article that
mentioned him by name did so in a deferential manner. The first of these
read:[61] "The remark that Lessing set his *Nathan* in Turkey might have
been joined by another one: that he made him a Jew. According to the
way in which the adversary presents the matter, perfect virtue ought to

be found chiefly among the Jews, at least in the major part of Europe, and in this respect their condition ought to be enviable. Yet, alas, we know of only One Mendelssohn, and he looks with sadness and horror upon the fetters of his brethren." The second passage recalled what Mendelssohn had once said[62] when one of Jacobi's friends had described in some detail the terrifying religious practices of certain peoples and expressed the view that they would be far happier if they believed nothing instead of worshipping such devilish beings. "The sage [Mendelssohn] contradicted this view. He said: These peoples derive from their worship at least a certain sublimity of thought, a certain development of the mind, and a salutary thrill in their entire soul, which provides ample compensation."[63]

But in conceding to Jacobi that he had misjudged his political views, Mendelssohn conceded no more than that. It would not have occurred to him to grant that Jacobi understood Lessing better than he did.

An Uneasy Correspondence

I

In February, 1783, Jacobi published *Objections to the Thoughts on a Noteworthy Treatise* in answer to Mendelssohn. On March 25, Elise Reimarus sent Jacobi an enthusiastic report on her visit to Mendelssohn the day before.[1] The last paragraph of her letter read:[2] "Toward you, dearest Jacobi, Mendelssohn harbors truly good feelings, and he is satisfied with your *Objections*. . . . and I did all we could to make you, if possible, still better known to him; for both of you certainly deserve to know each other *as you are*. Oh that you were here at this time!"

If Elise and the friend who accompanied her—probably Campe—felt the need to act as peacemakers, they must have been aware of some tension between the two men. As Dohm had already assured Jacobi in January,[3] Mendelssohn was by no means averse to friendly relations. It was obviously Jacobi who had to be persuaded to see his "adversary" *(der Gegner)*[4] objectively. The trouble was that he believed that he knew the nature of his adversary far too well to be impressed by any well-intentioned effort to make it possible for the two to know each other as they were. The very fact that Mendelssohn was "satisfied" with his *Objections* may have confirmed Jacobi in his suspicion that Mendelssohn had again missed the point, which was the radical critique of the Enlightenment.

In *Something that Lessing Said*[5] Jacobi had declared that the naked radicalism of a Hobbes or Machiavelli was preferable to the accommodations of the Enlightenment. In similar vein, he had said at the end of his *Objections*:[6] "The constant readiness to accommodate, which is so prevalent among us, is not to my liking. I even fail to understand the arrogance that dares to administer truth." What he meant was akin to what Hamann later wrote to him on July 22, 1785:[7] "Catholicism is nothing but despotism. Instead of Roman Catholicism there is now in the making a metaphysico-moral one, which has its seat in the very locality [Berlin] where such a hue and cry is raised about the papacy."

In a subsequent letter to Elise,[8] Jacobi spoke of the *morgue berlinoise* and the "magisterial, supercilious way" that was "rampant there" and had not left Mendelssohn "entirely uninfected"—as he put it somewhat cautiously, so as not to offend Elise. To both Jacobi and Hamann the Enlightenment of the Berlin school represented a theology and a philosophy of compromise that claimed an infallibility comparable to that claimed by the papacy and exhibited a self-assurance bordering on arrogance. The uncompromising attitudes of Hobbes and Machiavelli in politics and of Spinoza in metaphysics appeared to Jacobi to be far superior to the balanced "administration of truth" by the Berlin Enlightenment. What he admired in Lessing was the same uncompromising manner of thinking, which had despised the accommodations of the neologists far more than the rigidity of the orthodox. How then was he to react to the disclosure that Mendelssohn was "satisfied" with his *Objections* and, particularly, to the happy news conveyed by Elise that Mendelssohn was now about to "keep his word about 'Something on Lessing's Character.'" Could Jacobi, prejudiced as he was against Mendelssohn, share her enthusiasm and her prayer: "May Heaven grant him the requisite health and serenity of mind so that we may read yet once something about our friend that is worthy of the man"?

If Jacobi had wished to act in a straightforward manner, two ways were open to him. He could wait to see what Mendelssohn had to say and then come forward with a publication of his own. Or he could immediately make known the record of his talks with Lessing and the conclusions that he had drawn from them. He decided, however, to follow quite another course: he sent word to Mendelssohn that Lessing, toward the end of his life, had become a "Spinozist." Jacobi well knew that this piece of "information" would have the effect of compelling an alarmed Mendelssohn to attempt to refute the charge, which was tantamount to the charge of atheism. Jacobi would thus be provided with yet another opportunity to demonstrate his superior acquaintance with Lessing (and Spinoza) in a way reminiscent of the *mise en scène* surrounding the printing of Mendelssohn's *Thoughts* in the January issue of the *Museum*. If he failed to disclose Lessing's "Spinozism" in this manner, Jacobi supposed, he ran the risk of forfeiting such an opportunity, since Mendelssohn's forthcoming "Something on Lessing's Character" might otherwise omit reference to Lessing's metaphysical views. But by hinting that other people besides himself might have been let in on the secret, Jacobi made sure that Mendelssohn could not avoid discussing the matter!

Jacobi's desire to have another and more devastating go at Mendelssohn was motivated not merely by his disdain for the *morgue berlinoise* but also by a—perhaps unconscious—equation of the Enlightenment and Judaism.

On April 4, 1782, Jacobi had written to his friend Kleuker in Osnabrück:[9] "During my illness I tied up a few new metaphysical knots that look ugly enough. I shall tell you of them soon and shall also inform Lavater.—(On April 5.) If there is a God, there must be yet another revelation apart from the revelation of nature.... Here something dawns upon me that might greatly benefit the Christian doctrine." On October 10, 1781, he had confessed to Lavater:[10] "I know of no doctrine that seems to me more evident and more profoundly established than the doctrine of the Christian dispensation.... To be a Christian appears to me no more difficult than not to be an atheist." When he eventually published his counterblow to Mendelssohn, Jacobi concluded—"blessed and sealed"—it with a quotation from Lavater's "pious, angelic [*engelreinen*] mouth."[11] He felt as much drawn to Lavater as to Hamann, who in January and February, 1784, wrote his *Golgatha and Sheblimini,* in which he attacked Mendelssohn both as a philosopher of the Enlightenment and as a rabbinic upholder of the Mosaic Law. The philosophers, in Hamann's view, were as mistaken as the rabbis: they expected of reason what the Jews expected of the Law, namely, the knowledge of God. Both philosophers and rabbis "abused" the principles of sufficient reason and of contradiction, which could never reveal truth.[12] By the time of Jacobi's reply to Elise's letter (July 21, 1783), Mendelssohn's *Jerusalem* had been out almost three months, and the author's profile as both guardian of the Enlightenment and advocate of rabbinic Judaism had become more visible in its dual aspect than it had ever been before.

Interestingly enough, the earliest critical review (which may not have appeared in print) of the *Jerusalem* was written by Jacobi's uncle, Johann Friedrich Jacobi, who was superintendent in Celle. Hamann acknowledged an indebtedness to the elder Jacobi as his "precursor."[13] Mendelssohn was confronted, therefore, with a group of adversaries that included the two Jacobis, Hamann, and Lavater. In considering the younger Jacobi's reaction to Elise's letter, one has to give due weight to the entire syndrome of sentiments giving rise to his desire to take issue with Mendelssohn. As a clever tactician, Jacobi sought to entice Mendelssohn into rebutting the charge of Spinozism that Jacobi laid at Lessing's door so as to be able to move on to a broad attack on Mendelssohn himself. Had Jacobi simply disclosed Lessing's "Spinozism" to the public, he would have used up his ammunition and left Mendelssohn with the last word.

As matters turned out, Jacobi's stratagem succeeded only in part. Mendelssohn did fall into the trap and endeavored to interpret Lessing's alleged Spinozism in a way designed to render it innocuous (abandoning in the process his earlier plan to write on Lessing's character). Jacobi, on the other hand, was compelled to publish his own work in great haste and simultaneously with Mendelssohn's. But the only writings that could be termed polemical tracts in the proper sense of the term [i. e., Mendelssohn's *An die Freunde Lessings* and Jacobi's *Wider Mendelssohns Beschuldigungen*],— belonged to the second act of the drama that was unfolding.

Jacobi's reply to Elise's March 25 letter was not written until July 21.[14] He was unable to respond earlier, he explained, because he had wanted to talk to her about "something very important—the beliefs [*Gesinnungen*] finally held by our Lessing." She might convey them to Mendelssohn, if she deemed it right to do so. "Perhaps you know, and if you don't, I confide it to you under the rose of friendship, that in his last days Lessing was a decided Spinozist. Lessing could possibly have stated these beliefs to several people, in which case it would be necessary for Mendelssohn either to entirely evade certain matters in the memorial he wants to erect for him or to treat them at least in an extremely cautious manner. Perhaps Lessing was as explicit to his dear Mendelssohn as he was to me; perhaps he was not, because he had not talked to him for a long time and disliked writing letters. Let it be left to your discretion, my dear, whether or not you wish to disclose anything about this to Mendelssohn. At present I can not write in greater detail concerning the matter."

Jacobi could hardly have doubted that Elsie would pass this important piece of information on to Mendelssohn, especially in view of the possibility that the secret might already be known to others. His eagerness to have her share the news with Mendelssohn is betrayed by the fact that he twice stated that it was left to her discretion to do so. He also made sure that she would write to Mendelssohn by including in the final paragraph of his letter a request that was in fact addressed to Mendelssohn himself, in his unofficial capacity as literary coexecutor of Lessing's *Nachlass*.[15]

Jacobi had not miscalculated. On August 4, 1783, Elise wrote the following letter to Mendelssohn:[16]

> The two enclosed sheets are [a copy of] parts of a letter from the Düsseldorf Jacobi to me. I considered it necessary to pass them on to you, my dearest Mendelssohn, since only you are in a position to judge whether the public should be apprised of the information contained therein. I am very anxious to hear to what extent it is new to you and what you think of these last beliefs of our friend.
>
> I admit—and if it be calumny, may his sacred shade forgive me—that the words "in his last days" had made me suspect something entirely different, because shortly after his death even Lessing's best friends spoke a great deal about a divinitary and augural sense in him, which seemed to approach superstition. In this respect the word "Spinozist" was less dreadful to me.
>
> Yet what about it? With regard to this I am suspending my judgment until I hear yours. I am also keeping the entire matter strictly to myself. Should you desire to know more details about the matter, it is obvious that Jacobi will be glad to oblige, insofar as it can be useful to what you want to write *about Lessing's character* (not memorial!). You would do him a great favor, however, if you were willing or able to help him get hold of some of the manuscripts and books he mentioned, which are among the *Nachlass* of Lessing's papers and books kept in Berlin. . . .

As Mendelssohn put it later,[17] Jacobi's "offer" (*Antrag*), the information he had volunteered and was ready to augment, was "highly disagreeable" to him. He would undoubtedly have been happier if Elise had kept it to herself. One can read his indignation at the unwisdom of her action between the lines of some of his letters to her. When he asked her on August 8, 1784, to pass certain material and a letter on to Jacobi, and apologized for imposing this inconvenience upon her, he significantly added:[18] "You yourself have been the cause of it by having conveyed Herr Jacobi's challenge to me." On June 28, 1785, he wrote to her:[19] "Blame yourself, my dearest friend, if I bother you again with a bundle of manuscripts.... Since you have been the cause of all this scribbling [*Schreiberei*], you will have to put up with all the trouble that follows from it."

Mendelssohn considered Jacobi's piece of news, when he received it, as a "mere anecdote" that Jacobi might have picked up from somebody: some half-understood word or album inscription by Lessing could well have been exploited by some "hunter for anecdotes" *(Anekdotenkrämer)* in order to declare him to have been a Spinozist. The Germans, it seemed to Mendelssohn, had gotten into the habit of "classifying everything," and any conceivable circumstance was likely to be seized upon for purposes of putting a man under a certain rubric. But since this particular "anecdote" was clearly meant to "put Lessing on trial," and since he was about to write on Lessing's character, Mendelssohn felt that he had to look into the matter. To do this had not been part of his original plan, however, and he was therefore quite annoyed at having been drawn into "discussions and investigations" to which his mind was not attuned.

"Hence Herr Jacobi's statement was most unwelcome to me, and I insisted on a more detailed explanation as to how, on what occasion, and in what terms Lessing had indicated his Spinozism."[20] That is how, in his final utterance published posthumously in 1786, Mendelssohn would describe his immediate reaction to the information conveyed to him by Elise. The account he gave then tallies completely with the tone and temper of his initial reply to Elise on August 16, 1783, the opening paragraph of which read:[21] "What does this mean: 'Lessing was a decided Spinozist in his last days'? Must we eternally classify and put things under rubrics? How did Lessing express himself vis-à-vis Jacobi? Did he say in plain words: I consider Spinoza's system to be true and well founded? And which system of his? The one expounded in his *Tractatus Theologico-Politicus* or the one found in his *Principia philosophiae Cartesianae* or the one posthumously published in his name by Ludovicus Meyer [viz. the *Ethica*]? In case he affirmed the system of Spinoza that is generally held to be atheistic, I ask a thinker like Jacobi: did Lessing interpret the system in the way in which Bayle misunderstood it, or after the manner in which it has been better explained by others?—If Lessing was capable of agreeing with someone's system absolutely and without more closely defining his position, he was at the time either out of his senses or in one of those strange moods in which he would state some paradox that he himself rejected when in a serious frame of mind. In such a mood Lessing was capable of saying anything that was likely to incite his adversary for the sole purpose of making the debate more lively."

Mendelssohn thus repeated, with an added nuance, what he had suggested in his critical remarks on *Something that Lessing Said,* ignoring completely Jacobi's *Objections,* which had offered a rather different view of Lessing's love of paradox. Toward the end of the letter Mendelssohn reiterated his view of the matter: "I am returning to you Lessing's letters, which you had been kind enough to entrust to me.... Since I intend to write not about his genius but about his character, I cherish most those letters in which he concerned himself with unadulterated truth, following his natural bent and not being inclined to paradoxicalness and opposition. Once that particular mood got hold of him, any opinion, no matter how absurd, could be defended by him from love of acuteness; and in the heat of battle it sometimes seemed to represent his seriously held view. In such moments the gymnastic of the mind was more important to him than the simple truth."[22]

In this reply Mendelssohn considered yet another possibility of interpreting Lessing's alleged affirmation of Spinozism:[23] "Perhaps Lessing said something like this: 'Dear brother, the much maligned Spinoza may well have had a larger vision in some respects than all the clamorous people who proved their worth by shouting him down. His *Ethics* in particular contains excellent things, perhaps better ones than are found in many an orthodox moralistic work or in many a compendium of philosophy. His system is not as absurd as one believes it to be.' In the event that he betrayed sentiments like these, as I suspect my friend did—my dearest soul! I don't know how near or how far death stands behind me with the threatening scythe: yet I am ready at all times to put my signature under such a statement and to do so with all my heart, no matter what rubric I shall be placed under in consequence thereof." In other words, Mendelssohn would not mind being himself labeled a Spinozist if Spinozism was meant to denote the moral teachings of the *Ethics.*

Having unburdened himself of his initial, somewhat turbulent thoughts, Mendelssohn continued in a more sober vein: "Herr Jacobi is certainly not a man who only half inquires into a thing or understands only half of it; and a talk of this nature with Lessing is far too important to admit the possibility that its details might have been forgotten. I therefore greatly desire that your friend report to us, if he pleases, what, how, on what occasion, and on what account Lessing made this statement. For this is all that matters. For the time being, I persist in my astonishment and exclaim: *Lessing a decided Spinozist!,* just as Lessing and I once exclaimed: *Pope a Metaphysician!*"

If Mendelssohn actually suspected that Jacobi had learned the "news" at second hand from some "hunter for anecdotes," as he asserted later, he was polite enough not to say so, though the inquisitorial manner of his questioning betrayed his doubts. For the moment, at any rate, he was prepared to suspend judgment and even to face up to the remote possibility that the information was correct:[24] "As soon, however, as Herr Jacobi has convinced us in regard to this matter, I see no reason why we should conceal the last sentiments [*Gesinnungen*] of our friend and hold them back from posterity. In fact, we owe him no more and no less justice than he himself did to the Fragmentist [whose views he candidly disclosed]. In this case, too, truth cannot but gain. Should his arguments [in favor of Spinozism] be shallow, they will only serve the cause of truth; should they be dangerous, the good lady will have to make provision for her defense. Even our best friend's name is not meant to appear to posterity in a brighter light than he deserves. —Men like G[oeze], S[emler], and whatever their names may be will be glad and triumphant. Never mind! When I put pen to paper, when I write about the character of my friend Lessing, I place myself half a century ahead, when all partiality will have ended and all our present wrangling will at last be forgotten."

Mendelssohn had recaptured not only a sense of equanimity but even of serenity and good humor, as the subsequent passage shows: "Your fear, dearest Reimarus, that the words 'in his last days' might be followed by something far more 'dreadful' than the word 'Spinozist' has greatly amused me. Were you really afraid that Lessing might have become something even more dreadful than a Spinozist? Why, what if he had become both: Spinozist and Kabbalist at the same time? These systems are not so far apart that they completely exclude each other. Wachter[25] even maintained that Spinozism arose out of kabbalistic soil and is descended from kabbalistic doctrine. What is there that has not at some time coexisted in a paradoxical mind?—I would like to see your face, dearest Reimarus, if you visited me in my last hour and found me wearing an amulet around my neck and reading David Hume's *Dialogues* [*Concerning Natural Religion*]." Admittedly, Mendelssohn's humor was a little grim, and the repeated references to his death ("the threatening scythe" and the "last hour") appear in retrospect almost like a premonition of the approaching end—which was not to be unconnected with the Jacobi affair. Yet a playful note is unmistakable in this part of the letter.

What was it that enabled Mendelssohn to overcome his annoyance and completely regain his composure in the course of writing this letter to Elise? How can one explain his sudden readiness to acknowledge Lessing's Spinozism in his forthcoming essay, in the event that Jacobi could substantiate his allegation? What caused him to declare with almost brutal objectivity: "Even our best friend's name is not meant to appear to posterity in a brighter light than it deserves"? It may be surmised that several things combined to produce Mendelsson's startling bravura. There was, in the first place, his inevitable disapproval of Elise's (and her brother's) timidity: her suggestion that Mendelssohn was in a position to judge whether the public should be apprised of Lessing's Spinozism, with the implication that Mendelssohn might elect to suppress the truth, was bound to provoke the answer that the truth must on no account be suppressed. Mendelssohn's reference to Lessing's publication of the Reimarus *Fragments* was obviously intended as an argument ad hominem, and his good-humored banter about her fear was part of this reaction.

A further reason for Mendelssohn's bravura may be found in his need to demonstrate to Jacobi that the information provided had not thrown him off balance. The assurance that proper use would be made of the information, if it carried conviction, was calculated to show Mendelssohn's freedom from prejudice and bias. He could not afford to reject the alleged information out of hand. But it would have been more prudent of Mendelssohn to suggest that Jacobi publish the information first. His reason for not taking this simple course was probably twofold: he was afraid that a blunt public assertion of Lessing's Spinozism would damage Lessing's reputation, and he was confident that he would be able to interpret his friend's final views in a manner consonant with an essentially theistic philosophy. On April 22, 1783, Karl Lessing had sent Mendelssohn the theological writings found in his brother's *Nachlass*, including the manuscript of the fragment *The Christianity of Reason*, which Mendelssohn well remembered from the days of his youth.[26] As already remarked,[27] it was the sight of this old manuscript that inspired Mendelssohn to resume his plan to write "something on Lessing's character." It would appear that on learning from Elise what Jacobi had reported, Mendelssohn immediately associated Lessing's alleged Spinozism with the ideas expounded in the fragment. In his *Morgenstunden*[28] he quoted paragraphs 1–5 and 13–27 of the by then published fragment to show that in this early speculative effort Lessing had affirmed a "refined" form of pantheism that was as compatible with positive religion as the emanationist systems of the ancients had been. The fact that Lessing had described the notions expressed in the fragment as his "former fanciful ideas [*Grillen*]"[29] does not mean that he had abandoned them. It was Lessing's habit in letters to friends to refer even to his most serious writings—the *Nathan*, the theological treatises, and the *Education of the Human Race*— as trash, fancies, and scrawls (*Wisch, Grillen, Sudeleyen*). Throughout his life he was fond of metaphysical speculations of the kind found in *The Christianity of Reason*."[30] Mendelssohn had a perfect right, therefore, to associate the ideas of the fragment with Lessing's alleged "Spinozism."

The Spinozistic flavor of the fragment was also noticed, it seems, by Jacobi. On May 18, 1785, still prior to the publication of the *Morgenstunden*, he wrote to Hamann:[31] "Only four days ago I received Lessing's *Theologischer Nachlass* [edited by Karl G. Lessing] and I read it with great interest. In regard to my quarrel with Mendelssohn the essay (Number 12) on the Christianity of reason was most welcome to me." Jacobi was of course in no way inclined to interpret the fragment as an expression of a "purified pantheism." Mendelssohn was, however, and it was Mendelssohn's confidence in his ability to meet the challenge that enabled him to control his anger and to promise serenely not to suppress "the truth" about Lessing. The truth, he was confident, could be shown to be identical with his theory of Lessing's "purified pantheism."

Evidently, Mendelssohn was not trying to put a fresh complexion upon things when he declared, in his final statement *An die Freunde Lessings*, that Jacobi's piece of news had not astonished him:[32] "That I was astonished is surely not an account of facts but the reporter's [Jacobi's] surmise.[33] . . . I knew that there exists also a purified Spinozism that agrees very well with all that is practical in religion and morality, as I have shown at length in the *Morgenstunden*. . . . Finally, I also knew already that in his earliest youth our friend had been inclined toward pantheism, which he was not only able to combine with his religion but from which he had even sought to demonstrate the Athanasian creed. The passage from a youthful essay of this early writer, which I quote in the *Morgenstunden*, shows this most clearly, and he had given me this essay to read at the very start of our acquaintance. Hence, the news that Lessing was a Spinozist could neither astonish nor embarrass me."

Although this subsequent account cannot be fully credited—had not Mendelssohn claimed the right to persist in his "astonishment" until such time as Jacobi had convinced him of Lessing's Spinozism?—it accurately reflects the confidence he had felt in his ability to interpret the fact, should it be proved, in a completely innocuous way. After all, in his *Philosophical Dialogues* of 1755 he had already interpreted Spinoza himself in precisely the same manner in which he was going to explain Lessing's "Spinozism" in the *Morgenstunden* of 1785.[34] When he asked Jacobi (in his reply to Elise): "Did Lessing interpret the system in the way in which Bayle misunderstood it, or after the manner in which it has been better explained by others?" Mendelssohn meant by "others"—himself. This sentence alone would seem to leave no doubt that at the time of his reply to Elise he already had in mind applying to Lessing his concept of a purified Spinozism. He was careful, however, not to let this fact become known prematurely.

On September 1, 1783, Elise conveyed to Jacobi a summary of Mendelssohn's reply. She had evidently taken pains to smooth over its rough edges and tone down its occasional harshness. The result was a rather tame and courteous letter. By putting Mendelssohn's array of questions in the form of indirect speech she succeeded in making them sound less aggressive. She omitted whole sentences that she considered offensive or merely rhetorical. (The reference to the Reimarus *Fragments* was left out, probably because it was simply not to her own liking.) Her concluding paragraph read:[35] "As you see, dearest Jacobi, this is the result of the information conveyed by you, which I could not possibly conceal from Mendelssohn, and which you should not regret having promised to elaborate upon. For what would you say if Mendelssohn's publication on Lessing's character were to come out one day without saying anything about such important matters? You would then have to reproach yourself for having mutilated the cause of truth (for it, rather than our friend's cause, is at stake here). How I personally feel in anticipation of your statement in one way or another—this is irrelevant."

It was rather naive of Elise to apologize for having done precisely what Jacobi had left entirely to her discretion, and what, it seems clear, he had actually *wanted* her to do all along (though she had no way of knowing this). As her letter shows, she had accepted Mendelssohn's argument that the cause of truth had to prevail, come what might, but her last sentence indicated a certain uneasiness. Jacobi, too, could not help feeling a sense of discomfort when, two months later on November 4, 1783, he dispatched the long and weighty letter that contained the account of his talks with Lessing in the summer of 1780, a letter that was destined to become famous. The letter was addressed to Mendelssohn but sent to Elise with the request that she forward it. The covering letter to Elise reveals the state of his feelings at the time:[36]

> Today I am leaving my residence in the country in order to start the winter in town, though rather prematurely, for we have still the most beautiful weather. Yet regularity demands it. In order that, on top of everything, I should not also bring a bad conscience with me to the bad town, I send you herewith what, to my regret, I have been owing you for such a long time. You will not resent the fact that my letter is directed straight to Mendelssohn; and Mendelssohn will not take it amiss that I did not write the whole of it in my own hand. I leave it to you to convey to him my apologies on this account.
>
> Inform me by the Monday mail, if you can, that you received and forwarded the parcel, and also of your thoughts about the content. Tell me at a later date what I am supposed to know about Mendelssohn's reaction. I do not expect of him the very best of thanks for the trouble I took, because my way of looking at things is somewhat different from his, and the *morgue berlinoise*, the magisterial, supercilious way, which is rampant there and has not left even Mendelssohn entirely uninfected, cannot stand things of this sort. However, I am ready once and for all to bear whatever results from the appearance [*Schein*] of my being [*Sein*], and to manifest at all times my being alone as it truly is. This requires some courage and resignation, but in return one receives an inner peace that is not obtainable otherwise.

Thus Jacobi did not expect Mendelssohn to thank him for the "trouble" that he, Jacobi, had gone to, nor did he expect that his "way of looking at things" would be understood. He forgot that it had been he, Jacobi, who had chosen to alarm Mendelssohn with an unsolicited piece of news, and who had therefore no one to blame but himself for any trouble that might proceed from his action. Since he made no secret of his belief that Mendelssohn, as a prominent member of the *morgue berlinoise*, was quite incapable of even understanding him, Elise might well have wondered what the purpose of their correspondence was. She was, however, too noble and innocent a soul to suspect any dark or sinister motive, however strange and oracular his words may have seemed to her.

What Jacobi meant by the distinction between "appearance" and "being" he later discussed in a note *ad locum* in his self-defense *Against Mendelssohn's Accusations*:[37] Recently he had written something similar to a friend, except that he had used the term "renunciation of" (*Resignation auf*) instead of "submission to," and this had provoked a reply that he felt was worthy of being recorded. The unnamed friend was Hamann, and the relevant passage in Jacobi's letter to him read as follows:[38] "I must have told you more than once that renunciation of my being and of the appearance of my being constitutes my grand philosophy, and with it one does not need much of politics. In view of my lively temperament I have to seek above all that which best secures inner peace." In his note on the letter to Elise Jacobi gave the gist of Hamann's answer without indicating that it had criticized his professed retreat from being. This is what Hamann wrote:[39] "The essence [*das Herz*] of your philosophy, renunciation of being in the appearance of being, is as enigmatic to me as my 'learning even from an enemy' [*etiam ab hoste consilium*][40] is to you.... Renunciation of all appearance of being for the benefit of true being, this is how I translate your principle. One cannot resign from being, since it is not our property; yet one can [resign] from the appearance of being, because it is the property of art and politics. Inner peace is being. In appearance, all is changeable. It is a mere shadow and disquiet. Am I right? And is this not what you intended to say?" Jacobi agreed, and in his letter to Elise he had in fact anticipated this distinction between appearance and true being.

How fragile Jacobi's own sense of being was may be inferred from a letter he wrote to Goethe on April 28, 1784:[41] "I am what I became: tormented from my childhood on by a secret insuperable nausea at myself, at man, so that, increasingly deprived of hope, I often can hardly bear to be such a thing: a lie among lies, a dreaming [*Geträume*] of things dreamt; and to be still less when I believe myself to be awake." Similarly he had said in his *Allwill*:[42] "Appearance and shadow surround us. Not even the essence of our own existence do we know. We stamp everything with our image, and the image is a changing form: the ego [*Ich*] that we call our "self" is an ambiguous birth out of everything and nothing: our *own* soul is but an appearance ... yet an *appearance* approaching essence." The "existentialist" type of philosophizing, which tended to despair of ever knowing essence and being, so dominated Jacobi's thinking that the profound self-assurance that Mendelssohn derived from the Leibniz/Wolffian ontology seemed to Jacobi motionless and dead, a part and parcel of the *morgue berlinoise* whose "magisterial, supercilious essence" was the very antithesis of his insecurity and disbelief in himself. He could not help expressing it in his letter to Elise.

The letter that Jacobi sent Mendelssohn on November 4, 1783, contained thirty-six quarto pages, of which only the introduction (pages 1–3, line 19) and the concluding part (page 32, line 6 from the bottom to the end of page 36) were written in his own hand, while the bulk of the letter, covering his talks with Lessing, was copied from a *Vorlage* by somebody else.[43] It was pertinent to the subject, Jacobi remarked at the opening, to mention at the outset certain things about himself; this would make Mendelssohn somewhat better acquainted with him, and the rapport thus established would enable him [Jacobi] to summon the courage needed to speak his mind with complete frankness, and perhaps to forget what might cause him to be cautious or shy. It is difficult to understand why setting forth a factual account of a conversation with Lessing should have required "courage," especially after the central point at issue, the disclosure of Lessing's Spinozism, had already been made. One has to assume that the "courage" to speak with complete frankness was required for some other purpose, presumably for the harshness of Jacobi's introductory remarks, and also his remarks at the end of the report. In the introduction Jacobi said:

> If at any time there were only few people who struggled for truth with deep earnestness, truth revealed itself to each one of these in some way. I discovered this trail; I pursued it among the living and the dead; and the longer I did so, the more intimately I noticed that true profundity [*Tiefsinn*], like gravity in bodies, has a common direction. Proceeding as it does from different points of the periphery, this direction produces neither parallel lines nor lines crossing each other.
> It is different with acuteness [*Scharfsinn*], which I would like to compare with the chords of a circle, and which is often mistaken for profundity because it says profound things about form and externality. Here the lines cross each other as much as one wants, and sometimes they are parallels. A chord can be so close to the diameter that one holds it to be the diameter itself. In such a case, however, it only intersects a large number of radii, without even touching the ends of those which it seemed to be.—
> Where both are missing, i.e., where there is mere knowledge, so-called, without either acuteness or profundity, without a felt need for truth itself and without the enjoyment of it, can anything more nauseating be found?——Forgive me the stuff and nonsense of my imagery.—I now come to Lessing.[44]

Hamann, after reading this passage, wrote to Jacobi on December 1, 1784:[45] "Your comparison of profundity and acuteness with the diameter and the chord of a circle seems to me neither precise nor clear enough. My imagination has played differently with this figure. Profundity is needed for *truths*, which are all equal to one another and intersect the center [of the circle]. Acuteness shows *probabilities*, which are all diameters of smaller circles; they may touch a variety of opposite points of the periphery and may be parallels, but they never touch the center."

Jacobi had expressed himself more distinctly in a letter to Matthias Claudius on June 30, 1783:[46] "The inner similarity of the thoughts of all men who seriously seek the truth and are concerned about it is . . . most remarkable. All these people possess a certain profundity—which causes them to be profound and to find approximately the same thing.

Acuteness is something different but is often mistaken for profundity because it is, so to speak, profound concerning form. Pythagoras, Plato, and Spinoza were people totally unlike Aristotle and Hobbes. Inasmuch as we are sharp-witted we are nearly always at loggerheads with one another; profundity, however, makes us peaceable. The various radii of the same circle can never be in each other's way." Jacobi saw in Claudius a friend with whose ideas his own were in striking agreement not only in essentials but even in external forms of expression.[47]

In Jacobi's letter to Mendelssohn the distinction between acuteness and profundity was obviously intended to suggest why their ways of looking at things were so different. It was no mere coincidence that hitting the "center" was invariably the phrase used by Jacobi whenever he wanted to indicate where Mendelssohn's shortcomings lay. As in his article in the February issue of the *Museum,* and later in his comments on Mendelssohn's *Erinnerungen,* so in this letter, too, aiming at the center and not missing it is the criterion of profundity. Jacobi makes it abundantly clear that in his estimation Mendelssohn did not meet this requirement, since otherwise they would be in agreement. The "courage" to say this more or less openly was evidently not lacking in him; that he vindicated acuteness to his "adversary" is questionable. The sentence "Where both are missing . . . " (which was suppressed after the first edition of his treatise [*Über die Lehre des Spinoza in Briefen an den Herrn Moses Mendelssohn,* 1785] justifies the assumption that he considered the "knowledge" represented by Mendelssohn and the Enlightenment as "mere knowledge, so-called, without either acuteness or profundity, without a felt need for truth itself, and without the enjoyment of it." The abrupt transition from the cynical question "can anything more nauseating be found?" to the sentence "forgive me the stuff and nonsense of my imagery" corroborates this assumption. As the letter to Claudius shows, the imagery of the circle was anything but "stuff and nonsense" to Jacobi. The sentence to the contrary in the letter to Mendelssohn must therefore be considered disingenuous.

The concluding part of his letter was later commented upon by Jacobi in his tract *Against Mendelssohn's Accusations.*[48] He had felt a sense of embarrassment, he said, when faced with the task of answering Mendelssohn's pointed questions about the "character" of Lessing's Spinozism. In his view, the questions exhibited a lack of familiarity with Spinoza's works: "Was I to accuse the creditable and in many a respect venerable man of ignorance—of ignorance of the crassest sort on a matter concerning which he had posed questions with so much self-assurance? Or should I have approached him with delicate scorn? Neither way was becoming to me, and I therefore resorted to the stratagem of considering myself as having been insulted and of reproaching him on this account." In his letter Jacobi had written that the "specific questions" had "somewhat astonished" him because they had "presupposed such an ignorance"[49] on his (Jacobi's) part. Mendelssohn had asked, he recalled, which of Spinoza's systems Lessing had adopted and had referred to certain possibilities. Jacobi retorted with the biting remark that everyone who had even a nodding acquaintance with Spinoza knew that Descartes' *Principia* as demonstrated (i.e. as presented in geometrical form) by Spinoza had nothing to do with Spinozism. Nor did Jacobi know anything of a system of Spinoza published posthumously by Ludovicus Meyer, unless Mendelssohn had meant to refer to the *Opera posthuma*, in which case, however, it was inconceivable how he could have placed these in opposition to the *Tractatus Theologico-Politicus*, with which they were in complete agreement.

Jacobi was undoubtedly right in saying that Spinoza's presentation of Descartes was not to be confused with Spinozism. Mendelssohn had a copy of this work in his library[50] and could have gathered from a mere glance at Meyer's introduction that Spinoza did not share the ideas expounded in this treatise. Perhaps Mendelssohn wanted to put Jacobi to the test—not knowing how intensely Jacobi had studied Spinoza—or perhaps he had indeed forgotten some of what he had once known, his interests having long since taken him into other fields.[51] Mendelssohn was himself well aware that many details of his past researches had faded from memory, and he said just this quite candidly in a letter written at about the time that Jacobi's disconcerting letter reached him. A correspondent had asked Mendelssohn to contribute an essay on Leibniz to a projected "worthy memorial" to some "great Germans." In his reply of November 18, 1783, Mendelssohn proposed that Eberhard would be far better qualified for the task:[52] "However diligently I read and studied the writings of this school and, particularly, of its founder in my youth, I have lost touch with them during the last twenty and more years. Especially the historical aspects of his life and his works have completely slipped from my memory. I would therefore have to devote a great deal of time and energy to the humanities to be able to furnish an account of Leibniz' mind and character such as you, Sir, rightly demand." Mendelssohn would probably have written a similar letter had he been invited to write an essay on Spinoza.

However, while Mendelssohn was possibly in error when he referred to Spinoza's work on Descartes, his mention of the system posthumously published by Lodewijk Meyer could have referred only to the *Opera posthuma* (Amsterdam, 1677). According to Bayle, the *Opera* had been edited by Jarig Jelles and Lodewijk Meyer, but in fact Jelles and Jan Rieuwertsz were the editors.[53] Jacobi knew very well that Mendelssohn had been alluding to the *Opera posthuma* (which included the *Ethica*), for when Hamann asked him what was meant by Mendelssohn's reference, he replied that "assuredly nothing else but the *Ethics* [was] meant; for otherwise Mendelssohn would have had to mention it separately." To put Hamann's mind at rest, however, he was going to inquire of Mendelssohn through Elise Reimarus.[54] The perplexity that Jacobi exhibited in his reply to Mendelssohn's question was, therefore, entirely simulated. Nor was Jacobi in any way justified in his objection to Mendelssohn's asking whether Lessing's affirmation of Spinozism was related to the *Ethics* as a whole or to the specific concerns of the *Tractatus*. It was *not* true that Mendelssohn had implied that there was a contradiction between the two works.

To Mendelssohn's question concerning whether Lessing had interpreted the system in the way that Bayle had "misunderstood" it or after the manner in which it had been better explained by "others" (i.e., by Mendelssohn himself), Jacobi replied:[55] "There is a difference between understanding and not misunderstanding. Bayle did not misunderstand Spinoza's system insofar as its conclusions are concerned; all one can say is that he did not understand it far enough back—that he failed to see its reasons as conceived by the author. If Bayle misunderstood Spinoza, as your reproach has it, one would, in the same sense, have to say of Leibniz that he misunderstood him even more. . . . However, whereas Leibniz and Bayle did not misunderstand the system of Spinoza, those others who believed they had explained it better really misunderstood it; in other words, they twisted it. These are not the sort of people I fancy; and I vouch for the fact that Lessing did not fancy them either." This was an oblique but unmistakable reference to Mendelssohn. Jacobi said later[56] that Mendelssohn's "unfamiliarity" with Spinoza's writings had not surprised him, for he had long before read Mendelssohn's dialogue on Spinoza (in his *Philosophical Dialogues*). Jacobi did not know that in Lessing's judgment, too, Bayle had "least understood" Spinoza.[57] Having delivered his ungallant blow, Jacobi apologized in his final remark:[58] "That I have stated my complaints in such blunt and plain words and, perhaps, rather harshly must not be interpreted as wickedness by you, dear and noble-minded Mendelssohn. Toward a man whom I so much revere this tone was the only one becoming to me. I am, Sir, your most obedient servant Friedrich Heinrich Jacobi."

The main part of the letter can be discussed here only in broad outline.[59] It was intended to convince Mendelssohn that Lessing had indeed become a Spinozist, and the report of the conversations has a highly dramatic quality. It was on the second day of his visit to Wolfenbüttel that Jacobi gave Lessing a copy of Goethe's poem *Prometheus* to read. He assumed that Lessing would find its irreverence toward the gods on high objectionable, but Lessing confessed that he liked it, that its viewpoint conformed to his own: he no longer subscribed to the "orthodox conceptions of the deity." He found them distasteful. Lessing's creed was summed up in the ancient Greek formula *Hen kai Pan* ("One and All");[60] Goethe's poem tended in the same direction. Jacobi concluded from this remark that Lessing was also more or less in agreement with Spinoza, and Lessing admitted: "If I am to name myself after somebody, I know of no one else." Reading this passage, Mendelssohn surely must have wondered what had caused Jacobi to see in Lessing's approval of the poem an indication of Spinozism. On the following day, Jacobi's report continued, Lessing had resumed the discussion. He had noticed that Jacobi had been shocked by what he had told him the day before, and Jacobi did not deny that he had hardly suspected to find in Lessing a Spinozist or pantheist. Indeed, he had come there in the hope of receiving Lessing's help *against* Spinoza. In answer to Lessing's question whether he knew Spinoza, Jacobi said: "I believe that I know him as well as extremely few people know him." "Then you cannot be helped," Lessing told him. "Do instead become entirely his friend. There is no other philosophy beside Spinoza's." Jacobi agreed that once determinism was accepted, the final step toward "fatalism" (viz. the Spinozistic position affirming unpremeditated, blind necessity) was inevitable, and the rest followed by itself. Lessing was pleased with this answer and urged Jacobi to tell him what he considered to be the true "spirit" *(Geist)* of Spinozism, whereupon Jacobi took the opportunity of launching into a protracted exposition, the gist of which was as follows: Spinoza rejected all forms of emanationism that had sought to bridge the gulf between the finite and the infinite. He started out from the ancient principle *a nihilo nihil fit*, which thwarted any kind of endeavor to derive the finite from the infinite, since trying to do so implied the positing of something out of nothing. He therefore put an "immanent Ensoph" (viz. an immanent Infinite)[61] in place of the one from which things had been said to emanate, and posited an eternally immutable "cause of the world," which formed an indivisible unity with everything caused.

In continuing the report on his interpretation of Spinozism, Jacobi omitted Lessing's interposing remarks—the details having become blurred in his memory[62]—except for one:[63] Lessing observed that the most obscure point in Spinoza—already recognized as such by Leibniz *(Essais de Théodicée, #173)*—was the denial of intellect and will in the infinite cause, and Jacobi took great pains to explain this as essential for an appraisal of Spinozism: the immanent infinite cause could have no object of thinking and will, for to assume a capacity of forming a concept prior to any concept, or of forming a concept prior to its object (in which case the concept would be the cause of itself), or to assume a will that caused the act of willing, was absurd. Here Mendelssohn could read between the lines that Jacobi had denied the validity of his interpretation of Spinoza's world as an intradeical,[64] purely conceptual universe prior to the decree that, according to Leibniz, chose and made real the best of all possible worlds.[65] Jacobi had rejected the very possibility of a preexistent conceptual world as being compatible with Spinoza's system or, for that matter, with any kind of radical rationalism.

Why Jacobi should have held this view must have been rather puzzling to Mendelssohn. He could hardly have guessed that Jacobi's reasons had a private and personal flavor of the sort that is nowadays labeled "existentialist." One has only to compare the afore-mentioned statement with what Jacobi wrote to the princess of Gallitzin on March 14, 1782:[66] "Who can have the merest dark conception of a free act or thinking, of a concept not aroused by an *object;* of a concept prior to the object; of a concept prior to any concept; and of a will without an urge; of a voluntary, unconditioned thinking, acting and being.—Our consciousness develops from something as yet unconscious; our thinking from something that had as yet not thought; . . . our will from something that had as yet not willed; our rational soul from something that had as yet not been a rational soul. A mechanical lever—which as such need not be entirely absurd—seems everywhere to be the first. The ancients recognized it, without assigning an image to it, for to them it was the god of gods, before whom even Jupiter, the most high, bowed his head. . . . But how did I get into these ugly musings . . . dreams full of sickness and melancholy; a perverted eye, which of all colors bears least the color of hope." One can now understand how Jacobi could see in Lessing's consent to Goethe's *Prometheus* an affirmation of Spinozism: the god of gods, before whom Jupiter bows his head, is "all powerful time and eternal fate, my lord and thine," the *moira* of the Greeks, or in Spinoza's terms (as understood by Jacobi), the one, eternal substance prior to all intellect and will.

Jacobi's radical interpretation of Spinoza, which ignored the absolute and infinite Intellect (with a capital I) that knows all things clearly and distinctly at all times,[67] was meant to serve as a vehicle for his leap into faith. His "creed," he said, was not to be found in Spinoza, the apostle of "a poor salvation," for Spinoza's philosophy expressed a deeply felt wretchedness, "dreams full of sickness and melancholy." "I believe in an intelligent personal cause of the world," Jacobi told Lessing, who ironically retorted: "Oh, all the better. Now I am surely going to hear something entirely new." Jacobi came back at him: "Don't be too joyful in anticipation. I extricate myself from the dilemma by a somersault [*salto mortale*], while you are not used to finding particular pleasure in going head over heels."[68] At Lessing's request Jacobi proceeded to explain what he meant by his method. From fatalism he drew the direct conclusion that it and everything connected with it had to be wrong. For if only efficient causes and no final causes existed, as Spinoza taught, our thinking capacity would be limited to merely observing the mechanism of things: when Raphael painted the fresco known as *The School of Athens* and when Lessing wrote his *Nathan* they were merely watching a blind process that was going on. If one refused to accept this as true, one was bound to oppose Spinoza.

Lessing objected that it was by no means necessary to assume our will to be free and thinking to be the first and foremost principle. Extension, motion, and thought were obviously grounded in a higher power superior to these and were capable of a kind of enjoyment beyond all conception and distinct from any conceptual activity. Jacobi insisted that for Spinoza intelligence was the best part in all finite natures, and that if Spinoza had granted personality and life to the infinite substance he would have vindicated intelligence to it. Whereupon Lessing asked: "But how do you conceive your personal extramundane deity? According to Leibniz' ideas by any chance? I am afraid that Leibniz himself was a Spinozist at heart." Jacobi doubted this hypothesis, and Lessing admitted having gone a little too far. When he was asked, however, whether in his view Leibniz' principles had defeated Spinoza's, it was Jacobi's turn to break a lance for Leibniz' (and any serious metaphysician's) essential agreement with Spinoza. Jacobi was convinced that Leibniz' determinism was not really much different from Spinoza's fatalism, and that there was no philosophical system any closer to Spinozism than that of Leibniz. Surprisingly enough, Jacobi quoted Mendelssohn's *Philosophical Dialogues*—a work that he would later allege proved the author's lack of familiarity with Spinoza[69]—in corroboration of his thesis:[70] "Mendelssohn has publicly shown that the preestablished harmony [of Leibniz] is found [already] in Spinoza."[71] From this alone it followed that further points of agreement between the two thinkers had to be assumed. Lessing, who in a 1763 letter to Mendelssohn had disputed the legitimacy of Mendelssohn's claim that Leibniz' preestablished harmony had been anticipated by Spinoza,[72] apparently allowed Jacobi's remark to the same effect to pass without a word of criticism. Perhaps Lessing had been convinced by Mendelssohn's reply at the time,[73] or perhaps he did not consider this the occasion for going too deeply into the matter (which is more likely to have been the case). His earlier statement to Jacobi ("I am afraid that Leibniz himself was a Spinozist at heart") does not necessarily indicate that Mendelssohn had indeed convinced him on that score.[74]

According to Jacobi's report, Lessing had urged him to publicize "this parallelism" between Spinoza and Leibniz, seeing that "people still talked about Spinoza as if he were a dead dog." *Jacobi:* "They would still go on talking in this vein. To grasp Spinoza requires too long and too persistent an effort of the mind. And nobody has grasped him to whom a single line in the *Ethics* remained obscure. . . . Such a peace of mind, such heavenly bliss of intellect as this lucid, pure head created for himself could have been enjoyed by only a few." *Lessing:* "And you are not a Spinozist, Jacobi!" *Jacobi:* "No, on my word!" *Lessing:* "On your word? In that case your philosophy must mean that you turn your back on all philosophy." *Jacobi:* "Why must I have turned my back on all philosophy?" *Lessing:* "If so, you are a perfect skeptic." *Jacobi:* "On the contrary, I withdraw from a philosophy that makes perfect skepticism unavoidable." *Lessing:* "And you move—whither?" *Jacobi:* "Toward the light of which Spinoza says that it illumines itself and the darkness.[75] I love Spinoza because he, more than any other philosopher, has led me to the perfect conviction that certain things cannot be explained. . . . I must assume a source of thinking and acting that remains totally inexplicable to me. . . . He who does not wish to explain the incomprehensible but merely wants to know the borderline at which it starts and to recognize its existence gains, I believe, the largest space for authentic human truth." *Lessing:* "Words, dear Jacobi. Mere words! The borderline you want to fix cannot be determined. And on the other hand, you give free rein to dreaming, nonsense, and blindness." *Jacobi:* "I believe the border can be determined. I do not wish to fix it but merely to find and acknowledge the one that is already fixed. And so far as nonsense, dreaming, and blindness are concerned—" *Lessing:* "They prevail wherever confused ideas are found." *Jacobi:* "More so where false [*erlogene*] ideas are found. . . . For he who has fallen in love with certain explanations blindly accepts every consequence. . . . In my view it is the greatest merit of the searcher to disclose and reveal existence [*Daseyn*]."

Lessing argued no further: he saw himself confronted by a thinker who had made an "existential" decision and he was good-humored enough to admit that his adversary was not doing badly. *Lessing:* "Good, very good! I myself could do with all this; but I cannot use it in the same way. I quite like your *salto mortale,* and I can understand how a man with a head on his shoulders can go head over heels in order to get along. Take me with you, if this is feasible." *Jacobi:* "If you were only to tread on the elastic spot, the rest would follow." *Lessing:* "This, too, would require a leap that I must not impose on my old legs and my heavy head." The "elastic spot" as understood by Jacobi was the Spinozistic position. In his view it made the leap of faith inescapable. Lessing disputed this: one could remain on firm ground despite, and perhaps because of, one's Spinozism.

The question that was not really discussed in all this was the one question in which Mendelssohn was primarily interested: *what was Lessing's concept of Spinozism?* Jacobi's largely monological report made it quite clear how Jacobi understood Spinoza; it failed to shed much light on Lessing's view. What had attracted Lessing in Goethe's poem might simply have been its proud assertion of man's sense of having come of age,[76] which tallied with what he had proclaimed in *The Education of the Human Race.* The pantheism expressed in the formula *Hen kai Pan* was open to more than one interpretation. That Lessing urged Jacobi to adhere to Spinozism rather than use it as a springboard for a somersault into faith did not necessarily imply that Lessing was himself committed to a radical form of Spinozism à la Jacobi. It was quite possible that Lessing had merely played the role of the *advocatus diaboli.* Jacobi had handed him Goethe's poem as something likely to arouse annoyance and on hearing his approving remarks he had interpreted them as indicating a Spinozistic creed and as such regrettable ("a poor salvation"). Thus Lessing noticed at the outset Jacobi's opposition to Spinozism as a viable philosophy, and it would have been entirely consistent with his character to have posed as a Spinozist.[77] The jocularity of some of Lessing's remarks, especially his "kabbalistic" references to himself as divinity in the state of "contraction," which were quoted in this context, would support such a conjecture.

II

Mendelssohn received Jacobi's letter of November 4, 1783, together with a covering letter by Elise Reimarus and some observations by her brother, both dated November 11.[1] Elise wrote:

Here, my dear Mendelssohn, is Jacobi's reply. How far it will satisfy you I do not know, but it proves at least that Jacobi's judgment was not rendered on entirely flimsy grounds. That I transmitted your questions verbatim was necessary, I believe, to avoid generalities both on my part and in the answer; and the fact that he took them amiss you will, I think, in no way hold against him. On the whole this statement by Jacobi will perhaps enable you to add another shade of color to your portrayal of Lessing's character, which was after all your main concern.

Elise's reaction to Jacobi's disclosures was low-keyed and noncommittal: she was obviously anxious to reduce tension. Her brother took a more definite stand.

Jacobi's "story," Doctor Reimarus pointed out, left "almost no doubt" that Lessing had embraced Spinozism. The conjecture that Lessing's utterances vis-à-vis Jacobi had been due to mere "caprice" *(Laune)* or his pleasure in being paradoxical was untenable. Presumably Lessing had concealed his true beliefs from him and from Mendelssohn because he knew that they would disapprove of them. Once when asked by Doctor Reimarus about the meaning of the phrase *Hen kai Pan*, which Lessing had inscribed in some album, Lessing had answered abruptly that it had been a mere whim. Doctor Reimarus added that he now recalled several incidents that had puzzled him at the time but fit into the pattern revealed by Jacobi. He was inclined to see the reason for Lessing's Spinozism in a variety of factors—in his enjoyment of paradox, his spirited imagination, his ill-humor nurtured by passions. As a result, his clear judgment had been impaired. A kind of chronic skepticism had taken hold of him and produced the "phantom" *(Blendwerk)* of Spinozism. Doctor Reimarus expressed his confidence that Mendelssohn would find the best way to present the facts to the public without giving malevolent outsiders occasion to rejoice at seeing Lessing demasked as a Spinozist. He advised making the account as succinct as possible. Reimarus, too, considered Jacobi's report primarily as grist to the mill of Mendelssohn's projected essay on Lessing's character. At the same time he hoped that Mendelssohn would also write a book in refutation of Spinozism. He wished to see intellect and will demonstrated as attributes of the deity. The doctor concluded his letter with the sentence: "May peace be with you, my dear man! There is only *one* God, and Mohammed is no prophet." In other words, the One is not All, and the prophet of fatalism is no prophet.

Since Jacobi had addressed his letter to Mendelssohn and had sent it in an unsealed envelope to Elise to be forwarded by her, he might have expected a personal reply from Mendelssohn through the same channels. But Mendelssohn was in no hurry to write to Jacobi. On November 18 he addressed a letter to Elise and her brother giving his reaction to the report and asking Elise to convey his apologies to Jacobi for his not having replied as yet; he needed time, Mendelssohn explained, to make himself more fully acquainted with Jacobi's ideas. In a sense, however, this letter was actually intended for Jacobi, since Mendelssohn could properly assume that Elise would send Jacobi a précis of it, which in fact she did.

The letter started with a handsome compliment to his correspondent:[2] "I see clearly that I misjudged Herr Jacobi. I thought he was a *bel esprit* who as a pastime also took an interest in philosophical news; I find a man who has made thinking his main occupation and feels strong enough to tear himself away from the apron-strings and to pursue his own path." This was the first time that Mendelssohn had acknowledged Jacobi as a philosopher and, indeed, as an independent thinker. He was generous enough to admit that Jacobi had been justified in feeling a sense of indignation upon reading his questions. He was prepared to ask his forgiveness, should the tone in which Jacobi had brought home to him his error have failed to give him enough satisfaction. "I had not recognized the knight whom I so contemptuously challenged to a duel. He removed the visor; I realize whom I am facing, and in all humility I withdraw the gauntlet."

It is obvious that Mendelssohn wanted to avoid a quarrel with Jacobi and, above all, a premature publication of the report. And having withdrawn himself from the tournament, he expected the same amiability on the part of his adversary. At the same time, Mendelssohn did not conceal his sense of bewilderment at Jacobi's manner of philosophizing. He understood "not everything, perhaps only a minimal part" of what Jacobi had written. "At first sight, the hang of his ideas is still too perplexing to me; the wealth of imagery in his thoughts is too dazzling; and the gaps between them are so striking that I am left stupefied and groping for clarity." Mendelssohn immediately softened the harshness of this criticism by putting the blame on himself: "After fifty years [of age] the soul has deeply embedded its creases and does not admit new ones so easily."[3] Some months later, on August 1, 1784, when he sent his *Objections* to Jacobi, Mendelssohn would write in similar terms:[4] "After the fiftieth year our soul may not easily permit itself to be led along a new path.... This might be the reason why many a passage in your letter is incomprehensible to me, and why in some I miss the conclusiveness that would fit your ideas into your system."

The first impression had thus been decisive. In the letter of November 18, 1783, Mendelssohn could still pretend to expect to achieve a better understanding of Jacobi's ideas from "more frequent reading at greater leisure and with more effort." He admitted that "for the time being at least" Jacobi had answered his questions to his "complete satisfaction." He served notice, however, that before writing on Lessing's character he would have to ask Jacobi for an elucidation of several things stated in the report. His state of health, he implied, kept him from doing any sustained thinking on either Lessing or Spinoza at the moment. To be late was better than doing badly. "What use is going to be made of this conversation [of Lessing] with Herr Jacobi will depend principally on Herr Jacobi and the friendly advice given by the two of you."

It becomes increasingly clear that Mendelssohn now felt strong inhibitions against seriously pursuing his long-standing plan to write an essay on Lessing's character. He probably knew in his heart of hearts that the essay was not likely to be written. Renouncing the project now, however,

would have meant leaving the field to an adversary—an act of disloyalty
to the memory of his best friend. Lessing, in Jacobi's eyes, had been a
radical (i.e., atheistic) Spinozist. In Mendelssohn's view this was a travesty
of the truth. Believing that he possessed the key to the understanding
of Lessing's alleged Spinozism, Mendelssohn considered himself morally
obligated to persist in his plan, even if this meant no more than preventing
Jacobi from publishing his report in the foreseeable future. Mendelssohn
had therefore to stress his determination not to suppress any facet of
the truth about Lessing's character. Alluding to Doctor Reimarus' plea
for caution lest certain outsiders should have reason for rejoicing, Mendelssohn reaffirmed what he had already told Elise—and what he wanted
Jacobi to know:[5] "I still believe it to be necessary and useful to utter a
faithful warning to the devotees of speculative philosophy and to show
them by striking examples [such as Lessing's case] the kind of danger
to which they expose themselves if they abandon themselves to such pursuits
without any guidelines. Let those outside rejoice or be sad. We have no
intention of recruiting anybody or of luring him to our side. Nor are
we to form a party. We become traitors to the flag to which we have
sworn allegiance as soon as we try to make recruits or form a party."

Mendelssohn's disavowal of any intention to lure people to his "party"
may have been meant as a condemnation of Jacobi's effort to draw Lessing
into the camp of faith. For he referred later (in his *Objections*)[6] to Jacobi's
efforts to convince others of his philosophy as a proposal to "retreat to
the flag of faith." In his final utterance[7] he again mentioned Jacobi's past
effort to convert Lessing and his present effort to convert him and, in
this context he again used the term "flag of faith." It seems that Jacobi's
report had impressed him as the work of an enthusiast à la Lavater, of
a man against whom Mendelssohn had to affirm his continuing allegiance
to the "flag" of the Enlightenment. From the very start, then, the conflict
assumed in Mendelssohn's eyes the character of a test of strength between
the Enlightenment philosophy of reason and the recrudescence of blind
faith. This being the way he looked upon Jacobi from the outset, Mendelssohn's reply to the report must be seen as largely determined by tactical
considerations: he needed to gain time in which to produce a work interpreting Lessing's Spinozism (not his character), and he had to avoid provoking
Jacobi into publishing an account of his conversations with Lessing. Hence
Mendelssohn's repeated assurances that he was going to describe Lessing
with the utmost objectivity and even with a sense of indifference to whatever
aberrations from the truth Lessing might have indulged in toward the
end of his life:[8] "I attach, at any rate, little importance to what the greatest
man may say or do in his last hours, especially if he is so fond of swerves
as our Lessing was."

In the last part of his letter Mendelssohn addressed himself solely
to Doctor Reimarus' challenge that he write a book in refutation of
Spinozism:[9] "Alas, my friend! You certainly do not know the nervous debil-

ity that has kept me down so much for more than ten years. An effort of this kind would certainly blow up my brain." The worst part was that he had "nothing new, nothing striking" to say to "these people" (i.e., to contemporary pantheists). The old, well-known arguments against pantheism, which had lost none of their validity in his eyes, had become a matter of derision to the "sophists" of their century. What did not shoot across the mind and shake it like a thunderbolt no longer made an impression; and to restart the labors of Penelope by slowly yet firmly going over all the nooks and corners of sophistry in order to find the monster—for this he had no strength any more, if indeed he had ever had it. Of regaining it he had hardly any hope. He believed, however, that Doctor Reimarus was alert and strong enough to risk a contest *(Gang)* with these men. All Mendelssohn could do was to stand at his side as his shield-bearer, sharpening his arrows and handing them to him. As events proved, however, Mendelssohn did not play the role of a mere shield-bearer; in his *Morgenstunden* it was he who "risked a *Gang* with the pantheists." But the decision to undertake this effort would arise only under duress. The letter of November 18, 1783, concluded with the words: "Take care of yourselves and love in spirit and in truth your brother, Moses Mendelssohn.

A postscript intended to match Doctor Reimarus' read: "God is an only God, and who teaches truth and does the good is His prophet." Mendelssohn knew that this creed was shared by Elise and her brother, and he could therefore describe himself as their "brother" "in spirit and in truth." The entire letter is permeated with this sense of spiritual kinship. The opening address reads: "Revered sister and brother in spirit and truth!" It seems that the irruption of the strange and disconcerting figure of Jacobi into Mendelssohn's life had made him seek a heightened sense of reassurance through closer contact with his faithful friends in Hamburg, who were also Jacobi's friends. It was not the first time that he had found himself singled out for attack both as a philosopher and as a Jew. On this occasion the philosopher in him had to bear the brunt of the rather cleverly concealed but all the more brutal assault. The feeling that he was also under fire as a Jew could not be gainsaid but, for the time being, was more his personal impression than anything tangible.

What made the present situation different from all previous ones was that all of a sudden Mendelssohn had to defend not merely his own position but that of Lessing as well; that the complete mutual trust between him and his best friend, which he had always taken for granted, was being doubted, if not bluntly denied; and that thereby one of the most treasured possessions of his life, the unblemished record of his friendship with Lessing, was threatened—unless Jacobi's report could be shown to be biased. Perhaps drawing such melancholy conclusions from Lessing's adoption of Spinozism, assuming that Jacobi's account was accurate, was an overreaction. Outwardly, Mendelssohn himself had professed a sense of indifference to what his friend might have said toward the end of his life.

He had himself promised an uncensored report. Yet while he could do this on the strength of his conviction that the misunderstanding could be cleared up, a deep shadow had nevertheless fallen on a bright memory. It was shameful and insulting that something so shining and pure as his relationship with Lessing should be in need of verification.

On November 14, prior to receiving Mendelssohn's reply, Elise had written to Jacobi that her brother had found the report highly interesting and that both he and she had felt as if they were hearing Lessing and Jacobi talk viva voce. They were now convinced, she said, that Lessing had indeed turned toward Spinozism, and her brother had written a few lines to this effect to Mendelssohn. She suspected that Lessing had kept his views secret from Mendelssohn and her brother because he knew their attitude and was anxious to avoid a discussion. While they were averse to paradoxicalness, he had considered it "helpful" in his search for truth. In a debate with them Lessing would have been compelled to go "forward and backward" so as not to allow the "stubborn fellows" to drift away, and a discussion of this kind would not have been to his liking. "He fancied, however, the way you debated with him; it pleased both his mind and his mood of capriciousness. I can well imagine that he enjoyed your *salto mortale,* and I know, since he told me so, how fond he had become of you after he had made your personal acquaintance."[10]

Neither Doctor Reimarus nor Elise seem to have been especially perturbed by the thought that Lessing might have concealed his true opinion from them and from Mendelssohn. It apparently did not occur to them that even the surmise of such a possibility was bound to hurt Mendelssohn's feelings. But there was, after all, a vast difference between the complete trust Lessing had always placed in Mendelssohn's judgment and the circumspect manner in which he had treated Doctor Reimarus.[11] Considering the history of Mendelssohn's relationship with Lessing, the idea expressed by both Elise and her brother was hardly credible. Mercifully, Elise's letter to Mendelssohn did not support her brother's conjecture. But Mendelssohn would have been horrified to read what she did tell Jacobi—that the way he had debated with Lessing was most pleasing to him. One can sympathize with the two people who had to mediate between a pair of adversaries so far apart in their philosophy and temperament as Mendelssohn and Jacobi were; it was inevitable that in writing to the one they used nuances different from those employed in their letters to the other. Jacobi must have been pleased by their reaction to his account, notwithstanding the fact that the emphasis on Lessing's (and his own) love of paradox ran counter to the view he had expressed.[12] He was now waiting to hear from Mendelssohn, but all he received was a letter by Elise, dated December 5, 1783, which contained a résumé of Mendelssohn's reply to her and her brother.

In her December 5 letter[13] Elise again made every effort to avert the possibility of further friction between the two men. She therefore presented a rather emasculated version of what Mendelssohn had said.[14] The generous praise that Mendelssohn had bestowed on Jacobi was quoted in full, whereas his qualifying statements, such as his frank admission that he had understood little and had been stupefied by Jacobi's dazzling imagery and the gaps in his chain of reasoning, were left out entirely. The noncommittal voicing of the hope of perhaps understanding Jacobi better upon rereading him with more leisure and greater effort sounded differently the way she put it: "Since, however, your essay demands to be read again with more leisure and effort, he asks me to convey his apologies for taking his time in replying to your letter." She suppressed the mildly reproachful sentence expressing Mendelssohn's readiness to ask for Jacobi's pardon in the event that the tone in which Jacobi had brought his error home to him was not enough satisfaction. The metaphor of the knightly tournament was likewise dropped. Jacobi was informed, however, of Mendelssohn's assurance that he was going to consult with both him and the friends in Hamburg about the manner in which the report would be used. He was also told of Mendelssohn's unshaken resolve to avoid all partisanship and to present the full facts of Lessing's Spinozism as a warning to all devotees of unbridled speculation; he was not prepared to become a traitor to the flag of truth.

On December 24, 1783, Elise could report to Mendelssohn that Jacobi was "very satisfied" with what she had mentioned to him in her résumé and that she and her brother were even more satisfied with the entire letter, which promised them food for thought for a long time. Her note concluded with the words: "God keep you well, dear brother in truth. Amen!" She also asked Mendelssohn to hand to the bearer of her note, who needed no recommendation,[15] Jacobi's report about his conversations with Lessing, since her brother wished to read it again and promised to return it whenever Mendelssohn felt ready to use it. Attached to her note was a summary, in her hand, of Jacobi's last letter:[16]

> Amid my gouty headaches I found true joy in your letter of December 5. Mendelssohn's utterance that it was necessary and useful faithfully to warn the devotees of speculation . . . has given me exceedingly great pleasure.—You know the zeal with which I always insisted that one had the right and the duty to hang everything on the One peg of Truth. Surely Mendelssohn has no need to offer me apologies; to his reply, however, I am looking forward with great joy, and what he is going to ask of me I shall fulfil to the limit of my capacity.

It is hardly surprising that Jacobi could describe himself as being "very satisfied" with Mendelssohn's reaction. Elise's résumé, after all, must have given him the impression that his adversary had conceded total defeat! Had Elise been less selective, or had she sent him a copy of Mendelssohn's entire letter, Jacobi's joy would have been considerably reduced. He would have recognized the highly critical tone of the reply and been alerted to the fact that Mendelssohn was not insensitive to the unchivalrous manner in which he had been attacked by Jacobi. Elise's censorship having deleted the gentle reproach that Mendelssohn had administered to him, Jacobi must have been rather embarrassed by his foe's seeming readiness to accept all the blame; this would explain the sentence about there "surely" being no need for Mendelssohn to apologize to *him.* Jacobi's "joy"—the term sounds the keynote of his letter—was the result of Elise's editorial skill, and being based on half-truths, it was bound eventually to come to grief. There was a further irony in the fact that while Jacobi was waiting for Mendelssohn's personal answer and final questions, the corpus delicti—the report—was no longer even in Mendelssohn's possession: he had lent it to Doctor Reimarus, in whose safe keeping it would remain from January until the beginning of April, 1784.

Mendelssohn replied to Elise's note on January 5,[17] saying how pleased he was to learn that her brother wished to have another look at Jacobi's "essay." He obviously interpreted this desire as indicating a certain willingness to step into the breach and undertake the refutation of Jacobi. "I myself," he wrote, "find the task of refuting him highly unpleasant and annoying. On a new course, the most experienced navigator can hit a rock or be stranded on a sand-bank and founder. But when warning signals are displayed, he who nevertheless suffers shipwreck must either be a bad mariner or a mischievous one.—This was the case of Spinoza compared with Lessing or Jacobi.—Mere acuteness is sufficient if one wants to confuse and mix up ideas; and of this there is plenty in such adroit minds. Yet one who wishes to refute them is faced with the labors of Sisyphus."

The way in which Mendelssohn employed the simile of the navigator illustrates the shift that had occurred in his attitude. The experienced navigator who was wrecked when he set sail on a new course was Spinoza (on the new road from Descartes to Leibniz, Spinoza "fell into the immense abyss," as Mendelssohn had put it in his youthful *Dialogues,*[18] when he was seeking to evoke sympathy for the much abused fellow-Jew); there was no need to refute Spinoza, who had "innocently" gone astray and whose philosophy, Mendelssohn continued to believe, had already been disproved by Wolff. Lessing, on the other hand, was a mariner who ran aground because he was not versed in the art of philosophizing and so disregarded the warning signals; lured into Spinozism he may have been (this was, however, still a matter of interpretation) but he did not have to be refuted, since he was not a professional philosopher (though his intellectual acuteness was of the highest order). Jacobi's case was quite different. Jacobi knew the art and also possessed acuteness, but he was being mischievous when he proclaimed Spinozism as the only truly consistent philosophy. Failure to heed all warning signs, he wrecked his boat on the rock of Spinozism. That Jacobi was able to save his skin by a *salto mortale* was another matter. Jacobi, a member of the guild, had to be refuted. This was the task to be taken in hand by someone. Having expressed his horror at the thought of having to undertake the work of Penelope [that of refuting Spinozism], Mendelssohn was even less inclined to engage in the labor of Sisyphus [that of fighting Jacobi]. The mere prospect of having to "chew the cud" of first principles (substance, cause, truth, etc.) gave him, he declared, a feeling of nausea. To expound on all these "subtleties" would be a killing job.

The fact that the metaphysics of the "school" philosophy had been assailed lately by Kant may have aggravated Mendelssohn's distaste for going over the old ground again, though his own loyalty to Leibniz and Wolff had not been shaken. That Mendelssohn was well aware of the new situation in philosophy is attested by another remark in the very same letter: "It was very pleasant . . . to learn from Herr Rudolphi that your brother has no high opinion of the *Critique of Pure Reason*. For my part, I have to confess that I do not understand it. Whereas the résumé that Herr Garve has published in the [*Allgemeine deútsche*] *Bibliothek*[19] makes sense to me, others say that [even] Garve had failed to grasp it. It is therefore a welcome thought to me that I do not miss too much if I leave this world without having understood this work."

Thus it must have been with a sigh of relief that Mendelssohn passed Jacobi's report on to Doctor Reimarus: "You receive herewith Herr Jacobi's manuscript for use with G[od's] blessing. There is nobody here to whom I could have entrusted it for copying; and I have to ask you to let me have it back when your brother no longer wants it. There is no hurry, and he may keep it for at least a few months." His wish for God's blessing implied a silent prayer that Doctor Reimarus would absolve him from the task of having to refute Jacobi. The letter includes no mention of the old project, the essay on Lessing's character. Several newspapers had reported that a treatise by Mendelssohn on Lessing's life and works was soon to appear. Karl Lessing, who had read this news item in the *Gothaische gelehrte Zeitungen* (October, 1783) asked Mendelssohn on January 29, 1784, whether he could confirm it.[20]

Because Jacobi had put such great stress on the strictly confidential character of the information he had given to Elise "under the rose of friendship," it could properly be assumed, so it seemed, that only she, Doctor Reimarus, and Mendelssohn had been let in on the secret. But this was most certainly not the case. On November 22, 1783, Jacobi had sent Herder a copy of the report on the Jacobi/Lessing conversations, and also a copy of Mendelssohn's questions to Jacobi. (As Jacobi publicly admitted later,[21] the "essay" had been "in more than one good hand" two years prior to its publication. Since it was published in September, 1785, it must have been circulating among Jacobi's friends as early as the fall of 1783.) In a covering letter[22] Jacobi invited Herder to comment, if he should feel disposed to do so; every piece of information would contribute to the growth of their friendship, Jacobi declared, adding: "I want to tell you, if I may, my dear Herder, how the quiet and resolute resignation [*Ergebung*] to the authentic being of things, in truth and for the sake of truth, as pure as it can be had and given, constitutes the center of my philosophy and the very soul of my character." We may recall that a similar phrase was juxtaposed, in his letter to Elise on November 4, with his repudiation of the *morgue berlinoise*. In the letter to Herder his self-characterization was followed by an even broader attack on the Enlightenment.[23] Obviously Jacobi felt the need of a word of encouragement from a man like Herder, whom he considered an ally in the fight against Enlightenment thinking.

It was not until February 6, 1784, that Herder replied:[24] Having been immersed in his *Philosophy of History*,[25] he had completely forgotten to answer the letter, but Goethe, who had just heard from Jacobi, had reminded him of his duty.[26] In contrast to Jacobi, Herder saw in Lessing a "fellow-believer," insofar as his "philosophical creed" was concerned. Herder was not prepared, however, to accept Spinozism in the rather crude, fantastic, and undeveloped form imposed upon it by its historical position of dependence on Descartes.[27] He would therefore not call his own system, whose seeds could be found in antiquity, by the name of Spinozism. Spinoza had been the first to dare to combine those elements ("seeds") into a system, but in so doing he had had the misfortune of presenting it in the most awkward manner, thereby discrediting it in the eyes of Jews, Christians, and pagans alike. It seemed to Herder that Mendelssohn was right in declaring that Bayle had misunderstood Spinoza's system.[28] On the other hand, he maintained, no one (including Mendelssohn in his *Philosophical Dialogues*) had done justice to the system of *Hen kai Pan*, which to Herder was the essence of Spinozism. It was to be regretted that Lessing had failed to propound it. Herder himself was planning a work in which Spinoza, Shaftesbury, and Leibniz would be compared, and he hoped that Jacobi would permit him to make a copy of his report on the conversation with Lessing, which he had found "extremely interesting."

Thus, instead of expressing approval of Jacobi's position, Herder not only tended to support Mendelssohn but also asked for permission to use the report for his own purposes. Yet he warned Jacobi against allowing Mendelssohn to be the first to publish the ideas expressed by Lessing in the conversation; not knowing that Jacobi had already mailed the report to Mendelssohn, Herder wrote: "The letter [the report] may be dispatched to Mendelssohn, but you have to ask him not to publish it before you have made known whichever part of the conversation you choose. If he wants to refer to it polemically, let him do so; but it is your prerogative to reveal the discourse to the public. At all events, he [Mendelssohn] will refute you as much as him [Lessing], and I fail to see why both of you should lie prostrate before him as his footstool." This remark seems rather spiteful in tone, and hardly in tune with Herder's professed friendship for Mendelssohn, but in substance it expressed what any adviser would have suggested as the most obvious procedure. Jacobi's eagerness to foist the report on Mendelssohn without any strings attached had obviously arisen out of a desire to provoke Mendelssohn into making some utterance that he, Jacobi, could then attack.

On April 2, 1784, Elise informed Jacobi that Mendelssohn had lent the report to her brother, at his request, but that it was now being returned to Berlin. Mendelssohn had been ill, and so no time had been squandered. She assumed that Jacobi shared her and her brother's great annoyance at the recent publication of a tract by H. F. Diez[29] that defended and advertised Spinoza and, at the end, recalled with enchantment the times when there were noble-minded and great men who knew nothing of God. Referring to this "impertinent nonsense," Elise wondered what was in store for the search for truth if "such paradoxes" and "brilliant errors" became fashionable. She confessed that this newest work had so upset her brother that he now wished to see Lessing's Spinozism concealed by Mendelssohn insofar as the "sacredness of truth" permitted this. For disclosing "an example such as Lessing's" might have disastrous consequences.[30]

Doctor Reimarus himself wrote Mendelssohn a long letter (sixteen closely written quarto pages), dated June 14, 1784, offering his own "cursory and unsophisticated thoughts" on Jacobi's report.[31] It represented a notable effort to come to grips with Jacobi's assertion that Spinoza was irrefutable on purely philosophical grounds. The doctor admitted that certain points in both Spinoza and Jacobi had eluded him, and that he had found Jacobi's style and his way of thinking most baffling. It was his hope, however, that Mendelssohn would be pleased with some of his formulations and would go more fully into the matter. He deplored the new trends in philosophy, and mentioned the "strange" form of idealism taught by "the famous Kant." He was surprised to see that Herr Engel had taken so much trouble to study the *Critique of Pure Reason,* and in his opinion a man like Garve should not have been bothered with the task of writing a review. Tiedemann's examination of Kant's view of time and space[32] had only confirmed him in his judgment. Doctor Reimarus quoted Diez' concluding remark about the earlier periods that knew nothing about God and his statement that morality, according to Spinoza, had no other foundation than the social contract. He spoke, on the other hand, with much admiration of Mendelssohn's "psychological observations," which had appeared in Karl Philipp Moritz' *Magazin zur Erfahrungsseelenkunde,*[33] and noted that Mendelssohn's explanation of stuttering as being due not to a defect in the organs of speech but to over-hurried thinking had also been offered by a friend of Doctor Reimarus, a sagacious and lively man named Darwin, who was a physician in Lichfield, England. (This reference was, of course, to Erasmus Darwin [1731–1802], grandfather of Charles Darwin.) Doctor Reimarus' letter abounded in literary references of all sorts and ended on a humorous note, a parody of Jacobi's distinction between the "appearance" and the "true being" of his self: "Finally, and cordially, I express the wish that the phenomenon of your existence represent the appearance of a very cheerful and happy being and be diffused, at the same time, over other phenomena in order that we may have the perfect illusion of being true essences or things. Be thus assured that your existence gives great pleasure to J.A.H. Reimarus."

Mendelssohn's reluctance to undertake the Sisyphean labor of refuting Jacobi was overcome by the effect that this intrepid letter had upon him. The self-assured manner in which Doctor Reimarus had reasserted the validity of the well-tried metaphysical principles of the "school" against Jacobi's "baffling" way of thinking and Kant's "strange" idealism boosted Mendelssohn's spirit and challenged him to take a stand against Jacobi and in defense of the Enlightenment. Since his foe's philosophy was based on his interpretation of Spinoza, Mendelssohn considered it necessary to attack the so-called Spinozists rather than Spinoza, and he consulted with his "brother in spirit" about the procedure to be adopted. Was it better "to face a definite adversary and start from a certain point made by him, or better to strike in all directions to ward off all adversaries?" He personally preferred the first method, but he realized that the second might be more appropriate to the needs of the time.

On July 5, 1784, Elise informed Jacobi that she had received a letter from Mendelssohn acknowledging the return of the manuscript and announcing a change in his plan: "if he was well enough and had the leisure this summer, he might perhaps put aside 'Lessing's character' in order to risk a contest [*Gang*] with the Spinozists or devotees of All-One [*AllEiner*]," as he preferred to call them. Elise not only revealed to Jacobi the tactical considerations that Mendelssohn had discussed with her brother but was even naive enough to assume that Jacobi would share her feeling of joy and high expectation: "You must be glad that through your essay you provided the cause for such a useful work, though it was originally intended for (and will eventually serve) another purpose:—for it is certainly more important that the dazzling errors of our time be, for once, dispelled by the irresistible light of *pure reason* presented by so firm a hand." She admitted that she was looking forward just as ardently to the publication of Mendelssohn's "Character of our Lessing," which had been promised so long ago.[34]

Elise's letter of July 5, 1784, did not mention the possibility that before writing his new work Mendelssohn might seek still further clarifications from Jacobi, as Mendelssohn had actually indicated when writing to her and her brother on November 18, and as she had reported to Jacobi in an earlier letter dated December 5, 1783. The unqualified announcement of Mendelssohn's decision to "risk a contest" with him was bound therefore to please Jacobi.[35] How little he was convinced of the irresistibility of Mendelssohn's "pure reason" is shown by the fact that it was after receiving Elise's July 5 letter that he completed a long epistle to François Hemsterhuis, on which he had been working for several weeks; it included a dialogue between Spinoza and Jacobi (as a mouthpiece of Hemsterhuis' *Aristée*)[36] reaffirming his view of the invincibility of Spinoza as a philosopher and restating his own "viewpoint of faith" as the only alternative.[37] Jacobi was as confident as ever in the correctness of his position.

It came as something of a surprise to Jacobi, then, to receive a letter from Mendelssohn, dated August 1, 1784, seeking further clarification of Jacobi's ideas and arguments. The letter had been sent, with a covering note,[38] to Elise, who had forwarded it to Jacobi's Düsseldorf address, whence it had been mailed to Hofgeismar, a resort where Jacobi had been recuperating from an illness since the end of August.[39] In the first of three paragraphs in the letter Mendelssohn expressed appreciation of Jacobi's "kindness" in "forgiving" him the "precipitancy" with which he had formulated his questions. One was so used to coming across "philosophic masks and disguised faces" that inevitably one ran the risk of behaving like the Ethiopian in Shaftesbury's story,[40] who [after a carnival at Paris or Venice that had been his first exposure to Europe] took every genuine human face to be a mask. In the second paragraph he assured Jacobi that he had read his report more than once in order to acquaint himself with the "peculiar trend" *(eigenen Gang)* of his thoughts. It was not easy for someone beyond the age of fifty to let himself be guided along new paths. This might be the reason, he politely suggested, why he had found many a passage "entirely unintelligible" and had missed "conclusiveness" in others. He repeated here, in slightly attenuated form, what he had already said in his critical letter of November 18—and what had been suppressed in Elise's summary. The third paragraph read:

> Since, for the time being, I have given up my intention to write about Lessing [the draft has: "about Lessing's character"] and wish first to project something about Spinozism, you will appreciate how important it is to me to grasp your ideas accurately and to understand properly the arguments by which you endeavor to support this philosopher's system. I therefore take the liberty of placing my doubts [*Bedenklichkeiten*] and objections [*Erinnerungen*] before you in an essay, which I enclose. You have thrown down the gauntlet in chivalrous fashion; I take it up, and let us now fight out our metaphysical tournament, according to knightly usage, before the eyes of the lady who is held in high esteem by both of us . . .

Attached to Mendelssohn's letter were his "Objections to Herr Jacobi,"[41] in which he made the following points:

(1) The system of Spinoza could hardly be described as an answer to the problem of how the finite arose from the infinite. Positing the finite things within God was as difficult an assumption as deriving them from Him as a transcendent source of emanation. It was not correct to say that the emanationist theory violated the principle *a nihilo nihil fit*. Since Spinoza admitted the possibility of an infinite series, the origin of things by way of emanation did not imply a becoming of something out of nothing.

(2) Leibniz had found some obscurity in the way in which Spinoza spoke of God as possessing the attribute of thinking, yet having no intellect.[42]

Jacobi had interpreted Spinoza to mean that the infinite first cause could have no individual object of thinking or willing but was the "first universal *Urstoff* of intellect and will." In Mendelssohn's view the explanation was as difficult as the statement itself. Since Spinoza held thinking to be an attribute of the one true substance, how could its thinking be a mere formless matter without specific content? Were its own attributes and modifications not the proper objects of its thinking? So far as willing was concerned, Spinoza's denial was perfectly understandable: he considered free will as an undetermined arbitrary choice and rightly assumed that acts of will thus defined were incompatible with the infinite being of God. Yet why should Jacobi, who was a determinist, have denied the possibility of an eternally predetermined choice made by the infinite cause?

(3) Jacobi's statement that Spinoza's infinite substance did not exist per se and apart from particular things contradicted the conception Mendelssohn had formed of Spinoza's view. How could one understand that the One-formed-of-All was a mere togetherness? Was it nothing but a *collectivum quid* having no other substantiality than that of its constituent parts? Assuming this to be the case, did not the very notion of a collective entity, of an All *(Pan)*, presuppose an operation of the mind relating the isolated parts to a transcendental unity?[43] If this All was to be true, it had to subsist in a real transcendental unity that excluded all plurality, and we found ourselves unexpectedly back in the old-established doctrine of scholastic philosophy.

(4) The "greatest difficulty" of the Spinozistic system lay in its inability to arrive at the concept of the infinite by starting out from the finite. Wolff had already pointed out that no increase in extensive quantity could lead to an intensive quantity.[44]

Mendelssohn took this opportunity to comment also on some of Lessing's utterances as mentioned in Jacobi's report. Lessing's contention that the supreme being might be beyond the capacity of thinking was, Mendelssohn suggested, typical of his capriciousness; it was one of those vaultings by which he pretended to jump, as it were, beyond himself. For to assume the existence of something that not only transcended all conception but was completely unrelated to conceptual thinking was tantamount to such a leap. It had never occurred to him, Mendelssohn said of himself, to want to climb on his own shoulders to look farther afield. Though Jacobi had apparently not attached too much importance to this particular remark, he seemed on the other hand to agree with the attempt "to think something that was not a thought; to jump into a vacuum inaccessible to reason." For there was a passage in his manuscript[45] that Mendelssohn found completely incomprehensible: thinking, Jacobi had said, was not the source of substance but substance was the source of thinking; etc. It seemed to Mendelssohn that Jacobi had considered extension and motion to be the only objects of thought—an assumption à la Locke that a Spinozist did not need to share—ignoring the possibility that a thinking being might make itself the object of thought. "I make no remarks on a number of jokes with which our Lessing later entertained you and of which it is difficult to say whether they were intended as fun or philosophy. He was in the habit of pairing, in a frolicsome mood, the most heterogeneous ideas, with a view to finding out what kinds of offspring they would beget." Mendelssohn then cited a long list of things mentioned by Jacobi that fell in this category.

As for Jacobi's personal creed, Mendelssohn regarded his *salto mortale* as "a salutary device of nature": after having indulged in abstruse speculation for a while, one was well advised to try to return to normal by using one's *bon sens*. In other words, Mendelssohn minimized Jacobi's existential option for faith by explaining it away psychologically as a natural antidote for too many sterile metaphysical exertions. Yet this was not all. Mendelssohn connected Jacobi's leap of faith with his loyalty to Christianity, and contrasted it with his own rationalism, which was unchallenged by the religion he professed. Mendelssohn thus presented himself and Judaism as being in complete accord with the Enlightenment, and Jacobi and Christianity as submitting to a *sacrificium intellectus*. That Mendelssohn felt it necessary to introduce this comparison shows clearly that he saw in Jacobi another Lavater in disguise. He had been so frequently exposed to conversionist overtures of all kinds that he found it hard not to be suspicious when faced with an enthusiastic character like Jacobi. This is what he wrote:[46]

> Likewise, I shall not discuss the honest retreat to the flag of faith that you, on your part, propose. This proposal is entirely in the spirit of your religion, which imposes upon you the duty of suppressing doubts by faith. The Christian philosopher may amuse himself by teasing the naturalist and by raising knotty points that drive him from one corner into another and invariably elude his grasp when it seems surest. My religion knows of no duty to remove such doubts by any arguments except rational ones; it commands no [mere] faith in eternal truths. I have, therefore, an additional reason to seek conviction [by rational means].

Jacobi replied from Hofgeismar on September 5.[47] Mendelssohn's letter had not reached him, he said, until September 1, in the spa where he was undergoing treatment. His physical condition prevented him from answering immediately all the points that had been raised but, fortunately, a copy of a letter he had recently sent to François Hemsterhuis was in the hands of another visitor at the watering-place, the princess of Gallitzin, and he was able to enclose a replica made from this copy. For the time being it would convey to Mendelssohn a coherent presentation of his views and clear up many a misunderstanding.

The surmise—Jacobi called it "reproach"—that Jacobi considered extension and motion to be the only objects of thought had really startled him. He was at a loss to understand how such a notion could have been attributed to him. As soon as he was settled again back home, he was going to compare what he had written and what Mendelssohn had objected to, and fill in the gaps still left by the enclosed essay. "I know nothing about having thrown down the gauntlet. If it dropped from my hands and you wish to consider it as having been thrown down and choose to take it up, I am satisfied. I shall not turn my back but shall know how to save my skin as best as I can. However, what I stand for is not Spinoza and his system. It is expressed in Pascal's words:[48] *La nature confond les Pyrrhoniens, et la raison confond les Dogmatistes* [viz., neither skepticism nor the self-assured manner of the dogmatic philosopher are right: we know the truth but we cannot prove it by reason alone]. This is what I have clearly stated; hence also what and who I am. The fact that you mistake me for another is not due to my having hoodwinked you. The fight and its result will show that I employ no illicit tricks and have absolutely no intention of hiding. I commend myself to heaven, our lady [Elise], and the noble mind of my adversary."

Jacobi's letter shows how accurately Mendelssohn had characterized the situation when he wrote (in the note to Elise attached to his letter and "Objections"):[49] "I vouch for the fact that our letters will eventually become more and more extensive, obscure, ambiguous, quarrelsome, etc." One senses from Jacobi's outwardly polite but edgy letter that there was little chance of a narrowing of their differences. Mendelssohn had not been any more conciliatory. He had, however, been genuinely puzzled by Jacobi's stand on behalf of Spinoza as the only consistent dogmatist in metaphysics, and he had by no means mistaken Jacobi for a Spinozist. However, seeing that Jacobi had used Spinoza as a jumping-off point for his personal philosophy, Mendelssohn had every right to ask for clarification. His intention was to disprove the validity of Jacobi's interpretation of Spinoza and to establish his own interpretation as the one favored by Lessing. And, of course, the gauntlet had not accidentally "dropped" from Jacobi's hands. In warning Mendelssohn, through Elise, of Lessing's Spinozism, Jacobi had taken the initiative in setting the stage for a contest. In a sense, Jacobi acknowledged that the issue at stake was the interpretation of Spinoza: "So long as we disagreed about the nature of Spinozism," he would write in a later account of his reaction,[50] "we could not argue for or against the thing. By sending [Mendelssohn] the letter I had written to Hemsterhuis I believed that I had made a not entirely unimportant contribution."

Jacobi's reply and the attached "Copie d'une lettre à M. Hemsterhuis à la Haye"[51] reached Mendelssohn rather belatedly via Hamburg. As Elise explained in her covering letter of October 26,[52] the copying of the French text had had to wait until Jacobi's return to Düsseldorf, since no qualified copyist could be found in the spa; moreover, Elise had been suffering from gout, which had incapacitated her from writing for several months. Her main concern now was to convince Mendelssohn of Jacobi's friendly disposition toward him. To this end she quoted the following passage from

Jacobi's letter to her: "It is your task, Elise, to encourage the combatants. You are convinced of my zeal and of my thoroughly honest intentions. Do your best to impart to Mendelssohn a similar confidence in me. I did not want to write to him myself about things of this sort, and about the exceeding pleasure that his offer causes me, because I do not wish to change the tone that he has assumed and that I find altogether excellent." Elise added yet another quotation from an earlier letter of Jacobi's in reply to her announcement that Mendelssohn wanted first to write "a word in due season" (Elise's way of putting it in biblical language) against the Spinozists: "To me Mendelssohn's decision is the most agreeable one that he could have made, considering the enlightenment [*Aufklärung*] that his work will provide for us both directly and indirectly."

Elise felt that, having conveyed Jacobi's sentiments, she had done her part to "properly attune to one another two noble knights" worthy of her esteem. Mendelssohn was pleasantly surprised at so much kindness: "I am very glad," he wrote to Elise,[53] "that Jacobi does not disapprove of the tone that I dared to assume. I was afraid that I might have irritated him a little by the forward manner in which I approached him. We shall therefore continue to adhere to this old-German frankness." He obviously took Jacobi's words at face value, though it is hardly credible that Mendelssohn's adversary expected to receive any "enlightenment" from Mendelssohn's treatment of Spinozism. Jacobi wanted to encourage Mendelssohn to write on the subject only so as to afford Jacobi an opportunity to display his superior powers. That Mendelssohn might abandon the project, or at least omit all reference to Lessing, continued to worry Jacobi. On June 30, 1784, he had written to Herder:[54] "As I know from a reliable source,[55] Mendelssohn does not wish to suppress Lessing's utterances, but one of his friends, whom he greatly trusts [Doctor Reimarus], holds a different view. I realize that I am not completely trusted."

This was a rather odd "realization" on Jacobi's part, since the question in Doctor Reimarus' mind (as Jacobi knew) was not Jacobi's trustworthiness but the advisability of making Lessing's Spinozism known to the public. Knowing as he did from Elise's letter of April 2, 1784, how much averse she and her brother had been to letting the public in on the secret, Jacobi's plea for "confidence" was directed to them rather than to Mendelssohn. At this stage, however, there could be no further doubt that some form of literary contest was in the offing. The two combatants were ready and had accepted the romantic image of a knightly tournament before the lady they revered.

CHAPTER EIGHT

Guardian of the Enlightenment

The Contest

The contest between Mendelssohn and Jacobi, known as the *Pantheismus-streit*,[1] proved to be anything but a display of knightly chivalry. The mutual distrust and antagonism that had been building up was evidently too deeply felt to be kept under control. The documentary sources now at our disposal[2] clearly reveal the powerful emotions and motivations of the combatants on both sides.

We first turn our attention to Jacobi. He had promised to provide a more detailed answer to Mendelssohn's "Objections," but he took his time about it. He entered into a lively correspondence with Hamann, whose moral support he needed after Herder's failure to endorse a "leap of faith" as the antidote to Spinozism. While vacationing in Hofgeismar Jacobi had read Hamann's *Golgatha* with great enthusiasm. He had been immediately struck by a passage that described Mendelssohn as "a circumcised fellow-believer in the spirit and essence of pagan, naturalistic, atheistic fanaticism,"[3] and suspected that Hamann might have got wind—through Herder—of his, Jacobi's, report on the conversations with Lessing.[4] In Weimar, where he wound up his vacation, Jacobi found Herder and Goethe equally delighted with Hamann's spirited attack on Mendelssohn's *Jerusalem*.[5] On October 18, 1784, Jacobi sent Hamann a package containing his report on Lessing, Mendelssohn's "Objections," his letter to Hemsterhuis, and his correspondence with Herder. As he pointed out in a covering letter, he expected a great deal from Hamann's reaction to these documents, and he implored him: "Speak that I may see thee."[6]

It so happened that Jacobi did Hamann a great favor by sending him all this material. A friend of Mendelssohn's in Berlin had written to a friend of Hamann's in Königsberg complaining bitterly about the accusation of atheism made in the *Golgatha,* and Hamann was plagued by a sense of remorse at the rather drastic remark he had made (after some struggle against himself, as he admitted). He felt the need to probe the issue of atheism more deeply and also to study Spinoza. In this situation he gratefully accepted Jacobi's "confidence" as "a boon of Providence," as "grist to his mill" and "oil to his lamp."[7] He was not sure that it would benefit Jacobi as much as it would him, or that he could add much to what had already been said by Herder. It certainly helped him to come to grips with Spinoza's works (the discussion of which would play a notable part in their correspondence). On the other hand, their corresponding did enable Jacobi to expostulate with Hamann on the issues close to his heart and to receive a sympathetic, though critical, hearing. In the end Hamann grew rather tired of "the dear self-tormentor"—Jacobi—and began to wonder whether he could ever fully satisfy the man's *pia desideria.*[8]

The uneasiness that Hamann felt at having accused his "old friend Mendelssohn" of atheism led him to exaggerate its possible effect. Alluding to Elise's letter of April 2, 1784, a copy of which was attached to Jacobi's letter to Herder on June 30, Hamann wrote:[9] "If the great example of a Lessing [i.e. the disclosure of his Spinozism] is the cause of so many scruples there, how much more striking must it there appear to see Mendelssohn himself accused of 'atheistic fanaticism.' The hint that I received from Berlin was inexplicable to me so long as I lacked all this information. I suspect that my blind attack against my old friend Mendelssohn will provide additional encouragement to him to state his views on Spinozism." In a subsequent passage of the same letter to Jacobi he returned to the subject:[10] "Is it philosophy and religion or theologico-political enthusiasm, shrewdness, and vanity that makes my old friend Mendelssohn . . . so sensitive to the accusation of 'atticism,' unless I touched the sore point in blind simplicity, without knowing it."

He expected a sharp retort but was relieved when he learned of an incomparably fiercer assault upon Mendelssohn's *Jerusalem* that had been launched in the fall of 1784: Johann Heinrich Schulz (1739–1823), a clergyman and the advocate of an odd sort of religious atheism, had published a *Philosophic Contemplation on Theology and Religion in General and on the Jewish One in Particular.*[11] This scurrilous work poked fun at the Sinaitic revelation as a clever trickery on the part of Moses, and took Mendelssohn to task for having denounced atheism as undermining the moral fabric of society. The burden of Schultz' counterattack was an unbridled invective against Judaism as the source of all fanaticism and intolerance.[12] The author, who was known as the *Zopf-Schulz* because as a mark of protest against the establishment he wore a pigtail *(Zopf)* instead of the customary wig, differentiated between two classes of atheists: those like Spinoza who tried to define the ultimate "sufficient reason," and those like himself who were agnostics and content merely to affirm that "all things have a sufficient reason." On January 16, 1785, Hamann wrote to Jacobi:[13] *"Di bene fecerunt*

—that I shall have to fear no attack from my old friend Mendelssohn, since another preacher has arisen who did a ruder thing than the one 'in the wilderness' [viz. Hamann, who had designated himself thus on the title-page of *Golgatha*].[14] Schulz . . . has written a *Philosophical Contemplation* for the benefit of atheism, and the Israelite has achieved his desire to find a definite adversary[15] who is armed with sufficient reason; and I have achieved . . . [my desire] to be superseded and permitted to play the role of an idle spectator."[16]

The strange coincidence that he was being accused of atheism by Hamann and assailed for his stand against atheism by Schulz struck Mendelssohn as quite amusing. It was Isaac Euchel who, having returned to Königsberg from his journey to Copenhagen,[17] reported an earthy bon mot by which Mendelssohn had allegedly characterized his situation: he was in the position of a husband whose wife accused him of impotence and whose maid charged him with having made her pregnant. Euchel, who visited Hamann after his return, did not tell him the story, but Hamann heard it at third hand and immediately passed it on to Herder, Jacobi, and Scheffner, adding (no doubt on his own) that both the wife and the maid were, on the husband's admission, quite correct, and that the story was reminiscent of Father Abraham vis-à-vis Sarah and Hagar.[18] More serious and to the point, in terms of Jacobi's concern, was Hamann's assertion that there was no essential difference between Spinoza's *Causa sui* (the one substance that was both cause and effect) and the Wolffians' "sufficient reason." He was curious to see, Hamann wrote on January 16, 1785, what Mendelssohn could say in answer to his atheistic adversary. Hamann had repeated ad nauseam that philosophers and Jews shared a common ignorance: neither of them knew what reason and law were.[19] Experience and revelation were the indispensable "crutches or wings of our reason, if it was not to remain lame and merely creep along."[20]

As for the contest between Jacobi and Mendelssohn, Hamann agreed with Herder that all of the documentary material should be published without scruple.[21] On June 30, 1784, Jacobi had replied to Herder:[22] "Your desire that I publish my conversation with Lessing on its own, independent of [its present form as a letter to] Mendelssohn, I have turned over in my mind and, on reflection, I have come to the conclusion that I myself must not heed this advice. The form that this matter has taken on as a result of events must be retained. I shall allow the thing to proceed quietly on its historic course, without bothering about further developments and the outcome." There followed the passage about Mendelssohn's readiness to disclose Lessing's Spinozism. Jacobi still adhered to this policy. On December 30, 1784, he wrote to Hamann:[23] "He [Mendelssohn] will . . . not be slow to produce his essay against Spinozism, since he is afraid that what Herder desires might happen, be it only as a result of carelessness on my part."

Jacobi's correspondence with Hamann was destined to have an important bearing on the contest between Jacobi and Mendelssohn. We find echoes and actual quotations of sentences from it in the highly rhapsodic utterances through which Jacobi later asserted his position. On January 11, 1785, he wrote to Hamann:[24] "In your *Golgatha* I was particularly struck by the passage[25] in which you say: 'In view of the infinite disproportion between man and God ... man must either be granted a share in divine nature or the deity had to assume flesh and blood.' All theological and philosophical musing of my mind, too, has been placed for some time on the rack of this dilemma, as it were." In his reply to Mendelssohn's "Objections" Jacobi quoted this sentence in the name of "a preacher in the wilderness" (Hamann).[26] In his letter of October 18, 1784, he denied the possibility of working our way up the comprehension of the mysteries, if philosophy was our guide; yet he felt that the soul must have some capacity for cognizing God by "organizing it upward." Hamann saw no need for such "organizing" if there was already some capacity at work.[27] In his *Die Lehre des Spinoza*[28] Jacobi repeated his formulation. On July 22, 1785, Hamann urged Jacobi to read Herder's *Philosophical Lectures on the So-called New Testament,* a work over which he had "wept for joy," and Jacobi proved to be equally enthusiastic.[29] In the first edition of his *Die Lehre des Spinoza* Jacobi quoted a long passage ("The eye is the light of the body ...") from this work.[30]

One of the most significant results of Jacobi's close link with Hamann was the increasing influence of Lavater on Jacobi's thinking. Lavater had enthusiastically responded to *Golgatha,* though not all the artful allusions of Hamann's *cento* style[31] were intelligible to him.[32] Lavater and Hamann were in close touch with one another, and references to Lavater's works occurred frequently in Hamann's letters to Jacobi. One need not be surprised, therefore, to find that the concluding passage of Jacobi's work was a quotation from Lavater's *Pontius Pilatus,*[33] introduced (in the first edition) by the following words:[34] "At the risk of being called one of yours, let me ... , honest Lavater, bless my work with a word from your pious, angelic, and pure mouth and thus seal it [the work]." What happened during the late fall, winter, and early spring of 1784–1785 was the formation of an alliance between Jacobi, Hamann, Herder, and Lavater. On November 13, 1784, Hamann wrote to Lavater about the "good fortune" that had fallen to his lot: to have three "Jonathans" [most loyal friends], namely him, Herder, and Jacobi, was the greatest piece of luck imaginable.[35]

Mendelssohn did not stand too high in the estimation of this group. Herder, who had professed to be Mendelssohn's friend, reported to Hamann on February 28, 1785:[36] "Our past chamberlain, Herr Seckendorf ...returned last week from Berlin as Prussian ambassador to the [German] empire. He had talked with Mendelssohn, who is very curious about the continuation of my *Ideas*[37] and wished to sound him out as to what it was tending to. He is indeed afraid that enthusiasm is behind it and that in the end I shall produce a flamelet that, as he said, was not for us. He believes that all Christians are enthusiasts, and he holds this belief because, as I think, the arrow of your *Golgatha* has got stuck between his hide and flesh. It is strange that the metaphysicians, as for example your Kant, do not want any history even in history. . . ." Herder had promised to show the works of God as a blazing light, as a "flame and sun." Mendelssohn had reacted rather coldly to this announcement. Kant had been even more outspoken. In his review of Herder's *Ideen zur Philosophie der Geschichte der Menschheit*[38] he had advised Herder to curb the flights of his imagination, and the ensuing parts of Herder's work did not live up to the promise of the first volume (1784).[39] The "flame" did turn out to be a "flamelet," and there was indeed a great deal of "enthusiasm" behind it. Had Mendelssohn been able to read the letters that were passing between Herder, Lavater, and Jacobi on the one hand, and Hamann on the other, he would have found ample confirmation of his thesis that in these thinkers Christianity and *Schwärmerey* ("enthusiasm") went hand in hand. On April 23, 1785, Herder offered yet another unfriendly remark on the Jewish philosopher:[40] "It is good for Jacobi that he is kept busy; no discussion, however, is possible with Mendelssohn. In his nominal definitions everything he heeds is ready-made." On May 17 Hamann reported this remark straight away to Jacobi.[41] The gulf between the two adversaries was thus constantly widening, and the prospect of a serious contest in "knightly" fashion became increasingly remote.

On January 24, 1785, Hamann reported quite casually to his friend Scheffner:[42] "Only today did I receive an old letter from Plessing[43] [informing me] that Mendelssohn is working on a book entitled *Spinoza, or On the Existence of God.*" Plessing, who had been awarded the philosophical doctorate under the deanship of Kant in 1782 and had been in touch with Hamann, had spent part of the summer of 1783 in Berlin. Dohm, whose guest he was, had introduced him to Mendelssohn and other friends of the Enlightenment circle. It is possible that the news of Mendelssohn's forthcoming book had come to him from Dohm. Hamann does not seem to have bothered to pass the news on to Jacobi. The book mentioned by Plessing was, of course, the one that was later given the title *Morgenstunden, oder Vorlesungen über das Daseyn Gottes* ("Morning Hours, or Lectures on the Existence of God"). In a letter to Elise written at exactly the same time—on January 28, 1785—Mendelssohn announced that he was working on a book that was not merely an inquiry into Spinozism but was "a kind of revision of the proofs for the existence of God. . . ."[44] He mentioned no title, probably because he had not yet decided on one.

In his preface to *Morgenstunden*, Mendelssohn explained its title and, incidentally, the manner in which these "lectures" had originated. His sole motivation, he said, was his desire, born out of deep concern, to guide his son Joseph toward "a rational knowledge of God." He had had the boy read a great deal and "gather ideas," but now the time had come to bring "form and order" to the material collected and, to this end, instruct Joseph in "orderly and methodical reflection" on the subject. Mendelssohn had decided to devote the early morning hours to this purpose, for only during this part of the day could he muster the necessary serenity of mind. He had been pleased to have two additional young men of intelligence and amiable disposition participate in this venture: his son-in-law S[imon Veit Witzenhausen][45] and [Bernhard] W[essely].[46] The morning sessions consisted partly of free discussion and, whenever Mendelssohn felt in the mood, in lectures by him, which the students were allowed to interrupt for questions and debate. "In this way," Mendelssohn concluded his account, "originated the essays, the first part of which I herewith place before the public."[47]

Fortunately, we also possess some tangible evidence of the manner in which the *Morgenstunden* were written: four foolscap pages of the draft of the work have been preserved.[48] They contain about the last third of chapter fourteen, most of the text in the right hand column being written in a hand other than Mendelssohn's, while the left hand column and the last twenty-six lines on the right are additions written by Mendelssohn. It is obvious from the corrections in the main body of the text that what we have before us is a dictation subsequently checked and revised by Mendelssohn.[49] If one of his students acted as his secretary, as seems probable, what we have in this extant fragment is a specimen of the "lectures" that were delivered in the course. We may safely assume that the secretary was Joseph, notwithstanding the fact that Joseph's handwriting as we know it from a much later period[50] looks quite different. The stroke in our text bears some resemblance to that found on a page from Joseph's homework when he was still younger, which also contains his father's corrections.[51]

The letter that Mendelssohn wrote to Elise on January 28, 1785, contained more than the mere announcement of the progress of his work.[52] It was addressed mainly to Jacobi and reminded him of his promise to give a full reply to Mendelssohn's "Objections" as soon as he had returned home and found the necessary leisure. Had Jacobi forgotten him? How mindful he himself had been of Jacobi he hoped to demonstrate to him by a manuscript of perhaps twenty or more sheets. Against his will and only because of Elise [who had seen fit to convey to him Jacobi's sub rosa information] he was now immersed in "transcendental subtleties." His work proceeded at a snail's pace, for his nervous debility permitted no sustained effort, and his business consumed most of his time and energy. Therefore it was impossible for him to say just how soon he would be able to submit his manuscript to Jacobi. (This was a reference to the promise Mendelssohn had made in his letter of November 18: it would depend on Jacobi's as well as Elise's and her brother's advice what use was to be made of Jacobi's report on his conversations with Lessing.) Mendelssohn wondered whether Jacobi would allow him "to make public use of his philosophical letters." In his work so far he had treated the proofs for the existence of God. He intended, however, to enter into a discussion of the "special arguments of the Spinozistic system," and in this connection it would serve both his own convenience and many a reader's interest if he could draw on Jacobi's "lively presentation" and let him speak on Spinoza's behalf. He hoped to be informed soon whether this was agreeable to Jacobi, since he had to arrange his own presentation accordingly. On no account would he publish anything before having shown his work to Elise's brother. He was going to ask for his permission to insert in the appropriate place his "refutation of Spinozism" [viz. the relevant sections of his metaphysical treatise of June 14, 1784],[53] which had the great advantage of putting the case in simple terms without detriment to the profundity of the arguments.

Mendelssohn's request to Jacobi, though speaking of "philosophical letters" in the plural, was in fact only a petition for one new favor, namely the use of the Hemsterhuis letter. It was understood that the right to make use of the conversation with Lessing had already been granted to him on the assumption that Jacobi would be consulted prior to publication. This is how Elise interpreted the request. In her reply of February 4, 1785,[54] she expressed her sense of absolute certainty that Jacobi would raise no objection to the public use of his letter to H[emsterhuis]. It was, in fact, only in this letter (more precisely: in the dialogue contained in this letter) that Jacobi employed the dramatic device of letting Spinoza speak. In her letter Elise also assured Mendelssohn that her brother agreed with his proposal and was looking forward to his metaphysical work.

Elise had been right in her prediction. Immediately upon receipt of Mendelssohn's letter, which he had forwarded to him, Jacobi sent an affirmative reply straight to Berlin. In strange contradiction to his true feelings, of which we have received some inkling by now, his letter overflowed with kindness:[55] "I have not forgotten you, my revered—patron or friend—how may I call you? A rare concurrence of circumstances prevented me throughout four months from finding a moment of leisure, and treated me roughly, body and soul.[56] All this is about to depart; but it is a departure like the one of your ancestors from Egypt. During this entire month you must still excuse me; after that my notes to your "Objections" shall not be delayed much longer. In the meantime you herewith receive my full permission for the public use of my two letters on Spinozism. I cannot tell you how much I am pleased with your enterprise and bless your labors; and how impatiently I am looking forward to enjoying it. Take care of yourself, venerable man, and keep me in good remembrance."

Another spell of illness caused an unexpected further delay in Jacobi's work, but on April 26 he was able to send Mendelssohn a manuscript of thirty quarto pages copied by a calligrapher and signed by Jacobi, the title reading simply: "To Herr Mendelssohn Concerning the 'Objections' He sent Me."[57] The covering letter was clearly intended as an antidote to the extremely harsh introductory part of the "Notes" (as we shall call them here, using Jacobi's own expression in the previous letter):[58]

At my request, Elise will already have informed you what kind of new obstacles have again delayed my reply to your "Objections." I have been all the more concerned to satisfy you in regard to the subject matter itself. As for the opening part, I must ask you not to think by any chance that I had seriously taken amiss something you had done.—

Tonight I travel for a few days to Münster, and I am on this account very busy and distracted. Otherwise I would have liked to tell you one thing or another about the advantage one might derive from publicly presenting Spinoza's system in its true form and according to the necessary coherence of its parts. A ghost-like apparition of it has for some time been walking in Germany in all kinds of guises and is being looked upon by superstitious people and nonbelievers with equal reverence. I am referring not merely to mediocre minds but also to men of the first rank. Even Kant, when considering this X, permits his sentiments to operate in strange ways, assuming that he is the author of the little essay *Über das Fundament der Kräfte,* which I do not doubt.[59]

Perhaps we shall live to see that a fight arises over the dead body of Spinoza like the one that arose between the archangel and Satan over the dead body of Moses.[60] . . . I shall say more about all this when I have your reply and know whether you can agree with me about the concept of Spinoza's system: a doubt that I may hardly call thus. . . .

The introductory part of Jacobi's "Notes" shows clearly what he meant by his certainty that Mendelssohn would have to accept his interpretation of Spinozism:

Before looking for weak spots, one must first find, and keep in check, the adversary's blade. You were looking for mine and brandished your weapon in a circle without meeting any resistance; for my presence was not over against there. From the straight and quiet fort in which I was stationed, I want to advance against you and dare lunging into your circle with but one straight thrust. Only when your circle parries my thrust are we in combat. Without allegory: your "Objections" are based throughout on an error that you left unexplained. Since your idea of Spinoza's system did not agree with mine, one of us was obviously mistaken. Even though it was not worthwhile to inquire, or rather: although there could be no question which of the two of us was in error, the question had to be advanced if you were to give me the honor of entering into a discussion with me concerning this matter. To advance this question would have been all the more appropriate and harmless, in view of the fact that when reading the present essay you will certainly remember to what extent Spinoza's writings have faded from your memory, something you were bound to realize in some way already then. Suffice it to say that by omitting to weigh your concept of Spinozism against mine after consulting the text you in fact dodged the issue.

By now offering a second presentation of Spinozism, Jacobi hoped to make agreement possible on "the main thing" (i.e. Spinoza's doctrine itself); a useful debate on the merits of the doctrine could follow at a later stage. The self-assurance, if not arrogance, with which Jacobi claimed to be the authentic interpreter of Spinoza was not maintained vis-à-vis Herder, to whom he had sent a copy of his "Notes" on April 24:[61]

The enclosed essay Goethe will have already announced to you. I beg
of you, dear Herder, to read it not merely cursorily but with attention. . . .
Give me the little time required for such reading; and afterwards give
me another hour telling me, in case you are not convinced that my concept
of Spinoza's system is the true one, what justified in your view a different
one. . . . The inner consistency of this man's philosophy has struck me
again with particular force. . . . This firm connection, this living unity
I have tried to describe in the present essay. If I was hitherto convinced
of the correctness of my concept as I am convinced of the correctness
of the multiplication table, I am now almost equally certain that everyone
capable of judging this matter must become as convinced as I am after
having read this essay and having compared it with the text. —Dear
Herder! I do not write this to terrify you. You know too well your own
being to get frightened. It is I who should get frightened. You will understand how I would have to feel in case you told me again that I misunderstood Spinoza.

As this letter shows, it was only vis-à-vis Mendelssohn that Jacobi permitted himself the magisterial and menacing tone that we find in the opening
part of his "Notes."

In the main section of the "Notes" Jacobi made an attempt to condense
Spinoza's metaphysical doctrine into forty-four theses, with copious footnotes containing the textual evidence and some discussion. In the concluding part he took issue with Mendelssohn's rejection of faith as a substitute
for reason: "Dear Mendelssohn, we are all born in faith and must remain
in faith, even as we are born in society and must remain in society." There
was an "immediate certitude" that not only required no proofs but excluded
all proofs. Conviction based on proofs was a certitude at second hand:
it presupposed faith and derived its force from it. Faith itself was "a divine
force" and "the light that illumined the world."[62] Through faith we knew
of the existence of thinking beings other than ourselves and, indeed, of
ourselves; for without the "Thou" the "I" was impossible. This "revelation
of nature" compelled all men to believe and, through belief, to accept
eternal truths. The religion of the Christians *taught*—not: commanded—yet
another faith, one having to do with the finite, contingent nature of man
rather than with eternal truths. It instructed man in how to rise to a higher
consciousness, to a fulfilment that implied beatitude. Jesus, who had
achieved this fulfilment, "could therefore say in truth: I am the way, the
truth, and the life." The spirit of Christianity was man's awareness of
God brought about by a divine life. It afforded a peace greater than all
reason could provide. In it an incomprehensible love could be enjoyed
and contemplated. Quoting Hamann,[63] Jacobi spoke of the incarnation
in the sense of the living God manifesting himself by the arousal of love.
"Degenerate reason, which is impoverished (i.e., which has become speculative), can neither praise this practical way nor allow it to be praised." It
could merely "hobble behind" intuitively grasped truth and religious truth.
Jacobi concluded his affirmation of faith with the prayer: "May the spirit
of truth be with you and me."

On April 26, the day on which Jacobi had posted his "Notes" to Berlin, Elise also dispatched a letter to Mendelssohn.[64] Jacobi had informed her on February 22, she reported, that his promised "Notes" would soon be ready, but on April 5 he had explained that illness had made a delay inevitable. However, the draft, which was the hardest part of it, had been completed. Upon receipt of this letter and before Jacobi's "Notes" had arrived from Düsseldorf, Mendelssohn wrote to Elise on April 29:[65]

> I was just about to ask our common friend through you not to be in a hurry about the reply to my "Objections." I have decided to publish, after the Leipzig fair, Part One of my brochure. Though I deal in it primarily with pantheism, no mention has as yet been made of our correspondence. This I save for Part Two, for which there is plenty of time. Before replying to my "Objections" Herr Jacobi has to read first this Part One of my treatise; at the least, he will be able to reply to both at the same time, and my treatise will perhaps give him an opportunity to state his view more clearly. My "Objections" contain, besides, mere preliminary remarks, which are not sufficiently penetrating.
>
> I now have the manuscript copied for dispatch to you; but not for Herr Jacobi, whom I spare it until it appears in print. Your brother, on the other hand, must read everything in manuscript, for without his censorship nothing in this matter can appear publicly. Convey my regards to the amiable adversary and embrace the brother and umpire more than once on behalf of your brother and friend Moses Mendelssohn.

At first sight it might appear that this dramatic move violated the rules of the game. Yet such was not the case. Mendelssohn had not heard from Jacobi since February 11 (Elise had not notified him until now of Jacobi's two letters of February 22 and April 5) and it could therefore be suspected, even assumed, that Jacobi was again taking his time about writing the long-promised "Notes." In the meanwhile Mendelssohn had completed his *Morgenstunden* and he was anxious to see the work published. He had studiously refrained from including in it any reference to Jacobi's report on Lessing or to the letter to Hemsterhuis, and thus there was no obligation on his part to submit the manuscript to Jacobi. Mendelssohn had simply written a book on the proofs for the existence of God and on Spinozism—nothing more. He felt, moreover, that after reading it Jacobi would have a better understanding of his viewpoint and might write "Notes" substantially different from what he could have produced in response to the rather sketchy "Objections."

It was with a good conscience, therefore, that he asked Jacobi (through Elise) not to be in any hurry. The situation would have been quite different, of course, if he had known that the "Notes" were already on their way to him. The only point that might have puzzled his friends was the strictness with which he insisted that the manuscript not be shown to Jacobi. If his sole concern had been to supply his opponent with a more penetrating critique of Spinoza, Mendelssohn could have sent Jacobi the manuscript for his immediate use. Why had Jacobi to wait until the book was published?

Obviously, Mendelssohn was motivated by some tactical consideration that he had not stated openly in his letter. His secret purpose in publishing the *Morgenstunden* was to forestall any ill effects that the disclosure of Lessing's Spinozism might produce. The very heart of the book was the presentation of Lessing as a "purified Spinozist," in the sense in which Mendelssohn had ventured to interpret Spinoza himself in the *Philosophical Dialogues*. Its climax was the citation of Lessing's youthful fragment *The Christianity of Reason* as the decisive proof of the correctness of this interpretation. When Elise first reported to him the secret of Lessing's Spinozism, he could take the news with a fair amount of calm, as we have ventured to suggest, because he had already formed in his mind a connection between his late friend's early speculative effort and his own concept of a "purified Spinozism." The thought of elaborating this idea had been his carefully guarded secret, one that he was now prepared to share with Doctor Reimarus and Elise but could not prematurely reveal to his adversary.

Since Jacobi had sent his "Notes" straight to Berlin, Elise did not know that they had been delivered, and for some unknown reason she waited almost a month before she conveyed to him Mendelssohn's message not to be in a hurry. Her letter, which reached Jacobi on May 26,[66] mentioned Mendelssohn's intention to publish Part One of his "brochure" which, while dealing with pantheism, contained no reference to their correspondence. Part Two, she reported, would take care of this, but there was still plenty of time in which to discuss the matter. She also quoted Mendelssohn's request that before replying to his "Objections," Jacobi ought to read Part One of his treatise. Having informed Mendelssohn three months ago (in February) of his definite intention to send him the "Notes," Jacobi felt that the advice not to be in a hurry came rather late in the day, and he still hoped to hear from him a reply to the letter and manuscript that he had dispatched a month ago. Yet Mendelssohn made no haste to let him have an answer; how he felt about the situation was clearly expressed in a letter to Elise dated May 24, 1785:[67]

> I am sending you herewith, dearest Elise, part of the manuscript that I have decided to publish. Kindly read it yourself and submit it to our beloved brother for censorship.... I cannot let Herr Jacobi see the manuscript; he must first see Part One of the treatise in its complete form and in print. I will tell you why I consider this advantageous. The way I fare with Herr Jacobi is almost like the way Abraham de Moivre got on with Isaac Newton. The more he tries to explain things to me, the more incomprehensible he becomes. I already failed to understand— literally speaking—his letter to Hemsterhuis; and just now[68] I received from him an extensive German essay that was meant to serve as an interpretation of that letter and, at the same time, as a reply to my preliminary "Objections." I am ashamed to confess that I understand this essay still less. Where do we go from here? If we go on using different idioms, we shall never come to terms. Besides—I mention this *entre nous*—Herr Jacobi seems occasionally to become violent and hot-tempered, though this heat may be mere pretense in order to make the controversy more lively. In reality his heart could still be free of self-conceit and obstinacy.

Be this as it may; to avoid confusion I must first state my principles before I can enter into a contest with Herr Jacobi. I therefore publish Part One of my *Morgenstunden,* mentioning in it nothing about our correspondence, yet touching upon pantheism and trying to refute it. The correspondence and everything appertaining to Jacobi and Lessing in particular I save for the sequel that could appear some time afterwards.[69] In the meanwhile I [shall] perhaps come to understand Herr Jacobi better or ... [be] lucky enough to come to agree with him on certain points, so as to know from where to start. Before running a race, we must first meet at a certain place.

As this letter shows, Mendelssohn was well on his way to abandoning the contest altogether. Having read the "Notes" sent to him by Jacobi, he realized the hopelessness of ever meeting him on common ground. He frankly admitted his inability to grasp what his adversary was saying, and he was obviously annoyed at Jacobi's "self-conceit and obstinacy." Nevertheless, he still maintained the pretense that eventually the tournament might take place. For the time being all his interest was concentrated on the publication of the *Morgenstunden.* On June 18, 1785, Doctor Reimarus sent him an encouraging note in response to the part of the manuscript he had received, together with some random thoughts that had occurred to him when perusing it: "Mostly I found what I intended to write stated ·subsequently in the text, and I am fully aware that even that which I have written down is of little significance."[70] On June 28 Mendelssohn requested Elise to pass on to her brother the rest of the manuscript. His thanks would follow once he had heard the final judgment, which he awaited "with trembling." The question that troubled him was whether he had succeeded in avoiding undue subtlety without losing sight of all subtle points. The letter[71] indicated a radical departure from the stance that he had preserved until then, at least outwardly: "All this [i.e. Doctor Reimarus' judgment and Elise's approval] will not bring me together with our worthy Jacobi; that much I foresee. With his fiery spirit, I imagine, he will reject all my arguments as the well-known scholastic babble, and he will not consider it worth his trouble to reexamine it. He may even be cross with me for having opposed my dull philosophy of the compendia to the profound teachings of Spinoza. I am afraid that in the end we shall regale each other like the stork and the fox of the fable: the one serves drink in long-necked bottles, the other puts food on flat plates; invariably the host provides only what suits his mouth and allows the guest to starve. Be this, however, as it may. Herr Jacobi will, at any rate, learn in this fashion why I do not understand him; and why we must part company and bless each other before the sun rises."

Gone was the romantic dream of a knightly contest before the eyes of the noble lady. A new image, borrowed from the Bible (Gen. 32:27), was introduced: Jacob wrestling with the angel, who according to traditional Jewish interpretation, was Esau's daemon. Like Jacobi, Mendelssohn spoke now in biblical terms, and his true self became articulate. Jacob and Esau symbolize Israel and the Christian church.[72]

On July 28, 1785, Doctor Reimarus sent Mendelssohn the eagerly awaited final judgment of the *Morgenstunden*. His covering letter, a little essay in itself, opened with the words: "If I were to describe to you how pleased I am with your treatise as a whole and with numerous points in particular; how much I admire the exposition of Spinozism, etc., I would have to write at great length, most esteemed friend! Yet I have been asked to raise opposing viewpoints, and so I have put forward some real nonsense in opposition."[73] Even before this seal of approval had been received, Mendelssohn had taken the long overdue step of writing to Jacobi. His letter was dated July 21, 1785, and for tactical reasons it still kept alive the prospect of a contest:[74]

> Forgive me, dearest Herr Jacobi, my still leaving unanswered your two important essays, the French one for Hemsterhuis and the one in German for myself. Elise and Doctor Reimarus are my witnesses that, so far as my present debility permitted, I was not idle in the matter of our dispute, and if a Doctor Reimarus will not entirely condemn my work, the next catalogue of the Book Fair is going to confirm the testimonial accorded to it. I do not count, though, on convincing you of my view by this treatise. I cannot flatter myself with this belief, particularly as I have to confess to myself that many a passage in your essays (as well as in the writings of Spinoza himself) is completely incomprehensible to me. Yet I hope to establish the *status controversiae* [nature of the controversy] in the treatise that is to be submitted to your judgment in the near future, and thereby to start the dispute in a fitting manner. It will at least become apparent why it is that many things seem to me so utterly unintelligible and that the more you try to explain them to me, the more they elude my grasp.
>
> Now a request. I am a poor keeper of documents, and have lost among my papers the copy of my "Objections," which I know for sure that I have preserved somewhere. [But] I have been searching for it the last few weeks without success, and looking for lost papers is an altogether joyless labor. Perhaps you have it at hand and can let me have a copy without much trouble. You would thereby greatly oblige me, for I now intend to get ready for our contest, and to this end to reread your two essays with all possible attention and effort. For this purpose I need the "Objections" referred to in your reply. Take care of yourself, dearest man, and love me.

Jacobi answered this letter on August 2, 1785:[75] "A copy of your "Objections" made immediately after my return from Hofgeismar and still on hand has made it possible for me to fulfil at once the request expressed in your letter of July 21. May God give you strength, my dearest one, for the sake, also, of the hope you hold out for me. With the most sincere reverence, I am your most obliged Friedrich Heinrich Jacobi."

While the two adversaries sought to outdo each other in protestations of sincerity, the tension between them had risen to a high point. Mendelssohn, to all intents and purposes, had given up the contest and was bent on stealing a march on Jacobi by publishing his version of Lessing's Spinozism. He was no doubt afraid that his opponent might be tempted to anticipate him, and he felt it necessary, therefore, to maintain the fiction of a contest in the future. He made a grave mistake, however, in indicating his intention "to establish the *status controversiae*" in the treatise about to appear. What he meant to say was simply that—as he had put it in the letter written to Elise on May 24—before entering into a contest he had first to state his principles.

Jacobi misunderstood the ill-chosen phrase. He believed it to announce that Mendelssohn's forthcoming treatise—the *Morgenstunden*—was going to present him, Jacobi, as a Spinozist, as the *advocatus diaboli*, without giving the reader the benefit of knowing the background of the role he was playing—without its being made clear that Jacobi's advocacy of Spinozism as the one and only consistent speculative philosophy operated within a purely speculative frame of reference that was to be transcended by his leap of faith.[76] Mendelssohn actually had no intention of even mentioning Jacobi, let alone to fix his role in advance of the contest. But Mendelssohn had only himself to blame if his adversary misread the phrase. Having been kept in the dark about the treatise for two months, Jacobi was bound to become suspicious. Hamann had written on June 2 that Mendelssohn was working on a new book, the title of which had been variously given as "Morning Thoughts on God and Creation" and "On the Existence and Attributes of God."[77] He had reported further, on June 29, that the first part of Mendelssohn's *Morgenstunden* had allegedly left the press,[78] which Jacobi took to mean that the entire first volume was already in print[79] (in fact, however, the printing was still in progress as late as July 21).[80]

The information conveyed by Hamann led Jacobi to suppose that Mendelssohn had gone back on his word to consult with him (i.e. to let him see the manuscript) prior to publication. He assumed, not unnaturally, that the work in question dealt with the material that he had put at Mendelssohn's disposal. Holding this mistaken belief, as he did, Jacobi was understandably outraged by what he considered to be a flagrant breach of faith, and he began to consider publishing the entire correspondence on his own. Mendelssohn's letter of July 21 had the effect of making him decide to act. Unfortunately, the letter had failed to mention that the forthcoming book included no reference to their correspondence; perhaps Mendelssohn saw no need to reassure Jacobi on this point, since Elise's last letter to Jacobi had made this clear. But that letter had been written a long time ago and Jacobi, in the meantime, had begun to form in his mind a distorted picture of the situation. And he could find nothing to reassure him in the letter just received from Mendelssohn. On the contrary, the letter seemed to indicate that the reply to his essays would be given in the book. Mendelssohn's ambiguous remark about establishing the *status controversiae* was the last straw so far as Jacobi was concerned.

The book that Jacobi now proceeded to put together, in a mood of grim determination, proved to be a queer and rather shapeless cluster of disparate things. It contained, first and foremost, his long letter to Mendelssohn reporting on the conversations with Lessing, followed by Jacobi's letter to Hemsterhuis and his "Notes" on Mendelssohn's "Objections" (but not the "Objections" themselves). It presented, moreover, the texts of the letters, in summaries or verbatim, that had passed between him, Mendelssohn, and Elise. He had not bothered to ask for permission to publish this private correspondence, and Elise's identity was barely concealed by the fictitious name "Emilie." All this documentary evidence was linked together by a kind of running commentary in the form of a narration of events starting from Elise's letter of March 25, 1783, informing Jacobi of her visit to Mendelssohn the day before. The final part of the book consisted in a string of meditations, most of them quoted from a variety of sources—Job 28, Herder, Lavater. This section was rightly described by Karl Lessing as having a Lavaterian ring.[81]

Interspersed with the last part of the narrative was a succinct statement summing up Jacobi's position in six brief theses:

I. Spinozism is atheism.

II. The kabbalistic philosophy, *qua* philosophy, is nothing but undeveloped Spinozism or a confused new version of it.[82]

III. The Leibniz/Wolffian philosophy is no less fatalistic than Spinoza's philosophy, to whose principles it inevitably leads one back, if a persistent search is made.

IV. Every manner [of philosophizing that is bent upon the method] of demonstration ends in fatalism.

V. We can demonstrate only similarities; and every proof presupposes something already proven, the [very first] principle of which is revelation.

VI. The [prime] element of all human knowledge and action is belief (*Glaube*).[83]

Jacobi wrote a short preface to the work on August 28, 1785: he had named the book, in accordance with both the circumstances that had occasioned it and the major part of its contents, *On the Doctrine of Spinoza in Letters to Herr Moses Mendelssohn.* As he told Hamann on September 12, 1785,[84] he had felt very happy when he was writing the last few sheets. One wonders how he felt when, at the beginning of his narrative, he dealt this heavy blow to Mendelssohn:[85]

> Lessing wanted to persuade me to travel to Berlin without him, and became more urgent every day. His main motivation was Mendelssohn, whom he appreciated most among his friends. He was most anxious for me to make his personal acquaintance. In such a conversation I once expressed my astonishment . . . that a man of such bright and straight intelligence as Mendelssohn could have so zealously espoused the ontological proof for the existence of God,[86] as he had done in his treatise on evidence.[87] The excuses made by Lessing led me to the very question whether he had never asserted his own system versus Mendelssohn. "Never," was Lessing's answer. . . . "Only once I told him approximately

that which struck you in the *Education of the Human Race* [#73]. We could not agree with each other, and I left it at that."

The disclosure of Lessing's Spinozism contained in Jacobi's report had been a bitter pill for Mendelssohn to swallow, since it implied that despite their intimate friendship Mendelssohn had been left in the dark about certain of the beliefs of the man he had trusted most. Even so, Mendelssohn had not been unduly perturbed, since the interpretation of the *kind* of Spinozism subscribed to by Lessing remained an open question. This new piece of information was another matter: it seemed to be calculated to prove that notwithstanding Lessing's warm sentiments for Mendelssohn, there had been no real rapport between them in philosophical matters; that Lessing had given up even the attempt to convince his friend ("I left it at that"); and that Jacobi, not Mendelssohn, was the one who had enjoyed Lessing's full confidence. This was the trump card that Jacobi had been carefully withholding, waiting for the most propitious moment at which to display it. That moment had come at last.

Literary Activity: 1783–1785

The *Morgenstunden,* Moses Mendelssohn's last major work, would never have come into being had not the pressure of Jacobi's challenge wrested it from him. The kind of literary activity in which he engaged after the publication of *Jerusalem* in 1783 had been limited almost exclusively to short essays and even shorter notes.

The stage for this type of writing had been set by two events. In 1783 the *Berlinische Monatsschrift* had commenced publication, and in the same year a new learned society, the *"Berliner Mittwochsgesellschaft"* (also known as *"Freunde der Aufklärung"*) had been formed. Both of these establishments were entirely after Mendelssohn's heart, designed as they were to invigorate the forces of the Enlightenment in their struggle against all forms of reaction. The moving spirit in both enterprises was Johann Erich Biester, a classical scholar and head of the Royal Library. He edited the *Berlinische Monatsschrift* from its inception until 1791 jointly with Friedrich Gedike, a liberal clergyman and pedagogue, and afterwards until 1796 on his own. He was also the secretary of the learned society.[1]

Thanks largely to Biester's skill and determination, the new monthly became a powerful organ of the Enlightenment. Its religious orientation was deistic, its political creed a strong affirmation of the principles that had been the hallmark of the age of Frederick the Great. Tolerance ranked uppermost among them. If it erred, it was in the excessive zeal with which it pursued and sought to unmask real and suspected papism, Jesuitism, and enthusiastic charlatanism. It denounced Lavater as one who unwittingly served the purposes of the Jesuits, an accusation that called forth Jacobi's and Schlosser's protest in the *Deutsches Museum*. The monthly could flourish only so long as freedom of thought and expression were protected. When under Frederick's successor liberty was curbed by the notorious *Religionsedikt* of July 9, 1788, and with Johann Christoph von Wöllner, minister of justice and *chef* of the ecclesiastical *departement,* watching over the edict's rigorous application, the journal moved first to Jena and later to Dessau, where it was not subject to censorship but could not maintain its existence beyond 1796.[2]

While the *Berlinische Monatsschrift* was a public forum of discussion open to all and sundry, the Berlin Wednesday Society *(Mittwochsgesellschaft)* was a closed and indeed a secret group.[3] Its membership was not to exceed twenty-four, and the unanimous approval of members voting by ballot was required for election to membership. "Excellencies", i.e. noblemen of old standing [as distinct from newly created ones], were not eligible. Its meetings were held on Wednesday evening, twice a month in the period from Michaelmas (September 29) to Easter and once a month between Easter and Michaelmas. They started at half past six and lasted until eight, when dinner was served. At every session two lectures were delivered and discussed. A number of subjects were excluded: theology proper, jurisprudence, medicine, mathematics, philological criticism, and newspaper reports, but not matters arising from these disciplines that had a bearing on "enlightenment" and "human welfare." It was left to the choice of the speaker whether to deliver a full-fledged lecture (provided it was not too long and offered material for discussion), or simply to raise a number of points (which had to be in writing so as to make it possible to have them on permanent record), or perhaps even to read a passage from a book likely to stimulate discussion.

Members were expected to debate the issues dealt with by the speaker in rotation according to the order in which they happened to be seated, and not to speak again until the round was completed; the speaker, on the other hand, was entitled to reply to each discussant in turn. Minutes were kept of the main points made in the debate, and a record of them, edited by the speaker, was circulated among members along with the text of the lecture.[4] It was hoped to elicit in this way additional written responses *(vota).* To put the members entirely at their ease, every care was taken to ensure strict secrecy: *vota* were signed by numbers allotted to each name, and members were in honor bound not to divulge any opinion expressed to nonmembers, however trustworthy they might be.

The membership list, drawn up shortly after the society was established, included the names of many of Mendelssohn's closest friends: Ernst Ferdinand Klein, Johann Jakob Engel, Friedrich Nicolai, and Christian Wilhelm Dohm. Also belonging to the group were the most prominent theologians of the Berlin Enlightenment: the aged Johann Joachim Spalding, Johann Samuel Diterich, Wilhelm Abraham Teller—all three senior councillors of the consistory—and Johann Friedrich Zöllner, deacon at the Marienkirche and Diterich's son-in-law. Spalding and Diterich, it will be remembered, had crossed Mendelssohn's path as far back as the days of the Lavater affair. Other outstanding members were Karl Gottlieb Suarez, the eminent jurist who together with Klein had assisted the high chancellor von Carmer in the drafting of a new legal code for the Prussian states; Johann Karl Wilhelm Möhsen, personal physician to the king and a historian of the sciences (notably medicine) in the Mark Brandenburg; and Karl August von Struensee, an elder brother of the unfortunate Danish statesman Count Johann Friedrich Struensee and an economist of high rank.[5] The society lasted about fifteen years. It was probably dissolved toward the end of 1798 as a result of an edict against secret societies announced on October 20 of that year.[6]

Mendelssohn had never joined the purely social "Monday Club" (founded in 1749), of which Nicolai had been a member since 1756 and to which most educated people of all strata of society belonged. The motto of that club was "friendship and conviviality with the seasoning of a cheerful frugal meal."[7] Mendelssohn's observance of the Jewish dietary laws was of itself sufficient to preclude his membership in this club, but he was generally reluctant to join even learned societies. In 1762 Isaak Iselin had found it hard to persuade him to accept membership in the "Patriotic Society."[8] In 1785, when Joseph von Sonnenfels invited him join the newly founded "Society of the Sciences" in Vienna,[9] Mendelssohn accepted only with the proviso that he be under no obligation to contribute to any literary project; his "nervous debility" and his domestic duties, he explained, left him only a minimum of time and energy for philosophic pursuits.[10] It was not very much different when, toward the end of 1783, Biester asked him to become a member of the Wednesday Society. We learn of his first reaction from a letter by Biester that was quoted in part by Joseph Mendelssohn in his biography of his father:[11]

> When a little while ago I asked you in the name of the recently founded learned society to increase its membership, you refused, and did so for a reason that made your negative reply doubly painful to all of your friends.[12] Now the society has expressed a different desire and has instructed me to ask you to grant its fulfilment. A lecture delivered at a session is discussed not only on the spot; it subsequently circulates among all members in order to be more carefully considered, and is returned with the *vota* of the members attached to it. Now it is the general desire that we may occasionally be permitted to send the file[13] also to you, sir, so as to receive your opinion on a lecture deemed to be of sufficient importance. Will you permit this and be kind enough to give your *votum* from time to time? In this way you become an honorary member of the society, and have the right to attend the sessions whenever you so desire or find it convenient, or not to attend, as you please.

Mendelssohn accepted this proposal, as is evident from the *vota* he wrote. The six "notes" published from his *Nachlass*[14] and described as seemingly having been written for the "Philomathische Gesellschaft"[15] could not have been written for this particular society, which did not even come into being until 1800.[16] In actuality, the "notes" are unquestionably Mendelssohn's *vota* on lectures delivered in the *Mittwochsgesellschaft,* and the very first note (actually, *votum*) contains an unmistakable reference to the Wednesday Society:[17] "Such investigations [viz. dealing with the question of press censorship] are proper only for the closet, for secret societies like ours, where the enlightened part of the nation can put forward opinions among its own ranks in friendship and mutual confidence." He added: "In case the society should ever resolve to publish its *mémoires* [i.e. its proceedings], investigations of this kind would have to be among the first to be omitted." Before long the society did decide to publish some of its lectures in the *Berlinische Monatsschrift.* Mendelssohn's essay *On the Question: What Does Enlightenment Mean?* appeared in the issue of September, 1784,[18] after having been presented as a lecture to the society on May 16 of that year,[19] and of two shorter pieces by Mendelssohn published in the journal[20] one at least originated as a lecture read before the society.[21] The same was the case with Christian Gottlieb Selle's article in the December, 1784, issue of the journal,[22] for which Mendelssohn's *votum* has been preserved.[23]

Judging from the tone and temper of his *vota* and his essays, Mendelssohn felt entirely in his element as a member of this society. There he could speak his mind without any sense of inhibition, and the consciousness of being part of an intellectual fraternity was bound to strengthen his morale in the ongoing struggle with Jacobi. The extent to which he identified himself with the society can be sensed from the alacrity with which he participated in its activities. On one occasion at least he was glad to have an opportunity to refer a difficult question to the more competent tribunal of the society. On February 15, 1785, the baron von Monster intimated to him that he planned to acquire a small sovereign country, comprising three hundred acres of uncultivated and uninhabited land at the bank of a great river in Germany, for the purpose of establishing a "city state" for about a hundred Jewish families and an equal number of Christians. Under his rule every freedom, including exemption from taxes, was to be granted to the citizens. His sole ambition was to create a tiny island of true liberty and happiness. He hoped Mendelssohn would advise him in the drafting of a constitution, and that he would treat the matter in the strictest of confidence.[24] Replying on February 21, 1785, to this intriguing though somewhat utopian proposition, Mendelssohn wrote:[25]

> I am infinitely obliged to your Excellency for the confidence placed in me. Yet to be worthy of it, I ask your permission to entrust your great idea to a Society of Enlightened Friends, for whose discretion I vouch, and in whose insight and savoir faire I have more confidence than in my own.... your Excellency need not doubt that the men in question are of high repute and character. Privy Councillor Dohm is one of them; and though the others are not as famous as he in the literary field, they certainly are his equals in honesty and enlightened thinking.

Mendelssohn's first essay in the *Berlinische Monatsschrift*[26] was in answer to a request contained in a letter to Nicolai by a certain gentleman erroneously referred to as K.[27] The correspondent was Ludwig Julius Friedrich Höpfner (1743–1797), a professor in Giessen, who had been troubled by what he considered the inadequacy of the various definitions of free will; he now believed that he had found a satisfactory view in Christian Gottlieb Selle's *Primary Concepts [Urbegriffe] of the Quality, Origin, and Final Purpose of Nature* (1776). According to Selle,[28] motivations determine human action with the same necessity as a spring and weight determine the operation of a machine; the moral character of human acts remains unaffected. Höpfner wrote: "I [would] very much like to know what Moses Mendelssohn and Eberhard think about this subject." He suggested that the transmutation of morals into a kind of mechanics was apt to make for greater tolerance and less conceit. Started by Mendelssohn, a discussion ensued in which Eberhard and Selle also participated.[29]

Mendelssohn sought to clarify the issue by avoiding, in the first place, the use of the terms "necessity" and "will" and introducing, in their place, the distinction between efficient and final causes. All involuntary changes in the human body follow from efficient causes, whereas all voluntary actions derive from intentional purposes and are the results of choices made for ends considered to be good. I act involuntarily if my action is unrelated to any purpose. Since I conceive purposes in obscure, clear, or distinct fashion, as the case may be, my action may be said to be aroused, correspondingly, by instinct, urges, or motivating reasons. In the last case I act not merely voluntarily but with free will. The foreseeing of retribution has a bearing on the choice of ends and, thereby, on free-willed resolution. To call morals a system of mechanics is permissible only if the knowledge of good and evil is recognized, at the same time, as the first and last dynamic power. Are the fool and the knave synonymous terms, according to this view? In a sense, they are. The rabbis said:[30] "A man does not commit a sin unless a spirit of folly has taken hold of him." Yet there is a difference: the fool lacks knowledge of the true, the knave is ignorant of the good. One can be a good fool and hence lovable. The knave is not sure even of our pity, since we may consider suffering as his only cure. The fool, on the other hand, cannot be cured by suffering. Therefore he always deserves our pity. In essence, Mendelssohn upheld the Wolffian distinction between necessity and determination, which Höpfner had described as being unintelligible to him.

About a year later Mendelssohn replied in a similar vein to a letter dated April 2, 1784, from Professor Johann Christoph Schwab[31] of Stuttgart, who raised the question of the difference between the morally and the physically good.[32] Schwab referred to himself as a Wolffian, which delighted Mendelssohn:[33] "I am glad to find a philosopher in Germany who is not ashamed to be a Wolffian. I owe my first education in philosophy to the writings of this thinker; I have therefore remained biased in his

favor, and I shall always take pleasure in defending everything that flowed
from his pen." Among other topics Schwab had mentioned the problem
of freedom and necessity, but by now Mendelssohn was unwilling to debate
the matter further:[34] "It seems to me that [this] subject . . . has been exhaus-
tively treated. . . . The time has come to put it on the shelf. . . . One can
hardly expect anything new to be produced by any party." But this fore-
closure of further debate was not meant too seriously: Mendelssohn himself
returned to the psychological discussion of folly and knavery in an essay
that may have been read before the Wednesday Society—it is dated August
15, 1785—and was posthumously published in the *Berliner Monatsschrift*.[35]

Entitled *Are There Natural Dispositions to Vice?*, the posthumous essay
broke a lance for a happy medium between cold Stoicism and the "fire
of enthusiasm" as the best way of producing moral action. "The ability
to dissolve sentiments into rational deliberation and to make rational concepts sensual is, in my view, the great secret to be employed by one who
has the ambition to reach the heights of heroic virtue." Here Mendelssohn
repeated, with some fresh nuances, his basic theory concerning the necessary harmonization of the sensual and the rational.[36]

Man as a composite of intellect and sensuality was also the theme
of Mendelssohn's important essay *The Statue (Die Bildsäule)*, which he published in the *Berlinische Monatsschrift* in August, 1784, taking his cue from
an essay of the same title by Engel in the May issue.[37] Engel had tried
to show the absurdity of seeking to reduce the nonsensual to the sensual.
He had also rejected the notion that the "essence" of the soul was something
distinct from the totality of its qualities and forces. Mendelssohn went
beyond Engel in insisting upon the irreducibility of the rational to the
sensual and vice versa. He took issue with both the sensualism of Condillac
and Bonnet and the idealism of Berkeley. In 1754 the abbot Condillac
had published a *Traité des sensations*[38] in which he used the simile of an
animated statue to demonstrate the sensual origin of all representations
and notions arising in man. Condillac defended his theory vis-à-vis the
theologians by declaring that he was discussing the post-lapsarian condition
of the soul.[39] Diderot, d'Alembert, and Helvétius, who adopted his theory,
did so without any concessions to theology. The notion of man as a being
composed of two essentially different layers (reason and sense perception)
was radically questioned by the sensualists. Charles Bonnet, who as a good
Christian believed in the immortality of the soul, retained the concept
of man as a "mixed being" (*être mixte*), but as a physiologist he derived
all actions and conditions of the soul from the vibrations of sensual "fibers."
His *Essai analytique sur les facultés de l'Ame* (1760) developed a theory similar
to Condillac's.

Mendelssohn offered his observations on "the statue *à la Bonnet or
à la Condillac*" by analyzing a fictitous dream of an allegoical character:

> The son of sleep and poesy [viz. the dream] was kind enough to show
> me into a hall decorated with many automata of this kind. He bade

one of the statues step forward, walk up and down the hall, and, finally, sign and dance in a not at all disagreeable manner. The song pleased the ear, though the words would seem not to have been written by Metastasio[40] nor the melody composed by Gluck. The dance had not been invented by Noverre[41] either, but it appeared to be all the more natural and simple. Having had my fill of pleasure from this show, I called out: "Kindly genius, thank you for this lovely play; but reveal to me now the hidden machinery by means of which this Daedelian statue[42] is made capable of entertaining the senses in such a pleasant way. I wish not merely to enjoy myself but also, through your kindness, to gain insight in rational understanding." "In rational understanding?" asked the divine child. "Reason, a prudish matron, is hardly my friend. She has never been especially fond of my father [sleep]; and my mother [poesy], whose governess she claims to be, has advised me to show the lady outward respect but not to care much about her moods and harsh criticisms. Yet part of your wish may be granted."

If we de-allegorize the rest of the dream, the following notions emerge: Vision of space is closely related to touch. According to Pascal, the elements of geometry can be derived from vision of space, and Saunderson, the blind Cambridge mathematician,[43] showed the possibility of "optics" for the sightless based on touch. A line or a circle may be differently described according to the different "idioms" of the senses. It is wrong to borrow the terms valid for one kind of sense perception for the language of another, (e.g. to speak of a high or low sound or of a sharp taste); no sense can be reduced to another. Nor can sense perception be translated into the language of rational concepts without thereby losing its specific character. It is not correct to say that sound is but the vibration of a string, or that color is but a certain refraction of a beam of light. To explain the sensations of sound, color, smell, etc. in purely mathematical terms is to ignore their specific character.

In an early fragment "Affinity of the Beautiful and the Good" (ca. 1758)[44] Mendelssohn had already expressed the same view: "The musical triad is known to be nothing but a sensual perception of certain proportions; yet what we feel when hearing a triad differs widely from the consideration of certain proportions." The difference between sensation and scientific understanding, he had said, was the difference between the apperception of phenomena and true reality. The senses registered confusedly a total impression, while the intellect analyzed the elements of the impression and transformed them into clear and distinct notions. This Leibnizian differentiation between phenomena and reality had remained valid for Mendelssohn. The essay of 1784 added, however, a new perspective. Since his present point of departure was Condillac's attempt to derive all knowledge from sense perception, Mendelssohn tried to show, first, that the experience of the senses was *sui generis* and irreducible. Having arrived at this point, he was faced with the claim of the idealists that extension, figure, and motion were not different from sound, color, smell, taste, pain, thirst, and hunger. If sensations were subjective, why should the mathematical proportions associated with extension, figure and motion be referable to real objects outside ourselves?

In seeking to answer this question, Mendelssohn resorted to James Beattie, Thomas Reid, and "other friends of common sense who attacked the Bishop [Berkeley]." They had not allowed themselves to be led astray by "subtleties," and they trusted no speculation that was contradicted by common sense. There was nothing more evident to sound reason than Locke's distinction between primary and secondary qualities.[45] The bodies outside ourselves were really extended; they possessed real shape and real mobility; and by virtue of these primary qualities they produced the sounds, smells, and tastes perceived by our senses. To this view, Mendelssohn conceded, two objections might be advanced: (1) how could the perceptions of hearing, taste, and smell be said to be explained by translating them into the idiom of touch and sight? and (2) how could the quest for rational understanding be satisfied by the verdict of mere common sense? Mendelssohn realized that resorting to the authority of common sense was but a makeshift. He justified it by the assertion that whenever rational understanding was beyond reach, one had to be content with less. As for the first objection, he admitted that using the language of touch and vision in trying to explain the experiences of the other senses was like using a translation instead of the original text. But doing this, he argued, was still preferable to abandoning all effort, provided one did not mistake the translation for the original. From this vantage point it was not difficult for Mendelssohn to assail the sensualistic position: "What, however, are we to say about the forgetfulness of those who do not merely transform the rest of the senses into touch and sight, wishing to see the sound and touch the smell as it were, but also believe that they are able to explain all operations of intellect, reason, and imagination by reference to changes in the visible and touchable qualities of things?"

Mendelssohn's essay *On the Question: What Does Enlightenment Mean?*[46] was originally his contribution to a prolonged discussion in the Wednesday Society (it continued from January to May, 1784) in which practically all its members participated. The impulse to this debate had been provided by an almost casual footnote that had appeared in Johann Friedrich Zöllner's article "Is it Advisable to Rescind the Religious Sanction of Marriage?" The footnote read[47] "What is Enlightenment? This question, which is almost as important as [the question] what is truth, would seem to require an answer before one engages in enlightening activity." Kant, who was in no way connected with the society, responded to this challenge in his famous essay "Reply to the Question: What is Enlightenment?," which appeared in the December, 1784, issue of the *Berlinische Monatsschrift*.[48] In a postscript (dated September 30, 1784) he referred to Mendelssohn's answer to the question, which had been published before, as he had just then learned from a weekly: "It has not yet come to hand; otherwise, I would have held back the present one. It might now serve as an experiment to what extent chance can produce agreement in thought." As it happened, chance showed itself unwilling to produce much agreement.

The debate in the Wednesday Society had been initiated upon a proposal by Möhsen made on December 17, 1783. In a *votum* dated December 26 Mendelssohn had endorsed Möhsen's suggestion to discuss the issue and had offered the following guidelines for the conduct of the debate:[49]

> 1. I would hope that examples from history could be found of instances in which Enlightenment as such and unrestricted liberty in particular did actual harm to the public weal.
> 2. When considering the benefits and damages produced by Enlightenment and the revolutions that arose from it one should differentiate between the first years of crisis and subsequent periods. Those crises are sometimes only seemingly dangerous and, in fact, [may be] harbingers of improvement.
> 3. Even if it be true (as I really take for granted) that certain prejudices shared by a whole nation must be spared by all honest people in view of the circumstances, the question still remains: are their limits to be determined by laws and censors or are they, like the limits of prosperity, gratitude and sincerity, to be left to the discretion of every individual? Since they are variable by their very nature, their limit cannot be fixed by permanent laws, and to leave the decision to the whim of censors seems to me altogether more harmful than the most unrestricted freedom.
> 4. The discovery [of the hot-air-balloon, the forerunner of aviation] by Montgolfier [Joseph-Michael Montgolfier (1740–1810) and his brother Jacques Étienne (1745–1799)] will probably lead to great revolutions. Whether they will be for the good of human society nobody will as yet dare to decide. But who will on this account hesitate to promote progress? The discovery of eternal truths is as such good; it is for Providence to take care of them in the right direction.

Mendelssohn's *votum* in the actual debate was delivered on May 16, 1784. It opened with the following words, which were omitted in the printed essay so as to obliterate its provenience: "After the afore-going excellent observations [by the preceding speakers] I too make bold to lay down some definitions of terms and semantic distinctions that would seem to have some bearing on the subject." He did not confine himself to discussing the term "enlightenment" but treated the more comprehensive theme of "education" *(Bildung)*. He did so because to him "enlightenment" had become a word fraught with ambiguity. Enlightenment could be either specious or true.[50] Moreover, enlightenment was to him not merely an attitude of mind, as it was to Kant, but a clearly defined system of thought, one that Kant had abandoned but to which Mendelssohn was committed. This system—a modified version of the Leibniz/Wolffian philosophy, enriched by insights gained from the English empiricists, and fortified by the Scottish "commonsense" thinkers—had both an esoteric and an exoteric aspect. To secure it for posterity, as a vehicle of human happiness, Mendelssohn found it necessary to differentiate between the theoretical and practical elements that it embraced. In his view the term "enlightenment" did not cover both of these aspects, and he therefore distinguished between enlightenment and "culture." Together they constituted what he called "education."

Culture, Mendelssohn suggested, comprised the practical aspects of education: refinement and beauty in the crafts, arts, and social habits. Enlightenment, on the other hand, applied to the theoretical sphere: the attempt to gain a rational insight into the nature of things and their bearing on the vocation of man. The sciences imparted enlightenment to a language, whereas sociability, poetry, and oratory raised the level of culture. The two combined gave language the stamp of education. The French excelled in culture, the English in enlightenment; the Chinese had much culture but little enlightenment; the Greeks had both in ample measure. Were man an isolated individual, he would have no use for culture; he would need only enlightenment.[51] Different nuances of culture were required for different levels of society and for different professions. Qua man, every individual ought to share in a certain degree of enlightenment; qua member of society, the individual should aspire toward a level of enlightenment suited to his vocation. The enlightenment achieved by an individual qua man may conflict with the enlightenment beneficial to him qua citizen.

It would be a tragic situation, Mendelssohn went on to say, if a state were in danger of anarchy unless certain essential elements of enlightenment were repressed. In such cases political necessity would demand that fetters be imposed on the free exercise of reason and philosophy would have to remain silent. A situation of this kind would degrade man's essential humanity for reasons of political expediency. No objection could be raised, however, if certain "unessential" truths were concealed from the untutored in order to safeguard their religion and morality. The protagonist of enlightenment who was at the same time concerned about moral virtue would act with foresight and prudence: he would rather tolerate prejudice than insist on propagating truths dangerous to public morality. Misuse of enlightenment was likely to weaken moral sentiment and to give rise to obtuseness, egotism, irreligion, and anarchy. The greatest danger facing an educated nation was excessive prosperity which, like perfect health of body, was an unhealthy, sick condition.[52] For once having reached the pinnacle of well-being, the nation could rise no higher and was, therefore, in serious danger of falling down.

Kant, as is well known, defined Enlightenment as "man's release from his self-incurred tutelage" and as the "courage to use reason without direction from another." He and his contemporaries, he said, lived not in an enlightened age but in an age of enlightenment. The century of Frederick the Great had paved the road toward enlightenment by granting men freedom of conscience. Everything depended henceforward on the use that was made of this freedom. To renounce enlightenment and to accept tutelage was "violating the sacred rights of humanity." Kant was careful to distinguish between the private and the public use of reason. A minister of religion appointed to teach certain doctrines was not free to follow his own reason: the "domestic" or "private" character of the church imposed certain limitations. Qua scholar, however, even the clergyman, judge, or army officer had the right and duty to speak his mind. The public use of reason had to throw off all fetters. In sum, Kant's essay was a stirring manifesto on behalf of the freedom of conscience and expression.

Neither Kant's nor Mendelssohn's views went unchallenged. As for those of Kant, Hamann remarked that the simile of a minor's tutelage could hardly be reconciled with the accusation of "self-incurred" tutelage. To remind a professor of logic and a critic of pure reason of the rules of hermeneutics was, he realized, almost high treason: yet the term "self-incurred tutelage" was in fact a *contradictio in adjecto.* Inability implied no guilt, and might in certain cases result from the blindness of the guardian who arrogated all vision to himself.[53] Hamann's objection expressed a sentiment akin to Mendelssohn's in regard to the untutored.

Kant's distinctions between enlightenment and being enlightened and between the private and public uses of reason were characterized as strange and paradoxical by Johann Samuel Diterich, in a lecture before the members of the *Mittwochsgesellschaft.* Diterich's critique can be reconstructed in part from Mendelssohn's *votum* on his presentation.[54] Mendelssohn defended Kant's position with this stipulation: In certain circumstances even an accredited teacher must be permitted to advocate ideas contrary to the established norm, and to propose innovations. Though his acceptance of appointment as clergyman, judge, etc. implied a readiness to abide by the rules in force, he has the right and the duty to violate the agreement if he is convinced that his plea for innovation will win the approval of the community. However, he must be prepared to abstain from advocating his ideas if it becomes manifest that he was mistaken in his assumption. In such a case, the unsuccessful preacher of reform has to resign from office rather than go on trying to impose his views on an unwilling public. He must also be prepared to bear all consequences of his actions. With these stipulations in mind, Mendelssohn wrote, some of the wisest teachers of mankind had permitted themselves the propagation of novel ideas that they considered beneficial. Though he was anything but a reformer, Mendelssohn thus showed himself to be more daring and radical than Kant.

Mendelssohn's own essay was severely criticized by his friend Hennings in a letter dated October 21, 1784.[55] Hennings tacitly accepted the basic distinction between culture and enlightenment, but he was outraged by the suggestion that enlightenment could at times come into conflict with the duties of citizenship. The alternative to enlightenment was delusion, barbarism, or stupidity. There was nothing in between. He also assailed the differentiation between essential and nonessential elements in the vocation of man. There was no "more" or "less" in a vocation. Nor did he admit the possibility of any "misuse" of enlightenment. Could light be said to be occasionally dark? In a careful and lengthy reply, written on

November 27, 1784, by another hand,[56] Mendelssohn sought to dispel the misunderstandings that he felt underlay Hennings' criticisms, and added a number of interesting points;[57] his letter to Hennings deserves to be studied as a commentary on his essay.

Had Mendelssohn been free to divulge points raised in the discussions of the Wednesday Society, he might have mentioned a *votum* that he had written on May 23, 1784, a week after he had delivered his paper on the question "What does Enlightenment mean?" It concerned a lecture by Suarez[58] on censorship laws,[59] and made the point that restrictions on the freedom of literary expression could never be imposed by virtue of reason; only state power could resort to measures of this kind. But once censorship was deemed to be advantageous to the welfare of the people, public discussion of its guidelines would be self-defeating. It was equally foolish to declare in print that governing the populace by false prejudices was permissable. Mendelssohn referred here to a prize-essay written in response to the question posed in 1777 by the Berlin Academy: whether one could deceive a nation or leave it in its prevalent deceptions?[60]

On April 12, 1784, Mendelssohn wrote to Karl August, count of Oeynhausen-Gravenburg:[61] "About the *Jerusalem* two brochures of almost the same size as the treatise itself have already appeared. One of them has a local preacher, and the other is said to have a Hanoverian one, for its author. Both refute me but do so gently and modestly. I have less reason to be satisfied with the *Ritter* Michaelis." The two preachers referred to are Zöllner and August Georg Uhle (who published his polemical treatise anonymously). Hamann's *Golgatha und Scheblimini*, the most trenchant attack, had not yet appeared; it came out in August, 1784. A number of critical works were published in the next three years.[62] Among all his opponents, Zöllner was the only one who met Mendelssohn's basic thesis about the origin of compulsory rights on Mendelssohn's own ground.[63] It seems that after having published his critical analysis of the *Jerusalem*, Zöllner reverted to the theme of perfect and imperfect duties in a lecture delivered to the Wednesday Society. It appears that Selle also treated the subject from the same platform. For Mendelssohn's reply to Zöllner's *Aufsatz* (as distinct from his book), with its reference to Selle's theory,[64] is undoubtedly his *votum* on their presentations.

Zöllner advanced the following argument:[65] According to Mendelssohn's doctrine the state has the right to claim a part of the citizens' possessions because the citizens have surrendered their natural right of deciding how to dispose of their goods in cases of conflicting imperfect duties. Apart from questioning the propriety of the terms "perfect and imperfect duties," Zöllner asked: if the legal basis of the compulsory rights of the state was such an act of surrender, how was it possible to set any limit to state power and to secure the personal rights of the citizens?

In his *votum* on Zöllner's lecture, Mendelssohn noted that Zöllner, though still disagreeing on terminology, had come appreciably closer to his own view. The moral bond of society, he reemphasized, was a tacit contract. By accepting the benefits accruing from life in a society one tacitly accepted certain obligations. It was this fundamental principle that he had tried to establish. To determine the specific forms under which the social contract operated in the various systems of government was an entirely different question. To explain the origins of the various forms of government was still another matter.

According to Selle, all power of the magistrate rested upon the obligation to entrust oneself to the leadership of the wisest and best. In the state of nature this obligation was but an "inner" or imperfect duty, as Selle had admitted, and one had therefore to explain again how this imperfect duty became an enforceable one. Mendelssohn agreed with Selle that whenever the benefits of compulsory rule by an able leader outweighed its disadvantages, the renunciation of democratic rule was called for, it being understood that those dissatisfied with a monarchical or oligarchical system were at liberty to emigrate. The question which form of government was to be preferred had received the answer: the monarchical, if the ruler was a wise man. Mendelssohn proposed a different answer: the republican, if the people were wise. The right of self-government was the prerogative of society as a whole, and of each individual member, for as long as democracy worked. But when corruption and anarchy threatened to undermine the fabric of the state, then usurpation of power by wise and capable individuals was justified. Julius Caesar had been wrongly blamed by Brutus. The danger of despotism lay in the atrophy of the desire for freedom. The nation was apt to unlearn the use of political power and to lose the ability to stand on its own feet.

In his *Jerusalem*,[66] Mendelssohn had discussed the same question in similar vein. He turned to it anew in his *votum* on a lecture *Concerning the Best Constitution of the State*, which seems to have been read to the society by his friend Ernst Ferdinand Klein.[67]

The dangers inherent in the Enlightenment had been realized by Mendelssohn as early as 1759. In his very first contribution to the *Literaturbriefe*,[68] he had remarked that truth itself had turned into prejudice by the manner in which it had become accepted (i.e., by the easygoing fashion in which the sciences were being taught). He elaborated this theme in an essay that appeared in the February, 1785, issue of the *Berlinische Monatsschrift* and was originally his *votum* on Friedrich Gedike's paper "On Contemporary Enthusiasm," which had been read before the Wednesday Society in July/August, 1784.[69] The title of Mendelssohn's essay is: "Should One Obviate the Spread of Enthusiasm by Satire or by Some External Association?" Nothing was more harmful to true human welfare, he declared, than a "sham enlightenment" that caused everybody to mouth a mindless "stale wisdom" from which the animating spirit had "evaporated" long ago, and that made everybody deride prejudices "without discriminating between the true and false in them." The only means of promoting true enlightenment was not satire but—enlightenment. Wrong notions about God and Providence could not be exorcised by either derisive laughter or the fear of external power. It was natural for enthusiasts to band themselves together in associations. Fanaticism, Voltaire had aptly remarked, formed parties, while wisdom stood alone. Whenever a century inclined toward enthusiasm or superstition, it did so in response to some strongly felt need. The reason had to be sought in the preponderance of some shallow philosophy and in its corrupting influence on morality. In situations of this kind people were yearning for a return to childlike simplicity and infantile folly. They preferred to be surrounded by ghosts instead of facing a disenchanted "dead nature." Unbelief and superstition, the "twin evils" of their time, had not held sway to the same extent at the beginning of the century, when profundity of thought was the characteristic feature of German literature. The Leibniz/Wolffian philosophy had so clarified and solidified both concepts and terminology that sophistry had no chance of acceptance. Language itself refused to lend itself to its misuse by muddled thinking, be it atheistic or enthusiastic. Restoring German philosophy to its former glory, instead of giving currency to the idle talk of the French *philosophes*, might provide the necessary cure. The disease of sham enlightenment could be healed only by authentic enlightenment. Prejudice was not to be suppressed but to be illumined.

On an entirely different level from these *opera minora*, published in the *Berlinische Monatsschrift* or merely written as *vota* for the secret Wednesday Society, was Mendelssohn's treatise *"Causa Dei," or Providence Defended*, which was probably written in 1784 but was not meant for publication.[70] It is clearly addressed to a Jewish audience, speaking as it does of "our religion" and quoting sentences in Hebrew. Though unrelated to the *Morgenstunden*,[71] it might have originated, as that treatise did, in Mendelssohn's desire to guide his son Joseph toward "a rational knowledge of God."[72] If so, the work must have been designed for study by Joseph at a more mature age than fourteen (his age in 1784), for its intricate discussion of the problem of theodicy would have been beyond the boy's comprehension and his range of interest as well. Its literary form does not indicate any tutorial purpose: the use of dialogue and apostrophe, so characteristic of the *Morgenstunden*, is completely missing. Yet it seems highly probable that Mendelssohn was anxious to preserve for the future use of Joseph and his other children a kind of testament declaring his convictions on a subject that had engaged him throughout his adult life. His earliest known unfinished essay, *Of Chance Happenings* (1753), had touched on the subject, and as late as April 11, 1785, he would write to Nicolai:[73] "Do you know a certain J.C.G. Werdermann, who published a *New Essay on Theodicy* in the Librairie des Auteurs in 1784? The book seems to me worthy of attention." He had dealt with this theme in his correspondence with both Abbt and Hennings; in the third dialogue of the *Phaedon*, which for a long time he had been planning to rewrite; and in his *Annotations* on the correspondence with Abbt (1782).

In the first part of his Hebrew *Book on the Soul* he had promised (in 1769?) to deal with the problem of the justice of God in another place;[74] and in the second part, addressed to Hartog Leo, he had briefly discussed the questions of predestination, providence, and punishment.[75] Hartog Leo might have been the addressee of a treatise like *"Causa Dei,"* had it been written in Hebrew.[76]

In a letter to Jonathan Swift, written on August 2, 1731, Lord Bolingbroke said of Alexander Pope, as the author of *An Essay on Man:* "He pleads the cause of God (I am using Seneca's expression)."[77] Leibniz, too, had used Seneca's expression when he gave to the Latin Appendix IV of his *Essais de Théodicée*[78] the title *"Causa Dei...."* and Mendelssohn borrowed the name from him, translating it *"Sache Gottes."*[79] In juridical language *causa* may denote the "defense" by an advocate, and it was in this sense that Leibniz had used the term: in the preface to the *Essais de Théodicée* (#25) Leibniz expressed the hope that he would succeed in his polemic against Pierre Bayle, since he (Leibniz) represented "la cause de Dieu." Bayle, it should be recalled, had dealt a severe blow to natural theology by exposing its inability to account for the existence of evil in the world. The impossibility of a rational explanation of evil had been admitted by his orthodox opponent Pierre Jurieu. Yet Bayle, though outwardly advocating plain fideism and acceptance of the mystery, had played into the hands of atheism. For he had shown that Manicheanism—which, he suggested, had some affinity with the Christian concept of Satan—was rationally more acceptable than the orthodox doctrine declaring God to be the sole author of both good and evil.[80]

Leibniz had sought to restore the rationality of the orthodox faith and to justify even the eternality of punishment in Hell. He had defined the justice of God as "goodness tempered by wisdom" and had put the stress on wisdom: to the contemplative mind, which beholds the evidences of a universal order, evil loses its sting. Wolff had adopted Leibniz' solution of the problem.[81] However, the "school" philosophers shifted the emphasis from God's wisdom to God's goodness. They did this because to them the happiness of the human individual, not the manifestation of divine wisdom, was the ultimate purpose of God's creation. This new perspective can be clearly seen in Reimarus, Eberhard, Platner, Feder,[82] and most of all in Mendelssohn.[83]

Mendelssohn's *"Causa Dei"* was a highly felicitous attempt to show where he agreed and where he disagreed with Leibniz. Taking Leibniz' text as his *Vorlage,* he either quoted or paraphrased the major part of it paragraph by paragraph, adding or omitting words and sentences; reformulating what seemed to him obscure; eliminating references to Christian sources and substituting Hebrew citations whenever it suited him; modifying emphases; introducing a certain degree of sentimentality by stressing the divine concern for man's happiness; cutting out entire paragraphs of a christological character and replacing them by entirely new disquisitions; polemicizing strenuously against the doctrine of eternal punishment, which he described as unacceptable to "either our religion or our reason" (#60); abandoning the final sections of his *Vorlage* (#74–144) entirely, yet dealing with some of its points such as the doctrine of Satan and Adam's Fall in independent fashion—all this in the eighty-four paragraphs of his version of Leibniz' *"Causa Dei."* As a Leibnizian, Mendelssohn reflected (more or less) the treatment of the theme as presented in his *Vorlage;* as a critic, he followed not merely the prevalent trend of the eighteenth-century Enlightenment but also what he considered to be the Jewish doctrine vis-à-vis the Christian.

Mendelssohn's literary activities in this period were not limited to political and metaphysical writings. In 1783 there began to appear the first of the ten volumes of *Know Thyself, or Magazine of Experiential Psychology, a Reader for the Learned and Nonlearned, edited with the support of some Friends of the Truth by Carl Philipp Moritz.*[84] One of those who helped to plan this famous pioneering journal of psychology, and who contributed to it, was Mendelssohn.[85] He had suggested the ultimate form of the title and pointed out the need for giving due recognition to physiological factors. Most probably he also took part in drafting the "guidelines" published in the first number.[86] The new journal reflected not merely the anthropocentrism of the age, which had been reinforced by a secularized pietism. It was above all the personal creation of Moritz, a young man of genius, whose own neurosis compelled him to seek refuge in an objective, scientific approach to psychopathological phenomena.[87]

In his one-act drama *Blunt, or the Visitor* (1780) Moritz had already given expression to the traumatic experience of his childhood, which he would later elaborate in his autobiographical novel *Anton Reiser*—a work that has been compared with Goethe's *Dichtung und Wahrheit*[88]—and in *Andreas Hartknopf.* His magazine's preoccupation with child psychology was a direct reflection of his own personal problems. In his search for a positive father figure,[89] Moritz seems to have been greatly attracted to Mendelssohn, in whom he found what he had missed and needed all his life: a paternal friend "in whose presence the soul willingly opened itself." In the tribute he paid Mendelssohn,[90] Moritz praised him as a "true sage" remarkable on account of the strictness of his methodical mind, the severity of his physical and mental diet, the care with which he chose his words, and his good-natured trustfulness. "In being with him one felt happy. The very sight of him inspired and gave encouragement. Perhaps no one ever went away from him unimproved."

The project of a psychological journal was bound to appeal to Mendelssohn, whose entire literary *oeuvre* is shot through with flashes of psychological insight.[91] Goethe, in one of his letters, said of Mendelssohn:[92] "There are mixed sentiments that Mendelssohn so accurately draws and concerning which the rest of us have to keep silent." To Mendelssohn human nature had always been an object of fascination, to be observed with the utmost objectivity. In a sense, he shared Spinoza's view that "men, no less than everything else, act by the necessity of their nature."[93] A short essay of his entitled "Mood" *(Laune)*, which appeared in Moritz' *Magazine*,[94] advised the reader to engage in observing himself, if there is nothing else to do and there is danger of aimless daydreaming; by heeding this counsel one was assured of never being without an interesting occupation. An important study that Mendelssohn contributed to the *Magazine*[95] was occasioned by a pathological experience reported in the preceding number of the journal by none other than the famous Spalding, who had tried to account for it in physiological terms. Mendelssohn offered a purely psychological explanation, and he did so by outlining first a theory of human action that Garve judged to be "an excellent piece of philosophy."[96]

In every voluntary action, according to this theory, an interior mental cause produces an exterior physical effect, i.e. certain movements in the limbs of the body. At the point of transition from the mental to the corporeal an "efficient idea" (as distinct from inefficient, viz. merely speculative, ideas) provides an "organic impulse," which starts the bodily motions. How a transition from the mental to the physical is possible, how it can be reconciled with the assumption that new motions or even new directions of motion do not arise in nature, etc.—is not to be discussed here. If a voluntary motion is a composite of several simple ones, a series of organic impulses a, b, c, d will progress *pari passu* with a corresponding series of efficient ideas A, B, C, D. That is, the series of letters I write or of notes I play follows the mental pattern of them and comes to a stop when the purpose in mind is accomplished. A person learning to write or to play an instrument must make a conscious effort at every stage. Having repeated these actions long enough, one no longer needs to make a conscious effort to write each letter or play each note: the initial efficient idea will suffice to set the whole series in motion. The causal nexus between A, B, C, D and a, b, c, d does not cease even though the degree of consciousness accompanying this nexus diminishes to zero.

Thus Mendelssohn, who once had warned against the application of the infinitesimal calculus (Newton's *methodus fluxionum*) to "unextended quantities,"[97] now declares it to be also very fruitful in philosophy. By this method it is possible, he says, to demonstrate that the soul does not cease to think even in deep sleep, that remote objects still affect the senses, that not only violent passions but also psychic conditions in a state of normality have an effect on such bodily functions as digestion, blood circulation, etc.

When performing actions requiring no conscious effort we are able to pursue, at the same time, a heterogeneous series of speculative ("inefficient") ideas. It is also possible to pursue, at the same time, more than one series of efficient ideas. Thus a musician can use both hands and both feet to play his instrument and simultaneously think something unrelated to his playing—and talk as well. Mendelssohn considers it impossible, however, to pursue more than one series of distinct ideas without getting mixed up. It was likewise impossible in his view to continue an action once an idea of which one is conscious becomes so intensive that it attracts the soul's whole attention. In such cases the flow of *a, b, c, d* is impeded, the action comes to a standstill, and the soul has to make an effort to concentrate on the task in hand in order to provide again the organic impulse for action. Performing the task with a certain verve and velocity can usually prevent the intrusion of heterogeneous ideas. Two different efficient ideas must never be allowed to "collide" by being directed to one and the same organ. The result of such collision will be a sense of ambivalence and irritation in the organ concerned.

If this happens to the organs of speech, stuttering will inevitably follow. As Mendelssohn points out, the phenomenon of stuttering is not due to a deficiency in the vocal chords or to any physiological defect. It has purely psychological causes, as is evidenced by the fact that everyone is more or less subject to it when in a state of emotional turmoil. According to his "hypothesis," stuttering is but the result of a collision of some purposive idea and an intruding alien or anticipatory idea, both being of equal strength and both seeking simultaneously to affect the organs of speech. Situations conductive to such collision are emotional upsets, the use of a foreign tongue, stage fright, etc. The best way to prevent stuttering is through loud and slow reading, Mendelssohn suggests (from his own experience). He explains in similar fashion the giddiness of people under the influence of intoxicants and fever: the ideas follow upon each other too rapidly and the result is the incapacity of the bodily organs to act with a corresponding velocity. Moreover, different series of ideas will interfere and collide with each other. Dizziness, on the other hand, is said to be due to a merger of several series of inefficient ideas that jostle each other with such a degree of liveliness that the soul has difficulty mustering the strength to subject them to consciousness and so control them.

Mendelssohn applied this theory to the experience reported by Spalding, who had been attacked by a sudden incapacity to write and speak. (He felt a "tumultuous disorder" in one particular region of his mind, though his capacity for speculative thinking functioned properly as before.) Mendelssohn offered a running commentary on Spalding's account of his experience in the light of the hypothesis he had enunciated. He recalled that the paralytic attacks he had suffered in 1771 had shown similar symptoms: the series of speculative, inefficient ideas had remained unimpaired, whereas the series of efficient ideas was impotent to produce corresponding organic impulses. In a manner that vaguely anticipates elements of Freudian thinking,[98] Mendelssohn wrote:[99] The "unwelcome ideas" were "strangers" in the soul and intruded but accidentally. They had not yet been "naturalized" and were as yet unintegrated into any series of ideas. This is precisely why Herr S[palding] could not remember them later. In dreams we sometimes have the most vivid and efficient ideas; upon awakening we know that we had them but are unable to recall their content unless, perhaps, we happen upon an idea that is associated with them, and through which they had been aroused. The soul can recall only such absent ideas as become available through pulling the cord at its end, as it were. So long as this cord, this idea, is still missing, the rest cannot be recaptured. The soul is capable of remembering the past only by means of what is present to the mind. Mendelssohn compared the different series of ideas in the soul to citizens brought under proper control in a well-ordered state. And yet, he observed, the soul "does not rule in its interior commonwealth absolutely, and its commands are not carried out without demur. Its force has certain limits. At times, a certain idea attains to greater power and refuses to obey. It wishes to be active when it should not be. It dislodges [*verdrängt*] a purposive idea or impedes its functioning, which necessarily causes disorder and stagnation. . . . It is understandable that the recalcitrant idea will not always give way but will at times prevail . . . and produce an organic impulse that the ruling part of the ego totally disapproves."

Mendelssohn's essay here introduces, with remarkable emphasis, the concept of the "unconscious" in two senses of the term: (1) as the zero of awareness in purposive actions that, as a result of expertise, proceed almost mechanically; (2) as repressed ("dislodged") ideas that, being as yet "unwelcome," have been consigned to oblivion but become effective in dreams. The nature of these ideas is not further analyzed. It would be a mistake to see in them anything like Freud's "id." Yet the recalcitrant character of these ideas and the disturbing effect they have on the proper functioning of the "ego" point in the direction of asocial or otherwise reprehensible elements in the psyche.

It is intriguing to think that at a time when Jacobi and his friends were looking contemptuously upon Mendelssohn as a hopelessly petrified devotee of the Enlightenment, Mendelssohn was quietly helping a pioneering spirit like Moritz to break new ground in psychology.

Morning Hours

I

The *Morgenstunden* is the most systematic of Mendelssohn's major works. It has a single, well-defined theme, the existence of God, which it expounds step by step, starting from a discussion of the first principles of epistemology and culminating in the presentation of a novel argument in the last of the seventeen lectures. None of his previous writings had been so compact and methodical as this one. The *Philosophical Dialogues* and the letters *On the Sentiments* had roamed over many different areas. The prize-essay, though focused on a single question posed by the academy, had to probe the nature of four distinct disciplines. The *Phaedon* was partly a paraphrase or reworking of the Platonic *Vorlage,* partly an essay on the vocation of man; it certainly was not all of a piece. The *Jerusalem* was a particularly complex work. Only the *"Causa Dei"* had shown a unicity of purpose and closeness of argumentation comparable to the *Morgenstunden,* but it was an original work only to a very minor degree, since it followed in overwhelming measure its Leibnizian *Vorlage.*

The *Morgenstunden,* on the other hand, is wholly Mendelssohnian. In both literary form and philosophical content it is heavily indebted to no one other than to Mendelssohn himself. Though characterized in the subtitle as "lectures," the work makes ample use of the dialogue form, in which Mendelssohn had found his true medium. In designating the seven introductory lectures—those on truth, appearance, and error—as *Vorerkenntniss* ("Preliminary Notions"), he followed the precedent of his *"Causa Dei,"* in which he had stated in the opening paragraph: "This treatise will consist of two parts; the first will contain only *Vorerkenntnisse,* which have to be presupposed in the justification of God. The second contains the justification itself."[1] In developing his arguments in both the introductory and the main part he drew on his earlier writings, particularly the *Treatise on Probability* and the prize-essay, but he did so with a freshness and vitality that utterly belied the complaint about his "nervous debility" voiced in the preface.

In addition to restating and weaving together some of his older views, he put forward with equal gusto ideas of more recent vintage, especially his notion on the role of common sense. Only three out of the seventeen lectures dealt with Spinozism or pantheism—terms that he used interchangeably—notwithstanding the fact that the book was originally announced as a rebuttal of the *AllEiner,* i.e. of those who believed that All was One *(Hen kai Pan).* In the context of these three lectures Mendelssohn found it possible to discuss Lessing's Spinozism in a manner designed to take the sting out of any subsequent disclosure of the talks Lessing had had with Jacobi. The references to Lessing were the very heart of the book, of course, but to all intents and purposes this was the testament of an age, one that refurbished in the most impressive way the Enlightenment stance on the demonstrability of God's existence.

As the preface shows, Mendelssohn was quite aware of the risk he was taking in continuing to philosophize in a fashion no longer in vogue. His own philosophy, he said, still bore the odor of the "school" (viz. the Leibniz/Wolffian) in which he had brought himself up, and which had during the first half of the century tried to rule supreme, perhaps unjustifiably. Despotism of any sort inspired rebelliousness. The reputation of this school had declined in marked degree, Mendelssohn admitted, and in the process the prestige of speculative philosophy had been ruined altogether. Of late, it had become the order of the day, even among the finest representatives of German thought, to treat speculative philosophy with contempt. The tendency now prevailing was the quest for facts, for observation based on the evidence of the senses, and for a superabundance of experiments; general principles, by comparison, received scant attention. What defied the application of empirical methods was in danger of being considered unreal. Hence the increasing trend toward materialism on the one hand and enthusiasm *(Schwärmerey)* on the other: one either denied the reality of the invisible and untouchable or else sought to touch and visualize (through the mystical experience) what by its very nature could not become an object of sense perception.

The time was ripe, Mendelssohn suggested, to reverse this trend, and he expressed the hope that Kant's "profound mind" would bring about the desired "revolution" in thinking. In an earlier passage he had spoken of the "all-crushing Kant" *(des alles zermalmenden Kants)*[2]—a phrase destined to become famous—and now he assigned to his great contemporary the task of "rebuilding with the same mind with which he had torn down."[3] As for himself, he realized his limitations. With a candor worthy of a philosopher he recalled at the very beginning of his preface the disastrous effects that "a so-called nervous debility"[4] had had on his meditative capacity. During the last twelve to fifteen years he had been in a state of "utter inability to increase [his] knowledge."[5] It had been more difficult for him to read the writings of others than to do any thinking on his own. "I therefore know the works of the great men who have since excelled in metaphysics . . . only from insufficient reports by my friends or from learned reviews that are rarely much more instructive. Hence this discipline stands, so far as I am concerned, still at the point at which it stood about 1775." For this reason he had to be content, he declared, to bequeath to his friends and descendants "an account" of what he had "considered to be true in the matter." The "discourses" offered here contained what he had "previously read and thought on this important subject of our inquiry."

The extreme modesty with which Mendelssohn characterized both himself and the book did him great credit, no doubt, but is also misleading, if taken at face value. He himself went on to admit that despite the price he had to pay for occasional indulgence in philosophical reading he could never bear the thought of taking leave of philosophy, the faithful companion of his former years and his sole comfort in all adversities. Yet even this was an understatement, for throughout the years that had passed since 1771 Mendelssohn had done a great deal of reading and writing in various branches of philosophy. The metaphysicians whose works had become known to him, he said, only through the reports by friends, or through reviews, were Lambert, Tetens, Platner, and Kant;[6] it seems very likely, however, that his knowledge of the more recent works published of these authors was not entirely at second hand. For the philosophical syllabus that he drew up in 1774 at the request of van der Hoop[7] included not only Lambert's *Neues Organon* (1764), which Mendelssohn had reviewed in 1767,[8] but also his *Anlage zur Architektonik* (1771). Mendelssohn would hardly have suggested that both of these works be studied "above everything else and with all possible diligence" if he had not read them himself. J. N. Tetens' *Philosophische Versuche über die menschliche Natur und ihre Entwicklung* (1776 f.) has been shown to have an important affinity with Mendelssohn's notion about the essential oneness of reason and common sense.[9] Since Mendelssohn mentioned Tetens in the preface, it may be assumed that he had more than a nodding acquaintance with his work. Mention has already been made[10] of Mendelssohn's friendly relations with Ernst Platner, whose *Philosophische Aphorismen* (1776) he ordered through Nicolai as early as October 8, 1775. In a letter to Schwab, dated April 26, 1785, Mendelssohn admitted not having read Platner's *Aphorismen* "carefully,"[11] yet it is clear that he *had* read them.

Most important of all, Mendelssohn had made an honest effort, albeit a futile one, to come to grips with Kant's *Critique of Pure Reason* (1781). On April 10, 1783, he had written to Kant:[12]

> For many years I have been almost insusceptible [*wie abgestorben*] to metaphysics. My nervous debility prohibits all effort on my part, and in the meanwhile I amuse myself with less demanding work, samples of which I shall soon have the pleasure of presenting to you.[13] Your *Critique of Pure Reason* is to me also a criterion of health. As often as I flatter myself with the belief that I have gained more strength, I dare to approach this nerve-consuming work, and I have not entirely given up hope of still thinking it through in this life.

Kant did not abandon hope either—at least, not for some time—that Mendelssohn would prove helpful in promoting his difficult work. He had been disappointed when Markus Herz told him that for reasons of health Mendelssohn had "laid [his] book aside," and he had expressed the hope that this negative reply was not final[14] "Among all who can enlighten the world in this respect he [Mendelssohn] is the most important man, and I counted most on him, Herr Tetens, and you [Markus Herz]."

In answer to Mendelssohn's letter Kant wrote to him on August 16, 1783:[15] "I am not surprised that you consider yourself as almost insusceptible to metaphysics, seeing that nearly the entire intelligentsia seems to be insusceptible to it without taking into account any nervous debility (of which one cannot find the least trace in *Jerusalem*). However, the fact that, in place of it [metaphysics], a critique that merely endeavors to examine the groundwork of that edifice is unable to attract or hold your sagacious attention is a matter of regret to me, although it does not surprise me either."

As Kant explained, he had written the *Critique of Pure Reason*, the product of at least twelve years of reflection, within the short space of four or five months and had not managed to give it the final polish that would have made it more easily comprehensible. "Only few people have the good fortune to think for themselves and, at the same time, take account of the way others think, so as to present the subject in a manner suited to all. There is only one Mendelssohn." Kant then suggested that Mendelssohn might encourage others to examine the validity of three crucial points made in the *Critique:* (1) the distinction between analytical and synthetical judgments, and the difficulties involved in synthetical judgments a priori; (2) the contention that synthetical judgments a priori are possible only about the formal conditions of any possible experience; (3) the view that the only speculative cognition that is possible to us a priori is confined to objects of our experience and does not include the things in themselves.

The precision with which Kant laid the salient points of his work before Mendelssohn was bound to give him a more distinct view of the work as a whole. Details still remained blurred, and in his letter to Elise written on January 5, 1784,[16] Mendelssohn was honest enough to admit that he failed to understand Kant, although Garve's excerpt presented no difficulty to him. But this very statement presupposes that he had made an effort to understand the work itself—that he had not been content with secondhand information. The concept of "the thing in itself," which appears in the *Morgenstunden,*[17] was obviously borrowed from Kant, and so was the principle that no object can be real unless it conforms to a concept.[18] In his review of the *Morgenstunden,* in the *Allgemeine Literatur-Zeitung,* Christian Gottfried Schütz, who had become one of Kant's earliest followers, recalled Mendelssohn's assurance that the writings of men like Lambert, Tetens, Platner, and Kant were known to him only from reports or reviews, and he added: "One nevertheless believes . . . [that Mendelssohn's work shows] traces of the fact that he had before him the famous work by Herr Kant; on the other hand, these lectures show no traces of nervous debility. One might be tempted to regard what Herr Mendelssohn says about it as Socratic irony, were it [the nervous debility] not otherwise reliably known."[19] Kant's own judgment of the *Morgenstunden,* which will be discussed below, bears out Schütz' assessment.

The seven lectures on "preliminary notions" start with a discussion of "truth." The principle of contradiction enables us to distinguish the thinkable and the nonthinkable, but by what criterion do we differentiate between the real and the nonreal? My own thoughts, Mendelssohn said (with Descartes), I know to be real (i.e. to have an "ideal" [ideational] reality), while I myself, as the subject in which these thoughts occur, am real in an unqualified sense. In addition to the reality of the self and of the ideal reality of the self's thoughts, we may assume the reality of the external things of which the thoughts are representations. But how can this external reality be verified against the claims of the idealists? The problem of realism versus idealism is reserved for later discussion, but the realistic position is already affirmed at the outset. In the first place it is the senses that testify to an external reality. Once the existence of an external object is accepted, we may predicate certain qualities of the object and form propositions concerning it according to the rules of mathematics and logic. Moreover, we may conclude from the reality of a certain datum of experience the reality of concomitant data by dint of inductive inferences based on the rules of probability.

In lecture two Mendelssohn amplified the last point by recalling some of the things he had stated in his *Treatise on Probability*. A corollary of the tripartite division of reality is the threefold nature of cognition spoken of in lecture three: we know the data given in experience; we transform these raw data into rational knowledge by applying reasoning to them; and we are aware of the outside reality of the physical world.[20] All these kinds of knowledge are fraught with the danger of error and doubt. Neither our senses nor the use we make of our reasoning capacity are infallible. Knowledge is true if it results from a "positive" (i.e. nondefective) power of the soul. Deception by the senses and logical error are due to the same kind of mistake, that of wrong inductive inferences. Qua sense perception every experience can claim to give us an ideal reality, provided the senses do their job properly. A refracted image in the water and the vision of a rainbow have an ideal reality. It is only when I hastily draw inferences that I am apt to be misled. While my ideas are not deceptive qua ideas *(Vorstellungen)*, they may be mistaken if they are held to be representations *(Darstellungen)*, i.e. replicas of objective reality. This latter point is made in lecture four, which, from a literary point of view, has a particular charm and makes ample use of dialogue.

Lecture three touches on one of the central themes of the book: the close relationship between sound common sense and reason. In common sense, Mendelssohn suggests, unconscious rational processes are at work. There is therefore an element of reason in common sense, notwithstanding the fact that common sense is usually regarded as a function of the senses.[21] Reason, on the other hand, is but an exercise in the analysis of sense data. The difference between reason and common sense is that reason moves with slow, deliberate steps, while common sense rushes swiftly toward conclusions.[22]

In lecture five Mendelssohn returned to the Cartesian method of establishing indisputable reality. My thoughts, fears, hopes, etc.—all are covered by the term *cogito*—demonstrate my existence *(sum)*, and judging from the nature of my self-awareness, existence may be defined as a term denoting action and being acted upon *(actio* and *passio)*.[23] Some of my thoughts are not merely my subjective ideas *(Vorstellungen)* but representations *(Darstellungen)* of objective reality. In dreams, mental delusions and in a state of rapture the borderline between the subjective and the objective is blurred or lost sight of entirely. What is the criterion by which the two different realms can be distinguished? The answer given by Mendelssohn is: an association of ideas brought about by our mental faculties alone is subjective, but an association of ideas that reflects a causal nexus—a cause and effect sequence in accordance with the laws of nature outside ourselves—is objective and representative of external reality.

As lecture six points out, it is highly improbable that all my ideas are purely subjective. Both common sense and reason assure us of the objectivity of certain notions. Even animals possess this certitude. The geometer can prove that a straight line is the shortest connection between two points, but the cynic (Diogenes of Sinope)[24] rightly observed that this truth must be known also to a dog who darts toward his prey in a straight line. The idealist, as distinct from the egotist (solipsist), agrees with the dualist (realist)[25] that not all associations of ideas are subjective and that there exists an objective series of notions common to all thinking beings. What he denies is the right to assume the existence of external objects causing the series of objective thoughts. In the idealist's view extension and mobility are merely concepts that cannot be legitimately ascribed to an externally real matter. Mendelssohn tried to show that the area of disagreement between the idealist and the realist might be narrowed considerably if the meanings of the terms they used were properly analyzed. When the realist said that a thing was "extended" and "mobile," these words signified merely that a thing had such properties that it must be thought to be extended and mobile; to be A and to be thought to be A were the same thing. Hence in saying that matter was extended and mobile we merely asserted that there were prototypes *(Urbilder)* of our thoughts or mental images outside ourselves that appeared to every thinking being as extended and mobile.

In lecture seven Mendelssohn pursued this line of thought further in the direction of Kantianism.[26] If one was satisfied to know what the external *Urbild* caused us to think about it, it was futile to press for a knowledge of what this *Urbild* was "in itself." Wanting to know this was tantamount to wishing to know what was in fact not an object of knowledge. "We stand [here] at the limit not only of human knowledge but of knowledge as such; and we desire to reach beyond that limit without knowing whither. If I tell you what a thing effects and how it is affected, do not go on asking what it is. When I tell you what kind of conception [*Begriff*] you have to form of a thing, the further question, that of what the thing is in itself,[27] is meaningless." "I am afraid," Mendelssohn concluded, "that the famous controversy among the materialists, idealists, and dualists amounts in the end to a mere verbal dispute, which concerns the linguist more than it does the speculative philosopher."[28]

Before passing on to the main theme of the book (i.e., the "doctrine of God"), Mendelssohn emphasized yet another "preliminary notion," and one that promised to be of "great utility" in the discussion ahead: the customary division of the faculties of the soul *(Seelenvermögen)* into those of cognition and desire had to be enlarged. The sentiments of pleasure and displeasure, which were usually lumped together with desire, formed a group of their own. Mendelssohn here elaborated what he had noted down as early as 1776, giving particular stress to the notion of "disinterested pleasure," to use Kant's phrase in the *Critique of Judgment* (1790), which may well be indebted to Mendelssohn.[29] Between cognition and desire, Mendelssohn suggested, there lay the act of approbation, of applause, the soul's delight, which truly speaking was still a far cry from desire:[30] "We contemplate the beauty of nature and art with pleasure and delight, [and] without the least stirring of desire. On the contrary, it seems to be a special characteristic of beauty that it is contemplated with a quiet delight; that it pleases even if we do not own it and are ever so far removed from a desire to use it.... I shall call it [this particular faculty] 'capacity of approbation' so as to distinguish it... from [both] the cognition of truth...[and] the desire for the good. It represents, as it were, the transition from knowing to desiring and connects these two faculties by the most subtle gradation."

Mendelssohn distinguished the true and the false as the "matter" of cognition from the beautiful and the ugly, the good and the evil, as the "form" of cognition (i.e. of approval and disapproval). While there could be no more or less in the true and false, the objects of approval and disapproval were essentially subject to a comparative evaluation. Nothing was beautiful or ugly, good or evil, in an absolute and final sense. Everything may possibly become "the best" somewhere and sometime. For the very nature of these qualities (or values, to use a modern term) consists in their being given "preference" *(Vorzug)*.[31] The background for this assertion is unquestionably Leibniz' *Theodicy*. As the subsequent discussion shows, Mendelssohn equated the divine decree, which is ultimately responsible for all good and evil in the world, with the act of approbation. As in the sketch of 1776 so in the *Morgenstunden* Mendelssohn also differentiated between the objectivity of cognition and the subjectivity of approval, in the sense that in searching for true knowledge we seek to adapt our thinking to reality as it is, whereas the act of approbation tends to make reality conform to our standards.

Lecture eight introduces the principal theme of the book by stressing its "importance" for "man's happiness and peace of mind." "Without God, Providence, and immortality all the goods of life are of despicable value in my eyes, and our days on earth are ... like a pilgrimage in storm and rain without the comforting hope of finding shelter at night in an inn."[32] However, our partiality for a doctrine as consoling as the one embracing these truths must not interfere with the objectivity of our search for the truth. Johann Bernhard Basedow, it should be recalled, had tried to establish a new epistemological principle, "the duty to believe":[33] a proposition indispensable for securing human happiness must be accepted, Basedow declared, and since it could be demonstrated that human happiness was indissolubly connected with the belief in God, Providence, and immortality, it followed that this belief was mandatory. Mendelssohn disagreed. The concept of duty was inapplicable to the holding of opinions or convictions concerning the true and the false. Here impartial inquiry was the only obligation incumbent upon us. One could speak of "duty" only in respect of matters involving our faculty of approbation. Wishful thinking had no place when our goal was the truth. The task before us was, therefore, to *demonstrate* the existence of God. Once this task had been accomplished, we would be in a position to argue that an all-benign being could have approved and produced only the best and most perfect.

It may be safely assumed that in rejecting Basedow's notion of a "duty to believe" Mendelssohn also meant to repudiate, by innuendo, Jacobi's plea for a leap of faith, a plea that Mendelssohn could not discuss openly because the antecedents of the *Morgenstunden* were to be ignored in the book itself. But by insisting that "the spirit of inquiry" had to be kept alive and alert at all times, and that "blind faith" led to superstition and fanaticism, Mendelssohn certainly wished to imply that he, not Jacobi, was the true guardian of Lessing's legacy.[34]

Following these introductory observations, Mendelssohn proceeded to the heart of the matter by laying down seven *axiomata*. They summarized the most relevant insights gained in the preparatory section, adding merely the distinction between necessary eternal truths, accidental eternal truths, and historical truths. This threefold division, which we met already in the *Jerusalem,* is here connected with the differentiation between cognition and approbation. Necessary eternal truths cannot be nonreal, while accidental eternal truths (viz. the laws of nature) and temporal truths might be nonreal but for an act of approbation (i.e., for formal, not for material reasons).

The survey in lecture nine of the three methods of demonstrating the existence of God follows more or less the pattern familiar from the prize-essay on evidence. God's existence is inferred from the reality of a sensible world outside ourselves or from my own existence, and can also be shown by the a priori method (i.e., the ontological proof). In dealing with the objections to the a posteriori proofs Mendelssohn mentioned the idealists, egotists (solipsists), skeptics, and Spinozists. The answer to the doubts raised by these adversaries was to be found in common sense, and lecture ten gave Mendelssohn an opportunity to expound the relationship between reason, common sense, and speculative philosophy. As in the essay on Condillac's *Statue,* he related an "allegorical dream." In this one he belonged to a group touring the Swiss Alps. Their guides were a young and sturdy native of rather coarse intelligence and a tall, gaunt woman of serious disposition, with eyes cast down and features that betrayed an enthusiastic nature. At a crossroad they seemed to quarrel and then took different directions. Uncertain whom to follow, the party noticed a somewhat aged lady slowly approaching them. She explained that the guides, named Common Sense and Contemplation, often disagreed for a short while for petty reasons but were in the habit of returning, if the travelers refused to follow either of them, to have their dispute decided by her. Common Sense was usually right, and Contemplation yielded to the verdict; but when the judgment went against Common Sense, as it did occasionally, it had little chance of convincing the stubborn fellow that the other side had, for once, hit upon the truth. The travelers, however, knew that the old lady could be trusted. When one of the party asked her name, she answered: In this world I am called Reason, while heavenly beings——. Before she could finish her sentence, a terrific noise cut her short. A crowd of enthusiasts had gathered around Contemplation and had resolved to expel both Common Sense and Reason. With clamor and violent motions they closed in upon the group, which took fright—and the dreamer awoke.

The fictional dream narrated by Mendelssohn depicts in the form of a nightmare his extreme anxiety about the changing intellectual climate of the time. In his view, materialism on the one hand, and enthusiasm on the other, threatened both the authority of reason and the rightful claims of sound common sense. The gains of the Enlightenment, which were based on reason, and the simple truths of universal religion, which were anchored in common sense and not in the extravagancies of mystical faith, were both under attack by a clamorous crowd personified, in his mind, by Jacobi. Mendelssohn did not indulge, however, in "psycho-analyzing" his dream. He interpreted its meaning in the following way:[35] "Truly speaking, I am wont to use this rule for my guidance also when awake. Whenever speculation seems to lead me too far away from the high road of common sense, I pause and try to orient myself. I look back to the point from which we departed and seek to compare my two guides. Experience has taught me that common sense is usually right, and reason has to tip the balance very decisively in favor of speculation if I am to abandon common sense." Mendelssohn's resolve to check the flights of speculation[36] by sound common sense was praised by Kant when eventually he took his public stand in the Mendelssohn/Jacobi controversy. Kant's essay *What Does it Mean: To Orient Oneself in Thinking?*[37] said of Mendelssohn that he maintained "steadfastly and with just zeal" the need to orient oneself with the help of "authentic and pure human reason." He added, however, that Mendelssohn had allowed too much to the speculative faculty.

The idealistic position, which denies the objective reality of a material world, is contradicted by common sense, yet it has to be considered as weakening the force of the cosmological argument for the existence of God. The second proof, the one inferring the existence of an immutable necessary being ("God") from my own mutable being, is therefore to be preferred. Mendelssohn gave this Cartesian proof a new turn by applying the principle of approbation to the successive changes in temporal reality. Yet he refused to concede that idealism really invalidated the cosmological argument. Assuming that the walls of a room were covered with mirrors, each reflecting an object in a certain perspective, the constancy of the features seen in different perspectives proved the existence of an object that would be reflected in a supreme being, provided such a being existed, in the purest light and without any modifying admixture of perspective. The idealist was content to acknowledge the reflections in the various mirrors (i.e. minds) and considered the question of whether or not they corresponded to an object as irrelevant or unanswerable. Mendelssohn had previously admitted that the quest for the "thing in itself" was meaningless, and that the controversy between idealism and realism amounted to a mere verbal dispute. Here he sought to show that the presence in the mind of both a constant element (the truth) and of variables (perspectives) argued in favor of realism. God knows the *Urbild*, the "thing in itself," in its pure truth.

Lecture eleven discusses further objections to the cosmological argument. The question of how the possible became real had been answered in the epicurean school by invoking the principle of chance or the purely accidental. Here Mendelssohn interposed a personal remark:[38] "Since, as you know, I received my first tuition in the Hebrew tongue, I used to translate in my mind every significant term that I read or heard in another language into Hebrew. I found no genuine ancient Hebrew term for 'chance' or 'accident.' The word by which later authors rendered these notions signified originally something 'sent,' 'allotted,' 'occurring' to us—what a higher power has caused to come our way, and hence almost the opposite of chance and accident. What is 'allotted' and what is 'accidental' have in common only an absence of intent and causative action on the part of man, and this seems to have motivated the [Jewish] translators from the Arabic, who had to couch Greek notions in Hebrew words, to choose a word that bore some similarity with the original."[39] (There was never any inhibition on Mendelssohn's part to refer to his roots in Hebrew culture. On the contrary, he often took the opportunity to do so. The passage just quoted is also a clear indication of his scholarly approach to medieval Hebrew philosophical texts. He did not ignore the fact that some of the classical works had originally been written in Arabic.)[40] Continuing his analysis of the terms "chance" and "accident," he pointed out that they implied not merely the absence of all human intent and activity but also the denial of any purpose in chance happenings and the denial of any efficient cause in accidental events. In fact, however, even Epicurus admitted the necessity of a material cause and considered the atoms eternal. He also conceded efficient causes, viz. the motions of the atoms. What Epicurus denied was purposiveness, or final causes. All the beautiful, great, and sublime that we admire in nature was the product of blind chance, a theory that had been propagated anew by LaMettrie.

Before examining the validity of this view, Mendelssohn surveyed briefly the discussion about the possibility or impossibility of an infinite series of causes and effects. Some philosophers denied the eternity of the world *a parte ante* and assumed the existence of a necessary eternal Being as the first cause of all that exists. The chain of being must be fixed to the throne of the All-Powerful in order to achieve reality. Others saw in the denial of an infinite and independent series a *petitio principii*.[41]

In lecture twelve Mendelssohn attempted to answer the misgivings put forward by the defenders of an infinite series. Some philosophers, he pointed out, had inferred the existence of a necessary, immutable Being from the existence of contingent and mutable being, without presupposing the impossibility of an infinite series. The Leibnizians had done this with the help of the principle of sufficient reason, and Mendelssohn offered a succinct account of the way they had argued. He undertook, however, to reach the same conclusion with the aid of the principles he had enunciated. The reason for the existence of a contingent being or its dependence on a necessary Being cannot be found in its cognoscibility. For if this were the case, it would be real not merely somewhere and at some time but at all times and it would immutably remain the same, since as an object of cognition it is immutable and eternal. Its dependence on the necessary Being is rather to be found in the circumstance that it has become an object of the faculty of approbation. Only from this aspect can its mutability be reasonably accounted for and can it be understood why it becomes real now in this and now in that form. Hence the one true reason for the dependence of a contingent being from the necessary Being lies in an act of approbation and free choice by the latter. This necessary Being itself has the reason for its existence in its very essence, in its inner possibility, i.e. it exists because it is thinkable; its nonexistence is unthinkable and therefore an untruth. If this concept is properly developed, it leads to the a priori demonstration of the existence of a necessary Being from its mere conceivability. Mendelssohn left this proof for the last lecture. In the present context he was content to draw the following conclusions from the concept of the faculty of approbation: "All that is, is the best. . . . All thoughts of God, insofar as they aim at the best, become real. . . . God is the creator and preserver of the best universe."

Lectures thirteen, fourteen and fifteen interrupt the sequence of the arguments for God's existence by a discussion of Spinozism and Lessing. These lectures form a literary unit and will be treated as such. We conclude our account of the treatment of the principal theme by skipping to lectures sixteen and seventeen.

In lecture sixteen Mendelssohn first tried to define more clearly what he meant by the term "independent and necessary Being." Things whose reality did not follow from their conceivability were merely contingent, and insofar as their reality derived from the reality of other things they were dependent. Now, it had been shown that the totality of contingent beings, even assuming it represented an infinite series, was in the same position as individual contingent things: its reality could not be rationally explained because it did not follow from its conceivability. To make its reality intelligible we had to go on presupposing the reality of other things ad infinitum. We were therefore compelled to resort to the existence of an independent and necessary Being, an independent Being whose reality is conceivable without the presupposition of some other thing as its efficient cause; and of a necessary Being the conceivability of which is sufficient to account for its reality.

There was, however, Mendelssohn suggested, yet another way to prove the existence of God, a way that, so far as he knew, had not been proposed before. This proof goes as follows: I am not merely that which I distinctly perceive and know of myself. My existence comprises more than what I am conscious of, and even what I do know about myself is capable of being understood more precisely and in a more comprehensive manner. Neither our body nor our soul could exist if they were merely what we know of them distinctly. "Now I contend that not only must everything possible be thought as possible by some thinking being, but that everything real must also be thought real by some mind. What no thinking being conceives as possible is in fact not possible, and what no thinking being thinks real is in fact not real."

So far as the possible was concerned, Mendelssohn pointed out, the statement was readily acceptable. The thought of something that was merely possible or conceivable was by its very nature an ideal reality (i.e. a concept of a thinking being). Yet, he insisted, everything real had to be conceived and understood as true by some being. To every thing a concept had to correspond; every object had to be represented in some subject. A thing that was not conceived had no truth; truth carried not the least bit of evidence and hence was not truth unless some being was assured of it.

Once these propositions were admitted, it followed in the most obvious manner that there must exist a being that conceives everything appertaining to my existence in the most distinct, pure, and comprehensive way. Every limited knowledge failed to comprise all that belongs to my real existence. The consciousness and the distinct knowledge of a contingent being, nay of all contingent beings in their totality, grasped the existence of not so much as a single mote. In brief, no truth could be thought by contingent beings with the highest degree of knowledge either as possible or as real. Hence there must be *one* thinking being, *one* intellect, which thinks the totality of all possibilities as possible and the totality of all realities as real, and does so in the most perfect way. There is, therefore, an infinite Intellect. Mendelssohn added an extremely ingenious defense of this proof against the objection that while everything real had to be conceivable it did not follow that it had actually to be conceived by some thinking being.[42]

In his last lecture, the seventeenth, Mendelssohn made a valiant attempt to rescue the ontological argument, which Kant had subjected to attack as long ago as 1763 and, more recently, in his *Critique of Pure Reason*.[43] In his prize-essay Mendelssohn had presented a novel nuance of this argument based on Baumgarten's ontology,[44] and in 1778 he had taken it upon himself to reformulate the proof.[45] Though he knew only too well that some of his closest friends had remained unconvinced,[46] he clung to it tenaciously. Lecture seventeen of the *Morgenstunden* harked back to the treatment of the theme in the prize-essay but also took cognizance of the opposition that had developed since.

Having stated Descartes' and Leibniz' presentations of the ontological argument, Mendelssohn quoted the protest of "some adversaries":[47] "You [Mendelssohn] still build on ground whose solidity you have not properly investigated. You arbitrarily form an abstract notion and attribute all conceivable qualities to it. We cannot deny you the freedom to do so and permit the concept to be valid. Yet hardly have you gained our consent surreptitiously, than you reach for existence and say: in order to make the bundle complete, we have also to include this quality and must assign real existence to the concept. Is this not a disingenuous[48] procedure?"

Mendelssohn did not think so: "I believe I can justify . . . [my] procedure against all accusations of this kind." There was nothing arbitrary or surreptitious in his argument; the concept of the most perfect Being was inconceivable if it excluded reality. Mendelssohn realized that he could not silence his opposition merely by restating the old view, even though he had tried to refurbish it in an intervening passage: "Precisely here, the adversaries exclaim, lies the surreptitiousness. You take existence to be a quality of the thing, which supervenes upon all its possible qualities so as to call them into being. According to the definition of your school, you consider existence as a 'complement of essence' [*complementum essentiae*], as an addition, so to speak, to the possibility of a thing.[49] . . . But this presupposition cannot be conceded. Existence is no mere quality, no addition, no complement but is the positing of all qualities and characteristics of the thing, without which they remain mere abstract concepts." Mendelssohn was not at all impressed by this Kantian objection. Though he was ready to admit that existence was not a quality but the positing of all qualities, it could not be separated from the notion of the necessary Being without annihilating that notion.

It is not surprising that Kant considered the *Morgenstunden* an exercise in the very kind of dogmatic and purely speculative use of reason that his *Critique* had set out to demolish. He nevertheless cherished and praised the work as the most perfect paradigm of Enlightenment metaphysics. His appreciation was expressed in a letter to the Jena professor Christian Gottfried Schütz, who quoted it verbatim and in full at the end of his respectful and friendly review of the *Morgenstunden* in the *Allgemeine Literatur-Zeitung*:[50]

> Although the work of the worthy M[endelssohn] is to be considered in the main as a masterpiece of the self-deception of our reason . . . it is [nevertheless] an excellent work. Apart from the sagacious and novel things stated with exemplary clarity in the "Preliminary Notions" on truth, appearance and error—things that can very well be used in every philosophical lecture—it will prove of considerable value for the critique of human reason by its second section. For since the author . . . eventually arrives at the conclusion that nothing is conceivable unless it is actually conceived by some being and that no object can be real unless it be conceived; and since, moreover, he concludes that an infinite and active intellect must be real, . . . this extremely sharp-witted pursuance of the chain of our conceptions, to the extent that they embrace total being, offers a splendid opportunity, as well as a challenge, to subject our capacity of pure reason to a radical critique . . .
>
> As a result, pure philosophy is bound to gain, even assuming that after examination it turned out that illusion had interfered . . . One may also regard this final bequest of dogmatizing metaphysics as its most perfect

product, ... and as an enduringly valuable monument to the sagacity of a man who knows and controls the whole force of the mode of thinking that he has adopted ...

While Kant and some of his early followers (Schütz and Jakob) admired the *Morgenstunden* as the testament of an obsolete philosophy, others hailed it as a vigorous counterblast to Kant's work, as may be gathered from a letter written to Kant on March 26, 1786 by Ludwig Heinrich Jakob, his "disciple and admirer" in Halle:[51] "Mendelssohn deserved to have his treatise meet with applause, and I believe that everyone, including those who disagree with him, will gratefully acknowledge the lucid manner, so characteristic of him, in which he expounded the traditional arguments for the existence of God. Right at the outset, however, I heard some triumphal songs. Coming as they did more from the heart than from the head, they were all the more readily accepted. They attributed to Herr Mendelssohn a victory toward which, according to his own confession,[52] he had never aspired. Some reviewers, in fact, clearly indicated that in their view the Kantian *Critique* had been dealt a serious blow by this treatise." The *Gothaische Zeitung* had reported that Kant had decided to refute Mendelssohn's *Morgenstunden*,[53] and Jakob, who was anxious to try his hand at the subject, wondered whether it might not be a good idea if he, as an outsider, pursued this plan even if Kant adhered to his. The *Critique*, he pointed out, was still widely regarded as a "big animal" that inspired fear but not confidence, and the attachment to the old system was so strong that highly gifted philosophers condemned the *Critique* clandestinely, if not in public. Would Kant, Jakob inquired, have a look at his manuscript and tell him whether he considered it worthy of publication. Kant replied on May 26, 1786[54] that the newspaper report of his alleged intentions was not true and that pressure of other work prevented his undertaking to "refute the *Morgenstunden*." He welcomed Jakob's initiative, and promised to contribute to his work some remarks on a passage in Mendelssohn to which Jakob had drawn attention.

This promise was kept. Jakob's *Examination of Mendelssohn's "Morgenstunden"*[55] did indeed include "Some Remarks by Herr Professor Kant" (pp. xlix–lx).[56] The tone of these remarks, though still respectful, betrays Kant's annoyance at his adversaries' "rejoicing" (as Jakob had put it) in Mendelssohn's "victory." The unshaken confidence that Mendelssohn had in the demonstrability of the principal thesis of pure reason, Kant said, understandably tempted one to consider a "scrupulous critique" as unjustified and as refuted by his very performance. Jakob's work had shown the fallacy of such a facile assumption. All Kant wished to add was an exposure of two ways by which "the sagacious Mendelssohn" had tried to avoid the laborious business of adjudicating the self-contradictions of pure reason.

In the manner of some easygoing judges, Kant declared, Mendelssohn had sought either to compose the conflict by an amicable settlement or to dismiss it as lying beyond the competence of any court of justice. The first of these two methods was implied in Mendelssohn's favorite reduction of philosophical problems to mere verbal quibbles. Thus in one of his essays he had tried to resolve the old problem of freedom and necessity by distinguishing between two meanings of the word "must,"[57] which was like trying to hold the ocean back with a wisp of straw. The "subtle man" had used this very same "trick" throughout the *Morgenstunden*. Mendelssohn's second "maxim," Kant went on to say, consisted in his practice of arresting the process of inquiry at a certain stage and thereby simply "stopping the questioner's mouth." As evidence of this procedure Kant quoted Mendelssohn's contention that having established what a thing effected or how it was affected we could safely ignore the question of what the "thing in itself" was. Kant maintained that since we knew of a thing only its spatial relations, it was quite legitimate to ask what it was in itself. The rather drastic language used by Kant on this occasion was obviously designed to disqualify Mendelssohn's *Morgenstunden* as a serious challenge to his *Critique*. But that Kant should have felt the need to write his "remarks" at all illustrates the favorable impression that Mendelssohn's work had created in some circles, at least.

II

As the reader will recall, Mendelssohn's reason for undertaking the "sisyphean labor" of writing the *Morgenstunden* was far from being purely academic. Though originally announced as a refutation of Spinozism, the real concern of the work was the portrayal of Lessing in a manner calculated to neutralize, if not to nullify, the effect of any future disclosures by Jacobi. Mendelssohn kept this tactical consideration, which was the primary aim of the book, a closely guarded secret even from his best friends,[1] though by sending the manuscript to Doctor Reimarus[2] he made him, in a sense, a partner in his plan (but without breathing a word about it to the doctor). In his comments[3] Doctor Reimarus discussed Mendelssohn's critique of Spinozism but, strangely enough, remained silent on the author's interpretation of Lessing. Yet the preface of the *Morgenstunden* included a veiled reference to the "special reason that occasioned the present publication of this treatise" and would be explained in a subsequent volume. It is most unlikely that Mendelssohn seriously contemplated writing a sequel to the work. Having agreed to a "contest" with Jacobi, and having decided first to delineate his position, it was part of the game, as it were, to hold out the prospect of a second part of the book. But he made no definite promise: how soon the sequel would follow, could not yet be determined. It would depend, principally, on how Part One was received. As matters turned out, Jacobi's unexpected counterstroke necessitated the writing of a second book far sooner, and with far greater urgency, than Mendelssohn could have imagined. He was gravely mistaken in supposing that three chapters in the *Morgenstunden,* chapters thirteen, fourteen, and fifteen, dealing with Lessing and Spinozism, would dispose of this issue once and for all.

Chapter thirteen purports to be a straightforward "refutation" of Spinozism. Unlike Jacobi, who designated Spinozism as atheism, Mendelssohn defined it as pantheism or, to use a more adequate modern term, as panentheism. According to the Spinozists, Mendelssohn said, God was the only necessary and the only possible substance, and all else was but a modification of this substance. As modes of the one infinite substance, we and the sensible world outside us "lived and moved and had our being"[4] in God. This New Testament phrase is used twice in the same chapter,[5] and in quoting it Mendelssohn followed Spinoza himself, who in a letter to Heinrich Oldenberg[6] had written: "Like Paul, and perhaps also like all ancient philosophers, I affirm, albeit in a different way, that all things live and move in God; and I would dare to say that I agree also with the ancient Hebrews, insofar as it is possible to surmise from some of their traditions, which are, however, in many respects adulterated." Taking his cue from the formula *Hen kai Pan* mentioned in Jacobi's report, Mendelssohn summarized Spinozism in the sentence: "One is All, and All is One."[7] He went on to say that this doctrine had exercised a certain fascination upon both mystics *(Schwärmer)* and atheists, since it seemed to have a certain affinity to both kinds of error. That it could easily be mistaken for atheism was not surprising. Mendelssohn did not elaborate this point since there was no need to do so. The charge of atheism against Spinoza had been of long standing. As for the alleged closeness of Spinozism to the other extreme, he referred to Johann Georg Wachter's *Spinozism in Judaism,*[8] where it had been indicated that Spinoza's system had its origin and foundation in the kabbalistic *Schwärmerey.*

Wachter's *Spinozism in Judaism* was a polemical treatise directed against Moses Germanus (Johann Peter Speeth), a Swabian who had converted to Judaism and professed the belief that Spinoza's doctrine was based on the Kabbala. In later years Wachter became himself a devotee of Kabbala and wrote another work, *Elucidarius cabalisticus,*[9] which aimed at reconciling Kabbala and Spinozism. Mendelssohn knew both treatises.[10] In his letter to Elise dated August 16, 1783,[11] he quoted Wachter's thesis that Spinozism was an offshoot of kabbalistic teaching, a theory that had also been taken very seriously by Leibniz.[12] Jacobi was likewise convinced that Spinozism and Kabbala were closely related; when writing to Mendelssohn on April 26, 1785,[13] he compared the fight over the dead body of Spinoza to that of the archangel and Satan over the body of Moses, and he added the remark: "Those of the archangel's party look for light to Wachter's *Elucidarius cabalisticus.*" He had sent a copy of the *Elucidarius* to Herder, who replied on December 20, 1784, that although he had not yet had an opportunity to read the book, he was afraid that Jacobi had misjudged Spinoza:[14] "His only substance is the *ens realissimum* in which all that is truth, inner life, and existence is inwardly and radically united, . . . and as modifications of the highest, infinite, inner existence these attributes are conceivable only insofar as they partake of its nature and inasmuch as the only existent enduringly dwells in them." Herder's view of Spinoza was quite close to Mendelssohn's of purified Spinozism, and his final answer to Jacobi was given in his "Dialogues on Spinoza's System" entitled *God:*[15] "It seems to me that the [true] philosophy of Spinoza is as different from Kabbala as it is a futile effort to try to purify the latter by the former."

At what point, Mendelssohn asked, did Spinoza part company with the theists? The following propositions were shared by both schools: the necessary Being thinks itself as absolutely necessary, and it thinks the contingent beings as reduceable to an infinite series.[16] Disagreement starts as soon as the question is posed whether the contingent beings possess substantiality in the sense of separate existence, or whether they are mere modifications of the necessary substance. The theist (i.e., the follower of the Leibniz/Wolffian school), though admitting that finite beings depend on the infinite and are inconceivable without it, nevertheless holds that they have a separate existence—that they live and move and have their being not in God but outside him, as effects of his power. The Spinozist, who defines substance as separate as well as independent being, rejects the notion of more than one infinite substance and denies the substantiality of finite beings. Accepting Descartes' division of being into extension and thought, he speaks of these as the two attributes of infinite substance. Yet why should the term "substance" be used only in the sense of separate as well as independent, necessary being? Could one not distinguish between substantiality in the sense of separate existence and substantiality as independent as well as separate being? The theist did not ascribe substantiality of the second sort to finite or contingent existence. If Spinoza refused to call dependent being by the name of substance, the dispute resolved itself into a mere *Wortstreit,* and there was no real conflict.

Spinoza might have replied to Mendelssohn what he in fact had written in *Cogitata Metaphysica* (I, 3): "I am not accustomed to disputing about mere names."[17] However, in lecture fourteen Mendelssohn was able to refer to a passage in Spinoza's *Ethics* that in a way justified his "maxim"—as Kant would derisively call it—to seek to reduce conflicts to verbal disputes. The passage (II, 47, scholium), which he quoted in Latin, reads:[18] "Most controversies arise because people do not correctly explain their opinion or because they wrongly interpret the other person's opinion. For it is indeed the case that while they violently contradict each other, they either think alike or have something else in mind; so much so that the errors and absurdities assumed to exist in other people's minds do not exist." Mendelssohn may have overindulged in the application of his "maxim,"[19] but he could have invoked, in addition to Spinoza's, similar utterances by Leibniz, Wolff, and Lambert, among others.[20]

Continuing his critique of Spinoza, Mendelssohn made the following observation: Spinoza, like Descartes, had seen in extension the essence of matter and in thinking the essence of mind. He had regarded the totality of bodies as unified in a single substance, and he was able to do so because he had failed to take account of motion, which was the "form" of matter. But bodies had not only matter but also form, and the question had to be asked: what is the origin of motion in an organic matter and, particularly, in organic bodies that move in regular, designed fashion? It cannot be found in the whole, for the whole as such is motionless; qua a single substance, it can neither change its place nor be endowed with organization and figure. Hence the origin of motion can lie only in the parts as individual, separate beings. The whole must therefore be regarded as the mere aggregate of the parts, and the parts cannot be mere modifications of the one substance. If they were but modifications of the whole, they could have only such qualities as derived from the whole. An analogous objection could be raised to Spinoza's view of mind. He had considered merely the "material" aspect of thinking: truth and untruth had their origin in thinking as an attribute of the infinite substance. He had ignored the faculties of approbation and desire, which were the source of goodness and perfection, pleasure and displeasure, etc.

Whence could these "formal" aspects of mind derive if the whole was incapable of premeditation, planning, approbation, and desire. What was the origin of approving and desiring if individual beings had no separate, substantial existence but were merely modifications of the one substance from which these capacities were said to be absent? True, Spinoza denied free will and recognized only necessity. The problem raised might therefore be said not to constitute a valid objection. Yet in denying free will, Spinoza denied only what the determinists called the *aequilibrium indifferentiae*—the absolute freedom of choice in which no particular inclination tilts the perfect balance. He had no reason to deny freedom of choice that was motivated by the knowledge of good and evil.[21] Yet once he admitted (at least in finite beings) the distinction between good and evil, between the desirable and the nondesirable, etc., he had also to admit the distinction between the physically necessary and the morally necessary. Consequently, he was bound to concede that the attribute of thinking did not imply the attribute of approving, and that good and evil derived from a source other than the thinking of truth and untruth. "But where is this source to be found if no trace of it can be met with in the qualities of the one substance?" The epistemological distinction between the "matter" and the "form" of mental operations, which Mendelssohn had elaborated in the introductory lectures of the *Morgenstunden,* here paid him handsome dividends.

Mendelssohn recalled Wolff's refutation of Spinoza in Part Two of his *Theologia naturalis:*[22] An infinite series of finite beings represented nothing more than an extensive infinity. In terms of intensity it still remained finite. Yet only an intensively infinite power could be described as independent and requiring no other beings for its existence. Hence Spinoza would have to admit that, in addition to the totality of all finite beings, a single infinite Being must presumed to exist and to have infinite power.

Wolff's lucid and elaborate refutation of Spinoza, Mendelssohn remarked, had never been challenged, so far as he knew. He himself wished merely to offer another argument in proof of the thesis that an extensive infinite could not be independent but needed for its existence a power that was infinite, (i.e. an extramundane God). If for Spinoza the universe or the true substance was the totality of all material and thinking beings, this very concept presupposed the existence of a subject that embraced in its thinking the infinite variety of finite beings in the most perfectly distinct manner.

In the *Phaedon*[23] Mendelssohn had demonstrated the immateriality of the soul by pointing out that we had to presuppose the soul's activity in order to explain that an aggregate or any combination of parts into units presented itself to the mind. Isaak Iselin had suggested that this proof might also be used to show the immaterial nature and unity of God, and Mendelssohn had replied on September 10, 1767, that this "happy thought" *(glücklicher Einfall)* had much pleased him:[24] "I consider it possible and also very useful to implement it." He felt, however, the need for additional proof that God was not merely a "world soul," as might be inferred from this kind of reasoning. Our passage in the *Morgenstunden*[25] offered the implementation of Iselin's *Einfall* without any additional proof, which was deemed unnecessary because an infinite and perfect intellect that comprised the universe in all its aspects, with full clarity and as a unity, was more than a world soul: "That this limitless Mind must be of infinite power, separate in its existence and independent, is self-evident."

Lecture thirteen concludes with an expression of confidence that Spinoza, "this honest searcher for truth," would not have resisted the force of the argument had it been brought to his attention. He would have admitted that the unity of the infinite substance, with all its modifications both corporeal and spiritual, subsisted in a transcendent Mind that alone combined the variety of the parts into a system. Mendelssohn rejoiced in the prospect of being able to embrace a hypothetically converted Spinoza as a "friend" of the Leibniz/Wolffian doctrine.

The note of excessive optimism sounded at the end of lecture thirteen was an artful device intended to provide a cue for the opening of lecture fourteen: "By no means, my friend Lessing would have exclaimed, had he attended our last lecture; you are still far removed from the goal and you shout 'victory!' before you have conquered. Even assuming that all your objections to Spinoza were correct, in the end you would have refuted only Spinoza, not Spinozism." What follows is an imaginary dialogue between Lessing and Mendelssohn in which Lessing defends Spinozism in its "purified" form, as irrefutable from Leibnizian premises, and Mendelssohn, though attacking this claim, tries to show that the difference between them amounted to a mere "subtlety" having no practical consequences.

By presenting a fictitious dialogue between Lessing and himself Mendelssohn offered a counterpart to the Lessing/Jacobi discussion that was designed to take the wind out of Jacobi's sails should he ever publish his report. Mendelssohn was convinced that the fictitious dialogue he had written presented the authentic views of Lessing, whereas Jacobi's report of his conversations with Lessing, though presumably an accurate account of what had been said, gave a distorted picture; the report showed Lessing in a jovial mood and not in a serious frame of mind or ready to debate Spinozism on the same level of sophistication that had characterized his and Mendelssohn's debates on this subject. With Jacobi, Lessing had obviously been more interested in drawing out his partner than he was in seriously probing the issues. Otherwise he would hardly have remained silent when Jacobi took it for granted that, as Mendelssohn had "publicly shown," the Leibnizian doctrine of the preestablished harmony was prefigured in Spinoza, and when from this Jacobi inferred that additional Leibnizian notions might also have been anticipated by Spinoza.[26] As Mendelssohn knew only too well, Lessing had attacked this contention during his stay in Breslau when he had immersed himself in the study of Spinoza and begun to reëxamine the *Philosophical Dialogues*.[27] While Jacobi could judge Lessing's view of Spinozism only on the basis of what Lessing had chosen to reveal to him on a single occasion, Mendelssohn had the advantage of being able to recall their many talks on the subject in the early days—talks that had crystallized in the *Philosophical Dialogues*—and he could also reread the letters in which his late friend had expressed his revised opinions on various aspects of Spinozism. One such letter (unfortunately not extant) must have contained a copy (or at least an extract) from the fragment "On the Reality of Things Outside God,"[28] which dated from Lessing's Breslau period and affirmed the very position of purified Spinozism versus Leibnizianism that Mendelssohn would put into Lessing's mouth in lecture fourteen of the *Morgenstunden*.

Mendelssohn had not been unduly perturbed by Jacobi's disclosure of Lessing's Spinozism, it will be recalled, because he had immediately associated it with the purified Spinozism that Lessing had defended in the said fragment and propounded as his own view in the youthful essay *The Christianity of Reason*, the manuscript of which Karl Lessing had sent to Mendelssohn on April 22, 1783. As noted already, he had copied portions of this manuscript before returning it to Karl. But now the full text had become available in a volume containing Lessing's theological *Nachlass* that had appeared in spring, 1785.[29] Mendelssohn was therefore in a position to clinch his interpretation of Lessing by quoting a published text. Mendelssohn presented this documentary evidence at the end of lecture fifteen, as the climax of his proof.

In the fictitious dialogue, Lessing concedes the validity of the various objections to Spinoza that Mendelssohn has raised. The Spinozist or pantheist could admit the difference between the true and the good, between knowing and approving, and could recognize the necessity of seeing the source of both in the one infinite substance of divinity. He was also able to admit the difference between the extensive and the intensive infinite, and to agree that the necessary Being was infinitely powerful, perfect, and wise; that the divine intellect had a most distinct and comprehensive notion of all contingent beings in their infinite variety; and that it gave preference to the best series of possible worlds. In other words, Lessing is made to appear in complete agreement with the "theist" of the Leibnizian school, insofar as the concept of God is concerned.

The point of disagreement is said to relate to the objectivity of the world. While the theist asserted that God, having approved the best possible world, imparted to it objective existence in addition to its intradeical ideal existence, the pantheist denied the need to admit this. "How can you convince him," Lessing is made to ask, "of this objective existence outside the divine intellect? Who can prove that we and the world around us possess more than ideal existence in the divine mind; that they are more than mere thoughts of God and modifications of his primordial power?" "If I understand you correctly," Mendelssohn observes, "you admit, on behalf of your pantheist, an extramundane God but deny an extradeical world and make God an infinite egotist [solipsist], as it were." Lessing admits that this is indeed his view. His pantheism, he says, resembles a two-headed hydra. One head proclaims, All is One; the other, One is All. The monster could be killed only if both heads were cut off at the same time—a Herculean task.

At this point Mendelssohn attributed to Lessing an elaborate piece of reasoning that clearly reflects the incisive and lengthy argument found in Lessing's fragment "On the Reality of Things Outside God." Lessing had written:[30] "In whatever way I may try to explain to myself the reality of things outside God, I must confess that I fail to understand it. Let it [viz. the reality of a thing] be called the 'complement of possibility';[31] I ask: is there a concept of this complement of possibility in God, or is there not? Who would wish to affirm the second alternative? Yet if there is in him a concept of it, the thing itself is in him, and all things are real in him.

One might object that the concept that God has of the reality of a thing does not abolish the reality of the thing outside him. Does it not? In that case reality outside him must contain something that differentiates it from reality in his concept, i.e., in the reality outside him something must be found of which God has no conception. What an absurdity! But if nothing of the sort is true, and if the concept that God has of a thing contains everything that is found in its reality outside him, it follows that both realities are identical, and everything that is said to exist outside God exists in God. It is not different if one defines the reality of a thing as the totality of all possible determinations belonging to it.[32] Must this totality not also be in God's mind? What determination does the real have outside him if the archetype [*das Urbild*] were not also found in God? Consequently, this *Urbild* is the thing itself, and to say that the thing exists also outside this *Urbild* means doubling its *Urbild* in a manner that is as unnecessary as it is absurd."

Lessing pursued this point relentlessly and with impeccable logic. In reproducing the gist and to some extent even the terminology of this fragment, Mendelssohn put these words into Lessing's mouth:[33] "Since . . . all thoughts of God are true and adequate, no thought in God will be distinguishable from its *Urbild;*[34] or, rather, the thoughts of God . . . will themselves be, at the same time, their very own *Urbilder.* The inner and perpetual activity of the divine power of representation produces in himself imperishable images of contingent beings with the infinite series of their successive modifications and variations, and they are ourselves and the sensible world outside us. Viewed from this angle, pantheism, which you thought you had overthrown, seems to me completely rehabilitated. You wish to refute it? Show first that this is possible! If this is to be the case, it must be shown that the *Urbilder* outside God do not have the same predicates as the conceptions or images of them found in God. This you deny, however, according to your own system. For the thoughts of God must be true and adequate in the highest degree, and hence must contain all predicates that belong to their objects."

Mendelssohn rejected this argument. He believed that there were criteria by which the real things outside God could be distinguished from their images in the divine mind.[35] God has a perfectly accurate concept of the range of my limited consciousness, but this image of my consciousness in him is not affected by any limitations. God knows my weakness but he does not possess it. A question by Lessing, which again reflects the argumentation in the fragment,[36] is interposed here: "Has something to accede to the thought of God if it is to become real outside God?" Mendelssohn felt that this question went to the very heart of the matter, and he tried to answer it. Once again, his concept of approbation provided him with a key to the solution of a problem. God knows the best and approves of it with the highest degree of approbation, and since approval carries with it the desire to realize its object, the absolute power of God produces in himself predicates that are the best in an absolute sense. However, God also approves the relatively best and causes it to become real. Yet its reality, though known to God, is never part of him; for in him only the "absolutely best" can exist. The "relatively best" is admitted only as separate from his substance and as part of an extradeical series of contingent things. It belongs to the objective world. The real, objective, extradeical is, therefore, that which is only relatively the best: "Those thoughts of God that, preferentially, attain to existence do not owe their preference to their truth and thinkability; for their opposite is equally thinkable. . . . The thoughts of God that become real to the exclusion of others will therefore receive this preference on account of their relative goodness and utility insofar as they correspond to the idea of the perfect and best here and now."

Hence this visible world, Mendelssohn concluded, exists in God's mind not only as a thought of his but also as the totality of the relatively best and the most perfect. The pantheist had no reason to reject this modified interpretation of intradeical existence. If he admitted it (and the practical consequences that flow from it) his system would differ from that of the Leibnizian in no tangible manner. The only point of disagreement would be found in the "barren reflection" on whether God allowed his thought of the best in contingent things to radiate or emanate from him, or whether he kept its radiance within himself.

In discussing this subtle question one had to resort to imagery and so run the risk of losing oneself in either atheism or mysticism by reading too much into those metaphors. If this area of conflict between the theist and the "purified Spinozist" was ignored, there was hardly any cause for disagreement. The one was as conscious as the other of their dependence on God as the source of truth and goodness, and they both realized that their happiness was in proportion to their knowledge and love of God. "If my friend [Lessing], the defender of purified Spinozism, admits all this, as he would certainly have done by virtue of his principles, then morality and religion are safe, and this school differs from our system only in respect of a subtlety that can never become practical." In short, Lessing's defense of Spinozism should give rise to no misgivings. All he had stood up for was a purified version of Spinozism, a version lending itself to an interpretation hardly distinguishable from Leibnizian theism insofar as its moral and religious fiber was concerned.

By presenting Lessing as a Spinozist, albeit a "purified" one, Mendelssohn had made good his promise not to repress the truth. "Even our best friend's name is not meant to appear to posterity in a brighter light than he deserves," he had written to Elise on August 16, 1783, when he had received the first intimation of Lessing's talks with Jacobi.[37] He had confirmed his intention in his letter of November 18, 1783, and Doctor Reimarus' plea that he conceal Lessing's Spinozism to the extent that the "sacredness of truth" permitted[38] had failed to deflect him from his course. Yet in his heart Mendelssohn shared the doctor's[39] scruples, and he believed that he owed it to him, to himself, and above all to the memory of his late friend, to show him also in a different light. He knew that an unequivocal portrayal of Lessing as a Spinozist of sorts was bound to shock many people,[40] and although this in itself was no reason to add a rider to his fictitious dialogue, he felt that the picture he had drawn of Lessing would be lopsided if he failed to restore the balance by offering yet another interpretation. There was, after all, the possibility that in his defense of Spinozism vis-à-vis him—and all the more so vis-à-vis Jacobi—Lessing had merely played his favorite role as champion of the underdog without seriously meaning to subscribe to the doctrine in any shape or form. Mendelssohn himself had previously looked upon his friend's excursions into Spinozism as mere fanciful exercises, and Lessing had somewhat encouraged this estimate by self-deprecatingly describing them as his old "fancies" (*Grillen*).[41] Only the pressure of Jacobi's report had forced Mendelssohn to attach importance to the Spinozistic leanings that Lessing had seemingly betrayed. Yet was one really justified in taking them all that seriously?

It was considerations of this kind that prompted Mendelssohn to introduce in chapter fifteen "friend D.," who is said to have surprisingly turned up at the last morning session. Friend D. is, we suggest, none other than "the doctor" (i.e., Doctor Reimarus) who had urged the utmost caution in dealing with the subject, although (and indeed precisely because) he had no doubts concerning the veracity of Jacobi's report. In the fictitious discussion between him and Mendelssohn, which forms the content of chapter fifteen, friend D. is presented as the spokesman of a view of Lessing with which Mendelssohn would have loved to identify himself, and with which he had identified himself before Jacobi intruded on the scene. One senses the poignancy that Mendelssohn felt in not being able to offer friend D.'s interpretation of Lessing as his own. One becomes aware also of the pleasure it gave him to articulate, through D., in the most eloquent manner how he felt at heart—and what he wished he could believe.

"How could you make our Lessing a defender of such a mistaken and ill-reputed doctrine?," D. asks Mendelssohn, reproachfully. "Could you think of no other name upon which to lay such a suspect charge?" "You know," Mendelssohn replied, "that Lessing is invariably my first thought whenever I look for a judge in matters of this kind. With him I had philosophical conversations over a very long time; throughout many years we communicated our thoughts on these matters to one another, and we did so with an unbiased love of truth that admitted neither obstinacy nor partiality. It is he, therefore, whose image, sometimes from mere habit, still arises in my mind whenever a philosophical proposition is to be discussed." One notices here Mendelssohn's just concern to establish his credentials vis-à-vis Jacobi.

"I would still hesitate," says D., "to use his name on such an occasion. On no account would I wish to arouse the least suspicion against the religious principles of this excellent man. What? Lessing having been a defender of pantheism, a doctrine based on oversubtle sophistical reasons and, even if not directly subverting all truths of natural religion, making them, at least, highly problematical?" Friend D., like Doctor Reimarus, is a radical deist, as it turns out, and the initial could well stand for both *doctor* and *deist*. The issue at stake is now going to be formulated in this way: Was Lessing a pantheist or a deist in the sense in which the "Fragmentist" was a deist, i.e. a believer in the truths of natural religion?

D. continues: "To whom were the truths of the religion of reason more inviolate than to him, the champion of the Fragmentist and the author of *Nathan?* Germany knows no philosopher who expounded the religion of reason with such clarity . . . as the Fragmentist did. His loyalty to natural religion went so far that in his zeal for it he would not tolerate a revealed one. He believed that he had to put out all other lights so as to permit [our] illumination to emanate exclusively from the light of reason." The respectability of the unnamed Fragmentist could not have been expressed in stronger terms, but since he was described as a philosopher who had expounded the truths of natural religion with unmatched clarity, Mendelssohn's readers could hardly fail to identify the Fragmentist with Hermann Samuel Reimarus, known as the author of the *Treatises on the Foremost Truths of Natural Religion*.[42] Thus Mendelssohn had lifted the veil from the long-guarded secret of the Fragmentist's identity, and one understands all the better why he had wanted Doctor Reimarus to read his manuscript.[43]

Having made a valiant effort to rehabilitate the Fragmentist, "friend D." characterizes Lessing as having increasingly come to share his religious philosophy: "With the defense of the Fragmentist, Lessing seems also to have adopted his entire attitude [*Gesinnung*]. Admittedly, his earliest writings . . . show that he had always considered the rational truths of religion and morality to be sacred and inviolate. Yet after he made the acquaintance of the Fragmentist one notices in all of the essays that he wrote in defense of his friend or guest, as he called him, the same tranquil conviction that distinguished the latter, the same unbiased remoteness from all skepticism, the same straight course of sound common sense with respect to the truths of the religion of reason." How Mendelssohn, who had been exasperated by Lessing's brilliant but reckless theological polemics, could have written these lines is hard to understand. It is true that he put these words into the mouth of D., but Doctor Reimarus had suffered even more anguish than he had. Nor was it correct to say that Lessing had adopted the views of the Fragmentist. In many instances he had criticized them. Mendelssohn must have deliberately ignored these facts in order to permit D. to identify Lessing with radical deism in contrast to his own presentation of Lessing as a purified Spinozist.

D. is on infinitely firmer ground (and, in fact, echoes Mendelssohn's deep and cherished conviction) when he points out that in writing *Nathan the Wise* Lessing had given poetic expression to one of the "great truths" of natural religion: in this "masterpiece" Lessing had written a "magnificent poem in praise of Providence." Mendelssohn's reasons for believing this to be so and the enthusiastic manner in which he gave utterance to the belief have been discussed in a previous context;[44] since our earlier account drew heavily on D.'s speech in the *Morgenstunden*, we need only fill in some of the blank spaces. It was the "highest triumph of human wisdom," Mendelssohn said through his mouthpiece D., "to recognize the most perfect harmony between the system of final ends and the system of efficient causes, and to see, with Shaftesbury and Leibniz, that God's designs and his concurrence[45] extend to the most minute changes and events in inanimate and animate beings; . . . that everything produced in nature conforms as much to a divine purpose as it flows from his omnipotence." It was, therefore, more appropriate to revere God on account of the normal course of natural events than on account of miracles.

At this point in the dialogue Mendelssohn applauded this view and corroborated it by quoting the rabbinic dictum:[46] "Wherever you find the greatness and exaltedness of God [mentioned in Scripture], you find also his humility [*Herablassung*]," and by also citing Psalm 113:5–6. It is also Mendelssohn who mentioned Lessing's original intention to reply to Voltaire's *Candide*, that "satire upon Providence," by a sequel showing the ultimate good that resulted from the evils depicted. Lessing's *Nathan* could be regarded as "a kind of anti-Candide." D., on the other hand, was the one who recalled with sorrow the widespread resentment that *Nathan the Wise* encountered and the sense of loneliness and frustration that had afflicted Lessing's last days. A man who had paid so dearly for having been a protagonist of the religion of reason, D. suggested, ought not to be misused for the defense of a heretical doctrine. "You seem to think," Mendelssohn replied, "that Lessing's character was such that he would have been glad to see pantheism or Spinozism overthrown by me, no matter whether my arguments were good or bad."

D. admitted that such an assumption was wrong, and it was now Mendelssohn's turn to concede that his previous presentation of Lessing as a defender of purified Spinozism had to be taken with a grain of salt, that it had been in character for Lessing to espouse any doctrine under attack. The most erroneous proposition, the most absurd opinion, needed only to be contested by shallow arguments to be assured of a defense by Lessing, to whom the very spirit of inquiry was all-important. In that spirit he could well have taken up the cudgels on behalf of pantheism, and the more readily in view of the fact that, as he had shown, "refined" pantheism was consistent with the practical aspects of natural religion and morality. By quoting passages from Lessing's youthful essay *The Christianity of Reason* Mendelssohn sought to prove that Lessing had indeed conceived of pantheism in the "refined" manner outlined previously.

One is left with the impression that D. was allowed to prevail in the end; that what began merely as an attempt to present the older viewpoint gained sufficient momentum to take on a renewed vitality; and that Lessing's defense of purified Spinozism was declared ultimately to have been no more than yet another instance of his gallantry—except that in this particular case he would not have compromised his loyalty to natural religion. Much as Lessing may have toyed with Spinozistic notions, Lessing was no Spinozist.

This unexpected upshot of the inquiry was almost inevitable, given Mendelssohn's conviction that *Nathan the Wise* represented the acme of Lessing's spiritual pilgrimage: "He wrote *Nathan the Wise* and died. I cannot conceive of a work of the human mind that surpasses *Nathan* as much as this play surpassed in my eyes all he had written before. He could not rise higher without entering a region hidden from our physical eyes; and this he did." When Mendelssohn expressed these sentiments in the condolence letter to Karl,[47] he meant what he said. He considered *Nathan*, not *Education of the Human Race*, to be Lessing's testament. He hinted at this "small treatise that he published shortly before his death" in the last section of the *Morgenstunden* as a parallel to *The Christianity of Reason*. He had already expressed disagreement with its historical perspective in *Jerusalem*. He must have realized, as Doctor Reimarus did, that this little tract had indeed "moved the target" against which the elder Reimarus had shot his arrows. Yet he stubbornly refused to recognize the significance of *Education of the Human Race* in opening up new horizons beyond the concept of natural religion in which history had no place. Mendelssohn felt too close to the spirit of *Nathan* to be able to admit that it had been superseded by the later work, a work with which he was in actual disagreement. Being thus imbued with the belief that the *essential* Lessing was to be found in *Nathan,* that paean to Providence in the Leibnizian sense, Mendelssohn was bound to cling to the view that his late friend had not ceased to be his "brother in Leibniz."[48]

In Combat

Jacobi seems to have taken some pains to keep the news that *his* book was about to appear from reaching Mendelssohn. On August 31, 1785, Jacobi's friend Thomas Wizenmann[1] wrote to him from Duisburg:[2] "By the way, I can assure you, in order to put your mind at ease, that nowhere did I refer to Mendelssohn when mentioning your book, and that—as may be reliably stated—no one here has any close connection with the old sage."

There was no delay in the printing, and as early as September 2 Jacobi could send a copy of the work to Herder:[3] "Here, my dear one, you find my letters to Mendelssohn[4] in print. I am looking forward to what you have to say about the form, the last sheet, and the thing as a whole, which, it seems to me, has assumed an uncommon kind of unity.... I have made use of a large part of your annotations. The section on belief has been allowed to stand except for a few unimportant changes. What I say there is to me certain truth."

In his reply of September 16 Herder wrote:[5] "It [the book] has acquired a good measure of unity, and when reading the closing part, which I had not yet seen in the manuscript, your genius hovered over me like a beneficent good spirit. The scandal of Spinozism has now been made public; let us see how Mendelssohn will check it. You emerge from all this as a true, orthodox Christian; for you have an extramundane God, *comme il faut,* and you have saved your soul. With your axioms: 'Spinozism is atheism, etc.' you have fenced yourself about with stakes that he who wants to will have to run down. For the moment I keep out and stay at home with my 'Spinoza, Shaftesbury, and Leibniz.' "

Herder was obviously far from convinced by Jacobi's interpretation of Spinoza, and his remark about Jacobi's having saved his own soul has an ironical ring and anticipates what Mendelssohn would say later, with grim contempt, in his final answer to Jacobi.[6] How similar the reactions of Herder and Mendelssohn were is apparent from a letter that Herder wrote to Hamann in October, 1785:[7] "I hope you have received our Jacobi's Spinozism or anti-Spinozism, and, truly speaking, I must say, like Mendelssohn, that the more he [Jacobi] tries to explain, the more remote the matter becomes to me."

Hamann's reaction was quite different however. On September 5 Jacobi had sent him three copies of his work: one for Hamann himself, one for Theodor Gottlieb von Hippel,[8] and one "for whomever you want." Jacobi was most anxious, he told Hamann, to hear what impression "the thing as a whole" had made upon him.[9] On September 28 Hamann informed him that the parcel had arrived on the twenty-fifth and that he had already read the book three times:[10] "I am perfectly satisfied with your decision to forestall Mendelssohn and with the way you established the nature of the controversy [*statum causae*]. No matter how the book is received, your intention and procedure in this matter are right and interesting. . . . Your problem shall be the focal point of my *Metakritik* concerning the purism of language and reason."[11]

Goethe, who had also received a copy of the work, wrote to Jacobi that in his view the "historical form," i.e. the presentation of the material in chronological order, suited the book very well. He was less happy with the liberty Jacobi had taken in publishing one of his poems at the opening under his (Goethe's) name and in subsequently quoting, without a name, the poem *Prometheus:*[12] "Whether you did the proper thing in placing my poem with my name in front, in order that people should point their finger at me when coming across the still more scandalous *Prometheus,* you will have to make out with the spirit that bade you do it. Herder thinks it amusing that on this occasion I am joining Lessing at the stake."

As a precautionary measure, it should be noted, Jacobi had arranged for the *Prometheus* to be printed as a "carton," i.e. on two loose pages to be inserted by the binder (books were sold unbound, as a rule) if so desired. A notice attached on a special leaf read: "The poem *Prometheus* is to be stitched in between pages forty-eight and forty-nine. It has been printed separately so as to give everyone the choice of not having it in his copy if he prefers it that way. There was a further consideration that caused me to resort to this method. It is not altogether impossible that in this or that locality my treatise will be confiscated on account of *Prometheus.* I hope that in such localities it will be considered sufficient if the indictable page alone is removed. In case the poem is to be left out, pages eleven and twelve . . . are to be cut out, and the attached pages are to be substituted." The substitute page eleven contained the following footnote: "This poem, which speaks in very harsh terms against Providence, cannot, for good reasons, be reproduced here."

In a subsequent letter of September 26 Goethe added to his previous remarks:[13] "It was not the intention of my last letter to embarrass or somehow reproach you. Let us forget the matter and see what happens. The best thing would have been to print the *Prometheus* purely and simply, without any note and without the notice in which you suggest the possibility of a confiscation; moreover, the first poem might have been printed without my name."[14] Mendelssohn later said about this "carton":[15] "Herr Jacobi hesitated to print these verses without some safeguard, and he therefore inserted a harmless leaflet that readers of delicate conscience can have stitched in in place of the seductive verses. According to my taste, Lessing would have considered the warning more pernicious than the poison itself. One who can forfeit his religion under the influence of bad verse must surely have little to lose."

On September 30, 1785, Jacobi sent Mendelssohn an unbound copy of his book, with a covering letter reading as follows:[16]

> I hope, dearest Mendelssohn, that you will not disapprove the role I assumed in editing by themselves the essays that I addressed to you—at least that you will not bear me a grudge on this account. I shall not repeat here the reasons that motivated me. They are mentioned in the treatise itself.
>
> I did not include your "objections" because I believed myself free to deal as I pleased only with such material as belonged unquestionably to me alone. Besides, I was sure that the content thereof would be found in a much more elaborate form in your "Morning Thoughts," to which I am looking forward with inexpressible yearning. Since the "objections" were omitted, the entire introduction to my last essay was likewise omitted.
>
> Before long you will receive a bound copy of my treatise. I am sending you the enclosed one with the mounted post because I do not want you to learn about the existence of my treatise from the Book Fair catalog . . . Take care of yourself, dearest man, and continue to grant me your inestimable good will.

On October 4, 1785, Mendelssohn, who had not yet received this letter and knew nothing of Jacobi's book, in all innocence sent Jacobi a copy of the *Morgenstunden,* with an accompanying letter:[17]

> Receive herewith, dearest friend, the first part of my *Morgenstunden.* Though it does not expressly mention our dispute as such, it nevertheless takes it into consideration throughout. I had to start from first principles because I suspect that the reason that we understand one another so little lies in this area. I find myself too old and too stiff to leave off my shibboleth. I can no longer penetrate, by sheer effort, any philosophical language other than the one to which I have been accustomed for such a long time. The school in which I was educated has accustomed me to stick to distinctness so firmly that I am unable to take one single step once I lose sight of it.[18]
>
> Perhaps you succeed in noticing the points that matter in our dispute and can give me some light.[19] Have therefore the patience to let me declaim my whole lesson, and give me a friendly call whenever I am led astray. In this way, I think, we are bound either to get together[20] or, as you so well put it, to drift apart in the end. On my part, and I hope and pray on yours too,[21] the one as well as the other shall not happen without cordial affection and friendship.[22]

This was a truly modest and honest letter. Mendelssohn admitted his inability to follow Jacobi's thinking, which was no longer bound by the strict rules of the Leibniz/Wolffian school. Though still maintaining the fiction of a future contest, once some common ground was established, the letter does not sound too optimistic. It rather implies that they both might do better simply to accept the impossibility of their ever coming to terms. The final sentence puts the seal on this bleak prospect by expressing the—alas, vain—hope that they might be friends despite their differences. The straightforwardness of this letter contrasts sharply with the obviously hypocritical assurance in Jacobi's letter that he was looking forward to Mendelssohn's book "with inexpressible yearning." Yet Jacobi also seems to have wished to remain on amicable terms with his adversary. Each of them changed his attitude drastically upon reading the other's book.

The previously envisaged knightly contest—envisaged, at least, by Elise—gave way to a real battle. The two men would engage now in a bitter combat whose course would be watched with a great deal of concern by friends and foes alike. Anti-Semitic sentiments crept into some of the side-line commentary. Even Goethe, who disagreed with Jacobi's view of Spinoza,[23] would write to him on December 1, 1785:[24] "What do you think about the *Morgenstunden?* And about the Jewish tricks [*Pfiffen*] with which the new Socrates operates? How cleverly he introduced Spinoza and Lessing. Oh, you poor Christian, how badly will you fare once he has enveloped you by his whirring little wings! Are you getting ready for counteraction? And in what way?" In his reply Jacobi spoke not once but twice of the "rabbinic lectures" and described Mendelssohn as a "Jew" who was even "an arrant Jew (*Erzjude*)."[25] His anti-Semitic sentiment merged with his detestation of the "entire Berlin clique" that, he told Goethe in the same letter, shared Mendelssohn's sense of outrage and embitterment. He had not expected, he said, that the spirit of "pious fraud" that ruled this "species" would expose itself to such an extent.[26]

Hamann, who believed that the charge of atheism that his *Golgatha* had laid at Mendelssohn's door was ultimately responsible for the coming into being of the *Morgenstunden,* wrote to Jacobi on November 20, 1785:[27] "Perhaps I was the first who caused Rabbi Moses to take the jump in coming out with his lectures. The charge was thereby ipso facto refuted, and the job of cleansing his dead friend of the suspicion of Spinozism was made easier at the same time. Now he makes his entry into his Berlin-Jerusalem with two palm branches, and celebrates his triumph over both of us." Herder wrote to Hamann on January 2, 1786:[28] "Mendelssohn is too old and too classical a philosopher of the German nation and language to allow himself to be taught, and he is too crafty a Hebrew [*ein zu pfiffiger Ebräer*] to make it possible for an honest Christian to get on with him.[29] In his *Morgenstunden* he has treated[30] our Jacobi in such a cunning way and has tried to place his *shadow* of Lessing (for it is certainly not Lessing himself, whom he depicts there as a stag brought down) *hors de combat,* with the result that through shifting the pieces the game is as good as won by him. . . . It is strange that the concealed hatred against the Christians in the old man seems to come more to the surface with each day."

It is sad to observe the leading spirits of post-Enlightenment Germany—Goethe, Herder, Hamann, Jacobi—allowing anti-Semitic feelings to color their estimate of Mendelssohn, who sought merely to defend the legacy of the Leibniz/Wolffian school of which he believed Lessing had remained a partisan, and which he also found wholly compatible with Judaism. Mendelssohn's undeniable distaste for Jacobi's *Schwärmerey* stemmed not from "hatred" of Christianity but from an aversion to romantic and pietistic emotionalism. It also sprang from his suspicion that Jacobi's emphasis on "faith" was yet another conversionist attempt in disguise.[31]

When Jacobi's missile reached Mendelssohn, it hit him like a thunderbolt. In the words of his friend Engel:[32] "At first he would not believe in the existence of this book, and when, soon enough, its authenticity could no longer be doubted, its content seemed to him incredible." What upset him most at the outset, perhaps, was the fact that Jacobi had thwarted his own strategy. The simultaneous appearance of his book and that of his adversary was bound to deprive his presentation of Lessing of much of its effectiveness. Mendelssohn tried to persuade himself that this was not the case; thus he wrote to Nicolai on October 8:[33] "Have you read Jacobi's treatise *On the Doctrine of Spinoza*? What is your opinion of this strange, warped behavior? Fortunately, I have given the matter, unknowingly, a propitious turn in advance in my *Morgenstunden,* which permits the hope that this almost sneering procedure of the fanatical [*schwärmerischen*] party will no longer harm our Lessing." But the fact that Mendelssohn decided to publish an "Appendix," as it were, to Jacobi's work clearly shows how little trust he put in the *Morgenstunden* as a sufficient antidote to the "poison" that Jacobi had spread. Mendelssohn realized the inevitability of his publicly defending Lessing against what he considered a slur not merely on the man's religious convictions but also on his character.

Another reason for Mendelssohn's uneasiness was the excuse Jacobi gave for having rushed into print. According to Jacobi, Mendelssohn had gone back on his promise to let him see his manuscript before publication and had resolved to establish the nature of the controversy before proceeding with the contest. He, Jacobi, could not have permitted Mendelssohn to assign to him the role of *advocatus diaboli*, i.e. to make him appear to be a Spinozist. What troubled Mendelssohn was the charge that he had broken a promise. That the accusation was unjustified is borne out by the narrative of events given above.[34] The *Morgenstunden* did not refer to the correspondence between Mendelssohn and Jacobi, and hence Mendelssohn had been under no obligation to submit the manuscript to his opponent. Nor did the work include any reference to Jacobi's "role." Thus Jacobi's fear of being victimized was utterly groundless. Any unbiased reader could easily discover for himself that the suspicions that had allegedly given rise to Jacobi's book were not confirmed by the content of the *Morgenstunden*—a point that Mendelssohn would make very strongly in his ultimate reply.[35] However, the necessity of dispelling any possible lingering suspicion that he had acted in an improper manner was far from exhilarating. Perhaps the most poignant aspect of the new situation was the wound inflicted by Jacobi's allegation that there had been no real rapport between Lessing and Mendelssohn in philosophical matters. Considering that Lessing's friendship and trust in his judgment was what Mendelssohn had prized most highly, the "relevation" flung at him and the world by Jacobi was bound to hurt him deeply. The sheer cruelty of the act was underscored by Mendelssohn in his final answer to Jacobi, and he did this delicate job in masterful fashion:[36]

> At the beginning of his treatise he [Jacobi] relates: Lessing had indicated to him that he esteemed me most highly among his friends; he, Jacobi, had, however . . . expressed astonishment . . . that a man like myself should have espoused so zealously the proof for the existence of God from the idea of him, as I had done in the treatise on evidence; and Lessing's apologies on my behalf had induced Jacobi to pose the question whether he had never asserted his own system versus Mendelssohn. —"Never" was Lessing's answer. . . . "Once only did I tell him approximately what struck you in the *Education of the Human Race* (#73). We could not agree with each other, and I left it at that."
>
> Lessing, therefore, shows forbearance with my weakness, excuses my zeal for the metaphysical argumentation a priori, and conceals from me, the friend he esteems so highly, his true system—probably in order not to rob me of a conviction that, as he could see, allowed me to live in such tranquillity and happiness. This Herr Jacobi hears from Lessing's own mouth at the very time at which he confides his great secret to Jacobi—makes Jacobi his confident. Nevertheless, I am the first person on whom Herr Jacobi calls, in order to force upon me the dangerous secret that my friend had wished to spare me for so many years. Assuming that the reality of things corresponds to their appearance, I ask: who has evinced in this case more practical religion and more genuine piety, the atheist . . . or the orthodox Christian . . . ?

Mendelssohn could not admit the authenticity of Jacobi's report without at the same time denying a lifetime of personal and intimate experience. If it were true, Mendelssohn had said in an earlier passage,[37] that Lessing's conversations with Jacobi reflected his considered opinion, then his late friend would have to have been a most enigmatic character indeed, a curious mixture of hypocrisy and radicalism, of stubborn reserve and easy-going openness. Mendelssohn would have to be sorry both for him and for himself: "For I confess that it would humiliate me considerably had our friend Lessing deemed me unworthy of the confidence that another mortal was able to win in a few days of friendly conversation, and this after I had lived with him in the most intimate friendship for over thirty years; . . . searched with him incessantly for truth; and . . . discussed these important matters with him constantly by word of mouth and in writing. I confess to my weakness. I know no earthly being to whom I would not begrudge this privilege." The impossibility of acknowledging the veracity of Lessing's statement about him left Mendelssohn no choice than to regard the entire conversation as a good-humored attempt on Lessing's part to pull Jacobi's leg after having discovered that the man wanted to save his soul.[38] Mendelssohn had suspected this before, but he was now sure that this "hypothesis" was the only way to account for the erratic utterances that Lessing had permitted himself in the course of that strange conversation. What Lessing had said about him, Mendelssohn, was the last straw. He no longer had any doubt that Jacobi had been duped.

The agitated state of mind into which Mendelssohn was plunged by Jacobi's strange book ruled out any calm and relaxed appraisal of the matter. He had planned to devote himself exclusively to business for a period of several months after the *Morgenstunden* was out of the way; he needed this time of rest to recharge his batteries. After he received Jacobi's book considerations of health were brushed aside; Mendelssohn had but one all-consuming purpose: to erase the impression created by Jacobi's portrayal of Lessing (and of him). As Engel reported,[39] he now lived in a constant state of tension. Whereas he had been careful before to avoid any excitement in the evening, now he would talk about this subject with unusual vivacity through the late evening hours. One could sense that his heart and mind were incessantly engaged.

Mendelssohn's correspondence reflected his restlessness and his desire for moral support. On October 12, 1785, he sent complimentary copies of his *Morgenstunden* to his two princely patrons, Duke Leopold Friedrich Franz of Anhalt-Dessau and Duke Karl Wilhelm Ferdinand of Brunswick. The covering letter to Duke Leopold read as follows:[40] "I dare to place at the feet of the most serene ruler of my native country, the wise friend and protector of the good and beautiful, a treatise in which I resume the battle against the adversaries of natural religion. Their number is not small, and their party is to be reckoned with. Friends and foes of virtue seem to have joined forces to decry the reason of man.[41] . . . An indication of Your Serenity's approval would encourage me to continue in the exercise of my abilities . . ."[42] The letter to the duke of Brunswick sounded a different note: "When I had the privilege of presenting to Your Ducal Serenity my treatise on the immortality of the soul, you expressed the desire to see a similar tract dealing with the existence of God. Since then I have been occupied with this idea, and though my debility does not permit me as yet to hope that I have done full justice to this exalted notion, I am, nevertheless, pleased to place at the feet of Your Ducal Serenity an essay that might perhaps alert others to improve on mine."[43]

One of the first to receive a copy was the painter Johann Christoph Frisch. On October 8 Mendelssohn handed him the book together with the following epigram:[44] "Nature, guided by reason, inspires / the wise artist, when he works; / reason, guided by nature, delights him, / when he is resting." It was probably at about this same time that Mendelssohn wrote to his friend Doctor Zimmermann in Hanover:[45]

> I have taken the liberty of sending you, through the publisher[46] from Leipzig, a copy of my *Morgenstunden,* the subject matter of which I commend to your severest criticism, and the form of which I commend to your kind indulgence. The author of the classical work *On Solitude*[47] will know that the licking [viz. polishing] of the young thoughts is as trying to the mother as the act of giving birth....
>
> In the part that is to follow I had meant to indicate the circumstances that occasioned the publication of the *Morgenstunden*; but Herr Jacobi has forestalled me. He has publicly announced them under the title *On Spinoza's System,*[48] *in Letters to Moses Mendelssohn.* This little book is a rather strange monster. The head is Goethe's, the body is Spinoza's, and the feet are Lavater's.

The last phrase, which testifies to Mendelssohn's utter disgust with Jacobi's work, also occurs in the letter that he wrote, in a far more serious vein, to Kant:[49]

> I have taken the liberty of sending you, through the bookseller Voss & Son, a copy of my *Morning Hours, or Lectures on the Existence of God.* Though I no longer have the strength to study your profound writings with the effort required, I know nevertheless that we disagree in principles. Yet I also know that you bear with opposition and that you even prefer it to the mere echoing of your own views....
>
> I had it in mind to defer explaining the reason for the publication of these *Morning Hours* until the second part so as first to prepare the readers for certain statements that seemed to me somewhat dangerous in respect of their effect upon the reading public. Herr Jacobi has forestalled me and under the title *On the Doctrine of Spinoza, in Letters to Moses Mendelssohn* he has published a treatise which deals with that reason. In it he publishes a correspondence between him, a third person, and myself, in the course of which he (Jacobi) pursues the aim of making our Lessing into a declared Spinozist. Jacobi claims to have demonstrated Spinozism to him; that Lessing had found everything in agreement with his principles; and that he was glad to have met at long last, after a prolonged search, a brother in pantheism capable of shedding such a beautiful light on the system of the All-One or One-All.—
>
> As for [Jacobi] himself, he retreats in the end to [a position protected by] the cannon of faith, and finds salvation and security in a bastion of the soul-saving Lavater, out of whose "angelical and pure" mouth he quotes at the end of his treatise a comforting passage that can offer me no solace because I fail to understand it. All in all, this treatise by Herr Jacobi is a rare compound, an almost monstrous birth: the head is Goethe's, the body is Spinoza's, the feet are Lavater's.
>
> With what right one permits oneself nowadays ... the publication of a private correspondence without having asked for and obtained permission from the correspondents is incomprehensible to me. Moreover: Lessing is alleged to have confessed to him, i.e. Jacobi, that he had never revealed his true philosophical principles to me, his intimate philosophical friend of thirty years' standing. If this were true, how could Jacobi have brought himself to betray this secret of his late friend not only to me, from whom he [Lessing] had carefully concealed it, but to the whole

world? He saves his own skin, and leaves his friend naked and defenseless in the open field to become the prey or scorn of his enemies. I cannot put up with this conduct, and would like to know what righteous men think of it. I am afraid that philosophy has its *Schwärmer* [fanatics] who persecute others as violently, and are bent upon proselytizing even more, than the *Schwärmer* of positive religion.

This letter was a *cri de coeur* such as Kant had never before received from Mendelssohn. Since he admired the *Morgenstunden,* despite his fundamental objections, as his letter to Schütz proves,[50] he might have sent a note of appreciation to the author. Yet he left the letter unanswered and the copy of the book unacknowledged.[51] Kant seems to have been not entirely unhappy with the blow dealt to Mendelssohn. On October 3 Hamann reported to Jacobi:[52] "Kant is very satisfied with your presentation and with the content of the task as a whole [which you have set yourself]. He had never been able to make sense of Spinoza's system." On October 23 Hamann wrote:[53] "Kant . . . was very curious to read your treatise . . . and seemed to be pleased with the manner in which you put forward and presented the nature of the controversy [*statum causae*]." On November 3 Hamann informed Jacobi of further developments:[54] "The day before yesterday I visited Kant. He gave me the letter to read that Mendelssohn had sent to him on October 17[55] together with his lectures. I promised him not to misuse it, . . . [but] I must tell you confidentially that the people there [in Berlin] seem to be very much embittered and enraged by your little book. . . . Kant intends to contest Mendelssohn's views in the coolest fashion, which concerns me very much, and which I encouraged him to do. . . . Lavater is also mentioned in the letter: one finds in your Spinoza booklet [*Spinozabüchlein*], as Claudius calls it, Spinoza's head, Herder's trunk [*Torso*], and Goethe's toes."[56]

It is most surprising that Kant permitted himself the indiscretion of showing Hamann, whom he knew to be Jacobi's intimate friend, the letter that Mendelssohn had trustingly written to him. Jacobi reacted promptly. On November 17 he wrote to Hamann:[57] "So far as the Berlin people are concerned, I am quite satisfied if they find in my booklet Spinoza's head, Herder's trunk, and Goethe's toes, even assuming that by toes they mean claws or clutches. One might interpret this as the highest praise. For what more flattering thing could be said of an author than that he thinks with a head like Spinoza's, breathes as if from Herder's chest, and moves as if with Goethe's feet." Jacobi welcomed the news that Kant intended to contest Mendelssohn's *Morgenstunden,* but he was less pleased with the information that his own interpretation of Spinoza and the text itself made as little sense to "the author of the *Critique of Pure Reason*" as they did to Mendelssohn. In his next letter Hamann quoted Kant as having told him that he had never properly studied Spinoza.[58] On December 14 he reported having heard that Kant had abandoned his plan to refute Mendelssohn because the *Morgenstunden* did not actually bear on him personally, as he had originally assumed, and also because he was too busy with his own work.[59]

It would appear that a certain ambivalence in Kant's attitude toward Mendelssohn and, at the same time, a sneaking affection for Jacobi were responsible for Kant's failure to send the merest word of encouragement to Mendelssohn at the time when he needed it most. Biester's request that Kant take a stand in condemning "philosophical fanaticism" such as that expressed in Jacobi's book[60] fell on deaf ears. It was only after Mendelssohn's death that Immanuel Kant allowed himself to be persuaded to speak up for reason.

No one, apart from Mendelssohn, felt quite so dumbfounded and hurt by Jacobi's book as Elise Reimarus did. On October 4, the day on which, unsuspectingly, he had sent his *Morgenstunden* to Jacobi, Mendelssohn had also dispatched a complimentary copy to Elise.[61] In a letter dated October 17[62] she thanked him for the gift which, she pointed out, was sure to cause her some headache at times since its contents were far above her intellectual capacity. She added: "I have had no word from Jacobi for a long time, but I trust that you received the requested copy directly from him at the time. . . . Heaven give both of you strength and *patience* to meet each other in the chosen arena. To applaud from afar the winner or the reconciled friends is all a poor mortal like myself can do in the matter." In retrospect, these words make pathetic reading. On October 18, Elise had to write a postscript:

> I had hardly finished my letter when out of the blue, i.e. without a covering letter, without the least warning, I received, through Claudius, two bound little books, one for myself and one for our Doctor, entitled *On the Doctrine of Spinoza in Letters to Herr Moses Mendelssohn.* Already the mere sight of the title made my blood boil; but my resentment grew when I saw in the treatise itself not only every minute and irrelevant feature of a private correspondence but also every minute and irrelevant feature of a private conversation, including the private joking of our late friend, exhibited before the eyes of a scoffing or mourning public.
>
> How improperly, how crookedly even the best, most honest man acts when he becomes hot-tempered or thinks that he has to defend his affronted ego. That this has happened in Jacobi's case is apparent from the whole thing, especially from the passage in which he mentions the hope held out by you to see your *Morgenstunden* in manuscript, a hope you subsequently preferred to leave unfulfilled. —Yet I do not wish to recite ad nauseam details of this matter, which you may have already put aside with your characteristic smile.
>
> Only one thing, dearest Mendelssohn, is important to me: whether I have also to reproach myself for having been overactive in this matter, i.e. for having been too generous with the excerpts from your letters? I believed I could afford . . . to be so generous because I know this good and oversensitive man and because I realized how much importance he attached to every word in your letters that had a bearing on him. —In case I was mistaken, forgive the wrong judgment of a person *not* otherwise *guilty of loquacity.* Take care of yourself and, please, let me *soon* read a consoling word from your hand.

Elise was not wrong in sensing that, for all her impeccable intentions, she had played a very unfortunate role in this affair. Her excerpts from Mendelssohn's letters were injudicious in part, and the enthusiastic manner in which she wrote about Mendelssohn was bound to irritate Jacobi. She naively assumed that he was capable of sharing her admiration for him. Despite her uncommon intellectual powers she lacked psychological insight, savoir-faire, and diplomacy. In fact, Mendelssohn himself might also have managed the whole matter more prudently from the very start. He certainly was no match for Jacobi as a tactician. As it turned out, he paid a heavy price for allowing Jacobi's secret information to get under his skin. He could have dismissed it as being of no concern to him, instead of reacting in the way that he did. But at this moment there was no point in any self-reproach on either his or Elise's part. He was right, therefore, to try to put her mind at rest. Even so, he refused to acknowledge the justice of her effort to find a mitigating circumstance in Jacobi's sense of annoyance at not having been permitted to see the *Morgenstunden* before the manuscript was sent to the printer. His reply to Elise, dated October 21, read as follows:[63]

> I too, dearest Elise, find the precipitate action of Herr Jacobi most painful; and despite the exuberant kindness with which you know how to diminish his guilt, his recklessness remains unforgivable. The whole conduct of this man is so shifty and tangled that I cannot put up with it. If he can suspect me of publicly presenting him as a defender of atheism,[64] why did he seek my acquaintance? Why is he at first so trusting and afterwards, without rhyme or reason, so suspicious? If his self-love is so flammable, why does he approach the fire at such close quarters? . . .
>
> I do not like having anything to do with such people, dearest friend, and am firmly resolved to suspend henceforth all private correspondence with Herr Jacobi. What we have to say to one another shall be said in public. I shall reply in the near future and shall take heed not to pay back in the same coin. You can be perfectly assured that I shall not put pen to paper before I am completely free from all irritability. Yet he will have to hear a little of the truth; and the memory of our Lessing must be protected as much as my powers permit.
>
> Yet, how could it have entered your mind, my dearest, to impute part of the guilt to yourself? You did very well in communicating to him excerpts from my letters. Who could have been aware of such a thing in a man like him? Take care of yourself, revered friend! Compose yourself! I forgive Herr Jacobi as you do, but I cannot excuse him or desire any private contact with him.

On October 24, probably after receiving Mendelssohn's reply, Elise wrote a letter expressing her feelings to Jacobi.[65] She could not adequately describe, she said, with what surprise she had received the two copies of his book. "May I confess to you, dearest friend, that indignation was my immediate reaction?" It might be prejudice on her part, but she was shocked to find "our Lessing" exposed before a world that could neither understand nor judge him and did not deserve to see him without a veil. "Not that I disagreed with you and Mendelssohn that our friend had to be presented as a Spinozist, if he was one."[66] What had dismayed her was the detailed account of a confidential talk, including jocular remarks that, if broadcast, tended to sound like "blasphemies." Feelings of this kind had prevented her from at once thanking Jacobi for this "public monument" of his "friendship."[67] Now, however, she wished to thank him "in spirit and in truth."[68]

Unlike Mendelssohn, Elise obviously desired to remain on terms of friendship with Jacobi. Anticipating the argument that he could not have "sat still" while Mendelssohn was in the process of publishing his treatise without showing it to him, she made the following point: she was not going into the question of whether she would have preferred Mendelssohn to let him see the manuscript of the *Morgenstunden,* as he had originally intended.[69] However, she had had no reason to assume that Jacobi would take the action he took, for there had been a clear understanding that the *Morgenstunden* would deal merely with pantheism as such and omit all reference to the correspondence about Lessing. She had been convinced, moreover, that even in any future discussion of Lessing's Spinozism no details of the conversation (e.g. the poem) were to be made public—that these details were to be reserved for Lessing's most intimate friends or for "more sturdy stomachs."[70] She might have been mistaken in the latter respect, she conceded: "Yet, my dearest, can you take it amiss that I was shocked and indeed plunged into sadness and sorrow at the thought that a contest for truth between two of the noblest searchers for truth, who were Lessing's closest friends and mine, and who were supposed to hold out their hand to each other in public, has turned into a private quarrel that will make only the enemies of Lessing and of truth the final victors? Perhaps I innocently contributed a little spark towards this development."

She explained what she meant by this self-reproach: in her last letter (received by Jacobi on May 26) she might have offered a more explicit excerpt from Mendelssohn's to her (of April 29). She had, in fact, added the passage:[71] "At the least, he [Jacobi] will be able to reply to both at the same time, and my treatise will perhaps give him an opportunity to state his views more clearly.... I now have the manuscript copied for dispatch to you; but not for Herr Jacobi.... Your brother, on the other hand, must read everything in manuscript..." She had deleted this passage on the advice of her sister-in-law, and because she feared offending Jacobi by telling him that he was not to see the work before it was printed but that her brother was. Obviously Elise was unconscious of the completely confidential character of Mendelssohn's letter (her naïveté in this regard is simply staggering!). She went on to explain to Jacobi that she had refrained from trying to persuade Mendelssohn to send Jacobi the manuscript after all because it had been her impression that there was no further disagreement on this point, and also because her brother had had to go over the manuscript in great haste. She now left it to Jacobi to decide whether she had been wrong to keep quiet. She was anxious to know what he thought of the *Morgenstunden,* which had arrived only one day before his book. Her brother, who had also been "a little perplexed" when first setting eye on it (Jacobi's book), sent his thanks through her. Her letter concluded with the wishful thought that Jacobi and Mendelssohn might meet in the presence of her brother and that "this holy trinity" might determine how much the public was to be told. She expressed the hope that her sad forebodings of a break between the two men would be proved wrong: "By God and Lessing's shade, "she declared," this must not happen!"

Jacobi had every right to conclude from this letter that neither Elise's nor her brother's "respect and love" for him had been diminished as a result of his actions.[72] In his reply, dated November 7, 1785,[73] he tried to convince her that none of her objections were justified. The conversation with Lessing had *not* been a strictly confidential one: witnesses had been present even when the *Prometheus* was being discussed. To present Lessing as a Spinozist without going into details of the debate would have meant robbing the story of its content and the "seal of history." Mendelssohn *had* gone back on his word when, having affirmed his resolve to offer an objective account, he now sought to wrap up the truth in the mantle of a pious fraud. He hardly trusted his eyes, Jacobi said, when reading the preface and lectures thirteen, fourteen, and fifteen of the *Morgenstunden.* He had put the book aside and so far had not been able to bring himself to look at it again. Mendelssohn, he suggested, had obviously made a determined effort to hush up the truth by imputing to Lessing an innocuous Spinozism in the disguise of a still more innocuous pantheism. He, Jacobi, had had some inkling of this, and he therefore refused to abandon Lessing to any chance. Lessing was good enough for him just as he was. He would stand by him, a loyal and proud friend, so long as he lived. "The purified pantheism that he was supposed to take as a medicine for his recovery would have made him, in my view, a mere semi-thinker [*Halbkopf*]. I do not want to have him educated by Mendelssohn to be such a one after death."

When Jacobi wrote his self-defense against Mendelssohn's "recriminations," he started by quoting this letter. In her acknowledgment of this second book Elise admitted on May 9, 1786[74]—five months after Mendelssohn's death—that Jacobi's Lessing seemed to be "truer" [than Mendelssohn's] and that she "liked" him "better." She also confessed that from the start until now she had told both friends and foes of Jacobi that he had been misunderstood and that his intentions in respect of Lessing had been misjudged. "This is all. Incidentally (let it be considered a weakness), I must confess to you that the more I read about this matter, the more I am overwhelmed by deep sorrow. It hardly leaves me with any feeling except the wish that I could surrender a part of my life to undo the whole thing."

The contemptuous manner in which Jacobi dismissed Mendelssohn's interpretation of Lessing was by no means justified. It was an expression of his enormous conceit and took no account of the fact that his own closest friends—Goethe and Herder—doubted the validity of his interpretation of Spinoza. Mendelssohn's evaluation of the talks between Jacobi and Lessing was by far more competent than Jacobi's, who lacked an appreciation of the antithetical, hypothetical, and humoristic ingredients in Lessing.[75] Nor was the summary disparagement of the *Morgenstunden* as a whole to Jacobi's credit. On December 13, 1785, he wrote to Goethe[76] that the "rabbinic lectures" had caused him such boredom that he had to give up reading them, and that many people in Germany had fallen asleep over them. Yet philosophers like Kant, Schütz, and Garve had a high opinion of the book.

Garve, who after Mendelssohn's death would be wooed by Jacobi,[77] wrote on January 3, 1786, to Zollikofer in Leipzig:[78]

> I now come to two ... writings that have aroused your attention, no doubt, viz. those by Moses and Jacobi. About the latter's Moses is very angry. His letter to me about it shows a certain passion.[79] This treatise has, in fact, struck me, too, as rather strange. Firstly, why does Jacobi have to present Lessing if he wants to discuss Spinozism as such? This may be the principal reason for Mendelssohn's annoyance. He believes that the reputation of his late friend might suffer as a result. Besides, Jacobi should not have published a letter, which had been intended merely for Mendelssohn's information, without first asking for his permission.
>
> Yet these are private matters. What displeases me in particular is the revolting poem, the obscure manner in which the Spinozistic system is expounded, ... and the incomprehensible return to faith in God with the help of some revelation and tradition. —What an entirely different piece of work is Mendelssohn's! The light that strikes the reader even in [his] most abstract speculations makes everything not merely easy but also interesting. The books of this man are excellent for the training of the mind.... Some ideas of his are really new, and very well presented, e.g. the notion that all existing things must be known and conceived by some being....

And on January 14, Garve wrote to Christian Felix Weisse:[80] "Among my present readings Moses' and Jacobi's writings stand out. The first is light, the second darkness. The metaphysics of the first, though not always new, is always convincing, clear, and instructive. The other's metaphysics, which is supposedly extraordinarily novel, is partly incomprehensible, partly useless; for who wishes to strengthen faith in revelation, is ill-advised to undermine faith in God." Though neither Mendelssohn nor Garve really understood what Jacobi meant by faith and revelation, they were certainly justified in criticizing the oracular manner of his writing. The systematic mind of Mendelssohn also understandably rebelled against the "monstrous" nature of Jacobi's book, which was indeed a patchwork not deserving to be praised for its "historical form" by Goethe and others.[81] Hamann was more honest and more accurate when he called it "somewhat composite and piebald."[82]

The two combatants were getting ready for the real battle, but Hamann repeatedly urged Jacobi not to be in such a hurry. On October 23 he wrote to him that he could afford to take his time, for Mendelssohn was sure to do the same; in the interim Hamann would try to mobilize Kant against Mendelssohn.[83] On October 29 Hamann warned Jacobi that he had to expect attacks from Berlin, but again he counseled patience:[84] "Your game is great and honest; do not spoil it by any hasty move.... I wish you the utmost indifference to all confederates and seconders of the rabbi at Berlin." The advice was reinforced on November 3:[85] Jacobi should not allow himself to become exasperated by the hostility of the Berlin group but should be all the more composed. "People fail to understand you, and in this respect you share the same damnation with Kant and, perhaps, with the 'preacher in the wilderness.' "[86]

Mendelssohn, on the other hand, was hardly capable of exercising patience. He was itching to wipe out the blemish on Lessing's name and give the lie to Jacobi's testimony on Lessing's relationship with him. Little did he know how fast time was running out, but he gave himself no respite. Whatever vague plan he might have had for the second part of his *Morgenstunden*—he had never seriously contemplated such a sequel—now lay in a shambles. An entirely new book had to be conceived, and though he had promised Elise not to put pen to paper before regaining his tranquillity, he found he could not wait for this to happen. His last literary piece, which he called *To Lessing's Friends (An die Freunde Lessings)*, was written out of anguish and restlessness.

The Social and Domestic Scene

Had it not been for the upset caused by Jacobi's intrusion the year 1785 might have been a calm and happy one for Mendelssohn. After the tremendous labors of the period that culminated in the publication of the *Jerusalem,* he had tried to settle down to a more private kind of existence, away from the turmoil of public causes. Not that he wished to retire into an ivory tower: everything bearing on Jewish interests remained close to his heart. But the time for "activism" on his part was over, and he now tended to allow the hoped-for "improvements" to take shape by themselves.

Characteristic of the attitude he had now adopted is the reply he wrote on October 18, 1785, to Baron Leopold von Hirschen, who had invited him to contribute an essay to a publication pleading for Jewish civil rights and planned by him jointly with Friedrich Lebrecht Schönemann, "magister" of philosophy in Dessau:[1] "The letter with which you honored me, Sir, proves on the one hand that to one unbiased by prejudice it is a most evident truth that my nation can, like any other, be used to the advantage of the state; it shows on the other hand that the prejudice against my nation has struck roots that are too deeply embedded to be easily eradicated root and branch. I say 'root and branch' because it is invariably the nature of prejudices that the least particle left intact is like a seed, and all of a sudden a new trunk is restored. Every prejudice must therefore be resisted . . . repeatedly and emphatically so as to nip the flower in the bud. Now, it does not matter to men of searching mind who the author of a book is; they read it, examine the arguments, and do not withhold approval if it is merited. Yet in people of the average type arguments produce only a limited effect, and most of the impact comes from the established authority and unselfishness of the writer. For this reason it always gave me greater pleasure when I saw Christian prejudice against the Jews contested by a Christian rather than a Jewish author."

On the other hand, Mendelssohn offered helpful advice to Ephraim Veitel, court jeweller and one of the elders of the community, who had written a memorandum against the argument that Jews could not claim equal status since their religion debarred them from military service and from sharing in the defense of the country in times of national peril. Veitel made the point that the Jews of Prussia made themselves useful in many ways that amply compensated for what they failed to provide.[2] Veitel had submitted his memorandum to Mendelssohn, who replied on April 26, 1785,[3] that the arguments seemed "very good and to the point." They were bound to impress a fair-minded person and could do no harm, at any rate, since they were stated with as much modesty as thoroughness. However, they needed to be recast for the sake of greater clarity and might best be presented in French.

A letter that Mendelssohn wrote on January 11, 1785, to his cousin Elkan Herz offers eloquent testimony to his undiminished concern for the safeguarding of Jewish distinctiveness. The letter[4] opens with an elucidation of a juridical point concerning the validity of testaments "according to our [rabbinic] laws," which, Mendelssohn reminded his correspondent, had been fully explained in a special chapter of his *Ritual Laws of the Jews,*[5] a book he had published, he said, at the behest of the Berlin State Council, and which could be obtained in any bookstore. Having discussed the matter in question with the authority of a rabbinic scholar and in the manner of a concise halakhic responsum, he added: "Blessed be the judiciary in Prussian lands! Both daughters of [the late] Moses Chalfan have changed their religion and wish to bring about the nullification of his last will, which stipulates that an offspring be excluded from sharing in the settlement if he or she converts to another religion. They lost their case in court throughout all instances. I can send you copies of the verdicts passed, if you so desire."

The background of this eulogy of Prussian justice is, in brief, as follows: The wealthy Berlin Jewish banker and communal leader Moses Chalfan (Moses Isaac) had established a trust fund *(Fideikommiss)* of two hundred fifty thousand thalers for the benefit of his six children and declared in his last will that any of his offspring who did "not stay within the Jewish religion" forfeited their claim to both capital and interest. After his death in 1776 two of his daughters converted to Christianity, one of them marrying a Lieutenant von Runkel, the other the jurist von Bose. They nevertheless demanded their portion in the settlement. As Mendelssohn's letter relates, the Prussian courts upheld the validity of the testament. However, this was not the end of the story. The legal battle continued until December, 1787, when the concerned parties agreed to a compromise. The plaintifs had procured a testimonial by Professor O. G. Tychsen to the effect that conversion to Christianity, unlike atheism and freethinking, was compatible with staying within the Jewish religion, an opinion that was shown to be "absurd" in a countertestimonial furnished by Dean Teller.[6]

Mendelssohn's praise of Prussian justice was matched by the anger he felt at what he considered a perversion of justice in Austria. On October 4, 1783, he had written to Herz Homberg:[7] "Many thanks for all tolerance if its avowed purpose is still religious union! Because the emperor is tolerant, a wife is to be forced to live, contrary to the agreement entered into, in matrimony with a husband who wishes to bring up the children according to his changed [religious] principles!" This was, of course, a reference to the Arnstein case, which had been mentioned in the pseudo-Sonnenfels pamphlet and which Mendelssohn had cited in his *Jerusalem* as an instance of gross misuse of the idea of tolerance and as a violation of elementary legal concepts.[8] In both cases Mendelssohn's reaction was based as much on his legal philosophy as on Jewish sentiment. In each instance apostasy was involved. He blessed the law courts of his country because they had not permitted the flouting of the will of a Jewish father who had tried to stem, as much as lay within his power, what was to become a flood of desertions.

How little Mendelssohn trusted Joseph II's "tolerance," and how strongly he was in favor of a closing of the ranks, is evident from the well-known letter he dispatched to Herz Homberg on March 1, 1784:[9]

> So long as the system of [religious] union lies in ambush, this hypocritical tolerance seems to me even more dangerous than open persecution. In his *Lettres persanes*, Montesquieu, if I am not mistaken, had the pernicious idea that not harshness and persecution but gentleness and toleration were the best means of conversion. It appears to me that precisely this idea, and not wisdom and love of men, aspires now to become the ruling principle. If this be true, it would be all the more necessary for the small band of those who have no wish either to convert or to be converted to draw more closely together and form a solid unity. By what means? I am led back, again, to the necessity of the ceremonial law, unless we want doctrines to be transformed into precepts, and symbolic [i.e. dogmatizing] books to be written.

To be sure, Mendelssohn, who observed the "ceremonial" laws of Judaism throughout his life, saw the reason for so doing not merely in terms of their sociopolitical function. In the *Jerusalem* he had stressed the significance of Jewish "ceremonies" in various ways, and his deep respect for traditional

Judaism was unmistakable. David Friedländer reports that the young people who flocked to the hospitality of his home, particularly on sabbaths and festivals, debated many an issue in his presence and might have felt tempted to poke fun at the subtleties of talmudic argument and at the minutiae of Jewish law, which had of late become objects of derision among the more enlightened Berlin Jews. "Nevertheless, in Mendelssohn's presence they refrained from making such remarks in either a serious or a playful vein."[10]

These Jewish social gatherings at Mendelssohn's home, which had a marked educational effect, may be presumed to have continued to the very end of his life. They are mentioned at length not only by Friedländer, who became his disciple in 1771, but also by his son Joseph, who was only fifteen years old when his father died, but who still remembered them at the age of seventy-two.[11] Joseph also recalled the frequent late-afternoon visits of learned friends such as Engel, Moritz, Herz, and Friedländer, who were often joined by strangers of rank who happened to be passing through Berlin and were eager to make Mendelssohn's acquaintance. As a rule the conversation concerned subjects of a light nature, such as recent events in the news and current literary works.

Since Mendelssohn started his day, winter and summer alike, at five A.M., and devoted the first three to four hours to study or writing (if not to "lecturing" Joseph and his friends), he had to avoid all strain after returning from the factory, where he was wont to spend about six hours. Visitors were welcome to stay for a simple meal, Mendelssohn's own menu consisting, we are told, of water and sugar. He would stand behind a chair with a curved back, which he clasped with his right arm—his favorite posture. The talk during supper was always animated and witty, full of laughter, yet never lacking in dignity.[12] One of the visitors in January, 1785 (or December, 1784), about whom we happen to be informed, was the Austrian poet and dramatist Johann Baptist von Alxinger (1755–1792), who had become Herz Homberg's friend but, having no influence, could do nothing for him. On January 22, 1785, Mendelssohn wrote to Homberg:[13] "I like Alxinger. He is a young man of fine feelings, who has more common sense than the extravagant manner in which he expresses his sentiments would seem to indicate." After returning to Vienna, Alxinger wrote to Mendelssohn several times, assuring him of his "eternal devotion."[14]

An especially joyous occasion was the celebration of Mendelssohn's fifty-sixth birthday on September 6, 1785. It appears that his friends had arranged a large gathering at his home in honor of the event. For this is what he wrote to Herz Homberg on the very same day:[15]

> Forgive me for answering your letter . . . today, on my fifty-sixth birthday, and for having deferred my reply for such a long time. Today, on my birthday, having spent the morning very cheerfully and feeling well in the best, most friendly company that I might find in perhaps the whole

of Germany, I wish to allay the loving fears of an affectionate friend, who might have completed this amicable circle or might have been its very center. No, my dearest Homberg, thanks to Providence, I am still as well and sprightly as can be in the state of health known to you. I am alive, and hope to prove it to you by the time of the [imminent] fair. You are to get to read a little book of mine "On the Existence of God" [i.e. the *Morgenstunden*], which will demonstrate to you, apodictically, at least my present existence.

Just a month later Mendelssohn received Jacobi's book, which radically changed his mood and compelled him to devote his energies to formulating a fitting reply. During the trying period that followed, which ended only with his death, friendship again proved to be a great comforter. In September, 1785, Elise von der Recke and her traveling companion Sophie Becker, had come to Berlin, and the affection and reverence that these two remarkable ladies had for Mendelssohn brightened his last days.

Charlotte Elisabeth Constanze von der Recke (1754–1833), née countess of Medem and sister of the duchess of Courland, had passed through some years of emotional turmoil. In 1776 her marriage with the baron von der Recke had ended in divorce and she had thereafter led a quiet life in Mitau. But the death of her daughter and, shortly afterwards, that of her brother led in time to her becoming addicted to spiritualism. In 1779 she came under the spell of the notorious magician and hypnotist Alessandro Cagliostro, while at the same time considering Lavater her spiritual mentor (her correspondence with the Zürich deacon had commenced as early as 1775 and continued until February, 1785). She made a decisive break with both Cagliostro and Lavater, however, toward the end of her extended tour of Germany, when she allowed herself to be influenced by some prominent figures of the Enlightenment, especially Nicolai, who had been waging a relentless war against enthusiasm, crypto-Catholicism, and Jesuitism, and who saw in Cagliostro a secret emissary of the Jesuit order. Lavater had not supported Elise von der Recke in her admiration of Cagliostro's magical powers, but he was himself an adept of mystical experimentation, and Nicolai accused him as well as his friend Johann Konrad Pfenninger and the court preacher Doctor Starck in Darmstadt of rank spiritualism and crypto-Catholicism. It was inevitable, therefore, that Elise von der Recke's attitude toward Lavater should undergo a radical reversal. Their break led eventually to a bitter exchange of letters between her and her former father confessor, when in 1787 she published a sensational book demasking Cagliostro and showing herself, as Lavater put it, "possessed by the fanaticism of the Enlightenment mania."[16]

When Elise von der Recke arrived in Berlin in the early fall of 1785, she had already found in the veneration of Lessing's memory a new outlet for her emotionalism, and when she met Mendelssohn she was immediately captivated by his personality. On December 18 she sent him a pin that

Lessing had once worn in his coiffure; the other pins, which had been given to her as a "sacred relic," would now be worn by Nicolai, Sophie Becker, the duchess of Courland, and herself. To her, she said, this reminder of Lessing would serve as a constant exhortation to become worthy of Mendelssohn's friendship. With her letter she also enclosed a letter written to her by the countess of Brühl, which manifested the reverence of "this good soul" for him. She asked on her behalf that he "consecrate" a blank white page, which was attached, by inscribing it in his own hand.[17]

Elise's companion Sophie Becker (1755–1789), a member of a learned and enlightened family, also hailed from Courland. She would achieve a posthumous fame with her *Letters of a Courlander Female on a Trip through Germany*,[18] which was based on a diary she had kept during her travels with Elise von der Recke, and which was, likewise, posthumously published.[19] She died young, at the age of thirty-four, having been married to J. L. Schwartz, a government official and a man of letters, for only one year and having been the mother of a son for not much more than a month.[20] Her husband edited her and Elise von der Recke's poems.[21] This sensitive young woman, who arrived in Berlin at the closing stage of Mendelssohn's life, was beset by religious doubts and was happy to find a haven of refuge in his settled yet open mind. She put her thoughts in writing, and he responded to her in a most gracious and serene manner, never betraying in the least the anguish of soul that he himself felt at the time. His letters to Sophie Becker were, it seems, the very last letters that he wrote to anyone. They are worthy of this privilege.[22]

Sophie's first letter conveyed her brother's, rather than her own, religious scruples. Her eldest brother, Bernhard Becker, was preacher at Candau in Courland, and is known by some essays in the *Berlinische Monatsschrift* and in Voss' *Musenalmanach*.[23] He had written to his sister asking her to submit the following message to Mendelssohn:[24] "My brotherly kiss to Herr Moses, unless this indicates self-pride on my part. Tell him that my love for him has no limits. Alas, dear Sophie, I am an unbelieving theologian! To be sure, all men must belong to one of the classes into which—such is the world—all children of Adam are subdivided; but theologians are the most distorted sort of men." Sophie added: "Do nevertheless permit me to put his mind at ease by writing to him that you consider him exceptional and return the kiss." Mendelssohn replied:[25] "If your dear brother does not mind my grey beard, I shall certainly not allow his black coat to prevent me from pressing my breast to his, in which such a noble heart beats. . . . All in all, I am not so averse to the clergy as your brother seems to be. Every profession has its weak points; those of the clergy are more conspicuous because the profession as such is more venerable. In the words of a Hebrew author: the more noble a thing is in its perfection, the more repugnant it becomes in its corruption.[26] In the present condition of Germany the clergy is still the trustee of the entire culture and morality of the people. It alone maintains as much dignity as there is about philosophy and belles-lettres. The clergyman still reads, even if he is not retired. In all other professions men engage either in their business or play."

In her reply Sophie thanked Mendelssohn for expressing so well what she too had dimly felt. She had sent his letter to her brother on the understanding that he would return this "sacred deposit" to her. She wished, at the same time, to unburden her soul of "many an obscure notion" and of a variety of "feelings." She continued:[27]

> You have been the first of whom I could believe that you would understand me or offer some light where I fail to understand myself. Here I sit alone, and my mind is occupied with so many reflections on man's fate. . . . Suddenly, a Christmas carol[28] resounds in the street. How quickly my whole being is changed! I am a child again, and all the joys of this time that I once experienced reawaken with their religious associations. . . .
>
> These images appeared in such bright colors before my soul, and my involuntary tears seem to lament: They are no longer true! What a riddle I am to myself? Does my reason not proclaim with sufficient resonance and clarity: There was no truth there; here it lies and makes man happy without debasing his maker. By holding on to it you are freed from all the contradictions that confused even your childish mind at times. Yes, it says all this, but I feel as if there was an emptiness in my heart. . . .
>
> Dearest friend, how did you manage, with your feeling heart, to overcome the first false religious sentiments without having become in any way colder? . . . Now I cannot comprehend the thought of "God." I can only admire, be amazed, and fall silent when contemplating nature and its manifold active forces. My prayers no longer become words; for words suggest some thinkable object. My prayers are mere sentiments expressed solely by tears. Hence I find no more taste in public worship, and I remain cold when witnessing it. This is how my soul looks, dearest friend; only to you do I confess so openly. Advise me how to proceed in order to bring closer to my heart the God whom my reason adores in a grain of sand as much as in the sun. Sound common sense or pure reason appears to me rather too cold. The law of the Jews that prescribes the turning of the face toward Jerusalem in prayer proves rather strongly that the lawgiver knew the human soul. Alas! The universe is too vast for us; we do not find God in it. We have to fix our eyes upon a definite spot, as it were, to be able to speak to Him.

The question of reason versus sentiment in religion had never before been put to Mendelssohn in such a succinct and personal manner. His reply to Sophie's confession was truly a confession of his own and offers an invaluable insight into his personal piety. The letter, dated December 27, 1785, is important enough to be quoted in full:[29]

> Dearest Sophie! My maxim is to let no pleasure slip by that is bound up with any sort of representation. My reason must not act prudishly in spoiling my pleasure in the innocent enjoyments of this life. Philosophy is meant to make me happier than I would be without it. It must remain true to this vocation. I stay with her so long as she is a good companion;

when she pulls supercilious, frosty, or even sour faces and gets into a bad mood, I leave her alone and play with my children.

This is rather epicurean, you will say. Perhaps it is. I also choose from the systems of the philosophers invariably that which can make me happier and better at the same time. A philosophy that makes me disgruntled or indifferent to other people or to myself, or frosty toward the sentiment of the beautiful and good, is not my philosophy.

So far as popular concepts of religion are concerned, it seems to me that the pleasant sentiments that they evoke are, for the most part, founded upon an underlying truth that has been merely obscured by a false accretion. The omnipresence of God, for example, is over-sensualized in your religion and, according to some [theologians], it is reduced to the level of humanity. Yet truly speaking, we cannot, even according to reason, imagine the deity as *present* in a sufficiently strong and lively fashion. No anthropomorphism is adequate to communicate to us the enthusiasm that we ought to feel when conceiving of God. Therefore I adhere to popular concepts of religion until my reason is strong enough to furnish, in some other way, a replacement for the loss of those pleasant sentiments. I rejoice in every religious custom that does not lead to intolerance and hatred of men. Like my children, I am happy with every ceremony that has something true and good underlying it. I seek to cut out the untrue as much as I can, [but] I abolish nothing until I am able to substitute something better for its good effect.

If you should have enough patience, dearest Sophie, to read my *Morgenstunden*, you will notice the passage in which I deal with the difficulty of thinking the exaltedness of God in the closest connection with his all-merciful condescension, and where I attribute to our Lessing a great merit in regard to this important truth. It seems to me that in your present condition this thought might stand you in good stead. Your mind and heart will not be put to any undue strain to grasp this doctrine in its entire range of meaning, and to find in it true solace and peace.

You say that the philosopher does not pray—at least not aloud or in song but, at most, in thought. Dearest Sophie! When his hour comes and he is attuned to praying, the philosopher will, against his intent, burst into word and song. The most common man, it seems to me, does not sing in order that God may hear him and be pleased with his melodies. We sing for our own sakes, and this the wise man does just as the fool does. Have you ever read the Psalms with this idea in mind? To me it seems that many psalms are of the sort that they must be sung with true edification by the most enlightened people. I would again recommend to you my translation of the Psalms, would I not thereby betray too much of an author's weakness. This much is certain: the Psalms have sweetened many a bitter hour for me, and I pray and sing them as often as I feel the urge to pray and to sing.

Here we have a most vivid statement of Mendelssohn's creed. It has none of the "stiff pedantry and austerity" that Hegel was later to attribute to him and other representatives of the Enlightenment.[30] True, there are some of the unmistakable shibboleths of the *Aufklärung:* the denunciation of "false accretions" (viz. "superstitions") to the pristine truth of natural religion, the ultimate supremacy of reason, the stress on human happiness as the be-all and end-all of philosophizing. Yet Mendelssohn's creed represents an "enlightenment" tempered by a deep awareness of the intrinsic truth of popular religion.

The "ceremonies"—he is thinking, in particular, of the precepts of Judaism—enshrine precious truths and, what is still more important, they make religion into an emotional experience. They evoke a joy and happiness not easily obtainable by the exercise of pure reason. Again using Hegel's terminology,[31] we may say in contradiction to Hegel that in Mendelssohn's view the ceremonies prevent religious faith from becoming a "mere yearning." Nor does Mendelssohn look contemptuously upon anthropomorphism. On the contrary, he recognizes the need for anthropomorphic language when speaking of God, and he stresses the immanence of God as much as his transcendence. "Enthusiasm," an ugly word in the vocabulary of the period, is—rather surprisingly—acknowledged by Mendelssohn inasmuch as it merely expresses the sentiments appropriate to our notions about God. And prayer is seen to be the most powerful way of uttering man's religious sentiments.

All this is of course a far cry from naive popular religion. It signifies an attempt to humanize, rather than theologize, revealed religion, and it is fraught with all the ambiguities of the effort to transform the theology of revelation into a philosophy of religion. Yet in this moving letter it has a pathos of its own, and it reveals a reverent, mature, and almost esoteric approach to the reality of positive religion.

In her reply Sophie Becker wrote:[32] "How greatly I am obliged to you, dearest friend, for your letter. I shall try to make the best use of it, as well as of all your writings, for my peace and serenity." She could hardly have said more without the risk of sounding pretentious. Her letter conveyed to Mendelssohn an invitation by Elise von der Recke to visit her at any time convenient to him; being confined to her home on account of some indisposition, she would consider his visit a "medicine." The letter was dated December 30, 1785; three days earlier Sophie had recorded in her diary:[33] "Elise did not feel well during the whole day.... She is not at all in good shape. God help us to get back to Courland!"

It is not surprising that the patient was eager to be visited by Mendelssohn, for he had proved to be entertaining as well as inspiring company on several previous occasions. Sophie's diary had reported on September 29 that after a morning spent at the home of Chodowiecki, the famous painter and engraver, Elise, who had her sister the duchess with her, received after three that afternoon Moses Mendelssohn, the count of Stolberg, and another friend:[34] "The conversation became very interesting, and I feasted my eyes in seeing the amiable philosopher with the Jews' beard engaged in talk with some charming ladies. In the main the discussion dealt with the immortality of souls, with the question of whether an inborn state of feeling exists between children and parents, and with the death penalty." The duchess is said to have recalled an anecdote that proved to her the preexistence of the soul: we had a feeling of having existed before and, hence, of going to continue existing after death. "'Mendelssohn seemed to listen to this with pleasure, and he advised the duchess not to allow herself to be robbed of her natural and warm conviction by any learned babble on immortality."

On October 4 Sophie entered into her diary[35] an account of the preceding day. The weather had been beautiful, and the duchess had invited Mendelssohn and Ramler to visit her at her residence in Friedrichsfelde near Berlin. The gentlemen arrived a little earlier than expected, and while the duchess was getting ready to receive them, Sophie took them on a tour of the park. At dinner time Mendelssohn went to a nearby inn where he had ordered a frugal meal, for "on account of an undoubtedly very venerable reason this philosophical man never accepts an invitation to the meals of the Christians."[36] The diary continues: "We spent only a short time at dinner in order not to miss the man's company too long. Now we all sat in a circle around Dorothea [the duchess] while she talked about Italy and Ramler declaimed passages from *Nathan* and other writings. He included Bernhard's [Bernhard Becker's] poem in honor of the duchess' birthday, and I was pleased to hear Mendelssohn mutter to himself, 'A worthy poet.' Then we looked at drawings, and a few *Lieder* were sung and played. At five our dear guests took their leave, Mendelssohn saying, with radiant eyes: 'Today I have reveled in the spirit.'" It was on the following day, October 4, that he sent his *Morgenstunden* to Jacobi.

In her entry for October 10, 1785, Sophie mentioned a visit that Elise and she had paid to Mendelssohn in the company of Nicolai:[37] "Today there was a great deal of talk about Lessing, which was occasioned by the recently published letters of the privy councillor Jacobi to Mendelssohn. They were designed to refute Spinozism and to prove, at the same time, that Lessing had been in favor of it. Mendelssohn and Nicolai, who have an intimate knowledge of Lessing's mind and principles, consider this a plot by Lavater's party." We have here a clear echo of Mendelssohn's—and, as it turned out, also Nicolai's—theory that Jacobi, in true Lavaterian fashion, had tried to convert Lessing, and upon failing to do so, had tried to discredit him.

On October 11 Sophie spent half the forenoon reading Jacobi's *Letters*.[38] Later in the month Elise von der Recke and Sophie paid a visit to Hamburg, where they became very friendly with the Reimarus family. Highlights of their stay were a visit by Klopstock and meeting Karl Philipp Emanuel Bach, then seventy-three years old, who played his *Phantasien* and other pieces for them on two separate occasions.[39] An entry dated November 24 reads:[40] "Today we had again, at long last, the pleasure of visiting our beloved Mendelssohn in his house. The welcome he gave us testified to his inner joy on seeing us again. Nicolai accompanied us but had a dinner appointment with Governor Möllendorf and so had to leave after a short while. Again, there was much talk about Lessing. As Elise is about to return to Friedrichsfeld, I shall certainly avail myself of Moses' invitation to visit him on my own. In his presence the soul is so willing to open itself." On November 27 the diary records that in the afternoon—it was a Sunday—Mendelssohn came to see Elise, who was indisposed, and Sophie:[41]

> Jacobi's treatise, which is so eager to base everything, again, upon mere faith, and which presents reason as a will-o'-the-wisp, almost made Mendelssohn decide to show the difference between the old and the more recent theology. He meant to point out that the first Church Fathers recommended reason as a means of examining Christianity, and that they considered only the so-called mysteries of religion to be above (though not contrary to) reason, whereas the more recent theologians degraded the reasonableness of Christianity by disregarding it entirely. Yet Nicolai restrained him from doing this, out of a concern for his peace of mind.
>
> Elise told him what Spalding had preached today about the secret societies and fanaticism. She challenged him [Mendelssohn] to commit to writing and bequest to posterity, for the sake of truth, what concern for himself and his family prevented him from publishing now. "Good Heavens!" he said, "why should I take care of the Christians, when my own hearth is in such poor condition. True Judaism is no longer found anywhere. Fanaticism [*Schwärmerey*] and superstition exist among us to a most abhorrent degree. Were my nation not so stupid, it would stone me on account of my *Jerusalem,* but people do not understand me...."
>
> We then talked about the fact that religious tuition impressed upon Lutheran children that ... the despised condition of the Jewish nation was the most eloquent proof for the truth of Christianity.... Mendelssohn laughed and said: "Indeed, indeed, you regard us as living testimonies to your faith, and for this fanciful idea we have to thank a certain bishop, whose name I do not recall, for without it the Christians would have exterminated us long ago."[42]

The conversation recorded by Sophie Becker shows Mendelssohn in a rather grim mood. His annoyance with Jacobi's antirationalism had obviously reinforced his antipathy toward any kind of "fanaticism," including its Jewish variety. "True Judaism" as defined in his *Jerusalem* was of course to be found nowhere, since it represented a philosopher's vision rather than a historical reality. He was surprised at the absence of violent reaction on the part of the orthodox. On January 22, 1785, he had written to Homberg:[43] "That Fränkel[44] is more pleased with my *Jerusalem* than with my preface [to *Manasseh Ben Israel*] does indeed astonish me. I should have thought that, according to his principles [the *Jerusalem*] had put the lid on it." It was no doubt his proposal to curb rabbinic power, combined with his effort to present Judaism as a revealed legislation allied to natural religion (and hence bereft of all mystical elements), that he had expected to meet with fierce resistance. Yet no one had lifted a finger to "stone" him. Mendelssohn attributed this apathy to lack of comprehension and, ultimately, to fanaticism and superstition, which held the "nation" in their grip.

How Mendelssohn's mood could change is attested by his very last letter of December 27, his last to Sophie Becker. Mendelssohn's mood was also different on December 17 when, as the diary tells us,[45] Elise, Sophie, and Nicolai spent two hours of "the most pleasant conversation" at his home. The subject then under discussion was music, especially that of Gluck. Mendelssohn pleaded for simplicity in song and rejected coloratura, which Nicolai defended. Summing up the impressions conveyed by Sophie's diary, we may say that at a time of extreme tension the presence in Berlin of Sophie Becker and Elise von der Recke provided Mendelssohn with a happy antidote to the gloom into which he might otherwise have fallen.

However, there was yet another and perhaps more potent source of joy in Mendelssohn's life: his wife and children. All visitors were impressed by the domestic scene in the Mendelssohn household. When Elise Reimarus wrote to him on June 20, 1783, after her recent visit to his home, she concluded her letter with these words:[46] "Take care of yourself, dearest friend, and remember me not only to your dear wife and mother [in-law] but also to all your dear children, each one of whom I recall with pleasure. How good it was to be among all of you!" In her diary of October 1, 1785, Sophie wrote:[47] "He [Mendelssohn] has three very well-brought-up daughters, of whom the middle one is a most beautiful girl, and three sons, whose intelligence you could tell from their face." The entry for October 10 reads:[48] "At today's visit we also saw Mendelssohn's wife, whom I like very much and who seems to be a woman of a great deal of scholarly understanding. She takes a deep interest in everything her husband says." The youngest child, Nathan, who was not yet four, was Sophie's favorite. When writing to Mendelssohn on December 22, she enclosed a present for "my dear little Nathan,"[49] and in his reply Mendelssohn reported the child's reaction.[50] Mendelssohn seems to have been particularly fond of this bright little fellow, and a passing remark in a letter by Joseph, the eldest son,[51] about "our sweet Nathan" shows that these sentiments were shared by the rest of the family. Mendelssohn probably liked to play with this child of his old age, for in the *Morgenstunden*[52] he approvingly told the story of a king who did not mind receiving a foreign ambassador while playing hobby-horse with his children, and in his last letter he declared that as soon as philosophical reason became ill-tempered he was ready to abandon it and to play with his children.[53]

Yet neither Mendelssohn nor Fromet spoiled their children. In a letter that Joseph wrote to his sisters from Hamburg on September 15, 1785, he betrayed a certain shyness and a sense of distance vis-à-vis his parents, which must have stemmed from a strict and somewhat authoritarian upbringing:[54] "You, dearest sisters, are always the first to whom I write, and this for the following reason. True, it would be the proper thing and in response to my feelings to write first to our dear parents, but ... I am, at the moment, in an insufficiently sober mood to dare write to them. Reverence [*Ehrfurcht*] restrains me from writing everything that comes to my mind, and I prefer to wait until I can consider with less excitement what I am to write to them. You, however, my dear ones, are quite capable of standing any nonsense from me, and I am going to tell you all that my heart prompts me to say."

Whereas Joseph's attitude was one of laudable "reverence," his eldest sister Brendel seems to have been somewhat critical of her parents. A letter to Joseph written in her old age (on November 25, 1832), long after she had become Dorothea Schlegel and cut all her Jewish moorings, recalled past days spent during summer vacations in Alt-Strelitz at the home of good friends, the court agent Nathan Meyer and his wife, who later became Joseph's parents-in-law:[55]

> Hinni[56] is now the only one left from those gay childhood days when we were so often guests in Alt-Streliz in the parents' [the Meyers'] house. That house with its garden, sheep, and cows, horse and carriage; the greater freedom as well as the greater respect and attention with which we, the children, were treated compared with what we were used to in our paternal home; all this appeared to me like a world of fairies, and I remember every room, every pathway in the garden, and the little salon ... in which there was a picture of two wigged men painted grey in grey with the caption: Whig and Tory, two words I then came across for the first time and that were subsequently explained to me by our late father. All is still vividly before my eyes whenever I recall it, especially the lovely mother [Joseph's future mother-in-law] who was of such inimitable, dignified patience and gentleness, and ... [such] a striking contrast to our own somewhat impetuous, somewhat impatient mother.

If Brendel found some fault with her mother, she also realized in later years "that my obstinacy, my wilfulness, my impetuosity, my passionateness, my unfortunate restlessness, my dissatisfaction and fantasies, a certain sickly urge for the strange and unknown, caused me to drift."[57]

During Mendelssohn's lifetime there were no forebodings of such things to come. Brendel's marriage to Simon Veit (Witzenhausen), which took place on April 3, 1783 (Nissan 1, 5543), was an event celebrated with all the trimmings of a traditional Jewish wedding. A nuptial poem in honor of the occasion was composed by Joseph (Josel) Pick of Reichenau (Bohemia), whom Mendelssohn had appointed tutor to his children after Homberg had left.[58] Written in a flowery Hebrew style, it was addressed to the groom, describing him in the introduction as "the enlightened [*maskil*], precious, and lovely young man, the rabbinic scholar [*hatorani*], the honorable Rabbi Simon, son of the generous and wealthy leader, the *parnass* and *manhig*, the wise and understanding, the God-fearing honorable Rabbi Judah Witzenhausen." The bride was spoken of as "the precious and lovely young lady, the enlightened Brendel, daughter of the famed scholar, who engages in charity and acts of kindness, the wise and understanding, the God-fearing honorable Rabbi Moses."

How elated Mendelssohn was by this union can be seen from his letter to Herz Homberg on June 27, 1783:[59] "My daughter got married ... on Nissan 1. ... She lives with her incomparable Veit in a happy marriage. She could not have been happier if the son of the most wealthy man had condescended to take her as his wife." The epithet "incomparable" was not exaggerated. Veit was a young man of exceptional nobility of character and was capable, as the future showed, of the utmost self-denial and generosity.[60]

Brendel (Dorothea) was eighteen years old when she married Veit. Her sister Reikel (Recha) was seventeen, when in the fall of 1785 she became the wife of Mendel Meyer, son of Nathan Meyer of Alt-Strelitz. The couple seems to have been engaged for well over a year, for as early as June 26, 1784, Mendelssohn sent Mendel Meyer his "paternal blessing" in a very humorous letter that solicited the young man's support for a worthy cause and expressed the hope that he would be able to persuade both the duke, the "father of the country," and "his lordship, the father of his home," to make a contribution. The letter concluded:[61] "I remain yours graciously, in our garden at Moses' Rest [*zu Moses-Ruhe*], on the twenty-sixth of the month of roses in the year in which no rose desires to bloom as yet." On September 6, 1785, he wrote to Homberg:[62] "I believe I have already reported to you that I have given my consent to the marriage of my daughter Reikel to Mendel, son of the Mecklenburg-Strelitz court agent Nathan Meyer."[63] The youngest daughter Yente (Henriette) was only ten years of age when Mendelssohn died.[64]

Providing his children with a well-balanced education was one of Mendelssohn's major concerns. In his biography of his father Joseph reports:[65] "There remained six children, upon whose education he lavished his attention and a fortune. He entrusted their instruction in general subjects and in morals to private tutors, and he chose for this purpose men whose academic qualifications he had sufficiently tested and of whose [good] moral character he was convinced. From his letters to Homberg, who had been a private tutor appointed by him, it is evident how much he esteemed him as a man of learning. . . . After him Mendelssohn engaged a scholar by the name of Ensheim, who hailed from Alsace. Due to his excessive modesty, this man never published anything, but he was a profound thinker, steeped in abstract sciences and possessed of an unequalled gentleness and goodness of heart. Being [themselves] more advanced, his pupils were in a better position to appreciate him as a teacher and to sense his beneficial influence than they had been under Homberg. Long after he had left the house Ensheim's memory was cherished by the grown-up children in gratitude and love. Foreign languages, music, and drawing were taken care of through private lessons, and Mendelssohn had his older children instructed also in the cutting of quill-pens. . . . He arranged for his eldest son, when he was ten to twelve years old, to be taught Talmud and the Hebrew language. Later he sent him to a grammar school [*Gymnasium*]. Engel, out of friendship for Mendelssohn, undertook to instruct his eldest son in German style."

This brief account is neither complete nor entirely correct. It completely disregards the deep concern that Mendelssohn felt for the instruction of his children, particularly his sons, in the Bible. Joseph failed to mention that at the age of five he was already receiving Bible lessons from his father, who had translated the Pentateuch primarily for this purpose. Joseph may also have forgotten that from 1775 until 1780 the great Hebraist Solomon Dubno had been his tutor in Hebrew. His Jewish education in both Bible and Hebrew had thus commenced at the age of five.[66] Herz Homberg became Joseph's teacher in Jewish subjects in 1778 or 1779, when the boy was eight or nine years old, and remained at his post until 1782. His immediate successor was not Ensheim but Joseph Pick, who would later write the nuptial poem on the occasion of Brendel's wedding to Veit in 1783. The warm tribute that Joseph paid to Ensheim was certainly well deserved, but the information given about this remarkable man is woefully inadequate. Moses Ensheim (Moses Brisac or Metz) did publish some pieces of Hebrew poetry in *Ha-Me'assef* and *Recherches sur les calculs différentiels et intégrals* (Paris, 1799), a work held in esteem by Lagrange and Laplace. He was a friend of the Abbé Grégoire, whom he assisted in the writing of his prize-essay on behalf of the Jews. During the last years of his life Ensheim was a private tutor in the house of Abraham Furtado in Bayonne.[67]

Joseph did mention the instruction in philosophy received from his father when *Morgenstunden* was being written. Yet this was not the only occasion. On January 8, 1784, Mendelssohn wrote to Garve how pleased he had been to receive from him a complimentary copy of his German translation of Cicero's *De officiis,* which had been commissioned by the king. Garve, he said, had made "an important present to the Germans" by this work *On Duties,* and he had purposely delayed expressing his thanks because he had wanted first to test the value of this gift:[68] "Yet I did render thanks in a way in which Providence wishes to be thanked for its benefits: by receiving, enjoying, and sharing. In the morning hours that I devote to my thirteen-year-old son we read the *Duties,* comparing the translation with Cicero's text, and learn in this way." The pains that Mendelssohn took to train Joseph in clear thinking are manifest in the page of an exercise book[69] that contains four paragraphs in the lad's then still-clumsy handwriting. They set out to define the subtle differences between the meanings of what might seem to be synonymous terms: sympathy and pity; admiration and astonishment;[70] number and quantity; transgression, sin, and vice. The father made corrections and, in the last paragraph, reformulated his son's definitions in the margin of the page.

Mendelssohn's letters to Homberg offer invaluable insight into his attitude in educational matters, insofar as Joseph was concerned. Joseph was, undoubtedly the apple of Mendelssohn's eye, and he placed the highest hopes in him. His son Abraham, who was Joseph's junior by six years, was still too young to be a problem in this regard; he was a child of "extraordinary gifts," as the father noted, but the question of finding the right teacher for him was not a matter of concern for the time being.[71] On June 27, 1783, Mendelssohn reported to Homberg:[72] "Joseph is making good progress in his thinking. In his writing he is somewhat behind, though only in mechanical copy writing; his diction ... is good, painstaking, and also vivid." On October 4, when Joseph was already past his Bar-Mitsva, the father again expressed satisfaction with the lad's progress and diligence:[73] what mattered was not the amount of knowledge acquired but correct and penetrating thinking. Joseph's taste was also becoming more refined. Mendelssohn's only cause for complaint was the inflexibility of his son's character and the lack of gentleness in his whole being. "You know him: he was always of a mentality that would ten times sooner break than bend."

The next letter, which was probably written toward the end of 1783, made a startling announcement:[74] "My son Joseph has as good as shelved his Hebrew studies. After you left, he came unfortunately into the hands of a scholar who was an empty dialectician [*ba'al pilpul*];[75] and much as Joseph likes acumen and is inclined to argue a case, he has nevertheless no mind for dialectics [*pilpul*] proper." Mendelssohn was quite resigned to spare Joseph the training in this "sterile kind of acumen," and when Homberg was in charge of his tuition in Talmud it had been agreed that all *pilpul* would be shunned.[76] What he regretted was not his son's aversion to hairsplitting argumentation but the fact that his distaste for the teacher's instruction had made Hebrew studies generally repugnant to him. Assuming that Joseph had commenced studying the Talmud under Homberg at the age of nine, he had already had some four years of teaching in this subject. In a letter written about a year later, on November 20, 1784, Mendelssohn reported:[77] "My son Joseph attends a public lecture course in physics given by Doctor Marcus Herz, and one in chemistry by Mister Klaproth,[78] without my having as yet determined that he is to become a scholar. He has capabilities so far as the intellect is concerned, but languages are not his forte. He is very far behind even in Latin, and he has forgotten almost everything you taught him in Hebrew. I let him go his own way. As you know, I am not in favor of compulsion; and with this iron character, which would rather break than bend, nothing would be accomplished by compulsion anyhow. His sound common sense will, I am sure, guide him toward some goal."

It was by no means indifference, we gather from these remarks, that made Mendelssohn acquiesce in Joseph's turning his back on Hebrew studies. He simply realized the futility of exercising undue pressure on so stubborn a character as Joseph. Besides, Mendelssohn's philosophical principles were strictly opposed to any kind of compulsion: "Every compulsion," he had written,[79] "is in itself an evil." His trust in the power of common sense implied the hope that all would be well in the end, including Joseph's attitude toward religion. Almost another year later, on September 6, 1785, Mendelssohn could inform Homberg of some happy change:[80] "My son Joseph, my son-in-law Simon Witzenhausen, and the tutor of my son Abraham, Herr Moses Metz [Ensheim] read the *More* [*Nevukhim*] and compare the original diligently with the translation."[81] Ensheim's personality had made a sufficient impression on Joseph to draw him back to Hebrew studies. Obviously, he had not forgotten all his Hebrew, and the study of the *Guide of the Perplexed* in both Hebrew and Latin seems to have excited his curiosity. How firmly the fifteen-year-old Joseph was still attached to traditional mores, observances, and sentiments is documented by a letter that he wrote to the two older sisters on September 15, 1785, during a visit to Hamburg.[82] The letter is written in Hebrew characters, bears the Hebrew date, starts with the abbreviation of the pious formula "With the help of God," and mentions *Hol Ha-Mo'ed Sukkot* as the date originally fixed for his return. He was being urged, he mentioned in the letter, to stay on until the fair but unless he received "an express command from our dear parents" he would not wish to remain longer than about a week or two after the *Sukkot* festival.

The question of Joseph's future career occupied Mendelssohn's mind to a large degree. In the letter written to Homberg toward the end of 1783 he told him:[83] "As yet we have decided nothing about his future manner of living. I am still uncertain what to recommend to him. His talents and good dispositions for the profound sciences justify the expectation that he will accomplish excellent results in this sphere. As a Jew, however, he can only practice medicine, and for this profession he has neither the inclination nor the natural gift. To commit him to business is premature, it would seem. Therefore, let him first of all learn everything to which he feels inclined. His fitness for becoming a merchant will . . . not be spoiled thereby. If need be, let him do as his father had to do: muddle his way through now as a scholar, now as a merchant, though he may run the risk of becoming neither the one nor the other in a full sense." By the time of Joseph's trip to Hamburg, it had been decided that he should go into business, a decision that was proved right by his immense success as the founder (jointly with his brother Abraham) of the famous banking-house Mendelssohn & Comp.[84]

Joseph arrived in Hamburg, with a letter of introduction from his father to Elise Reimarus, on September 1, 1785.[85] Mendelssohn wrote to Elise again on October 4, when sending her his *Morgenstunden:*[86] "You no sooner said goodbye to my physical son, for whose kind reception I still owe you thanks, than my spiritual son [the *Morgenstunden*] is already knocking at your door asking to be admitted. . . . My son Joseph will stay a few days in Strelitz; I am longing to see him back. It is a matter of deep regret to me that I have to withhold him from the sciences in order to make him a slave of Mammon. For medicine he has no inclination; and as a Jew he must become a physician, a merchant, or a beggar." In her reply of October 17 Elise assured Mendelssohn how much joy the visit of his "physical son" had given her. As for the young man's career, she tried to console the father:[87] "Why . . . do you regret that you must commit him to business? Anyway, cause him here, too, to follow in his father's footsteps and to combine, as you do, the earthly with the spiritual vocation. Let business be the breadwinner, while the Muses are free. With a head on his shoulders such as his there is no danger that he will become a slave of the former, and every mortal is supposed to have to contend with some kind of drag."

Elise's words must have been balm to Mendelssohn's soul, for deep down in his heart he cherished the hope that Joseph would continue the work that he had left unfinished. Only once had he permitted himself to express this fond hope. When on September 1, 1784, he thanked Doctor Zimmermann for the gift of his book *On Solitude* and praised it as a happy blend of common sense and humor, he added the following paragraphs:[88]

> I wish some blessed child of Providence were to attack, in a work of the very same quality, atheism, which is both the precursor and successor of enthusiasm *(Schwärmerey)*. It would have to be a man in control of the sublime seriousness of reason as well as of the most tender warmth of sentiment and of all the gentleness of a rich, though not luxuriant imagination. In one word, if I am to picture to myself the ideal man for such a task: one who would do for the cause of God[89] what Winckelmann[90] did for paganism. A man of this description would write a counterpart to your work of art, and the malaise that is becoming rampant on all sides would thereby be remedied effectively.
>
> For my part, I can for the time being express only a pious wish and have to let the matter rest at that. I feel much too weak to accomplish so exalted a task. However, I want to collect the material for it as long as Providence grants me life. Perhaps, someday, a more fortunate mortal will make use of this material. And perhaps—the very contemplation of it is giving comfort and strength to my heart—perhaps this more fortunate one is my son!

Joseph was not destined to fulfil this hope, but he did live up to Elise's prediction that he might combine business with devotion to the Muses.[91] The care that his father had lavished on his education also paid dividends in another respect. He and his sister Reikel (Recha) were the only ones of Mendelssohn's children to resist the lure of baptism in an age of transition during which social and cultural pressures played havoc with the new generation.

The End

The upshot of *To Lessing's Friends,* Mendelssohn's last and most impassioned piece of writing, was the assertion that Jacobi, a true disciple of Lavater, had tried in vain to convert Lessing to his antirational stance of faith, and having failed, had depicted him as a Spinozist, atheist, and blasphemer; that, moreover, Jacobi's overtures to Mendelssohn had been animated by the same conversionist zeal.

The suspicion that Jacobi was a religious enthusiast advocating a "return to the flag of faith" had already been expressed by Mendelssohn in his

"Objections" of August 1, 1784. The new element in the thesis now advanced was the charge that by publishing his book Jacobi had publicly "accused" Lessing of Spinozism, atheism, and blasphemy. In trying to clear his late friend's good name of these imputations, Mendelssohn had only to draw the full implications from his basic assumption that Jacobi was an enthusiast à la Lavater. The idea that Jacobi must have sought to "convert" Lessing provided Mendelssohn with a kind of Ariadne's clue in his attempt to disentangle fiction and truth in Jacobi's "Report." It explained to his full satisfaction the roles played by both Jacobi and Lessing in their talks:[1]

> In my endeavor to remove all these perplexities and seeming contradictions [in Lessing's behavior during his conversations with Jacobi] I see only one way of picturing to myself the course of events, and though it might be merely a hypothesis, it nevertheless appears to me, in view of Herr Jacobi's manifest aim, very natural and in keeping with the characters of the persons concerned.... Herr Jacobi obviously aims to lead his fellowmen, who have lost their way in the wilderness of speculation, back to the straight and sure path of faith. All his talks with Lessing (as well as his correspondence with Hemsterhuis, with our lady friend, and with me) tend in this direction.
>
> So far as, in the first place, Lessing is concerned, Jacobi perhaps did not himself believe that Lessing had entrusted a special secret to him but considered him [Lessing] a man of unstable principles capable of asserting one thing today and another tomorrow.... He held him to be a mistaken sophist lost in his subtleties, as one who sees truth and error in the same light or in the same obscurity; who ultimately prizes wit as much as philosophy; and who, given the mood, seems to regard blasphemy as evidence of a strong mind. Jacobi believed our friend to be in such a deplorable state of mental confusion, and he magnanimously resolved to cure him of his ills. As a skillful physician he took the risk of first aggravating the illness so as to be able to cure it the more effectively later. He introduced Lessing deeper and deeper into the labyrinth of Spinozism and lured him into the thorn-hedges of pantheism in order to make the single exit, which he meant to show him, all the more agreeable. This exit, as we now see clearly enough, is a retreat to the flag of faith. [Jacobi] wanted to convince [Lessing] that, as he put it, certain things could not be explained; that one should, nevertheless, not ignore but accept them as they were; and that one should retreat from philosophy, which left no choice but perfect skepticism. To Lessing's eager question: "Retreat—whither?" the answer is given: "Toward the light of which Spinoza says that it illumines itself and the darkness;" and thus Spinoza himself was to lead Lessing back to the path to truth, from which he [Spinoza] had caused him to depart to such an extent.
>
> Our friend, who may quickly have sensed the honest intention of Herr Jacobi, was roguish enough to confirm him in the view he had formed of him. In part, he may have relished the play, in part he might have enjoyed the acumen with which Jacobi knew how to present and defend Spinoza's doctrine. You know that our friend found more pleasure in hearing an absurd proposition cleverly argued than in hearing the truth badly defended. Therefore he perfectly simulated the attentive disciple; he contradicted nothing and agreed with everything; and he merely sought to keep the discussion going by some jocular remark, whenever it tended to come to a halt....

I pursue my hypothesis, for it appears increasingly natural to me. Jacobi realized that his experiment with Lessing had failed. However, motivated as he was by the same pious intention, he believed that he had to make an example of Lessing as an edifying warning to all other wiseacres. . . . Unless they want to follow Lessing, Leibniz, Wolff, and all the other metaphysical demonstrants in becoming determinists and hence (according to Jacobi) fatalists, Spinozists, and atheists, or unless they want to abandon themselves to extreme skepticism, let them in good time go after the light that illumines also the darkness. "Every proof presupposes something already proven, the very first principle of which is revelation;" and, as he further states, "the prime element of all human knowledge and action is belief."

Since Herr Jacobi does not know me, I too may have been described to him as such a wiseacre, as one who concedes too much to reason and nothing to faith, who labors under the illusion that he can accomplish everything with the help of metaphysical demonstrations (e.g., that by his quiddities he can exorcise spirits or render ineffective the machinations of secret societies). Hence [Jacobi's] earnest endeavor to cure me as well of this illness, if possible. Hence he permitted himself to reveal to me the secret that our friend allegedly wished to hide from me. The good and honest aim of guiding me to the bosom of faith, though not justifying everything, can at least excuse a great deal.

I had, right in the beginning, suspected something of this kind, having experienced very often such well-intentioned attempts by my contemporaries. I therefore made it clear to Herr Jacobi in my reply [in the "Objections"] that the cure was doomed to failure in my case, and that in respect of doctrines and eternal truths I recognized no conviction that was not founded on reason. Judaism prescribes faith in historical truths, in facts on which the authority of our positive ritual law is based. The existence and authority of the Supreme Lawgiver, however, must be cognized by reason, and here no revelation and no faith are applicable, according to the principles of Judaism. Judaism is not a revealed religion but a revealed law. As a Jew, I said, I had special reason to seek conviction through rational arguments.

By exposing Jacobi as a kind of missionary and interpreting Lessing's part in the reported conversations as an exhibition of sheer playfulness Mendelssohn artfully contrived to achieve two purposes: he cleared Lessing of all charges and he simply brushed aside as pure nonsense any suggestion of a lack of rapport in philosophical matters between himself and his late friend. By innuendo he attributed the revelation of the "secret," the most upsetting passage in Jacobi's book, to pious deceit inspired by conversionist zeal. What is astonishing in the section just quoted is not the bitter irony or the forensic skill of the presentation—all this could have been expected—but the seriousness with which Mendelssohn treated Jacobi's suspected attempt to convert him. It reads almost as if he was repeating the gist of what he had told Lavater, throwing in for good measure the main thesis of the *Jerusalem*.

There can be little doubt that Mendelssohn identified Jacobi with the Swiss deacon, Lavater, that most sinister figure in Mendelssohn's life. In a footnote attached to the quotations from Jacobi concerning revelation and faith Mendelssohn actually pointed out that the prooftext offered by Jacobi was a passage from Lavater,[2] and at the end of *To Lessing's Friends*[3] he wrote: "Things being what they are, I believe that little can be accomplished by discussion and that the best course to follow is to part company. Let him [Jacobi] return to the faith of his fathers, subdue stammering reason by the triumphant power of faith, crush rising doubts ... by authoritative dicta, bless and seal his childlike return with words from the 'pious, angelic, and pure mouth of Lavater....' I, for my part, continue in my Jewish unbelief, attribute to no mortal an 'angelic and pure mouth,' would not wish to depend even on the authority of an archangel, where eternal verities, on which man's happiness is founded, are concerned; and I have no choice but to stand on my own feet or fall; or rather, since 'we are, all of us, born in faith,' as Herr Jacobi says, I too return to the faith of my fathers, which according to the primary meaning of the word [the Hebrew word *emuna*] does not consist in belief in any doctrine or opinion but signifies confidence and trust in the attributes of God."

Thus the shadow of Lavater thus lies heavily on this, the last of Mendelssohn's publications, and it seems that to a considerable degree his animus against Jacobi drew its power and heat from a reactivation, as it were, of the Lavater phobia in his psyche. The internal evidence to this effect in *To Lessing's Friends* is supported by other testimonies. Mention has already been made of an entry in Sophie Becker's diary, the entry for October 10, according to which Mendelssohn and Nicolai considered the whole thing "a plot by Lavater's party."[4] Further testimony is provided by the report on a visit paid to Mendelssohn on December 13, 1785, three weeks before his death, by Johann Friedrich Reichardt, musical director of the Berlin Opera. Although Reichardt's report—about which more will be said later—was undoubtedly tendentious, it does reveal a great deal about Mendelssohn's thinking at the time. It shows, among other things, how obsessed Mendelssohn was with the idea that Lavater was behind it all. Reichardt, who was a friend of Jacobi's but was also on cordial terms with Mendelssohn, wrote on January 29, 1786:[5]

> Mendelssohn received me on December 13 at five P.M. in an extremely jovial mood with the words: I am glad you came. A copy of my *Morgenstunden,* which I had promised to send you to London, has been waiting to be delivered for a long time. You had left London far too soon. *I* [Reichardt]: I regard this a most welcome present. I hear that your *Morgenstunden* is related to a treatise that Jacobi gave me. *M:* Then you know Jacobi's treatise? What do you think of it? *I:* I was just about to ask you the very same question. *M:* I can find in it only one purpose. Jacobi wants to convert me, and he wanted to convert Lessing at the time. *I:* This sounds funny enough. However, it is still more unlike Jacobi than allowing himself to be converted is likely in your case.—Both of us laughed heartily at this fanciful idea. Yet he continued to defend this strange hypothesis by mentioning several of the things that are set forth in his treatise [*To Lessing's Friends*]. He said among other things: Why does [Jacobi], on top of everything, adduce Lavater after having done what,

according to his belief, he had to do? And, with that familiar delicate ironic smile of his, he added: It is certain, dear Reichardt, that Jacobi and Lavater are engaged in a common plot.[6]

Mendelssohn was of course quite right to suspect that Jacobi was hand in glove with Lavater, and if he had had any inkling of the enthusiastic tone of their correspondence he would surely have been all the more convinced that some sinister plot was involved. Nevertheless, he did misjudge the situation, for Jacobi had never had any intention of converting either Lessing or Mendelssohn. Was Mendelssohn, then, the victim of a morbid obsession caused by the traumatic experience inflicted upon him long ago by Lavater, whose influence on Jacobi could not be gainsaid, and whose very name revived dark shadows of the past? This may have been the case to some extent, but there was a certain substance to his imaginings. Nicolai, as we know from Sophie's diary, shared Mendelssohn's theory of a Lavaterian plot, and Nicolai had his own good reasons, which were known to Mendelssohn, for considering such a plot to be possible.

In 1784 there had been a protracted and acrimonious correspondence between Nicolai and Lavater concerning Lessing.[7] It centered on the following issue: In March, 1782, a new periodical called *The Churchly Messenger for the Friends of Religion in all Churches* had started publication in Dessau and Leipzig under the editorship of Lavater's intimate friend Pastor Johann Konrad Pfenninger of Zürich, and under the sponsorship of Lavater, who not only helped to raise funds for the project but also solicited news items. The first issue of the journal had included some so-called "extracts from some very trustworthy letters from Brunswick concerning Lessing's death." These extracts, quoted—allegedly—from four letters (dated February 16, March 21, April 25, and May 31, 1781), spoke in the most malicious, brutal, and insulting way about Lessing's last hours, his burial, the causes of his death, and his mother's grief at having given birth to a son who had so grievously injured religion. The unnamed writer depicted Lessing as a veritable demon who had refused, on his death bed, to see the venerable Abbot Jerusalem, and who had uttered blasphemies to his physician and to his Jewish friend Alexander Daveson. The Israelites had been his favorite nation. In his *Nathan the Wise* the hero was a Jew, while the Christians were rogues and knaves.

This revolting piece seems to have been procured by Lavater, who had shown the fiercest animosity toward Lessing even prior to his death. Nicolai asked the Brunswick professor Eschenburg to make discreet inquiries into the matter and eventually published, in the *Allgemeine deutsche Bibliothek,* an anonymous article by Eschenburg, which concluded with the following condemnatory statement: "It seems to me that the fiction presented bears too obviously the mark of falsification and of the lowest kind of slander to have appeared probable and publishable ... to men such as the editors of the *Churchly Messenger* wish and ought to be. And to go as far as designate these letters as 'very trustworthy'! What could have motivated, what could have justified Messrs. Lavater and Pfenninger to do a thing like this? If the wretched person who was stupid or malicious enough to patch up these reports has the courage to reveal his identity, I shall appear under my name and accuse him of untruthfulness."

Pfenninger remained silent but Lavater sent Nicolai a declaration disclaiming responsibility for what was published in the journal but not indicating any disapproval of the contents of the abusive letters—an omission that Nicolai was not slow to notice. He returned the declaration to Lavater, who had asked him to insert it in the next issue of the *Bibliothek,* and in a letter that minced no words put the question to him: "Do you consider them [the "inhuman reports about Lessing's death"] to be shameless lies or don't you? Do not beat about the bush but say Yes! or No!" On April 28, 1784, Lavater simply repeated that he had nothing to do with those "excerpts." Nicolai again refused to accept this dodging of the issue: "When speaking about this matter," he wrote Lavater on May 15, "you ought to have spoken about it with disgust. You owed this to the memory of a very honest man." Indignantly, Lavater rebuked Nicolai on June 2 for having condemned Pfenninger, "the best, most honest man," for his having published a piece of news that had been transmitted to him with the assurance of its trustworthiness.

Lavater's continuing refusal to answer yes or no to a simple question caused Nicolai to write to Lavater on June 15: "I ask you once again, Herr Deacon, whether you consider it right that the honor of so great, so learned, so good a man as Lessing be tarnished after his death? . . . And do you blame me because a contributor to the *Bibliothek* said what half of the German people believed (and what is most probably true), namely that you and your friends are participants in the *Churchly Messenger.*" Lavater wrote yet another evasive reply on October 2, and Nicolai made yet another attempt to elicit a clear statement from the deacon, but Nicolai's letter, dated October 26, was returned to him on November 20. Diplomatic relations between Nicolai and Lavater had ceased, never to be resumed.

Another year passed before Pfenninger, not Lavater, publicly revoked the "letters" as "untrustworthy." He did this in the November/December, 1785, issue of his journal, the last issue to appear. Lavater's role in the launching of the *Churchly Messenger* has not been entirely clarified, but Pfenninger did not deny that he had received the slanderous "letters" through him. Nicolai, at least, took it for granted that this had indeed been the case, and Mendelssohn may be presumed to have shared his view. From it there was but a small step to his "hypothesis" concerning Jacobi's motivation in presenting Lessing in a way that Mendelssohn considered defamatory. Since Lavater had been responsible for the publication of those malicious "letters," and since Jacobi was Lavater's intimate friend, it seemed very plausible to infer that Jacobi's portrayal of Lessing as a "Spinozist, atheist, and blasphemer" was part of one and the same plot. Lessing's jocular reference to himself as the deity in a state of "contraction," which had been reported by Jacobi as part of his banter,[8] now assumed the character of "blasphemies" such as those imputed to him in the *Churchly Messenger*. It also appeared plausible to assume that Jacobi had intended originally to "convert" Lessing and was now attempting to convert Mendelssohn.

To return to Reichardt's discussion with Mendelssohn on December 13, 1785:[9] Reichardt tried to disprove the allegation that Jacobi and Lavater were plotting something. Mendelssohn, he insisted, was misjudging both men. Lavater had tried to convert him, to be sure, but his sole purpose had been the promotion of Mendelssohn's salvation and felicity. Jacobi, on the other hand, was far removed from any such intention. Jacobi had quoted Lavater at the end of his book not to offend Mendelssohn's sensibilities but to show Lavater's Berlin detractors where his own sympathies lay. "Upon my word!," Mendelssohn exclaimed. "In that case he utterly missed his aim, so far as I and my friends are concerned." According to Reichardt's report, Mendelssohn said this amid "hearty laughter" and seemed to be in a jovial mood, laughing a great deal more in the later course of the conversation. Reichardt obviously, and for good reasons, misinterpreted Mendelssohn's behavior. As Doctor Marcus Herz would remark in his *Reply*,[10] this repeated "hearty laughter" at points in the discussion that were hardly occasions for mirth was strange and out of character. It testified to the nervous tension that Mendelssohn was suffering and that he sought to overcome in order to put his visitor at ease. In defending Lavater, Reichardt had spoken rather tactlessly of the "noble, dear Lavater," who had been treated so "abominably" in Berlin—a dig, no doubt, at Nicolai in particular—and Mendelssohn had scarcely any choice than to laugh it off.

Reichardt continued his account: "When I saw him treat the whole matter so lightly, I said to him: Seeing I find you so much less displeased with Jacobi's treatise than some mischief-makers had told me you were (contrary to what I know about your character), I need not hesitate to deliver a message that Jacobi has asked me to give you." With his customary politeness and remarkable composure Mendelssohn declared his willingness to listen: "Give it me! Be assured that I am not upset. I am most anxious to know what it really was that caused Jacobi's dissatisfaction with me." In other words, Mendelssohn wanted to learn what had caused Jacobi to rush into print.

Mendelssohn's curiosity on this point may seem naive, and in a sense it was. Yet it also shows how convinced he was of the propriety of his having published the *Morgenstunden* without first showing the manuscript to Jacobi. In *To Lessing's Friends* Mendelssohn stated his case clearly and emphatically.[11] What may need some clarification is the fact that whereas Mendelssohn denied the justification of Jacobi's hasty disclosure of the documents of the case, he boldly proclaimed that his own original plan had been to clarify first the issue of Spinozism without any reference to the correspondence, leaving the publication of the correspondence for Part Two of the *Morgenstunden,* which might appear a year later. He even quoted his letter to Elise (May 24, 1785) to prove that this had been his intention.[12] It might seem rather strange that he openly vindicated to himself the right to publish the letters but disputed Jacobi's right to do the same, notwithstanding the fact that the core of this correspondence was Jacobi's own report on his conversations with Lessing. There would seem to be more than a kernel of truth in Matthias Claudius' question:[13] "Yet, seriously speaking, how can Herr Mendelssohn consider it unjust to Lessing that Herr Jacobi published the conversation and the correspondence? Does he himself not say in several places and on page seventy-nine[14] in bold letters that he wishes to make use of the correspondence in Part Two of the *Morgenstunden?*"

In order to understand Mendelssohn's attitude in the matter one has first to bear in mind that Jacobi had imposed the news of Lessing's alleged Spinozism upon Mendelssohn and, by revealing the news sub rosa, had given Mendelssohn the impression that the subject was highly confidential. When asked for further clarification, Jacobi had offered it in the form of a letter to Mendelssohn, and Jacobi had subsequently given his consent to Mendelssohn's use of this report. When Jacobi published his book, he included in it not only his own report, which he had previously given Mendelssohn permission to use, but also a great deal of private correspondence whose publication had not been authorized by either Mendelssohn or Elise. In so doing Jacobi acted in a completely illegal manner. Mendelssohn, in contrast, had adhered strictly to his previous assurances. His plan to publish Jacobi's report as Part Two of the *Morgenstunden* was the ultimate stage in a development that had begun with his original plan to write "something on Lessing's character." The cancelation of the original project and its replacement by another were the direct result of Jacobi's much-resented intrusion. Mendelssohn's new plan envisaged, at least on paper, the use of Jacobi's report, and Jacobi's permission for such use had been obtained. There was, then, nothing at all irregular in Mendelssohn's conduct, and the question that Mendelssohn put to Reichardt was perfectly in order: he wanted a satisfactory explanation of Jacobi's behavior. Mendelssohn's own conscience was clear.

Mendelssohn's question gave Reichardt the opportunity to deliver Jacobi's message: "He asked me to tell you that he was somewhat perplexed when you considered it necessary to establish publicly [and] in advance the viewpoint from which to look at a thing about which you had received information from him; concerning which you expected clarification to be furnished by him; and in respect of which you had challenged him to a contest. [He further asked me to tell you] that he was no less struck by the fact that you did not let him see the manuscript, to which you had referred him previously . . . and that he had to learn from others that it was already in print and contained everything that could be objected to Spinozism; moreover, that these objections had been put into the mouth of Lessing in a manner that was most detrimental to your opponent [Jacobi]; finally, that he could not have remained entirely indifferent to the way in which you saw fit in the book to take him in hand, along with your boys, to teach him correct thinking. It had hurt him above all, he said, that your manner of presentation was not entirely free of the pious deceit so frequently employed by the so-called enlighteners and defenders of sound reason in Berlin . . ."

Reichardt continued: "Mendelssohn listened . . . in his usual manner, without interrupting me, something of which few people are capable and which always seemed to me one of the most prominent features of his noble mind and heart. After a brief silence he said: 'A mask? Of this, at least, I am not conscious.' " He obviously interpreted the accusation of "pious deceit" in the sense of wearing a "mask." And this charge he firmly rejected.

It is likely that the term "mask" lept to Mendelssohn's mind at this point because he had chosen as the motto of his *To Lessing's Friends* the passage from Shaftesbury to which he had alluded in his letter to Jacobi of August 1, 1784.[15] Shaftesbury had written that an Ethiopian suddenly transported to Paris or Venice at carnival time, when everyone wore a mask, might mistakenly assume at first that this was how Europeans looked; but if he should carry the jest too far and laugh just as heartily at the sight of a natural face, he would become ridiculous. For to see in a man of sobriety and sense "one of those ridiculous Mummers" was surely "a silly presumption." By quoting this passage Mendelssohn had no doubt meant to characterize the way in which Jacobi had mistaken Lessing's frolicsome utterances as indicative of his true opinions, while considering his natural face a mere mask. The motto now assumed a new significance to him: Jacobi saw in *all* men of sobriety and sense, and particularly in the men of the Berlin Enlightenment, only "ridiculous Mummers" who wore masks *all* the time. Thus the motto had become even more apposite than before.

Reichardt, having no way of knowing what was going through Mendelssohn's mind, simply replied: "I myself do not know your treatise [the *Morgenstunden*], and I have merely passed along Jacobi's message." "For this I thank you," Mendelssohn replied, "and you can rest assured that it offended me as little as did Jacobi's treatise. Of the first part of the message I already had some presentiment. I recently said to my family: it seems that in this matter I shall again face the charge, which one of my friends recently expressed, by saying that in my elementary education I had not been imbued with any proper notion of honor and *point d'honneur*."

Mendelssohn thus conceded quite unnecessarily and without real justification that the way he had treated Jacobi had not been gentlemanly. This remark did not imply any sense of guilt. He had been well within his rights. He admitted, however, that he might have considered the matter of withholding the manuscript from Jacobi as involving a point of honor, since the original understanding had been to the effect that the manuscript would be shown to Jacobi prior to publication. Even so, this admission was too generous and out of place, for the gentlemen's agreement had concerned only a manuscript containing material supplied by Jacobi, and the agreement had become invalid when Mendelssohn changed his plan. In *To Lessing's Friends* Mendelssohn rightly ignored the remark he had made off-handedly to Reichardt in a weak and tense moment, and defended the course of action he had taken, while condemning Jacobi's.

Reichardt, unfortunately, felt not the least compunction in immediately reporting Mendelssohn's remark to Jacobi. On December 23 Jacobi, in turn, wrote to Hamann:[16] "Today I received a letter from Reichardt. Mendelssohn told him that 'his misbehavior [!] toward me amounted, in the main, to what his friends had already previously reproached him for: that he had no proper notion of honor and *point d'honneur,* and that one could recognize in this the way he had been brought up.' " If ever there was a man who had a sense of "honor" it was Moses Mendelssohn, and it is regrettable that this remark, if indeed it ever fell from his lips, should actually have been taken seriously and broadcast by the man to whom it had been confided.

The conversation with Reichardt was eventually cut short when Fromet reminded her husband that it was time for him to take his usual evening ride. Little Nathan insisted on joining his father, and while waiting for the child to get ready, Mendelssohn, holding the hat in his hand, leaned forward against the table and said with a smile: "A mask?" He then turned to his visitor and said: "Dear Reichardt, let Jacobi know that I have already written a few sheets that will shortly be published as an appendix to his book. He will receive them as soon as they are out, and I hope he will be satisfied with them and get as little angry about them as I am on account of his book, though I fail to understand why he rushed into print and why, indeed, he sent word to me about the matter in the first place, after what he had heard about me from Lessing."

Now that the conversation was drawing to a close, Mendelssohn spoke his true mind: Jacobi would find the answer to his question in the new book [viz. *To Lessing's Friends*], which—was this meant ironically?—should cause him little annoyance. He saw no justification for Jacobi's haste in publishing the correspondence. Above all, why had Jacobi seen fit to bother him with his disclosures, if he believed himself to have heard Lessing say that he had never revealed his true mind to his friend Mendelssohn? This last point was the one most deeply felt. When Reichardt tried to defend Jacobi, Mendelssohn was not to be taken in: "A man of Jacobi's caliber ought to have found out very quickly when Lessing was serious and when he was not. He should also have realized that I could not be expected to follow him on his new paths and teachings at this time of my life. I grew old in Leibnizian and Wolffian philosophy, and simply cannot take a single step forward in a new language—but about all this you will find something in my book."

Reichardt had no opportunity to continue the discussion, though he shared the ride in the carriage. They drove first to pick up David Friedländer, and the conversation turned to a variety of other subjects. It was arranged that Mendelssohn, Fromet, and the children would visit Reichardt some evening in the next few days, but it subsequently turned out that the date suggested by Mendelssohn was inconvenient for Reichardt because of a rehearsal at the opera that had been fixed for that evening. The following Sunday, which he proposed instead, was unacceptable to the Mendelssohns, who had already invited friends to come for an evening of reading. The visit was therefore postponed indefinitely.

Saturday, December 31, 1785, was a bright but bitterly cold day. Mendelssohn had decided to deliver the manuscript of the just-completed new book to the publisher. So eager was he to get rid of this manuscript that he personally took it to Voss, who was both his publisher and friend. Being an observant Jew, he must have waited until the termination of the sabbath in the late afternoon before embarking on this errand. He could have ordered a carriage, but being in a great hurry he chose to walk and over Fromet's protests left the house without his overcoat. Upon returning home, he complained of feeling unwell.[17] What followed is perhaps best told in the words of Doctor Marcus Herz, whose moving account of Mendelssohn's last days was included in Engel's preface to Mendelssohn's last work, *An die Freunde Lessings,* which was posthumously published on January 24, 1786:[18]

> Only on Monday [January 2, 1786] had I learned by chance that the pious man was not well and kept indoors. I hastened to see him and found him standing in front of a chest of drawers and occupied with his ledger accounts. "How are you, my dear Moses? Are you sick?"—"I caught a cold on Saturday," he replied, "when I took my treatise about the Jacobi affair to Voss. I am glad to have gotten this annoying matter off my mind." He uttered the last sentence with a disgust and ill-humor that were out of character and cut me to the heart. In fact, throughout his life nothing seems to have caused him so much emotional upset, or rather any comparable upset of an essentially emotional character, as this matter about his Lessing. "You have no idea," he continued, "how weak my memory has become of late. My ledger is in complete disarray. Now there is some error here, now there, and so I have to stand up and strain myself to put things right." He also complained of a general weakness, but he attached no great importance to his indisposition. His pulse was normal and he had no trouble breathing. Yet he had a bad cough, which he tried to alleviate by a harmless household medicine and by taking sugar frequently. Sugar was his favorite dainty, despite the warnings he was given against it. He used to say that the only bad thing about sugar was that one could not take it with sugar. We then spoke about the present state of medicine, of which he was well aware, and about the intellectual capacities and subsidiary sciences that were

required of a great medical practitioner. I left him without any prescription, since his body could no longer stand any medicine whatever.

On Tuesday morning I found him wrapped in a fur coat and sitting on the sofa beneath the bust of his Lessing. As one could immediately see, his illness and debility had worsened. "Today I am really and truly sick, dear Doctor," he said. "My cough does not leave me alone; I cannot eat, did not sleep, and feel very weak." Nevertheless he talked to me with perfect clarity of mind about the talents of his youngest son, who happened to be in the room. His pulse was somewhat weak and agitated. I persuaded him to take at certain intervals a spoonful of a very mild assuaging and cooling drink.

At five P.M. he lay on the sofa running a rather high temperature, but [his] breathing easier and his mind more serene than had been the case in the morning. At nine P.M. the temperature had gone down to almost normal, and the breathing had also improved. He pointed, however, to a spot in the chest where he felt pangs, which he attributed to flatulence. I agreed with Doctor Bloch that he be given an enema, and that warm compresses be put on the sensitive spot. We agreed to open a vein if the pangs persisted. He was in a rather serene mood when we told him that too many people were in the room. He replied somewhat humorously that Achard's[19] experiments had shown this kind of air to be the healthiest. We then bade him good night.

On Wednesday morning at seven A.M. his son came to me in a state of consternation, asking me to see his father at once, since he was very restless. I rushed there and found him on his sofa, no longer beneath Lessing's bust, which had been placed opposite him on the chest of drawers.

I was shocked at the sight of him. His eyes no longer had their penetrating radiance. His face was sunken and pale. He received me, in his friendly way, by grasping my hand: "Do not take it amiss, dear Doctor, that I have troubled you so early. I have had a miserable night. Although the pangs have stopped as a result of the compresses, I feel completely exhausted by the several voidances I have had. I am full of anxiety and restlessness. I have a sensation as if something was driving upward from the abdomen, and my chest is congested."

His pulse was almost normal, though a little weak, without the least irregularity. After some minutes' reflection I confessed my embarrassment: "I really do not know, dear Herr Moses, what to do with you, since you cannot stand any medicine. Everything causes you flatulence and anxiety; the smallest dose upsets you." "I will sit up," he said, "perhaps this will help." He lifted himself up with considerable strength, sat down on the nearest chair, rose again after half a minute, seated himself on the sofa, and said: "I now feel somewhat easier."

Yet his appearance grew steadily worse, and while I went into the open adjacent room to tell his wife and son-in-law about his condition, and to ask for an assistant to be called, I heard some noise coming from the sofa. I ran back, and there he lay, having dropped down a little from the seat, the head bent backward, with some foam on the mouth; breathing, pulse, and life had ceased. We tried in several ways to revive him, but in vain. There he lay without any prior death-rattle, without convulsion, with his usual friendliness on his lips as if an angel had taken him with a kiss from the earth.

His death was a natural one and such as occurs very rarely. It was due to an apoplectic stroke from weakness. The light went out because the lamp lacked oil. Given his constitution, only a man of his wisdom, self-control, moderation, and peace of soul could have kept the flame burning for fifty seven years.

In the first moment of terror I immediately grasped his head and remained, petrified, in this position for God knows how long. To sink down beside him and pass away together with him was the most ardent desire I had then or shall ever have.

Thus Moses Mendelssohn died peacefully on the morning of January 4, 1786 (Shevat 5, 5546).

The sad news spread quickly throughout Berlin. Sophie Becker's diary recorded on that day:[20] "We were getting up early, when I received a note from the duchess, the first line of which filled me with horror: 'Our great, wise Mendelssohn passed away this morning.' What a strange revolution was wrought in my soul, and soon also in Elise's, by reading these few words! He, whom we loved so dearly and who only some days ago sat so cheerfully in our midst, has departed so suddenly from us and has left so many orphans behind."

The loss was keenly felt by the Jewish community, whose pride and glory Mendelssohn had been. The leaders of Berlin Jewry ordained that as a special mark of respect all Jewish shops and offices would be closed until after the funeral.[21] Ordinarily interment would have taken place on the same day, but probably in deference to Mendelssohn's misgivings about early burial it was postponed until the day following.

On January 5 Sophie wrote in her diary:[22] "Now Moses rests with his fathers. At ten A.M. the body, accompanied by many hundreds of his nation, was taken to its resting place." The coffin was carried by his best friends,[23] and "many scholars and statesmen, many young people who knew and revered him, and almost all Jewish householders in Berlin were present when the body was committed to earth."[24] No record seems to have been preserved of the eulogies delivered at the funeral, but the grief felt by Mendelssohn's Jewish friends and admirers was well expressed in a Hebrew dirge written by Hartwig Wessely.[25]

The dirge glorified the achievements of the deceased and took comfort in his immortality: "Death, thou hast felled the tree but its fruit remaineth. / Not all didst thou destroy, only some part. / The writ of his wisdom is engraved upon the tablet." A poem bewailing Mendelssohn's death in both Hebrew and German was composed by Simon Höchheimer.[26] It described Mendelssohn as "Moses, the man of God,[27] the prince of the House of Jacob, the shepherd of Israel; the mighty man, leader, spokesman and protector of his people." The sorrow of Mendelssohn's Christian friends was voiced in an "elegiac cantata" written by Karl Ramler and set to music by Bernhard Wessely.[28] In it Sulamith and Eusebia, representing the Jewish community and the Christian world respectively, lament in turn over the death of the man who was the embodiment of "wisdom, virtue, and the love of men"; who had given the lie to the erroneous belief of the nations that wisdom and virtue had departed from the Jewish nation; who occupied the highest rank in Israel and was among the first and foremost of the human race. Mendelssohn, like Socrates, had remained loyal to the faith and customs of his people. Ramler reiterated this praise in the lines he wrote for Mendelssohn's bust: "Moses Mendelssohn, wise like Socrates; loyal to the faith of his fathers; like him he taught immortality; and he immortalized himself like him."[29]

When Herder received the news, he wrote to Jacobi on January 15:[30] "Because I greatly love the goddess Nemesis, I do unto you as you do unto me, and I write only when I have to send a letter. . . . You undoubtedly already know that Mendelssohn is dead. All feud has now come to an end. He died from apoplexy on the fourth, and I would be glad if he had left his essay unfinished. It is always unpleasant to quarrel with the dead. The goddess [Nemesis] has removed him and probably he [now] knows—though it is more likely that he still does not know—what he is up against. His death has doubly struck home because for the last few weeks I have been surrounded by monuments of death. We poor shadows on earth! . . . whither does the philosophy of our dreams venture to soar?" Herder was, at this time, preoccupied with his essay on *Nemesis, an Instructive Symbol,* and he was also refashioning the older Lessing-oriented essay *How the Ancients Depicted Death.*[31] Nemesis was to him the goddess of "measure and restraint," and akin to the rule of reason and *Humanität.* One senses, however, precious little humane feeling in Herder's cool and rather self-pitying reaction to the death of the man whom he had admired, hated, befriended, and deserted in turn. How much more humane than the Greek symbol of Nemesis as the cause of Mendelssohn's death had been Marcus Herz' poetic metaphor of the angel's kiss by which he had been taken from earth, a variation of the rabbinic saying about the death of the righteous by a kiss of God.[32]

Goethe sent Jacobi a short letter in February, 1786, which contained the following sentences:[33] "Mendelssohn's death was most unexpected. Those left behind will now fight on behalf of the deceased, and they have, therefore, an easy game." Again, not a word of regret, though Goethe seemingly had great respect for Mendelssohn. In his *Xenien* of 1794–1797 he wrote about him, next to Sulzer and Haller:[34] "Indeed, you see me immortal!—'Have you not long ago proved this / In the *Phaedon.*'—My friend, be glad that you see it!" And in part three of *Dichtung und Wahrheit,*[35] which was written in 1814, he recalled the effect produced some thirty years before by his poem *Prometheus:* "It served as the fuse of an explosion that disclosed and brought up for discussion the most intimate relationships of some worthy men: relationships that, unknown to themselves, lay dormant in an otherwise highly enlightened society.

The rupture was so violent that as a result of it, in conjunction with certain accidental happenings, we lost one of our most worthy men, Mendelssohn." As late as 1822 Goethe would write to Zelter in similar vein:[36] "You probably remember that the good man Mendelssohn died as a result of a premature publication of *Prometheus*." No offense was meant by this humorous diagnosis thirty-six years after the event. At the time of the event, however, Goethe's reaction, like Herder's, was rather callous.

Nor did Kant respond to the news of Mendelssohn's death in the way one might have expected, if Hamann's report to Jacobi on January 15, 1786, can be trusted:[37] "Kant thinks that the Christians have lost nothing, while his [Mendelssohn's] own nation has sustained an all the greater loss, since he is said to have been a great asset to them in commercial matters and public concerns owing to his sound practical judgment." Rather inconsistently Hamann added: "He [Kant] is much taken in by his [Mendelssohn's] literary style, and he admired his *Jerusalem*, at the time, as an irrefutable book." It seems hardly credible that Kant should have felt—let alone have made a statement to the effect—that by Mendelssohn's demise the Christian world had lost nothing. He surely knew better.[38]

Hamann was himself obviously quite upset by the news of Mendelssohn's death. The letter he sent to Jacobi on January 11 reflects the change of mood he underwent in the process of writing it (that is, before and after he learned about the sad event):[39]

> At noon I received the *Morgenstunden* back.... This afternoon I started reading all over again but instead of the spirit and the truth I found *bona verba, praetereaque nihil*. One of the two of us must be blind, either the Jewish philosopher or I. His seeking and finding the truth is pure jugglery. There is nothing to be said for finding when one has [already] placed the thing [just] where one wants to discover it.
>
> My son just came home with the news of Mendelssohn's death, which deeply moved me and reawakened my old friendship, which does not seem to have suffered shipwreck. [In my attacks] I aimed less at him than at the silly admirers and Chaldeans who will not fail to labor for his apotheosis. Assuming that the dead still bother about our quarrels, I hope that he will agree with me more than with them. In the beyond, he is now closer to truth than either of us is.

In his January 15 letter Hamann mentioned that he had intended eventually to make his private peace with Mendelssohn. He added:[40] "I therefore tortured myself with the foolish idea of doing for the son what I had believed I owed to the father. I meant to express my sincere condolence to him and the family, having once enjoyed the hospitality of his home; and to reaffirm, as an old friend, my recent warning to the father to beware of the pestilential 'wisdom,'[41] to remain faithful to Moses and the Prophets, and to prefer their testimony to all mathematical and metaphysical speculations. He is still a boy of about fourteen years of age.[42] The fanciful idea passed out of my mind, however, as suddenly as it had entered it."

Epilogue

On January 24, 1786, barely three weeks after Mendelssohn's death had occurred, his final answer to Jacobi, the little tract *To Lessing's Friends* appeared in print. It contained not only his closely argued "hypothesis" about the true character of Jacobi's discussions with Lessing but also the "Objections" he had offered before[1] and Jacobi's harsh reply,[2] neither of which had been published in the latter's book. It was a strange experience to hear the voice of the deceased again, from beyond the grave, as it were, and to see the combat continued. Additional fuel to the controversy was unintentionally provided by Johann Jakob Engel's editorial preface, in which Doctor Marcus Herz' report on Mendelssohn's last illness and death was quoted in full. The preface opened with a tribute to the dead author:[3]

> How much the world of learning, philosophy, and German literature lost by the demise of a Mendelssohn is known to all to whom these areas are important; but how little does this suffice to describe the irreparable and immeasurable loss sustained by his friends! What shone in public before the eyes of the world was but the smallest part of the man's worth: not even his mind can be fully appreciated by what is found in his books, replete though they are with broad knowledge, good taste, and acumen. How much less his moral goodness, friendliness, modesty, and all the great and amiable virtues of his character! . . .

Engel then spoke about the cause of his death:[4]

> The immediate cause of his justly and universally lamented death was the very thing that caused this tract to be written.—If [strenuous] reflection disagrees . . . with the "machine" [i.e. the human body], the profound, intense reflections of a Mendelssohn were bound to have a pernicious effect on a machine so infirmly, so unhappily constructed as his. Nevertheless, this excellent man had gone on working steadily without any noticeable detriment to his health, so long as his labors were of a purely speculative nature. It was only when Lavater's challenge affected his heart as well that he suddenly became aware of the most terrifying consequences of the strain under which he lived. Without the strength of soul that this true, practical sage exercised in denying himself for years all physical and intellectual enjoyment, death would have overtaken him long ago. Of physical enjoyments he continued to deprive himself steadfastly until the end. . . .
>
> He could not do for long, however, without the intellectual pleasure of reading, and without the even more alluring one of writing. Having been tempted to write a series of smaller essays, and having done so in his best hours without incurring harm, he allowed himself to indulge in more. He began to pursue his former favorite ideas, and had one allowed him to pursue his own path, and had one not again forced him out of the sphere of quiet speculative thinking, he would, despite these exertions, probably have kept himself alive for many more years.

The following paragraph described feelingly the fatigue that the writing of the *Morgenstunden* had caused, and the profoundly disturbing effect that the appearance of Jacobi's book had produced. Doctor Herz' testimony completed the story.

The *Berlinische privilegirte Zeitung* (known also as *Vossische Zeitung*) carried a review of Mendelssohn's posthumous work on the very day of its appearance. It was written by Karl Philipp Moritz and ended with these words: "He became a victim of his friendship with Lessing and died as a martyr defending the suppressed prerogatives of reason against fanaticism and superstition.—Lavater's importunity dealt his life the first blow. Jacobi completed the work." The review was reprinted on January 27 in the *Hamburger unpartheyischer Correspondent*, and it produced a sensational effect.[5] Reichardt published an account of his visit to Mendelssohn on December 13, 1785, with the avowed object of disproving the charge as expressed both in Engel's preface and, more bluntly, in Moritz' review: Reichardt had found Mendelssohn by no means gravely upset but rather in a jovial mood. He also opposed Doctor Herz' story by quoting what Mendelssohn's widow had told him on the occasion of his visit to the family a few days after her husband's death: "On Wednesday [January 4] he still took his breakfast in a cheerful frame of mind; the same morning he was gone."[6]

Both Engel and Doctor Herz were upset by the embarrassingly harsh manner in which Moritz had articulated what Engel's preface had seemed to imply. They therefore hastened to answer Reichardt in a way designed to rectify the impression created. On February 11 the *Hamburger unpartheyischer Correspondent* published declarations by them and by David Friedländer, all bearing the date February 7. While Herz and Friedländer had notified Moritz in advance, Engel had failed to do so. His reply hardly tried to conceal his anger at having been exposed by Moritz, on whom he now tried to fix the entire blame.[7] Doctor Herz was more circumspect in his answer. He suggested that Reichardt must have misunderstood what he had heard from the widow, since the facts, of which he had first hand knowledge, were to the contrary. Reichardt had also completely misjudged Mendelssohn's state of mind. There could be no doubt that the affair had hurt him deeply. (David Friedländer's declaration made the same point.) Herz added, however, a clear statement dissociating himself and Engel from the charge that had been leveled [by Moritz] against Jacobi: neither of them nor "any person of sound common sense" could go beyond saying that the publication of Jacobi's book had caused Mendelssohn an emotional upset *(Gemüthskränkung)*. Nowhere in the preface had Engel declared that this had brought about Mendelssohn's death. True, he was hurt and he made a strenuous effort to vindicate Lessing and himself. It was also true that his nerves, enfeebled as they had been for a long time, were further weakened by the strain. All this was an effect of the remote cause, the appearance of Jacobi's treatise. Yet what would have happened if, in addition, he had not caught a chill? He would have returned to normal after a few weeks' rest. In fact, however, he exposed himself

to severe weather, caught a bad cold, and his already weakened body suc-
cumbed. He would probably have withstood the illness had his body not
been debilitated by previous strain. Death was caused by the conjunction
of the predisposing cause, his debility, and the efficient cause, the cold.
Causing a predisposition for death could not be construed to be equivalent
to causing death. Otherwise, given the universal nexus between everything
in the world, every man would be every day the killer of thousands of
his fellow-men.

Moritz reproduced the statements by Reichardt, Doctor Herz and
Friedländer in the *Vossische Zeitung* of February 11. Stubbornly adhering
to his view, he commented on Doctor Herz' distinction: "No matter whether
an efficient or a merely predisposing cause is spoken of, hopefully everyone
will congratulate himself that in this critical case he is not in Herr Jacobi's
shoes, seeing he was to such a high degree the predisposing cause of Mendelssohn's death, as is evident from Herr Engel's preface and the posthumously published work." Engel's disavowal of any charge against Jacobi
aroused Moritz' fierce anger when it came to his notice later. He replied
to it on Feburary 22 in the *Hamburger unpartheyischer Correspondent,* declaring
that he had merely rephrased Engel's words, yet in essence and figuratively
speaking, what he had said he still believed to be true. Moritz' concluding
sentence reads: "I hereby declare that the words on account of which
I am blamed most by those least entitled to do so were but an expression
of the indignation felt by me about the Jacobi controversy as the accidental
cause of Mendelssohn's death. Such indignation cannot be disapproved
even by Herr Jacobi, who must surely feel aggrieved at having been, albeit
accidentally, the cause of Mendelssohn's demise." Others who attacked
Moritz were the Hamburg theologian J. H. D. Moldenhawer and the *Jenaer
allgemeine Literaturzeitung.*[8] The question whether Jacobi had indeed caused
Mendelssohn's death was widely discussed.

Another of Jacobi's friends, the poet Matthias Claudius in Wandsbeck,
wrote in his review of *To Lessing's Friends:*[9] "And this step, the publication
of the *Letters about Spinoza,* was the immediate cause of Herr Mendelssohn's
death, as Professor Engel says in the preface. I am sorry, and I am sure
others will be, if this was the case. However, the publication of the talks
[between Jacobi and Lessing] could have been prevented by Herr Mendelssohn, had he responded trustfully to [Jacobi's] trustfulness. Nor had he
himself wished to suppress the conversation. . . . for he had written in his
own hand: 'Let the unphilosophical ones rejoice or be sad. We remain
imperturbable.'[10] And now someone became—it does not matter how—so
perturbed over it that it caused his death. Yet, according to the preface,
he is said to have been a 'true, practical sage'!—I gladly excuse 'someone'
as a human being and Professor Engel as a friend; but 'wisdom' I cannot
admit, nor can I allow it to be cheapened. It seems to me that everything
here is *tout comme chez nous.* And wisdom is not *chez nous.* A great gulf
is fixed between it and ourselves." Claudius added: "Yet Herr Mendelssohn
might have died without the *Letters.* I hope so, for the sake of all concerned."

The cynicism displayed here is indeed remarkable. First the charge that Jacobi caused Mendelssohn's death is almost relished as evidence of a foolish sort of disturbance, far removed from wisdom, and also as following upon a self-incurred predicament. Jacobi is pictured as the trusting man, whose confidence was not reciprocated. In the end the hope is expressed that Mendelssohn was going to die anyway.

Doctor Marcus Herz was particularly disgusted with this reaction. On Feburary 27, 1786 he wrote to Kant:[11] "What do you think about the tumult that has started, since Moses' death and concerning it, among preachers and geniuses, exorcisers of the devil, clownish poets, enthusiasts, and musicians, led by the privy counsellor at Pimplendorf?[12] If only a man like you were to shout at this rabble once in a stern voice: 'Be quiet!'—I bet it would be scattered like chaff before the wind. Above all, I wished the wantonness of that insipid rhymester at Wandsbeck[13] were punished, in whose entire life and thinking the final words of his childish verse-lines are the only things that rhyme. How, with deliberate malice, he misunderstands our Moses, for whom he [once] had a certain fondness [*tendre*], in order to deprive him of his fame and reputation!"[14]

The debate was joined by the young and gifted Thomas Wizenmann, whose critical investigation of Jacobi's and Mendelssohn's philosophies created something of a stir.[15] Wizenmann had studied philosophy and theology in Tübingen, where Ploucquet had been one of his teachers. Oetinger's works, he wrote in an autobiographical letter to Hamann,[16] had deepened his understanding of the "philosophy of the Bible," while Herder had opened his eyes to biblical history. As a vicar in Essingen he had read Mendelssohn, Locke, Leibniz, Wolff, and Boehme. He planned to refute Mendelssohn's *Phaedon,* in which he thought he had discovered "sophisms." Even so, he must have retained his respect for the author and his work, for as a private tutor in Barmen he wrote "a little ode about Mendelssohn's death," which he presented to one of his students, a young lady, who was eagerly studying Mendelssohn's writings on her own.[17] The ode depicted a shadowy figure rising in the somber light of the moon and lost in quiet meditation: "This is the shade of the wise man [i.e. Mendelssohn], who indefatigably pursued the light of truth while on earth; full of divinations of God and immortality, he went along his path. . . . Harken, behind him lament is heard! I can hear deep sorrow voiced over the loss sustained. . . . All around, sighs resound in Germany's fields [*Gefilden*]. He is being lamented by noble and brave young men who found strength through him when wrestling with error and truth; and he is lamented also by Germany's daughters, who thanks to him gathered hope of life eternal."

This same young man, Wizenmann, wrote on Feburary 9 to his friend Hausleutner:[18] "Mendelssohn is dead, as you know. The bitter rumors spread on this occasion about Jacobi will likewise be known to you. They are like dust before the wind, and they refute themselves. He left behind a treatise addressed to Lessing's friends, which we await impatiently.

Perhaps it will offer me an opportunity to espouse, for once, the concept of faith with the necessary emphasis. I hope this quarrel will turn out to be interesting and useful." As soon as Mendelssohn's book was available, Wizenmann began work on his analytical essay, which in time grew to be quite a substantial volume. Its salient point was the contention that Mendelssohn had been inconsistent. On the one hand, he had put his trust in the demonstrative method; on the other, he had admitted that speculation had to orient itself with the help of sound common sense. By making this concession, Wizenmann argued, Mendelssohn had, in essence, affirmed Jacobi's viewpoint, according to which no philosophical proof of the existence of God was possible and that our possession of the truth was safe against all skepticism. "That the one [Jacobi] speaks of belief [*Glauben*], while the other [Mendelssohn] follows the guidance of sound common sense, is only a terminological difference, and both agree that conviction of the truths of religion is possible and real even without demonstration."[19]

Wizenmann pointed out that Mendelssohn seemed to have understood and approved Jacobi's thesis when he wrote in his "Objections" that the *salto mortale* of faith was "a salutary device of nature"—that, having indulged for a while in abstruse speculation, one was well advised to return to normality by using one's *bon sens*.[20] What divided Mendelssohn's philosophy from Jacobi's was its assumption that the existence of God was capable of rational demonstration. Jacobi, who denied this possibility, resorted to the evidence provided by inner experience: the divine within man was the source of all knowledge of truth. Wizenmann, on the other hand, preferred to rely exclusively on the testimony of the Bible, being himself unaware, as he later put it,[21] of an immediate inner experience of the divine. The final part of his book affirmed the superiority of historical truth as manifested in the Bible to the eternal metaphysical truths as proclaimed by Mendelssohn as the spokesman of the Enlightenment. Here Wizenmann showed himself the true disciple of Hamann, whose radical critique of Mendelssohn's *Jerusalem* he reiterated.[22]

Wizenmann completed his work on April 19, 1786, the day on which Jacobi wrote the preface to his *Against Mendelssohn's Accusations Concerning the Letters about the Doctrine of Spinoza*.[23] A short time prior to this date he had sent Jacobi the finished part of his manuscript. In his preface Jacobi paid the young man a most enthusiastic tribute:[24] "An extraordinary measure of good fortune has fallen to my lot. The present treatise was completed and more than half of it was already in print, when [your] *Critical Investigation of the Results of Jacobi's and Mendelssohn's Philosophies* was brought to my notice. It presents with admirable clarity my true opinion in its total and fundamental aspect, and it reveals an independent thinker of the first rank, a man in the noblest sense of the word."[25]

Jacobi's own work, in contrast, was a polemical treatise of the worst sort. Had he been less vain, less self-righteous, and less contemptuous of Mendelssohn, Jacobi might have defended himself in a calm and factual manner that would have served his purpose quite well. Thus it would not have been difficult for him to show that Mendelssohn's "hypothesis" had overshot its mark; that he had not tried to "convert" either Lessing or his Jewish friend; that his purpose had not been to put Lessing on trial by accusing him of atheism and blasphemy; that, in short, Mendelssohn's understandable indignation had caused him to see ghosts where there were none. On the other hand, it would have been more difficult for Jacobi to explain why he felt that he had to impose the news about Lessing's Spinozism upon Mendelssohn in such an odd way, leaving Elise Reimarus hardly any choice. It was so much easier, as the book itself demonstrates, simply to decry the "clamor in all newspapers" over his importunity and to declare that there was hardly a man alive who was less importunate than he; to quote Elise's rather naive letter in which she excused herself for having passed the secret on; and finally to quote his own letter resignedly pointing out, in a self-pitying, self-righteous tone, that he hardly expected any thanks for all the "trouble" he had gone to, and castigating the *morgue berlinoise*.[26] Jacobi would also have been a little hard put to refute objectively the assumption that the "Spinozism" professed by Lessing was identical with the speculative ideas formulated by him on certain previous occasions, occasions of which Mendelssohn had firsthand knowledge and Jacobi knew nothing. It was infinitely simpler to reject this assumption out of hand, as an insult to Lessing's intelligence.[27]

Typical of the arrogance with which Jacobi treated his dead adversary were the two engravings reproduced in his book, one as a frontispiece and the other on the last page. The frontispiece shows an anatomist examining a human skull, disregarding a fury above him in the sky, who waves a banner inscribed "The Good Cause" with one hand and hurls down arrows and snakes with the other. Commenting on this picture, Jacobi deplores the despotism of the utilitarians (viz. the men of the Enlightenment) who object to the analysis of truth if it contradicts what they consider to be reason.[28] Even more characteristic is the second picture, which shows an ostrich egg lying in the sand, and starlings, crows, and other birds of similar breed trying to peck and crush it, while the ostrich [presumably Jacobi himself] calmly observes the attack from behind a bush. Jacobi's contempt for Mendelssohn and his supporters is most clearly expressed in the final paragraph, which precedes this picture:[29]

> Let this treatise too be sealed with words of Lavater (my fellow-thief on the cross). . . .[30]
>
> "There are unconvincible, utterly deformed characters. The more distinctly they see, the more loudly they exclaim: What a darkness! The more precisely one addresses them, the more stubbornly they complain of vexatious imprecision. Never believe that you may win them over by simplicity and sincerity. They know only deformity. They are true visionaries of all that is crooked and ignoble. . . ."

The very opening of Jacobi's book bespoke his callousness:[31] "I shall present documents and submit facts, and I shall nowhere fail to show the sacred seal of truth, the clear imprint of which caused my adversary to blush and turn so pale." Without any compunction, he attributed Mendelssohn's death to the shattering impression that his, Jacobi's, "sacred seal of truth" had made upon him. Perhaps the best comment on Jacobi's treatise is found in a letter dated May 5, 1786, in which Goethe summed up his reaction to it:[32]

> I read your booklet with sympathy but not with joy. It is, to all intents and purposes, a polemical treatise of a philosophical kind, and I have such an aversion to all literary quarrels that I would hardly enjoy one even if Raphael painted and Shakespeare dramatized it. You had to write these sheets; this I realize, and I expected them. Yet I wished you had presented the facts in a simpler way. I cannot approve all the passion that you displayed; nor are the many wrappings and appendages of much use when one is engaged in a fight. The shorter, the better....
>
> Furthermore, dear brother, in all sincerity, the ostrich egg does not please me at all. I might let it pass in the form of words, had it not, in addition, been impressed as a seal at the end. If your foes have only a shred of cleverness, they will attack the long-necked author who in infinite self-conceit looks out of the bushes and, sheltered in the shade, enjoys his superiority over magpies and ravens....
>
> When self-assurance expresses itself in contempt for others, be they even the least ones, it becomes obnoxious. An easygoing man may poke fun at others and may humiliate and disparage them since, at some time, he holds himself up to ridicule. One who has self-respect would seem to have renounced the right to despise others. After all, what are we, any of us, to think of ourselves so highly?

In defending himself against the accusation of being an "enthusiast," Jacobi invoked the name of Immanuel Kant. If denying the demonstrability of God and having recourse to faith amounted to enthusiasm, would Kant, "that Hercules among thinkers," not incur the same charge in even greater measure? He quoted some passages from the *Critique of Pure Reason*[33] in which Kant had stated that faith in God and immortality was only "morally" certain, that it was bound up with moral goodness, and that the "essential purposes of human nature" were accessible to all men and not merely to philosophers. Jacobi was cautious enough to point out that he did not mean to "lower" the Kantian philosophy to his own level or to "raise" his philosophy to that of Kant.[34] The reference to Kant was enough, however, to alarm Mendelssohn's friends. The situation obviously called for a clear statement by Kant himself, who had so far remained silent.[35] What was at stake was the cause of the Enlightenment itself.

On June 11, 1786, Johann Erich Biester, coeditor of the *Berlinische Monatsschrift,* addressed a long and urgent letter to Kant. It had the merit of placing the issue in proper perspective:[36] The Mendelssohn/Jacobi controversy, Biester declared, concerned, in the main, two points, viz. the truth of the facts alleged by the warring parties on the one hand, and the larger philosophical issue on the other. The factual aspect could be summed up in these questions: was Lessing an atheist, and did Mendelssohn first admit and then suppress the fact? Biester confessed that he considered it highly probable that Lessing had inclined toward atheism. Yet Mendelssohn's conduct in the whole affair could be properly judged only by someone who was intimately acquainted with his character and had at his disposal all letters that had been exchanged between the parties concerned. The letters, he suggested, ought to be presented in their entirety and in chronological order.[37] He personally felt, however, that the factual problem was somewhat irrelevant. In his view it did not matter whether Lessing was an atheist or whether Mendelssohn had betrayed a certain weakness. Biester was obviously not interested in biographical facts, and was therefore prone to treat this particular aspect of the controversy rather cavalierly. He stressed all the more the second point, which alone (he knew) would make some impression on Kant: the "philosophical enthusiasts" were bent on undermining and deriding all rational knowledge of God; they praised and almost deified the "unintelligible Spinozistic vagaries"; and they recommended the adoption of some positive religion as the only course open to men of reason. At a time when fanaticism on the one hand and a coarse dogmatic atheism on the other had taken hold of many people, it was most desirable that men of universally recognized authority should guide the public aright. The issue at stake was not Moses Mendelssohn but truth and reason. Only a Kant could utter an effective warning against the current danger, especially now when "the strange Jacobi" had, in the most indiscreet fashion, dragged Kant into the discussion. How could the rank and file discriminate between error and truth when they were told by Jacobi that Kant was on his side?

This appeal had the desired effect. On August 8, 1786, Biester acknowledged with thanks Kant's "excellent essay on the Jacobi/Mendelssohn controversy."[38] The title of the essay *(What Does it Mean: To Orient Oneself in Thinking?)* took its cue from "the principle that the late Mendelssohn, so far as I know, professed explicitly only in his last writings,[39] viz. the maxim of the necessity to orient himself in the speculative use of reason . . . with the help of a certain directive called by him *sensus communis* or sound reason or simple common sense."[40] The article, which appeared in the October, 1786, issue of the *Berlinische Monatsschrift*,[41] not only took a firm stand on the question of reason versus enthusiasm (as Biester had requested) but also went out of its way to acknowledge the merits of Mendelssohn as a philosopher and even to repudiate Jacobi, without specifically referring to him. Kant left no doubt that he had more respect for Wizenmann ("the sagacious author of the *Resultate*") than for Jacobi, but he rejected Wizenmann's claim that there was hardly any difference between Jacobi's affirmation of "belief" and Mendelssohn's stress on common sense. In Mendelssohn's case, Kant pointed out, it was in fact only reason, not "a presumed inner sense of truth" nor "any enthusiastic intuition called belief," that was invoked. What Mendelssohn had "steadfastly and with just zeal" advocated as a means of orientation was "authentic and pure reason." His only mistake had been to vindicate to pure reason more than it could accomplish.[42] Though the proofs of "the worthy Mendelssohn" in the *Morgenstunden* were not demonstrative, they were "by no means without value."[43] Mendelssohn's "sagacity," Kant declared, would have caused him to admit the limits of pure reason had he lived longer and had it been granted to him to retain the nimbleness of mind that he had possessed in his younger days, and which had enabled him to adapt old-established views to the progress of the sciences. No one, however, could take from him the merit of having insisted on seeking the ultimate criterion of truth in reason alone.

It was a far cry from this evaluation of Mendelssohn by Kant to Jacobi's statement that Mendelssohn, though clear-minded, was "no metaphysician" and lacked the impulse "to inquire into other systems, to imbibe and digest them."[44] Having paid a handsome tribute to Mendelssohn, Kant went on to deplore the trend of thinking manifested by the other party. If in matters of a metaphysical nature the primacy of reason was denied, Kant pointed out, then enthusiasm, superstition, and even atheism were given free rein. Mendelssohn's adversaries, he suggested, seemed to aim at the overthrow not only of speculative reason but also of rational beliefs. They appeared to espouse a different kind of faith to suit each individual's preference. The establishment of Spinoza's concept of God as the only rational one and its subsequent rejection clearly indicated that this was the intention.[45] Kant concluded his essay with a fervent appeal to all men of intellectual caliber to respect reason and thereby to safeguard freedom of thought.[46]

Mendelssohn would have been pleased with the tenor of Kant's powerful and timely utterance, which completely chimed with his trust in reason, though it denied the validity of his proofs. Kant's essay fixed Mendelssohn's place in the history of philosophy as that of a guardian of the Enlightenment. It also served as a catalyst in the then prevalent situation. By raising his voice above the din of battle Kant produced the incidental result that his own philosophy began to attract more attention and recognition. The reaction to Jacobi's attacks upon Mendelssohn's speculative dogmatism was a more widespread awareness of the limitations of pure reason as shown by Kant. The philosophical ethos gained new strength: Jacobi's and Hamann's manner of philosophizing declined in respectability and Kant's philosophy took the field.[47] On the other hand, the study of Spinoza by Jacobi, Herder, and Goethe ushered in a new era in the appraisal of that much-maligned Jewish philosopher.[48] But it was Mendelssohn who had given the first stimulus to this development, for it was Mendelssohn who had originally introduced Lessing to Spinoza and had immortalized his and Lessing's discussions of the subject in the very first work he published. The interpretation that Jacobi had given to Lessing's Spinozism had not been accepted by Mendelssohn, nor had he lost his admiration for Spinoza as a result of Jacobi's interpretation of him. In his last work, *To Lessing's Friends,* he had written:[49]

> Lessing is a follower of Spinoza? So what? What bearing do speculative propositions have on a man? Who would not himself be glad to have Spinoza for a friend, although he was a Spinozist? Who would refuse to do justice to Spinoza's genius and excellent character? ... [Besides,] I knew that there was a purified Spinozism ... [and that] this purified Spinozism was quite compatible with Judaism in particular; that, irrespective of his speculative doctrine, Spinoza could have remained an orthodox Jew, had he not contested authentic Judaism in other writings of his, and had he not thereby withdrawn from the Law.

Among his friends Mendelssohn's death had caused not only poignant feelings but also a sense of obligation to perpetuate his memory. His oldest friend, Friedrich Nicolai, who knew him so well and had shared in so many of his endeavors, was the first to put pen to paper. On January 7, 1786, only three days after the sad event, he wrote a biographical sketch for publication in the *Allgemeine deutsche Bibliothek.*[50] Drawing on a rich store of personal recollections and evaluating both happenings and achievements, he presented a vivid story of extraordinary merit. The sketch acquainted the world for the first time with some of the details about Mendelssohn's early years in Dessau and Berlin, described the friendship with Lessing as the decisive event in his life, characterized his philosophical works as distinguished by a combination of charm, lucidity, and thoroughness, and spoke about their partnership in the various literary journals they had edited.[51] Nicolai preferred to remain silent about the cause of his "grave illness," the history of which presented "a great deal of psychological information." As for the more recent controversy, he expressed the opinion that Jacobi had misunderstood Lessing. Of particular interest is Nicolai's report about the plans Mendelssohn had had in mind for Part Two of the *Morgenstunden:* he had intended to apply the concept of God in its significance for human society, i.e. to show the relevance of the concept for natural law and morality. The rights and duties of men were in his view related to the divine perfection. He had discussed details of this idea with him many a time, Nicolai revealed. This piece of information corroborates the view that Mendelssohn had no serious intention of devoting Part Two of the *Morgenstunden* to the Jacobi Letters, if indeed he actually intended to publish a second part.

An appreciation of Mendelssohn by Johann Erich Biester appeared in the *Berlinische Monatsschrift.*[52] Mendelssohn, he said, had been "the pride and ornament" of Berlin. The best minds cherished his wise counsel, for he possessed the rare gift of being able immediately to grasp the essential point of a problem and was able to elucidate the most abstract ideas in an easy way. Among those who consulted him were men of all walks of life, including statesmen, artists, and merchants. He could discuss the existence of God with the same facility with which he explained a new design in a silk fabric. He was a happy counterpart to his friend Lessing, whose brilliant and sometimes terrifying fireworks he well knew how to evaluate and to interpret. His own enduring merits might be summed up as follows. By his style of writing he had imparted a new gracefulness to German philosophical literature. Together with Lessing and Nicolai he had laid the foundation for unbiased and frank literary criticism in Germany. He had been a pioneer in German aesthetics, by following the lead of the British empiricists. His own nation the Jews, Germany, and humanity at large owed him a major portion of their moral and intellectual education. His love for the Jewish nation and its heritage had produced his important translations of two biblical books. Finally, his impeccable conduct, his righteousness, and his zeal for truth had compelled recognition of the fact that even a non-Christian, even a Jew, could be a good man, a man of religion, and one capable of promoting virtue and religion even among Christians. Not so long ago many of the most distinguished citizens had considered this an impossibility; Mendelssohn's living example had made such narrow-minded intolerance obsolete.

In a letter to Engel (dated February 12, 1786), Christian Garve paid this tribute to Mendelssohn:[53] "To me, too, Moses' death came as a great and painful loss. From him I first learned philosophy, for his letters *On the Sentiments* were the first book of this kind to impress me. I continued to learn from him in particular. In the way in which he set forth his ideas there was such neatness, such fullness without superfluity, such profundity combined with the utmost lucidity and grace, that no one I know of matches him."

The Berlin Society of Patriots and Admirers of Great Men had, on June 1, 1785, announced a plan to erect a monument in memory of Leibniz, Lambert, and Sulzer. The idea had been proposed by Johann Georg Müchler, the suggestion being that the monument take the form of a pyramid placed in the Berlin Opera square and showing on its faces portrait medallions of the three men.[54] When Mendelssohn died, some of his friends felt that the monument should have the shape of a four-sided obelisk, the fourth side to have a medallion with his picture. The society accepted this proposal and made an announcement to this effect on February 17, 1786.[55] Biester's essay in the March number of the *Berlinische Monatsschrift* carried the following note:[56] "We wish to take this opportunity of informing our readers that the pyramid that is to be erected in the Berlin Opera square, and for which subscriptions are invited, will have Moses Mendelssohn's portrait side-by-side with Leibniz', Lambert's, and Sulzer's." The flow of contributions was disappointing, however, and on March 14 a new appeal was published above the signatures of Engel, Biester, Nicolai, Friedländer, Isaac Daniel Itzig, and Marcus Herz.[57] In order to raise more funds a memorial concert was arranged at which Ramler's poem *Sulamith and Eusebia* was performed as a cantata set to music by Bernhard Wessely.[58] The concert was announced on May 16,[59] and it took place on May 23.[60]

It does not seem to have appreciably helped toward providing the necessary funds.

However, the fact that the entire project was eventually abandoned was not due, it seems, to lack of financial means but to anti-Jewish prejudice. In a letter to Friedländer, dated February 18, 1786, and published in the *Berlinische Monatsschrift*, the Prussian General Johann Andreas von Scholten, an ardent admirer of Mendelssohn, wrote in the course of his glowing praises of the man:[61] "I do not wish to forestall any inventive genius, but Leibniz and Sulzer would not feel ashamed to receive into their memorial another group: Mendelssohn presenting Lessing with the vindication of his honor, and Lessing ready to embrace him. I fear, however, that even among our learned men there will perhaps be some who look askance because they cannot forgive our philosopher that he was circumcised and wore a beard." Von Scholten, who had spontaneously conceived the idea of including Mendelssohn and Lessing in the projected monument, had at once foreseen the difficulties that would in the end defeat the plan.[62]

A year or so after Mendelssohn's death an article, "Rural Memorial for Moses Mendelssohn" by Carl Wilhelm Hennert, lecturer at the school of forestry, appeared in the *Berlinische Monatsschrift*.[63] It was obviously inspired by a desire to offset the shelving of the Berlin project with some cheering news: the friends of the late Moses Mendelssohn would be pleased to learn that there were men in Germany who, without laying claim to being learned, revered the memory of this great philosopher quietly, without any noise, and who erected monuments to him in rural surroundings. In the spring of 1786, the author reported, he had visited the forester [Johann Caspar] Jung in Baruth, Saxony, in whose library he noticed a collection of all of Mendelssohn's works. The man told him that the *Phaedon* had so moved him that he felt the urge to meet Mendelssohn in person. He called on him when an opportunity presented itself and was most cordially received. In the summer of 1776 Mendelssohn and his wife paid him a return visit in Baruth on their way to Dresden. Mendelssohn stayed there for several days, working every morning on his Psalms translation in the garden. There, on the bank of a brook, Jung showed Hennert a stone-walled seat between two pillars. It bore the inscription: "Herr Moses Mendelssohn's Seat on August 12, 1776."

Another project that foundered at the time concerned the publication of Mendelssohn's collected writings and his biography. The idea had first occurred to Doctor Marcus Bloch[64] but was subsequently taken up by Mendelssohn's widow, who with remarkable energy proceeded to carry it into effect. In April, 1786, she put the following announcement in the *Berlinische privilegirte Zeitung*, where it appeared on May 18:[65] "I herewith inform the public that I have entrusted to some friends of my late husband the editing of his hitherto unpublished writings as well as the collection of his scattered printed works, both large and small. These friends will arrange

the printing of all his works with the rightful publishers, whose names
will be announced in due course, and the edition will be accompanied
by a biography written by an author held in universal esteem." An amplified
version of the project was given in an editorial note by Biester attached
to von Scholten's article in the *Berlinische Monatsschrift*:[66] "According to
an announcement by Mendelssohn's widow, to which further publicity is
given here in order to obviate any unlawful reprinting, an authorized
edition of the scattered printed writings of the late Moses Mendelssohn
is being prepared. It will include an important segment of his correspondence and a biography written by a universally esteemed author.
For this reason everyone who has in his possession letters or any [other]
autographs of the deceased is kindly requested to make them available
in the interest of this public-spirited endeavor."

It seems that David Friedländer approached a number of individuals
with this particular request, for in his article, which was addressed to Friedländer, von Scholten wrote:[67] "I am sending you herewith at your request
some letters of our late friend, on condition that they be returned to me."

The zeal with which Fromet pursued her task is attested, and some
welcome further information about the project is provided, by a highly
interesting letter that has only recently come to light. It was written on
November 18, 1788, by Mendelssohn's daughter Brendel, who signed her
name "B. Veit, geb. [née] Mendelssohn" (she later became Dorothea von
Schlegel). The addressee was most probably the writer Christian Friedrich
von Blankenburg in Leipzig, whom Brendel had visited together with her
friend Henriette Herz. The letter reads as follows:[68]

> I wanted to send you the copy of my father's essay, which I had prom-
> ised you. . . . However, it was impossible for me to do so. My mother keeps
> these things with both hands. I cannot get out of her as much as a single
> small page. A strong effort is now being made, though, to edit the entire
> *Nachlass* of the deceased [*des seeligen*]; the correspondence with Lessing . . .
> belongs to the younger Lessing [Karl], who will presumably publish it;
> he produced a letter from my father in which he consigned it to him. . . .
>   What is still left over concerning the Lavater correspondence is said
> to be important but will not be published. It is said to be too frank,[69]
> and one is afraid that it might do harm to his reputation. I for one
> fail to see this point. Among thinking and noble-minded people . . . frank-
> ness can hardly be damaging, and reputation in the eyes of others is
> not worth the effort. . . . In brief, Mendelssohn's friends do not wish
> to publicize this piece of writing.
>   The rest, viz. essays on various philosophical subjects and several
> letters of which copies are available . . . will be taken care of by Doctor
> Biester. . . . Nicolai and Voss will come to an agreement as publishers.
> Probably it will appear as early as the coming Easter fair.

This letter, which incidentally reveals Brendel's independence of mind
and gives a hint of her impatience with her mother,[70] indicates some of
the problems that confronted the editor. A certain timidity guided the
selection of the material. We also gather that Biester was in charge of

the edition. The biographer chosen was most probably Engel. Biester did not feel competent to undertake this task; as if in answer to a challenge, he declared in his appraisal of Mendelssohn in the *Berlinische Monatsschrift:*[71] "To become Mendelssohn's biographer one must have been his friend over many years." Engel fulfilled this requirement. Unfortunately, for reasons now unknown, the project never got off the ground.[72]

The first Mendelssohn biography to appear as a book was the anonymously published work by Friedrich Wilhelm von Schütz (Hamburg, 1787).[73] It was written with warm feeling for its hero and offered a great deal of information. The only puzzling feature of the book was its motto: "The man was noble but through his last undertaking his name became a monument to posterity." It is difficult to assume that the second part of the sentence (introduced as it is by the word "but") implied criticism of Mendelssohn's stand against Jacobi, for the author concluded the account of his life by saying:[74] "From youth on he had loved to strive for truth. The striving for truth was also the path on which death overtook him. Hence his friends may rightfully declare: the man died a noble death." Yet the motto described itself as a variation of some lines found in Shakespeare's *The Tragedy of Coriolanus* (Act V, Scene iii): "The man was noble, / But with his last attempt he wiped it out, / Destroy'd his country, and his name remains / To the ensuing age abhorr'd." Why von Schütz had to choose for his motto a strange and meaningless adaptation of this particular text remains an enigma.

A different and unusual kind of biography was published in the same year by Carl Philipp Conz (1762–1827), a native of Würtenberg and friend of Friedrich Schiller, who in 1804 became professor of classical languages in Tübingen.[75] It took the form of a "lyric-didactic poem in four cantos" entitled *Moses Mendelssohn, Sage and Man*[76] and was modeled after the manner in which Karl Friedrich Kretschmann (1738–1809), the "bard," had depicted the poet Ewald Christian von Kleist.[77] In his preface (dated March 13, 1787) Conz wrote: "The death of our late sage has left none unaffected. It put me, like all who are impressed by his immortal achievements as a man and as a philosopher, into a tender, inspiring sadness, and so I vowed to set him a modest memorial. Thus the idea of this poem matured in my soul. I could not hope, and not even desire, to contribute something to the preservation of his memory among us; this would have been an insult to Germany [where his memory is secure]. Nor did I wish to write a mere panegyric. Hence I resolved to combine the didactic poet and the panegyrist and to present in poetic form his ideas about some of the most important philosophical truths." Actually Conz went far beyond this plan, producing also a biography of Mendelssohn in which the events of his life from the cradle to the grave appear in poetic transfiguration.

A *Sketch of the Life and Character of Mendelssohn* by Daniel Jenisch, the Berlin preacher, preceded the minor essays of the deceased in a little volume edited by Johann Georg Müchler in 1789.[78] Jenisch justified his undertaking by pointing out that until such time as Professor Engel redeemed his promise to write a full biography an effort such as this was called for. In Holland, where Mendelssohn had many admirers, Gerrit Brender á Brandis, a historian of literature, published in 1788 a well-informed and well-written biography, together with a Dutch translation of selected essays and letters.[79]

In terms of Jewish intellectual history great significance must be attached to the *Life of Mendelssohn* written in Hebrew by Isaac Euchel.[80] Published in 1788, it was not only a remarkable piece of research and a beautiful specimen of Haskala literature but also a document testifying to the role that Mendelssohn had assumed in the estimation of the group that Euchel represented. The first instalment of the biography had appeared in the periodical *Ha-Me'assef,* the literary organ of the Maskilim. To this group Mendelssohn was a charismatic leader during his lifetime and after. The slogan "From Moses [Maimonides] until Moses [Mendelssohn] there arose no one as wise and understanding like Moses," which varied the old epigram hitherto applied to Maimonides, had been coined and published even before Mendelssohn's death.[81] The veneration of Mendelssohn, the "unique one," who was a new Moses, increased after his death.[82] A contributor to *Ha-Me'assef* described as "one of the poets"—his identity still remains a riddle[83]—eulogized Mendelssohn in two Hebrew lines of verse adapted from Alexander Pope's famous praise of Newton: "Nature and Nature's Laws lay hid in the night / God said, Let Newton be! and all was Light." In the Hebrew writer's glorification of Mendelssohn, the harbinger of Enlightenment to his people, the phrase runs: "Truth and Religion lay hid in night since time immemorial / God said, Let Moses be! and there was Light." Euchel described his effort as being directed toward "research in the history of a righteous and wise man, who throughout his earthly existence walked before us to illumine the path of truth, and who 'in his death did not take everything away' from us but left behind a blessing destined to spread out for generations to come." He invited the reader to examine with him the qualities of a man who was high above the multitude, thereby to know both him and the mercies of his Maker, who had appointed him an "ensign to the nations."

Through Euchel's emotionally charged account the saga of Mendelssohn's astonishing endurance and rise to fame was again brought home to his people. The story of the man appeared as a divinely guided chain of events: he had been sent by God to free the minds of the Jewish nation from the fetters of inertia, to be a teacher and guide such as was needed for their good.[84] The biography ended with these words:[85]

> This was the portion that this great man received from God. He was a gift of God to his contemporaries. His wisdom and his deeds were equally serving the good until the day on which he departed from us. One seeking wisdom will seek it in his books. One seeking faith will take it from his utterances. A soul longing to choose the upright path

will walk in his footsteps. Then the light of Israel will break forth like the dawn of morning, and Israel's honor will be great among the nations. Let the upright sages of our generation see this, and let them rejoice in the heritage he left us: the Tora of God and the songs of His holy ones rendered distinctly, their meaning explained; Israel's faith purified and strengthened, made safe against attack; plenty of consolation to oppressed souls by the understanding that God on high rewards those who fear Him with the goodness stored up with Him for all eternity. He is blessed, his portion is blessed, and his work is blessed! "Let me die the death of the righteous, and let my end be like his."

Notes

———❦———

ABBREVIATIONS USED IN THE NOTES

ADB	*Allgemeine deutsche Biographie* (Leipzig, 1875–1912; reprinted 1971)
AZJ	*Allgemeine Zeitung des Judentums* (Leipzig, 1837–1922)
Biedermann, *Gespräche*	*Gotthold Ephraim Lessings Gespräche nebst sonstigen Zeugnissen aus seinem Umgang*, ed. Flodoard Freiherr von Biedermann (Berlin, 1924)
BLBI	*Bulletin des Leo Baeck Instituts* (Tel-Aviv, 1957 . . .)
Danzel, *Lessing*	Th[eodor] W[ilhelm] Danzel, *Gotthold Ephraim Lessing, sein Leben und seine Werke*, volume 1 (Leipzig, 1849); volume 2 by G[ottschalk] E[duard] Guhrauer (sections one and two, Leipzig, 1853, 1854)
Dep. RvM	"Depositum Robert von Mendelssohn," i.e., autographs of letters from and to Moses Mendelssohn and other Mendelssohn autographs in the possession of Robert von Mendelssohn, lent to the Staatsbibliothek Stiftung Preussischer Kulturbesitz, Berlin
EJ	*Encyclopaedia Judaica*, ed. Jakob Klatzkin, 10 volumes (Berlin, 1928–1934)
Euchel, *Toledot*	Isaac [Abraham] Euchel, *Toledot Rabbenu Ha-Hakham Moshe Ben Menahem* (Berlin, 1788; new edition, Vienna, 1814)

Festschrift Martin Philippson	*Beiträge zur Geschichte der deutschen Juden, Festschrift zum siebzigsten Geburtstage Martin Philippsons* (Leipzig, 1916)
Frühschriften	Alexander Altmann, *Moses Mendelssohns Frühschriften zur Metaphysik untersucht und erläutert* (Tübingen, 1969)
Gedenkbuch David Kaufmann	*Gedenkbuch für David Kaufmann*, eds. M. Brann and F. Rosenthal (Breslau, 1900)
GGA	*Göttingische Anzeigen von gelehrten Sachen* (Göttingen, 1753 ff.)
Geiger, *Briefe*	Ludwig Geiger, "Briefe von, an und über Mendelssohn," *Jahrbuch für jüdische Geschichte und Literatur*, 20 (Berlin, 1917): 85–137
Graetz, *Geschichte*	H. Graetz, *Geschichte der Juden von den ältesten Zeiten bis auf die Gegenwart*, vol. 10 (2nd ed.); vol. 11 (1870)
GS	*Moses Mendelssohn's gesammelte Schriften*, ed. G. B. Mendelssohn. In 7 volumes (Leipzig, 1843–1845)
Hamann Briefwechsel	*Johann Georg Hamann Briefwechsel*, eds. Walther Ziesemer and Arthur Henkel (Wiesbaden, 1955 ff.)
HAR	*Histoire de l'Académie Royale des Sciences et Belles Lettres* (Berlin, 1746–1771)
Harnack, *Geschichte*	Adolf Harnack, *Geschichte der Königlich preussischen Akademie der Wissenschaften zu Berlin*. In 3 volumes (Berlin, 1900)
JJLG	*Jahrbuch der jüdisch-literarischen Gesellschaft*, vols. 1–22 (Frankfurt am Main, 1903–1932)
JubA	*Moses Mendelssohn Gesammelte Schriften Jubiläumsausgabe.* Jointly with F. Bamberger, H. Borodianski, S. Rawidowicz, B. Strauss, L. Strauss edited by I. Elbogen, J. Guttmann, E. Mittwoch. Vols. 1, 2, 3.1, 7, 11, 14, 16 (Berlin, 1929–1938). Reprinted and continued under the editorship of Alexander Altmann (Stuttgart, 1971 ff.)
Kant, *Werke*	*Immanuel Kants Werke*, ed. Ernst Cassirer. In 11 volumes (Berlin, 1922–1923)
Kayserling, *Mendelssohn*, 1st ed.	M[eyer] Kayserling, *Moses Mendelssohn. Sein Leben und seine Werke. Nebst einem Anhange ungedruckter Briefe von und an Moses Mendelssohn* (Leipzig, 1862)

Kayserling, *Mendelssohn*	M[eyer] Kayserling, *Moses Mendelssohn. Sein Leben und Wirken*. Second revised edition (Leipzig, 1888)
Kayserling, *Ungedrucktes*	M[eyer] Kayserling, *Moses Mendelssohn. Ungedrucktes und Unbekanntes von ihm und über ihn* (Leipzig, 1883)
Klausner, *Historiya*	Josef Klausner, *Historiya shel Ha-Sifrut Ha-'Ivrit Ha-Hadasha* (Jerusalem, 1952)
LBH	*Carl Robert Lessings Bücher- und Handschriftensammlung.*, ed. Gotthold Lessing. In three volumes (Berlin, 1914–1916).
L–M	*Lessings Sämtliche Schriften*, ed. K. Lachmann; 3rd ed. by F. Muncker (Stuttgart and Leipzig, 1886–1924)
Marburg File	A collection of letters and notes from Moses Mendelssohn to Friedrich Nicolai, discovered by Richard Wolff, Marburg, in the thirties of this century, and quoted here from typewritten copies and, partly, from xerographs of the original letters; now edited by Alexander Altmann, in conjunction with Werner Vogel, under the title, *Neuerschlossene Briefe Moses Mendelssohns an Friedrich Nicolai* (Stuttgart, 1973)
Meyer, *Bibliographie*	Herrmann M. Z. Meyer, *Moses Mendelssohn Bibliographie* (Berlin, 1965)
MGWJ	*Monatsschrift für Geschichte und Wissenschaft des Judentums* (Breslau, 1851–1939)
Nachlass Hennings	Collections of letters from and to August Hennings, in the possession of the Staats- und Universitätsbibliothek, Hamburg
Nicolai-Briefe	Letters from and to Friedrich Nicolai, in the vast and (for the most part) unpublished collection at the Staatsbibliothek Preussischer Kulturbesitz, Berlin
NZZ	*Neue Zürcher Zeitung* (Zürich)
PAAJR	*Proceedings of the American Academy for Jewish Research* (New York, 1932 ff.)
PMLA	*Publications of the Modern Language Association of America* (New York, 1885 ff.)
REJ	*Revue des Études Juives* (Paris, 1880–1936; n.s. 1937 ff.)

Verzeichnis

Verzeichniss der auserlesenen Büchersammlung des seeligen Herrn Moses Mendelssohn (Berlin, 1786), ed. Herrmann Meyer, Publication no, 5 of the Son-cino-Gesellschaft (Berlin, 1926)

ZGJD

Zeitschrift für die Geschichte der Juden in Deutschland, ed. Ludwig Geiger (Braunschweig, 1887–1890); ed. Ismar Elbogen, Aron Freimann, Max Freudenthal (Berlin, 1929–1938)

Chapter One: Years of Growth
Childhood in Dessau (pages 3–15)

1. See Max Freudenthal, *ZGJD,* 2 (1930):84. A more elaborate version of the present chapter is found in Alexander Altmann, "Moses Mendelssohns Kindheit in Dessau," *BLBI,* 10, No. 40 (1967):237–75.

2. See *GS,* 5:524–27.

3. See Elieser Landshuth, *Toledot Anshey Shem U-Fe'ulotam* (Berlin, 1884), 55 f.; Max Freudenthal, *Aus der Heimat Moses Mendelssohns* (Berlin, 1900), 164 f., 239 f.

4. Mendelssohn's ancestry on the maternal side has been traced back, as far as fourteen generations, to Rabbi Joseph ben Yohanan, known as Joseph Ha-Gadol, rabbi of Paris (born ca. 1305). See Gerhard Ballin, "Die Ahnen des Komponisten Felix Mendelssohn Bartholdy," *Genealogie,* ed. Gerhard Gessner and Heinz Reise, 16 (1967):646–55. For further references see Altmann, "Kindheit in Dessau," 243, note 19.

5. See Max Freudenthal, "Die Mutter Moses Mendelssohns "*ZGJD,* 1 (1929):192–200.

6. *JubA,* 16:142; cf. Kayserling, *Mendelssohn,* 3 f., note 1; Freudenthal, ibid., 195. Elkan (Elhanan) Herz was the son of Naphtali Herz, whose wife Gittel was presumably Moses Mendelssohn's maternal aunt. See *JubA,* 16:xxxvi.

7. Mendelssohn's Hebrew and Yiddish letters have been published by Haim Borodianski (Bar-Dayan) in *JubA,* 16. Of his extensive correspondence only a fraction (216 letters, partly written and partly received by him) has been preserved. For an evaluation of these letters and their stylistic character, see *JubA,* 16:ix–xxxi, and Borodianski's Yiddish essay, "Moses Mendelssohn in his Yiddish Letters," *Historische Schriften,* ed. A. Tscherikover (Warsaw, 1938), 1, 296–345.

8. *JubA,* 16, letter 127, p. 150 f.

9. Landshuth, *Toledot,* 36.

10. See Gershom Scholem, *Shabbatai Tsevi* (Tel-Aviv, 1957), 2:673, note 3.

11. A full account of his life is found in Freudenthal's *Aus der Heimat . . . ,* 37–114. See also Selma Stern, *The Court Jew* (Philadelphia, 1950), 57 ff., 251 f.

12. See Jacob Katz, *Masoret U-Mashber* (Jerusalem, 1958), 240 (English edition: *Tradition and Crisis: Jewish Society at the End of the Middle Ages,* New York, 1961, 206); Selma Stern, *The Court Jew,* 223 ff.; David Kaufmann and Max Freudenthal, *Die Familie Gomperz* (Frankfurt am Main, 1907), 37; Azriel Shochet, *'Im Hilufey Tekufot* (Jerusalem, 1960), 90; a comprehensive view of the commercial role of the court-Jews is given by Heinrich Schnee, *Die Hoffinanz und der moderne Staat* (Berlin, 1953–1955, 1963).

13. Freudenthal, *Aus der Heimat . . . ,* 123.

14. Freudenthal, *Aus der Heimat . . . ,* 19, 121 ff., 128–39.

15. See Altmann, "Moses Mendelssohns Kindheit," 253 f.

16. Isa. 32:9.

17. For a discussion of this phrase see Freudenthal, *ZGJD,* (1929) 1:194, note 8 and Altmann, "Moses Mendelssohns Kindheit," 252. The Hebrew inscription is found in Freudenthal's essay, "Die Mutter Moses Mendelssohns," 200.

18. See L-M, 19:46.

19. *JubA,* 16, letter 88, p. 105. The date May 18, 1764, given in the editor's note (p. lvi) is obviously in error.

20. Euchel, *Toledot,* 6.

21. Daniel Jenisch, "Skizze von dem Leben und Charakter Mendelssohns," *Moses Mendels-*

sohns kleine philosophische Schriften, ed. Johann Georg Müchler (Berlin, 1789), 7. For the variations of the report, see Altmann, "Moses Mendelssohns Kindheit," 255 ff.

22. For references, see Altmann, "Moses Mendelssohns Kindheit," 254 f.

23. See Freudenthal, *Aus der Heimat . . .* , where the Hebrew text of the inscription is easily legible on the photographic reproduction of the tombstone opposite p. 34.

24. B[enjamin] H[irsch] Auerbach, *Geschichte der israelitischen Gemeinde Halberstadt* (Halberstadt, 1866), 189; Kayserling, *Mendelssohn,* 4; Freudenthal, *Aus der Heimat . . .* , 217.

25. Euchel, *Toledot,* 6.

26. Ibid.

27. See Freudenthal, *Aus der Heimat . . .* , 219–22, 259; Shochet, *'Im Hilufey Tekufot,* 198–231, especially p. 207.

28. See Altmann, "Moses Mendelssohns Kindheit," 259 f., where Freudenthal's elaborate account of the activities of the Wulffian Press in its various domiciles is used.

29. See Simeon Günzburg, *Rabbi Moshe Hayyim Luzzatto U-Veney Doro, Osef Iggerot Ve-Te'udot* (Tel-Aviv, 1937); Yesha'yahu Tishby, *Netivey Emuna U-Minut,* 1964, 169–203.

30. Euchel, *Toledot,* 7; Kayserling, *Mendelssohn,* 5; Joseph Mendelssohn *(GS,* 1:7) merely reported that his father "mentioned very often that he owed much, very much indeed, to Maimonides."

31. See Max Freudenthal, "Rabbi David Fränckel," *Gedenkbuch David Kaufmann,* 573–78; David Kaufmann, "Aus Moses Mendelssohns Frühzeit," *AZJ,* 55 (1891): 476–78. Cf. Altmann, "Moses Mendelssohns Kindheit," 261 ff.

32. See Louis Ginzberg, *Geonica,* 1 (New York, 1909), 73.

33. See the historical survey in Louis Ginzberg's *A Commentary on the Palestinian Talmud,* 1 (New York, 1941), li–lvi.

34. Volume 1: Dessau, 1743: volume 2: Berlin, 1757; volume 3: Berlin, 1760–1762.

35. The "bound-up testimony" was, according to a passage in *Zohar Hadash,* Midrash Ruth quoted by Fränkel in Preface 2, an allusion to the Palestinian Talmud. See Altmann, "Moses Mendelssohns Kindheit," 264.

36. See Freudenthal, "Rabbi David Fränckel," 579–86.

37. Ibid.

38. Viz. *She'elot U-Teshuvot Rivash* (Responsa of Rabbi Isaac ben Sheshet), Riva, 1559. The young Moses' inscription was discovered by the Prague rabbi, Dr. Nathan Grün, and published by him in 1875. A facsimile reproduction of the entire page, which contains more than the bare text, was published by Fritz Bamberger in his beautiful edition of Mendelssohn autographs, *Denkmal der Freundschaft* (Berlin, 1929), folio 1. The facsimile has been republished, together with a transcription of the Hebrew text and a German translation, in Altmann, "Moses Mendelssohns Kindheit," 267 f.

39. Bamberger, *Denkmal,* note to folio 1 made it plausible that the young Mendelssohn presented Fränkel with the volume that he had inscribed originally as belonging to him.

40. For an evaluation of the mentality and style of the inscription, see Altmann, "Moses Mendelssohns Kindheit," 269 f.

41. *GS,* 5:526.

42. *GS,* 4.2:136 f.

43. *GS,* 5:673.

44. *GS,* 5:206. By the German philosophers said to engage in rabbinic casuistry, Nicolai meant particularly Kant and Fichte. See Altmann, "Moses Mendelssohns Kindheit," 258, note 78.

45. L.F.G. von Gökingk, *Friedrich Nicolai's Leben und literarischer Nachlass* (Berlin, 1820), 146, note.

46. See Landshuth, *Toledot,* 23–26, 35–38; Selma Stern, *Der preussische Staat und die Juden* (Tübingen, 1962), 2.1:141 f.

47. See Altmann, "Moses Mendelssohns Kindheit," 273 ff.

The Early Years in Berlin (pages 15–25)

1. See [Friedrich Nicolai,] *Beschreibung der Königlichen Residenzstädte Berlin und Potsdam,* 3rd ed. (Berlin, 1786), 1:lxx: "Berlin has 15 gates, 268 streets and squares, 36 bridges, and 33 churches." The lively scenes at the gates are described by Ernst Consentius, *Alt-Berlin Anno 1740* (Berlin, 1911), 147–52.

2. The anecdote first appeared in Sigismund Stern, *Geschichte des Judentums von Mendels-*

sohn bis auf die neuere Zeit (Breslau, 1857), 58, and was taken over by Kayserling, *Mendelssohn,* 1st ed., 8, and by Graetz, *Geschichte,* 11:4. Jacob Auerbach, "Moses Mendelssohn und das Judenthum," *ZGJD,* 1 (1887):10, note 1, considered it apocryphal. Otto Zarek, *Moses Mendelssohn* (Amsterdam, 1936), 73–75, retold it with a great deal of imaginative embellishment.

3. See Ludwig Geiger, *Geschichte der Juden in Berlin* (Berlin, 1871), 1:52 f.; 2:83 ff., 87 ff.; Selma Stern, *Der preussische Staat und die Juden,* 2.1:21, 146 f.; Josef Meisl (ed.), *Protokollbuch der jüdischen Gemeinde zu Berlin* (Jerusalem, 1962), xxvii. In 1784 the Jewish population in Berlin was 3,372. See Nicolai, *Beschreibung,* 2:605.

4. See Meisl, *Protokollbuch,* xxvii.

5. A facsimile is found in *Jüdisches Lexikon,* ed. Georg Herlitz and Bruno Kirschner (Berlin, 1927), 1:871.

6. See Meisl, *Protokollbuch,* 155, No. 157.

7. See Ismar Freund, *Die Emanzipation der Juden in Preussen* (Berlin, 1912), 2:22–60, where the text of the revised "General-Privilegium und Reglement" of Apr. 17, 1750 is reproduced.

8. Our account is based on C. F. Koch, *Die Juden im Preussischen Staate* (Marienwerder, 1833), 32–38.

9. The *Privileg* of 1730 excluded daughters from the right of inheriting protected status, but an amendment enacted that same year gave them this right if there was no male heir. See Selma Stern, *Der preussische Staat und die Juden,* 2.1:144 f.

10. See Geiger, *Geschichte,* 2:84. A more specified list is given in Ulrich's anonymous work, *Über den Religionszustand in den preussischen Staaten seit der Regierung Friedrichs des Grossen* (Leipzig, 1779), 4:328.

11. He is variously referred to as Chajim Bomburg (Euchel, *Toledot,* 8), Bamberger (Joseph Mendelssohn, *GS,* 1:8, omitting the first name), and Heimann Bamberger (Kayserling, *Mendelssohn,* 8; Sebastian Hensel, *Die Familie Mendelssohn* (Leipzig, 1924), 1:19). His full name was Hayyim ben Löb Bamberg. According to Kayserling, who cites no source, he lived in the Probstgasse, near the Molkenmarkt.

12. See Meisl, *Protokollbuch,* xxxii ff.; Jacob Katz, *Tradition and Crisis,* 82.

13. In the Minute-Book *(pinkas)* of the Berlin community his name appears in the tax assessment lists of the years 1742, 1745, 1748, etc. through 1764, the year in which he died. His election as one of the four administrators of charity took place in 1747. His signature is found under a number of documents dealing with synagogal matters. See Meisl, *Protokollbuch,* 134 f., 146–52, 155, 157. For all references concerning him see the index, p. 491, *s.v.* Hayyim B-B (Bamberg).

14. *Toledot,* 8.

15. See the text of his letter of appointment and its reconfirmation in Landshuth, *Toledot,* 37, 39 f.

16. On the Beth Hamidrash see Meisl, *Protokollbuch,* lvf.; on Naftali Levin see *JubA,* 16:lxxx; Kayserling, *Ungedrucktes,* 38 f.

17. *JubA,* 16, letter 188, p. 212 f.

18. *GS,* 1:8.

19. See Nicolai, *Beschreibung,* 1:14 f.

20. On Ramler's and Lessing's lodgings see Arno Hach, "Verschollener Dichterwinkel," *Vossische Zeitung,* Nov. 23, 1930. A description of the streets of Berlin is found in Nicolai, *Beschreibung,* 1:10 ff. A street map is attached at the end of the volume. A steel engraving by Finden after a drawing by Stock of the Mühlendamm seen from the Molkenmarkt with Veitel Heine Ephraim's *Palais* on the right is reproduced in this volume.

21. See above, note 11.

22. See Nicolai, *Beschreibung,* 1:10 f.

23. A picture of the interior from the engraving by Goblin is found in this volume. The synagogue was completed and consecrated in 1714. For its history see Meyer Kayserling, "Die Synagoge zu Berlin," *Jeschurun,* ed. Samson Raphael Hirsch, 3:173–83. For a description of it, see Albert Wolf, "Das jüdische Berlin gegen Ende des 18. Jahrhunderts," *Gedenkbuch David Kaufmann,* 631 f.

24. See G. C. Küster, *Altes und neues Berlin* (Berlin, 1752), 2:1027 ff. (quoted by Geiger, *Geschichte,* 2:46 f.).

25. A picture of the curtain is reproduced in *EJ,* 4:231.

26. The service held in the chief rabbi's house on sabbath mornings had to start not later than 5 A.M. so as not to interfere with the main service in the synagogue (see Meisl,

Protokollbuch, liii, lv). The synagogue, the Beth Hamidrash, and the house of the chief rabbi were all situated in the Heydereuthergasse (see Landshuth, *Toledot*, 39). On the general rabbinic privileges, which included the right to hold services at his Beth Hamidrash (or at his home) and to confine visits to the synagogue to alternate sabbaths and festivals, see Jacob Katz, "*Le-toledot ha-rabbanut be-motsa'ey yemey ha-beynayim*," *Sefer Zikaron le-Binyamin de Vries* (Jerusalem, 1969), 281–94, especially 284.

27. See Geiger, *Geschichte*, 1:21 ff.; 2:43–48; Kayserling, "Die Synagoge zu Berlin," 175–81.

28. See Selma Stern, *Der preussische Staat und die Juden*, 2.1:126; Meisl, *Protokollbuch*, xxiv ff., xlix.

29. The organization of the community (*kehilla*) in Berlin followed the prevalent pattern. See the chapter on communal organization in Katz' *Tradition and Crisis*, 79–90.

30. See Selma Stern, *Der preussische Staat und die Juden*, 2.1:126.

31. Landshuth, *Toledot*, 6–13.

32. Ibid., 23–26.

33. Ibid., 20–34.

34. In his reply to Michaelis; see below, p. 467.

35. Quoted by Selma Stern, *Der preussische Staat und die Juden*, 2.1:152.

36. On the gradual development of "common ground," see Jacob Katz, *Tradition and Crisis*, 245–59, and *Exclusiveness and Tolerance* (Oxford, 1961), 156–68.

37. See Isaac E. Barzillay, "The Italian and Berlin Haskala," *PAAJR*, 29 (1960–1961):19 f.

38. Ibid.

39. *GS*, 5:204 f.; Kayserling, *Mendelssohn*, 11 f.; *EJ*, 8:638 f.

40. According to Kayserling, *Mendelssohn*, 11, note 2, a fragment of this copy was in the possession of Professor Abraham Berliner (1833–1915). After Berliner's death his library was sold to the Städtische Bibliothek, Frankfurt am Main. My efforts to trace the fragment have been unsuccessful.

41. See Adolf Jellinek, "Biographische Skizzen," *Literaturblatt des Orients*, 7 (1846):260 f.

42. *GS*, 1:10; 5:206.

43. Louis Lewin, *Geschichte der Israelitischen Kranken-Verpflegungs-Anstalt zu Breslau* (Breslau, 1926), 36 f., 124, note 49; Elisabeth Kupka, "Die ersten jüdischen Ärzte im preussischen Breslau," *Jüdische Familien-Forschung*, 8(1932):439 f.

44. JubA, 16, letter 267, p. 288. Kisch died on June 5, 1803. See Guido Kisch, "Die Prager Universität und die Juden," *Jahrbuch der Gesellschaft für Geschichte der Juden in der cechoslovakischen Republik*, 6 (1934):94, note 74. Borodianski (*JubA*, 16, xcv) denied the identity of Dr. Kisch, Mendelssohn's early mentor, and Dr. Kisch mentioned in Letter 267. He assumed that there were two Prague physicians named Abraham Kisch, and that the one who had been Mendelssohn's tutor died in 1760, since the death of a certain Abraham Kisch in that year is attested. Professor Guido Kisch, by his discovery that Dr. Abraham Kisch died in 1803, was able to disprove Borodianski's surmise. There was only one physician of this name. See also Friederich Thieberger, "Moses Mendelssohn und Prag," *B'nai B'rith, Monatsblätter der Grossloge für den cechoslovakischen Staat*, 8 (1929), no. 7, quoted by Meyer, *Bibliographie*, p. 154 f., no. 1088; 292.

45. See Nicolai's report in *GS*, 5:205, 207.

46. *GS*, 5:526.

47. See David Kaufmann and Max Freudenthal, *Die Familie Gomperz* (Frankfurt a.M., 1907), 164–200; Borodianski, *JubA*, 16:xxxvii.

48. See Friedrich Nicolai, *Anekdoten von König Friedrich II. von Preussen und von einigen Personen, die um Ihn waren* (Berlin & Stettin, 1788–1789). Mendelssohn figures largely in these anecdotes. See also Bruno Strauss, "D'Argens und Moses Mendelssohn," *Vossische Zeitung*, Nov. 18, 1928 (quoted by Meyer, *Bibliographie*, p. 82, no. 435). For a fuller account of the man see Newell Richard Bush, *The Marquis d'Argens and his Philosophical Correspondence, A Critical Study of d'Argens' Lettres juives, Lettres cabalistiques and Lettres chinoises*, Dissertation Columbia University, New York, N.Y., 1953; Elise Johnston, *Le Marquis d'Argens, Sa Vie et ses oeuvres* (Paris, 1929).

49. See Richard H. Popkin, "Manicheanism in the Enlightenment," *The Critical Spirit: Essays in Honor of Herbert Marcuse*, ed. Kurt H. Wolff and Barrington Moore, Jr. (Boston, 1967), 41 ff.

50. See Kaufmann and Freudenthal, *Die Familie Gomperz*, 174 ff.

51. Published by Theodor Wilhelm Danzel, *Gottsched und seine Zeit* (Leipzig, 1848), 333; see Kaufmann and Freudenthal, *Die Familie Gomperz*, 175, note 4.

52. Neither Nicolai *(GS,* 5:205, 207) nor Kaufmann and Freudenthal *(Die Familie Gomperz,* 177 f.) suggests any date for the start of Mendelssohn's participation in Heinius' course. Our surmise is based on an evaluation of Gumpertz' circumstances.

53. Euchel, *Toledot,* 10 f.

54. See Friedrich Nicolai, "Etwas über den verstorbenen Rektor Damm und Moses Mendelssohn," *Neue Berlinische Monatsschrift,* ed. J.E. Biester, 3 (1800): 339 f.

55. *GS,* 5:526.

56. *JubA,* 11, letter 3, p. 12.

57. See p. 41 f.

58. Kaufmann and Freudenthal, *Die Familie Gomperz,* 183 ff.

59. The work appeared in Hamburg (1765) and Vilna (1836).

60. A description of the work is given by Kaufmann and Freudenthal, *Die Familie Gomperz,* 197 ff.

61. *JubA,* 14:111 f.

62. To see in the *Ma'amar Ha-Mada'* a "polemical tract" and a "program for a new time," as Eschelbacher did, is to exaggerate its importance. See Joseph Eschelbacher, "Die Anfänge allgemeiner Bildung unter den deutschen Juden vor Mendelssohn," *Festschrift Martin Philippson,* 176.

63. *JubA,* 16, letter 101, p. 124 f.

64. *JubA,* 16, letter 105, p. 127 f.

65. *JubA,* 11, letter 114, p. 220.

The Budding Philosopher (pages 25–36)

1. *GS,* 5:206.

2. Johann Gustav Reinbeck, *Betrachtungen über die in der Augspurgischen Confession enthaltene und damit verknüpfte Göttliche Wahrheiten* . . . Part One (Berlin & Leipzig, 1740).

3. Reinbeck, *Betrachtungen,* xlvi.

4. Reinbeck, *Betrachtungen,* xlvii.

5. *GS,* 5:206 f.

6. *JubA,* 1:64 f.

7. *JubA,* 7:8.

8. *JubA,* 1:64.

9. JubA, 11, letter 178, p. 295 f. (Feb. 22, 1762). Translated: "The qualities of this volume / Are wit, good taste, imagination galore / French sophistry / And sheet-lightning of reason."

10. *GS,* 5:288, 309.

11. Christian Wolff's German metaphysics is entitled: *Vernünfftige Gedancken von Gott, der Welt und der Seele des Menschen;* his German ethics is named: *Vernünfftige Gedancken von der Menschen Thun und Lassen.*

12. *JubA,* 1:32.

13. *GS,* 4.1:503 f. *(Literaturbrief,* no. 21, Mar. 1, 1759).

14. *JubA,* 11, letter 79, p. 176

15. *JubA,* 1:30.

16. *JubA,* 1:13 f.

17. See Bruno Strauss, *JubA,* 11:446.

18. *JubA,* 1:14.

19. *GS,* 4.2:72

20. *GS,* 4.2:68. Cf. below, p. 71 f.

21. *JubA,* 11, letter 81, p. 181.

22. *GS,* 4.1:331.

23. *JubA,* 11, letter 81, p. 181.

24. *GS,* 3:413 ff., reprinted from *Berlinische Monatsschrift,* 5:133 ff.

25. *GS,* 4.1:262; *JubA,* 1:14; see G.E. Guhrauer, *Gottfried Wilhelm Freiherr von Leibniz, Eine Biographie* (Breslau, 1846), 2:331 ff.

26. *GS,* 4.1:501.

27. *JubA,* 1:21–27; see *Frühschriften,* 38–59.

28. *GS*, 4.1:504 *(Literaturbrief*, no. 22, Mar. 1, 1759).
29. *Histoire de l'Académie Royale des Sciences et Belles-Lettres*, 25 vols. (Berlin, 1746–1771). See Harnack, *Geschichte*, 1.1:309–11, 481.
30. *JubA*, 1:3–5.
31. See Fritz Bamberger, *JubA*, 1:x f.
32. See above, p. 27.
33. *JubA*, 2:363.
34. André Pierre Le Guay de Prémontval, *Du Hazard sous l'empire de la Providence* (Berlin, 1755); see *Frühschriften*, 3 f., 68 f.
35. *GS*, 3:5.
36. Letter to Michaelis (Oct. 16, 1754), L-M, 17:40; see Erich Schmidt, *Lessing, Geschichte seines Lebens und seiner Schriften*, 4th ed. (Berlin, 1923), 1:250.
37. Pierre Bayle, *Dictionnaire Historique et Critique*, new ed. (Paris, 1820), 13:417 (article on "Spinoza").
38. Pierre Poiret, *Cogitationes rationales de deo, anima et malo* (Amsterdam, 1685), 490.
39. Bayle, *Dictionnaire*, 13:418 f.
40. Ibid., 440–44 (note N, ii–iv).
41. *JubA*, 1:15 f.
42. See *JubA*, 1:564: *Lesarten* 351, lines 17–20 ("blinder Religionseifer").
43. *JubA*, 1:16.
44. *JubA*, 1:14 f.
45. *JubA*, 1:15. Wolff's refutation of Spinoza is found in his *Theologia naturalis* (Verona, 1738), #671–716.
46. Wolff, *Theologia naturalis*, #714–16.
47. *JubA*, 1:17.
48. *HAR*, 1754 (Berlin, 1755), 121–42.
49. Ibid., 130.

Lessing (pages 36–50)

1. *Allgemeine deutsche Bibliothek* (Berlin & Stettin, 1786), 65.2:627; quoted by Biedermann, *Gespräche*, 40, no. 33.
2. *GS*, 5:207.
3. Viz. during his first stay in Berlin from November, 1748, until the end of 1757.
4. Karl G. Lessing, *Gotthold Ephraim Lessings Leben . . .* , First Part (Berlin, 1793), 166 f. Taking his cue from this report, Kenneth Keeton, "Berliner Montags-Klub," *Germanic Review*, 36 (1961):149, suggested that Mendelssohn and Lessing played chess prior to the weekly sessions of the Monday Club, of which Lessing was a member and which Mendelssohn, who was not a member, may be assumed to have frequented as a guest. However, all this is pure conjecture on Keeton's part.
5. See *JubA*, 16, letters 50 and 52, p. 67 (*JubA* 11, letters 159 and 162, p. 278). Mendelssohn tried his best to find him a suitable position. Hess eventually succeeded after May, 1762. See *JubA*, 16, letters 50, 66, 70, and 84, pp. 67, 83, 85, and 102 (*JubA*, 11, letters 162, 185, 188, and 207, pp. 278, 304, 305 f., and 334). Graetz mistakenly attributed Mendelssohn's meeting Lessing to Hess (see Borodianski, *JubA*, 16:xlix).
6. *Allgemeine deutsche Bibliothek*, 65. 2:627.
7. See Danzel, *Lessing*, 1:223–31.
8. See Karl Borinski, *Lessing* (Berlin, 1900), 1:14.
9. See Bruno Strauss, "Moses Mendelssohn und seine Zeit," *Moses Mendelssohn. Zur 200-jährigen Wiederkehr seines Geburtstages*, ed. Encyclopeadia Judaica (Berlin, 1929), 7.
10. See Hans Schmoldt, *Der Spinozstreit*, Dissertation, Berlin, 1938 (Würzburg, 1938), 17 f., where, however, only the vaguest conjectures are offered.
11. See *Frühschriften*, 27.
12. See Erich Schmidt, *Lessing, Geschichte seines Lebens und seiner Schriften*, 4th ed. (Berlin, 1923), 1:251 f.
13. *JubA*, 1:1–39.
14. *GS*, 1:13 f.; Euchel, *Toledot*, 15 f.
15. Joseph Mendelssohn rightly rejected Nicolai's assertion that it was the letters *On the Sentiments* that was written first. See *Frühschriften*, 1, note 5.
16. *JubA*, 1:231.
17. See *Frühschriften*, 1–4.

18. *Staats- und Gelehrte Zeitungen des Hamburgischen unpartheyischen Correspondenten,* 1755, no. 26; see *JubA,* 1:xviii; *JubA,* 11:390.
19. *JubA,* 11, letter 6, p. 15. Lessing was in Potsdam at the time.
20. *Berlinische privilegirte Zeitung,* 1755, no. 26; reproduced in *Lessing Gesammelte Werke,* ed. Paul Rilla (Berlin, 1955), 3:142 ff.
21. On Lessing's later doubts concerning Mendelssohn's Spinoza interpretation, see *Frühschriften,* 21–24, and below, pp. 50 f., 620, 691.
22. *GS,* 5:205, note.
23. *JubA,* 11, letter 25, p. 53.
24. On the translation "industry" and its sloppiness in eighteenth-century Germany, see Friedrich Nicolai's satirical novel *Leben und Meinungen des Herrn Magisters Sebaldus Nothanker* (1773–1776; ed. Heinz Stolpe, Berlin, 1960), 85–95.
25. On Christian Nicolaus Naumann see Bruno Strauss, *JubA,* 11:385.
26. The review appeared in *GGA,* 1755, no. 64 (May 29):586 ff.
27. See Danzel, *Lessing,* 1:246–52.
28. Lessing is said to have been influenced by English sentimental comedy (Sir Richard Steele's *The Conscious Lovers* and similar works), which tended to idealize human types. See Paul P. Kies, "Lessing's Relation to Early English Sentimental Comedy," *PMLA,* 47 (1932): 807–26; quoted by Karl S. Guthke, *Der Stand der Lessing-Forschung* (Stuttgart, 1965), 42 f.
29. See Erich Schmidt, *Lessing,* 1:146: Michael A. Meyer, *The Origins of the Modern Jew* (Detroit, 1967), 16 f., 185.
30. *JubA,* 11, letter 3, pp. 9–13; notes pp. 387–89.
31. Section 1, no. 6 (L-M, 6:159–66).
32. L-M, 6:166.
33. See Danzel, *Lessing,* 1:234 f.
34. *Berlinische privilegirte Zeitung.*
35. *JubA,* 11, letter 7, p. 15 f.; see *Frühschriften,* 138, note 1.
36. *GGA,* 1755, no. 118:1107 f.
37. Michaelis seems to have noticed the autobiographical character of the passage quoted above, p. 27 f.
38. *Über die Empfindungen* (Berlin, 1755): *JubA,* 1:41–123; reprinted, with revisions, in Mendelssohn's *Philosophische Schriften* (1761, 1771, 1777; see *JubA,* 1:541). The thoroughly revised text of the 1771 edition is found in *JubA,* 1:233–330.
39. *JubA,* 1:43 f. When Mendelssohn republished the letters in his *Philosophische Schriften,* he exchanged the name Palemon for Theocles, another figure in Shaftesbury's *Rhapsody,* which, as he explained to Elkan Herz (JubA, 16, letter 129, p. 153; Nov. 15, 1771), served there as spokesman for deistic principles.
40. Wilhelm Dilthey, *Das Erlebnis und die Dichtung,* 12th ed. (Göttingen, 1921), 40.
41. See *Frühschriften,* 92.
42. Ibid,. 109 f.
43. See Rudolf Hunziker, "Briefe von Johann Georg Sulzer," *NZZ,* Feb. 24, 1929 (no. 351); Mar. 3, 1929 (no. 397); Mar. 10, 1929 (no. 448); Mar. 15, 1929 (no. 487).
44. Johann Georg Sulzer, "Recherches sur l'origine des sentimens agréables et désagréables," *HAR,* 1751 (Berlin, 1753): 80, 83, 85, 87. See *Frühschriften,* 97 f.
45. *Briefe deutscher Gelehrter,* ed. Wilhelm Körte (Zürich, 1804), 1:255. In a letter to Bodmer, dated June 1, 1761, Sulzer wrote (p. 349 f.): "The Jew, Lessing's friend, is called Moses, a rare genius who should mix with other people, though, than Lessing and Nicolai."
46. *JubA,* 11, letter 10, p. 17.
47. *JubA,* 1:56, 73 (248, 267). See Fritz Bamberger, *JubA,* 1:608 f. Sulzer is mentioned by name in Mendelssohn's draft, "Von dem Vergnügen," *JubA,* 1:128. See *Frühschriften,* 102 ff., 125.
48. *JubA,* 2:27–33.
49. Ibid., 29. Concerning the dating of the critical notes, see *Frühschriften,* 108 ff.
50. MS 5 of the Lavater collection at the Zentralbibliothek, Zürich.
51. See Bamberger, *JubA,* 2:xi f.
52. See Harnack, *Geschichte,* 2:306; Leo Strauss, *JubA,* 2:xv–xx; *Frühschriften,* 184–90.
53. *Essay on Man,* 1:45–46. An excellent bibliography on the theme of the "Golden Chain of Being" *(catena aurea)* is offered in Bernard McGinn's doctoral dissertation (1969): *The Golden Chain: A Study of the Symbolic Theology of Isaac of Stella* (Brandeis University, 1969).
54. See *Frühschriften,* 189.

55. Ibid., 200 ff.
56. *GS*, 5:195.
57. See Lessing's letter to Mendelssohn (Feb. 18, 1755), *JubA;* 11, letter 6, p. 14: "Your refusal to disclose your name was my principal reason," viz. for not submitting the manuscript to the academy. Apart from this "principal" reason, Lessing obviously had other reasons as well.
58. Ibid.
59. Ludwig Hirzel, *Wieland und Martin und Regula Künzli* (Leipzig, 1891), 116; see Harnack, *Geschichte,* 1.1, 407.
60. *JubA*, 11, letter 12, p. 21.
61. *JubA*, 11, letter 16, p. 27 f.
62. See Karl G. Lessing, *Lessings Leben,* 1:162 f.
63. It had been announced in the *Berlinische privilegirte Zeitung* (Mar. 29, 1755), and the catalog of publications planned by Voss for Easter, 1755, listed it as having already appeared by then. Mendelssohn inquired about the progress of the edition in his letter of Feb. 17, 1775 (*JubA*, 11, letter 5, p. 13 f.). Lessing recalled this project as late as 1778, in a letter to Elise Reimarus dated December 16 (L-M, 18:295).
64. *JubA*, 2:83.
65. *Lessing Gesammelte Werke,* ed. Rilla, 3:153 f.
66. *JubA*, 11, letter 11, p. 18.
67. *JubA*, 11, letter 15, p. 26.
68. *Johann Jacob Rousseau Bürgers zu Genf Abhandlung von dem Ursprunge der Ungleichheit unter den Menschen und worauf sie sich gründe: ins Deutsche übersetzt mit einem Schreiben an den Magister Lessing und einem Briefe Voltairens an den Verfasser vermehret* (Berlin, 1756).
69. *JubA*, 2:90 f.
70. *JubA*, 2:105.
71. See Leo Strauss, *JubA*, 2:395 commenting on p. 105, lines 33–34.
72. *JubA*, 2:90 f.
73. *JubA*, 2:33.
74. *GS*, 5:586.
75. In a letter to J. A. Ebert, dated Nov. 7, 1769 (L-M, 17:306).

The Metaphysician (pages 50–65)

1. See Harnack, *Geschichte,* 1.1:311.
2. *GS*, 5:168 f.
3. *GS*, 5:174–77; see *Frühschriften,* 21–24.
4. *JubA*, 1:3–19 (337–55); see *Frühschriften,* 8–29.
5. See *Frühschriften,* 20 ff.
6. Ibid., 10.
7. The phrase is Frederick Pollock's; see his *Spinoza* (1912), 331.
8. For an analysis of Mendelssohn's interpretation of Spinoza in the *Dialogues* see *Frühschriften,* 29–38.
9. It was edited for the first time by L. Duten in *Opera Omnia,* vols. 2 and 6 (Geneva, 1768).
10. *Essais de Théodicée,* 1:195.
11. *JubA*, 1:356–66.
12. *JubA*, 1:27 f.
13. C. J. Gerhardt (ed.), *Die philosophischen Schriften von G. W. Leibniz* (Berlin, 1875–90), 7:371 f.; for a discussion of this dialogue see *Frühschriften,* 60–82.
14. See *Frühschriften,* 31.
15. See *GS*, 4.1, 499 f.; *Frühschriften,* 82 f.
16. For an analysis of this work, see *Frühschriften,* 85–183.
17. Dep. RvM, B II, no. 4; published in *JubA*, 1:123–31.
18. See *Frühschriften,* 121 f.
19. Ibid., 111 f.
20. Ibid., 116 ff.
21. Spinoza had already said (in a letter to Hugo Boxel) that the things in themselves or in relation to God are neither beautiful nor ugly.

22. See *Frühschriften*, 129.
23. Ibid., 132 f.
24. *JubA*, 1:381–424.
25. *JubA*, 11, letter 42, p. 105.
26. *JubA*, 11, letter 43, p. 108.
27. Samuel von Pufendorf, *The Officio Hominis et Civis juxta Legem Naturalem Libri Duo* (Lund, 1673), chap. 5.4
28. Cicero, *De senectute*, 72. The simile of the sentry who must not leave his post is also found in Bahya ibn Pakuda's *Hovot Ha-Levavot*, 4.4 (p. 198, line 10 in A. S. Yahuda's edition of the original Arabic text; p. 310 in A. Tsifroni's Hebrew edition).
29. Jeremy Taylor, *Doctor Dubitantium, or the rule of Conscience* (London, 1660); John Sym, *Lifes Preservative* (London, 1637).
30. See *Frühschriften*, 140.
31. Ibid., 141, 144–47.
32. Ibid., 148 f.
33. *JubA*, 11, letter 38, p. 84 f.; *Frühschriften*, 153 ff.
34. *JubA*, 14:193.
35. See *Frühschriften*, 161.
36. Ibid., 162 f.
37. Mishna, Hagiga, 1:8.

The Bel Esprit (pages 65–74)

1. See Martin Sommerfeld, *Friedrich Nicolai und der Sturm und Drang* (Halle, 1921).
2. See L.F.G. von Göckingk, *Friedrich Nicolai's Leben und literarischer Nachlass* (Berlin, 1820), 16–19; Nicolai, *Über meine gelehrte Bildung . . .* (Stettin & Berlin, 1799), 40.
3. *JubA*, 11, letter 23, p. 39.
4. *JubA*, 11, letter 27, p. 55. See also Nicolai's letter to Lessing, *JubA*, 11, letter 28, p. 57 and Bruno Strauss' note, p. 407. The "Bibliothek" is the *Bibliothek der schönen Wissenschaften und der freyen Künste* (see below, p. 69 f).
5. Arno Hach, "Verschollener Dichterwinkel," *Vossische Zeitung*, Nov. 23, 1930. Hach's account has to be corrected in part in light of documentary evidence provided by Theodor Zondek, "Moses Mendelssohns Hypothekenbrief," *BLBI*, 9, no. 35 (1966): 278–83. On Jan. 29, 1762, the house Spandauerstrasse 68 had been acquired from the Hegelin estate by the Royal *commissarion* and *Waagenmeister* Johann Michael Hensel, from whom Rösel Meyer, née Ephraim, wife of Aaron Meyer (Joresch), bought it on Nov. 6, 1765, having received from her father Veitel Heine Ephraim a mortgage of four thousand thalers at four percent. Moses Mendelssohn signed the deed on her behalf. On May 11, 1773, he became the mortgagee by payment of this sum, while Rösel remained the owner of the property until Mendelssohn's widow bought it from her. Zondek seems to assume that Mendelssohn moved into the house only after it had been acquired by Rösel Meyer, but it is highly probable that his occupancy of the house dated from the beginning of his married life in 1762. In his letters to his fiancée Fromet written in March of this year (*JubA*, 11: 309, 311) he announced that by Passover the house would be vacated [viz. by the previous tenants].
6. For references see Bruno Strauss, *JubA*, 11:407.
7. The book reviews written by Mendelssohn are published in *GS*, 4.1:157–599; 4.2:3–560.
8. *GS*, 5:217.
9. *JubA*, 1:85. See Ludwig Goldstein, *Moses Mendelssohn und die deutsche Ästhetik* (Königsberg, 1904), 24, 70–86.
10. See below, p. 270.
11. *GS*, 5:218.
12. *JubA*, 2:187–96; see Haim Borodianski's introduction, xxxvi–xli.
13. *JubA*, 11, letter 48, p. 118 f.
14. Bruno Strauss, *JubA*, 11:425.
15. *JubA*, 11, letter 75, p. 167.
16. *JubA*, 11, letter 75, p. 167 f.
17. Nachlass Hennings, no. 22, letter 8, fol. 12*v* (June 29, 1779).
18. The Hebrew text and the German translation were printed as a pamphlet, and the

German version was reproduced in a Berlin weekly on Oct. 11, 1756 (see Eliezer Landshuth, *Toledot Anshey Shem U-Fe'ulotam* (Berlin, 1884), 49–51). It opens with the words: "Herr, der die Welt mit deiner Allmacht regierest."

19. *Danklied über den rühmlichen Sieg . . .* (see Meyer, *Bibliographie*, p. 32, no. 87; Landshuth, *Toledot*, 52). Reproduced by M. Kayserling, *Zum Siegesfeste. Dankpredigt and Danklieder von Moses Mendelssohn. Eine Reliquie.* Berlin, 1866, 16–18.

20. The sermon appears to be lost. It was most probably never published. See Bruno Strauss, JubA, 11:440. Kayserling, *Mendelssohn*, 1st ed., 145, note 2, believed a copy to be extant but admitted, in the pamphlet *Zum Siegesfeste*, p. iv f., his failure to obtain it, and made no further reference to the matter in the second edition of his Mendelssohn biography.

21. See Landshuth, *Toledot*, 53 (reproduced by Kayserling, *Zum Siegesfeste*, 19–21); *Dankpredigt über den grossen und herrlichen Sieg . . . bey Leuthen . . . Gehalten . . . von Daniel Hirschel Fränkel, Oberland-Rabbiner. Ins Deutsche übersetzt. Berlin. Gedruckt bey Friedrich Bernstiel . . . 1757.* See Landshuth, *Toledot*, 55. Kayserling, *Zum Siegesfeste*, 1–15, republished the sermon.

22. Strangely enough, his name was given as Daniel Hirschel (instead of David) Fränkel.

23. *JubA*, 11, letter 74, p. 166 f.; see Strauss' note, p. 440.

24. *JubA*, 11, letter 75, p. 167.

25. On the development of the new style of preaching see *Studies in Nineteenth Century Jewish Intellectual History*, ed. Alexander Altmann (Cambridge, Mass., 1964), 65–116.

26. See the text published by Kayserling, *Zum Siegesfeste*, 5, 13 f.

27. Parallels of this saying are either anonymously stated or ascribed to R. Jehuda bar Joseph. See M. Margaliot, ed., *Midrash Vayikra' Rabba* (Jerusalem, 1953), 190, note 4.

28. *GS*, 2:411–51. On this treatise and its date of composition see below, p. 666 ff. Mendelssohn translated "*concursus*" as "*Mitwirkung*."

29. *GS*, 5:167; 173.

30. See *GS*, 5:221 ff.; Meyer, *Bibliographie*, p. 33, no. 93.

31. Reported by Nicolai, *GS*, 5:224, who also asserted that the "Sermon on Peace" was published soon thereafter in both Hebrew and German by Hartog Leo. Landshuth, *Toledot*, 61, seems to merely have copied this information. Nothing is known of a bilingual edition of the sermon. Nicolai may have confused it with the Hebrew-German edition of the hymn composed for the occasion by Hartog Leo and translated by Mendelssohn (see Meyer, *Bibliographie*, p. 38, no. 130, where the title is given). The "Sermon on Peace" (see Meyer, *Bibliographie*, p. 37, no. 129) is reproduced in *GS*, 6:407–15. A Hebrew translation of it (by Euchel?) appeared in *Ha-Me'assef*, 1789, 14–23.

32. *Hamann Briefwechsel*, 2, 249 f.

33. MS 5 of the Lavater collection in the Zentralbibliothek Zürich; see below, p. 201.

34. See *GS*, 6:393 ff.; 398 ff.

35. His work includes translations of Hamlet's monologue (3:1, "To be, or not to be") and a poem by Pope (see *GS*, 6:391 ff.); also a rewriting of an *Ode in Praise of God* by a contemporary Jewish poet, Ephraim Kuh (1731–1790); see *GS*, 6:396 ff. Cf. Kayserling, *Der Dichter Ephraim Kuh* (Berlin, 1864); Arthur Galliner, *BLBI*, 5, no. 19 (1962): 196 ff.

36. *JubA*, 11, letter 50, p. 135 (May 29, 1757).

37. See *GS*, 4.1:155–496. The review of Klopstock's *Der Tod Adams* should have been included (see Goldstein, *Mendelssohn und die deutsche Ästhetik*, 16; *JubA*, 11:432).

38. It is found in *Bibliothek*, 1.1, 17–68; reedited by Robert Petsch, *Lessings Briefwechsel mit Mendelssohn und Nicolai über das Trauerspiel* (Leipzig, 1910), 1–42. See now Jochen Schulte-Sasse, *G. E. Lessing, M. Mendelssohn und F. Nicolai, Briefwechsel über das Trauerspiel* (Munich, 1972).

39. *JubA*, 11, letter 28, pp. 57–60.

40. *JubA*, 1:110.

41. That Lessing used Mendelssohn's definition of fear has been stressed by Jürgen Ricklefs, "Lessings Theorie vom Lachen und Weinen," *Dankesgabe für Albert Leitzmann* (Jena 1927), 25 and note 35 (quoted by Bruno Strauss, *JubA*, 11:412) and by Max Kommerell, *Lessing und Aristoteles* (Frankfurt am Main, 1957), 80.

42. *JubA*, 2:86. See Bruno Strauss, *JubA*, 11:412.

43. *JubA*, 11, letters 33, 35, 36, and 38, pp. 66 f., 72 f., and 86. For an analysis, see J. G. Robertson, *Lessing's Dramatic Theory* (Cambridge, 1939; New York, 1965), 356–68. The reply quoted is found on p. 86.

44. See also Mendelssohn's essay *On the Sources and Connections between the Fine Arts and*

the Sciences (JubA, 1:178), in which the idea of the need for choosing the "fertile moment" is already found.

45. See O. F. Walzel, *Vom Geistesleben alter und neuer Zeit* (Leipzig, 1922), 243; Fritz Bamberger, *JubA,* 2:xli–xlv.

46. Erich Schmidt, *Lessing,* 4th ed. (Berlin, 1923), 1:252.

47. A description of the original manuscript, bibliographical references, and textual notes is given in *JubA,* 2:352–55. A critical edition of the text is found on pp. 231–58.

48. See Bamberger, *JubA,* 2, xliii f.

49. See Hermann Hettner, *Geschichte der deutschen Literatur im achtzehnten Jahrhundert* (Berlin, 1961), 1:464–69.

50. *GS,* 4.2, 461–564.

51. Mendelssohn's initials were D, M, P, Z, and K, in turn. See Göckingk, *Nicolai's Leben,* 27; Emil Neidhardt, "Moses Mendelssohns Anteil an den Briefen, die neueste Litteratur betreffend," *Festschrift des Gymnasiums Erfurt* (Erfurt, 1891), 1–36. Readers were sometimes quite puzzled as to the identity of the reviewer. See Otto Hoffmann (ed.), *Herders Briefwechsel mit Nicolai* (Berlin, 1887), 23; R. M. Werner, "Gerstenbergs Briefe an Nicolai nebst einer Antwort Nicolais,"*Zeitschrift für deutsche Philologie,* ed. Hugo Gering and Oskar Erdmann, 23 (1891): 48: "That Herr Moses is the author of the critical review of [Anna Louisa] Karschin's poems [in *Literaturbriefe* 272–76; see *GS,* 4.2:420–44] would not have occurred to me."

52. *GS,* 4.2:141–58. Other instances of Mendelssohn's use of fictional devices are found in *GS,* 4.2:134 ff., 159, 292 ff.

53. E.g., Lorenz Withof is compared with Pope and Young *(GS,* 4.1:158; 4.2:159 f.).

54. *GS,* 4.2:163.

55. *GS,* 4.2:66–98.

56. See above, p. 68.

57. *GS,* 4.2:67–72.

58. *GS,* 4.1:230 f.; 4.2:29 f.

59. *GS,* 4.1:315 f.; see also his review of Baumgarten's*Aesthetica,* Part Two in *GS,* 4.2:375 ff.

60. *GS,* 4.2:247ff.

61. *GS,* 4.2:149.

62. *GS,* 4.2:48–51.

63. *GS,* 4.2:337–40.

64. Cf. Liselotte Richter, *Philosophie der Dichtkunst: Moses Mendelssohns Ästhetik zwischen Aufklärung und Sturm und Drang* (Berlin, 1948), 14–21.

65. See Robertson, *Lessing's Dramatic Theory,* 57, 136 f., 145–48, 152–58, 250.

66. Ibid., 252 f.

67. *Hamburgische Dramaturgie,* section 96 (quoted by Robertson, *Lessing's Dramatic Theory,* 458).

68. See Danzel, *Lessing,* 2.2:92 f.

69. F. H. Jacobi in a letter to Heinse (Oct. 20, 1780); see Biedermann, *Gespräche,* 244.

70. Ibid.

71. See below, p. 332.

72. See Rudolf Haym, *Herder* (Berlin, 1954), 1:143 f.

73. *GS,* 4.1:499–506.

74. *GS,* 4.1;538–69.

75. See *JubA,* 3.1:135, 148 f.

76. *GS,* 4.1:512–22; see A. E. Gaisinovich, "C. F. Volff i Evseevich o razvitii organizmov," Proceedings of the Academy of Sciences of the U.S.S.R. (Moscow), 1961, 265 ff.; see also pp. 8, 178, 187 f. I am indebted to Dr. Haim Bar-Dayan for having brought this work to my notice.

77. *GS,* 4.2:176–97.

A Learned Society (pages 74–83)

1. *JubA,* 11, letter 19, p. 36.

2. *GS,* 5:214 f.

3. Son of the famous Leonhard Euler (1707–1783).

4. Friedrich Nicolai, *Neue Berlinische Monatsschrift,* 24 (1810): 168.

5. Geiger, *Briefe,* 129 f.

6. See, also for the following account, Max Birnbaum, "Moses Mendelssohn, der Seidenfabrikant," *Gemeindeblatt der Jüdischen Gemeinde zu Berlin,* 19 (1929): 452–54, and Nicolai, *Beschreibung der Königlichen Residenzstätte Berlin und Potsdam,* 3rd ed. (Berlin 1786), 510 f.

7. *GS,* 5:171.

8. See L.F.G. von Göckingk, *Friedrich Nicolai's Leben . . .* (Berlin, 1820), 73 ff.; Erich Schmidt, *Lessing,* 4th ed. (Berlin, 1923), 1:245 f. That Mendelssohn was not a member of the Montag-Klub is apparent from the fact that none of the extant membership lists contains his name. Lessing joined the club in 1751, Nicolai in 1756.

9. "Gedanken von der Wahrscheinlichkeit," first published anonymously in *Vermischte Abhandlungen und Urtheile über das Neueste aus der Gelehrsamkeit,* 3 (Berlin, 1756): 3–26; reprinted under the title "Uber die Wahrscheinlichkeit" in Mendelssohn's *Philosophische Schriften,* vol. 2 (Berlin, 1761, 1771, 1777); and reproduced in *GS,* 1:349–69 and *JubA,* 1:147–64; 495–515.

10. *GS,* 5:215 f.

11. See Richard Maria Werner, "Nicolai und seine Freunde über Mendelssohn," *ZGJD,* 1 (1887): 130.

12. See *Frühschriften,* 209 ff.

13. According to Nicolai's report, the person concerned was Lord Middleton, a Scotsman, who was an admirer of Mendelssohn and translated the letters *Über die Empfindungen* into English. This translation was never published. Only French, Dutch, and Italian versions appeared (see Meyer, *Bibliographie,* 31 f.).

14. *JubA,* 11, letter 31, p. 63.

15. For a detailed account see *Frühschriften,* 213–51.

16. See above, p. 55.

17. *JubA,* 11, letter 38, p. 88.

18. *JubA,* 11, letter 39, p. 96.

19. See above, p. 55.

20. *JubA,* 11, letter 43, p. 109.

21. *JubA,* 11, letter 77, p. 169–74.

22. Both letters are lost (see *JubA,* 11:161).

23. *JubA,* 11, letter 71, p. 164; letters 74 and 75, pp. 167 and 169; see note, p. 437.

24. *JubA,* 1:231, 325.

25. *JubA,* 2:305.

26. *GS,* 2:253–58.

27. See the comprehensive bibliography in J.G. Meusel, *Das Gelehrte Deutschland,* 5 (Lemgo, 1797): 302 ff. and the biographical note in *JubA,* 11:397.

28. Mendelssohn's coeditorship is attested by Müchler's letter to Georg August von Breitenbauch published in *LBH,* 2:197, no. 2446; Geiger, *Briefe,* 129 (see *JubA,* 2:xxiv).

29. Bamberger's notes (*JubA,* 2:397–402) illustrate the point.

30. *JubA,* 2:113–20.

31. *JubA,* 2:121–24.

32. *JubA,* 2:400.

33. *JubA,* 2:128–31.

34. *JubA,* 2:133–43.

35. Other articles by Mendelssohn that appeared in the *Chamäleon* contain further "Reflections" *(Gedanken)* and Socrates' "Dialogue with Euthydemus on the Fear of God and on Justice" (*JubA,* 2:131 f., 144f.).

36. On this poem, its editions, and its translations, see Salo W. Baron, *A Social and Religious History of the Jews,* 7 (New York, 1958): 168, 300 (note 46).

37. The "Elegie an die Burg Zion gerichtet" and the excerpt from *Prüfung der Welt* appeared in *Beschäftigungen,* vol. 2, no. 2:111–14; 115–18 and are reprinted in *GS,* 6:425–35. The editorial remark *(GS,* 6:425) that the translation of Bedershi's chapters was first published in *Ha-Me'assef* (1784) is mistaken. So is the statement (p. 429) that Ha-Levi's elegy first appeared in Christian Gottlob Meyer's German edition of Solomon Dubno's *'Alim Li-Terufa (see Meyer, Bibliographie,* p. 51, no. 249 and below, p. 376 f.). Müchler reprinted both pieces in his edition of *Moses Mendelssohns kleine philosophische Schriften* (Berlin, 1789), 155–70, and mentioned their earlier publication in his preface.

38. See above, p. 39.

39. In the preface of his edition of Mendelssohn's smaller philosophical writings cited at the end of note 37.

40. See Waldemar Kawerau, "Friedrich Gabriel Resewitz, Ein Beitrag zur Geschichte der deutschen Aufklärung," *Geschichts-Blätter für Stadt und Land Magdeburg*, 20 (Magdeburg, 1855): 151–59.

41. *Über meine gelehrte Bildung* (Berlin & Stettin, 1799), 44 (quoted by Bruno Strauss, *JubA*, 11:404).

42. Nicolai-Briefe, vol. 60, no. 50 (unpublished).

43. Nicolai-Briefe, vol. 60, no. 94 (unpublished).

44. Nicolai-Briefe, vol. 60 (no number; unpublished).

45. Published in *Sammlung vermischter Schriften zur Beförderung der schönen Wissenschaften*, vol. 2, no. 1 (1759) and vol. 3, no.1 (1760).

46. *GS*, 4.2:52-54; 335–48.

47. See above, p. 73.

48. See *Frühschriften*, 173–76.

49. See Alexander Altmann, "Eine neuentdeckte Moses Mendelssohn-Korrespondenz zur Frage des Selbstmords," *Zeitschrift für Religions- und Geistesgeschichte*, 20 (1968): 240–58; and *Frühschriften*, 165–73.

50. See Altmann, *Eine neuentdeckte . . . Korrespondenz*, 242.

51. See *Frühschriften*, 174.

52. "Wir wollen uns lieben, aber nicht wie sich die Weltlichen lieben" (*JubA*, 11, letter 24, p. 41).

Kohelet Mussar (pages 83–91)

1. See *JubA*, 14:iv.

2. See *JubA*, 14:289.

3. See *GS*, 4.1:176 f., 189.

4. *GS*, 4.1:303 ff.

5. *JubA*, 14:iii, xii.

6. Simon Höchheimer, *Über Moses Mendelssohns Tod* (Vienna & Leipzig, 1786), 68; see *JubA*, 14:iv. On Mendelssohn's friendship for Höchheimer, see Kayserling, *Mendelssohn*, 516; Fritz Bamberger, *Denkmal der Freundschaft*, note on fol. 14.

7. *JubA*, 14:289.

8. This negative result is the only conclusion one may draw from Jacob Toury's strenuous effort to solve the riddle. See his article in *Kiryat Sefer*, 43 (1968): 279-283; *BLBI*, 10, no. 38–39 (1967): 95–110; 11, no. 41 (1968): 60 f., in reply to Herrmann M.Z. Meyer's article, *BLBI*, 11, no. 41:48–59.

9. Euchel, *Toledot*, 13.

10. See below, p. 366.

11. *Ha-Me'assef* (1785), 90–93, 93–95, 103–105.

12. Issachar Edelstein, "*Ha-Hibbur Kohelet Mussar*," *Festschrift zum 50 jährigen Bestehen der Franz-Josef-Landesrabbinerschule in Budapest*, ed. Ludwig Blau, (Budapest, 1927), 60 f. rightly rejected Graetz' view that only the essays published in *Ha-Me'assef* were by Mendelssohn. He went, however, to the other extreme in suggesting that Mendelssohn merely inspired his friends to contribute to *Kohelet Mussar*, while not himself writing at all.

13. See Josef Meisl, *Protokollbuch der jüdischen Gemeinde Berlin* (Jerusalem, 1962), 492; Toury, *Kiryat Sefer*, 43:281 and *BLBI*, 10: 102f. On Hebrew writers by the name of Soldin, who lived in Denmark and revered Mendelssohn from the distance, see D. Simonsen, "Mendels-sohniana aus Dänemark, " *Festschrift Martin Philippson*, 219 f.

14. See Meisl, *Protokollbuch*, 492; Toury, *Kiryat Sefer*, 43:281; *BLBI*, 10:103 f.

15. *JubA*, 16, letter 132, p. 156; letter 136, p. 160.

16. On Tobias Boaz see D.S. van Zuiden, *De Hoogduitsche Joden in 's-Gravenhage . . .* (The Hague, 1913), *passim*.

17. See *JubA*, 16, letter 188, p. 212 f.; lxxx; Kayserling, *Ungedrucktes*, 39 f.

18. *JubA*, 14:1–3.

19. *JubA*, 14:3–7.

20. Mendelssohn quotes Jehuda Ha-Levi's *Kuzari*, 4:25, where the Hebrew language is said to have been created by God, whereas all other languages owed their origin to conventional devices. Mendelssohn upheld this view in the introduction, *Or Li-Netiva*, to his Pentateuch edition (*JubA*,14:214 ff.).

21. *JubA*, 14:11–15.

22. *JubA*, 14:15–18.

23. *JubA*, 14:18–21.

24. This passage clearly indicates that Dr. Gumpertz was not coeditor, as has been surmised by Toury.

25. By mistake Mendelssohn wrote "Samuel ibn Tibbon."

26. This sums up Jehuda ibn Tibbon's statement in the preface to his translation of Bahya ibn Pakuda's *Duties of the Heart:* "It is impossible to express the thoughts of our hearts succinctly and eloquently in Hebrew, while we are capable of it in Arabic, which is adequate to the purpose, elegant in expression and readily available to those who speak it." See A.S. Halkin, "The Medieval Jewish Attitude to Hebrew," *Biblical and Other Studies,* ed. Alexander Altmann (Cambridge, Mass., 1963), 237.

27. This work, having been originally written in Hebrew, should not have been included in the list.

28. A pseudo-Aristotelian Arabic treatise translated into Hebrew by Abraham ben Hasday (see M. Steinschneider, *Die hebräischen Übersetzungen des Mittelalters und die Juden als Dolmetscher* (Berlin, 1893; Gratz, 1956), #144.7, p. 267 f.).

29. The Hebrew term used by Mendelssohn is *imrey no'am.*

30. On the *Epistle* mentioned see Steinschneider, *Die hebräischen Übersetzungen,* #530, p. 860 f.

31. Translated under the title *Ben Ha-Melekh Ve-Ha-Nazir* by Abraham ben Hasday.

32. See Mendelssohn's remarks in his review (1757) of Withof's *Moral Poems, GS,* 4.1:158.

33. It may be assumed that Euchel's account *(Toledot,* 13) was based on information supplied by Mendelssohn. Dubno, who was also well informed, merely alluded to the opposition by saying that the enterprise came to an early end "for some reason."

Chapter Two: Maturity and Fame
Marriage and Family Life (pages 92–100)

1. For the rules and customs governing the institution of marriage in the pre-Enlightenment era, see Jakob Katz, *Tradition and Crisis: Jewish Society at the End of the Middle Ages* (New York, 1961), 135–48.

2. *JubA*, 11, letter 104, p. 206 f.

3. Viz. Johann Georg Hamann; see *GS,* 4.2:315 f.

4. *JubA*, 11, letter 217, p. 345 f.

5. *JubA*, 16, letter 3, p. 3–letter 87, p. 104 (in Hebrew characters; transliterated into German: *JubA*, 11, letter 103, p. 205–letter 210, p. 336 f.). The correspondence is interspersed with many letters to and from other people. Fromet's letters are unfortunately lost. A separate edition of *Moses Mendelssohn Brautbriefe,* with an introduction by Ismar Elbogen, appeared in no. 49–50 of the *Bücherei des Schocken Verlags* (Berlin, 1936). Haim Borodianski transliterated the slightly Judeo-German text of the original into German.

6. See Elbogen, *Brautbriefe,* 8–11; Katz, *Tradition and Crisis,* 268.

7. *JubA*, 16, letter 76, p. 93 *(JubA,* 11, letter 197, p. 318); *JubA*, 16, letter 78, p. 95 *(JubA,* 11, letter 200, p. 324).

8. *JubA*, 16, letter 46, p. 62 (JubA, 11, letter 155, p. 273). See also *JubA*, 16, letter 49, p. 65 *(JubA,* 11, letter 158, p. 276).

9. *JubA*, 16, letter 77, p. 94 *(JubA,* 11, letter 199, p. 323).

10. *JubA*, 16, letter 79, p. 96 *(JubA,*11, letter 202, p. 328 f.).

11. *JubA*, 16, letter 11, p. 15 (JubA, 11, letter 112, p. 219).

12. *JubA*, 16, letter 15, p. 19 f. *(JubA,* 11, letter 116, p. 224).

13. *JubA*, 16, letter 29, p. 38 *(JubA,* 11, letter 131, p. 242).

14. *JubA*, 16, letter 36, p. 50 *(JubA,* 11, letter 140, p. 225).

15. *JubA*, 16, letter 37, p. 52 *(JubA,* 11, letter 142, p. 257 f.).

16. Ibid.

17. *JubA*, 16, letter 25, p. 32 *(JubA,* 11, letter 127, p. 236 f.).

18. *JubA*, 16, letter 36, p. 50 *(JubA,* 11, letter 141, p. 255 f.). The authorship of this poem could not be established. Translated into English, it reads: Happy, happy is childhood / which the Lord instructs and takes under his protection / As in a quiet valley / at the edge of a pure shadow / a young lily, the beloved of nature / believes to be protected against the wind from the North.

19. *JubA*, 16, letter 33, p. 45 *(JubA,* 11, letter 136, p. 250).

20. *JubA*,16, letter 26, p. 33f. (*JubA*, 11, letter 128, p. 238 f.). On the medallion see Bruno Strauss, *JubA*, 11:468.

21. Mendelssohn's *Philosophische Schriften* appeared in the fall of 1761.

22. *JubA*, 16, letter 29, p. 38 f. (*JubA*, 11, letter 131, p. 243).

23. *JubA*, 16, letter 4, p. 5 (*JubA*, 11, letter 105, p. 209); *JubA*,16, letter 17, p. 21 (*JubA*, 11, letter 118, p. 225); and *passim*.

24. *JubA*, 16, letter 59, p. 75 (*JubA*, 11, letter 173, p. 287).

25. *JubA*, 16, letters 4, 8, 17, 38, pp. 6 13, 21, 54 (*JubA*, 11, letters 105, 109, 118, 144, pp. 209, 217, 225, 260). The critical review appeared in *Literaturbrief* 171 and is reproduced in *GS*, 4.2:278–83.

26. *JubA*, 16, letter 21, p. 27 (*JubA*, 11, letter 123, p. 232).

27. *JubA*, 16, letter 23, p. 30 (*JubA*, 11, letter 125, p. 234 f.).

28. See *Literaturbrief* 167 (*GS*, 4.2:267 f.). Cf. *JubA*, 11:467.

29. *JubA*, 16, letter 13, p. 16 (*JubA*, 11, letter 114, p. 220). For references to the *Lettres de Mylady Catesby* see JubA, 16, letter 8, p. 13 and letter 17, p. 21 (JubA, 11, letter 109, p. 217, and letter 118, p. 225).

30. *JubA*, 16, letter 20, p. 25 (*JubA*, 11, letter 122, p. 229).

31. *JubA*, 16, letter 26, p. 34 (*JubA*, 11, letter 128, p. 239).

32. See Meisl, *Protokollbuch*, p. 76, no. 80 and p. 429; Moritz Stern, *Beiträge zur Geschichte der Juden in Berlin* (Berlin, 1909), 1:6.

33. Stern, *Beiträge*, 1:5; Graetz, *Geschichte*, 11:5.

34. See *GS*, 1:37; Albert Wolf, "Das jüdische Berlin . . . ," *Gedenkbuch David Kaufmann*, 633 ff.; Bruno Strauss, *JubA*, 11:471.

35. *JubA*, 16, letter 38, p. 53, and letter 39, p. 55 f. (*JubA*, 11, letter 144, p. 259 f., and letter 145, p. 261 f.). Joseph Mendelssohn (*GS*, 1:37) referred to this humorous passage in the correspondence with Fromet. This provides clear evidence that he knew the *Brautbriefe*. According to Elbogen (*Brautbriefe*, 15), the correspondence remained in Hamburg after Fromet's death (1812) and did not come into the Mendelssohn family archive until 70 years later. Joseph, who wrote his father's biography in 1841–1842 (see *BLBI*, 11, no. 42:81, 83, 88–99), obviously made use of the letter, which he must have found among the *Brautbriefe*. Borodianski seems to have overlooked the passage in the biography when he suggested (*JubA*, 16:xvii) that neither he nor his son, Prof. Georg Benjamin Mendelssohn (who edited the *GS*), knew anything of this correspondence.

36. See Wolf, "Das jüdische Berlin," 633 ff.

37. *Über Mendelssohns Bart*, 21.

38. *JubA*, 16, letter 40, p. 56 (*JubA*, 11, letter 146, p. 262).

39. *JubA*, 16, letter 19, p. 24 (*JubA*, 11, letter 120, p. 228). See also *JubA*, 16, letters 31, 32, 34, pp. 41, 42, 46 (*JubA*, 11, letters 133, 135, 138, pp. 245, 247, 252). An engraving showing Veitel Heine Ephraim's *Palais* is reproduced in this volume.

40. They involved the supply of low grade coins at the time of the Seven Years' War. See Nicolai's note, *GS*, 5:220.

41. *JubA*, 16, letter 62, p. 78 (*JubA*, 11, letter 179, p. 296). The immediately following letter of March 2 fully explains Mendelssohn's reasons for refusing the offer.

42. *JubA*, 16, letter 21, p. 27 (*JubA*, 11, letter 123, p. 231 f.). See also *JubA*, 16, letter 32, p. 42 (*JubA*, 11, letter 135, p. 247 f.) and the letter to Naftali Herz, *JubA*, 16, letter 1, p. 1 (*JubA*, 11, letter 91, p. 192).

43. All dates given here are taken from a stenciled copy of the Family Tree put at my disposal by Prof. Peter N. Witt, himself a member of the Mendelssohn family. The date mentioned in *JubA*, 16:lvi has to be corrected.

44. *GS*, 5:315.

45. *JubA*, 16, letter 236, p. 257.

46. *JubA*, 16, letter 141, p. 170 (Feb. 9, 1773).

47. *GS*, 5:362.

48. See *JubA*, 16:lxi.

49. *JubA*, 16, letter 141, p. 170.

50. So it is stated in the Family Tree, p. 5. Meyer, *Bibliographie*, 304, has 1768 or 1774 (without giving the month and day).

51. *JubA*, 16, letter 188, p. 212 f.

52. *JubA*, *16* letter 193, p. 216.

53. *JubA*, 16, letters 212 and 215, pp. 242 and 244; lxxxvi. In the Family Tree (p. 10) the name of the child is given as Busgen(?).

54. Quoting the rabbinic phrase from Berakhot 31b.

55. *GS*, 5:674. Joseph Swa is mentioned in Mendelssohn's financial accounts (Marburg File under "E"): "Obligation von HE. Joseph Swa in Ld'or 20–." He is said to have been a clerk in the banking firm of Moses Isaac [Chalfan]; see Theodor Zondek, "Moses Mendelssohns Hypothekenbrief," *BLBI*, 9, no. 35 (1966): 281. In 1820 Friedländer wrote to Karl August Böttiger, editor of the *Deutscher Merkur:* "For more than thirty years Moses Mendelssohn was on friendly terms with the mathematician Swa, without ever asking him to which religion he belonged" (quoted by Meyer, *Bibliographie*, p. 88, no. 492). Rabbi Samuel was resident tutor in the Mendelssohn household (see *JubA*, 16, letters 193, 196, 200, pp. 216, 222, 230).

56. *JubA*, 16, letters 147, 148, 152, 170, pp. 172, 173, 176, 194.

57. *JubA*, 16, letter 124, p. 144 f.

58. *GS*, 5:191 f.

59. *JubA*, 16, letter 150, p. 174 f.

60. *JubA*, 16, letter 173, p. 197.

61. *JubA*, 16, letter 172, p. 196.

62. Karl Gotthelf Lessing, brother of Gotthold Ephraim Lessing, who lived in Berlin from 1765 until 1779.

63. The philosopher Johann Jakob Engel, Mendelssohn's close friend.

64. *JubA*, 16, letter 194, p. 217 f.

Thomas Abbt (pages 100–112)

1. *Confusionem linguarum, quae Babelica audit, non fuisse poenam generi humano a Deo inflictam* (Halle, 1758). The biblical treatises are described by Friedrich Nicolai (ed.), *Thomas Abbts Vermischte Werke*, 6 (1781): vi–viii, and in greater detail by Annie Bender, *Thomas Abbt, Ein Beitrag zur Darstellung des erwachenden Lebensgefühls im 18. Jahrhundert* (Bonn, 1922), 36–39.

2. See above, p. 68.

3. *JubA*, 11, letter 92, p. 193. See also Nicolai's letter to Lessing, L–M, 19:165.

4. *JubA*, 2:93. Concerning Iselin see Hermann Hettner, *Geschichte der deutschen Literatur* . . . (Berlin, 1961), 1:594–97, and Bruno Strauss, *JubA*, 11:500 f.

5. See *Literaturbrief* 67 (Nov. 8, 1759): *GS*, 4.1:582–85.

6. *Literaturbrief* 138 (Jan. 1, 1761): *GS*, 4.2:214–19.

7. François de Salignac de la Mothe Fénelon (1651–1715), archbishop of Cambrai and a mystical theologian.

8. Timur i Leng (Tamerlane), restorer of the Mongol empire, who invaded Persia in 1381 and India in 1398.

9. *Literaturbrief* 181: *GS*, 4.2:284–92.

10. *Von dem Nationalstolze* (Zürich, 1758, 1760, and 1768; Vienna, 1766).

11. In the *Bibliothek der schönen Wissenschaften und der freyen Künste*, 4.1 (1758): 551–78; *GS*, 4.1:439–57. Mendelssohn reviewed the second edition in *Literaturbrief* 143 (Feb. 5, 1761): *GS*, 4.2:224–28.

12. *GS*, 4.2:224.

13. See Bender, *Thomas Abbt*, 57.

14. *GS*, 4.1:443.

15. See Arthur Marmorstein, *The Doctrine of Merits in Old Rabbinic Literature* (London, 1920).

16. *GS*, 4.2:287. On Ibn Gabirol's phrase and the prominence it achieved in Kabbala see Gershom Scholem, *"Ikevotav shel Gabirol ba-Kabbala"* (*"Traces of Gabirol in the Kabbala"*), *Me'assef Soferey Erets Yisra'el*, 1940: 163 ff.

17. See his letter to *Kriegsrath* von Segner (Apr. 3, 1761) in *Abbts Vermischte Werke*, 6 (1781): 55 f.

18. Letter to Blum, in *Abbts Vermischte Werke*, 5 (1780): 107.

19. *Abbts Vermischte Werke*, 6:57.

20. His first review appeared on Mar. 5, 1761. See *GS*, 5:234, note 2.

21. *JubA*, 11, letter 93, p. 194 f.; letter 97, p. 197–200.

22. *JubA*, 11, letter 98, p. 200 ff.

23. It attacks Mendelssohn's main proof against the rationality of suicide; see above, p. 63 f., and *Frühschriften*, 155–58.

24. *GS*, 1:182–86; *JubA*, 1:318–24 (note p). The original form of the criticized passage is found in *JubA*, 1:96; for its amended form see *JubA*, 1:292.

25. *Abbts Vermischte Werke*, 3:14–22. Abbt's second note is reproduced in *GS*, 5:240; *JubA*, 11, letter 99, p. 202 f. Nicolai published Mendelssohn's replies in *Abbts Verm. Werke*, 3:22–28. Mendelssohn's reply to the second objection is reproduced in *GS*, 5:241; *JubA*, 1:519. See also Bruno Strauss, *JubA*, 11:460.

26. *JubA*, 11, letter 223, p. 359. On Nicolai's garden see above, p. 66.

27. *Abbts Verm. Werke*, 5:178.

28. *GS*, 5:301.

29. *JubA*, 11, letter 218, p. 350 f.

30. *JubA*, 11, letters 176 and 213, pp. 291, 341.

31. From November, 1760, until Easter, 1765, Lessing stayed in Breslau. Mendelssohn's last letter to him during that period is dated Aug. 1, 1763, and Lessing's last letter to Mendelssohn from Breslau was written on Apr. 17, 1763. The above statement is imprecise.

32. Using the biblical phrase, Exod. 32:32.

33. *GS*, 5:346.

34. From Easter, 1765, until June, 1766, Lessing was again in Berlin.

35. *GS*, 5:350.

36. See above, p. 70 f.; Danzel, *Lessing*, 2.1:10.

37. See the editorial note, *GS*, 5:367.

38. *GS*, 5:367.

39. *GS*, 5:301.

40. See the full-length portrait of Möser in Friedrich Meinecke, *Die Entstehung des Historismus* (Munich, 1959), 303–54.

41. See above, p. 103.

42. He described them as similar to "wooden blocks attached to keys to prevent their getting lost," and found deep symbolic meaning in them. Goethe spoke of Möser as the very incarnation of common sense, and as one worthy of being a contemporary of Lessing, the very representative of the critical spirit. He quoted with approval Möser's essay *On the Superstitions of our Ancestors* (see Inselverlag edition of Goethe's works, 2:84–88).

43. Justus Möser was the author of *Harlekin or Defense of the Grotesque-Comical* (1761); see Bruno Strauss, *JubA*, 11:474.

44. The review was the joint work of Abbt, Nicolai, and Mendelssohn. It appeared as *Literaturbrief* 204–06. Abbt's covering letter to Möser is found in *Justus Möser Briefe*, ed. Ernst Beins and Werner Pleister (Osnabrück, 1939), 109 f. For earlier editions see Bruno Strauss, *JubA*, 11:497. The "Harlekin" is already referred to in Abbt's first letter from Rinteln (see *JubA*, 11, letter 148, p. 265, and Mendelssohn's reply, letter 154, p. 272).

45. See *JubA*, 11, letter 189, p. 322; *Möser Briefe*, 230.

46. Volume 1: Ancient History (Halle, 1766). Nicolai described the work in *Abbts Verm. Werke*, 6:xxv–xxxiii.

47. See Nicolai, *Abbts Verm. Werke*, 6:xxvi.

48. See Meinecke, *Historismus*, 313 f. For Möser's comments on the project, see *Möser Briefe*, 184 f., 189 f.

49. *GS*, 5:362.

50. *GS*, 5:368. Möser's *History of Osnabrück* had then not yet appeared. Its publication commenced in 1768.

51. *Abbts Verm. Werke*, 5:208. For some inexplicable reason Abbt's last letter to Mendelssohn was omitted from the reproduction of the Mendelssohn/Abbt correspondence in *GS*, vol. 5. The editorial note on p. 368 ignores the letter.

52. *GS*, 5:342.

53. *GS*, 5:284. The work criticized was Abbt's *Leben und Charakter Alexander Gottlieb Baumgartens* (1763). The letter containing the criticism is dated Feb. 9, 1764.

54. Letter to Abbt, dated July, 1764 (*Möser Briefe*, 165): " . . . to tell you that your metaphors, which Moses criticizes, are all derived, and excessively so, as though visualized through a magnifying glass."

55. *Möser Briefe*, 233.

56. *JubA*, 11, letter 217, p. 350 (July 21, 1762).

57. E.g., *gleichalterig; einen Satz zur Wahrheit stempeln;* see *GS,* 5:231 f.

58. See Rudolf Haym, *Herder* (Berlin, 1954), 1:198–201; Bender, *Thomas Abbt,* 75.

59. See Werner Krauss (ed.), *Die französische Aufklärung im Spiegel der deutschen Literatur des 18. Jahrhunderts* (Berlin, 1963), cxliii ff.

60. *GS,* 5:320. Abbt worked on this book from 1762 to 1764 (see Nicolai, *Abbts Verm. Werke,* 6:xxiii). It was first published in 1765 (later editions in 1767, 1772, 1790).

61. *Abbts Verm. Werke,* 3:47 (quoted by Krauss, *Französische Aufklärung,* cxliv; see also cxlvii).

62. *GS,* 5:330 f.

63. *Möser Briefe,* 230 (Feb. 11, 1767).

64. *JubA,* 11, letter 217, p. 347.

65. Hamann made a remark to this effect in one of his letters; see *F. H. Jacobi's Werke* (ed. F. Roth), 4.3 (Leipzig, 1819): 140.

66. *JubA,* 11, letter 16, p. 30; see Anthony, earl of Shaftesbury, *Characteristicks of Men, Manners, Opinions, Times in three Volumes,* the sixth edition, 1:61 (1737); see also *JubA,* 11, letters 16 and 49, pp. 29 f., 130.

67. *JubA,* 1:356 ff.

68. *JubA,* 11, letter 154, p. 270 f.

69. According to Fritz Bamberger, *JubA,* 1:619, and Bruno Strauss, *JubA,* 11:475, two versions of the draft of the Shaftesbury translation are extant in Mendelssohn's own handwriting. I have been able to locate only one version, that in the possession of Herr Robert von Mendelssohn. This version is not contained in Dep. RvM.

70. The words used are: *Höhnerey, Höhnung, Spott, spöttische Weise, Munterkeit, Rallirie, Ralliiren.*

71. *JubA,* 11, letter 176. p. 290. It is unknown which of Shaftesbury's works Abbt translated.

72. *JubA,* 11, letter 178, p. 296.

73. See note 69 above.

74. *GS,* 5:382; 3:263, 402.

75. *JubA,* 11, letter 201, p. 328 (Apr. 28, 1762); letter 225, p. 362 (Dec. 26, 1762).

76. *JubA,* 11, letter 217, p. 346 f. (July 4, 1762).

77. *JubA,* 11, letter 217, p. 346.

78. See *Neue Berlinische Monatsschrift,* 3 (1800): 338 ff.; Kayserling, *Mendelssohn,* 56 f.

79. See Ferdinand Schwarz, "Briefe Moses Mendelssohns an Isaak Iselin," *Basler Jahrbuch 1923,* ed. August Huber and Ernst Jenny, p. 65.

80. They are in the possession of Mr. Eric Warburg, who kindly placed photocopies of them at my disposal. The fragments cover the following passages: *Republic,* I, 2, 328D; I, 4, 330B; I, 9, 336A; I, 11, 337D.

81. On this forerunner of *Sturm und Drang,* see Hettner, *Geschichte,* 2:82–90. Nicolai had tried to win his cooperation for the *Allgemeine deutsche Bibliothek* (see Max Kirschstein, "Briefe Nicolais an Gerstenberg," *Euphorion,* 28.3 (1927): 22 ff.

82. Nicolai's memory played him false; *The Moralists, or a philosophical Rhapsody* (1709) had not been translated by Mendelssohn.

83. R. M. Werner, "Gerstenbergs Briefe an Nicolai . . .," *Zeitschrift für deutsche Philologie,* 23 (1918): 52.

The Prize-Essay *(pages 112–130)*

1. *Beurtheilung der Schrift die im Jahre 1755. den Preiss von der Academie zu Berlin erhalten hat . . .* (Frankfurt & Leipzig, 1757).

2. It was first published in *GS,* 4.1:76 ff., and is reproduced in *JubA,* 2:159 ff.; see p. 350.

3. Shaftesbury, *Characteristicks,* 1:72.

4. *JubA,* 2:160.

5. *GS,* 4.1:508 ff.

6. See Harnack, *Geschichte* 1.1:407 ff.

7. *GS,* 4. 1:585–96.

8. Harnack, *Geschichte,* 2:306 f.

9. An analysis of the then prevailing situation is given in *Frühschriften,* 252 ff.

10. *JubA,* 11, letter 198, p. 321.

11. The letter is lost (see *JubA*, 11, letter 212, p. 340) but from Abbt's reply (*JubA*, 11, letter 213, p. 341 f.) it is clear that it had dealt only with his desire to leave Rinteln.

12. According to Jewish custom, a bridegroom versed in talmudic lore delivers a learned discourse prior to his wedding.

13. Marburg File, no. 7.

14. Nicolai-Abbt Letters at the Fürstliche Hofkammer Bückeburg, Hausarchiv, Sig. A XXXV/18–95.

15. *Abbts Vermischte Werke*, 4:36; quoted by Bruno Strauss, *JubA*, 11:506 f.

16. *Abbts Verm. Werke*, 3:74, 102 ff., 106 ff., and *passim*.

17. See *Frühschriften*, 271–78, 288.

18. *JubA*, 11, letter 217, p. 347 f.

19. *JubA*, 11, letter 218, p. 352.

20. *JubA*, 11, letter 223, p. 360.

21. *JubA*, 11, letter 225, p. 362. Abbt seems to have considered December 20 as the deadline.

22. *GS*, 5:271.

23. *GS*, 5:272 f.

24. *GS*, 5:170.

25. Letter to Segner written in Geneva on June 11, 1763; see *Abbts Verm. Werke*, 6:71 f.

26. *Akten der Kgl. Preussischen Akademie der Wissenschaften*, I.iv:31 (quoted by Leo Strauss, *JubA*, 2:xlvi); Harnack, *Geschichte*, 1.1:411.

27. "Précis du discours qui a remporté le Prix," *Dissertation qui a remporté le Prix proposé par l'Académie Royale des Sciences et Belles-Lettres de Prusse sur la Nature, les Especes, et les Degrés de l'Evidence avec les Pieces qui ont concouru* (Berlin, 1764), i–xx.

28. Ibid., xx. Translated: "I believe [that I] have faithfully discharged the task of an abbreviator and given a fair idea of the things [discussed in the prize-essay]. But I could not convey [an idea as to] the style of this dissertation, which is very elegant and reveals one of the most beautiful writers of Germany."

29. Quoted by Kayserling, *Mendelssohn*, 133.

30. See Haym, *Herder*, 1:48.

31. Kant, *Werke*, 9:33 (June 28, 1763).

32. *GS*, 5:273 ff. A vivid description of a theater party at Ferney is contained in Abbt's letter to Segner, dated June 19, 1763; see *Abbts Verm. Werke*, 6:75 f.

33. According to the editor's note, *GS*, 5:273, a reprint appeared 1764 in Berlin. Meyer, *Bibliographie*, p. 37, no. 128, lists the Geneva edition as undated but carrying the information: "se vend à Berlin chez Frédéric Nicolai 1764." Abbt's letter as published in *GS*, 5:273 ff. represents only a fraction of the original letter. From Mendelssohn's reply of November 20 (*GS*, 5:277) it can be inferred that Abbt had sent his translation to Mendelssohn.

34. *GS*, 5:277.

35. *GS*, 5:274. It is safe to assume that Abbt had congratulated Mendelssohn on his victory, since Mendelssohn's reply deals with the subject.

36. *GS*, 5:278.

37. *GS*, 5:283.

38. *GS*, 5:304.

39. For a full analysis of the prize-essay, see *Frühschriften*, 263–391.

40. *JubA*, 2:269–72.

41. Kant, *Werke*, 2:176 f., 180.

42. For references see *Frühschriften*, 273.

43. *JubA*, 14:70.

44. For references, see *Frühschriften*, 274 f.

45. Ibid., 278 f.

46. Mendelssohn was referring to Resewitz' argument, with which he had already taken issue in the *Literaturbriefe* (see *GS*, 4.2:336 ff.).

47. *JubA*, 2:290 f.

48. *GS*, 4.2:491 f.; 501 f.

49. *GS*, 5:322. Vulcan was the Roman god of fire.

50. See *Frühschriften*, 293.

51. Ibid., 298.

52. *Novum Organum*, 1:44.

53. *Guide of the Perplexed,* 1:31.
54. *JubA,* 2:297 f; see *Frühschriften,* 306 f.
55. *Guide,* 1:57.
56. See Alexander Altmann, "The Divine Attributes," *Faith and Reason,* eds. R. Gordis and Ruth B. Waxman (New York, 1972), 9–32. Mendelssohn rejected negative theology in a note inserted in the second edition of his *Phaedon* (176): *GS,* 2:114 f.; *JubA,* 3.1:362 f.
57. For references to Baumgarten's ontological concepts, see *Frühschriften,* 310–13.
58. Ibid., 316–24.
59. Ibid., 330–35.
60. Ibid., 335–41.
61. III. ix:16–17; IV. iii:18.
62. For references see *Frühschriften,* 342 f.
63. Ibid., 347 f.
64. Ibid., 348 ff.
65. Ibid., 350 f.
66. *JubA,* 1:169, 429.
67. See *Frühschriften,* 252 f.
68. *JubA,* 2:181–85.
69. Christian Wolff, *Vernünfftige Gedancken von der Menschen Thun und Lassen,* new ed. (Halle, 1752), #12; 19.
70. *JubA,* 2:317.
71. Lucretius, *De rerum natura,* 6:26.
72. See *Frühschriften,* 358 ff.
73. Ibid., 360–66.
74. Ibid., 368–72.
75. See for the following *Frühschriften,* 372–91.
76. Ibid., 379 f.
77. See above, p. 63.

Correspondence on the Vocation of Man (pages 130–140)

1. *GS,* 5:279.
2. Johann Gottlieb Fichte, *Sämtliche Werke* (Berlin, 1845–1846), 5:231.
3. *GS,* 5:282 f.
4. *GS,* 5:285–88.
5. See *Spaldings Bestimmung des Menschen (1748) und Wert der Andacht (1755),* newly ed., with an introduction, by Horst Stephan (Giessen, 1908), 15–31.
6. *GS,* 5:288 f.
7. *GS,* 5:309.
8. *GS,* 5:292.
9. *GS,* 5:294 f. See John Locke, *Essay Concerning Human Understanding,* II.xx, 2; xxviii, 5.
10. *GS* 5:298 f.
11. *GS,* 5:289–91.
12. Abbt pretended that he had not reported the whole story: "I could go on copying from it for a long time; about some inventions of the general to keep his people under control, especially to prevent their running away, . . . but I want to be sparing with my quotations" (*GS,* 5:291).
13. *GS,* 5:296.
14. *GS,* 5:296 ff.
15. *GS,* 5:305 ff.
16. *GS,* 5:308.
17. Christian Wolff, *Vernünfftige Gedancken von Gott, der Welt und der Seele des Menschen* (Frankfurt & Leipzig, 1738), #1027–34; Idem, *Der vernünfftigen Gedancken von Gott . . . Anderer Theil* (Frankfurt am Main, 1735), #391–94; Idem, *Vernünfftige Gedancken von den Absichten der natürlichen Dinge* (Halle, 1752), #14.
18. *Guide,* 3:13 (interpreting Prov. 16:4).
19. *GS,* 5:307 ff., 323 f.
20. Leibniz, *Monadology,* #84–90, and in other writings of his.
21. *JubA,* 2:88 f. See Jean-Jacques Rousseau, *Oeuvres Complètes,* ed. Bernard Gagnebin

and Marcel Raymond 3 (1964): 142, 154, 219.

22. *JubA*, 11, letter 18, p. 34. See the note by Bruno Strauss, p. 401 f.; Martin Rang, *Rousseaus Lehre vom Menschen* (Göttingen, 1959), 178–91; Frederic C. Tubach, "*Perfectibilité*: der zweite Diskurs Rousseaus und die deutsche Aufklärung," *Études Germaniques*, 15 (1960); 144–51.

23. *GS*, 5:312 f.; see Mendelssohn's note, p. 378 f.

24. *GS*, 5:315; see above, p. 98.

25. The weakness of his eyes about which he complained in a letter to Nicolai on May 15, 1764 (Marburg File, no. 10) was probably due to his emotional state.

26. *GS*, 5:320.

27. *GS*, 5:323 f.

28. *GS*, 5:321.

29. *GS*, 5:325.

30. *GS*, 5:326.

31. GS, 5:347.

32. See *Les Oeuvres de Mr. de Maupertuis* (Berlin-Lyons, 1753), 1:15.

33. Christian Wolff, *Vernünfftige Gedancken von den Würckungen der Natur* (Halle, 1746).

34. *Les Oeuvres*, 1:7. On Mendelssohn's use of the psysico-theological proof, see *Frühschriften*, 322 f.

35. In part two of his *Critique of Judgment* (1790; 2nd ed., 1793); Kant, *Werke*, 5:437 ff.

36. *GS*, 5:348 f.

37. *GS*, 5:352.

38. See *GS*, 5:353 f.; *Justus Möser Briefe*, ed. Ernst Beins and Werner Pleister (Osnabrück, 1939), 193 f.; for biographical data see *GS*, 5:443 f. (editorial note).

39. *Abbts Vermischte Werke*, 5:193.

40. No longer extant.

41. *Abbts Vermischte Werke*, 5:196–200; likewise in *GS*, 5:363–65 (where the latter part is omitted altogether). The full text of Mendelssohn's letter to Abbt, dated June 11, 1766, has been discovered by me among the Nicolai-Briefe (Nachtrag 2, B. a. 2) in the "Staatsbibliothek der Stiftung Preussischer Kulturbesitz," Berlin. The passage omitted by Nicolai in his edition (*Abbts Vermischte Werke*, 3:395 ff.)—he actually crossed it out in the original!—and therefore missing in GS, 5:362 after line 18, is published here, in translation, for the first time.

42. *Abbts Vermischte Werke*, 5:197 f.; *GS*, 5:364 (June 26, 1766).

43. *Abbts Vermischte Werke*, 5:205; *GS*, 5:367.

44. Mendelssohn probably meant to say that a Jew must find it as incongruous to achieve merit under the then prevalent social conditions as a prince must find it hard to reconcile his power with greatness of soul.

45. *Abbts Vermischte Werke*, 5:207 (Aug. 28, 1766); omitted in *GS*, vol. 5.

46. The count sought to encourage Mendelssohn to adhere to his plan. When Mendelssohn sent him a complimentary copy of the *Phaedon*, the count not only acknowledged the gift in highly flattering terms but also renewed his invitation. On May 17, 1767, he wrote: "During the last year you exchanged letters with the late Abbt about a plan that gave rise to the pleasant hope of my making your personal acquaintance. I shall be very glad to hear from you that you persevere in the decision then taken" (*LBH*, 3:41f., no. 4538).

The Phaedon (pages 140–158)

1. *JubA*, 11, letter 88, p. 190. See Alexander Altmann, "Die Entstehung von Moses Mendelssohns *Phädon*," *Lessing Yearbook*, I, (Munich, 1969), 200–33.

2. See *JubA*, 11:452 f.

3. *JubA*, 11, letter 94, p. 195.

4. *JubA*, 11, letter 100, p. 203.

5. *JubA*, 11, letter 101, p. 204.

6. See above, pp. 22, 25, 69, 119.

7. *Socratische Denkwürdigkeiten für die lange Weile des Publikums* (Amsterdam, 1759). See now Fritz Blanke, *Johann Georg Hamann Sokratische Denkwürdigkeiten* (Gütersloh, 1959).

8. *GS*, 4.2:99 f.

9. *Die letzten Gespräche des Socrates und seiner Freunde* (Zürich, 1760).

10. *GS*, 4. 2:106, 152 f.; *JubA*, 11:493.

11. 19 (Zürich, 1761): 147–51.

12. See Lutz Geldsetzer, *Die Ideenlehre Jakob Wegelins* (Meisenheim am Glan, 1963), 88 f., 95.

13. Otto Hoffmann (ed.), *Herders Briefe an Joh. Georg Hamann* (Berlin, 1889), 102.

14. See his letter to Abbt (Apr. 7, 1762), *JubA*, 11, letter 194, p. 314.

15. See the above-quoted (p. 111) passage on Plato.

16. The quotation is imprecise but conveys the meaning; see Plato, *Symposium*, 215B, 216D, 221 E f.

17. See the references in *JubA*, 3.1:xxi–xxiii.

18. See *Literaturbrief* 119: *GS*, 4.2:125–33.

19. *GS*, 4.2:129.

20. Thomson's *Socrates* in Fatema's translation (Amsterdam, 1749) is briefly dismissed.

21. JubA, 3.1:35, lines 5–36, line 29.

22. See above, p. 111.

23. Campe Collection (No. 10) in the Staats- und Universitätsbibliothek, Hamburg; reproduced by Max Grunwald in *AZJ*, 61 (1897):43, and in *JubA*, 3.1:3–4.

24. See JubA, 11, letter 195, p. 316, and the note, p. 494; Jacob Keller, "Zur Geschichte von Mendelssohns *Phädon*," *Euphorion*, ed. August Sauer, 5 (1898): 685–94.

25. JubA, 11, letter 212, p. 337–40. On Moser see Bruno Strauss' note, p. 489. Mendelssohn's attitude toward him became increasingly critical. In the unpublished part of his letter to Abbt, dated June 11, 1766, he urged Abbt to write a severe review of Moser's *Reliquien* (1766). He wondered how Herr von Moser, who had "really become wholly intolerable," had managed to acquire a high reputation as a writer, etc. See Nicolai-Briefe, Nachtrag II, B. a. 2.

26. *JubA*, 11, letter 214, p. 343 f.; published first in *LBH*, 3:340 ff., no. 6100, which escaped the notice of the editor, *JubA*, 11:504.

27. *JubA*, 11, letter 220, p. 354 f.

28. Quoted here from the original letter in the possession of the Staatsarchiv Basel: Isaak Iselin-Archiv 28, fols. 258–61; the reproduction of the letters by Ferdinand Schwarz ("Briefe Moses Mendelssohns an Isaak Iselin," *Basler Jahrbuch 1923*) misreads the text in many places.

29. Iselin-Archiv 28, fol. 262; Schwarz, "Briefe," 67.

30. In the essay cited in note 1 of this section I argued for the assumption that in November, 1763, Mendelssohn sent Iselin the first *two* dialogues. I have since convinced myself that this was not the case. Leo Strauss, *JubA*, 3.1:xv–xvi had left the question open.

31. Wolff, *Vernünfftige Gedancken von Gott, der Welt und der Seele des Menschen* (1738), #926 f.; cf. Leo Strauss, *JubA*, 3.1:xv.

32. See *GS*, 5:344, 370.

33. *Nachlass* Zimmermann in the Niedersächsische Landesbibliothek Hanover, A II, letter 45 (Oct. 28, 1767), fol. 1–2.

34. Iselin-Archiv 13, fol. 85; quoted in part by Jakob Keller, *Euphorion* 5:691.

35. *JubA*, 3.1:80.

36. *JubA*, 3.1:79.

37. *GS*, 4.2:534. The similarity between Mendelssohn's thought and Dusch's poem has been mentioned by Leo Strauss, *JubA*, 3.1:79.

38. The German phrase *"unter der Feder habe"* implies no more than the fact that Mendelssohn had commenced writing the *Phaedon* some time ago; it does not indicate that he had recommenced work some time ago.

39. *GS*, 5:343 f.

40. *GS*, 5:366.

41. *JubA*, 3.1:7 f.

42. Marburg File, no. 15. Spalding, to whom the *Phaedon* owed so much, does not appear on the list but may be presumed to have received a complimentary copy. On Nov. 26, 1767, he sent Mendelssohn the most recent edition of his *The Vocation of Man* (see *LBH*, 2:288, no. 3016).

43. See Bruno Strauss, *JubA*, 11:505 f.

44. See Hermann Hettner, *Geschichte der deutschen Literatur* (Berlin, 1961), 1:306 f.

45. *JubA*, 11, letter 56, p. 141; see Bruno Strauss' note, p. 428. On Mendelssohn's letter to Gleim in March, 1765, see p. 432; on their friendship cf. Kayserling, *Mendelssohn*, 172 f.

46. See Hettner, *Geschichte*, 1:565 f.

47. See Meyer, *Bibliographie,* 39–41; Leo Strauss, *JubA,* 3.1:xxx, xxxiii.
48. *GS,* 4.2:559; Marburg File, no. 20.
49. Marburg File, no. 23.
50. *GS,* 5:684 f.
51. See the listing of the translations in Meyer, *Bibliographie,* 41–44.
52. The *Verzeichnis* lists only two older works, viz. *Demonstratio immortalitatis animae rationalis authore Kenelmo* (Frankfurt, 1664) and *A Discourse concerning the certainty of a future and immortal State* (London, 1706); also a subsequent work, *De immortalitate animarum dissertatio auctore Planco* (1770); see p. 27, no. 186, 189; p. 48, no. 572.
53. Vol. 31 (Amsterdam, 1757): November issue.
54. See above, note 37.
55. See Benno Böhm, *Sokrates im achtzehnten Jahrhundert* (Leipzig, 1929), 220 f.
56. *JubA,* 3.1:8 f.
57. 1767, no. 124:985.
58. Nicolai-Briefe, vol. 60, no. 25, Sept. 16, 1767 (unpublished except for a partial quotation by Leo Strauss, JubA, 3.1:415).
59. "Auch ist es etwas wider das Costume gehandelt."
60. *Allgemeine deutsche Bibliothek,* 9.1 (1769): 128–38; the relevant passage is quoted by Leo Strauss, *JubA,* 3.1:415.
61. *JubA,* 3.1:149 f.
62. See Böhm, *Sokrates,* 223.
63. *JubA,* 3.1:9.
64. See Leo Strauss, *JubA,* 3.1:xxi ff., 399, 401.
65. Ibid., 399 ff.
66. *Les Oeuvres de Platon traduites en françois,* II (Paris, 1701); see Leo Strauss, *JubA,* 3.1:400, 401, 403.
67. It was announced, together with Mendelssohn's *Phaedon,* in Christian Adolf Klotz' *Deutsche Bibliothek,* 1769.
68. See Leo Strauss, *JubA,* 3.1:399–408.
69. R. M. Werner, "Gerstenbergs Briefe an Nicolai nebst einer Antwort Nicolais," *Zeitschrift für deutsche Philologie,* 23 (1891): 48.
70. Iselin-Archiv 28, fol. 269; Schwarz, "Briefe," 75.
71. Max Kirschstein, "Briefe Nicolais an Gerstenberg," *Euphorion,* 28.3 (1927): 345 f.
72. Werner, "Gerstenbergs Briefe," 56.
73. 1767, no. 124:986.
74. See Leo Strauss' judgment, JubA, 3.1:xxx.
75. *JubA,* 3.1:9.
76. Goethe edition Inselverlag, 12:21–24.
77. 1767: 985–92.
78. 6.1 (1768): 80–107; 6.2:313–39. Garve's authorship is attested by David Friedländer; see *JubA,* 3.1:409.
79. The page numbers refer to *JubA,* 3.1 and Plato's *Phaedon,* respectively.
80. *De continuitatis lege, et ejus consectariis* (Dissertation Rome, 1754); *Philosophiae naturalis Theoria redacta ad unicam legem virium in natura existentium* (Vienna, 1759).
81. *GS,* 4.1:538–69.
82. See Garve, *Neue Bibliothek der schönen Wissenschaften und der freyen Künste,* 6.2 (1768): 325.
83. See Leo Strauss, *JubA,* 3.1:405, 420, 423 f.
84. *Enneads,* 4: 7: 2; see Emile Bréhier (ed. and tr.), *Plotin, Ennéades,* 4 (Paris, 1927): 190 and introduction, p. 179.
85. See the summing-up in *JubA,* 3.1:xxvii f.
86. Garve, *Neue Bibliothek,* 6.2:328.
87. 1767: 992. See also Resewitz, *Allgemeine deutsche Bibliothek,* 9.1: 131 f.
88. *JubA,* 1:143 f.
89. Garve, *Neue Bibliothek,* 331 f.; Mendelssohn's proof was cited with approval by Resewitz, *Allgemeine deutsche Bibliothek,* 9.1:133 f.
90. See above, p. 147.
91. This was noted by Garve, *Neue Bibliothek,* 6.2:323.
92. See Leo Strauss' quotation of the relevant passage from Resewitz' review in *JubA,* 3.1:415.

93. On Cooper's work see Benno Böhm, *Sokrates,* 79 ff.
94. See Böhm, *Sokrates,* 223–26, where the similarities between Mendelssohn and Cooper's Socrates are pointed out. For Hemsterhuys see p. 223, note 1.
95. The manner in which Mendelssohn partly followed and partly modified Cooper's account is analyzed by Leo Strauss, *JubA,* 3.1:392 ff.
96. *JubA,* 2:20–25; see Fritz Bamberger's notes, p. 372 ff.

Questions and Answers (pages 158–179)

1. P. Klauswitz, "Wie Moses Mendelssohn von der Einquartierung befreit wurde," *Mitteilungen des Vereins für die Geschichte Berlins,* 11 (Berlin, 1894): 120 f. I owe this reference to Herr Heinrich Hümpel of Berlin.
2. See Josef Meisl, (ed.), Protokollbuch der jüdischen Gemeinde Berlin (Jerusalem, 1962), 477; *JubA,* 16:xl.
3. See Max Birnbaum, "Moses Mendelssohn, der Seidenfabrikant," *Gemeindeblatt der Jüdischen Gemeinde zu Berlin,* 19 (1929): 452–54; based on O. Hintze, *Acta Borussica: Die Preussische Seidenindustrie im 18. Jahrhundert* (Berlin, 1892).
4. *LBH,* 2:277 f., no. 2946.
5. The reference is probably to Fromet's unmarried sister Gitel; see *JubA,* 16, letter 199, p. 228; lxxxiv.
6. Daughters of the banker Daniel Itzig.
7. See *Hamann Briefwechsel,* 2:272; 3:5; Dep. RvM, C II, no. 24; Fritz Bamberger, "Four Unpublished Letters to Moses Mendelssohn," *Living Legacy, Essays in Honor of Hugo Hahn,* ed. Bernhard N. Cohn (New York, 1963), 97, 88, note; Hermann Hettner, *Geschichte der deutschen Literatur* (Berlin, 1961), 1:684.
8. Bruno Strauss, "Drei ungenannte Empfänger Mendelssohnscher Briefe," *ZGJD,* 1 (1929): 249 f.; Arthur Warda, *Briefe and und von Johann Georg Scheffner* (Munich & Leipzig, 1918), 1:487.
9. Warda, *Briefe,* 2 (1926): 327.
10. Quoted by Leo Strauss, *JubA,* 3.1:414, from a manuscript in the Niedersächsische Landesbibliothek, Hanover.
11. Iselin-Archiv 28, fol. 266–69; Ferdinand Schwarz, "Briefe Moses Mendelssohns an Isaak Iselin," *Basler Jahrbuch* 1923, 70–75.
12. See *JubA,* 3.1:134 f., 147 f.
13. See *JubA,* 3.1:136, 149, 414; xxiv.
14. See Johann Georg Meusel, *Lexikon der vom Jahr 1750 bis 1800 verstorbenen Teutschen Schriftsteller,* VIII (Leipzig, 1808), *s.v.*; Moritz Steinschneider, "Mathematik bei den Juden," *MGWJ,* 49, n.s. 13 (1905): 723–28; Haim Borodianski (Bar-Dayan), "Moses Mendelssohn and his Yiddish Letters," (in Yiddish), *Historische Schriften,* ed. E. Tscherikower, 1 (Warsaw, 1929), 340.
15. See *Fortsetzung und Ergänzungen zu Christian Gottlieb Jöchers allgemeinem Gelehrten-Lexikon,* 3 (Delmenhorst, 1810): 1715.
16. *Tekhunat Ha-Shamayim,* edited, without the knowledge and permission of the Author, by Moses ben Yekutiel of Tiktin (Amsterdam, 1765).
17. See Steinschneider, "Mathematik bei den Juden," 727.
18. GS, 5:446–49. The identity of the unnamed addressee of the letter was first suggested by Jakob Auerbach, *ZGJD,* 1 (1887): 8, note.
19. See the essay "Raphael Lewi, Ein jüdisches Lebensbild," reprinted from a well-informed anonymous article in the *Hannoversche Morgenzeitung* (?) by Julius Fürst in *Der Orient,* 7, no. 33: 256 ff. (see Steinschneider "Mathematik bei den Juden," 723).
20. See G.E. Guhrauer, *Gottfried Wilhelm Freiherr von Leibniz,* (Breslau, 1846; Hildesheim, 1966), 2:369.
21. See Fürst, *Der Orient,* 258.
22. Ibid.; Jakob Auerbach, *ZGJD,* 1:7–8.
23. See D. Simonsen's article in *Dansk biografisk Leksikon,* 15:201–05; quoted by him in his essay "Mendelssohniana—aus Dänemark," *Festschrift Martin Philippson,* 218; see also Max Grunwald, "Aus dem Nachlass Augusts von Hennings," *MGWJ,* 53, n.s. 17 (1909): 83, 229.
24. See Meyer, *Bibliographie,* p. 41, no. 167.
25. Quoted by Simonsen, "Mendelssohniana," 218.

26. Simonsen refers to L. Koch, *Oplysningstiden i den danske Kirke* [The Period of Enlightenment in the Danish Church] 1770–1800 (Copenhagen, 1915); see "Mendelssohniana," 218f.

27. *GS*, 5:450–53; Hensler's letter to Nicolai and Nicolai's to Mendelssohn are reproduced *GS*, 5:449 f.

28. *GS*, 5:453 f.

29. His letters to and from Mendelssohn are found in *GS*, 5:460–84.

30. *GS*, 5:466 f.

31. Mendelssohn (*JubA* 3.1:132; 145; see 413) quotes the Latin translation by Marsilius Ficinus, which differs slightly from the Greek text of *Enneads*, 4: 7: 3.

32. I could not trace the source from which Mendelssohn took this principle.

33. The text reads *nicht bloss* ("not only"), which must be due to a slip of the pen or to a misprint.

34. *GS*, 5:478.

35. *GS*, 5:476.

36. *GS*, 5:483.

37. Mendelssohn's last major effort in applied mathematics was his *Versuch, eine vollkommen gleichschwebende Temperatur durch die Construction zu finden* (published in 1761; *JubA*, 2:187–196; see Borodianski's observations, p. xxxvi–xli; Meyer, *Bibliographie*, p. 38, no. 131; p. 67, no. 392). See above, p. 67.

38. *Kritische Wälder, oder Betrachtungen über die Wissenschaft und Kunst des Schönen.* Only the first three *"Wäldchen"* appeared in Herder's lifetime. The fourth, a fragment, was published in the fourth volume of *Herders Sämmtliche Werke,* ed. Bernhard Suphan (Berlin, 1878). The term *Wäldchen* ("small forest") is used by Herder in the sense in which the Latin word *silva (sylva)* designates random thoughts gathered in a book (see Rudolf Haym, *Herder* [Berlin, 1954], 1:244, where Quintilian [M.F. Quintilianus, *Institutiones Oratoriae*, 10.3.17] is mentioned).

39. Cf. the passages quoted by Haym, *Herder*, 1:143 f.

40. *J. G. von Herders sämmtliche Werke: Fragmente zur deutschen Literatur*, First Series (Karlsruhe, 1821), 122.

41. Ibid., 156 f.

42. See Haym, *Herder*, 1:228 f.

43. So Wieland said in a letter to Zimmermann, quoted by Hettner, *Geschichte*, 2:25.

44. See above, p. 108; Haym, *Herder*, 1:198–202.

45. *Hamann Briefwechsel*, 2:395; see also 404 f.

46. Ibid., 420.

47. Horace, *Ars poetica*, 191.

48. Otto Hoffmann (ed.), *Herder's Briefwechsel mit Nicolai* (Berlin, 1887), 35.

49. Ibid., 43.

50. The original letter (6 pages, undated, and without address or signature) is extant in the Nationale Forschungs- und Gedenkstätten der klassischen deutschen Literatur, Weimar, which kindly placed a photostatic copy at my disposal. The letter is reproduced in modernized orthography and with the omission of many italics in *Herders Briefe*, ed. Wilhelm Dobbek (Weimar, 1959), 28–36.

51. *GS*, 5:484–91 (see the notes by Nicolai and the editor, p. 484).

52. *Monadology*, #61–63.

53. C. J. Gerhardt (ed.), *Die philosophischen Schriften von G. W. Leibniz*, 6:539 f.

54. Mendelssohn followed here Sulzer's view; see above, p. 56, and *Frühschriften*, 96 ff.

55. The reading found in Nicolai's copy (see *GS*, 5:488, note 4) seems to be the correct one.

56. Hoffmann, *Herder's Briefwechsel mit Nicolai*, 43.

57. Ibid., 47 f.

58. Ibid., 53.

59. It is published in Emil Gottfried von Herder (ed.), *Herder's Lebensbild* (Erlangen, 1846), 2:108–15. An editorial note (p. 108) states erroneously that the Mendelssohn letter to which Herder replied is no longer extant.

60. The final paragraph of Herder's letter made reference to that affair.

61. Kant, *Werke*, 9:78.

62. See *JubA*, 3.1:xxxiii.

63. Marburg File, no. 34.

64. Reproduced in *GS*, 5:370–408.

65. See above, p. 145 f.
66. *Herder's Lebensbild,* 2:111 f.
67. *GS,* 5:390 ff.
68. *Berlin und Wien—gegen ein ander gehalten* (Frankfurt & Leipzig, 1784).
69. See *JubA,* 3.1:372; Meyer, *Bibliographie,* p. 19, no. 55.
70. *Moses Mendelssohns Abhandlung von der Unkörperlichkeit der menschlichen Seele* (Vienna, 1785); the work appeared in three different impressions in the same year and by the same publisher (see *JubA,* 3.1: 371; Meyer, *Bibliographie,* p. 59, nos. 320–22).
71. By Leo Strauss, *JubA,* 3.1:xxxviii.
72. See Fritz Arnheim, "Moses Mendelssohn und Luise Ulrike von Schweden," *ZGJD,* 3 (1889): 283 f.
73. Ibid.
74. The count acknowledged receipt of the manuscript and commented on it in a letter to Mendelssohn dated Oct. 15, 1774 *(LBH,* 3:42 f., no. 4539): One had to be grateful to d'Alembert for having stimulated this piece of writing. Mendelssohn acknowledged the return of the manuscript in his letter of Feb. 11, 1775 *(GS,* 5:533); see *LBH,* 3:43, no. 4540.
75. See *JubA,* 3.1:xxxvii.
76. Ibid., 186 and the note, p. 427 f.
77. Ibid., 187.
78. Ibid., 165–67; *GS,* 5:465–67.
79. Kant, *Werke,* 5:282 f.

Cognate Hebrew Writings (pages 179–193)

1. See above, p. 162.
2. *GS,* 5:449.
3. *JubA,* 16, letter 98, p. 119.
4. Using the well-known phrase from Rabad of Posquières' gloss on Maimonides, *Mishne Tora, Hilkhot Teshuva,* 3:7.
5. See above, p. 140.
6. See Leo Strauss, *JubA,* 3.1:432, note on p. 212, lines 26 ff. We conclude from this passage that the essay could not have been written before 1769. Borodianski thinks it was written in 1767/68 (see *JubA,* 14:vi).
7. Reproduced in *JubA,* 14:121–44, where the title is given as *Ha-Nefesh.* The correct title is stated in the reprint edition (Stuttgart, 1972), cv.
8. *JubA,* 16, letters 89–91, pp. 106–13.
9. *JubA,* 14:315.
10. A German translation of this treatise by Friedländer himself is said to have appeared in the same year; see Meyer, *Bibliographie,* p. 63, no. 356.
11. Ibid., p. 63, no. 358. Both translations are inadequate. A new German translation of both treatises is offered in JubA, 3.1:201–33.
12. *JubA,* 14:125.
13. See Alexander Altmann, *Saadya Gaon: The Book of Doctrines and Beliefs* (Oxford, 1956), 147; S. Weil (ed.), *Das Buch Emunah Ramah ... von Abraham Ben David Halevi* (Frankfurt am Main, 1852), 42 f.; Hebrew text, 33. Maimonides equated *nefesh, ruah,* and *neshama* with the animal soul, the vital spirit, and the hylic intellect respectively (see *Guide of the Perplexed,* 1:40, 41, 70). For kabbalistic interpretations of these three terms, see G. Scholem, *Major Trends in Jewish Mysticism* (New York, 1946), 240 f.
14. *Rosh Ha-Shana* 11a; Hullin 60a; *Guide,* 2:30.
15. Viz. in Mendelssohn's treatise, "Sache Gottes oder gerettete Vorsehung," *GS,* 2:411–51; see below, pp. 666–68.
16. 3:12.
17. In *Sache Gottes.*
18. *JubA,* 14:127; transl. *JubA,* 3.1:208 f.
19. *JubA,* 7:96.
20. *Mishne Tora, Hilkhot Teshuva,* 3:6; 8:1; 8:5; see also Maimonides, *Commentary on the Mishna, Sanhedrin,* ix, x.
21. Nahmanides, *Torat Ha-Adam, Sha'ar Ha-Gemul* in *Kitevey Rabbenu Moshe Ben Nahman,* ed. Hayyim Dov Cheval, 2 (Jerusalem, 1963):285, 291 f. While Nahmanides rejected

Maimonides' notion of the death of the soul as a punishment for grave sins, he upheld the doctrine of eternal punishment in hell. See *Sha'ar Ha-Gemul*, 285. His repudiation of Maimonides' concept is shared by Bahya ben Asher, *Commentary on the Tora*, Lev. 18:29; Isaac Abrabanel, *Commentary on the Tora*, Num. 15:22.

22. *JubA*, 16, Letter 98, p. 119.

23. Wessely published a tract on the subject in *Ha-Me'assef*, 1788, which also appeared separately, with an epilogue by him, under the title, *Ma'amar Hikkur Din*, ed. Shabbatai Janow (Berlin, undated).

24. Isa. 7:15, 16.

25. Ps. 58:9.

26. *JubA*, 14:44-46.

27. *Avot* 3:19.

28. Combining Eccl. 9:2 (slightly varied) and Mal. 3:18.

29. Varying Gen. 8:25.

30. *JubA*, 14:131 f.; transl. *JubA*, 3.1:215.

31. The Hebrew text (*ha-tsofe u-mabit . . .*) reflects the well-known phrase from the *Mussaf 'Amida* for the New Year's service.

32. Prov. 10:12.

33. See Leo Strauss' notes, *JubA*, 3.1:433–37.

34. *JubA*, 14:138 f.; transl. *JubA*, 3.1:225.

35. *JubA*, 14:139; transl. *JubA*, 3.1:226.

36. Varying Job 26:14.

37. *JubA*, 14:141 ff.; transl. *JubA*, 3.1:229 ff.

38. See *Frühschriften*, 31 ff., 240 ff., 248 f., 366 f.

39. *JubA*, 14:143; transl. *JubA*, 3.1:232.

40. See Mendelssohn's "Counterreflections," *JubA*, 7:72 ff.

41. The surmise that the correspondence belongs to the same period as the first treatise (see *JubA*, 14:vi) is not supported by any evidence.

42. See above, p. 179.

43. See JubA, 16, letter 98, p. 118 f.; Aaron Wessely was clerk in the silk factory owned by Moses Ries, the father-in-law of Mendelssssohn's employer Isaac Bernhard.

44. *JubA*, 16, letter 61, p. 77 (*JubA*, 11, letter 175, p. 289).

45. *JubA*, 16, letter 40, p. 57 (*JubA*, 11, letter 146, p. 263).

46. *JubA*, 16, letter 43, p. 58 (*JubA*, 11, letter 149, p. 266).

47. *JubA*, 16, letter 44, p. 61 (*JubA*, 11, letter 151, p. 269).

48. *JubA*, 16, letter 61, p. 77 (*JubA*, 11, letter 175, p. 289).

49. That Mendelssohn and Hartwig Wessely had not met has already been noticed by Klausner, *Historiya*, 1:112, note 1, whereas Kayserling, *Mendelssohn*, 305, maintained that they had. Klausner's assumption that Wessely was appointed to the Amsterdam post sometime between 1750 and 1760 (*Historiya*, 109) is purely conjectural.

50. There is no difficulty in assuming that for a number of years as a young man, commencing at the age of twenty-five, Wessely studied under Eybeschütz. Klausner, *Historiya*, 107, note 6, seems to consider this improbable. For the biographical data mentioned here, see Klausner, ibid., 104 ff.

51. *JubA*, 16, letter 98, p. 118 f.

52. Isa. 44:5.

53. Gen. 49:21. A commentary on Genesis called *Imrey Shefer* was written by Wessely in later years (see Klausner, *Historiya*, 118).

54. Varying Isa. 65:25.

55. Varying the meaning of Isa. 9:6 and 37:32.

56. The phrase occurs frequently in the Bible.

57. Isa. 5:21.

58. Gen. 37:30.

59. Gen. 27:12.

60. Varying Isa. 40:12.

61. Mal. 3:18.

62. Varying Ps. 28:5.

63. *Bava Batra* 16a.

64. Deut. 32:5.

65. Varying Gen. 45:26.

66. We read *'erko* instead of *'erki,* and *'otsmo* instead of *'otsmi,* as otherwise no satisfactory sense can be obtained. The biblical references are Job. 28:13 and Ps. 139:15.

67. Klausner's statement *(Historiya,* 111) that Wessely lived in Amsterdam until 1769, when his father called him to Copenhagen in order to make sure that he got married, is disproved by the fact the correspondence under review took place in 1768.

68. *JubA,* 16, letter 99, p. 120–23. The beginning of the letter is missing (see JubA, 16:lx).

69. See Wessely's *Bi'ur* on Lev. 19:17, where this point is made.

70. Daniel 12:3.

71. Ps. 119:25.

72. Varying Isa. 14:13.

73. Varying Ps. 57:2.

74. *Fédon, Hu' Sefer Hash'arat Ha-Nefesh Le-Ha-Hakham Ha-Shalem Rabbenu Moshe Mi-Dessau Ha-Nikra' Mendelssohn,* tr. Yishai Beer (Berlin, 5647/1787).

75. The pages of the preface are unnumbered. The paragraph quoted is found on the second page.

76. JubA, 16, letter 182, p. 206 f; see p. lxxix.

77. A manuscript copy of David ben Phoebus Wagenaar's *Phaedon* translation is extant in the Bibliotheca Rosenthaliana, Amsterdam (MS. Ros. 263). The Librarian, Dr. L. Fuks, who kindly sent me xerographic specimen copies of some pages, mentioned that at the end of the MS, on the back flyleaves, a brouillon of an undated letter of the translator to Hartwig Wessely has been added.

Chapter Three: The Turning Point: The Lavater Affair
"Juif de Berlin" (pages 194–201)

1. See Jacob Katz, *Tradition and Crisis* (New York, 1961), 254, where this particular aspect of what Katz termed "the neutral society" is underlined.

2. On the history and semantic character of this term, see Ismar Elbogen, "Die Bezeichnung 'jüdische Nation,' " *MGWJ,* 63, n. f. 27 (1919): 200–08.

3. Dep. RvM, C ii, no. 24.

4. The phrase first occurs in a note to the French translation of Mendelssohn's essay *Reflections on the Sources and Connections of the Fine Arts and of Belles-Lettres (JubA,* 1:165–90) in the *Journal étranger,* February, 1761 (see *JubA,* 11:508). The title-page of Georges Adam Junker's French translation of the *Phaedon* (Paris, 1772, 1773) adds to the name of the author the epithet, "Juif à Berlin" (see Meyer, *Bibliographie,* p. 42, nos. 171–73).

5. *GS,* 5:326.

6. *GS,* 5:344 (alluding to Exod. 32:20).

7. *GS,* 5:191.

8. See above, p. 113.

9. Quoting Ps. 42:2.

10. Viz. the "Fast of Gedalya," which follows immediately after the two days of Rosh Hashana, the Jewish New Year.

11. Marburg File, no. 13.

12. Marburg File, no. 38.

13. See above, p. 45.

14. *Hamann-Briefwechsel,* 2:33 (letter to Johann Gotthelf Lindner, July 2, 1760).

15. *JubA,* 1:75 (270).

16. Sota 47a (combined with Deut. 32:39).

17. *JubA,* 1:106 (302); Hagiga 1:8.

18. Über die Frage: was heisst aufklären?" *Berlinische Monatsschrift,* 4 (1784): 193–200; *GS,* 3:399–403; p. 403.

19. Yadayim 4:6 ("according to the degree of their being cherished is the degree of their impurity").

20. Sota 3a; see L. F. G. von Göckingk, *Nicolai's Leben und literarischer Nachlass* (Berlin, 1820), 201. The essay *(Über Freiheit und Nothwendigkeit)* was first written as a letter to Nicolai; see Göckingk, ibid., 197–201; published in *Berlinische Monatsschrift,* 2 (1783) :1–11; *JubA,* 3.1:346–50 (the rabbinic quotation is found on p. 349).

21. J. J. Engel (ed.), *Der Philosoph für die Welt*, 2 (Leipzig, 1777): 49–64; reprinted in the revised edition, 1 (Berlin, 1801): 295–314.

22. No. 35 (Apr. 26, 1759): *GS*, 4.1:529 f.

23. *GS*, 4.2:134–41.

24. Johann Jacob Rabe, *Mischnah oder Text des Talmud*. Translated from the Hebrew (Onolzbach [Ansbach], 1760). The work appeared in six volumes (1760–1763).

25. *Literaturbrief* 186 (Sept. 18, 1761): *GS*, 4.2:292–99.

26. *Abbts Vermischte Werke*, 5 (1780): 108.

27. *Der Prediger Salomo . . . von dem Verfasser des Phädon. Aus dem Hebräischen übersetzt von dem Übersetzer der Mischnah* (Anspach, 1771). On Mendelssohn's publication of his commentary on Kohelet, see below, p. 242.

28. See Friedrich Roth (ed.), *Hamann's Schriften*, 1 (Berlin, 1821) :102; *JubA*, 11, letters 177 and 181, pp. 293 and 300. In a letter to Nicolai, dated Dec. 21, 1762 (*Hamann Briefwechsel*, 2:182), Hamann sent regards to Mendelssohn, "den ich durch ein Missverständnis mich gefreut habe hier persönlich näher kennen zu lernen." This remark is rather puzzling, since nothing is known about a trip to Königsberg by Mendelssohn during the latter half of 1762.

29. See above, p. 141.

30. Nos. 166–170 (June 4–18, 1761); *GS*, 4.2:260–78.

31. The name Kulm is explained by Hamann as an acrostic for *Karacter* (character), Lessing, Moses (*Hamann Briefwechsel*, 2:131).

32. No. 192 (Oct. 22, 1761): *GS*, 4. 2:311–23.

33. Ibid., 312.

34. Ibid., 316 f.

35. *JubA*, 11, letter 177, pp. 291, 294 (Feb. 11, 1762).

36. Isa. 11:6 (quoted by Mendelssohn in Hebrew).

37. *JubA*, 11, letter 181, p. 299 (Mar. 2, 1762).

38. *JubA*, 11, letter 189, p. 307 (Mar. 21 or 25, 1762).

39. *JubA*, 11:299 f., 307.

40. See above, p. 81.

41. *JubA*, 11, letter 148, p. 264.

42. *GS*, 5:343.

43. *JubA*, 11, letter 198, p. 319 f.; see the full documentation in Bruno Strauss, *JubA*, 11:495.

44. See *LBH*, 3:69 f., no. 4698. The letter was written on June 27, 1767. Its opening paragraph praised the "naturalness and strength" of language in the *Phaedon* and declared the book worthy to be read with attention. It "said something new" and helped the reader to clarify his ideas on the subject.

45. Published by L. Geiger, *ZGJD*, 1 (1887): 253 ff.; *LBH*, 3:70 f., no. 4699; see *JubA*, 3.1:406.

46. See *JubA*, 3.1:395, 401, 406.

47. The duke replied on Aug. 4, 1767 (*LBH*, 3:72 f., no. 4700) that a philosopher brought up on the teachings of revelation was apt to be virtuous through the combined light of reason and Holy Scripture. As for Mendelssohn's request for the rest of his notes, they were appreciative, not critical, and might "irritate" him by the repetition of praise. A second letter by Mendelssohn to the duke (written on Apr. 9, 1768) was in the possession of Baron von der Tann, who agreed to lend it to Felix Mendelssohn Bartholdy for the duration of his life. Felix promised in return to procure for the baron some other autograph of his grandfather. See Karl Ernst Henrici, *Auktionskatalog* 109, no. 311 (Berlin, June, 1926): Felix Mendelssohn Bartholdy Dokument, München, Nov. 2, 1831. I owe this piece of information to Dr. Rudolf Elvers, curator of the Mendelssohn-Archiv, Berlin.

The Prehistory of the Lavater Affair (pages 201–209)

1. Poet and minister of state (1744–1789).

2. See Julius Forssmann, *J. K. Lavater und die religiösen Strömungen des achtzehnten Jahrhunderts* (Riga, 1935), 23–35.

3. Translated here from the original text in the diary (MS 5 of the Lavater collection at the Zentralbibliothek, Zürich), which is quoted—not always correctly—by Leo Weisz, "Aus Lavaters Tagebüchern," *NZZ*, no. 1034, Mar. 21, 1961. Weisz also gives excerpts from

Lavater's letters to his parents. The relevant parts of the letter to Breitinger are reproduced by Simon Rawidowicz, *JubA*, 7, p. xii.

4. According to an ancient biography, Aesop, the famous author of fables, was physically deformed.

5. The diary gives the full text of this ode. It is also quoted by Hamann in a letter to Lindner dated Mar. 31, 1764 *(Hamann Briefwechsel*, 2:249 f.). The ode was presented to the king when he entered the city, as Hamann reports in his letter. It is not identical with Hartog Leo's *Friedenslied*, which Mendelssohn translated from the Hebrew and which was chanted at the service in the synagogue.

6. *Bibliothek der schönen Wissenschaften und der freyen Künste*, ed. Christian Felix Weisse.

7. Strangely enough, Leo Weisz imputed to Füssli the remark that one might, with greater justification, call Mendelssohn the greatest poet of his time; according to Weisz, Mendelssohn replied that he had merely talent, not genius, etc. This represents a flagrant mutilation of what is actually contained in the MS.

8. The ode to the king was presented at the second visit when belles-lettres were discussed.

9. Quoted by Weisz, *NZZ*, Mar. 21, 1961, no. 1036.

10. See *JubA*, 7:xxvii.

11. *JubA*, 7:327.

12. Øjvind Andreasen (ed.), *Aus den Tagebüchern Friedrich Münters* (Copenhagen & Leipzig, 1937), 1:41; see below, p. 503.

13. Nicolai-Briefe, vol. 60, no. 40.

14. Friedrich Nicolai, *Gedächtnisschrift auf Johann August Eberhard* (Berlin & Stettin, 1810), 23. On Spalding's annoyance with Eberhard see below, p. 503.

15. See Weisz, *NZZ*, Mar. 21, 1961, no. 1036.

16. *GS*, 3:90 f.; *JubA*, 7:59.

17. *GS*, 3:39 f.; 56; *JubA*, 7:7 ff., 30.

18. *GS*, 3:105; *JubA*, 7:63.

19. *GS*, 3:90 f.; *JubA*, 7:59.

20. *GS*, 5:501 f. See also Mendelssohn's letter to Lavater dated Jan. 15, 1771 (discussed below, p. 260 f.).

21. Maimonides did refer to the Christian religion in his *Guide of the Perplexed* 1:50, in his *Epistle to Yemen*, ed. Abraham S. Halkin (New York, 1952), 12–18 (English translation, pp. iii–v), and in his *Mishne Tora, Hilkhot Melakhim*, 11:3–4 (see the Amsterdam edition of 1702). He rejected Jesus and Paul, and he considered Paul to have been the real founder of Christianity. Mendelssohn was obviously unaware of these passages. He probably knew the *Epistle to Yemen* in Rabbi Jacob Emden's edition of it in his *Sefer Ha-Pedut Ve-Ha-Purkan* (Altona, 1769, fol. 6a–18a), in which the anti-Christian references are suppressed. The editions of the *Mishne Tora* known to Mendelssohn were, it seems, those from which, owing to Christian censorship, all traces of anti-Christian utterances had been obliterated.—Isaac Orobio de Castro (ca. 1620–1687) was the "erudite Jew" with whom the Arminian theologian Philipp van Limborch (1633–1712) debated the issue of Judaism versus Christianity; see *Philippi a Limborch de Veritate Religionis Christianae Amica Collatio cum Erudito Judaeo* (Gouda, 1687). A brief characterization of this debate is found in Hans Joachim Schoeps, *Israel und Christenheit, Jüdisch-christliches Religionsgespräch in neunzehn Jahrhunderten* (Munich & Frankfurt am Main, 1961), 97–114. Mendelssohn had a copy of the 1687 treatise in his library (see *Verzeichnis*, p. 14, no. 212).

22. See Jacob Katz, *Exclusiveness and Tolerance* (Oxford, 1961), 90.

23. Ibid., 167.

24. The significance of Lavater's chiliastic speculations as a motivating force in his approach to Mendelssohn had been perceived first by Nicolai (see below, p. 207). Having pursued the clue provided by Nicolai, I was glad to find that the results of my inquiry were in agreement with the findings of Barukh Mevorach, "The Background of Lavater's Appeal to Mendelssohn," *Zion*, 30 (1965): 158–70.

25. Johann Caspar Lavater, *Aussichten in die Ewigkeit, in Briefen an Hrn. Joh. Georg Zimmermann*, First Part (Zürich, 1768); Second Part, 1769; Third Part, 1772; 2nd ed. of all three parts, 1773.

26. Lavater, *Aussichten*, 1:93, 97.

27. Cf. Mevorach, "The Background . . .," 161–64.

28. *Aussichten*, 2:xvii ff.

29. Viz. to Zimmermann, to whom the *Aussichten* were addressed.

30. The gnostic heretic (c. 100 C.E.).

31. Karl C.E. Ehmann (ed.), *Briefwechsel zwischen Lavater und Hasenkamp* (Basel, 1870). See also Lavater's anonymously published *Geheimes Tagebuch von einem Beobachter seiner Selbst* (Leipzig, 1773) and its sequel, *Unveränderte Fragmente aus dem Tagebuch eines Beobachters seiner Selbst* (Leipzig, 1773).

32. *Briefwechsel . . .*, 43. A letter by Lavater, dated May 30/June 1, 1773 mentions "a very learned and pious Jew leading a life of privacy," who considered the writings of Jakob Boehme as authentic Kabbala, was an avid reader of the New Testament in Syriac, and was presumed to be "a secret worshipper of Jesus." The editor's note (p. 88) identifies this Jew with a certain Cappel (Koppel) Hecht in Frankfurt a Main. F. C. Oetinger, the Swabian mystic, referred to Koppel Hecht as a Kabbalist aware of the affinity of Jakob Boehme's teaching to Kabbala; see G. Scholem, *Major Trends in Jewish Mysticism*, rev. ed., 238. Scholen gives 1729 as the year of Hecht's death.

33. See his letter to Lüdke, dated Feb. 10, 1770, *JubA*, 7:328.

34. *JubA*, 7:327 f.

35. *Gotthold Ephraim Lessings Briefwechsel mit Karl Wilhelm Ramler, Johann Joachim Eschenburg und Friedrich Nicolai, nebst einigen Anmerkungen über Lessings Briefwechsel mit Moses Mendelssohn* (Berlin & Stettin, 1794), 301.

36. See below, p. 424–26.

37. In two vols., Geneva, 1769.

38. See Raymond Savioz, *La Philosophie de Charles Bonnett de Genève* (Paris, 1948).

39. See Heinrich Maier, "Lavater als Philosoph und Physiognomiker," *Johann Caspar Lavater 1741–1801, Denkschrift zur Hundertsten Wiederkehr seines Todestages* (Zürich, 1902), 370.

40. For bibliographical references see Simon Rawidowicz, *JubA*, 7:clxxiv, note 21; 458; Savioz, *La Philosophie*, 340–49.

41. *Palingénésie*, 1:206 ff.; 301 ff.; 308 ff.; 2:145.

42. Ibid., 2:145 ff.

43. Ibid., 2:151 f.

44. Ibid., 2:173 f.

45. Ibid., 2:195.

46. Ibid., 2:194–97.

47. Ibid., 2:254 f.

48. Lavater, *Aussichten*, 2nd ed., p. 4. The reference is to Johann Andreas Cramer's *Die Auferstehung; eine Ode* (Leipzig, 1748; Zürich, 1768). Cramer (1723–1788) was a scholar, preacher, and poet of repute.

49. Vol. 2, chaps. xvi–xxii.

50. *Herrn Carl Bonnets . . . philosophische Untersuchung der Beweise für das Christentum. Samt desselben Ideen von der künftigen Glückseligkeit des Menschen. Aus dem Französischen übersetzt, und mit Anmerkungen herausgegeben von Johann Caspar Lavater* (Zürich, 1769), pp. iv–v.

Lavater's Challenge and Mendelssohn's Reply (pages 209–223)

1. *Herrn Carl Bonnets . . . philosophische Untersuchung*, 2–5; *JubA*, 7:3.

2. *GS*, 3: 81; *JubA*, 7:297.

3. It concerned the relation of Mishna Betsa 2:3 to Mishna Mikva'ot 10:6 (see Emden, *Lehem Shamayim* [Wandsbeck, 1768], fol. 100a). Mendelssohn's letter to Emden is reproduced in *JubA*, 16, letter 108, p. 130 f.

4. *JubA*, 16, letter 109, p. 132.

5. *She'ilat Yavets* (Altona, 1770), fol. 87b f.; see Borodianski's note, *JubA*, 16:lxii.

6. See Alexander Altmann, "Briefe Karl Gotthelf Lessings an Moses Mendelssohn," *Lessing Yearbook* I (Munich, 1969), 9–59.

7. L–M, 19:320.

8. A sarcastic allusion to Lavater's *Vistas of Eternity*.

9. The reference is to Jacob Frank (1726–1791), who proclaimed himself as the last incarnation of the Messiah and was said to have performed miracles in 1755 (see Graetz, *Geschichte*, 10:417 ff.; S.A. Horodetzki's article in *EJ*, 6:1071–80).

10. Nicolai's *Allgemeine deutsche Bibliothek*, the literary organ of the Berlin Enlightenment.

11. On Jan. 2, 1770, Lessing wrote to Nicolai: "How is our Moses? I pity him for being so much embarrassed by a man whom he should not have allowed to obtain his friendship surreptitiously. Lavater is an enthusiast fit for a mental asylum to a surpassing degree. He

no longer makes a secret of his ability to produce miracles, for in his view the gift of miracle performance is the mark of a true Christian" (L–M, 17:310).

12. Cf. Lüdke's letter to Lavater, dated Jan. 23, 1770 (*JubA*, 7:312): "Having discussed the matter several times with him [Mendelssohn]... I did not notice the least irritability in him (it is obvious that he merely conceals it)."

13. *GS*, 3:105 f.; *JubA*, 7:61 ff., 378.

14. *JubA*, 7:xxxiv.

15. The doctrine that the preservation of the Jews is meant to furnish testimony to the truth of the Christian faith was introduced by St. Augustine; see Bernhard Blumenkranz, *Die Judenpredigt Augustins* (Basel, 1946), 175–81.

16. The point made here was reiterated by Mendelssohn toward the end of his life; see below, p. 722.

17. *Gelehrter Briefwechsel zwischen D. Johann Jacob Reiske, Conrad Arnold Schmid und Gotthold Ephraim Lessing*, Second Part (Berlin, 1789), 207 f. (L–M, 19, letter 280, p. 323).

18. *Gelehrter Briefwechsel*, 2:210 (L–M, 17:306).

19. Otto Hoffmann (ed.), *Herder's Briefwechsel mit Nicolai* (Berlin, 1887), 51.

20. Ibid.

21. L–M, 19:327.

22. Published, with some omissions and changes in spelling, in *GS*, 3:137–76; a critical edition by Simon Rawidowicz is found in *JubA*, 7:65–107.

23. *GS*, 3:128 f.; *JubA*, 7:299 f.

24. This may be inferred from the prince's reply quoted above. Mendelssohn's letter is lost.

25. The view that the "Counterreflections" were written in 1770 (see *JubA*, 7:xciv) is therefore untenable.

26. See Rawidowicz' description, *JubA*, 7:378 f.; a specimen page is reproduced in *JubA*, 7, opposite p. 104.

27. *JubA*, 16, letter 129, p. 153 (Nov. 15, 1771).

28. *Schreiben an den Herrn Diaconus Lavater zu Zürich von Moses Mendelssohn* (Berlin & Stettin, 1770). The "letter" is dated Dec. 12, 1769.

29. *JubA*, 7:297 f.,   30. *JubA*, 7:10.

31. *JubA*, 7:8.

32. *JubA*, 7:8 f.

33. *JubA*, 7:9 f.

34. *JubA*, 7:93 f.

35. *JubA*, 7:63.

36. Spinoza, *Tractatus Theologico-Politicus*, chap. 5.

37. See Abraham Lichtenberg (ed.), *Kovets Teshuvot Ha-Rambam Ve-Iggerotav* (Leipzig, 1859), 2, fol. 23d–24a.

38. *JubA*, 7:11.

39. It has been suggested (*JubA*, 7:456) that Mendelssohn might have had in mind certain passages in Emden's *Lehem Shamayim*. The reference could possibly be also to Emden's *Migdal 'Oz*, the third part of his commentary on the Prayer Book (Altona, 1748), in which the strictly rational character of the moral law is defended against Maimonides (see *JubA*, 16, letter 154, p. 179).

40. *JubA*, 16, letter 154, p. 178. See below p. 294 f.

41. *JubA*, 16, letter 155, pp. 179–83; see Jacob Katz, *Exclusiveness and Tolerance* (Oxford, 1961), 175, note 5.

42. This work is listed in *Verzeichnis*, p. 6, no. 90.

43. JubA, 16, letter 154, p. 178.

44. See above, p. 147.

45. *JubA*, 7:12.

46. See Paul Hazard, *The European Mind 1680–1715* (Cleveland & New York, 1963), 23.

47. *Jean-Jacques Rousseau, La "Profession de Foi du Vicaire Savoyard,"* critical edition by Pierre-Maurice Masson (Fribourg-Paris, 1914), 379 ff.; English translation by Olive Schreiner: *Profession of Faith of a Savoyard Vicar* (New York, 1889), 95–100.

48. *JubA*, 7:95.

49. *JubA*, 7:12.

50. *JubA*, 7:73. Cf. Rousseau, *Profession*, 379 ff., where the incomprehensibility of the gospels to distant nations is strongly argued.

51. *JubA*, 7:90 f.

52. Jean François Marmontel, *Bélisaire* (1767), quoted here from the edition by N. Wanostrocht (London, 1805), 194–200 (chap. 15). The four points raised by the censor of the Sorbonne were discussed by Johann August Ernesti in his *Neue Theologische Bibliothek*, 9, no. 6 (1769): 509–22.

53. *JubA*, 7:12.

54. Johann August Eberhard, *Neue Apologie des Sokrates oder Untersuchung der Lehre von der Seligkeit der Heiden* (Berlin & Stettin, 1772; 2nd rev. ed., 1776; vol. 2, 1778; 3rd ed. of Vol. 1, 1788). A detailed presentation of the Marmontel controversy is found in vol. 1, pp. 2–17 (1st ed.).

55. Mendelssohn praised it in his letter to Winkopp, dated Mar. 24, 1780 (*GS*, 5:565 f.).

56. See Ernesti's review in his *Neueste Theologische Bibliothek*, 2, no. 7 (1772): 621–35. Eberhard's work is discussed by Benno Böhm, *Sokrates im achtzehnten Jahrhundert* (Leipzig, 1929), 266 ff., and by Henry E. Allison, *Lessing and the Enlightenment* (Ann Arbor, 1966), 40–42.

57. Cf. Allison, *Lessing*, 186 ff.

58. *JubA*, 7:13.

59. *JubA*, 7:13 f.

60. *JubA*, 7:14.

61. *JubA*, 3.1:18 f., 25.

62. See below, p. 660 ff.

63. Nachlass Hennings, no. 22, letter 30, fol. 78r–v; reproduced (but wrongly dated) by Kayserling, *Mendelssohn*, 1st ed., 536 f. See below, p. 663 f.

64. *JubA*, 7:14 f.

65. See Mendelssohn's letter to Bonnet (Feb. 9. 1770), *JubA*, 7:317.

66. An anonymously published work by Bonnet (London, 1755), from which he quoted frequently in his subsequent works, without ever disclosing his authorship.

67. *JubA*, 7:15 f.

68. *JubA*, 7:16 f.

First Reactions . . . (pages 223–234)

1. *GS*, 1:20; 5:594.

2. *JubA*, 7:298 f. For the date of arrival see *JubA*, 7:316, line 1.

3. *JubA*, 7:306 f.

4. The entire correspondence between Bonnet and Lavater and between Bonnet and Mendelssohn has been published by Rawidowicz (*JubA*, 7:295–374) as part of the appendix "Briefe und Dokumente." The most important letters are reproduced in French by Raymond Savioz, *Mémoires autobiographiques de Charles Bonnet de Genève* (Paris, 1948), 267–89, as arranged by Bonnet and with his explanatory narrative and observations.

5. *JubA*, 7:311.

6. Cf. Meyer, *Bibliographie*, p. 44, nos. 198–99.

7. The verses quoted are from the end of Gellert's poem *Die beiden Wandrer*; see *C.F. Gellerts sämmtliche Schriften* (Leipzig, 1769), 1:274–76. The *Velten* and *Kunzen* mentioned in the text stand for the Valentines and Konrads, Velt being the short form for Valentine, and Kunz being the short form for Konrad; the names are used like Tom, Dick, and Harry in English.

8. See *JubA*, 7:lxxx f., clxxii, notes 157–58; Leo Weisz, "Georg Christoph Lichtenberg und Johann Caspar Lavater," *NZZ*, Apr. 1, 1962, no. 1279/2.

9. Michaelis' letter has been published by L. Geiger, *Briefe*, 95 f. Mendelssohn acknowledged receipt of the complimentary copy of the book on April 8 (see his letter in Kayserling, *Mendelssohn*, 1st ed., 507 f.). The undated letter by Mendelssohn (GS, 5:504 ff.; see below, p. 243 f.) was not in reply to Michaelis' of January 27, as suggested in *JubA*, 7:clxxii, note 159.

10. *GS*, 1:20; *JubA*, 7:lxxvi.

11. Arthur Warda and Carl Driesch, eds., *Briefe an und von Johann George Scheffner*, 4 (1931): 50. The date of the letter is Dec. 28, 1769.

12. Arthur Warda, ed., *Briefe an und von George Scheffner*, 2 (1926): 346.

13. Goethe edition, Inselverlag, 3:645.

14. See above, p. 212.

15. Hoffmann, *Herder's Briefwechsel mit Nicolai*, 54.

16. Emil Gottfried von Herder (ed.), *Johann Gottfried von Herder's Lebensbild* (Erlangen, 1846), 2:115; see also the letter to Hartknoch, p. 125 f.

17. Viz. Mendelssohn, who lived on the other side of the Alps, seen from Zürich.

18. *Hamann Briefwechsel*, 3:1 f.

19. La *"Profession de Foi du Vicaire Savoyard,"* critical edition by Pierre-Maurice Masson (Fribourg-Paris, 1914) 374 f.; Olive Schreiner, *Profession of Faith of a Savoyard Vicar* (New York, 1889), 93 f. On Rousseau's attitude toward the Jews, see Masson's extensive note on pp. 375–79.

20. Nicolai-Briefe, vol. 60, no. 40 (unpublished).

21. L–M, 19:341.

22. See above, p. 223.

23. *JubA*, 7:310 f.

24. *JubA*, 7:312.

25. *JubA*, 7:313.

26. *JubA*, 7:99–103.

27. *JubA*, 7:315 f.

28. Warda, *Briefe*, 1:503.

29. Georg Joachim Zollikofer, neologistic preacher and one of the leading figures in Enlightenment theology.

30. *JubA*, 7:326 f.

31. *JubA*, 7:328 f.

32. *JubA*, 7:330 ff.

33. *JubA*, 7:329 f.

34. *JubA*, 7:334 ff.

35. For the date see *JubA*, 7: clxiv, note 4. The letter was written a few days before March 10.

36. *JubA*, 7:333.

37. See *JubA*, 7:342.

38. *GS*, 3:90–92; *JubA*, 7:59 f., 378.

39. *JubA*, 7:315.

40. See above, p. 204, where Mendelssohn's account is quoted in full.

41. *JubA*, 7:312.

42. See above, p. 226 f.

43. *JubA*, 7:59 f.

44. *GS*, 5:172.

45. Having approved the fourth addendum and rejected the fifth as superfluous. The contents of these addenda remain obscure.

46. *Lessings Briefwechsel mit Ramler, Eschenburg und Nicolai*, 300 f., note 3.

47. Ibid., 300.

48. *JubA*, 16, letter 118, p. 139.

49. *JubA*, 7:341.

50. *JubA*, 7:342–45.

51. Marburg File, no. 17.

52. *JubA*, 7:338.

53. *JubA*, 7:345.

54. *JubA*, 7:clxv, note 55.

55. *Antwort an den Herrn Moses Mendelssohn zu Berlin, von Johann Caspar Lavater. Nebst einer Nacherinnerung von Moses Mendelssohn* (Berlin & Stettin, 1770).

56. *Lessings Briefwechsel mit Ramler . . .*, 299 f.

57. Ibid., 301, note.

Reverberations of the Conflict (pages 234–242)

1. *Gedanken über die Zumuthung des Herrn Diaconus Lavater an Herrn Moses Mendelsohn (sic) ein Christ zu werden, in einem Schreiben eines guten Freundes an einem (sic) andern* (Hamburg, 1770).

2. *JubA*, 7:332.

3. *JubA*, 7:339.

4. L–M, 17:323 (May 17, 1770), 373 (Feb. 16, 1771).

5. *JubA*, 7:345.

6. Johann Balthasar Kölbele, *Kleiner Versuch über die Wunder nach Houttevillischem Bonnetischem und Hollmännischem Leitfaden mit einigen Zusätzen über die Mendelssohnische und Kölbelische Religionsstreitigkeit* (Frankfurt am Main, 1772), 282.

7. Johann Balthasar Kölbele, *Zweytes Schreiben an Herrn Moses Mendelssohn insonderheit über den ehemaligen Mendelssohnischen Deismus, über das Mendelssohnische Kennzeichen einer Offenbarung, und kürzlich über die Glaubwürdigkeit der Evangelischen Geschichte* (Frankfurt am Main, 1770).

8. A monograph about him was published as a *Privatdruck*, in 150 copies dedicated to the "Frankfurter Bibliophilen-Gesellschaft," by Heinrich Voelcker and Georg Schlosser: *Johann Balthasar Kölbele . . . Ein Frankfurter Schriftsteller zu Goethes Jugendzeit* (1924).

9. Voelcker and Schlosser, *Kölbele*, 16, 20 f.

10. Johann Buxtorf I (1564–1629) wrote an *Epitome radicum Hebraicarum et Chaldaicarum* (Basel, 1607), later known as *Lexicon Hebraicum et Chaldaicum*.

11. Kölbele's second letter is quoted here from its reproduction in *Sammlung derer Briefe, welche bey Gelegenheit der Bonnetschen philosophischen Untersuchung der Beweise für das Christenthum, . . .gewechselt worden* (Frankfurt am Main, 1774), 114 f.

12. *Flüchtige Vergleichung zwischen der Weltweisheit und Messkunde, wobey zugleich die über die Berlinische Preisfrage von der metaphysischen Evidenz herausgekommene Schriften kürzlich beurteilet werden* (Frankfurt am Main, 1765).

13. *JubA*, 7:49.

14. Viz. John Barclay's (1582–1621) *Argenis* (1622), a political allegory published in Rome; François de Salignac de la Mothe Fénelon's (1651–1715) *Les Aventures de Télémaque* (1699), a political satire; and the novels of Samuel Richardson (1689–1761). See Kölbele, *Pflichten des Christlichen Dichters in dem Dramatischen . . .* (Frankfurt am Main, 1769), 47, 63; see Voelcker and Schlosser, *Kölbele*, 18, where these references are interpreted as indications of Kölbele's literary models.

15. See the preceding note. Kölbele, who was not overly modest, described himself as having struck a happy medium between Richardson and Klopstock (see his *Pflichten*, 63).

16. See above, note 6.

17. L–M, 17:323 (May 17, 1770).

18. Kant, *Werke*, 9:79 f.

19. *Frankfurter gelehrte Anzeigen vom Jahr 1772, Erste Hälfte*, republished in *Deutsche Literaturdenkmale des 18. Jahrhunderts*, ed. Bernhard Seuffert (Heilbronn, 1882), 208. On the question of Goethe's possible authorship, see L. Geiger, "Die Juden und die deutsche Literatur," *ZGJD*, 1 (1887):343 f.

20. *Göttingische Anzeigen*, 1770 (March 31), no. 39: 330 f. The heading "Frankfurt am Mayn" does not indicate that the reviewer lived in that city (as is assumed in *JubA*, 7:lxxii) but that Kölbele's letter had appeared there. This is clear from other headings (e.g. "Berlin und Stettin" in the case of works published by Nicolai).

21. No. 5, Jan. 11, 1770, 44 f. The author of this review was the theologian Gottfried Less, professor in Göttingen and author of a *Kompendium der theologischen Moral* (1767), who was sympathetic to Kölbele (see *JubA*, 7:lxxii).

22. *GS*, 5:504.

23. *GS*, 3:63 f.; *JubA*, 7:41.

24. *JubA*, 7:316–26; see Bonnet's letter of January 12 (*JubA*, 7:305–10).

25. Such a charge had been leveled against Bonnet in the anonymous *Institutions leibnitiennes ou Précis de la Monadologie* (Lyon, 1767), whose author was the abbé Sigorgne. See Raymond Savioz, *Mémoirs autobiographiques de Charles Bonnet de Genève* (Paris, 1948), 354.

26. *La Palingénésie*, 2:189–94 (chap. 17). In a note to his German translation, Lavater quoted, in support of this theory, abbé Houteville's definition of miracle as forming part of the general order and of the economy of divine designs; see his *Herrn Carl Bonnet's . . .philosophische Untersuchung der Beweise für das Christentum . . .*, p. 56 f. in the 1773 edition.

27. *JubA*, 7:320; 77 ff. Gegenbetrachtungen; for references see Rawidowicz' notes, 469 f. On the subject, see Joseph Heller, "Maimonides' Theory of Miracle," *Between East and West*, ed. A. Altmann (London, 1958), 112–27; Harry A. Wolfson, *Religious Philosophy, A Group of Essays* (Cambridge, Mass., 1961), 204 ff.

28. See Manasseh ben Israel, *Nishmat Hayyim* (Amsterdam, 1652; Lemberg, 1858), 2:4.

29. See Rawidowicz, *JubA*, 7:clxxii, note 7.

30. *JubA*, 7:16, 31, 309 f.

31. See Jehuda Ha-Levi, *Kuzari*, 1:25, 87; 4:11.
32. *JubA*, 7:86–88.
33. *Mishne Tora, Hilkhot Yesodey Ha-Tora*, 8:1.
34. *JubA*, 7:323–25.
35. *GS*, 3:65; *JubA*, 7:43.
36. 1770 (May 17), no. 59: 514 f. Mendelssohn's undated draft of a letter to Michaelis (see below, p. 243) shows that the assumption of his authorship is correct.
37. *GS*, 5:504.
38. *GS*, 5:504 f.

Literary Concerns . . . (pages 242–263)

1. Reproduced in *JubA*, 14:145–207. For a brief characterization of the work see Borodianski, *JubA*, 14:vii; his annotations to the text are found on pp. lxxvii–lxxxiii; the various editions are listed on p. lxxvii; see also Meyer, *Bibliographie*, p. 49, nos. 231–35.
2. See Borodianski, *JubA*, 14:vii.
3. *JubA*, 14:160.
4. L–M, 19:352. When the Psalms translation finally appeared in 1783, Karl Lessing wrote to Mendelssohn on June 14 of that year: "About your Psalms I will say nothing, for I now read one or two every day. What one admires one cannot judge" (Dep. RvM, C II, no. 4; published in Alexander Altmann, "Briefe Karl Gotthelf Lessings an Moses Mendelssohn," *Lessing Yearbook* 1 (Munich, 1969): 22.
5. *GS*, 5:692. A literary analysis of Mendelssohn's Psalms translation is found in Simon Rawidowicz' elaborate essay on the subject published (in Hebrew) in his collected Jewish studies edited by Benjamin C. I. Ravid *(Iyyunim Bemahashevet Yisrael)*, 2 (Jerusalem, 1971), 118–40.
6. L–M, 19:352.
7. The undated version is published in GS, 5:504 ff., the dated one in Kayserling, *Mendelssohn*, 1st ed., 509–12.
8. See above, p. 241 f.
9. This would explain the omission of both the date and the address.
10. Gerlach Adolph Freiherr von Münchhausen (1688–1770), prime minister of Hanover since 1765 and the ruling authority at the University of Göttingen.
11. Kayserling, *Mendelssohn*, 1st ed., 509.
12. Dep. RvM, C II, no. 13.
13. It appeared as part six of Michaelis' *Deutsche Übersetzung des alten Testaments* (1771).
14. Dep. RvM, C II, no. 13. Both Mendelssohn and Michaelis expressed the hope that they would meet in Pyrmont, the popular watering place. See below, p. 278.
15. See *JubA*, 1:544–99 *(Lesarten)*.
16. *JubA*, 1:231 f.
17. Henry Home Lord Kames (1696–1782), *Elements of Criticism*, Vols. 1–3 (Edinburgh, 1762).
18. *GS*, 5:277.
19. *JubA*, 1:488 f.
20. See Ludwig Goldstein, *Moses Mendelssohn und die deutsche Ästhetik* (Königsberg, 1904), 117–22.
21. See *GS*, 5:506 ff.; J. Wille, *De litterator R.M. van Goens en zijn kring* (1937). In an unpublished letter to Nicolai, dated October 1, 1770 (Marburg File, no. 20), Mendelssohn wrote: "Herr van Goens mentions in his preface to *The Sublime* a translation of my treatise *Over de zedelijke gevoelens* [On the moral sentiments] by his friend Petsch. This I would like to see. The treatise takes its title not from me but from Herr Abbt [viz. from Abbt's French version of Mendelssohn's *Rhapsody*, which he entitled *Recherches sur les Sentiments Moreux;* see above, p. 117]. If only Petsch did not translate the entire treatise from Abbt's French instead of the German!" Cf. Mendelssohn's reference to Petsch in his letter to van Goens, *GS*, 5:508.
22. *LBH*, 3:273 f., no. 5687.
23. *GS*, 5:507. Mendelssohn published a brief review of the Dutch edition in the *Allgemeine deutsche Bibliothek* (reproduced in *GS*, 4.2:560). The second edition of van Goens' translation gave rise to a severe attack upon him by clerical circles who accused him as a secularist who highly esteemed "public denigrators of the true Christian religion." A philippic to this

effect appeared in *De Nederlandsche Bibliotheek* (Amsterdam, de Bryn, 1774), which caused Utrecht University to proscribe the *Bibliotheek* on Mar. 13, 1775. See W.P.C. Knuttel, *Verboden boeken in de Republiek der Vereenigde Nederlanden. Beredeneerde catalogus* (The Hague, 1914), no. 61. I owe this information to Mr. Daniel Swetschinski.

24. Garve published his important critique of Lessing's *Laokoön* during his period as professor in Leipzig (1770–1772). See Danzel, *Lessing*, 2.1:84.

25. Marburg File, no. 18.

26. *JubA*, 7:348–51; Raymond Savoiz, *Mémoires autobiographiques du Charles Bonnet de Genève* (Paris, 1948), 283–85.

27. *Recherches Philosophiques sur les Preuves du Christianisme.* Nouvelle édition ... , 1770. A revised edition of this work appeared in 1771; announced in the *Göttingische Anzeigen*, (Sept. 3, 1770), no. 106, and reviewed by Ernesti in his *Neueste Theologische Bibliothek*, no. 3 (1772): 319 ff.

28. See Bonnet's letter to Lavater, dated Jan. 29, 1771 (*JubA*, 7:365).

29. *JubA*, 7:354 f.

30. Ibid.

31. Johann Friedrich Wilhelm Jerusalem (1709–1789), leading theologian of the Enlightenment.

32. L–M, 17:366.

33. See the penetrating interpretation of the much-debated passage by Edward S. Flajole, S. J., "Lessing's Attitude in the Lavater-Mendelssohn Controversy," *PMLA*, 73, No. 3 (June, 1958): 201–14.

34. See Bonnet's refutation of the charge in his notes on Mendelssohn's letter to Lavater, *JubA*, 7:373; Savioz, *Mémoires*, 289. He mistakenly referred to Mendelssohn's objections as having been published as early as December, 1769, whereas they only appeared in the epilogue at the end of April, 1770.

35. The same explanation is offered by Rawidowicz, *JubA*, 7:lxxxviii; see his detailed account of Mendelssohn's relations with Bonnet, pp. lxxxi–xciii.

36. See *JubA*, 7:363–74; Savioz, *Mémoires*, 285–89.

37. Savioz, *Mémoires*, 289.

38. A survey of the pamphlets that appeared is given by Rawidowicz, *JubA*, 7:lvi–lxxi.

39. *Sammlung derer Briefe, welche bei Gelegenheit der Bonnetschen ... Untersuchung ... gewechselt worden* (Frankfurt am Main, (1774), 87–168.

40. Prov. 24:4.

41. Johann August Ernesti, *Neue Theologische Bibliothek*, 10, no. 8 (1769): 751, in his review of Mendelssohn's *Letter to Lavater:* "Besides, this treatise confirms the judgment one has passed on contemporary Judaism, namely, that it is mere naturalism."

42. Prov. 14:23.

43. *JubA*, 16, letter 127, p. 150 f.

44. See above, p. 216.

45. *Sammlung derer Briefe*, 32.

46. See above, p. 241.

47. *Sammlung derer Briefe*, 118.

48. *JubA*, 16, letter 120, p. 142.

49. *Betrachtung über das Schreiben des Herrn Moses Mendelssohn an den Diaconus Lavater zu Zürich* (Leipzig, 1770). Its author was August Adolf Beyschlag (see JubA, 7:clxx, note 110; Meyer, *Bibliographie*, p. 46, no. 213).

50. *Sammlung derer Briefe*, 112, note 1.

51. See *JubA*, 7:lvii.

52. In its most pregnant sense, the term "sanctification of the Holy Name" (*Kiddush Ha-Shem*) denotes the act of submission to martyrdom that the Jewish law prescribes in certain situations. See the chapter "The Martyrs" in Jacob Katz, *Exclusiveness and Tolerance* (Oxford, 1961), 82–92.

53. Using the phrase found in *Mishna Avot*, 2:4.

54. *JubA*, 16, letter 125, p. 148.

55. L–M, 19, letter 333, p. 397; Kayserling, *Mendelssohn*, 221.

56. On Lessing's librarianship see Heinrich Schneider, *Lessing* (Bern, 1951), 53–93; his letter to the father: L–M, 17, letter 266, p. 330; on Mendelssohn's reaction to seeing the Library and learning of Lessing's discovery see Karl G. Lessing, *G.E. Lessings Leben ...* , *1* (Berlin, 1793), 318 f.

57. See L–M, 17, letters 276 and 279, pp. 346 and 348; L–M, 19, letter 344, p. 406 f. *(GS*, 5:184 ff.); letter 351, p. 425 *(GS*, 5:186 f.); L–M, 17, letter 291, p. 364 *(GS* 5:187 f.); letter 295, p. 373; L–M, 18, letter 629, p. 303 f.

58. See Karl Aner, *Die Theologie der Lessingzeit* (Halle, 1929), 351 ff.; Henry E. Allison, *Lessing and the Enlightenment* (Ann Arbor, 1966), 185 f.

59. In 1814 the original MS was presented to the then Hamburg City Library (now Staats- und Universitätsbibliothek Hamburg) by Dr. Johann A.H. Reimarus, and it is still extant there. Reimarus also gave a copy of it to the university library in Göttingen. This copy, which is still preserved there, contains also the last "book" of volume one, which was never included in the original manuscript, probably because the author had intended to give it some final polish but had died before carrying out his intention. Since it was not put together with the rest of the bundle of manuscripts of the *Schutzschrift*, it was overlooked by the son when he sent the entire *Konvolut* to the binder. A replica of the complete Göttingen manuscript is found also in the Staatsarchiv, Hamburg, which received it from its previous private owner. It is this copy that David Friedrich Strauss used for his publications about Reimarus. In addition, the Staatsarchiv, Hamburg, possesses 13 large and small fragments of earlier drafts, which are partly earlier and partly later than the fragments edited by Lessing. The final text as contained in the Hamburg and Göttingen manuscripts is now being edited for the first time under the auspices of the Joachim-Jungius Gesellschaft der Wissenschaften, Hamburg. I am grateful to Prof. Dr. Hellmut Braun, director of the Staats- und Universitäts-bibliothek, Hamburg, for the above information, conveyed to me in a letter dated Dec. 10, 1970. See also Benedict Brandl, *Die Überlieferung der Schutzschrift des Hermann Samuel Reimarus* (Pilsen, 1907); Hartmut Sierig, ed., *Hermann Samuel Reimarus Vorrede zur Schutzschrift ... Facsimile* (Göttingen, 1967).

60. See Lessing, *Anti-Goeze* VI (L–M, 13:176); *Von dem Zwecke Jesu und seiner Jünger* (L–M, 13:219).

61. See Lessing's letter to Duke Karl of Brunswick (July 20, 1778), L–M, 18, letter 601, pp. 274–76; *GS*, 5:185 f.; 189. Lessing was ordered by the duke to return the manuscript (see L–M, 21, letter 753, p. 214; July 13, 1778). This copy of the manuscript is lost, as Professor Braun informed me (see above, note 59).

62. See Lessing's letter to Elise Reimarus (May 25, 1779), L–M, 18, letter 652, p. 319 f., and her reply, L–M, 21, letter 806, p. 259 f.

63. "Von Duldung der Deisten," L–M, 12:254.

64. In his letter of November or December, 1770, Dr. Reimarus addressed Lessing as "Dearest Friend" (L–M, 19, letter 345, p. 408).

65. See the notes Lessing sent to Dr. Reimarus on Aug. 22, 1769; Sept. 30, 1769; Apr. 10, 1770 (L–M, 17, letters 236, 240, and 258, pp. 269 f., 299 f., and 318 f.).

66. Quoted by Heinrich Sieveking, "Elise Reimarus (1735–1805) in den geistigen Kämpfen ihrer Zeit," *Zeitschrift des Vereins für Hamburgische Geschichte*, 39 (Hamburg, 1940): 98; Sieveking sought to prove that the manuscript was not given to Lessing by the Reimarus family but was found by him in the ducal library. His arguments are far from convincing.

67. L–M, 19, letter 345, p. 411 f.

68. Sieveking, "Elise Reimarus," 101, must have overlooked this passage in Dr. Reimarus' letter when arguing that if he had given Lessing the manuscript, he might have suggested that Lessing consult it. This is just what Dr. Reimarus did suggest.

69. See L–M, 21, letter 743, p. 196 f. (Mar. 19, 1778); letter 751, p. 207 f., 211 f., (June, 1778); L–M, 18, letter 597, p. 267 ff. (Apr. 6, 1778); L–M, 21, letter 792, p. 248 f. (Mar. 13, 1779); letter 803, p. 257 (May 18, 1779).

70. *GS*, 5:186 (L–M, 19, letter 344, p. 408).

71. *GS*, 5:189 (L–M, 17, letter 291, p. 365 f.).

72. *Vom Zwecke Jesu und seiner Jünger*, Part 2, #49 (L–M, 13:304 f.).

73. "Von Duldung der Deisten," L–M, 12:262–66.

74. Facsimile edition by Sierig (see note 59), fol. 96 f.

75. *GS*, 5:184 f. (L–M, 19, letter 344, p. 407 f.).

76. *GS*, 5:188 f. (L–M, 17:365).

77. *GS*, 5:188 (L–M, 17:364 f.). See Edward S. Flajole, S.J., "Lessing's Retrieval of Lost Truths," *PMLA*, 24.1 (March, 1959): 52 ff.

78. *GS*, 5:189 (L–M, 17:366). See Edward S. Flajole, S.J., "Lessing's Attitude in the Lavater-Mendelssohn Controversy," *PMLA*, 73.3 (June, 1958): 201–14, whose interpretation of the passage we follow.

79. *JubA,* 7:301; quoted by Flajole, "Lessing's Attitude," 210.

80. *GS,* 5:187 (L–M, 19, letter 351, p. 425).

81. See *JubA,* 7:xlvi–l; Flajole, "Lessing's Attitude," 210; Leo Weisz, "Johann Caspar Lavaters Tagebuchstreit," *NNZ,* Feb. 8, 1961, nos. 454; 456.

82. *GS,* 5:227, note 20.

83. The Latin text is reproduced in *JubA,* 7:353.

84. *JubA,* 7:354.

85. See Weisz,, "Tagebuchstreit," no. 454.

86. See above, p. 230; Weisz, *NNZ,* Mar. 21, 1961, no. 1036.

87. *JubA,* 7:356.

88. *JubA,* 7:356 f.

89. *JubA,* 7:357.

90. *JubA,* 7:358–60.

91. This was assumed by Rawidowicz, *JubA,* 7:xlvii.

92. E.g., both in the diary (see above, p. 201) and in the Latin report Mendelssohn's "modesty" (piety) toward his Jewish brethren is mentioned; in both places his admiration for his peers is stressed.

93. See Weisz, *NZZ,* Mar. 21, 1961, no. 1036, end.

94. JubA, 7:361 f. (Jan. 15, 1771). See above, p. 205.

95. His next letter was written on Apr. 14, 1775. It was concerned with an entirely different matter; see below, p. 426 f.

96. *Freymüthige Gedanken über des Herrn Moses Mendelssohn Sendschreiben an den Herrn Diaconus Lavater. An einen Freund in Sachsen* (Leipzig, 1771).

97. "Die *Freymüthigen Gedanken* sind mir, ich darf es Ihnen nicht verhehlen, an einigen Stellen recht durch die Seele gegangen: o Gott! ist das deine Weise, die Wahrheit auszubreiten?" (*JubA,* 7:356). It seems that Lavater disapproved of the author's radicalism, yet was deeply stirred by it.

98. *Freymüthige Gedanken,* 38.

99. *Sammlung derer Briefe,* 95, 152, 154.

100. See above, p. 226.

101. *Sammlung derer Briefe,* 166 and passim. For an evaluation of the Josephus passages concerning Jesus, see now Paul Winter, "Josephus on Jesus," *Journal of Historical Studies,* I, no. 4. (Princeton, N.J., 1968): 289–302. Kölbele's references to Rousseau are found in *Sammlung derer Briefe,* 94 f., 144, 152 f., 159.

102. A medieval work of strongly anti-Christian tendency, which exists in several recensions. See Samuel Krauss, *Das Leben Jesu nach jüdischen Quellen* (Berlin, 1902); Joseph Klausner, *Jesus of Nazareth, His Life, Times and Teaching* (New York, 1929), 47—54.

103. *Sammlung derer Briefe,* 95, 101, 149.

104. Ibid., 154.

105. *JubA,* 7:362.

106. *JubA,* 7:362 f.

107. Otto Justus Basilius Hesse, *Schreiben des Herrn Moses Mendelssohn in Berlin an den Herrn Diaconus Lavater in Zürich nebst Anmerkungen über dasselbe* (Halle, 1770). Mendelssohn's letter to Hesse is reproduced in *GS,* 5:513 ff.

108. Hesse, *Schreiben,* 81.

Chapter Four: Changes in the Pattern of Life
The Strange Illness (pages 264–271)

1. Minutes of the academy session of Feb. 7, 1771, quoted by Harnack, *Geschichte,* 1.1:470, note 1.

2. *LBH,* 2:294, no. 3044. The date (February 17) given in *GS,* 1:24 is incorrect.

3. The minutes of the academy session of Feb. 14, 1771, indicate that the proposal had been sent to the king.

4. L–M, 20:15.

5. L–M, 20:25.

6. *LBH,* 2:294, no. 3045. The account of events given by Kayserling, *Mendelssohn,* 227 f., obfuscates both the chronological sequence and Sulzer's role. As Arend Buchholtz, *LBH,* 2:294, put it, and Geiger, *Briefe,* p. 100, repeated after him, "Sulzer hat . . . das Wesentlichste verschwiegen."

7. Harnack, *Geschichte,* 1.1:470, note 1.

8. Ibid.

9. Harnack (ibid.) wrote: "The king's refusal can be explained as due only to Mendelssohn's being Jewish."

10. *GS,* 3:420. Emanuel Mendes d'Acosta (da Costa), a physician and a geologist, was elected a fellow of the Royal Society in 1740 and became its librarian in 1763; see M. Kayserling, *Biblioteca Española-Portugueza-Judaica* (Strasbourg, 1890), 39; Idem, *Mendelssohn,* 333, note 1. His works include a *Natural History of Fossils* (London, 1757); see Cecil Roth, *Magna Bibliotheca Anglo-Judaica* (London, 1937), 410, 412, 413.—The *Gesellschaft naturliebender Freunde* was founded in 1773. Only "friends of nature" active in research, the collection of natural curiosities, or both were eligible for regular membership, which was limited at a maximum of twelve and entailed obligatory attendance at the weekly sessions. During Mendelssohn's lifetime ten volumes of papers appeared (1775–1785). It seems that until the end of the century Marcus Elieser Bloch, one of the founders of the society, remained the only Jew among its regular members. See Dietrich L.G. Karsten, "Zur Geschichte der Gesellschaft Naturforschender Freunde in Berlin am 9ten Juli 1798 dem 25jährigen Stiftungsfeste derselben vorgelesen," in *Jahrbücher der preussischen Monarchie unter der Regierung Friedrich Wilhelms des Dritten* (September, 1798), 9–24; V.H. Schmidt and D.G.G. Mehring, *Neuestes gelehrtes Berlin,* 1–2 (Berlin, 1795). I owe this information to Herr Heinrich Hümpel, Berlin.

11. *GS,* 5:679 f.

12. L–M, 20:15.

13. Marburg File, no. 20.

14. See above, p. 139 f.

15. *GS,* 5:445.

16. Letter from Karl Gottlieb Bock to Johann George Scheffner (Sept. 9, 1793), published by W. Dorow, *Krieg, Literatur und Theater* (Leipzig, 1845), 215 f.; reprinted in Arthur Warda, ed., *Briefe an und von Johann George Scheffner,* 1 (1918): 63.

17. L. Geiger and R.M. Werner, "Briefe von, an und über Mendelssohn," *ZGJD,*1 (1887): 109. The identity of the addressee is unknown.

18. Kant, *Werke,* 9:76–79.

19. Kant, *Werke,* 9:90–93.

20. *JubA.* 1:362 f.; see *Frühschriften,* 56 f.

21. A critical appraisal of Kant's dissertation, rejecting Kant's charge that Leibniz was guilty of a circular argument, is found in a 2-page manuscript in Dep. RvM, D I, no. 4. The handwriting is not Mendelssohn's, but this fact does not preclude his authorship.

22. As early as 1766 Kant had agreed to enter into regular correspondence with Mendelssohn (see Kant, *Werke,* 9:54), but it was Herz who brought them together.

23. Kant, *Werke,* 9:106.

24. M.E. Bloch, *Medicinische Bemerkungen* (Berlin, 1774), 60 ff.; *GS,* 3:438 (Mendelssohn's own description of the symptoms). That the attacks started in the early spring ("since Purim"), 1771, is attested by Mendelssohn's letter to Elkan Herz, which was written on July 22, 1771. See *JubA,* 16, letter 127, p. 150.

25. Bloch, *Bemerkungen,* 60: "The symptoms first occurred about 13 years ago." Bloch's account, though published in 1774, must have been written in 1771, for the story breaks off at the point of the improvement after the first two months of therapy. Therefore, the year of the very first attacks was 1758.

26. See Bloch, *Bemerkungen,* 64 ff.

27. See above pp. 243, 251; Eduard Bodemann, *Johann Georg Zimmermann, Sein Leben und bisher ungedruckte Briefe an denselben . . .* (Hanover, 1878), 66 f.

28. Dep. RvM, D II, no. 4.

29. Bloch, *Bemerkungen,* 69.

30. *JubA,* 16, letter 127, p. 150; Kayserling, *Mendelssohn,* 235, mistranslated the Hebrew words *kelal u-khelal* (at all) by "im allgemeinen" (in general).

31. Letter to Dr. Ernst Platner (unpublished Moses Mendelssohn autograph I/599, Staatsbibliothek Stiftung Preussischer Kulturbesitz, Berlin). On Platner see below, p. 302.

32. Unpublished autograph, Collection Darmstaedter, 2a 1767 (2), Staatsbibliothek Stiftung preussischer Kulturbesitz, Berlin.

33. *G.E. Lessings Briefwechsel mit Friedrich Nicolai,* ed. Nicolai (1794), 349, 354 f.

34. *Lessings Briefwechsel mit Nicolai,* 301.

35. I am grateful to Dr. Aaron Brand-Auraban of Jerusalem for his kindness in appraising

the extant clinical reports of Mendelssohn's illness, and for suggesting the above-mentioned diagnosis in a letter to me, dated Apr. 15, 1970.

Ups and Downs: A Chronicle of Events (pages 271–286)

1. See Josef Meisl, *Protokollbuch der jüdischen Gemeinde zu Berlin* (Jerusalem, 1962), xliv f., xlix.

2. Ibid., 258 f., no. 253.

3. Ibid., 315; no. 315; 322, no. 322; 342, no. 321. On the office of *tovim*, see xxxi.

4. The rhymed Hebrew text of the document was first published by Elieser Landshuth, *Toledot Anshey Shem U-Fe'ulotam* (Berlin, 1884), 64. It is reproduced in *JubA*, 14:384, and Meisl, *Protokollbuch*, 211 f., no. 209.

5. L–M, 20, letter 380, p. 31.

6. Viz. Nebuchadnezzar; see Daniel 4:30, 31.

7. Corneille de Pauw, *Recherches sur les Américains*, 2 vols. (Berlin, 1768, 1770, 1772). The autograph of Michaelis' letter of Dec. 27, 1770, unpublished, is extant in Dep. RvM, C II, no. 13.

8. Dep. RvM, C II, no. 14.

9. Albrecht von Haller (1708–1777), the famous physiologist and poet, had suggested that circumcision was meant to prevent masturbation.

10. Published by Kayserling, *Mendelssohn*, 1st ed., 512–14.

11. Probably a misspelling of Gumprich.

12. *Herder's Briefwechsel mit Nicolai*, ed. Otto Hoffmann (Berlin, 1887), 61.

13. Kant, *Werke*, 9:101.

14. Karlsruhe, 1788, p. 263 ff.

15. P. 269; see also Eduard Bodemann, *Johann Georg Zimmermann, Sein Leben und bisher ungedruckte Briefe an denselben* (Hanover, 1878), 67.

16. See Bodemann, ibid.; Kayserling, *Ungedrucktes*, 9; Idem, *Mendelssohn*, 236.

17. Dep. RvM, C II, no. 43.

18. Not identical with Johann Georg Jacobi, the anacreontic poet, as Kayserling, *Ungedrucktes*, 10, assumed.

19. A reference to Mendelssohn's commentary on Kohelet, a German translation of which by Johann Jacob Rabe *(Der Prediger Salomo*, Anspach, 1771) had just appeared.

20. Bodemann, *Zimmermann*, 287 f.; Kayserling, *Ungedrucktes*, 9–12, reproduced the entire letter and inferred the date from the last sentence. His dating is confirmed by Zimmermann's letter of November 6.

21. It seems that Mendelssohn mentioned Zimmermann's letter to Nicolai, who thereupon confessed that he had been the source of Jacobi's information.

22. Johann David Michaelis, *Teutsche Übersetzung des alten Testaments, mit Anmerkungen für Ungelehrte*, Part 6 (Göttingen & Gotha, 1771).

23. Concerning the latter psalm (Ps. 110), *GS* 3:364.

24. See Bruno Strauss, *Moses Mendelssohn in Potsdam am 30. September 1771. Eine kleine Aufklärung* (Berlin, 1929), where the historical features of the story, as distinct from its legendary elements, are established in masterly fashion.

25. See Friedrich Nicolai, *Anekdoten von König Friedrich II. von Preussen* (Berlin, 1788), 3rd fasc., 278.

26. It is reproduced in Strauss' booklet and as an illustration to Horst Behrend's essay, "Daniel Chodowiecki," *Jahrbuch der Stiftung Preussischer Kulturbesitz* (Köln & Berlin, 1964/65), facing p. 160. For the earliest reproductions see Meyer, *Bibliographie*, p. 179, p. 58; L. Geiger, "Eine bildliche Darstellung Moses Mendelssohns," *ZGJD*, 5 (1892): 105 f.

27. L–M, 20, letter 418, p. 81. In September, 1771, Lessing had spent almost three weeks in Hamburg and the rest of the month in Berlin, leaving the city on September 30, the very day on which Mendelssohn made his memorable trip to Potsdam. See L–M, 17: 397 f., 400 f.; 20:66 f., 69.

28. Bodemann, *Zimmermann*, 301; Kayserling, *Ungedrucktes*, 12.

29. See Fritz Arnheim, "Moses Mendelssohn und Luise Ulrike von Schweden," *ZGJD*, 3 (1888): 283 f. Cf. above, p. 178.

30. *Herder's Briefwechsel mit Nicolai*, 69.

31. Ibid., 72. On Herder's prize-essay see Rudolf Haym, *Herder* (Berlin, 1954), 1:428 ff., 495.

32. Marburg File, no. 22. On Mar. 14, 1772, Nicolai wrote to Zimmermann: "Herr Moses begins to show some improvement. Yesterday he even dared to read the whole of Lessing's new tragedy." See Bodemann, *Zimmermann*, 301. During the winter of 1771/72 Lessing had written the tragedy *Emilia Galotti* and his brother Karl had helped with proofreading and valuable suggestions. The author was particularly curious to know Mendelssohn's reaction. Having inquired on Mar. 1, 1772, whether Ramler, Moses, and Nicolai had read any part of *Galotti*, and having been somewhat displeased with Ramler's "squinting" review, Lessing wrote on April 22: "I would, indeed, have preferred to read a verdict by our Moses. His remark about the prince's character makes a rather good point." On March, 12, it seems, Karl had reported to him, at considerable length, a conversation in which Mendelssohn had shown himself deeply moved by Emilia and the drama as a whole but had expressed some reservations about the character of the prince: he thought he had detected a certain shift in his portrayal. Karl had disagreed, but Lessing found the criticism justified: he recalled having written the first act at a time when he was as yet unsure about the part the prince would play in the end. See L–M, 18:22, 35; 20:146 f.

33. Bodemann, *Zimmermann*, 286 (slightly abridged; likewise in Kayserling, *Ungedrucktes*, 12 f.; *Mendelssohn*, 236). The original of the letters is found in the Niedersächsische Landesbibliothek, Hanover, Letters by Mendelssohn to Zimmermann, fol. 1r.

34. A humorous reference to the Moabit district of Berlin.

35. The popular watering place near Hameln, Lower Saxony.

36. *JubA*, 16, letter 136, p. 160.

37. Kayserling, *Mendelssohn*, 1st ed., 516 f.

38. Dep RvM, C II, no. 15.

39. Kayserling, *Mendelssohn*, 1st ed., 514–16.

40. Nicolai-Briefe, vol. 18.

41. *JubA*, 16, letter 147, p. 172.

42. *GS*, 5:191 f.

43. *JubA*, 16, letter 148, p. 173 f.

44. *JubA*, 16, letter 151, p. 175.

45. *Briefwechsel zwischen Christian Garve und Georg Joachim Zollikofer* (Breslau, 1804), 95 f.

46. *JubA*, 16, letter 152, p. 176.

47. See Kayserling, *Mendelssohn*, 1st ed., 518 f.; Michaelis' reply is found in Geiger, *Briefe*, 107 f.

48. L–M, 20, letter 543, p. 279.

49. L–M, 21, letter 565, p. 24.

50. *GS*, 5:517 ff.

51. See *GS*, 5:524 ff., note. On the medal, see Meyer, *Bibliographie*, p. 176, p. 14.

52. *GS*, 5:424–527.

53. Geiger, *Briefe*, 92 f., 108 ff.

54. Landesbibliothek, Hanover, Letters ... fol. 2r; quoted by Kayserling, *Mendelssohn*, 176, from Bodemann, *Zimmermann*, 286. See also Kayserling, *Ungedrucktes*, 20.

55. Marburg File, no. 53: Sept. 4, 1781. In a letter dated Jan. 28, 1773 (*LBH*, 2:322 f., no. 3178), Wieland had "greeted" Mendelssohn "in the holy name of friendship" and invited him to become a contributor to *Der Teutsche Merkur*, which he was about to launch as editor.

56. See Biedermann, *Gespräche*, 258 f.

57. *JubA*, 16, letter 170, p. 194 f.

58. *JubA*, 16, letter 172, p. 196.

59. *GS*, 5:405 f.

60. *GS*, 5:406 f. The countess died on June 16, 1776, her 33rd birthday. The count died on September 10, 1777, at the age of 53. A picture of the count, put at my disposal by the Niedersächsisches Staatsarchiv, Bückeburg, is reproduced in this volume.

61. *JubA*, 16, letter 172, p. 196.

62. See Haym, *Herder*, 1:408 f.; 495 ff., 762. Mendelssohn's notes on his correspondence with Abbt were reviewed by Herder in *Teutscher Merkur* (August, 1782). Herder disapproved of Mendelssohn's description of the count as "the finest Greek soul in a rough Westphalian body." In Herder's view, the count's features were most noble and attractive. See Haym, *Herder*, 1:493 f.

63. Haym, *Herder*, 1:652.

64. See Albert Wolf, "D. Chodowiecki und Moses Mendelssohn," *Ost und West,* 3 (1903): 829–843; Idem, "Das jüdische Berlin gegen Ende des 18. Jahrhunderts in Abbildungen und Medaillen," *Gedenkbuch David Kaufmann,* 635. The count wrote to Mendelssohn on Oct. 15, 1774: "We [the countess and I] received with indescribable pleasure your excellent portrait, the likeness of a man in whom Europe reveres wisdom, virtue, and learning" *(LBH,* 3:42, no. 4539). Mendelssohn had sent the portrait at the specific request of the countess *(LBH,* 3:45, no. 4543).

65. "A good and wise man, one of thousands the like of whom Apollo raised up when consulted [by oracle]." *Herders Briefe an Johann Georg Hamann,* ed. Otto Hoffmann (Berlin, 1889), 90 (Nov. 14, 1774); 108 f. Frau von Ompteda seems to have maintained contact with Mendelssohn, as a letter from Zimmermann to Mendelssohn dated January, 1778 (Dep. RvM, C II, no. 44) suggests.

66. Quoted by Kayserling, *Mendelssohn,* 243. In December, 1774, Zimmermann wrote to Sulzer: "Herder and I were together last summer in Pyrmont. Mendelssohn, whom I hold in such respect, was also there. Herder and Mendelssohn met, each in his own way, with the highest acclaim, but it was remarkable that each of these two men found the other somewhat repulsive." See Bodemann, *Zimmermann,* 67, 242.

67. Quoted by Kayserling, *Mendelssohn,* 243 f.

68. Published for the first time in *JubA,* 3.1:305–07; see lvii f., 385, 457–60.

69. Cf. above, p. 31.

70. Marburg File, no. 20 (Oct. 1, 1770). Reid's work had appeared in 1764.

Hebraica and Judaica *(pages 286–295)*

1. See above, pp. 243 f.; 274 f.

2. See above, p. 208.

3. *GS,* 5:516.

4. We could not trace the English commentary on the Pentateuch referred to by Mendelssohn. The emendation of Gen. 4:7 suggested there was based on the Septuagint reading. It is found in C. J. Ball, *The Book of Genesis* (1896); see B[enno] Jacob, *Das erste Buch der Tora Genesis* (Berlin, 1934), 139.

5. *GS,* 5:517 ff.

6. Mendelssohn's cryptic remark becomes intelligible in the light of a passage in Karl Lessing's letter to his brother written on Apr. 17, 1773 (L-M, 20:249): "That through Kennicot's work a fragment by Livy came to be unearthed, nobody will put down to his credit.... From this whole incident I but infer the truth that Providence causes even our most useless activities to turn out for the good."

7. *Olaf Gerhardi Tychsen Tentamen de variis codicum hebraicorum veteris testamenti manuscriptorum generibus, a Judaeis et Non-Judaeis descriptis* (Rostock, 1772); Idem, *Befreyetes Tentamen von den Einwürfen der Herren Bruns Dathe, Michaelis, nebst Beurtheilung Kennicots paradoxer Sätze* (Rostock & Leipzig, 1774).

8. See *Verzeichnis,* p. 29, no. 213; p. 37, no. 324.

9. *JubA,* 16, letter 111, p. 133; lxiii; see Siegfried Silberstein, "Mendelssohn und Mecklenburg," *ZGJD,* 2 (1930): 166.

10. Tychsen's copy of Mendelssohn's commentary on Kohelet contained the inscription "Donum Auctoris Mosche Dessau (dicti Mosis Mendelssohn) praesentat. O. d. 18. Feb. 1770. O. G. Tychsen, Bützow, 1770." See Silberstein, "Mendelssohn und Mecklenburg," *ZGJD,* 1 (1929): 275. Tychsen, who was prone to make purely imaginary assertions, may have invented this presentation. See Silberstein *ZGJD,* 2:166. Tychsen is to be given credit for his remarkable effort to obtain the famous David Oppenheim Collection of Hebrew manuscripts and books for Rostock University. He tried to persuade the duke, who took Hebrew lessons with him, to purchase this unique library and kept up a lively correspondence on this subject with the Altona Dean G. C. Adler, the Mecklenburg courtier Cornelius, and Prof. Giovanni Bernardo de Rossi in Parma. See Siegfried Silberstein, "Zur Geschichte der Oppenheimerschen Bibliothek," *Mitteilungen der Soncino-Gesellschaft,* No. 7–10/March, 1931: 9–26.

11. The full story of the edict has been told, on the basis of fresh archival evidence, in Silberstein's article, *ZGJD,* 1 (1929): 233–44; 278–86.

12. *JubA,* 16, letter 131, p. 154 f.

13. The text has been published by Silberstein, *ZGJD,* 1 (1929): 284 ff. It is entitled "Schema zu einer Vorstellung an den Landesherrn." This memorandum is referred to in Mendelssohn's letter to the Schwerin community (*JubA,* 16, letter 133, p. 157, line 13) as *tofes ha-bakasha.* The note *ad loc.* (p. lxix) is superseded by Silberstein's publication of the text.

14. The memorandum referred to *Sanh.* 46a, where Deut. 21:23 is cited as prooftext.

15. See Silberstein, *ZGJD,* 1 (1929): 237 f.

16. *JubA,* 16, letter 133, p. 156 f.; for earlier publications of this letter and its German translation see *JubA,* 16:lxix.

17. Mendelssohn referred to the passage in *Semahot* 8:1, where cases of seemingly dead people returning to life are reported.

18. *Nidda* 69b.

19. *JubA,* 16, letter 134, p. 157 f. (June 26, 1772).

20. *JubA,* 16, letter 135, p. 159.

21. *JubA,* 16, letter 137, p. 161 ff.

22. Emden referred to a treatise of his on the subject, viz. the *Sefer ve'Iggeret le'ammitah shel Tora* (*JubA,* 16:162).

23. *JubA,* 16, letter 138, p. 164 ff.

24. *JubA,* 16, letter 139, p. 166 ff.

25. Prov. 4:24.

26. Lit.: "rearing a dog [in his house]."

27. Prov. 9:8.

28. Jer. 8:19.

29. Mendelssohn regarded himself as a "disciple" of Emden. His letter of June 30, 1772, referred to Emden as "my teacher." On Emden's influence upon Mendelssohn, see Heinz Mosche Graupe, *Die Entstehung des modernen Judentums* (Hamburg, 1969), 88 f.

30. 2 Samuel 15:1; 1 Kings 1:5; see *JubA,* 16, letter 154, p. 178 f.

31. For passages from the *Zohar* and other kabbalistic writings see Reuben Margaliot, *Sha'arey Zohar* (Jerusalem, 1957), 192. According to David Ibn Abi Zimra, the most celebrated rabbinic authority in the first half of the sixteenth century, delay of burial prevents the soul from entering into transmigration; see his *Metsudat David* (Zolkiew, 1862; reprinted in Israel, 1964), no. 552; *Responsa* (Warsaw, 1882), no. 1179.

32. See above, p. 215.

33. It appeared first in the *Rostocker Wanderer* (September, 1772); see *JubA,* 16:lxix.

34. See Silberstein, *ZGJD,* 1 (1929): 238–44.

35. For the bibliography on the burial issue see Moshe Pelli, *Moses Mendelssohn: Bonds of Tradition* (Israel, 1972), index, s.v. *halanat ha-metim* (Hebrew).

36. *JubA,* 7, 11; see above, p. 217.

37. Maimonides, *Mishne Tora, Hilkhot Melakhim,* 8:10. Cf. above, p. 217 f., where Mendelssohn's treatment of this theme is discussed in the context of his *Letter to Lavater.*

38. *JubA,* 7:10 f., 75 f.

39. Ferrara, 1556; republished Westmead, Farnborough, Hants., 1969 [no pagination or division into chapters], end of paragraph commencing: *ve-ha-kelal ha-'oleh.*

40. Maimonides seems to have relied on a rabbinic source which has come to light again only in recent times, viz. *Mishnat Rabbi Eli'ezer,* ed. H. Enelow (New York, 1934), 121; see Jacob Katz, *Exclusiveness and Tolerance* (Oxford, 1961), 175, note 5.

41. On Eberhard see above, p. 220.

42. See Julius Guttmann, *Dat U-Mada'* (Jerusalem, 1955), 200 f.; Katz, *Exclusiveness and Tolerance,* 174–77.

43. *Tosefta Sanhedrin* 13:2; *Sanhedrin* 105a.

44. *JubA,* 16, letter 155, p. 179–83.

The Chronicle Continued (pages 295–312)

1. Nicolai-Briefe, vol. 5.

2. Marburg File, no. 28.

3. Marburg File, nos. 28, 29.

4. Marburg File, nos. 31, 32.

5. See Friedrich Nicolai, *Leben und Meinungen des Herrn Magisters Sebaldus Nothanker,* ed. Heinz Stolpe (Berlin, 1960), 495 ff.

6. *GS,* 5:529 f.
7. *GS,* 5:532 f.
8. See below p. 332.
9. See Schneider, *Jerusalem Aufsätze,* 14.
10. Gotthold Ephraim Lessing, ed., *Philosophische Aufsätze von Karl Wilhelm Jerusalem* (Braunschweig, 1776), 113 f.
11. *GS,* 5:196 f. (L–M, 18, letter 477, p. 172). On Apr. 28, 1776, Lessing had sent three copies of Jerusalem's essays to his brother Karl: one for him, "the second for Herr Moses, with my regards," the third for Doctor Herz (L–M, 18, letter 463, p. 161 f.).
12. Herz' further critical remarks were dispatched to Lessing by his brother Karl on June 22, 1776 (L–M, 21, letter 644, p. 106). Herz had dealt with Jerusalem's theory of the sentiments in a letter to Lessing writen in the early spring of 1775. See Mendelssohn's references to this letter in his communication to the count of Schaumburg-Lippe *(GS,* 5:535 f.), which is to be dated May 20, 1775; see Bruno Strauss, "Drei ungenannte Empfänger Mendelssohnscher Briefe," *ZGJD,* 1 (1929): 246. Herz had had an opportunity to read Jerusalem's essays when Lessing sent the proofs to Mendelssohn before he went on his trip to Italy; see Heinrich Schneider, *Lessing* (Bern, 1951), 104. Lessing's letter to Marcus Herz, which accompanied the complimentary copy of the published essays sent through his brother on Apr. 28, 1776 (L–M, 18, no. 464; note 1), replied to Herz' criticism.
13. L–M, 21, letter 640, p. 103; see Schneider, *Lessing,* 105, 282; Idem, *Jerusalem Aufsätze,* 15.
14. See above, p. 282.
15. Flodoard Freiherr von Biedermann, "Zu Lessings Gesprächen," *Lessing-Buch,* ed. Josef Jellinek and Paul Alfred Merbach (Berlin, 1926), 15–20 (quoted by Schneider, *Lessing,* 37 f.).
16. Biedermann, *Gespräche,* 258 f.
17. See Bruno Strauss, "Drei ungenannte Empfänger Mendelssohnscher Briefe," *ZGJD,* 1 (1929): 245–49. For a biography of the count, see G. Jansen, *Rochus Friedrich Graf zu Lynar* (Oldenburg, 1873), and Anton Friedrich Büsching, *Beyträge zu der Lebensgeschichte denkwürdiger Personen . . . ,* 4 (Halle, 1786): 73–218.
18. See *GS,* 5:534 f.
19. 26:277–81; reproduced in *GS,* 4.2:561–64.
20. Dep. RvM, C II, No. 11; published by Bruno Strauss, *Drei ungenannte Empfänger,* 247 f.
21. Bruno Strauss identified the count of Lynar as the addressee of the letter (reproduced on p. 245), which was first published in 1858 (see ibid.), and subsequently published by Kayserling, *Mendelssohn,* 1st ed., 552 ff. and in *JubA,* 3.1:315 ff.
22. The term used by Mendelssohn is *Genie* (Baumgarten's *ingenium;* see *Frühschriften,* 351). Cf. *JubA,* 3.1:451, where the closeness of the term to the French *génie* is stressed, and a number of references to Mendelssohn's use of it are given. We might paraphrase the present passage: The ideas have to be congenial to a man's personality.
23. See *JubA,* 3.1:462 (317.5)
24. Nicolai-Briefe, vol. 46.
25. The count's *Miscellanies* could not be traced.
26. See below, note 28.
27. Marburg File, no. 32.
28. *GS,* 5:534 ff. The date (May, 20, 1775) has been established by Bruno Strauss *(Drei ungenannte Empfänger,* p. 246) from the original letter in the Schaumburg-Lippe Princely House Archive, Bückeburg.
29. See *JubA,* 3.1:385. It seems that Mendelssohn requested the copy from Nicolai for his own use and sent the original of the essay to the count, who possibly returned it to him after his secretary had made a copy.
30. See above, p. 178.
31. *GS,* 5:533 f. The date is found in the count's reply of Mar. 9, 1775 *(LBH,* 3:93, no. 4540).
32. See *LBH,* 3:43, no. 4540.
33. *GS,* 5:530 (Oct. 3, 1774).
34. See *ADB, s. v.* Platner, Ernst P.
35. Dep. RvM, C II, no. 25.
36. Dep. RvM, C II, no. 26.

37. Dep. RvM, C II, no. 27.

38. Marburg File, nos. 26, 33, 42.

39. Moses Mendelssohn Autograph I/599, Staatsbibliothek Stiftung Preussischer Kultur-besitz, Berlin.

40. Marburg File. no. 34.

41. *JubA*, 3.1:273 f.

42. See above, p. 70 f.

43. The three entries are reproduced in *JubA*, 3.1:273–77.

44. *Philosophische Versuche über die menschliche Natur und ihre Entwicklung* (Leipzig, 1776), 625 ff.

45. Fritz Bamberger (ed.), *Moses Mendelssohn: Denkmal der Freundschaft* (Berlin, 1929), folio 8.

46. Ibid., folios 13, 16; see Bamberger's note on folio 8; *GS*, 5:389; 2:300.

47. Lecture 7, end *(GS,* 2:300).

48. See Wilhelm Windelband, *Lehrbuch der Geschichte der Philosophie* (ed. H. Heimsoeth), (Tübingen, 1957), 15th ed., 438.

49. *JubA*, 16, letter 191, p. 215.

50. *JubA*, 16, letter 193, p. 216.

51. *JubA*, 16, letter 195, p. 219.

52. *JubA*, 16, letter 198, p. 225.

53. *JubA*, 16, letters 197–200, pp. 224–27, 229.

54. *JubA*, 16, letter 244, p. 276; Kayserling, *Mendelssohn*, 1st ed., 504.

55. *JubA*, 16, letter 200, p. 229; Kayserling, *Mendelssohn*, 259.

56. *JubA*, 16, letter 196, p. 220 f.

57. *JubA*, 16, letter 200, p. 229.

58. Kant, *Werke*, 9:158.

59. *Hamann Briefwechsel*, 3:365.

60. Ibid., 3:375.

61. Ibid.

62. Ibid.

63. "Abschiedsgruss an Moses Mendelssohn," *Königsbergische Gelehrte und Politische Zeitung* ("Kantersche Zeitung"), Aug. 21, 1777, no. 67:266.

64. *JubA,* 16, letter 203, p. 233.

65. The entire documentation of the case is found in Ludwig Ernst Borowski (ed.), *Moses Moses Mendelssohns und Georg David Kypkes Aufsätze über jüdische Gebete und Festfeiern* (Königsberg, 1791). Mendelssohn's testimonial is reproduced on pp. 53–62; it is reprinted in *GS,* 6:418–24. See also L. Geiger, *Geschichte der Juden in Berlin,* (Berlin, 1871), 2:133; B[enjamin] H[irsch] Auerbach, *Geschichte der israelitischen Gemeinde Halberstadt* (Halberstadt, 1866), 167 ff., 185.

66. Joseph ben Abraham Haltern (1737–1818) became a contributor to *Ha-Me'assef.* He translated poems by Gellert, Lessing, Ramler a.o. into Hebrew, See *JubA,* 16:xcix.

67. L–M, 18, letter 577, p. 254 f.

68. L–M, 21, letter 726, p. 178 ff.

69. L–M, 18, letter 577, p. 255.

70. L–M, 21, letter 729, p. 179 f.; concerning the letter to Nicolai see L–M, 18:256, note 2.

71. "Ernst und Falk. Gespräche für Freymäurer," L–M, 13:339–68; 387–411; 15:484–90.

72. See Heinrich Schneider, *Lessing,* 185 f.

73. See above, p. 279.

74. Karl G. Lessing, *G. E. Gotthold Ephraim Lessings Leben . . . ,* 1 (Berlin, 1793) 299 f.; quoted by Kayserling, *Mendelssohn,* 263 f. The conversation must be dated July, 1773 (not 1777), as Schneider, *Lessing,* 182 f. has shown.

75. Our account of Lessing and Freemasonry is based on Schneider, *Lessing,* 166–86.

76. See Jacob Katz, *Jews and Freemasons in Europe, 1723–1939* (Cambridge, Mass., 1970), 25. For the Masonic career of Ephraim Hirschel, see below p. 352.

77. *GS,* 4.2:561 f.

78. See Schneider, *Lessing,* 173.

79. Ibid., 178.

80. Ibid., 185. See below, p. 559 f.

81. L–M, 21, letter 727, p. 179 f.

82. A further passage of this letter is quoted below, p. 559 f.
83. L–M, 21, letter 729, p. 183.
84. L–M, 18, letter 583, p. 258.
85. See Schneider, *Lessing,* 278, note 23.
86. See above, p. 273.
87. Kayserling, *Ungedrucktes,* 61.

Some Philosophical Preoccupations (pages 313–329)

1. *Betrachtungen über das Universum* (Erfurt, 1777; 6th edition: Mannheim, 1819).
2. See *GS,* 5:540, note; Jakob Müller, *Carl Theodor von Dalberg, der letzte deutsche Fürstbischof* (Würzburg, 1874).
3. The letter is lost, but its main content can be reconstructed from Mendelssohn's reply, *GS,* 5:536–39.
4. *Hamann Briefwechsel,* 3:372.
5. The autograph of Mendelssohn's letter is extant in the Staatsbibliothek Stiftung Preussischer Kulturbesitz, Berlin (1:418). It is dated June 10, not June 9, as given in *GS,* 5:536, and a comparison of the autograph with the text printed in *GS,* 5:536–39 shows that the editor allowed himself considerable freedom in changing the wording.
6. *GS,* 5:540.
7. See Bruno Masch, *Karl von Dalbergs Philosophie des Universums,* Dissertation Bonn (Bonn, 1929), 15–58.
8. See above, p. 59; *Frühschriften,* 122 f.
9. *GS,* 3:360.
10. I have not been able to establish whether Dalberg incorporated Mendelssohn's remarks in the next or any subsequent edition of his work.
11. Dep. RvM, C II, no. 45.
12. Concerning de Luc's letters to Zimmermann, see *JubA,* 3.1:xxxviii.
13. The Hague & Paris, 1779. Zimmermann's letter makes it clear that from the very start de Luc had intended to incorporate his *Traité* in the *Lettres.* Originally, they were to form an appendix. Later he decided to make the *Traité* part of the *discours* of the *Lettres.* The description given in *JubA,* 3.1:xxxix is not entirely correct.
14. Quoted in French by Zimmermann.
15. Dep. RvM, C II, no. 46.
16. Quoted in French by Zimmermann. The text of the letter (dated Dec. 16, 1778) has been published by Eduard Bodemann, *Zimmermann . . .* (Hanover, 1878), 68. On Oct. 31, 1777, Zimmermann had written to de Luc: "Je viens de voir et j'aurai cette après-dinée chez moi le plus grand philosophe de l'Allemagne, Mr. Moise Mendelssohn. Voilà un homme qui m'entend et qui m'a expliqué en deux mots pourquoi les plus grands physiciens n'entendent jamais ou rarement un médecin" (Bodemann, ibid.).
17. *GS,* 5:550.
18. See *GS,* 5:550, note 1. The text appeared first in *GS,* 4.1:124–27, and is reproduced in *JubA,* 3.1:197–99.
19. See *JubA,* 3.1:428.
20. *JubA,* 3.1:176 ff., 180, 429.
21. *GS,* 3:385–99.
22. See *JubA,* 3.1:xxxix.
23. *GS,* 5:552–54.
24. *JubA,* 3.1:xxxix.
25. Johann Caspar Lavater, *Physiognomische Fragmente, zur Beförderung der Menschenkenntniss und Menschenliebe* (Leipzig & Winterthur, 1775–1778); English translation: *Essays on Physiognomy,* trans. by T. Holcroft, 4 vols. (1804).
26. Part four, book 18 (Inselverlag edition of Goethe's works, 3:773 ff.).
27. See *JubA,* 3.1:xlix.
28. See Werner Milch, *Die Einsamkeit, Zimmermann und Obereit im Kampf um die Überwindung der Aufklärung* (Frauenfeld-Leipzig, 1937), 145.
29. See Leo Weisz, "Georg Christoph Lichtenberg und Johann Caspar Lavater, I. Die Judentaufen," *NZZ,* Apr. 1, 1962, no. 1279/2.
30. See *JubA,* 3.1:xlix–l.
31. See Milch, *Die Einsamkeit,* 145 f.

32. See *GS*, 5:546.

33. For a full account of the controversy see Franz H. Mautner, *Lichtenberg, Geschichte seines Geistes* (Berlin, 1968), 179–208.

34. *GS*, 5:548; Dep. RvM, C II, No. 45, p. 3; *JubA*, 3.1:liii f.

35. See below, p. 334 f. (Hennings report to Elise Reimarus); *JubA*, 3.1:lv.

36. They were published by L. F. G. von Göckingk in his *Friedrich Nicolai's Leben und literarischer Nachlass* (Berlin, 1820), 184–96 (omitting three paragraphs that were quoted by Nicolai in his review of Lavater's work in *Allgemeine deutsche Bibliothek*, 29.2:386–400; see *JubA*, 3.1:liv f.). The entire essay is reproduced in *JubA*, 3.1:321–28. From Mendelssohn's note to Nicolai on Feb. 19, 1777 it appears that the essay was written in the early part of 1777. This assumption tallies with Nicolai's remark in a letter to Lichtenberg dated Apr. 15, 1778 (see *JubA*, 3.1:liv) that Mendelssohn's essay had been written "a year and a half ago."

37. The use of the term "machine" for organic beings, which goes back to La Mettrie's "L'Homme-Machine," became popular even among opponents of materialism. See *Moses Mendelssohn an die Freunde Lessings* (Berlin, 1786), p.v: "his so infirm, so unfortunately constructed machine" (Engel's preface about Mendelssohn).

38. *JubA*, 3.1:325 f.

39. *JubA*, 3.1:328. Lichtenberg agreed with Mendelssohn's distinction between the pleasant beauty of lines and proportions *(Verhältnisschönheit)* and beauty as signifying inner qualities *(Ausdrucksschönheit)*. See Mautner, *Lichtenberg*, 194 f.

40. First published in *JubA*, 3.1:287 ff.; see xlvi f., 384.

41. Johann Caspar Lavater, *Physiognomische Fragmente*, 1st ed. (Leipzig & Winterthur, 1775), 243 f.

42. See Boie's letter to a friend (Jan. 1, 1778) in Geiger, *Briefe*, 123 f.

43. See *JubA*, 3.1:li–lv.

44. 29.2:379 ff.

45. See *JubA*, 3.1:liv f.

46. Geiger, *Briefe*, 124.

47. Dep. RvM, C II, no. 45.

48. Dep. RvM, C II, no. 46.

49. *GS*, 5:546–50.

50. See Fritz Bamberger's observation, *JubA*, 3.1:liv.

51. *JubA*, 3.1:lvi f.

52. Dep. RvM, C II, no. 37.

53. "Das Daseyn Gottes *a priori* erwiesen," Dep. RvM, B II, no. 11.

54. [Johann Daniel Schumann,] *Neue Bestätigung des Schlusses von der Möglichkeit des allervollkommensten Wesens auf dessen Wirklichkeit nebst einigen Erinnerungen gegen Mendelssohn's neue Wendung dieses Beweises* (Clausthal, 1771). Schumann's authorship is attested by Johann Georg Meusel, *Lexikon der vom Jahr 1750 bis 1800 verstorbenen Teutschen Schriftsteller*, 12 (Leipzig, (1812): 558. The essay was reviewed in the *Allgemeine deutsche Bibliothek*, 21:1 (1774): 208–10. The reviewer pointed out that the "unnamed author" had failed to invalidate Mendelssohn's proof. It may be safely assumed that Mendelssohn was aware of the identity of the author.

55. *Über die Evidenz der Beweise für die Wahrheit der christlichen Religion* (Hanover, 1778). The work actually appeared in 1777, as is evident from the fact that Lessing's reply came out in that year.

56. "Über den Beweis des Geistes und der Kraft, An den Herrn Direktor Schumann zu Hannover," *Lessing Gesammelte Werke*, ed. Paul Rilla (Berlin, 1956), 8:9 ff. Schumann replied to Lessing in *Antwort auf das aus Braunschweig an ihn gerichtete Schreiben über den Beweis des Geistes und der Kraft* (Hanover, 1778). Lessing took no notice of this rejoinder.

57. *Zur elementarischen Bibliothek. Das Methodenbuch für Väter und Mütter der Familien und Völker* (Altona & Bremen, 1770; 2nd ed. 1772; 3rd ed. 1773).

58. See Hugo Göring (ed.), *J. B. Basedows Ausgewählte Schriften* (Langensalza, 1880), 150, note 1 [editor's note]. Mendelssohn's name is mentioned in a more general context together with Bonnet, Reimarus, and [Johann Friedrich Wilhelm] Jerusalem (p. 147).

59. Dep. RvM, C I, no. 3.

60. Basedow asked Mendelssohn in the same letter to inform some friends that they could obtain copies of the "beginning of the work" (viz. the *Elementarwerk)* and copper-plates from the publisher, Mylius, in case they wished to promote its sale. The *Elementarwerk* appeared in 1774. Hence the letter could not have been written before 1774.

61. Kant, *Werke*, 9:78.
62. Dep. RvM, D I, no. 2.
63. See *Biografisch woordenboeck van Protestantsche godgeleerden in Nederland*, ed. J. P. de Bie and J. Loosjes (The Hague, 1931), 412–18.
64. *GS*, 5:550 f.
65. For the above information and a xerographic copy of the volume concerned I am indebted to Dr. A. J. W. Huisman, librarian of the Bibliotheek der Rijksuniversiteit te Leiden.
66. "Argumenti, quo Cartesius, eumque secuti Existentiam Dei A priori ex idea entis perfectissimi ac necessarii probare conati sunt, Modesta Disquisitio."
67. *Dissertationes . . . Legati Stolpiani . . .*, 2:7: Johann Albert Fabricius, *Delectus argumentorum & syllabus scriptorum, qui veritatem religionis Christianae adseruerunt*, chap. 10, p. 325 ff.
68. *Dissertationes . . .*, 10.
69. *Dissertationes*, p. 50, line 10 – p. 51, line 25 is a Latin version of *JubA*, 2, p. 300, line 4 – p. 301, line 9; *Dissertationes*, p. 56, line 6 – p. 57, line 10 renders *JubA*, 2, p. 301, line 11 – line 39.
70. *Dissertationes*, 52 f.
71. *GS*, 5:551.
72. The essay is found on pp. 207–86 of *Dissertationes*, 2, and is entitled: "Onderzoek, om Gods Bestaan van vooren te betoogen, zynde een Antwoord, aan de Heeren Bestuurders van 't Stolpiaans Legaat, op the Vraag: Kan, uit het Denkbeeld van een Noodzaakelyk Wezen, 't week de voorheen bewezene Eigenschappen bezit, deszelfs dadelyk Bestaan van vooren (a priori) worden betoogd?"
73. Page 244 f.
74. *GS*, 5: 551.
75. Ibid.
76. Bodemann, *Zimmermann*, 288–90; Kayserling, *Ungedrucktes*, 13 ff. The original of the letter is found in the Niedersächsische Landesbibliothek, Hanover, Letters by Mendelssohn to Zimmermann, fol. 4r–5r.
77. Dep. RvM, C II, no. 44 (Zimmermann to Mendelssohn, January 1778).
78. *GS*, 4.1:120; facsimile reproduction in Fritz Bamberger, *Denkmal der Freundschaft*, fol. 9 (see note). The original is now owned by Professor Robert Alexander Bohnke, Tübingen (a great grandson of Joseph Mendelssohn).
79. Marburg File, no. 43.
80. Dep. RvM, C II, no. 22 (Sept. 4, 1778).
81. See Meyer, *Bibliographie*, 177 ff.
82. *GS*, 1:36. See Joseph's letter to his nephew Felix Mendelssohn Bartholdy, published by Alexander Altmann in *BLBI*, 11, no. 42 (1968): 83.
83. The painting is owned by Dr. Cécile Lowenthal-Hensel, Berlin.

Friends in Unexpected Quarters (pages 329–345)

1. See Joachim Hild, *August Hennings, ein schleswig-holsteinscher Publizist um die Wende des 18. Jahrhunderts* (Erlangen, 1932), 22. On the interval of a year between the date of Reimarus' letter of introduction and its presentation by Hennings see *GS*, 5:532.
2. Dep. RvM, C II, no. 29.
3. A reference to Mendelssohn's letters *On The Sentiments;* see above, p. 62–65 and *Frühschriften*, 138–83.
4. Dep. RvM, C I, no. 19 (Jan. 6, 1775).
5. Nachlass Hennings, no. 22, letter 1, fol. 2r; *GS*, 5:532 (Jan. 20, 1775).
6. See note 1 above.
7. See Max Grunwald, "August von Hennings, der Freund Moses Mendelssohns," *Jahrbuch für Jüdische Geschichte and Literatur*, 11 (1908): 128 f. On Voltaire's anti-Semitism see Arthur Hertzberg, *The French Enlightenment and the Jews* (New York, 1968).
8. See Hild, *Hennings*, 1–22.
9. See Grunwald, *August von Hennings*, 130 f.
10. Dep. RvM, C I, no. 19 (Jan. 6, 1775).
11. For this phrase see *GS*, 4.1:89; *JubA*, 2:415.
12. See above, p. 297 f.
13. Nachlass Hennings, no. 32, p. 539 (quoted by Hild, *Hennings*, 24, note 44). For Hennings' reaction to *Werther*, see Hild, ibid.

14. Geiger, *Briefe*, 123 f.

15. Nachlass Hennings, no. 45, fol. 112*v*–113*r*.

16. Ibid., 128*v*. At this writing, an edition of Elise Reimarus' correspondence with Hennings is being prepared by Dr. Eva Horvath, Hamburg. I am obliged to Dr. Horvath for having permitted me to consult the Nachlass Hennings, No. 45 (the Dresden–Hamburg letters), on which she was working at the time of my visit to the State and University Library, Hamburg.

17. See above, p. 74.

18. L–M, 19:408–12.

19. Lessing had sent Dr. Reimarus a copy of his *Berengarius Turonensis* (1770).

20. See above p. 253 f.

21. See above, p. 254 ff.

22. Dr. Reimarus' letter to Lessing was written in November or December, 1770. In November, 1770, Mendelssohn wrote to Lessing that he had not yet found the time to read the manuscript (see *GS*, 5:184 f.).

23. See Hild, *Hennings*, 24 ff.

24. See Dep. RvM, C I, no. 20 (Mar. 7, 1775) and no. 21 (Mar. 14, 1775).

25. Dep. RvM, C I, No. 23; Nachlass Hennings, no. 22, letter 2, fol. 2*v*–3*r* (copy).

26. Nachlass Hennings, no. 22, letter 3, fol. 4*r*–*v;* Kayserling, *Mendelssohn*, 1st ed., 520.

27. Nachlass Hennings, no. 45, letter 14, fol. 42*r*.

28. Ibid., letter 16, fol. 48*r*.

29. Ibid., letter 28, fol. 98*v*–99*r*.

30. Hennings disagreed with him both politically and philosophically; see Hild, *Hennings*, 31 f. and *passim*.

31. Nachlass Hennings, no. 45, letter 33, fol. 113*r*.

32. Lavater, *Physiognomische Fragmente* 2 (1776): 53: "in *Basedow*—den unverdrossnen, redlichen, thätigen, tiefen Durchforscher? die Leibwache der Vernunft?"

33. Nachlass Hennings, no. 45, letter 36, fol. 126*r*–127*r* (Aug. 21, 1776).

34. Lichtenberg's essay in the *Almanach*, in which he first indicated his critical attitude, appeared in October, 1777. See above, p. 317 f.

35. Dep. RvM, C I, no. 24; Nachlass Hennings, no. 22, letter 4, fol. 5*r*–7*r* (copy).

36. Albrecht von Haller, *Briefe über einige noch lebenden Freygeister Einwürfe wider die Offenbarung*, Part 1 (Bern, 1775). Parts 2 and 3 appeared in 1776; a revised edition of all three parts (containing 22 letters) was published in 1778.

37. New ed. (1771); see Haller, *Briefe* (1778), letter 1, p. 11.

38. Nachlass Hennings, no. 45, letter 33, fol. 113*r*.

39. See Haller, *Briefe* (1778), letter 13, p. 92; letter 16, p. 194 ff., 197; and passim.

40. J. G. Zimmermann, *Das Leben des Herrn von Haller* (Zürich, 1755).

41. Kayserling, *Ungedrucktes*, 15; the original is found in the Niedersächsische Landesbibliothek, Hanover, Letters of Mendelssohn to Zimmermann, fol. 5*r*.

42. Dep. RvM, C II, no. 45 (Mar. 3, 1778).

43. *GS*, 5:549 (May 12, 1778).

44. See Werner Milch, *Die Einsamkeit, Zimmermann und Obereit . . .* (Frauenfeld-Leipzig, 1937), 144.

45. *Gedichte von einem pohlnishen Juden* (published anonymously in Mietau & Leipzig, 1772; 96 pp.); *Anhang zu den Gedichten eines pohlnischen Juden* (Mietau & Leipzig, 1772; 32 pp.).

46. L–M, 20, letter 400, p. 57.

47. See Daniel Jacoby, "Ein jüdischer Dichter des 18. Jahrhunderts," *AZJ*, 64 (1900): 356 f.

48. Quoted ibid.

49. Goethe, Inselverlag edition of his works, 12:45–47.

50. *JubA*, 16, letter 140, p. 169. The conjecture that Behr was a relative of Fromet (*JubA*, 16:lxx) is not supported by any evidence.

51. See *EJ*, 6:915 f.; Jacobi, *Ein jüdischer Dichter*, fails to mention his conversion and gives 1781 as the year of his death. The latter event occurred in 1817.

52. *Gedichte von einem pohlnischen Juden*, 68 f.

53. Kayserling, *Mendelssohn*, 203, quotes the stanza mentioning Cerberus and suggests that it refers to Kölbele.

54. Nachlass Hennings, no. 45, letter 36, fol. 125*v*–127*v*.

55. Hennings misspelled the name "Meinert." Christoph Meiners (1747–1810) was a pro-

fessor in Göttingen. He published a digest of psychology (1773), a history of religion entitled *Versuch über die Religionsgeschichte der ältesten Völker, besonders der Egyptier* (Göttingen, 1775), and a 2-volume history of the sciences in ancient Greece and Rome (Lemgo, 1781). All three works were in Mendelssohn's library (see *Verzeichnis*, pp. 23, 36, 37).

56. What Mendelssohn may have alluded to was the passage in David Hume, *Essays and Treatises on Several Subjects*, 4, new ed. (London, 1760): 272 in the essay, "The Natural History of Religion," sect. iv: "The only point of theology in which we shall find a consent of mankind almost universal, is, that there is invisible, intelligent power in the world. But whether this power be supreme or subordinate, whether confined to one being, or distributed among several . . . , there is the widest difference in the popular systems of theology."

57. See *Frühschriften*, 228 f.

58. Johann Georg Palitzsch (1723–1788), a Saxon farmer who had acquired, through self-study, a high degree of scientific knowledge, particularly in astronomy, and became a corresponding member of the St. Petersburg Academy and the London Royal Astronomical Society. He constructed astronomical instruments for his own use, cultivated a botanical garden, and was also quite at home in Wolff's philosophy (see *ADB*, 25:80 f.).

59. Adrian Z. Zingg (1734–1816), a draughtsman and engraver, had been appointed professor of engraving and member of the Academy of Arts in Dresden. He enjoyed a considerable reputation among his contemporaries (see *ADB*, 45:323). His drawing of Mendelssohn is mentioned nowhere except here.

60. Nachlass Hennings, no. 45, letter 38, fol. 129*v*–130*r*.

61. Moses Mendelssohn and the "prophet" Lessing.

62. Nachlass Hennings, no. 45, letter 41, fol. 138*v*.

63. Ibid., letter 42, fol. 146*r*–148*v*.

64. Johann Esaias Silberschlag (1716–1791), a Protestant preacher of traditional piety who was opposed to all reform but also cultivated the natural sciences (see *ADB*, 34:314 ff.).

65. One might have expected some mention of Mendelssohn's latest definition of the beautiful as that which is "approved" without being an object of desire (see above, p. 304 f). Mendelssohn apparently failed to bring it up in his conversations with Hennings.

66. See *Sallustius Concerning the Gods and the Universe*, ed. with prolegomena & translation by Arthur Darby Nock (Cambridge, 1926), p. 14 ff. (no. 8). Hennings will have used the French translation by J. H. S. Formey (Berlin, 1748); see Nock, p. cxxii, where this version (which is accompanied by the Greek text) is mentioned.

67. See Hild, *Hennings*, 41.

68. *Über die Vernunft* (Berlin, 1778). For the biographical data, see Hild, *Hennings*, 30–34.

69. Nachlass Hennings, no. 79, fol. 23*r* f.

70. See above, pp. 309–12.

71. Nachlass Hennings no. 79, fol. 27*r*.

72. Nachlass Hennings no. 22, letter 5, fol. 7*r*–8*r*; reproduced by L. Geiger, *ZGJD*, 1 (1887):112.

73. Nachlass Hennings, no. 79, fol. 39*r*.

74. Nachlass Hennings, no. 22, letter 5, fol. 7*v*–8*r*; Geiger, *ZGJD* 1 (1887):112.

75. Nachlass Hennings, no. 22, letter 6, fol. 8*r*–*v*.

76. Nachlass Hennings, no. 79, fol. 80*v*.

77. Nachlass Hennings, no. 79, fol. 107*v*.

78. Dep. RvM, C I, no. 25.

79. Nachlass Hennings, no. 79, fol. 72*r*.

80. August Hennings, *Olavides, herausgegeben und mit einigen Anmerkungen über Duldung und Vorurtheile begleitet* (Copenhagen, 1779).

81. See Hild, *Hennings*, 36–45.

82. Ibid., 45–48.

83. Dep. RvM, C I, no. 26.

84. Nachlass Hennings, no. 22, letter 8, fol. 11*r*–*v*; reproduced in Kayserling, *Mendelssohn*, 1st ed., 522.

85. Bloch, *Medicinische Bemerkungen* (Berlin, 1774), 63; reported in Mendelssohn's name by Zimmermann, *Über die Einsamkeit*, 3 (Leipzig, 1785): 182.

86. Marburg File, no. 34.

87. Nachlass Hennings no. 22, letter 3, fol. 4*v*–5*r*; see Kayserling, *Mendelssohn*, 1st ed., 520.

Chapter Five: The Teacher
The Avant-Garde of Haskala (pages 346–368)

1. Mordecai Gumpel (Levison) was one such exception. See Heinz Moshe Graupe, "Mordechai Gumpel (Levison)," *BLBI*, 5, no. 17 (1962): 4–5.

2. *JubA*, 11, letter 88, p. 189.

3. See Josef Meisl, *Protokollbuch der jüdischen Gemeinde zu Berlin* (Jerusalem, 1962), 516; Lewin, *JJLG*, 15:73; *JubA*, 11:452 ff.

4. See above, p. 267, 323; for his biography see the fragment of the story of his life and illness written by himself shortly before his death and published in *LBH*, 2:100 ff., no. 1899; *Sulamith* (ed. David Fränkel), 3.2 (1811): 77–97.

5. Fritz Bamberger, *Moses Mendelssohn. Denkmal der Freundschaft* (Berlin, 1929), fol. 5.

6. Kant, *Werke*, 9:77 ff.

7. Ibid., 90. Another paragraph of the same letter has been quoted above, p. 267 f.

8. Quoted by Meyer, *Bibliographie*, 78, from *Sulamith* (see above, note 4).

9. The reference is to Christian Gottlieb Selle (1748–1800), author of *Philosophische Gespräche* (Berlin, 1780).

10. Kant, *Werke*, 9:194 f.

11. It is incomplete and undated; see ibid., 197 ff.

12. Ibid., 198.

13. Nicolaus Tetens (1736–1805).

14. See Max Dessoir, *Geschichte der neueren deutschen Psychologie* (1902), 233–38 and passim.

15. Berlin, 1777.

16. Kant, *Werke*, 9:159.

17. For a discussion and bibliography on the much debated question of authorship, see Salo W. Baron, *A Social and Religious History of the Jews*, 8 (New York, 1958): 239, and 391, note 23; J. Pagel, "Maimuni als medizinischer Schriftsteller," *Moses Ben Maimon*, ed. W. Bacher, M. Brann, D. Simonsen, 1 (Leipzig, 1908): 244.

18. 1 (1783):43 ff.

19. Published in *Berlinische Monatsschrift*, 24: 335–39.

20. *GS*, 5:555 (Feb. 11, 1780).

21. *GS*, 5:556 ff. (Feb. 14, 1780).

22. *GS*, 5:558–62 (Feb. 28 and Mar. 3, 1780).

23. *GS*, 5:589–97 (undated); *JubA*, 3.1:353 f.; see the editor's note, *GS*, 5:589; also *JubA*, 3.1:lxiii.

24. *JubA*, 3.1:354.

25. Kant, *Werke*, 9:179. Cf. L–M, 21:234: "D. Herz liest jetzt ein Collegium über Logik und Metaphysik, das der Minister von Zedlitz, einige Räthe und viele andere Männer und junge Leute hören."

26. Included by Johann Jacob Engel in his preface to *Mendelssohn an die Freunde Lessings* (Berlin, 1786), xii–xxii.

27. An enlarged edition of the treatise appeared as a separate publication (Berlin, 1788). See Meyer, *Bibliographie*, p. 97, no. 538. It was published in Euchel's Hebrew translation under the title *Mikhtav ol Mehabrey Ha-Me'assef* (Berlin, 1789).

28. Kant, *Werke*, 9:342.

29. See the biography by Ludwig Geiger in *ADB*, 7:393–99.

30. See J. A. Ebert's letter to Lessing, dated Oct. 21, 1770 (L–M, 19, letter 333, p. 397).

31. Kayserling, *Mendelssohn*, 220 f. The "Herr Friedländer" mentioned in Ebert's letter was probably a Jewish resident of Brunswick.

32. Kant, *Werke*, 9:79 f.

33. Ibid., 99.

34. Ibid., 151, 233, 284.

35. See Euchel, *Toledot*, 6; L.F.G. von Göckingk, *Friedrich Nicolai's Leben* . . . (Berlin, 1820), 146, note (quoted above, p. 9); *Frühschriften*, 209.

36. See above, p. 181.

37. See Meyer, *Bibliographie*, p. 40, nos. 154, 156. Friedländer sent copies to Goethe and Zelter (see Kayserling, *Mendelssohn*, 427, note 3).

38. See Meyer, *Bibliographie*, 10.

39. Ibid.; Simon Rawidowicz, "Mendelssohns handschriftliche Glossen zum More Nebukim," *MGWJ*, 78, n.s. 42 (1934): 195 ff.

40. 8:523–50. The essay contains a commentary on Ps. 110. A scrutiny of Mendelssohn's translation and Friedländer's commentary was published by Christian Gottlieb Perschke (Berlin, 1788); see Meyer, *Bibliographie*, p. 59, no. 317.

41. See Meyer, *Bibliographie*, p. 49, no. 233; p. 63, no. 359c.

42. 3.3 (Berlin, 1800): 132–47; rev. ed. 1 (Berlin, 1801): 315–34. Mendelssohn's *Proben rabbinischer Weisheit* appeared in 3.2 (1800): 49–64; revised edition 1 (1801): 295–314. Friedländer actually continued Mendelssohn's *Proben*.

43. See Meyer, *Bibliographie*, p. 74 f., no. 411. 34, 36, 45.

44. 21(1809): 28–35; see Meyer, *Bibliographie*, p. 77, no. 417. 20.

45. The letter is addressed to Moses Moser (1797–1838), one of the founders of the Verein für Kultur und Wissenschaft des Judentums, and a friend of Heinrich Heine; it was published by Albert Wolf in *MGWJ*, 50, n.s. 14 (1906): 370–73.

46. He is discussed below, p. 352–54.

47. See Klausner, *Historiya*, 1:165.

48. *Zeh Sefer Zekher Tsaddik* (Amsterdam, 1909).

49. See Jacob Katz, "Moses Mendelssohn und E. J. Hirschfeld," BLBI, 7, no. 28 (1964): 295–311; Idem, *Jews and Freemasons in Europe, 1723–1939* (Cambridge, Mass., 1970), 27–53 and passim.

50. Kayserling, *Mendelssohn*, 335, described Mendelssohn as having suggested the creation of the school, whereas J. M. Jost, *Geschichte des Judenthums und seiner Sekten*, 3 (Leipzig, 1859), 317, wrote: "How far Mendelssohn participated in it we do not know. We find neither him nor Wessely mentioned in this connection, but both undoubtedly approved the enterprise."

51. See Moritz Steinschneider, "Hebräische Drucke in Deutschland," ZGJD, 5 (1892): 166.

52. See Mordechai Eliav, *Ha-Hinukh Ha-Yehudi Be-Germaniya Bi-Tekufat Ha-Haskala Ve-Ha-Emantsipatsia* (Jerusalem, 1960), 67, 79.

53. See Steinschneider, "Hebräische Drucke," 165 f., 171. A facsimile reproduction of the *Lesebuch* was published by the Soncino-Gesellschaft, Berlin, 1927 (see Meyer, *Bibliographie*, p. 53, nos. 259, 260).

54. See Steinschneider, "Hebräische Drucke," 168.

55. Ibid., 167.

56. Ibid., 162. Satanov's works are listed in chronological order on pp. 162–82. Klausner, *Historiya*, 1:169–77, presents them in systematic order.

57. For the biographical data mentioned see Klausner, *Historiya*, 1:165–69. Satanov died on Dec. 25, 1804 (not in 1805, as stated by Klausner); see Steinschneider, "Hebräische Drucke," 162.

58. Beer-Bing's Hebrew translation of the *Phaedon* and Friedländer's edition of the *Sefer Ha-Nefesh* appeared as late as 1787.

59. *Sefer Ha-Middot*, 143.

60. Satanov published these works in Koretz. He seems to have returned to Podolia in 1780 and to have stayed there for at least two years. See Klausner, *Historiya*, 1:166. Steinschneider, "Hebräische Drucke," 163, found it "incomprehensible" that the two works appeared in Koretz.

61. Klausner, *Historiya*, 1:170 f.; Steinschneider, "Hebräische Drucke," 167, 169 f.

62 Steinschneider, "Hebräische Drucke," 164, 170 f.

63. "Hebräische Drucke," 162 f.; Klausner, too, found mitigating circumstances in judging the man; see *Historiya*, 1:63 f.

64. *Toledot*, new edition (Vienna, 1814), 139 (quoted by Klausner, *Historiya*, 1:166, note 4).

65. See B.H. Auerbach, *Geschichte der israelitischen Gemeinde Halberstadt* (Halberstadt, 1866), 179, quoting Dubno's letter to Wolf Heidenheim. Cf. below, p. 403 f.

66. *Sefer Mirkevet Mishne 'al Ha-Rambam* (Frankfurt an der Oder, 1751).

67. Frankfurt an der Oder, 1766; see Steinschneider, "Hebräische Drucke," 168.

68. See Gershom Scholem, "Shetey Ha-'Eduyot Ha-Ri'shonot 'al Havurot Ha-Hasidim Ve-Ha-Besht," *Tarbits*, 20 (1949): 228–40, where the significance of Solomon Helma's work, and likewise of Moses Satanov's *Mishmeret Ha-Kodesh*, for our knowledge of the earliest phase of Hasidism is discussed.

69. See Isaac Eisenstein-Barzilay, "The Background of the Berlin Haskala," *Essays on Jewish Life and Thought Presented in Honor of Salo Wittmayer Baron* (New York, 1959), 184.

70. See the letter to Heidenheim, quoted by Auerbach, *Geschichte*, 182 f.

71. The first edition had appeared in Amsterdam, 1743. For an evaluation of this work see Fischel Lachower, *Toledot Ha-Sifrut Ha-'Ivrit Ha-Hadasha,* 1 (Tel-Aviv, 1946): 34 ff.

72. Kayserling, *Mendelssohn,* 1st ed., 549.

73. *JubA,* 14:243.

74. In 1780, when Joseph was ten years old, he received lessons from Dubno only once a week, on Fridays. See *JubA,* 16, letter 237, p. 260.

75. *JubA,* 16, letter 193, p. 216; letter 196, p. 222.

76. *JubA,* 16, letter 202, p. 231 f.; letter 204, p. 234 f.

77. *JubA,* 16, letter 118, p. 139.

78. Kayserling, *Mendelssohn,* 304, note 1 denied Mendelssohn's authorship of the riddle. He was obviously unaware of Dubno's reply. See also Haim Bar-Dayan's (Borodianski's) additional note to *JubA,*14:cii, line 34, in the reprint edition of *JubA,*14 (Stuttgart, 1972), refuting E. Carmoly's (*Ben Chananja,* 6 [1863]:157–62) view that the riddle was the one sent him by Avigdor Levi in 1770 (see below, p. 367). As Bar-Dayan points out, the genre of riddle was rather popular among Hebrew writers of the latter half of the eighteenth century.

79. *JubA,* 16, letter 230, p. 254.

80. A good portrayal of Jewish life in Amsterdam in the second half of the eighteenth century is offered in H.G. Enelow's essay, "Isaac Belinfante, an eighteenth-century bibliophile," *Studies in Jewish Bibliography and related Subjects in Memory of Abraham Solomon Freidus* (New York, 1929), 5–30.

81. See below, p. 378 f.

82. *Levanon (Gan Na'ul),* 1 (Amsterdam, 1765), 10 ff. On the meaning of *hokhma* as understood by him see above, p. 191.

83. See *JubA,* 16: lxxix. The titlepage indicates 1775 as the year of publication.

84. *Masekhet Avot 'Im Perush Yeyn Levanon* commenting on 1:2 and 3:21 (fols. 8b and 71a of the Warsaw edition of 1884).

85. Wessely saw these two ways of faith indicated by the prepositions *le* and *be* with which the verb *ha'amin* (to believe) is used in biblical Hebrew. See *Yeyn Levanon,* 183a–b.

86. See below, p. 718 ff.

87. See H.J.D. Azulai, *Shem Gedolim* (Warsaw, 1864), 1:68a, 69b.

88. Fol. 2a–b in the Warsaw edition.

89. Cf. Cant. 5:1; 4:15.

90. Varying *Gen. Rabba* 55:8 to read: *ahava megalgelet ha-shura.*

91. On Nahmanides' acquaintance with the *Wisdom of Solomon,* see Gershom Scholem, *Ursprung and Anfänge der Kabbala* (Berlin, 1962), 364 f.

92. *Sefer Hokhmat Shelomo . . . Ve-Ha-Ramban zal be-Hakdamato le-ferush Ha-Tora kera'o be-shem Hukhmata Rabbata di-Shelomo Malka* (Berlin, 1780).

93. These three hymns, and a fourth by a certain Isaac Friedland, are reproduced at the beginning of the book.

94. Ex. 2:6.

95. The early poem was published by Gabriel Isaak Polak in *Bikkurim,* ed. Naphtali Keller, 2 (Vienna, 1865): 201–10; the late one appeared in Meir Letteris' *Avney Nezer* (see Klausner, *Historiya,* 1:109, note 1).

96. He held the view that the *Wisdom of Solomon* had originally been written by a Jew in imitation of Proverbs. He recalled that Robert Lowth had made an attempt to reconstruct the original Hebrew text from the Greek version (see *GS,* 4.1;196 f.). With Lowth, he assumed that the Greek text was a translation from the Hebrew.

97. See S.J. Fünn, *Kenesset Yisra'el* (Warsaw, 1886),197; Idem, *Kirya Ne'emana* (Vilna, 1915), 146; *EJ,* 3:1111 f.

98. On the Gaon's educational principles see *Sefer 'Aliyot Eliyahu* (Warsaw, 1901), 28 f., 59 ff. See also Israel of Shklov, *Sefer Pe'at Shulhan* (Safed, 1836), preface. Other pertinent statements by the Gaon are quoted by Israel Jacob Dienstag, *Rabbenu Eliyahu Me-Vilna* (New York, 1949), 39 f. On the pursuit of secular knowledge among Polish and Lithuanian Jews see Isaac Eisenstein-Barzilay, "The Background of the Berlin Haskala," 184 f.

99. *'Aliyot Eliyahu,* 46, note 31.

100. Ibid., 43–50.

101. According to Joseph Mendelssohn's testimony, Homberg joined his father's circle in about 1778/79; see Homberg's letter quoted by Alexander Altmann in "Moses Mendelssohn's Gesammelte Schriften, Neuerschlossene Briefe zur Geschichte ihrer Herausgabe," *BLBI,* 11, No. 42 (1968): 106, and *GS,* 5:653. Fünn, *Kenesset,* 271, likewise accepted "1778 or 1779"

as the year of Homberg's return to Berlin. Kayserling, *Mendelssohn*, wrote "about 1779" in the 1st edition (p. 311), and "1779" in the second (p. 314). Klausner, *Historiya*, 1:212, adopted the rather arbitrary decision taken in Kayserling's second edition.

102. Quoted from Joseph Mendelssohn's letter to Homberg (Mar. 12, 1841), published in *Ost und West*, ed. Rudolf Glaser (Prague, 1841), and reproduced in Julius Fürst's *Der Orient*, 2 (Leipzig, 1841): 135 f.; see Altmann, "Neuerschlossene Briefe," 107 ff. On Mar. 2, 1841, Joseph Mendelssohn wrote to Heyman Golowicz (Jolowicz) in Culm: "Do you know that Herz Homberg is still alive and that he lives in Prague? ... Surely, from this man I can receive the finest material for the biography" [of Moses Mendelssohn, which Joseph was then writing] (autograph in the possession of Alexander Robert Bohnke, Tübingen; a copy is found in the Staatsbibliothek Stiftung Preussischer Kulturbesitz, Berlin, Autogr. I/410). On Golowicz, see Altmann, "Neuerschlossene Briefe," 88 f., 92, 112 ff.

103. *GS*, 5:654.

104. Alluding to the talmudic statement that "one who teaches Tora to his fellow-man's son, becomes his father, as it were" *(Sanhedrin* 19b).

105. *JubA*, 14:247.

106. See the preface *(JubA*, 14:304 ff.).

107. It has an elaborate new preface *(JubA*, 14:306–13).

108. See Mendelssohn's letter to Homberg (July 16, 1782), *GS*, 5:660. Jaroslav was among the Breslau subscribers to Mendelssohn's Pentateuch. See *JubA*, 14:371.

109. See Klausner, *Historiya*, 1:74 f.

110. Kant, *Werke*, 9:176 f.

111. Ibid., 183.

112. *Salomon Maimon's Lebensgeschichte. Von ihm selbst geschrieben und herausgegeben von K.P. Moritz*, 1 (Berlin, 1792): 268 ff. Abbreviated English translation: Solomon Maimon, *Autobiography*, ed. Moses Hadas (New York, 1947), 60 f.

113. *Lebensgeschichte*, 2 (Berlin, 1793): 152 ff.; ed. Hadas, 73.

114. 1:262; ed. Hadas, 57.

115. Kant, *Werke*, 9:415.

116. 2:158; ed. Hadas, 75. The correspondence is lost; see *JubA*, 16, lxxxix.

117. 2:158 f.; ed. Hadas, 75 f.

118. The Polish Jew (the "wild Pole") who once came rushing into Mendelssohn's room and threw at him a bundle of writings that explained the Ten Sefirot of the Kabbala in terms of the "most modern philosophy" was certainly not Solomon Maimon, as Kayserling *(Mendelssohn*, 431) assumed.

119. *GS*, 5:661. See *Lebensgeschichte*, 2:160–65. The "noble friend L. in Berlin" is the addressee of Maimon's epistolary essay "On Truth," published in *Berlinisches Journal für Aufklärung*, 5.1: (1789) 67–84, and reprinted in Salomon Maimon, *Gesammelte Werke*, ed. Valerio Verra, 1 (Hildesheim, 1965): 599 ff.

120. Kant, *Werke*, 9:384 f.

121. Maimon's observations on Mendelssohn's character *(Werke*, 2:168 ff.) are largely based on impressions received when he was visiting Mendelssohn and noticed his reactions to other visitors.

122. *Lebensgeschichte*, 2:232 ff.

123. Hermann Samuel Reimarus, *Über die vornehmsten Wahrheiten der natürlichen Religion* (Hamburg, 1754).

124. The translation seems to be lost. The Hebrew version that appeared in Königsberg, 1845, is by Joseph Herzberg (see Meyer, *Bibliographie*, p. 60, no. 327).

125. *Lebensgeschichte*, 2:252.

126. 2:168 ff (chap. 12).

127. 1:172 f.

128. *Berlinische Monatsschrift*, 14 (1789): 171–79; reproduced in *Gesammelte Werke*, ed. Verra, 1:589–97.

129. Published by Isaac Abraham Euchel, together with Moses Narboni's commentary on *Guide*, part I, Berlin, 1791; see Steinschneider, "Hebräische Drucke," 175.

130. *JubA*, 16, letter 272, p. 291. Mendelssohn expressed himself more distinctly in a letter to Avigdor Levi, dated Apr. 22, 1784 *(JubA*, 16, letter 273, p. 292): "Someone here has anticipated me in printing a *Bi'ur* on Psalms, in which he wants to indicate, in Hebrew, the reasons underlying my translation. Moreover, the German translation is to be printed in Hebrew characters. I permitted him to do this. I believe that he will do a good job.

I cannot apply myself to the task because my time and energy are otherwise occupied. Should he miss my true meaning at times, no harm will be done. One day I intend to do the work myself, please God, should Christian critics dare to defend their usual interpretation in opposition to me."

131. See the review in *Ha-Me'assef*, 7.2:158 f. For a characterization of Loewe's childhood, see Euchel's epistolary preface, in which a few stanzas of Loewe's poem in praise of his teachers are quoted.

132. *Ha-Me'assef*, 1785: 116–21, 137–42. See Meir Letteris' biography of Euchel in *Ha-Me'assef*, 1784, republished in Vienna, 1862, 41 ff.

133. See J[eremias] Heinemann, ed., *Moses Mendelssohn. Sammlung theils noch ungedruckter, theils in anderen Schriften zerstreuter Aufsätze und Briefe von ihm, an und über ihn* (Leipzig, 1831), 120 ff. The quoted passage is taken from the second of two fragments by David Friedländer recording talks ("*Unterhaltungen*") with Mendelssohn that Friedländer published first in the periodical *Jedidja*, 2.1 (Berlin, 1818): 14–21, 143–76, and later in his book, *Moses Mendelssohn. Fragmente von ihm und über ihn* (Berlin, 1819).

134. Wessely's *Imrey Shefer* (Lyck, 1868–71); see Klausner, *Historiya*, 1:118.

135. H. Vogelstein, "Handschriftliches zu Isaak Abraham Euchels Biographie," *Festschrift Martin Philippson*, 228. Since Euchel left Königsberg on May 8 (ibid., p. 227), he could have arrived in Berlin by the middle of May and the debate with Wessely could have taken place before June 1. It can hardly be assumed that Euchel attacked Wessely after having been favored with this token of friendship.

136. *JubA*, 16, letter 275, p. 294.

137. Vogelstein, "Handschriftliches," 225.

138. Concerning him see S. J. Fünn, *Kirya Ne'emana*, 178 f.

139. *JubA*, 16, letter 92, p. 113 f.

140. Cant. 5:14.

141. Cf. Lam. 4:7.

142. Cant. 5:14.

143. Cant. 3:10.

144. I Chron. 12:34.

145. Quoted by Fünn, *Kirya Ne'emana*, 178.

146. Eccl. 12:10.

147. *JubA*, 16, letter 118, p. 139. See, however, *JubA*, 16, letter 202, p. 231 f. (referred to above, p. 355) and Gabriel I. Polak, *Ben Gorni* (Amsterdam, 1851), xviii, 39 f.

148. *JubA*, 16, letter 159, p. 186 ff.

149. *JubA*, 16, letter 160, p. 189 f. Mendelssohn correctly perceived that the obscurity of the phrase was due to the literalness of the Hebrew rendition of the Arabic original.

150. See below, pp. 381, 396 f., 400.

151. *JubA*, 16, letter 267, p. 287.

152. *JubA*, 16, letter 273, p. 292 ff. Cf. Kayserling, *Ungedrucktes*, 41–50.

The German Translation of the Pentateuch (pages 368–383)

1. See above, p. 242.

2. See above, pp. 243 f., 274 f.

3. *JubA*, 14:243 f.

4. Deut. 6:7.

5. Viz. substituting idiomatic German phrases for idiomatic Hebrew.

6. Viz. departing from traditional ways of interpretation whenever the context (*hemshekh ha-'inyan*) demanded a different exegesis. For an elaborate account of Mendelssohn's exegetical principles, see Edward R. Levenson's doctoral dissertation on the subject (Brandeis University, 1972): *Moses Mendelssohn's Understanding of Logico-Grammatical and Literary Construction in the Pentateuch: A Study of his German Translation and Hebrew Commentary (The Bi'ur)*.

7. p. 355.

8. See above, p. 98.

9. *JubA*, 16, letter 227, p. 251.

10. *JubA*, 14:326 f.

11. *JubA*, 14:viii.

12. *JubA*, 14:242.

13. Cf. Lam. 1:9; Jer. 50:32.

14. Cf. Isa. 28:11.
15. Elijah Levita (1469–1549). The translation referred to appeared in Constance, Switzerland, in 1544. It was the work of Michael Adam, a Jewish convert to Christianity, who coedited this Judeo-German Bible together with Paulus Fagius. See *GS*, 7:xx–xxii; *JubA*, 14:ccii. Mendelssohn was misled by the statement of the bibliographer Shabbatai Strim ("Meshorer Bas"), author of *Sifetey Yeshenim*, who described this Bible translation as Levita's work. A reference to this statement occurs in our passage. The Constance Bible is described by W. Staerk and A. Leitzmann, *Die jüdisch-deutschen Bibelübersetzungen von den Anfängen bis zum Ausgang des 18. Jahrhunderts* (Frankfurt am Main, 1923), 114 ff.
16. Berlin, 1760. The phrase of the title is taken from Job 36:2.
17. Varying Isa. 7:16.
18. Ez. 29:6.
19. Elyakim ben Ya'akov of Komarno (Galicia), *Melammed Siah* (Amsterdam, 1710), a dictionary of the Tora and the Five Scrolls, explaining the meaning of the words in German. The *editio princeps* also contains the biblical text. The dictionary was republished several times (Dyrenfurth, 1718; Fürth, 1726 and 1737; etc.).
20. Moses ben Issachar Halevi (Strelitz), *Be'er Moshe* (Prague, 1605; 1612; etc.), another dictionary of the Tora and the Five Scrolls. Many editions include the text, and some even include Rashi's commentary.
21. *JubA*, 16, letter 227, p. 251 f.
22. *JubA*, 14:243 f.
23. Literally: "of parable and figurative expression" *(mashal u-melitsa)*. In the letter to Avigdor Levi the corresponding sentence reads: "for the benefit of Jewish children who seek an explanation of Scripture and a translation into German that is superior to the misleading Bibles of the Gentiles."
24. The phrase "argue with me" is not found in the letter.
25. In the letter: "in brief language easily comprehensible to the reader." Since the stipulation of brevity was not observed by Dubno, Mendelssohn tactfully omitted it from the introduction.
26. The letter does not contain this sentence.
27. See above, p. 355.
28. See *GS*, 3:399–403.
29. See Bertha Badt-Strauss, "Elise Reimarus und Moses Mendelssohn," *ZGJD*, 4 (1932): 179.
30. *JubA*, 16, letter 277, p. 252.
31. *JubA*, 14:245.
32. Viz. Gentile translations (*JubA*, 14:244); "Gentile productions" (*JubA*, 16:252).
33. *JubA*, 16:252; with slight variations: *JubA*, 14:244.
34. See David Friedländer's letter to Joseph Elias of Vilna, dated Shevat 4, 5543/1783, in: S. J. Fünn, *Soferey Yisra'el* (Vilna, 1871), 138 f. That Mendelssohn's loss amounted to 3000 *Reichsthaler* was erroneously stated by Samson Bloch in his letter to Jehuda Wahrmann, *Kerem Hemed*, 2:85 (Vienna, 1836). The total cost of production was 3500 *Reichsthaler* (see *JubA*, 14:247).
35. *JubA*, 14:247.
36. Ezra 3:9.
37. See *JubA*, 16, letter 242, p. 241; letter 252, p. 281; letter 267, p. 287.
38. *JubA*, 14:268. See also *JubA*, 16, letter 242, p. 275.
39. *JubA*, 16, letter 248, p. 279; for the date see Jacob Katz, *Zion*, 29 (1964):127.
40. I Sam. 28:21; Ps. 121:1; Isa. 50:6.
41. Ez. 47:12.
42. *JubA*, 14:327.
43. Amos 8:12.
44. Ps. 40:5; see Mendelssohn's translation, which we have followed, *GS*, 6:189.
45. Amos 5:7.
46. Literally: "They please themselves in the brood of aliens" (Isa. 2:6).
47. See above, p. 371.
48. Florence, 1750; Berlin, 1761.
49. Printed first in his *Shetey Yadot* (Venice, 1618); as a separate publication Amsterdam, 1659; Berlin, 1745.
50. Mantua, 1742–1744.

51. *JubA*, 14:329 f., 245, xciii.
52. As Haim Borodianski (Bar-Dayan), *JubA*, 14:viii, indicates, this fact is corroborated by a letter that Joseph Mendelssohn wrote to Heymann Golowicz (Jolowicz).
53. See the detailed analysis in Edward R. Levenson's dissertation (quoted above, note 6).
54. See above, p. 80.
55. *JubA*, 14:242.
56. A facsimile reproduction of the entire pamphlet is found in *JubA*, 14:321–68. The place for the insertion of the price was left blank in the prospectus (see *JubA*, 14:331). The price was probably fixed after printing had started. It is mentioned in a letter to Hennings (see below, p. 388) and in another to Pinchas Kopenhagen (*JubA*, 16, letter 252, p. 281).
57. A German translation of the prospectus by Christian Gottlob Meyer, a Jewish convert to Christianity, was published in Göttingen (1780). The preface is dated Aug. 12, 1779 (see Kayserling, *Mendelssohn*, 289, note 1; *JubA*, 14:xcii; Meyer, *Bibliographie*, p. 51, no. 249).
58. The letter ordering the copies was written, in Hartknoch's own hand, on Feb. 2, 1779 (Dep. RvM, C i, no. 18).
59. See the list of subscribers reproduced in *JubA*, 14:369–83.
60. *Theologische Bibliothek*, 1 (Leipzig, 1782):156; see also his review of the complete edition of the Pentateuch in *Theologische Bibliothek*, 3.1 (1784):4 f., where the same point was made.
61. 44.1 (1780): 227–55. The author of the review was Johann Bernhard Köhler (see *GS*, 5:583, note 2).
62. Cf. his letter to Herder dated Mar. 15, 1781 (*GS*, 5:583 f.).
63. Published by Mendelssohn at the opening of the Second Book [Exod.] of the Tora (Berlin, 1781).
64. Deut. 33:2.
65. According to medieval Neoplatonic Jewish writings, Divine Wisdom or Intellect (with which the "preëxistent Tora" is identified) resides above both the souls of the spheres and the hierarchy of the intelligencies or angelic choirs. For the concepts involved see Louis Ginsberg, *The Legends of the Jews*, 6:63; Harry A. Wolfson, *The Problem of the Souls of the Spheres from the Byzantine Commentaries on Aristotle through the Arabs and St. Thomas to Kepler* (Dumbarton Oaks, 1961); Alexander Altmann, *Studies in Religious Philosophy and Mysticism* (London and Ithaca, N. Y., 1969), 53–66 and passim.
66. For this midrashic motif see Altmann, *Studies*, 128–39.
67. *Mishna, Avot*, 6:9, and in numerous similar utterances.
68. Possibly alluding to the mystical notion of the Tora as a living organism in which Divinity is manifested. See Gershom Scholem, *Zur Kabbala und ihrer Symbolik* (Zürich, 1960), 64–72.
69. For an analysis of this particular motif, see Altmann, *Studies*, 41–72.
70. See Charles Duschinsky, *The Rabbinate of the Great Synagogue, London from 1756–1842* (Oxford, 1921), 31 ff., 37. Lewin had been chief rabbi of London from 1756 until 1764. When occupying the rabbinate in Halberstadt, he won the respect of the poet Gleim, who in a letter written to F. E. Boysen in August, 1770, expressed his admiration of the "Berlin Socrates," Mendelssohn. The letter is quoted in Abraham Geiger's *Jüdische Zeitschrift für Wissenschaft und Leben*, 10 (1872): 232 and in Elieser Landshuth's *'Ateret Tsevi* (Berlin, 1884), 19; see also Duschinsky, *The Rabbinate*, 38.
71. See Duschinsky, *The Rabbinate*, 38, note 38.
72. See the Hebrew text published by Landshuth, *'Ateret Tsevi*, 17 f.
73. Gen. 27:7.
74. Prov. 11:15.
75. Literally: "who understands Assyrian for his going (*le-'ashuro*)," a pun on Prov. 14:15.
76. Num. 11:18.
77. A pun on Ex. 8:20.
78. Viz. the translation by Yekuti'el Blitz; see above, p. 369.
79. Viz. the translation by Josel Witzenhausen, which took only nine years to complete (1678–1687); see above, p. 370. Lewin seems to have considered both versions equally poor, while Mendelssohn rightly regarded the one by Blitz as below the standard of the other. His judgment has been confirmed by Staerk and Leitzmann, *Bibelübersetzungen*, 161–64.
80. Prov. 22:18.
81. Job 21:16.
82. Isa. 25:1.
83. See above, note 46.

84. Isa. 8:14.
85. Job 28:10.
86. Prov. 24:5.
87. Prov. 31:23.
88. Using the phrase *yad-va-shem* (Isa. 56:5).
89. Ps. 45:18.
90. Isa. 43:9.
91. Ps. 89:22.
92. See below, p. 483 f.
93. A recent study, "Mendelssohn, Wessely, and the Rabbis of their Time" (in Hebrew) by Moses S. Samet in *Studies in the History of the Jewish People and the Land of Israel in Memory of Zvi Avneri*, ed. by A. Gilboa, B. Mevorach, U. Rappaport, A. Shochet (Haifa, 1970), 233–57, confirms the findings at which I had arrived independently in my own investigation of the subject. Most of the sources drawn upon by Samet coincide with those that had been used by me. They clearly prove that Graetz' presentation of events in his *Geschichte der Juden*, Vol. 11, note 1, can no longer be accepted. In certain respects, however, my evaluation of the happenings in Altona differs from Samet's, who did not have access to some of the material (hitherto unpublished) that I had been able to use. The sources concerned are particularly important for an assessment of Mendelssohn's attitude toward the rabbis who opposed him.
94. The letter is lost but its date and content can be inferred from Mendelssohn's reply (*JubA*, 16, letter 227, p. 251 ff.).
95. *JubA*, 16, p. 253, lines 2–3.
96. *JubA*, 16, letter 227, p. 251 ff.; in German transliteration: *GS*, 6:447 ff.
97. Quoted above, p. 371–73; the account was later incorporated in the introduction, *Or Li-Netiva*.
98. Mendelssohn's phrase for Judeo-German is *leshon yahadut-deitsch*.
99. Viz. the inverted writing of the letter *nun* in Num. 10:35, 36.
100. *Noda' Bi-Yehuda*, Prague, 1776, fol. 77b f. (see *JubA*, 16:lxxxviii); Warsaw, 1891, Vol. 1, fols. 39b–40a (Section Yoreh De'a, responsum 74).
101. The Peace of Teschen had been proclaimed on May 13, 1779.
102. Read: *le-hashivenu* [instead of *le-hashiveni*] *davar*, which accords with the plural forms used throughout the sentence. Since Mendelssohn had not approached Landau, he could not have expected a reply addressed to him personally.
103. The text of the *haskama* was published by Gabriel I. Polak, *Ben Gorni* (Amsterdam, 1851), 44 f.
104. The quoted passage occurs in the *haskama* given to Sussmann Glogau as reproduced in *Ha-Me'assef* (1786), 142–44; summarized rather freely, and without any reference to sources, by Yekuti'el A. Kamelhar, *Mofet Ha-Dor* (Pietrekov, 1934; reprinted in Israel, 1968), 62 f.
105. *Mishna*, Avot, 1:6.
106. The authenticity of the above text can hardly be questioned, since the stated reasons completely agree with what is also otherwise known of Landau's attitude toward Mendelssohn's translation and toward him personally. See below, p. 398, and Samet, *Studies*, 243. The editor of *Ha-Me'assef* (1786:141 f.) criticized the bad Hebrew of the *haskama* and suggested that Landau had merely added his signature to the scribbling of one of his students. Mendelssohn himself found fault with the phrase "the translator deepened his language" *(he'emik sefatho)*; see *JubA*, 16, letter 277, p. 295.
107. His biography is found in Eduard Duckesz, *Ivvah Le-Moshav* (ed. Eisig Gräber, Cracow, 1903), 63–74.

Obstacles on the Road (pages 383–405)

1. The Mendelssohn/Hennings correspondence is extant in Nachlass Hennings, no. 22 and Dep. RvM; the Reimarus letters are found in Nachlass Hennings, no. 79.
2. See above, p. 344.
3. See *JubA*, 16, letter 213, p. 243. The friend was probably Nathan Meyer Katz, court agent of the duke of Mecklenburg (see *JubA*, 16:lxix).
4. See his letter to Fromet, *JubA*, 16, letter 230, p. 254.
5. Nachlass Hennings, no. 22, letter 8, fol. 9*v*–11*r*; Kayserling, *Mendelssohn*, 1st ed., 521 f.

6. Fürst lived in Copenhagen and seems to have kept in close contact with Hennings.

7. Dep. RvM, C I, no. 25.

8. Dep. RvM, C 1, no. 26. Samet, *Mendelssohn, Wessely, and the Rabbis of their Time,* (see note 93 of the preceding section), 238, mistakenly assumed that both Hennings' letters were lost. It is clear from Hennings' letter of June 22 that the situation in Altona was rather menacing.

9. Nachlass Hennings, no. 22, fol. 13r ff.; Kayserling, *Mendelssohn,* 1st ed., 524 f.

10. The hypothetical case is derived from Hennings' *Olavides* (see above, p. 343 f).

11. Christian VII (1749–1808), who was mentally unstable and only nominally the king of Denmark; his brother, Prince Frederick conducted all affairs pertaining to royalty.

12. The French text is quoted by Kayserling, *Mendelssohn,* 1st. ed., 293 f. (p. 296 f. of the 2nd ed.).

13. Dep. RvM, C I, no. 27.

14. Dep. RvM, C I, no. 30. The letter is undated but must have been written shortly after the previous one, since Elise Reimarus forwarded both of them together to Mendelssohn; see her letter quoted below, note 16.

15. Hennings was mistaken. Mendelssohn's translation was printed in the ordinary Hebrew square script, not in cursive Rashi script.

16. Nachlass Hennings, no. 79, fol. 151r f. The date is illegible.

17. Viz. her brother and sister-in-law.

18. See Graetz, *Geschichte der Juden,* 11:589; S. Samet, "Mendelssohn, Wessely, and the Rabbis of their Time," 236 f. and note 25. Samet's statement that this report is not mentioned in any contemporary source is obviously incorrect.

19. Nachlass Hennings, no. 22, letter 11, fol. 20r. See below, p. 392. The evidence at our disposal disproves Graetz' assumption that a ban had been proclaimed by the chief rabbi of Altona and that Prince Frederick's hesitancy was due to this fact. Kayserling, *Mendelssohn,* 297, does not seem to share Graetz' view. Yet he makes no clear statement on the issue.

20. Nachlass Hennings, no. 22, letter 10, fol. 15r–17v; Kayserling, *Mendelssohn,* 1st ed., 525 ff.

21. *JubA,* 14:367.

22. He later became superintendent general in Gotha; see J[eremias] Heinemann, *Moses Mendelssohn. Sammlung theils noch ungedruckter, theils in anderen Schriften zerstreuter Aufsätze und Briefe . . .* (Leipzig, 1831), 26; Meyer, *Bibliographie,* 51 f., no. 251.

23. Kayserling, *Mendelssohn,* 301 f.

24. Reprinted in *GS,* 6:119–24 and in other places; see editorial note, ibid., and Kayserling, *Mendelssohn,* 302, note 1.

25. Marburg File, no. 45.

26. Lit.: "translation." Mendelssohn seems to have felt that some new feature had to compensate for the failure to offer extracts from the commentary.

27. The Song of Deborah was appended to the editor's preface (pp. xii–xvi). See Meyer, *Bibliographie,* 52. The edition bears the title: *Die fünf Bücher Mose, zum Gebrauch der jüdisch-deutschen Nation nach der Übersetzung des Herrn Moses Mendelssohn. Erstes Buch. Berlin und Stettin, bey Friedrich Nicolai,* 1780.

28. Nachlass Hennings, no. 79, fol. 167r–v.

29. Ibid., fol. 169r–v.

30. Dep. RvM, C I, no. 29 (Sept. 7, 1779).

31. See the letter to Avigdor Levi quoted above, p. 374.

32. Nachlass Hennings, no. 22, letter 11, fol. 18r–20v; published by L. Geiger, *ZGJD,* 1 (1887):113–15; see also Bertha Badt-Strauss, "Elise Reimarus und Moses Mendelssohn," *ZGJD,* 4 (1932): 178.

33. See, e. g., *JubA,* 7:13 f., 75.

34. In the missing letter or in one of his essays.

35. Nachlass Hennings, no. 22, letter 12, fol. 20v–21r (Sept. 20, 1779).

36. Quoted by Kayserling, *Mendelssohn,* 296.

37. Dept. RvM, C I, no. 29.

38. Pastor Johann Melchior Goeze, Lessing's fierce antagonist (see below, p. 561 and passim), and Pastor Krohn of the Church Maria Magdalena in Hamburg. Only the latter figures in the list of Hamburg subscribers.

39. Nachlass Hennings, no. 79, fol. 164r.

40. Dep. RvM, C I, no. 31.

41. Quoted by Elise Reimarus in her letter to Hennings on Sept. 7, 1779, Nachlass Hennings, no. 79, fol. 172r.

42. Ibid.

43. Nachlass Hennings, no. 79, fol. 172v–173v.

44. On this belated impact of Mendelssohn's work see Klausner, *Historiya*, 1:69. Mendelssohn's translation and the *Bi'ur* were widely used in the secular schools established by the Maskilim in Eastern Europe and even in the old-time *Hadarim*, especially those in the western provinces of Austria. See M. N. Zobel, *Kiryat Sefer*, 18 (1941–1942):130, who refers to Eisik Hirsch Weiss' memoirs; Perez Sandler, *Ha-Bi'ur la-Tora shel Moshe Mendelssohn ve-si'ato* (Jerusalem, 1940), 163, note 7; Mordechai Eliav, *Ha-Hinukh Ha-Yehudi Be-Germaniya Bi-Yemey Ha-Haskala Ve-Ha-Emantsipatsia* (Jerusalem, 1960), 37 ff.

45. Nachlass Hennings, no. 79, fol. 169r.

46. Ibid., fol. 209v.

47. Ibid., fol. 202v.

48. Ibid., fol. 218v.

49. Dep. RvM, C I, no. 29.

50. Dep. RvM, C I, no. 31.

51. Nachlass Hennings, no. 79, fol. 224r.

52. Nachlass Hennings, no. 22, letter 13, fol. 21r–22r; Kayserling, *Mendelssohn*, 1st ed., 528 (where the first part is omitted).

53. See above, p. 389.

54. On Rector Damm, see above, p. 112, and below, p. 565.

55. The term "first instalment" *(erste Ablieferung)*, used in the letter to Hennings, also appears in the letter to Avigdor Levi of Apr. 17, 1780, where it is explained by the addition: "consisting of the Book [of] Genesis" *(bestehend in Sefer Bereshith)*.

56. Nachlass Hennings, no. 22, letter 14, fol. 23r.

57. Ibid., letter 15, fol. 23r.

58. *JubA*, 16, letter 236, p. 257.

59. *JubA*, 16, letter 242, p. 275.

60. *JubA*, 16, letters 240, 242, p. 274 f.

61. *JubA*, 16, letter 248, p. 279; first published by Avigdor Levi in *Iggeroth . . . Rabbi Moshe Dessau* (Vienna, 1794) as letter 5; reproduced in German characters in *GS*, 6:452 f. The letter must have been written between June and September, 1781 (see Jacob Katz, *Zion*, 29:127, and below, p. 461).

62. *Ha-Ga'on Av Beth Din de-kehilatkhem, nero ya'ir.*

63. Esther 9:26.

64. See above, p. 374.

65. For the identification of the correspondent in Fürth, see Leopold Löwenstein, "Zur Geschichte der Juden in Fürth," *JJLG*, 6 (1908):201.

66. See *JubA*, 14:378.

67. Graetz' assumption to this effect has been disproved by Löwenstein, "Zur Geschichte," 200 f.

68. Ibid., 201.

69. Avigdor Levi, *Iggeroth*, 11v (quoted by Graetz, *Geschichte*, 11:589).

70. Graetz' doubts about the trustworthiness of Levi's testimony are unfounded.

71. See above, p. 382.

72. See above, p. 383.

73. Prague, 1813, preface, p. 3 a–b.

74. The author of the biography was Jacob Landau, and the manuscript was shown to Jeiteles by his brother Samuel. See Jehuda Löb Jeiteles, *Mevo' Lashon Aramit*, 3 a–b.

75. Ex. 33:8; *Kiddushin* 33b.

76. Viz. his translation of the Tetragrammaton by "the Eternal One" *(der Ewige)*.

77. Ex. 34:30; i.e. to attack Mendelssohn openly.

78. Cf. *Berakhot* 28b.

79. Isa. 57:19.

80. Cf. Ex. 34:29–35. Jeiteles' statement and part of his quotation are cited by N. Brüll, *Jahrbücher für jüdische Geschichte und Literatur*, 3 (1877):210 f., in refutation of the view that

Landau issued a ban against Mendelssohn's translation. Brüll, who had first subscribed to this view (*Jahrbücher*, 3:137), revised it in light of the evidence discovered by him. Graetz had left it undecided whether a formal ban was proclaimed. See also Löwenstein, "Zur Geschichte," 201, note 2; Louis Lewin, "Aus dem jüdischen Kulturkampfe," *JJLG*, 12 (1918):174, note 2; Samet, "Mendelssohn, Wessely, and the Rabbis of their Time," 240–44.

81. See below, p. 486 f.

82. See below, p. 403 f.

83. *JubA*, 16, letter 237, pp. 258–61.

84. *Sefer Shemot*, 1781, introduction. The remaining part of Dubno's introduction was published by Fünn in *Ha-Karmel*, 4 (1879):391 f. See *JubA*, 16:xc. Fünn possessed many of Dubno's unpublished manuscripts; see Simcha Assaf, *Kiryat Sefer*, 1 (1924–1925):68, note 1.

85. See Mendelssohn's remarks about the pettiness of some of the grammarians' (including Dubno's) researches, in his letter to Moses Fischer (Mar. 6. 1784), *JubA*, 16, letter 272, p. 291.

86. See below, p. 418.

87. *JubA*, 16:260.

88. See Fünn, *Soferey Yisra'el* (Vilna, 1871), 138 f.

89. *JubA*, 16, letter 242, p. 275.

90. *JubA*, 14:245–47.

91. See above, p. 371.

92. Fünn, *Soferey Yisra'el*, 139.

93. See above, note 88.

94. See Fünn, *Soferey Yisra'el*, 139 (end of Friedländer's letter); *Idem, Kirya Ne'emana*, 225. Dubno praised Joseph Elias for his hospitality; see his *Birkat Yosef* (Dierenfurth, 1783).

95. Fünn, *Kirya Ne'emana*, 225 f.

96. Gabriel Isaak Polak, *Ben Gorni*, 42 f.

97. A copy of the *herem* against the Hasidim proclaimed in Vilna on Av 20, 5541/1781 and a copy of a letter sent by Rabbi Samuel ben Avigdor jointly with some 20 rabbis and *parnassim* to the principal communities of Lithuania dated Av 23 (which was signed by the Gaon of Vilna on the 24th) were dispatched to Brody and came into the possession of Solomon Dubno. The manuscript (now at the Hebrew National and University Library, Collection Schwadron: Solomon Dubno, no. 4, 1r–2v) contains, on fol. 2v, the following entry in Dubno's hand: "The copy that came to Brody contained only a few signatures but I copied them [sc. those missing] in Vilna on Thursday of the week of [the perikope] *Behar* on Iyyar 13, 5543/1783." It is clear from this document that in the summer of 1781 Dubno was in Brody. The letter was first published in *Mahashavot Kesilim* (Slonim, 1860), reprinted by Simon Dubnow in *Devir*, Vol. 1 (Berlin, 1923), and presented in abbreviated form in Dubnow's *Toledot Ha-Hasidut*. See Mordechai Wilensky, *Hasidim U-Mitnagedim* (Jerusalem, 1970), 1:101–10.

98. Cant. 8:8.

99. *Berakhot* 33b.

100. Fünn, *Soferey Yisra'el*, 141 f.

101. See Polak, *Ben Gorni*, 43–51; Fünn, *Kirya Ne'emana*, 166, note; 177; 225 f.

102. See Polak, *Ben Gorni*, 43. According to S. Stanislawski (*Woschod*, 1803, x–xi), Dubno's manuscripts may have been preserved in Vilna and Amsterdam (see *EJ*, 6:101).

103. The manuscript had been put at his disposal by Mendelssohn; see *JubA*, 14:246.

104. B. H. Auerbach, *Geschichte der israelitischen Gemeinde Halberstadt* (Halberstadt, 1866), 178 ff. reports that he had been shown Dubno's letter when he visited Heidenheim "toward the end of the twenties," and that the latter had permitted him to make a copy of it. Auerbach (ibid.) published a German version of the rather extensive letter, which deals with a variety of subjects. Here we quote only the passage relevant to the theme under discussion. The authenticity of the letter need not be questioned.

105. Num. 16:26.

106. See Samet, *Mendelssohn, Wessely, and the Rabbis of their Time*, 235 f., who first called attention to this fact but drew the unwarranted conclusion that Dubno's letter represents a "forgery" by B. H. Auerbach. There can be little doubt, however, that 1777 was the year of Hirz' death, although no evidence is quoted by Ya'akov 'Adini (ed.), *Dubno: Sefer Zikaron* (Tel-Aviv, 1966), 93, whose testimony Samet accepts. Corroborative evidence may be found in the fact that a rabbinic ordinance *(takkana)* recorded in the *pinkas* of the Dubno community under the date of Tishri 26, 5538/1778, already bears the signature of Hirz' son, Ze'ev Wolf, who succeeded him as head of the local Beth Din. The last *takkana* signed by the

old man is dated Heshwan 12, 5535/1775. See Hayyim Ze'ev Margaliot, *Dubno Rabbati* (Warsaw, 5670/1910; reprinted in Israel, 5728/1968), 111; 115.

Completing the Work (pages 405–420)

1. Cf. *JubA*, 16, letter 236, p. 257.
2. Cf. *JubA*, 16, letter 242, p. 275.
3. *JubA*, 14:246.
4. *JubA*, 14:247.
5. Ibid.
6. Schwadron Collection: Solomon Dubno, no. 2, fol. 1r–4v; published by Haim Borodianski (Bar-Dayan) in *JubA*, 16:263–73 (see xc–xci).
7. Simcha Assaf, *Kiryat Sefer*, 1 (1924–1925):69 suggested Hirschel Lewin as the addressee; Borodianski considered the text as part of a letter to Hartog Leo (*JubA*, 16:261 ff.).
8. *JubA*, 16:264 (4th paragraph).
9. Strangely enough, Sandler, who recognized this note as coming from Dubno and who also noticed the close affinity between our text and the corresponding passages in the *Bi'ur*, failed to see that we are dealing here with Dubno's comments on Mendelssohn's *Bi'ur*. He seems to have assumed that Dubno copied notes written by somebody else: "This passage gives the impression of being copied, and it may be assumed that it was copied by Dubno." See Perez Sandler, *Ha-Bi'ur la-Tora shel Moshe Mendelssohn ve-si'ato* (Jerusalem, 1940), 84 f. and note 29. It appears that in the letter wrongly attributed to Hartog Leo, the first three sections (*JubA*, 16:261–63) likewise represent notes written by Dubno at different times and for different reasons.
10. *JubA*, 16:267 (1st paragraph).
11. *JubA*, 16:264 (2nd paragraph). See *Bi'ur* on Exod. 28:6.
12. *JubA*, 268 f.; *Bi'ur*, Exod. 29:7.
13. *JubA*, 16:266 (second paragraph); *Bi'ur*, Exod. 28:20.
14. Of the 40 chapters of the book, about three fourths had already been completed.
15. On Sept. 22, 1780, he stated that writing the introduction had taken him 10 weeks. Assuming that the introduction was finished by the middle of September, the process of composition must have started about July 1.
16. *JubA*, 14:330.
17. *JubA*, 14:247 f.
18. *JubA*, 16, letter 237, p. 258.
19. *JubA*, 16, letter 272, p. 291.
20. Sandler's theory to this effect (*Ha-Bi'ur*, 16 ff.) is highly conjectural.
21. See Franz Rosenzweig's essay, "Der Ewige" in his *Kleinere Schriften* (Berlin, 1937), 182–98, in which the significance of Mendelssohn's rendering of the Tetragrammaton is evaluated.
22. Rosenzweig was obviously unaware of Mendelssohn's practice of putting glosses by Dubno within square brackets and marking them by an asterisk. Hence he failed to recognize Dubno's authorship of the first gloss and only "surmised" that the second was part of "the materials left" by Dubno ("Der Ewige," 186, note 1).
23. Following Job 10:17. For *tsava'* in the sense of "fixed time for service," see Job 7:1.
24. The passages quoted are *Midrash Genesis Rabba*, 3:6; Sa'adya Gaon, cited from an unnamed source by Nahmanides ad loc. (not from *Emunot ve-De'ot*), and Maimonides, *Guide*, 1:63 (cited by Nahmanides).
25. See *Frühschriften*, 306.
26. Cf. Rosenzweig, "Der Ewige," 185.
27. *De sacra poesi Hebraeorum, praelectiones academicae Oxonii habitae* (Oxford, 1753); English translation by G. Gregory (Boston, 1815): lecture 19.
28. *GS*, 4.1:171–210.
29. See *JubA*, 16, letter 239, p. 274; *Verzeichnis*, p. 45, no. 530.
30. Lowth refers to "Azarias, a Jewish rabbi, not indeed a very ancient, but a very approved author," and quotes a passage of his *Imrey Bina*, chap. 60, from a Latin translation (Mantissa Dissert. ad Librum Cosri, p. 418). He failed to mention that his criticism of dei Rossi's theory (p. 271) had been anticipated by dei Rossi himself (*Imrey Bina*, Berlin, 1794, 258a). Nor did he acknowledge his indebtedness to dei Rossi when pointing out (p. 47 f.) that it was a particular quality of Hebrew poetry to retain "much of its native dignity" even in literal

translation—something that could not be said of Greek and Latin poetry. See dei Rossi, *Imrey Bina,* 258b.

31. Don Isaac Abrabanel's short survey of three types of Hebrew poetry in his commentary on Isaiah, chap. 5 (mentioned by dei Rossi) cannot be considered a precedent.

32. See Jehuda Moscato's commentary *Kol Yehuda, ad loc.; David Cassel, Das Buch Kusari* (Leipzig, 1869), 174, note 5. The view that the metrical system was foreign to Hebrew was opposed by Moses ibn Ezra; see Benzion Halper, *Shirat Yisra'el* (Leipzig, 1924).

33. *JubA,* 2:169. On the question of date see Fritz Bamberger, xxx–xxxv.

34. Similarly in his *Remarks on Lessing's Draft of the Laokoon, JubA,* 2:247 and elsewhere; see Bamberger, *JubA,* 2;xxx–xxxv.

35. Azarya dei Rossi, *Imrey Bina,* 307b; Lowth, *De sacra poesi,* 47 (lecture 3).

36. *JubA,* 16, letter 239, p. 274.

37. For the imagery of cedar and hyssop, see I Kings 5:13.

38. Micah 6:6.

39. Ps. 102:15.

40. Cant. 7:10.

41. I Chron. 17:16.

42. I Sam. 29:4.

43. The identity of Dr. Mires, the transmitter of the letter, has not been established.

44. Kayserling, *Mendelssohn,* 1st ed., 549. The date of the letter refutes the assumption (Meyer, *Bibliographie,* p. 57) that the third volume appeared in 1782.

45. See M. N. Zobel, *Kiryat Sefer,* 18 (1941–1942) 130. Whether the Gaon of Vilna actually praised Wessely's commentary is rather doubtful. See Sandler, *Ha-Bi'ur,* 138, note 8; Zobel, ibid.

46. *Juba,* 14:247.

47. Ps. 18:36.

48. Klausner, *Historiya,* 1:116 gives 1778–1780 as the approximate date. It seems more likely, however, that the event occurred in 1778, since Wessely must have started work on the commentary no later than 1779 and was exposed to his plight before he was commissioned to do so. Friedrichsfeld, *Zekher Tsaddik,* 15 ff., gives no date whatever.

49. See Klausner, *Historiya,* 1:116 and note 3.

50. Part of it (viz. the first four pericopes) is published under the title *Imrey Shefer* (ed. *Mekitsey Nirdamim,* Lyk, 1868–1871). For the story of this edition see Klausner, *Historiya,* 1:118.

51. See below, p. 486.

52. Ibid.

53. Ps. 111:10.

54. *Sifra', ad loc.; Sanhedrin* 27b.

55. Leibniz expressed a similar view in his *Essais de Théodicée,* 1, B. 40.

56. Nahmanides, likewise, holds that divine reward and punishment operate through natural agencies and therefore represent "hidden miracles."

57. See *GS,* 2:424.

58. *JubA,* 14:247.

59. Not to be confused with Shalom (ben Jacob) Cohen, the well-known Hebrew poet and editor, who came to Berlin in 1789.

60. See above, p. 359 f.

61. JubA, 16, letter 263, p. 286; see p. xcv and Fritz Bamberger, *Moses Mendelssohn. Denkmal der Freundschaft* (Berlin, 1929), f. 10.

62. *GS,* 5:656.

63. *GS,* 5:659.

64. *GS,* 5:660.

65. *GS,* 5:661.

66. *GS,* 5:662.

67. *GS,* 5:666.

68. See Zobel, *Kiryat Sefer,* 18:131.

69. *JubA,* 14:267.

70. *GS,* 3:362.

71. The *Jerusalem* was written in August, September, and October, 1782; see below, p. 510.

72. *JubA,* 14:267.

73. See below, p. 473 f.

74. *GS*, 3:201 f.

75. *JubA*, 14:267.

76. *GS*, 5:662,

77. The printer was Adolf Georg Starcke, then a "young beginner" (see Mendelssohn's letter to Friedländer, *JubA*, 16, letter 217, p. 245 f.), whose firm attained to great prominence.

78. *GS*, 5:692.

79. Dep. RvM, C II, no. 34. See below, p. 475 f.

80. *GS*, 5:611–13. The letter (undated) must have been written at the beginning of April, 1783.

81. The subtitle of the *Jerusalem*.

82. *GS*, 5:665.

83. Nathan Arnstein (1748–1838), son-in-law of Veitel Heine Ephraim and resident as a banker in Vienna (see *JubA*: 16, xciii).

Chapter Six: Political Reformer
Spokesman of his People (pages 421–449)

1. See above, p. 159.

2. See above, p. 786, note 3.

3. See above, p. 349.

4. Quoted by Kayserling, *Mendelssohn*, 258.

5. See Kant, *Werke*, 9:168 f., 171 f.

6. Ibid., 175.

7. This hitherto unknown letter was made available to me by the late Professor Bruno Strauss, who had discovered and owned it. He sent me a copy on Feb. 21, 1965.

8. Johann Georg Büsch (1728–1800), son of a Hamburg preacher, taught mathematics at the Hamburg gymnasium and in 1767 established a trade school in his native city (see *ADB*, 3:642 f.). He was a friend of Lessing; see Heinrich Lüdtke, *Lessings Beziehungen zur Niederelbe mit Berücksichtigung Altonas 1729–1929* (Altona, 1929); quoted by Heinrich Schneider, *Lessing*, 278. In 1770 or thereabouts Büsch had devised a scheme of a compulsory credit insurance to protect business firms against losses from bankruptcy. He submitted his plan to the Prussian government, which consulted Mendelssohn as to its feasibility. Mendelssohn's memorandum on the subject expressed so many doubts that the government dropped the matter. The minister of state who approached Mendelssohn was the baron von der Horst. See J. G. Büsch, *Sämtliche Schriften* (Vienna, 1814), 2:193 ff. The text of Mendelssohn's memorandum has not come to light, although in 1932 Dr. Bruno Kirschner made every effort to trace it. The Mendelssohn Archive of the Leo Baeck Institute, New York, preserves the following letters on the subject: (1) one from Kirschner to Franz von Mendelssohn, giving a précis of the facts; (2) one from Kirschner to Simon Rawidowicz, posing the question whether there existed any letters or diary notes by Mendelssohn on the conversations he had with Büsch concerning the scheme when they spent some time together at Pyrmont in 1773; and (3) a letter from Bruno Strauss to Kirschner, dated Aug. 11, 1932, which makes these points: It was very believable that Mendelssohn would have been consulted by von der Horst, the link between them being Johann August Eberhard, who had served as resident tutor in the household of von der Horst since 1759 in Halberstadt, had accompanied the baron to Berlin in 1763, and had remained in his service until the end of 1768. When Zedlitz inquired of Mendelssohn about Büsch in 1775, he had every justification for turning to him.

9. See *Friedrich August Wolf, Ein Leben in Briefen*, ed. Siegfried Reiter (Stuttgart, 1935), 160. The late Bruno Strauss drew my attention to this letter.

10. Robert Wood, *Essay on the Original Genius of Homer* (1769). This work became known in Germany through Christian Gottlob Heyne's laudatory review in the *Göttingische Anzeigen* (1770, no. 32) and, subsequently, through Michaelis' translation of the revised edition (1778).

11. On Wolf's conflict with Heyne and on Nicolai's objections, see Richard Volkmann, *Geschichte und Kritik der Wolfschen Prolegomena zu Homer* (Leipzig, 1874).

12. *GS*, 5:492 f.

13. *GS*, 5:491 f.

14. *GS*, 5:494.

15. See above, p. 299–301. For the identification of the anonymous writer with the count of Lynar, see Bertha and Bruno Strauss, "Wer ist der 'Mann von Stande'? Eine Untersuchung

zu Moses Mendelssohns Briefwechsel und zur Geschichte der Judenstaatsprojekte," *Occident and Orient; being studies . . . in honour of Haham Dr. M. Gaster's 80th birthday . . .*, ed. Bruno Schindler (London, 1936), 518–25. Bruno Strauss had previously shown that the recipient of Mendelssohn's letter of Feb. 12, 1775 was the count of Lynar; see *ZGJD*, 1 (1929): 245 ff.; cf. above, p. 807, notes 17 and 21.

16. See Bertha and Bruno Strauss, ibid., 523.

17. See above, p. 343 f.

18. *GS*, 5:493 f.

19. For this original meaning of the term "statistics," see *Encyclopaedia Britannica* (1964), 21:345.

20. Isaac Pinto, *Réflexions critiques sur le premier chapitre du septième tome des oeuvres de M. de Voltaire, au sujet des Juifs* (1762); cf. Graetz, *Geschichte*, 11:54 f., 58 f.

21. Isaac Pinto, *Précis des arguments contre les matérialistes* (Amsterdam, 1774).

22. *GS*, 5:527 f.

23. See above, p. 287 f.

24. See above, p. 288 f.

25. See above, p. 261.

26. See Kayserling, *Mendelssohn*, 272.

27. See above, p. 307–09.

28. See above, p. 309 f.

29. *JubA*, 16, letter 205, p. 236 f.

30. See above, p. 275 f.

31. See above, p. 338 f.

32. See above, p. 339.

33. See Kayserling, *Ungedrucktes*, 56 ff., where the story of Mendelssohn's stay in Dresden is told in some detail (see also 2nd ed., 247 ff.), which may be apocryphal in part. Dassdorf's annotated edition, *Winckelmann's Briefe an seine Freunde*, appeared in two volumes (Dresden, 1777, 1780). Concerning Dassdorf, see *GS*, 5:543, note 2.

34. See *GS*, 5:543. A letter by Mendelssohn to Dassdorf, dated Aug. 16, 1779, is preserved in facsimile reproduction (see Meyer, *Bibliographie*, p. 18, no. 54b).

35. *GS*, 5:543 f.

36. Cf. *JubA*, 16, letter 206, p. 237, where Mendelssohn speaks of several letters by the baron von Ferber offering such an assurance. This may, however, have been hyperbolic language used by Mendelssohn to give added confidence to the addressee, Samuel Halberstadt. The text of the letter is quoted below.

37. *GS*, 5:544 f.

38. Cf. the last paragraph of the letter: "My heart is too full, my mind [*Gemüth*] too disturbed, and incapable of composed deliberation" (*GS*, 5:545).

39. *JubA*, 2:8.

40. *JubA*, 16, letter 206, p. 237.

41. Job 13:13; Jer. 20:9; Job 4:2.

42. Cf. Gen. 43:14; Exod. 32:14; Isa. 18:2.

43. See Kayserling, *Ungedrucktes*, 60; Idem, *Mendelssohn*, 272.

44. Isaac Euchel, *Toledot* (Vienna, 1814), 139 (not in the older edition).

45. The reading *me'eyn* in the text is probably a misprint for *me-'inyan*.

46. Ephraim Veitel Ephraim, son of Veitel Heine Ephraim, was court jeweller and elder of the community (see *JubA*, 16:lii; Meyer, *Bibliographie*, p. 269; *GS*, 5:630 f.). The report must have been written when he was still alive, i.e. before his death on Oct. 14, 1803. Euchel died on June 14, 1804; the second edition of his Mendelssohn biography appeared posthumously.

47. Not identical with Abraham Marcuse of Strelitz, as stated in *JubA*, 16:lxi; see *ZGJD*, 2 (1930): 165.

48. See Simon Dubnow, *Die neueste Geschichte des jüdischen Volkes* (Berlin, 1920), 1:54 f.

49. *GS*, 3:186.

50. Dep. RvM, C I, no. 26.

51. Nachlass Hennings, no. 22, letter 9, fol. 14*r–v*; Kayserling, *Mendelssohn*, 1st ed., 525.

52. Dep. RvM, C I, no. 27.

53. Kayserling, *Mendelssohn*, 1st ed., 488.

54. See above, p. 343 f.

55. See Kayserling, *Mendelssohn*, 1st ed., 488.

56. See *Allgemeine deutsche Bibliothek*, 39.2 (1780): 483–86. The only reference to Hennings'

public spirit occurs in the following sentence: "Herr Hennings has so much knowledge and talent, so much warm feeling for what is true, good, noble, and salutary to mankind, that one has to wish that he will continue on the course he has commenced to follow."

Cooperation with Dohm (pages 449–461)

1. See M. Ginsburger, *Cerfberr und seine Zeit* (1906); David Sinzheim, *Yad David* (Offenbach, 1799), introduction. For the historical data see Graetz, *Geschichte,* 11:62 ff.

2. Christian Wilhelm Dohm, *Über die bürgerliche Verbesserung der Juden* (Berlin & Stettin, 1781), 78 f.

3. Ibid., 193 f.

4. See below, p. 455 ff.

5. See Dohm, *Über die bürgerliche Verbesserung,* 185, note.

6. This is also the view expressed by Graetz, *Geschichte,* 11:66 f. W. Gronau, *Christian Wilhelm von Dohm nach seinem Wollen und Handeln, Ein biographischer Versuch* (Lemgo, 1824), 84 f., imprecisely states that Dohm was a participant in the editing (*Redaktion*) of the memorandum and had taken care of its composition *(Abfassung)*.

7. See Dohm, *Über die bürgerliche Verbesserung,* 78, note.

8. See Gabriel Hemerdinger, "Le Dénombrement des Israélites d'Alsace," *REJ,* 42 (1901): 254 ff.

9. See Gronau's biography (referred to in note 6) and Franz Reuss, *Christian Wilhelm Dohms Schrift "Über die bürgerliche Verbesserung der Juden" und deren Einwirkung auf die gebildeten Stände Deutschlands,* Dissertation Leipzig (Kaiserslautern, 1891), 8–16.

10. See above, p. 828, note 19.

11. See Gronau, *Dohm,* 39.

12. Ibid. 44–84.

13. Nicolai's part in persuading him is attested by Dohm's letter to Nicolai dated Jan. 9, 1782; see Ludwig Geiger, "Aus Briefen Dohm's an Nicolai," *ZGJD,* 5 (1890):76.

14. Gronau, *Dohm,* 27, 33.

15. Ibid., 82 f.

16. See Dohm, *Über die bürgerliche Verbesserung der Juden, Zweyter Theil* (Berlin & Stettin, 1783) [henceforth: Dohm, 2], 169.

17. Dohm, 2:71.

18. *Deutsches Museum,* 1778 (Oct.): 289–324.

19. *Denkwürdigkeiten meiner Zeit . . . oder Beiträge zur Geschichte* (Lemgo & Hanover, 1815), 2:266.

20. Ibid., 283 f.

21. Ibid., 282 f., note 7; 284, note 8; 4 (1819):484, note 31.

22. Excerpts from Dohm's letters to Nicolai were published and discussed by L. Geiger, *ZGJD,* 5 (1890):75–91. Dohm's letters to Mendelssohn are extant in Dep. RvM, C I, nos. 6–13, and are published, in an annotated edition, by Alexander Altmann in *The Salo W. Baron Jubilee Volume,* English section (Jerusalem, 1973).

23. Geiger, *ZGJD,* 5 (1890) :75 f.

24. "*Rath*"—more precisely: "*Oberkonsistorialrath*"—and "*Probst*" (Dean) Wilhelm Abraham Teller, the well-known theologian of the Berlin Enlightenment.

25. Dep. RvM, C I, no. 6.

26. Geiger's conjecture that publication was delayed until 1782 is unfounded.

27. Dep. RvM, C I, no. 8.

28. Dohm liked to address Mendelssohn, respectfully, in the third person.

29. See Gronau, *Dohm,* 30 f., 53.

30. *Wöchentliche Nachrichten von neuen Landcharten, geographischen . . . und historischen Büchern,* 9 (1781): 299–302, 319–20, 331–35. See Volkmar Eichstädt, *Bibliographie zur Geschichte der Judenfrage* (Hamburg, 1938), p. 8, no. 90.

31. Dep. RvM, C I, no. 7.

32. A publishing firm that printed works at the author's expense.

33. See above note 27.

34. It is found on p. 214 of the French version and on p. 239 f. of Dohm, 2.

35. Dep. RvM, C I, no. 9.

36. Published by the *Librairie des auteurs et des artistes,* Dessau (see Eichstädt, *Bibliographie,* p. 8, no. 93).

37. 1:17 f.; 22 f.; see Graetz, *Geschichte,* 11:74, note.

38. See above, p. 450.
39. Dep. RvM, C I, no. 6.
40. Dep. RvM, C I, no. 11.
41. P. 165, line 18–p. 166, line 17.
42. Wilhelm Dohm, *Über die bürgerliche Verbesserung der Juden,* First Part (1783), p. 133, line 14–p. 134, line 7.
43. *GS,* 3:201 (quoting Job 2:6; *Bava Batra* 16a).
44. See Geiger, *ZGJD,* 5(1890):77. Geiger's assumption that the words "Hierbei die Schrift von Wessely" refer to Hartwig Wessely's *Divrey Shalom Ve-Emmet* (1782) is mistaken. For the latter work, see below, pp. 478–80.
45. *Anmerkungen zu der Schrift des Herrn Dohm, über die bürgerliche Verfassung der Juden* (Altona, 1782), 32 pp. In 1778 Unzer had taken up Lessing's defense against his orthodox opponents. See Heinrich Schneider, *Lessing,* 228, and below, p. 565.
46. In a footnote to the addendum (p. 134).
47. Geiger seems to assume this because Mendelssohn claimed free copies (as mentioned in Dohm's Nov. 4, 1782, letter to Nicolai.) He ignores the circumstance that the reference is to part 2 of the treatise, to which Mendelssohn had contributed a section (pp. 72–77).
48. The term is used by Graetz, *Geschichte,* 11:74.
49. See below, p. 460.
50. Dohm, 2:72 ff.
51. *GS,* 3:181 f.
52. Jacob Katz, "The Term 'Jewish Emancipation': Its Origin and Historical Impact," *Studies in Nineteenth Century Jewish Intellectual History,* ed. Alexander Altmann (Cambridge, Mass., 1964), 15 f., observed that Mendelssohn "characteristically dropped the term *bürgerliche Verbesserung,* substituting in its stead *bürgerliche Aufnahme.*" The term *Aufnahme* corresponds to the old juridical term *jus recipiendi.* Michaelis' review of Dohm's treatise uses the phrase *aufgenommen;* see *Orientalische und Exegetische Bibliothek,* 19(1782):2; reproduced in Dohm, 2:32.
53. Michaelis saw in Dohm's plea on behalf of the poor among the Jews clear evidence that his treatise had not been "paid for by rich Jews." Concerning the charge leveled against Lessing, see below, p. 578 f.
54. Geiger, *ZGJD,* 5 (1890):76–79.
55. Dep. RvM, C I, no. 10.
56. Edited and annotated by Fritz Bamberger, "Four Unpublished Letters to Moses Mendelssohn," *Living Legacy, Essays in Honor of Hugo Hahn* (1963),. 93 f.
57. See above, p. 454.
58. P. 22 ff. Hissmann described the Jews as an incorrigible race.
59. Dep. RvM, C I, no. 12.
60. Eichstädt, *Bibliographie,* records no such review.
61. 19 (1782):1–40.
62. See Geiger, *ZGJD,* 5(1890):77.
63. *Orientalische und Exegetische Bibliothek,* 19 (1782):21 (Dohm, 2:50). The term *Lästerschrift* is found on p. 9 (Dohm, 2:39).
64. Dohm, 2:31–71.
65. Dohm, 2:300–46.
66. See Gerson Wolf, "Der Prozess Eisenmenger," *MGWJ,* 19 (1869):430, where the text of the king's letter is published.
67. Dohm, 2:112–50.
68. I found this note in the Felix Mendelssohn Bartholdy *Nachlass* ("Grüne Bücher," 29/3, depositum at the Bodleian Library, Oxford).
69. See Geiger, *ZGJD* 5 (1890): 77, 79.
70. Dep. RvM,C I, no. 13.
71. Johann Friedrich Poppe (1753–1843), who had just then been appointed professor at the Königlich Joachimsthalersches Gymnasium in Berlin.

A Momentous Event . . . (pages 461–474)

1. See Dohm's letter to Nicolai quoted above, p. 453.
2. See S. Dubnow, *Weltgeschichte des jüdischen Volkes* (Berlin, 1928), 7:372 f.
3. See Volkmar Eichstädt, *Bibliographie zur Geschichte der Judenfrage* (Hamburg, 1938), 15.

4. See Jakob Katz' essay in *Zion*, 29 (1964):127 f., where the principal bibliographical references are given.

5. *JubA*, 16, letter 248, p. 278 f.

6. Gen. 24:50.

7. Katz, *Zion*, 29:128 f., expressed a different view.

8. Marburg File, no. 47.

9. Dohm, 2:137 f.

10. See above, p. 459 f.

11. *Orientalische und Exegetische Bibliothek*, 19(1782):28; Dohm, 2:57. A similar stipulation was contained in the earlier version of the edict issued for Bohemia (see Dubnow, *Weltgeschichte*, 7:374 f.; Katz, *Zion*, 29:127).

12. *Orientalische . . . Bibliothek*, 19:22; Dohm, 2:51. A similar view has been expressed by Dubnow, *Weltgeschichte*, 7:375; Idem, *Die neueste Geschichte des jüdischen Volkes* (Berlin 1920): 30 f.

13. Dohm, 2:182–85, 363–76. Cf. Peter Philipp Wolf, *Geschichte der Veränderungen . . . unter der Regierung Joseph II.* (Germanien, 1795), 239 ff., where the "improvement of the civil condition of the Jews " and the "mistreatment of the deists" are discussed.

14. Dohm, 2:184.

15. *GS*, 5:613.

16. The view that Mendelssohn was perturbed by some anti-Jewish measures (see Katz, *Zion*, 19:130) is unfounded.

17. *GS*, 5:639f. The periodical (named *Judenbibliothek*) appeared in two issues (Leipzig, 1786–1787). See Geiger, *Geschichte der Juden in Berlin*, 2:132 f.

18. See *GS*, 3:182, where the title of the periodical is quoted, and p. 203, where the title of the treatise is given in an abbreviated German translation.

19. See Kayserling, *Mendelssohn*, 375; Ludwig Geiger, *ZGJD*, 1 (1887):123; *Meyer, Bibliographie*, p. 53, no. 262. Joseph Mendelssohn seems to have attributed the translation to his father (see *GS*, 1:28, where the title page is misquoted). That Mendelssohn was not himself the translator is attested by Hartwig Wessely's "Second Epistle: *Rav Tuv Le-Vet Yisrael*" (Berlin, 1782); see below, p. 484 f.

20. See Meyer, *Bibliographie*, 284, *s.v.*

21. Simon Höchheimer, *Über Mendelsohns* [sic] *Tod* (Vienna & Leipzig, 1786), 71.

22. Part of this note has been quoted above, p. 462.

23. Marburg File, no. 47.

24. *GS*, 3:202.

25. Nachlass Hennings, no. 22, letter 25, fol. 50; reproduced by L. Geiger in *ZGJD*, 1 (1887):119.

26. *Manasseh Ben Israel, Rettung der Juden. Aus dem Englischen übersetzt. Nebst einer Vorrede von Moses Mendelssohn. Als ein Anhang zu des Hrn. Kriegsraths Dohm Abhandlung: Über die bürgerliche Verbesserung der Juden* (Berlin & Stettin, 1782); reproduced in *GS*, 3:177–254.

27. *Salomon und Joseph II* (Vienna, 1781); see *Ha-Me'assef*, 1784 (German supplement). On Isaac Alexander (c. 1722–c. 1800) see M. Kayserling, *MGWJ*, 16 (1867):161–67. Mendelssohn had little respect for him; see *JubA*, 16, letter 248, p. 279, xcii.

28. *GS*, 3:179.

29. JubA,11, letter 16, p. 28; *JubA*, 1:194, 498.

30. Viz., the anonymous author (Hermann Samuel Reimarus) of the "fragments" on natural religion that were published by Lessing.

31. Friedrich Eberhard von Rochow stated in a letter to Mendelssohn, dated May 9, 1782 (Dep. RvM,C II, no. 33; see below, p. 492–96), that the Fragmentist had, in fact, been preceded by Basedow.

32. See below, p. 577 f., 697.

33. *GS*, 3:180.

34. See the passage, *GS*, 3:181, where distinct reference is made to the "difficulties" raised by "the nation that was to be educated" *(der zu bildenden Nation)*.

35. Dohm, 2:152.

36. *Orientalische . . . Bibliothek*, 19: 11–16; Dohm, 2:40–45.

37. Mendelssohn referred to the interpretation of Cant. 2:7 (3:5) found in *Midrash Rabba* ad loc. and Ketuvot 111a, which he called "mystical."

38. *GS*, 3:182.

39. *GS*, 3:185; see above, p. 430 f.

40. Dohm, 2:72–74.

41. *GS,* 3:182 f.
42. GS, 3:187.
43. Cf. Michaelis' argument (*Orientalische . . . Bibliothek,* 19:16; Dohm, 2:45).
44. See *GS,* 3:245 f. (ch. 6).
45. See Mendelssohn's reference to Justi in a letter to Abbt (*GS,*5:271).
46. On Sonnenfels see below, p. 504.
47. See Wilhelm Roscher, *Geschichte der Nationalökonomik in Deutschland* (München, 1874), 444–65; 533–52; Robert A. Kann, *A Study in Austrian Intellectual History* (New York, 1960), 175 ff., 324.
48. Dohm, 2:159 f.
49. *GS,* 3:189.
50. The article expressing this view had appeared in *Ephemeriden der Menschheit,* October, 1782, no. 10:423; see *GS,* 3:301. Its author was the Swiss economist G. Beckmann; see Eichstädt, *Bibliographie,* 8, no. 90, where yet another article by the same writer in *Physikalisch-ökonomische Bibliothek,* 12 (1782): 124–29, is listed.
51. See above, p. 431 ff.
52. Cf. the Aristotelian distinction between making *(poiein)* and doing *(prattein)* in *Ethica Nicomachea,* 608a, 17.
53. "Nicht nur wer mit Händen arbeitet."
54. Dohm, 2:248–99.
55. See *JubA,* 2:292; 320.
56. *GS,* 4.1:128–31.
57. See the survey of the various legal positions offered by Dohm, 1:126–29, note.
58. See Geiger, *Geschichte der Juden in Berlin,* 2:123 ff.
59. See S. Rawidowicz, *JubA,* 7:cxlv–cl. The work is reproduced in *GS,* 6:1–118; *JubA,* 7:109–251 (with valuable notes by Rawidowicz).
60. See Dohm, 1:124–27.
61. *GS,* 3:193.
62. See Jacob Katz, "A State Within a State, The History of an Anti-Semitic Slogan," *The Israel Academy of Sciences and Humanities Proceedings,* 4.3 (Jerusalem, 1969): 38.
63. *GS,* 3:193 f., 197.
64. See Ismar Elbogen, "Die Bezeichnung 'jüdische Nation'," *MGWJ,* 63, n.s. 27 (1919): 207.
65. See above, p. 450, 455 f.
66. See Selma Stern, *Der Preussische Staat und die Juden,,* 1.1:113.
67. See above, p. 465, and below, pp. 478, 480–86.
68. *GS,* 3:197 f.
69. *GS,* 3:234–37.
70. *GS,* 3:199.
71. *GS,* 3:194 f.
72. *GS,* 3:201.
73. See Kayserling, *Mendelssohn,* 298 ff., 378. The communal records of the case were found by Jacob Katz in the Jewish Historical Archives in Jerusalem (see Katz, *Zion,* 29:115, note 27). A second hand copy of the letter of rebuke sent by the government to Chief Rabbi Raphael Kohen (published by Kayserling, *Mendelssohn,,* 299 f.) is extant in the Staatsbibliothek Preussischer Kulturbesitz, Berlin.
74. *Über den Missbrauch der geistlichen Macht und weltlichen Herrschaft in Glaubenssachen durch Beyspiele aus dem jetzigen Jahrhundert ins Licht gesetzt* (Berlin, 1781).
75. See Gronau, *Dohm,* 90 f.
76. See the references in Eichstädt, *Bibliographie,* 7, nos. 84–87.
77. The case was mentioned (with anti-Jewish bias) as late as 1789 in the *Chronic von Berlin;* see Eichstädt, *Bibliographie,* 187, no. 2358–9.
78. Here the term "nation" is clearly used in the sense of "religious community."
79. *GS,* 3:201 f.

The Issue of Educational Reform (pages 474–489)

1. See A.F. Pribram, *Urkunden und Akten zur Geschichte der Juden in Wien,* 1 (Vienna & Leipzig, 1918): 496.
2. Ibid.

3. Ibid., 497. In Germany, Jewish children were admitted to primary and high schools; cf. Mendelssohn's letter to Campe, *GS*, 3:420.

4. *Normalschulen* and *Realschulen*.

5. Reproduced by Pribram, *Urkunden*, 513 f. The decree, though preceding the proclamation of the Edict of Tolerance in Lower Austria, was issued to all states within the Austrian monarchy.

6. Pribram, *Urkunden*, 514 f., quoting G[erson] Wolf, *Geschichte des Unterrichtes der israelitischen Jugend in Wien*, 10 f.

7. See G. Wolf, *Geschichte der Juden in Wien* (Vienna, 1876), 87.

8. Pribram, *Urkunden*, 515.

9. See above, p. 352.

10. See below, p. 488.

11. Dep. RvM, C II, No. 34.

12. See Eduard Winter, *Ferdinand Kindermann Ritter von Schulstein (1740-1801) der Organisator der Volksschule und Volkswohlfahrt Böhmens. Ein Lebensbild nach archivalischen Quellen* (Augsburg, 1926). Schulstein became Bishop of Leitmeritz in 1790.

13. See Winter, *Schulstein*, 69.

14. Ibid., 132.

15. Mentioned by Charles L. Ozer, "Jewish Education in the Transition from the Ghetto to Emancipation," *Historia Judaica*, ed. Guido Kisch, 9 (New York, 1947): 86 f. No source reference is given.

16. *gesellschaftlichen*.

17. See Winter, *Schulstein*, 167.

18. Ibid., 132.

19. See Wolf, *Geschichte der Juden in Wien*, 86 f.

20. See Naphtali Herz Wesel [Hartwig Wessely], *Divrey Shalom Ve-Emmet* (Vienna, 1826), 81–86 ("Third Epistle").

21. For an appreciation of Morpurgo see Yitshak Rivkind's article in *Studies in Jewish Bibliography and Related Subjects in Memory of Abraham Solomon Freidus* (New York, 1929), 138–59 (Hebrew Section). Morpurgo's ambition to produce an anthology of medieval Hebrew poetry remained unfulfilled (see p. 147 f.).

22. Rivkind, *Studies*, 142.

23. See Graetz, *Geschichte*, 11:96; *JubA*, 16:xcii.

24. *JubA*, 16:xcii.

25. *JubA*, 16, letter 254, p. 281 f., xciii.

26. See Wessely's letter to the leaders of Trieste Jewry dated Iyyar 23, 5542/1782, ed. Reggio, *Kerem Hemed*, 1 (Vienna, 1833): 5.

27. Quoted here from the Vienna edition of 1826 (see note 20 above), which also contains the three epistles written by Wessely in defense—though with considerable modifications—of his original plea.

28. Graetz and others suggested March as the month of publication, but in view of the fact that the opposition had gained momentum and reached its peak around Passover, which commenced on March 29, some weeks prior to this date must be allowed. See Mordechai Eliav, *Ha-Hinukh Ha-Yehudi Be-Germaniya Bi-Yemey Ha-Haskala Ve-Ha-Emantsipatsia* (Jerusalem, 1960), 40, note 6. Jost, Zinberg, Ozer and Eliav assume that the pamphlet appeared in January; see Ozer, *Historia Judaica*, 9:87, note 19, where the literature on the subject is quoted.

29. *Divrey Shalom Ve-Emmet* (henceforth quoted as *DSVE*), 4. The rabbinic statement is found in *Lev. Rabba*, 9:3; *Seder Eliyahu Rabba* (ed. M. Friedmann), p. 1 (abbreviated); cf. *Pesahim*, 118a.

30. *DSVE*, 6.

31. See his "Second Epistle," *DSVE*, 37 f.

32. Ibid., 4.

33. See above, p. 217.

34. *Ha-nimusiyot, ha-limmudiyot, ve-ha-tiv'iyot*.

35. *Lev. Rabba*, 1:15. M. Margaliot (ed.), *Midrash Wayikra' Rabba*, I (Jerusalem, 1953), p. 32, note 5, has shown this statement to be a gloss from *Seder Eliyahu Rabba*, chap. 6. It is mentioned by Wessely, *DSVE*, 4 f.

36. Wessely had offered this interpretation of the *Lev. Rabba* passage as early as in his commentary on *Avot, Yeyn Levanon* (1774, 138b), as he recalled in his "Fourth Epistle" *(DSVE*, 216).

37. Wessely, *DSVE*, 11 f.
38. Ibid., 15 f., 20.
39. Ibid., 18.
40. Ibid., 13–15.
41. See his comparison of the linguistic deficiency of the German Jews with the mastery of the vernacular by the Jews of Italy, France, England, Turkey, and the Arab countries: *DSVE,*16 f.
42. *Sheney Luhot Ha-Berit,* section on *Shavu'ot* (fol. 181b in the Fürth edition of 5524/1764).
43. [Shabbatai Sheftel Horovitz], *Vavey Ha-'Amudim,* ch. 5 (fol. 8a in the Nuremberg edition of 5522/1762). For similar criticisms of the educational system by prominent authorities see Ozer, *Historia Judaica,* 9:152 ff.
44. Wessely, *DSVE*, 39 f.; see also the "verdicts" *(pesakim)* of the three Venetian rabbis, reproduced in Wessely's "Third Epistle" *(DSVE,* 97).
45. *DSVE,* 20 f.
46. See the detailed account by Eliav, *Ha-Hinukh,* 47–50.
47. See Ozer, *Historia Judaica,* 9:148–51; Eliav, *Ha-Hinukh,* 50 f. For a penetrating analysis see Ernst Simon, "The Pedagogical Philanthropinism and Jewish Education," in the *Mordecai Kaplan Jubilee Volume* (New York, 1953), 149–87 (Hebrew Section).
48. *Derushey Ha-Tselah* (Jerusalem, 1966), no. 39, fol. 53a–54a, pp. 105–07.
49. See Wessely's private letter, ed. Reggio, *Kerem Hemed,* 1:6.
50. The full text of this sermon was published by Louis Lewin, "Aus dem jüdischen Kulturkampfe," *JJLG,* 12 (1918): 182–94.
51. *Kerem Hemed,* 1:5; *JubA,* 16:281.
52. Wessely, *DSVE,* 23–69.
53. The first pamphlet had been addressed to the Jewish communities under Austrian rule.
54. *Kerem Hemed,*1:7.
55. See Wessely, *DSVE,* 77 ("Third Epistle").
56. Ibid., 131–220.
57. Ibid., 66; 82, note 2; 119, note 1.
58. Ibid., 30; 93, note 2.
59. The sentence is omitted in the text published by Reggio but occurs in a copy of the letter discovered by M. Güdemann. See *MGWJ,* 19, n.s. 2 (1870): 478–80.
60. See Graetz, *MGWJ,* 20, n.s. 3:465–69; Lewin, *JJLG,* 12:194–97.The Gaon occupied no rabbinic post.
61. See the emendation of the Reggio text *(ha-rabbanim* for *ha-rabim)* by Graetz, *Geschichte,* 11:591.
62. *Kerem Hemed,* 1:6.
63. Rivkind, *Studies,* 151. Morpurgo's letter to Rabbi Israel Benjamin Basan of Reggio (Sivan 17, 5542) quotes this information (ibid., 150).
64. Lit.: "after having had it suspended on an iron chain in the courtyard of the synagogue." See Lewin, *JJLG,* 12:188.
65. Ibid., 192.
66. See Mordecai Wilensky, *Hasidim U-Mitnaggedim* (Jerusalem, 1970), 1:42. The Polish word *Kuna* used in the letter from Vilna dated Iyyar 8, 5532/1772, denotes an "iron chain fastened to the wall" of the synagogue (ibid., 43, note 45). David Tevele spoke of the very same thing (see note 64).
67. About Wessely's rehabilitation see Moses S. Samet, "Mendelssohn, Wessely, and the Rabbis of their Time" (in Hebrew), in *Studies in the History of the Jewish People and the Land of Israel in Memory of Zvi Avneri,* ed. by A. Gilboa, B. Mevorach, U. Rappaport, A. Shochet (Haifa, 1970), 255. As for the argument from the Gaon's fondness of the *Bi'ur* on Leviticus, see ibid., 246.
68. Graetz' note on Güdemann's article, *MGWJ,* 19, n.s. 2:480, mentioned only that a letter by the Gaon giving such advice was said to exist. He did not testify that he had seen this letter "with his own eyes," as stated by Samet, *Mendelssohn, Wessely ...,* 248.
69. See Wilensky, *Hasidim,* 1:101, 107 (note 1). During the first phase (1772), hasidic writings, which then existed only in the form of unpublished manuscripts—the *Toledot Ya'akov Yosef* (1780) was the first hasidic book to be printed—had been burned in Vilna in the manner described by David Tevele (ibid., 1:42 f.; above, notes 64 and 66). A hasidic tradition ascribes

the burning of *Toledot Ya'akov Yosef* also to Ezekiel Landau (cf. Wilensky, *Hasidim* 1:42, note 44).

70. See Israel Zinberg, *Toledot Sifrut Yisrael*, 5 (1959), 327; Eliav, *Ha-Hinukh*, 46; Samet, *Mendelssohn, Wessely* . . ., 246.

71. The book *Toledot Ya'akov Yosef* was most probably burned in the summer of 1781, whereas Wessely's pamphlet appeared as late as 1782. Apart from David Tevele's statement in his sermon, and in a letter he is alleged to have written to Amsterdam (see Ozer, *Historia Judaica* 9:142 f.), there is only Wessely's report and an utterance by Chief Rabbi Pinhas Ha-Levi Horowitz to this effect ("I have heard that in many holy congregations these books [sc. by Wessely] were burned, and that in Vilna this was done publicly"). Both these testimonies merely reecho David Tevele's mistaken statement. For the context of Horowitz' reference, see below, p. 485 f. There is no evidence that the pamphlet was burned in Posen.

72. See Wessely's second letter to the Trieste community, dated June 28, 1782 (Rivkind, *Studies*, 152). According to a note by David Friedländer, written in his old age, in March, 1820 *(GS,* 5:593), the rabbi of Lissa was acting in concert with Shelomo Dov Berusch, the rabbi of Glogau; see Graetz, *Geschichte*, 11:591. Wessely's testimony, which mentions only the rabbis of Lissa and Posen, may perhaps be considered the more reliable, since it was written at the time, See Samet, *Mendelssohn, Wessely* . . ., 250 f.

73. See Kayserling, *Mendelssohn*, 311.

74. *GS*, 5:594.

75. See above, p. 223.

76. Kayserling, *Mendelssohn*, 312.

77. Kayserling (ibid., 311) was certainly right in his assumption that Mendelssohn had intervened. Samet's objections are unfounded.

78. See M. Freudenthal, "R. Wolf Dessau," *Martin Philippson Festschrift*, 207 f. Wolf Dessau had previously published a Hebrew commentary on the Book of Job, called *Pesher Davar*. He was a friend of the Dessau philanthropinists, and was esteemed highly by both Mendelssohn and Wessely. See also JubA, 16, letter 190, p. 214. Mendelssohn's letter of July 11, 1782, is reproduced in *GS*, 5:600 ff.

79. Should read: "Words of Peace and Truth." The same misquotation is found in Zedlitz' second letter. If Mendelssohn was the source of Zedlitz' information, as we assume he was, it is no mere coincidence that the same error is found also in Mendelssohn's reference to the work.

80. *der vernünftigere Theil der Nation.* This phrase reflects Wolf Dessau's expression, *von dem einigermassen verständigen Theile unserer Nation*, which he had used in the emended preface of his manual on the Jewish religion; see Freudenthal, "R. Wolf Dessau," 207 f., where the text is quoted.

81. Wessely, *DSVE*, 66.

82. Ibid., 77, 130. The "Fourth Epistle," entitled *Rehovot*, appeared in 1785.

83. Rivkind, *Studies*, 152.

84. Ezekiel Landau's letter (undated) was published by S. Assaf, *Mekorot Le-Toledot Ha-Hinukh Be-Yisra'el*, 1 (1925): 239, quoted by Samet, *Mendelssohn, Wessely* . . ., 252. Samet (ibid.) has drawn attention to yet another letter alleged to have been written by Landau to Lewin in 1782, in which both Wessely and Mendelssohn are vilified. This letter appears to be unauthentic.

85. See above, p. 473.

86. See Jacob Katz, *Zion*, 29 (1964): 115 f. and note 30. Johann Georg Meusel, *Das Gelehrte Teutschland*, 1, 5th ed. (Lemgo, 1796), 637, had already noted that Cranz' *Über den Missbrauch der geistlichen Macht* (1781) appeared in two parts.

87. Wessely, *DSVE*, 79.

88. See above, p. 484.

89. Wessely, *DSVE*, 40.

90. Ibid., 28, 35, 37, 64.

91. Ibid., 51.

92. Ibid., 67–69.

93. That Horowitz acted in league with David Tevele of Lissa is attested by the letter he wrote to him on Tammuz 6, reporting on the action he had taken and promising more of the kind; see the passage quoted by Samet, Mendelssohn, Wessely . . ., 248. It is likely that he had also been approached by Ezekiel Landau (ibid., 246).

94. Author of the *novellae* on the Talmud, entitled *Hafla'a* and of many other works.

95. The day is observed as a minor fast-day (Yom Kippur Katan).

96. Quoted by Graetz, *MGWJ*, 20, n.s. 3 (1871): 467 f. and Markus Horovitz, *Frankfurter Rabbinen*, 4 (Frankfurt am Main,, 1885), 53–59; ed. by Josef Unna (Jerusalem, 1969), 223–29. Both Graetz and Horovitz had excerpted a manuscript of the sermon put at their disposal by the chief rabbi of Copenhagen, Professor Dr. Wolff, son of Rabbi Sender Wolf of Darmstadt, who was studying at the time in Frankfurt, was present when the homily was delivered, and made a copy from the original text entitled *Tokhahat Mussar;* see Graetz, *MGWJ*, 20, n.s. 3:466, note 1; Horovitz, *Frankfurter Rabbinen*, 53, note 1; ed. Unna, 224, note 4. Efforts to trace Sender Wolf's manuscript have been unsuccessful.

97. See above, p. 414 f.

98. Wessely, *DSVE*, 62–65.

99. Cf. *Sanhedrin*, 71b.

100. *Tselah 'al Berakhot* (Prague, 1791). Although the volume appeared as late as 1791, its completion in 1783 is attested by Landau's own remark to this effect in *Tselah 'al Pesahim* (Prague, 1783), fol. 116; see Samet, *Mendelssohn, Wessely ...*, 241, note 55.

101. *Berakhot*, 28b. Landau's interpretation of this passage has been omitted in many subsequent editions. A survey of the large variety of interpretations bestowed upon the term *higgayon* is found in Naphtali Wieder's *The Judean Scrolls and Karaism* (London, 1962), 236–39.

102. *Derushey Ha-Tselah* (Jerusalem, 1966), no. 14, fol, 24a f., p. 47f. The year in which the sermon was delivered is not stated. Judging from its references to contemporary trends, it could not have been earlier than 1782, the year in which Joseph II's educational reforms, aiming at making the Jews more "useful" citizens, were introduced.

103. See S.H. Lieben, "Rabbi Eleasar Fleckeles." *JJLG*, 10 (1912):1–33.

104. *'Olat Hodesh Ha-Sheni* (subtitle: *'Olat Tsibbur),* Prague, 1787, no. 1.

105. *ke-garzina ha-ba'a be-aharona;* see *Lam. Rabba*, introduction.

106. Here the clumsy term that occurs in Landau's *haskama* for Sussmann Glogau (see above, p. 382), crops up again. Had Fleckeles drafted the haskama, perhaps? A suspicion that Landau had left its writing to one of his disciples was voiced in *Ha-Me'assef,* 1786.

107. *Hotem Tokhnit* (Vienna, 1797), 25–32.

108. *Sendschreiben an die deutschen Juden* (written in German and published as an appendix to *Ha-Me'assef,* 1788). Samet, *Mendelssohn, Wessely ...*, 242, interpreted Fleckeles' attack as having been directed primarily against the use of German characters in the anonymous edition [by Löffier] of the book of Genesis and in Mendelssohn's translation of the Psalms (1783). There are no grounds on which to base such an interpretation. Samet's assumption that the German-lettered edition of Genesis appeared without Mendelssohn's knowledge is mistaken. See above, p. 389.

109. See above, p. 475 f.

110. *GS,* 5:611–13. The letter must have been written in March, 1783.

111. A good-natured reference to Schulstein's emphasis on the supposed need to teach Jews the "social virtues."

112. Dep. RvM, C II, no. 36.

113. *Lesebuch für jüdische Kinder* (Prague, 1784). See *JubA*, 16:xcviii.

114. *Nachricht von dem Ursprunge und Fortgang der deutschen jüdischen Hauptschule zu Prag* (Prague, 1785). See Winter, *Schulstein*, 69, note 1.

115. *JubA*, 16, letter 281, p. 298 f.

116. *JubA*, 16, letter 282, p. 299 f.

117. *JubA*, 16, letter 277, p. 295 f.; *GS*, 6:451, letter 5, where the word *meiner* (line 1) has to be changed to *der*. As for the year in which this letter was written, see *Ha-Me'assef*, 1786, p. 144. Rabbi Hanokh was probably Hanokh Rocknitz of Vienna; see *JubA*, 16:xcvii; *JubA*, 14:375.

118. See above, p. 382 f.

The Summer of 1782 (pages 489–513)

1. *GS,* 5:655 f.

2. See above, p. 480–86.

3. See above, p. 483 f.

4. A brief account of the challenges presented to Mendelssohn in response to the preface

is found in Alexander Altmann, "A New Evaluation of Moses Mendelssohn's *Jerusalem* in the Light of Biographical Data," (in Hebrew), *Zion*, 33 (1968):50 f.

5. Cf. above, p. 464. The copy of the letter extant in Nachlass Hennings, no. 22, letter 25, fol. 50r–56v, contains numerous corrections in Hennings' hand, applied by him when he planned to publish his correspondence with Mendelssohn. It has been published in its original form, with some minor deviations, by L. Geiger in *ZGJD*, 1 (1887):119–23. The quotations given here follow the original text.

6. Hennings' *Über Duldung* (Copenhagen, 1780) appeared as a separate reprint of a chapter contained in his *Philosophische Versuche* (Copenhagen, 1779–1780). See Joachim Hild, *August Hennings . . .* (Erlangen, 1932), 60.

7. See Voltaire, *Traité sure la tolérance*, ch. 12; Arthur Herzberg, *The French Enlightenment and the Jews* (New York, 1968), index, q. v. Voltaire, anti-Semitism of.

8. *GS*, 3:226–38.

9. See above, p. 473.

10. A reference to the *'Aleynu* prayer quoted by Manasseh ben Israel and commented on by Mendelssohn *(GS*, 3:235 f.). See above, p. 307 ff.

11. Quoted by Bertha Badt-Strauss (with no indication of the source) in her beautiful essay, "Elise Reimarus und Moses Mendelssohn," *ZGJD*, 4 (1932):180.

12. See L. Geiger, *ZGJD*, 1 (1887):123.

13. Quoted by Bertha Badt-Strauss, "Elise Reimarus," 181 (no source reference given).

14. Dep. RvM, C II, no. 33.

15. *ADB*, 28:727–34.

16. See above, p. 466.

17. *GS*, 3:187 f.

18. *GS*, 3:193.

19. *GS*, 3:187.

20. *GS*, 3:193.

21. See above, p. 475 f.

22. Dep. RvM, C II, no. 34, p. 6.

23. They appeared under the title, *Vermischte Abhandlungen über Gegenstände der Gesetz-gebung und Rechtsgelehrsamkeit*, 1, Leipzig, 1779; 2 and 3, Leipzig, 1780. The entire work is reviewed in *Allgemeine deutsche Bibliothek*, 51.1 (1782):153–55. For the data mentioned here see Klein's autobiographical essay in M. S. Lowe, ed., *Bildnisse jetzt lebender Berliner Gelehrten mit ihren Selbstbiographieen*, 2 (Berlin, 1806), 45 f.

24. Lowe, *Bildnisse*, 46.

25. Ibid., 53.

26. Ibid., 46 f.

27. The essay is entitled *Von dem Erfüllungseide der Juden gegen die Christen*. It is referred to by Christian Wilhelm Dohm, *Über die bürgerliche Verbesserung der Juden*, 2 (Berlin & Stettin, 1783):308. The subject had aroused some interest. In his *Beantwortung der Frage: Ob die Zulassung eines Judeneydes wider einen Christen bedenklich sey?* (Halle, 1778), Philipp Jacob Heisler had argued against anti-Jewish prejudice expressed in Estor's treatise *Von der Misslichkeit der Judeneyde* (1753). Klein was not the only jurist to plead for fair treatment of Jews.

28. Klein's letter of inquiry is unfortunately lost, and Mendelssohn's reply as reproduced (probably from the draft) in *GS*, 5:606–09, is undated. The editor (ibid.) was right in suggesting "c. 1782" as the year but wrong in placing the letter after Klein's of Aug. 29, 1782. For the letter was referred to by Mendelssohn in one of his marginal notes to Klein's letter June 5 to him (JubA, 7:265). It could hardly have been written prior to Klein's coming to Berlin in the winter of 1781, for it presupposes a personal acquaintance of the two men. The only possible assumption is that Klein wrote his inquiry shortly after his return to Breslau. According to his statement in Lowe, *Bildnisse*, 47, he spent the *summer* of 1782 on leave of absence in Breslau. This need not be taken too literally: he seems to have left Berlin toward the end of April. Mendelssohn *(GS*, 5:606) refers to his letter of inquiry as one of the fifth of this month, which we take to mean May 5. He referred to his own letter of reply on June 5 (JubA, 7:265), at which time he and Klein were working on the proposals. The rabbinic sources referred to—but not spelled out—in Mendelssohn's reply to Klein are the following: *Talmud Nedarim*, 27a–b; Maimonides, *Mishne Tora, Hilkhot Shevu'ot*, 3:1; *Bet Yosef on Tur, Yore De'a*, #232; *Shulhan 'Arukh, Yore De'a*, #232:14. Heisler's *Beantwortung* is mentioned by Mendelssohn *(GS*, 5:606–07). It seems that Dohm, when writing the passage

on Jewish law concerning compulsory oaths (Dohm 2:331 ff.), had the draft of Mendelssohn's letter to Klein before him.

29. For details, see L. Geiger, *Geschichte der Juden in Berlin*, 2:72 f., 265–80; Leopold Zunz, *Gesammelte Schriften*, 2 (Berlin, 1876): 241–64; *EJ*, 9:533–41.

30. All documents mentioned are reproduced in *JubA*, 7:257–76.

31. *JubA*, 7:255 f.

32. See the source references given by Rawidowicz, *JubA*, 7:488 f.

33. See the references to Zacharias Frankel's critical remarks in *JubA*, 7:488.

34. *JubA*, 7:258.

35. *JubA*, 7:264 f.

36. See *JubA*, 7:clviii f., 490.

37. *JubA*, 7:279; *GS*, 5:605.

38. *JubA*, 7:277. For the sequel of Klein's and Mendelssohn's cooperation in the matter of Jewish oaths see *JubA*, 7:clix f., 280–93. The final outcome was the government order of May 1, 1786, which contained an appreciative reference to Mendelssohn's help.

39. Dep. RvM, C I, no. 49; *JubA*, 7:278.

40. *GS*, 3:279.

41. *Schreiben an Garve über den Unterschied der Zwangs- und Gewissenspflichten* (Berlin, 1789); see Lowe, *Bildnisse*, 56.

42. See Kayserling, *Mendelssohn*, 456, and *Erste Beilage zur Königlich privilegierten Berlinischen Zeitung*, Apr. 13, 1862, no. 88:3–4; Lowe, *Bildnisse*, 59.

43. Lowe, *Bildnisse*, 85. The others were Shaftesbury, Sulzer, Jacobi, Kant and Fichte.

44. Lowe, *Bildnisse*, 53, where Mendelssohn figures among a galaxy of Berlin scholars (Spalding, Engel, Dohm, Selle, *et. al.*) who became Klein's friends.

45. Lowe, *Bildnisse*, 14 f.

46. A letter from Klein to Mendelssohn dated Dec. 2, 1783, addresses him as "Dearest Friend" and thanks him for his efffort to place an essay by Klein in the newly established *Berlinische Monatsschrift:* Dep. RvM, C I, no. 50.

47. Marburg File, no. 51.

48. *M. Tulli Ciceronis Epistularum ad Familiares Libri Sedecim*, V, xii, 1: epistula enim non erubescit ("for a letter does not blush").

49. In large octavo on handmade paper with rough edge.

50. *GS*, 5:649 f.

51. *JubA*, 11, letter 10, p. 19.

52. See above, p. 242 ff.

53. Nachlass Hennings, no. 11, fol. 161r.

54. "Grüne Bücher," 11:78, Depositum at the Bodleian Library, Oxford; published in Alexander Altmann, "Moses Mendelssohn's gesammelte Schriften, Neuerschlossene Briefe zur Geschichte ihrer Herausgabe," *BLBI*, 11, no. 42 (1968):80. As shown in this essay, it was Felix Mendelssohn Bartholdy whose initiative led to the publication of his grandfather's collected works in the Leipzig edition of 1843–1845. Joseph Mendelssohn had considered such a plan thirty years earlier (see Hanns Günther Reissner, "Mendelssohn-Miszellen," *BLBI*, 12, nos. 46–47 [1969]: 212 f.), but nothing had come of it.

55. *Das Forschen nach Licht und Recht in einem Schreiben an den Herrn Moses Mendelssohn auf Veranlassung seiner merkwürdigen Vorrede zu Manasseh Ben Israel* (Berlin, 1782).

56. See [Josef von] *Sonnenfels gesammelte Schriften*, 8 (Vienna, 1786): 105 f.

57. *GS*, 5:656; 660.

58. See *JubA*, 14:376. Dr. Münter was involved in polemic with Hennings. In a letter to Hennings, written on June 20, 1780, Mendelssohn expressed disapproval of his friend's immoderate tone vis-à-vis Münter. See Nachlass Hennings, no. 22, letter 17, fol. 27v; Kayserling, *Mendelssohn*, 1st ed., 529.

59. Øjvind Andreasen, ed., *Aus den Tagebüchern Friedrich Münters, Wander- und Lehrjahre eines dänischen Gelehrten*, 1, 1772–85 (Copenhagen & Leipzig, 1937): 37–51; Idem, ed., *Aus dem Briefwechsel Friedrich Münters, Europäische Beziehungen eines dänischen Gelehrten 1780–1830*, 1 (Copenhagen & Leipzig, 1944) :390–92. See Jacob Katz, "To whom was Mendelssohn replying in his *Jerusalem?*," *Zion*, 29 (1964) :112– 32, where this material was first utilized in the service of Mendelssohn research.

60. *Aus dem Briefwechsel*, 1:390 f. On the basis of Münter's remark in the letter and his entries in the diary Katz was able to present a most convincing case for the assumption that the author of the anonymous pamphlet *Das Forschen . . .* was Sonnenfels and not August

Friedrich Cranz, as had been assumed by several historians. However, in a note published in *Zion*, 36 (1971): 116–17, Katz disclosed fresh evidence that had come to light and, accordingly, modified his view. See below, p. 511 ff.

61. *Aus den Tagebüchern*, 1:51.

62. Ibid., 1:37 f.

63. Ibid., 1:41.

64. Ibid., 1:42; see Katz, *Zion*, 29:118, where the consistency of Teller's attitude is shown.

65. Geiger, *Briefe*, 114.

66. For Sonnenfels' pedigree see Hans Jäger-Sustenau's essay on the subject in Heinz F. Friedrichs, ed., *Genealogisches Jahrbuch*, vol. 10 (Neustadt/Aisch, 1970). On Michel Hasid see Max Freudenthal's study, *MGW*, 76, n.s. 40 (1932): 370–85.

67. See R. A. Kann, *A Study in Austrian Intellectual History* (New York, 1960): 146–258.

68. See Alfred F. Pribram, *Urkunden und Akten zur Geschichte der Juden in Wien*, 1 (Vienna & Leipzig, 1918): 487 f., 491 f.

69. In 1810 he became president of the Vienna Academy of Creative Arts. Beethoven dedicated a piano sonata (op. 28) to him.

70. See *Sonnenfels gesammelte Schriften*, 1 (1783), introduction.

71. Ibid., 3 (1783), Dedicatory Address: 234 f.

72. Ibid., 3:259. The passages quoted here appeared originally in his *Der Mann ohne Vorurtheil*, 3 (Vienna, 1767).

73. Reviewed in *Allgemeine deutsche Bibliothek*, 51.2 (1782): 564 f., as one of "41 Viennese pamphlets that appeared on the occasion of the pope's stay in Vienna, including some others" (pp. 561–609).

74. Published in *Sonnenfels gesammelte Schriften*, 9 (1786): 215–42. Sonnenfels' *Fragment* is quoted in the anonymous tract *Die Reise des Pabstes zum Kaiser, Nebst einer kurzen Erzählung von der Veranlassung dazu* (?, 1782):156 f.

75. *Allgemeine deutsche Bibliothek*, 51.2 (1782):572–77.

76. *Das Forschen*, 3–9.

77. The phrase actually used by Mendelssohn (see *JubA*, 7:7, 12) was "the religion of my fathers."

78. *Das Forschen*, 10 f.

79. Deut. 27:26; *Das Forschen*, 18. The "harshness" of the Mosaic Law had been stressed in Socinianism. The ground was thereby prepared for the view that the Old and New Testaments had hardly anything in common. See Leo Strauss, *Spinoza's Critique of Religion* (New York, 1965), 65, 278, note 39.

80. *GS*, 3:306 f.

81. The Gospel according to St. John, 4:21, 24; *Das Forschen*, 24 f.

82. A characteristically biblical phrase *(helek ve-nahala)*.

83. *Das Forschen*, 27–30.

84. Ibid., 31 f.

85. Ibid., 33 f.

86. Ibid., 34–37.

87. Ibid., 40 f.

88. Ibid., 41.

89. Thus formulated in the first draft of *Jerusalem*, no. 3 (see below, p. 515).

90. *Das Forschen*, 41–47.

91. The following specimens may serve as an illustration: *verhülte(m)*, pp. 5, 6; *Dekke*, p. 6; *Sazungen*, p. 10; *Kezer*, p. 12; *Fal*, p. 12; *Wal*, p. 17; *Flek*, p. 28; *Fus*, p. 28; *glüklich*, p. 31; *füren*, p. 44; *Plaz nemen*, p. 45.

92. *GS*, 3:274–76, note.

93. See Katz, *Zion*, 29:126.

94. Ibid., 127–30.

95 Carelessly substituting "truth" for "right"; see *GS*, 3:308; 5:612.

96. *GS*, 5:661.

97. *GS*, 5:612.

98. See above, p. 420.

99. "die dem Vorgeben nach zu Wien abgefasst sein soll."

100. GS, 3:275.

101. *GS*, 5:613.

102. Geiger, *Briefe*, 116.

103. See his elaborate "Entwurf zu einer Privatvereinigung für Männer von Wissenschaften" (read Sept. 12, 1784) in *Sonnenfels gesammelte Schriften,* 9 (1786): 287–357.

104. *GS,* 5:622 (Jan. 21, 1785).

105. See Jacob Katz, *Zion,* 36 (1971): 116–17.

106. *Die Ehre Hamburgischer Staats-Bürger ohne Unterschied der Nationen nebst einem Anhang: Herr D. Niemann gegen die Juden. Zweite Beilage zur Stimme der Menschheit* etc. von Cranz (Altona, 1798), 12. A xerographic copy of this treatise was kindly sent to me by Professor Katz immediately upon its discovery in December, 1971.

107. *Aus dem Josephinischen Wien. Geblers und Nicolais Briefwechsel während der Jahre 1771–1786,* ed. Richard Maria Werner (Berlin, 1888), 118. The date of the letter is May 2, 1784.

108. Cranz had attacked Nicolai in his *Bockiade* and *Die Neue und vermehrte Bockiade in Briefen über den Ton in der Litteratur . . . des heutigen Jahrhunderts* (Berlin, 1781), 42 ff.

109. See *ABD,* 4:564–66; Cranz, *Beytrag zur Chronika von Berlin . . ., Erstes Stück,* 4th ed. (Berlin, 1781), 5, 13.

110. See W. Gronau, *Christian Wilhelm von Dohm . . .* (Lemgo, 1824), 90–94.

111. See the glowing tribute he paid to Mendelssohn in his *Annalen oder Neue geheime deutsche Correspondenz in Briefen für subscribierte Freunde mit deutscher Freiheit geschrieben von dem Verfasser der Gallerie der Teufel* [sc. Cranz]. *Zweiter Band fürs Jahr 1786 gedruckt in Terra Incognita,* 11–17.

112. See Katz' suggestion to this effect in *Zion,* 36 (1971): 116–17.

113. See above, p. 485.

114. See Katz, *Zion,* 29:115.

115. In *Die Ehre Hamburgischer Staats-Bürger,* 3–12, he freely admitted this.

116. *Supplement zum Ersten Stück der Chronika von Berlin in einem Sendschreiben an den Weltmann in Berlin . . . von dem Verfasser der Bokiade* (Berlin, 1781), 42.

117. *Die Ehre Hamburgischer Staats-Bürger,* 11.

118. In his *Charlatanerien in alphabetischer Ordnung als Beyträge zur Abbildung und zu den Meinungen des Jahrhunderts,* 2nd ed. (Berlin, 1780), Cranz had overstepped the boundaries of propriety in his scurrilous portrayal of the patriarch Abraham's matrimonial life (pp. 5–9), and in his denigration of the Bible (pp. 13–23).

119. *Supplement zum Ersten Stück der Chronika von Berlin,* 8–10, 18–23.

120. *Beytrag zur Chronika von Berlin,* Drittes Stück (Berlin, 1781), 31.

121. *Das Forschen,* 44.

122. Cranz, *Annalen oder Neue geheime deutsche Correspondenz,* 12 f.

Jerusalem I (pages 514–531)

1. *Jerusalem oder über religiöse Macht und Judentum* (Berlin, 1783); *GS,* 3:255–362. For the various editions and translations see Meyer, *Bibliographie,* 54 f., to which is to be added *Jerusalem and Other Jewish Writings by Moses Mendelssohn,* translated and edited by Alfred Jospe (New York, 1969). *Die Psalmen.* Übersetzt von Moses Mendelssohn (Berlin, 1783); *GS,* 6:125–366; for later editions see Meyer, *Bibliographie,* 57.

2. *Hamanns Schriften,* ed. Gustav Adolph Wiener, 8.1 (1842):353. For a new and splendidly annotated edition of the text, see Lothar Schreiner, *Johann Georg Hamanns Golgatha und Scheblimini* (Gütersloh, 1956). Hamann's work first appeared in the summer of 1784.

3. Lit., "bewildered" (*verstörten*) but intended, primarily, in the sense of "destroyed" (*zerstörten*).

4. It seems that the choice of the title *Jerusalem* was not made until shortly before the publication. The letter to Schulstein early in 1783 (*GS,* 5:612) used the subtitle, while the letter to Redlich on April 4 (ibid., 613) mentions for the first time the full name of the book. There would have been no reason to suppress mention of the main title in the letter to Schulstein, if it had already been adopted at the time.

5. The autograph is in the possession of Prof. Fritz Bamberger, who kindly put a xerographic copy at my disposal.

6. *JubA,* 1:127–31; see above, p. 56 ff.

7. *JubA,* 3.1:3–4; see above, p. 143 f.

8. For a characterization of Mendelssohn's working method, see *Frühschriften,* 90–92.

9. *JubA,* 7:64 f.; see above, p. 211 f.

10. Canzius, *Disciplinae morales omnes* (Leipzig, 1739), nos. 2236, 2240, 2246. See *Verzeichnis,* p. 24, no. 128.

11. Chap. 32 and 35. Mendelssohn used the Latin edition: *Thomae Hobbes opera* (Amsterdam, 1668); see *Verzeichnis*, p. 10, no. 112.

12. Published here for the first time.

13. The corresponding sentence in *Jerusalem, GS*, 3:257 reads: "Und unermesslich sind die Übel, die aus der Misshelligkeit dieser moralischen Wesen [sc. State and Church] bisher entstanden sind . . ." The *Vorlage* for this statement is found in one of Mendelssohn's excerpts from Canz: *Infinita enim mala sunt, quae ex illorum triplicis generis jurium abusu nascuntur*. The third genus, according to Canz, is the individual conscience (beside state and church).

14. *JubA*, 7:91.

15. *GS*, 5:665.

16. *GS*, 5:676.

17. Kant, *Werke*, 9:233 f.

18. For analytical studies, see Julius Guttmann, "Mendelssohns Jerusalem und Spinozas Theologisch-Politischer Traktat," *48. Bericht der Hochschule für die Wissenschaft des Judentums* (Berlin, 1931), 31–67; in Hebrew translation: Julius Guttmann, *Dat U-Mada'* (Jerusalem, 1955), 192–229; Fritz Bamberger, "Mendelssohns Begriff vom Judentum," *Korrespondenzblatt des Vereins zur Gründung und Erhaltung einer Akademie für die Wissenschaft des Judentums*, 10 (1929): 4–19; reprinted in *Wissenschaft des Judentums im deutschen Sprachbereich*, ed. Kurt Wilhelm (Tübingen, 1967); Simon Rawidowicz, "Zur Jerusalem Polemik," *Festschrift Armand Kaminka zum 70. Geburtstag* (Vienna, 1937), 103–15; Idem, "Ha-Pilosofia shel Yerushalayim," *Sefer Bialik*, ed. Jacob Fichmann (Tel-Aviv, 1934), 99–140; now included in Simon Rawidowicz, *Iyyunim Bemahashevet Yisrael: Hebrew Studies in Jewish Thought*, ed. Benjamin C.I. Ravid, 2 (Jerusalem, 1971): 70–117; Nathan Rotenstreich, "On Mendelssohn's Political Philosophy," *Leo Baeck Institute Year Book*, 11 (London, 1966):28–41.

19. See the list in Volkmar Eichstädt, *Bibliographie zur Geschichte der Judenfrage* (Hamburg, 1938), 10–12, to which should be added (under no. 115) *GGA*, 1783 (September 27), 157:1569-80; Johann Christoph Doederlein, *Auserlesene Theologische Bibliothek*, 2.12 (Leipzig, 1784): 885–921; *Zürcher Bibliothek*, 1.1 (quoted by Christian Siegmund Krause, *Über kirchliche Gewalt*, Berlin, 1786, 8 f.). The author of the anonymous *Gedanken über Moses Mendelssohns Jerusalem . . .* (Bremen, 1786)—see Eichstädt, *Bibliographie*, no. 135—was Gotthelf Andreas Regenhorst; see Meyer, *Bibliographie*, p. 56, no. 290. The probably earliest, though unpublished, reply to the *Jerusalem* came from Johann Friedrich Jacobi, superintendent in Celle, who was an uncle of Friedrich Heinrich Jacobi. It was read by Hamann; see Schreiner, ed., *Golgatha*, 17.

20. *GS*,5:676.

21. *GS*,5:675 f.

22. See Bamberger, "Mendelssohns Begriff vom Judentum," 522 f.

23. Montesquieu, *De l'esprit des lois*, 5:14.

24. Friedrich Schiller's description of church despotism as creating "*die Ruhe eines Kirchhofs*" ("the quiet of a churchyard") might have been suggested by the Mendelssohn passage. On Schiller's acquaintance with Mendelssohn, see *Frühschriften*, 379.

25. See *GS*, 3:258, 265, 285.

26. In 5 vols, 1714–1736; 5th ed., 1756–1789.

27. See above, p. 515.

28. #2246.

29. See Mendelssohn's excerpts from #2236 and #2240 as well as the critical remarks interjected by him.

30. Cf. Franz Rosenzweig, *Hegel und der Staat* (Berlin, 1920; reprint: Aalen, 1962), 1:227: "Wieweit Hegel unmittelbar beeinflusst ist von der kollegialistischen Richtung des Kirchenrechts, die auch hinter Mendelssohns Schrift steht und damals überhaupt (Landsberg, *Geschichte der deutschen Rechtswissenschaft*, III, i, 308) allgemein in Aufnahme gekommen war, wage ich nicht zu bestimmen."

31. On public and private worship see *Leviathan*, 2:31.

32. *Leviathan*, 1:15.

33. *GS*, 3:260 f. See Hobbes, *Leviathan*, 1:15.

34. *GS*, 3:261. Cf. Mendelssohn's characterization of Hobbes in *JubA*, 2:98 (392).

35. Among the excerpts from *Leviathan* on the sheet attached to his draft, Mendelssohn noted down the passages that assign the right of punishing dissidents not to the ministers of Christ but to the civil authorities, who are given also the right of excommunication; see *Leviathan*, pt. 3, chap. 42.

36. Spinoza, *Tractatus Theologico-Politicus,* chap. 19; Rousseau, "Du Contract Social," *Oeuvres complètes,* ed. Gagnebin-Raymond (1964), 3:468; Emmerich de Vattel, *Le Droit des Gens* (1758), 1, chap. 12, #129, 133, quoted by Krause, *Über kirchliche Gewalt,* 39, note. Krause (ibid.) refers also to Boehmer and Lossius.

37. See *Oeuvres complètes,* 3:469.

38. See below, p. 536 f. where we follow, in the main, Julius Guttmann's essay (quoted above, note 18).

39. See *The Works of John Locke* (London, 1823; reprint: Aalen, 1963), 6:5 ff. ("A Letter Concerning Toleration," First Letter); Mendelssohn quotes Locke's definition of the commonwealth (state) GS, 3:261.

40. GS, 3:262. The exact title of the work is *De potestate summi pontificis in rebus temporalibus* (1610).

41. Mendelssohn seems to have had in mind, primarily, the arguments that Hobbes had advanced against Bellarmin *(Leviathan,* 3:42).

42. GS, 3:263. Translations of *Jerusalem* texts are, in part, reprinted here, by permission of Schocken Books Inc., from *Jerusalem and Other Jewish Writings by Moses Mendelssohn,* translated and edited by Alfred Jospe. Copyright © 1969 by Schocken Books Inc.

43. *JubA,* 2:32; *JubA,* 3.1:113 f.

44 *GS,* 5:382.

45. *Anmerkungen zu Abbts freundschaftlicher Korrespondenz* (Berlin, 1782), 28 (*GS,* 5:296).

46. Nachlass Hennings, no. 22, letter 26, fol. 57r–65r; Mendelssohn's reply, ibid., letter 27, fol. 65v–67r; *GS,* V, 597–600.

47. *Oeuvres complètes,* 3:465 (*Du Contract Social,* iv).

48. *GS,* 3:265.

49. See *Frühschriften,* 372–91. The "four means" discussed there are designed to transform moral duty into "inclination" or part of our nature.

50. *GS,* 3:267.

51. Ibid.

52. See Guttmann, "Mendelssohns Jerusalem," 53–59.

53. Cf. Christian Wolff, *Vernünfftige Gedancken von der Menschen Thun und Lassen* (Halle, 1752), 108: "ein blosses Spielwerk."

54. *GS,* 3:268 f.

55. *GS,* 3:269.

56. 1783, no. 157:1572.

57. *JubA,* 2:292. See *Frühschriften,* 290.

58. See R. Hoffmann, *Die staatsphilosophischen Anschauungen Fr. Chr. Wolffs mit besonderer Berücksichtigung seiner naturrechtlichen Theorien,* Dissertation Leipzig (Leipzig, 1916), 28 ff.

59. Geiger, *Briefe,* 109. See also Mendelssohn's own statement in a letter to Abbt (*GS,* 5:316 f.).

60. *GS,* 4.1:128–31; *GS,* 3:195 ff.

61. *GS,* 3:279, note (see above, p. 500).

62. *Adam Fergusons Grundsätze der Moralphilosophie.* Übersetzt und mit einigen Anmerkungen versehen von Christian Garve (Leipzig, 1772). Ferguson's work had appeared in 1769.

63. *JubA,* 2:92; *GS,* 4.2:523 f. Rousseau himself had characterized the concept of the natural state as a mere hypothesis (see *Oeuvres complètes,* 3:1302).

64. See *JubA,* 2:426, where relevant passages from Cumberland's *De legibus naturae* are quoted.

65. *JubA,* 2:320.

66. *GS,* 3:270.

67. *Essais de Théodicée,* 2, Appendix 2, #12.

68. *JubA,* 2:292.

69. *GS,* 3:270.

70. *GS,* 3:271. See also Locke, *Of Civil Government,* 2:5; Garve, *Fergusons Grundsätze,* 174 f.; Kant, "Die Metaphysik der Sitten," *Werke,* 7:73, where the third category of natural property agrees with the third listed by Mendelssohn. Wolff, *Jus Naturale,* 2, #7–9, did not admit private property for the *status naturalis originarius* as distinct from the *status naturalis adventitius;* see Hoffmann, *Die Anschauungen Wolffs,* 29 ff.

71. *GS,* 3:269.

72. *GS*, 3:271; cf. *GS*, 5:313; 378 f.; 677 (in answer to an objection by the physician and poet Isaaco Luzzatto).

73. *GS*, 3:272.

74. Ibid. The identical view (probably also going back to Ferguson) had been expressed in 1773 by Samuel Johnson, as reported by James Boswell in his *Life of Johnson* (1791): "Sir, you must consider that we have perfect and imperfect obligations. Perfect obligations, which are generally not to do something, are clear and positive, as 'thou shalt not kill.' But charity, for instance, is not definable by limits. It is a duty to give to the poor, but no man can say how much another should give to the poor. . . ."

75. Garve, *Fergusons Grundsätze*, 414 f.

76. GS, 3:272 f., 276, 278 f., 288.

77. *GS*, 3:276 f.

78. *GS*, 5:669.

79. *GS*, 3:278 f.; Geiger, *Briefe*, 88 f. (letter to Garve); Garve, *Fergusons Grundsätze*, 177, 417 ff.

80. GS, 3:280 f. On Mendelssohn's motivation in discussing the issue of marriage contracts, see Katz, *Zion*, 29:126 f.

81. *GS*, 3:281.

82. *GS*, 3:266 f.

83. *GS*, 3:281; *GS*, 4.2:138 f.; *GS*, 5:669. Objections to this theory of social contract raised by Johann Friedrich Zöllner, *Über Moses Mendelssohn's Jerusalem* (Berlin, 1784), were repudiated by Mendelssohn in his *votum*, "Über vollkommene Pflichten, in Beziehung auf Zöllner's Schrift," *GS*, 4.1:135–45, see below, p. 664 f.

84. Here Mendelssohn makes a radical break with the prevalent division of duties. Christian Wolff, *Vernünfftige Gedancken von der Menschen Thun und Lassen* deals in section 3 (pp. 451 ff., #650 ff.) with "Pflichten des Menschen gegen Gott." Alexander Gottlieb Baumgarten, *Ethica Philosophica* (Halle, 1740, 1751) differentiates between three kinds of obligations, viz. those to religion, ourselves, and others (see *Frühschriften*, 358, note, 40). Francis Hutcheson, *A Short Introduction to Moral Philosophy* (Glasgow, 1764), 77 ff. discusses "Our Duties toward God."

85. GS, 3:282 f. Here Mendelssohn anticipates Kant's position; see *Die Religion innerhalb der Grenzen der blossen Vernunft* (1793; 2nd ed., 1794), Book Four, Part One: Kant, *Werke*, 6:302: "Religion (subjectively regarded) is the recognition of all our duties as divine commandments." "There are no special duties toward God in a universal religion; for God cannot receive anything from us; we cannot produce any effect upon him or for him."

86. *GS*, 3:283.

87. *GS*, 3:283 f.

88. See Zöllner, *Über Mendelssohns Jerusalem*, 134 f.; Doederlein, *Bibliothek*, 2.12:897; *GGA*, 1783, no. 157: 1574, where Mendelssohn is said to have confused the concepts of God, religion, and Church.

89. *GS*, 3:284 f.; cf. *GS*, 5:592.

90. See Zöllner, *Über Mendelssohns Jerusalem*, 136–47; Doederlein, *Bibliothek*, 2.12:897 f.; [August Georg Uhle], *Über Herrn Moses Mendelssohns Jerusalem, politisch religiöse Macht, Judenthum und Christenthum* (Berlin & Leipzig, 1784), 55–58.

91. *Orientalische und exegetische Bibliothek*, 22 (1783): 63–68.

92. Viz. the concept of *sekhar batala* (*p. Nedarim*, 38c), also called *agar batala* (*Ketuvot* 105a). See Adolf Altmann, "Die Besoldung rabbinischer Funktionen als Usus und Recht," *Jeschurun*, ed. Josef Wohlgemuth, 15 (1928): 444–51.

93. *Nedarim* 37a; *Bekhorot* 29a.

94. *GS*, 3:284.

95. Cf. the similar expression in Locke, *A Letter Concerning Toleration*, First Letter, 11 f.

96. Ibid., 10.

97. Spinoza, *Tractatus*, chap. 20; see also chaps. 7 and 19.

98. *GS*, 3:285.

99. Locke, *A Letter Concerning Toleration*, First Letter, 12 ff.

100. Ibid., 47.

101. *JubA*, 2:21 f.; see Fritz Bamberger's note, p. 375 f., where the relevant works are quoted.

102. *GS*, 3:287.

103. Doederlein, *Bibliothek*, 2.12:900; [Uhle], *Mendelssohn's Jerusalem*, 61.

104. Mendelssohn mentions twice that the state has to watch the situation only "from afar." The meaning of this term is probably the same as in *JubA*, 1:55 and 527, where the artist is advised to allow the rules of his art to become consciously operative only "from afar, as it were." In the creative process, the artist must not be burdened with overly detailed rules. Analogously, the state should not concern itself with theological minutiae but should pay attention to broad principles only. See *GS*, 3:287, where this very point is made.

105. See *GS*, 5:529, 533.

106. *GS*, 3:287–92.

107. *Orientalische . . . Bibliothek*, 1783. no. 22:69 ff.

108. Ibid., 1783, no. 332: 165–70.

109. Michaelis hastened to add that the person concerned was not the bishop of London (Robert Lowth). In view of his own admiration of Lowth (see above, p. 412 f.), Mendelssohn must have been relieved to know that it was someone else that had made the statement reported by Michaelis. He took umbrage, however, at the reason given for keeping the bishop's identity undisclosed; see *GS*, 3:376.

110. Marburg File, no. 55.

111. Cf. *GS*, 3:375, the last 3 lines.

112. GS, 5:706; 3:374–85. The *Göttingische Anzeigen*, 1784 (March 11), no. 41, would not let matters rest at that but published a vitriolic denunciation of Mendelssohn's reply: his defense had made the accusation "even harder" and the "winning modesty" of his character had not only been absent but seemed to have given way to an offensive self-aggrandizement. Eberhard sadly remarked in a letter to Mendelssohn (Apr. 1, 1784) that this latest act had appreciably added to the "measure of Michaelis' sins."

113. *GS*, 3:296.

114. Hosea 11:4.

Jerusalem II (pages 531–552)

1. See the letter to Herz Homberg quoted above, p. 489.

2. *GGA*, 1782 (Sept. 14), no. 111:893.

3. *GS*, 3:299–306.

4. *GS*, 3:307.

5. The German translation given here (*GS*, 3:308) differs slightly from the one in Mendelssohn's Psalms translation (*GS*, 6:194).

6. [Uhle], *Mendelssohns Jerusalem*, 120 f.

7. *GS*, 3:352.

8. Ibid., 308.

9. Ibid., 308 f.

10. Kant, *Werke*, 6:315, note.

11. *GS*, 3:309 ff. Some Christians were troubled by the conjecture that the Jews possessed such documents; cf. Rousseau's statement quoted above, pp. 226, 238 f.

12. *GS*, 3:311 f.

13. Literally, "through nature and thing," a hendiadys.

14. *JubA*, 16, letter 127, p. 151; see above, p. 249.

15. *JubA*, 7:10–12.

16. *JubA*, 7:73, 75, and passim.

17. *GS*, 3:315.

18. *JubA*, 16, letter 154, p. 178; see above, p. 294 f.

19. Zöllner, *Über Mendelssohns Jerusalem*, 158 f.

20. Doederlein, *Bibliothek*, 906 f.

21. See Guttmann, "Mendelssohns Jerusalem," 40 f. (*Dat U-Mada'*, 198 f.).

22. See above, pp. 29–32.

23. *GS*, 3:319.

24. See Guttmann, "Mendelssohns Jerusalem," 43 (*Dat U-Mada'*, 201 f.).

25. *GS*, 3:316 f.

26. *GS*, 3:317.

27. *GS*, 3:319. The same view is expressed in Mendelssohn's *Bi'ur* on Exod. 20:1.

28. Chap. 14; cf. chap. 1; see Guttmann, "Mendelssohns Jerusalem," 38 f. (*Dat U-Mada'*, 197).

29. *Tractatus,* chap. 3; see also *Short Treatise,* 2, xxiv:10.
30. *GS,* 3:319.
31. See *Mekhilta,* ad loc.; Abraham ibn Ezra's commentary ad loc.; Jehuda Ha-Levi, *Kuzari,* 1:15–25; Nahmanides' commentary ad loc.; cf. the survey in Samuel David Luzzatto's commentary on the Pentateuch (Tel-Aviv, 1965), 317 ff. Mendelssohn's *Bi'ur* on Exod. 20:1 reflects the same view.
32. *GS,* 3:320.
33. Originally, Leibniz distinguished between *vérités éternelles* and *vérités de fait* (rational truths and empirical truths) only in the sense that man's imperfect intellect could not perceive the rational necessity of the empirical facts; for God, on the other hand, the distinction was not valid (see "*Meditationes de cognitione, veritate et ideis*" (1684), C. J. Gerhardt, ed., *Die philosophischen Schriften von G. W. Leibniz* (Berlin, 1875–90), 4:426). He later acknowledged the metaphysical character of the distinction, however, probably in order to avoid any Spinozistic implications. For the passage in the *Jerusalem* referred to, see *GS,* 3:312 ff.
34. Leibniz, *Essais de Théodicée,* 1, A, #3; Mendelssohn, *GS,* 3:312; *Frühschriften,* 321 ff.
35. *GS,* 3:315.
36. Zöllner, *Über Mendelssohns Jerusalem,* 150 f.
37. See below, p. 546 f.
38. Nachlass Hennings, no. 22, letter 26, fol. 60r–v.
39. Ibid., letter 27, fol. 66r–67r; reproduced in *GS,* 5:598 f.
40. *GS,* 4.1:150–53.
41. *GS,* 5:495 ff. (Mar. 13, 1770).
42. Eccl. 3:7.
43. *GS,* 3:317 f.
44. See below, p. 560 f.
45. The charge that the Old Testament was unaware or only dimly conscious of the soul's immortality and was, therefore, inferior to Christianity was frequently made in the polemics of the medieval church. It had been taken up by the Socinians; see Guttmann, "*Mendelssohns Jerusalem,*" 37 (*Dat U-Mada',* 196).
46. Ibid., 33 (*Dat U-Mada',* 192).
47. *Die Erziehung des Menschengeschlechts,* #18, 32.
48. Ibid., #51, 53, 85, 86, 89.
49. See Karl Löwith, *Weltgeschichte und Heilsgeschichte* (Stuttgart, 1952); and Alexander Altmann, "Franz Rosenzweig on History," in *Studies in Religious Philosophy and Mysticism* (London, England & Ithaca, N.Y., 1969), 276–80.
50. For an analysis of Lessing's doctrine see Henry E. Allison, *Lessing and the Enlightenment* (Ann Arbor, 1966), 147–61.
51. *GS,* 3:312.
52. See his letter to Hennings, quoted above, p. 539.
53. *GS,* 3:318.
54. "Über den Gemeinspruch: Das mag in der Theorie richtig sein, taugt aber nicht für die Praxis" (1793): Kant, *Werke,* 6:392 ff.
55. "Der Streit der Fakultäten" (1798), 2: Kant, *Werke,* 7:391–407 (see, in particular, p. 405). Both works of Kant are referred to by Moritz Brasch, *Moses Mendelssohns Schriften . . .* (Leipzig, 1880), 2:427 f., note.
56. *GS,* 3:283.
57. According to a view recorded in the Talmud (*Avoda zara* 9a–b; *Sanhedrin* 97a–b), the messianic era was to commence with the advent of the year 5000 after the world's creation, and was to last for a period of two-thousand years, but it had been delayed on account of the sins of Israel. Mendelssohn probably wished to allude to this view when he expressed the hope that the first year of the sixth millennium (which coincides with the year 2240 of the Common Era) might usher in the long overdue messianic age.
58. *GS,* 3:323, note.
59. *GS,* 3:321.
60. *Zohar,* II, 99a–b; see G. Scholem, *Zur Kabbala und ihrer Symbolik* (Zürich, 1960), 77–79; 269.
61. *GS,* 3:321 ff.
62. See M. Freudenthal, "R. Wolf Dessau," *Festschrift Martin Philippson,* 184–212. The title of the commentary on Job is *Pesher Davar* (Berlin, 1777). The other work is entitled

Jüdische Religionsstütze oder Grundsätze der jüdischen Religion (Dessau, 1782). The full name of the author was Wolf Abraham Nathan of Dessau.

63. *GS,* 5:602 f.

64. *JubA,* 7:95. Cf. p. 340 f.

65. This has already been noted by Rawidowicz, *JubA,* 7:480; see Albo, *'Ikkarim,* 2:4.

66. *Temura,* 14b.

67. *GS,* 3:324 ff. Mendelssohn had expressed similar sentiments in a review of Ramler's *Odes (GS,* 4.2:541) as early as 1768.

68. Quoted by Arno Borst, *Der Turmbau von Babel,* 3.2 (1961): 1442 f.

69. See Theodor L. Haering, *Hegel, Sein Wollen und sein Werk* (Leipzig & Berlin, 1929), 154.

70. See Mendelssohn's remarks in his letter to Herz Homberg (Sept. 22, 1783), *GS,* 5:668.

71. See *JubA,* 2:104–09: *GS,* 4.1:585–99.

72. See *Or Li-Netiva, JubA,* 14:214 f.

73. See Borst, *Turmbau,* 3.2:1441 f.

74. *GS,* 3:327 ff. The treatment of Mendelssohn's theory of language in his *Jerusalem* was excerpted from an older manuscript in which he had sketched his ideas on the subject; see his letter to Herz Homberg of Sept. 22, 1783 *(GS,* 5:668). It seems that it was this manuscript that he had shown to Johann Jacob Engel, who in turn had submitted it to Johann Christoph Adelung (1732–1806), the great German linguist. When returning the manuscript to Engel on Dec. 23, 1780, Adelung had remarked on the similarity of several of his and Mendelssohn's views and had expressed the hope that Mendelssohn would elaborate his "system" and apply it to the Hebrew language (Geiger, *Briefe,* 133). In an unpublished letter of May 19, 1781 (a copy of which was placed at my disposal by the late Professor Bruno Strauss), Eberhard reported to Mendelssohn that when visiting Adelung in Leipzig he had found him occupied with research into the origin of language and that Mendelssohn's thoughts on the subject, which he remembered having read (a reference, probably, to the same manuscript), were sure to benefit Adelung.

75. See Borst, *Turmbau,* 3.2:1476–1501.

76. See James C. O'Flaherty, *Unity and Language: A Study in the Philosophy of Johann Georg Hamann* (Chapel Hill, N. C., 1952); Harold Stahmer, *"Speak That I May See Thee": The Religious Significance of Language* (New York, 1968).

77. *GS,* 3:329–32.

78. Plutarch, *De Iside et Osiride,* chap. 71.

79. Hosea 13:2.

80. For the reaction of Hellenistic Jewish writers, especially Philo of Alexandria, to myth and idolatry, see Harry A. Wolfson, *Philo,* Third Printing (Cambridge, Mass., 1962), 1:3–34.

81. *JubA,* 2:21 f. The Plutarch passage concerned is found in *De Iside,* ch. 11, 355D; *De Superstitione,* ch. 1, 164E; ch. 2, 165C (quoted by Wolfson, *Philo,* 1:32, note 40).

82. *GS,* 3:332–49.

83. The observation quoted from Christoph Meiners' *Versuch über die Religionsgeschichte der ältesten Völker, besonders der Egyptier* (Göttingen, 1775), 101 *(GS,* 3:333, 335) would hardly seem to corroborate Mendelssohn's view.

84. *GS,* 3:339 f.

85. As Guttmann, "Mendelssohns Jerusalem," 44 *(Dat U-Mada',* 202 f.), has shown, Mendelssohn had questioned this view in his "Counterreflections" *(JubA,* 7:74).

86. In the rabbinic tradition, idolatry is held to have commenced in the age of Enosh; see *Targum Jonathan* on Gen. 4:26; *Mekhilta, Ba-Hodesh,* ch. 6; *Sifrey, 'Ekev,* #43; Maimonides, *Mishne Tora, Hilkhot 'Avoda Zara,* ch. 1.

87. *GS,* 3:341.

88. *Guide,* 3:29; 31.

89. *GS,* 3:340.

90. Ps. 73:17.

91. *GS,* 3:326, 340–42, 350.

92. Ibid., 320.

93. Ibid., 351.

94. See Gerhard Oestreich, "Die Idee des religiösen Bundes und die Lehre vom Staatsvertrag," *Zur Geschichte und Problematik der Demokratie, Festgabe für Hans Herzfeld* (Berlin, 1938), 11–32.

95. *GS*, 3:353.
96. *The Works of John Locke* (London, 1823), 6:37 ff.
97. *GS*, 3:350 f.
98. Ibid., 352.
99. Ibid., 355.
100. *Sanhedrin* 14b, 52b, 87a; *Bava Kama* 15b; *Avoda Zara* 8b; see *Encyclopedia Talmudit*, ed. S.Y. Zevin (Jerusalem, 1956), 7:354 f., 376 f.
101. *GS*, 3:353.
102. Ibid., 356; see also *JubA*, 7:89.
103. Zöllner, *Über Mendelssohns Jerusalem*, 183 f.
104. [Uhle], *Mendelssohns Jerusalem*, 174.
105. See Katz, *Zion*, 29:129 f.
106. Cf. *GS*, 5:660, where Mendelssohn expressed some doubt whether Sonnenfels would be able to keep his promise to help Homberg.
107. *JubA*, 7:98.
108. Cf. Ezek. 34:23, 37:24, where the reference is, however, only to Israel.
109. Isa. 11:9.
110. *GS*, 3:235 f.
111. Ibid., 358.
112. *Orientalische . . . Bibliothek*, 1783, no. 22:95.
113. *GS*, 5:669 f.
114. *GS*, 3:361 f.

Chapter Seven: Strains and Stresses
Friendship with Lessing: The Last Phase I (pages 553–569)

1. "Leibniz von den ewigen Strafen," L–M, 12:461–87.
2. See Mendelssohn's "Counterreflections," *JubA*, 7:72 f.; on Eberhard see above, pp. 220, 295. Mendelssohn's opposition to the notion of eternal punishment had been anticipated by the vigorous stand of a seventeenth-century Amsterdam rabbi, Issac da Fonseca Aboab, whose treatise *Nishmat Hayyim* (1636) attacked the traditional view but did so from a mystical stance, viz. that of Lurianic Kabbala.
3. 1, B #74; 133; 2, B, #266; Appendix 4 *(Causa Dei)*, #56–59.
4. L–M, 11:470.
5. See Henry E. Allison, *Lessing and the Enlightenment* (Ann Arbor, 1966), 86–91.
6. L–M, 20, letter 513, p. 218.
7. L–M, 20, letter 523, p. 245.
8. L–M, 18, letter 387, p. 82 f.
9. L–M, 20, letter 525, p. 249.
10. L–M, 20 letter 527, p. 252. See above, p. 270.
11. See above, p. 279.
12. L–M, 18, letter 389, p. 86. The report must have been added to the letter after Lessing had returned from Brunswick, since we know for sure that Mendelssohn arrived in Brunswick on July 16 and stayed there until the 19th.
13. *GS*, 5:565. On Winkopp see *GS*, 5:571–75. That his doubts concerned, in particular, the doctrine of eternal punishments is attested by his second letter of Apr. 24, 1780; see Dep. RvM, C II, no. 40.
14. *GS*, 5:565 f.
15. See below, p. 666 ff.
16. *GS*, 2:431 f. (#60); 441 f. (#77). Mendelssohn had already expressed his objections to the doctrine of eternal punishments in his "Counterreflections" (see note 2 above).
17. See *JubA*, 7:96, 16:119, 3.1:208.
18. "Des Andreas Wissowatius Einwürfe wider die Dreieinigkeit" (1773), L–M,12:71–99.
19. See Allison, *Lessing and the Enlightenment*, 91 ff.
20. *Defensio Trinitatis per nova reperta logica;* see C. J. Gerhardt, ed., *Die philosophischen Schriften von G.W. Leibniz* (Berlin, 1875–1890) 4:111–25.
21. *GS*, 5:192 f. (L–M, 21, letter 557, p. 5 f.).
22. L–M, 12:85.
23. See above, p. 47; below, pp. 591, 610, 691.

24. *GS,* 5:194 f. (L–M, 18, letter 409, p. 110; written on May 1, 1774).
25. "Von Duldung der Deisten," L–M, 12:254–71.
26. So named after its place of publication. In a letter to George August von Breitenbauch (*JubA,* 11:53) Mendelssohn had recommended this translation of the Pentateuch. Lessing, too, had shown an early interest in the work. See Bruno Strauss, *JubA,* 11:407.
27. See above, p. 253 f.
28. See above, p. 254 f.
29. L–M, 21, letter 583, p. 42 f. (Nov. 1, 1774).
30. L–M, 18, letter 416, p. 118 (Nov. 11, 1774).
31. L–M, 21, letter 586, p. 46.
32. See above, p. 297.
33. "Ein Mehreres aus den Papieren des Ungenannten, die Offenbarung betreffend," L–M, 12:303–450.
34. Quoted by Heinrich Sieveking, "Elise Reimarus (1735–1805) in den geistigen Kämpfen ihrer Zeit," *Zeitschrift des Vereins für Hamburgische Geschichte* 39 (Hamburg, 1940): 103; see also Lessing, *Gesammelte Werke* (ed. Rilla), 9:684 f.
35. Quoted by Sieveking, "Elise Reimarus," 104.
36. Ibid.
37. L–M, 21, letter 710, p. 161.
38. L–M, 18, letter 565, p. 244 (May 25, 1777).
39. See above, p. 310 f.
40. *GS,* 5:199 (L–M, 21, letter 726, p. 180). The preceding passage of the letter has been quoted above, p. 311. Mendelssohn was referring to Lessing's utterance in his letter to him; see L–M, 18:256, note 2.
41. L–M, 21, letter 743, p. 197.
42. L–M, 18, letter 597, p. 269 (Apr. 6, 1778).
43. See above, p. 540.
44. L–M, 18, letter 539, p. 221 (Jan. 8, 1777).
45. *Freywillige Beyträge zu den Hamburgischen Nachrichten aus dem Reiche der Gelehrsamkeit* (ed. Ziegra), no. 63, February 1778; reproduced in Erich Schmidt (ed.), *Goezes Streitschriften gegen Lessing* (Stuttgart, 1893), 41 f.
46. [Anon.], *Die Auferstehungsgeschichte Jesu Christi gegen einige im vierten Beytrage . . . gemachte neue Einwendungen vertheidiget* (Brunswick, 1777); Goeze's review appeared in *Freywillige Beyträge,* nos. 61–63, February, 1778 (*Goezes Streitschriften,* 23–42).
47. *Über die Evidenz der Beweise für die Wahrheit der christlichen Religion* (Hanover, 1778).
48. *Streitschriften,* 189 f.
49. *Über den Beweis des Geistes und der Kraft. An den Hrn. Direktor Schumann zu Hannover* (Brunswick, 1777); L–M, 13:3–8.
50. For a succinct account of Lessing's theological polemic, see Allison, *Lessing and the Enlightenment,* 101–20. Also see Hartmut Sierig, *Über den garstigen Graben* (Hamburg, 1967). Henry Chadwick published *Lessing's Theological Writings,* selections in translation with an introductory essay (London, 1956).
51. *Eine Duplik* (Brunswick, 1778); L–M, 13:19–90.
52. L–M, 18, letter 594, p. 265 (Feb. 25, 1778); Karl's letter: L–M, 21, letter 739, p. 189 (Feb. 7, 1778).
53. Niedersächsische Landesbibliothek, Hanover: Mendelssohns Letters to Zimmermann, fol. 5*v;* first published by E. Bodemann, *Joh. G. Zimmermann, Sein Leben und bisher ungedruckte Briefe* (Hanover, 1878), 289 f.; see also Kayserling, *Ungedrucktes,* 15.
54. *Eine Parabel . . .* (Brunswick, 1778); L–M, 13:91–103; *Axiomata . . .* (Brunswick, 1778); L–M, 13:105–37; L–M, 18, letter 595, p. 266.
55. *Freywillige Beyträge,* nos. 55–56 (1778); reproduced in Goeze's *Etwas Vorläufiges . . .* (reprinted in *Streitschriften,* 11–23).
56. Johann David Michaelis, *Einleitung in die Schriften des Neuen Testaments,* 2nd ed., 73.
57. See *Streitschriften,* 57.
58. L–M, 21, letter 741, p. 190 f.
59. See Dr. Reimarus' letter, L–M, 21:197 (Mar. 19, 1778).
60. no. 71; see *Streitschriften,* 192 f.
61. *Streitschriften,* 104.
62. Similar views had been expressed in England by deistic writers like Thomas Woolston

(1670–1733) and Anthony Collins (1676–1729). See Friedrich G. Lüdke's review of Lessing's *Vom Zwecke Jesu und seiner Jünger* in *Allgemeine Deutsche Bibliothek*, 40.1 (1780): 357.

63. *Von dem Zwecke Jesu und seiner Jünger. Noch ein Fragment des Wolfenbüttelschen Ungenannten* (Brunswick, 1778); L–M, 13:215–327.

64. See Matthew 5:22.

65. *Lessings Schwächen*, no. 2 (*Streitschriften*, 105).

66. *Allgemeine deutsche Bibliothek*, 40.1(1780): 385.

67. L–M, 21, letter 750, p. 204 f.

68. *Streitschriften*, 56.

69. *Beytrag zum Reichs-Postreuter*, no. 19 (*Streitschriften*, 201).

70. *Reichs-Postreuter*, nos. 30 and 75 (*Streitschriften*, 202; 84).

71. *Reichs-Postreuter*, no. 45, June 15, 1778 (*Streitschriften*, 205).

72. Johann Friedrich Kleuker, *Einige Belehrungen über Toleranz, Vernunft, Offenbarung . . .* (Frankfurt, 1778); see Lüdke's review, 40.1:390–98.

73. See *GS*, 5:340 f.; letter to Hennings, Mar. 14, 1780 (Nachlass Hennings 22, letter 13, fol. 22r); Friedrich Nicolai, "Etwas über den verstorbenen Rektor Damm und Moses Mendelssohn," *Neue Berliner Monatsschrift*, 3(1800): 338–63; Georg Alexander Kohut, *Moses Mendelssohn und Rector Damm* (New York, 1892); Meyer, *Bibliographie*, p. 171, no. 1366.

74. See Walter Grossmann's introduction to the facsimile edition of Edelmann's *Sämmtliche Schriften* (ed. W. Grossmann), 9 (Stuttgart, 1969), v–xxvi.

75. Nachlass Hennings 22, letter 10, fol. 16r; reproduced in Kayserling, *Mendelssohn*, 1st ed., 526.

76. See Heinrich Schneider, *Lessing* (Bern, 1951), 228, 300.

77. L–M, 18, letter 615, p. 290.

78. [Anon.], *Epistel an den hochehrwürdigen Hrn. Hauptpastor Göze in Hamburg, von 'n Layen 'n Hauptschlüssel zu den von Gotthold Ephraim Lessing herausgegebenen Fragmenten und Streitschriften . . .* [no year nor place of publication]; described by Lüdke, in *Allgemeine deutsche Bibliothek*, 39.1(1779):78, as "a plain, utterly stupid [*erzdummes*], vile lampoon." See also Lüdke's review (40.1:398), in which the assertion of Mendelssohn's authorship is rejected.

79. L–M, 21, letter 773, p. 233 (Oct. 23, 1778).

80. Kayserling, *Mendelssohn*, 1st ed., 549 f. Herder repudiated the rumor of Mendelssohn's authorship of the fragments; see Rudolf Haym, *Herder* (Berlin, 1954), 2:178.

81. Nachlass Hennings 22, letter 17, fol. 27v; Kayserling, *Mendelssohn*, 1st ed., 528 f.

82. *D. Joh. Salomo Semlers Beantwortung der Fragmente eines Ungenannten, insbesondere vom Zwecke Jesu und seiner Jünger* (Halle, 1779); *Allgemeine deutsche Bibliothek*, 40.1:416–28 (signed "Agm."). Resewitz' authorship of this review is apparent from both its style and content, which bear striking resemblance to what is found in the letter to Nicolai. Lüdke's review appeared in *Allgemeine deutsche Bibliothek*, 39.1:36–78; 40.1:356–416.

83. Nicolai-Briefe, vol, 60, no. 94.

84. The work appeared in Constantinople (1710) and contains Nahmanides' disputation with the (convert) Pablo Christiani (Fra Paolo), which Wagenseil published in a Latin translation. The Hebrew text was reedited by M. Steinschneider (*Vikuah Ha-Ramban*, Stettin, 1860) and is reproduced in H.D. Cheval, ed. *Kiteve Rabbenu Moshe ben Nahman* (Jerusalem, 1963), 1:299–320.

85. *Freywillige Beyträge*, Oct. 27, 1778; see *Streitschriften*, 193 f.

86. *Lessing Werke* (ed. Rilla), 9:778 f., note 2.

87. L–M, 21, letter 753, p. 214 f.

88. L–M, 18, letters 599 and 601, pp. 271 ff., 274 ff.; L–M, 21, letter 759, p. 220 f.

89. L–M, 21, letter 754, p. 214 ff. (July, 1778).

90. L–M, 21, letter 758, p. 220.

91. Biedermann, *Gespräche*, 209 f.

92. L–M, 18, letter 602, p. 276 f.

93. *Nöthige Antwort auf eine sehr unnöthige Frage . . .*; L–M, 13:329–36. For Goeze's questions see his *Lessings Schwächen*, no. 2 (Hamburg, 1778); reproduced in *Streitschriften*, 124.

94. L–M, 21, letter 760, p. 321.

95. L–M, 18, letter 609, p. 282 f.

96. L–M, 18, letter 18, p. 125 (Aug. 2, 1778); L–M, 21, letter 761, p. 222 f. (Aug. 3, 1778).

97. L–M, 21, letter 762, p. 223 f.

Friendship with Lessing: The Last Phase II (Pages 569–582)

1. So Joseph Mendelssohn in the biography of his father, *GS,* 1:21.
2. See Zelter's letter to Goethe, Jan. 19, 1826 (Biedermann, *Gespräche,* 51 f.); *GS,* 1:22; 5:226 f. Danzel, *Lessing,* 2.2:208, note 4, dismissed Zelter's report as an apocryphal anecdote related by David Friedländer. However, there is independent evidence from Sara von Grotthus' letter to Geothe, May 25, 1814 (Biedermann, *Gespräche,* 259).
3. L–M, 21, letter 807, p. 261.
4. Thus Danzel, *Lessing,* 2.2:207: "Nathan is Lessing himself, not, as is always being maintained, his Jewish friend Mendelssohn."
5. L–M, 18, letter 617, p. 292 (Nov. 7, 1778).
6. L–M, 18, letter 611, p. 285 f.
7. L–M, 21, letter 764, p. 225.
8. From Strelitz; see Mendelssohn's letter to Elkan Herz, Aug. 25, 1778, *JubA,* 16, letter 213, p. 243 (cf. above, p. 383).
9. L–M, 21, letter 765, p. 226 f. (Aug. 25, 1778).
10. L–M, 21, letter 754, p. 215.
11. L–M, 21, letter 765, p. 226.
12. L–M, 18, letter 615, p. 289 f.
13. See Elise's letter to Hennings, Sept. 25, 1778 (Biedermann, *Gespräche,* 210).
14. L–M, 18, letter 613, p. 287.
15. L–M, 16:444.
16. L–M, 18, letter 650, p. 319 (May 18, 1779).
17. L–M, 18, letter 657, p. 322 f. (Aug. 13, 1779).
18. Biedermann, *Gespräche,* 218.
19. On the various senses of the "analogy," see Peter Demetz, *Gotthold Ephraim Lessing: Nathan der Weise,* Ullstein Series, no. 5025 (Frankfurt am Main & Berlin, 1966), 140 f.
20. L–M, 18, letter 617, p. 292 f.
21. L–M, 18, letter 619, p. 294.
22. See Demetz, *Nathan der Weise,* 129.
23. L–M, 18, letter 622, p. 296 f. (Dec. 18, 1778).
24. Dec. 7, 1778; Dec. 19, 1778 (up to p. 74); Jan. 15, 1779 (pp. 75–116); Feb....; Mar. 13, 1779 (return of pp. 148–72); Mar. 16, 1779 (pp. 172–202); ...(the rest). See L–M, 18, letters 619, 623, 631, 635, 636, pp. 294, 297 f., 304 f., 307 (note 2); L–M, 21, letter 791, p. 248.
25. See L–M, 21, letter 783, p. 241 (Jan. 9, 1779).
26. Dep. RvM, C I, no. 15.
27. L–M, 18, letter 637, p. 308 f.
28. See L–M, 18, p. 308, note 3.
29. Friedländer apparently gave no indication of the story referred to by Mendelssohn.
30. L–M, 21, letter 800, p. 253 f.
31. L–M, 16:444 f.
32. In his essay *Über naive und sentimentalische Dichtung* (1795/6), Schiller criticized *Nathan the Wise* on this account (see *Schillers sämtliche Werke,* ed. J. Wychgran, 12:127, note 1). Berthold Auerbach defended Lessing against Schillers strictures; see Hermann Hettner, *Geschichte der deutschen Literatur im achtzehnten Jahrhundert* (Berlin, 1961), 1:728. In his *Dichtung und Wahrheit,* Goethe praised *Nathan's* "serene naïveté" (*heitere Naivität*), as Danzel, *Lessing,* 2.2, 208, noted.
33. *Morgenstunden,* xv (*GS,* 2:366).
34. See Demetz, *Nathan der Weise,* 212. The various versions of the parable are recorded on pp. 200–16.
35. On the fragmentization of the parable in later versions, including Lessing's, see Heinz Politzer, "Lessings Parabel von den drei Ringen," *The German Quarterly,* 31.3(May, 1958): 161–77.
36. 3:7.
37. See Yitshak Baer, *Sefer Shevet Yehuda le-Rabbi Shelomo ibn Verga* (Jerusalem, 1947), 78–80. According to Baer (p. 14 f.), Ibn Verga's story is based on both a 13th-century collection, *Le Cento Novelle Antiche* and Boccaccio's *Decameron,* as shown in his *Untersuchungen über Quellen und Komposition des Shebet Jehuda* (1923). A German translation of Ibn Verga's version is found in August Wünsche, "Der Ursprung der Parabel von den drei Ringen," *Les-*

sing–Mendelssohn Gedenkbuch (Leipzig, 1879), 338 ff. (reproduced in Demetz, *Nathan der Weise,* 200 f.).

38. L–M, 13:8–17.

39. English translation by William A. Steele, *Lessing: Laocoön, Nathan the Wise, Minna von Barnhelm* (London, 1930).

40. *JubA,* 7:44 f.

41. *GS,* 5:503 f.

42. See Lessing's letter to Elise, Sept. 6, 1778: "Yet if you look up, in Boccaccio's *Decameron,* the story of the Jew Melchizedek, which will form the heart of my play,..." (L–M, 18, letter 613, p. 286 f.).

43. no. 79; referred to by Henry E. Allison, *Lessing and the Enlightenment* (Ann Arbor, 1966), 146.

44. See Leibniz, "Considérations sur les Principes de vie...," in C. J. Gerhardt, ed., *Die philosphischen Schriften von G. W. Leibniz* (Berlin, 1875–1890), 6:542; Leibniz, *Essais de Théodicée,* 2, B, #247 (Gerhardt, 6:137); cf. *Frühschriften,* 14; Allison, *Lessing,* 146 f., 200, note 91.

45. *Morgenstunden,* xv (*GS,* 2:362).

46. Horace, *Epist.,* 1, 2, 4.

47. *Morgenstunden,* xv (*GS,* 2:366).

48. The preface to *Manasseh Ben Israel* (*GS,* 3:180); cf. above, p. 465.

49. 4:4.

50. *GS,* 3:358.

51. *GS,* 3:360. Cf. Mendelssohn's letter to Count Dalberg, *GS,* 5:541 (see above, p. 314).

52. L–M, 16:444.

53. See above, p. 40 f.

54. See Danzel, *Lessing,* 2.1:209.

55. L–M, 21, letter 825, p. 276.

56. L–M, 18, letter 669, p. 329–31; letter 672, p. 334; letter 674, p. 334 ff. For the refutation see L–M, 13:379–86. For further details, see Karl G. Lessing, *G.E. Lessings Leben* ..., 1 (Berlin, 1793): 416.

57. See L–M, 21, letter 811, p. 263.

58. L–M, 21, letter 829, p. 280.

59. L–M, 18, letter 665, p. 327 f.

60. *Morgenstunden,* xv (*GS,* 2:366 ff.).

61. Karl G. Lessing, *Lessings Leben,* 1:407.

62. Ibid., 413.

63. Fliess, born in 1745, was a doctor of medicine, a landowner, and later *Kammerrat* in Berlin (see Meyer, *Bibliographie,* p. 271); L–M, 21, p. 289, note 2).

64. See Nicolai's note, *GS,* 5:228; Meyer, *Bibliographie,* 327.

65. *GS,* 5:201 (L–M, 21, letter 840, p. 289).

66. L–M, 18, letter 674, p. 334 ff.

67. *Yoricks empfindsame Reise,* a German version of Laurence Sterne's *A Sentimental Journey Through France and Italy* (1768).

68. *GS,* 5:202 f. (L–M, 18, letter 703, p. 361 f.).

69. See Karl G. Lessing, *Lessings Leben,* 1:406.

70. L–M, 18, letter 598, p. 269 f.

71. *GS,* 2:407 f.

72. L–M, 21, letter 877, p. 318, note 4; *GS,* 5:582; quoted below, pp. 582–83.

A Projected Essay on Lessing's Character (pages 582–593)

1. See Heinrich Schneider, *Lessing* (Bern, 1951), 74.

2. *GS,* 5:580 ff.; first published by Karl G. Lessing, *G.E. Lessings Leben* (Berlin, 1793), 1:449–52, and reproduced in numerous places; see Meyer, *Bibliographie,* p. 240, no. C.93.1, and Alexander Altmann, "Briefe Karl Gotthelf Lessings an Moses Mendelssohn," *Lessing Yearbook,* 1 (Munich, 1969) :10, note 6. The text of the letter extant in Dep. RvM, D II, no. 3 is neither a fragment, as it is mistakenly described there, nor the original, as erroneously stated in my article in *Lessing Yearbook,* 1. On its second page, the Paris address of Mendelssohn's daughter Henriette ("Hotel Sebastian") is written by another hand. The letter is undated.

3. See Rudolf Haym, *Herder* (Berlin, 1954), 2:177 f.

4. Herder's work is entitled: *Maran-Ata, Das Buch von der Zukunft des Herrn.*

5. Kayserling, *Mendelssohn*, 1st ed., 541 f.; quoted from *Aus Herder's Nachlass* (ed. Heinrich Düntzer and Ferdinand Gottfried von Herder), 2:217 f.

6. *Älteste Urkunde des Menschengeschlechts,* 1 (1774); 2 (1776). Mendelssohn's admiration for this work is attested by Zimmermann: "Moses Mendelssohn told me that he had found in Herder's *Älteste Urkunde* . . . treasures of profound truth that he had not understood before, and an entirely novel oriental spirit in explaining Holy Scripture, that no one had attained previously." See *Hannoversches Magazin*, vol. 44 (1779); Eduard Bodemann, *Johann Georg Zimmermann, Sein Leben und bisher ungedruckte Briefe an denselben* (Hanover, 1878), 79.

7. *Lieder der Liebe* (1778). The original of Mendelssohn's letter to Herder (June 20, 1780) is found in the A. Schwadron Collection of the Hebrew University and National Library, Jerusalem (Moses Mendelssohn File 1). It is reproduced in facsimile in *Jüdisches Lexikon* (ed. G. Herlitz and B. Kirschner), vol. 4, on a separate sheet inserted between columns 96 and 97; it is printed in Kayserling, *Mendelssohn*, 1st ed., 542 f.

8. See Rudolf Haym, *Herder*, 2:157 f.

9. Kayserling, *Mendelssohn*, 1st. ed., 543–46.

10. Nicolai had published a devastating review of Herder's *Älteste Urkunde* in *Allgemeine-deutsche Bibliothek* (see Haym, *Herder*, 1:648 f.).

11. The letter as printed in *GS*, 5:582–87, contains some editorial changes; see the note by Heinrich Düntzer and F.G. von Herder in their edition of *Briefe an Herder von Lavater, Jacobi, Forster u. A.* (Frankfurt am Main, 1858), p. 224; reproduced by Kayserling, *Mendelssohn*, 1st ed., 546; Haym, *Herder*, 2:178, note 41. The letter has never been published in its original form.

12. *GS*, 5:580.

13. The original draft of the letter and the note are extant in "Depositum Berlin," 68, Mendelssohn–Archiv Stiftung Preussischer Kulturbesitz, Berlin; they are copied in Marburg File, no. 46.

14. Published by Alexander Altmann in *Lessing Yearbook*, 1 (Munich 1969): 40 f.

15. See O. von Heinemann, ed., *Zur Erinnerung an Gotthold Ephraim Lessing, Briefe und Aktenstücke . . .* (Leipzig, 1870), 189.

16. Ibid., 195–208.

17. Ibid., 158.

18. See Altmann, *Lessing Yearbook*, 1:42 f., where the humorous dubbing of the operation as "Salomon Moses Levische Handlung" (see letter no. 1, p. 11) is explained. It should be added that the name as such was rather common. See Josef Meisl, ed., *Protokollbuch der jüdischen Gemeinde zu Berlin* (Jerusalem, 1962), 519: Moses Salomon Levi (Halfan); [F.W. von Schütz], *Leben und Meinungen Moses Mendelssohn* (Hamburg, 1787), where the list of subscribers contains the name Moses Salomon Levi in Königsberg.

19. *Lessing Yearbook*, 1:11.

20. Ibid., 12–14.

21. The letters written to Mendelssohn by Karl G. Lessing from Jan. 21, 1782, to Oct. 24, 1785 (Dep. RvM, C II, nos. 1–6, 8–10) were published, with annotations and an evaluation of their significance, by Alexander Altmann in *Lessing Yearbook*, 1:9–59.

22. 1784 is given as the year of publication on the title pages of both volumes.

23. See Altmann, *Lessing Yearbook*, 1:43 f.

24. See above, p. 412.

25. Kayserling, *Mendelssohn*, 1st ed., 531 f. Ludwig Geiger, *ZGJD*, 1 (1887):117 f. In Nachlass Hennings 11, fol. 169*v*–170*r*, the passage of the letter is reproduced. The date is erroneously given as Oct. 17, 1780.

26. Kayserling, *Mendelssohn*, 1st ed., 546 f.

27. Marburg File, no. 50.

28. *Lessings Leben*, 2 (1795):14 ff.; Kayserling, *Mendelssohn*, 1st ed., 563 ff.

29. Of the 10 letters mentioned by their dates, 6 are lost, viz. those of August, 1761, August, 1767, October, 1768, April, 1772, July, 1776, and March, 1779. Lessing's letters to Mendelssohn mentioning Herder are also lost.

30. See *GS*, 5:598 ff. 3:413 ff.; 4.1:150 ff.; see above, p. 539 f.

31. Quoted by Kayserling, *Mendelssohn*, 367, from *Nieder-Lausitzsches Magazin*, 38:37.

32. Quoted by Kayserling, *Mendelssohn*, 368, note 1.

33. Reproduced in *Herder's Werke,* 15 (Zerstreute Blätter), ed. Heinrich Düntzer (Berlin, 1875): 61–79. For an evaluation see Haym, *Herder,* 2:179–82.

34. See above, p. 49.

35. Kayserling, *Mendelssohn,* 1st ed., 547 ff.

36. *Lessing Yearbook,* 1, letter no. 2, lines 51–55, p. 13; 46.

37. Ibid., letter no. 3, lines 1–14, p. 15 f.; 46.

38. Ibid., 47, 58, note 29; *GS,* 2:369; see above, pp. 47, 557.

39. The letter is lost, but its content can be reconstructed in part from Karl's reply of May 8, 1783; see *Lessing Yearbook,* 1:46 f.

40. Dep. RvM, B II, no. 15. Mendelssohn could have copied these paragraphs only in April–May, 1783, after receipt of the theological *Nachlass,* not after its publication in the spring of 1785; see *Lessing Yearbook,* 1:47 f.

41. Letter no. 3, lines 61–68, p. 17.

42. Published by Jacobi in his *Über die Lehre des Spinoza in Briefen an den Herrn Moses Mendelssohn* (Breslau, 1785), 1 f.

43. *GS,* 5:691 ff.

44. Dep. RvM, A, no. 1.

45. *GS,* 6:127.

46. Nachlass Hennings 11, fol. 156r; Kayserling, *Mendelssohn,* 1st ed., 533.

47. Read: "last spring."

Jacobi's Attitude ... (pages 593–603)

1. "David Hume über den Glauben, oder Idealismus und Realismus, Ein Gespräch" (1787), *Friedrich Heinrich Jacobi's Werke,* 2 (Leipzig, 1815): 183 f.

2. Theodore Bestermann (ed.), *Studies in Voltaire and the Eighteenth Century,* Vol. 45: Lettres inédites de F.H. Jacobi publiées par J.Th. de Booy et Roland Mortier (Geneva, 1966). This edition comprises 72 letters from Jacobi to Rey written during the years 1763–1771. It sheds light, for the first time, on the period of Jacobi's development from his return to Düsseldorf to his becoming acquainted with Wieland. The correspondence was conducted in French.

3. Ibid., 128 f.

4. Ibid., 136.

5. Ibid., 145.

6. Ibid., 149 f.

7. Ibid., 151.

8. Ibid., 152.

9. Ibid., 158.

10. Ibid., 64. The editors suggest that the criticized translator was M[onsieur Abel] Burja, whose *Phaedon* translation was edited twice in 1722. For the French versions see Meyer, *Bibliographie,* 42.

11. *Friedrich Heinrich Jacobi's auserlesener Briefwechsel,* 1 (Leipzig, 1825): 83.

12. Cf. Hermann Hettner, *Geschichte der deutschen Literatur im achtzehnten Jahrhundert* (Berlin, 1961), 1:675.

13. *Jacobi's auserlesener Briefwechsel,* 1:91. Mendelssohn's lines were found in *Abbt's vermischte Werke,* 3:50 f. (*GS,* 5:250).

14. Quoted by Ludwig Geiger, "Die Juden und die deutsche Literatur," *ZGJD,* 1 (1887): 335, from *Briefe Goethes an Frau von Stein* (ed. Fielitz), 436.

15. *Vermischte Schriften von Friedrich Heinrich Jacobi,* part one (Breslau, 1781; 2nd edition: Karlsruhe, 1783). Part two never appeared.

16. See Ludwig Geiger, *ZGJD,* 4 (1890): 304.

17. April and May, 1779.

18. See Jan Ulbe Terpstra, *Friedrich Heinrich Jacobi's "Allwill"* (Groningen, 1957).

19. See Ferdinand Deycks, *Friedrich Heinrich Jacobi im Verhältnis zu seinen Zeitgenossen, besonders zu Goethe* (Frankfurt am Main, 1848), 53; Heinz Nicolai, *Goethe und Jacobi, Studien zur Geschichte ihrer Freundschaft* (Stuttgart, 1965).

20. L–M, 18 letter 650, p. 319.

21. L–M, 21, letter 816, p. 266 f.

22. Rudolf Zoeppritz, *Aus F.H. Jacobi's Nachlass* (Leipzig, 1869), 1:27–43. For the reference to Mendelssohn see p. 28 f.

23. L–M, 21, letter 872, p. 312.

24. L–M, 18, letter 700, p. 358; L–M, 21, letter 875, p. 317.

25. *Jacobi's auserlesener Briefwechsel*, 1:317; see also Jacobi's letter to Sophie Laroche, Zoeppritz, *Aus Jacobi's Nachlass*, 1:47.

26. *Jacobi's auserlesener Briefwechsel*, 1:334.

27. See below, pp. 652 f., 703.

28. Jacobi, *Über die Lehre des Spinoza . . .* 2nd rev. ed., 4.

29. *Jacobi's auserlesener Briefwechsel*, 1:325–28.

30. When Jacobi presented Herder with a copy of the same book, he did so through Matthias Claudius; see Rudolf Haym, *Herder*, 2:305.

31. Dep. RvM, C I, no. 10; see Alexander Altmann, "Letters from Dohm to Mendelssohn," *Salo W. Baron Jubilee Volume* (Jerusalem, 1973).

32. Zoeppritz, *Aus Jacobi's Nachlass*, 1:50.

33. Ibid., 1:48.

34. Johann Georg Müller, ed., *Johannes von Müllers sämmtliche Werke*, 25 (Stuttgart & Tübingen, 1833): 13–45.

35. *Etwas das Lessing gesagt hat, Ein Commentar zu den Reisen der Päpste nebst Betrachtungen von einem Dritten* (Berlin, 1782).

36. Viz. Justinus Febronius, the pseudonym chosen by Johann Nicolaus von Hontheim (1701–1790), historian, theologian, and auxiliary bishop of Trier, who demanded the limitation of papal power in his *De statu ecclesiae et legitima potestate Romani Pontificis* (1763, 1765).

37. *Etwas*, 11 f.

38. Ibid., 12 f.

39. *Jacobi's auserlesener Briefwechsel*, 1:344–50.

40. "Gedanken Verschiedener bey Gelegenheit einer merkwürdigen Schrift," *Deutsches Museum*, 1. 1 (Leipzig, January, 1783): 3–9.

41. *Jacobi's auserlesener Briefwechsel*, 1:350 f.

42. *Friedrich Heinrich Jacobi wider Mendelssohns Beschuldigungen . . .* (Leipzig, 1786), 33 f.

43. *Jacobi's auserlesener Briefwechsel*, 1:351.

44. *Hamann Briefwechsel*, 5:243.

45. The section written by Mendelssohn starts with the words, "Auch geht unser Verfasser" (p. 8) and continues to the end of the article (see *Jacobi wider Mendelssohns Beschuldigungen*, 33, note). Dohm contributed the passage from "Lessing selbst mag" (p. 7) to "von Fürst und Volk gehandelt" (p. 8).

46. "Erinnerungen gegen die in den Januar des Museums eingerückte Gedanken über eine merkwürdige Schrift," *Deutsches Museum*, 1.2 (February, 1783): 97–105.

47. First published in *Moses Mendelssohn an die Freunde Lessings* (Berlin, 1786); subsequently by Jacobi in the second revised edition of his *Über die Lehre des Spinoza* (Breslau, 1789), 164 ff.

48. 1.2:98

49. *Etwas*, 98. The motto of Jacobi's treatise reads: "Dic cur hic? respice finem! Which Leibniz renders: Où en sommes nous? venons au fait! Nouv[eaux] Ess[ais], p. 255." Justus Möser's gloss (on p. 14 ff.) is a passage from his treatise, *Von dem wichtigen Unterschiede des würklichen und förmlichen Rechts*.

50. *Museum*, 1.2:99.

51. *Etwas*, 26–31.

52. *Museum*, 1.2:100 f.

53. *Museum*, 1.2:101.

54. See Jacobi's letter to Hamann, Oct. 18, 1784, *Hamann Briefwechsel*, 5:243.

55. *Museum*, 1.2:101, note.

56. See above, p. 600.

57. Kayserling, *Mendelssohn*, 1st ed., 563; see above, p. 589.

58. *GS*, 2:368

59. In *Wider Mendelssohns Beschuldigungen* (1786), 34.

60. *Jacobi's auserlesener Briefwechsel*, 1:357 f.

61. *Museum*, 3.2:103.

62. Ibid., 103 f.

63. Cf. *JubA*, 2:21 f.

An Uneasy Correspondence I (pages 603–621)

1. See above, p. 591 f.
2. Jacobi, *Über die Lehre des Spinoza,* 2nd rev. ed. (1789), 4.
3. See above, p. 602.
4. It is by this term that Jacobi persistently referred to the anonymous critic (Mendelssohn) in his *Objections.*
5. *Etwas,* 82 ff.
6. *Museum,* 1.2:105.
7. *Jacobi's Werke,* ed. Friedrich Roth (Leipzig, 1812–1825), 4.3:67.
8. *Jacobi wider Mendelssohns Beschuldigungen,* 13.
9. *Jacobi's auserlesener Briefwechsel,* 1:342 f.
10. Ibid., 332.
11. Thus in the first edition (1785) of his *Über die Lehre des Spinoza*; in the second edition (1789), p. 256, changed to "pious, sincere mouth" *(frommen, aufrichtigen Munde).*
12. See Lothar Schreiner, ed., *Johann Georg Hamann Golgatha und Scheblimini* (Gütersloh, 1956), 69 f.
13. Schreiner, *Golgatha,* 17.
14. Dep. RvM, A, no. 2 (enclosure); copy by an unknown hand; reproduced, without the final paragraph, in *Über die Lehre des Spinoza,* 2nd ed., p. 4 ff.
15. Dep. RvM, A, no. 2 (enclosure), last paragraph: Jacobi requested the return of the manuscript of a comedy *(Die Poeten)* by Lang, of which he was the owner; also of a number of letters that he had lent to Lessing, and those he had written to him; finally, of Hemsterhuis' *Lettre sur les Desirs,* which belonged to the princess of Gallitzin.
16. Dep. RvM, A, no. 2.
17. *An die Freunde Lessings* (1786), 8 f. *(GS,* 3:6).
18. *GS,* 5:709.
19. *GS,* 5:717.
20. *An die Freunde Lessings,* 10f. *(GS,* 3:6 f.).
21. Dep. RvM, A, no. 3 (copy); reproduced *GS,* 5:693–98.
22. *GS,* 5:698.
23. *GS,* 5:694 f.
24. *GS,* 5:695.
25. Johann Georg Wachter, *Der Spinozismus im Judenthumb, oder die von dem heutigen Judenthumb und dessen geheimen Kabbala Vergötterte Welt* (Amsterdam, 1699); Idem, *Elucidarius cabalisticus sive reconditae Hebraeorum philosophiae recensio* (Rome, 1706).
26. See above, p. 47; *GS,* 2:369; 5:192–95.
27. See p. 591.
28. *GS,* 2:369–72.
29. *GS,* 5:195 (May 1, 1774).
30. See Johannes Schneider, *Lessings Stellung zur Theologie vor der Herausgabe der Wolfenbüttler Fragmente,* [Dissertation Amsterdam] (The Hague, 1953), 112.
31. *Hamann Briefwechsel,* 5:444.
32. *An die Freunde Lessings,* 6–9 *(GS,* 3:5 f.).
33. Jacobi, *Über die Lehre des Spinoza* (1785), 4. The sentence, "Mendelssohn erstaunte ..." was omitted in the second edition. See Heinrich Scholz, *Die Hauptschriften zum Pantheismusstreit zwischen Jacobi und Mendelssohn* (Berlin, 1916), 69, note b.
34. See *JubA,* 1:17 f.; *Frühschriften,* 29–33.
35. Jacobi, *Über die Lehre des Spinoza,* 2nd ed., 9–13.
36. The covering letter is reproduced, in part, in Jacobi's *Über die Lehre des Spinoza,* 2nd ed., 13 f. and, in full, in his *Wider Mendelssohns Beschuldigungen,* 12–14.
37. *Wider Mendelssohns Beschuldigungen,* 14 f.
38. *Jacobi's Werke,* 4.3:175 (Feb. 28, 1786).
39. Ibid., 184 f. (Mar. 15, 1786).
40. See Jacobi's letters of Feb. 15, 1786 (ibid., 158) and Feb. 28, 1786 (ibid., 175).
41. Max Jacobi, ed., *Briefwechsel zwischen Goethe und F. H. Jacobi* (Leipzig, 1846), 70.
42. See Jan Ulbe Terpstra, ed., *Jacobi's "Allwill"* (Groningen, 1957), 292.
43. The original letter is extant in Dep. RvM, A, no. 4a; reproduced with some slight changes in Jacobi, *Über die Lehre des Spinoza* (1785), 7–48; 2nd ed. (1789), 14–68; *Jacobi's Werke,* 4.1:47–94; Scholz, *Hauptschriften,* 72–105.

44. Quoted here after the original letter, which is reproduced with one minor variation in the 1st edition of Jacobi's *Über die Lehre des Spinoza*. The 2nd edition has after the words "Menge Radii": "ohne aufzuhören eine Sehne zu sein," but omits the aggressive sentence: "Wo beydes mangelt... gefunden werden."

45. *Hamann Briefwechsel*, 5:271.

46. *Jacobi's auserlesener Briefwechsel*, 1:362 f.

47. Ibid.

48. *Wider Mendelssohns Beschuldigungen*, 35 f.

49. So in the original letter (Dep. RvM, A, no. 4a, p. 33, line 1).

50. See *Verzeichnis*, p. 16, no. 253.

51. Cf. T. C. van Stockum, *Spinoza-Jacobi-Lessing* (Groningen, 1916), 14.

52. A xerographic copy of Mendelssohn's letter was put at my disposal by Baron Hugo von Mendelssohn Bartholdy. The present owner of the original is unknown. The addressee of the letter was Anton von Klein (1748–1810), professor of poetry and philosophy in Mannheim, who edited *Leben und Bildnisse grosser Deutschen* (5 vols., 1785–1805).

53. See Carl Gebhardt, ed., *Spinoza Opera* (Heidelberg, 1925), 2:314.

54. *Hamann Briefwechsel*, 5:270 (Dec. 1, 1784); 5:300 (Dec. 30, 1784). Jacobi had, confidentially, sent Hamann his correspondence with Mendelssohn. Elise conveyed the question to Mendelssohn as late as Apr. 26, 1785, as her letter of that date (Dep. RvM, A, no. 16, p. 1) shows. Mendelssohn seems to have ignored the question.

55. The text of the original letter (p. 34 f.) differs in minor linguistic respects from the printed one (Scholz, *Hauptschriften*, 104).

56. *Wider Mendelssohns Beschuldigungen*, 35.

57. Karl G. Lessing, *Lessings Leben*, 1:246; cf. Wilhelm Dilthey, *Das Erlebnis und die Dichtung*, 12th ed. (1921), 101; van Stockum, *Spinoza...*, 14.

58. Original letter, p. 36 (Scholz, *Hauptschriften*, 105). The paragraph (Scholz, 104, bottom): "Die Anrede: 'Lieber Bruder...' [see above, p. 608] ist von Lessing nicht an mich gehalten worden" is not found in the original letter. In its place are three lines that Jacobi made illegible by deletion.

59. For a full analysis, see Alexander Altmann, "Lessing und Jacobi: Das Gespräch über den Spinozismus," *Lessing Yearbook*, 3 (Munich, 1971), 25–70. See also Reinhard Schwarz, "Lessings 'Spinozismus,'" *Zeitschrift für Theologie und Kirche*, 65.3 (July, 1968): 271–90, and Friedemann Regner, "Lessings Spinozismus," ibid., 68.3 (September, 1971): 351–75.

60. Lessing considered this formula to have been "the inscription of a temple of the ancients" (see *Hamann Briefwechsel*, 5:271, 301 f.). It occurs in a sentence of Heraclitus as recorded by Hippolytus (see Diels, *Die Fragmente der Vorsokratiker*, 2nd ed., 1:69), and it was used by Giordano Bruno (see Jacobi, *Über die Lehre des Spinoza*, 2nd ed., 306; Scholz, *Hauptschriften*, 223). On the profound echo that this formula found in Herder, Hamann, Goethe, and later in Hegel, Hölderlin, and Schelling, see Renate Knoll, *Johann Georg Hamann und Friedrich Heinrich Jacobi* (Heidelberg, 1963), 52 f. and passim.

61. For a discussion of the kabbalistic terms in Jacobi's letter, see Altmann, *Lessing Yearbook*, 3:29–32.

62. Original letter, p. 32 (Scholz, 102).

63. Original letter, p. 8, note (Scholz, 79, note).

64. We are using the term coined by Harry A. Wolfson, "Extradeical and Intradeical Interpretations of Platonic Ideas," *Religious Philosophy, A Group of Essays* (Cambridge, Massachusetts, 1961), 27 ff.

65. See above, p. 52.

66. Rudolf Zoeppritz, *Aus F. H. Jacobi's Nachlass* (Leipzig, 1869), 1:52 f.

67. Spinoza, *Korte Verhandeling*, 1:9, #3.

68. An allusion to Lessing's famous statement in his *On the Proof of the Spirit and the Power*.

69. See above, p. 617.

70. Original letter, p. 15 (Scholz, 85).

71. See above, p. 51 f.; *Frühschriften*, 8–29.

72. *GS*, 5:168 ff.; see *Frühschriften*, 21–24.

73. *GS*, 5:174–77.

74. See Altmann, *Lessing Yearbook*, 3:52 f. Lessing's critique was resumed by Karl Heinrich Heydenreich, *Natur und Gott nach Spinoza* (Leipzig, 1789), 1:90–102.

75. *Ethica*, 2:43, scholion.

76. "Hast du nicht alles selbst vollendet, Heilig glühend Herz."
77. For a discussion of Lessing's position, see Altmann, *Lessing Yearbook*, 3:40–58.

An Uneasy Correspondence II (pages 621–637)

1. Dep. RvM, A, no. 4b and 4c.
2. *GS*, 5:699–704.
3. Dr. Reimarus' letter has at the end: "1783, Nov. 11, when I reached the age of 54." Mendelssohn's letter concludes: "Berlin, Nov. 18, 1783, likewise in the first quarter of my 54th year."
4. See Jacobi, *Über die Lehre des Spinoza*, 2nd ed., 77 (Scholz, *Hauptschriften*, 109 f.).
5. *GS*, 5:701 f.
6. See *Moses Mendelssohn an die Freunde Lessings*, 51 (*GS*, 3:22); Jacobi, *Über die Lehre des Spinoza*, 2nd ed., 91 (Scholz, 118).
7. *An die Freunde Lessings*, 23 f., 27 f. (*GS*, 3:11, 13).
8. *GS*, 5:702.
9. *GS*, 5:703 f.
10. See *Jacobi wider Mendelssohns Beschuldigungen*, 18 f.; *Werke*, 4. 2, 188.
11. The cryptic manner in which Lessing answered Dr. Reimarus' question about the authorship of *The Education of the Human Race* (see above, p. 560) is a case in point.
12. Viz. in his article in *Deutsches Museum*, 1.2 (see above, p. 601 f.).
13. Published by Jacobi in *Wider Mendelssohns Beschuldigungen*, 19–22, and subsequently in the second edition of his *Über die Lehre des Spinoza*, 68–71 (*Werke*, 4.2, 190–92; Scholz, 105 f.).
14. As published by Jacobi, the text of Elise's letter contains several dashes that might indicate some omissions on his part. A comparison of the text with Mendelssohn's letter makes it almost certain, however, that the dashes were put in by Elise.
15. As Mendelssohn's reply of Jan. 5, 1784 (*GS*, 5:705 f.) shows, the person concerned was L.C.G. Rudolphi, who resided in Hamburg and became prominent as a man of letters and as a pedagogue (see *GS*, 5:705 f., editor's note).
16. Elise's note and her summary of Jacobi's letter are extant in Dep. RvM, A, no. 6.
17. *GS*, 5:705 f.
18. *JubA*, 1:14; see *Frühschriften*, 7 f.
19. See *GS*, 5:706, note 1.
20. See Altmann, *Lessing Yearbook*, 1:24; 25, note 4.
21. *Wider Mendelssohns Beschuldigungen*, 48.
22. *Jacobi's Werke*, 3:481 f.
23. Ibid., 482–84.
24. See Wilhelm Dobbek, ed., *Herders Briefe* (Weimar, 1959), 226–30.
25. The first Part of Herder's *Ideen zur Philosophie der Geschichte der Menschheit* was published in April, 1784. Parts 2, 3, and 4 followed in August, 1785, April, 1787, and November, 1791, respectively.
26. On Dec. 30, 1783, Goethe had informed Jacobi that Herder was going to write to him. The subject of Jacobi/Lessing had shortly before been discussed among friends in Weimar (see *Briefwechsel zwischen Goethe und Jacobi*, 67).
27. As Herder explained in *Gott* (1787), he considered the designation of extension as an "attribute" of God to be a mistake. Spinoza himself, he pointed out, had admitted in his *Letters* (nos. 69–72) that the nature of matter was insufficiently defined by the term "extension." Not God but the corporeal world was extended. See *Herders sämtliche Werke: Zur Philosophie und Geschichte*, 8 (Karlsruhe, 1820): 142 ff.
28. We conclude from this reference that Jacobi had sent Herder a copy of Mendelssohn's letter. In *Gott*, Herder dealt at length with Bayle's misunderstanding of Spinoza (see *Werke* . . ., 8:102 ff.).
29. H. F. Diez, *Benedikt von Spinoza nach Leben und Lehren* (1783); see Scholz, 107 and note 13.
30. *Über die Lehre des Spinoza*, 51; 2nd ed., 71 f.; *Wider Mendelssohns Beschuldigungen*, 24 f. (Scholz, 107).
31. Dep. RvM, A, no. 8.
32. In *Hessische Beiträge*, 1:113 ff.
33. See below, p. 669 ff.

34. *Über die Lehre des Spinoza*, 2nd ed., 74 f. (Scholz, 108 f.).
35. See his statement in *Über die Lehre des Spinoza*, 2nd ed., 74 f. (Scholz, 109).
36. Frans Hemsterhuis, *Aristée ou De La Divinité* (Paris, 1779).
37. *Über die Lehre des Spinoza*, 1st. ed., 56–113, 2nd ed., 100–57; Scholz, 123–40.
38. *GS*, 5:709.
39. The draft of the letter in Mendelssohn's hand is extant in Dep. RvM, A, no. 9 (a). Its reproduction in *GS*, 5:707–09 omits phrases that were deleted by Mendelssohn but are of considerable interest. The fair copy sent to Jacobi contained further changes, which are indicated by the editor. Jacobi published the letter in his *Über die Lehre des Spinoza*, 2nd ed., 76–78 (Scholz, 109 f.).
40. *Essay on the Freedom of Wit and Humor*, part 2, sect. 1; quoted in full by Mendelssohn as the motto of his *An die Freunde Lessings* (Berlin, 1786), xxiii–xxiv (*GS*, 3:2).
41. A copy in an unknown hand is found in Dep. RvM, A, no. 9 (b) and another in no. 20, pp. 10–16; published by Mendelssohn in his *An die Freunde Lessings*, 36–56 (*GS*, 3:16–24), and by Jacobi in his *Über die Lehre des Spinoza*, 2nd ed., 78–96.
42. *Essais de Théodicée*, 1, B., #173.
43. Cf. the same argument in Mendelssohn's *Phaedon*, *JubA*, 3. 1:89–99.
44. *Theologia naturalis*, 2, #671 ff. The text of Wolff's critique of Spinoza is reproduced in Scholz, *Hauptschriften*, xlii–lix; the particular point referred to is found on page lii. Mendelssohn had mentioned it as early as 1755 in his *Philosophische Gespräche* (*JubA*, 1:16).
45. As the extant copies of Mendelssohn's "Objections" (see note 41) show, Mendelssohn here quoted p. 17 of the letter he had received from Jacobi (Dep. RvM, A, no. 4a). When reproducing his "Objections" in his *An die Freunde Lessings*, he referred to p. 26 of the letter as published by Jacobi in his *Über die Lehre des Spinoza*.
46. *An die Freunde Lessings*, 51f. (*GS*, 3:22); Jacobi, *Über die Lehre des Spinoza*, 2nd ed., 90 f. (Scholz, 118).
47. The original letter in Jacobi's hand is extant in Dep. RvM, A, no. 10a; published in *Über die Lehre des Spinoza*, 2nd ed., 96–98 (Scholz, 121 f.).
48. *Pensées de Pascal*, art. 21.
49. *GS*, 5:709 (Aug. 8, 1784).
50. *Über die Lehre des Spinoza*, 2nd ed., 157 f. (Scholz, 136 f.).
51. Dep. RvM, A, no. 10b (27 quarto pages); the title is written in Jacobi's hand.
52. Dep. RvM, A, no. 11.
53. *GS*, 5:711 (Nov. 15, 1784).
54. See *Jacobi's Werke*, 3:492.
55. Viz. from Elise's letter of Apr. 2, 1784.

Chapter Eight: Guardian of the Enlightenment
The Contest (pages 638–653)

1. See Heinrich Scholz, *Die Hauptschriften zum Pantheismusstreit zwischen Jacobi und Mendelssohn* (Berlin, 1916). The account given by Fritz Mauthner, *Jacobis Spinoza Büchlein* (München, 1912), is rather tendentious.
2. Some important sources, such as Jacobi's correspondence with Hamann and Herder and hitherto unpublished letters from Dep. RvM, are used here for the first time.
3. Lothar Schreiner, ed., *Johann Georg Hamann Golgatha und Scheblimini*, 154.
4. See his letter of Dec. 30, 1784, to Hamann (*Hamann Briefwechsel*, 5:300).
5. *Hamann Briefwechsel*, 5:241; see also Herder's letter to Hamann, 248 f.
6. Ibid., 5:241; *Jacobi's Werke*, ed. Friedrich Roth (Leipzig, 1812–1825), 1:378.
7. *Hamann Briefwechsel*, 5:263 f.
8. Letter to Herder (Feb. 3, 1785), ibid., 5:351.
9. Ibid., 5:270 (Dec. 1, 1784).
10. Ibid., 5:274.
11. *Philosophische Betrachtung über Theologie und Religion überhaupt und über die jüdische insonderheit* (Frankfurt am Main, 1784; 2nd ed. Frankfurt & Leipzig, 1786).
12. An account of Schulz' work is found in *Bibliothek der Deutschen Aufklärer des achtzehnten Jahrhunderts*, ed. Martin von Geismar [Bruno Bauer], vol. 3 (1846).
13. *Hamann Briefwechsel*, 5:325.
14. *Golgatha und Scheblimini. Von einem Prediger in der Wüsten.*
15. An allusion to Mendelssohn's stated preference as mentioned in Elise's letter of July 5, 1784; see above, p. 632.
16. Hamann expressed the same feeling of relief to other friends; see *Hamann Briefwechsel*,

5:341 (Johann Georg Scheffner); 351 (Herder); 375, 377 (Franz Kaspar Buchholtz).

17. See above, p. 365 f. Obviously, Euchel returned via Berlin, where he saw Mendelssohn again.

18. *Hamann Briefwechsel,* 5:330, 402, 405, 409.

19. Ibid., 5:326 f.

20. Ibid., 5:265.

21. Ibid., 5:266.

22. *Jacobi's Werke,* 3:491 f.

23. *Hamann Briefwechsel,* 5:300.

24. Ibid., 5:319.

25. In Schreiner's edition, p. 142 f. Cf. above, p. 630.

26. Scholz, *Hauptschriften,* 170 f.

27. *Hamann Briefwechsel,* 5:242, 265.

28. Scholz, *Hauptschriften,* 186.

29. *Jacobi's Werke,* 4.3:65 f., 77 f. Herder's *Philosophische Vorlesungen über das so genannte Neue Testament* [vol. 1] appeared in Leipzig in 1785.

30. See Altmann, *Lessing Yearbook,* 1:38, note 2.

31. Viz. forming sentences from various utterances of other authors (Latin *cento,* Greek *kentron*=patchwork).

32. *Hamann Briefwechsel,* 5:243, 245.

33. Part 4, chap. 6; see Jacobi, *Wider Mendelssohns Beschuldigungen,* 126.

34 *Über die Lehre des Spinoza,* 212–15; slightly changed in the second edition, 256–58 (Scholz, 199–201).

35. *Hamann Briefwechsel,* 5:260.

36. Ibid., 5:388.

37. Herder's *Ideen zur Philosophie der Geschichte der Menschheit,* 1 (1784).

38. *Jenaische allgemeine Litteraturzeitung,* 1785, no. 4 (Kant, *Werke,* 4:179–90).

39. See Rudolf Haym, *Herder,* 2:248 f.

40. *Hamann Briefwechsel,* 5:426.

41. Ibid., 5:439.

42. Ibid., 5:341.

43. Friedrich Victor Lebrecht Plessing (1749–1806); see *ADB,* 26:277 ff. Plessing and Dohm visited Mendelssohn on July 14, 1783 (Marburg File, no. 54).

44. See below, note 52.

45. See below, p. 724.

46. Bernhard Wessely, composer and a nephew of Hartwig (1768–1826). See below, p. 741.

47. *GS,* 2:236.

48. They are owned by Prof. Fritz Bamberger, who kindly put a photostatic copy at my disposal. The text corresponds, with a few minor variations, to the passage in *GS,* 2:357, line 15 from the bottom of the page ("*quia homines . . .*")–360, line 14 from the bottom of the page ("ergossen habe"). The draft ends abruptly on line 5 of page 4 with the beginning of a sentence ("Man sieht") that does not appear in the printed text. The four pages are a fragment marked as folios 9 and 10 of the draft.

49. One has to distinguish between corrections made by the scribe and changes applied by Mendelssohn. It is clear that when deleting *refera* and substituting for it *re vera* the scribe had misunderstood the dictation at first.

50. E.g., from his correspondence with his nephew Felix Mendelssohn Bartholdy and Prof. Johannes C.E. Buschmann in the years 1840–1845. See Alexander Altmann, "Moses Mendelssohn's gesammelte Schriften: Neuerschlossene Briefe zur Geschichte ihrer Herausgabe," *BLBI,* 11, no. 42 (1968): 73–115.

51. A photostatic copy of this page was put at my disposal by its owner, the late Prof. Bruno Strauss. (The original is now in the possession of the Leo Baeck Institute, New York.) There can be no doubt that the writing is Joseph Mendelssohn's when he was in his early teens, for a note in Joseph's familiar script entered on the back reads: "geschrieben von Joseph M—die Correcturen sind eigene Handschrift v M.M." The difference between the script on this page and that in the fragment of the *Morgenstunden* is easily accounted for by the intervening period. For the content of the page see below, p. 726.

52. A copy of the letter is extant in Dep. RvM, A, no. 12. Jacobi published a summary of it in his *Über die Lehre des Spinoza* (1785) and quoted the major part of it in the second edition, 159–61. The full text is reproduced in *GS,* 5:712–14.

53. See above, p. 631. The editor's note (2) in *GS*, V, 713, is mistaken.

54. Dep. RvM, A, no. 13.

55. The original letter is extant in Dep. RvM, A, no. 14 (Feb. 11, 1785). It is referred to but not quoted in Jacobi's *Über die Lehre des Spinoza*, 2nd ed., 161 (Scholz, 139).

56. See *Hamann Briefwechsel*, 5:319, 371.

57. "An Herrn Moses Mendelssohn, über desselben mir zugeschickte Erinnerungen"; Dep. RvM, A, no. 15b; reproduced with omissions in the first edition of *Über die Lehre des Spinoza* (pp. 117–66), and in full in the second edition (pp. 164–220). The aggressive openning part (omitted in Jacobi's first edition) was published by Mendelssohn in his *An die Freunde Lessings*, 58–60 (*GS*, 3:25 f.).

58. The original letter is extant in Dep. RvM, A, no. 15a; published with omissions in Jacobi's second edition (pp. 162–63). Scholz, *Hauptschriften*, 139–40, filled in only some of the lacunae.

59. Jacobi was mistaken in attributing the *Betrachtungen über das Fundament der Kräfte* . . . (Königsberg, 1784) to Kant. He expressed this erroneous view also in a letter written, on the same day, to Hamann (see *Hamann Briefwechsel*, 5:428). As Hamann informed him (440, 448), he had been told by Kant that the author was a certain Herr von Elditten of Wickerau, Prussia. See also Kant's letter to Christian Gottfried Schütz (*Werke*, 9:269). On behalf of her brother, Elise asked Mendelssohn on April 25, 1785 (Dep. RvM, A, no. 16) whether he knew this work; if not, it deserved to be known by him. Mendelssohn replied on July 21, 1785, that he had found it disappointing (*GS*, 5:718). He was not so easily misled as Jacobi, and would never have attributed it to Kant.

60. On Jan. 12, 1785, Goethe had written to Jacobi: "I do exercises in Spinoza; I read and reread him, and I wait with great expectation for the fight over his dead body to begin" (see Max Jacobi, ed., *Briefwechsel zwischen Goethe und Jacobi* (Leipzig, 1846), 83).

61. *Jacobi's auserlesener Briefwechsel*, 1, 377 f.

62. Dep. RvM, A, no. 15b, pp. 28–29. The last sentence is missing in the printed texts.

63. See above, p. 641.

64. The original letter is extant in Dep. RvM, A, no. 16.

65. *GS*, 5:714 f.

66. *Über die Lehre des Spinoza*, 2nd ed., 221 (Scholz, 172).

67. The draft of the letter in Mendelssohn's own hand (Dep. RvM, A, no. 17) was published, with slight changes, by Mendelssohn in his *An die Freunde Lessings*, 77–79 (*GS*, 3:32 f.). The letter as sent to Elise (*GS*, 5:715 f.) contained more alterations.

68. In the draft: "a few days ago." This was an understatement. Jacobi's letter must have been received at least three weeks earlier.

69. In the draft: "a year later."

70. Dep. RvM, A, no. 18. Enclosed with the covering note are six and a half pages commenting on the sentence, "God knows, chooses and effects the best," which sums up the content of chapter xii. The pages that contained at least 6 notes on passages in chapters iii, iv, v, and vi are no longer extant. Those notes were printed by Mendelssohn, together with additions of his own, as an appendix to the *Morgenstunden*. The "profound philosopher" in whose name he presented them was undoubtedly Dr. Reimarus. Testimony to this effect is provided by the latter's preface to his treatise *Über die Gründe der menschlichen Erkenntniss und der natürlichen Religion* (Hamburg, 1787), which states: "The late Mendelssohn requested me to let him know my view of the work he was about to publish. Having received a copy of the first part, I had to peruse it in haste and, without expressing an opinion on his system as a whole, I noted down several points that were quoted by him in the appendix" (cited by Leo Strauss in his forthcoming edition of the *Morgenstunden* in *JubA*, 3.2).

71. *GS*, 5:717 f.

72. See Gerson D. Cohen, "Esau as Symbol in Early Medieval Thought," *Jewish Medieval and Renaissance Studies*, ed. Alexander Altmann (Cambridge, Mass., 1967), 19–48.

73. Dep. RvM, A, no. 19. The notes attached to Dr. Reimarus' letter of July 28, 1785, are lost. Unlike some of the earlier notes that he contributed they were not included in the appendix to the *Morgenstunden*. Dr. Reimarus explained in the preface to his *Über die Gründe* . . . (see above, note 70) that several of his annotations concerning the part of the *Morgenstunden* that he reveived in the second batch could not be included since printing was already in progress when they arrived (quoted by Strauss, *JubA*, 3.2). This explanation does not sound convincing, for by July 21 only the first three sheets had been delivered to the press, and Reimarus' notes reached Mendelssohn by the end of the month; it would

not have been difficult to accomodate them in the appendix. Most probably Mendelssohn considered them unsuitable for inclusion.

74. *Über die Lehre des Spinoza,* 2nd ed., 230 ff. (Scholz, 181 f.); reproduced from Jacobi's work (retaining the fictitious name "Emilie" for Elise) in *GS,* 5:720 f.

75. The original is extant in Dep. RvM, A, no. 20. Cf. *Über die Lehre des Spinoza,* 2nd ed., 232 (Scholz, 182).

76. See *Über die Lehre des Spinoza,* 2nd ed., 233 f. (Scholz, 182).

77. *Hamann Briefwechsel,* 5:448; see *Über die Lehre des Spinoza,* 2nd ed., 230 (Scholz, 180).

78. *Hamann Briefwechsel,* 5:466.

79. *Über die Lehre des Spinoza,* 2nd ed., 230 (Scholz, 180 f.).

80. See *GS,* 5:720.

81. See Altmann, *Lessing Yearbook,* 1:36, lines 3–4; 38, note 2.

82. Taking "Spinozism" to be a generic term for a type of philosophy found among many nations and in many periods of history. In support of this thesis Jacobi referred to [Jan Baptiste] van Helmont's (1577–1644) *Opuscula philosophica* (Amsterdam, 1690) and Johann Georg Wachter's *Elucidarius cabalisticus* (Rome, 1706).

83. For a discussion of the development of Jacobi's philosophy of belief, see Arthur Frank, *Friedrich Heinrich Jacobi's Lehre vom Glauben* (Halle, 1910), and *Günther Baum, Vernunft und Erkenntnis, Die Philosophie F. H. Jacobis* (Bonn, 1969).

84. *Jacobi's Werke,* 4.3:77.

85. *Über die Lehre des Spinoza* (1785), 3 (Scholz, 68 f.).

86. Literally, "the proof for the existence of God from the idea."

87. Viz. the prize essay; see *Frühschriften,* 310–16.

Literary Activity: 1783–1785 (pages 653–671)

1. See *GS,* 1:30 and below, note 3.

2. See Joseph Hay, *Staat, Volk und Weltbürgertum in der Berlinischen Monatsschrift von Friedrich Gedike und Erich Biester (1783–96),* [Dissertation Breslau, 1913], (Berlin, 1913), 6–11.

3. Our hitherto scant knowledge about this society and Mendelssohn's part in it has now been considerably enlarged by Heinrich Hümpel's discovery of a file of manuscripts containing the society's standing rules (in Biester's hand) and a diary of activities, including the texts of some of the lectures that were delivered and written opinions *(vota)* about them. The presentation of this material is to be part of a doctoral dissertation to be submitted by Hempel to the Free University of Berlin under the title: "Die Entstehung des Vereinswesens in Berlin im 18. Jahrhundert: Bürgertum und Organisation." I am much obliged to the author for having placed at my disposal (in a letter dated Aug. 19, 1971, and during my stay in Berlin in July, 1972) the results of his research and their full documentation, and for permitting me to make use of the former. Apart from the dissertation, an edition of the extant lectures of the society is being prepared by Hümpel jointly with Professor Norbert Hinske, Trier. My references are to the letter mentioned above and to material I was shown.

4. Hümpel letter of Aug. 19, 1971.

5. For the complete list see *GS,* 1:30, note. Three more members were elected in 1784 (Hümpel letter), bringing the number up to 24.

6. Hümpel letter. Another *"Mittwochs-Gesellschaft,"* founded by Prof. Ignaz Fessler in 1796 and dissolved in 1798, arranged lectures that were open to the public. It, too, had a broad humanitarian outlook and stressed the equality of Jews and Christians. See M. Oesfeld, "Zur Geschichte des Berliner Montags-Klubs," *Zeitschrift für preussische Geschichte und Landeskunde* (ed. Constantin Rössler), 16 (Berlin, 1879): 351, where it is erroneously stated that it was founded by Fessler and Bartholdi in 1795. The mistake has been pointed out to me by Heinrich Hümpel.

7. See Oesfeld, "Geschichte," 328 f.; L.F.G. von Göckingk, *Friedrich Nicolai's Leben und literarischer Nachlass* (Berlin, 1820), 73–84.

8. See above, p. 144.

9. *GS,* 5:620 ff.

10. *GS,* 5:622 f.

11. *GS,* 1:30. No date is given.

12. Mendelssohn was probably referring, as usual, to his nervous debility and domestic preoccupations.

13. *"Kapsel."*

14. *GS*, 4.1:132–53.
15. Editorial note, *GS*, 4.1:132.
16. Hümpel letter, quoting S.M. Lowe, *Bildnisse jetztlebender Berliner Gelehrten mit ihren Selbstbiographien* (Berlin, 1806–1807), no. 5: Lazarus Bendavid, p. 71.
17. *GS*, 4.1:132 f.
18. 4:193–200; *GS*, 3:399–403.
19. See below, p. 660 f.
20. *Berlinische Monatsschrift*, 5 (February, 1785): 133–37; 7 (March, 1786): 193–204; reproduced in *GS*, 3:413–15, 406–12.
21. See below, p. 665.
22. 4:565–75: "Versuch eines Beweises, dass es keine von der Erfahrung unabhängige Vernunftbegriffe gebe."
23. *GS*, 4.1:134 f.
24. *GS*, 5:623 ff.
25. *GS*, 5:626 f.
26. 2 (July, 1783): 4–11; *GS*, 3:370–74; *JubA*, 3.1:346–50 (see 386 f., 463 f.).
27. A copy of this letter is extant in Dep. RvM, D II, no. 2, dated Sept. 28, 1780; reproduced in *GS*, 3:368–70. The *Berlinische Monatsschrift* printed the letter under the heading "K. an Nicolai," and the editor of *GS*, 3, followed suit.
28. Christian Gottlieb Selle (1748–1800) was the personal physician to Frederick the Great and a prolific writer in the fields of medicine, physics, chemistry, and philosophy. His *Philosophische Gespräche* and *Grundsätze der reinen Philosophie* appeared in 1780 and 1788 respectively. He revered Kant but not uncritically (see Kant, *Werke*, 9:346 f.), and Kant held him in high esteem (ibid., 195).
29. Eberhard: *Berlinische Monatsschrift*, 2 (September, 1783):276–81; Selle: 2 (October, 1783): 294–306.
30. *Sota*, 3a.
31. About him, see *GS*, 5:631, editor's note.
32. *GS*, 3:403–06.
33. *GS*, 5:631 f. (Apr. 26, 1785).
34. *GS*, 5:633.
35. 7 (March, 1786): 193–204; *GS*, 3:406–12.
36. See *Frühschriften*, 372–91.
37. Engel: *Berlinische Monatsschrift*, 3 (May, 1784): 396–407; Mendelssohn: 4 (August, 1784): 130–54. Mendelssohn's essay is reproduced in *GS*, 3:385–99.
38. *Oeuvres Philosophiques de Condillac*, 1:219–317 (Paris, 1947).
39. Ibid., 1:7 ("Essai sur l'origine des connoissances humaines").
40. Gluck's librettist.
41. Jean Georges Noverre (1727–1810), a famous French choreographer.
42. The Greeks were wont to attribute statues of unknown origin to Daedalus.
43. Nicholas Saunderson (Sanderson), 1682–1739.
44. "Verwandtschaft des Schönen und Guten," *GS*, 4.1:78–82; *JubA*, 2:181–85; see 404 f.
45. John Locke, *An Essay Concerning Human Understanding*, 1.2.8.
46. See note 18.
47. *Berlinische Monatsschrift*, 2 (1783):516.
48. 4:481–94; Kant, *Werke*, 4:169–76.
49. Information supplied by Heinrich Hümpel in July, 1972.
50. See below, p. 665 f.
51. This sentence seems to echo Maimonides' statement: "Supposing a human individual is isolated . . . all his moral virtues will be in vain, unemployed and unneeded, without in any way perfecting the individual" *(Guide of the Perplexed*, 3:54; see also 3:51, where it is said that the solitary life is conducive to intellectual perfection). Though Mendelssohn preferred moral "culture" to purely intellectual "enlightenment," he adopted Maimonides' view that morality made sense only in the context of society. His intensive study of the *Guide*, part 3, is attested by the glosses he entered in his copy; see Simon Rawidowicz, "Mendelssohns handschriftliche Glossen zum More Nebukim," *MGWJ*, 78, n.s. 42 (1934): 196–202.
52. Cf. *GS*, 4.1:151.
53. *Hamann Briefwechsel*, 5:289 f., 294 f.
54. *GS*, 4.1:146–48.

55. Nachlass Hennings 22, letter 29, fol. 74r–76v; inaccurately reproduced in *ZGJD*, 1 (1887): 125 ff.

56. Except for the last few lines, in which Mendelssohn explained that his eyes had been failing him for some weeks.

57. Nachlass Hennings 22, letter 30, fol. 76v–78v.

58. Presented to the *Mittwochsgesellschaft* on May 5, 1784 (Hümpel letter).

59. *GS*, 4.1:132–34 ("Über die Freiheit seine Meinung zu sagen").

60. According to rumors reported by Karl Lessing (L–M, 21: 182), Frederick II, the Great, in a jesting mood, had commanded the academy to pose this question. G. W. F. Hegel (*Phänomenologie des Geistes*, ed. J. Hoffmeister, [Hamburg, 1952], 392) mentioned this "public question [as to] whether it is permitted to deceive a people."

61. Karl August Graf von Oeynhausen-Gravenburg (1738–1793), Portuguese ambassador in Vienna from 1780 until 1784, was married to the Portuguese poetess D. Leonor d'Almeida Marquesa de Alorno (1750–1839). When the count informed Mendelssohn of the pleasure that the countess had derived from reading his *Phaedon*, Mendelssohn promised to send her his *Annotations* on his correspondence with Abbt. A copy of this letter, dated Dec. 3, 1783, and the original of a second one, dated Apr. 12, 1784, have been preserved in the palace of the Marquesa de Fronteira in Benfica, Lisbon. Copies of both letters (and a letter by Dr. Marion Ehrhardt, who discovered the correspondence and wrote the above items of information on Feb. 6, 1967) are in the possession of the Staatsbibliothek Stiftung Preussischer Kulturbesitz, Berlin, Autogr. I/509/1–2; Tgb. Hs. 67/164–13.2.

62. See Meyer, *Bibliographie*, 55–56.

63. Johann Friedrich Zöllner, *Über Moses Mendelssohn's Jerusalem* (Berlin, 1784).

64. *GS*, 4.1:135–45.

65. Zöllner, *Mendelssohn's Jerusalem*, 92 f.

66. *GS*, 3:266.

67. *GS*, 4.1:150–53. Klein is quoted in the last paragraph.

68. Letter 20 (Mar. 1, 1759); *GS*, 4.1:501.

69. 5:133–37; *GS*, 3:413–15.

70. "Sache Gottes oder die gerettete Vorsehung," published from the *Nachlass* in *GS*, 2:411–51; see Leo Strauss, "Zu Mendelssohns 'Sache Gottes oder die gerettete Vorsehung,' " *Einsichten Gerhard Krüger zum 60. Geburtstag* (Frankfurt am Main, 1962), 363 f.

71. Strauss, *Einsichten*, 364 f.

72. Ibid., 366.

73. Marburg File, no. 57.

74. *JubA*, 14:127; 3.1:230 ff.

75. *JubA*, 14:142 ff.; 3.1:230 ff.

76. Hartog Leo died before March, 1784 (see *JubA*, 16:lvii), which makes it all the more unlikely that the treatise was written for him.

77. *Pope's Works* (ed. W. Elwin and W. J. Courthope), 7:244 f.

78. C. I. Gerhardt, ed., *Die Philosophischen Schriften von G. W. Leibniz*, 6:437 ff.

79. "Sache Gottes oder die gerettete Vorsehung."

80. See Richard H. Popkin, "Manicheanism in the Enlightenment," *The Critical Spirit, Essays in Honor of Herbert Marcuse*, ed. Kurt H. Wolff and Barrington Moore, Jr. (Boston, 1967), 31–54.

81. See Christian Wolff, *Theologia Naturalis*, #1067.

82. See Eduard Zeller, *Geschichte der deutschen Philosophie seit Leibniz*, 2nd ed. (Munich, 1875), 252–66.

83. See the analysis of Mendelssohn's position in Leo Strauss' essay, *Einsichten*, 361–75.

84. *Magazin der Erfahrurgsseelenkunde, als ein Lesebuch für Gelehrte und Ungelehrte*. Mit Unterstützung mehrerer Wahrheitsfreunde herausgegeben . . ., Berlin, 1783–1793.

85. See Hugo Eybisch, *Anton Reiser. Untersuchungen zur Lebensgeschichte von K. P. Moritz und zur Kritik seiner Autobiographie* (Leipzig, 1909), 110.

86. 1.1:31–38. There is a striking similarity between the leading ideas of Mendelssohn's essay (see below) and the first five paragraphs of the *Grundlinien*.

87. See Adam John Bisanz, *Die Ursprünge der "Seelenkrankheit" bei Karl Philipp Moritz* (Heidelberg, 1970), 100–05.

88. By Clara Menck, *Anton Reiser. Ein Psychologischer Roman* (*Insel-Almanach auf das Jahr 1961*), 52 ff.; quoted by Bisanz, *Ursprünge*, 112.

89. See Bisanz, *Ursprünge,* 118 ff.

90. In his periodical *Denkwürdigkeiten* (1786), 1:17–24, 49–53, 97–101, 129–33; quoted by Eybisch, *Anton Reiser,* 110, 122, 312.

91. See Jacob Kellner, "Freud und Mendelssohn. Zur Vorgeschichte des psychoanalytischen Denkens," *BLBI,* 5 (1962), no. 19:171–88.

92. Letter to Ph. E. Reich, Feb. 20, 1770; quoted by Kellner, "Freud und Mendelssohn," 180.

93. Spinoza, *Ethica,* 5, Prop. x, note; cf. 3, introduction.

94. 2.3:122–24.

95. 1.3:46–75; reprinted in *GS,* 3:423–42.

96. See *Briefwechsel zwischen Christian Garve und Georg Joachim Zollikofer* (Breslau, 1804), 338.

97. *GS,* 4.1:504 f.; 4.2:201; *Frühschriften,* 267, 269.

98. See Kellner, "Freud und Mendelssohn."

99. *GS,* 3:440–42.

Morning Hours I (pages 671–686)

1. *GS,* 2:413, #1. Leibniz' *Causa Dei,* #1, has the simpler wording: "prior [sc. pars] praeparatoria magis, altera principalis censeri potest."

2. *GS,* 2:235.

3. Ibid., 237.

4. Mendelssohn had obviously resigned himself to the futility of diagnosing his illness.

5. This is a rather vague and also inaccurate dating. The illness started in 1771, some 14 years prior to 1785.

6. *GS,* 2:235.

7. See above, p. 284 ff.

8. *GS,* 4.2:501–20; see *GS,* 5:322; *Frühschriften,* index, *s. v.* Lambert.

9. See Leo Strauss' note *ad locum* in his forthcoming edition of the *Morgenstunden* in *JubA,* 3.2.

10. See above, p. 302 f.

11. *GS,* 5:633.

12. Kant, *Werke,* 9:212 f.

13. The reference is to the *Jerusalem.*

14. Kant, *Werke,* 9:198 (undated).

15. Ibid., 231 ff.

16. *GS,* 5:706; see above, p. 629.

17. *GS,* 2:293.

18. Ibid., 374 f.

19. [Jenaische] *Allgemeine Literatur-Zeitung,* Jan. 2 and 9, 1786, nos. 1 and 7: 2–6, 50–56. Schütz' authorship is attested by the fact that the review quotes a letter evaluating the *Morgenstunden;* the letter is reproduced without indication of authorship, but it is identical with Kant's letter to Schütz (see Kant, *Werke,* 9:285 f.; cf. also pp. 280, 287). Schütz had moved away from his youthful enthusiasm for Mendelssohn as "the philosopher of Germany" (see above, p. 159 f.), but he had retained his respect for him.

20. This tripartite division of knowledge is hardly derived from Locke's division of knowledge into intuitive, demonstrative, and sensitive *(An Essay Concerning Human Understanding,* 4.2.14).

21. Mendelssohn was here probably thinking of Hutcheson's various "senses" (especially of the moral sense) and his own previous use of the term (see *Frühschriften,* 344–56).

22. This description of common sense is reminiscent of Aristotle's term *anchinoia,* which denotes an inborn sagacity to guess the middle term of a syllogism in an "imperceptible time" *(Anal. Post.* I, 34, 89 b 10). On the development of this concept in the Stoa and Plutarch, see F[azlur] Rahman, *Prophecy in Islam* (London, 1958), 66.

23. Mendelssohn seems to have borrowed this definition of existence from Georg Bernhard Bilfinger, *Dilucidationes Philosophicae* ... (Tübingen, 1727); see J. C. F. Bornträger, *Über das Daseyn Gottes in Beziehung auf Kantische und Mendelssohnsche Philosophie* (Hanover, 1788), 2 f.

24. In a note ad locum prepared for his forthcoming edition of the *Morgenstunden* in *JubA,* 3.2, Leo Strauss mentions that, according to Eduard Zeller *(Philosophie der Griechen,* 5th ed., 2.1:289, note 2), Diogenes' remark is quoted by Simplicius, *De coelo* (ed. Heiberg,

148, 18–20). One might add that Mendelssohn quoted directly from Simplicius, it seems, for he had ordered Simplicius' commentaries on Aristotle and on Epictetus' *Enchiridion*, in a note (undated) to Nicolai; see Marburg File, no. 42. See also *Verzeichnis*, p. 4, no. 57.

25. The terminology used by Mendelssohn reflects Wolff's *(Psychologia rationalis, #36, 38, 39)*; see Leo Strauss, *JubA*, 3.2 ad locum.

26. In his review, Schütz quoted the passage concerned with approval; see also Ludwig Heinrich Jakob's letter to Kant (Kant, *Werke*, 9:291). Kant himself *(Werke*, 4:483 f.) undertook to show that Mendelssohn's statement was unacceptable to him.

27. "Was dieses Ding an und für sich selbst sey."

28. Kant vigorously denied the reducibility of this conflict, and of others of similar importance, to the level of mere *Wortstreit*. In his view, philosophical disagreements of a serious nature invariably concerned the ideas themselves, not merely the way in which they were phrased *(Werke*, 4:482).

29. See above, p. 304; Ludwig Goldstein, *Moses Mendelssohn und die deutsche Aesthetik* (Königsberg, 1904), 229 ff.

30. *GS*, 2:295 ff.

31. There is a certain resemblance between Mendelssohn's concept of the "good" as that which is "preferred" and Franz Brentano's notion of "preferential love"; see Alexander Altmann, *Die Grundlagen der Wertethik: Wesen, Wert, Person, Max Schelers Erkenntnis- und Seinslehre in kritischer Analyse* (Berlin, 1931), 65 f., where Brentano's notion and its influence on Scheler are discussed.

32. *GS*, 2:303 f.; cf. *Jerusalem, GS*, 3:287.

33. See Johann Bernhard Basedow, *Philalethie* (Altona, 1764), 2:311 f.; Idem, *Theoretisches System der gesunden Vernunft* (Altona, 1765), 3:76 ff.; 87; 4:144; *Methodenbuch*, 7, #14 *(J. B. Basedows Ausgewählte Schriften*, ed. Hugo Göring (Langensalza, 1880), 143).

34. In his "Hauptzüge" (see Karl G. Lessing, *G. E. Lessings Leben*, 2:14–19; Kayserling, *Mendelssohn*, 1st ed., 563–65) he had repeatedly characterized Lessing by his spirit of inquiry. Cf., in particular, *Morgenstunden*, xv *(GS*, 2:368): "Geist der Untersuchung war bei ihm Alles."

35. *GS*, 2:318.

36. In the dream, contemplation is described as having something like wings at the back of her head.

37. "Was heisst: sich im Denken orientieren?", *Berlinische Monatsschrift* 8 (October, 1786), 304–30; *Werke*, 4:349–66.

38. *GS*, 2:326.

39. For a discussion of the terminology see Harry A. Wolfson, "Hallevi and Maimonides on Design, Chance and Necessity," *PAAJR*, 11 (1941), 105, note 2.

40. See *JubA*, 16, letter 160, p. 189 *(GS*, 5:523, incomplete).

41. See *Frühschriften*, 40–59, 316–24.

42. Cf. *GS*, 4.2:500.

43. *Der einzig mögliche Beweisgrund zu einer Demonstration des Daseins Gottes* (Königsberg, 1763); *Werke*, 2:76–81 (see *Frühschriften*, 355 ff.); *Kritik der reinen Vernunft*, Elementarlehre, 2,2:2:3.

44. See *Frühschriften*, 310–16.

45. See above, pp. 322–27.

46. See Biester's letter to Kant (Kant, *Werke*, 9:306): "He was well aware of the fact that neither Herz nor Engel were satisfied with his a priori proof for the existence of God."

47. *GS*, 2:385 f.

48. "*sycophantisch*."

49. See *Frühschriften*, 311 f.; Kant, *Werke*, 2:80.

50. Jan. 9, 1786, no. 7:55. Schütz introduced his quotation of Kant's letter with these words: "We conclude this review with the judgment of a man who, for a long time, has established himself as a perfect spokesman in this field. We hope he will forgive us if we place it here before our readers." See note 19 above.

51. Kant, *Werke*, 9:290–93.

52. In the preface.

53. See Kant, *Werke*, 9:290 f., 303.

54. *Werke*, 9:303 f.

55. Ludwig Heinrich Jakob, *Prüfung der Mendelssohnschen Morgenstunden oder aller spekulativen Beweise für das Dasein Gottes in Vorlesungen* (Leipzig, 1786).

56. Kant, *Werke*, 4:481–85.

57. See *GS*, 3:370 ff.; cf. above, p. 657.

Morning Hours II (pages 686–698)

1. In his letter to Nicolai dated Oct. 8, 1785 *(GS,* 5:634) Mendelssohn upheld the fiction that the neutralizing effect of his presentation of Lessing was unpremeditated.

2. He sent it in three instalments, viz., on May 24, June 28 *(GS,* 5:715, 717), and prior to July 21, 1785 (see *GS,* 5:719 f.; cf. Dep. RvM, A, no. 19, July 28, which contains Dr. Reimarus' evaluation of the complete manuscript).

3. See above, p. 650.

4. Acts 17:28.

5. *GS,* 2:339, 342.

6. Ep. 21 in the 1677 edition of the *Opera posthuma,* p. 449; now counted as Ep. 73.

7. *GS,* 2:340, 342.

8. See above, p. 609. In his *Über meine gelehrte Bildung* . . . (Berlin & Stettin, 1799, p. 43), Nicolai reported that Mendelssohn had explained to him his "excellent ideas about the kabbalistic philosophy of the Hebrews." In Mendelssohn's view, the "strange" and "obscure" character of this "oriental philosophy" was due to both the lack of a philosophical terminology in classical Hebrew and the luxuriant growth of imagery in that language. The underlying sense was perfectly consistent, while the elaboration of the literal meaning in equally imaginative commentaries had produced the most absurd and enthusiastic notions, and had led many a Christian adept of occultism completely astray. Mendelssohn, Nicolai maintained, had convincingly shown how Spinoza, by combining kabbalistic doctrine with Cartesian philosophy, had arrived quite naturally at the notion of God as the one substance of which the world was but a modification. See Meyer, *Bibliographie,* p. 113, where Nicolai's report is quoted in full.

9. See above, p. 855, note 25.

10. See *Verzeichnis,* p. 44, no. 500; p. 52, no. 651.

11. *GS,* 5:696.

12. See *Essais de Théodicée,* 1, A, #9; 2, B, #372. Unknown to Mendelssohn, Leibniz had written "animadversiones" on Wachter's *Elucidarius.* A. Foucher de Careil edited these notes under the title *Réfutation inédite de Spinoza par Leibniz* (Paris, 1854), and subsequently under the title "Remarques critiques de Leibniz d'après le manuscrit original de la Bibliothèque de Hanovre" in his book *Leibniz, Descartes et Spinoza* (Paris, 1862).

13. Dep. RvM, A, no. 15a (quoted, with some omissions, above, p. 645).

14. Wilhelm Dobbek, ed., *Herders Briefe* (Weimar, 1959), 240 ff.

15. *Gott, Einige Gespräche über Spinoza's System* . . . (*Sämmtliche Werke,* 8 [Karlsruhe, 1820], 227).

16. See *Frühschriften,* 35 f.

17. See Harry A. Wolfson, *Spinoza* (Cambridge, Mass., 1961), 1:190, where similar sentences by medieval authors are quoted (in addition to Spinoza's).

18. *GS,* 2:357.

19. See *GS,* 5:547 f.; *JubA,* 3.1:329 ff.; *GS,* 4.1:134, 136, 146, etc.

20. See Leibniz, *Théodicée,* 1, B, #168; Wolff, *Vernünfftige Gedancken von den Kräfften des menschlichen Verstandes* (Halle, 1749), pp. 66, 203, 207; J.H. Lambert, *Neues Organon,* 1 (Leipzig, 1764; ed. Hans-Werner Arndt, Hildesheim, 1965), 398; Hume, *An Enquiry Concerning Human Understanding,* section 8, part 1.

21. Mendelssohn had offered this view of Spinoza's position as early as 1755 in his *Philosophische Gespräche*—without, however, adducing any proof. See *Frühschriften,* 31 f.

22. Part 2, sect. 2, chap. iv, #671 ff., pp. 346 ff. (Verona, 1738); reproduced in German translation by Heinrich Scholz, *Die Hauptschriften zum Pantheismusstreit* . . . (Berlin, 1916), xlii–lix.

23. *JubA,* 3.1:92 f. (see above, p. 154 f.).

24. Staatsarchiv Basel: Isaak Iselin-Archiv 28, fol. 269 (*Basler Jahrbuch,* 1923, 74). Cf. Leo Strauss, *JubA,* 3.1:408.

25. *GS,* 2:347 f.

26. See W. Dilthey, *Das Erlebnis und die Dichtung,* 12th ed. (1921), 103 f.; T. C. van Stockum, *Spinoza–Jacobi–Lessing* (Groningen, 1916), 46 f.

27. See above, p. 50 f.; 620.

28. "Über die Wirklichkeit der Dinge ausser Gott," L–M, 14:292 f.; see Alexander Altmann, *Lessing Yearbook*, 3:53 ff. "
29. See above, p. 591 f.
30. L–M, 14:292 f.
31. See Christian Wolff, *Ontologia*, #174.
32. Alexander Baumgarten, *Metaphysica*, #55. On both definitions, see *Frühschriften*, 311 f.
33. *GS*, 2:353.
34. In this instance *Urbild* denotes simply the object to which the concept conforms, not the archetypal idea in God's mind.
35. While Lessing applied the term *Urbild* to the concept of a thing in the divine mind, Mendelssohn, who wished to differentiate between the intradeical and extradeical existence of things, called the extradeical, real thing *Urbild* and its ideal existence in God's intellect by the term *Bild* ("image"). He thus reversed the traditional terminology without, however, intending to deny that the intradeical concept of a thing was in fact the archetype of the real thing. His unorthodox terminology is clearly designed to rebut Lessing's argument, and should not be construed to have any further purpose.
36. Viz. the sentence: "In that case reality outside him must contain something that differentiates it from conceptual reality."
37. See above, p. 609.
38. See above, p. 631.
39. Elise was wont to refer to her brother by this term.
40. Karl Lessing wrote to him on Oct. 19, 1785, after having read the *Morgenstunden:* "When I came upon your interpretation of Spinozism, I was not a little annoyed to find that you had made your friend its defender. Not because it is such a great misfortune to be a Spinozist but because you had no other reason for so doing than the few sentences in his theological *Nachlass*." See Alexander Altmann, *Lessing Yearbook*, 1:32–33.
41. See above, p. 47.
42. *Abhandlungen über die vornehmsten Wahrheiten der natürlichen Religion* (Hamburg, 1754).
43. That Mendelssohn here offered a clue to the identity of the Fragmentist has already been noticed by Gottfried Fittbogen, *Die Religion Lessings* (Leipzig, 1923), 241, note 1.
44. See above, p. 577 f.
45. *Mitwürkung* (Leibniz' *concursus*); see above, p. 68 f.
46. Viz. Rabbi Yohanan's in *Megilla*, 31a. In *Sache Gottes*, #2 (*GS*, 2:414) it is quoted (in Hebrew) in the name of R. Yohanan.
47. See above, p. 582.
48. *GS*, 5:170.

In Combat (pages 698–712)

1. 1759–1787; more about him below, p. 747 f.
2. See Alexander Freiherr von der Goltz, ed., *Thomas Wizenmann der Freund Friedrich Heinrich Jacobi's in Mitteilungen aus seinem Briefwechsel und handschriftlichem Nachlasse* (Gotha, 1859), 2:116.
3. *F.H. Jacobi's auserlesener Briefwechsel*, 1:389 f.
4. Viz. *Über die Lehre des Spinoza in Briefen an den Herrn Moses Mendelssohn* (Breslau, 1785).
5. Dobbek, ed., *Herders Briefe*, 225 f.
6. *An die Freunde Lessings* (Berlin, 1786), 18.
7. Dobbek, *Herders Briefe*, 260.
8. See A.H.F. Schlichtegroll, ed., *Biographie des Königl. preuss. Geheimen Kriegsrates zu Königsberg Theodor Gottlieb von Hippel* (Gotha, 1807).
9. Jacobi, *Werke*, ed. Friedrich Roth (Leipzig, 1812–1825), 4.3:77.
10. Ibid., 80 f.
11. Cf. J.G. Hamann, "Metakritik über den Purismus der Vernunft," published by F.T. Rink, *Mancherley zur Geschichte der metacritischen Invasion* (Königsberg, 1800), 120–34.
12. Max Jacobi, ed., *Briefwechsel zwischen Goethe und Jacobi*, 88.
13. Ibid., 89.
14. The first poem, which followed the motto and bore Goethe's name, was the full text of "Edel sey der Mensch / Hülfreich und gut . . ." (omitted after the first edition).
15. *An die Freunde Lessings*, 16 f.

16. Quoted here from the original (Dep. RvM, A. no. 21); reproduced by Rudolf Zoeppritz, ed., *Aus F.H. Jacobi's Nachlass*, 1:62 f.

17. The draft of this letter in Mendelssohn's own hand is extant in Dep. RvM, A, no. 22, I; it contains a fair number of corrections. It is reproduced in its corrected form in *GS*, 5:722 f.

18. Mendelssohn wrote first: "that I fear to drown if for a moment..."

19. There follows a deleted sentence: "I have so far not succeeded."

20. Deleted: "in friendship."

21. The phrase "and I hope... too" is added in the margin.

22. Deleted: "true esteem."

23. Max Jacobi, *Briefwechsel*, 94 (Oct. 21, 1785).

24. Ibid., 95.

25. Ibid., 96, 97, 101.

26. Ibid., 101.

27. Jacobi, *Werke*, 4.3:110 ff.

28. Otto Hoffmann, ed., *Herders Briefe an Hamann* (Berlin, 1889), 223 f.

29. Both Herder's and Goethe's letters contrast Mendelssohn's alleged *Pfiffigkeit* ("craftiness") with a poor/honest Christian's mentality.

30. The German text uses an untranslatable expression of rudeness.

31. *An die Freunde Lessings*, 27 ff.

32. Ibid., vii f.

33. *GS*, 5:634.

34. See above, pp. 647 f., 650 f.

35. *An die Freunde Lessings*, 79–83.

36. Ibid., 19–21.

37. Ibid., 12 ff.

38. Ibid., 21–27.

39. Ibid., vii–xi.

40. The draft in Mendelssohn's hand (Dep. RvM, A, no. 22, II) varies slightly from the final letter as reproduced in *GS*, 5:635 f., where the deviations are noted.

41. In the draft: "The fight I have to wage is a hard one... to make man's reason hateful and suspect."

42. In his reply, dated Nov. 20, 1785, the duke of Anhalt-Dessau wrote: "I note with satisfaction that reason has found its defender in a man whom Germany has long named one of her first sages. Complete your noble work and be sure of victory over your adversaries, and of the world's acclamation" (*LBH*, 3, no. 4306, p. 4).

43. Of this letter only the draft is extant. It is written on the same sheet as the draft of the letter to the duke of Anhalt-Dessau. The duke's reply, dated Oct. 21, 1785, reads: "A work by you on so sublime a subject is the most interesting gift to humanity. It affords me real pleasure to be able to express to you my reverence and perfect esteem" (*LBH*, 3, no. 4407, p. 23).

44. Staatsbibliothek Stiftung Preussischer Kulturbesitz, Berlin, Autogr. I/608.

45. Niedersächsische Landesbibliothek, Hanover, Letters by Mendelssohn to Zimmermann, fol. 8r; published by Eduard Bodemann, *Zimmermann...* (Hanover, 1878), 291; Kayserling, *Ungedrucktes*, 19.

46. Christian Friedrich Voss & Son, Berlin.

47. Viz. Zimmermann, who had just completed the publication of his work *Über die Einsamkeit* (vols. 1–2, Leipzig, 1784; vols. 3–4, Leipzig, 1785).

48. *Über Spinoza's Lehrgebäude;* a misquotation of the title.

49. The draft (Dep. RvM, A, no. 22, IV) is reproduced in *GS*, 5:637 f.; Kant, *Werke*, 9:274 ff. The draft is dated Oct. 16, 1785, and so is the letter. In Hamann's letter of Nov. 3, 1785, to Jacobi (Jacobi, *Werke*, 4.3:95) October 17 is erroneously given as the date.

50. See above, p. 684 f.

51. See Dr. Marcus Herz' remark in his letter to Kant (*Werke*, 9:288).

52. Jacobi, *Werke*, 4.3:82.

53. Ibid., 89.

54. Ibid., 113.

55. See note 49.

56. Hamann's memory played him false in reporting the sentence.

57. Zoeppritz, *Aus Jacobi's Nachlass*, 1:71. In his postscript (p.76) Jacobi wrote: "If you

could somehow enlighten me where in my Spinoza booklet Goethe's toes are to be found, I would deem it a favor. The *Prometheus* is by him, as can presumably be guessed, but this gives me no sufficient clue."

58. Jacobi, *Werke*, 4.3:114 (December 3, 1785).

59. Ibid., 116.

60. Kant, *Werke*, 9:277.

61. *GS*, 5:721 f.

62. Dep. RvM, A, no. 23.

63. A copy of the letter in an unknown hand is found in Dep. RvM, A, no. 24; reproduced in *GS*, 5:723 f. ˙

64. The handwritten copy reads: "als ein Sachwalter des I.," which makes no sense. The editor of *GS* (5:723, note **) misread *I* for *T*, and suggested that the correct reading might be *S* for *Spinoza*. It seems more probable that *I* is a slip of the pen and should read *A* for *Atheismus*.

65. A version of the letter based on a copy made by Hamann is reproduced by Zoeppritz, *Aus Jacobi's Nachlass*, 1:66 f.; see Scholz, *Hauptschriften*, lxxxvi, note 1. An abbreviated version of is found in Jacobi's *Wider Mendelssohns Beschuldigungen* (Leipzig, 1786), 55 f. A typewritten copy of a more elaborate version is extant in a collection of letters by and to Elise Reimarus in the possession of the Staats- und Universitätsbibliothek, Hamburg (letter no. 3, pp. 3–7). There are indications that this text represents the draft of the letter. Our account follows this original version.

66. Slightly different in the printed version.

67. In the printed version: "of your friendship toward me."

68. In the printed version: "I could not thank you immediately . . . in the manner in which you deserve it and as I can do only if you convince me that the consequences will not be as bad as I anticipate."

69. Elise here ignored the fact that the *Morgenstunden* did not deal with the Jacobi correspondence and that the original promise had therefore become invalid.

70. In the printed version: "or for the more sturdy ones in the nation."

71. See above, p. 647.

72. See *Jacobi wider Mendelssohns Beschuldigungen*, 56 f.

73. Ibid., 2–10; revised in Jacobi, *Werke*, 4.2:177 ff.; Scholz, lxxxvii–xc.

74. Letter no. 4, pp. 7–8, of the collection referred to in note 65.

75. See the view expressed by Heinrich Scholz, *Hauptschriften*, lxvii–lxix.

76. Max Jacobi, *Briefwechsel*, 96.

77. See *Jacobi's auserlesener Briefwechsel*, 1:397 ff. (Apr. 27, 1786).

78. *Briefwechsel zwischen Christian Garve und Georg Joachim Zollikofer . . .* (Breslau, 1804), 373 f.

79. Cf. *Briefe von Christian Garve an Christian Felix Weisse* (Breslau, 1801), 1:227 f. (Nov. 17, 1785).

80. Ibid., 232.

81. E.g. by Thomas Wizenmann; see von der Goltz, *Wizenmann*, 2:124, where Wizenmann's letter of Dec. 10, 1785, to Hausleutner is quoted: "Compare . . . the historical in Jacobi's letters with the way in which Mendelssohn introduces the Spinozist as interlocutor through Lessing."

82. Jacobi, *Werke*, 4.3:113.

83. Ibid., 90.

84. Ibid., 91 f.

85. Ibid., 94 f.

86. Viz. Hamann, *Golgatha und Scheblimini. Von einem Prediger in der Wüsten.*

The Social and Domestic Scene (pages 712–729)

1. Dep. RvM, B I, no. 6; inaccurately reproduced in *GS*, 5:639 f.

2. The memorandum (20 folios) is extant in a copy from the original in the Staatsbibliothek Stiftung Preussischer Kulturbesitz, Berlin, Rep. 94 (unpublished; the surmise about its contents in Kayserling, *Mendelssohn*, 336, is mistaken).

3. A copy of Mendelssohn's letter is attached to the memorandum; reproduced in *GS*, 5:630 f.

4. *JubA*, 16, letter 279, p. 296 f.

5. *Ritualgesetze der Juden* . . . (Berlin, 1778); *JubA*, 7:109–251; see above, p. 470.
6. See L. Geiger, "Vor hundert Jahren," *ZGJD*, 3 (1889), 205–08, 395.
7. *GS*, 5:671.
8. *Das Forschen* . . . , 38 f.; *Jerusalem, GS*, 3:274 ff.; Katz, *Zion*, 29 (1964): 126 f.
9. *GS*, 5:677.
10. J. Heinemann, ed., *Moses Mendelssohn, Sammlung theils noch ungedruckter, theils in anderen Schriften zerstreuter Aufsätze und Briefe von ihm, an und über ihn* (Leipzig, 1831), 116.
11. See his biography of the father, *GS*, 1:44 (written in the summer of 1842) and his letter to Herz Homberg of Mar. 12, 1841, published by Alexander Altmann, *BLBI*, 11 (1968), no. 42:107 ff.
12. *GS*, 1:52 f.
13. *GS*, 5:682.
14. *LBH* 2:3 f., no. 1211; Geiger, *Briefe*, 121 f.
15. *GS*, 5:683.
16. See Heinrich Funck, "Briefwechsel zwischen Lavater und Frau von der Recke," *Euphorion* (ed. Josef Nadler), 25.1 (Leipzig & Vienna, 1924): 52–63; Paul Rachel, *Elise von der Recke*, 2 vols. (1902).
17. Dep. RvM, C II, no. 28. Elise von der Recke had a very special reason for being devoted to Lessing's memory: when *Nathan the Wise* appeared, the verses "Begreifst Du aber, / Wie viel andächtig schwärmen leichter, als / Gut handeln ist! Wie gern der schlaffste Mensch / Andächtig schwärmt . . ." had suddenly released her from her addiction to Cagliostro (see Danzel, *Lessing*, 2.2:205).
18. *Briefe einer Curländerin auf einer Reise durch Deutschland* (Brunswick, 1791).
19. G. Karo and M. Geyer, eds., *Vor hundert Jahren. Elise von der Reckes Reisen durch Deutschland 1784-86 nach dem Tagebuche ihrer Begleiterin Sophie Becker* (Stuttgart, n.d.).
20. See L. F. G. von Goekingk, "Sophiens Denkmal," *Deutsche Monatsschrift*, 1 (Berlin, 1790):67–86.
21. J. L. Schwarz, *Elisens und Sophiens Gedichte* (1790).
22. Published first by Goekingk, "Sophiens Denkmal," 81–86; reproduced in *GS*, 5:642–44, 647–50. Two letters by Sophie to Mendelssohn are found in Dep. RvM, C I, nos. 4–5.
23. See Goekingk, "Sophiens Denkmal," 68.
24. Dep. RvM, C I, no. 4 (Dec. 22, 1785).
25. *GS*, 5:642 ff. (Dec. 23, 1785).
26. Paraphrasing *Mishna, Yadayim*, 4:6 *(le-fi hibbatan tum'atan);* see the same paraphrase in *GS*, 3:403.
27. *GS*, 5:645 f.
28. The letter was written on December 24.
29. *GS*, 5:647–50.
30. *Hegels Sämmtliche Werke, Jubiläumsausgabe* (ed. H. Glockner), 19:529–31.
31. Ibid., 1:281; 16:345.
32. Dep. RvM, C I, no. 5.
33. Karo-Geyer, ed., *Vor hundert Jahren*, 229.
34. Ibid., 191.
35. Ibid., 192 ff.
36. *Briefe einer Curländerin*, 2:172 (quoted by Kayserling, *Mendelssohn*, 494). The diary says merely that Mendelssohn had his meal at an inn (p. 193).
37. *Vor hundert Jahren*, 196.
38. Ibid.
39. Ibid., 200–05.
40. Ibid., 216.
41. Ibid., 218.
42. See above, p. 212.
43. *GS*, 5:682.
44. Viz. Joseph Jonas Fränkel (1721–1793), chief rabbi of Breslau. See *JubA*, 7:278 and above, p. 499.
45. *Vor hundert Jahren*, 225.
46. Dep. RvM, A, no. 1.
47. *Vor hundert Jahren*, 192.

48. Ibid., 196.
49. Dep. RvM, C I, no. 4.
50. *GS*, 5:644; see also 646 f.
51. *JubA*, 16:309 (Sept. 15, 1785).
52. *GS*, 2:363.
53. *GS*, 5:648.
54. *JubA*, 16:306.
55. A copy of the letter was kindly put at my disposal by Prof. Felix Gilbert.
56. Hinni (Henriette) Mendelssohn, Joseph's wife and the daughter of Nathan Meyer.
57. Letter to Simon Veit, Aug. 28, 1819; see Theodor Zondek, "Dorothea Schlegel und Simon Veit," *BLBI*, 5 (1962) no. 20:303; see also Josef Körner, "Mendelssohns Töchter," *Preussische Jahrbücher*, Vol. 214 (2) (1928): 174; Adolph Kohut, *Moses Mendelssohn und seine Familie* (Dresden & Leipzig, 1886), 82–95.
58. See Marcus Brann, *Die schlesische Judenheit vor und nach dem Edikt vom 11. März 1812* (Breslau, 1913), 13, note 4. Brann published the poem in *Otsar Ha-Sifrut* (ed. S. E. Gräber), 2:433 ff. (Cracow, 1888).
59. *GS*, 5:667. We catch a glimpse of the cultural atmosphere in the home of the newlywed from Henriette Herz' memoirs, in which the weekly *Lesegesellschaften*—the "earliest" she attended—are recalled: "As a rule some part of a drama was read.... Mendelssohn was a regular and attentive listener. How we prowled around him to catch a word indicating how he judged the reading! How elated we were when he uttered approval!" See J. Fürst, ed., *Henriette Herz. Ihr Leben und ihre Erinnerungen*, 2nd ed. (Berlin, 1858), 104 f.
60. See Zondek, "Dorothea Schlegel," 302–04; Fürst, *Henriette Herz*, 114.
61. *JubA*, 16, letter 276, p. 294 f.
62. *GS*, 5:685 f.
63. The marriage was of short duration; see Kohut, *Mendelssohn und seine Familie*, 95.
64. About her see Körner, "Mendelssohns Töchter," 176–82; Kohut, *Mendelssohn und seine Familie*, 95–101.
65. *GS*, 1:53 f., 32.
66. See above, pp. 355, 369.
67. See J. Schirmann's article in *EJ*, 6:673 f.; *AZJ*, 3, no. 75 (June 22, 1839):306.
68. Geiger, *Briefe*, 87 f.
69. See above, p. 643.
70. Cf. *JubA*, 11, letters 36 and 38, pp. 74 f., 82 f., 417.
71. *GS*, 5:663. Abraham would become the father of Felix Mendelssohn Bartholdy.
72. *GS*, 5:667.
73. *GS*, 5:670.
74. *GS*, 5:673.
75. This remark can refer only to Joseph Pick, though he was a man of "fine education" and became tutor in the household of Simon Hirsch, *Obervorsteher* ("president") of the Breslau community, and a follower of Mendelssohn's (see Brann, *Die schlesische Judenheit*, 13, note 4).
76. See above, p. 15.
77. *GS*, 5:680.
78. Martin Heinrich Klaproth (1743–1817); see *GS*, 5:680, note 2.
79. *GS*, 4.1:141.
80. *GS*, 5:685.
81. Viz. Johannes Buxtorf, Jr.'s Latin version (Basel, 1629) of Maimonides' *Guide of the Perplexed*.
82. *JubA*, 16:306–09.
83. *GS*, 5:673 f.
84. See W. Treue, "Das Bankhaus Mendelssohn," *Mendelssohn Studien*, ed. Cécile Lowenthal-Hensel (Berlin, 1972), 1:34 ff.
85. *GS*, 5:721.
86. *GS*, 5:721 f.
87. Dep. RvM, A, no. 23.
88. Niedersächsische Landesbibliothek, Hanover, Letters from Mendelssohn to Zimmermann, fol. 7r–7v; published by Bodemann, *Zimmermann*, 290 f.; Kayserling, *Ungedrucktes*, 16–18.

89. A reminiscence of Leibniz' *Causa Dei* and his own "Sache Gottes."

90. Johann Joachim Winckelmann (1717–1768), celebrated author of a *History of Ancient Art* (1764).

91. For glimpses of Joseph's character, see Altmann, *BLBI,* 11 (1968) no. 42:73–115. A portrait of Joseph at a mature age is reproduced in this volume.

The End (pages 729–743)

1. *An die Freunde Lessings,* 21–27 (*GS,* 3:10–13).
2. Ibid., 27, note (*GS,* 3:13, note).
3. Ibid., 84 *(GS,* 3:35).
4. See above, p. 721.
5. *Beyträge zum gelehrten Artikel des Hamburgischen unpartheyischen Correspondenten,* Zweytes Stück, Feb. 1, 1786; quoted here from its reproduction in *Erste Beylage zum 18ten Stück der Königl. privilegirten Zeitung,* Feb. 11, 1786.
6. "Jacobi steckt mit Lavatern unter einer Decke."
7. See *LBH,* 2:154–66; Leo Weisz, "Lavaters Polemik gegen Lessing," *NZZ,* Dec. 17, 1961 no. 4864/124.
8. *Über die Lehre des Spinoza* (1785), 33, 36; 2nd ed., 45, 51; Heinrich Scholz, *Die Hauptschriften zum Pantheismusstreit . . .* (Berlin, 1916), 92, 95.
9. *Erste Beylage . . .*
10. Ibid.
11. *An die Freunde Lessings,* 79 ff. (*GS,* 3:33 f.).
12. Ibid., 1 f., 78 f. (*GS,* 3, 3, 32 f.). For the letter, see *GS,* 5:716, and above, p. 648 f. In his letter of Apr. 29, 1785 (*GS,* 5:714) Mendelssohn had said that for the publication of part 2 there was still "plenty of time."
13. Asmus [pseudonym for Matthias Claudius], *Zwey Recensionen etc. in Sachen der Herren Lessing, M. Mendelssohn und Jacobi* (Hamburg, 1786), 12.
14. *GS,* 3:32 f.
15. GS, 5:708; see above, p. 633. The motto is found in *An die Freunde Lessings,* xxiii–xxiv *(GS,* 3:2).
16. Jacobi, *Werke,* ed. Friedrich Roth (Leipzig, 1812–1825), 4.3:125.
17. *Erste Beylage . . .* : Reichardt in the name of Fromet; Dr. Marcus Herz' report in Engel's preface to *Moses Mendelssohn an die Freunde Lessings,* xiv.
18. Herz' report in Engel's preface, xiii–xxii.
19. Franz Karl A. Achard (1753–1821), famous chemist and a member of the Berlin Academy.
20. G. Karo and M. Geyer, eds., *Vor hundert Jahren . . .,* 232.
21. Euchel, *Toledot,* 109; *Berlinische privilegirte Zeitung,* Jan. 10, 1786, no. 4; [F. W. von Schütz], *Leben und Meinungen Moses Mendelssohn . . .* (Hamburg, 1787), 142; Joseph Mendelssohn *(GS,* 1:55) stated that the shops remained closed for the whole day.
22. *Vor hundert Jahren,* 233.
23. *Berlinische privilegirte Zeitung,* Jan. 10, 1786.
24. *GS,* 1:55.
25. Published in *Ha-Me'assef,* Adar, 5546/1786.
26. *Über Moses Mendelsohns [sic] Tod* (Vienna & Leipzig, 1786), 80–98. The preface is dated Aug. 6, 1786.
27. Deut. 33:1.
28. Karl Wilhelm Ramler, "Sulamith und Eusebia, eine Trauerkantate auf den Tod Moses Mendelssohns," *Berlinische Monatsschrift,* 7 (1786): 481–89; reproduced in Ramler, *Poëtische Werke* (Berlin, 1800), 2:35–42.
29. The bust was placed in the Jüdische Freyschule.
30. Wilhelm Dobbek, *Herders Briefe* (Weimar, 1959), 266.
31. See Rudolf Haym, *Herder,* 2:359–64.
32. *Bava Bathra,* 17a; *Berakhot,* 8a; Deut. Rabba, 11, end; Cant. Rabba, 1:1. Schiller's poem "Die Götter Griechenlands" (1788), echoing Lessing's "Wie die Alten den Tod gebildet," also uses the motif of death by a kiss: "Ein Kuss nahm das letzte Leben von der Lippe, Seine Fackel senkt ein Genius."
33. Max Jacobi, *Briefwechsel zwischen Goethe und Jacobi* (Leipzig, 1846), 102.
34. *Werke* (Inselverlag), 14:386.

35. Book 15; *Werke* (Inselverlag), 3:679 f.

36. *Briefwechsel zwischen Goethe und Zelter*, 3:87 (quoted by Kayserling, *Mendelssohn*, 518, note 4).

37. Jacobi, *Werke*, 4.3:142.

38. In 1820 David Friedländer found it necessary to refute a crudely anti-Jewish statement attributed to Kant; see Friedländer, *Beitrag zur Geschichte der Verfolgung der Juden im 19ten Jahrhundert durch Schriftsteller. Ein Sendschreiben an die Frau Kammerherrin von der Recke . . .* (Berlin, 1820).

39. Jacobi, *Werke*, 4.3:158f.

40. Ibid., 142.

41. Viz. the "strange wisdom" (Prov. 5–7), representing an impious philosophy. The "warning" was implied in Hamann's *Golgatha*.

42. Joseph Mendelssohn was then fifteen years old.

Epilogue (pages 744–759)

1. On Aug. 1, 1784; see above, pp. 633–35.

2. Dated Apr. 21, 1785; see above, p. 645.

3. *Moses Mendelssohn an die Freunde Lessings, Ein Anhang zu Herrn Jacobis Briefwechsel über die Lehre des Spinoza* (Berlin, 1786), iii f.

4. Ibid., iv–xi.

5. See the account in Hugo Eybisch, *Anton Reiser. Untersuchungen zur Lebensgeschichte von K. P. Moritz und zur Kritik seiner Autobiographie* (Leipzig, 1909), 123–27.

6. See note 5 of the preceding section ("The End").

7. See Eybisch, *Anton Reiser*, 126, 312, note 36, where Nicolai's remark to this effect is quoted.

8. Ibid., 125–27, 286 f.

9. Asmus [Matthias Claudius], *Zwey Recensionen . . .* (Hamburg, 1786), 19 f.; written in Feburary, 1786.

10. In Mendelssohn's letter to Elise and her brother, written on Nov. 18, 1783 (*GS*, 5:701 f.), the sentence "We remain imperturbable" (*"Wir bleiben unbekümmert"*) did not occur. It was inserted by Elise in her report to Jacobi. See *Über die Lehre des Spinoza*, 2nd ed., 70–71; *Wider Mendelssohns Beschuldigungen*, 9; Heinrich Scholz, *Die Hauptschriften zum Pantheismusstreit . . .* (Berlin, 1916), 9.

11. *Werke*, 9:288.

12. A mocking corruption of "Pempelfort" (near Düsseldorf), where Jacobi spent part of the year.

13. Instead of "Wandsbeck" where Claudius lived.

14. Mendelssohn's daughter Brendel seems to have admired Claudius, for her brother Joseph had to promise her to visit the poet (the "Wandsbecker Bote") when in Hamburg (*JubA*, 16:307).

15. *Die Resultate der Jacobischen und Mendelssohnschen Philosophie; kritisch untersucht von einem Freywilligen* (Leipzig, 1786); published anonymously.

16. See Alexander Freiherr von der Goltz, ed., *Thomas Wizenmann . . .* (Gotha, 1859), 2:176 ff.; the letter is dated July 4, 1786.

17. Published by Wizenmann in his "Letter" to Kant in *Deutsches Museum* (February, 1787), 127; quoted by von der Goltz, *Wizenmann*, 2:130 f., note 1.

18. Von der Goltz, *Wizenmann*, 2:137.

19. Ibid., 140, quoting Wizenmann's "Letter" to Kant, *Deutsches Museum* (February, 1787), 119 ff., where a summary of his work is offered. Cf. *Die Resultate*, 46 ff.

20. *Die Resultate*, 58 f.; see above, p. 635.

21. *Deutsches Museum* (February, 1787), 118f.

22. *Die Resultate*, 236–43.

23. *Friedrich Jacobi wider Mendelssohns Beschuldigungen betreffend die Briefe über die Lehre des Spinoza* (Leipzig, 1786).

24. Ibid., vi f.

25. Jacobi later deleted this passage when preparing the edition of his works; see von der Goltz, *Wizenmann*, 2:150, note 1.

26. *Wider Mendelssohn's Beschuldingungen*, 11–14.

27. Ibid., 8, 28–31.

28. Ibid., 116–21. The anatomist shown on the engraving was the famous Sömmering of Mainz (see ibid., 119; von der Goltz, *Wizenmann*, 2:154).

29. *Wider Mendelssohns Beschuldigungen*, 126 f.

30. Lavater, *Pontius Pilatus*, 4.6:6 (reference by Jacobi).

31. *Wider Mendelssohns Beschuldigungen*, 1 f.

32. Max Jacobi, *Briefwechsel*, 104 f.

33. Kant, *Werke*, 3:555–57; *Wider Mendelssohns Beschuldigungen*, 101–04.

34. *Wider Mendelssohns Beschuldigungen*, 104, note.

35. Only in a private letter of Apr. 7, 1786, had Kant replied to Herz (*Werke*, 9:295): "Jacobi's fancy [*Grille*] is nothing serious but merely an affected *Genieschwärmerey* to make himself a name. It is hardly worthy of an earnest refutation. Possibly I will publish something in the *Berlinische Monatsschrift*, in order to expose this jugglery."

36. Kant, *Werke*, 9:304–10.

37. We believe this desideratum to have been fulfilled by the account offered in the present work.

38. Kant, *Werke*, 9:314.

39. Kant referred parenthetically to *Morgenstunden*, 165–66 (*GS*, 2:318) and *An die Freunde Lessings* [erroneously quoted as "*Briefe an Lessings Freunde*"], 33, 67 (*GS*, 3:15, 28).

40. Kant, *Werke*, 4:351; see above, pp. 676, 679 f.

41. Pages 304–30; Kant, *Werke*, 4:351–66.

42. *Werke*, 4:352.

43. Ibid., 356, note 1.

44. *Wider Mendelssohns Beschuldigungen*, 45. Jacobi's claim that Lessing had agreed with this characterization is refuted by the fact that, as Jacobi himself reported to Wilhelm Heinse shortly after his visit to Wolfenbüttel, Lessing had described Mendelssohn as "the brightest mind, the most excellent philosopher, and the best literary critic of our century"; see Rudolf Zoeppritz, *Aus F. H. Jacobi's Nachlass*, 1:28 f.

45. Kant, *Werke*, 4:361 f.

46. Ibid., 363–66.

47. See Daniel Jenisch's letter to Kant (May 14, 1787), *Werke*, 9:323.

48. See *Frühschriften*, 24–28.

49. *GS*, 3:5 f.

50. 50.2:624–31. A handwritten copy is found in Dep. RvM, A, no. 25.

51. Nicolai referred to his earlier article in *Göttingisches Magazin*, 3, no. 36, 393 ff., where he had already dealt with Mendelssohn's participation in the *Literaturbriefe* in particular.

52. 7 (March, 1786):204–16.

53. Dep. RvM, A, no. 28.

54. See Simon Höchheimer, *Über Moses Mendelsohns [sic] Tod* (Vienna & Leipzig, 1786), 10; C.G.M. Denina, *La Prusse littéraire sous Fréderich II* (Berlin, 1791), art. Müchler; quoted by Joseph Mendelssohn, *GS*, 1:55; Julius F. Knüppel, Carl C. Nenke, and Christian L. Paalzow, *Büsten Berliner Gelehrten und Künstler* (Leipzig, 1787), 204 f.

55. Höchheimer, see preceding note.

56. 7:216.

57. It appeared in the *Haude- und Spenersche Zeitung;* see *GS*, 1:56.

58. See above, p. 741.

59. *GS*, 1:55.

60. Kayserling, *Mendelssohn*, 519.

61. "Über Moses Mendelssohn, Schreiben des Königl. preussischen Generals von Scholten an den jüdischen Kaufmann D[avid] F[riedlander] in Berlin," *Berlinische Monatsschrift*, 7:398–406 (ibid., p. 405).

62. Meyer, *Bibliographie*, p. 127, no. 731 (h) quotes the article "Müchler, Johann George" in Knüppel, Nenke, and Paalzow, *Büsten*, 203–05, as evidence of Müchler's opposition to the inclusion of Mendelssohn's medallion in the monument. The article merely indicates, however, that the king refused permission and adds the authors' (not Müchler's) view that despite his merits in "learning, enlightenment, and German literature" Mendelssohn did not belong to the same "class" as Leibniz, Lambert, and Sulzer; but that it was nevertheless to be desired that Mendelssohn should not be "entirely forgotten" and that a monument to him should be erected in some other location.

63. 10 (1787):552–56.

64. See Kayserling, "Moses Mendelssohn-Denkmal," *AZJ*, 50 (1886):3.

65. Ibid. On Mar. 7, 1786, Dr. Reimarus had written to Nicolai: "I have been told that the late Mendelssohn's correspondence is to be published [marginal note in Nicolai's hand: I know nothing about it]. What I wrote [to Mendelssohn] about philosophical matters may be printed, but publishing views on people who are still living . . . you will certainly consider distasteful, and in this case, too, you will prevent this" (*LBH*, 2, no. 2770, p. 241 f.).

66. 7 (1786):403.

67. Ibid.

68. See J.A. Stargardt Catalogue 595 (1971):84, no. 278.

69. See above, p. 213 f.

70. See above, p. 724.

71. 7 (1786):211 f.

72. For subsequent efforts see Kayserling, *AZJ*, 50 (1886):3 f. The story of the Leipzig edition (1843–1845) has been told in my essay on the subject in *BLBI*, 11 (1968), no. 42: 73–115. Concerning the vicissitudes of the Jubilee edition (Berlin, 1929–1938),see my *"Geleitwort"* to volume 1 (1971) of the new edition (Stuttgart, 1971 ff.), which is scheduled to comprise 20 volumes.

73. *Leben und Meinungen Moses Mendelssohn nebst dem Geiste seiner Schriften in einem kurzen Abrisse dargestellt.* Only 12 of the 66 subscribers were Jews.

74. Ibid., 143.

75. He is described by Gustav Schwab, *Schillers Leben in drei Büchern* (Stuttgart, 1859), 462 ff.

76. M.C.Ph. Conz, *Moses Mendelssohn, der Weise und der Mensch. Ein lyrisch-didaktisches Gedicht in vier Gesängen* (Stuttgart, 1787).

77. For Conz' dependence on Kretschmann see Karl Heinrich Jördens, *Lexikon deutscher Dichter und Prosaisten*, 3:555 (Leipzig, 1808).

78. *Moses Mendelssohns kleine philosophische Schriften. Mit einer Skizze seines Lebens und Charakters* (Berlin, 1789). For yet another early biography (1790) see Meyer, *Bibliographie*, 71, no. 403 d.

79. *Wijsgeerige verhandlingen, brieven en gesprekken, van Moses Mendelszoon. Uit het hoogduitsche vertaald, en met antekeningen, en het leven van den autheur, verrijkt, door G. Brender á Brandis* (Leiden, 1788).

80. *Toledot Rabbenu Moshe ben Menahem* (Berlin, 1788). Euchel had begun to publish his work in *Ha-Me'assef*, 1787.

81. By Abraham Meldola in *Ha-Me'assef* (1785), 81; see Moshe Pelli, *Moses Mendelssohn: Bonds of Tradition* (Tel-Aviv, 1971), 92 (Hebrew). The slogan was first applied by Johann Jakob Rabe; see above, p. 197.

82. See Pelli, *Bonds of Tradition*, in which the full documentation is to be found.

83. See now Moshe Pelli, *"Rik'ah u-mehabrah shel imrat-kanaf 'al Moshe Mendelssohn,"* *Bizaron*, 63.4 (1972): 184–88. The epigram was first published in *Ha-Me'assef* 3 (1786):161 [177].

84. *Toledot*, 3.

85. *Toledot*, 126 f.

Index of Subjects
and Names